AF572113

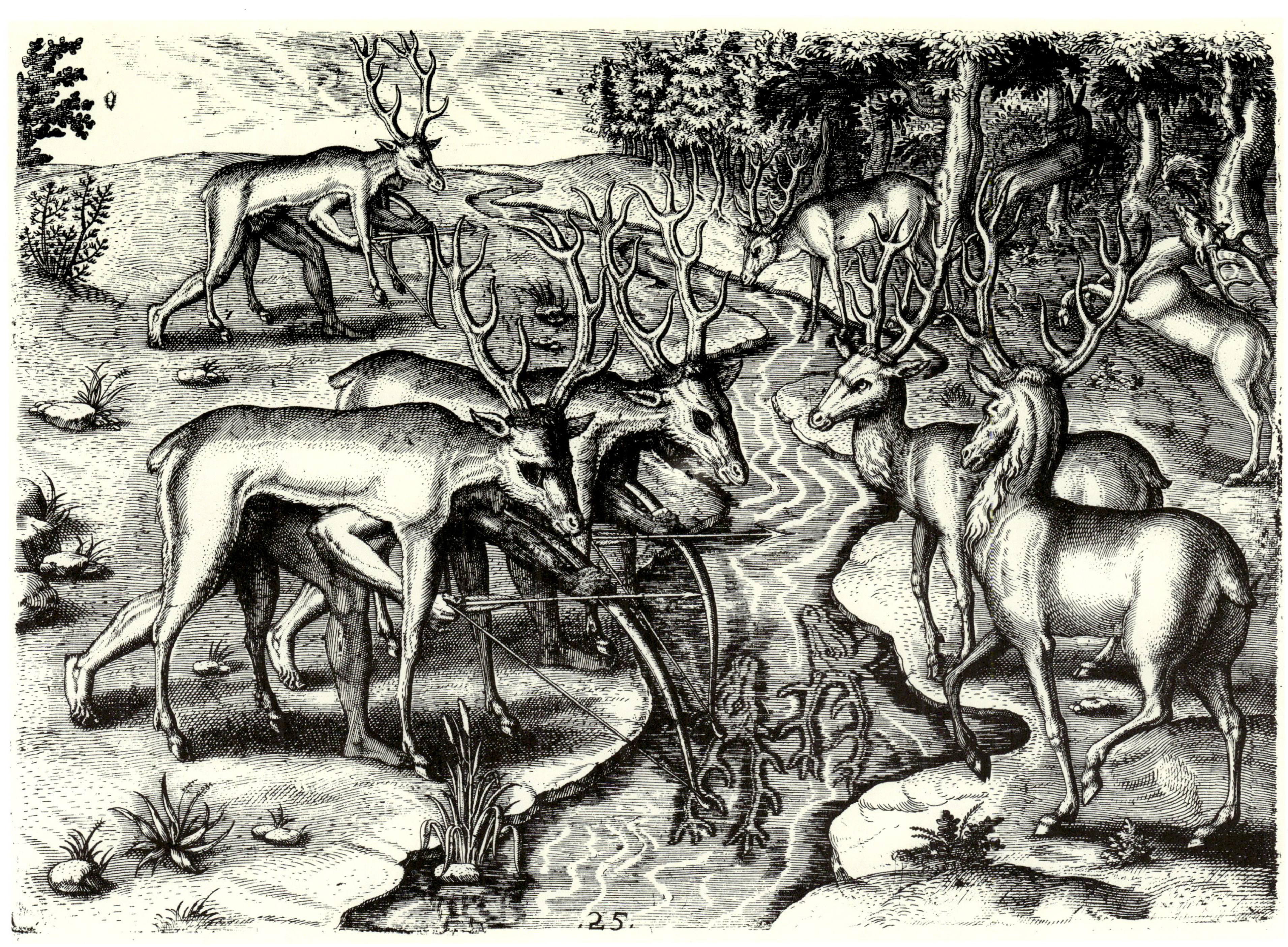

DEER HUNTING. THEODOR DE BRY, *VOYAGES TO AMERICA,* VOL. 2, PLATE 25. ENGRAVING AFTER A DRAWING BY JACQUES LE MOYNE, FRANKFURT, 1591.

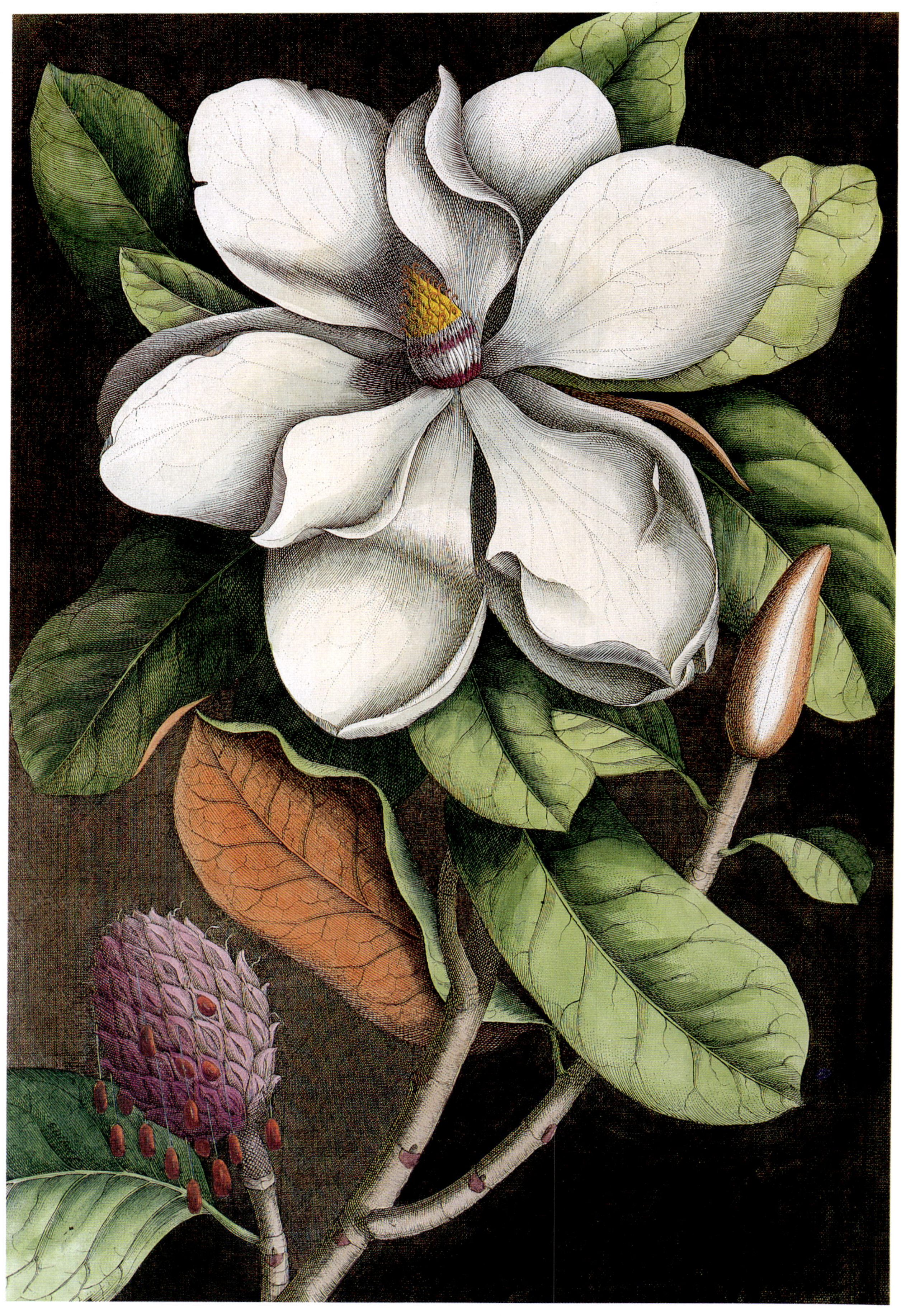

THE LAUREL TREE OF CAROLINA. MARK CATESBY, *THE NATURAL HISTORY OF CAROLINA, FLORIDA, AND THE BAHAMA ISLANDS,* VOL. 2, PLATE 61. HAND-COLORED ETCHING AFTER A DRAWING BY GEORGE EHRET, LONDON, 1731-1743.

NATIVE GRACE

Prints of the New World

1590-1876

BY W. GRAHAM ARADER III INTRODUCTION BY WENDY SHADWELL

THOMASSON-GRANT
CHARLOTTESVILLE, VIRGINIA

Published by Thomasson-Grant, Inc.:
Frank L. Thomasson III and John F. Grant, Directors;
C. Douglas Elliott, Vice-President, Product Development;
Megan R. Youngquist, Art Director;
Carolyn M. Clark, Senior Editor;
Jim Gibson, Production Manager.
Designed by Melissa W. Livingston
Edited by Owen Andrews
Text by Mary Boxley Bullington
Introduction by Wendy Shadwell
Curatorial Consultants: Tom McLaughlin, Roberta Tygart

Library of Congress Catalog Card Number: 88-40128
ISBN 0-934738-47-5
Color separations by Pioneer Graphic through CGI (Malaysia) Sdn. Bhd.
Printed and bound in Japan by Dai Nippon Printing Co. Ltd.
95 94 93 92 91 90 89 88 5 4 3 2 1

Any inquiries should be directed to Thomasson-Grant, Inc.,
One Morton Drive, Suite 500, Charlottesville, Virginia 22901,
telephone (804) 977-1780.

Library of Congress Cataloging-in-Publication Data
Arader, W. Graham, 1950-
Native grace.
1. North America in art—Catalogs. 2. Prints—Catalogs. 3. Arader, W. Graham, 1950- —Art collections—Catalogs. 4. Prints—Private collections—United States—Catalogs. 5. Printmakers—Biography.
I. Title.
NE962.N67A74 1988 769'.49973 88-40128
ISBN 0-934738-47-5

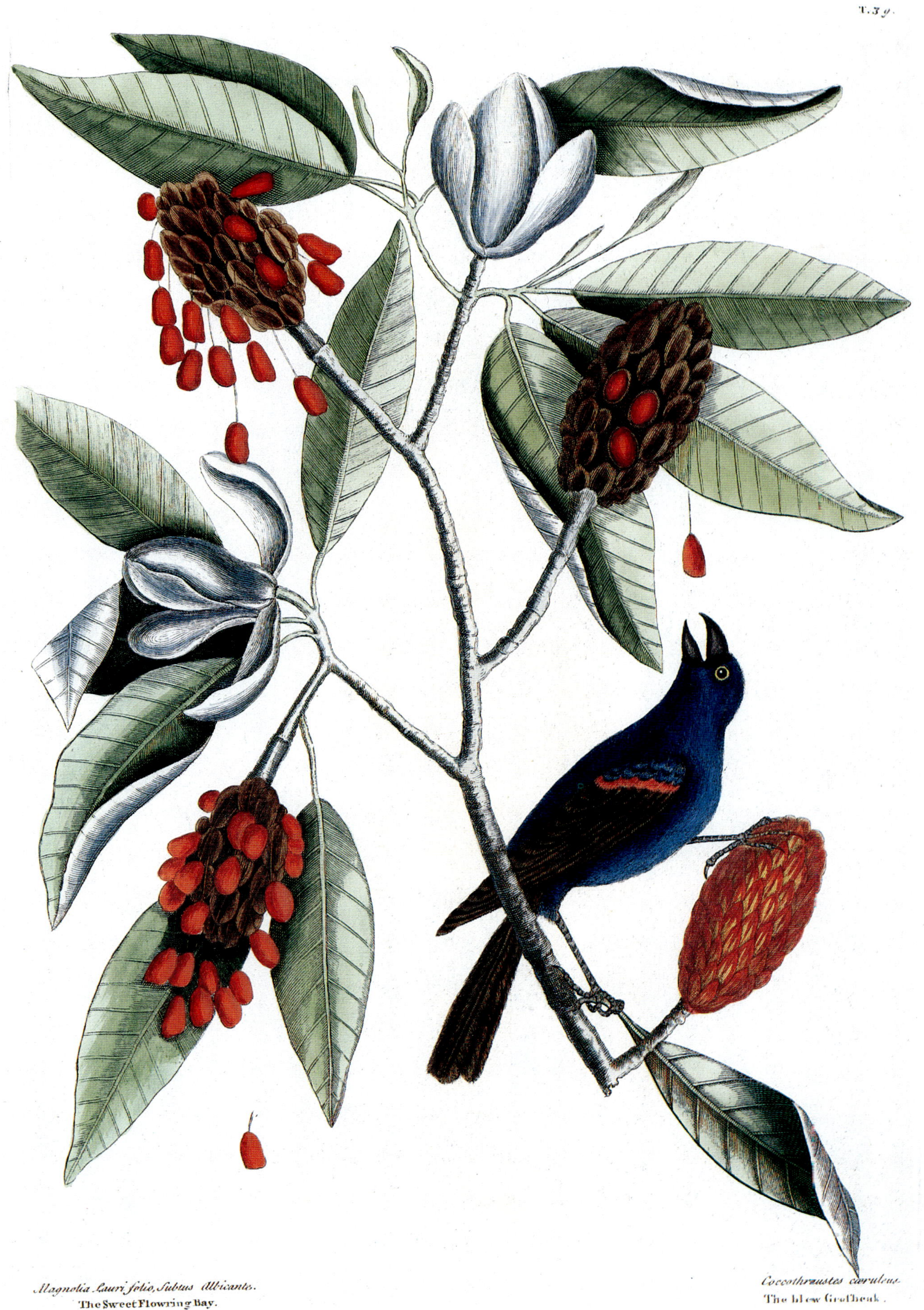

THE BLUE GROSBEAK. THE SWEET FLOWERING BAY. MARK CATESBY, *THE NATURAL HISTORY OF CAROLINA, FLORIDA, AND THE BAHAMA ISLANDS,* VOL. 1, PLATE 39. HAND-COLORED ETCHING, LONDON, 1727-1731.

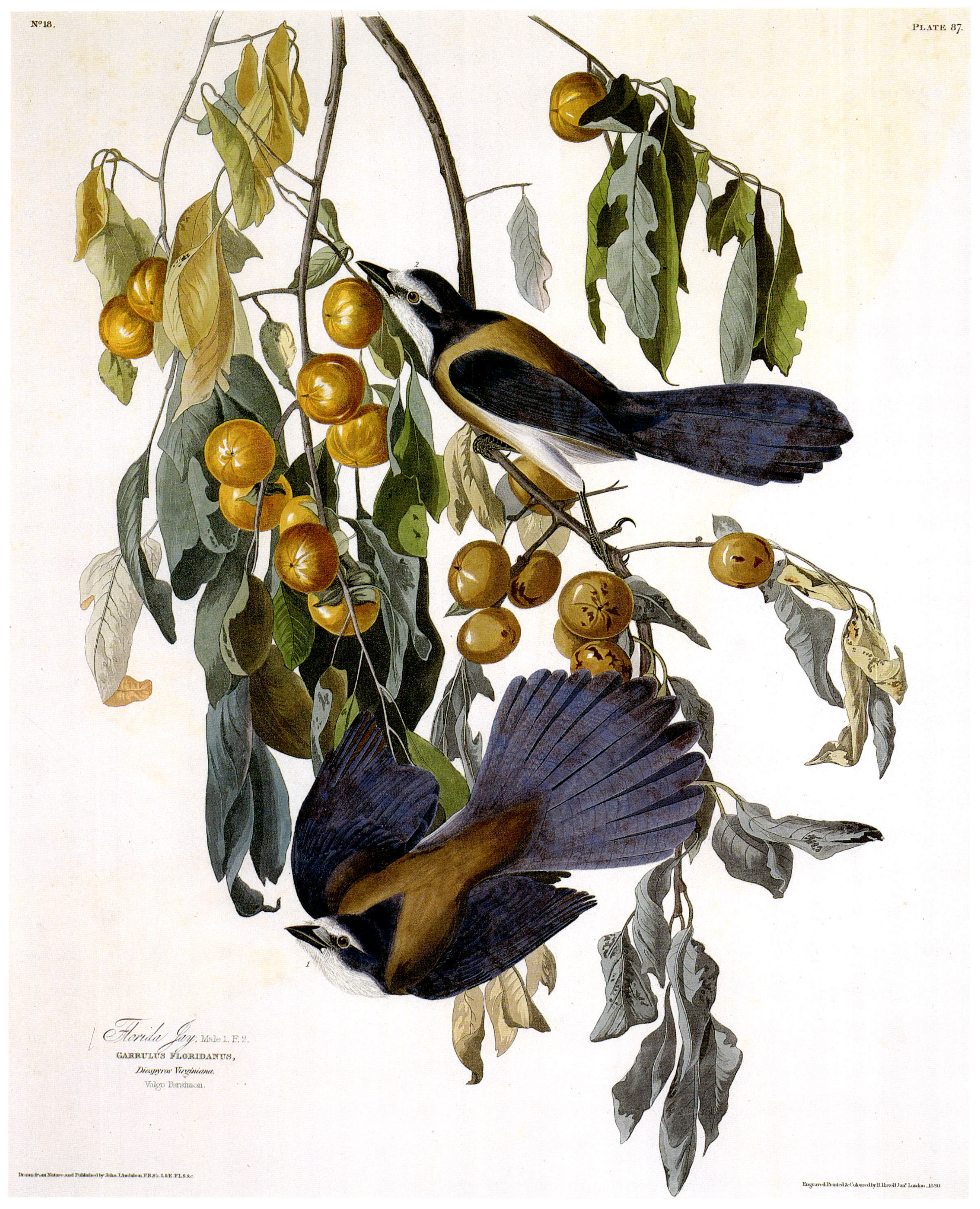

FLORIDA JAY. JOHN JAMES AUDUBON, *THE BIRDS OF AMERICA,* VOL. 1, PLATE 87. HAND-COLORED ETCHING AND AQUATINT, ROBERT HAVELL, LONDON, 1827-1830.

TABLE OF CONTENTS

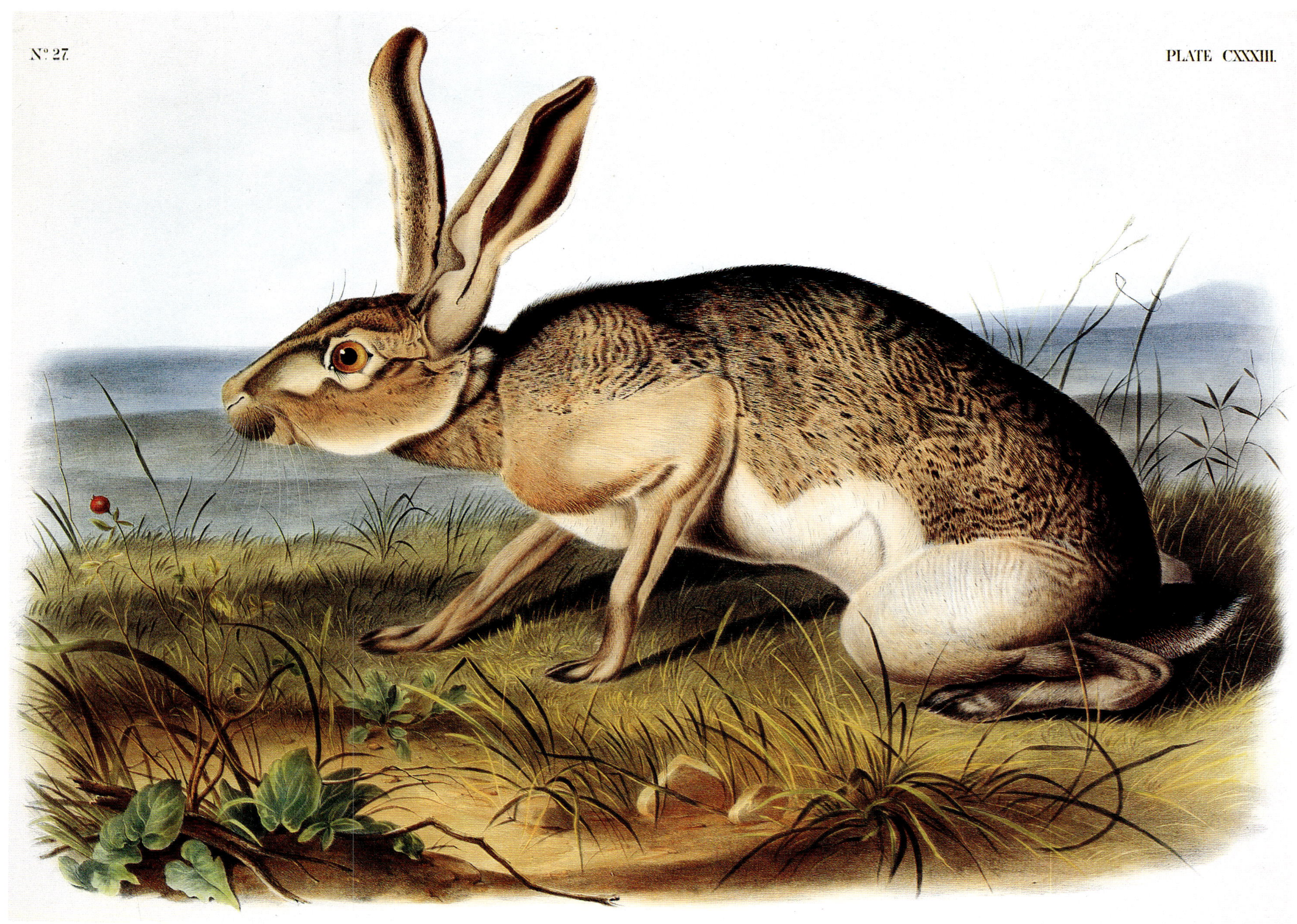

TEXIAN HARE. JOHN JAMES AUDUBON, *THE VIVIPAROUS QUADRUPEDS OF NORTH AMERICA,* VOL. 3, PLATE 133. HAND-COLORED LITHOGRAPH AFTER A PAINTING BY JOHN WOODHOUSE AUDUBON, JOHN T. BOWEN, PHILADELPHIA, 1848.

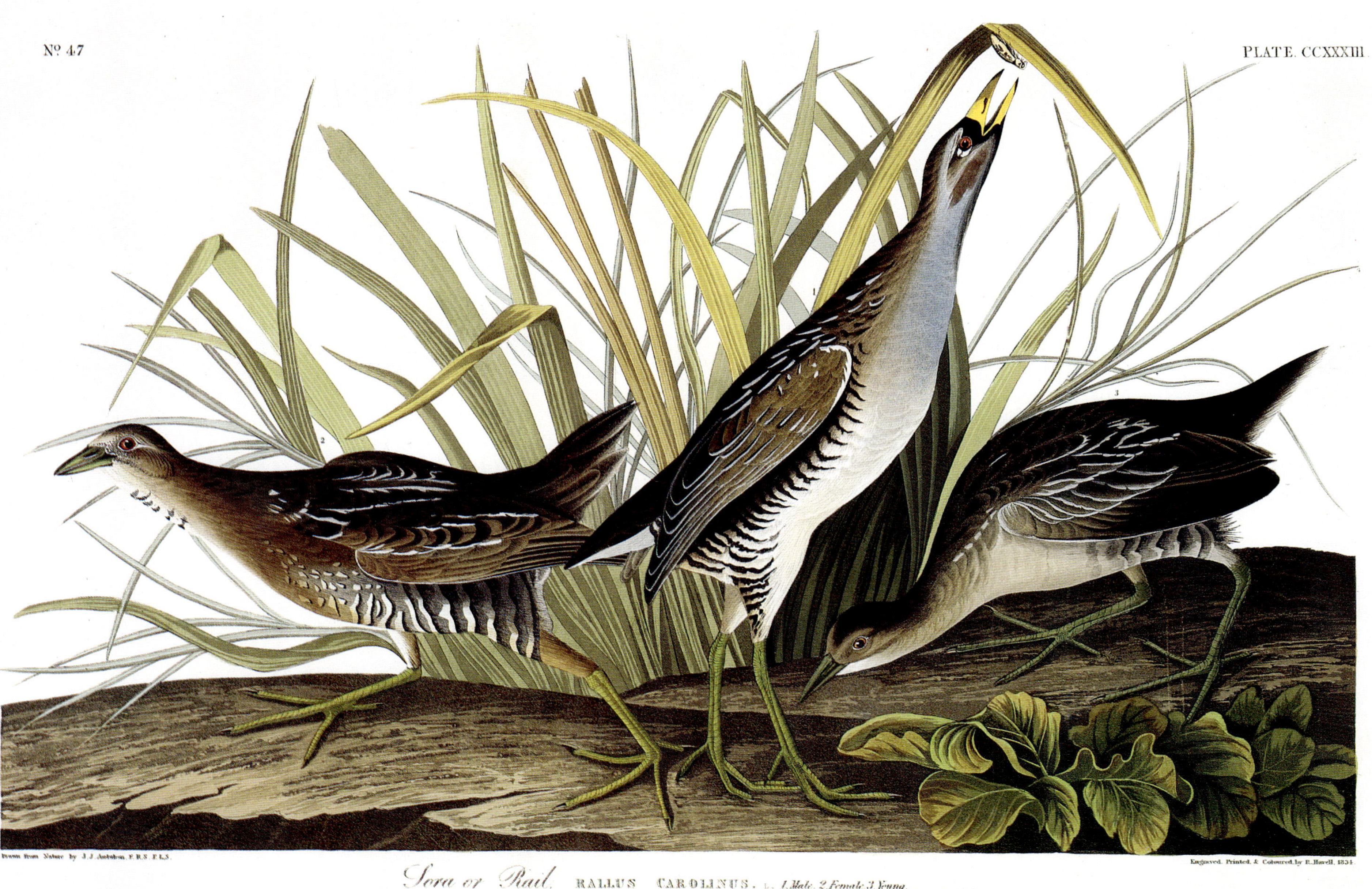

SORA OR RAIL. JOHN JAMES AUDUBON, *THE BIRDS OF AMERICA,* VOL. 3, PLATE 233. HAND-COLORED ETCHING AND AQUATINT, ROBERT HAVELL, LONDON, 1834-1836.

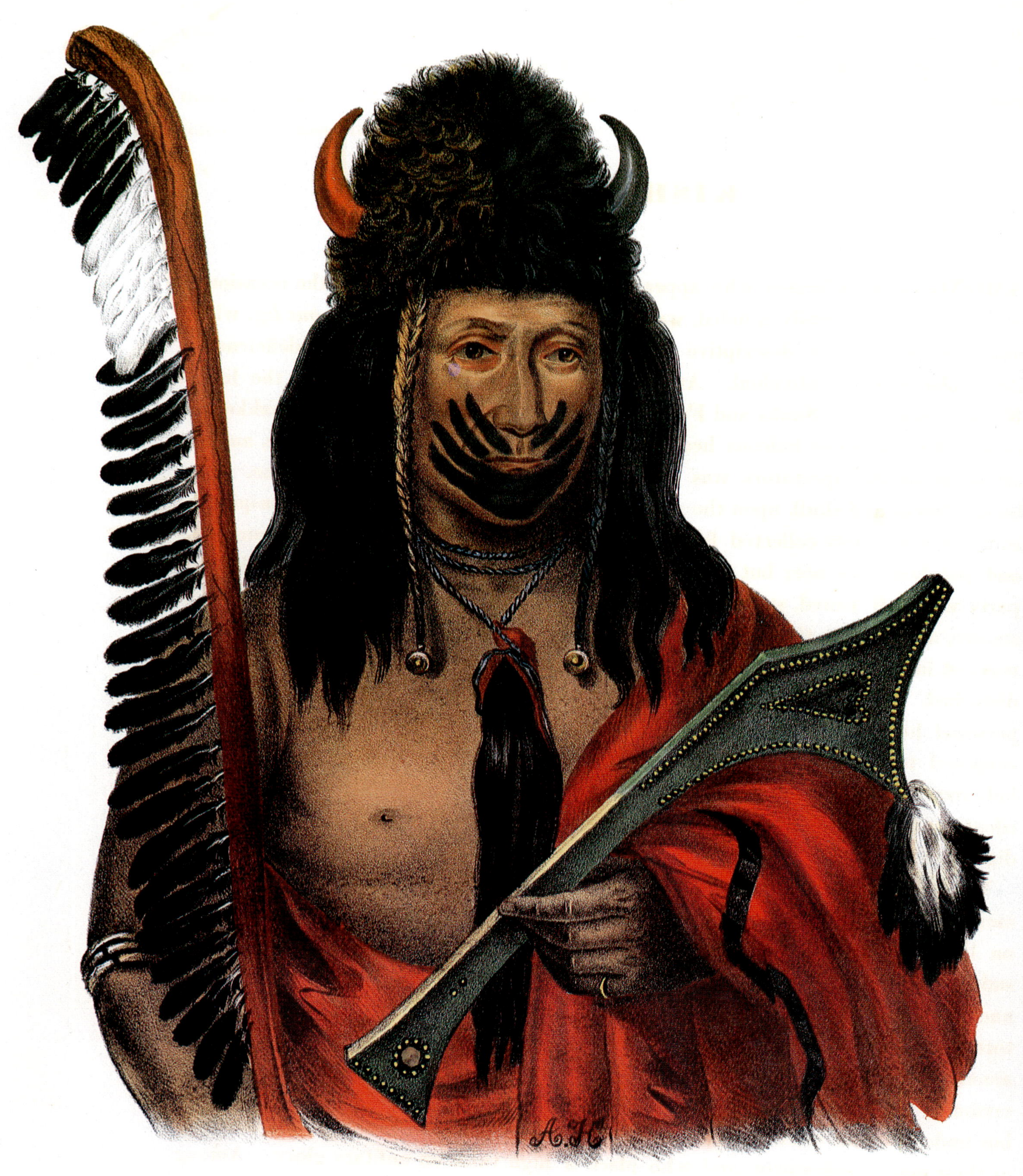

KISH-KE-KOSH, A FOX BRAVE. THOMAS McKENNEY AND JAMES HALL, *THE HISTORY OF THE INDIAN TRIBES OF NORTH AMERICA,* VOL. 2. HAND-COLORED LITHOGRAPH AFTER A PAINTING BY GEORGE COOKE, JOHN T. BOWEN, PHILADELPHIA, 1838-1842.

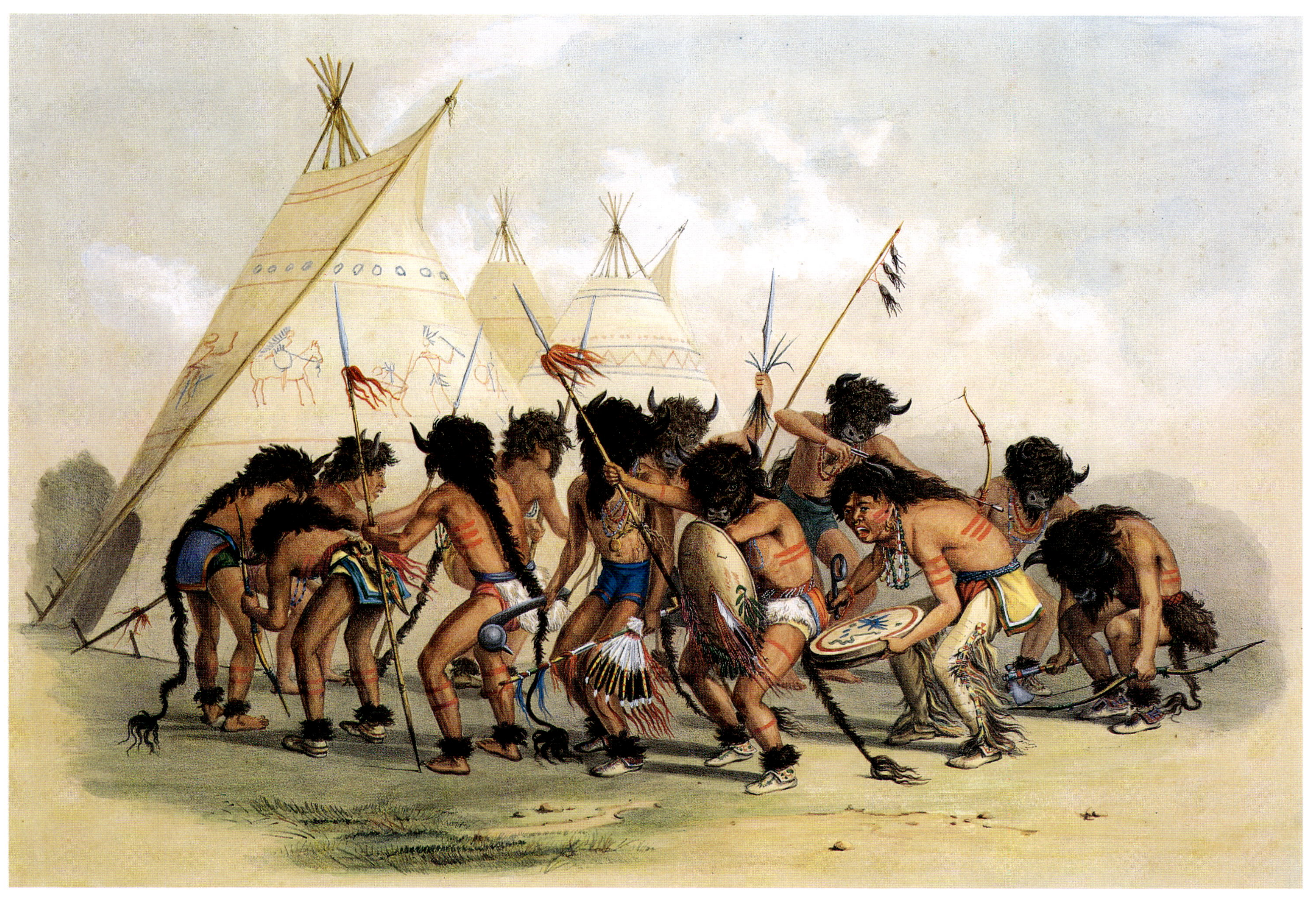

BUFFALO DANCE. GEORGE CATLIN, *NORTH AMERICAN INDIAN PORTFOLIO,* NO. 8. HAND-COLORED LITHOGRAPH, DAY & HAGHE, LONDON, 1844.

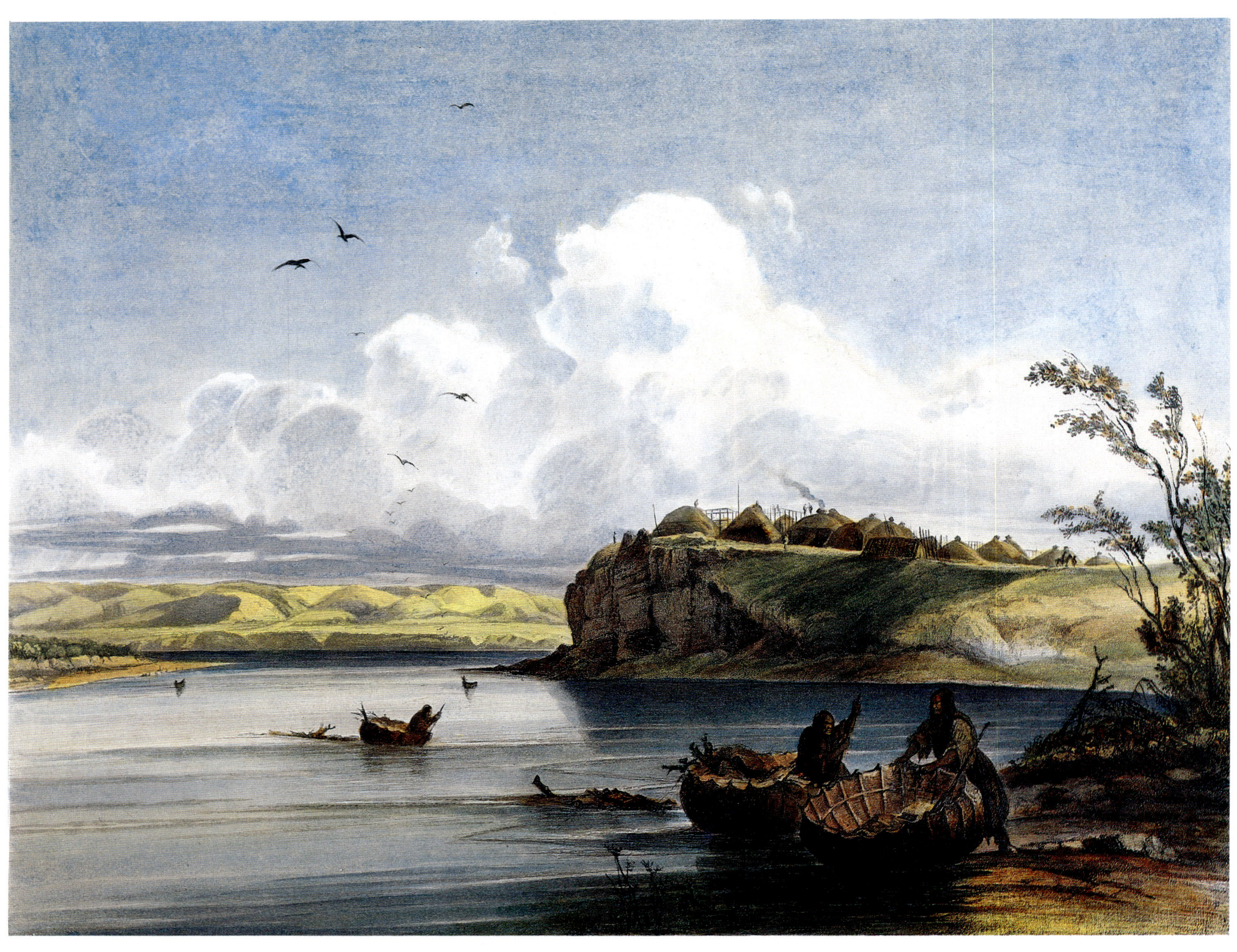

MIH-TUTTA-HANGKUSCH. A MANDAN VILLAGE. KARL BODMER, *ATLAS* TO *TRAVELS IN THE INTERIOR OF NORTH AMERICA,* BY PRINCE MAXIMILIAN OF WIED, PLATE 16. HAND-COLORED AQUATINT, BOUGEARD, PARIS, 1836-1842.

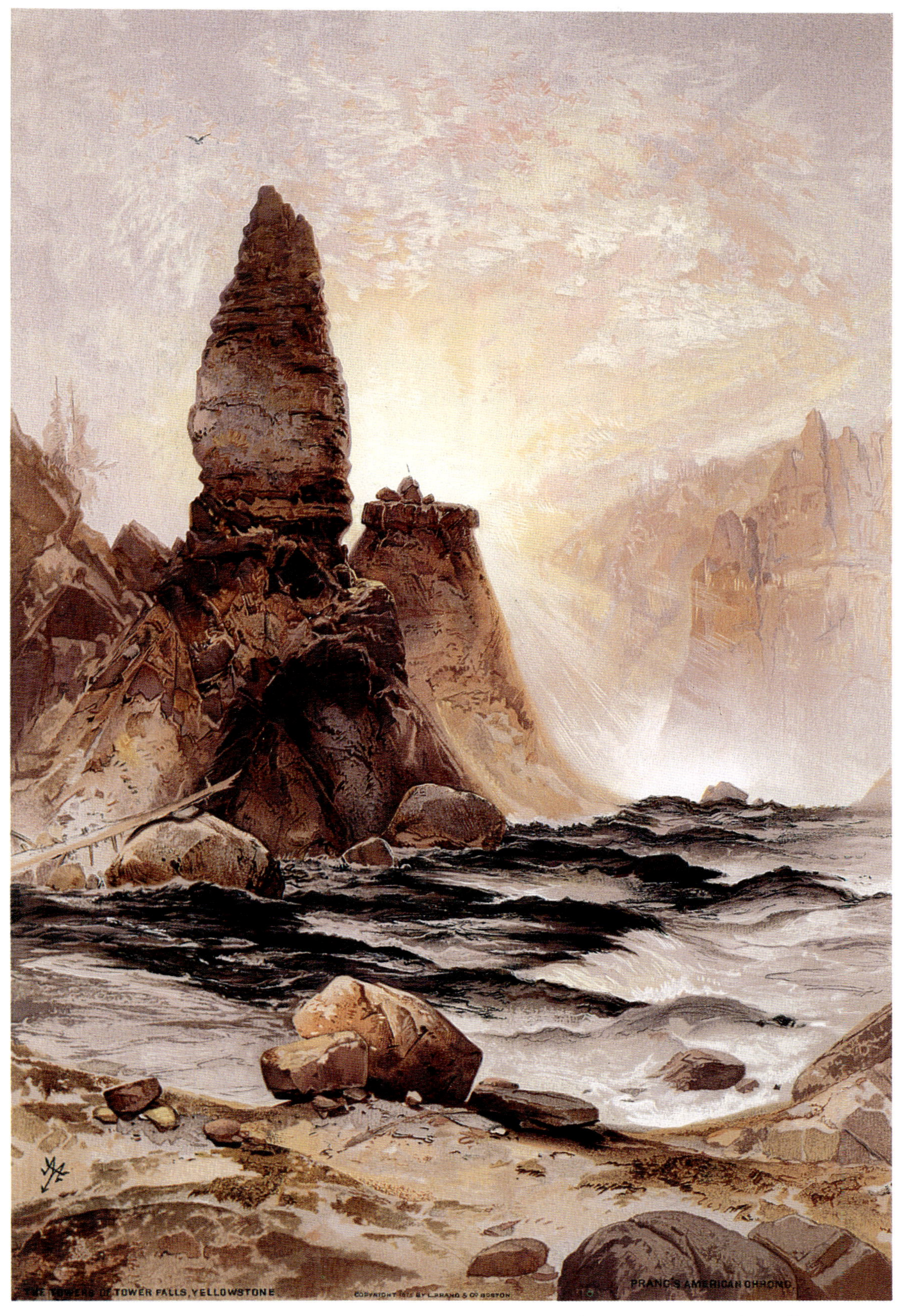

THE TOWERS OF TOWER FALLS, YELLOWSTONE. FERDINAND V. HAYDEN, *THE YELLOWSTONE NATIONAL PARK.* CHROMOLITHOGRAPH AFTER A PAINTING BY THOMAS MORAN, LOUIS PRANG, BOSTON, 1876.

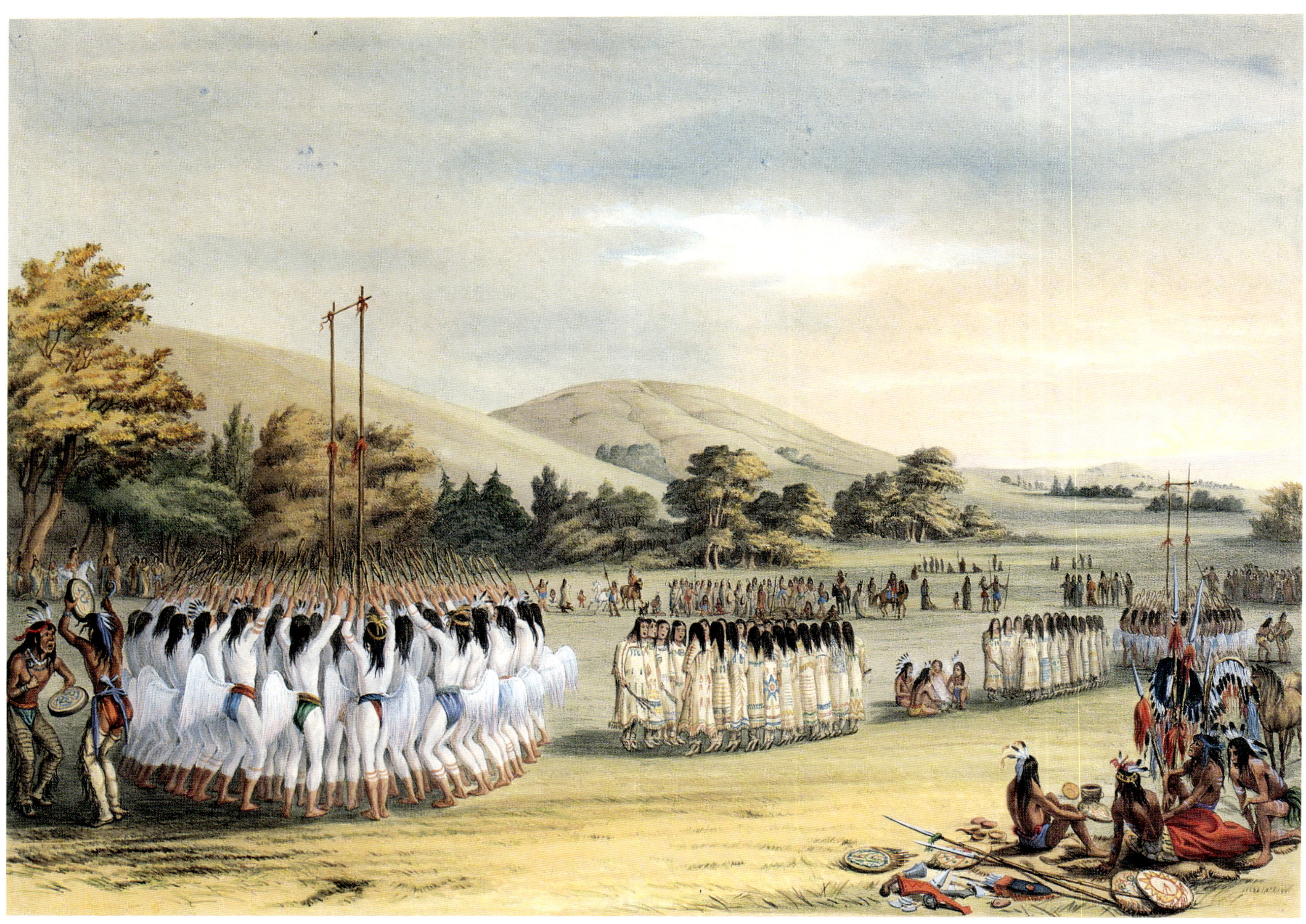

BALL-PLAY DANCE. GEORGE CATLIN, *NORTH AMERICAN INDIAN PORTFOLIO,* NO. 22. HAND-COLORED LITHOGRAPH, DAY & HAGHE, LONDON, 1844.

INTRODUCTION

As the frontier of the New World advanced from the Atlantic coast to the Rocky Mountains over the course of three centuries, the explorers who pushed westward encountered peoples, animals, plants, and landscapes no European had ever seen before. Conscious of their role as pioneers, many recorded the wonders they saw in journals, sketches, and paintings, so that people in Europe, and later on America's settled east coast, could experience something of the frontier's abundance and strangeness. To spread these fascinating images more widely, a further step was often taken, the reproduction of explorers' artwork in prints, beautifully engraved and bound in books.

The seven publications represented in this book contain some of the finest and most appealing of these prints. Brought together here, they reflect both the history of printmaking and the history of the exploration of America. The artists and engravers who depicted American subjects brought a variety of purposes to their work, purposes which reflected changing ideas about the New World. In the 16th century, intending to encourage colonization, some expeditions came equipped with a staff artist such as the Frenchman Jacques Le Moyne at Fort Caroline in Florida and the Englishman John White at Roanoke Island in North Carolina. Despite the failure of both colonies, Theodor de Bry's engravings of White's and Le Moyne's watercolors, published in 1590 and 1591, convey an impression of a land of plenty, inhabited by dignified, genial, tractable savages.

With the settlement of the easternmost part of the continent came naturalists such as Mark Catesby, Alexander Wilson, and John James Audubon, who were determined to discover, record, and make prints of North American plants and animals—especially birds. The variety of birds in America and the brilliance of their plumage delighted 18th- and 19th-century naturalists. Where earlier explorers described the flora and fauna of the new continent in terms of their value as resources for subsistence or profit, these men took a more purely scientific interest in the character and habits of the land's nonhuman life.

Early in the 19th century, some Americans and Europeans realized that North American Indians were threatened with extinction. Moved by their plight, George Catlin, Thomas McKenney, and Prince Maximilian of Wied sought to record Indian ways in detailed, engaging narratives and illustrations.

By the late 19th century, people began to feel the impulse to preserve the landscape's original character as well. After the Civil War, explorers reached the most inaccessible spots in the country where, overwhelmed by natural wonders like Yellowstone, they resolved to protect them always. Thanks to the prints made from Thomas Moran's watercolors, and to his contemporary Albert Bierstadt's oil paintings, the American public became aware of that unique, pristine environment, and the first ripples of conservationism started edging from shore to shore.

The term *print*, as it is used today, refers to a wide range of methods for making multiple copies of an image, from serigraphic or screen printing to photographic reproduction from negatives. The prints gathered in this book can be more narrowly defined. All were originally impressed on paper with a copper plate or lithographic stone. Shown together, they permit an informal survey of printing technology from the 16th to the 19th century.

We begin with Theodor de Bry's scenes of Virginia and Florida. Like most late 16th-century European prints, they are line engravings, a form of intaglio printing, in which the lines to be reproduced are cut below the main surface of the plate. To make a line engraving, the engraver incises the lines of a design into a soft copper plate with a pointed instrument called a burin. The printer inks the plate, wipes the surface clean, lays a piece of dampened paper on it, and runs plate and paper through a press. Pressure forces the paper down into the crevices where it picks up ink and forms the image.

In the 1730s, Mark Catesby used etching, an intaglio technique developed in the early 16th century, to make prints of his watercolors of the flora and fauna of the southern Atlantic coast of North America. To etch, the artist coats a plate with a hard wax ground, then draws designs in the coating with a needle or an échoppe, a steel cylinder with one end cut at an angle. Because the coating is softer than copper, the etcher can work more spontaneously than an engraver working directly on a copper plate. When the plate is subjected to acid, the acid eats into the metal wherever the protective wax has been scratched away, and cuts lines which will hold ink. The plate can then be printed like a line engraving. To reduce the cost of his project, Catesby taught himself how to etch.

Copper engraving and etching still prevailed when Robert Havell engraved the watercolors of Audubon's *Birds* in London between 1827 and 1838, after taking over the project from William Home Lizars of Edinburgh. Havell combined both methods with aquatint, a technique developed in the 18th century which provides black-and-white tone. For an aquatint, the engraver first dusts the surface of the copper plate with rosin powder and heats the plate to fix the coating. The plate then receives an acid bath. As the acid bites into the metal around the specks of partially melted rosin, it creates a pitted surface which will print a distinctive grainy pattern. The longer the acid stays on the plate, the deeper the pitting becomes and the darker the grain will be. If the engraver wants certain areas to remain unmarked, he coats these with an acid-resistant varnish before using the etching acid. Successive acid baths bring about the desired gradations from black to white. Although Audubon frequently criticized the hand coloring of *Birds*, he was satisfied enough with Havell's engraving to write: "I am perfectly confident that the birds were ever so beautifully and softly represented on copper."

By the mid-1800s, the practice of combining several techniques to achieve special effects had become increasingly common. Karl Bodmer's illustrations of western American scenery and Indians, engraved in Paris, used aquatint and etching, a frequent pairing. With all intaglio techniques, some prints were left just as they came from the press, images in black ink on white paper. Others were hand colored and therefore fetched a higher price. Audubon's *Birds* and Bodmer's western scenes are outstanding examples of the beauty of hand-colored intaglio printing at the peak of its development. After 1840, as cheaper and quicker lithographic techniques were perfected, intaglio printing gradually lost its popularity.

Lithography, in which prints are made from a stone "support" rather than a metal plate, derives its name from *lithos*, the Greek word for stone. An unsuccessful Bavarian actor and playwright, Alois Senefelder, invented the technique in 1798 while experimenting with different ways to print his plays cheaply. His method is based on the fact that oil and water repel each other. To make a lithograph, the printer first draws with a greasy crayon on a slab of porous stone such as limestone. The stone absorbs some of the grease; the printer washes off the rest and immerses the stone in water. Wherever the stone has not absorbed crayon grease, it absorbs water. To print, the artisan rolls the ink, an oily, greasy compound, across the support's surface. The ink adheres to the greasy image, but not to the moist, unmarked stone. When the stone and a piece of paper go through a press, ink transfers from the greasy areas to the paper.

Unlike intaglio plates, which transfer ink to paper from lines and patterns cut into the plate's surface, lithographic stones print from a smooth surface. Hence lithography, the forerunner of all modern printing techniques, is called a *planographic* process, from the Latin *planus*, meaning flat or smooth. Because a lithographer can capture both line and tone, the technique is better suited than engraving to reproducing oil and watercolor paintings. Its quickness, simplicity, and cheapness also helped it to replace the older technique.

The plates for McKenney and Hall's *The History of the Indian Tribes of North America* were made and hand colored in Philadelphia by a series of lithographers and colorists, including John T. Bowen. Audubon saw these prints, and hired Bowen in 1840 to lithograph a smaller, less costly octavo edition of *The Birds of America*. Bowen also lithographed Audubon's *The Viviparous Quadrupeds of North America* a few years later. Day & Haghe of London lithographed and hand colored Catlin's much shorter work, *The North American Indian Portfolio*, and following Day & Haghe's prints, the New York lithographer James Ackerman prepared an American edition the next year.

In the first half of the 19th century, an assembly line method was often used to color prints. Following a model supplied by the artist, each watercolorist applied a single color freehand and passed the print on to the next worker. John T. Bowen's firm is reported to have had up to 25 colorists working at once, many of them women. Gradually, however, less laborious methods were developed for coloring prints. Chromolithography, the most successful of these, used several stones, each inked with a different color, to print a composite image. Thomas Moran's spectacular views of the Rocky Mountains, printed in 1876, show the method at its best, and are the only prints reproduced in this book from originals colored on the press, not by hand.

Moran's printer, Louis Prang of Boston, led the development of this technique, widely used in the second half of the 19th century both for reproducing works of art and for commercial purposes. Skillfully translated into chromolithographs, paintings such as William Harnett's "The Old Violin" and Winslow Homer's "The North Woods" graced parlors nationwide, giving the populace the opportunity to enjoy art in their homes. Advertisers as diverse as P.T. Barnum's Greatest Show on Earth and Old Valley Forge Fire Copper Whiskey distributed chromolithographed posters and trade cards. In addition, greeting cards, billheads, certificates, rewards of merit, religious and sentimental mementoes, and calendars poured from chromolithographic presses in ever-increasing quantities.

The relationship of a finished print to the original work falls anywhere between two extremes. At one extreme, the print *is* the original work; the artist creates the image on the plate, achieving expression directly through printing techniques. At the other, an engraver meets the demand of art lovers by replicating some masterpiece in print form as faithfully as the medium will permit.

The prints reproduced here follow the originals upon which they are based, but not painstakingly. In some cases, the originals were not intended to be reproduced as prints. The engraver worked independently, shaping and changing the material to improve its artistic qualities and enhance its appeal. In others, the artist had publication in mind from the start, and made plates for the prints himself, or worked closely with the printer to modify weak, improbable, or shocking images.

Furthermore, while the original watercolors and drawings from which these prints derived are often masterful images in their own right—the watercolors of Audubon and Bodmer are notable examples—in most cases, the originals were not created specifically to be regarded as final versions. The artist-explorers who traveled through the New World rarely had leisure to perfect their illustrations on the spot. They worked under the stress of enemy attacks, illness, bitter weather, and short provisions. Observing how these images evolved into finished prints, we gain insight into the unique nature of the collaboration between an artist and a printer.

Many of John White's watercolors, based on his stay at Roanoke Island in 1585, survive today at the British Museum. When we compare them to their published versions engraved by Theodor de Bry, de Bry's tendency to idealize Indian faces and postures becomes clear. The purpose of de Bry's publication, after all, was to encourage the settlement and economic development of potentially lucrative colonies. Too vivid a depiction of savage and possibly threatening natives could have been counterproductive. The tendency to adapt images of America to suit European notions was not confined to the 16th century; European printmakers were still softening and classicizing American landscapes as late as 1828.

While we cannot say for certain that White expected his drawings to be made into prints, Catesby, like Audubon, Bodmer, and Moran after him, went to the wilderness to gather sketches for later published works. In the preface to *The Natural History of Carolina, Florida, and the Bahama Islands*, Catesby expressed his desire for realistic depictions, explaining how he colored his prints by hand with watercolors and gouaches that would both be durable and resemble the tints of nature. Aware of his artistic idiosyncrasies, he wrote: "As I was not bred a Painter, I hope some faults in Perspective, and other niceties, may be more readily excused."

In fact, Catesby achieved considerable success in drawing his subjects to scale, and in pairing mammals, birds, snakes, and insects with the plants they frequented. In the few cases where he has made improbable pairings of flora and fauna, his purpose may have been to reduce the total number of plates. When he defies the laws of perspective, as in his depiction of a bison and a bristly locust tree (see page 33), he may be indulging a playful logic that permits him to show his readers an unusually large animal without sacrificing a detailed view of a plant's flowers and leaves.

Audubon began painting watercolors of birds long before he thought of publishing them, and even after he decided on his ambitious project to portray every American bird, he spent several years traveling and painting in the United States before making arrangements with a publisher. Unable to find one in Philadelphia, he went to Great Britain, where he also raised funds for publication. During the ten years it took to make the engravings, he traveled unceasingly, crisscrossing eastern North America in search of additional species, overseeing the engraving in London, and seeking subscribers in the United States, Great Britain, and France.

All of the known Audubon watercolors for *The Birds of America* are at the New-York Historical Society. Audubon certainly strove for accuracy in his images. Because he wanted to represent the birds life-size, he insisted on "double elephant" folio paper, over two feet wide and three feet long. Audubon did not, however, insist on doing all of the preliminary work himself. Some of the backgrounds in the watercolors were supplied by other artists working with Audubon. Some were added by the engraver Havell, who generally served Audubon well.

George Catlin did not intend to publish his paintings of western American Indians. He hoped that Congress would purchase his gallery and Indian artifacts as a monument to a vanishing race and way of life. Disappointed when Congress refused, he took the collection to London where its exhibition initially caused a sensation. After its popularity faded, Catlin sought to recapture public attention with a publication, and engaged a superior London lithographic firm, Day & Haghe, to produce *The North American Indian Portfolio*, some 14 years after his first trip west to paint.

The western paintings he turned over to Day & Haghe are now at the Smithsonian Institution's National Museum of American Art. They reveal his often uncertain draftsmanship, which the lithographers worked wonders to overcome. Vague outlines of men, horses, and buffaloes became convincing bodies with volume and the appearance of motion, and details of the landscape were enhanced and refined. Catlin evidently approved of these transformations; he gave the English lithographs, not his original paintings, to James Ackerman as models for the 1845 American edition.

Karl Bodmer, the Swiss artist hired by Prince Maximilian of Wied for his 1833 expedition to study the Plains Indians, involved himself as closely with the engraving and printing of his work as Audubon or Catesby, supervising the engravers and colorists from a Paris studio as they produced the 81 aquatints with etching that illustrated Prince Maximilian's *Travels in the Interior of North America*. The originals, acquired by the Joslyn Art Museum of Omaha in 1962 after over a century in the Wied family archives in Coblenz, make it possible to study the sources of each print. We find, for example, that the striking and fearsome "Pehriska-Ruhpa, Moennitarri Warrior in the Costume of the Dog Danse," showing the warrior full-length in a threatening crouch with a scowl on his face (see page 106), differs sharply from the watercolor portrait, where his expression and posture are calmer. Other changes in this image are more perplexing. The costume has been redrawn to correspond exactly with the prince's description of the Dog Dance costume of the Mandans, a different tribe. We can only speculate about why Bodmer made this alteration and why the prince approved of it.

After the success of Thomas Moran's first paintings of the Yellowstone, publisher Louis Prang expressly commissioned views of western scenery from the landscape painter so that his firm could chromolithograph them. Moran was in a superb position to produce watercolors that could be translated into chromolithographs; as a youth, he received training in wood engraving, etching, and lithography before beginning his career as a painter in oils and watercolors. His initial sketches for *The Yellowstone National Park* have been compared to a chromolithographer's key plate, a diagram that could be analyzed for the composition of its colors, separated into individual color patterns, transferred to the multiple chromolithographic plates required for each print, and reassembled in print form on the presses. How well Moran succeeded is indicated by the fact that the English art critic John Ruskin, who had hitherto spoken of chromolithographs only to disparage them, purchased a set of the Moran prints.

Originally, the prints presented here were intended to be enjoyed in book form, usually in conjunction with a narrative. De Bry's, Catesby's, and McKenney and Hall's images illustrate text on adjacent pages. Thomas Moran's western chromolithographs were bound with F.V. Hayden's *The Yellowstone National Park*. Audubon's *Birds of America* accompanied *Ornithological Biography* and Bodmer's *Atlas* supplemented Prince Maximilian's *Travels in the Interior of North America*, but the prints were issued separately from the text. Catlin published *The North American Indian Portfolio* independently of his *Letters and Notes on the North American Indians*.

Many of the publishing projects, especially the more ambitious ones, were issued in parts. Audubon's *Birds* appeared five plates at a time; McKenney and Hall's *The Indian Tribes of North America*, six plates at a time, with biographies of the Indians portrayed. Subscribers received portions sporadically: McKenney's project took eight years to be completed, Audubon's took ten, and Catesby's took twenty. It was the subscriber's responsibility to bind the prints into volumes.

Who, then, were these subscribers, rich enough to afford such lavish productions, and patient enough to wait decades for them? In some cases, their names have been recorded; in others, we can only speculate. The first edition of Hariot's *A briefe and true report*, published by Richard Hakluyt without illustrations, was meant to promote English settlement on the Carolina coast. Ironically, a supply expedition, returning to the embryo colony on Roanoke Island shortly after de Bry published the illustrated *report*, found it deserted. The work was popular nonetheless; its readers must have included not only those interested in colonizing the New World, but curious individuals who had no intention of leaving the comforts of home.

Prince Maximilian's 300,000-word narrative and Bodmer's 81 aquatints represent the most extensive published record of the American west as it looked when Indians flourished there. The prince sought to make his work widely available: it was issued first in German, then in French and English. In *Across the Wide Missouri*, Bernard De Voto, a noted American scholar, called the work "a permanent landmark in the study of America," and it doubtless found a place in many educational institutions, learned societies, and noble libraries across Europe and in this country.

We know a tremendous amount about the first owners of Audubon's *Birds of America*, thanks to records kept by the Audubon family and the industry of Dr. Waldemar Fries, the eminent Audubon scholar. Audubon enrolled 161 subscribers in his enormously expensive undertaking, and his sales were limited to the wealthiest patrons. One, the Prince of Massena, regretfully informed Audubon that he should not expect more than six or eight names in Paris. In the end, 79 Europeans appeared on Audubon's list, beginning with Queen Adelaide of Great Britain, running through many dukes and lords, and ending with Sir John Hastley. Audubon also found 82 subscribers in America, including the Boston Athenaeum, Columbia College, and Stephen Van Rensselaer of Albany.

Between 175 and 200 complete sets of *Birds* were printed. The exact number is hard to determine; because subscribers died or withdrew during the lengthy course of publication, fewer prints were required from the later plates. Today, 133 sets can be found in the United States, 52 more than originally subscribed for here. Sets once caged in European libraries have returned to the birds' homeland. The New-York Historical Society's *Birds of America*, for example, was originally in the library of the Duke of Newcastle.

George Tomko, Curator of the Roberson Center for the Arts and Sciences, has written that many prints which were once intended as adjuncts to narratives about the New World have now become the most significant part of the work. The language of the narratives seems charming and remote. Consider the conclusion of Hariot's description of the Englishmen's arrival in the New World: "Suche was our arrivall into the parte of the world, which we call Virginia, the stature of bodee of wich people, theyr attire, and maneer of lyvinge, their feasts, and banketts, I will particullerlye declare unto you." The images, however, make an immediate appeal, transcending the time that separates us from the southeastern Algonquians or from an Osage chief as they did the space that separated the audience for whom they were published from the splendors of Yellowstone or the mysteries of the Carolina shoreline. Through them, we encounter North America as it looked under the care of native Americans—a kind of Eden, untouched by the material demands of European culture.

Wendy Shadwell
Curator of Prints
New-York Historical Society

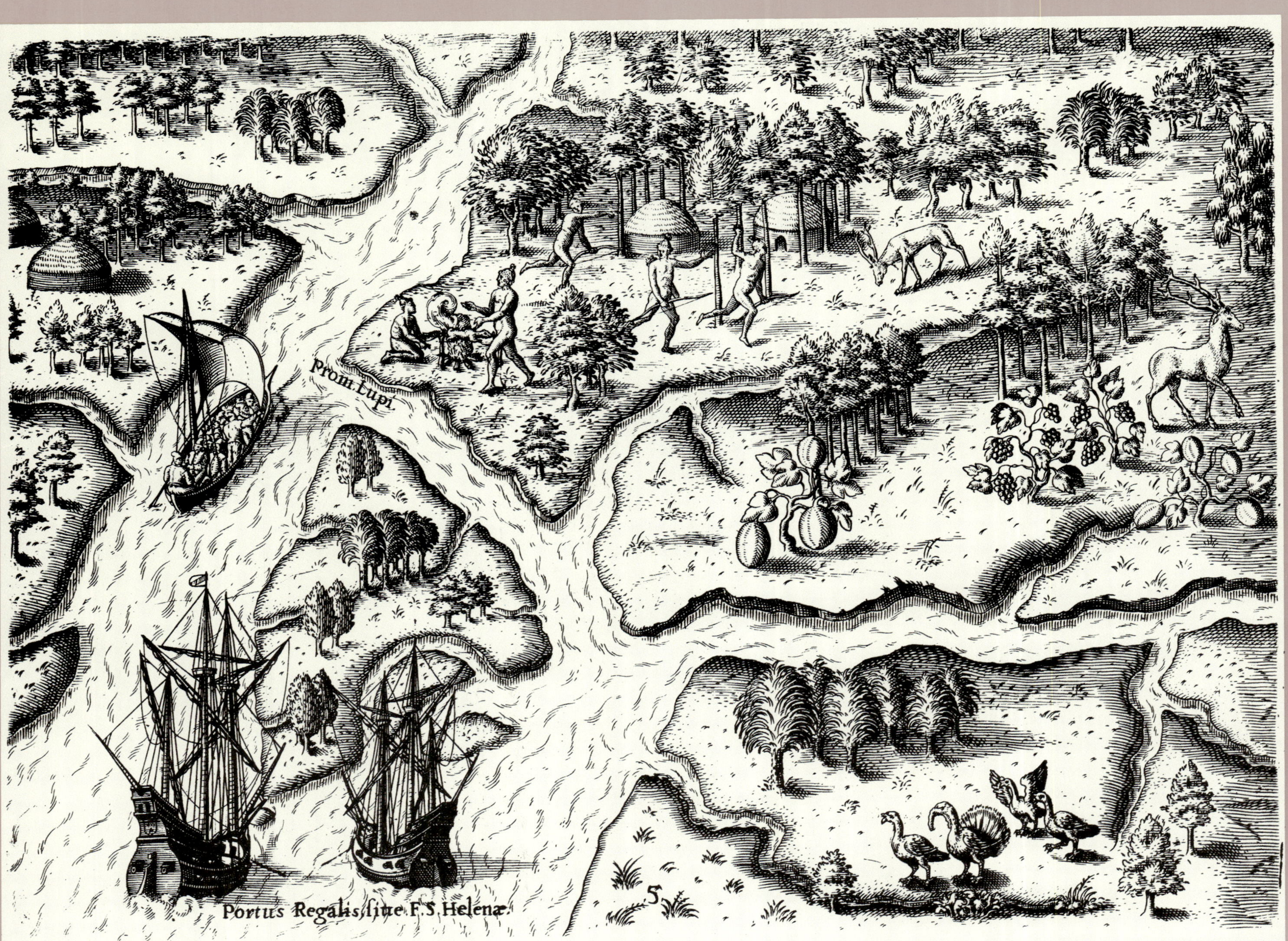
Prom. Lupi
Portus Regalis, ſiue F. S. Helenæ.
5

THEODOR DE BRY (1528-1598)

As the 16th century, the great age of European explorers, drew to a close, book printers met public curiosity about the voyagers' exploits with an outpouring of exotic narratives. The 14-volume series, *Grands et petits voyages*, begun by the Flemish engraver Theodor de Bry in 1590 and continued by his sons until 1634, was a distinguished achievement in this genre. The first two volumes included something altogether new: line engravings of America based on paintings and drawings by eyewitnesses.

Illustrators of previous narratives, relying on imagination, portrayed the new continents as an earthly paradise peopled by demons or Greek gods. De Bry, by contrast, based his engravings on the work of two colonists, survivors of failed English and French expeditions. Their depictions of the Algonquians of North Carolina and the Timucua of Florida show an attention to Indian culture that would go unmatched until the 19th century.

FRENCH ARRIVING AT PORT ROYAL. THEODOR DE BRY, *VOYAGES TO AMERICA,* VOL. 2, PLATE 5. ENGRAVING AFTER A DRAWING BY JACQUES LE MOYNE, FRANKFURT, 1591.

In 1562 and 1564, the French sought to establish footholds in Spanish La Florida—today's southeastern United States. Here Le Moyne reconstructs what the 1562 adventurers reported seeing as they sailed up Port Royal River near present-day Beaufort, South Carolina. Turkey, geese, squash, grapes, and deer represent the new land's abundance; in the background, Indians roast a young wolf.

Born in Liege to a wealthy family, the Protestant de Bry fled to Germany in 1570, when Flanders' Spanish Catholic rulers banned the new doctrine and confiscated the property of its adherents. De Bry settled in Frankfurt, working as a goldsmith, engraver, and publisher.

De Bry's personal history naturally predisposed him to be interested in accounts of Protestant settlement of the New World. Scholars suggest that in 1586 or 1587 he may have come across René Goulaine de Laudonnière's narrative of the French Huguenots' 1564 attempt to colonize Florida at a site across the St. Johns River from today's Jacksonville. Reading Laudonnière, de Bry could have learned that a colonist named Jacques Le Moyne de Morgues had painted a series of watercolors of Florida Indians. When the Spanish destroyed the colony in 1565, the artist was one of the few to escape.

In 1587, de Bry traveled to London, where Le Moyne had settled, and met Laudonnière's English translator, the geographer Richard Hakluyt, hard at work on his compendium, *The Principal Navigations...of the English Nation*. Hakluyt appears to have directed the engraver to Le Moyne, who was reluctant to sell his work, much of which had been produced from memory after his return to Europe.

A publisher and bookseller as well as an artist and engraver, Le Moyne may have planned to publish his paintings himself. In 1588, however, he died, and de Bry was able to buy the pictures and a narrative from his widow. De Bry published them in 1591 with Laudonnière's report as the second volume of his series.

Meanwhile, de Bry more quickly obtained and published the drawings of John White, cartographer, draftsman, and veteran of two colonizing expeditions sent by Sir Walter Raleigh to Roanoke Island in the 1580s. De Bry's first volume also featured *A Briefe and true report of the new found land of Virginia* by Thomas Hariot, a mathematician and scientist who worked with White to make a comprehensive record of the resources and native people encountered by the first expedition. Unfortunately, many of Hariot's notes and White's drawings and maps were lost when the colony was abandoned in July 1586. As the colonists were rowed out to the main vessels, the weather proved so "boysterous" that, to avoid sinking, the sailors threw much of the baggage overboard.

Raleigh sent a second expedition to Roanoke in 1587 and appointed White as its governor. White left the colony after a few months to bring more supplies from England, leaving behind his daughter and son-in-law, who had recently become the parents of Virginia Dare, the first English child born in America. Because White happened to reach England in the midst of preparations to fight the Spanish Armada, over two years passed before a ship could be spared for a journey to Roanoke. It was during this detainment that he met de Bry and sold him one of two sets of his watercolors and maps.

In 1590, the year de Bry published his volume on Virginia, the governor reached Roanoke only to find the colony abandoned and its inhabitants vanished—including his daughter and grandchild. No clues indicated what had happened to them. Beset by stormy weather, White's crew lost interest in the search after a ship's boat capsized, drowning a captain and six sailors. The fate of the Lost Colony remains a mystery.

When de Bry brought out Le Moyne's volume on Florida in 1591, he also printed a second edition of the volume on Virginia in French, Latin, and German. De Bry may have considered the Florida volume artistically finer than the Virginia one; he told his French readers that its copper engravings were "more numerous and more beautiful." At the same time, White's Algonquians seemed to have a finer nature; de Bry thought them "sweet and peaceful" in contrast to Le Moyne's "cunning, wicked, bellicose, vindictive" Timucua. Perhaps de Bry's opinions reflect the difference between Le Moyne's emotional, highly wrought manner and White's more restrained depictions.

De Bry's faithfulness to his originals preserves both the objective and stylized aspects of Le Moyne's and White's work. Le Moyne's portrayal of a deer hunt and White's depiction of the Secota village (see pages 1 and 26) realistically show the daily life of the Indians. Yet distinct classical overtones mark Le Moyne's picture of grieving widows requesting help from their king and White's portrait of "a great Lorde of Virginia" (see pages 23 and 24); the idealized figures of the chiefs lend them heroic stature, and their warpaint and tattoos assume the appearance of Roman armor.

De Bry incongruously closed *A Briefe and true report* with engravings of the Picts of Scotland, based on drawings by White and Le Moyne. His aim, he writes, was to show "how that the Inhabitants of the great Bretannie have bin in times past as savage as those of Virginia." He seems to have admired the Indians, for he comments in his envoi to the reader that although deprived of the true knowledge of God, the natives "still pass us in sober feeding and dexterity of wit, in making without any instrument of metal things so neat and so fine, as a man would scarcely believe the same, unless English had made proof thereof by their travels into the country." De Bry's copper engravings of the Indians, equally fine and neat, testify to the respect they inspired in him.

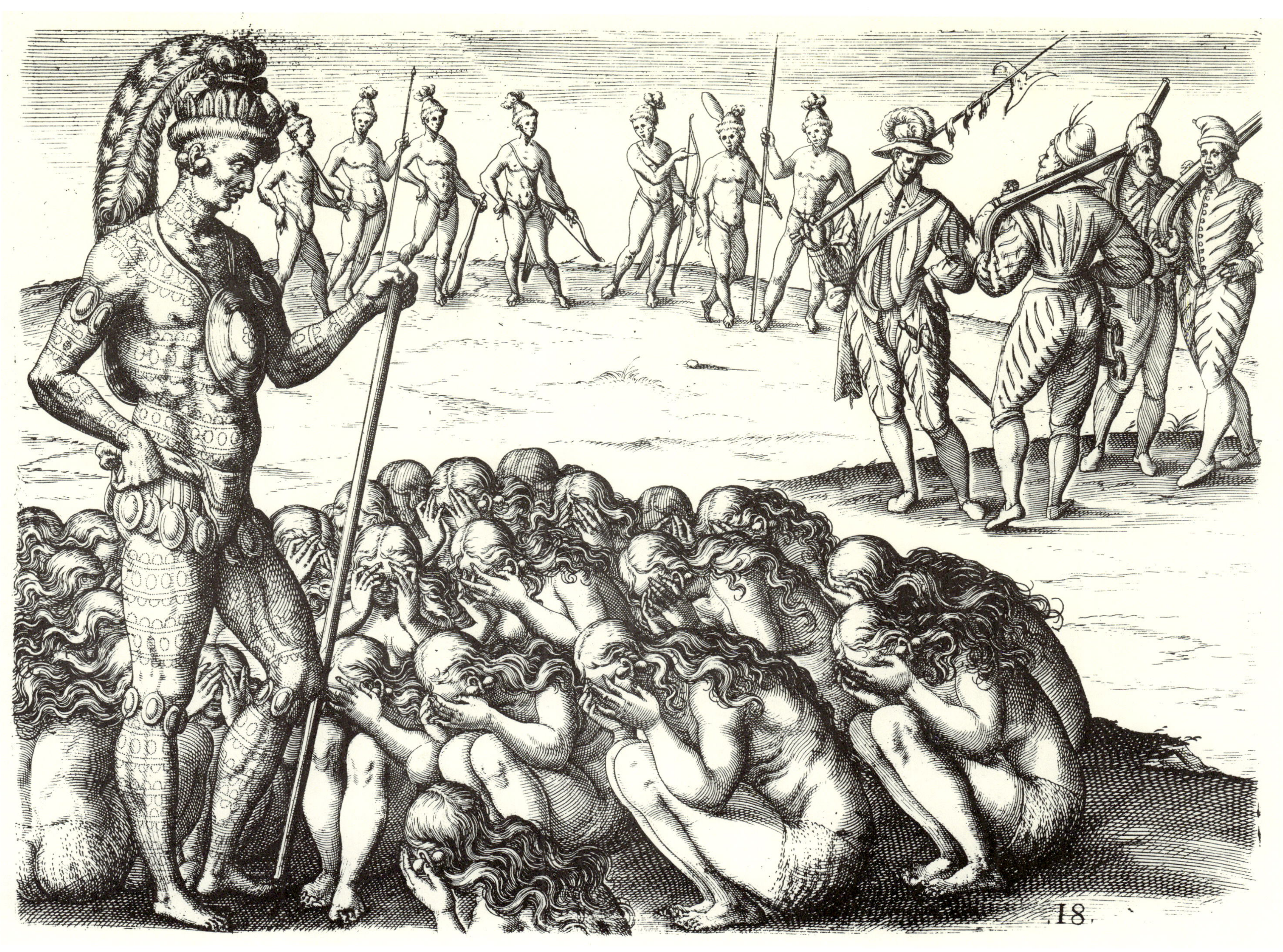

WIDOWS SUPPLICATING THEIR CHIEF. THEODOR DE BRY, *VOYAGES TO AMERICA,* VOL. 2, PLATE 18. ENGRAVING AFTER A DRAWING BY JACQUES LE MOYNE, FRANKFURT, 1591.

The second French expedition went to the St. Johns River in Florida. These Timucua widows seek revenge, shelter, and permission to marry again when their mourning period ends. Northern Renaissance artistic conventions mark Le Moyne and de Bry's work, evident here in the ordered foreground and background and stylized, repetitious treatment of the kneeling women's outlines and postures.

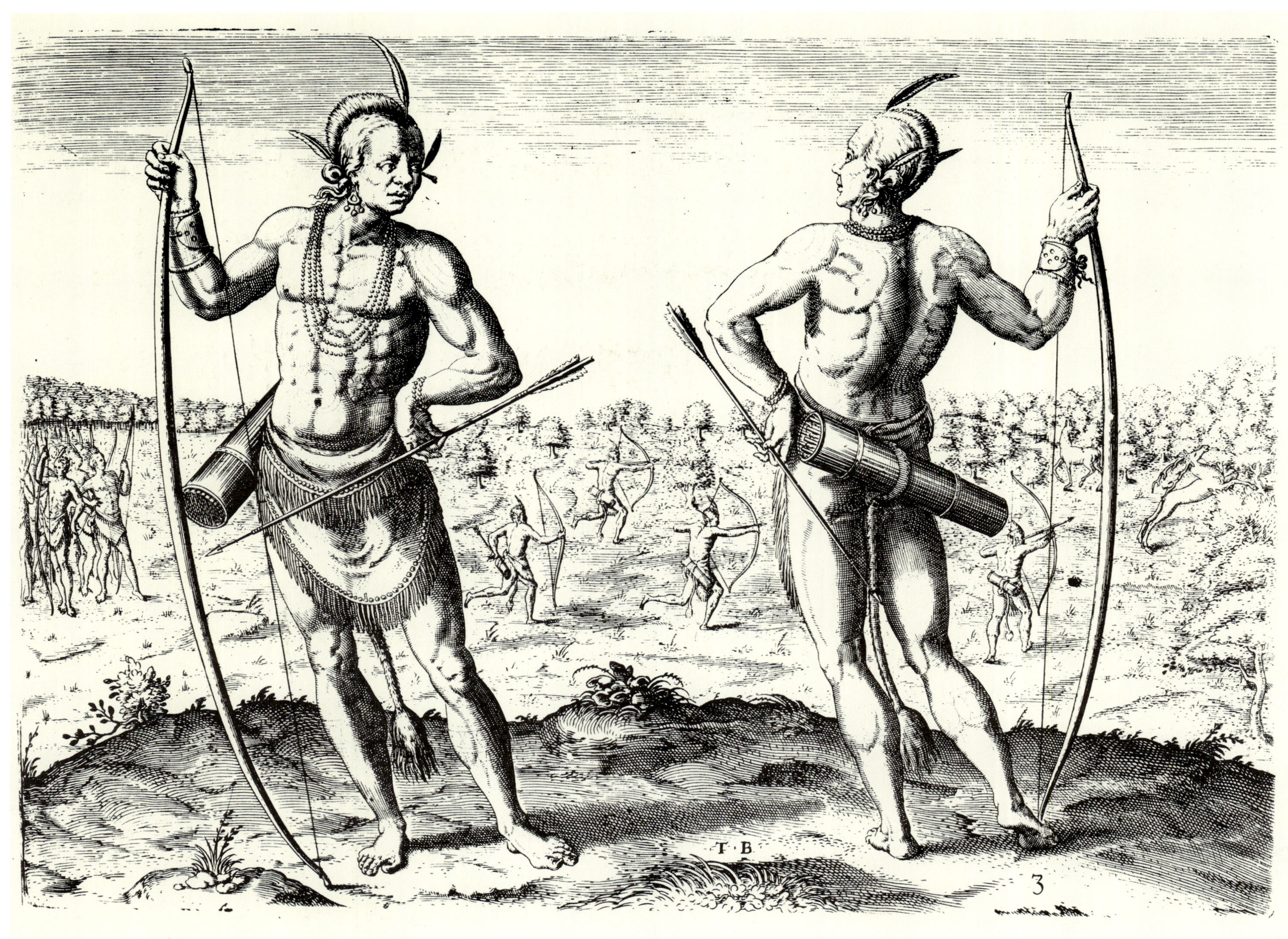

A WEROAN OR GREAT LORDE OF VIRGINIA. THEODOR DE BRY, *VOYAGES TO AMERICA,* VOL. 1, PLATE 3. ENGRAVING AFTER A DRAWING BY JOHN WHITE, LONDON, 1590.

White showed this Algonquian warrior only from the front; de Bry adds the second view and makes the warrior's features much more muscular, poised, and fierce. The accompanying text describes warriors' customary adornment: they wore necklaces of beads or copper, arranged animal skins around their waists so that the tail hung down behind, and painted themselves "in the most terrible manner" for battle.

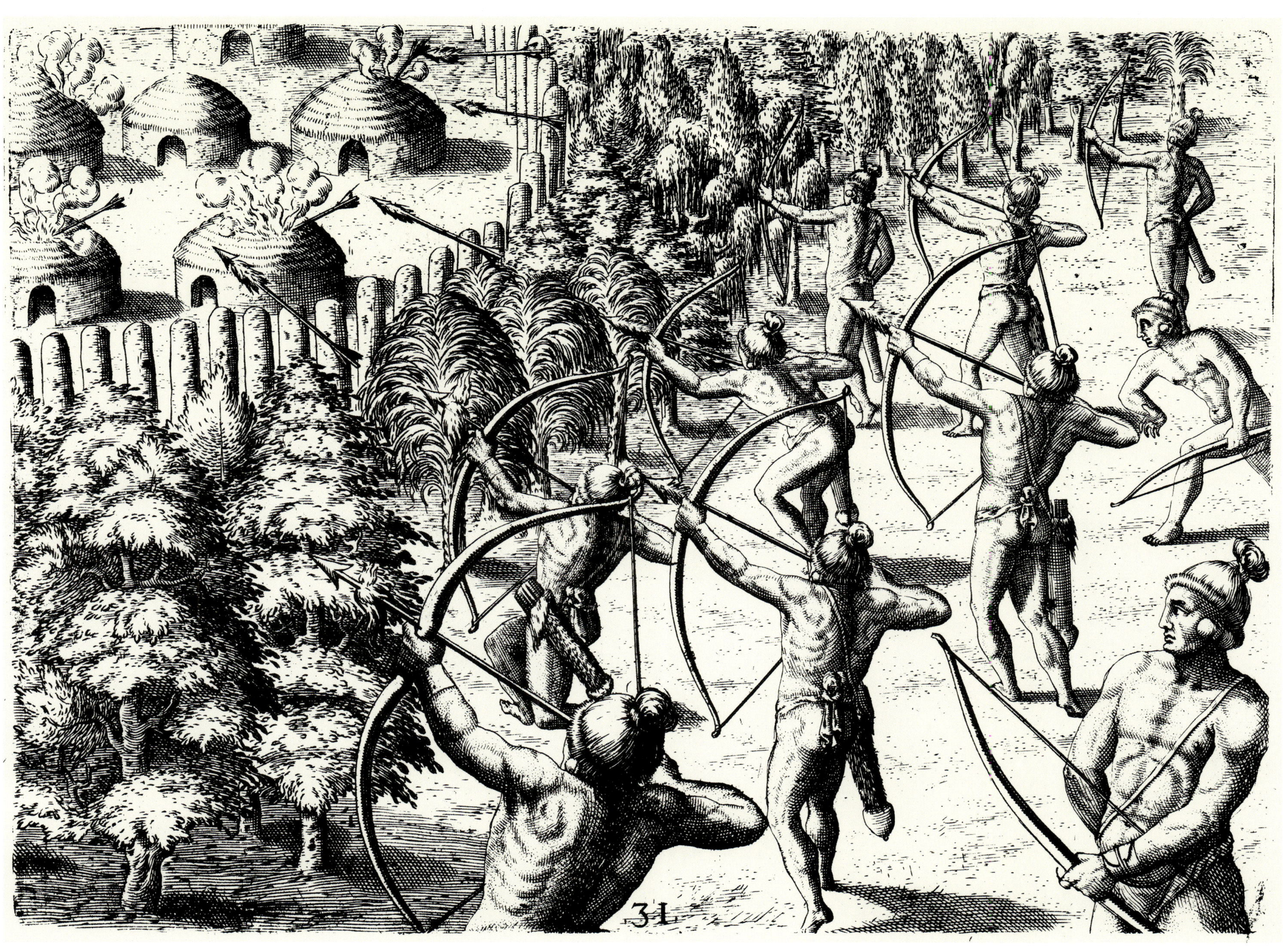

HOW ENEMIES DESTROY FORTRESSES AT NIGHT. THEODOR DE BRY, *VOYAGES TO AMERICA,* VOL. 2, PLATE 31. ENGRAVING AFTER A DRAWING BY JACQUES LE MOYNE, FRANKFURT, 1591.

The unreal impression created by de Bry's distortion of perspective belies the brutality of Timucua warfare. Le Moyne describes how the archers' flaming arrows instantly ignited the thatched roofs of enemy huts; elsewhere he reports that Timucua warriors could not leave a battlefield until they had scalped their enemies and severed their arms and legs.

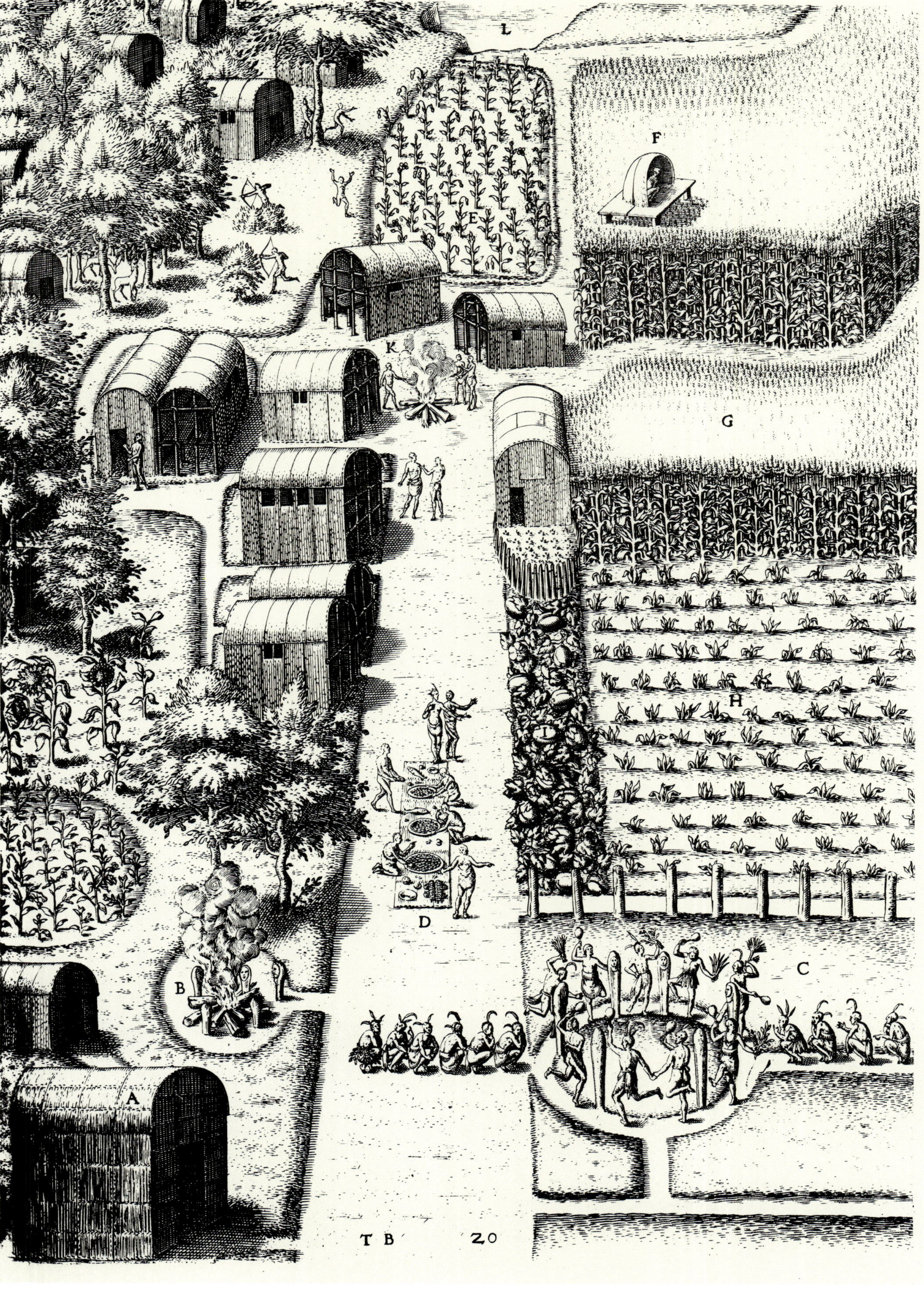

THE TOWNE OF SECOTA.
THEODOR DE BRY, *VOYAGES TO AMERICA,* VOL. 1, PLATE 20. ENGRAVING AFTER A DRAWING BY JOHN WHITE, LONDON, 1590.

Secota, on the Carolina coast, was one of the first towns in North America to be illustrated. A *marks the chief's tomb;* B, *a place of prayer;* C *and* D, *areas for dances and feasts;* E, *tobacco and sunflower gardens;* F, *a platform from which villagers scared birds and animals out of the gardens;* G *and* H, *corn gardens;* I, *a pumpkin garden;* K, *a fireplace for solemn feasts; and* L, *a river.*

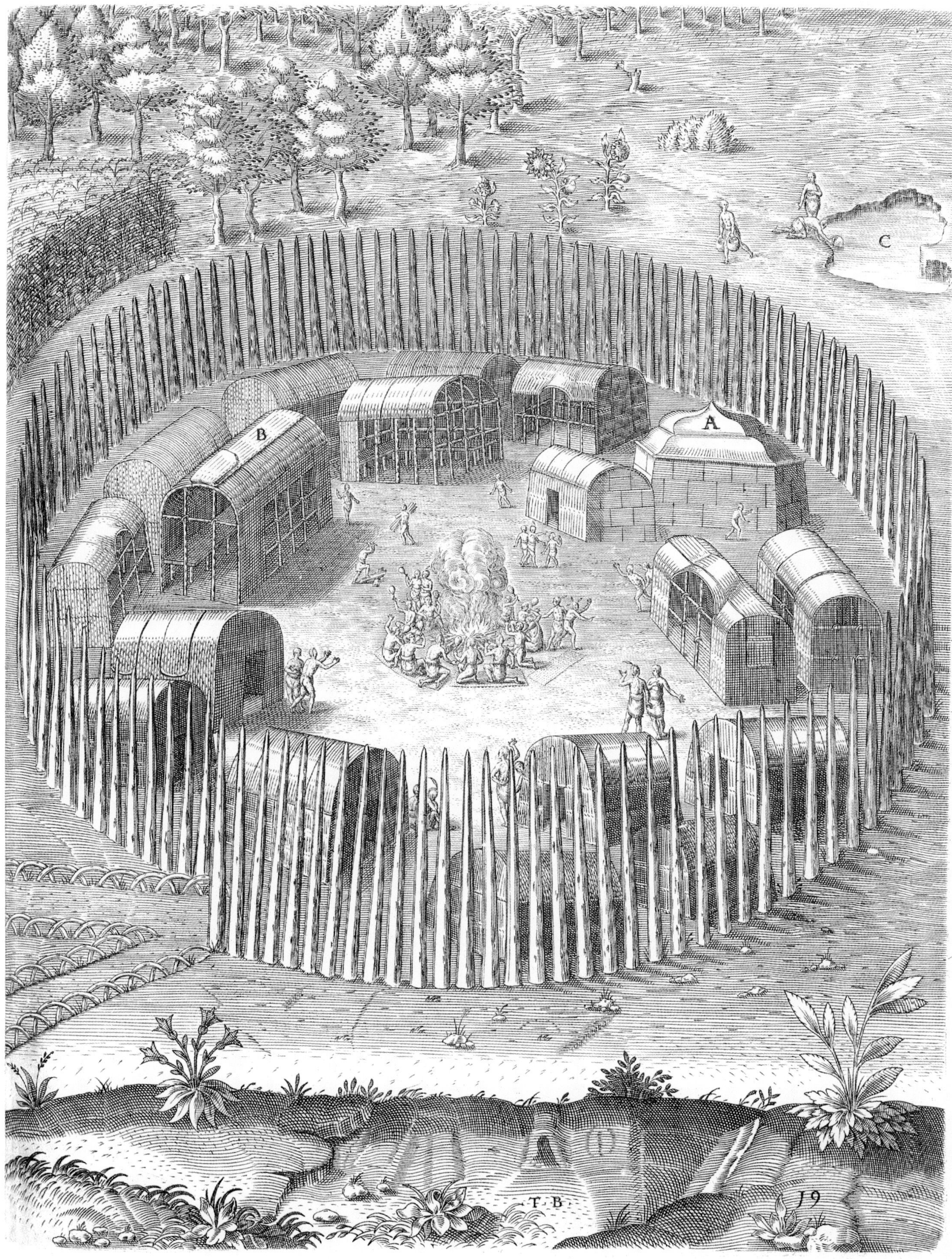

THE TOWNE OF POMEIOOC. THEODOR DE BRY, *VOYAGES TO AMERICA,* VOL. 1, PLATE 19. ENGRAVING AFTER A DRAWING BY JOHN WHITE, LONDON, 1590.

The Raleigh expedition reached the coast of the Carolinas on June 20, 1585. Exploring Pamlico Sound, they found the small town of Pomeiooc. De Bry believed that Algonquian villages were less well defended and cared for than those of the Timucua. Here he depicts pole houses covered with skins raised for light and lowered for warmth.

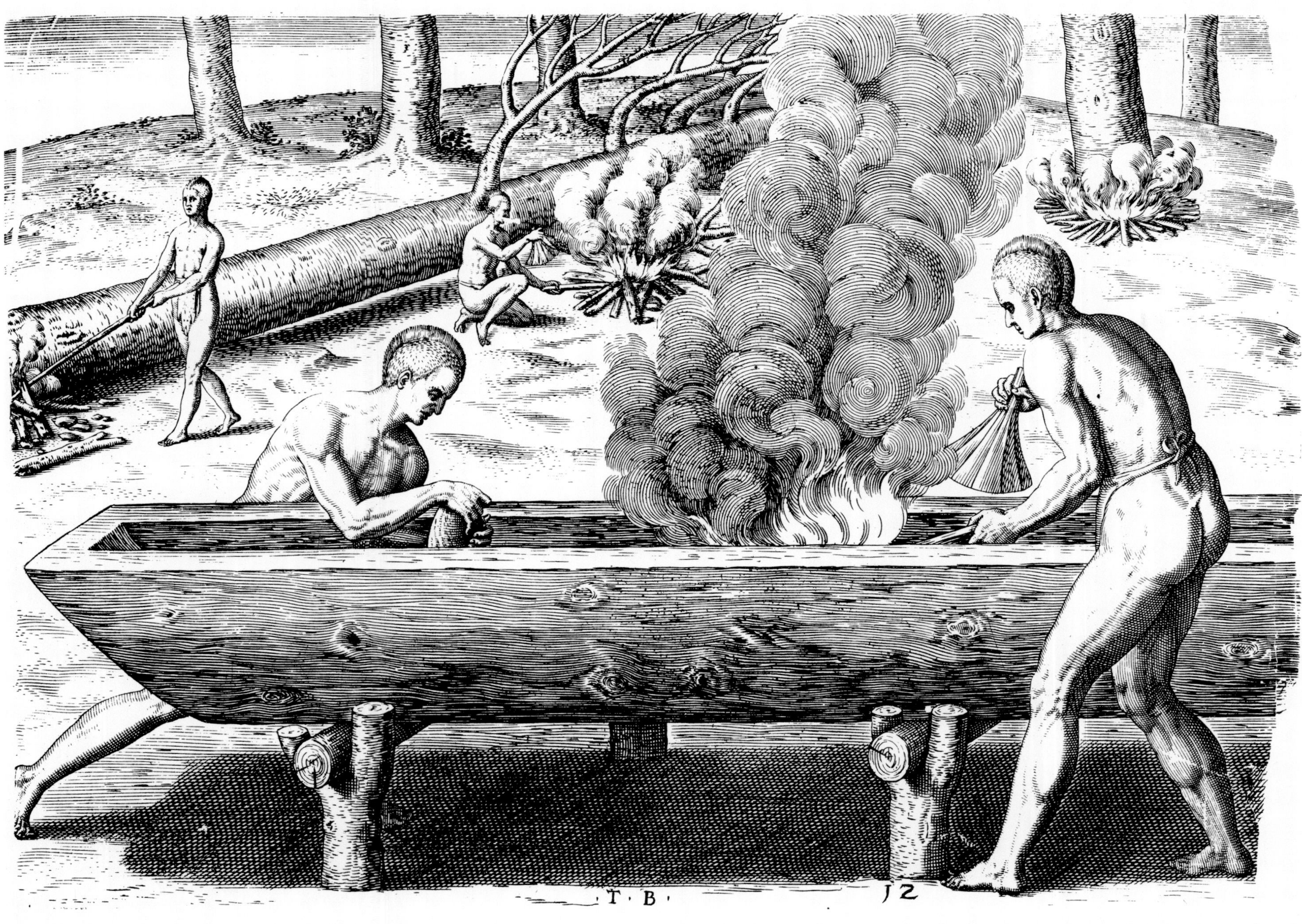

THE MANNER OF MAKINGE THEIR BOATES. THEODOR DE BRY, *VOYAGES TO AMERICA,* VOL. 1, PLATE 12. ENGRAVING AFTER A DRAWING BY JOHN WHITE, LONDON, 1590.

To make a canoe, Algonquian Indians first felled a suitable tree by setting fire to its roots, then hollowed the trunk, alternately burning layers and scraping the charred wood with seashells. De Bry found the effectiveness of this simple method "wonderful."

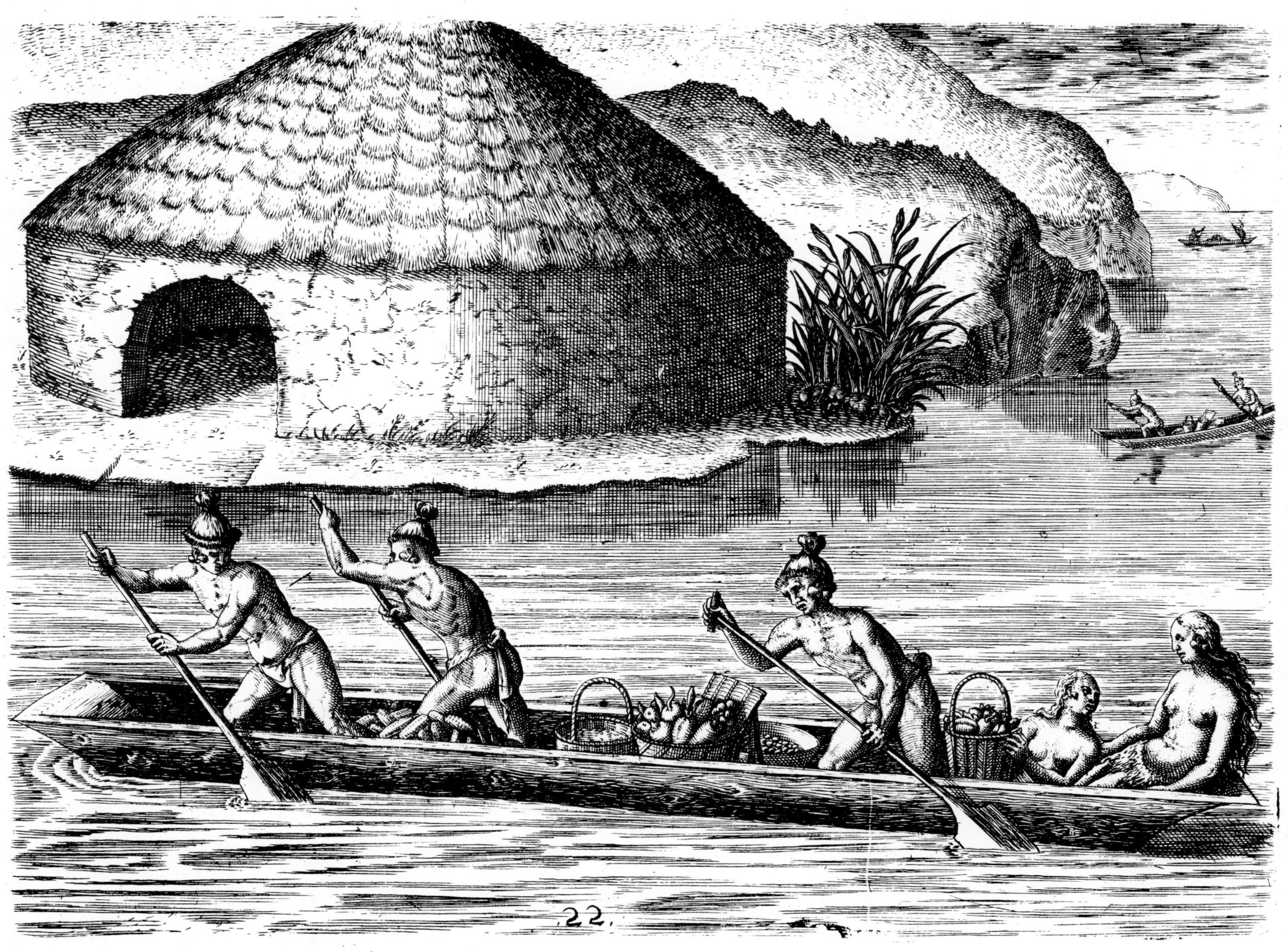

FLORIDIANS TAKING THE HARVEST TO STOREHOUSES. THEODOR DE BRY, *VOYAGES TO AMERICA,* VOL. 2, PLATE 22. ENGRAVING AFTER A DRAWING BY JACQUES LE MOYNE, FRANKFURT, 1591.

Inside the rounded storehouses, built of earth and small stones and roofed with branches and clay, temperatures remained cool, preserving boatloads of fruit which the Timucua brought from nearby islands twice a year. According to Le Moyne, who considered the Timucuas' communal spirit admirable, no permission was needed for individuals to take food from the storehouses.

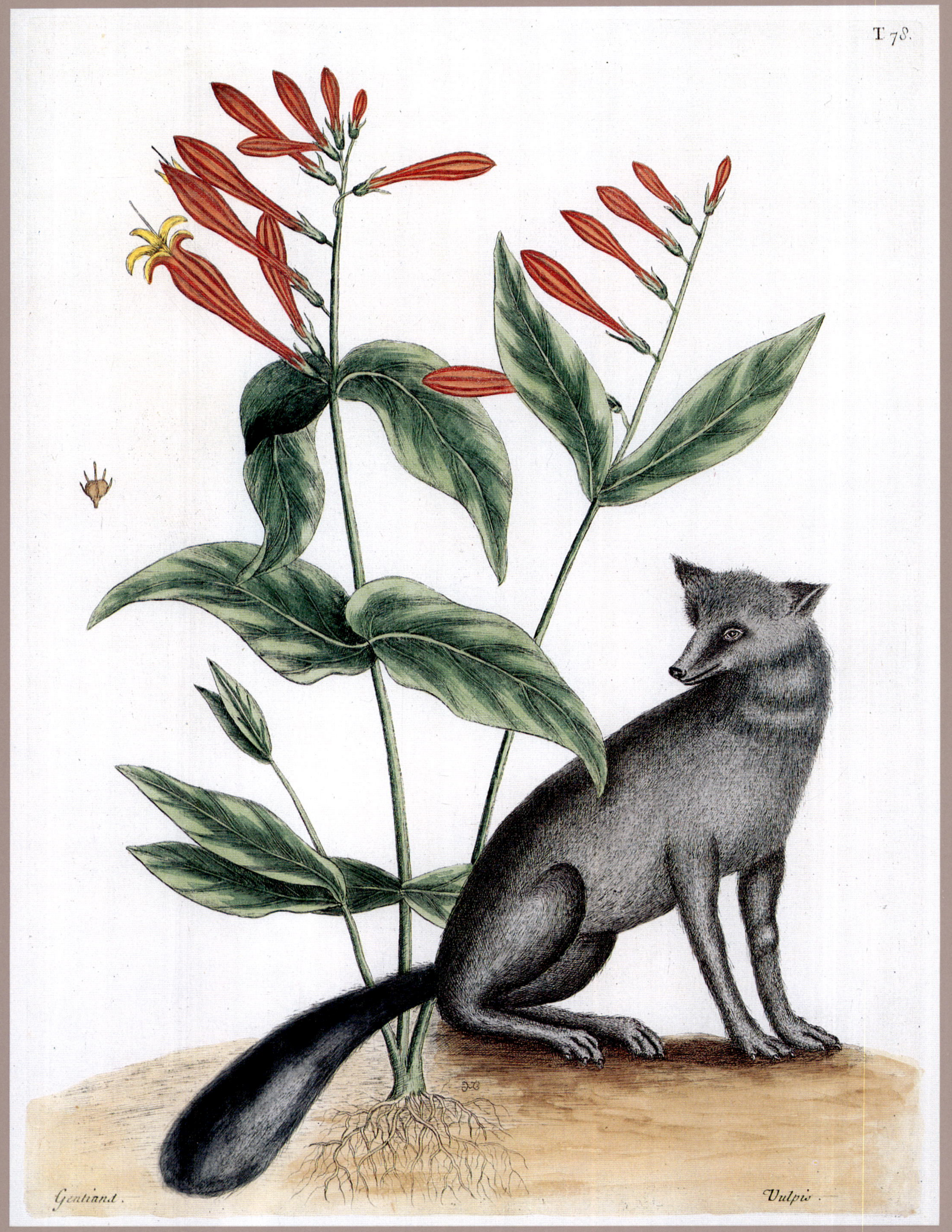
T 78.
Gentiana.
Vulpis.

MARK CATESBY (1682/3-1749)

Mark Catesby's *Natural History of Carolina, Florida, and the Bahama Islands* is in every sense the lifework of this precise and witty English naturalist. He spent ten years in England's American colonies, first as a casual observer and botanical collector, then as a commissioned scientific researcher and painter, gaining as deep a knowledge of New World life forms as any of his English contemporaries. He gave another 20 years to his monumental book, writing the text, etching the illustrations, and in the first edition, hand coloring a majority of the prints himself. The result, the first comprehensive study of American plants and animals in English, won fame in its time as a model of the spirit of scientific inquiry which Catesby's age revered, and lives on now as a delightful testament to the genius of its creator.

Born in Essex, the fourth child of a prosperous lawyer, Mark Catesby found nature fascinating from his earliest days. He was fortunate to grow up near three experts in different aspects of the science of plants. His maternal uncle, Nicholas Jekyll, an antiquarian and horticulturist, maintained botanical gardens at his ancestral Essex home, Castle Hedingham. Through Jekyll, young Catesby came to know Jekyll's neighbor and friend, Dr. Samuel Dale, who established the modern science of pharmacology. Nearby, too, lived John Ray, the leading English naturalist of the period. With a colleague, Ray developed the concept of *species* and set out to catalogue all living things, a lifelong pursuit which helped lay the foundations for Carl Linnaeus' taxonomic revolution in the 18th century.

THE GRAY FOX. THE INDIAN PINK. MARK CATESBY, *THE NATURAL HISTORY OF CAROLINA, FLORIDA, AND THE BAHAMA ISLANDS,* VOL. 2, PLATE 78. HAND-COLORED ETCHING, LONDON, 1731-1743.

Catesby, the first European to produce a large-scale study of North American birds and animals, accurately noted that gray foxes live in trees. The medicinal uses of plants deeply interested botanists of Catesby's time. Of the Indian pink or pinkroot flowering next to the fox, he writes, "A Decoction made of this Plant is good against Worms."

Catesby had not yet conceived of his own ambitious project when he went to America for the first time at the age of 30 in 1712. Inspired perhaps by Ray or Dale, he was eager to see the native plants and animals of other countries. He settled in Williamsburg at the house of his older sister Elizabeth, whose husband, Dr. William Cocke, knew many important Virginians. Soon Catesby was advising William Byrd II of Westover on the restoration of the estate's vast gardens. They hunted and explored the region; Byrd recorded in his journal that on September 12, 1712, Catesby shot a bear cub eating grapes in a tree.

During his seven-year stay, Catesby visited many plantations along the rivers around Williamsburg. On one occasion, he boated up the James to the foothills of the Blue Ridge. While he roamed and admired, he gathered specimens and seeds to send to Dale and other English naturalists who no doubt discussed the shipments with each other. By the time Catesby returned to England in 1719, the name of this "curious Botanist" was familiar to several patrons of scientific study and Fellows of the Royal Society.

Soon Catesby began making plans for a second, more deliberate journey to America. With Dale's help, sponsors were found, including the Duke of Chandois and Sir Francis Nicholson, the new governor of South Carolina.

Catesby sailed for Charleston in February 1722 to begin nearly three years of collecting and painting in the Carolinas, Georgia, and Florida, and a fourth in the Bahamas. He particularly enjoyed the Carolina uplands, where he owed much to the friendliness of the Indians: "I not only subsisted on what they shot, but their first care was to erect a bark hut, at the approach of rain to keep me and my cargo from wet." His sponsors were often less accommodating, demanding more specimens and disputing the division of the shipments they received. Preparing these shipments took time and trouble. Catesby observed in a letter from Charleston that his drying plants molded if they were not turned every day. Since he shipped many animal specimens in jars of spirits, sailors sometimes broke into them for the sake of the drink, undeterred by dead lizards and snakes.

Upon his return to England in 1726, Catesby hoped to have his watercolors engraved in Paris or Amsterdam. While his sponsors at the Royal Society agreed that the drawings should be published, they would not pay for the engraving. To make ends meet, he went to work for one of these patrons, Thomas Fairchild, at his nursery in Hoxton, and after Fairchild's death, for Christopher Gray at Fullerton Gardens. Long after Catesby left America, employment as a nurseryman gave him access to the exotic American plants he used in his engraved compositions.

To make publication affordable, Catesby decided to etch his drawings himself, studying techniques with the French-born watercolorist and etcher Joseph Goupy. In May of 1729, he displayed his first 20 plates at the Royal Society. In 1733, shortly after the completion of the first volume, he was elected a fellow. He maintained a modest, steady flow of income for the project by selling the prints in groups of 20 as he completed them. Volume I of the first edition was finished in 1731, and Volume II in 1743. In 1747, he issued an appendix of 20 additional plates, bringing the total to 220. Catesby's subtle coloring makes the first edition far more valuable than later editions colored by other artisans.

Catesby's work reveals his delight in the natural world. He wryly describes the flying fish in the Atlantic who "escape their Enemies in the Water" only to be "caught in the air by voracious Birds," and the now-extinct parrots of Carolina who made "great destruction" in the autumn orchards and whose "Guts is certain and speedy poison to Cats." He tells of flamingos nesting on hillocks "on which they sit with their legs extended down, like a Man sitting on a Stool." Of migrating land crabs in the Bahamas, he writes: "They have been known to enter in at a Window, and on a Bed, where People who never before had seen any, were not a little surprized."

Catesby apologized to his readers for errors in perspective and for the flatness of his pictures. In fact, he was an innovator; he drew from fresh specimens whenever possible and portrayed birds flying or making characteristic movements rather than in conventional static profiles. He was also one of the first to depict birds and animals in full compositions with plants suggestive of natural habitats. The appeal of his writing has rarely been matched by later naturalists, and his work set standards for the portrayal of North American wildlife which would not be surpassed until the 19th century, when Alexander Wilson and John James Audubon went into the field.

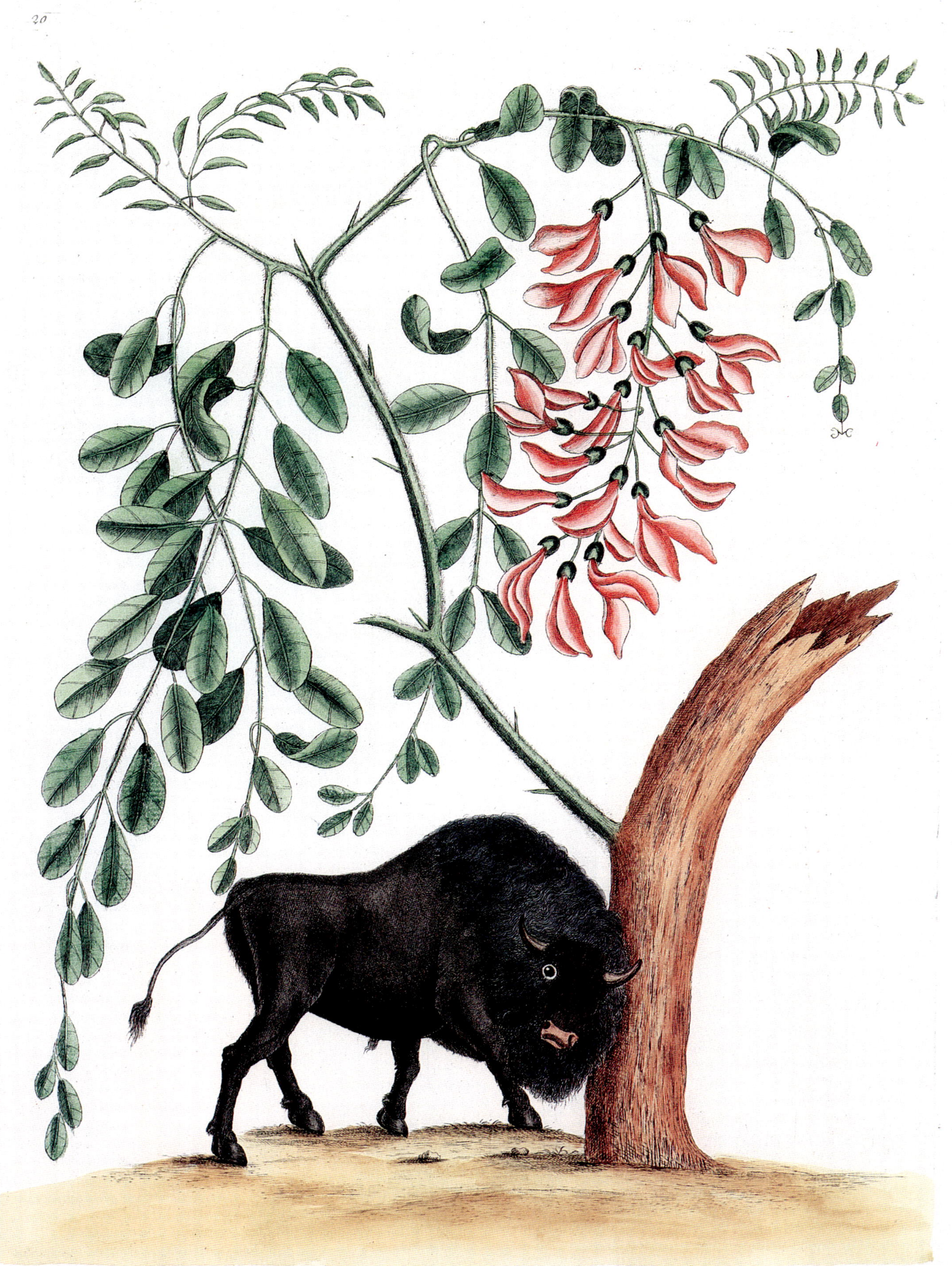

BISON. BRISTLY LOCUST. MARK CATESBY, *NATURAL HISTORY,* APPENDIX, PLATE 20. HAND-COLORED ETCHING, LONDON, 1743-1747.

The last bison in the East were shot before 1800, but in the 1720s, when Catesby explored the southeastern piedmont, they were still plentiful. At the only site where he identified this locust, Catesby also found bison droppings and other signs of the animals' activities. When he returned to obtain locust seeds, the trees were gone; "ravaging Indians had burned the Woods many Miles around."

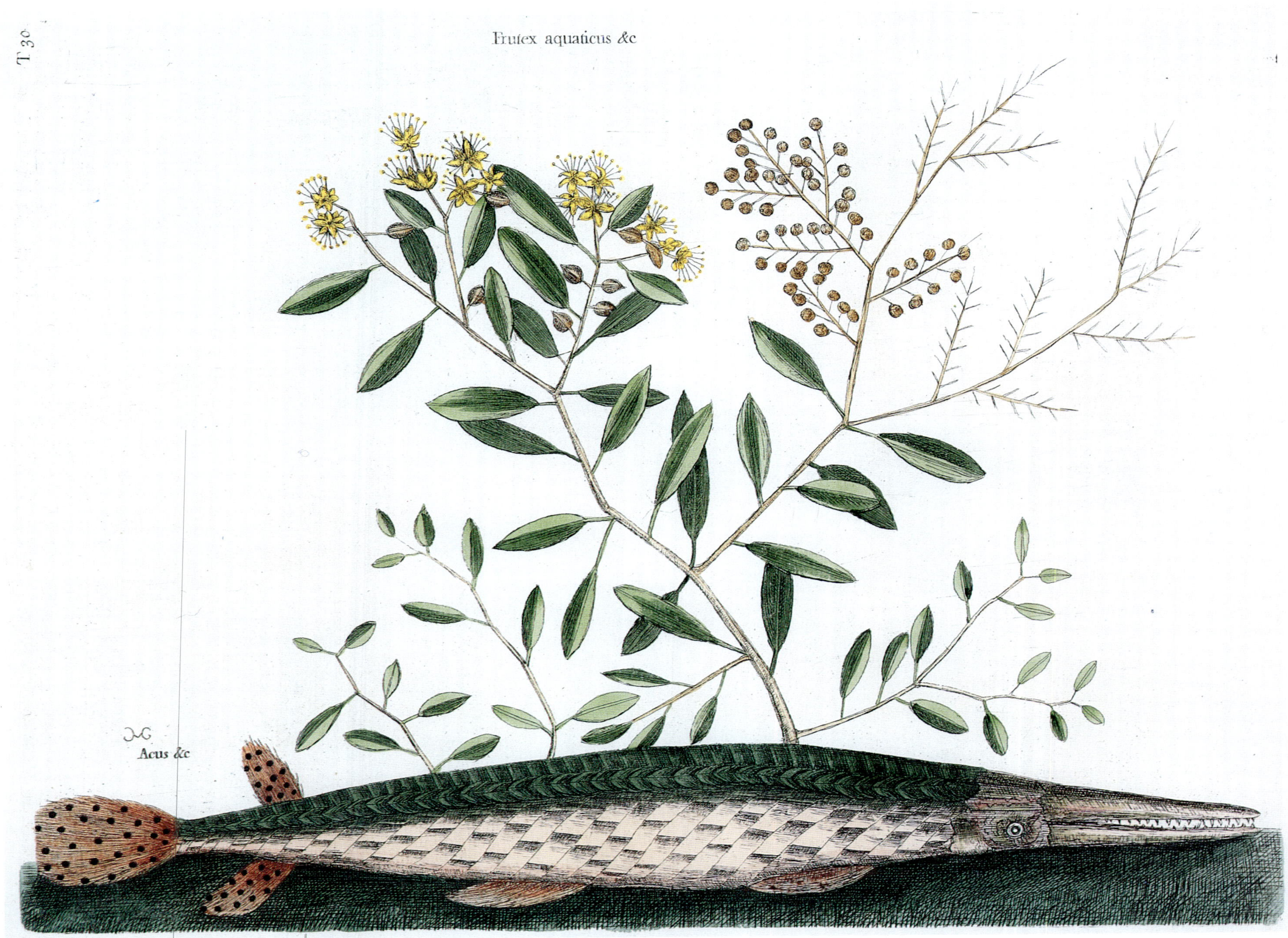

THE GREEN GAR-FISH. MARK CATESBY, *NATURAL HISTORY,* VOL. 2, PLATE 30.
HAND-COLORED ETCHING, LONDON, 1731-1743.

Sir Hans Sloane, a patron of the Natural History *whose own collections later formed the basis of the British Museum, possessed a set of John White's drawings from Roanoke Island. Catesby copied several of these, including* The Green Gar-Fish, The Globe Fish, *and* The Land Crab. *The garfish, he notes, grows to a length of at least three feet.*

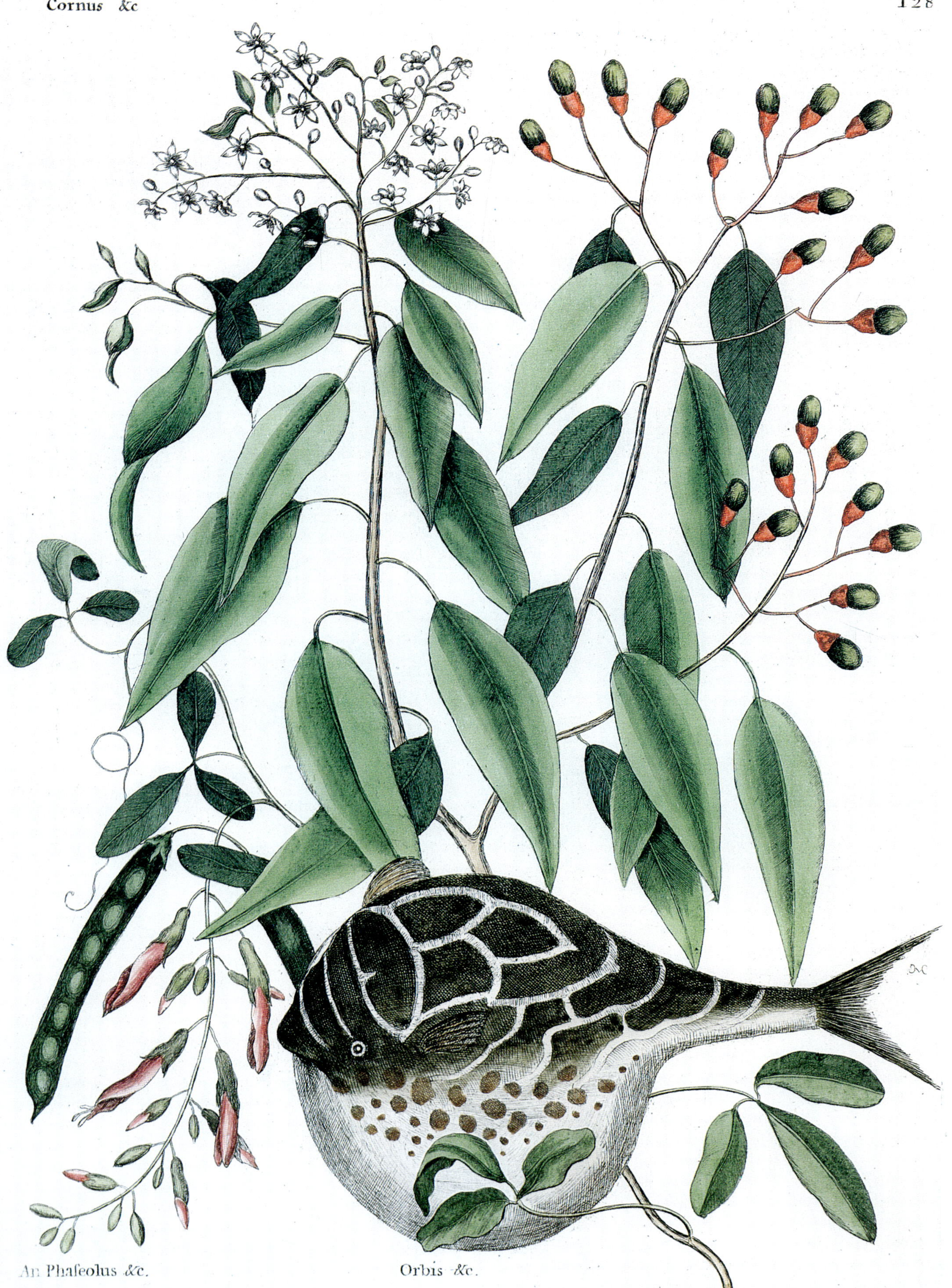

THE GLOBE FISH. SASSAFRAS. MARK CATESBY, *NATURAL HISTORY,* VOL. 2, PLATE 28. HAND-COLORED ETCHING, LONDON, 1731-1743.

Catesby's globefish is almost certainly based on a John White drawing. Globefish or puffers, found in the coastal waters of the Carolinas and the Bahamas, are normally shaped like other fish; they only inflate themselves and float upside-down to the surface when they perceive a threat.

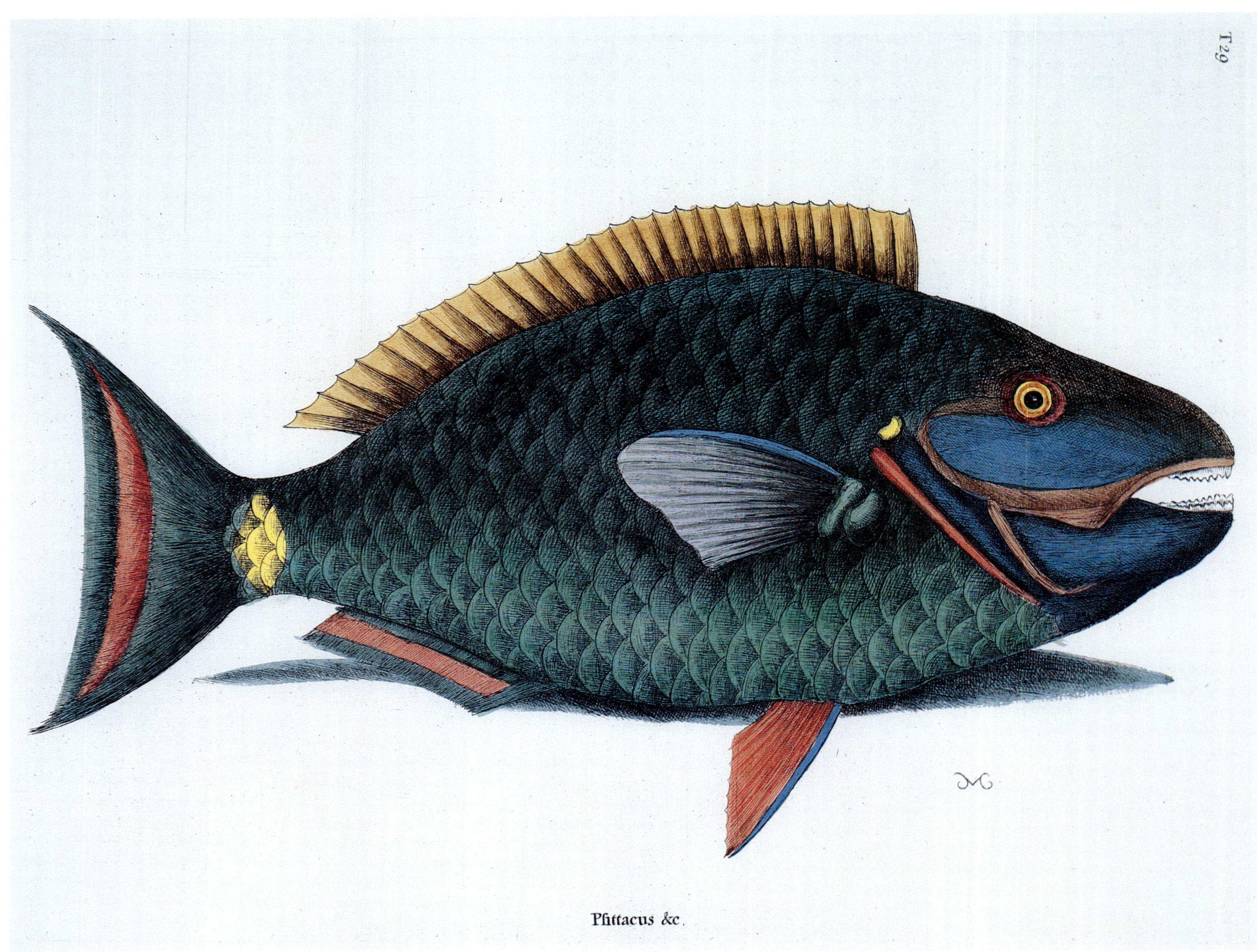

THE PARROT FISH. MARK CATESBY, *NATURAL HISTORY,* VOL. 2, PLATE 29. HAND-COLORED ETCHING, LONDON, 1731-1743.

To keep color in his fish specimens, which rapidly became "dull and sordid" when taken from the ocean, Catesby placed them in pails of water while he sketched them. Known for its bright colors and extremely strong jaws and teeth, the parrotfish is capable of chewing coral. Catesby describes its mouth as "paved" with teeth and emphasizes them in the drawing.

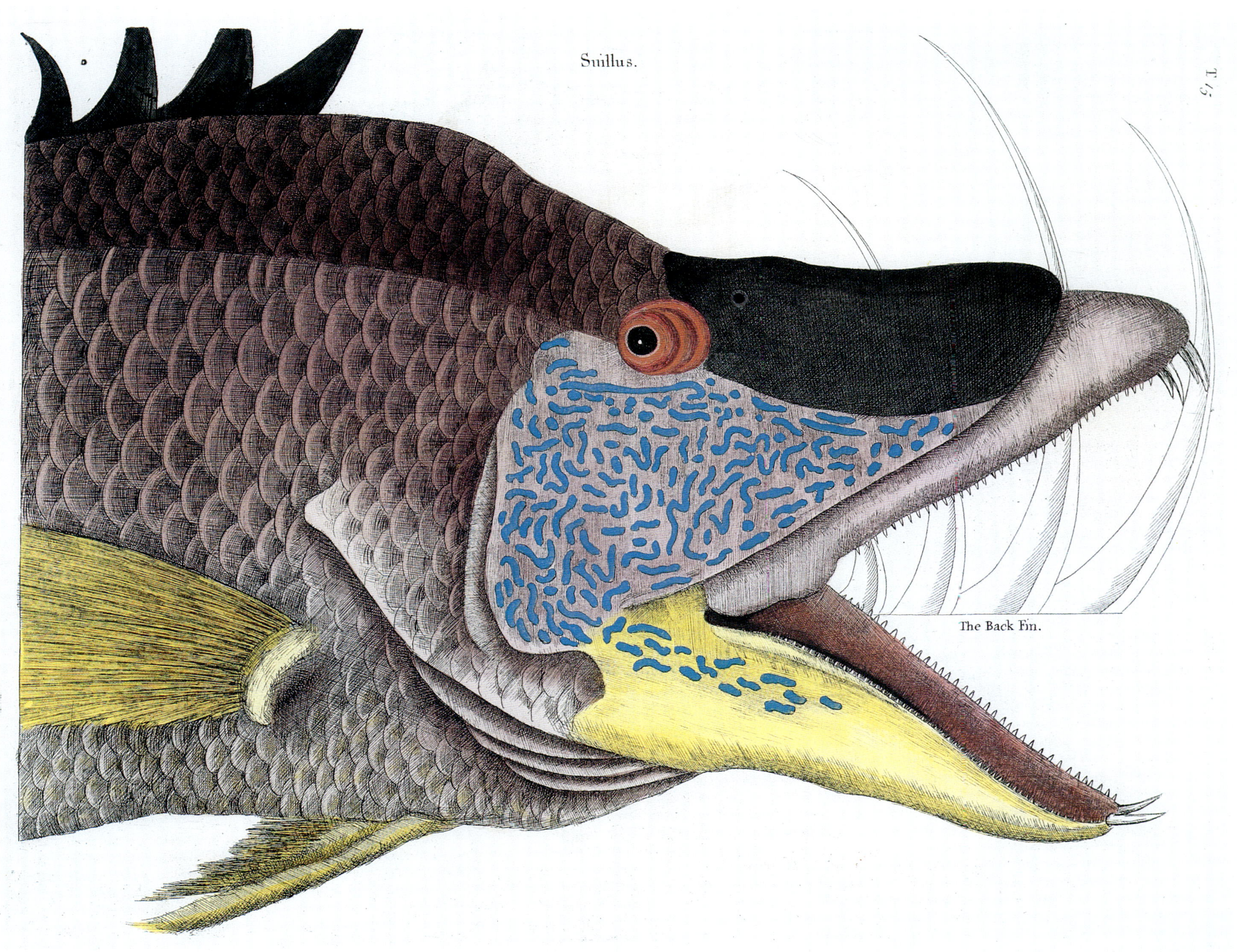

THE GREAT HOG-FISH. MARK CATESBY, *NATURAL HISTORY,* VOL. 2, PLATE 15.
HAND-COLORED ETCHING, LONDON, 1731-1743.

Catesby based this drawing on a specimen some four feet long. By filling the page with only half the fish, he dramatically conveys its bulk. However, his reason for omitting the tail is strictly scientific: because it was "cut off before I had it, I cannot say of what form it was." The back fins, which will not fit at the drawing's top, form an intriguing pattern behind the fish's mouth.

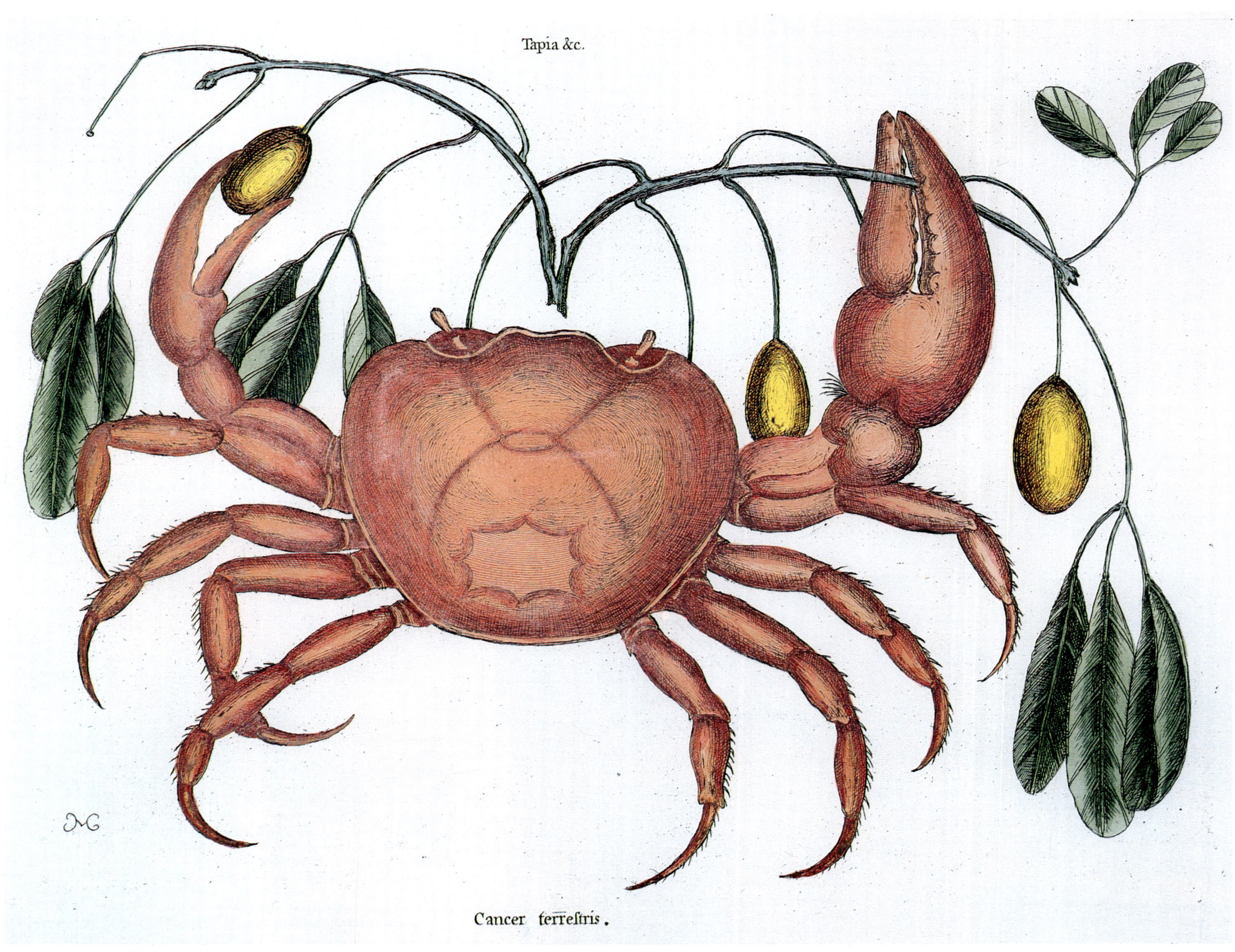

THE LAND CRAB. MARK CATESBY, *NATURAL HISTORY,* VOL. 2, PLATE 32. HAND-COLORED ETCHING, LONDON, 1731-1743.

Catesby neatly balances his crab, copied from one of White's finest sketches, with a black-mangrove branch and fruit, widespread in Caribbean swamps. He describes how land crabs "annually descend the hills in large numbers, to lay their eggs near the sea," and how they supplemented the meager diet of West Indian slaves, "who on many of the islands would fare very hard without them."

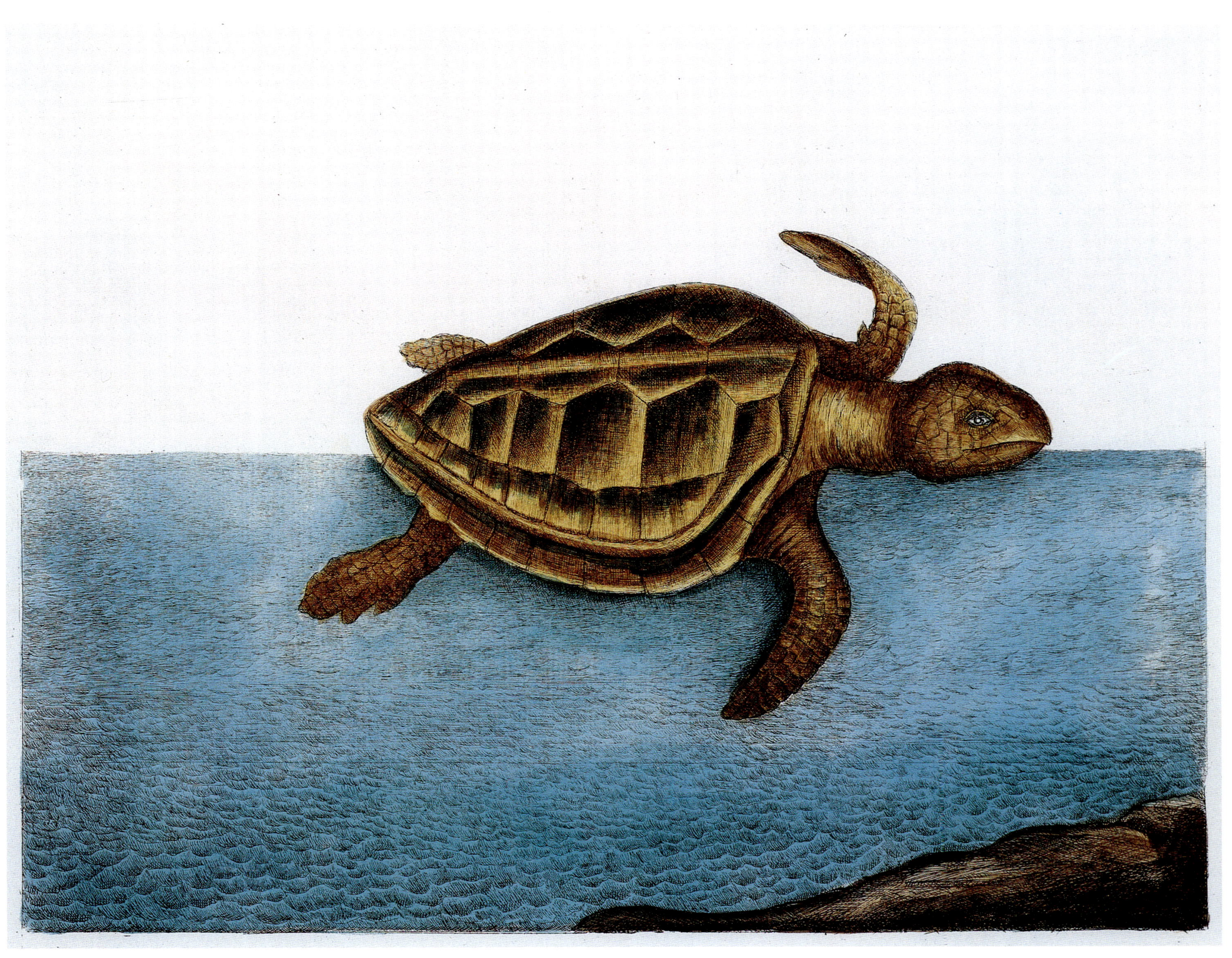

THE LOGGERHEAD TURTLE. MARK CATESBY, *NATURAL HISTORY,* VOL. 2, PLATE 40. HAND-COLORED ETCHING, LONDON, 1731-1743.

The loggerhead turtle, a marine species which Catesby once spotted 1,000 miles from land, weighs as much as 280 pounds. Fascinated by West Indian methods of hunting large turtles, Catesby notes that the plentiful loggerheads, "the boldest, most voracious, and foulest feeders of all the turtles," had rank flesh and were rarely pursued.

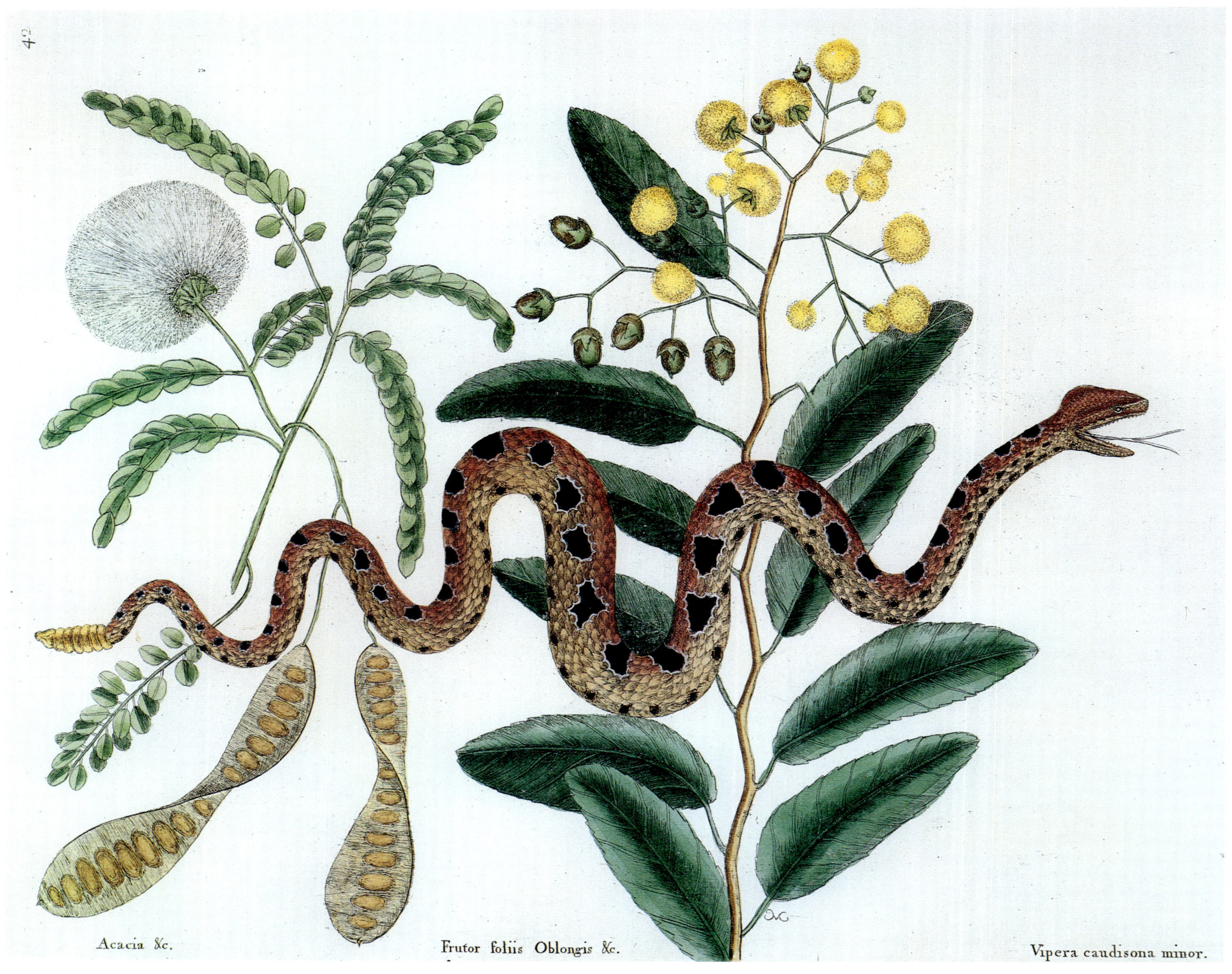

THE SMALL RATTLE-SNAKE. MARK CATESBY, *NATURAL HISTORY,* VOL. 2, PLATE 42. HAND-COLORED ETCHING, LONDON, 1731-1743.

Traveling through snake-infested regions, Catesby heard many snakebite remedies. He agreed with the Indian belief that a wound's seriousness was determined by its location and the snake's size. The Indians, he writes, "know their destiny the minute they are bit; and when they perceive it mortal, apply no other remedy, concluding all efforts in vain."

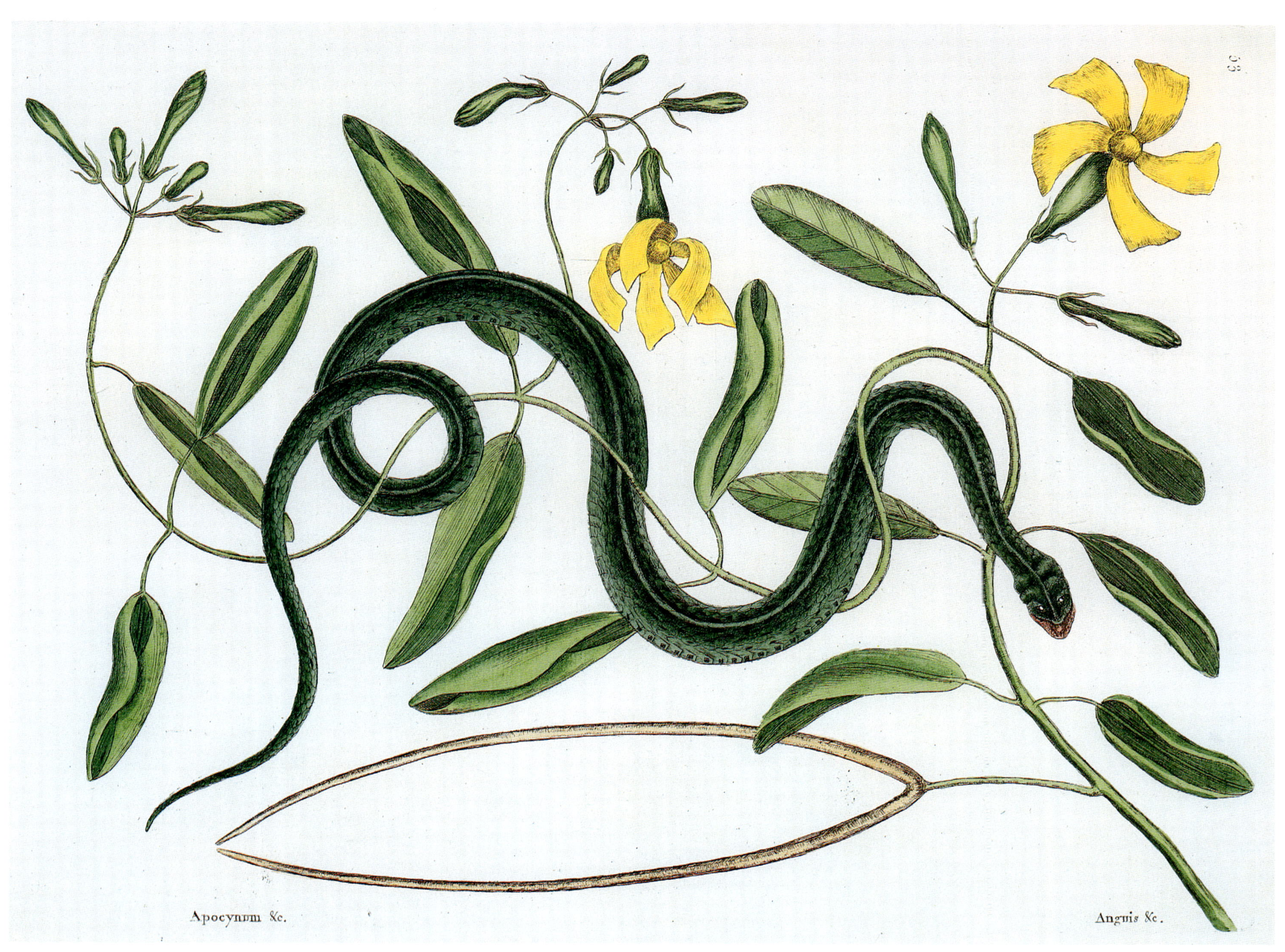

THE GREEN SPOTTED SNAKE. MARK CATESBY, *NATURAL HISTORY,* VOL. 2, PLATE 53. HAND-COLORED ETCHING, LONDON, 1731-1743.

Catesby found snake identification perplexing; he "would willingly avoid mistakes by describing the same snake twice." The difficulty arose because a number of species change their markings when they shed their skins. A painstaking observer, he learned this "by assisting many of them to strip off their old coats." The snake's expression of gleeful villainy typifies Catesby's style.

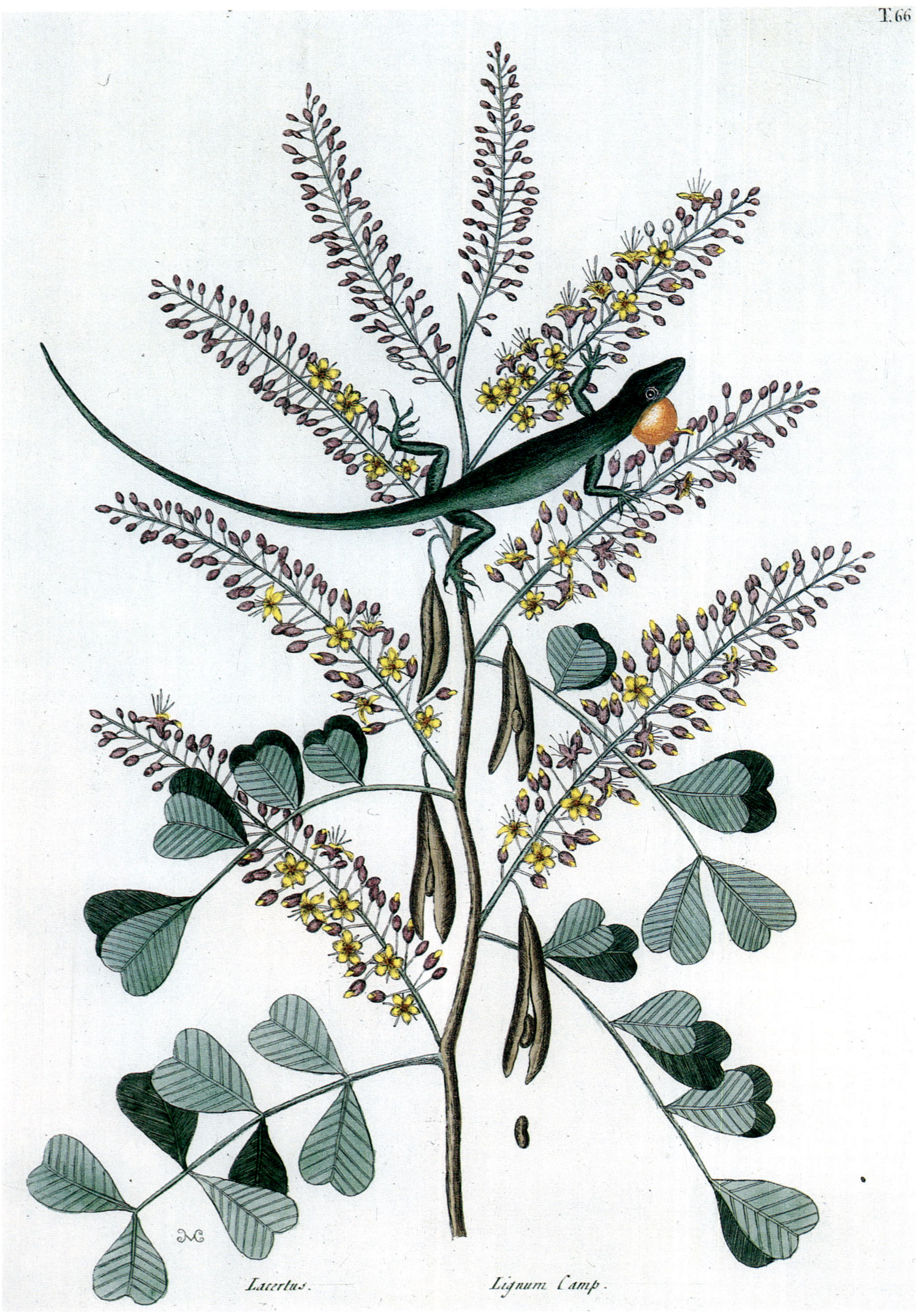

THE GREEN LIZARD OF JAMAICA. MARK CATESBY, *NATURAL HISTORY,* VOL. 2, PLATE 66. HAND-COLORED ETCHING, LONDON, 1731-1743.

Catesby portrays this American chameleon with its throat swelled, a signal for both predators and potential mates. It perches on a logwood, a tropical tree which produces a useful black or brown dye. The dye, Catesby notes, had been the cause of several conflicts between Spaniards and Englishmen.

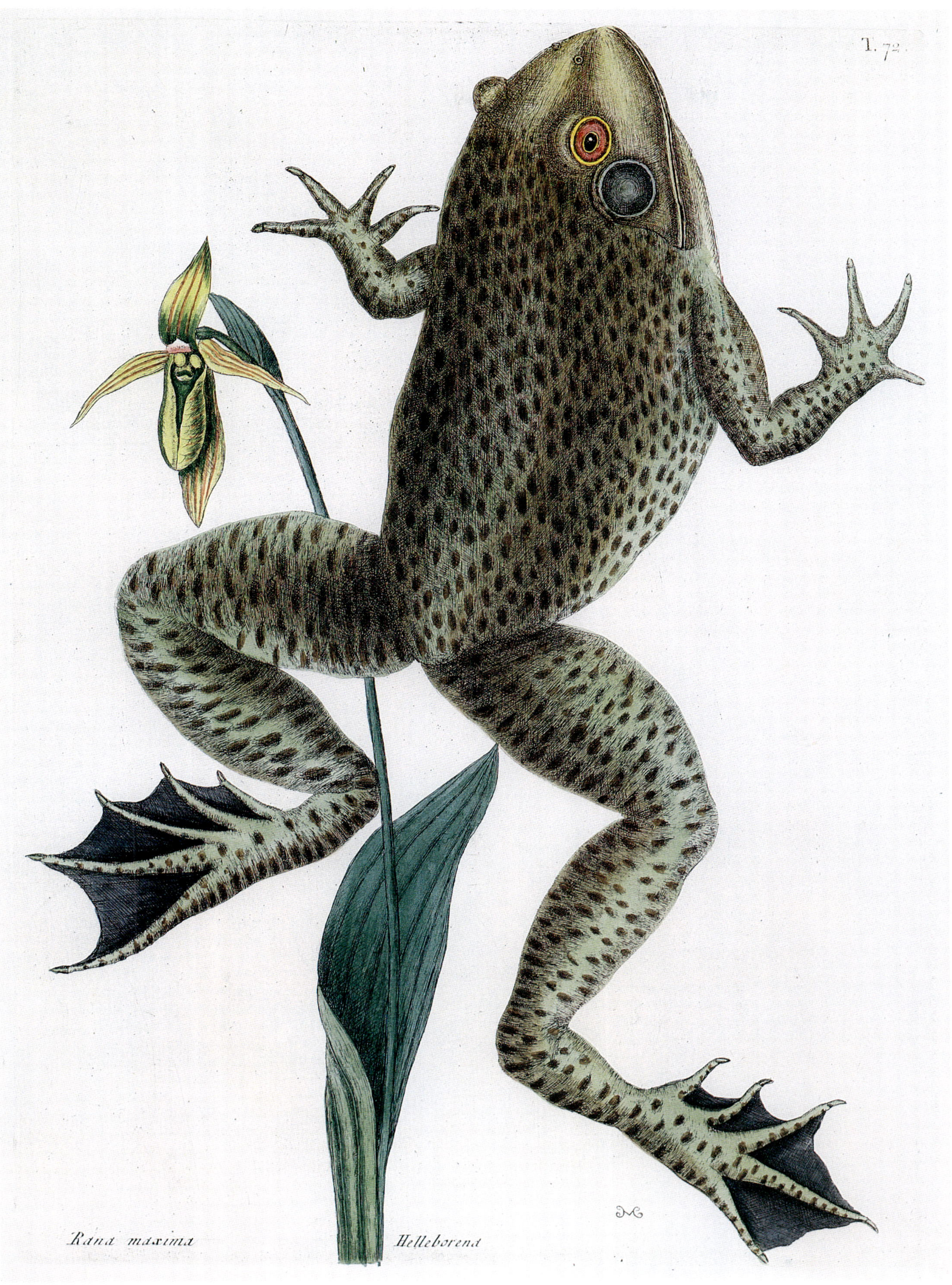

THE BULL FROG. THE LADY'S SLIPPER OF PENSILVANIA. MARK CATESBY, *NATURAL HISTORY*, VOL. 2, PLATE 72. HAND-COLORED ETCHING, LONDON, 1731-1743.

The bullfrog's Latin name, Rana catesbeiana, *honors Catesby's work. Here he shows a specimen about a foot long but writes that it "is smaller than many of these frogs I have seen." The accompanying lady's-slipper, he reports, "flowered in Mr. Collinson's garden in 1738"—one example of the many American flowers successfully cultivated in England and sketched there by Catesby years after his travels.*

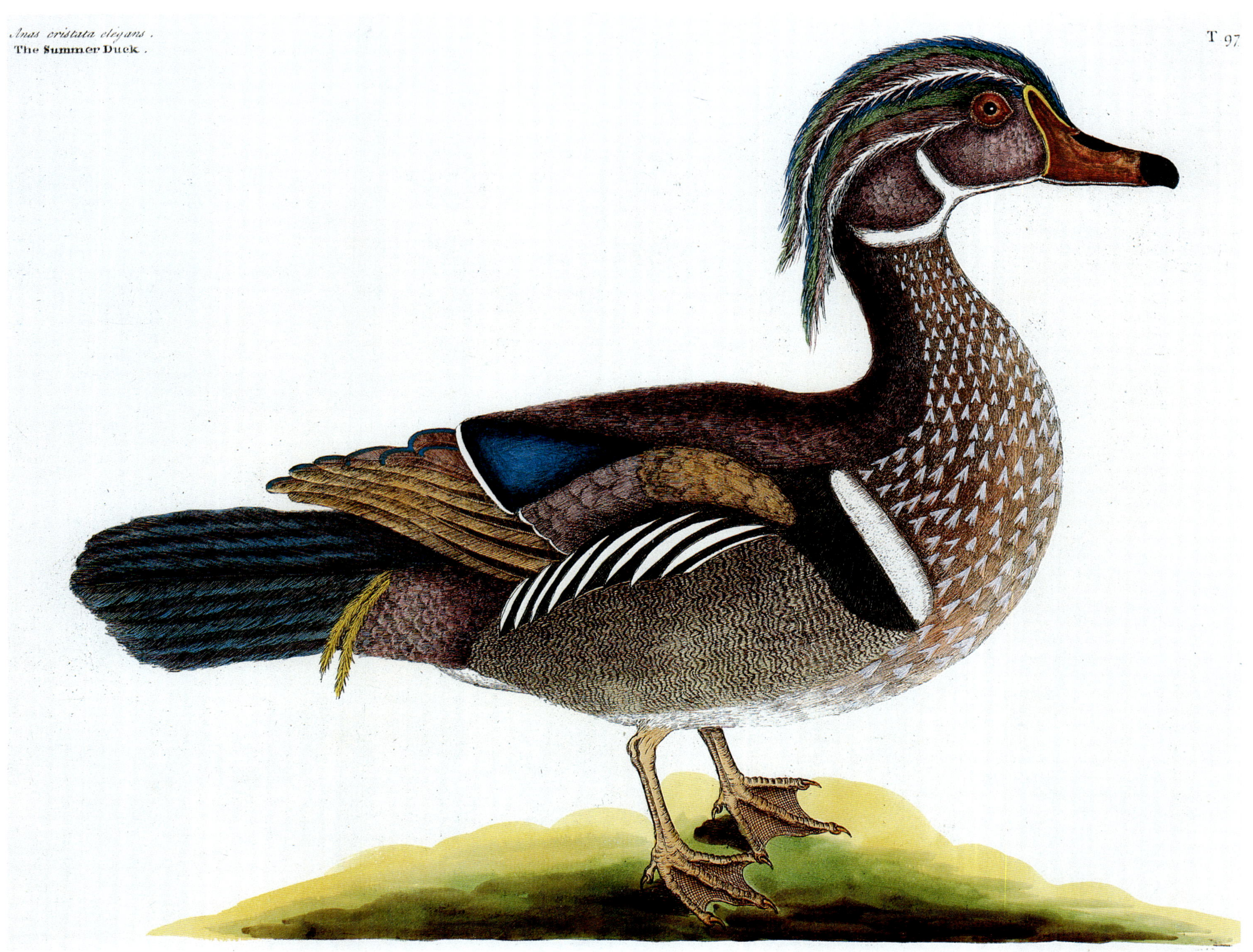

THE SUMMER DUCK. MARK CATESBY, *NATURAL HISTORY,* VOL. 1, PLATE 97. HAND-COLORED ETCHING, LONDON, 1727-1731.

The brilliantly colored wood duck still thrives in woodland swamps, rivers, and ponds throughout the eastern and central United States. Catesby notes its habit of nesting in holes in tall trees, but he believed that the hen flew from the nest with her young on her back; in fact, the ducklings tumble to the ground.

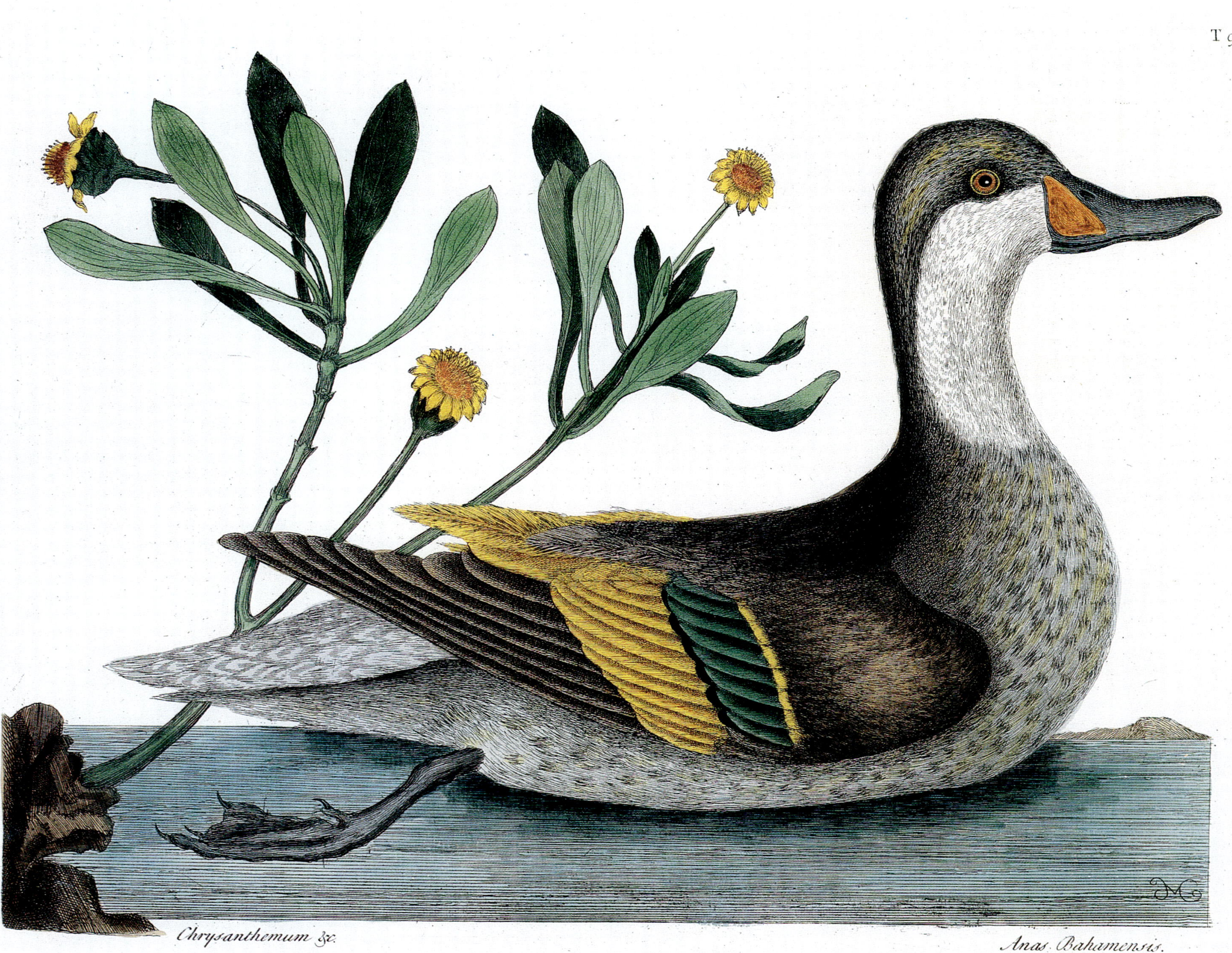

THE ILATHERA DUCK. MARK CATESBY, *NATURAL HISTORY,* VOL. 1, PLATE 93. HAND-COLORED ETCHING, LONDON, 1727-1731.

This image, regarded as one of Catesby's most successful, is made more remarkable by his scant opportunities to observe this duck, now known as the Bahama or white-cheeked pintail. As he reports, "These birds frequent the Bahama Islands, but are not numerous. I never having seen but one, which was a drake." A sea ox-eye or sea-bush grows in the background.

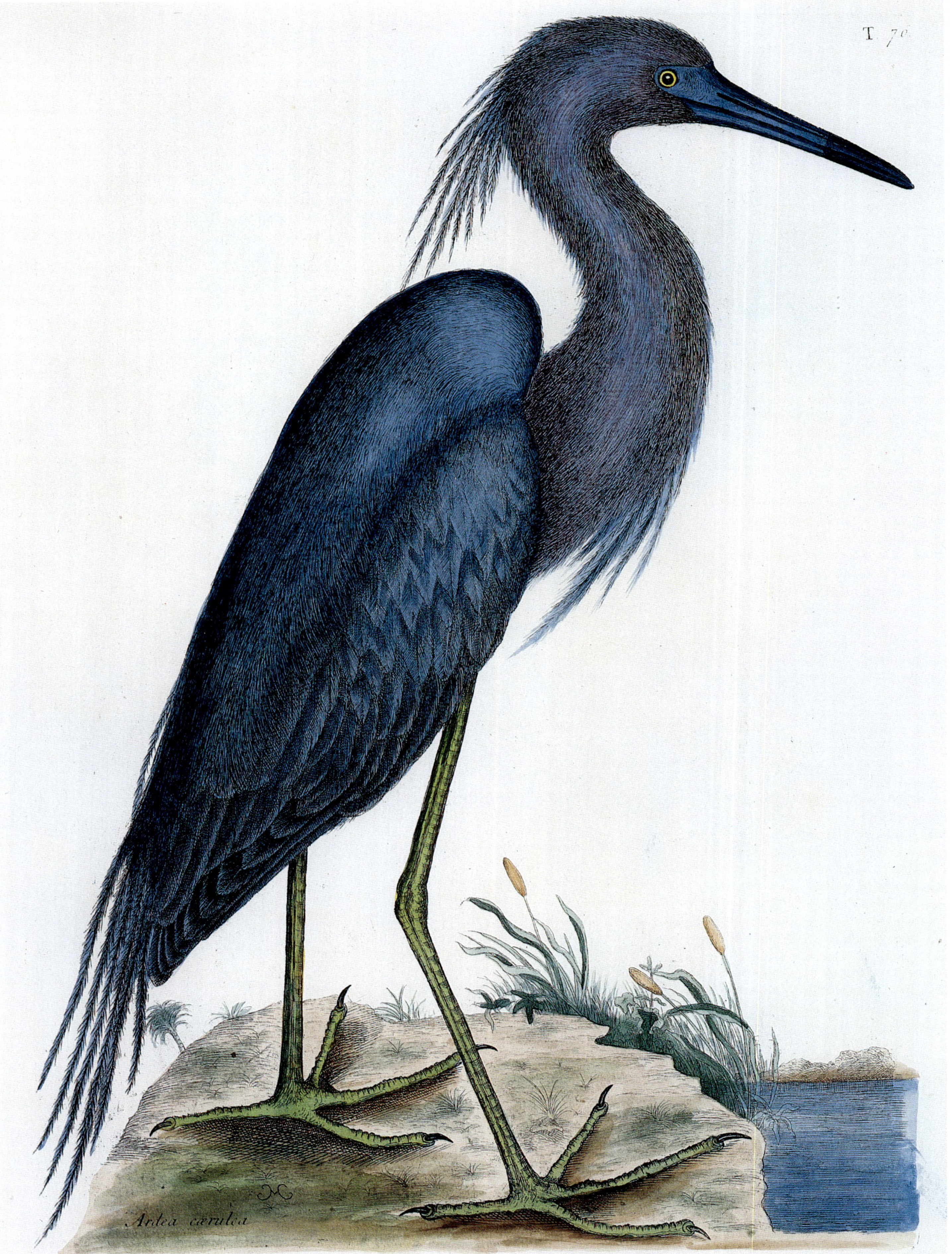

THE BLUE HERON. MARK CATESBY, *NATURAL HISTORY,* VOL. 1, PLATE 76. HAND-COLORED ETCHING, LONDON, 1727-1731.

The blue heron, which breeds in marshes throughout the south Atlantic states, is another bird Catesby saw infrequently. With typical candor he writes, "Whence they come, and where they breed, is to me unknown." However, Catesby was one of the first naturalists to grasp the principle of bird migration, described in his paper for the Royal Society entitled "Of Birds of Passage."

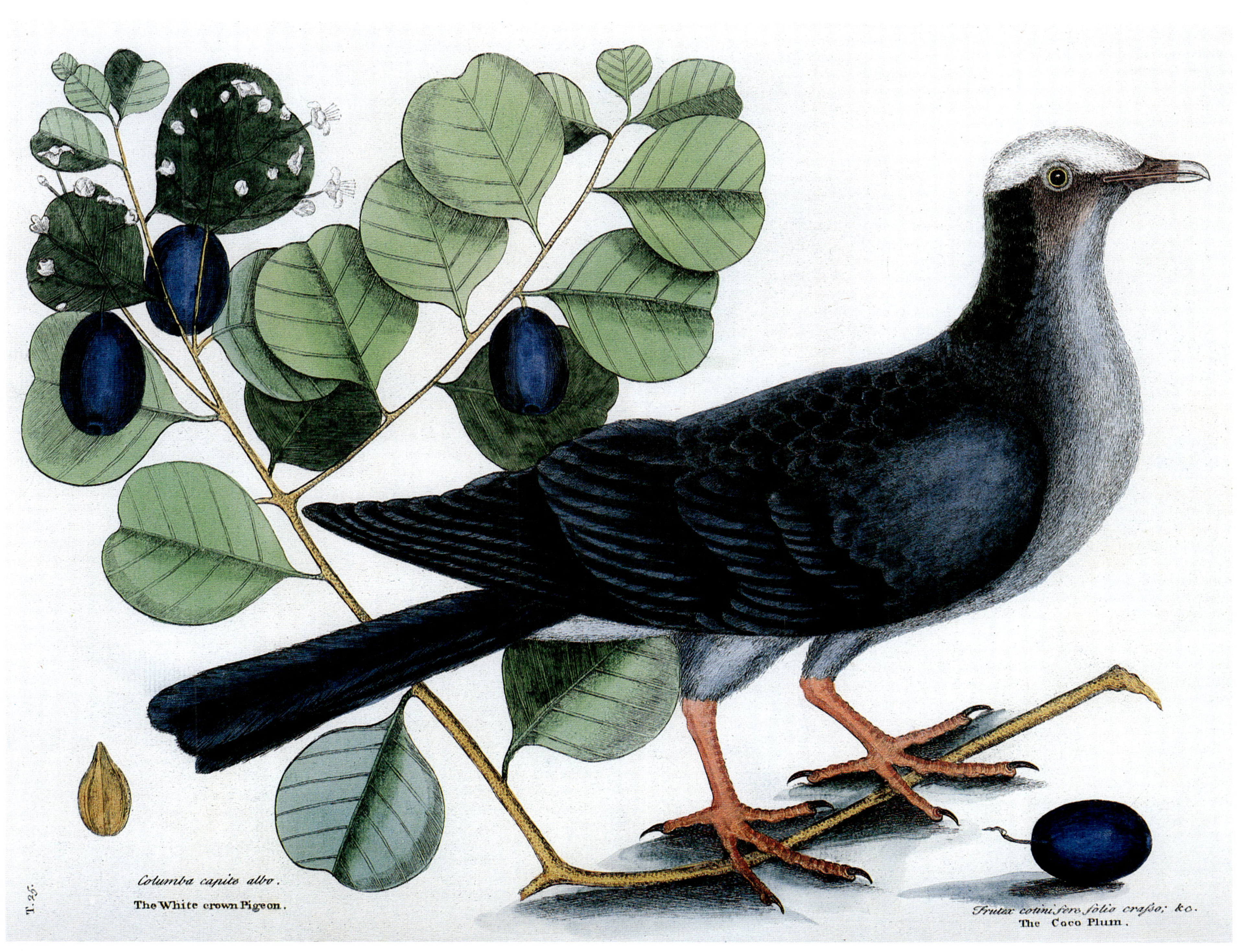

THE WHITE CROWN PIGEON. THE COCO PLUM. MARK CATESBY, *NATURAL HISTORY,* VOL. 1, PLATE 25. HAND-COLORED ETCHING, LONDON, 1727-1731.

Catesby notes that the white-crowned pigeon, which breeds throughout the West Indies, was hunted in great numbers by islanders, as it is today. The coco-plum neatly balancing this composition is an edible fruit to which Catesby ascribes a "sweet luscious taste."

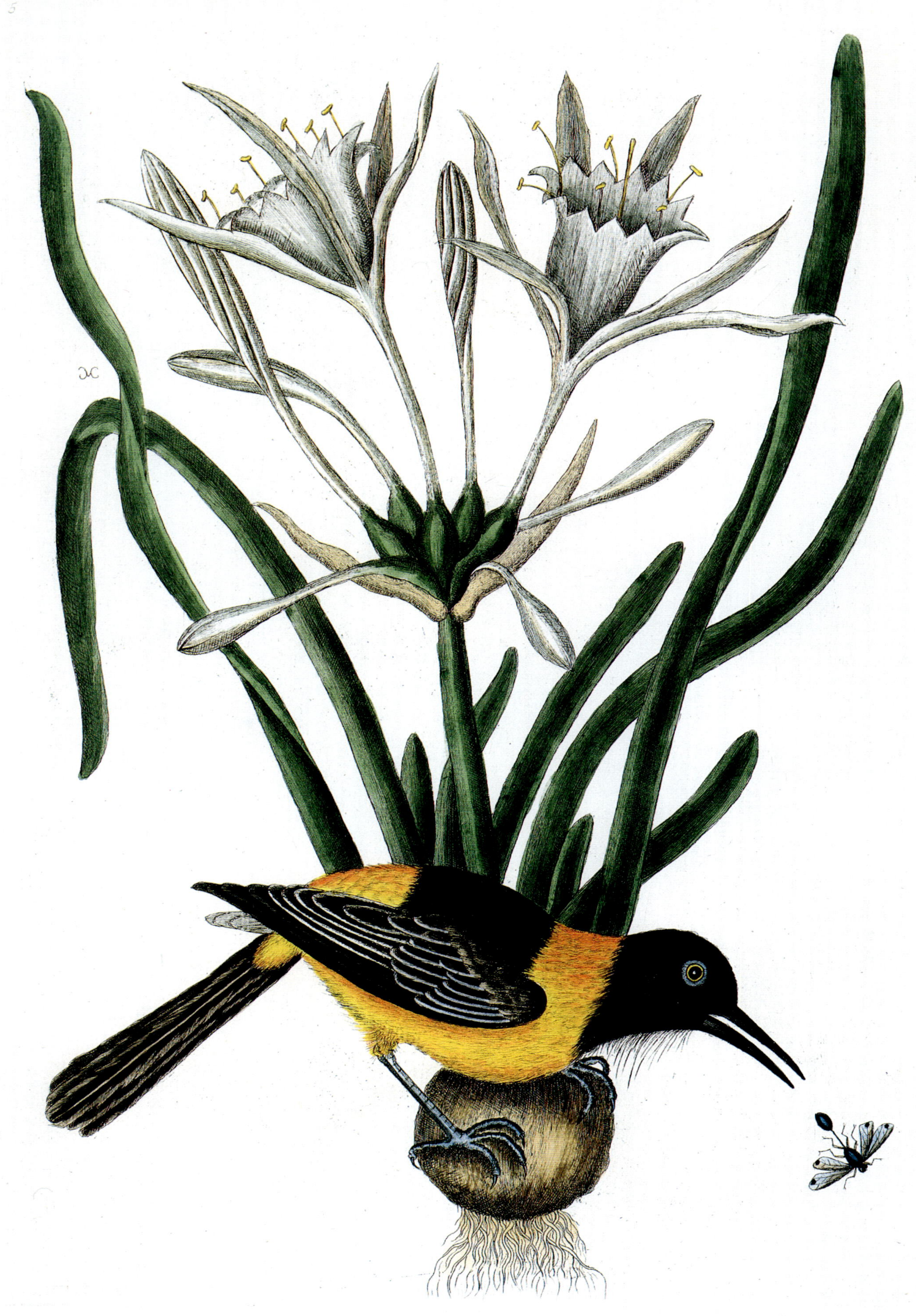

THE YELLOW AND BLACK PYE. MARK CATESBY, *NATURAL HISTORY,* APPENDIX, PLATE 5. HAND-COLORED ETCHING, LONDON, 1743-1747.

In 18th-century Charleston, yellow and black pyes, now called troupials, were "often kept in cages for their docility and antic gestures." Catesby devotes far more of his accompanying text to the wasp at lower right. He was charmed by the singing sounds these insects make as they add clay to their nests and impressed by their ability to capture and carry spiders eight times their weight.

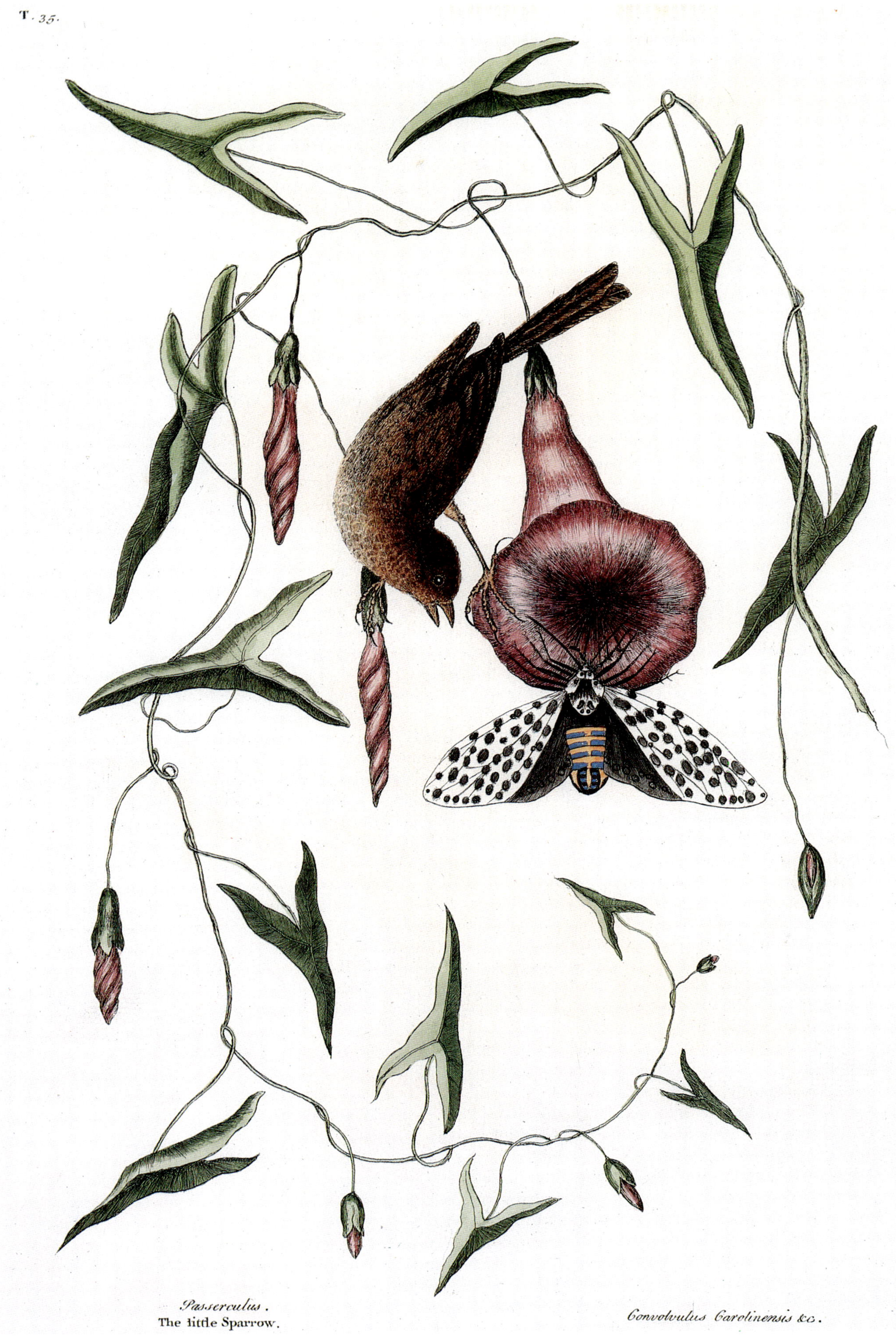

THE LITTLE SPARROW. THE PURPLE BIND-WEED OF CAROLINA. MARK CATESBY, *NATURAL HISTORY,* VOL. 1, PLATE 35. HAND-COLORED ETCHING, LONDON, 1727-1731.

Although Catesby frequently observed it "hopping under bushes...near houses in Virginia and Carolina," this bird is one of a handful in the Natural History *which modern ornithologists have not identified. It perches improbably on a type of morning-glory from which, according to Catesby, Indians extracted a juice to repel rattlesnakes.*

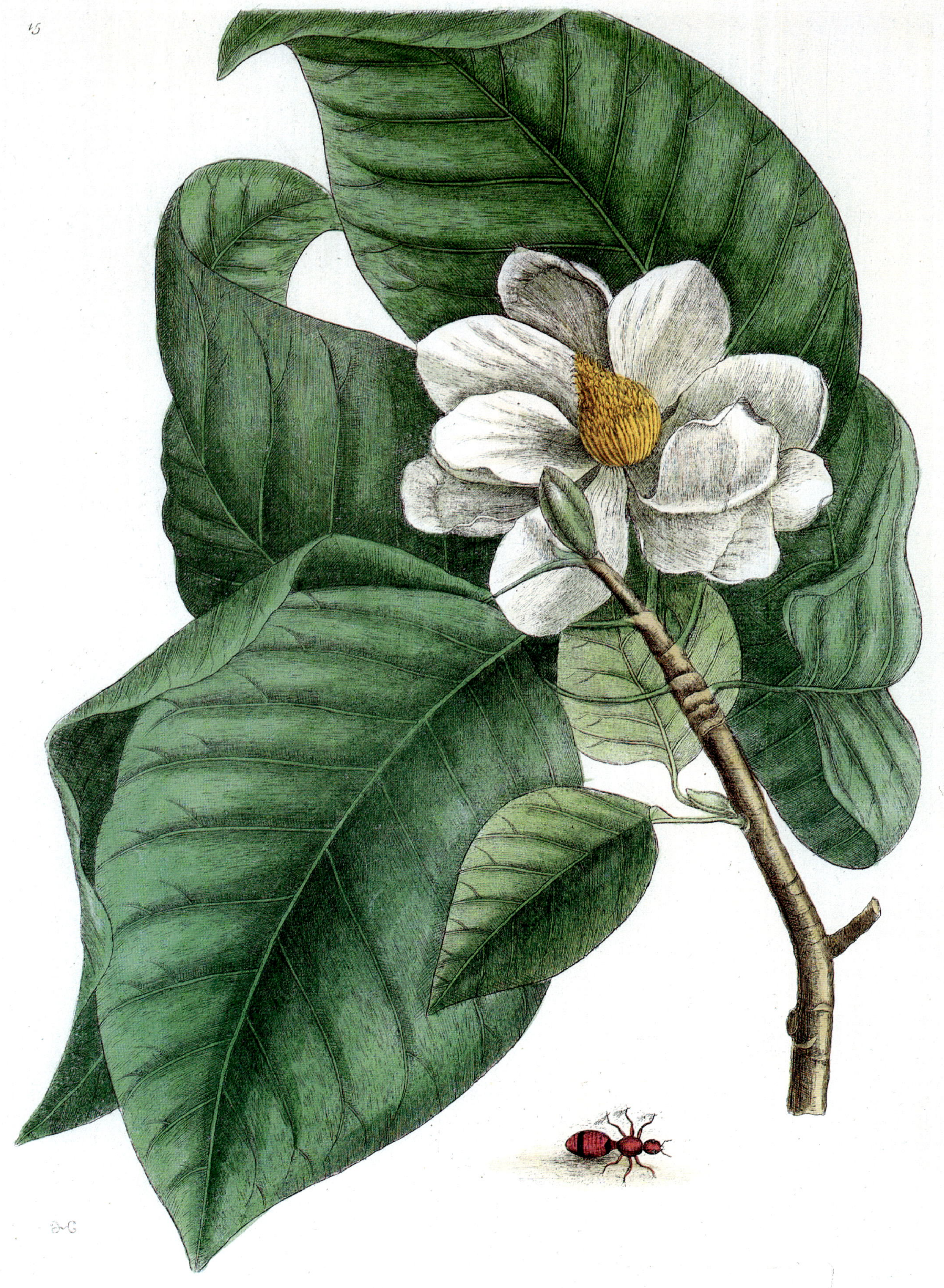

THE VELVET ANT. MARK CATESBY, *NATURAL HISTORY,* APPENDIX, PLATE 15. HAND-COLORED ETCHING, LONDON, 1743-1747.

To demonstrate the remarkable formal differences found in nature, Catesby contrasts the very dissimilar shapes of an ant and a sprig from a cucumbertree. The ants, he reports, "are mostly seen running very nimbly on sandy roads in the hottest Summer weather." Their shells are so hard that they survive being stepped on by men or cattle; to those who go barefoot, they give a powerful and painful sting.

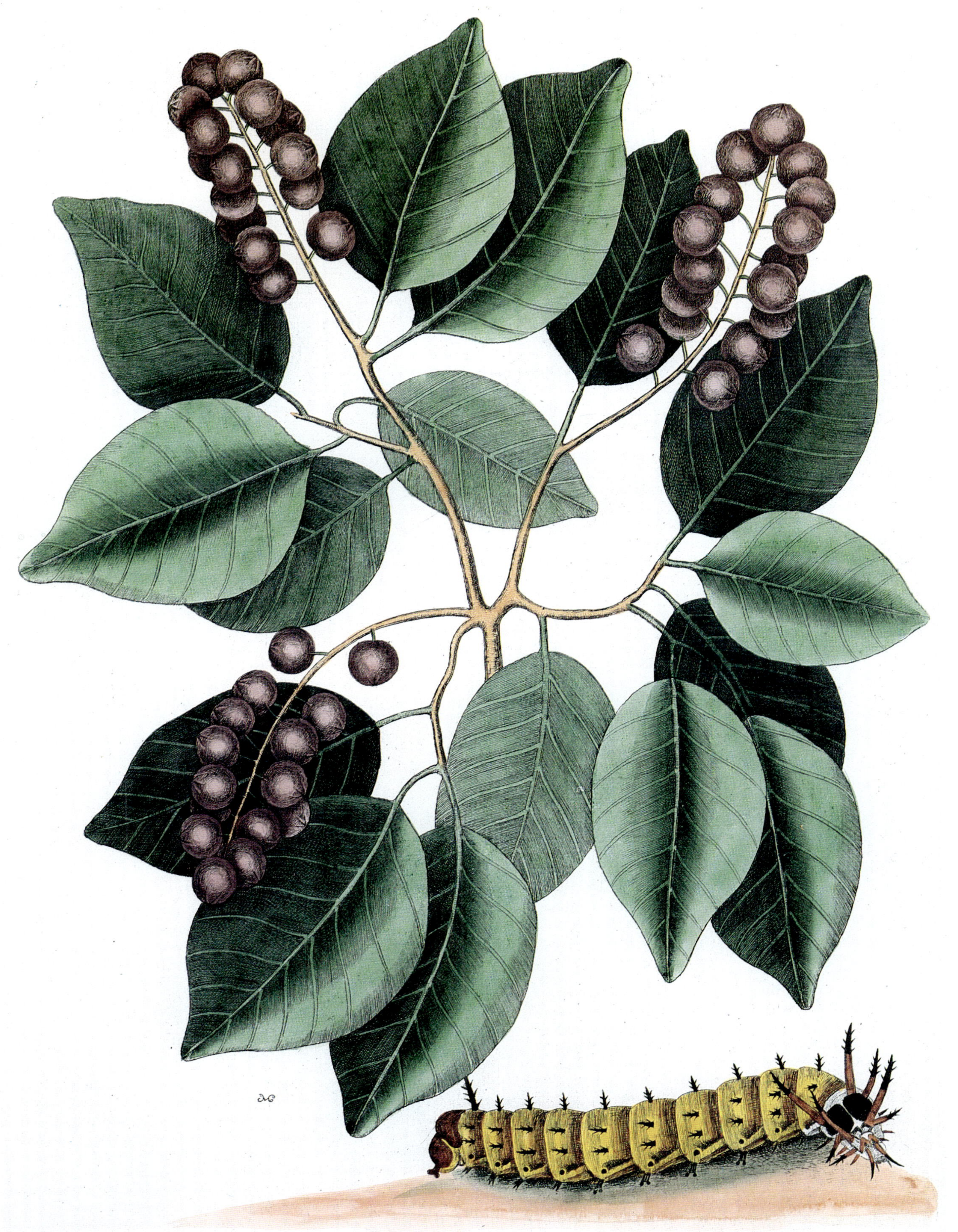

PIGEON-PLUM. THE GREAT HORNED CATTERPILLAR. MARK CATESBY, *NATURAL HISTORY,* VOL. 2, PLATE 94. HAND-COLORED ETCHING, LONDON, 1731-1743.

In this felicitous juxtaposition of improbable companions, the pigeon plum perfectly balances the mass, lines, and tonality of the caterpillar beneath it.

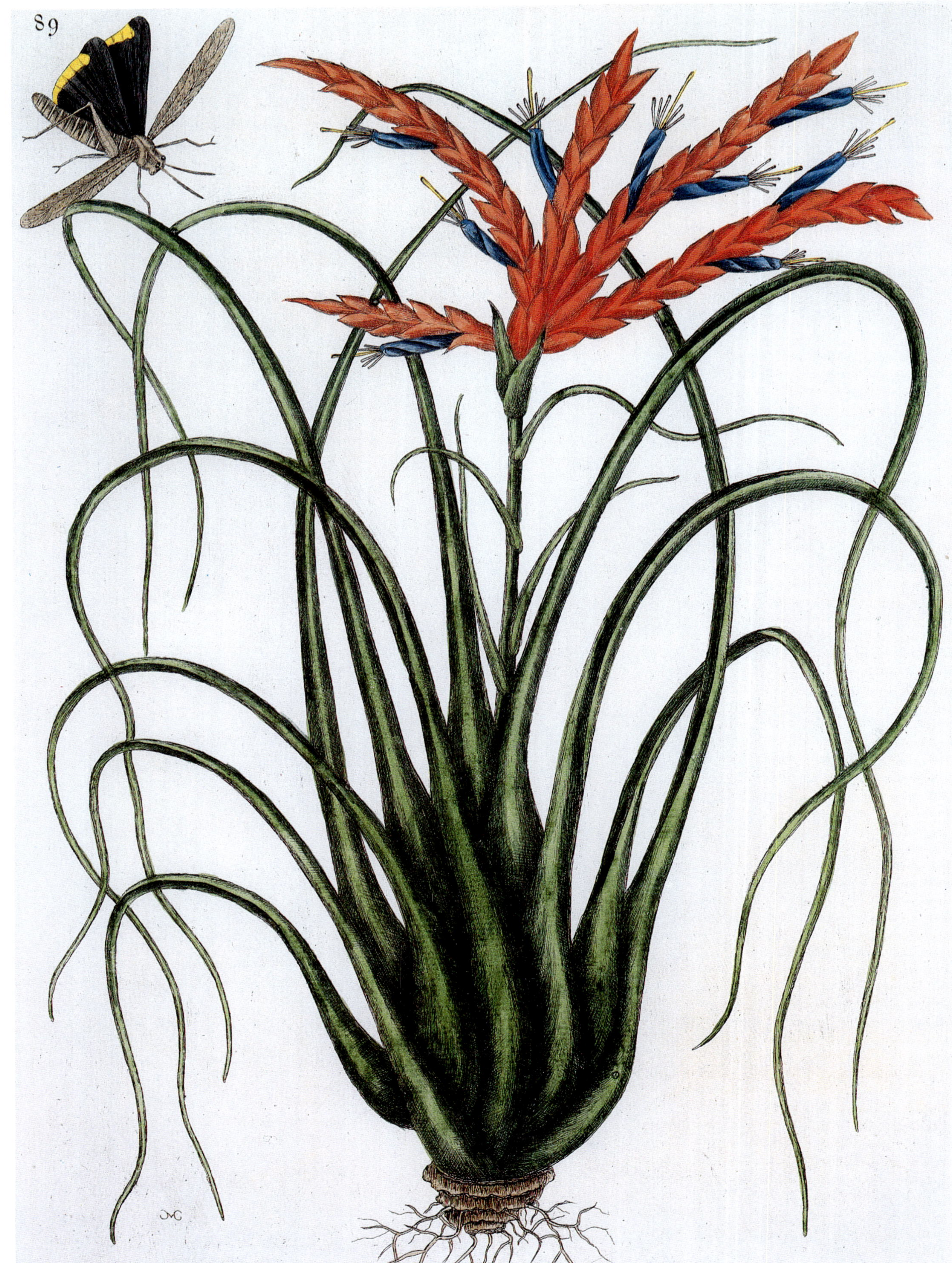

THE WILD PINE. THE CRICKET. MARK CATESBY, *NATURAL HISTORY,* VOL. 2, PLATE 89. HAND-COLORED ETCHING, LONDON, 1731-1743.

Of the wild pine, which grows on other trees throughout the Bahamas, Catesby writes: "What recommends this useful and very singular Plant is, that its hollow leaves, lapping over one another, are so closely placed, that one Plant will contain two quarts of clear water. In many countries between the Tropicks, *that are destitute of water, having neither springs nor rivers, these Plants abound, and are of great benefit in relieving the thirsty in distress."*

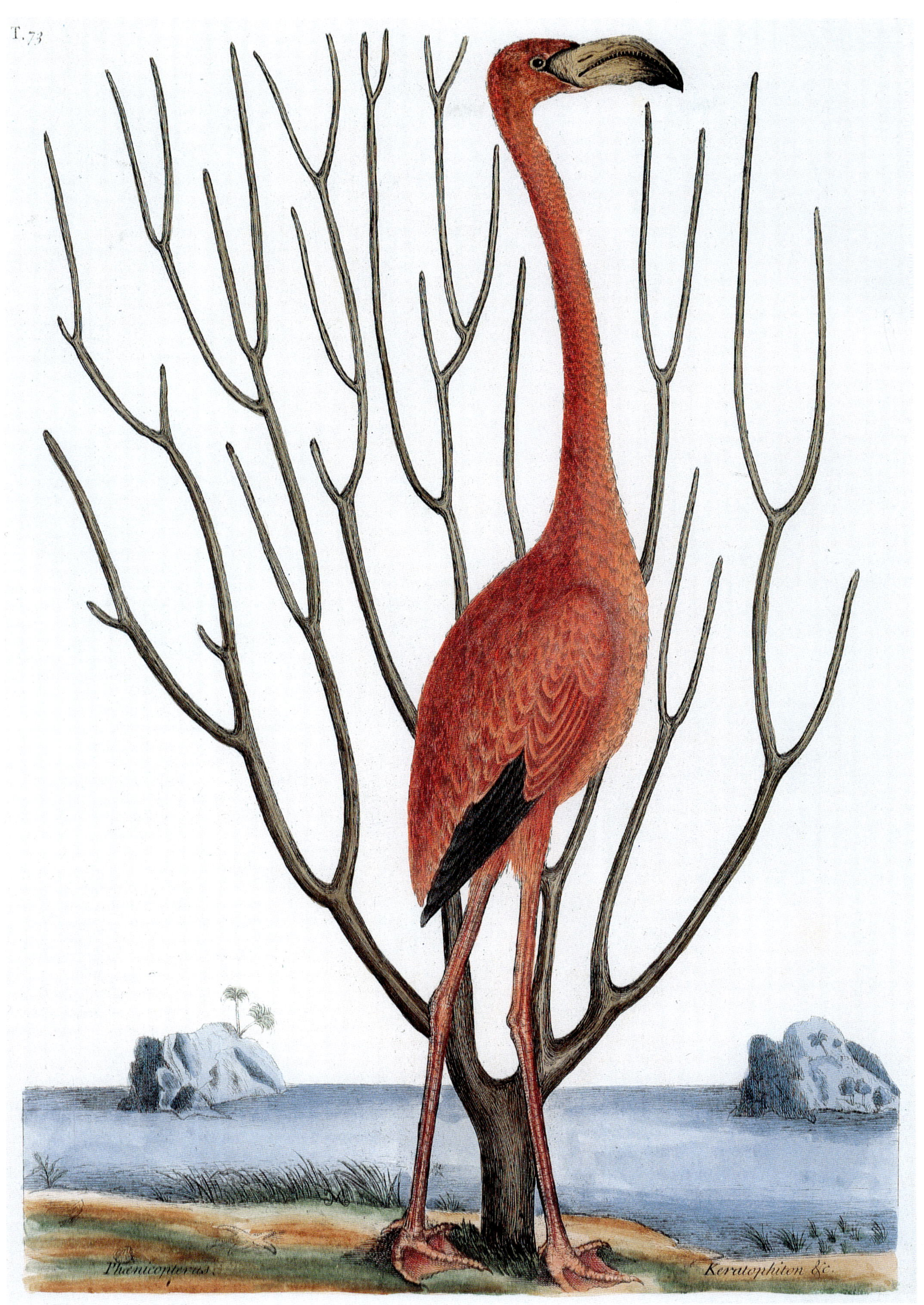

THE FLAMINGO. MARK CATESBY, *NATURAL HISTORY,* VOL. 1, PLATE 73. HAND-COLORED ETCHING, LONDON, 1727-1731.

Catesby observed flamingos in the Bahamas and writes that because they did not startle at the sound of a gun, they could be slaughtered easily by the hundreds. Intrigued by the "singular form" of the bird's bill, he devoted a second plate to drawing it in detail. The skeletal plant in the background is a type of gorgonian coral, shown here out of the water.

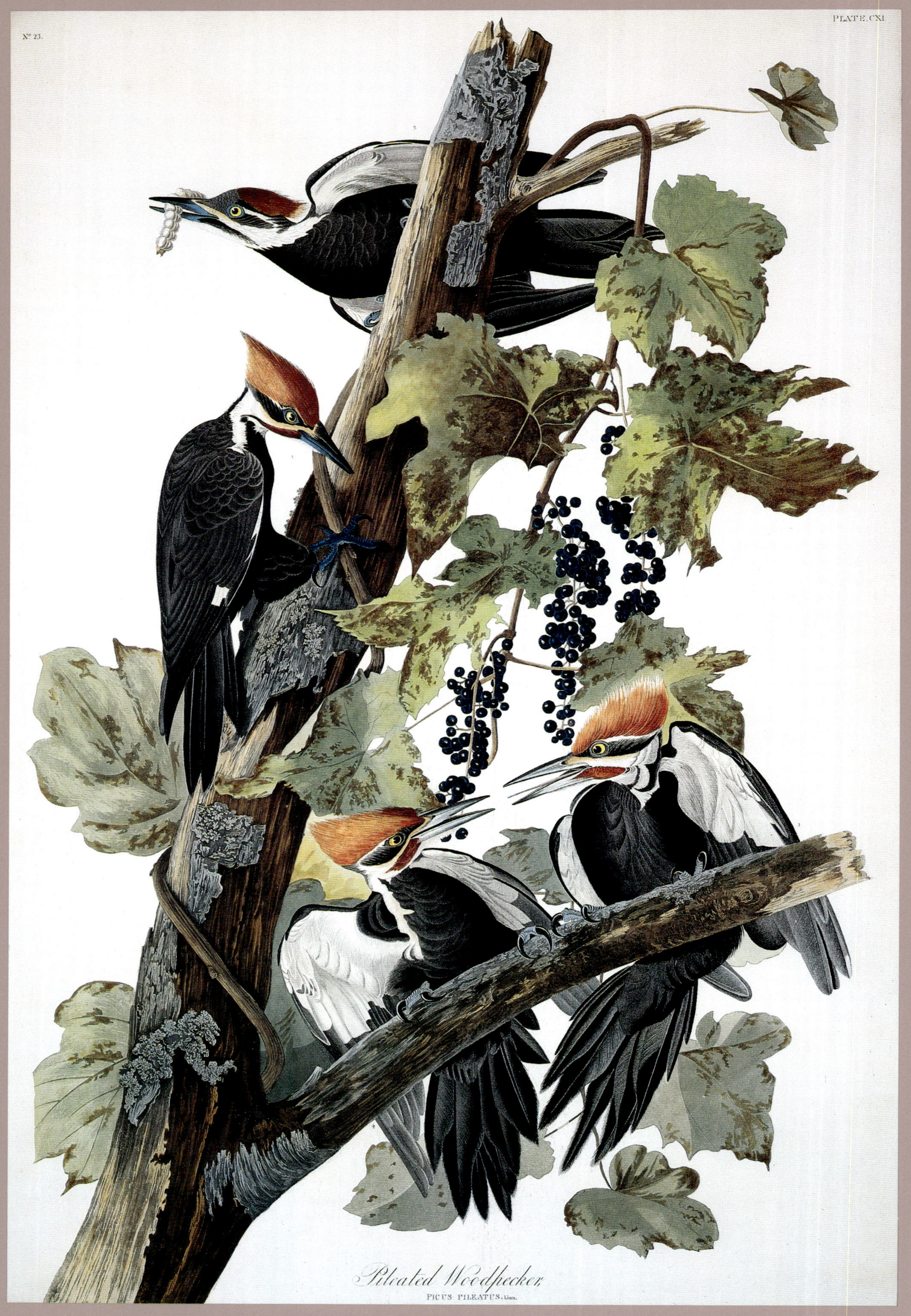
No 23.
PLATE CXI
Pileated Woodpecker,
PICUS PILEATUS, Linn.

JOHN JAMES AUDUBON (1785-1851)

PILEATED WOODPECKER. JOHN JAMES AUDUBON, *THE BIRDS OF AMERICA*, VOL. 2, PLATE 111. HAND-COLORED ETCHING AND AQUATINT, ROBERT HAVELL, LONDON, 1831-1834.

Though pileated woodpeckers were common in Audubon's time, he had difficulty shooting a specimen. Finally he gave up chasing the wily bird. Taking "a circuitous route," he hid in the woodpecker's path, "waited till it came up," and fired a successful shot. Here Audubon shows an adult pair and two young males.

Vain, often naive in his dealings with people, sometimes astonishingly ungrateful to those who helped him, John James Audubon was also a man abounding in energy, whose passion for the outdoors and for drawing birds was matched by his determination to publish his watercolors in grand style. In three monumental works, *The Birds of America*, its companion text *Ornithological Biography*, and *The Viviparous Quadrupeds of North America*, Audubon brilliantly represented the birds and animals of a continent still largely wild and open.

Though Audubon claimed that as a youth he received instruction in the atelier of Jacques-Louis David, his training in art and science was haphazard at best. Born in Santo Domingo (now Haiti), the illegitimate son of a French lieutenant and his mistress, Audubon spent his boyhood on a farm on the Loire, hunting and drawing wild birds—much to the detriment of his schoolwork. As a young man, he was befriended by a number of naturalists, including the noted systematist Charles d'Orbigny.

In 1803, at the age of 18, he emigrated to America to manage Mill Grove, his father's farm in Pennsylvania. There he continued his pursuit of birds, conducting some of the world's first experiments with banding. He also practiced wiring freshly killed specimens, a technique which enabled him to sketch birds in lifelike postures while their feathers were still bright, lending his work unprecedented vitality and drama.

Several years later, Audubon and a business partner, Ferdinand Rozier, set up a dry goods store first in Louisville, then in Henderson, Kentucky. Audubon's poor business sense and his habit of neglecting work to roam the woods led to his bankruptcy in 1819, when he was jailed briefly for debt.

In March 1810, while Audubon was a storekeeper in Louisville, he chanced to meet the bird painter Alexander Wilson, an encounter which may have inspired the hapless merchant to turn his beloved recreation into a career. Wilson was looking for subscribers to his *American Ornithology*, the first work exclusively devoted to American birds, and stopped in at Audubon's store with two portfolios under his arm.

Twenty years afterward, Audubon wrote that he was preparing to sign up when his partner interrupted him. "My dear Audubon," Rozier said in French, "what induces you to subscribe to this work? Your drawings are certainly far better, and again, you must know as much of the habits of American birds as this gentleman." Audubon did not sign. Years later, the Philadelphia naturalist George Ord, about to publish a posthumous edition of Wilson's nine-volume work, accused Audubon of scientific errors and, not without justification, of plagiarizing some of Wilson's birds. It was chiefly Ord's hostility to Audubon which caused the artist to go to England to find a publisher.

At the age of 35, Audubon began the watercolors for *The Birds of America* in earnest. Determined to carry out his "Great Idea" of publishing a comprehensive work presenting all the American birds life-size in their natural habitats, he traveled down the Ohio and Mississippi to New Orleans in 1820, first by flatboat, then by keelboat, specifically to kill and paint birds. He was to remain in the

Mississippi basin for the next three years, working on his project and teaching French, music, and dancing to planters' children.

The book Audubon had in mind when he went to England in 1826 to find a publisher was a daunting labor for any engraver. Ignoring the advice of friends, patrons, and publishers, he insisted on aquatints that would present his birds life-size. Thus the sumptuous "Double Elephant" folio, printed from copper plates more than two feet wide and three feet long, and painstakingly colored by hand, came to be.

William Home Lizars, an Edinburgh engraver, took on the gargantuan task in 1826, but completed only ten plates before his colorists went on strike. Fortunately, Audubon found Robert Havell in London to finish the work. Havell, a landscape artist whose plates are considered far superior to Lizars', turned Audubon's exquisite watercolors into elegant engravings, sometimes hand coloring them himself.

Published in four volumes, *The Birds of America* took over 11 years to complete and cost $1,000 per copy. To finance this project, Audubon had to find—and keep—approximately 180 subscribers, no easy task. When he showed his first five plates to the members of the Academie Royale des Sciences in Paris, the price startled them as much as the work pleased them. "*Quel ouvrage!*" they exclaimed. "*Quel prix!*" Not one could afford it.

Audubon was criticized in his day for the charged ambience of his work. Scholars commonly observe three stylistic phases in *Birds*, all of which testify to the artist's persistent fascination with predation and feeding. His early phase (roughly the first 150 plates) displays a spirited, dramatic style and lavish floral decoration. In the engraving of mockingbirds, for example, a rattlesnake attacks the birds' flower-entwined nest (see page 61). Audubon's enemies claimed that snakes could not climb trees and that the viper's fangs would not have curved inward as shown. Audubon was right on both counts.

The flowers and plants in at least 50 of these plates are the work of Joseph Mason, a 13-year-old pupil who shared Audubon's hardships and poverty during the 1820 expedition to Louisiana. A capable artist who became disillusioned with the life they led, Mason left Audubon in August 1822, and in later years, when *The Birds of America* was published, he complained bitterly about Audubon's failure to give him credit for his work.

Audubon's second phase, covering approximately Plate 151 to Plate 370, reveals a mature artist in complete control of his technique. Many of the backgrounds in these plates, especially the landscapes and city views, are the work of the Swiss-born artist George Lehman, who accompanied Audubon on his expedition down the south Atlantic coast to Florida in 1831. The long-billed curlew with Charleston in the distance (see page 68) typifies their collaboration.

In Charleston, Audubon met the Reverend John Bachman, who later conceived the idea and wrote the text for *The Viviparous Quadrupeds of North America*. An amateur naturalist, the Lutheran minister invited Audubon and Lehman to stay with him, taking the artists hunting in the nearby marshes. At Bachman's house, Audubon met Maria Martin, Bachman's sister-in-law and future wife. Martin's delicate drawings of flowers and insects appear in both the second and third phases.

With notable exceptions, the plates in the third phase lack the virtuosity of the earlier work. Many of the birds, drawn from purchased bird skins, are wanting in vitality, and the backgrounds in these plates seem repetitive. In order to include many new birds from the far west without enlarging the work beyond all reason, Audubon occasionally found it necessary to perch several species on a single branch.

In 1841, three years after Havell finished engraving *Birds*, Audubon began an ambitious new pictorial work, *The Viviparous Quadrupeds of North America*. After working 14-hour days on the project for two years, the 58-year-old artist went out to the Missouri River on his last expedition in the spring of 1843, accompanied by the naturalist Edward Harris and the young artist Isaac Sprague. The specimens they gathered on the eight-month trip were brought home pickled in barrels of rum. During this excursion, Audubon, who was not averse to killing 25 brown pelicans to draw a single male, was shocked at the mindless slaughter of the buffaloes. He also criticized George Catlin for romanticizing the Indians, ravaged as they were by smallpox and alcoholism.

Seventy-six of the 150 lithographs in *Quadrupeds* come from Audubon watercolors, chiefly of small mammals, while the larger mammals are based on oils by his son John Woodhouse Audubon. John's older brother Victor painted some of the backgrounds. Acclaimed in the United States and Europe as the most important book to date on American mammals, *Quadrupeds* presented many new species and confirmed Audubon's versatility.

Audubon did not live to see the completion of Bachman's three-volume text for *Quadrupeds* in 1854. A year before the plates were completed in 1848, he developed symptoms of senility, and on January 27, 1851, at the age of 66, he died on his farm on the Hudson.

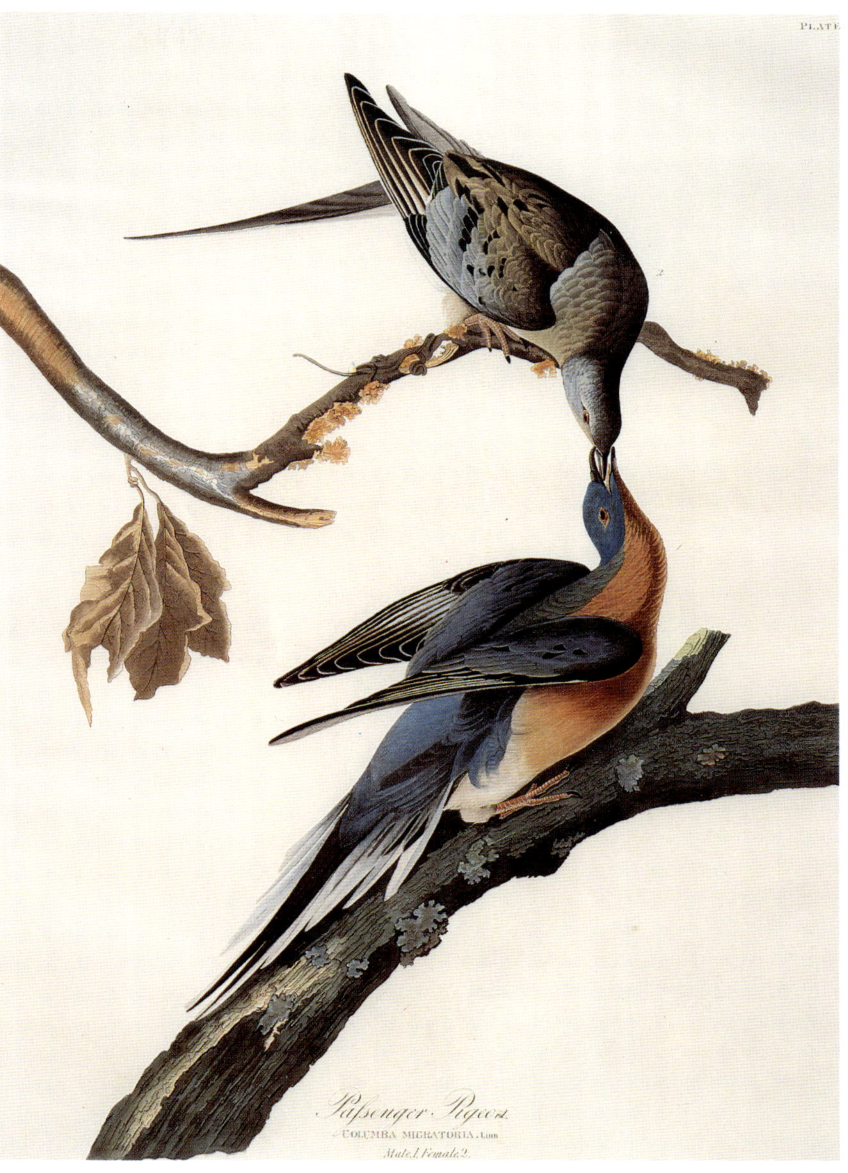

PASSENGER PIGEON. JOHN JAMES AUDUBON, *THE BIRDS OF AMERICA,* VOL. 1, PLATE 62. HAND-COLORED ETCHING AND AQUATINT, ROBERT HAVELL, LONDON, 1827-1830.

In Audubon's day, passenger pigeons were so numerous that during migration "the light of noon-day was obscured as by an eclipse." Wanton slaughter drove the species to extinction by 1914.

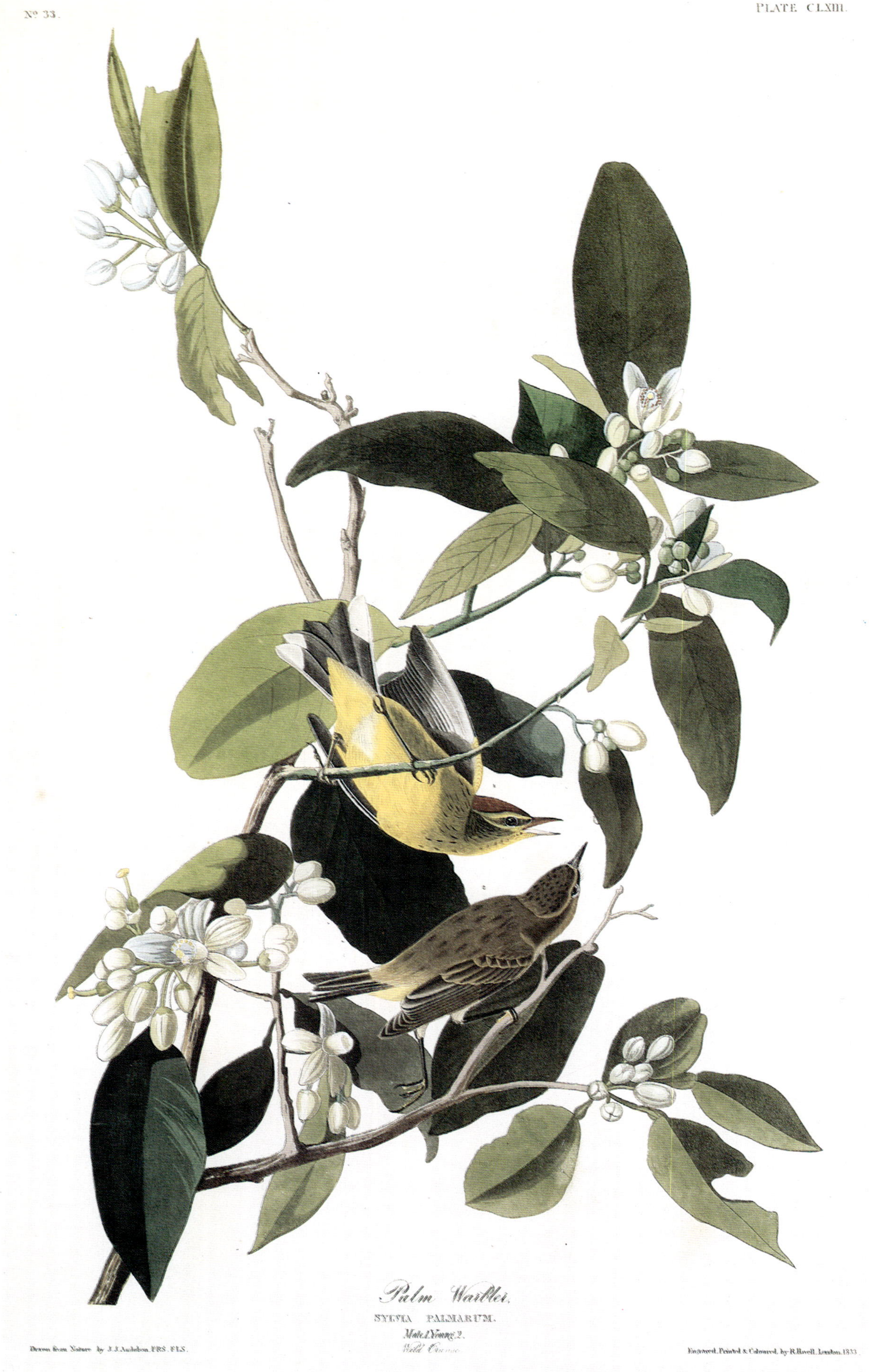

PALM WARBLER. JOHN JAMES AUDUBON, *THE BIRDS OF AMERICA,* VOL. 2, PLATE 163. HAND-COLORED ETCHING AND AQUATINT, ROBERT HAVELL, LONDON, 1831-1834.

Because Audubon's smaller birds could hardly fill the large sheet size of the double-elephant folio, he ornamented some of the extra space with beautiful depictions of the birds' natural settings. This plate is a collaboration; Audubon drew the birds, and George Lehman drew the wild orange tree branch.

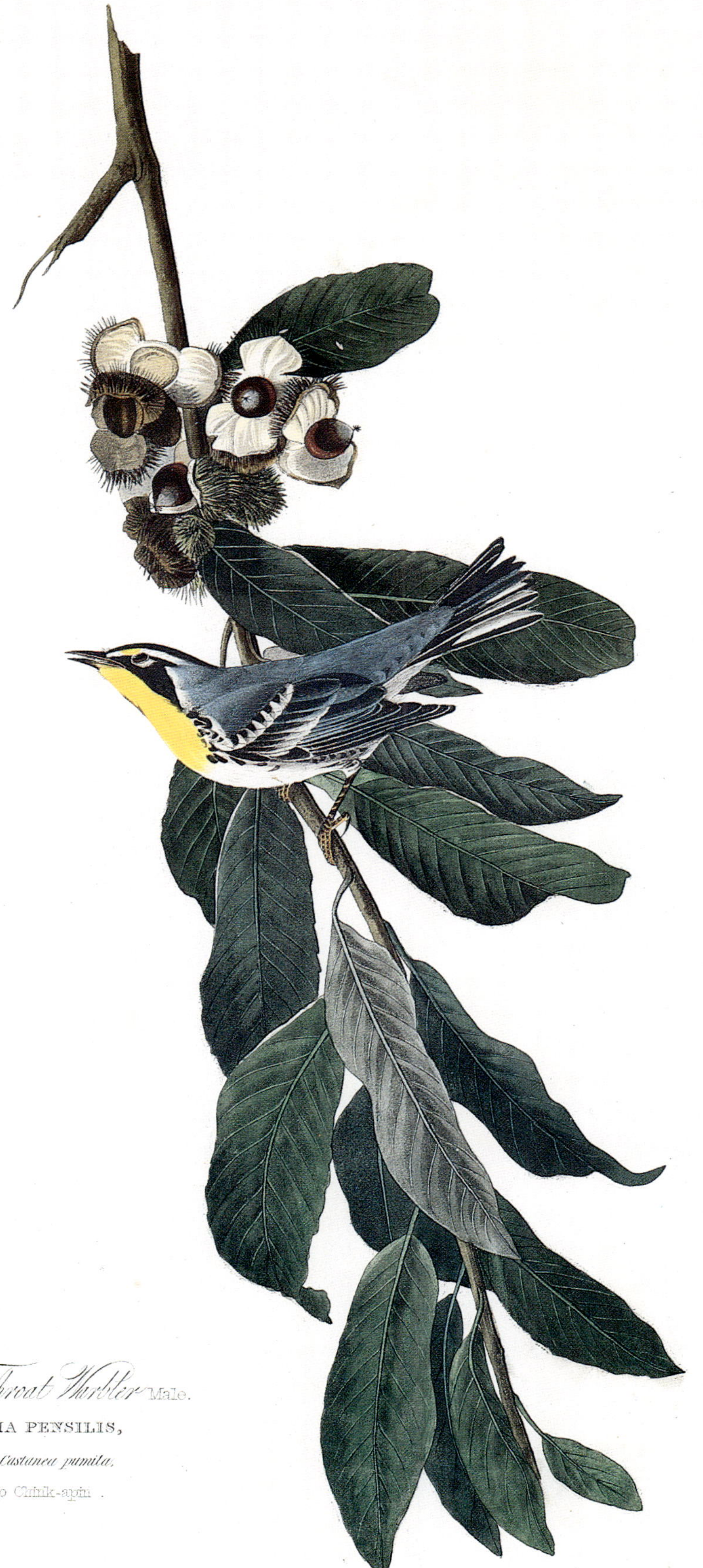

YELLOW THROAT WARBLER. JOHN JAMES AUDUBON, *THE BIRDS OF AMERICA*, VOL. 1, PLATE 85. HAND-COLORED ETCHING AND AQUATINT, ROBERT HAVELL, LONDON, 1827-1830.

Audubon writes that he shot his specimens of this bird as they sat in "a large Chinquapin," the tree depicted here. He praises the warbler's song: "As it is heard in all parts of our most dismal Cypress Swamps, it contributes to soothe the mind of a person whose occupation may lead him to such places."

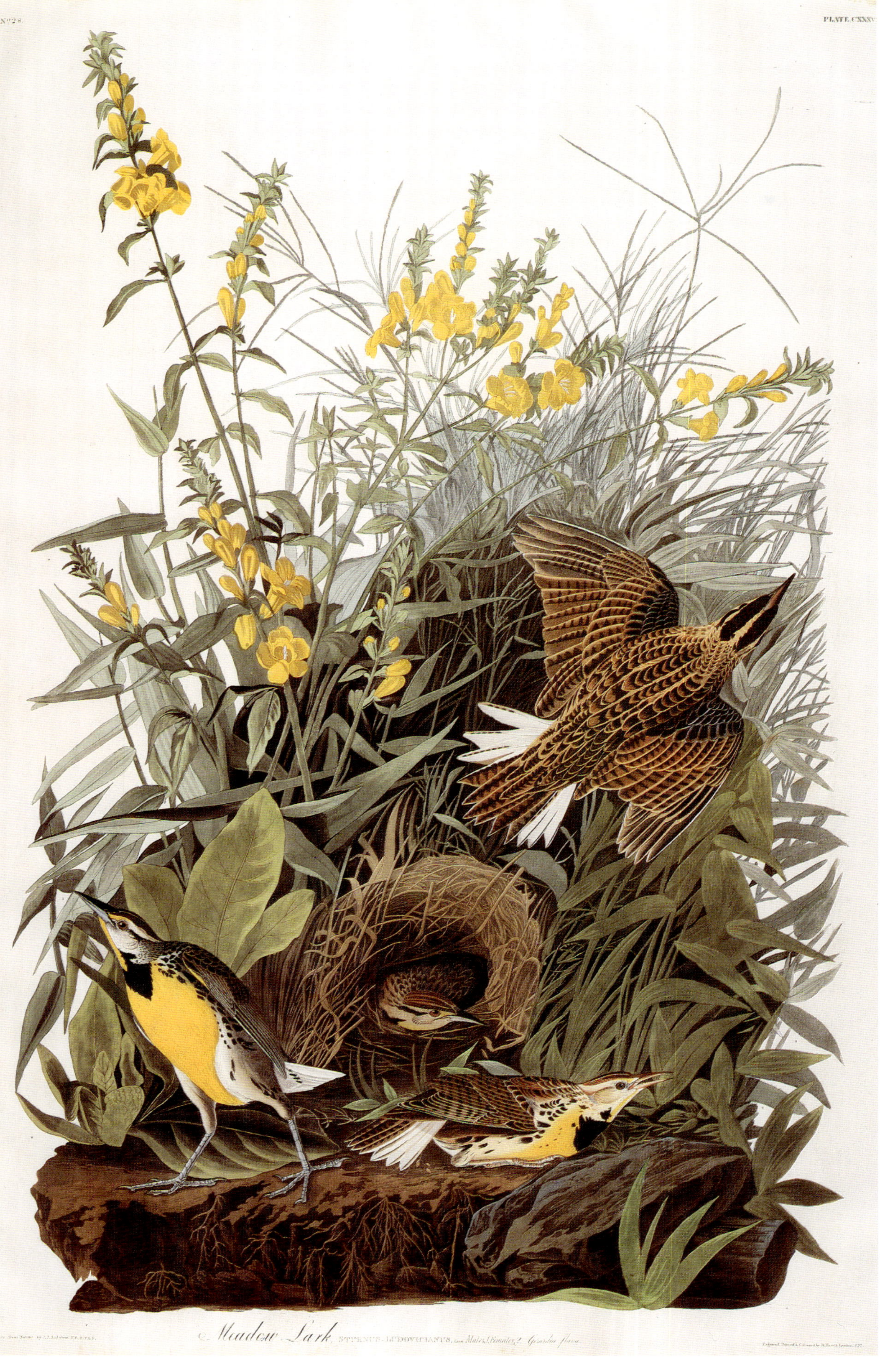

MEADOW LARK. JOHN JAMES AUDUBON, *THE BIRDS OF AMERICA,* VOL. 2, PLATE 136. HAND-COLORED ETCHING AND AQUATINT, ROBERT HAVELL, LONDON, 1831-1834.

This highly regarded Audubon study benefits, like the Palm Warbler, *from the technique of George Lehman, who drew the false foxglove on which the bird perches. The eastern species is portrayed; Audubon did not encounter the western meadowlark until he traveled up the Missouri to collect specimens for* Quadrupeds.

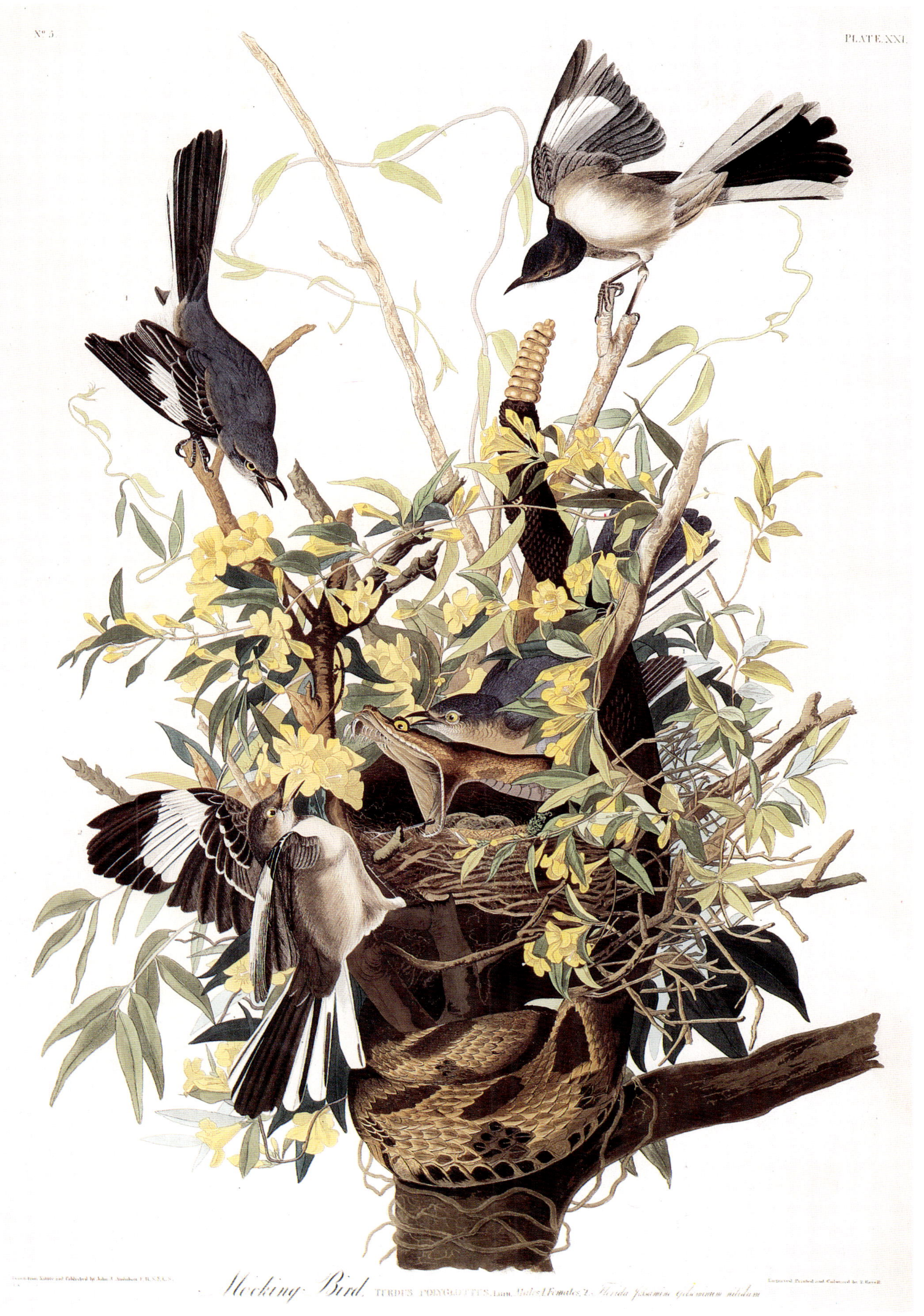

MOCKING BIRD. JOHN JAMES AUDUBON, *THE BIRDS OF AMERICA,* VOL. 1, PLATE 21. HAND-COLORED ETCHING AND AQUATINT, ROBERT HAVELL, LONDON, 1827-1830.

When snakes climb to a mocking-bird nest, writes Audubon, "not only the pair to which the nest belongs, but many other Mocking Birds from the vicinity, fly to the spot, attack the reptiles, and in some cases are so fortunate as to either force them to retreat, or deprive them of life." Here the lush jasmine vine nearly obscures the battle.

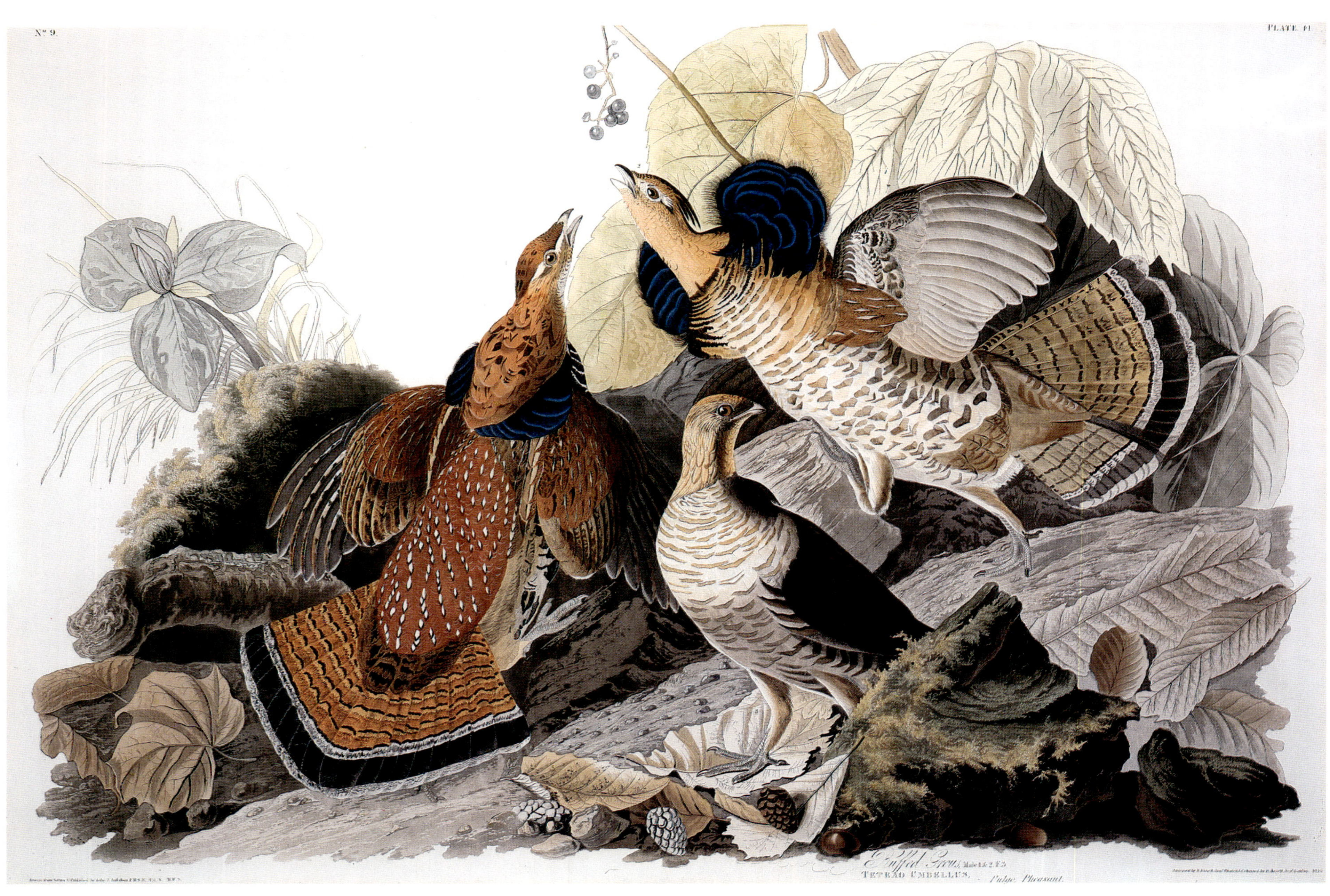

RUFFED GROUSE. JOHN JAMES AUDUBON, *THE BIRDS OF AMERICA,* VOL. 1, PLATE 41. HAND-COLORED ETCHING AND AQUATINT, ROBERT HAVELL, LONDON, 1827-1830.

Strong pyramidal composition shows the front and back feathers of two males to their full advantage. Audubon relished the flavor of grouse and admired the graceful movements of the bird, "which walks with an elevated, firm step, opening its beautiful tail gently," often displaying "the velvety tufts of its neck."

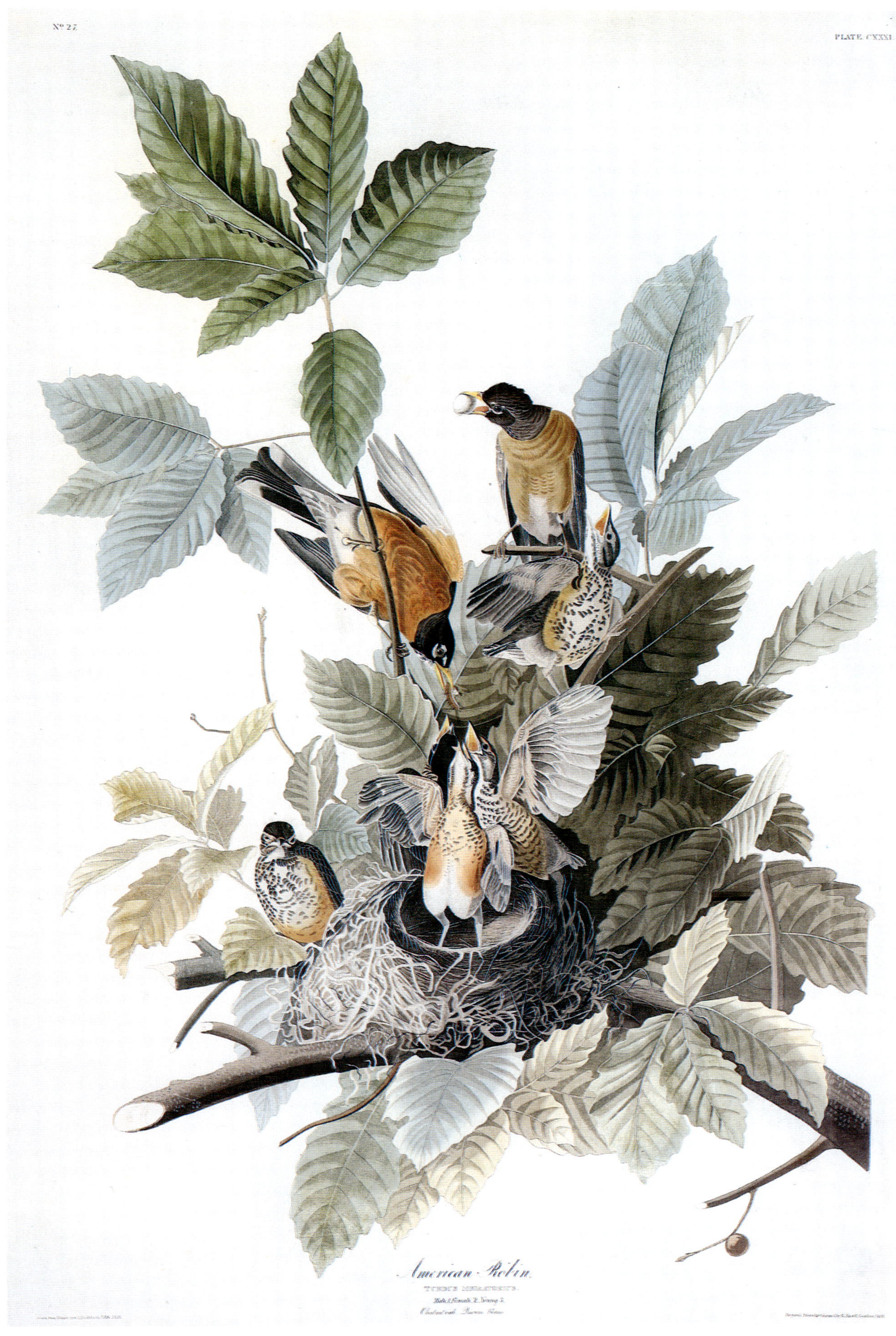

AMERICAN ROBIN. JOHN JAMES AUDUBON, *THE BIRDS OF AMERICA,* VOL. 2, PLATE 131. HAND-COLORED ETCHING AND AQUATINT, ROBERT HAVELL, LONDON, 1831-1834.

Audubon's study of the American robin is rich in details such as the delicate but durable construction of the nest and the feeding of the young. The adults' red breasts contrast boldly with the fledglings' spotted ones.

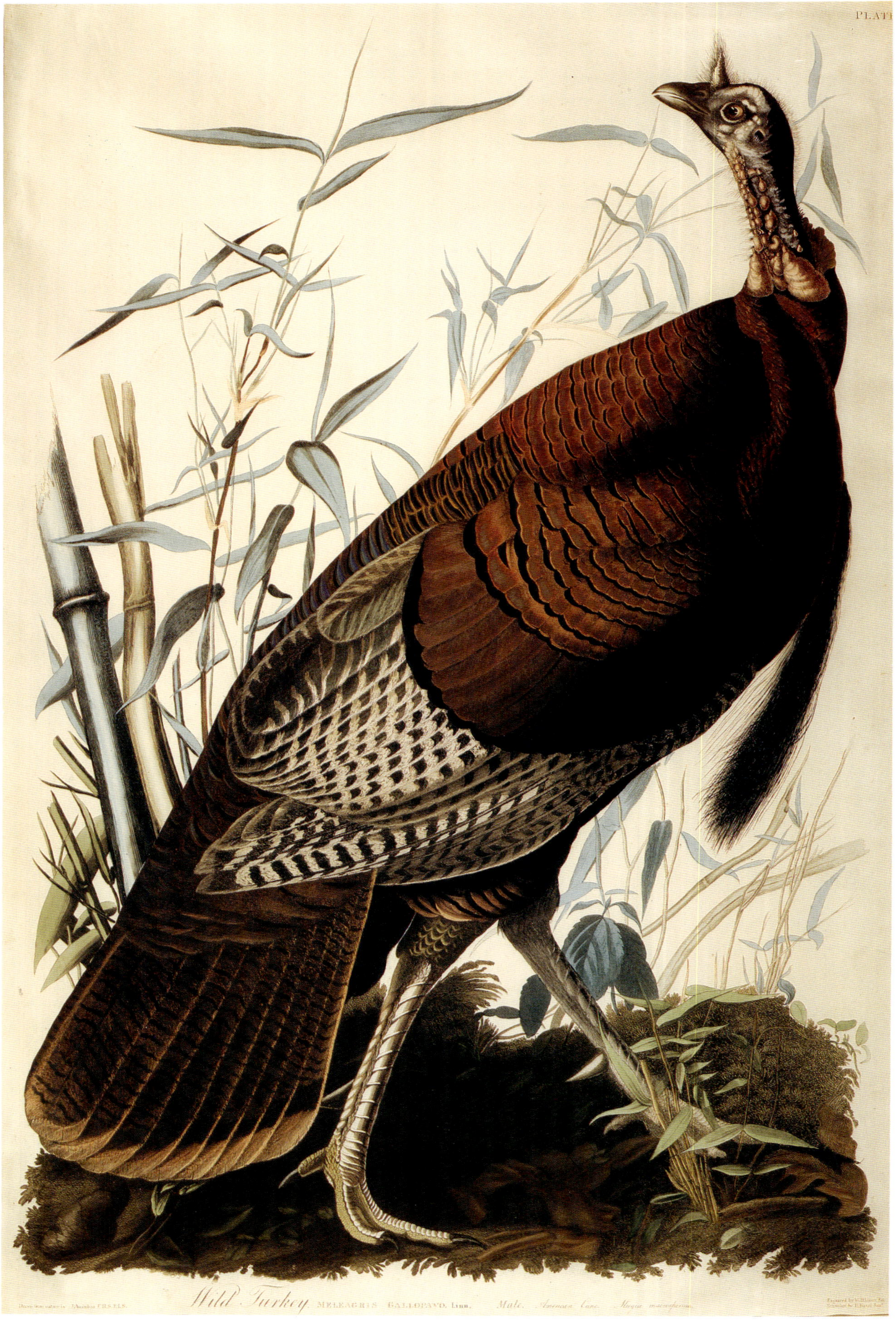

WILD TURKEY. JOHN JAMES AUDUBON, *THE BIRDS OF AMERICA,* VOL. 1, PLATE 1. HAND-COLORED ETCHING AND AQUATINT, WILLIAM LIZARS, EDINBURGH, 1826; RETOUCHED BY ROBERT HAVELL, LONDON, 1827.

After much discussion, Audubon and his first engraver, William Lizars, settled on the wild turkey as the opening plate of Birds. *It was a happy choice; Audubon's* Wild Turkey *has become a classic American print. American cane is shown in the background.*

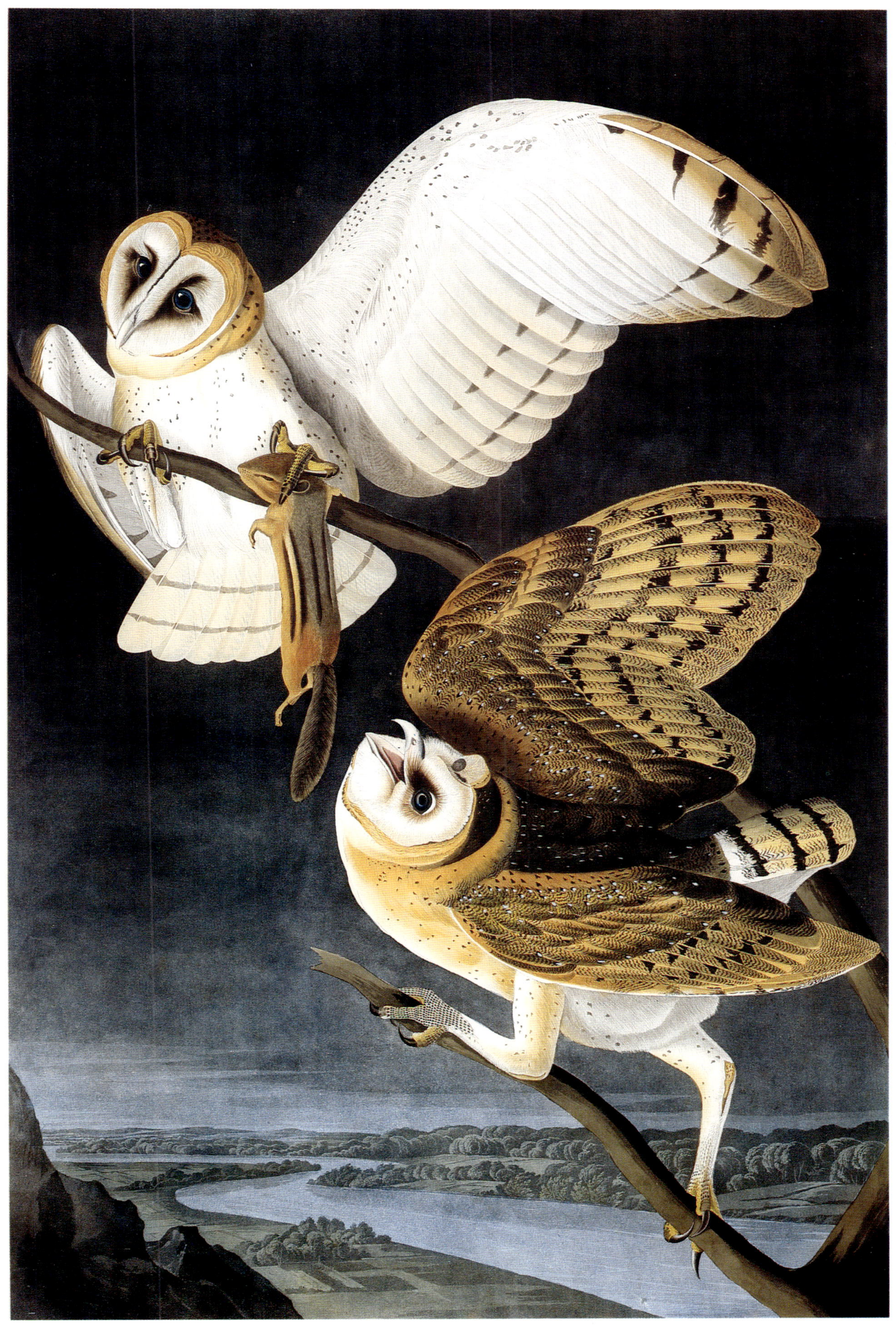

BARN OWL. JOHN JAMES AUDUBON, *THE BIRDS OF AMERICA,* VOL. 2, PLATE 171. HAND-COLORED ETCHING AND AQUATINT, ROBERT HAVELL, LONDON, 1831-1834.

Audubon's original watercolor sketch shows only the two owls and their prey. The night sky and countryside, probably added at Havell's shop, enhance Audubon's chilling portrayal of these nocturnal predators as they prepare to eat the squirrel pinned under the upper bird's powerful talon.

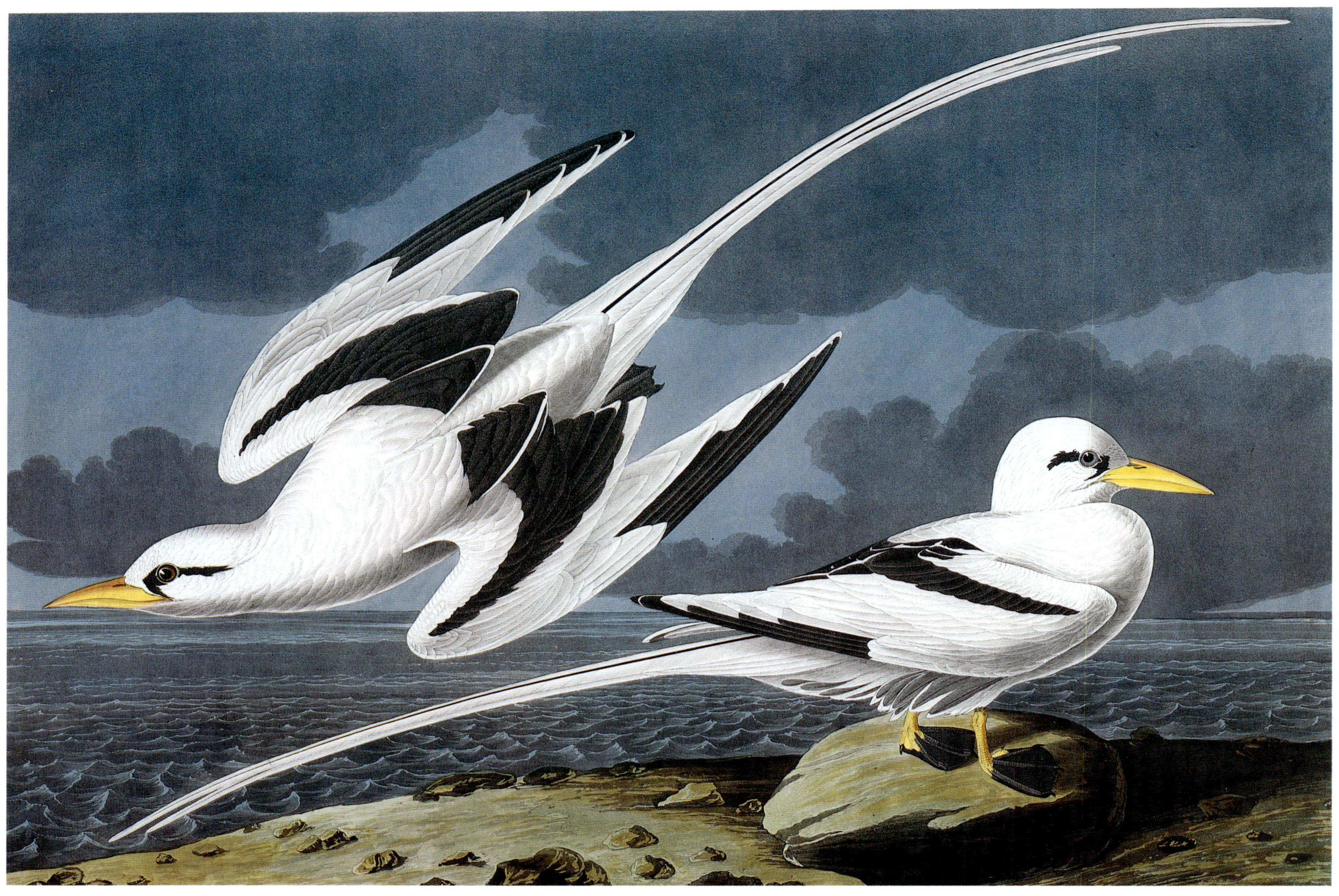

TROPIC-BIRD. JOHN JAMES AUDUBON, *THE BIRDS OF AMERICA,* VOL. 3, PLATE 262. HAND-COLORED ETCHING AND AQUATINT, ROBERT HAVELL, LONDON, 1834-1836.

Native to Bermuda, the Bahamas, and other ocean islands, these graceful sea birds make shallow dives from the air to seize small fish and squid. Audubon based his watercolor on two specimens sent to him from the Dry Tortugas in 1832.

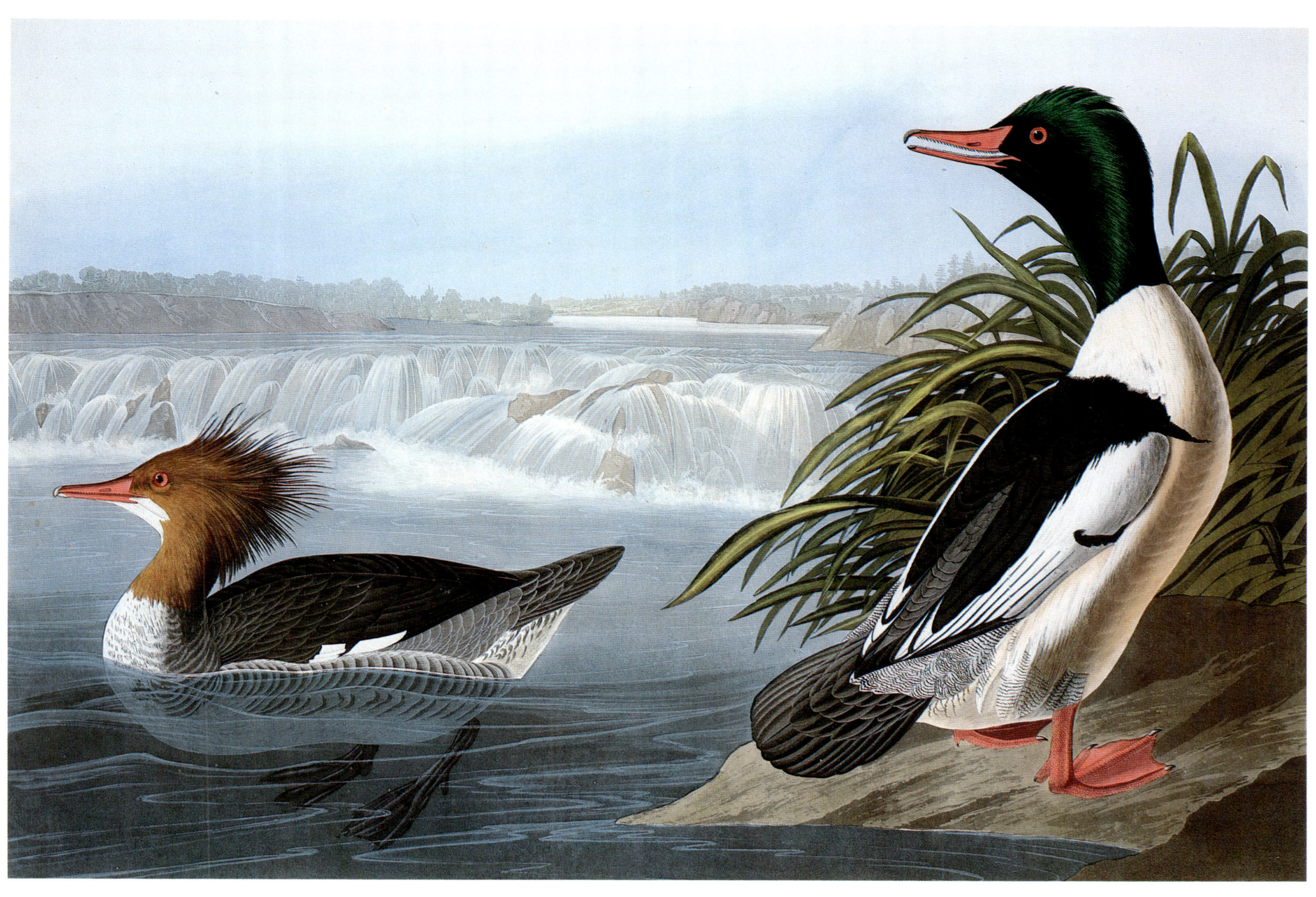

GOOSANDER. JOHN JAMES AUDUBON, *THE BIRDS OF AMERICA,* VOL. 4, PLATE 331.
HAND-COLORED ETCHING AND AQUATINT, ROBERT HAVELL, LONDON, 1836-1838.

The goosander is a fish-eating species known today as the common merganser. This male and female are before Cohoes Falls in the Hudson Valley. The engraver lavished particular care on the male's ruddy crest.

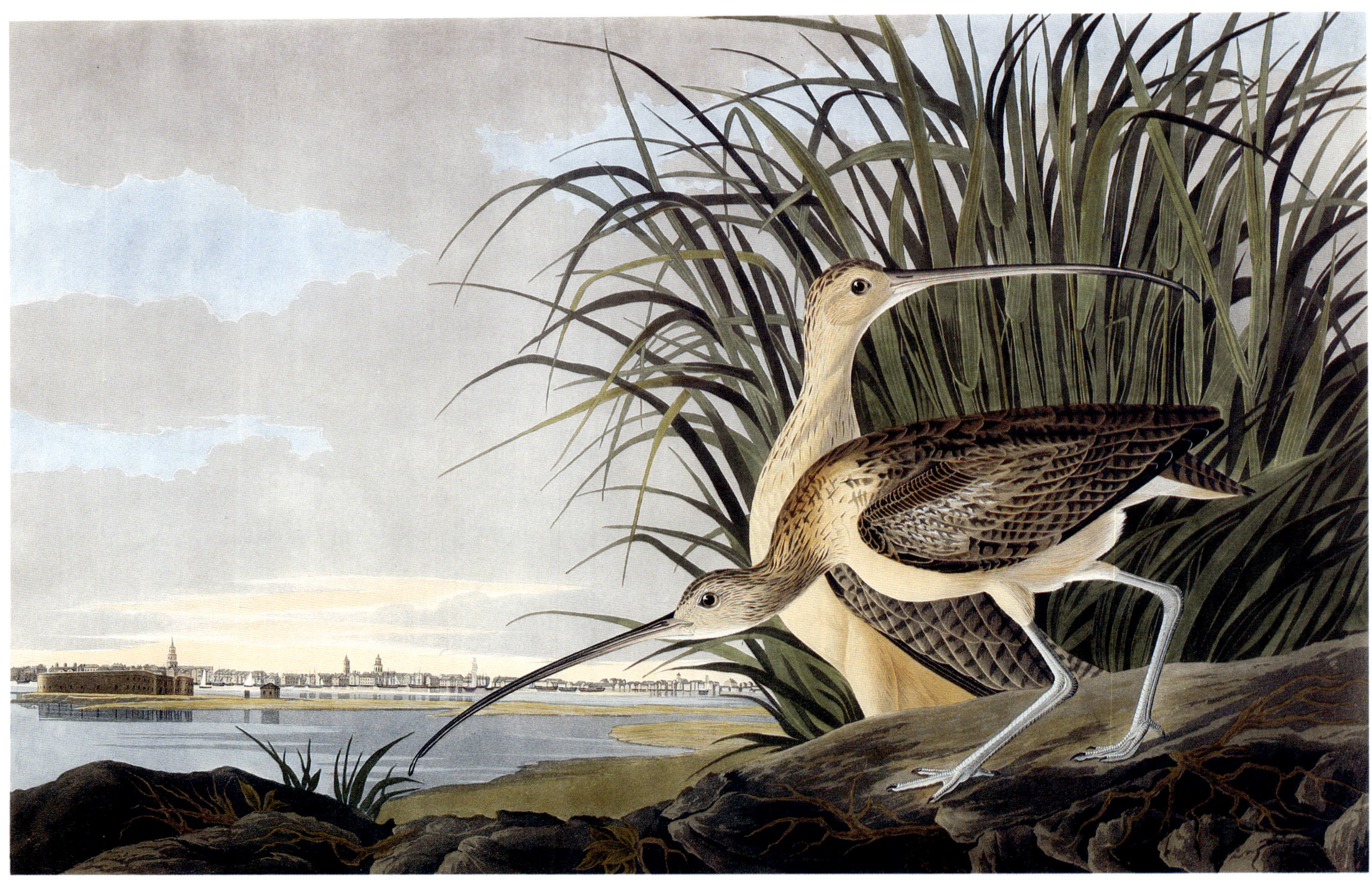

LONG-BILLED CURLEW. JOHN JAMES AUDUBON, *THE BIRDS OF AMERICA,* VOL. 3, PLATE 231. HAND-COLORED ETCHING AND AQUATINT, ROBERT HAVELL, LONDON, 1834-1836.

This image, showing Charleston in the background, commemorates Audubon's 1831 and 1832 sojourns with the Reverend John Bachman in South Carolina. An amateur naturalist, Bachman later wrote the text for Audubon's Quadrupeds. *Audubon's sons Victor and John married two of Bachman's daughters.*

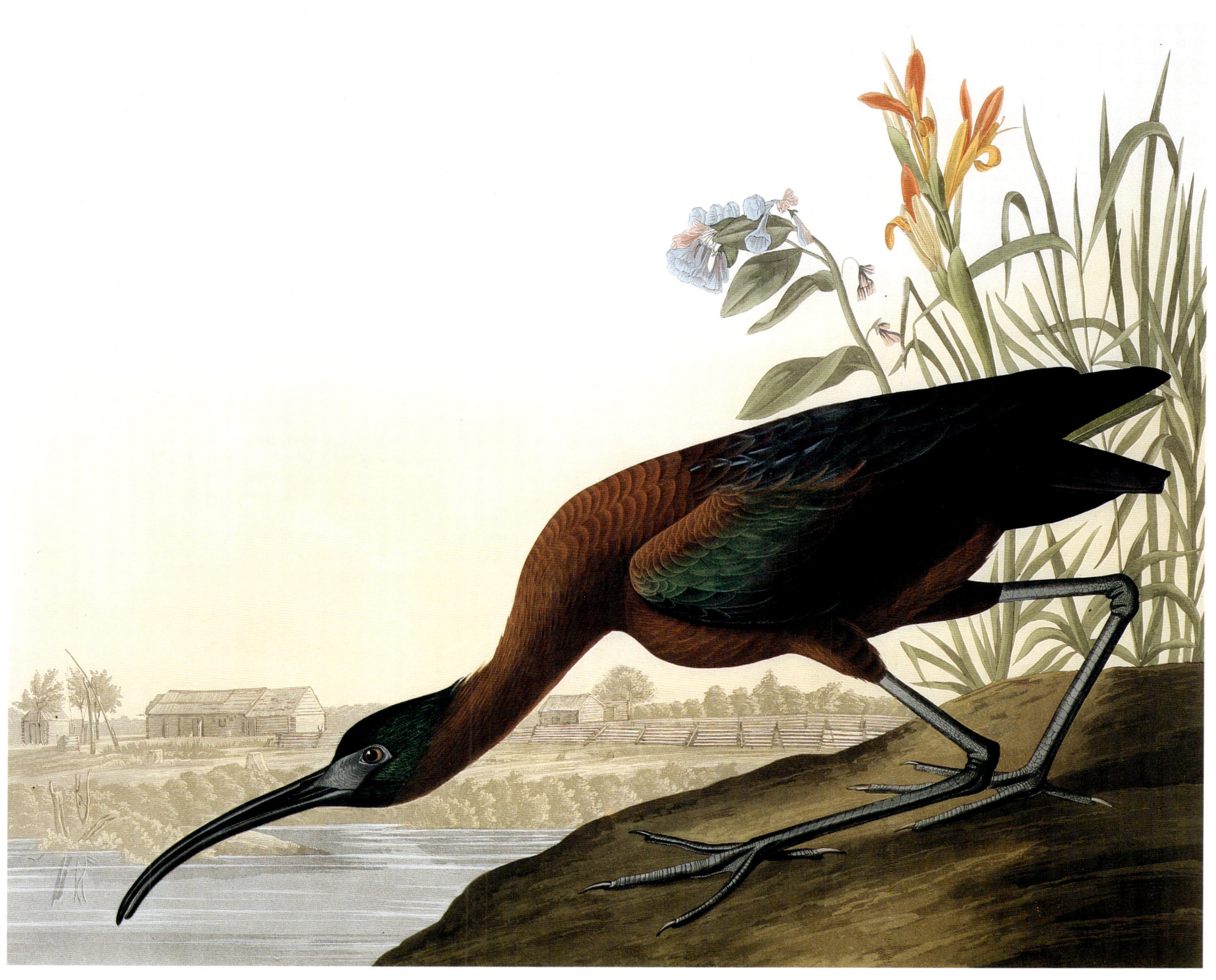

GLOSSY IBIS. JOHN JAMES AUDUBON, *THE BIRDS OF AMERICA,* VOL. 4, PLATE 387. HAND-COLORED ETCHING AND AQUATINT, ROBERT HAVELL, LONDON, 1836-1838.

Like the long-billed curlew, the glossy ibis appears before a Carolina landscape drawn by George Lehman. The ibis' strong coloring and its precisely rendered physical details contrast with the soft tints of the flowers and the farm across the river.

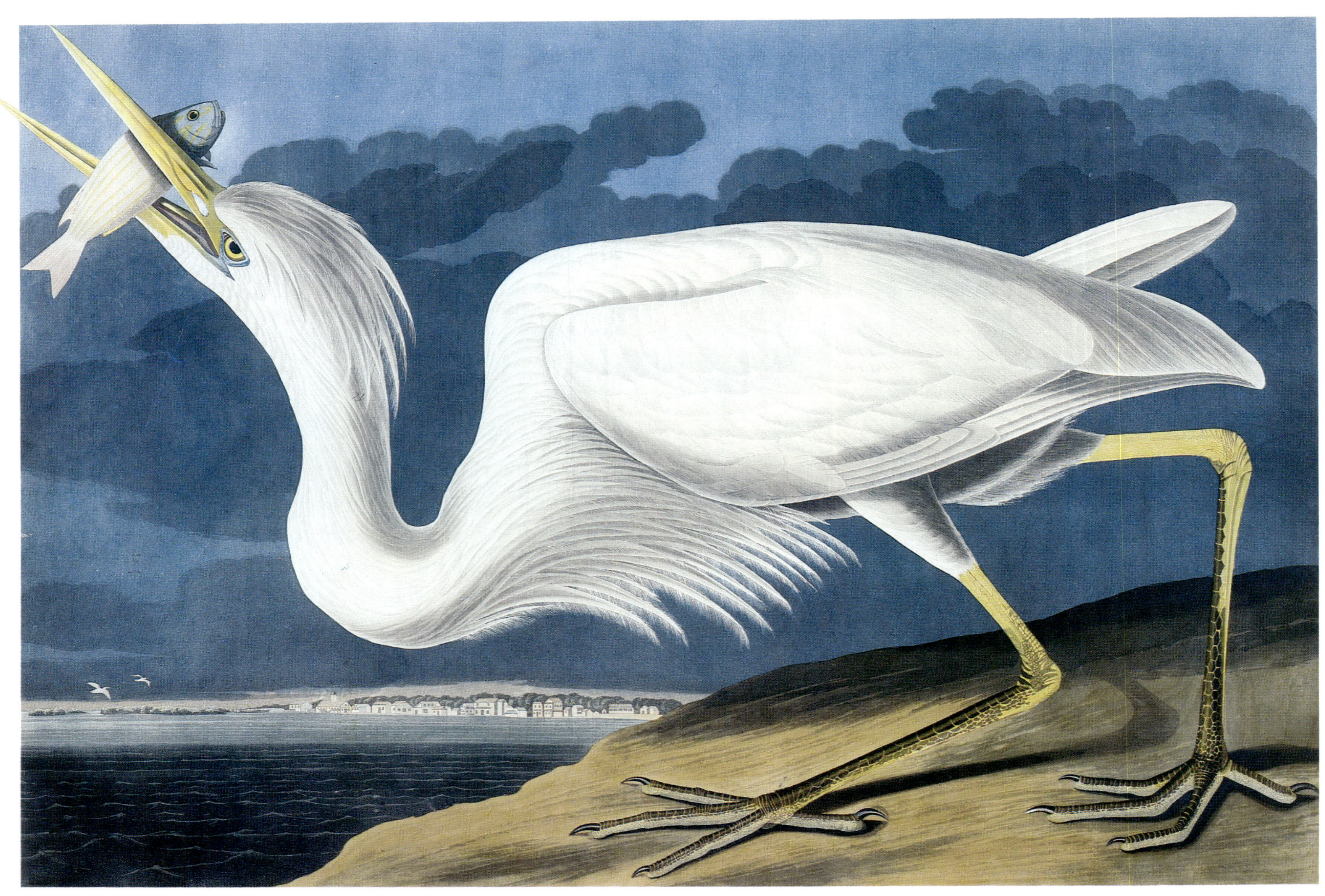

GREAT WHITE HERON. JOHN JAMES AUDUBON, *THE BIRDS OF AMERICA,* VOL. 3, PLATE 281. HAND-COLORED ETCHING AND AQUATINT, ROBERT HAVELL, LONDON, 1834-1836.

Audubon's male great white heron, resplendent in spring plumage, clutches a hapless fish in his bill before swallowing it. Nature's violence, suggested by the bird's feeding and the ominous sky and sea, threatens to overwhelm the town of Key West, drawn by George Lehman.

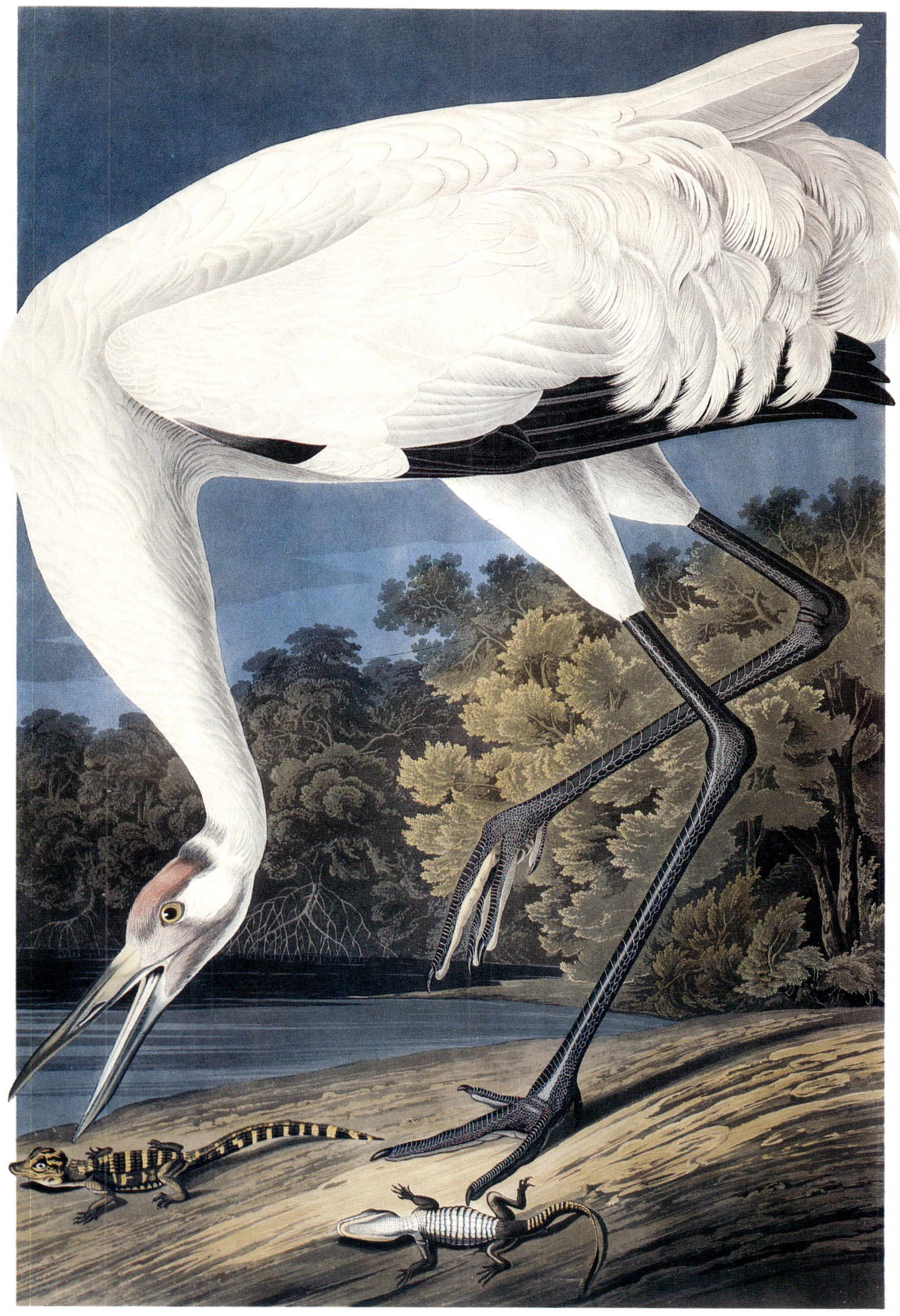

HOOPING CRANE. JOHN JAMES AUDUBON, *THE BIRDS OF AMERICA,* VOL. 3, PLATE 226. HAND-COLORED ETCHING AND AQUATINT, ROBERT HAVELL, LONDON, 1834-1836.

The inspiration for this image was Audubon's 1822 sighting of nine whooping cranes attacking a group of young alligators in a Louisiana bayou. Now threatened by extinction, this crane is one of the largest species depicted in Birds. *To convey the bird's dimensions, Audubon permits its outline to escape the edge of the plate.*

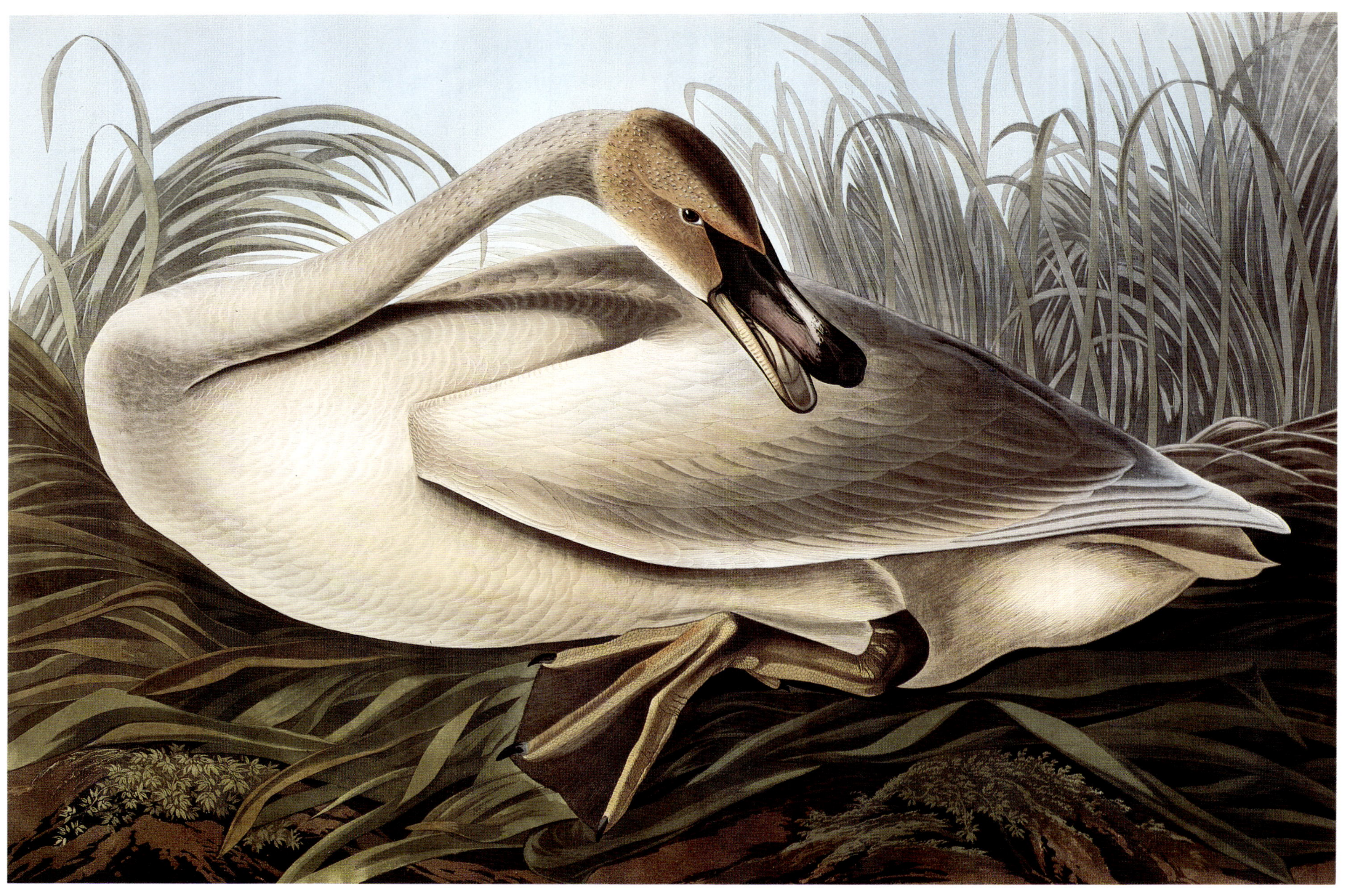

TRUMPETER SWAN. JOHN JAMES AUDUBON, *THE BIRDS OF AMERICA,* VOL. 4, PLATE 376. HAND-COLORED ETCHING AND AQUATINT, ROBERT HAVELL, LONDON, 1836-1838.

Audubon captures the dusky coloring of a yearling trumpeter before it grows the white feathers of adulthood. Against the muted greens and browns of marsh reeds, the bird's subtle tones impart a tranquil mood rarely found in Audubon's work.

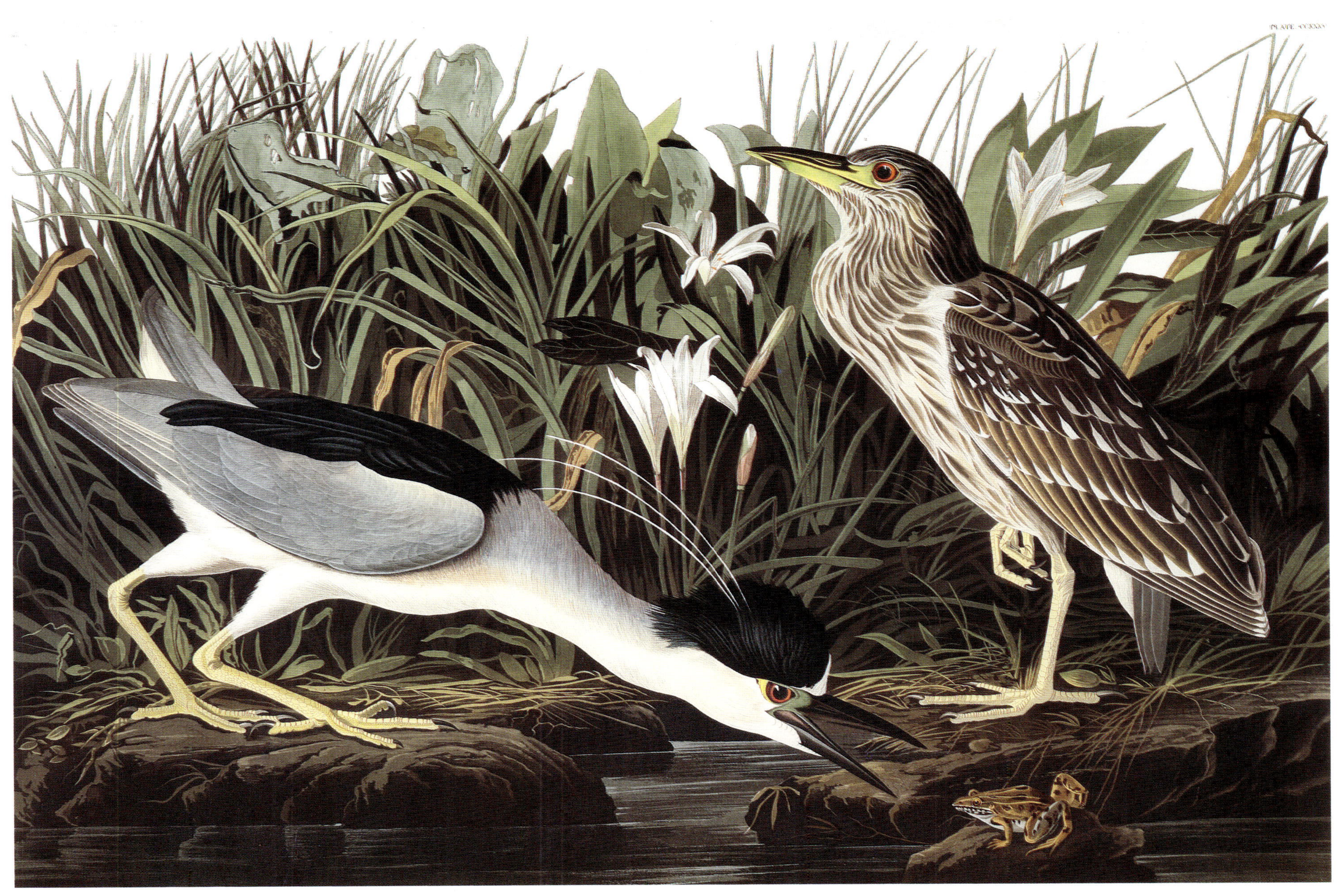

BLACK-CROWNED NIGHT HERON. JOHN JAMES AUDUBON, *THE BIRDS OF AMERICA,* VOL. 3, PLATE 236. HAND-COLORED ETCHING AND AQUATINT, ROBERT HAVELL, LONDON, 1834-1836.

Audubon completed a watercolor of the night heron near Charleston, where the birds wintered on the Ashley River. The long white plumes in the male's crest indicate that it is breeding season. George Lehman probably produced the background with its delicate zephyr lilies.

N°2.

PLATE VII.

CAROLINA GREY SQUIRREL. JOHN JAMES AUDUBON, *THE VIVIPAROUS QUADRUPEDS OF NORTH AMERICA,* VOL. 1, PLATE 7. HAND-COLORED LITHOGRAPH, JOHN T. BOWEN, PHILADELPHIA, 1845.

Here Audubon suggests the inquisitive character of the Carolina grey squirrel which "is remarkable for its fondness of 'sights,' and will sometimes come down from the highest branch of a tree to within three feet of the ground to take a view of a small scarlet snake...not much larger than a pipestem."

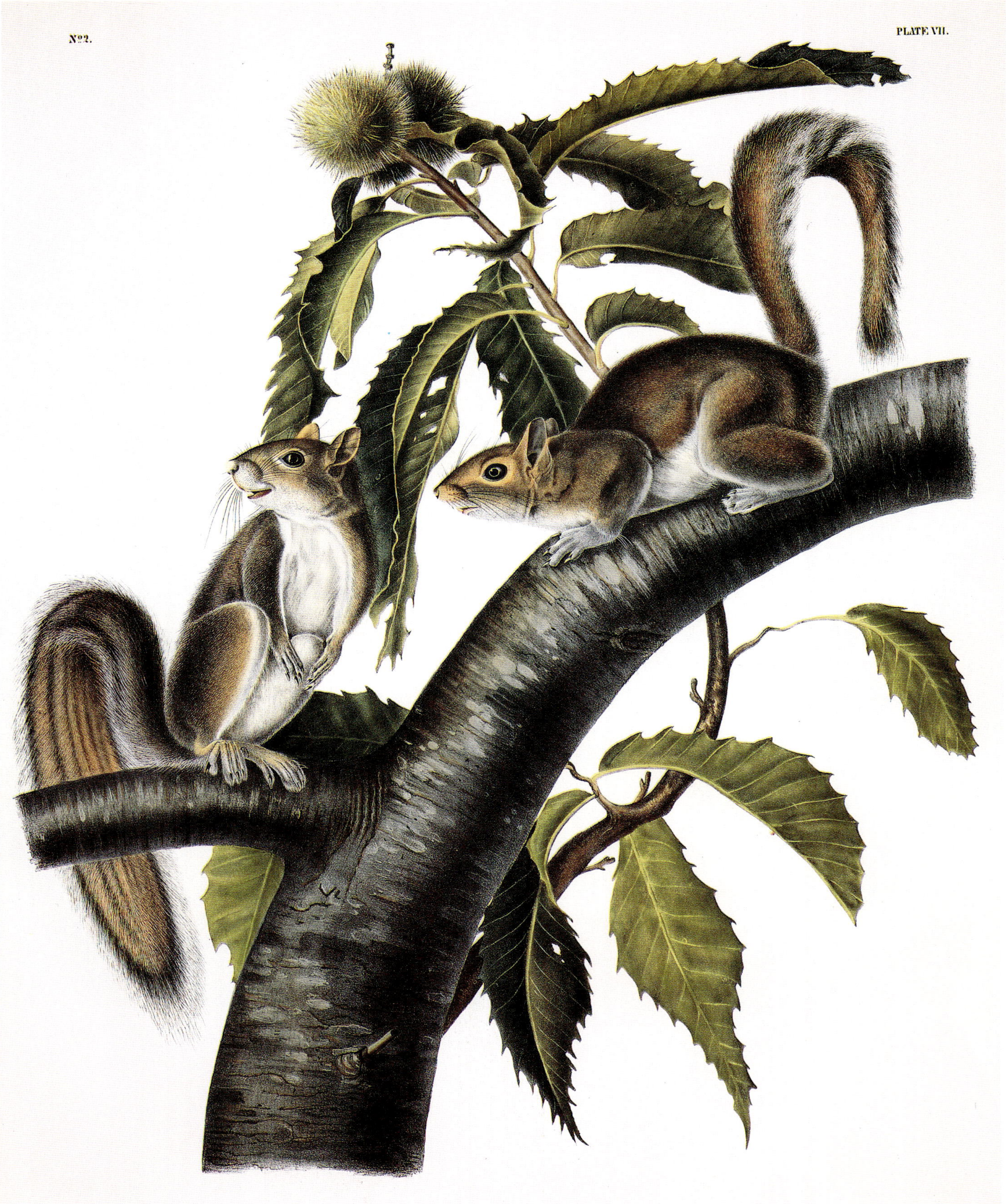

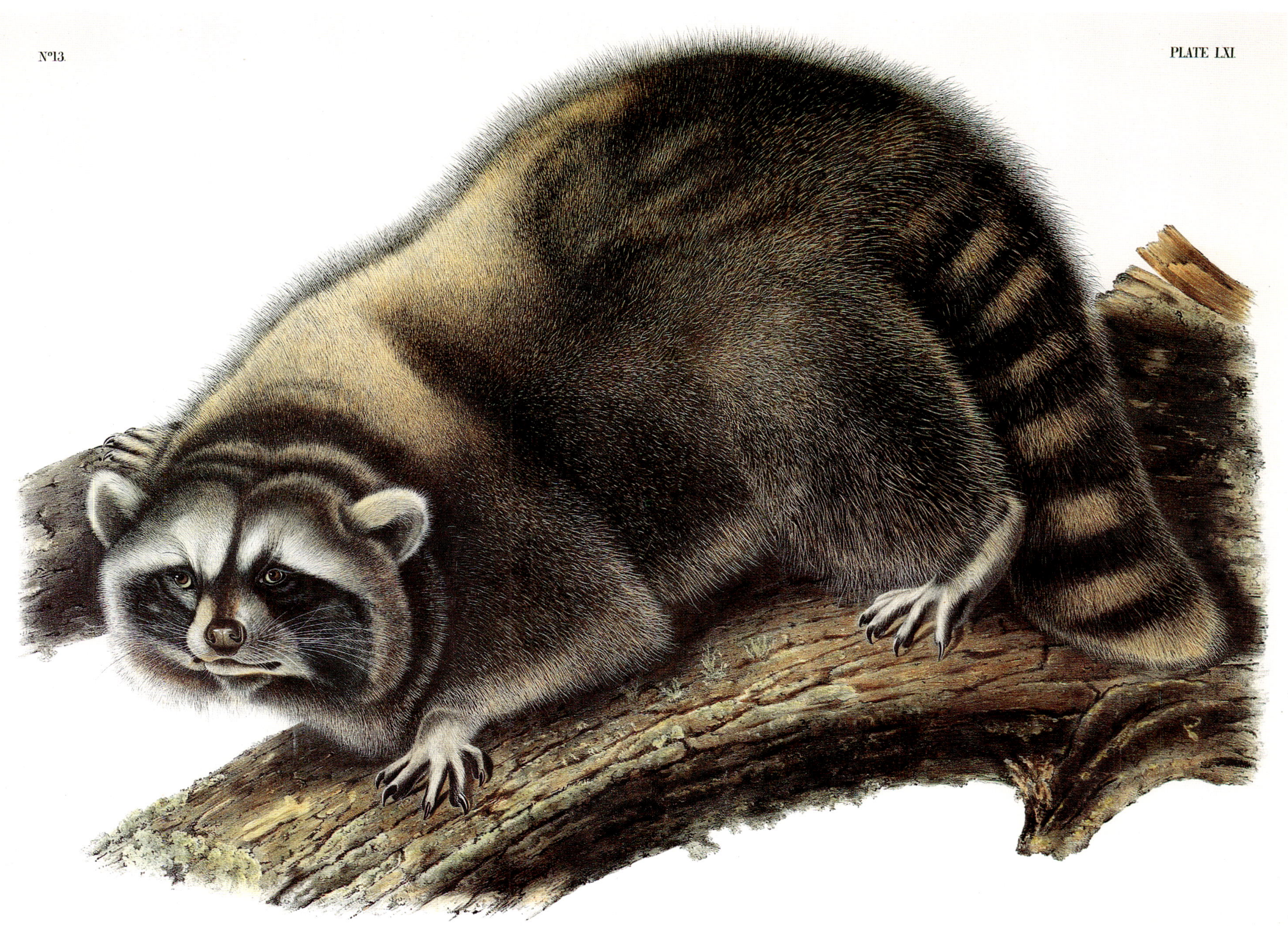

RACCOON. MALE. JOHN JAMES AUDUBON, *QUADRUPEDS,* VOL. 2, PLATE 61.
HAND-COLORED LITHOGRAPH, JOHN T. BOWEN, PHILADELPHIA, 1846.

Audubon, his sons, and their lithographer John Bowen wanted the lithographs in Quadrupeds *to be as fine and accurate as the aquatints in* Birds. *In this study of a raccoon, each hair is delineated, and the tree bark is as precisely detailed as in* Birds.

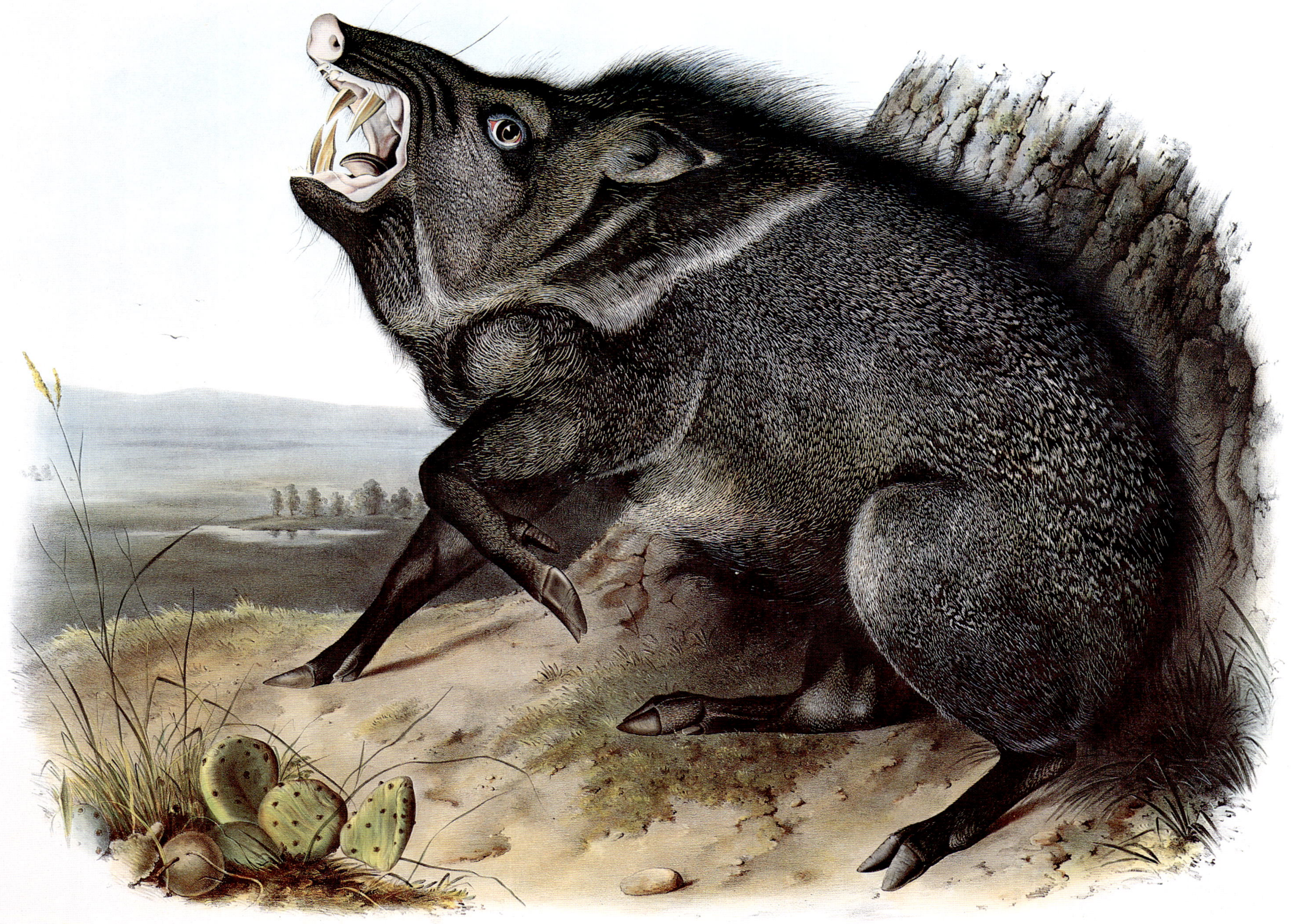

COLLARED PECCARY. MALE. JOHN JAMES AUDUBON, *QUADRUPEDS,* VOL. 1, PLATE 31. HAND-COLORED LITHOGRAPH, JOHN T. BOWEN, PHILADELPHIA, 1845.

Audubon emphasizes the incongruity between the peccary's large, humped torso and slender legs. Echoing his vigorous compositions in Birds, *he makes the animal appear more aggressive than it is.*

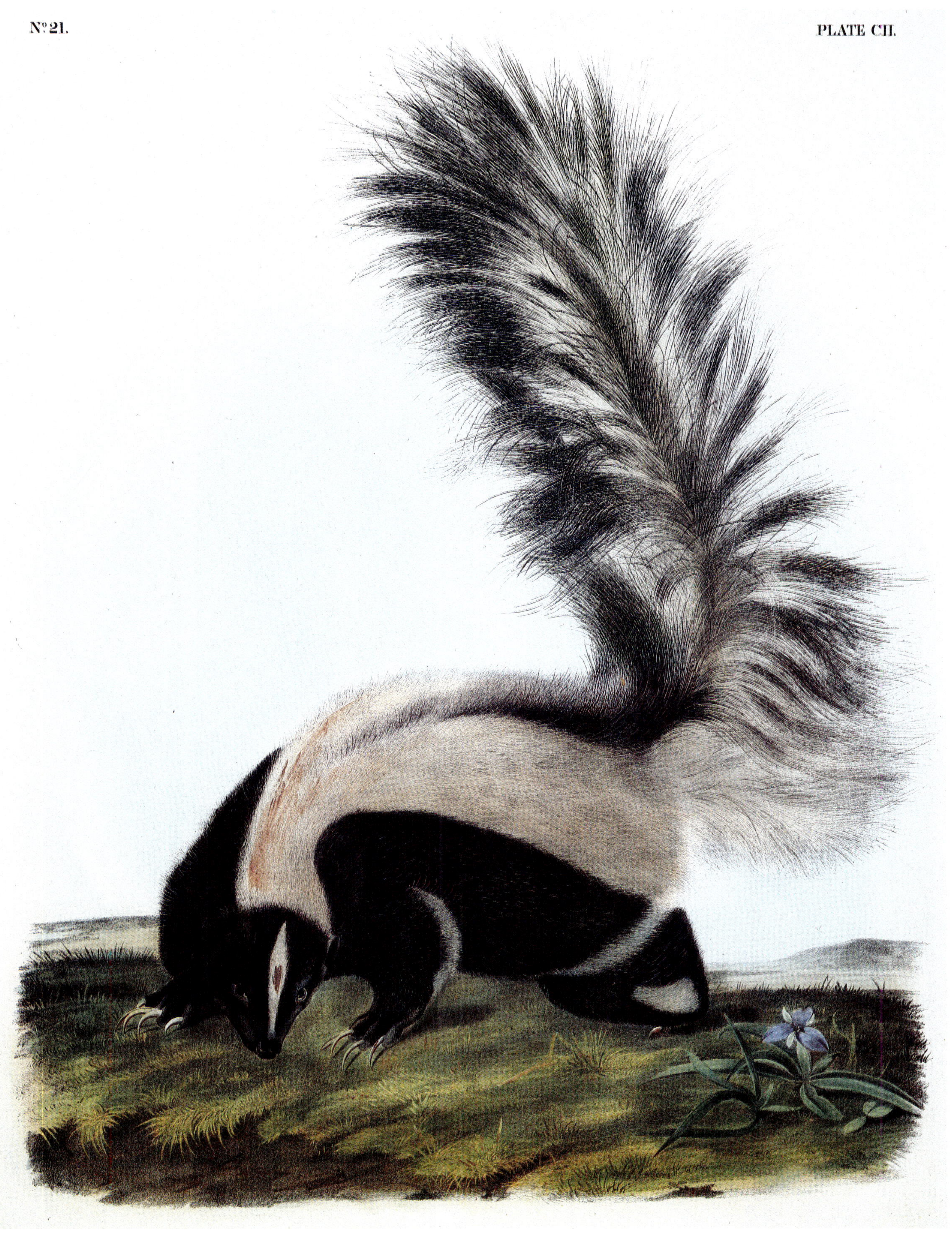

LARGE TAILED SKUNK. MALE. JOHN JAMES AUDUBON, *QUADRUPEDS,* VOL. 3, PLATE 102. HAND-COLORED LITHOGRAPH AFTER A PAINTING BY JOHN WOODHOUSE AUDUBON, JOHN T. BOWEN, PHILADELPHIA, 1848.

The large-tailed or hooded skunk, a western species, was painted by Audubon's son John Woodhouse Audubon, who completed the studies for Quadrupeds *after his father's eyesight failed in 1846. John Woodhouse notes that country dwellers in Texas used skunk tails as plumes for their hats.*

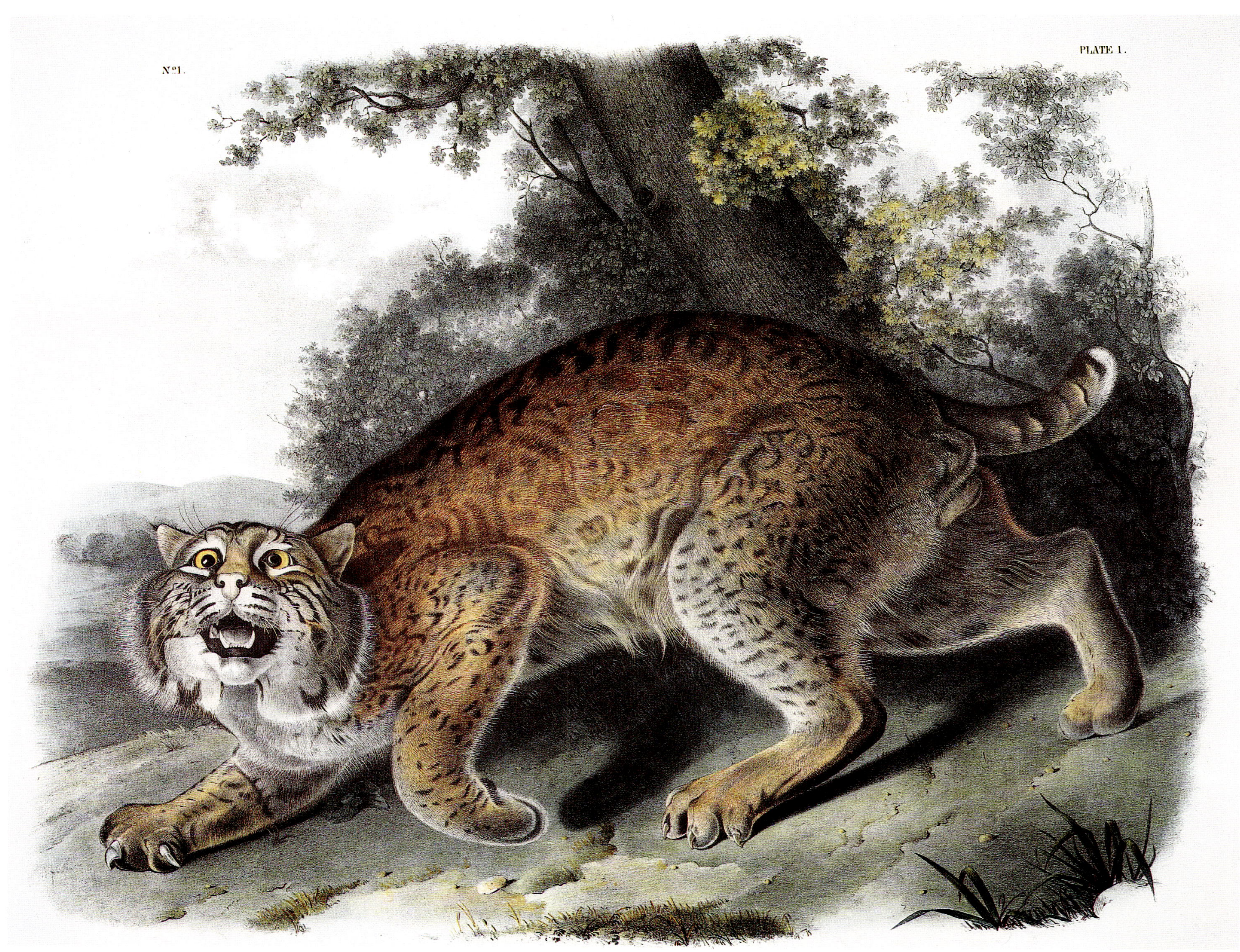

COMMON AMERICAN WILD CAT. MALE. JOHN JAMES AUDUBON, *QUADRUPEDS,* VOL. 1, PLATE 1. HAND-COLORED LITHOGRAPH, JOHN T. BOWEN, PHILADELPHIA, 1845.

Audubon admired the bobcat's speed and courage. "When hard pressed by fast dogs, and in open country, he ascends a tree with the agility of a squirrel, but the baying of the dogs calling his pursuers to the spot, the unerring rifle brings him to the ground, when not mortally wounded, he fights directly with the pack until killed."

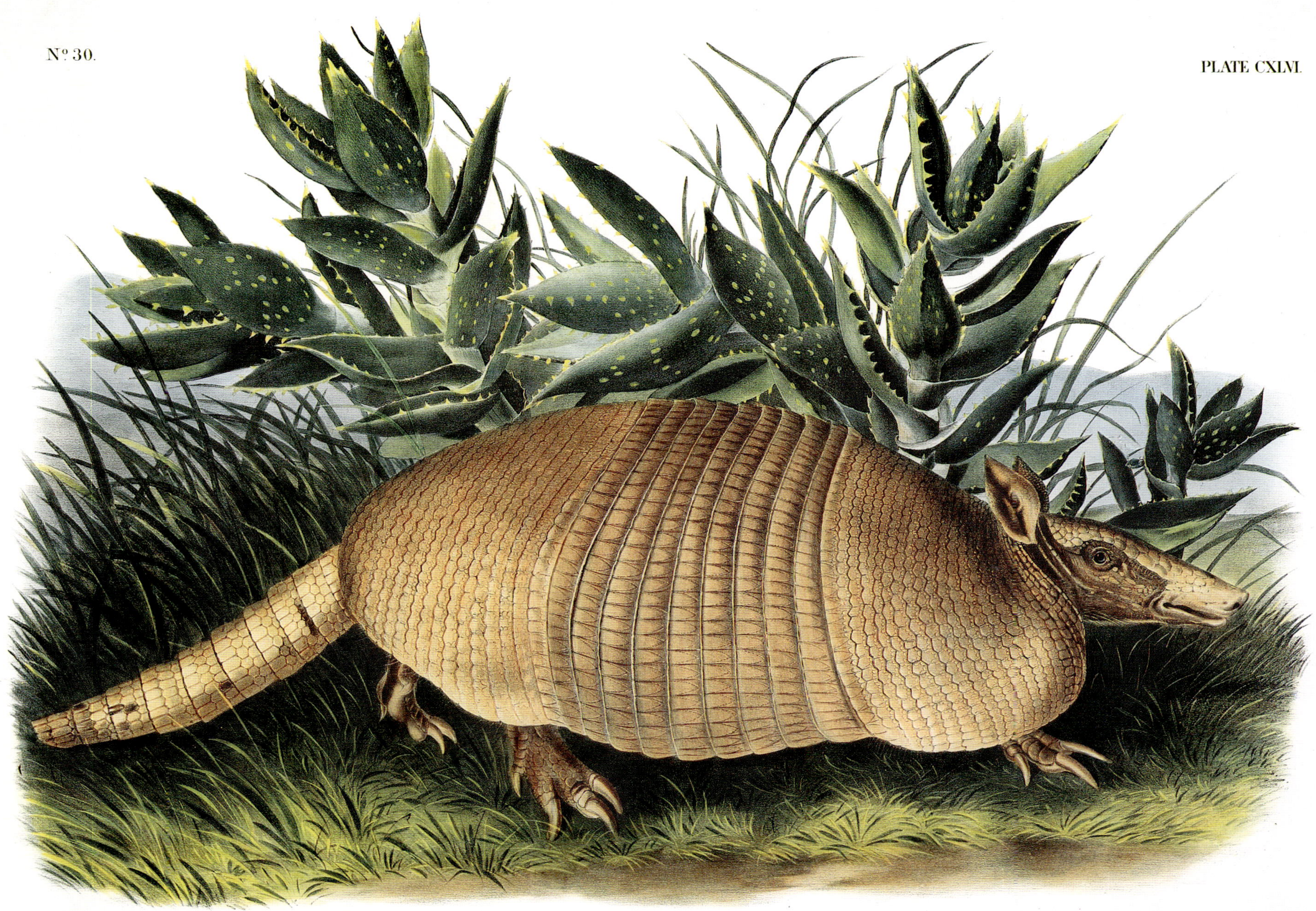

NINE BANDED ARMADILLO. MALE. JOHN JAMES AUDUBON, *QUADRUPEDS,* VOL. 3, PLATE 146. HAND-COLORED LITHOGRAPH AFTER A PAINTING BY JOHN WOODHOUSE AUDUBON, JOHN T. BOWEN, PHILADELPHIA, 1848.

John Woodhouse Audubon also drew the nine-banded armadillo. In the text to Quadrupeds, *John Bachman describes it as resembling "a small pig saddled with the shell of a turtle." A skilled digger, the animal "on being much alarmed rolls itself up, and does not attempt to fly." It is the only furless creature included in the work.*

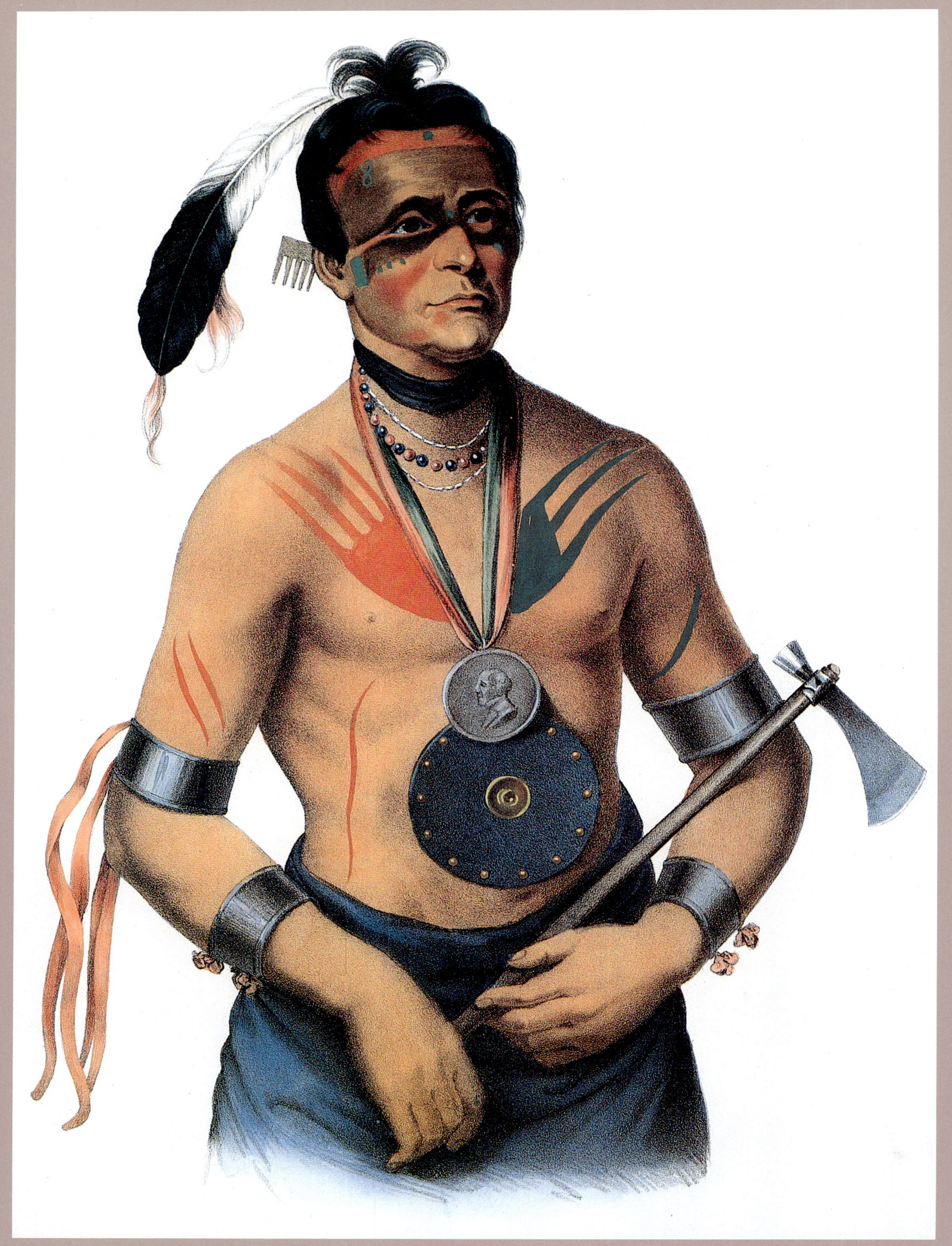

THOMAS McKENNEY (1785-1859)

Colonel Thomas McKenney was neither artist, engraver, nor writer, but rather a government official who looked beyond paperwork to the tragic predicament of his charges, the Indians of the United States. Superintendent of Indian Trade from 1816 to 1820, and head of the Bureau of Indian Affairs from 1822 to 1830, McKenney had the foresight to commission portraits of Indian leaders before war, disease, famine, drink, and forced removals from their lands ravaged the tribes. Based on these portraits, McKenney and Cincinnati writer James Hall later produced *The History of the Indian Tribes of North America,* remarkable for its detailed lithographs of leading Indians dressed in an astonishing variety of garb.

McKenney's fascination with Indian culture surfaced early in his government career. In 1817, he instructed his field agents to buy artifacts "relating to our aborigines...for the inspection of the curious and for the information of future generations long after the Indians will have been no more." Thus he began to assemble a museum in his office in the War Department.

HOO-WAN-NE-KA, A WINNEBAGO CHIEF. THOMAS McKENNEY AND JAMES HALL, *THE HISTORY OF THE INDIAN TRIBES OF NORTH AMERICA,* VOL. 2. HAND-COLORED LITHOGRAPH AFTER A PAINTING BY JAMES OTTO LEWIS, JOHN T. BOWEN, PHILADELPHIA, 1838-1842. *Hoowanneka (Little Elk) is shown as he appeared when he addressed President Monroe in 1824, wearing a silver peace medal given to him by President Madison. Hoowanneka's tribe fought for the British in the War of 1812, but he sought reconciliation with the United States after England neglected to include her Indian allies in peace negotiations. The Winnebagos lived around Lake Michigan's Green Bay.*

His interest in preserving the memory of the Indians suggests that he was resigned to their demise. But McKenney tried to act on their behalf, jeopardizing his career by doing so. Initially, he supervised government trading posts where Indians sold furs for blankets, pots, and other European wares. Most officials felt no compunction about cheating Indians, but Colonel McKenney insisted on supplying them with good merchandise. A supporter of temperance, he kept alcohol out of his trading posts, seeing it as the greatest threat to Indian survival. This infuriated John Jacob Astor, owner of the American Fur Company, who insisted that he could not outbid competing Canadian fur traders without offering the whiskey Indian hunters demanded. Through Astor's influence, McKenney became the target of Congressional investigations aimed at driving him from office.

McKenney sought other means to improve the Indians' condition. Enlisting the aid of missionary societies, the colonel prodded Congress into signing the Indian Civilization Act of 1819, a bill requiring the government to pay the Indians $10,000 a year to create and maintain schools for their children. The state of Georgia, which in 1811 had asked President Madison to "extinguish" the rights of the Cherokees and the Creeks to their lands, protested. "If you enlighten the Indians, as to the value of their possessions...you increase the difficulty of obtaining their consent to part with them."

Beginning with Thomas Jefferson, American presidents had increasingly espoused a policy of shifting Indians westward from lands desired by settlers. Motivated both by personal convictions and political expediency, McKenney became a leading proponent under Presidents John Quincy Adams and Andrew Jackson of the systematic removal of the Civilized Nations of the South to lands west of the Mississippi.

McKenney believed removal would give the tribes time to absorb the virtues of white culture before confronting its vices. In 1827, he persuaded the reluctant Creeks to send a delegation west to look at the new lands, naively assuring them that they would never be forced off their property. However,

Andrew Jackson, elected in 1828, cared nothing for McKenney or his assurances; he abruptly dismissed the colonel in 1830. The same year, Jackson initiated the forced removal of southern tribes, an exodus so brutally administered that it became known as the Trail of Tears.

Throughout his tenure in office, McKenney's Indian collection grew, including a unique portrait gallery. In the 1820s, the federal government had begun bringing large delegations of Indians to Washington. To commemorate their visits and document a race he feared would soon be extinct, McKenney commissioned portraits of these chieftains and warriors from Charles Bird King, known for his paintings of statesmen. Using government funds, McKenney paid the artist $20 for busts and $27 for full-length oils. Other portraits came from McKenney's treaty expeditions to Illinois and Wisconsin in 1826 and 1827, during which he hired the Detroit artist James Otto Lewis. The colonel was later castigated in Congress for wasting money on useless "pictures of the wretches."

Before his dismissal, McKenney had begun trying to publish his gallery. Out of office, he pursued the project from his new home in Philadelphia, where he edited the *Commercial Herald*. Ironically, he now had no legal right to the portraits he had gathered so assiduously; they belonged to the Department of War. He managed to convince John Eaton, Secretary of the Department of War, to quietly send him a few portraits at a time in Philadelphia, and he hired the artist Henry Inman to make copies in oil. Inman also copied some Indian portraits McKenney discovered at the American Philosophical Society.

Publication was further slowed by the difficulty of identifying the Indians pictured and by McKenney's chronic lack of funds. Fortunately, James Hall agreed to buy out Samuel F. Bradford, the first of several publishers to invest in the expensive project. A distinguished jurist who helped bring law and order to frontier Illinois before retiring to Cincinnati, Hall wrote biographies for the *History* which portrayed not only individual Indians and their culture, but their betrayal. Hall also tried to interest George Catlin in contributing his work to the book, but Catlin felt he could make a better book on his own.

The printing of the plates for the *History* proved another protracted, arduous task. In 1829, McKenney had contracted with Cephas G. Childs of Philadelphia to produce the book's lithographs. By the time the first volume appeared in 1837, Childs' company changed owners three times. Throughout these changes, the firm retained the lithographer Albert Newsam, who prepared most of the volume's 48 plates. The last six were the work of John T. Bowen's much larger company, which went on to lithograph the second and third volumes.

First completed in 1844, the *History* went into several editions, but failed to enrich McKenney and Hall. With some justification, Hall blamed the price—$120 for the three-volume set—for confining it "to public libraries or the collections of wealthy persons." Irretrievably impoverished, McKenney spent his old age moving from hotel to hotel up and down the eastern seaboard, lecturing small audiences on the sad plight of once-magnificent tribes.

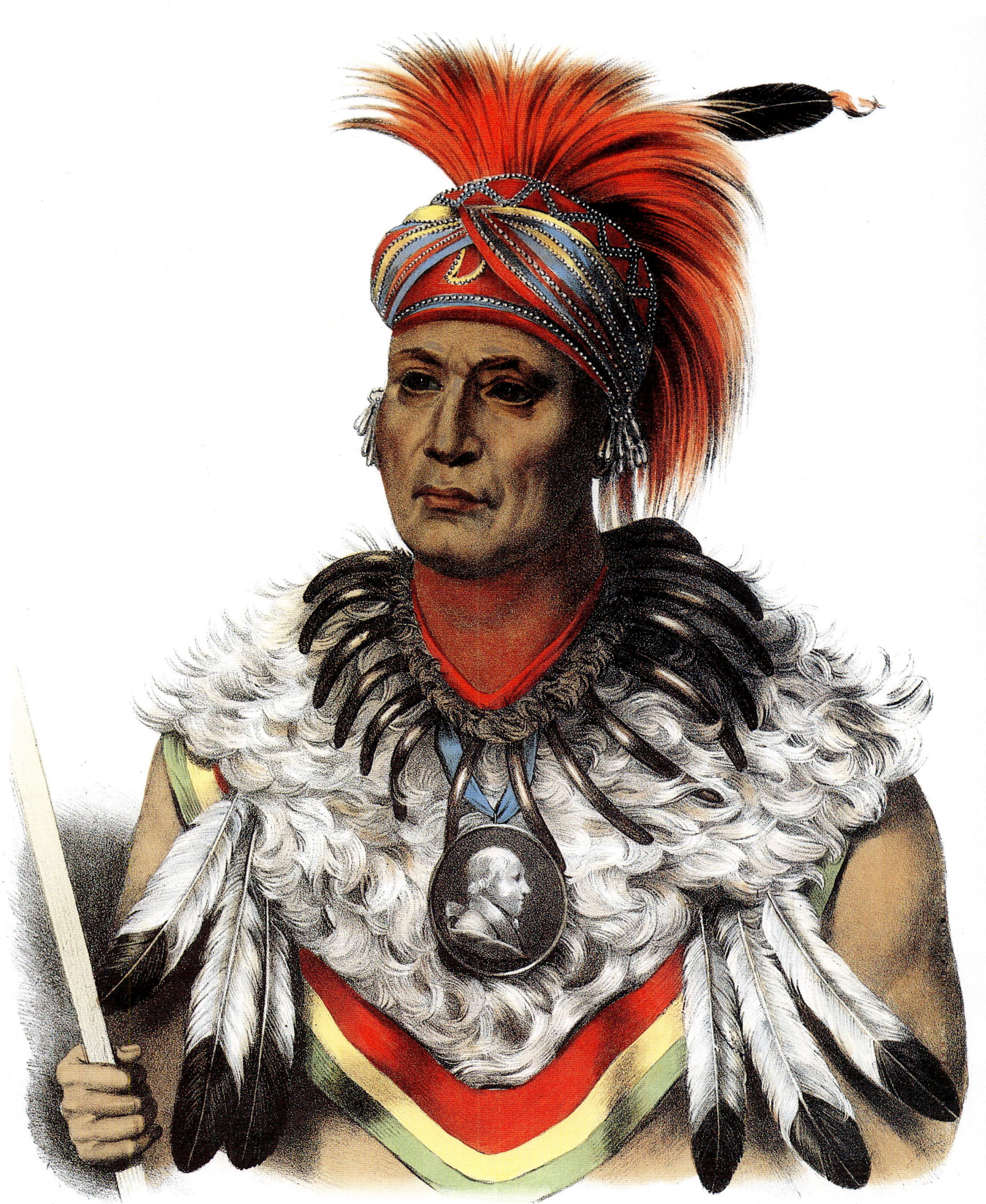

WA-PEL-LA, CHIEF OF THE MUSQUAKEES. THOMAS McKENNEY AND JAMES HALL, *HISTORY,* VOL. 2. HAND-COLORED LITHOGRAPH AFTER A PAINTING BY CHARLES BIRD KING, JOHN T. BOWEN, PHILADELPHIA, 1838-1842.

This Musquakee chief visited Washington in 1837 with a delegation led by Keokuk (see following page). Later that year, speaking to the Governor of Massachusetts, Wapella showed a strangely generous attitude toward the invasion of Indian America by white settlers: "I am happy to meet my friends in the land of my forefathers...I am very happy that this land has induced white men to come upon it."

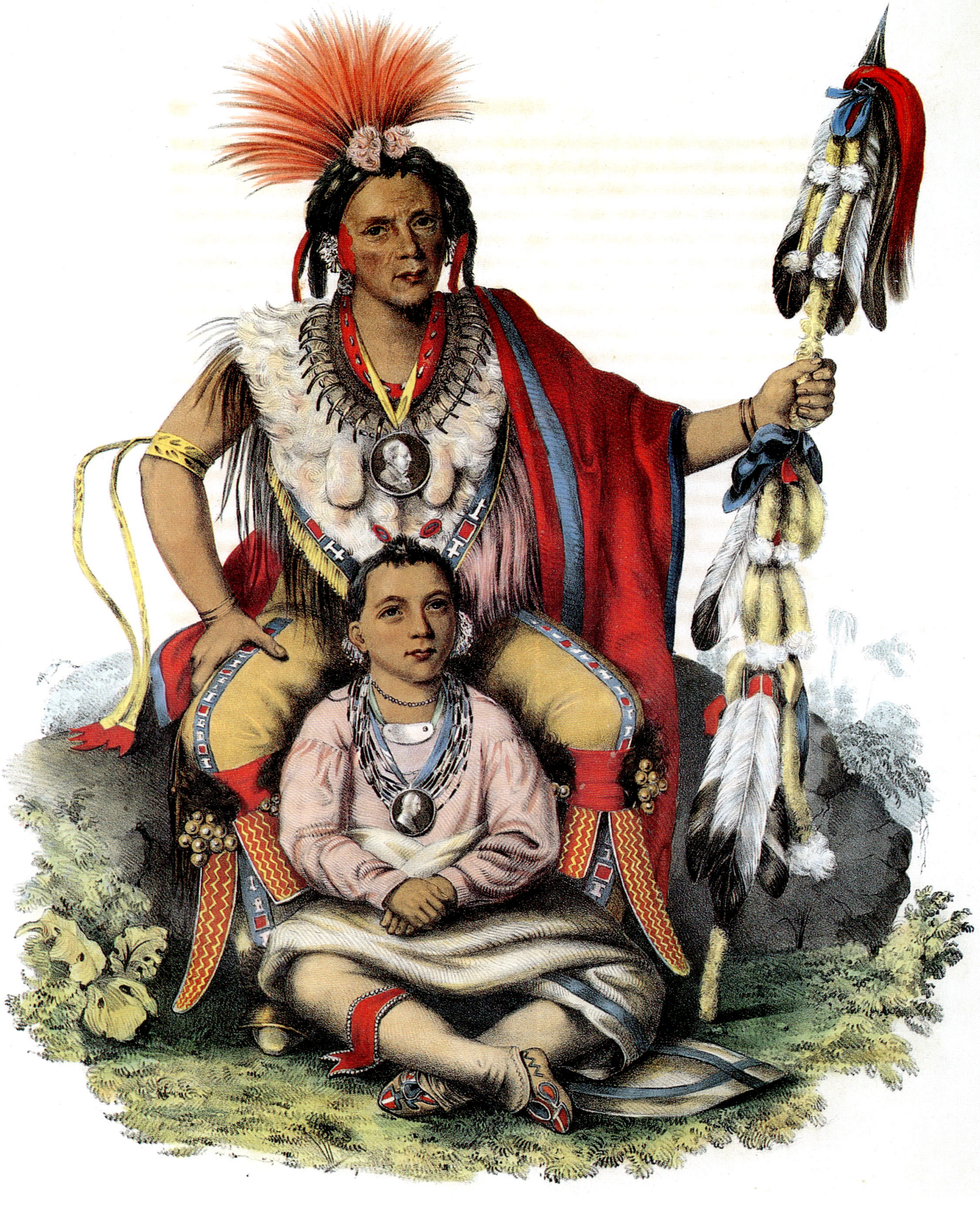

KEOKUK, CHIEF OF THE SACS AND FOXES. THOMAS McKENNEY AND JAMES HALL, *HISTORY,* VOL. 2. HAND-COLORED LITHOGRAPH AFTER A PAINTING BY CHARLES BIRD KING, JOHN T. BOWEN, PHILADELPHIA, 1838-1842.

Keokuk, the most respected Indian of his time, led the Sauk, Fox, and Musquakee tribes, who lived along Illinois' Rock River. Indians were disingenuously encouraged to view the president as their Great Father; like Hoowaneka and Wapella, Keokuk wears a presidential peace medallion. At Washington in 1837, when this portrait was painted, his delegation signed a treaty ceding over a million acres to the United States.

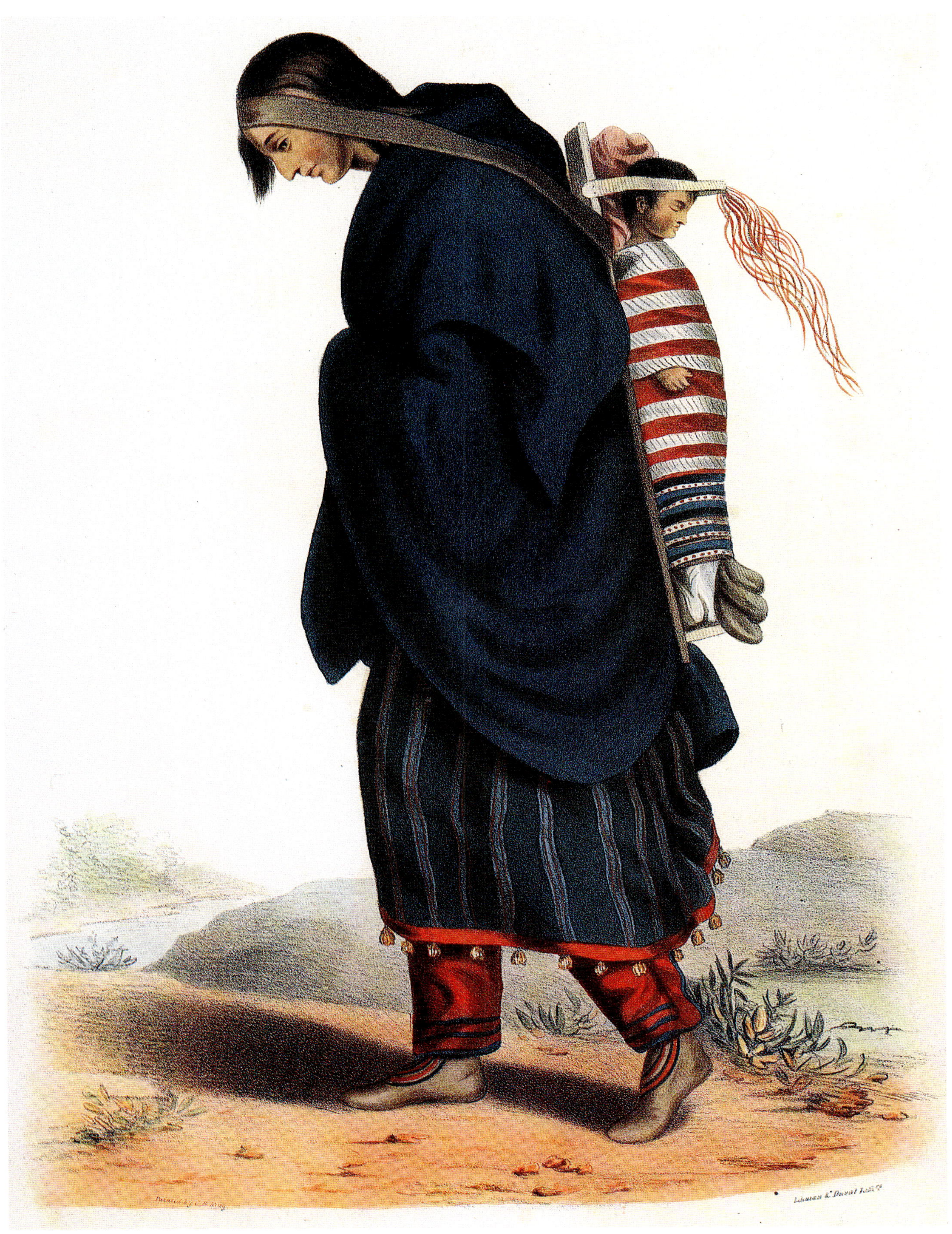

CHIPPEWAY SQUAW & CHILD. THOMAS McKENNEY AND JAMES HALL, *HISTORY,* VOL. 1. HAND-COLORED LITHOGRAPH AFTER A PAINTING BY JAMES OTTO LEWIS, LEHMAN AND DUVAL, PHILADELPHIA, 1836-1837.

Introducing this plate, James Hall writes: "the life of the Indian woman, under the most favorable circumstances, is one of continual labor and unmitigated hardship.... They are servants rather than the companions of man." Elsewhere Hall describes the cradle in which Indian infants were carried, saying that the "little prisoner" placed his heels on a footrest "covered with the softest moss."

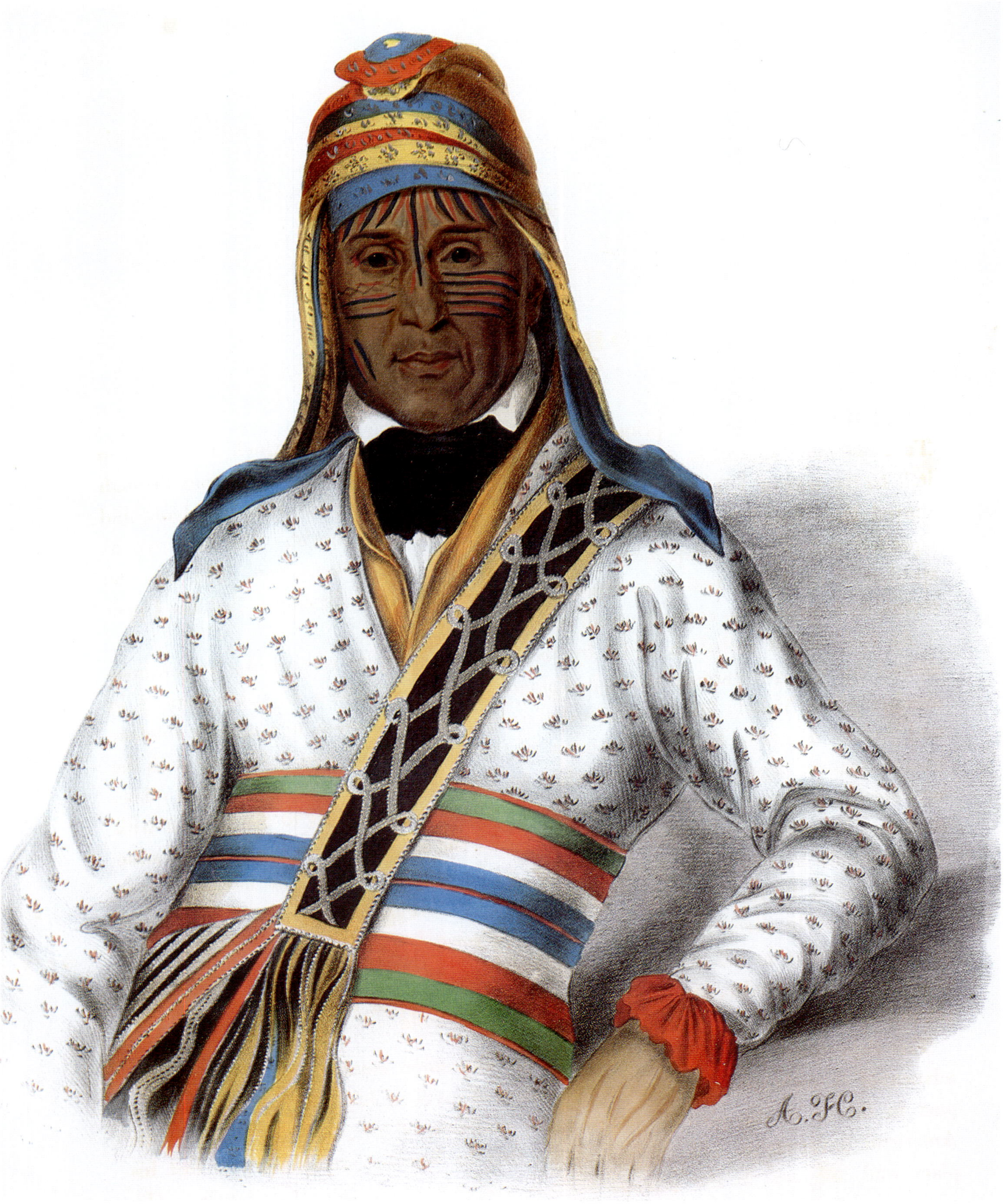

YOHOLO-MICCO. A CREEK CHIEF. THOMAS McKENNEY AND JAMES HALL, *HISTORY,* VOL. 2. HAND-COLORED LITHOGRAPH AFTER A PAINTING BY CHARLES BIRD KING, JOHN T. BOWEN, PHILADELPHIA, 1838-1842.

Yoholo Micco, a generous, eloquent chief of the Creek nation in eastern Alabama, supported two policies pursued by McKenney: the gradual incorporation of Indian tribes into white civilization, and their removal to lands west of the Mississippi. As his tribe traveled to Arkansas, he died "of the fatigues attending the emigration."

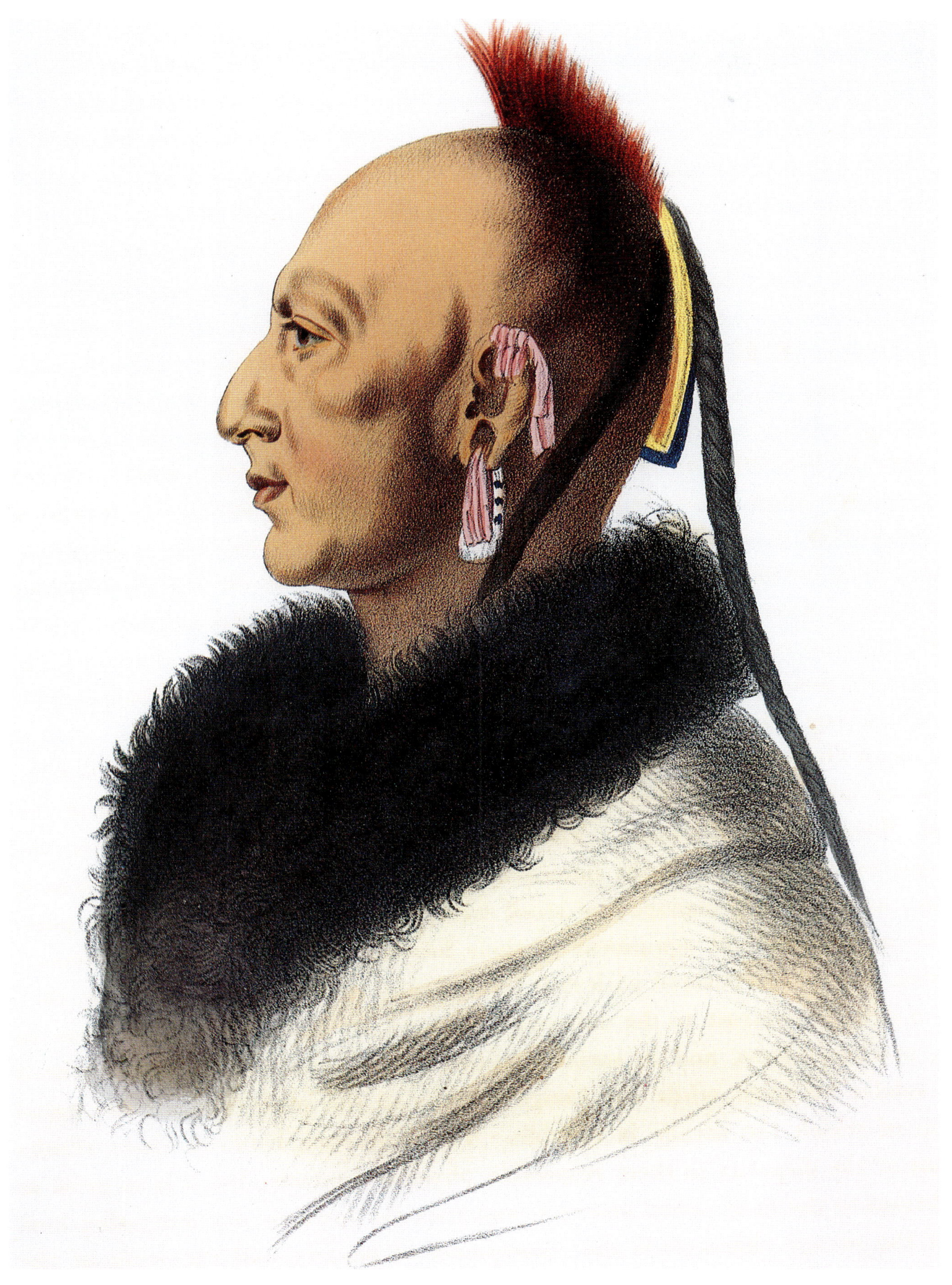

LE SOLDAT DU CHENE, AN OSAGE CHIEF. THOMAS McKENNEY AND JAMES HALL, *HISTORY,* VOL. 2. HAND-COLORED LITHOGRAPH AFTER A PAINTING BY CHARLES DE SAINT-MEMIN, JOHN T. BOWEN, PHILADELPHIA, 1838-1842.

"The Soldier of the Oak" was portrayed at Philadelphia on a visit to President Jefferson in 1805 or 1806. Hall reports that Le Soldat won his name by fighting against several enemies from the shelter of a large oak. At its height, his tribe ranged the rich prairies and oak bluffs of Arkansas, Missouri, and Kansas.

SHAR-I-TAR-ISH, A PAWNEE CHIEF. THOMAS McKENNEY AND JAMES HALL, *HISTORY,* VOL. 2. HAND-COLORED LITHOGRAPH AFTER A PAINTING BY CHARLES BIRD KING, JOHN T. BOWEN, PHILADELPHIA, 1838-1842.

Sharitarish traveled from the Platte River to Washington in 1821 to meet President Monroe. His elder brother, a more important chief, had refused the invitation, claiming that to journey that far showed too much respect for a ruler who commanded fewer braves, owned fewer horses, and maintained fewer wives. Sharitarish returned "with enlarged views of the numbers and power of the white men."

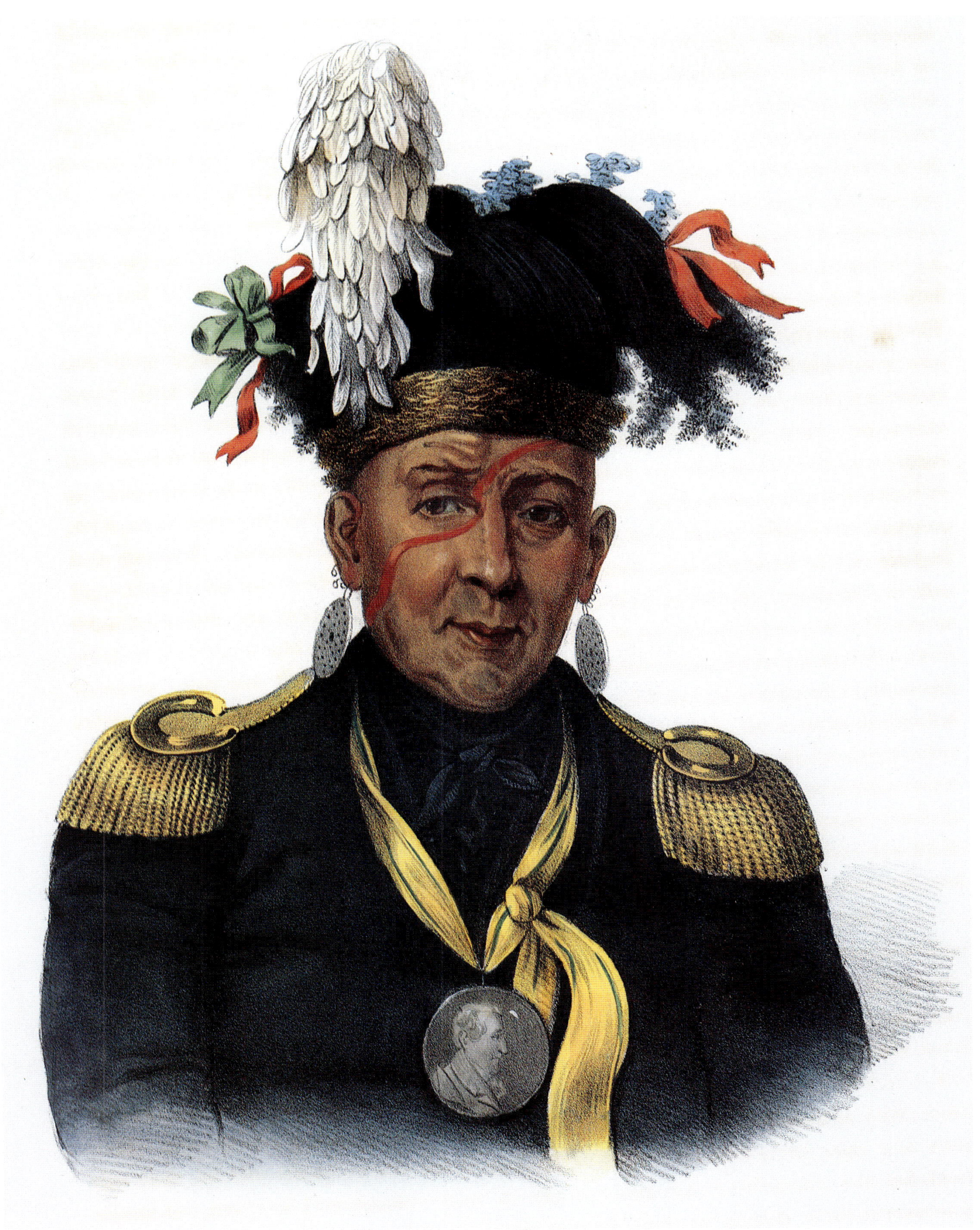

WA-BAUN-SEE, A POTTAWATOMIE CHIEF. THOMAS McKENNEY AND JAMES HALL, *HISTORY,* VOL. 2. HAND-COLORED LITHOGRAPH AFTER A PAINTING BY CHARLES BIRD KING, JOHN T. BOWEN, PHILADELPHIA, 1838-1842.

Wabaunsee, whose tribe lived along the Kankakee River in Illinois, negotiated with the United States government for years before agreeing to lead his tribe to Missouri. King brilliantly portrays the toll of balancing two radically different cultures. Although Wabaunsee was a man of integrity and courage, the military garb he wears here undercuts his character by suggesting a confusion of identities and hopes.

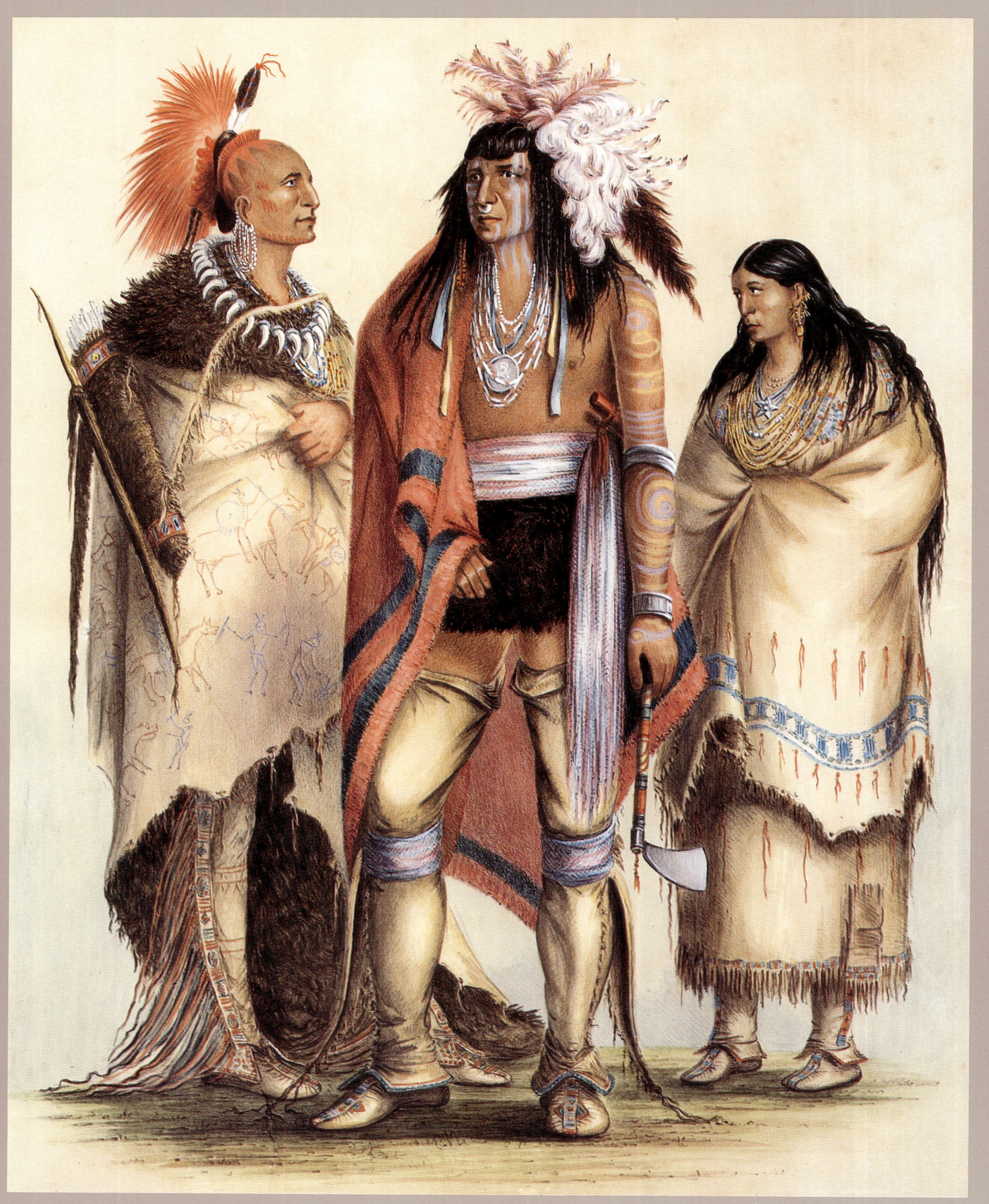

GEORGE CATLIN (1796-1872)

In his *Letters and Notes on the North American Indians,* George Catlin wrote: "Nowhere has Nature presented more beautiful scenes than those of the vast prairies of the West. Of man and beast, no nobler specimens than the Indian and the buffalo—joint and original tenants of the soil, and fugitives together from the approach of civilized man. They have fled to the great plains of the West, and there, under an equal doom, they have taken up their *last abode,* where their race will expire, and their bones will bleach together." Artist, writer, explorer, ethnographer, lecturer, and showman, Catlin devoted his life to recording for posterity "the living manners, customs, and character of a people who were rapidly passing away from the face of the earth."

Largely a self-taught artist, Catlin was born in Wilkes-Barre, Pennsylvania, the fifth of 14 children. At the urging of his father, a country lawyer, he went to law school and practiced briefly, but sold his law library in 1823 and moved to Philadelphia to become a painter of miniatures.

NORTH AMERICAN INDIANS. GEORGE CATLIN, *NORTH AMERICAN INDIAN PORTFOLIO,* NO. 1. HAND-COLORED LITHOGRAPH, DAY & HAGHE, LONDON, 1844.

This plate brings together portraits of Indians from different tribes: Tal-lee, an Osage, Not-to-way, an Iroquois, and an unidentified woman. In contrast to McKenney and Hall's formal depictions with their emphasis on costume, Catlin's compositions, created directly from field observations, celebrate the Indians' alertness, agility, and physicality.

Catlin soon learned full-length portraiture as well, and was elected in 1824 to the Pennsylvania Academy of Fine Art, whose members included Thomas Sully and Charles Willson Peale. But Catlin yearned for a subject to which he could "devote a whole life-time of enthusiasm." One day he encountered a delegation of Indians on their way to Washington "arrayed and equipped in all their classic beauty, with shield and helmet—with tunic and manteau—tinted and tasselled off, exactly for the painter's palette!" He resolved to become the historian of their race.

To raise money for a journey to the Missouri River, where Indian ways of life had yet to be seriously altered by contact with whites, Catlin continued painting society portraits and also traveled to upstate New York to paint Indians on reservations. In 1830, at the age of 34, he set out for St. Louis on the first of six annual trips to territories known only to Indians and fur traders. He intended to reach "every tribe... on the Continent of North America."

In St. Louis, the artist introduced himself to General William Clark, veteran of the Lewis and Clark expedition. Now governor of the Missouri Territory and superintendent of Indian Affairs in the West, Clark was impressed with Catlin's project. He introduced the artist to tribal delegates and took him to treaty councils at Prairie du Chien and Fort Crawford.

In the spring of 1832, Catlin made his most memorable trip, up the Missouri to the mouth of the Yellowstone aboard the American Fur Company's steamboat (also called the *Yellowstone*), through lands where Indians lived largely undisturbed by whites. He worked tirelessly during the 86-day journey, roughing out as many as six Indian portraits a day. Depicting the faces with care, he would sketch in the bodies in a few quick strokes, planning to refine them later.

Among his 66 portraits from that summer is the second of a pair he made of Wi-Jun-Jon (see page 93). The first shows Wi-Jun-Jon as Catlin saw him in St. Louis before the young Assiniboine went to Washington, the second shows how he dressed after he returned. When Wi-Jun-Jon told his tribesmen tales about the white man's world, they thought he was concocting fabulous lies and ceased to respect him as a warrior. Only a powerful, dangerous medicine man could tell such lies. Jealous braves, conspiring to kill him, did not trust an ordinary bullet. Instead, one of them loaded his rifle with the straightened handle of an iron pot and fired it through Wi-Jun-Jon's skull.

On this journey, Catlin also visited the Mandans, soon to be wiped out by smallpox, and witnessed their brutal initiation rite, the O-Kee-Pa, in which young men were suspended from beams by splints forced under the tendons of their chests or shoulders. Catlin also painted many of the dances and hunts central to Indian life. Fascinated by the ball-play, an intertribal game arranged months in advance in which up to a thousand young warriors took part, he went to as many of these contests as possible.

After his final trip to the prairies in 1836, Catlin began preparing his "Indian Gallery," including 470 oil paintings and a vast collection of artifacts, for public display. In September 1837, Catlin's gallery opened to acclaim in New York. He later toured Washington, Philadelphia, and Boston with his show, lecturing on the Indians' plight. While the public loved Catlin's sensational stories and exotic paintings, he failed to win political support for the Indians. When Congress failed to buy his gallery, he took his exhibition to London, hoping to sway European sentiment on the Indians' behalf.

In February 1840, the "Indian Gallery" opened at the Egyptian Hall in Piccadilly. That fall, Catlin added costumed white men performing Indian dances and ceremonies. Later, to spur flagging public interest, he made the show more authentic by hiring visiting troupes of Ojibwa and Iowa Indians for the dances. Attendance briefly improved, and the Ojibwas were invited to perform for Queen Victoria in 1843. But Catlin's use of the Indians also brought charges that he was exploiting their cause for personal gain.

In 1841, aided by Sir Charles Murphy, the queen's Master of the Household, Catlin published his *Letters and Notes*. Reviewers praised them, but sales lagged. Three years afterwards, hoping to boost his finances, he published *Catlin's North American Indian Portfolio,* a series of 25 lithographs skillfully adapted from his most popular paintings by Thomas McGahey for Day & Haghe. Catlin selected the originals, supervised the printing, and assisted with the hand-coloring. Day & Haghe brought out five editions that year, adding six more prints. An American edition of the original 25 prints, lithographed by James Ackerman in New York, appeared in 1845.

By 1845, Catlin could no longer win sizable English audiences to his gallery. He moved with his family to Paris, where King Louis Philippe invited him to exhibit in the Louvre. Even so, his fortunes did not improve. Catlin's wife died of pneumonia that summer, and his little boy of typhoid the following year. When smallpox killed two members of his troupe on a tour of Belgium, the surviving Indians returned home. Meanwhile, Louis Philippe had commissioned him to depict La Salle's exploration of the Mississippi. But in the Revolution of 1848 that ousted the Citizen King, soldiers bayoneted the just-finished canvases.

Back in London, Catlin mortgaged his gallery and sold copies of his oils to raise money, but in 1852, after

Congress failed again—this time by a single vote—to buy the gallery, he went bankrupt. Fortunately, the locomotive manufacturer Joseph Harrison paid Catlin's creditors $40,000 and preserved the collection, including 507 oil paintings, at his boiler works in Philadelphia.

Catlin returned quietly to Paris. In 1853 or 1854, he sailed to Venezuela to hunt for gold. During the next seven years, he painted the tribes of the Amazon Valley, the Andes, and coastal Peru, eventually making his way up the Pacific coast to the Northwest and to the Aleutian Islands and Siberia. His *Last Rambles Among the Indians of the Rocky Mountains and the Andes* (1868) records his travels.

Now deaf, Catlin spent the 1860s in Brussels working on his new pictures and painting from memory the Indian Gallery he had lost. In 1870, an exhibition of about 600 new paintings in New York failed, closing after five weeks. However, an old friend of Catlin's, Joseph Henry, had become the new secretary of the Smithsonian Institution. He invited the artist to bring his show to the Smithsonian, providing him with a small studio in a turret of the museum's castle-like headquarters. There Catlin continued to work until Bright's disease disabled him two years before his death.

Six years after Catlin died in 1872, Joseph Harrison's widow gave Catlin's original gallery to the Smithsonian. The tepees, robes, and other artifacts had been ruined by smoke and water in several fires at the boiler works, but 80 percent of the paintings survived. Today, just as Catlin had hoped, they provide a vivid record of the Indians of the Great Plains.

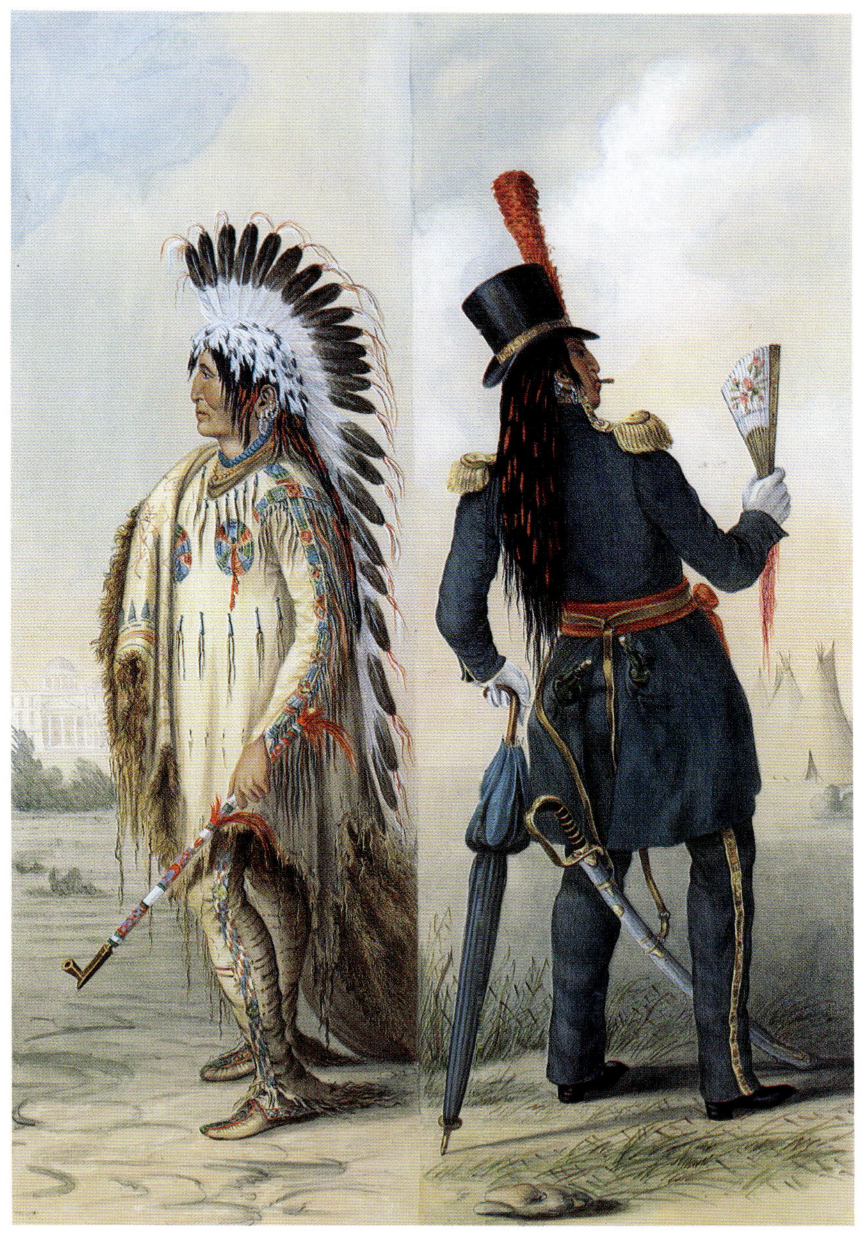

WI-JUN-JON. AN ASSINIBOIN CHIEF. GOING TO WASHINGTON. RETURNING TO HIS HOME. GEORGE CATLIN, *INDIAN PORTFOLIO,* NO. 25. HAND-COLORED LITHOGRAPH, DAY & HAGHE, LONDON, 1844.

Here Catlin comments wryly on white society's corruption of the Indian. Wi-Jun-Jon went to Washington a respected warrior and returned a whiskey-swigging dandy whose vanity kept him from participating in ordinary tribal life. Wi-Jun-Jon's name means The Light; Catlin's mistranslation, Pigeon's Egg Head, suggests his disdain for this debased leader.

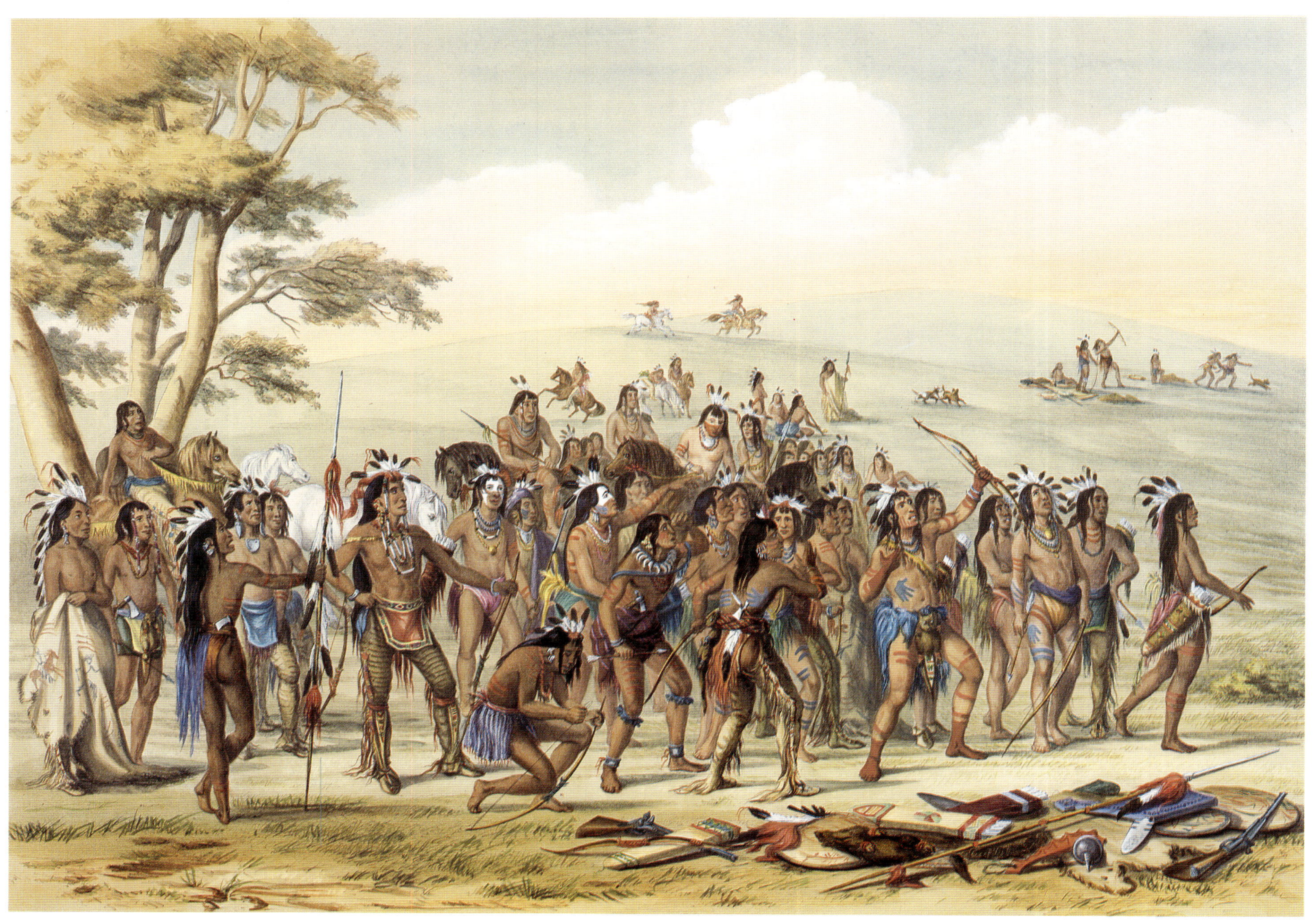

ARCHERY OF THE MANDANS. GEORGE CATLIN, *INDIAN PORTFOLIO,* NO. 24.
HAND-COLORED LITHOGRAPH, DAY & HAGHE, LONDON, 1844.

In his Letters and Notes, *Catlin describes the Mandans' "game of arrow": the young men, "having paid, each one, his 'entrance fee,' such as a shield, a robe, or other article, step forward in turn, shooting their arrows into the air, endeavouring to see who can get the greatest number in the air at one time, thrown from the same bow."*

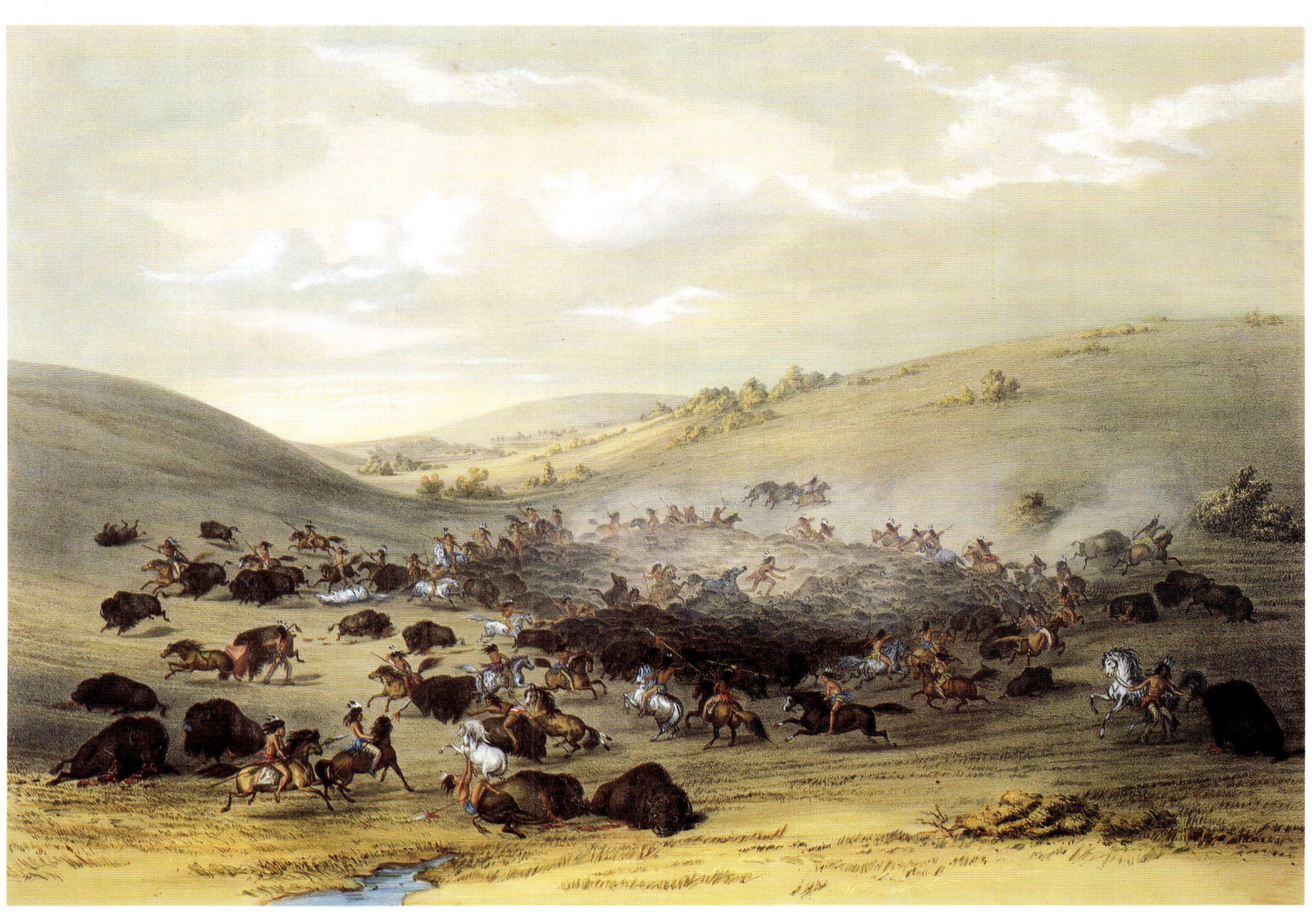

BUFFALO HUNT, SURROUND. GEORGE CATLIN, *INDIAN PORTFOLIO,* NO. 9. HAND-COLORED LITHOGRAPH, DAY & HAGHE, LONDON, 1844.

Men armed with arrows had to cooperate closely to hunt buffalo. Forming a circle around the grazing herd, they slowly rode toward the center and forced the animals into a constricted area. To prevent buffalo from escaping, each hunter sought to maintain the same pace unerringly.

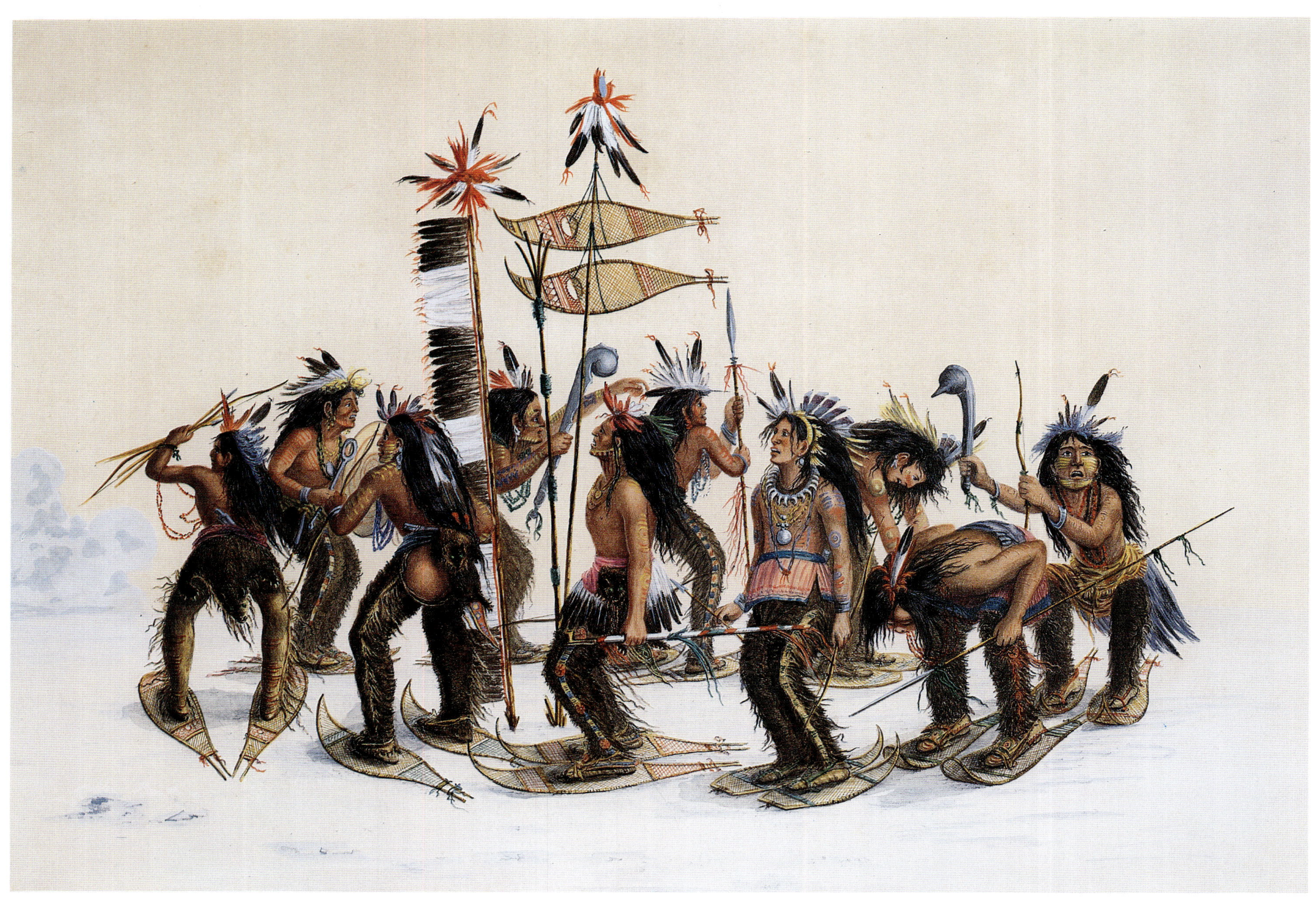

THE SNOW-SHOE DANCE. GEORGE CATLIN, *INDIAN PORTFOLIO,* NO. 14. HAND-COLORED LITHOGRAPH, DAY & HAGHE, LONDON, 1844.

Because winter snow made bison hunting easier, the first snowfall each year inspired the Ojibwa to thank the Great Spirit with dancing and singing. Hunters in snowshoes would drive a beast toward deep drifts. As it bogged down, they skimmed swiftly over the surface for the kill.

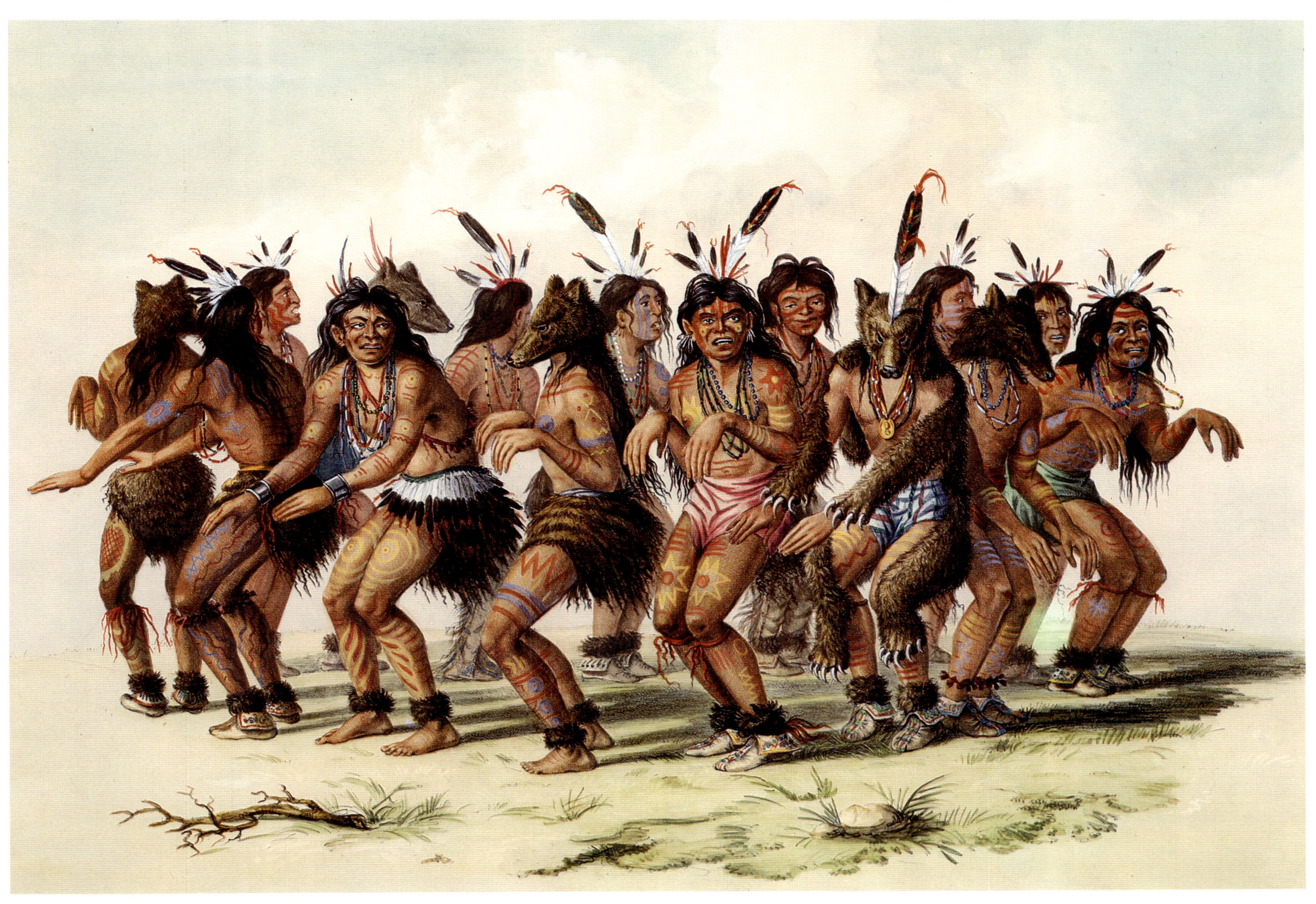

THE BEAR DANCE. GEORGE CATLIN, *INDIAN PORTFOLIO,* NO. 18. HAND-COLORED LITHOGRAPH, DAY & HAGHE, LONDON, 1844.

"The Sioux," writes Catlin, "all like the fine pleasure of a bear hunt, and also participation in the bear dance...in which they all join in a scng to the Bear Spirit; which they think holds somewhere an invisible existence, and must be consulted and conciliated before they can enter upon their excursion with any prospect of success."

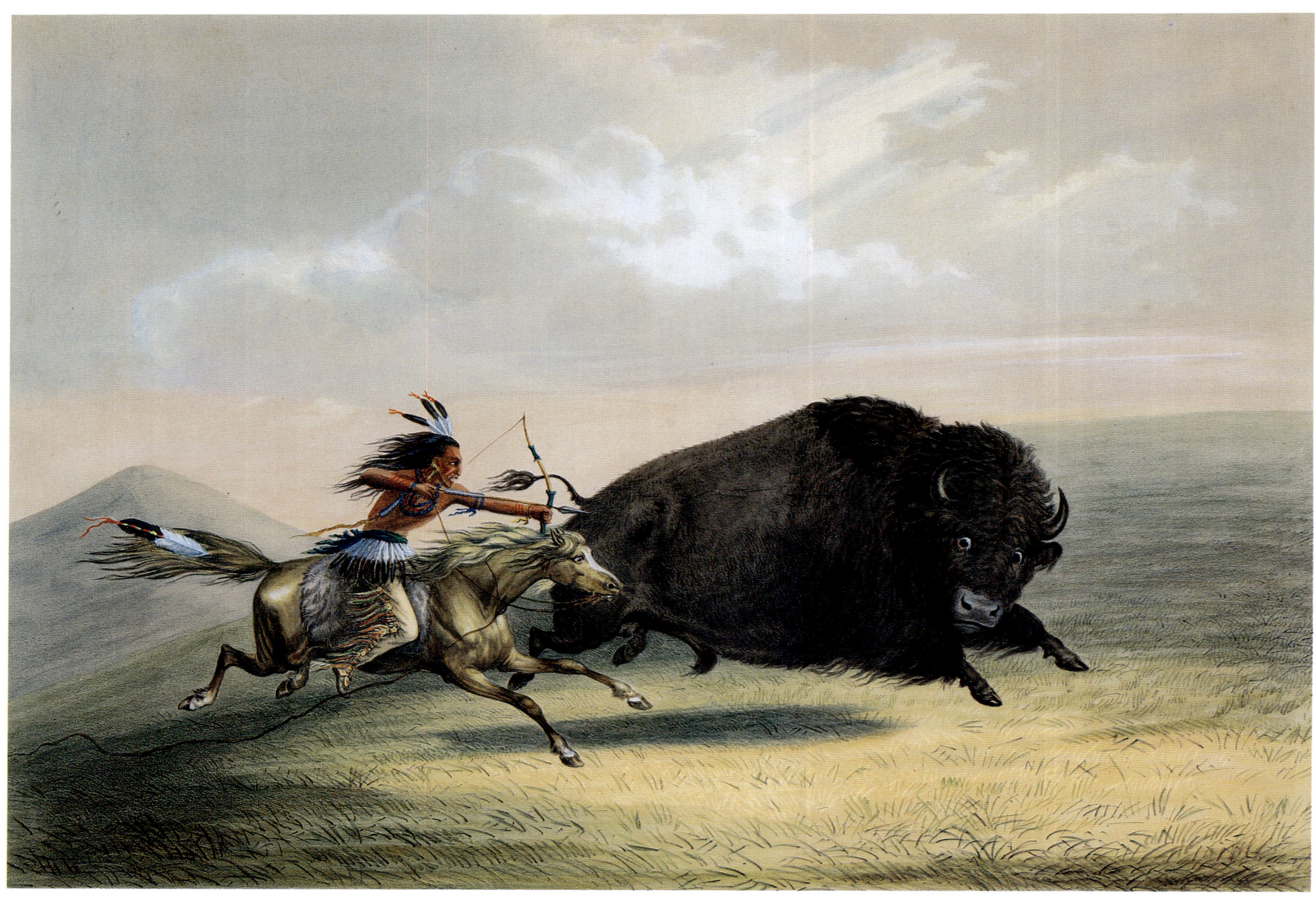

BUFFALO HUNT, CHASE. GEORGE CATLIN, *INDIAN PORTFOLIO,* NO. 5. HAND-COLORED LITHOGRAPH, DAY & HAGHE, LONDON, 1844.

Indian ponies were trained to respond to signals from the rider's legs, freeing his hands for bow and arrows. One of Catlin's greatest images, the Buffalo Hunt *captures a climactic moment as three beings fully exert themselves. Both animals are in the air; not a hoof touches the ground.*

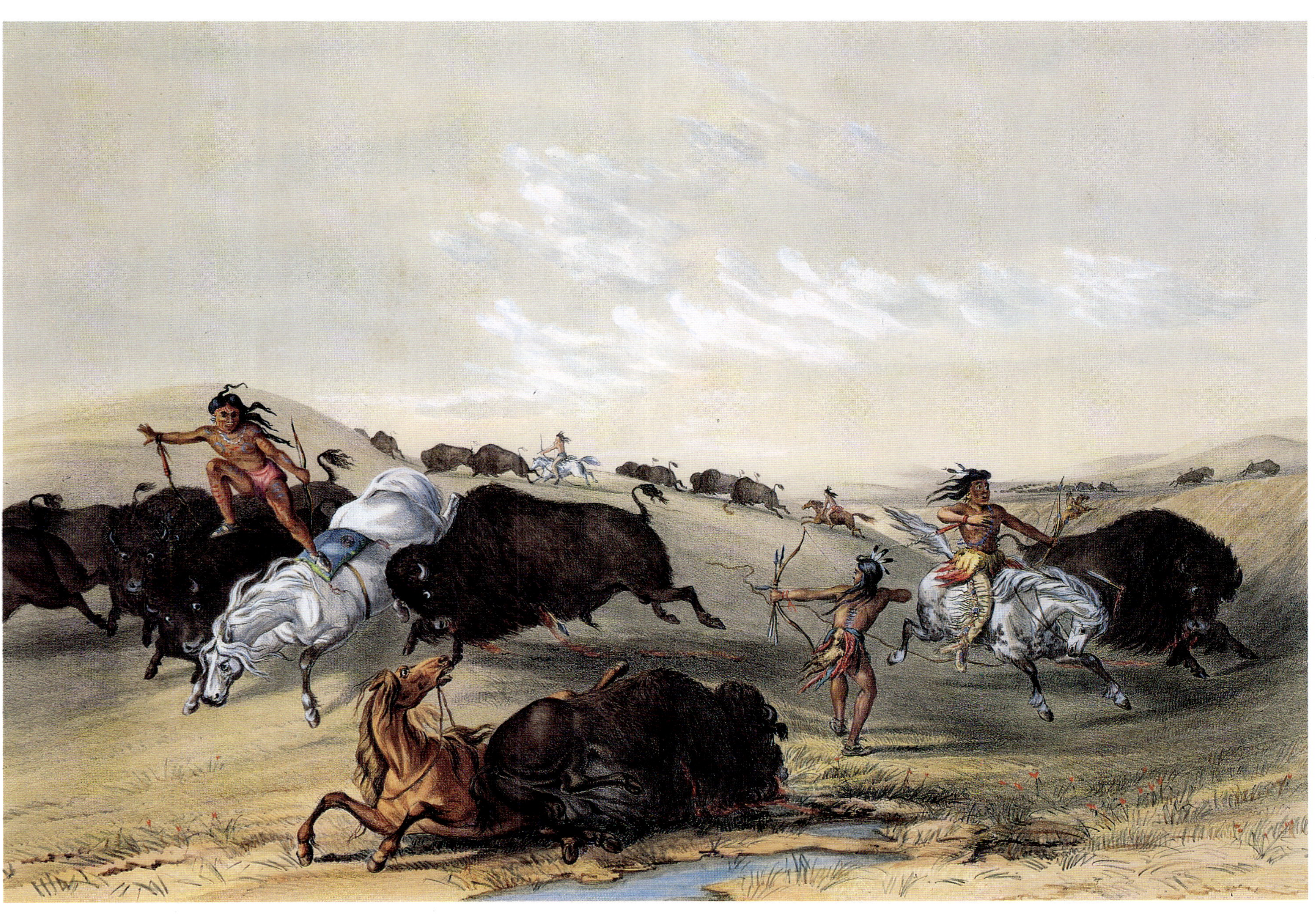

BUFFALO HUNT, CHASE. GEORGE CATLIN, *INDIAN PORTFOLIO,* NO. 7. HAND-COLORED LITHOGRAPH, DAY & HAGHE, LONDON, 1844.

Catlin's depictions of buffalo hunts were so much improved by his lithographers' careful drafts-manship that he often modeled later oils on their prints. Here the normally timid buffalo fight their attackers; one gores a pony as its rider deftly escapes.

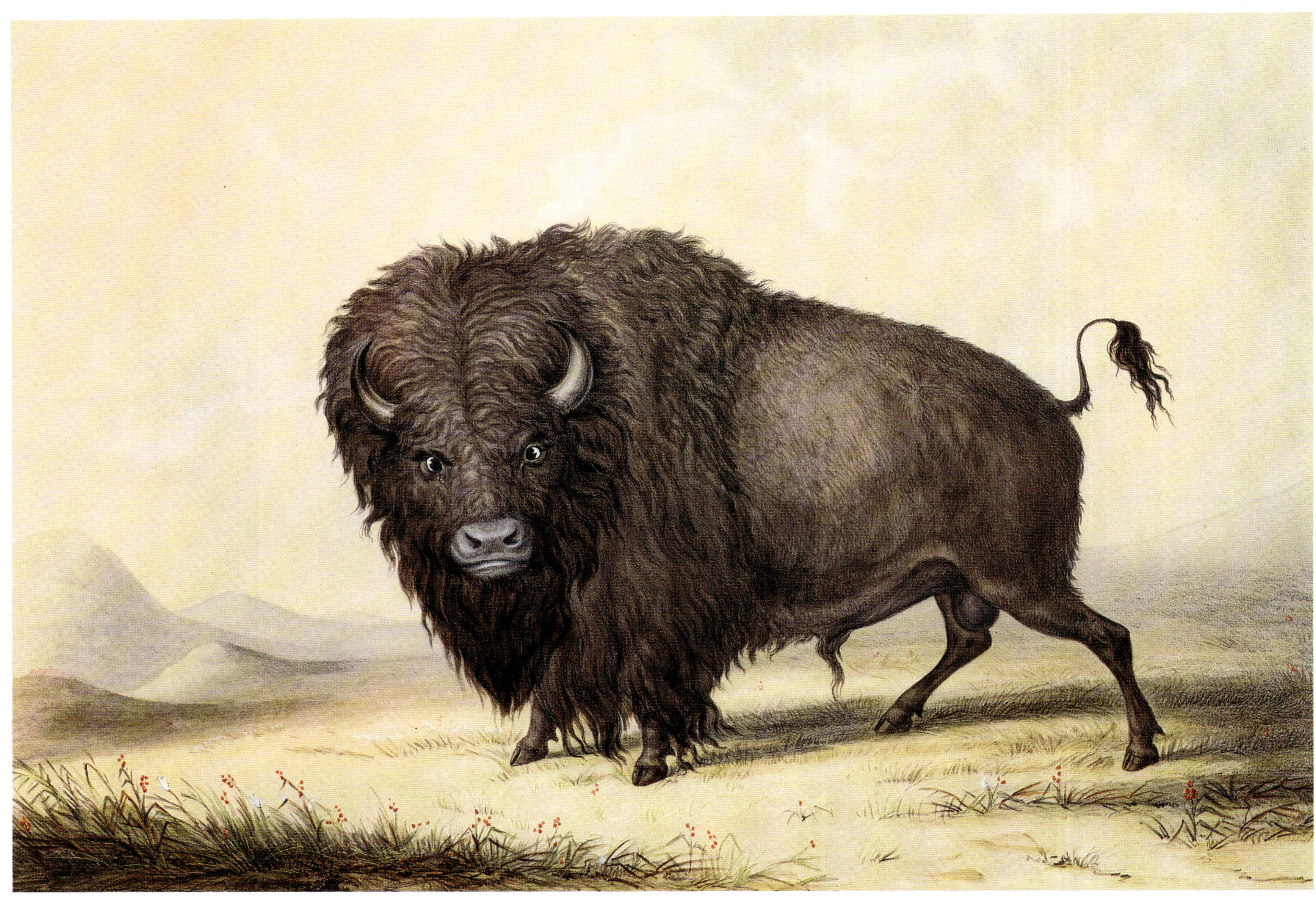

BUFFALO BULL, GRAZING. GEORGE CATLIN, *INDIAN PORTFOLIO,* NO. 2. HAND-COLORED LITHOGRAPH, DAY & HAGHE, LONDON, 1844.

Catlin writes passionately about whites' wasteful slaughter of bison, making the animal a symbol of the doomed prairies and Indian tribes. Catlin's depiction of this powerful bull suggests its wariness as it looks up from grazing.

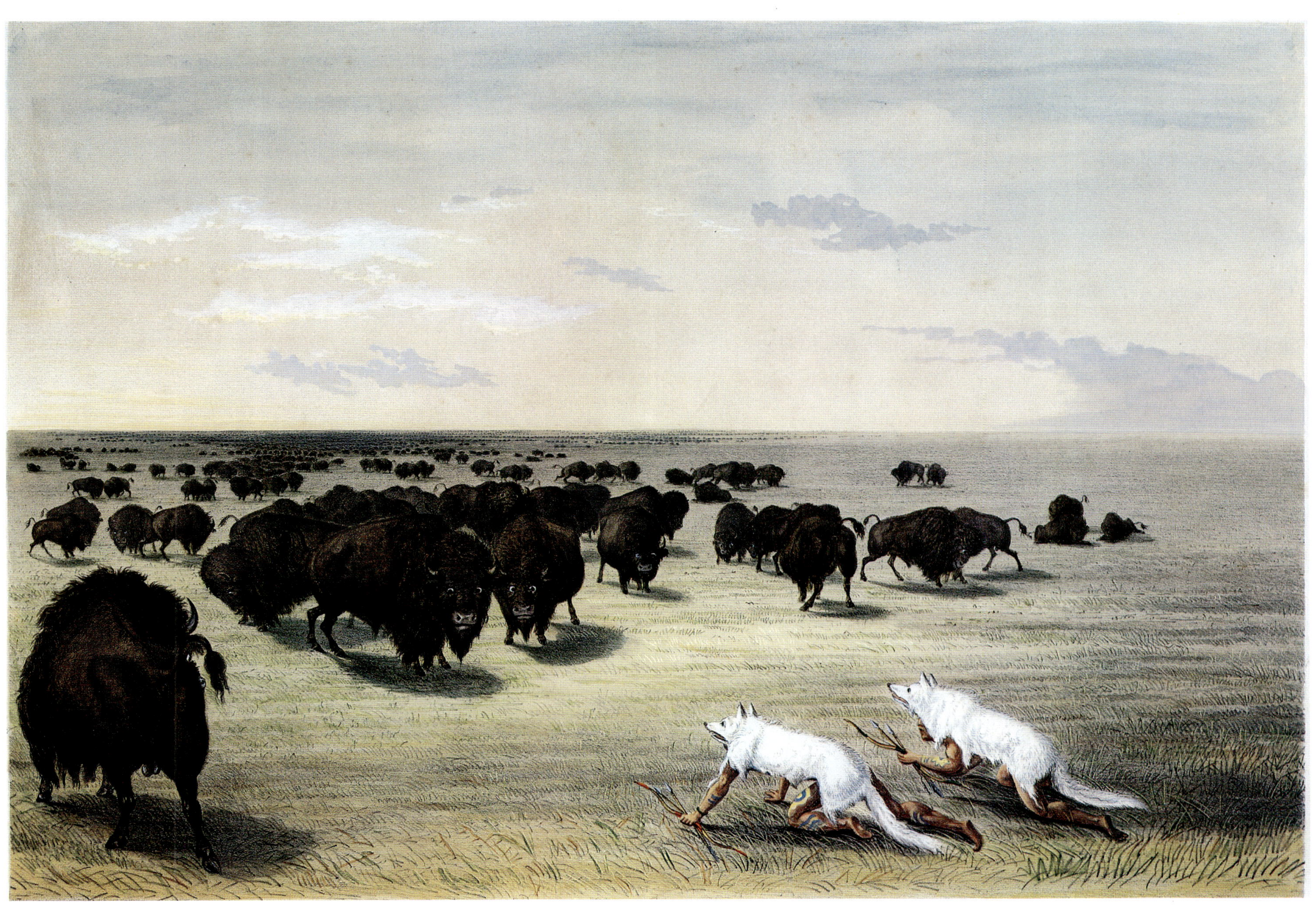

BUFFALO HUNT, UNDER THE WHITE WOLF SKIN. GEORGE CATLIN, *INDIAN PORTFOLIO,* NO. 13. HAND-COLORED LITHOGRAPH, DAY & HAGHE, LONDON, 1844.

Catlin's sympathetic depiction of this buffalo herd is reflected in his journals: "The poor buffaloes have their enemy man, besetting and besieging them at all times of the year, and in all the modes that man in his superior wisdom has been able to devise for their destruction."

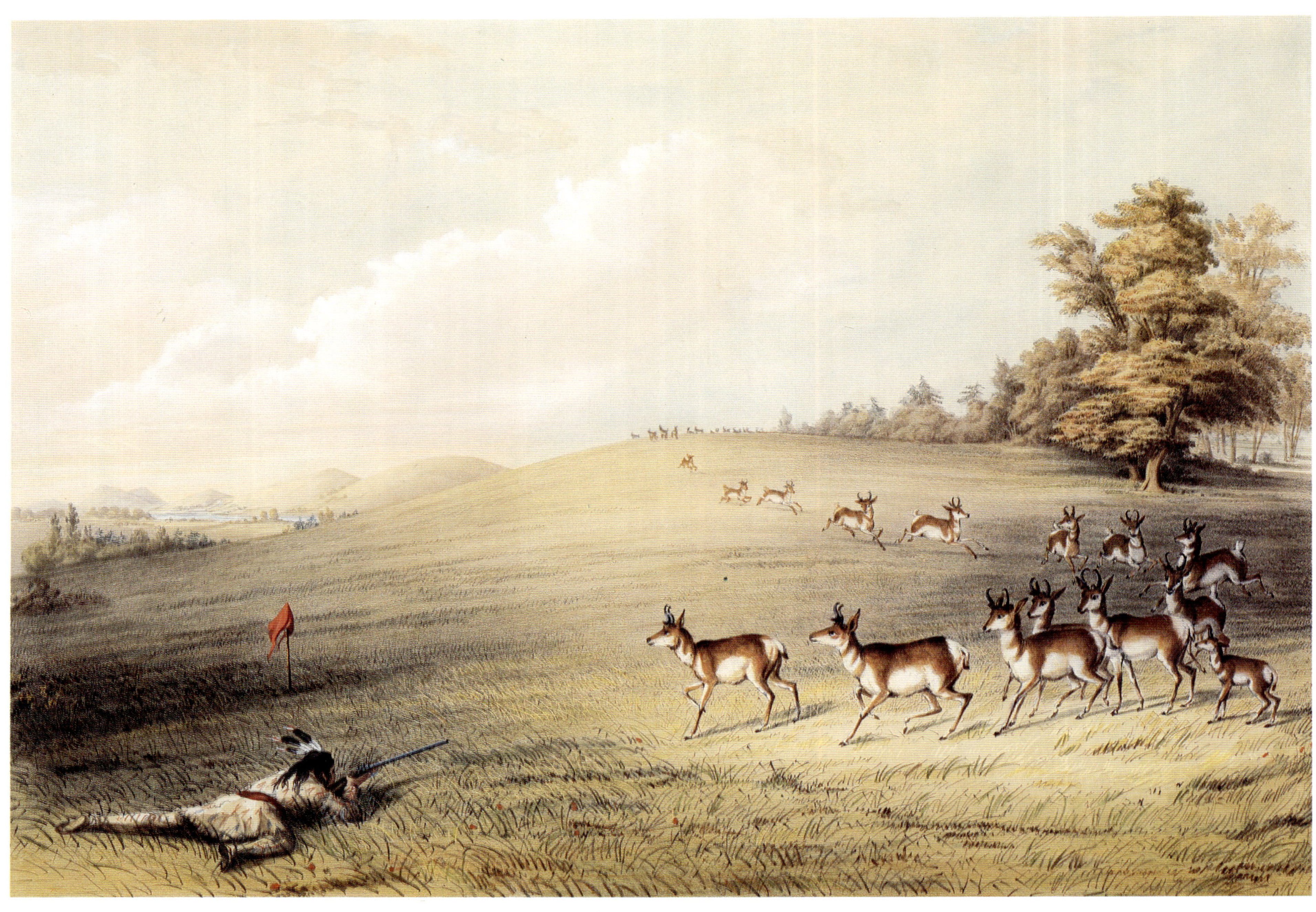

ANTELOPE SHOOTING. GEORGE CATLIN, *INDIAN PORTFOLIO,* NO. 20. HAND-COLORED LITHOGRAPH, DAY & HAGHE, LONDON, 1844.

In Letters and Notes, *Catlin describes how Indians killed antelopes, which can outrun a pony. Taking advantage of antelopes' natural curiosity, the hunters fastened a red flag to a pole and lay in wait until the timid but inquisitive creatures came within range.*

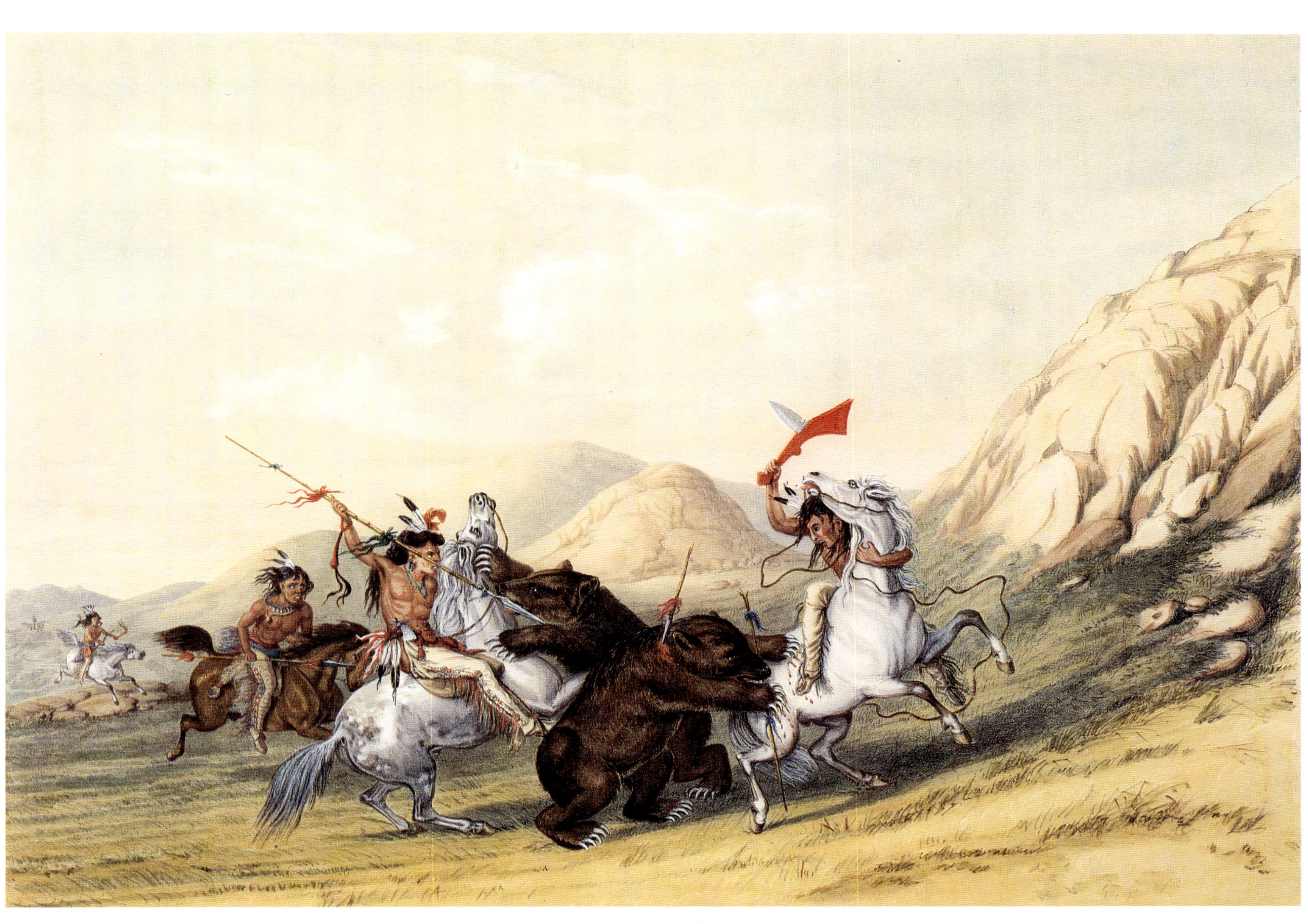

ATTACKING THE GRIZZLY BEAR. GEORGE CATLIN, *INDIAN PORTFOLIO,* NO. 19. HAND-COLORED LITHOGRAPH, DAY & HAGHE, LONDON, 1844.

The Sioux prized bear meat and used bear grease to anoint their hair and bodies. When a hunter killed a grizzly bear, he became entitled to wear a necklace made from the claws of this cunning and dangerous animal. Although many of these prints are based upon scenes which Catlin painted in the field, the original for this image was completed in a studio.

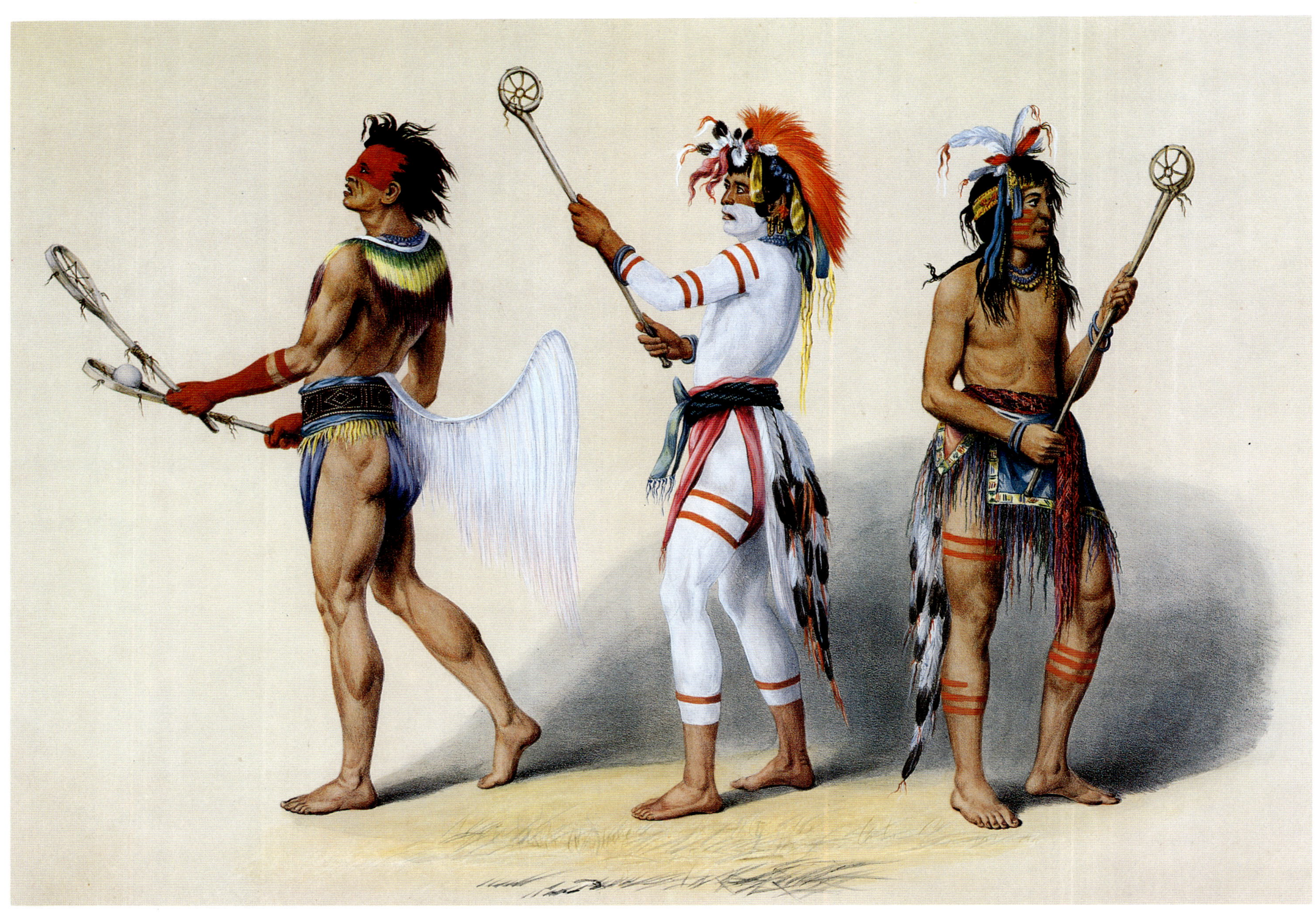

BALL PLAYERS. GEORGE CATLIN, *INDIAN PORTFOLIO,* NO. 21. HAND-COLORED LITHOGRAPH, DAY & HAGHE, LONDON, 1844.

A Choctaw (left), an Eastern Sioux (center), and a Sioux (right) display their lacrosse attire. The Choctaw, whose tribe had recently been removed from ancestral lands in Alabama and Mississippi, wears a mane of dyed horsehair and a tail of either horsehair or quills.

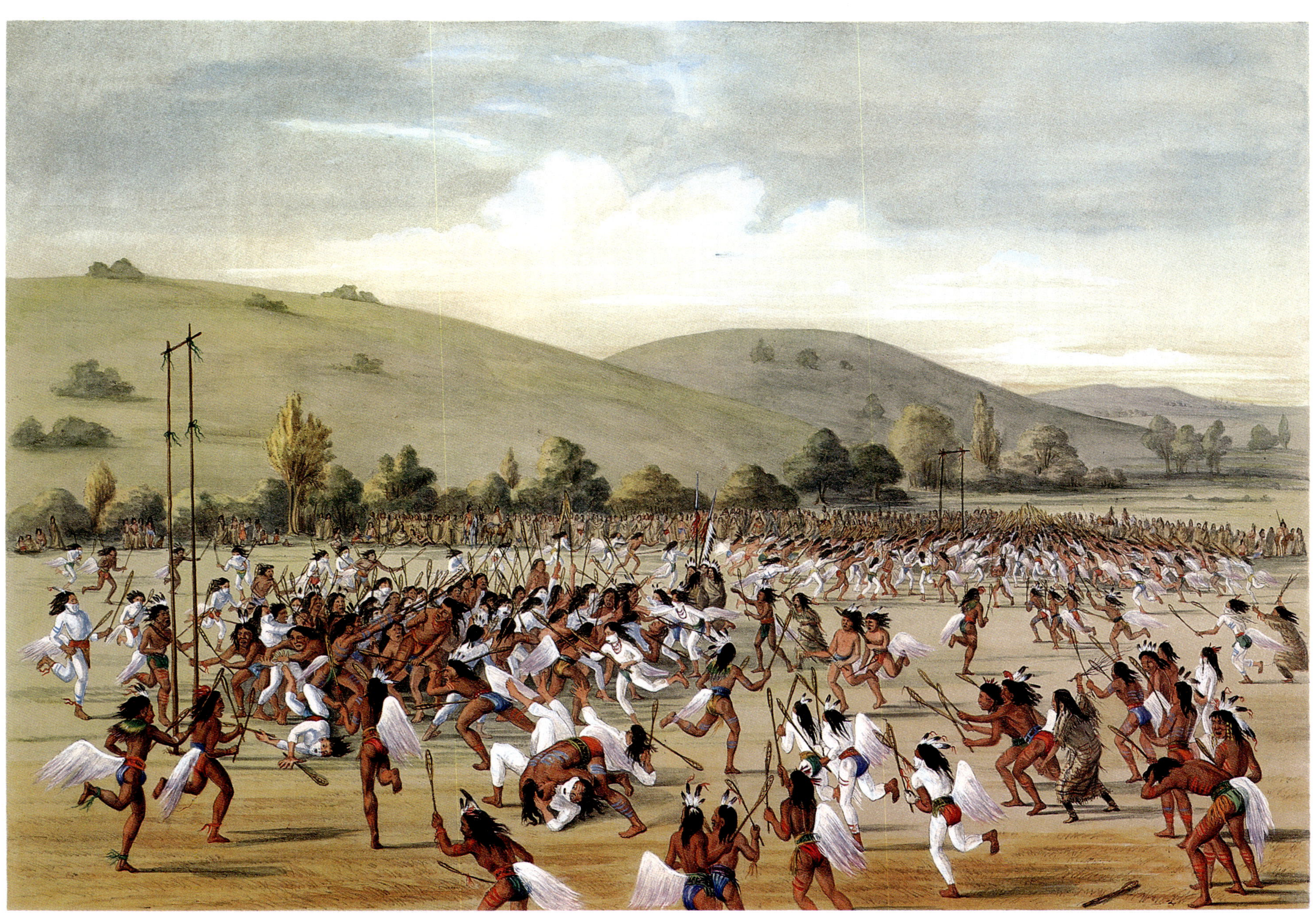

BALL PLAY. GEORGE CATLIN, *INDIAN PORTFOLIO,* NO. 23. HAND-COLORED LITHOGRAPH, DAY & HAGHE, LONDON, 1844.

To announce the next playing of this boisterous game, runners were sent to tribal villages months in advance. According to Catlin, some 600 players would participate, "running together and leaping, actually over each other's heads, and darting between their adversaries' legs, tripping and throwing, and foiling each other in every possible manner, and every voice raised to its highest key in shrill yelps and barks!"

Tab. 28

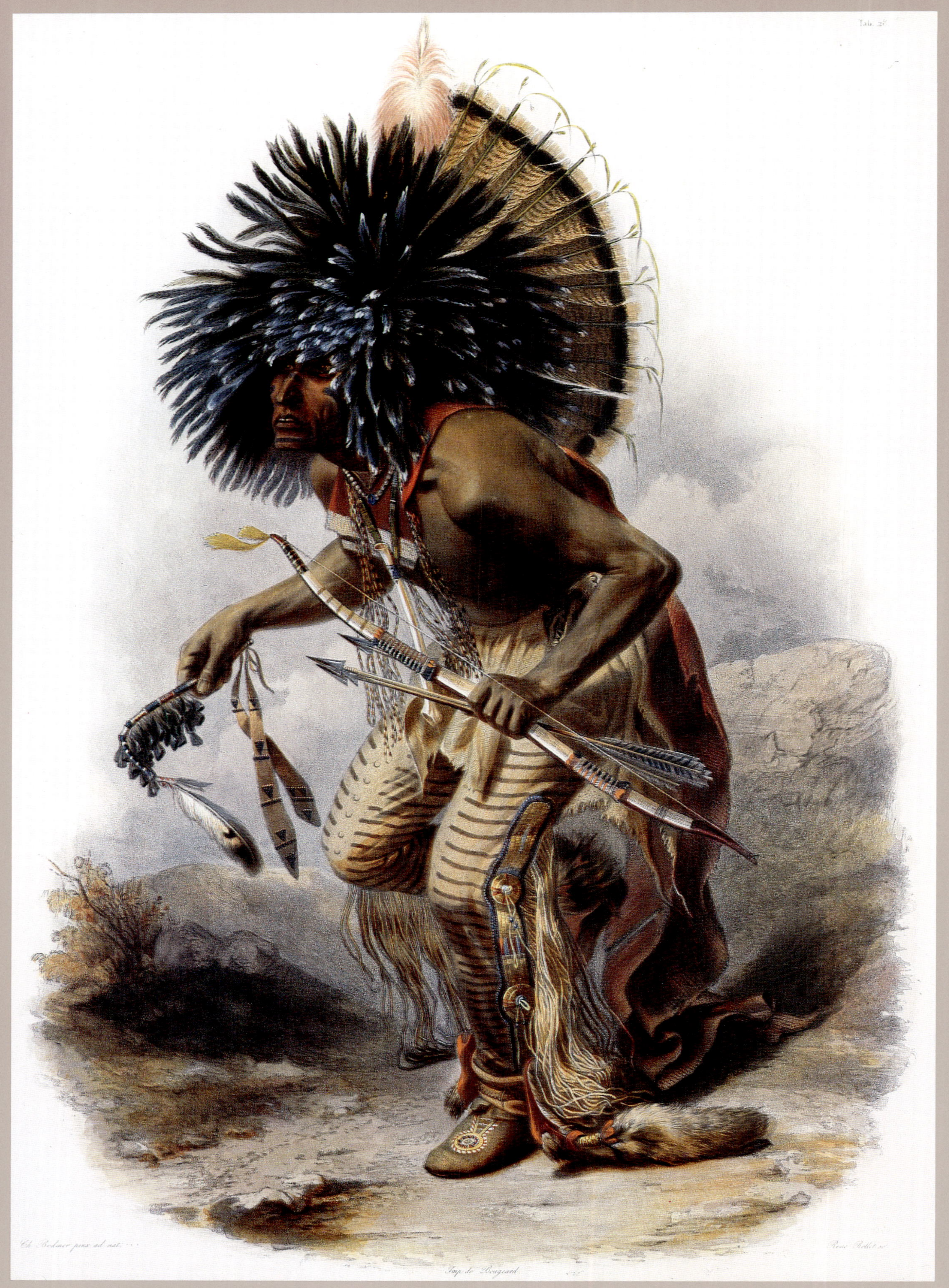

Ch. Bodmer pinx ad nat.

Imp. de Bougeard

Rene Rollet sc.

KARL BODMER (1809-1893)

George Catlin's Indian Gallery and his *Letters and Notes* might be our most complete record of the tribes of the Great Plains were it not for a learned German nobleman and an obscure Swiss artist. In 1833, a year after Catlin traveled up the Missouri in the American Fur Company's steamboat, the *Yellowstone*, Prince Alexander Phillip Maximilian of Wied and the 23-year-old Karl Bodmer boarded the same vessel in St. Louis for a longer trip on the same river. Together they were to create the most detailed study of the Plains Indians ever produced, *Travels in the Interior of North America*, based on the prince's journals and accompanied by 81 hand-colored aquatints from Bodmer's watercolors and sketches.

A naturalist and scholar who emulated the great scientific explorer Alexander von Humboldt, Maximilian deplored the scarcity of information available on the native people of North America, and resolved to fill the gap. The Missouri River journey would be his second adventure in the New World. After distinguishing himself in the Prussian army during the Napoleonic Wars, the prince had explored Brazil's coastal forests with two other German scientists between 1815 and 1817.

PEHRISKA-RUHPA, MOENNITARRI WARRIOR IN THE COSTUME OF THE DOG DANSE. KARL BODMER, PLATE 23, *ATLAS* TO *TRAVELS IN THE INTERIOR OF NORTH AMERICA.* BY PRINCE MAXIMILIAN OF WIED. HAND-COLORED AQUATINT, BOUGEARD, PARIS, 1836-1842.

No finer full-length portrait of an American Indian exists. Although Pehriska-Ruhpa was a Minatarre, Bodmer paints him in the costume of the "dog band" society of the neighboring Mandans. When the band met, three members who were designated "true dogs" were obliged, "if anyone throws a piece of meat... onto the ground, saying, 'There, dog, eat,' to fall upon it, and devour it raw, like dogs or beasts of prey."

His book about that expedition established his scientific reputation, but its engravings, based on his own drawings, dissatisfied the prince, to say nothing of his brother and sister, who found the original sketches so inept that they redrew them for publication. For his new venture, Maximilian decided to hire an artist whose work could supply the "fine portfolio of plates" he felt was essential "for a faithful and vivid picture of these countries and their original inhabitants." Karl Bodmer soon came to his attention.

Born in Zurich in 1809, Bodmer learned drawing, painting, and engraving from his uncle, Johann Jakob Meyer. In 1828, Bodmer moved to Coblenz, near Maximilian's estate on the Rhine, to make a living depicting the Rhine Valley's romantic scenery for travelers. Early in 1832, he met the prince and soon agreed to join the expedition. He would paint whatever Maximilian requested, and the prince would pay his expenses.

They arrived in Boston on July 4, 1832. Delayed by a cholera epidemic and an illness of the prince, they did not reach St. Louis until April 1833. There General William Clark, who had been so helpful to Catlin, introduced Maximilian and his artist to Indian delegations, and to all St. Louis' leading citizens, with whom the prince thoroughly discussed wilderness travel.

The pair began working their way upstream aboard the *Yellowstone* on April 10. At that time, a few Indian agencies and fur trading posts hundreds of miles apart along the Missouri's 2,500-mile course served as meeting places for Indians and whites. Between outposts, the prince and Bodmer rarely encountered natives. As the *Yellowstone* inched across sandbars or was hauled through driftwood islands by the entire crew, the prince often went ashore to hunt or to gather specimens, and Bodmer painted dozens of views of the river, compiling what now stands as a unique record of the Missouri in its wild state.

At each outpost—Bellevue, Fort Clark, Fort Union, Fort McKenzie—Bodmer spent long days portraying the remarkable representatives of Sioux, Crow, Mandan, Hidatsa, Assiniboine, Blackfeet, and other tribes who came to trade with the fur company or simply to meet the exotic visitors. More painstaking than Catlin, Bodmer often spent a day or two on a painting, entertaining his sitters with a music box, tobacco, and small gifts.

Most sat patiently and were pleased with the results, though uncomfortable situations sometimes arose. Of Haschato the orator, the prince wrote, "It was not easy to bargain with him, as he estimated his handsome person very high, and was much offended at our refusal to paint him at such an extravagant price." On another occasion, a Minatarre warrior, irked when the artist refused to give him the finished portrait, got even by sketching a portrait of Bodmer. Other Indians were superstitious about having their likenesses depicted at all. According to Maximilian, Bodmer persuaded leery would-be sitters at Fort McKenzie by telling them that "none of the men whose portraits he had drawn, had been lately killed or wounded."

Beyond Fort Union, Catlin's stopping place the previous year, the Missouri became impassable to steamboats, and the prince and Bodmer boarded a keelboat which brought them to Fort McKenzie, the American Fur Trading Company's westernmost outpost, on August 9. Here, as 800 Indians gathered to exchange furs for rifles, cloth, and other goods, the travelers witnessed skirmishes just outside the fort between the Piegan Blackfeet and their neighbors the Cree and the Assiniboine. Bodmer later reconstructed one of the battles for Plate 42 (see page 121).

After a month, disturbed by these Indian troubles, the prince's party returned downriver to winter at Fort Clark near a Mandan village. It was a difficult time for them. Their lodgings were so cold that Bodmer's paints and Maximilian's ink froze, and their food was so poor and scanty that the prince developed scurvy and might have died had the cook not diagnosed his illness and prescribed a diet of wild onions.

Despite the hardships, Bodmer painted some of his most arresting portraits during these months. His precise depictions and the prince's careful observations have provided an invaluable record of the Mandans, who were virtually wiped out by smallpox four years later.

The pair returned to Europe in 1834. Maximilian retired to Coblenz to write his *Travels*, while Bodmer went to Paris to supervise the engraving of the plates. To fill out the composition of each plate, he often combined sketches, sometimes pairing Indians from unlikely tribes. Eighty-one aquatints resulted: 33 small "vignettes," to be bound with the text, and 48 larger prints to be bound separately. In the end, both sets were bound separately.

First published in German, *Travels* later appeared in English and French. Although buyers could choose between a costly edition with hand-colored prints and a cheaper black-and-white version, the work never turned a profit. Bodmer's illustrations, however, remain his finest achievement and are thought by many to be the most beautiful engravings ever made of the Great Plains and its native inhabitants. The dignity and strangeness of Plains Indian life awakened talents in this meticulous draftsman that rarely mark his later work.

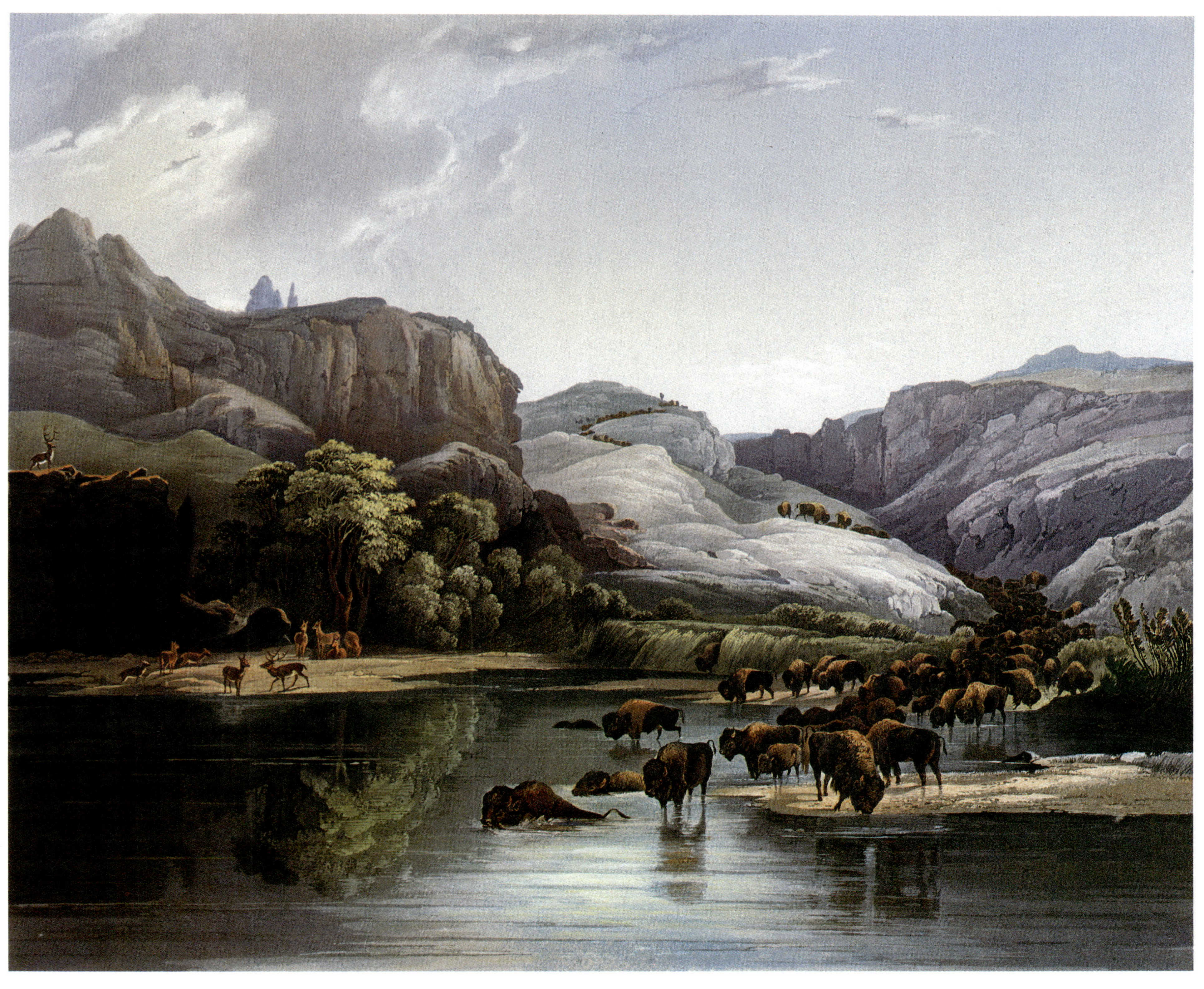

HERDS OF BISONS AND ELKS ON THE UPPER MISSOURI. KARL BODMER, *ATLAS,* PLATE 47. HAND-COLORED AQUATINT, BOUGEARD, PARIS, 1836-1842.

Bodmer's acute sense of color and light is well displayed in this Badlands landscape, first sketched in September 1833 as the prince's party sailed downstream from Fort McKenzie in a small boat. To avoid startling the herds, the prince ordered the crew to stop rowing, and as the boat drifted noiselessly, the animals continued coming down to the water, giving Bodmer an excellent chance to make observations.

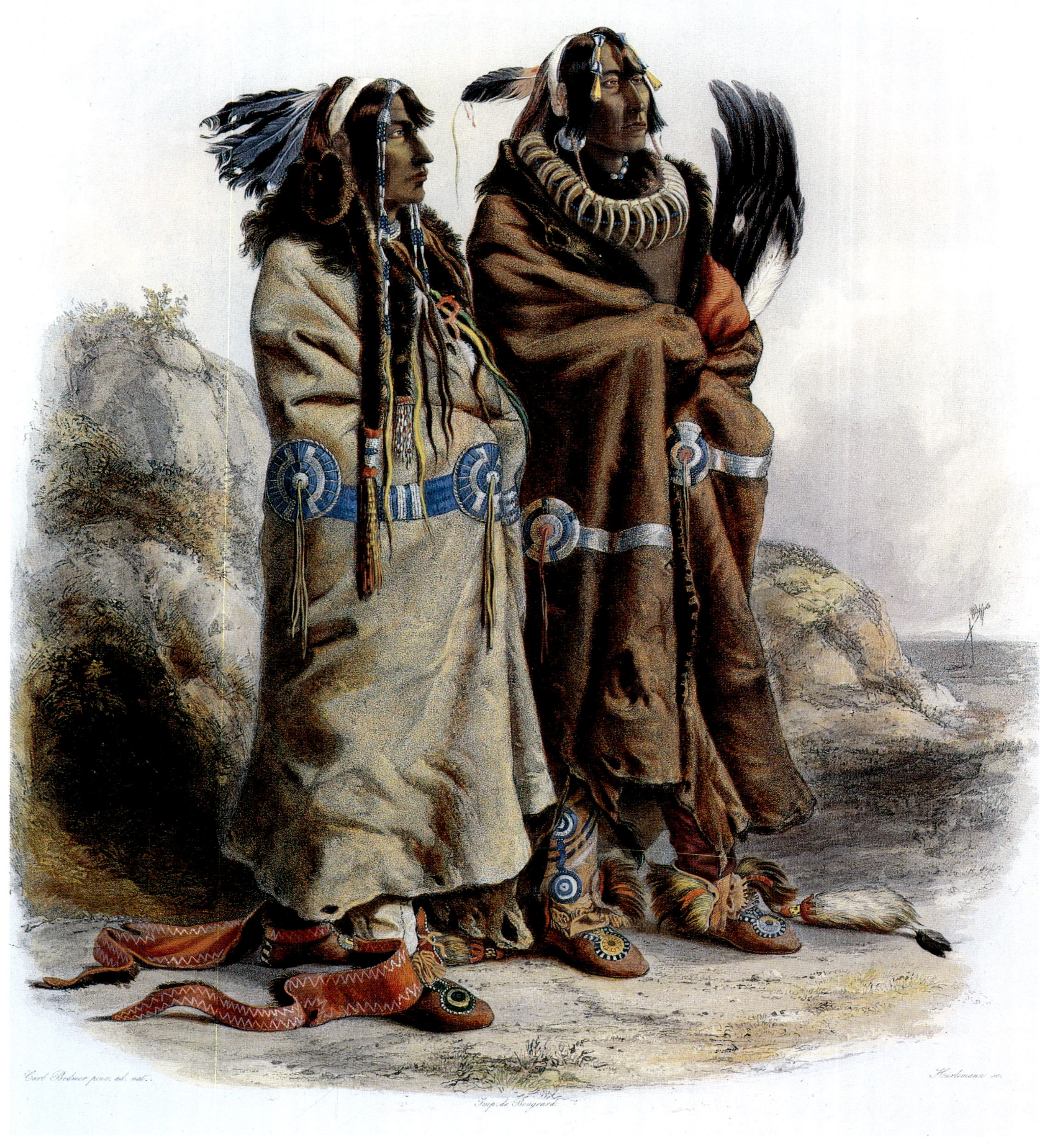

SIH-CHIDA AND MAHCHSI-KAREHDE. MANDAN INDIANS. KARL BODMER, *ATLAS,* PLATE 20. HAND-COLORED AQUATINT, BOUGEARD, PARIS, 1836-1842.

Sih-Chida visited Bodmer and the prince almost daily during their winter at Fort Clark. He passed the evenings making drawings; his manner and "delicacy of feeling" impressed Maximilian. Mahchsi-Karehde, a warrior, was "the tallest man among the Mandans." Bodmer's exacting attention to details of attire is matched by his successful rendering of the braves' self-possession and integrity.

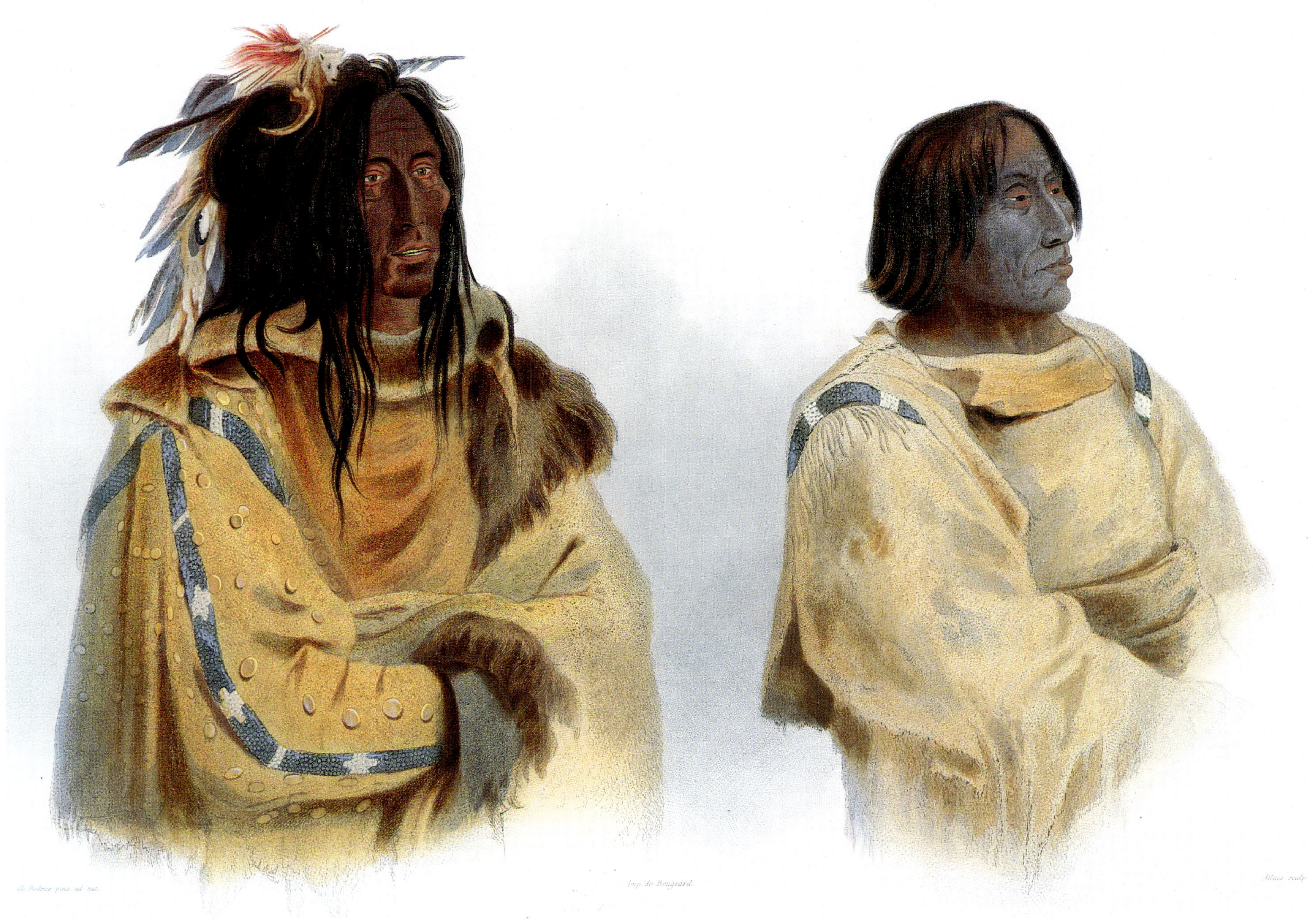

MEHKSKEME-SUKAHS. BLACKFOOT-CHIEF. TATSICKI-STOMICK. PIEKANN-CHIEF. KARL BODMER, *ATLAS,* PLATE 45. HAND-COLORED AQUATINT, BOUGEARD, PARIS, 1836-1842.

Bodmer's portrait of Mehkskeme-Sukahs (Iron Shirt) and Tatsicki-Stomick (Middle Bull) demonstrates his ability to reveal depths of character in his subjects. Although both chieftains preferred American military costume, they agreed to the prince's request that they sit for their portraits in traditional garb.

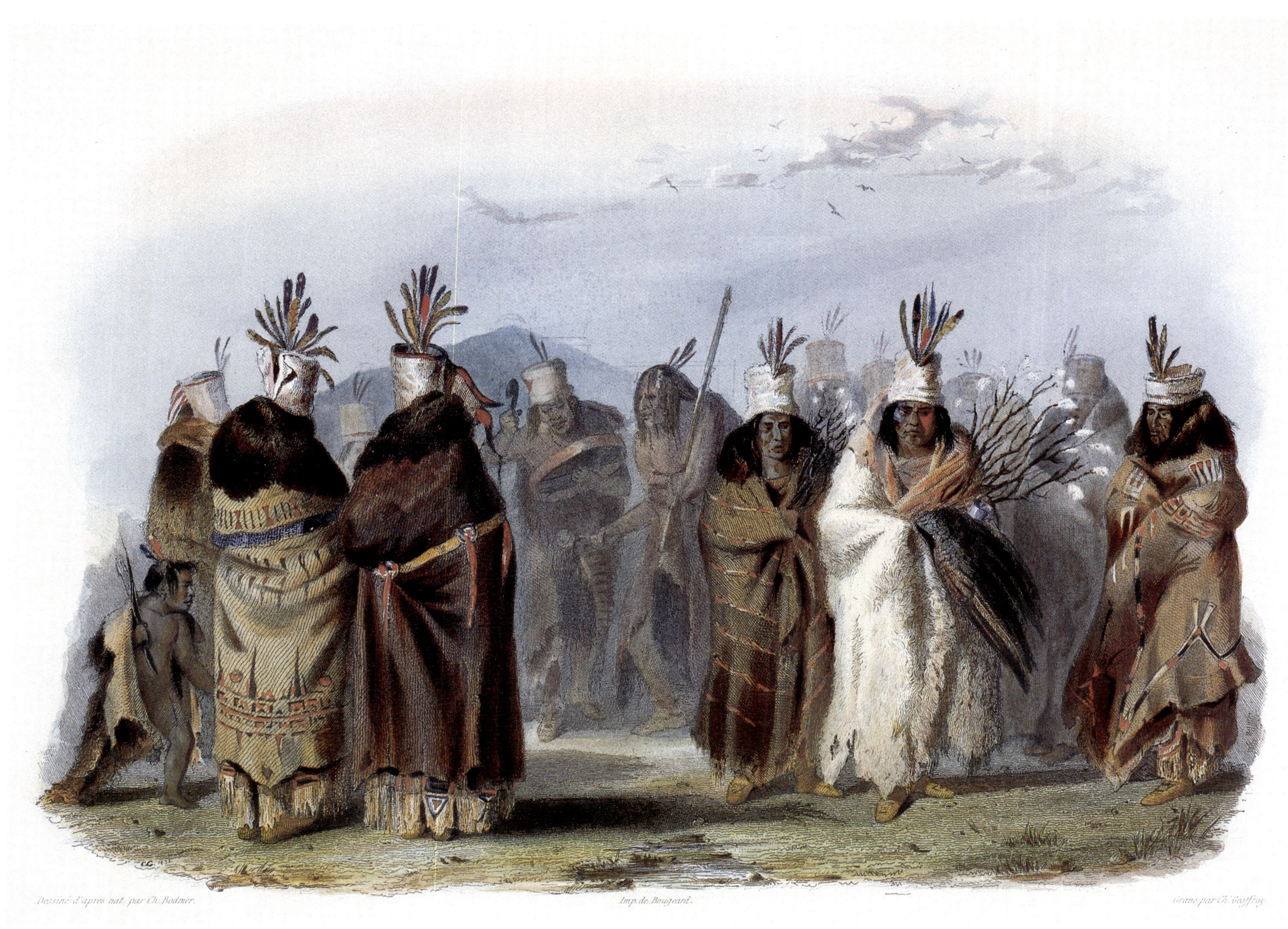

PTIHN-TAK-OCHATA. DANCE OF THE MANDAN WOMEN. KARL BODMER, *ATLAS,* VIGNETTE 28. HAND-COLORED AQUATINT, BOUGEARD, PARIS, 1836-1842.

Mandan women, like Mandan men, were divided into four classes "according to their age." The eldest women belonged to the white buffalo cow society. On Christmas Day of 1833, 17 members of this society came to Fort Clark from Mih-Tutta-Hangkusch and performed for the prince. "In their dances," Maximilian reports, "they rock from side to side, always remaining on the same spot."

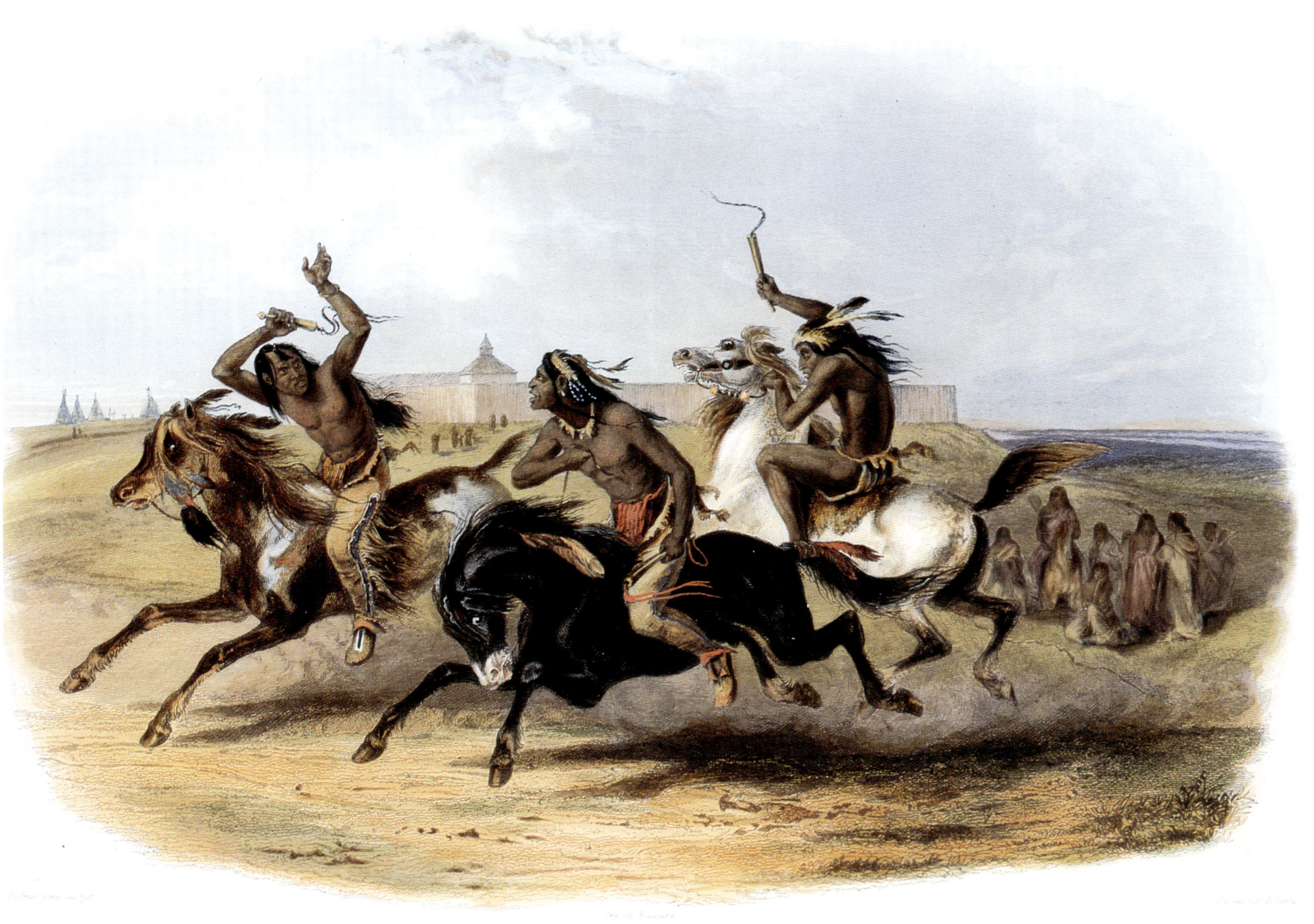

HORSE RACING OF SIOUX INDIANS NEAR FORT PIERRE. KARL BODMER, *ATLAS,* VIGNETTE 30. HAND-COLORED AQUATINT, BOUGEARD, PARIS, 1836-1842.

At Fort Pierre, near present-day Pierre, South Dakota, the prince's group transferred from the steamboat Yellowstone *to the smaller* Assiniboin. *While they waited for rains to raise the river, they encountered a number of Sioux Indians. Although Bodmer's study of young warriors at play is more carefully constructed than similar works by Catlin, the image seems completely spontaneous.*

ABDIH-HIDDISCH. A MINATARRE CHIEF. KARL BODMER, *ATLAS,* PLATE 24. HAND-COLORED AQUATINT, BOUGEARD, PARIS, 1836-1842.

Abdih-Hiddisch's odd European hat, calculating glance, strong muscles, and scalp make this one of Bodmer's most unsettling portraits. In fact, Abdih-Hiddisch, a highly respected elder, was on friendly terms with the prince throughout the winter of 1833-1834 and visited on many successive evenings to tell the history of his tribe.

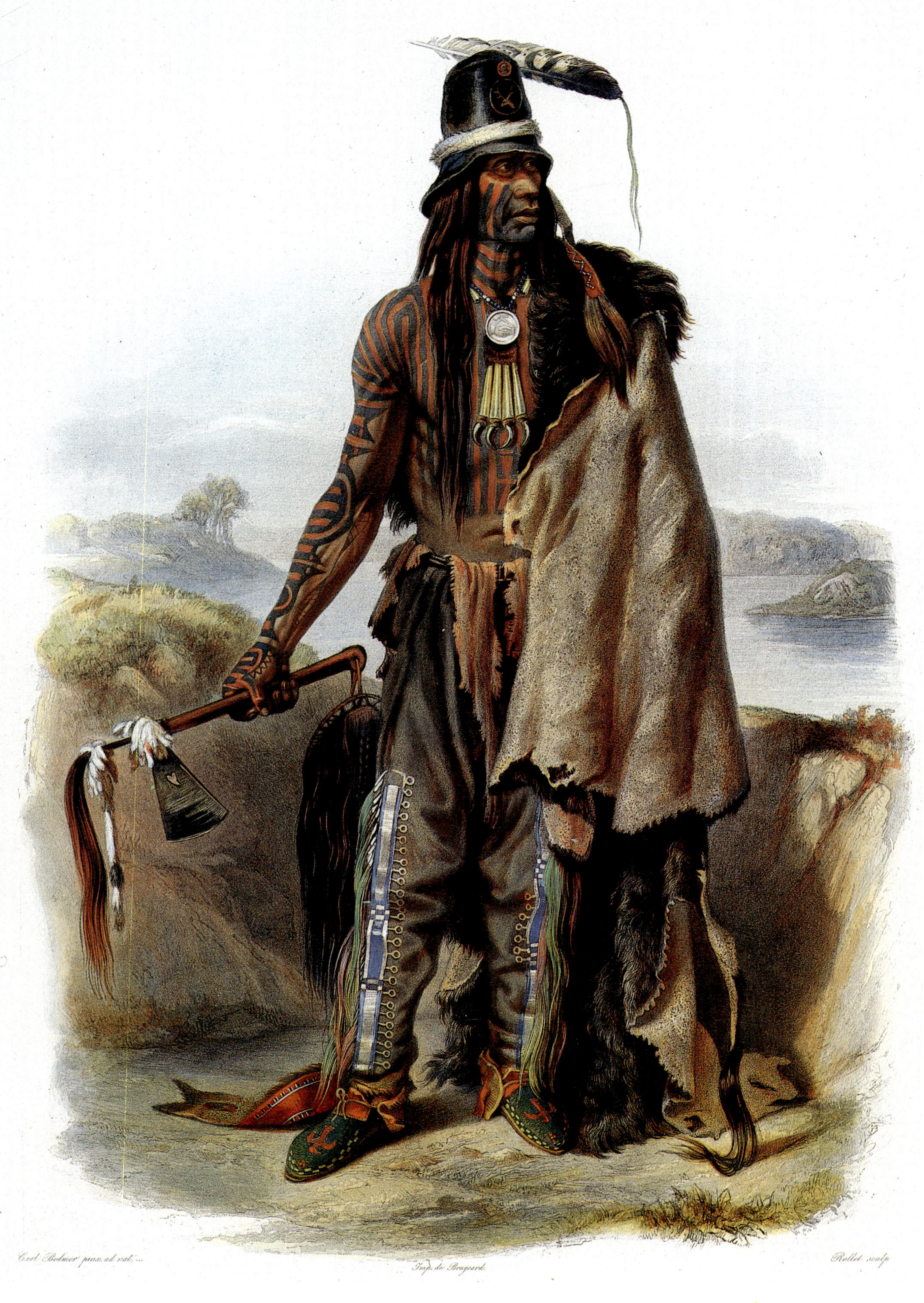

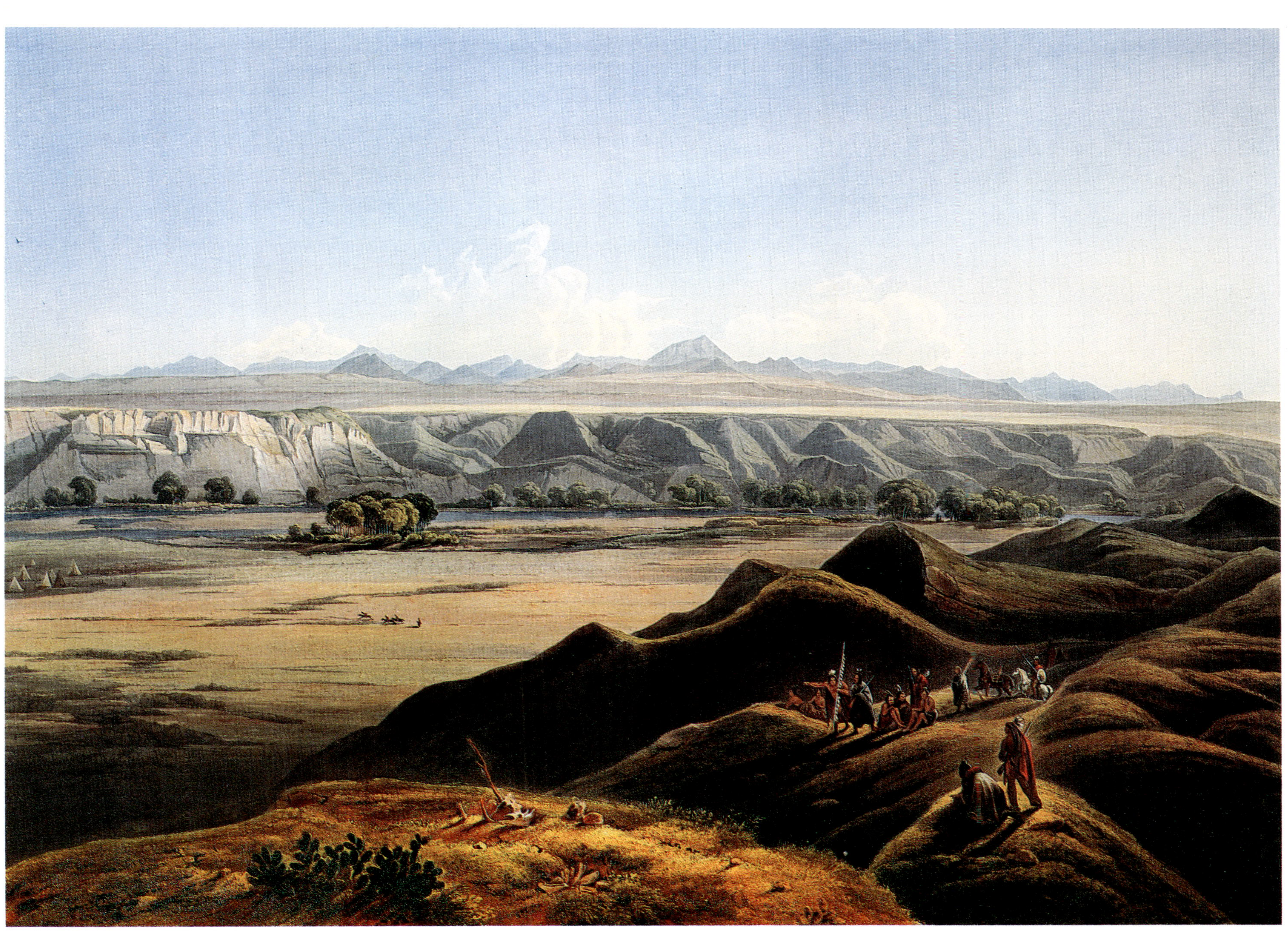

VIEW OF THE ROCKY MOUNTAINS. KARL BODMER, *ATLAS,* PLATE 44. HAND-COLORED AQUATINT, BOUGEARD, PARIS, 1836-1842.

At Fort McKenzie, the westernmost point in his journey, Prince Maximilian mistakenly supposed that these peaks to the southwest, now called the Highwoods, were the Rocky Mountains, which he and Bodmer never actually reached.

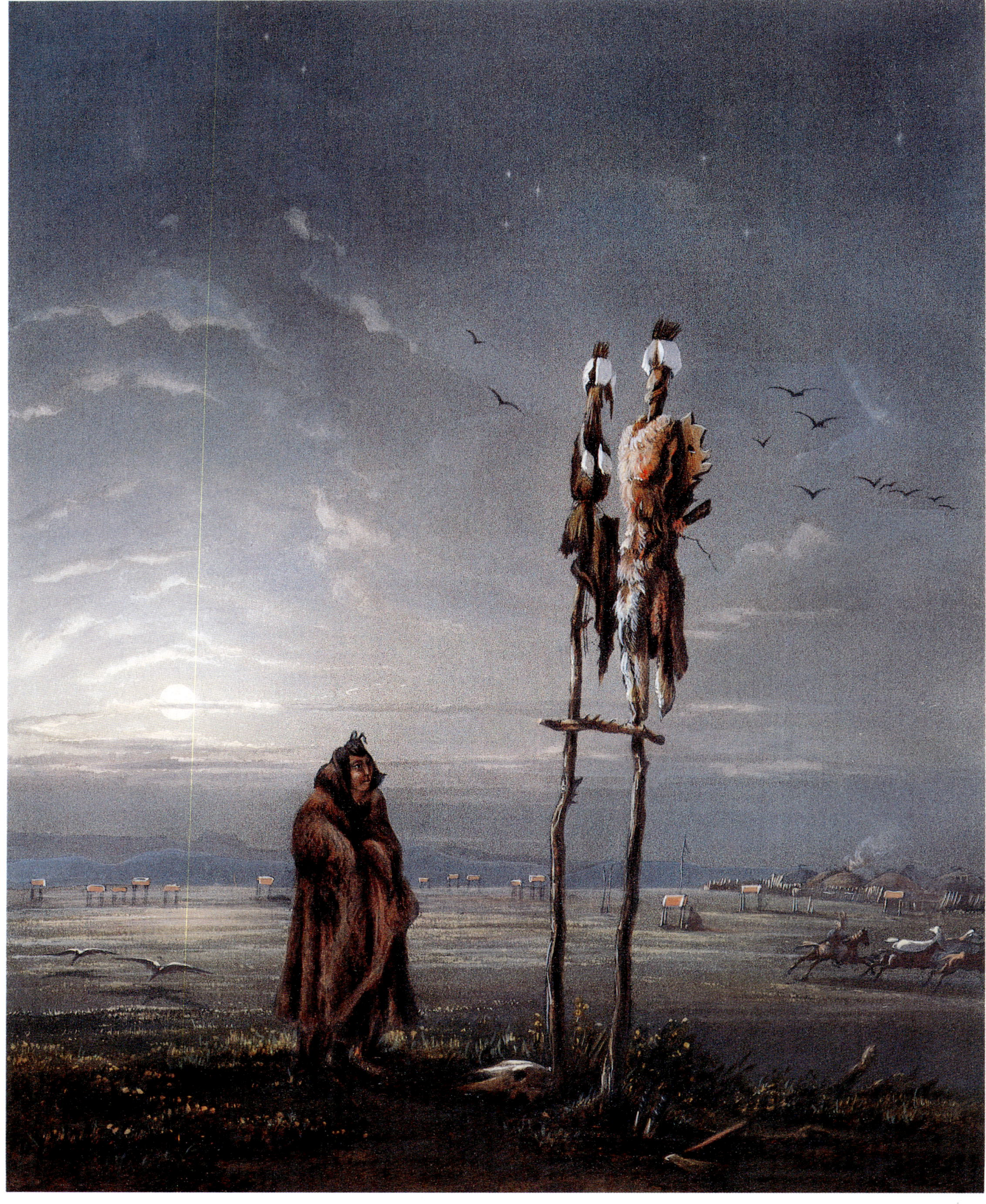

IDOLS OF THE MANDAN INDIANS. KARL BODMER, *ATLAS,* PLATE 25. HAND-COLORED AQUATINT, BOUGEARD, PARIS, 1836-1842.

These two poles represent the sun and the moon, referred to in Mandan mythology as the Lord of Life and the One Woman Who Never Dies. When Bodmer painted this shrine, the Mandan supplicant at left had been standing in prayer for several days, a common practice among Plains Indians.

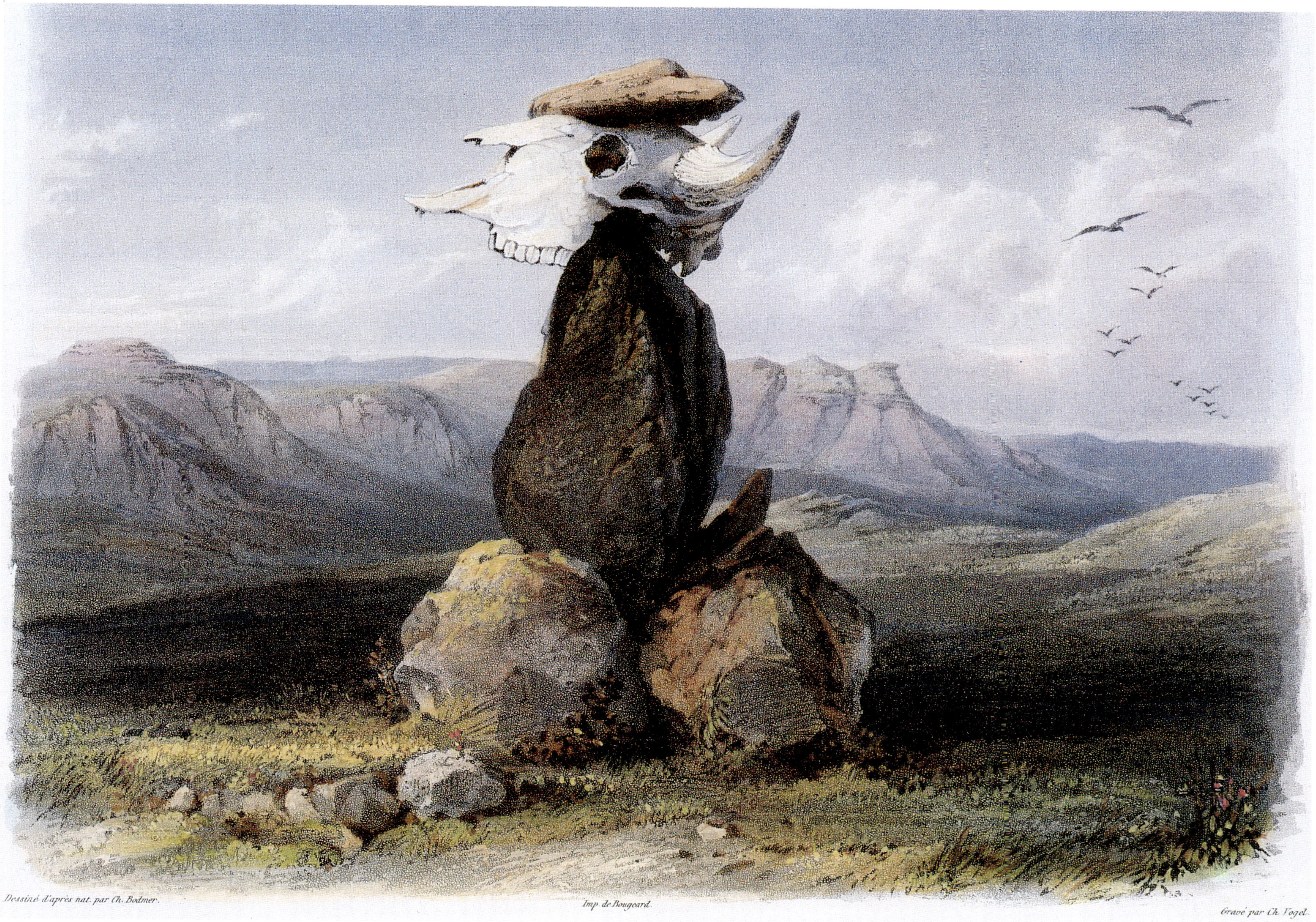

Dessiné d'après nat. par Ch. Bodmer. Imp. de Bougeard. Gravé par Ch. Vogel.

MAGIC PILE ERECTED BY THE ASSINIBOIN INDIANS. KARL BODMER, *ATLAS*, VIGNETTE 15. HAND-COLORED AQUATINT, BOUGEARD, PARIS, 1836-1842.

Exploring the area around Fort Union in June 1833, Bodmer and the prince found an Assiniboine magic pile. The Assiniboines believed that these constructions attracted the bison upon which they depended for food, shelter, clothes, and bone implements. Alien as the magic pile must have seemed, Bodmer presents it without exaggerating its potential eeriness.

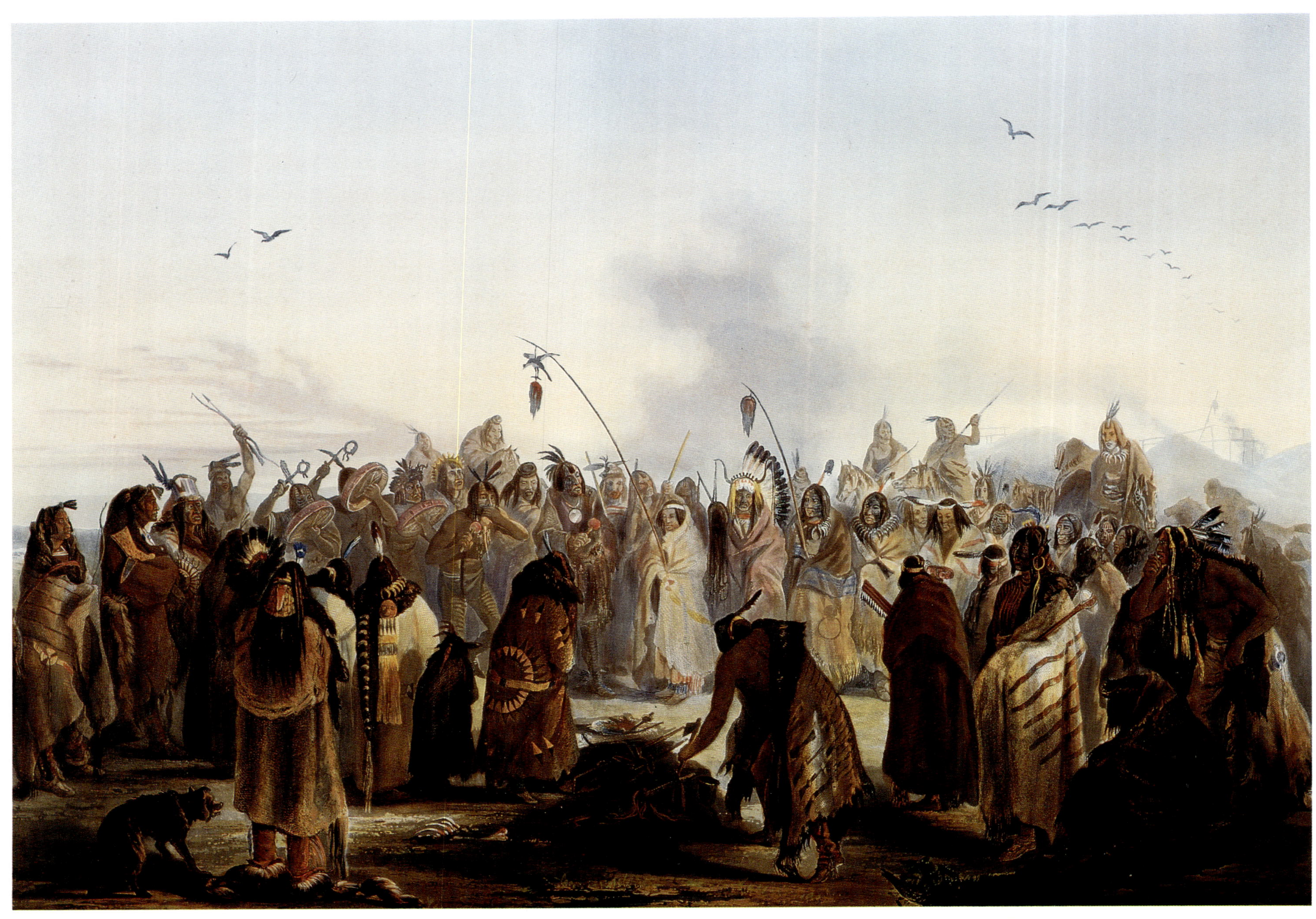

SCALP DANCE OF THE MINATARRES. KARL BODMER, *ATLAS,* PLATE 27. HAND-COLORED AQUATINT, BOUGEARD, PARIS, 1836-1842.

Ridiculing the enemy was an important rite when Indians went to war. Here Minatarre women perform a dance of derision, holding enemy scalps at the ends of long sticks. This was considered the ultimate insult to slain warriors' spirits, since women were not regarded highly.

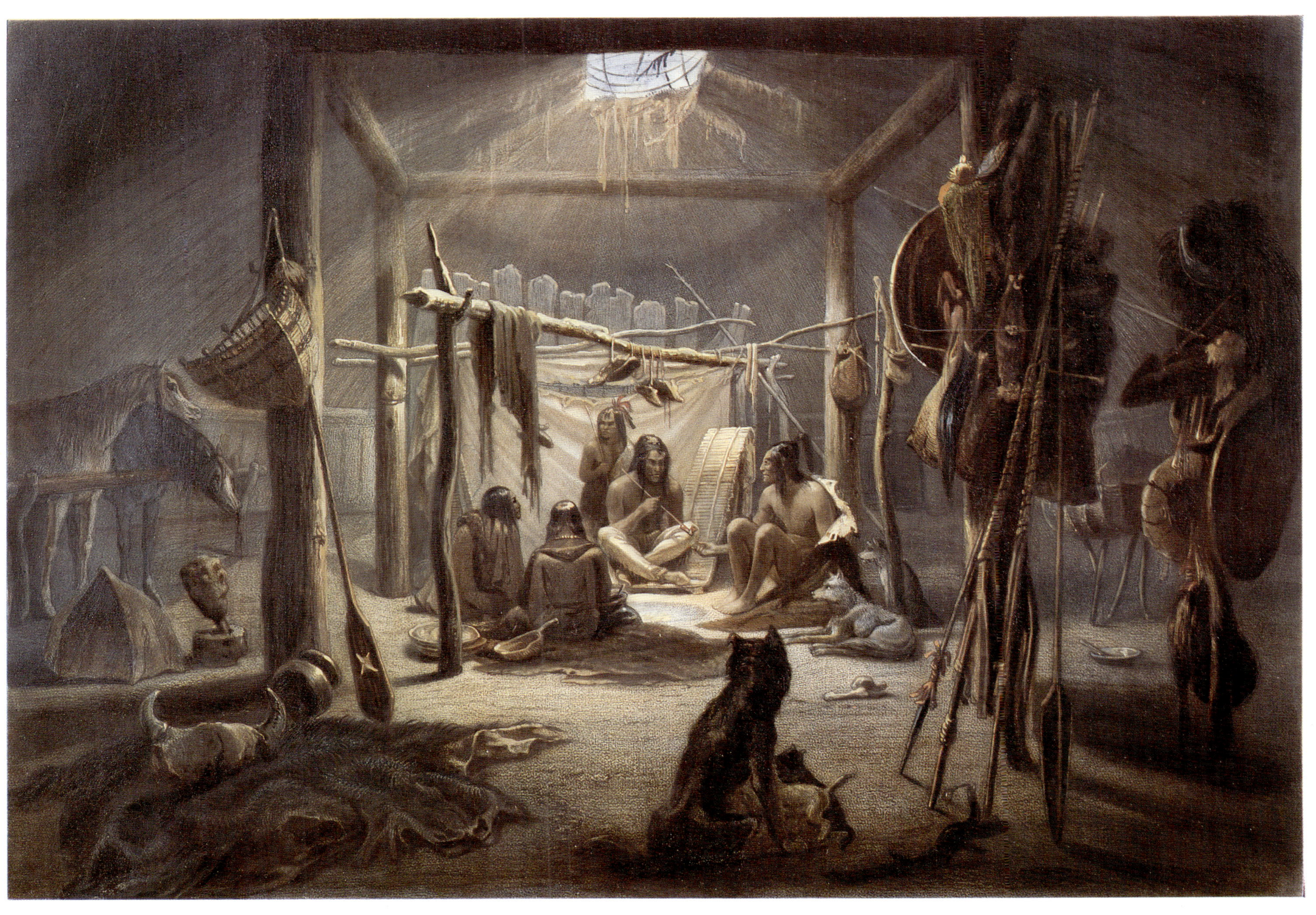

THE INTERIOR OF THE HUT OF A MANDAN CHIEF. KARL BODMER, *ATLAS,* PLATE 19. HAND-COLORED AQUATINT, BOUGEARD, PARIS, 1836-1842.

Records of Mandan domestic customs are extremely rare. Bodmer's print, from a sketch which he compiled during the winter of 1833-1834, catalogues the utensils, weapons, and medical paraphernalia integral to Mandan life.

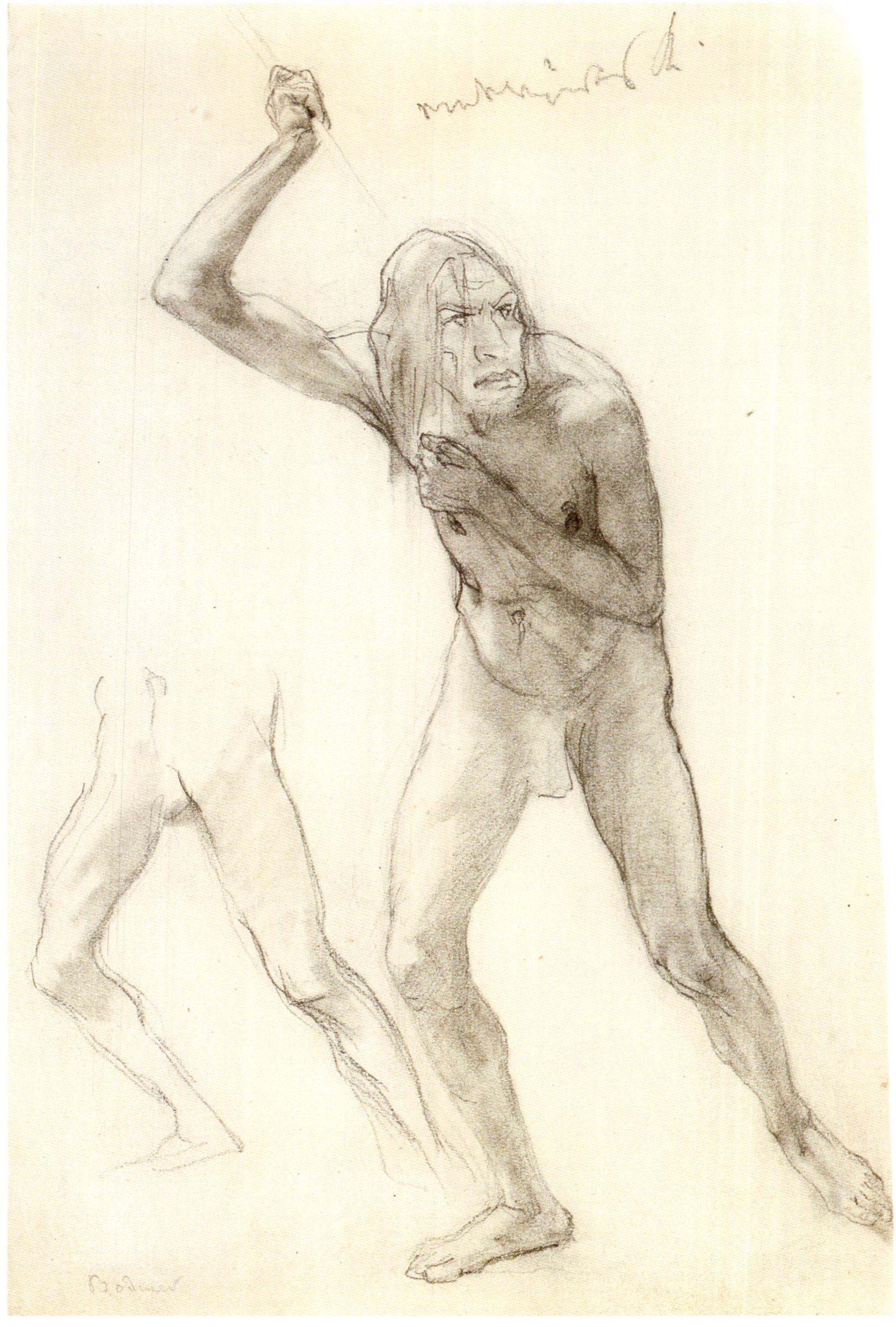

SKETCH FOR *FORT McKENZIE, AUGUST 28th, 1833* (SEE FOLLOWING PAGE). KARL BODMER.

As Bodmer witnessed an Assiniboine attack on the Piegan Blackfeet tribe encamped at Fort McKenzie, he made this rapid sketch, which he later used for the engraving. During the battle, 600 Assiniboine warriors massacred sleeping Blackfeet men, women, and children before being driven off. The prince himself may have fired a few shots from the palisade.

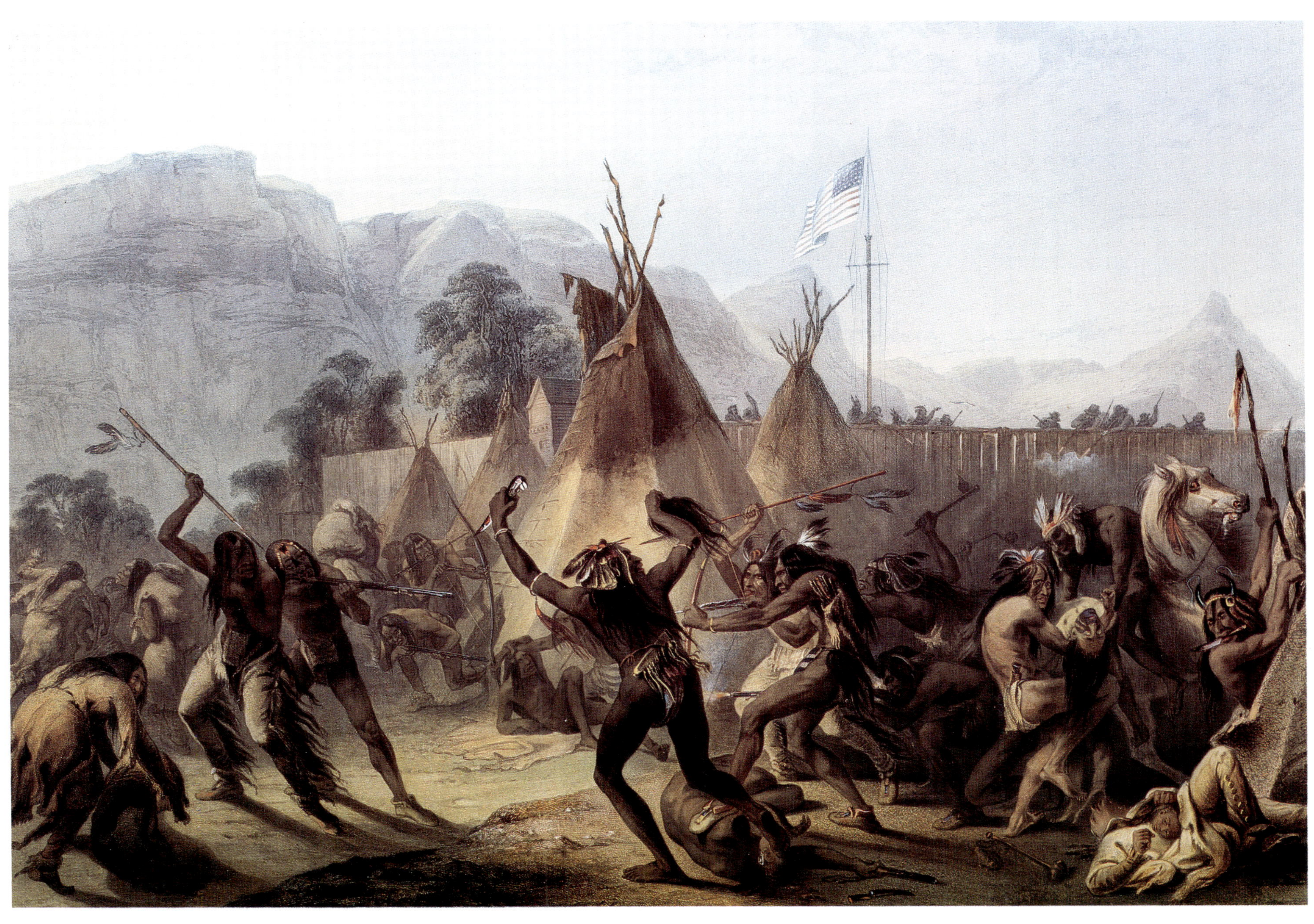

FORT McKENZIE, AUGUST 28th, 1833. KARL BODMER, *ATLAS,* PLATE 42. HAND-COLORED AQUATINT, BOUGEARD, PARIS, 1836-1842.

Although Bodmer and Prince Maximilian stayed inside the fort throughout the battle, Bodmer selects a point of view in the midst of the action to create a sense of chaos and to convey the fierce, awkward postures of both attackers and victims. The figure from the sketch occupies the left foreground.

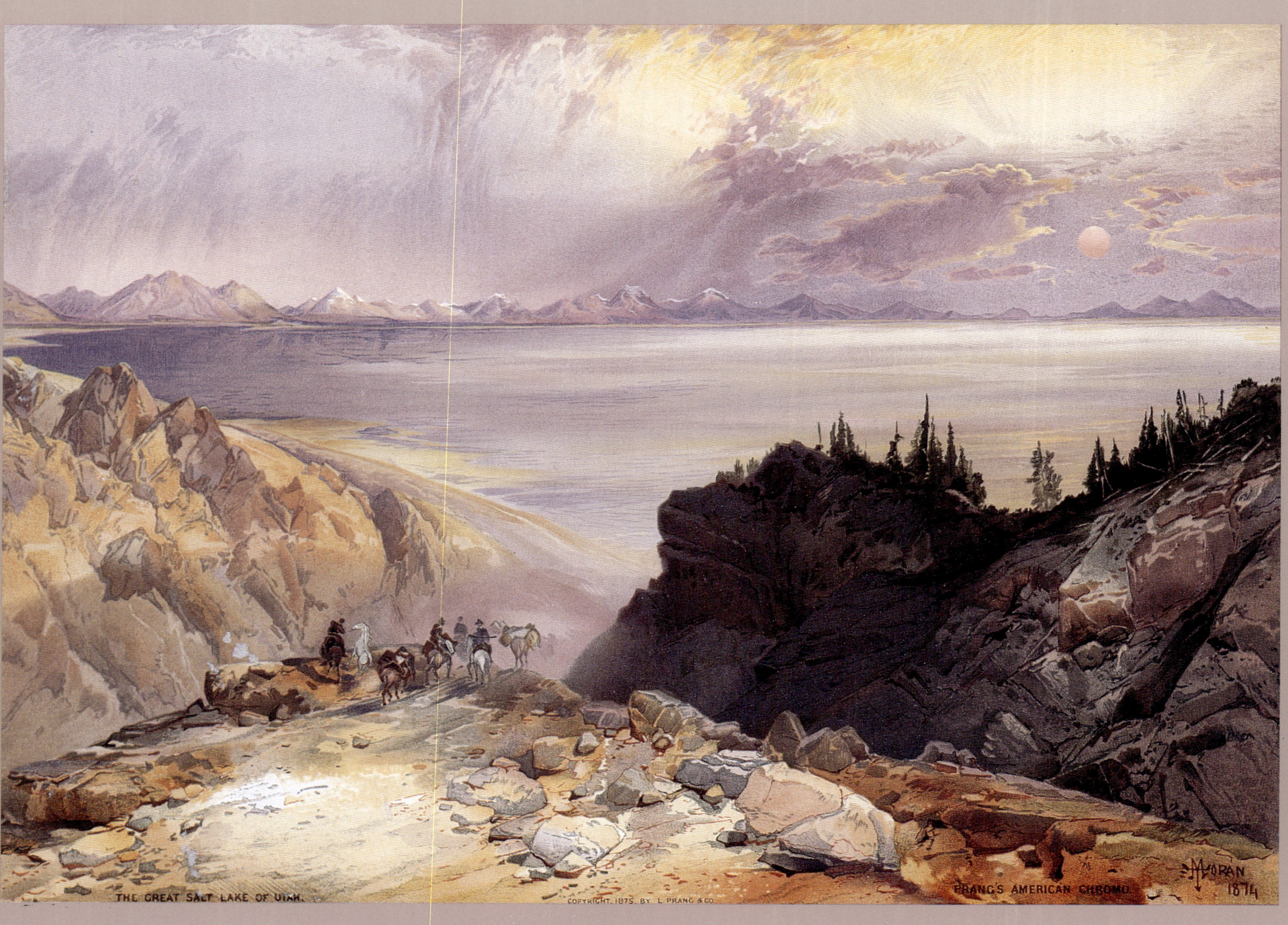
THE GREAT SALT LAKE OF UTAH.
COPYRIGHT. 1875. BY L. PRANG & CO.
PRANG'S AMERICAN CHROMO.
MORAN
1874

THOMAS MORAN (1837-1926)

Some early depictions of the Far West's natural wonders were the creation of an artist who had yet to see them. In 1870, *Scribner's Monthly* commissioned the landscape painter and printmaker Thomas Moran, then living in Philadelphia, to illustrate an article on the Yellowstone by Nathaniel P. Langford. Langford had led an exploring party into the region that summer to verify reports of fabulous geysers, hot springs, and canyons. Moran was dissatisfied with his illustrations, based on rough sketches made by the explorers, but Langford's story captured his imagination. Although the 34-year-old artist had never lived away from civilized comforts, he resolved to paint the wilderness firsthand—a decision which would be the making of his artistic career.

A few months after illustrating Langford's article, he read in a newspaper that Ferdinand V. Hayden of the United States Geological Survey was preparing an official expedition into the Yellowstone country. Moran immediately obtained a letter of introduction to Hayden and headed west uninvited. To pay his way, he borrowed money from an editor at *Scribner's* and from Jay Cooke, owner of the Northern Pacific Railroad, who foresaw lucrative tourism at Yellowstone.

THE GREAT SALT LAKE OF UTAH. FERDINAND V. HAYDEN, *THE YELLOWSTONE NATIONAL PARK.* CHROMOLITHOGRAPH AFTER A PAINTING BY THOMAS MORAN, LOUIS PRANG, BOSTON, 1876.

Thomas Moran's sensitivity to color and appetite for grand scenes made him the ideal painter of the Rocky Mountains and the Southwest. This print matches F. V. Hayden's description of the Great Salt Lake: "Its maximum beauty is reached when the setting sun sends its slanting rays across the valley and the lake, and lends an air of enchantment to the entire region."

William Henry Jackson, the survey's photographer, recalled in 1936 that when the "frail" and "artistic" Moran caught up with the expedition in Virginia City, Montana, he appeared unfit for the rigors of exploration. But he quickly adapted, cushioning his saddle with a camp pillow and wolfing down bacon, though at home he avoided all fats. In addition to producing his own sketches, Moran helped Jackson maneuver his unwieldy equipment and select views to photograph. These efforts repaid themselves; Jackson's photographs became a continual resource for Moran as he completed western paintings in his studio at home.

The expedition, the peak of Hayden's distinguished surveying career, also brought Moran into the public eye. During the 1871-1872 session of Congress, as Langford and others lobbied to make Yellowstone the country's first national park, Jackson's photographs and Moran's watercolors circulated among the legislators. Congress not only voted for the park, but bought Moran's seven-by-twelve-foot oil painting *The Grand Canyon of the Yellowstone* for exhibition in the Capitol.

Busy with commissions to finish sets of watercolors from his first expedition for Jay Cooke and the British industrialist William Blackmore, Moran remained in the East the following summer, except for a brief trip with his wife to Yosemite in August. In the fall, a highly successful New York exhibition of Moran's watercolors for Blackmore confirmed his position as a leading painter of western scenery.

When Moran returned to the West in 1873, he turned down an invitation to join Hayden again, deciding to travel this time with Major John Powell, the courageous one-armed explorer of the Colorado River's ferocious rapids, on a survey of Indian life on the plateaus of Utah, Arizona, and Nevada. Working with the expedition photographer John K. Hillers, he obtained more photos for studio work, and at the expedition's climax, overlooking the Grand Canyon from the Kaibab Plateau, he sketched while a thunderstorm brewed in the mile-deep abyss. From these sketches, he later painted

The Chasm of the Colorado, one of his largest and most dramatic works, purchased by Congress to be hung with *The Grand Canyon of the Yellowstone.* The painting's hues and atmospheric effects led one reviewer to call it "a glimpse of another planet."

The next fall, as Moran began work on material from the Powell expedition, the Boston publisher Louis Prang offered to issue chromolithographs of a dozen or more of his western views. Moran signed a contract in December and supplied Prang with 24 watercolors in the next two years, 15 of which were published with F.V. Hayden's *The Yellowstone National Park, and the Mountainous Regions of Portions of Idaho, Nevada, Colorado, and Utah* in 1876. Many critics have placed these among the finest examples of American chromolithography; their delicate tints and bold compositions preserve the excitement of Moran's first four western journeys.

Moran's early training had prepared him both for translating his sketches into prints and for painting grandiose scenery. Born in 1837 in Lancashire, England, he immigrated to the United States with his family when he was seven. They settled in Philadelphia, and when he was 15, Moran apprenticed himself to the wood engravers Scattergood and Telfer.

While Moran learned many special techniques at the engravers', he wanted to be a painter, not an illustrator. When he was 18, he fell seriously ill with pleurisy and was able to cancel his apprenticeship. After he recovered, he set up a studio with his brother Edward, who was to become a well-known painter of marine subjects. Older painters encouraged them, including John Hamilton, who introduced Thomas to the work of the great English landscape painter J.M.W. Turner. Turner's sense of space, color, and light and his feeling for the spiritual significance of nature were to be major influences on Moran's mature art.

His paintings of the West made him something of a celebrity in that region, where Hayden named a 12,600-foot peak in the Grand Tetons after him in 1872. In 1892, at the age of 55, he traveled with William Henry Jackson, his friend from the Hayden expedition, to the Grand Tetons, the Yellowstone, and the south rim of the Grand Canyon. The painter described their struggles with a hailstorm, hunger, and gumbo clay in an article published in *The Century Illustrated* (January 1893). To his wife, he wrote, "I have been made much of at all the places in the park as the great and only 'Moran,' *the* painter of the Yellowstone and I am looked at curiously by all the people at the Hotels."

A follower of the romantic school, unaffected by newer artistic movements such as impressionism, Thomas Moran sought to capture the spirit of places and would transpose details to achieve a more striking final effect. His friend John Ruskin, who purchased a set of the Prang prints, criticized the emotionalism of Moran's later work. Moran felt, however, that a literal rendering of details could not convey the sublime effect of magnificent scenery. His drawings, paintings, lithographs, and etchings celebrate not only the physical grandeur of the West, but that grandeur's spiritual impact, overwhelming in its otherness and energy.

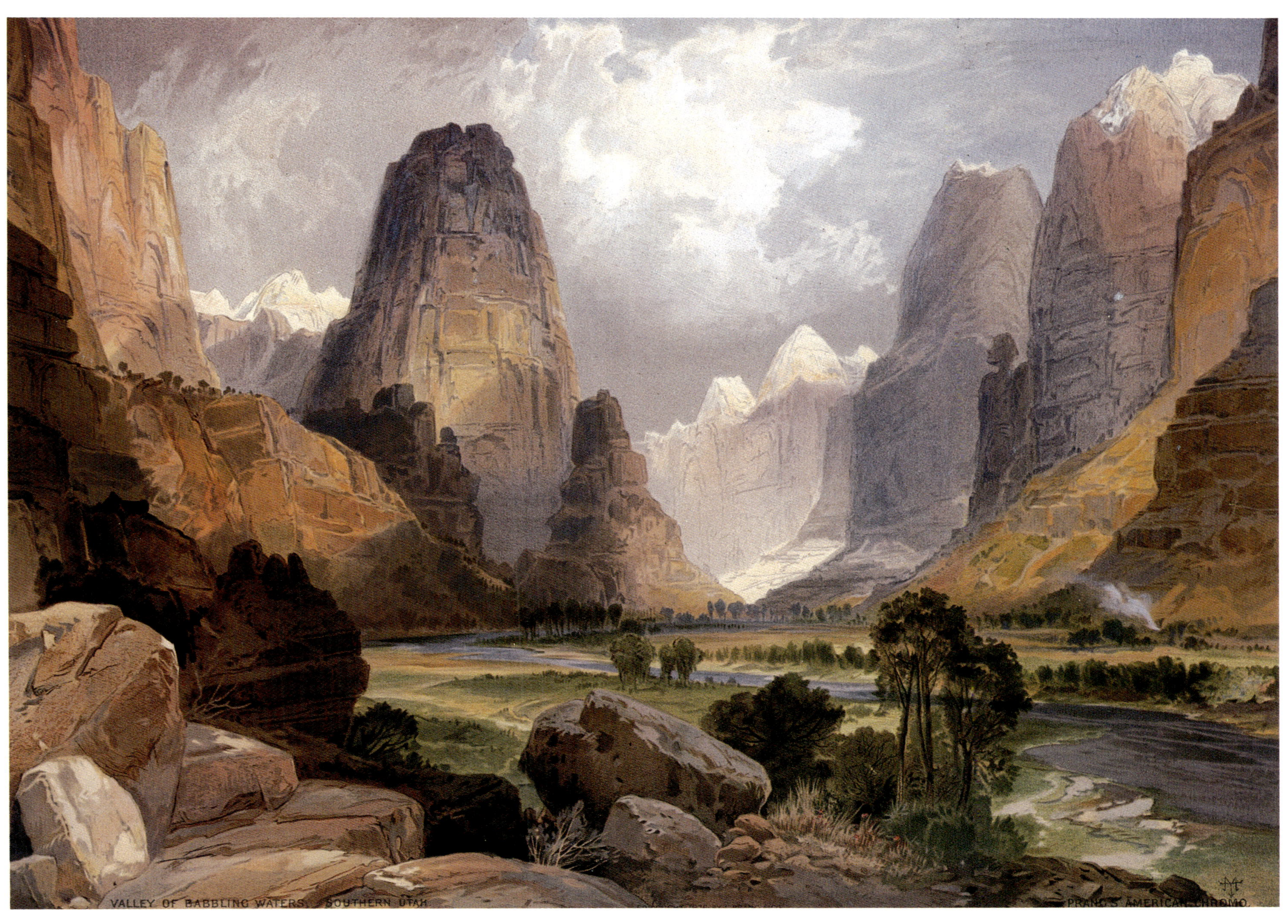

VALLEY OF BABBLING WATERS, SOUTHERN UTAH. FERDINAND V. HAYDEN, *THE YELLOWSTONE NATIONAL PARK.* CHROMOLITHOGRAPH AFTER A PAINTING BY THOMAS MORAN, LOUIS PRANG, BOSTON, 1876.

On Major John Wesley Powell's 1873 expedition to investigate claims of wrongdoing against Indians in Utah and Colorado, Moran visited this portion of Zion Canyon on the Virgin River, now part of Zion National Park. In this print, as in most of Moran's work, humans are scarcely present—a campfire smokes at lower right.

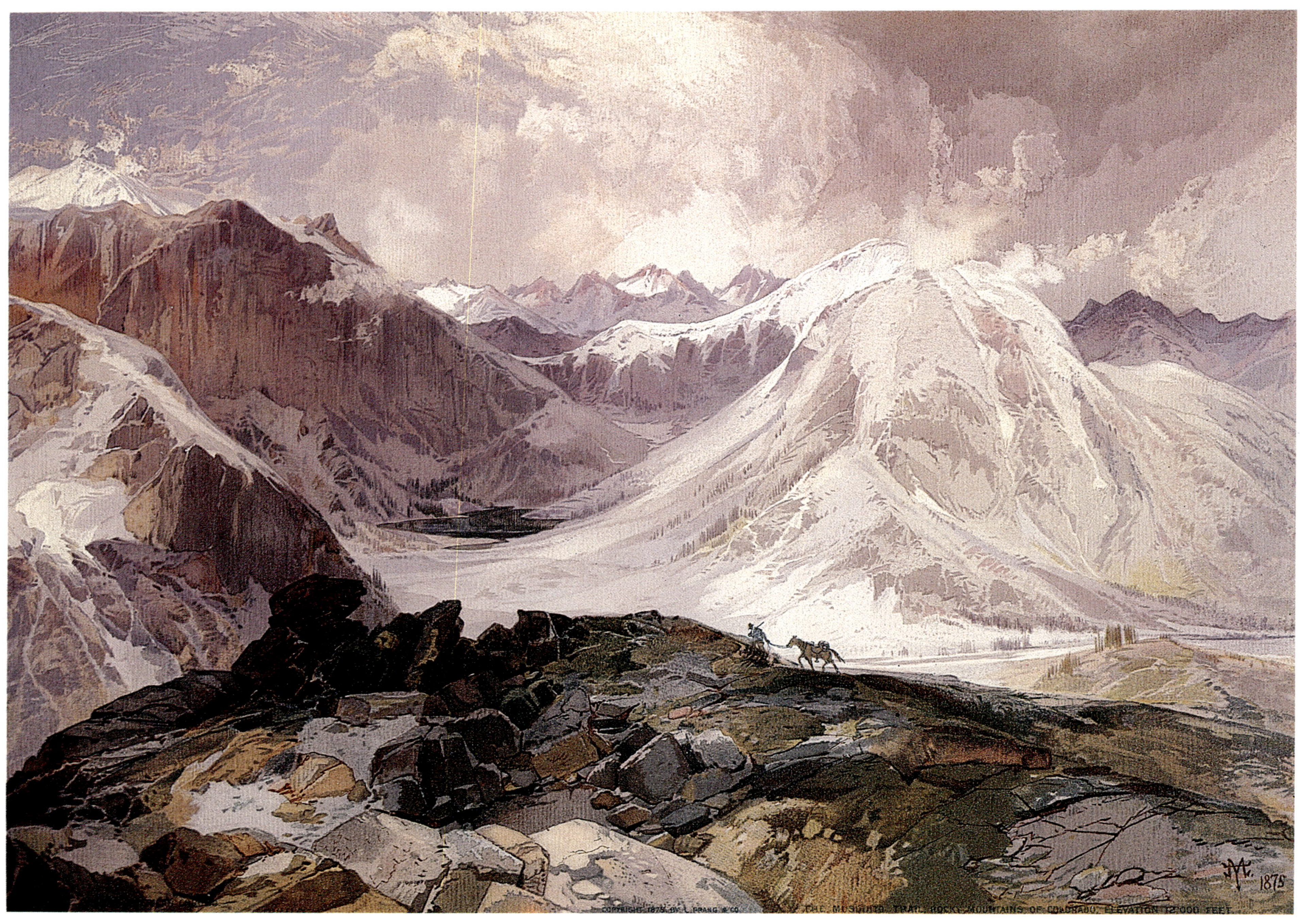

THE MOSQUITO TRAIL, ROCKY MOUNTAINS OF COLORADO, ELEVATION 12,000 FEET. FERDINAND V. HAYDEN, *THE YELLOWSTONE NATIONAL PARK.* CHROMO-LITHOGRAPH AFTER A PAINTING BY THOMAS MORAN, LOUIS PRANG, BOSTON, 1876.

Moran traveled on the Mosquito Trail in the summer of 1874 with one of Hayden's surveys, bound for the Mount of the Holy Cross. On one slope of this mountain, two snow-filled crevasses formed a huge cross which fascinated pious 19th-century Americans. After seeing a photograph of the cross taken by William Henry Jackson the previous summer, Moran had become determined to paint it.

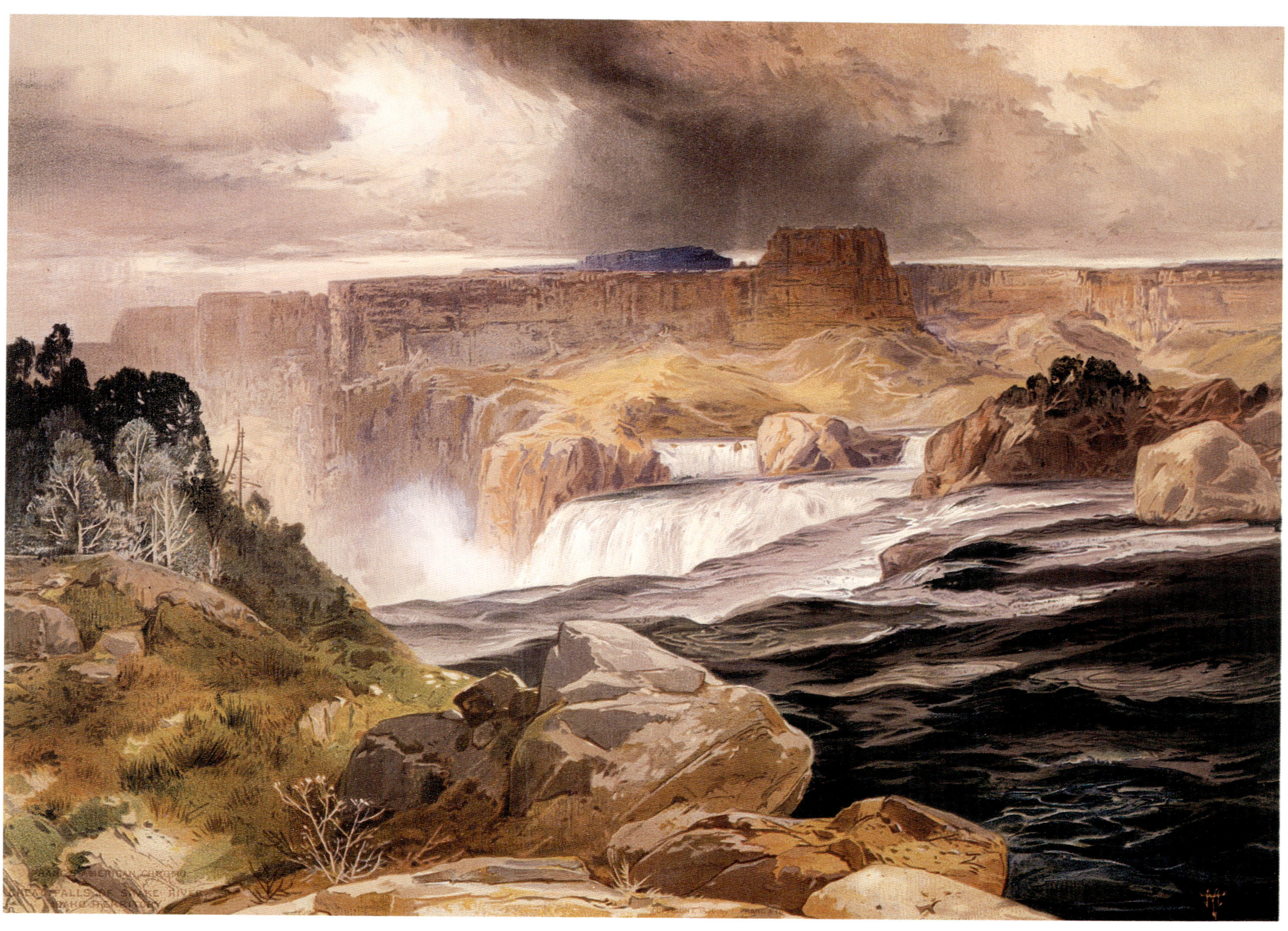

GREAT FALLS OF SNAKE RIVER, IDAHO TERRITORY. FERDINAND V. HAYDEN, *THE YELLOWSTONE NATIONAL PARK.* CHROMOLITHOGRAPH AFTER A PAINTING BY THOMAS MORAN, LOUIS PRANG, BOSTON, 1876.

Crisscrossing the mountains of the West on their ambitious surveys, geologists of Moran's era marveled at the forces of erosion and the short lives of mountains in the vastness of geological time. Moran's depiction of rushing water and turbulent sky emphasizes the mutability of the natural scene.

Johann Friedrich Naumann // Die Vögel Mitteleuropas //

Die Andere
Bibliothek

Johann Friedrich Naumann

Die Vögel Mitteleuropas

Eine Auswahl.
Herausgegeben und mit einem Essay
von Arnulf Conradi

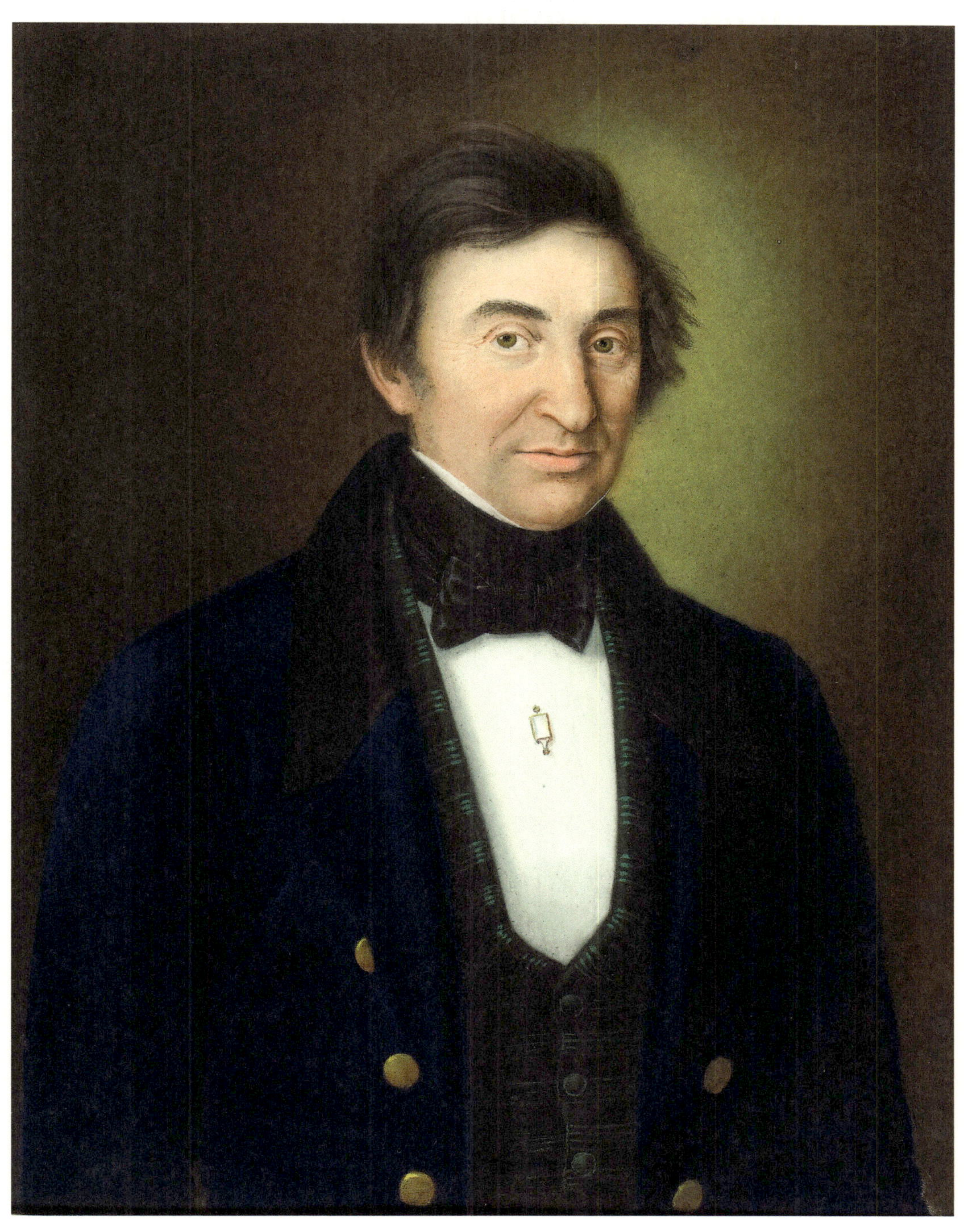

Johann Friedrich Naumann

// INHALTSVERZEICHNIS //

// EIN VERGESSENES GENIE //

Wo steckt er nur — dieser Brief von Goethe? Oder sind die bewundernden Worte über Johann Friedrich Naumanns Werk bloß mündlich gefallen? Nein, es ist wahrscheinlicher, daß es ein schriftliches Lob gegeben hat. Und wenn ein so aufrechter Mann wie der Theologe Eduard Baldamus, Lehrer am Gymnasium von Köthen und enger Freund Naumanns, davon berichtet, daß sich der verehrte Vogelforscher im Alter über nichts so gefreut habe wie über die anerkennenden Worte Goethes, verbietet sich jeder Zweifel. Niemals hätten Männer wie Baldamus oder Naumann sich so etwas aus den Fingern gesogen. Aber so sehr man auch gesucht und geforscht hat — was genau Goethe zu Johann Friedrich Naumanns *Naturgeschichte der Vögel Deutschlands* gesagt hat, wann er es gesagt hat, es ist nicht festzustellen. Auch der Direktor des schönen kleinen Naumann-Museums im Schloß zu Köthen, Wolf-Dieter Busching, hebt bedauernd die Hände. Nach nichts werde er öfter gefragt, aber er wisse es auch nicht. Vielleicht liegt der Brief auf dem Dachboden irgendeines Naumann-Nachfahren, oder er steckt in einem Buch, das in einem Antiquariat oder einer Bibliothek verstaubt.

Johann Friedrich Naumann fehlte es aber keineswegs an Ehrungen. Zu seiner Zeit war er ein berühmter Mann. Vogelkundler aus dem In- und Ausland besuchten ihn auf seinem Gut Ziebigk bei Köthen. Der Herzog von Köthen-Anhalt ernannte ihn nach Vollendung des achten Bandes seiner *Naturgeschichte* zum Professor und schmückte ihn kurz vor seinem Tode mit den Ritterinsignien des Bärenordens, was immer das sein mochte. Die Universität Breslau oder Halle — da sind sich die Biographen nicht einig — verlieh Naumann den Ehrendoktor, einen *doctor philosophiae honoris causa*. Der Rötelfalke, den er bestimmte, trägt bis heute den wissenschaftlichen Namen *falco naumanni*, und die Zeitschrift der Ornithologischen Vereinigung, die Naumann auf ihrer Gründungssitzung zum Vorsitzenden, später zum Ehrenvorsitzenden wählte, bekam den Titel »Naumannia«. Er war korrespondierendes oder Ehrenmitglied einer ganzen Reihe von wissenschaftlichen Vereinigungen, darunter der »Naturforschenden Gesellschaft zu Halle«, auch der zu Berlin, oder der »Allgemeinen schweizerischen Gesellschaft für die gesamten Naturwissenschaften«. Baldamus spricht an einer Stelle sogar von einem »Naumann-Kult«.

Naumann lebte in einer Zeit des naturwissenschaftlichen Aufbruchs, und er zählte zur Avantgarde dieser großen Bewegung. Überall in Europa blickte man plötzlich mit Interesse auf die Natur, forschte, reiste, entdeckte, katalogisierte, klassifizierte. Rückblickend kann man sagen, daß diese Bewegung, die in England wohl am lebhaftesten war und am systematischsten vonstatten ging, ein paar Jahrzehnte später zur Evolutionstheorie Darwins führte, welche die Naturforschung auf eine neue Grundlage stellte.

Naumann wurde damals fraglos als der größte Ornithologe Deutschlands angesehen. Seine grundlegende Leistung war die *Naturgeschichte der Vögel Deutschlands*, deren letzter Band im Sommer 1844 erschien. Darwins *Entstehung der Arten* wurde 1859 publiziert.

Fünfundzwanzig Jahre hat Naumann mit unerbittlichem Fleiß an seinem zwölfbändigen Hauptwerk gearbeitet, und auch nach Abschluß der *Naturgeschichte* lieferte er unermüdlich immer neue »Nachträge«, die Korrekturen oder Ergänzungen enthielten.

Auf Naumann gehen viele Vogelnamen zurück, etwa: »Dorngrasmücke«, »Sperlingskauz«, »Waldohreule«, »Waldkauz«, »Schellente«, »Sand-, Fluß- und Regenpfeifer«, um nur einige zu nennen. Alle 380 Illustrationen zeichnete und stach er selbst in Kupfer. Die Vorlagen in Aquarell sind atemberaubend. Nahm er die Kolorierung nicht selbst vor, so überwachte er sie genau. Nie zuvor hat es ein vergleichbar gründliches, mit soviel Sachkenntnis und persönlicher Erfahrung geschriebenes

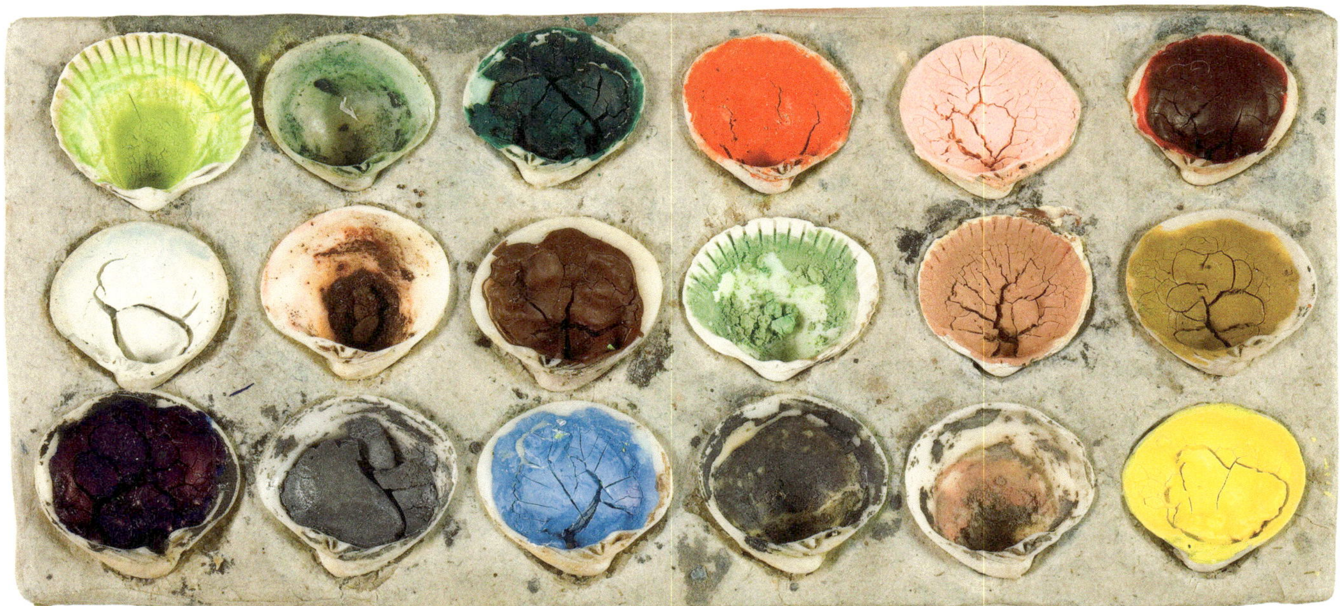

Buch über die deutsche Vogelwelt gegeben, und man mußte bis ins 20. Jahrhundert warten, um auch nur annähernd Gleichwertiges zu sehen. Naumann wurde mit seinem Werk zum Begründer der wissenschaftlichen Ornithologie in Deutschland. Der sprachliche Glanz seines Werks blieb unübertroffen.

Seine Korrespondenz mit Wissenschaftlern wie Coenraad Jacob Temminck oder Christian Ludwig Brehm, dem Vater des »Tierleben«-Verfassers Alfred Brehm, war, wie damals üblich, ebenso höflich wie umfangreich, und er unterhielt Freundschaften mit Ornithologen oder einfach begeisterten Vogelfreunden wie Heinrich Boie aus Holstein, dem Grafen Friedrich Albert von der Schulenburg oder Alexander Robert Baron von Loebenstein, der auf einem Rittergut in Lohsa bei Hoyerswerda saß. Mit dem Vogelforscher Eugen Ferdinand von Homeyer, der sich mit der Vogelwelt Pommerns beschäftigte, tauschte er Briefe und Vogelbälge. Ornithologen von europäischem Rang wie Prinz Charles Lucien Bonaparte oder John Gould pilgerten nach Ziebigk, um Naumann persönlich zu begegnen.

Er selbst reiste nicht viel. Sein Mangel an Bargeld verdammte ihn zu Seßhaftigkeit. Er fuhr mal nach Leipzig oder Berlin, er kam im Sommer 1819 an die Küste Holsteins und nach Sylt, 1835 reiste er mit einem Freund, dem Apotheker Ludwig August Neubert, neun Wochen durch Ungarn, und 1840 fuhr er nach Helgoland. Auf Einladung besuchte er gelegentlich Freunde, meist begüterte Adlige, die ihm

Naumanns Aquarellkasten

die Reise ermöglichten. Viel mehr konnte er sich nicht leisten, was er oft beklagte.

Um so mehr freute er sich über den Besuch verwandter Seelen. Am 18. August 1843 stand der englische Ornithologe John Gould unangemeldet vor seiner Haustür:

»Von der Freude, diesen lieben berühmten Mann in meiner Behausung zu sehen und vor mir zu haben, war ich so ausserhalb aller Contenance, dass ich mich auf die geläufigsten englischen Namen und manche einzelne, mir sonst wohlbekannte Wörter und Redensarten nicht besinnen konnte. Wie viel konnte ich von dem Mann in der, wenn auch nur kurzen, Zeit lernen, hätten wir uns nur ordentlich mittheilen können! Ein mir befreundeter Prediger, welcher recht viel Englisch versteht, wohnt zwar nur 1 Stündchen von hier und hätte sehr gern den Dolmetscher zwischen uns gemacht, wär er nur gleich dagewesen. Mit vieler Herzlichkeit schied der grosse Ornithologe, und mit dem Versprechen, Temminck, welchen er auf der Rückreise besuchen will, einen Gruss von mir zu überbringen, fuhr er wieder fort.«

An diesen Besuch knüpft sich eine Anekdote, die Eduard Baldamus überliefert hat. Sie wirft ein Licht auf Naumanns Bescheidenheit. John Gould wurde in einer deutschen Zeitung anläßlich seines Besuchs als »der größte Ornithologe Europas« bezeichnet. »Der größte Ornithologe Europas«, empörten sich Naumanns Freunde. »Das sind Sie!« — »Ach, ich Armer«, erwiderte Naumann, »ich bin zufrieden, wenn man mir einen Platz im Parterre gestattet.«

Aber selbst dieser Platz im Parterre war ihm auf Dauer nicht vergönnt. In Deutschland ist er ganz in Vergessenheit geraten, und eher als in Berlin oder Leipzig wird man in London auf ihn angesprochen. Das liegt sicher auch daran, daß es in Deutschland verhältnismäßig wenige Leute gibt, die sich für Vögel interessieren. Jeder dritte Engländer, heißt es, nennt sich selbst einen »birder«, und in den USA sind es 40 Millionen, die dem Hobby des »birdwatching«, des Vogelbeobachtens, nachgehen. Dabei ist Deutschland mit seinen Wäldern, Flußlandschaften und Seenplatten und vor allem mit seinen unvergleichlichen Wattgebieten vor der schleswig-holsteinischen und niedersächsischen Nordseeküste eigentlich ein Land, das jeden Bewohner auf die Vogelwelt seiner Umgebung neugierig machen sollte.

Während Naumanns »Konkurrenten« und Zeitgenossen, der Engländer John Gould und der Amerikaner John James Audubon bleibenden Ruhm genießen, der sich auch in den hohen Preisen ihrer Vogelstiche ausdrückt, waren Blätter von Naumann vor kurzem noch auf Berliner Flohmärkten zu finden. Dabei sind Naumanns Vogelbilder denen, die unter dem Namen Gould erschienen sind, sicher gleichwertig und können sich, was Genauigkeit und Eleganz angeht, ebenso mit denen Audubons messen, auch wenn ihnen die Wucht und Dramatik der Darstellungen des Amerikaners fehlen. Naumann arbeitete leider in einem kleineren Format. Sowohl sprachlich wie wissenschaftlich war er beiden jedoch weit überlegen.

Auf jeden Fall teilte Naumann mit Gould und Audubon die Liebe zur Natur, die Jagdleidenschaft und das wissenschaftliche Interesse an der Vogelwelt. Diese drei stellten nicht nur die Ornithologie auf eine neue wissenschaftliche Basis — sie waren sich auch in ihrem künstlerischen Ehrgeiz nah. Ihnen war es ein Anliegen, die Vögel in ihrer Vitalität und natürlichen Umgebung darzustellen. Dafür brachen Naumann und Audubon — ohne voneinander zu wissen — mit der alten Methodik der Vogeldarstellung. Sie lehnten es ab, präparierte, also ausgestopfte, Vögel abzuzeichnen, und ließen nur das frische, meist gerade geschossene Exemplar gelten. Audubon fixierte den Vogel mit Draht in der gewünschten Haltung auf einem Holzbrett und zeichnete ihn dann ab. Wir wissen nicht, wie Naumann gearbeitet hat, aber er muß eine ähnliche Methode angewendet haben. »Ich habe niemals ein ausgestopftes Exemplar gezeichnet [...]«, schrieb Audubon, »die Natur muss zuerst lebendig gesehen und genau studiert werden, bevor man versuchen kann, sie wiederzugeben.« — »Ich habe ohne Ausnahme mit frischen Exemplaren nach der Natur gearbeitet«, schrieb Naumann. Gould, der seine Karriere als Gärtner und dann als Ausstopfer von Vögeln, als »Taxidermist«, begann, blieb bei der alten Methode der Abbildung von ausgestopften Vögeln.

Keiner der drei war Akademiker. John Gould lernte von seinem Vater, der Gärtner in den Royal Gardens von Windsor war, das Entscheidende: die Liebe zur Natur. Naumanns Vater war da ein anderer Lehrmeister: Er liebte die Jagd und das Herumstreifen in der freien Natur, war selbst Vogelbeobachter und -fänger und verfaßte ein Buch über die Vögel Mitteldeutschlands. Früh erkannte er das zeichnerische Talent seines ältesten Sohnes und förderte es nach Kräften.

John James Audubon hatte eine Lehre in einer Kunstschule hinter sich, welche das aber war, bleibt unklar. Er behauptete, er habe bei Jacques-Louis David in Paris gelernt. Da er aber dann und wann zu »tall tales« neigte und vieles erzählte, was offensichtlich nicht so ganz der Wahrheit entsprach, nimmt man eher an, daß er in einer unbedeutenderen Institution in Nantes unterrichtet wurde.

John Gould — er lebte von 1804 bis 1881 — ist übrigens einer dieser interessanten Fälle, die erst heute, im Zeitalter des Feminismus, aufgearbeitet werden. Der wichtigste Schritt in seiner Karriere war 1829 die Heirat mit der jungen Elisabeth Coxen, einer Hauslehrerin und enorm begabten Zeichnerin und Malerin. Die Bilder, die Gould berühmt machten, sind mit »J. and E. Gould« gezeichnet, manchmal auch nur mit »J. Gould«. Die entscheidende Frage ist natürlich: Welchen Anteil hatte Elisabeth an der gewaltigen künstlerischen Produktion ihres Mannes? Die offizielle Version lautete: Er zeichnete — sie machte die Lithographien. Aber hat das wirklich jemand geglaubt? Der große Vogelmaler, von dem manche Zeitgenossen meinten, er stelle selbst Audubon in den Schatten, war nur ein mittelmäßig begabter Zeichner. Das weist Isabella Tree in ihrer Biographie John Goulds ziemlich überzeugend nach.

Offenbar verhielt es sich so, daß Gould nur rohe Skizzen zur Stellung des Vogels machte — Skizzen, die dann seine Frau in die wunderbaren Vogelbilder verwandelte, die Goulds Ruhm begründeten. Gould selbst war eher ein Produzent, ein Impresario, ein Verleger als ein Künstler, aber es gelang ihm, noch lange über seinen Tod hinaus, die Arbeit seiner geduldigen, fleißigen Frau im Dunkel zu halten. Nimmt man auch noch seine Zusammenarbeit mit Edward Lear, H.C. Richter oder Joseph Wolf hinzu, ist es schwer, einem paradoxen Urteil auszuweichen: John Gould ist ein berühmter Vogelmaler, der in Wirklichkeit kein einziges Bild gemalt hat.

John James Audubon, der von 1785 bis 1851 lebte, hatte einen kühnen Plan: Er wollte alle Vögel des nordamerikanischen Kontinents in natürlicher Größe malen, und das schaffte er — fast. Einige Arten im Westen des Landes, den er nicht bereiste, entgingen ihm. Für dieses Unternehmen fand er vor allem in England Subskribenten. Den Engländern erschien er als Inbegriff des Amerikaners. Der Maler John Symes hat ihn 1826 in einer bezeichnenden Pose dargestellt: Er trägt einen schwarzen, pelzbesetzten Jagdrock, schräg vor der Brust hält er die Flinte. Die Adlernase, das wallende schwarze Haar, der entschlossene Blick deuten mehr auf den Entdecker und Jäger als auf den Künstler. Obwohl er sich eines riesigen Formats, des sogenannten Double Elephant Folios (ungefähr 120 x 90 cm) bediente, hatte er Mühe, große Vögel wie den Flamingo unterzubringen. Die Adler stellte er mit angezogenen Flügeln dar, so daß man glaubt, sie würden im nächsten Moment abstürzen. Von Kritikern wurden sie schon mal als »flying footballs« tituliert.

Audubons leidenschaftliche Liebe zu Vögeln, zur Natur in ihrer ungezähmten Wildheit, spricht aus seinen Bildern. E.P. Richardson, der Audubon ebenso wie Robert Hughes zu den größten Malern Amerikas zählt (nicht etwa nur den Vogelmalern), sagt in seinem Buch *Painting in America*: »Vögel sind sein Gegenstand, aber sein Thema ist die Natur — wild, grandios, vielfältig und unendlich schön.«

Vor allem im zwanzigsten Jahrhundert, in dessen Verlauf Naumann in Vergessenheit geriet, stieg Audubons Ruhm unaufhaltsam. Die größte Naturschutzorganisation in den USA nannte sich »Audubon-Society«. Vollständige Exemplare der *Birds of America* — die meisten liegen in Museen — sind Millionen wert. Von den 200 Exemplaren der Double Elephant Folio-Edition sind, so nimmt man an, etwa 120 erhalten. Viele von ihnen wurden auseinandergenommen, weil sich die Besitzer bessere Einkünfte erhofften, wenn sie die Drucke einzeln verkauften. So kann man heute in einigen Galerien in New York oder Chicago, manchmal auch in London Blätter erstehen. Die Kühnheit der Darstellung, die Komposition der Bilder ist noch immer atemberaubend. John James Audubon ist ohne Zweifel der größte aller Vogelmaler.

Der junge Johann Friedrich Naumann wuchs auf Gut Ziebigk bei Köthen im Herzogtum Anhalt auf. Seit Generationen befand sich dieses Gut im Besitz der Familie Naumann. Ein Hans Naumann erwarb es nach dem Dreißigjährigen Krieg und gab es an seinen Sohn Michael weiter. 1772 ging der Besitz von der Witwe eines Theodor Andreas Naumann an deren Sohn Johann Andreas über, der dafür seiner Mutter und jeder seiner drei Schwestern 500 Taler zahlte und seiner Mutter überdies Naturalien im Wert von 40 Talern jährlich schuldete.

Dieser in vieler Hinsicht bemerkenswerte Mann war der Vater Johann Friedrichs. »In dem verderblichen dreissigjährigen Kriege 1636«, schrieb er, »kaufte einer meiner Vorfahren allhier ein verwüstetes und verlassenes Ackergut, samt einem schönen anmuthigen Busche. Durch seinen Fleiss brachte er mit Hülfe seiner Kinder dieses verwüstete Gut wieder in Stand, und übergab es seinem einzigen Sohne. Dieser fing nun erst an, die Früchte seiner und seines Vaters saurer Arbeit zu geniessen; er suchte sich nun auch neben seinen Arbeitsstunden eine Gemüthsergötzung zu machen. Die schöne anmuthige Lage dieses Dorfes, welches auf der einen Seite das Feld hat, und auf der anderen mit Gebüschen, Wiesen und Teichen abwechselt, mag ihn wohl gereizt haben, sein Vergnügen am Vogelfangen und Jagen zu suchen; er legte daher verschiedene Vogelheerde, wovon man jetzt noch Spuren siehet.«

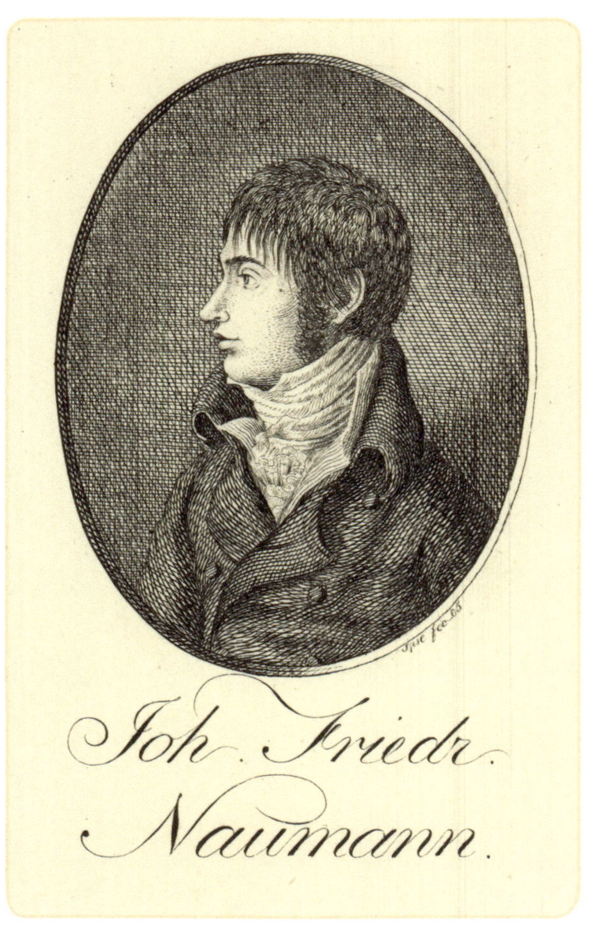

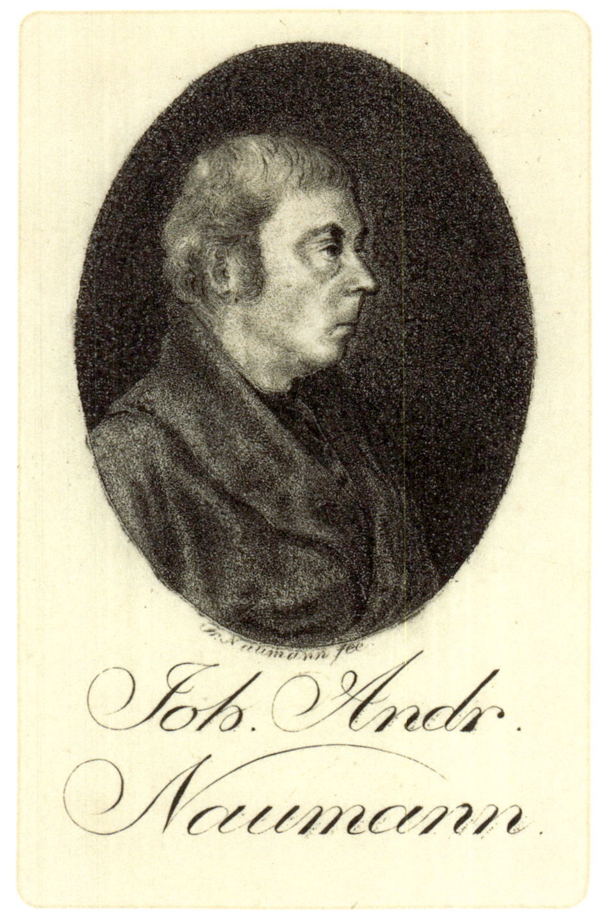

Das Interesse für die Vögel wurde also schon dem Vater Johann Friedrichs gewissermaßen in die Wiege gelegt. »Ob diese meine Vorfahren gleich keine Naturforscher waren«, fuhr der alte Naumann fort, »so wurden sie doch aus Erfahrung gute Vogelkenner; die Söhne lernten vom Vater, und sammelten noch eigene Erfahrungen dazu.«

Das Land um Ziebigk ist flach wie ein Tisch, die Elbe war natürlich unreguliert und trat im Frühjahr oft über die Ufer. Johann Friedrich Naumann klagte in seinen Briefen manches Mal über seine überschwemmten Äcker und Felder. Diese weiten Feuchtgebiete aber zogen riesige Schwärme von Wasservögeln an, und man kann sich durchaus vorstellen, daß die reiche Vogelwelt direkt vor ihrer Haustür die ornithologische Leidenschaft des ganzen Naumann-Stammes weckte und wachhielt. »Die Liebe zu den schönen Luftbewohnern schien bei mir so stark eingewurzelt zu sein, dass es mir unmöglich war, die Vögel mit gleichgültigen Augen anzusehn, und in meinen Jünglingsjahren wurde dieselbe mir zur Leidenschaft«, schrieb Johann Andreas in seinem liebenswürdigen Deutsch.

Der alte Naumann war Autodidakt. Er verfaßte drei Bücher, darunter ein 1791 veröffentlichtes und für ihn sehr bezeichnend tituliertes: *Der philosophische Bauer oder Anleitung, die Natur durch Beobachtung und Versuche zu erforschen.* Ein philosophischer Bauer war er in der Tat und Denker einer Generation, der es noch möglich war, ihren Wissensdurst und aufklärerischen Eifer mit einer tiefen Frömmigkeit zu vereinen. Schon fünfzig Jahre später war das für die Generation, der Charles Darwin angehörte, nicht mehr so einfach. Johann Andreas war aber nicht nur ein spekulativer Kopf, er war auch ein tüchtiger Landwirt und offenbar ein hochbegabter Handwerker und Bastler.

1754–58 hatte er die Städtische Reformierte Knabenschule in Köthen besucht. Als sein Vater früh starb, durfte er die Schulbildung zunächst fortsetzen, aber mit vierzehn Jahren wurde er von der Mutter, die ihn in der häuslichen Wirtschaft brauchte, nach Ziebigk zurückgerufen. Er hatte den Katechismus gelernt, dazu Lesen, Schreiben und Rechnen, Briefeschreiben (wie ausdrücklich erwähnt wird) und ein wenig Griechisch und Latein. Auf das Gut zurückgekehrt, arbeitete er in der Landwirtschaft mit, seine tüchtige Mutter (alle Naumann-Frauen scheinen sehr tatkräftig gewesen zu sein) ließ ihm dennoch reichlich Zeit, seinen Vorlieben, der Jagd und dem Vogelfang, nachzugehen. Er trieb sich viel in den Wäldern der Umgebung herum, ein befreundeter Richter erlaubte ihm, in seinem Revier zu jagen.

»Ich liebte die Einsamkeit, und hatte niemals Wohlgefallen an Umgang, wenn es nicht mit einem erfahrnen Vogelsteller, Jäger oder Künstler war.« Künstler? Wen meinte er damit? Wahrscheinlich Leute, denen die Zeichnung und Kolorierung von Vögeln leichter fiel als ihm. In der Vorrede seines Buches über die Vögel Norddeutschlands nennt er auch den eigenen Sohn, Johann Friedrich, der die Illustrationen machte, einen jungen Künstler.

»Wenn ich allein war«, fuhr er fort, »liess ich meinen Gedanken freien Lauf, und gewöhnte mich immer, diejenige Arbeit, die ich vorhatte, vorher in meinen Gedanken durchzugehen oder etwas neues zu erfinden. Dies hatte nachgehend immer seinen guten Nutzen, und wenn mein Vogeltag glücklich vonstatten ging, so schätzte ich mich den glücklichsten Menschen in der Welt und bekümmerte mich im geringsten nicht um die Lustbarkeiten anderer junger Leute.«

Es ist kein Wunder, daß er erst spät eine Frau fand. Sein Wissensdurst und seine Experimentierlust waren unerschöpflich. Freunde und ehemalige Mitschüler besuchten ihn und fütterten seinen wachen Geist mit Büchern und Hinweisen auf Schriften, die ihm seine Arbeiten erleichterten. So wurden, wie er schrieb, die Sonntagsstunden nach dem Gottesdienst und die langen Winterabende zu Studierstunden:

»Ich machte mir das Merkwürdigste aus der Mathematik, Physik, und Chemie bekannt, schaffte Instrumente an, machte Versuche, und kam endlich dahin, dass ich mir mein Hausgeräth, Jagdzeug, Schiessgewehr und andere nützliche Dinge selbst verfertigte.«

Er gebraucht hier das Wort »merkwürdig« im alten Sinne, also gleichbedeutend mit »wissenswert«. Johann Andreas Naumann, der grüblerische, experimentierfreudige Bauer hätte durchaus als Vorbild für den Vater des Adrian Leverkühn in Thomas Manns *Doktor Faustus* dienen können.

Diese glückliche Lebensphase endete, als 1777 die Mutter starb. Johann Andreas war 32 Jahre alt und musste sich nun ganz der Landwirtschaft widmen. Das Vogelfangen und die Jagd traten für eine Weile in den Hintergrund. Er war mit ganzem Herzen Landwirt und kam der schweren Arbeit mit Freude nach. Ohne Zweifel hatte er auch darin eine glückliche Hand — und ihm blieben einige Jahre die für die Landwirtschaft schädlichen und für die Vogelbeobachtung so günstigen Überschwemmungen seines Landes erspart. Nun nahm er sich vor zu heiraten und machte sich mit der ihm eigenen Umsicht auf die Suche nach einer Frau.

»... ich hatte jetzt meine Freude an der Wirthschaft; ich sah mich nach einer Gattin um, traf 1779 auch eine so gute Wahl, dass ich an derselben eine wahre Gehülfin hatte und sie machte sich eine Freude daraus, meine Geschäfte indessen zu besorgen, wenn ich auf dem Vogelheerd oder auf die Jagd gieng.«

Neben dem Vogelherd, den man sich als einen Ort vorstellen muß, zu dem durch Fütterung und gute Lage viele Vögel gelockt wurden, die der Vogelsteller dann mit Netzen oder Schlingen zu fangen versuchte, baute er sich eine kleine Hütte, in der er sich Notizen machte über die beobachteten, erlegten oder lebendig gefangenen Vögel. Dort entstand seine schon erwähnte Schrift, *Der philosophische Bauer*, die er 1791 im Eigenverlag veröffentlichte. »Meine Frau besorgte indessen die Wirtschaft.« Der glückliche Mann!

Ziebigk war und ist eine Idylle — man kann das Gutshaus heute besichtigen, und über den Gartenzaun hinweg sieht man das klassizistisch gestaltete Gartenhäuschen, in dem Johann Friedrich im Sommer gerne arbeitete und schrieb. Neben der Landwirtschaft, die sowohl der alte Naumann als auch sein Sohn Johann Friedrich mit großem Ernst betrieben, denn sie mußte die Familie ernähren, ging es im Gutshaus meist um Vögel. Der früh verwitwete Vater (er trauerte tief um seine »getreue Gehülfin«) brachte oft Vögel mit nach Hause, die er verletzt oder geschwächt aufgefunden hatte, um sie gesund zu pflegen und zu zähmen.

Eine Zeitlang lebte ein Vertreter der seltsamen Triele — dickköpfige Vögel mit großen gelben Augen — bei der Familie. »Mein Vater besass einen lebenden Triel, welcher in seiner Wohnstube herumlief und ihm durch sein sanftes, zutrauliches Wesen viel Vergnügen machte ...«, schrieb Johann Friedrich. »Mein Vater kehrte selten mit leeren Händen von seinen Spaziergängen zurück, und der Vogel, dies wissend, kam ihm immer schon an der Thür entgegen [...] und nahm ihm das Mitgebrachte aus der Hand. Er hatte erstaunend viele liebenswürdige Eigenschaften, wurde aber, weil er die Stube sehr verunreinigte, etwas lästig, und war den Frauensleuten im Haus ein Greuel.« Dieser Abscheu wurde erwidert. »Vor Frauenzimmern, ohne Ausnahme, fürchtete er sich erschröcklich«, schrieb Johann Andreas. Damit er die Fliegen wegfing, ließ der alte Naumann einen Fliegenschnäpper in seiner Stube frei herumfliegen, auch eine Maßnahme von zweifelhaftem hygienischem Nutzen.

Früh nahm er die drei Söhne Johann Friedrich, Carl Andreas und Gottfried Lebrecht mit auf die Jagd, lehrte sie den Vogelfang und gab ihnen von seinem reichen Wissen über die Welt der Vögel soviel wie möglich mit. Besonders bei den beiden Älteren, Johann Friedrich und Carl Andreas, fiel das auf fruchtbaren Boden. Schon im Alter von zehn Jahren gingen sie zu seiner Freude mit Flinte, Netz und Schlingen äußerst geschickt um. Johann Friedrich hat sich und Gottfried Leberecht (wahrscheinlich auch Carl Andreas, aber das Bild ist nicht erhalten) im Alter von elf beziehungsweise dreizehn Jahren gezeichnet und auf einem Kupferstich verewigt. Man sieht die beiden Kinder mit Flinten herumlaufen, die fast so lang sind wie sie selbst. Es waren Vorderlader, und es kann für die Kleinen nicht einfach gewesen sein, sie zu laden und abzufeuern, geschweige denn zu treffen. Sie machten mit ihrem Vater weite Ausflüge — etwa zum Eislebener Salzsee, wo ihnen ein befreundeter Besitzer zu jagen erlaubt hatte. »Heil dem edlen Manne!«

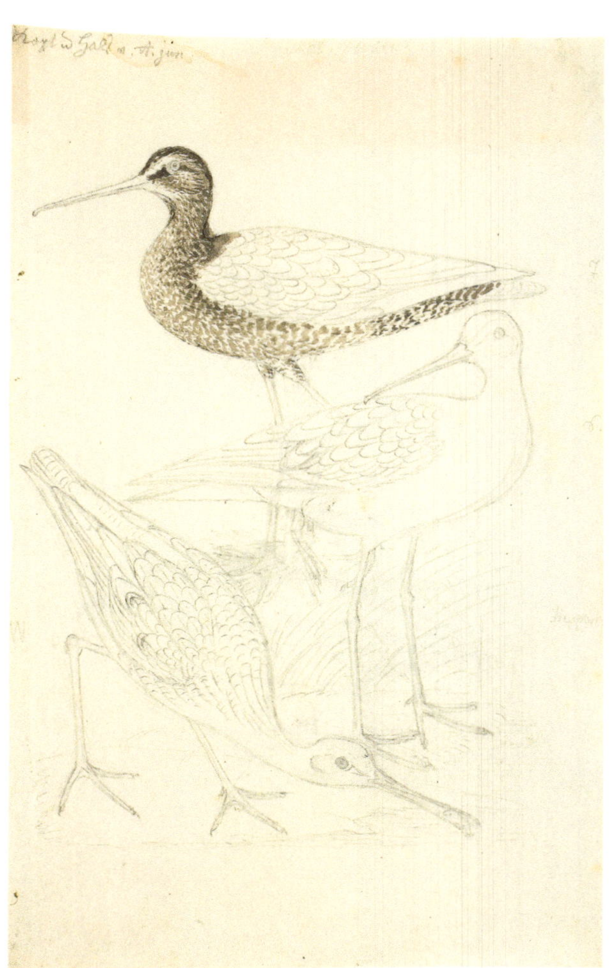

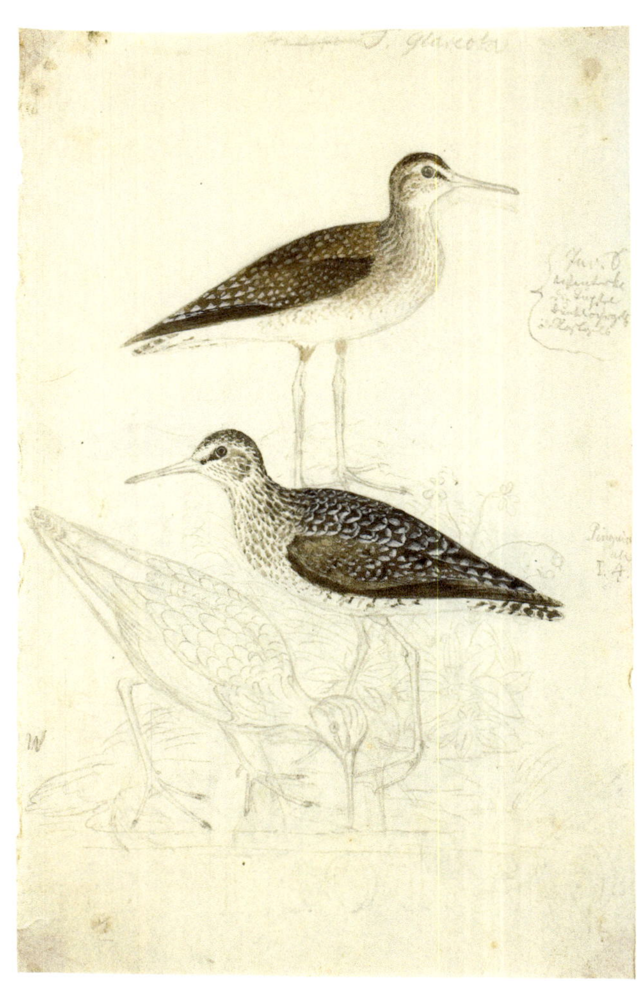

Sie streiften durch Feuchtgebiete an Elbe, Saale und Mulde, immer auf der Suche nach seltenen oder unbekannten Vögeln.

Der alte Naumann kam auf die Idee, einen großen Teich mit Schilf und Röhricht anzulegen, um am Wasser brütende Vögel anzulocken. »Mein Vater pflanzte das Rohr mit allem Fleiss an, um Rohrsänger herbeizulocken«, schreibt Johann Friedrich, »weil er sie recht aus der Nähe zu beobachten wünschte.«

Es gelang ihm eben nicht leicht, die unbedeutenden Fischteiche, aus Liebe zur Ornithologie, in Rohrteiche umzugestalten. Sonst hat man gewöhnlich Not, aus Rohrteichen Fischteiche zu machen; hier war es gerade umgekehrt. Diese Idee hatte indes in der Ausführung die besten Folgen. »Rohrsänger aller Arten fanden sich auf unseren Teichen ein, sobald das Rohr sie immer mehr und mehr überzog, und bald nisteten mehrere darin.«

Dunkler Wasserläufer (Studie)
Bruchwasserläufer (Studie)

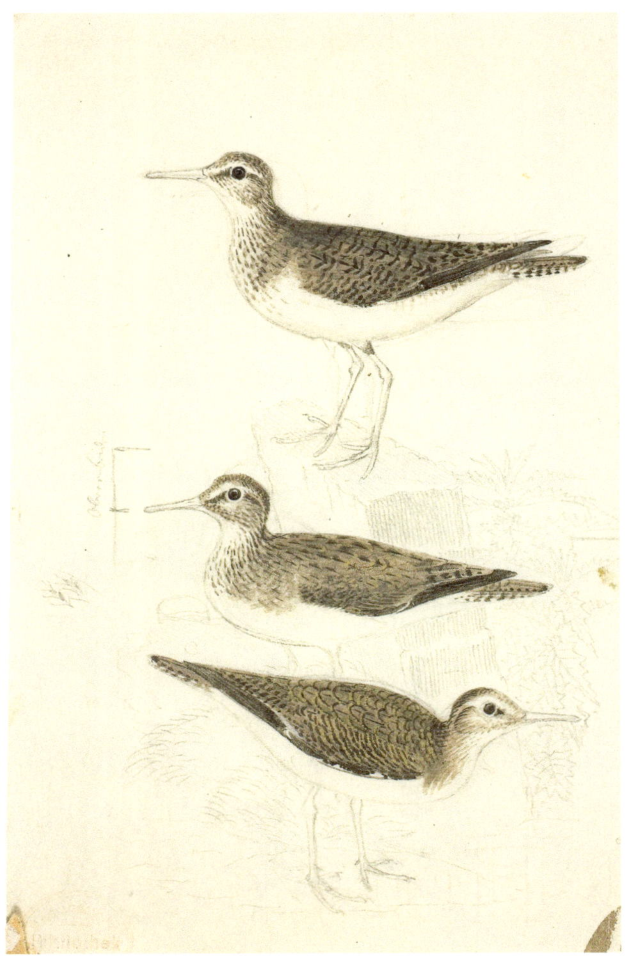

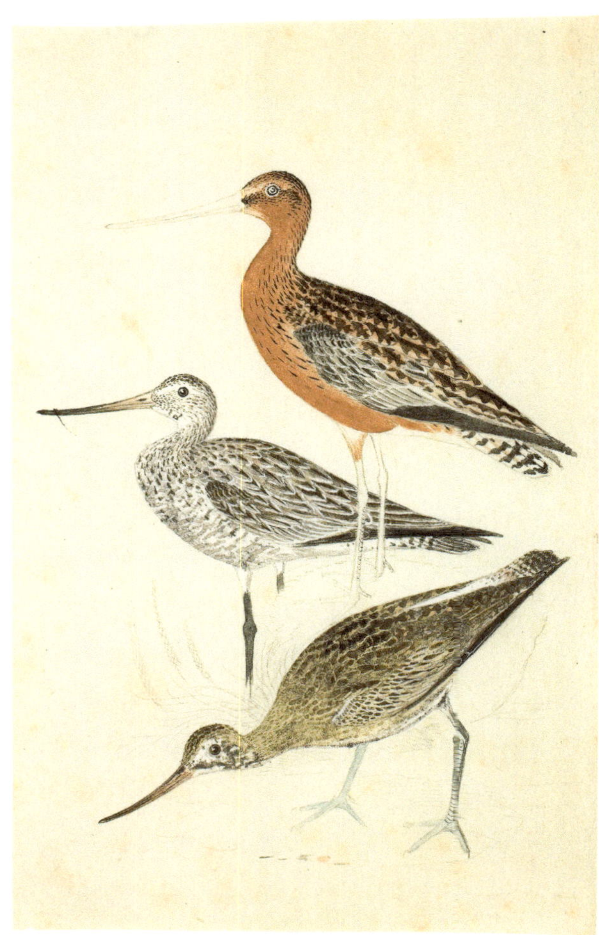

Zu den vielen Experimenten und Erfindungen des alten Naumann zählte auch das Beringen von Vögeln — ihm ging es dabei vor allem darum, die (uns auch heute noch erstaunenden) krassen Unterschiede in der Gefiederfärbung der Mäusebussarde zu verstehen. Und er kam einem Phänomen auf die Spur, das »Zugunruhe« genannt wird. Bei der Beobachtung gefangengehaltener Pirole fiel ihm auf, daß sie in ihrer Voliere Ende Juli oder im frühen August unruhig wurden. Diese Unruhe hielt bis zu acht Wochen an, woraus der geniale Kauz schloß, daß Pirole einen langen Zug nach Afrika unternahmen. Es dauerte 160 Jahre, bis seine Schlußfolgerung von einem deutschen Ornithologen, Eberhard Gwinner, bestätigt wurde. Darauf weist der englische Professor Tim Birkhead in seinem 2008 publizierten Buch *The Wisdom of Birds* hin. Gwinner wurde für seine Forschungen 1974 der Erwin-Stresemann-Preis zugesprochen, und Birkhead fügt netterweise an,

Flußuferläufer (Studie)
Pfuhlschnepfe (Studie)

er hoffe, daß Gwinner in seiner Dankesrede den alten Naumann nicht vergessen habe.

Johann Andreas Naumann versuchte, die Vögel zu malen, die er beobachtet oder geschossen hatte, überließ das aber bald Johann Friedrich, der darin großes Talent bewies:

»Der Älteste von meinen drei Söhnen, zeigte grosse Lust und Fähigkeit zum Zeichnen und Malen, ich ließ ihm Unterricht geben, und wenn ich einen seltenen Vogel gefangen oder geschossen hatte, malte er denselben ab. Wir fingen endlich an, eine Sammlung von allen Vögeln, die unsere Gegend durchfliegen, zu unserem Vergnügen zu machen, da mir endlich einige gute Freunde den Rath gaben, dieselben in Kupfer stechen zu lassen, und davon eine Naturbeschreibung herauszugeben. Dieses überlegte ich, und als ich vorher verschiedene Naturgeschichten gelesen, und befunden, dass noch immer Dunkelheit und Verwirrung darinnen herrscht, es hauptsächlich aber an Erfahrungen mangelt; so glaubte ich, dass dieses Werk wohl nicht überflüssig sein werde.«

Da spricht der Widerwille des erfahrenen Jägers und Waldläufers gegen die Stubengelehrsamkeit, den auch Johann Friedrich und sein Bruder Carl Andreas später teilen sollten. Es war der Beginn von Johann Andreas Naumanns ornithologischer Schriftstellerei und zugleich der von Johann Friedrichs Vogelmalerei. Der Titel des Werks war, wie damals üblich, lang und erschöpfend: *Ausführliche Beschreibung aller Wald-, Feld- und Wasser-Vögel, welche sich in den Anhaltinischen Fürstenthümern und einigen umliegenden Gebieten aufhalten und durchziehn.* In seiner »Vorrede« schrieb Johann Andreas: »Die Bewohner der Lüfte, die Vögel, sind der Gegenstand, womit ich meine Leser zu unterhalten und zum Lobe des Allgewaltigen aufzumuntern gedenke. Mit einem Worte, ich, ein Ungelehrter, überreiche einem verehrungswürdigen Publiko, eine auf vieljährige Erfahrung gegründete Naturgeschichte der einländischen Land- und Wasservögel [...] Mein Sohn hat die sämmtlichen Vögel nach der Natur gemalt.«

»Nach der Natur« und eben nicht nach den ausgestopften Exemplaren, die alle anderen Vogelmaler der Zeit außer dem großen Audubon als Vorlage nutzten. Die präparierten Vögel in den zeitgenössischen Sammlungen und Museen verloren schnell ihre leuchtenden Farben, sie verstaubten und wurden oft in atypischen Haltungen montiert, die mit der Lebhaftigkeit der Vögel in der Natur nichts mehr gemein hatten.

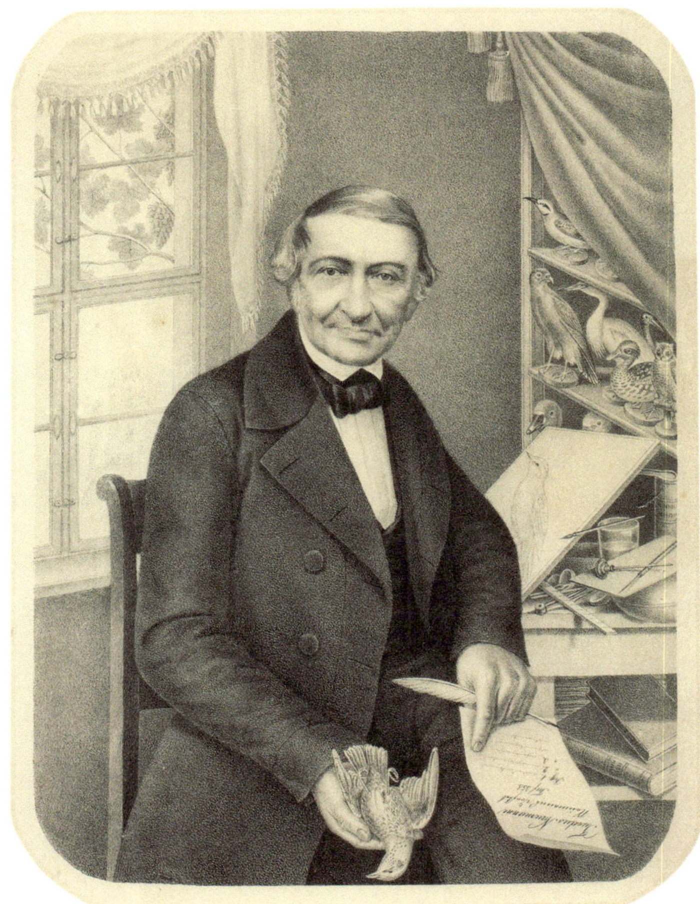

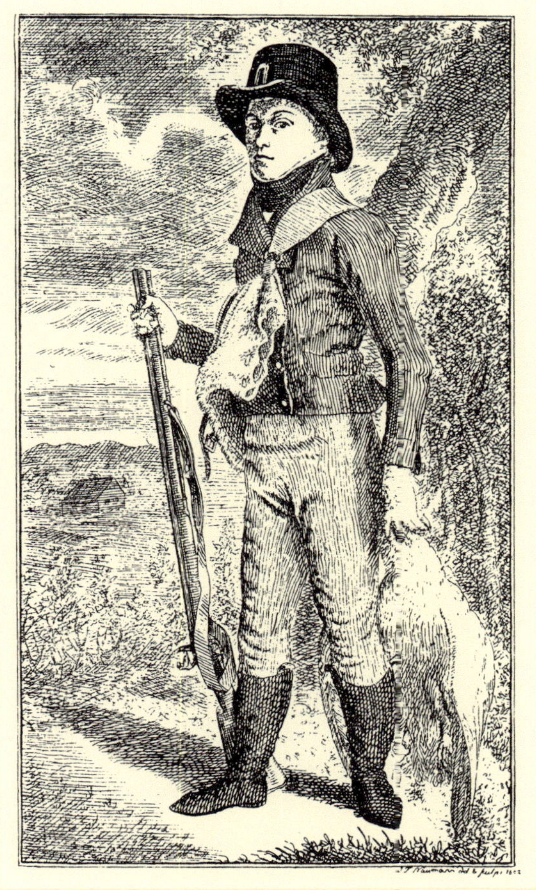

Als 1798 der zweite Band erschien, wurde der Titel geändert. Jetzt gab Johann Andreas seinem Unternehmen einen umfassenderen Anspruch, und das programmatische Ziel, die Vögel möglichst natürlich abzubilden, spiegelte sich darin: *Naturgeschichte der Land- und Wasser-Vögel des nördlichen Deutschlands und angränzender Länder, nach eigenen Erfahrungen entworfen, und nach dem Leben gezeichnet von Johann Andreas Naumann.* »Nach dem Leben gezeichnet«, das ist entscheidend, aber der Künstler war nicht Johann Andreas, sondern Johann Friedrich. Dieser, der sich zum Teil auf die Forschungen seines Vater stützte und sie in sein späteres Werk einarbeitete, erweiterte den Gegenstand erneut: *Naturgeschichte der Vögel Deutschlands* war schließlich der Titel seines Lebenswerks, das gewissermaßen aus dem des Vaters herauswuchs. Auch die Kupferstiche, die er für das Buch des Vaters geschaffen hatte, übernahm er.

Johann Friedrich Naumann an seinem Arbeitstisch
Gottfried Leberecht Naumann, 13 Jahre alt

Wie später sein berühmter Sohn lehnte auch der Vater die damals um sich greifende Manie ab, immer neue Arten und Unterarten der Vogelwelt einzuführen. Er hielt sich an seine Beobachtungen in der Natur, die für ihn das Maß der Dinge waren. Diese Abgrenzung von der »Bücherweisheit« vieler Vogelkundler ist ihm so wichtig, daß er sie im Nachwort seiner *Wald-, Feld- und Wasservögel der Anhaltinischen Fürstenthümer* einem autobiographischen Abriß voranstellt:

»Damit nun der geneigte Leser überzeugt werde, dass ich meine Beschreibungen der Vögel nicht aus Büchern, sondern alle nach eignen Erfahrungen, treu nach der Natur entworfen habe und dass ich nicht Bücherforscher sondern Naturforscher bin, so halte ich nicht für überflüssig, demselben meine Lebensgeschichte hier in der Kürze mitzuteilen.«

Und in der Vorrede schreibt er auch über die Bilder seines Werkes, daß sie »alle sehr genau nach der Natur entworfen und durch die Hand eines jungen Künstlers in Kupfer gestochen und illuminirt worden sind [...]«

Sein Sohn Johann Friedrich, der junge Künstler, schrieb später über seine frühe Mitarbeit an den Büchern des Vaters: »Als ich 1790 nach Dessau auf die Schule kam, gab mir mein seliger Vater das Exemplar seines ›Vogelstellers‹ mit, um mir es zu binden und mit weißem Papier in Quart durchschiessen zu lassen, damit ich die im Fertigen beschriebenen Vögel dazu malen könne, wozu er mir grösstenteils die Vögel in Natur frisch zusandte, oder auch, wo das nicht möglich war, sie selbst malte und nachher die Abbildungen kopieren und hier eintragen liess; doch ist das letztere nur bei wenigen der Fall gewesen. Ich habe darnach, wenig über zehn Jahre alt, schon angefangen, Vögel nach der Natur zu malen und zwar ohne weitere Anleitung als das wenige, was mir mein seliger Vater hinsichtlich der Stellung und dergleichen anratend empfahl.«

Man muß sich das so vorstellen: Zum einen erhielt das begabte Kind durch Boten oder die Post tatsächlich frisch geschossene, wohl oft blutige Vögel, die es unverzüglich abmalte. Zum anderen schickte der Vater seine ungelenken Zeichnungen, die der Sohn dann nach eigener Anschauung verbessernd abzeichnete. Mit dem dritten Band, das meint zumindest der Naumann-Biograph Peter Thomsen, wird auch die literarische Mitarbeit des Sohnes erkennbar. »Der Ausdruck wird flüssiger«, schreibt Thomsen, »Beziehungen auf andere Werke lassen sich [...] häufiger erkennen.« Dieser Band erschien im Jahre 1799, da ist Johann Friedrich neunzehn Jahre alt. Es ist die ungewöhnliche Zusammenarbeit eines hochbegabten Sohnes mit dem originellen Vater — getragen von gegenseitigem Respekt vor der Leistung des anderen. Auch die ersten selbstgeschriebenen Bände seines Werkes ließ Johann Friedrich noch unter dem Namen des Vaters erscheinen.

Der philosophische Bauer, Grübler, Forscher, Landwirt, Jäger und Handwerker starb am 16. Mai 1826. So einer ließ sich nicht auf dem Friedhof beerdigen — auf eigenen Wunsch wurde er mit kirchlicher Erlaubnis in dem Wäldchen begraben, das zu seinem Besitz gehörte. Wenig später schrieb sein Sohn Johann Friedrich in einer distanzierten und doch ergreifenden Passage an seinen Freund Lichtenstein:

»Der merkwürdige Mann wählte sich schon früh seine Ruhestätte, in seinem Wäldchen, an einem seiner Lieblingsplätze, früher ein Vogelheerd, an welchem der Grabhügel und die umstehenden Bäume mit Epheu umkränzt sind, was er längst dort pflanzte und pflegte. Beim Geflüster der Abendlüfte im jungen Grün der Bäume geleiteten ihn nun die schmelzenden Melodien seiner Schützlinge, der äusserst zahlreich dort wohnenden Nachtigallen, Drosseln und viel anderer befiederter Sänger mit ihren Abendliedern zur Ruh.«

Johann Friedrich Naumann war wie sein Vater zuerst Landwirt und konnte sich wie der Alte nur in den Mußestunden — vor allem im Winter — der Ornithologie widmen. Aus seinen Briefen spricht deutlich, daß er sich der ständigen Gefährdung des Anwesens durch Überschwemmung und Krieg sehr bewußt war. Er hatte die napoleonischen Kriege und ihre Verwüstungen miterlebt, die lastenden Abgaben und Steuern in Kriegszeiten, die mühsamen Aufbauarbeiten nach Unruhen und Wirtschaftskrisen. Mehr als einmal stand Ziebigk vor dem Ruin. Aber der jüngere Naumann war ebenfalls ein tüchtiger, unerschrockener Mann, und er war von beharrlichem Fleiß, der sich auch darin ausdrückte, daß Naumann neben der Landwirtschaft, der Jagd und der Ornithologie noch ein tätiges Interesse am Obstanbau, an der Pflanzenzucht und an Schmetterlingen entwickelte.

Johann Friedrichs Schulausbildung war nicht besser oder gründlicher als die des Vaters. Mit zehn Jahren wurde er auf die »Fürstliche Hauptschule« in Dessau geschickt, aber nachdem er fünfzehn geworden war, holte ihn der Vater zurück nach Hause, weil er seine Hilfe brauchte. Die Schule, die sehr fortschrittlich im rousseauschen Geist geführt wurde, also unter Betonung der »guten Natur« des Kindes, sah den Lehrer als väterlichen Freund, und diese humane Auffassung der Pädagogik hat Johann Friedrich wohl mehr geprägt als der Stoff, den er in seiner fünfjährigen

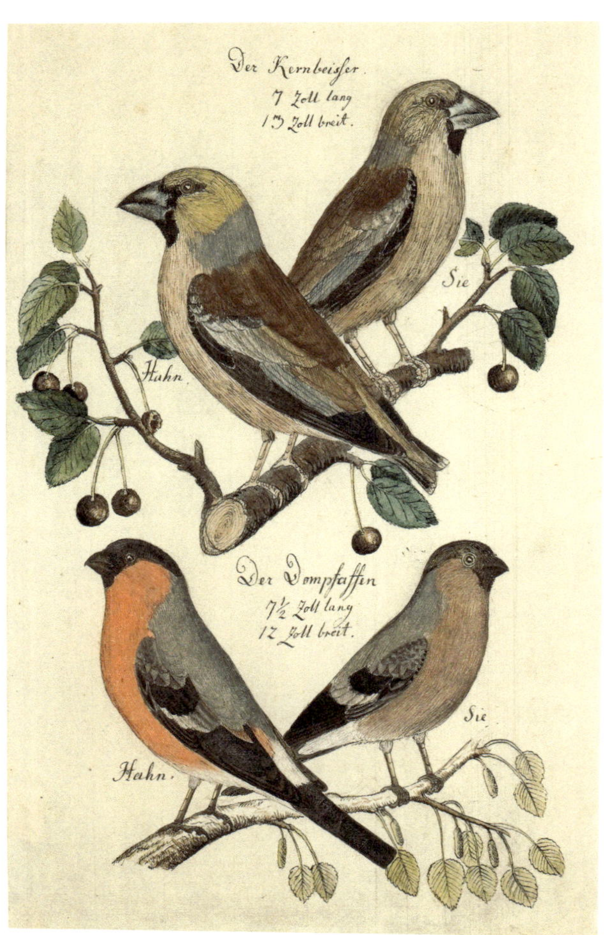

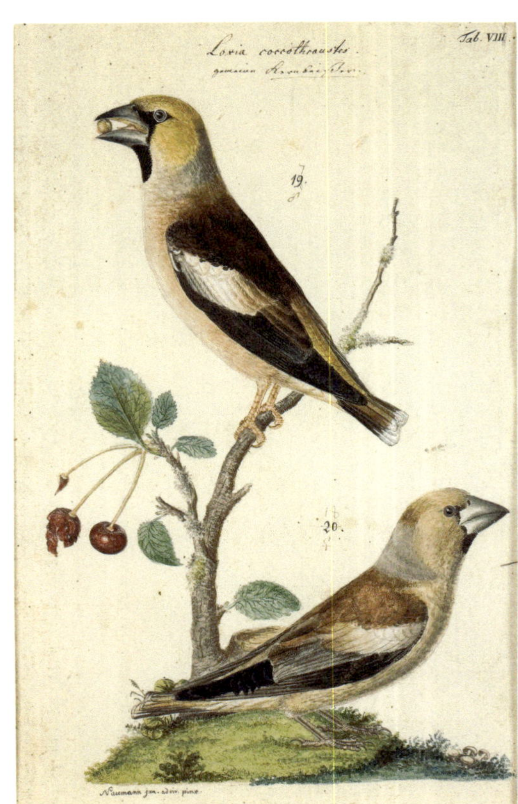

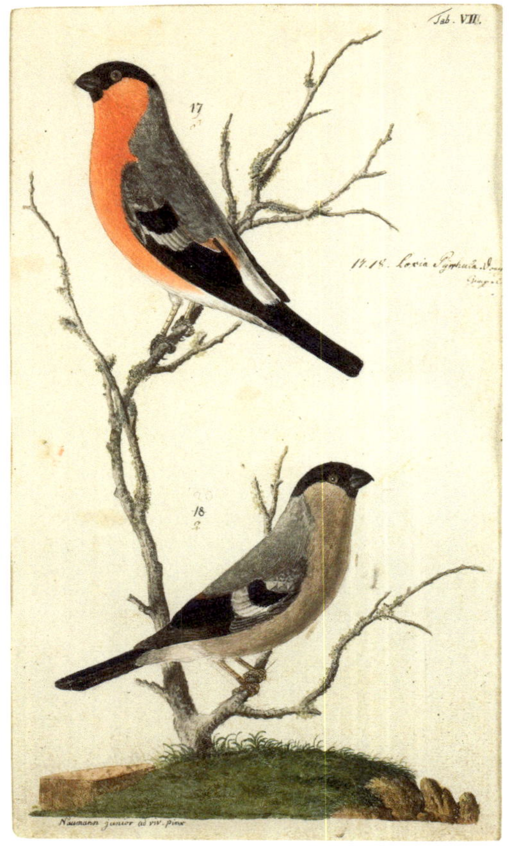

Obere Bildreihe: Kernbeißer
Untere Bildreihe: Gimpel

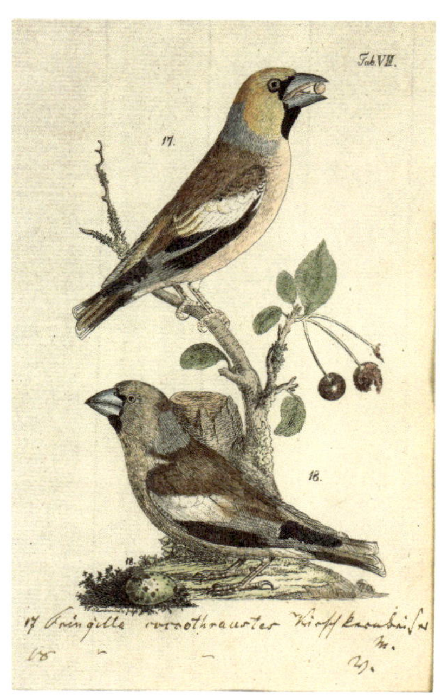

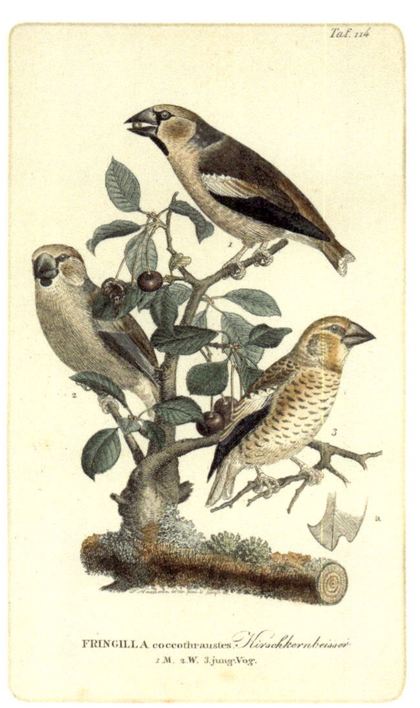

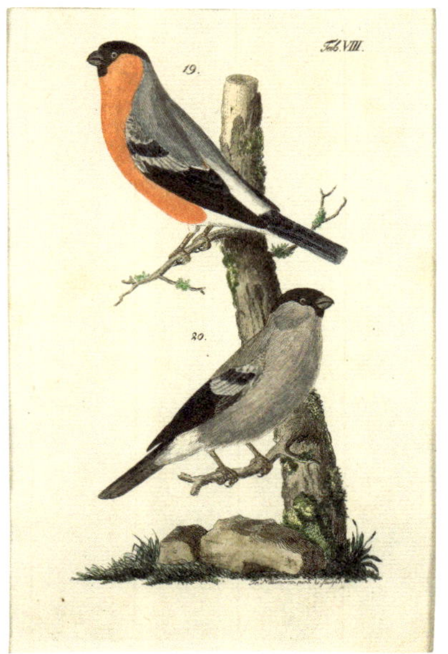

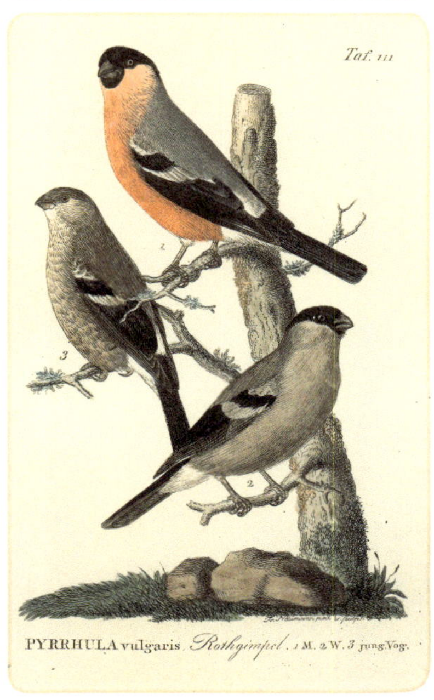

Diese Bildfolge zeigt den Fortschritt in Naumanns Malweise. Fallen die in der Jugend entstandenen Blätter (S. 26) noch relativ flach und zweidimensional aus, wirken die später entstandenen Bilder (S. 27) aufgrund der Beobachtung von Licht und Schatten vollendet räumlich und lebendig. Die kleineren Aquarelle (auf dieser Seite) dienten schließlich als Vorlage für die Kupferstiche ganz rechts.

Schulzeit zu bewältigen hatte. Er war anfangs einer der besten Schüler, litt dann aber häufig unter Krankheiten, die ihn zurückwarfen.

Thomsen schildert ihn einmal als »schmächtigen Jüngling«, wovon aber bei dem Erwachsenen kaum noch die Rede sein kann, denn was er als Landwirt, Wissenschaftler und Jäger leistete, setzte eine eiserne Konstitution voraus. Immerhin bekam er auf der Fürstlichen Schule die Grundlagen von Physik und Geographie vermittelt, ein wenig Latein, auch Rechnen, Buchführung und Haushaltslehre, was ihm bei der Führung des Gutes sicher half. Aber wie sein Vater war auch er ein großer Autodidakt — was immer ihm gerade nützlich erschien, brachte er sich selbst bei, und wenn er zu einem Vogel nur einen englischen Beitrag fand, lernte er eben so viel Englisch, daß er den Sinn des Textes erfassen konnte.

Wichtig für ihn wurde, daß er im Gegensatz zu seinem eigenbrötlerischen Vater schon früh den Kontakt zu verwandten Geistern suchte. Er ließ sich in literarischer wie in künstlerischer Hinsicht beraten, führte einen umfangreichen Briefwechsel mit anderen Ornithologen und weitete auf entscheidende Weise seinen Horizont aus. Seine Mitarbeit am Werk des Vaters wurde immer umfangreicher, mit ihm zusammen verfaßte er die »Nachträge«, welche die gröbsten Fehler des Vaters korrigierten. Um nur zwei Beispiele zu nennen: Johann Andreas war noch von zwei Amselarten ausgegangen, der »Grauen« und der »Schwarzen«, und er hatte den Waldlaubsänger noch nicht von Fitis und Zilpzalp unterschieden.

Auf die ständigen ökonomischen Schwierigkeiten der Naumanns ging auch die Entscheidung zurück, schon 1804 vom Folioformat der Illustrationen auf das kleinere Oktav überzugehen. Diese Entscheidung hat mit Sicherheit dazu beigetragen, daß die wunderbaren Stiche Naumanns von der Nachwelt kaum noch wahrgenommen wurden. Verglichen mit den großen Formaten aus der Gouldschen »Werkstatt« und vor allem den Riesenbildnissen John James Audubons wirkten sie sehr zurückgenommen und bescheiden.

Überdies gingen die Kupferplatten der Foliotafeln, wie Johann Friedrich am 19. Mai 1816 an den holländischen Ornithologen Temminck schrieb, durch einen Unglücksfall verloren. Wenn es denn ein »Unglücksfall« war. Einiges spricht auch dafür, daß der perfektionistische Naumann mit den frühen Bildern im Folioformat (etwa 190 sind im Druck erschienen) unzufrieden war und sie selbst vernichtete oder abschleifen ließ. Aber auch die neuen Oktavplatten wurden nach dem Druck der einzelnen Bände der *Naturgeschichte der Vögel Deutschlands* abgeschliffen, um sie für

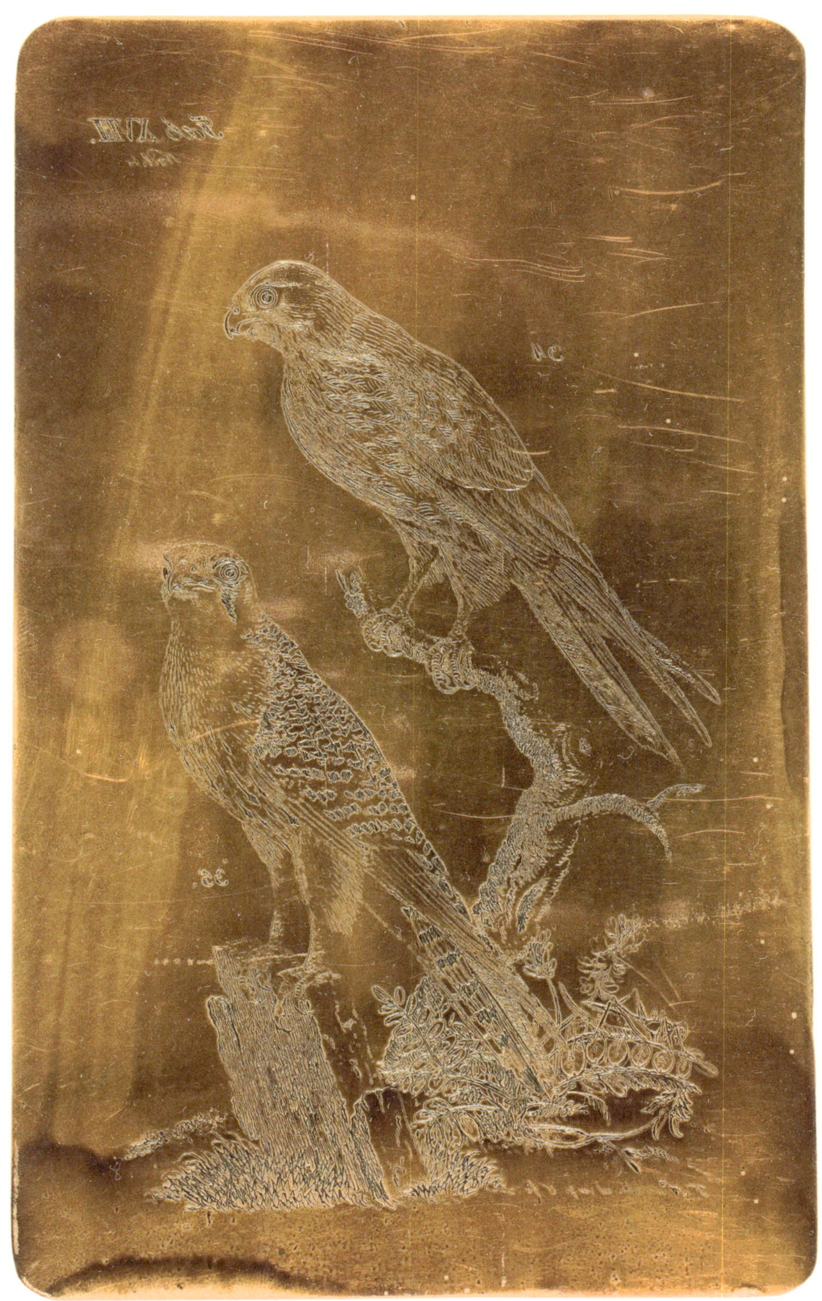

neue Bilder wieder verwenden zu können. Auch das ein wahrhaft schrecklicher Verlust, der auf den ständigen Geldmangel Naumanns zurückging. So mußte der große Nachdruck des Naumannschen Werkes, den Carl Richard Hennicke von 1897 bis 1905 veranstaltete, mit Vogeldarstellungen anderer Künstler illustriert werden.

Kupferstichplatte, Rotfußfalke

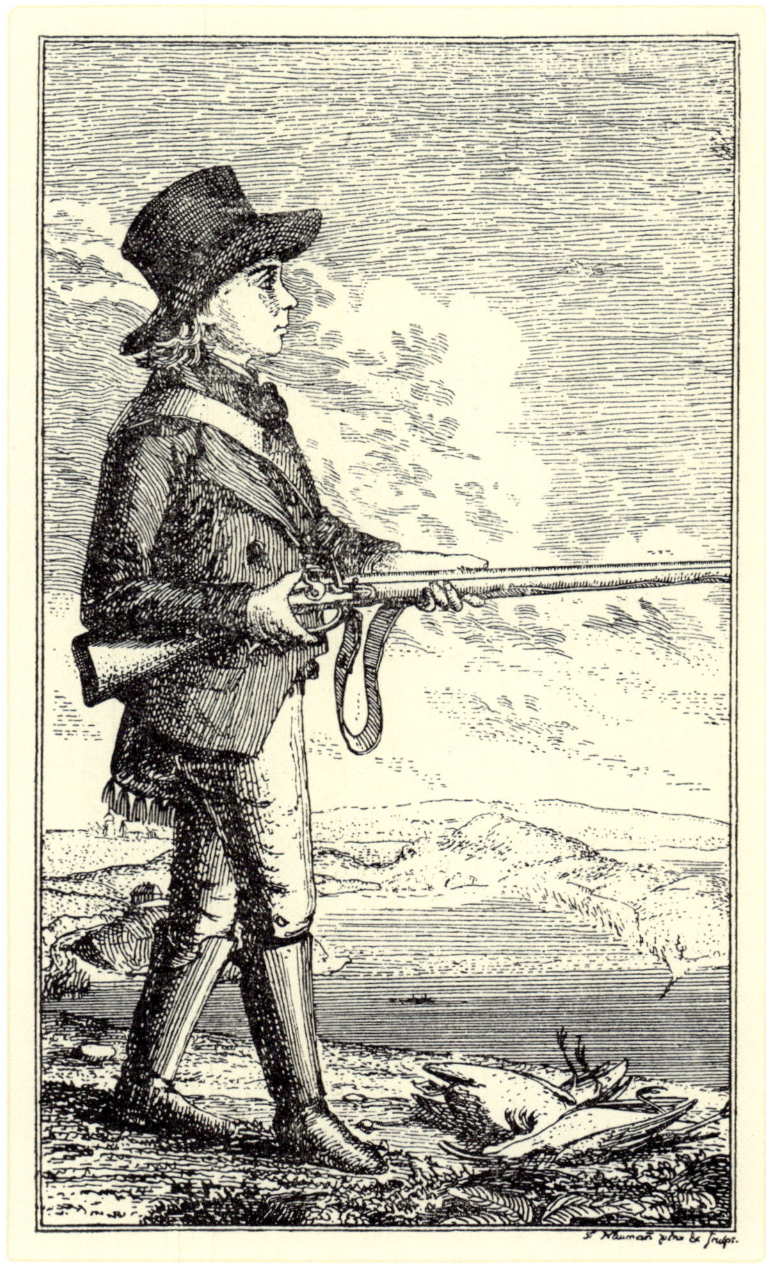

In der Zeit der Napoleonischen Kriege — 1806 schlug das französische Heer die Preußen bei Jena und Auerstedt — fand der damals sechsundzwanzigjährige Johann Friedrich seine Zukünftige. Im August desselben Jahres besuchte er seinen Freund Ernst Friedrich Böttiger, der Hauslehrer bei der Familie Troitzsch war. Dort lernte er die achtzehnjährige Marie Juliane Troitzsch kennen. Es war Liebe auf den

Carl Andreas Naumann im Alter von elf Jahren

ersten Blick, und Johann Friedrich hielt bald um ihre Hand an. Die Eltern waren nicht ganz so überzeugt, verlangten eine Wartezeit, willigten aber schließlich ein, und am 8. Oktober 1807 wurde geheiratet. Eine Woche vor der Hochzeit übergab Johann Andreas Naumann seinem ältesten Sohn das Gut — allerdings unter einer Bedingung. Johann Friedrich mußte seinen Geschwistern jeweils 1900 Taler auszahlen — eine für die damaligen Verhältnisse hohe Summe, die Johann Friedrich nur aufbringen konnte, weil seine Frau eine stattliche Mitgift erhielt. Zwei Jahre später bekamen Johann Friedrich und Juliane einen Sohn, den sie Friedrich Julius nannten — eine Kombination ihrer Namen —, und zwei weitere Jahre später eine Tochter, Alwine. Juliane, die eine ausnehmend tüchtige Hausfrau und Mutter war, gebar ihrem Mann elf Kinder, von denen fünf früh verstarben. An Johann Friedrichs geistigen und wissenschaftlichen Interessen nahm sie wenig Anteil.

Die ornithologische Arbeit mußte nun erstmal zurückstehen. Wichtiger war es, die Landwirtschaft nach den Wirren der Napoleonischen Kriege wieder instand zu setzen. Erst nach acht Jahren veröffentlichte Naumann das erste Buch unter eigenem Namen. Es war merkwürdigerweise eine Abhandlung über die Taxidermie, das Ausstopfen erlegter Tiere und Vögel, auch eine Kunst, die sich Naumann selbst beigebracht hatte. Darin liegt eine gewisse Ironie, denn Naumann war zusammen mit Audubon einer der ersten Vogelmaler, die ausgestopfte Exemplare als Vorlage für ihre Arbeit strikt ablehnten. Seine umfangreiche Sammlung an ausgestopften Vögeln sollte Naumann später für eine sicher willkommene stattliche Summe an den anhaltinischen Herzog verkaufen. Sie ist noch heute in ihren alten Vitrinen in den Räumen des Naumann-Museums im Köthener Schloß zu besichtigen. Ausgestopfte Tiere spielten für die meßwütige Wissenschaft jener Zeit eine wichtige Rolle. Naumann wurde auch zum »Inspektor« dieser Sammlung ernannt und erhielt dafür ein kleines monatliches Gehalt.

Als Naumann wieder halbwegs sicheren Boden unter den Füßen hatte, begann er an der Erweiterung des väterlichen Werks über die deutschen Vögel zu arbeiten. Einen wichtigen Gehilfen fand er in seinem jüngeren Bruder Carl Andreas. Dieser war der beste Schütze und scharfsinnigste Beobachter von den drei Söhnen des großen Jägers Johann Andreas. Der Vater nannte ihn deshalb in Briefen und in einer Einleitung schon früh seinen »Leibjäger«.

»Ohnerachtet er erst das zwölfte Jahr erreicht hat«, schrieb der Alte, »so hat er doch schon seit zwei Jahren fast alle Strapazen und Nachtwachen mitgemacht, und seinem Posten jederzeit so gut vorgestanden, dass ich viele meiner gesammelten Vögel seiner Aufmerksamkeit und Fleisse zu verdanken habe.«

Carl Andreas wurde Herzoglicher Förster und Jagdbeamter in Kleinzerbst, und er unterstützte den älteren Bruder nach Kräften bei dessen vogelkundlichen Arbeiten. 1836 stattete Johann Friedrich ihm in der Vorrede des achten Bandes der *Naturgeschichte der Vögel Deutschlands* seinen Dank ab:

»Mit einer angeborenen Beobachtungsgabe, einer ungemeinen, von früher Jugend an geübten Bekanntschaft mit dem Fluge, dem Betragen, den Stimmen der Vögel, dazu mit einer Jagd- und Schießfertigkeit, die ihresgleichen (im vollen Sinne des Ausdrucks) nicht leicht finden möchte, begabt, zu allen diesen Eigenschaften auch mit dem unermüdlichsten Jagdeifer, mit der regsten Forschungslust und einer unbegrenzten Liebe zur Naturkunde ausgerüstet, entging ihm nicht leicht ein seltener Vogel, welcher sich in jener Gegend niederliess, und sehr viel hat ihm meine Sammlung — jetzt im Besitz meines Durchlauchtigsten Landesherren —, sehr viel hochschätzbare Beiträge an Beobachtungen dieses Werk zu verdanken [...] Sein täglich geübtes Falken-Auge unterscheidet schon in weiter Ferne seinen Gegenstand, der leiseste Ton einer ihm nicht bekannten Vogelstimme spannt seine Aufmerksamkeit, die geringste Abweichung in den Bewegungen eines fliegenden Vogels fesselt seine Neugierde.«

Carl Andreas muß viel von seinem originellen, knorrigen, ja ein wenig skurrilen Vater gehabt haben. Zugleich war dieser Förster in Kleinzerbst, der Leidenschaft und Beruf vereinte, offenbar ein sehr glücklicher Mensch. Sein Verhältnis zur Natur und insbesondere zu den Vögeln erinnert sowohl an Audubon, der, wie er einmal in seiner *Ornithological Biography* schrieb, so gern mit den Gefiederten sprechen würde, als auch an seinen älteren Bruder, der wiederholt das »Seelenleben« der Vögel erwähnte. Alle drei nähern sich damit einem gewissen Anthropomorphismus — den Vögeln zugeschriebene menschliche Eigenschaften. Über die Wirtsvögel des Kuckucks äußert Naumann einmal die überraschende Ansicht, daß diese genau wüßten, der viel zu große Zögling, der dicke junge Kuckuck, könne unmöglich ihr Nachwuchs sein. Aber sie hätten ihn nun einmal adoptiert, was sollten sie anderes tun, als ihn durchzufüttern? Vielleicht hat Naumann damit sogar recht, denn Vögel sind außerordentlich intelligent.

Zurück zum Förster Carl Andreas. Carl Richard Hennicke, der Herausgeber der Neuauflage von Naumanns *Naturgeschichte der Vögel Deutschlands,* gibt im ersten

Band, der 1897 erschien, eine wunderbare Anekdote wieder, die Eduard Baldamus überliefert hat:

»Die originelle Biderbheit seines Wesens äußerte sich auch in seiner Sprache, die zuweilen reich an kühnen Bildern war. ›Na, was hast du denn hier zu suchen, Rosenrote?‹ redete er einst in Baldamus' Gegenwart eine Rabenkrähe seines Reviers an. ›Warum Rosenrote?‹ fragte jener. ›Ja, ich nenne sie die Rosenrote, weil sie rosenrot schreit; ich habe auch eine Himmelblaue hier.‹ — ›Aber was soll das denn heißen, Förster?‹ — ›Na, wenn Sie das nicht unterscheiden können, dann kann ich's Ihnen auch nicht erklären.‹

In seiner dichterischen Anschauung lebte alles, sprach alles und er mit allem. Die scherzhafte Behauptung, daß er die Sprache der Tiere verstehe, war insofern nicht aus der Luft gegriffen, als die aus der fortgesetzten Beobachtung erworbene intime Vertrautheit mit den Sitten und Gewohnheiten der Tiere, die sich in der Stimme, in einem einzelnen Ton, in der Haltung, in den Gebärden und anderem, in den Uneingeweihten gänzlich entgehenden Zügen offenbaren, ihm eine große Sicherheit in der Deutung all dieser Dinge verlieh. Baldamus sagte, ihm würden die hochinteressanten Tage der Jagd mit dem vielleicht *größten aller Vogelbeobachter* ewig im Gedächtnis bleiben und er könnte eine Menge ähnlicher Anekdoten mitteilen. Schade, daß er's nicht getan hat, rufen wir Epigonen aus!«

(Sollte jemand über das anfängliche »Biderbheit« gestolpert sein: es ist ein historisierender Rückgriff auf das Althochdeutsche und bedeutet einfach Biederkeit. Bieder ist jemand, der Rechtschaffenheit und Unkompliziertheit mit Anstelligkeit verbindet.)

Vielleicht war dieser Carl Andreas tatsächlich, wie Baldamus sagt, der beste Vogelbeobachter aller Zeiten. Er ist eigentlich eine Nebengestalt in der Geschichte seines Bruders, aber so faszinierend, daß ich es nicht lassen kann, noch zwei Begebenheiten einzuschieben, die ein Licht auf seinen Scharfsinn, sein phantastisches Einfühlungsvermögen und seine Gutmütigkeit werfen. Beides sind Jagdgeschichten, und sie werden dieses Mal von Baldamus selbst erzählt:

»Von seiner feinen, den Jäger so sehr fördernden Beobachtungsgabe nur ein Beispiel. Ein Sonntagsjäger hatte bei der Schnepfensuche in seinem Wald eine Schnepfe geschossen, wurde aber ob dieser Behauptung von seinen Kollegen, etwas geübteren Schützen, um so mehr ausgelacht, als alles Suchen nach dem gefallenen Vogel vergeblich war. Carl Andreas war auf dem anderen Ende der Schützenkette, vernahm von dem angeblich glücklichen Schusse, horchte und sagte dann: ›Ja, sie ist ihm wirklich ins Blei geflogen, er hat sie geflügelt‹, und ging nebst anderen Schützen über hundert Schritte zurück direkt auf eine grüne Stelle zu, blickte nach oben, bückte sich dann und zog die flügellahme Schnepfe aus dem Gestrüpp hervor. ›Der klagende Fink da oben hat's mir gezeigt‹, erklärte er den verwunderten Zuschauern, ›der dumme Kerl hält sie für eine Eule; ich brauchte nur der Richtung seines Blicks zu folgen, um ihr Versteck zu finden.‹«

Carl Andreas war kein Freund des »Schreibervolks«, wie er es nannte, hatte aber große Achtung vor seinem gelehrten Bruder, der »nur wirklich Beobachtetes, keine Stubengelehrten-Phantasien niederschrieb«. Die Dorfgemeinschaft, in der der Förster lebte, verehrte und liebte ihn wegen seines Gerechtigkeitssinnes und seiner Milde. Einmal wurde er bei einer Treibjagd von Schrotkugeln im Gesicht getroffen. »Im ersten Schreck und Schmerz stiess er einige heftige Worte aus«, schreibt Baldamus, »rief aber sofort den herbeieilenden Schützen zu: ›Ein Hundsfott, wer mir sagt, wer mich geschossen hat! Ich könnte einen Hass auf den Unglücklichen werfen, der mich um die Augen gebracht hat‹, fügte er ruhig hinzu. Glücklicherweise war die Befürchtung grundlos; aber Carl Andreas ist gestorben, ohne den Namen des Täters je erfahren zu haben.« Der große Jäger und Vogelkenner starb im Jahre 1856.

Im Rahmen seiner umfangreichen Korrespondenz mit anderen Vogelkundlern und Sammlern kam Johann Friedrich Naumann in Kontakt mit dem holländischen Ornithologen Coenraad Jacob Temminck, der 1815 sein *Manuel d'Ornithologie, ou tableau systématique des Oiseaux qui se trouvent en Europe* veröffentlichte. (Er schrieb auf französisch.) Auf Temmincks Bitte hin schickte Naumann ihm einige seiner Oktavtafeln, und Temminck war so begeistert, daß er eine Zusammenarbeit vorschlug. »[...] ces petites gravures surpassent tout ce que j'ai vu dans ce genre; il est impossible d'imiter plus exactement la nature, et si toutes vos autres petites planches répondent à cet échantillon, que je viens de recevoir, alors je ne vois rien de plus parfait qu'une collection complète des oiseaux d'Europe, ainsi figurées.«

Temminck war ein wohlhabender Mann — sein Vater war Schatzmeister der Ostindischen Kompanie gewesen und ebenfalls ein Vogelsammler. Mit der Absicht, Naumann für ein gemeinsames Werk über die Vögel Europas zu gewinnen, lud er ihn ein, nach Amsterdam zu kommen. Aber daraus wurde nichts — zum Glück, muss man rückblickend sagen —, die Reise scheiterte an vielen Hindernissen, wurde immer wieder verschoben und schließlich aufgegeben. So machte Johann Friedrich sich daran, seine eigenen *Vögel Deutschlands* zu schreiben, zu zeichnen, zu stechen und zu kolorieren. Wäre er auf das großzügige und sicher verlockende Angebot des Holländers eingegangen, hätten wir dieses unvergleichliche Werk wahrscheinlich nicht.

Aber es ist bezeichnend, daß der weltläufige, gelehrte Temminck, der fast alles gekannt haben muß, was es im damaligen Europa an Vogelillustrationen gab, Naumanns Bilder über alles stellte, was er bislang gesehen hatte, und diese Lobpreisung mit dem Angebot einer Zusammenarbeit untermauerte. Naumann muß sich über diese Anerkennung gefreut haben, aber letztlich war er klug genug, sich nicht unter die Fittiche eines anderen großen Ornithologen zu begeben, sondern in seiner abgeschiedenen, immer bedrohten, aber glanzvollen Eigenständigkeit zu verharren. Er war diplomatischer und auch kommunikativer als sein Vater, dessen Genügsamkeit und Unabhängigkeit hatte er sich jedoch bewahrt.

Der Korrespondenz mit Temminck verdanken wir einen wunderbaren Einblick in den Alltag der Naumanns. Folgender Brief an Temminck stammt aus dem Jahre 1816:

»Ich bin Besitzer von einem kleinen Landgute, das mich und meine Familie nährt, aber weder erlaubt, grossen Aufwand zu machen, noch etwas mehr übrig lässt, als was zu den nothwendigsten Bedürfnissen des Lebens gehört.

Ich muss alles in der Oekonomie Vorfallende besorgen, ja leider oft selbst Hand anlegen; mir Leute halten zu können, reichen die Einkünfte nicht. Meinen Garten, in welchem ich eine Baumschule und an 700 Arten fremder Gewächse kultiviere (ich bin auch Botaniker), muss ich größten theils selbst bearbeiten, und so bin ich auch Mechaniker u. verfertige mir alle nicht zu groben Geräthschaften zur Land- und Gartenwirtschaft u. auch meine Jagdflinten u. andre Dinge von Holz, Knochen u. Metall selbst.

Sie finden mich daher immer beschäftigt, bald bin ich Tischler, bald Schlosser und Büchsenmacher oder Drechsler, oder arbeite als Gärtner in meinem Garten oder bin Aufseher bei meinen Arbeitsleuten auf dem Felde [...]

Die Kupferplatten schleift und poliert mein alter Vater, und er druckt sie auch während des Winters ab, wozu er sich die Presse selbst gebauet hat. So sind denn nun, wenn im Winter die Feld- und Gartenarbeiten ruhen, die Arbeiten für unser Werk, als Zeichnen, Malen, Stechen, Drucken, Beschreiben der Vögel, unsere liebsten Beschäftigungen. Bloss der Druck des Textes u. das Illuminiren der Kupfer machen wir nicht selbst, das letztere geschieht nach von mir gemachten Vorlegeblättern. Der Winter ist denn auch die Zeit, in welcher ich naturhistorische Werke, Reisen und die neuesten Zeitschriften mit Musse studiren kann.«

Nach der lang ersehnten Reise an die Küste Norddeutschlands, nach Holstein und Sylt, die er im Jahre 1819 unternahm (sein Bericht darüber ist in diesem Band wiedergegeben), begann er die Arbeit an der *Naturgeschichte der Vögel Deutschlands.* Er war bislang davon ausgegangen, die Naturgeschichte des Vaters durch Nachträge allmählich ergänzen zu können, bis alle Vögel Deutschlands darin aufgenommen wären. Aber nun verwarf er diesen Plan und entschied sich für ein kühneres Vorhaben. Zwar sollten die Erkenntnisse des Vaters einbezogen werden, wie er in der Vorrede schrieb, aber das Ganze sollte von Grund auf neu konzipiert werden:

»Aufgefordert von Freunden und Verehrern der vaterländischen Ornithologie, und durch ein Zusammentreffen besonderer Umstände, entschloss ich mich zu der Bearbeitung eines solchen Werkes, wobei ich die früheren Arbeiten und Erfahrungen meines Vaters aus seiner *Naturgeschichte der Land- und Wasservögel des nördlichen Deutschland usw.*, an welchem Werke ich späterhin selbst Mitarbeiter war, und was von 1796 bis 1817 heftweise erschien und mit viel Beifall aufgenommen wurde, zum Grunde lege, oder vielmehr eine neue Auflage davon erscheinen lasse. Obschon der ganze Schatz jener Erfahrungen dieser neuen Auflage zur Basis dient, und die meinigen, seit mehr als zwanzig Jahren theils auf Reisen, theils an der Seite meines Vaters mühevoll gesammelt, ihr beigefügt, also das Praktische dieses deutschen Werks ansehnlich vermehrt werden soll; so wird es doch die hier mit ihm auf das Sorgfältigste verbundene Theorie der Wissenschaft, diese erste Stütze des Neulings, so umwandeln, dass die neue Ausgabe der alten nur in der Wahrheit, dem innern Gehalt nach gleich bleiben, aber von aussen her, in Hinsicht der Zusammenstellung der Materialien und das Ordnen derselben, ihr nicht mehr ähneln wird.«

Daraus sprechen sowohl die Pietät dem Vater gegenüber als auch die Entschlossenheit, ganz neu anzusetzen. Er stellte sich ein vierbändiges, handliches Werk vor und machte sich auf die Suche nach einem Verlag. Der junge Leipziger Verleger Ernst Fleischer hatte ihn 1817 in Ziebigk aufgesucht, und mit ihm schloß er nun einen Verlagsvertrag, der vorsah, daß die vier Bände (wie immer in verschiedenen »Lieferungen«) in den Jahren 1818 bis 1821 erscheinen sollten. Er wollte die meisten der für das Werk des Vaters verwendeten Tafeln wiederverwenden. Aber die Arbeit

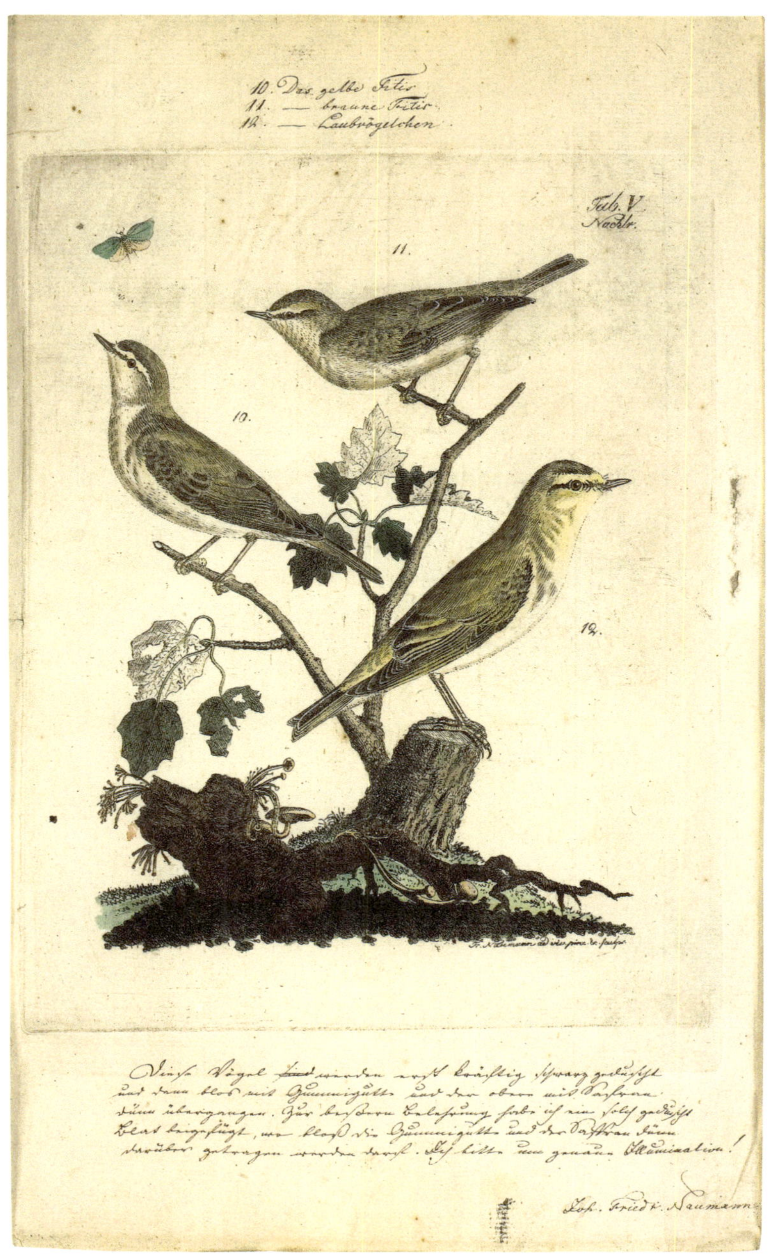

zog sich länger hin, als er angenommen hatte, und um es sich ein wenig leichter zu machen, überließ er die Kolorierung der Stiche einem Mitarbeiter. Die ökonomische Situation des Gutes war schwierig, auch das trug dazu bei, daß Naumann nicht recht vorankam. Die Hoffnungen der anhaltinischen Landwirte auf eine Verbesserung ihrer Lage wurden bei der Inthronisierung des neuen Herzogs im Jahre

Fitis, Zilpzalp, Waldlaubsänger — mit handschriftlicher Anweisung für die Kolorierung des Kupferstichs von Johann Friedrich Naumann

1818 enttäuscht: Auch dieser Herrscher änderte nichts an den hohen Abgaben und den Frondiensten, die viele Bauern zum Aufgeben zwangen. Immerhin erteilte er seinem berühmten Untertan Johann Friedrich Naumann die ungewöhnliche Erlaubnis, überall in Anhalt-Köthen Vögel zu schießen.

Eine der inhaltlichen Fragen, mit denen Naumann zu kämpfen hatte, betraf die Klassifizierung. Die gesamte Vogelkunde der damaligen Zeit litt unter diesem ungelösten Problem. Wie viele Vogelarten (Spezies) gab es, und wie waren sie zu ordnen? Gegen Ende des 17. Jahrhunderts zählten die englischen Naturforscher Ray und Willughby etwa 500 Arten, nahmen aber mit britischem Realismus an, daß es noch eine Menge unentdeckter Spezies gebe. Charles Lucien Bonaparte (ein Neffe Napoleons, der zu Naumanns Zeiten lebte und diesen in Ziebigk besuchte) kam bereits auf etwa 7000 Arten. Bis Anfang des 20. Jahrhunderts stieg die Zahl auf 19 000, weil selbst bei kleinsten Abweichungen neue Spezies ausgerufen wurden. Erst um 1940 einigte sich die wissenschaftliche Welt auf das, was eine Spezies definiert, und die Zahl der Vogelarten fiel auf 8600. Heute geht man von etwa 10 000 existierenden Vogelspezies weltweit aus.

Naumann sträubte sich also ganz zu Recht gegen die zu komplizierten und immer neu entworfenen Systeme verschiedener »Naturphilosophen«, wie er sie nannte, darunter auch der strenge Christian Ludwig Brehm oder Friedrich Boie, der ältere Bruder von Heinrich, der ihn auf den Franzosen Savigny verwies. Dem wollte Naumann nicht folgen. Er wandte sich vor allem gegen die Einführung stets neuer Arten und Unterarten. An Boie schrieb er:

»Warum will man denn eines einzigen kleinen Unterschiedes willen im Bau des Nasenloches oder eines anderen Theils wegen sogleich eine neue Gattung (*Genus*), wenn die Art übrigens in allem mit den anderen Arten übereinstimmt? [...] Das System, welches ich annehme, habe ich praktisch geprüft; es ist nach meiner Überzeugung hinreichend für Deutschland, das Weitere will ich gern anderen überlassen.« Er machte natürlich ein paar Fehler, aber im Großen und Ganzen hat ihm die Geschichte Recht gegeben.

Bald sah er ein, daß es mit vier Bänden nicht getan war, und so brachte es die *Naturgeschichte der Vögel Deutschlands* im Lauf von fünfundzwanzig Jahren auf zwölf Bände. Der fünfte Band war 1826 vervollständigt, dann trat eine längere Pause ein. Krankheiten und Todesfälle innerhalb der Familie hielten ihn auf, so daß erst 1833 die Lieferung des sechsten Bandes folgte, dann allerdings kam schon 1834 der siebente. Die Arbeit am achten unterbrach er, um eine seiner seltenen Reisen zu unternehmen — nach Ungarn. Ermöglicht wurde sie von einem neuen Freund Naumanns, dem Arzt und Apotheker Ludwig August Neubert, der ihn auch begleitete. Naumanns Ruhm war inzwischen bis nach Ungarn vorgedrungen, und er wurde dort mit großer Ehrerbietung empfangen. In einer ungarischen Zeitschrift hieß es: »Unsere Stadt [Pest] ist so glücklich, seit längerer Zeit Herrn Johann Friedrich Naumann hier zu sehen, der als berühmtester Ornithologe beinahe in der ganzen gebildeten Welt bekannt ist [...]« Naumann blieb neun Wochen. Nach Ziebigk zurückgekehrt und beglückt von der Vielfalt der ungarischen Vogelwelt, schrieb er einen Aufsatz mit dem Titel »Ornithologische Reise nach und durch Ungarn«, der 1837 in Wiegmanns *Archiv für Naturgeschichte* abgedruckt wurde.

Der neunte Band erschien 1838. Er bereitete Naumann einiges Kopfzerbrechen, denn es ging um die Möwen und Seeschwalben, und er hatte nur wenig unmittelbare Erfahrung mit Seevögeln. Deshalb wollte er unbedingt noch einmal ans Meer, am liebsten nach Helgoland, denn die Insel war ihm von befreundeten Vogelkundlern immer wieder empfohlen worden. »Ich gestehe, dass ich mit Zagen an die Bearbeitung der Sternen [Seeschwalben] und Meven [Möwen] gehe, weil der Scrupel hier gar zu viele sind, und die meisten sich nur in der lebenden Natur beseitigen lassen, durch vergleichende Beobachtungen eines ganz geübten Forschers. Was ich im Stande war, habe ich getan, aber es ist leider nicht viel, weil ich nicht die Zeit darauf verwenden konnte und nicht oft genug solche Orte zu besuchen vermochte, an welchen sich so manches hätte in's Reine bringen lassen.«

1840 brach er nach Helgoland auf. Es gab jetzt eine Eisenbahnstrecke von Köthen nach Magdeburg, und von Magdeburg aus konnte man nach Hamburg fahren und von dort weiter mit dem Dampfschiff nach Helgoland. Naumann war begeistert von Helgoland — er beobachtete dort nicht nur die Seeschwalben und Möwen, sondern auch die Lummen, die er im elften Band zu bearbeiten hatte. »Schwerlich möchte für Deutschland ein zweites Plätzchen aufzufinden sein, das, hinsichtlich unserer vaterländischen Vögelkunde, zu einer solchen Fundgrube für die Wissenschaft werden könnte oder bereits geworden ist, als das kleine Felseneiland Helgoland.«

Im Sommer 1844 war es schließlich vollbracht, auch der zwölfte Band konnte gedruckt werden. Sehr zur Freude des Verlegers Philipp Mainoni, der die Nachfolge von Ernst Fleischer angetreten hatte. Die bereits vorliegenden Bände hatten sich

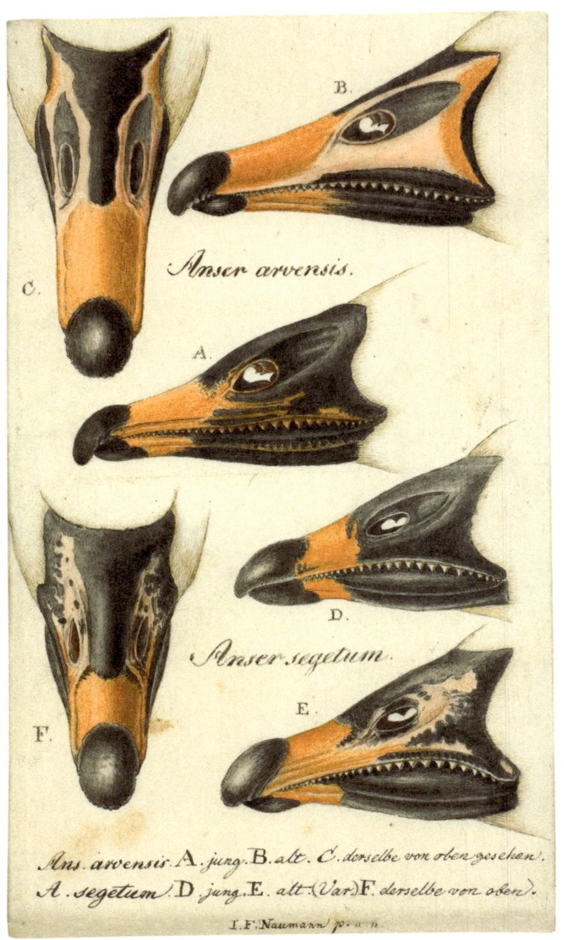

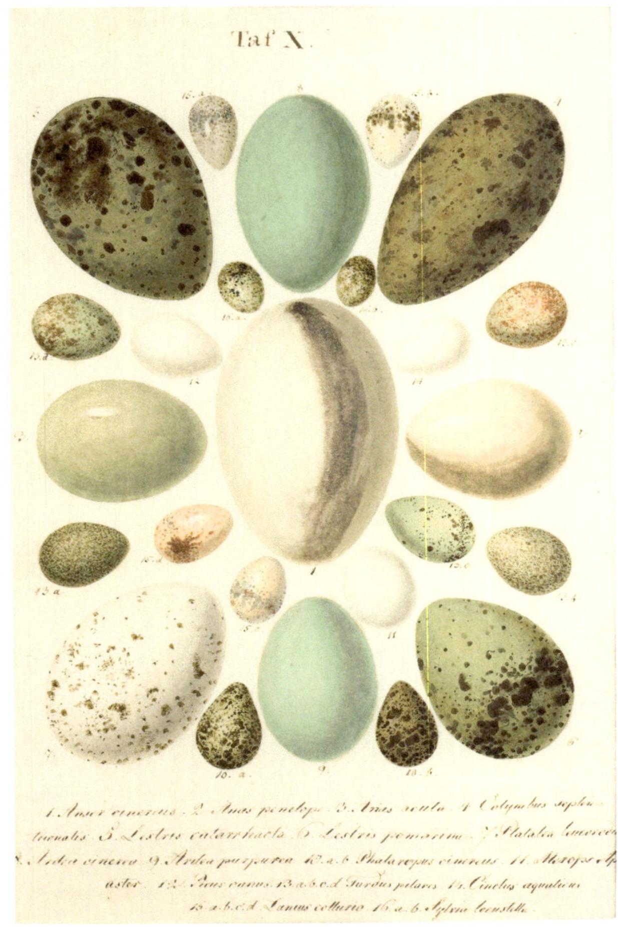

aufgrund des wachsenden Ruhms ihres Verfassers gut verkauft, so daß der Verleger von sich aus das Honorar erhöhte.

»Es muss mir in der Tat die grösste Freude gewähren, mit Hülfe des Höchsten, endlich im vorliegenden zwölften Theile den Schluss meiner Naturgeschichte der Vögel Deutschlands errungen zu haben«, schrieb Naumann, »eines Werkes, für das ich mein ganzes Leben gelebt, in welchem ich seit einem Vierteljahrhundert meine Erfahrungen niedergelegt habe.«

Diese zwölf Bände waren in der Tat Johann Friedrichs Lebenswerk, eine erstaunliche Leistung in wissenschaftlicher, sprachlicher und künstlerischer Hinsicht. Naumann war auf dem Stand der Wissenschaft seiner Zeit, und man weiß nicht, was man mehr bewundern soll: die Kraft und Kreativität seines sprachlichen Ausdrucks oder die Schönheit und Natürlichkeit seiner Vogelbilder.

Studie von Gänseschnäbeln
Tafel mit fünfundzwanzig Vogeleiern

Über die Grundlagen seiner Arbeit, die »Ingredienzien des Forschers«, schrieb der aufrechte Baldamus voller Verehrung, aber ohne Übertreibung: »Naumann war Beobachter wie keiner, und wurde darin vielleicht nur teilweise von seinem Bruder Carl Andreas übertroffen. Ein fester, abgehärteter Körper, Kunstfertigkeit der Hände, ein scharfes Auge, ein gebildetes Ohr, ein klarer Verstand, ein treues Gedächtnis, verbunden mit scrupulösester Wahrheitsliebe und Gewissenhaftigkeit, und das alles vereinigt und zugespitzt in der Liebe zur Natur, welche zum unwiderstehlichen Beobachtungstriebe wird: das sind die Ingredienzien, welche den praktischen Forscher bilden. Ein so organisierter Geist musste früh einsehen, dass keine einzelne Wissenschaft oder Kunst ohne Zusammenhang mit dem übrigen denkbar ist. Und so hatte er denn von Jugend auf das lebendigste Interesse für alles Göttliche und Menschliche. Das eifrigste Selbststudium ergänzte nach und nach die Lücken seiner Schulbildung. Das Gesamtgebiet der Naturwissenschaften zog ihn vor allem mächtig an. Um die neueren Werke seiner speziellen Studien lesen zu können, trieb er auch neuere Sprachen, und seine auserlesene, wenn auch nicht grosse Bibliothek beweist am besten, wie das ›nicht unter Bücher begraben sein mögen‹ keineswegs als ausgesprochene Scheu vor der Buchgelehrsamkeit zu verstehen ist.«

Die Darstellungen der Vögel waren klar und elegant, von großer Grazie und Natürlichkeit, der Hintergrund und die abgebildeten Pflanzen entsprachen immer dem Habitat jedes Vogels. »Die ornithologische Vollkommenheit dieser Naumannschen Tafeln«, schreibt Claus Nissen in seinem 1953 erschienenen Werk *Die illustrierten Vogelbücher,* »die zu den lebendigsten und sorgfältigsten Vogeldarstellungen überhaupt zählen und keine einzige Kopie, sondern nur Originale nach lebenden oder frisch geschossenen Stücken enthalten, ist von den anderen Werken jener Zeit nicht erreicht worden [...] Die sorgfältige Ausmalung macht diese *Naturgeschichte der Vögel Deutschlands* [...] rein äußerlich zum schönsten deutschen Vogelbuch, das unter bibliophilen Gesichtspunkten wohl eine Auferstehung mittels heutiger Reproduktionstechniken verdienen könnte. Es hat immerhin Goethe, der auch auf diesem Gebiet einige Kennerschaft besaß, zu fast begeisterter Anerkennung hingerissen.« Man kommt nicht umhin, noch einmal zu betrauern, daß die Kupferplatten, die einen Neudruck ermöglichen würden, für immer verloren sind.

Aber wie sich bei einem Besuch des kleinen Naumann-Museums im Köthener Schloß herausstellte, existiert noch ein großer Teil der Aquarelle, die Naumann als Grundlage für seine Kupferstiche dienten. Sie sind zu einem Arbeitsbuch provisorisch zusammengebunden, dem man die Spuren von Naumanns Arbeit noch ansieht. In den Farben von erstaunlicher Frische, zeigen diese Aquarelle, was für ein großer Künstler Naumann gewesen ist. Viele der Äste oder Steine, auf denen die Vögel sitzen, sind nur mit dem Bleistift angedeutet, so daß man Naumanns Arbeitsweise nachvollziehen kann. Manche der Hintergründe sind dagegen wunderbar ausgearbeitet, tauchen in dieser Form aber nicht in den Kupferstichen auf. Dieses in schmucklose, verschmutzte Deckel gebundene Arbeitsbuch Johann Friedrich Naumanns ist eine aufregende Entdeckung, denn bisher kannte außer dem Direktor des Naumann-Museums kaum jemand diese Aquarelle. Sie sind noch nie veröffentlicht worden. Wir stellen in diesem Band zum ersten Mal achtzig von ihnen vor.

Ich kann mir vorstellen, daß Goethes Begeisterung ebensosehr Naumanns Sprache wie dessen Fähigkeit als Maler galt. Denn stilistisch vollbrachte Naumann Wunder sowohl in der Schilderung von Gestalt und Federkleid jedes behandelten Vogels als auch in der Wiedergabe des Gesangs und der Rufe. Nie zuvor und nie danach hat jemand so klar und schön, so sprachschöpferisch und treffend über Vögel geschrieben. Hier ist, um nur ein Beispiel zu geben, die Beschreibung des Gänsesägers. Wenn Naumann vom »alten Männchen« spricht, meint er damit einfach den erwachsenen Vogel.

»Ein ausserordentlich schönes Geschöpf ist das alte Männchen in seinem Pracht- oder Hochzeitskleide, in welchem das Rot am Schnabel und den Füssen in höchster Lebhaftigkeit prunkt. Der Kopf mit seiner einfachen, buschigen und gerundeten Holle und der Hals bis gegen die Mitte seiner Länge herab sind tief schwarz, mit prächtigem, goldgrünem Schiller, welcher in verschiedenem Lichte etwas ins Violette und Stahlblaue spielt, dieser Glanz jedoch nicht stärker als bei dem alten Männchen der gemeinen Schellente, mit dem auch der ganze Bau des Kopfputzes übereinstimmt; das Übrige des Halses, Kropf, Brust und Bauch, die Tragefedern und von der Schulterpartie ein breiter Streifen längs dem Flügel weiss mit sanftem Anhauch einer lieblichen reinen Aurorafarbe, welcher an den unteren Teilen des Rumpfes am deutlichsten, am After und der unteren Schwanzdecke aber stets matter erscheint; der Oberrücken und die hintere größere Hälfte der Schulterpartie der Länge nach, nebst ihrer langen, über die Hinterschwingen sich legenden Spitze, samtschwarz; der Unterrücken und Bürzel hell schieferblaugrau, an den Seiten des letzteren und des Bauches in abwechselnd schiefergraue und weisse Wellenlinien, Zickzacks und Pünktchen sich auflösend; die Oberschwanzdecken schieferblaugrau, zunächst den schwarzen Schäften etwas dunkler, ebenso die Schwanzfedern, jedoch noch dunkler, aber ihre untere Seite hell silberblaugrau und hier mit weissen Schäften.«

Eines der besten Beispiele für die Wiedergabe eines Gesanges findet sich im Text dieses Buches, wo es um das Lied der »Nachtigall der Sumpfgebiete«, des Sumpfrohrsängers, geht. Auch die Schilderung der Rufe des Großen Brachvogels, ebenfalls im Text, ist wunderschön. Hier ist die Amsel oder Schwarzdrossel:

»Das Männchen hat einen lauten, vortrefflichen Gesang und gehört unter die vorzüglichsten Singvögel unseres Landes. Dieser Gesang hat mehrere Strophen, die sie in kurzen Intervallen aufeinander folgen lassen, worunter aber leider einige zirpende und heisere Töne mit hellpfeifenden abwechseln, aber ein lautes flötenartiges Tra-tütratatö, das man auch mit den Worten: David, Hans David vergleicht, sich besonders auszeichnet und weit hörbar ist. Sie beleben durch diesen etwas melancholischen Gesang besonders die stillen Abende des ersten Frühlings auf eine höchst angenehme Weise, singen zwar auch am Tage, besonders am frühen Morgen, doch meistens erst recht anhaltend gegen Abend, in der Dämmerung, bis es völlig Nacht geworden, in dieser aber nicht oder doch nur höchst selten. Vom März bis in den Juli singen sie ununterbrochen, am meisten an solchen Abenden, denen ein warmer oder schwüler Tag vorherging [...] Es gewährt einen unvergleichlichen Genuss, nach einem heiteren Frühlingstage den Abend in einem schönen Laubholzwalde zuzubringen, wo die eben eintretende nächtliche Stille nur noch von den melancholischen Gesängen der Amsel und der Singdrossel unterbrochen wird; dies Konzert ist so anmutig, dass es manchen erfreut, der sonst nicht gewohnt ist, auf dergleichen Dinge zu achten.«

Solche Passagen lassen sich bei fast jeder beschriebenen Vogelart finden — man ist tatsächlich geradezu in Verlegenheit, wenn man Beispiele aussuchen soll. Sie ließen sich beliebig ergänzen.

Schon 1846, zwei Jahre nach Veröffentlichung der *Naturgeschichte der Vögel Deutschlands,* erschien Heft 1 der Nachträge, Heft 2 folgte 1847, die Hefte 3, 4 und 5 wurden 1851 veröffentlicht. Interessant ist, daß Naumann in den Heften 6 und 7 bei den Illustrationen zu Steindrucken überging — jene Technik, die Goulds Werkstatt angewandt hatte. Seit 1826 hatte Naumann damit experimentiert, war aber nie zufrieden — die Klarheit des Kupferstichs sagte ihm mehr zu.

1850 wurde die Gesellschaft Deutscher Ornithologen gegründet. Sie wählte Naumann zu ihrem Ehrenvorsitzenden. Eine neue ornithologische Zeitschrift, die ein

Jahr zuvor, 1849, ins Leben gerufen worden war, trug den Titel »Naumannia«. Die zweite Versammlung der neuen Gesellschaft fand im September 1846 in Dresden statt. Naumann hielt einen Vortrag über die Abnahme der Vogelarten in Mitteldeutschland — schon damals ein Thema, das die Vogelkundler beschäftigte.

Von dieser Reise kehrte Naumann krank zurück, und er erholte sich nur langsam. An der dritten Versammlung, dieses Mal in Halle, konnte er jedoch wieder teilnehmen. Die politischen Wirren des Jahres 1848 warfen ihre Schatten voraus, und zu Naumanns Kummer waren nur dreizehn Ornithologen erschienen. In den Auseinandersetzungen um eine liberale Verfassung für das anhaltinische Herzogtum stand Naumann auf seiten der Reformer. Wie Baldamus offenbar einem frühen Biographen namens Röhl berichtete, konnte Naumann nichts mehr erregen als Frömmelei und religiöse Intoleranz. »Wo diese sich auch zeigten, da trat der sonst so freundliche und ruhige Mann mit einer Entschiedenheit, ja, man möchte sagen mit einer Heftigkeit auf, die seinem Charakter sonst völlig fremd war.« Als der alte Herzog starb und sein Nachfolger auf dem Thron, Alexander Karl von Anhalt-Bernburg, die von der Ständeversammlung mühsam erkämpfte neue Verfassung annullierte, kam es im März 1849 zu Unruhen, die schließlich zum Einmarsch preußischer Truppen führten.

Naumann war jetzt fast siebzig Jahre alt, und wie er dem Pastor Zander schrieb, brachten ihm »die Märzerrungenschaften Lärm aller Art und schlaflose Nächte sonder Zahl«. Es folgten ein paar ruhige Jahre, aber dann verschlechterte sich sein Gesundheitszustand deutlich. »Ich habe unterdessen mein 75tes Lebensjahr angetreten«, schreibt er 1854 an seinen Freund von Loebenstein, »bin bisher, Gott Lob, gesund geblieben, habe aber in den letzten Jahren bedeutend an Kräften, sowohl des Körpers, wie des Geistes abgenommen. Alles geht langsamer von statten und immer langsamer, bis es endlich gar aufhören wird, wie z. B. mit der Jagd.«

Im Winter desselben Jahres schickte er Baldamus fast schon einen Abschiedsbrief.

»Mein theurer Freund!

Alles hienieden ist vergänglich! Ich bin völlig Invalid! Kaum daß ich noch schreiben könnte, wenn ich nicht eine gute helle Stunde dazu abpaßte. Vom Zeichnen und Malen kann keine Rede mehr sein. O, das ist traurig! Das rechte Auge ist das kranke; aber es wirkt auch auf das gesunde linke, sodass ich oft ganz confus werde, zumal auch dieser Umstand den Kopf einnimmt und die Gedanken so abgestumpft hat, dass ich zuweilen dämmere wie ein Träumender [...]«

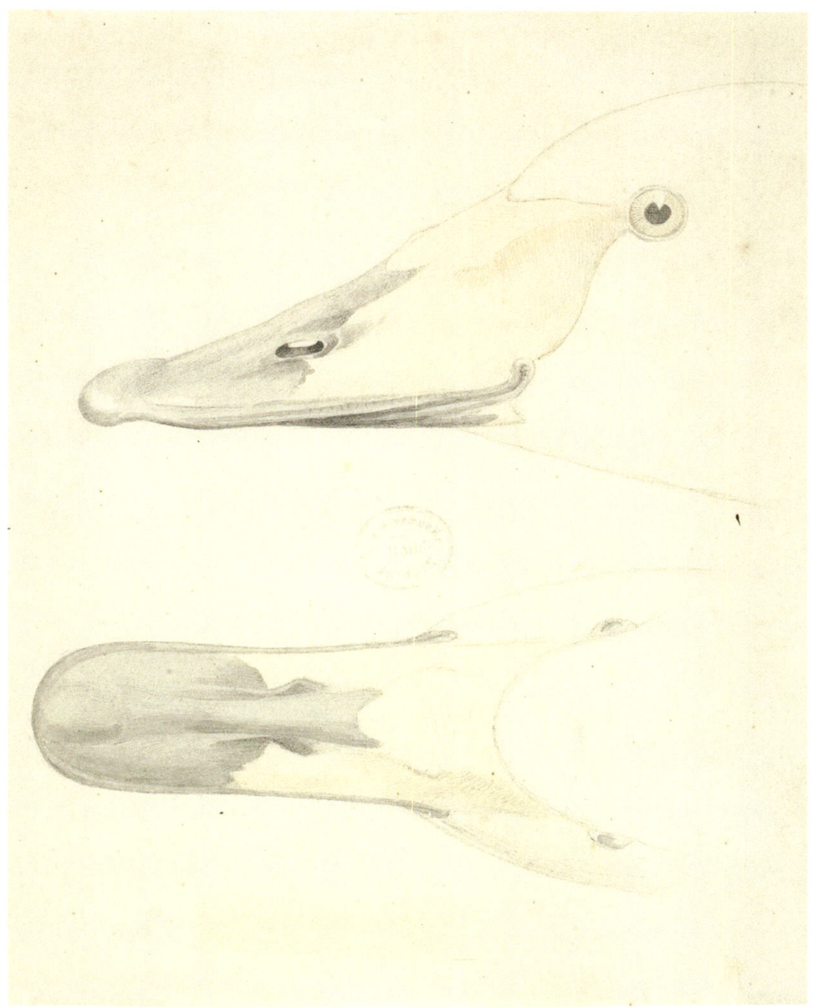

Sein Trost war die Musik. Bei Thomsen heißt es: »Seine besonderen Lieblinge waren Haydn, Mozart, C. M. von Weber, später auch Beethoven und Mendelssohn. Er selbst blies die Flöte, seine Söhne Julius und Edmund spielten Geige, der Lehrer Bernsdorf Klavier, und so erfüllten unserer Meister unsterbliche Töne an manchem Abend das still gewordene Haus.«

Das letzte Treffen der Ornithologengesellschaft, an dem Naumann teilnahm, war ihm zuliebe nach Köthen einberufen worden. Wie sehr er inzwischen in Ornithologenkreisen verehrt wurde, mag man daran ermessen, daß im Versammlungssaal eine mit Lorbeer bekränzte Büste von ihm aufgestellt worden war. Aber nur am ersten Tag beteiligte er sich an den Diskussionen um die akute Frage »Was ist eine Spezies?«,

Schnabelstudie vom Singschwan

dann kehrte er erschöpft nach Ziebigk zurück. Er starb am 15. August 1857. Der »liebe Mann und große Forscher«, wie Brehm ihn nannte, war tot.

»Naumann ist tot«, begann Pastor W. Pässler aus Brambach seinen Nachruf, »der Trauerruf geht durch die ornithologische Welt. Wer Naumann auf der Versammlung in Köthen gesehen, musste darauf vorbereitet sein, binnen kurzem die Trauerkunde von seinem Ableben zu vernehmen; gleichwohl lässt sie bei allen einen schmerzlichen Nachhall zurück.«

Zum hundertsten Geburtstag von Johann Friedrich Naumann, im November 1880, setzte die Naumann-Stiftung ihm ein Denkmal im Schloßgarten von Köthen. Geschaffen hatte es der Bildhauer Heinrich Pohlmann. Es trug seine Büste und an den Seiten auf runden Platten die Bildnisse des Vaters, Johann Andreas', und des Bruders, Carl Andreas'. Im Zweiten Weltkrieg wurde das Denkmal zerstört, die Kupferplatten eingeschmolzen. Heute steht dort wieder eine Büste. Auf dem einfachen weißen Quader, der sie trägt, steht: Professor Dr. Johann Friedrich Naumann, 1780–1857. Wie beim alten Denkmal wird an den Seiten ganz zu Recht an den Vater und den Bruder erinnert. Aber weder die Büste noch das Museum in Köthen haben etwas daran ändern können, daß heute kaum noch jemand weiß, wer dieser große Ornithologe und Vogelmaler war. Johann Friedrich Naumann ist ein vergessenes deutsches Genie.

Arnulf Conradi

Das Vorwort stützt sich auf die folgenden Werke:
Tim Birkhead: *The Wisdom of Birds,* London 2008 // Carl Richard Hennicke, Hg., Johann Friedrich Naumann: *Die Vögel Mitteleuropas,* Gera 1897–1905 // Isabella Tree: *The Ruling Passion of John Gould. A Biography of the Bird Man.* London 1991 // E. P. Richardson: *Painting in America,* New York 1956 // Howard Hughes: *American Visions,* New York 1997 // Marshall B. Davidson im Vorwort zu *The Original Water-Color Paintings of John James Audubon,* New York 1997 // Peter Thomsen: *Johann Friedrich Naumann, der Altmeister der deutschen Vogelkunde.* Leipzig 1956

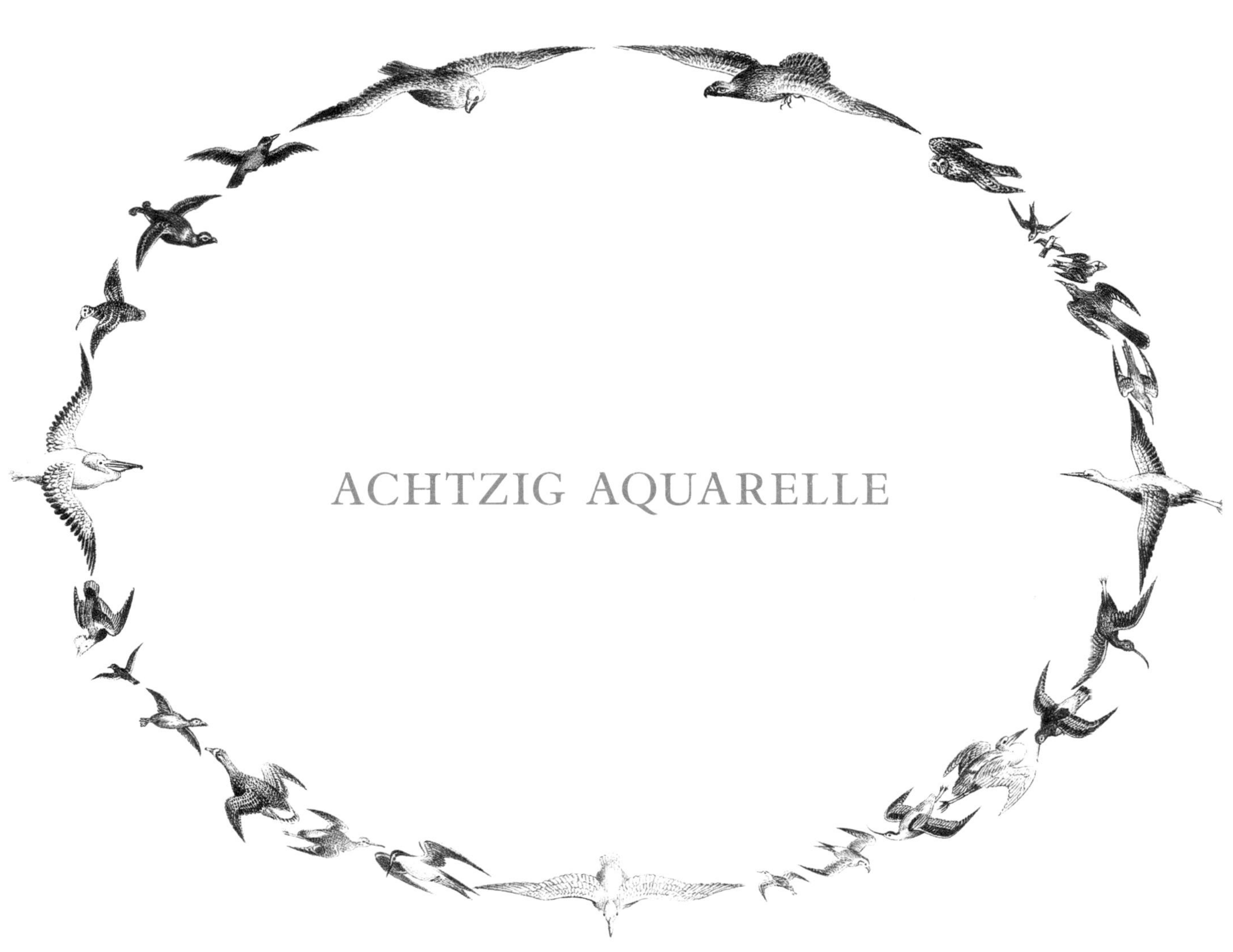

ACHTZIG AQUARELLE

Kaiseradler

~~Falco Aquila D. ... Adler~~

Falco imperialis. Königl. Adler

N 2

(20.)

Nach einem alten verschnittenen, viele Jahre auf dem Schloß zu Cöthen gehaltenen, auch bei Harzgerode am Harz im Tellereisen gefangenen Exemplar, ergänzend — gemalt v. J. F. Naumann 1799.

IV. 10.

Fischadler

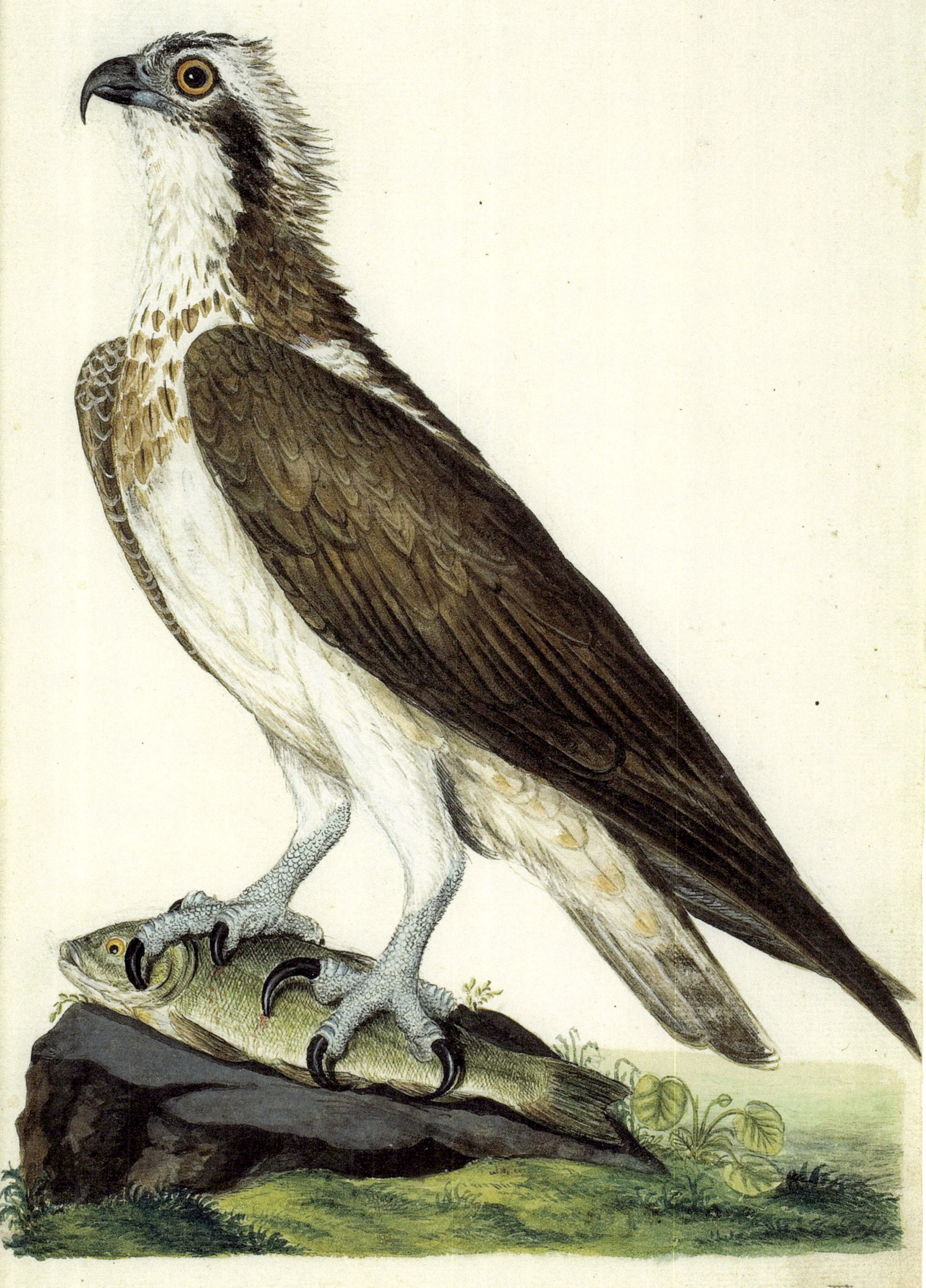
Falco Haliaetos L.
4
IV. 11.

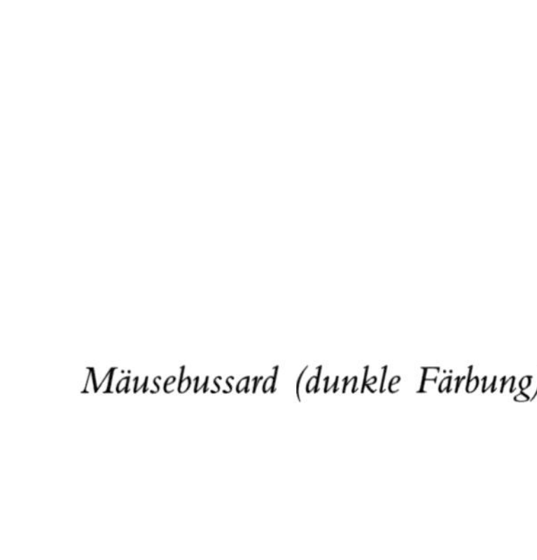

Mäusebussard (dunkle Färbung)

Falco Buteo Mäusebussard, d. dunkle Var.

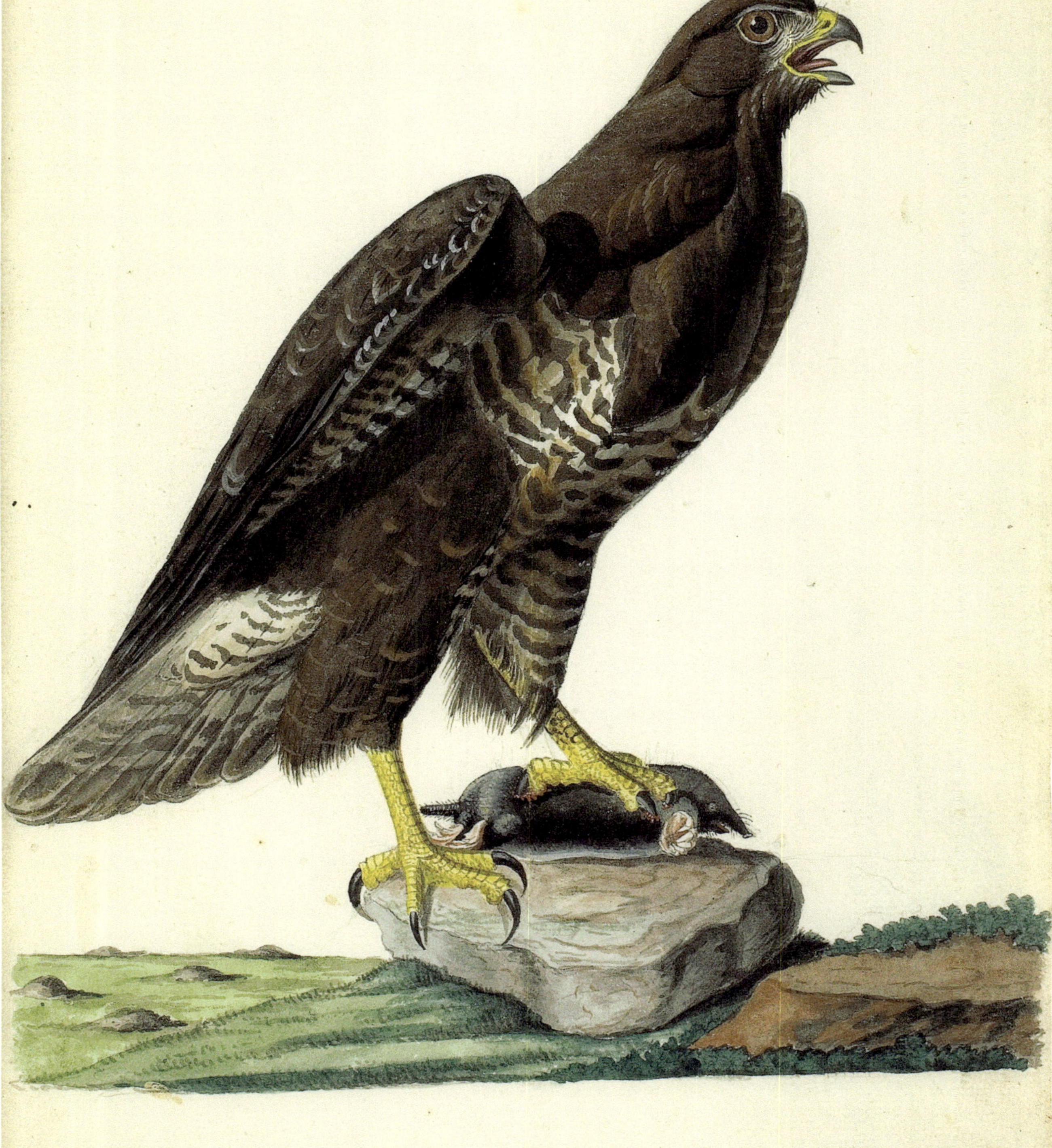

IV.24

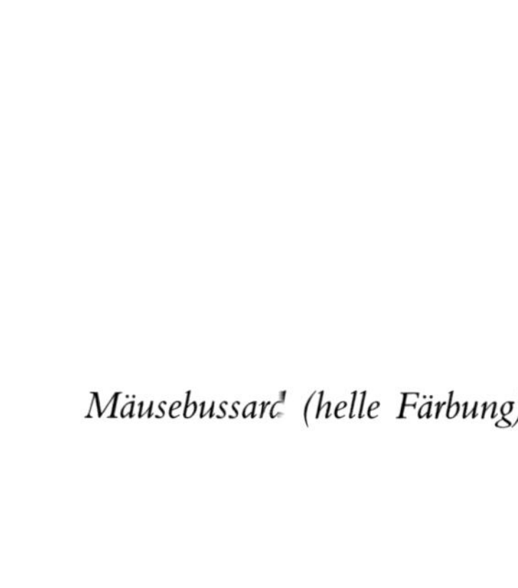

Mäusebussard (helle Färbung)

Falco Buteo. Mäusebussard. F. [illegible] Var. F. albidus, auctor.

IV25

Roh-weihe (♂)

14

Falco aeruginosus, L. Rohrweihe. (mas) sehr altes ♂.

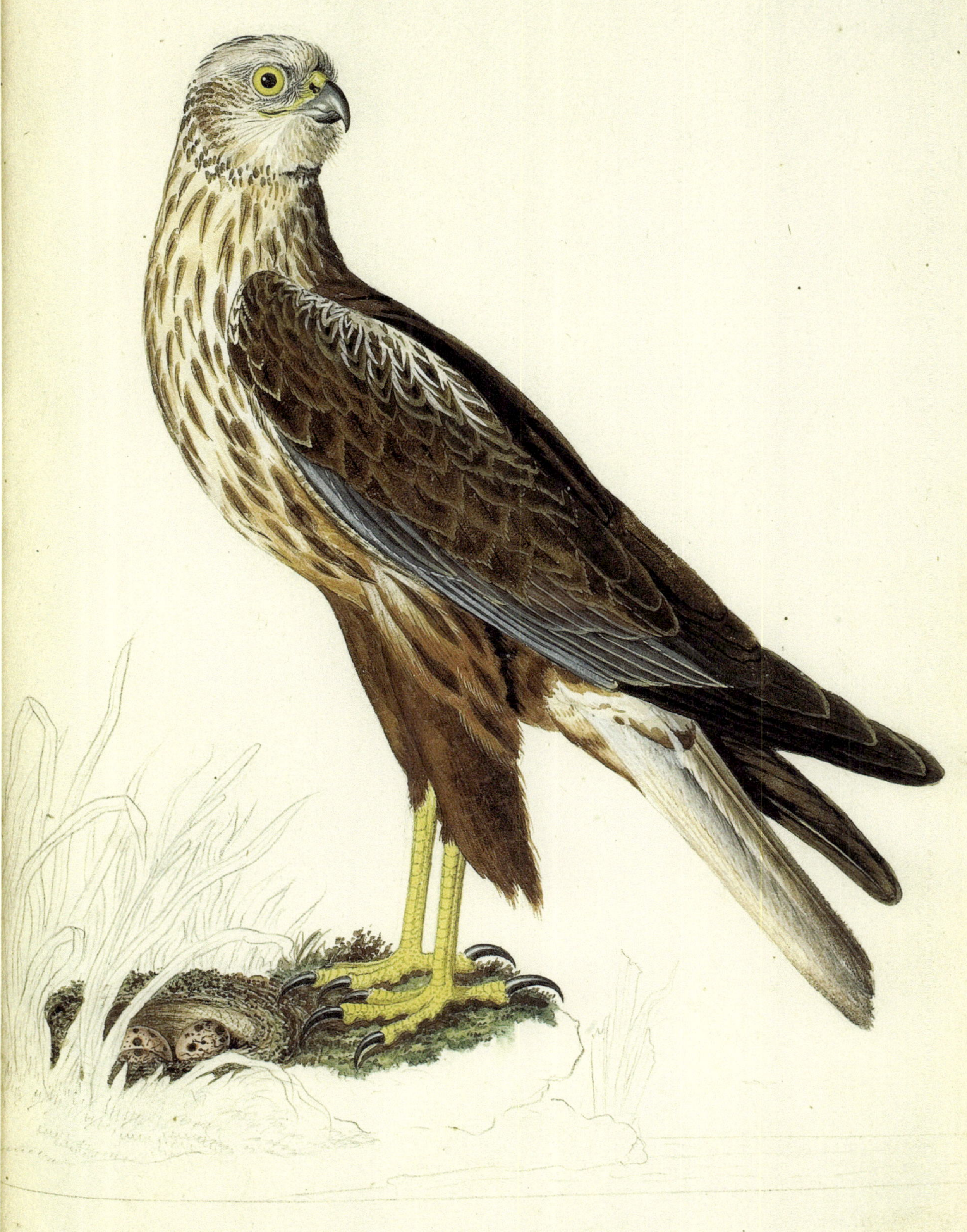

IV.22.

Rohrweihe (♀)

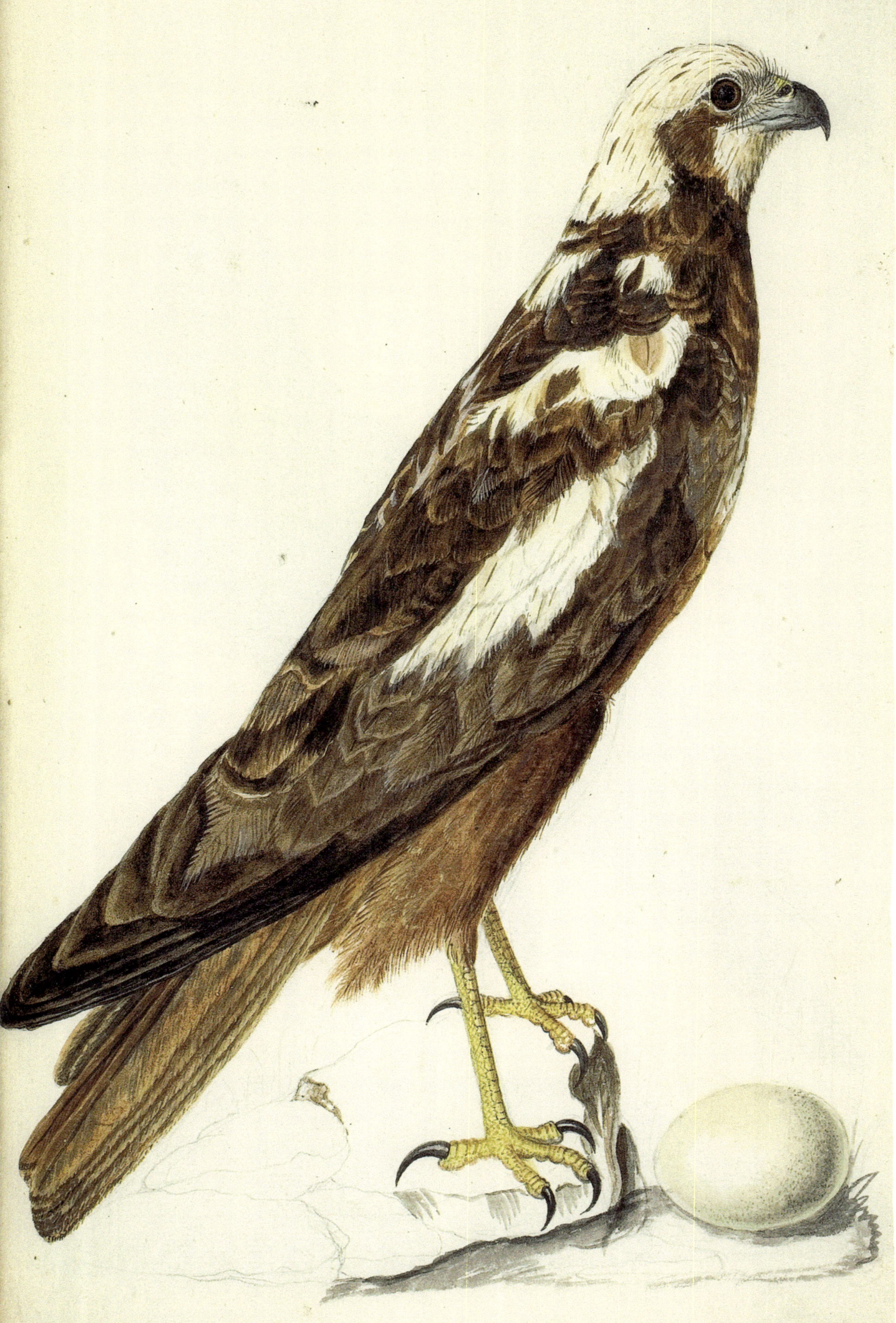
15
Falco aeruginosus. L. Rohrweihe. (fem.) alt.
IV.22.

Wanderfalke (♂)

Falco Subbuteo major. B. (mas.) Blaufalk. F. peregrinus, ad. ♂.

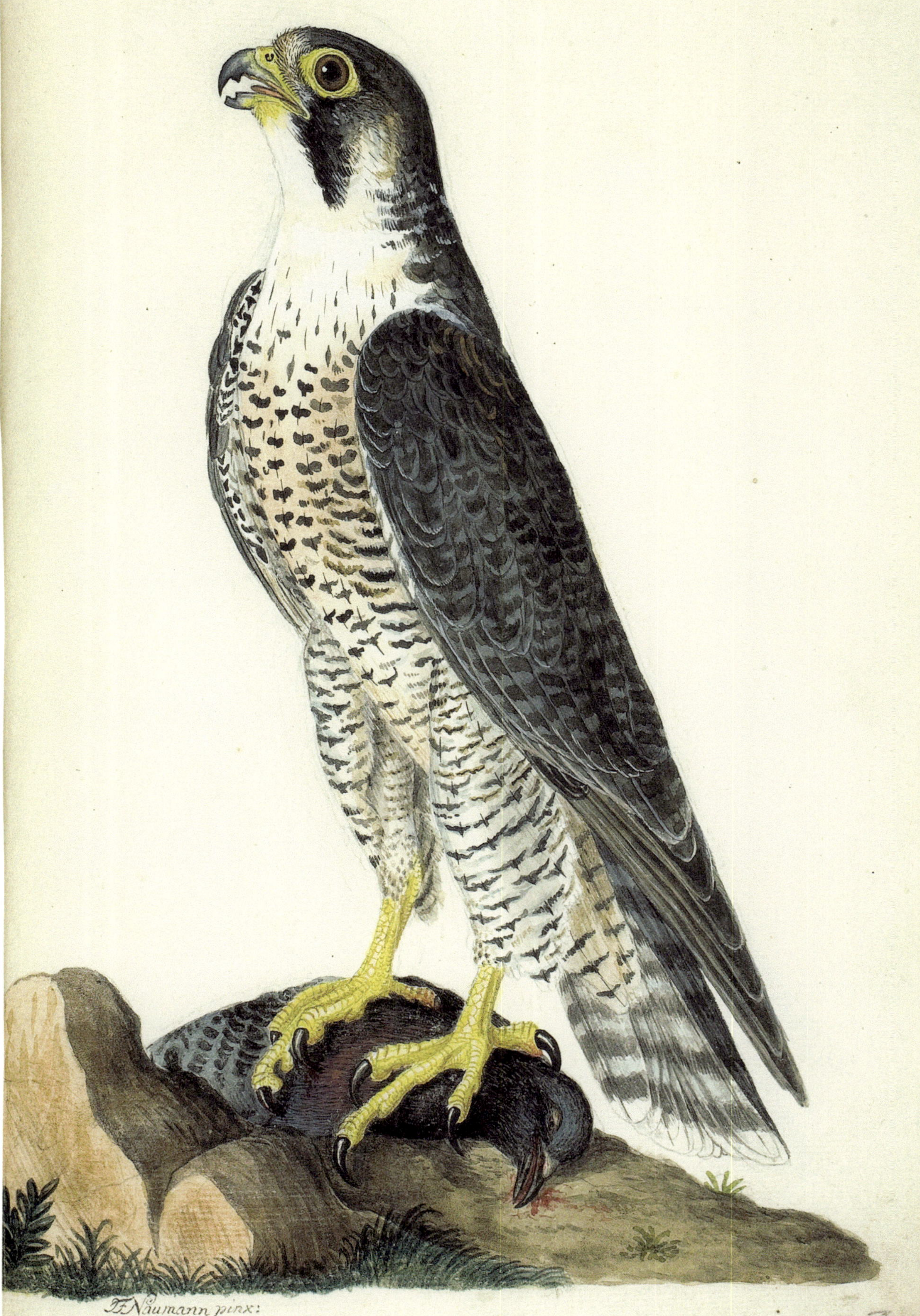

Sperber (♂)

Falco Nisus. L. Sperber (mas)

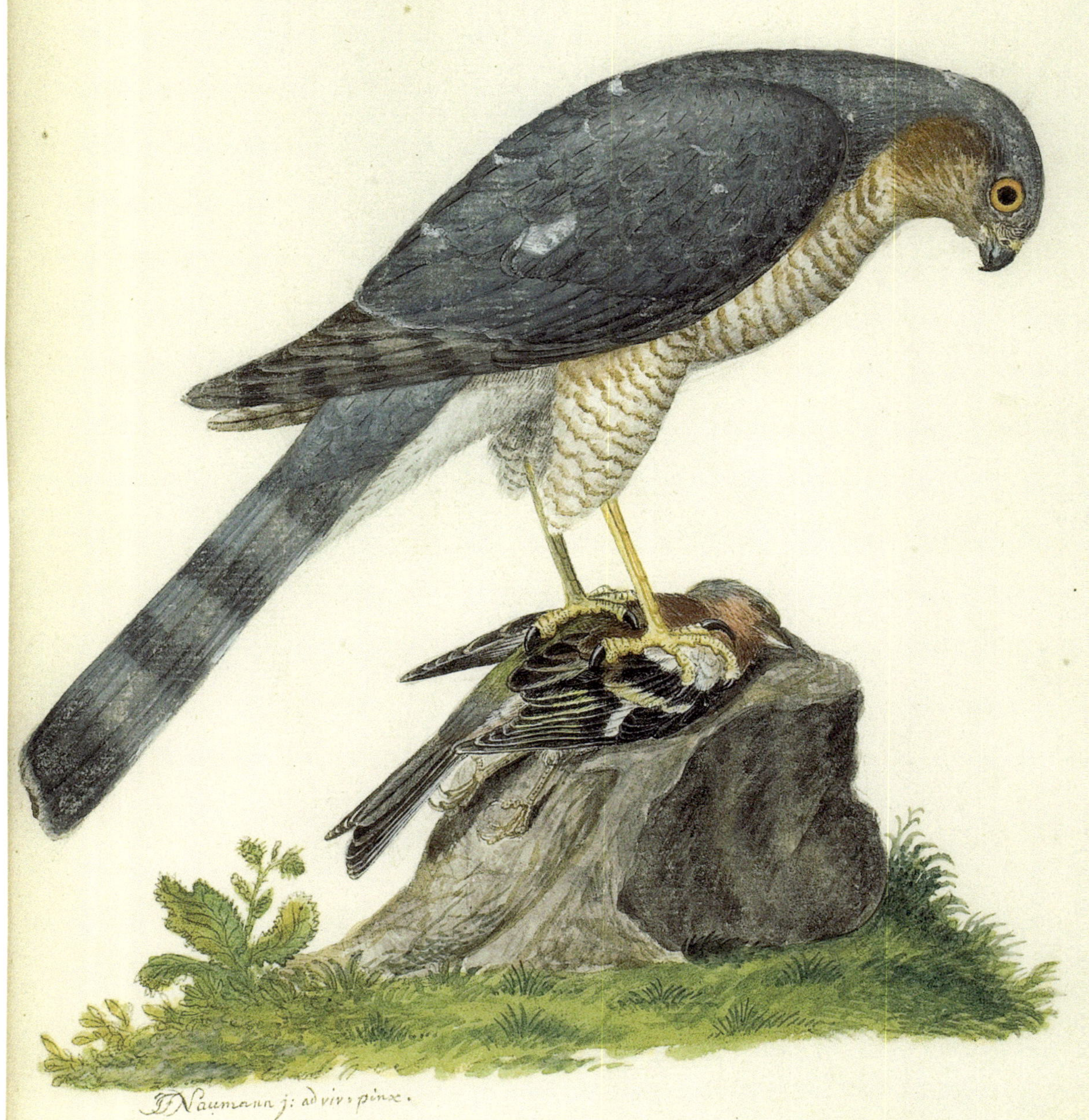

J.F. Naumann j: ad viv: pinx.

IV. 18

Turmfalke (♂)

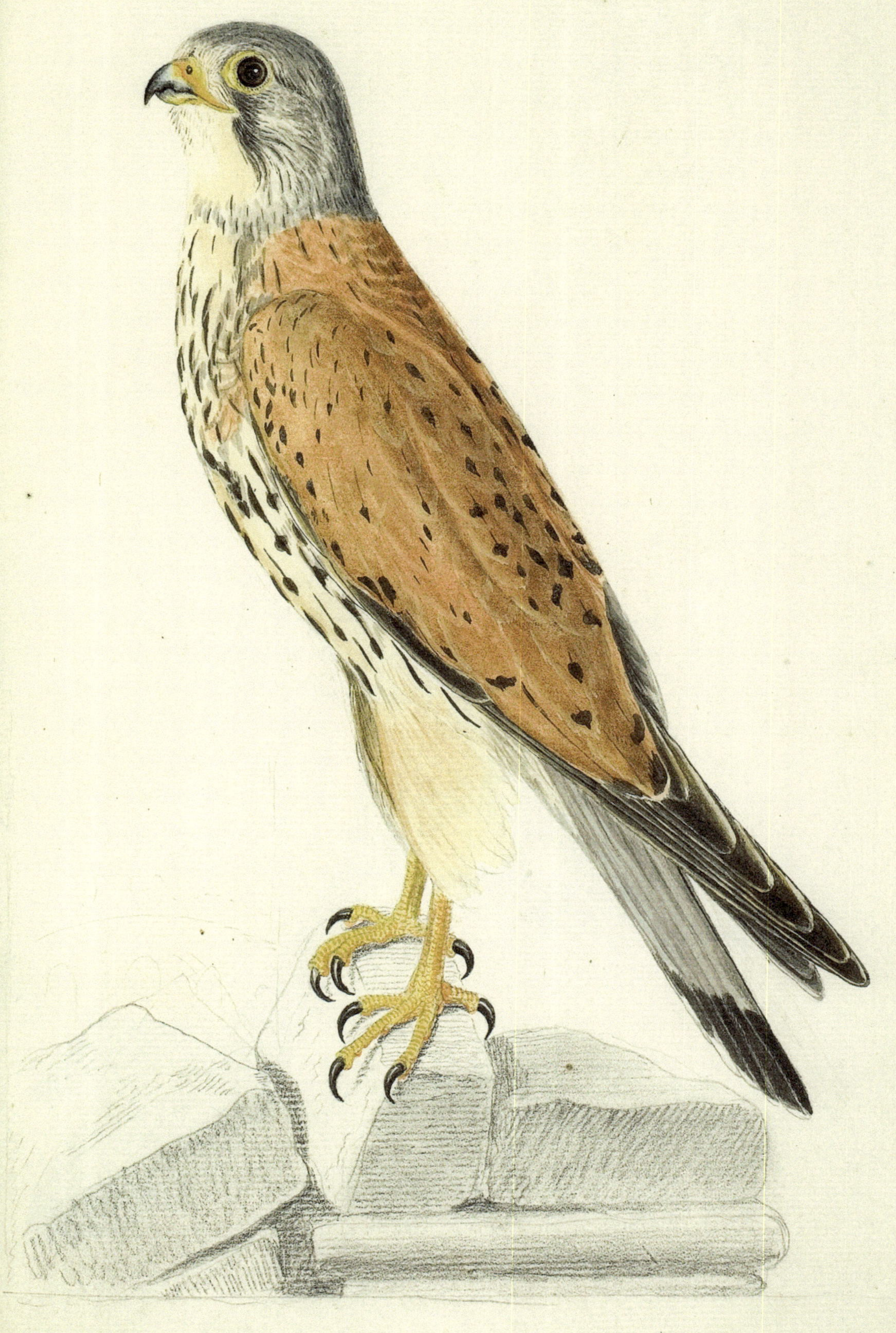
29
Falco Tinnunculus. h Kirchenfalke (mas) alt.
TP. 20.

Uhu (♀)

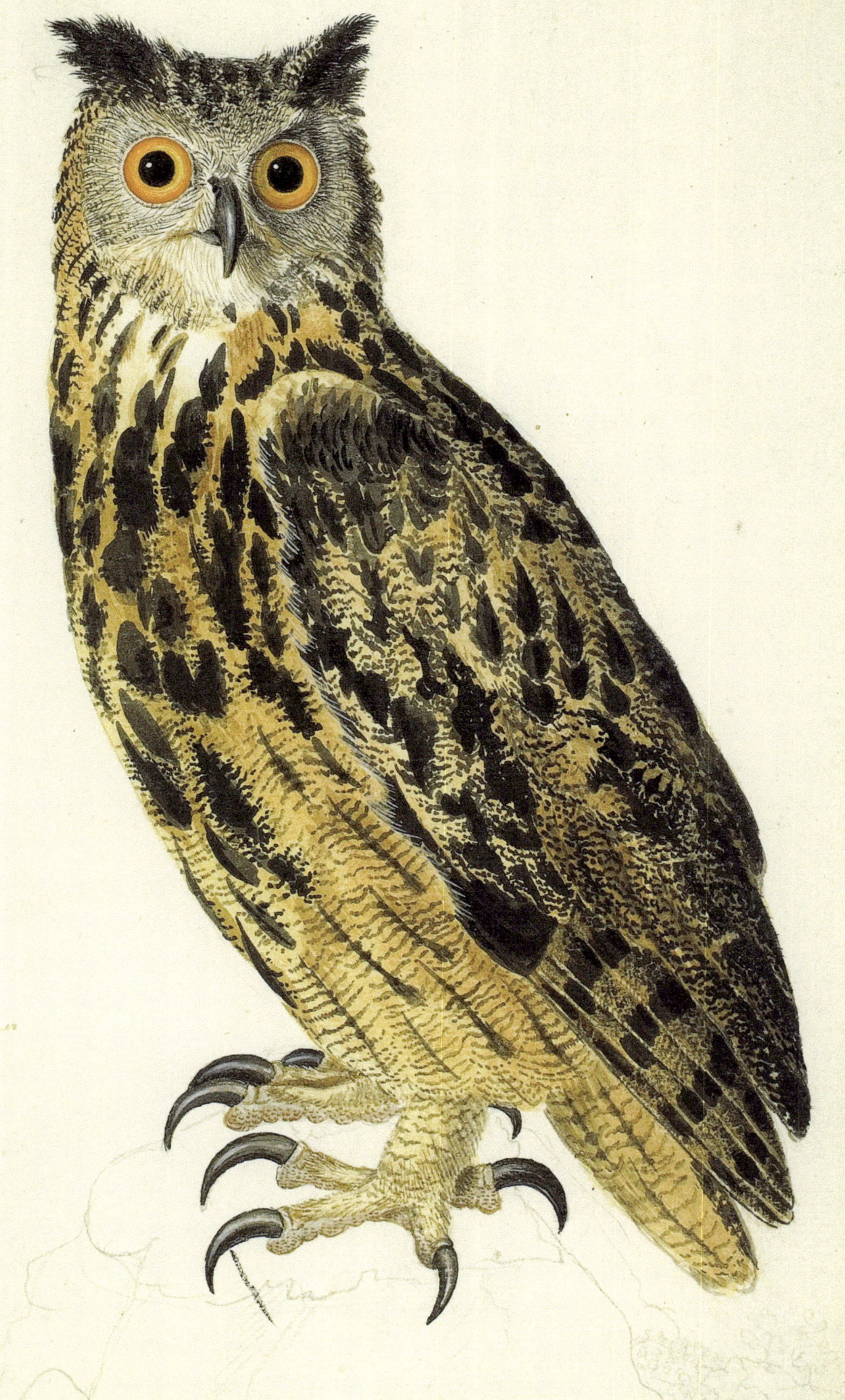
32
IV.28.

Waldohreule (♀)

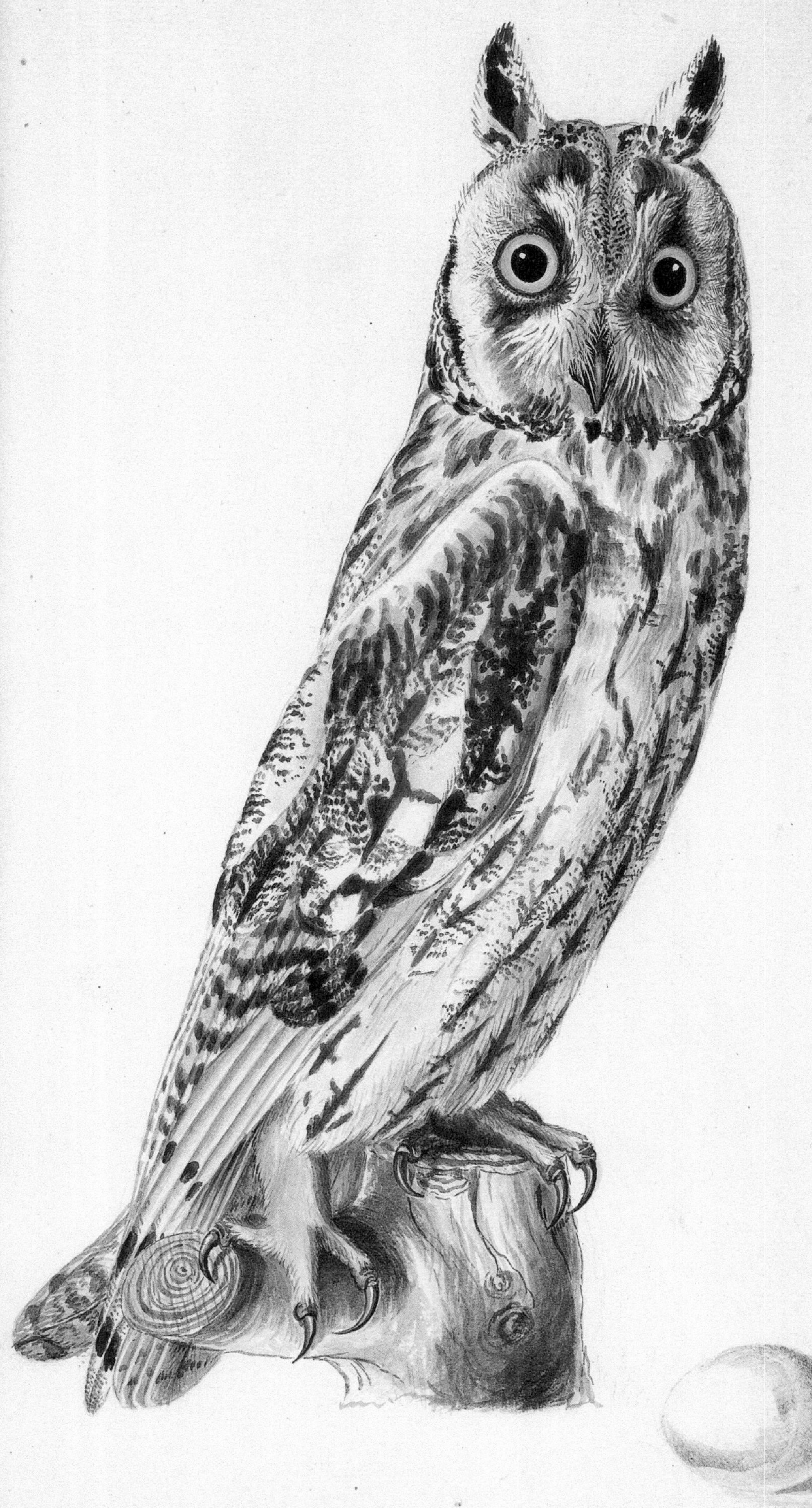
Strix Otus. Wald-Ohreule ♀
33
IV. 29.

Waldkauz (♂)

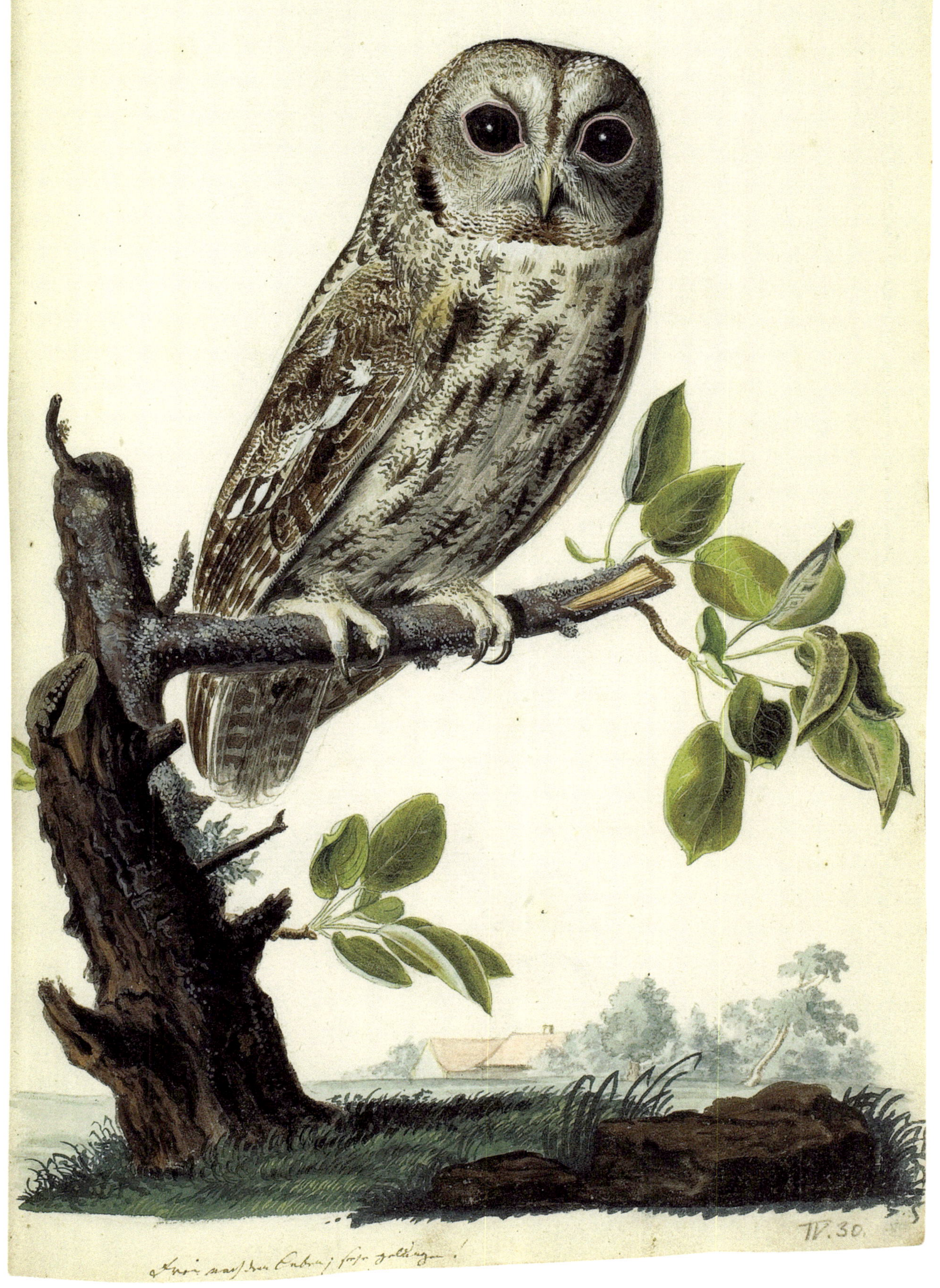
35
Strix Aluco. Waldkauz. alt. ♂
IV. 30.

Schleiereule (♂)

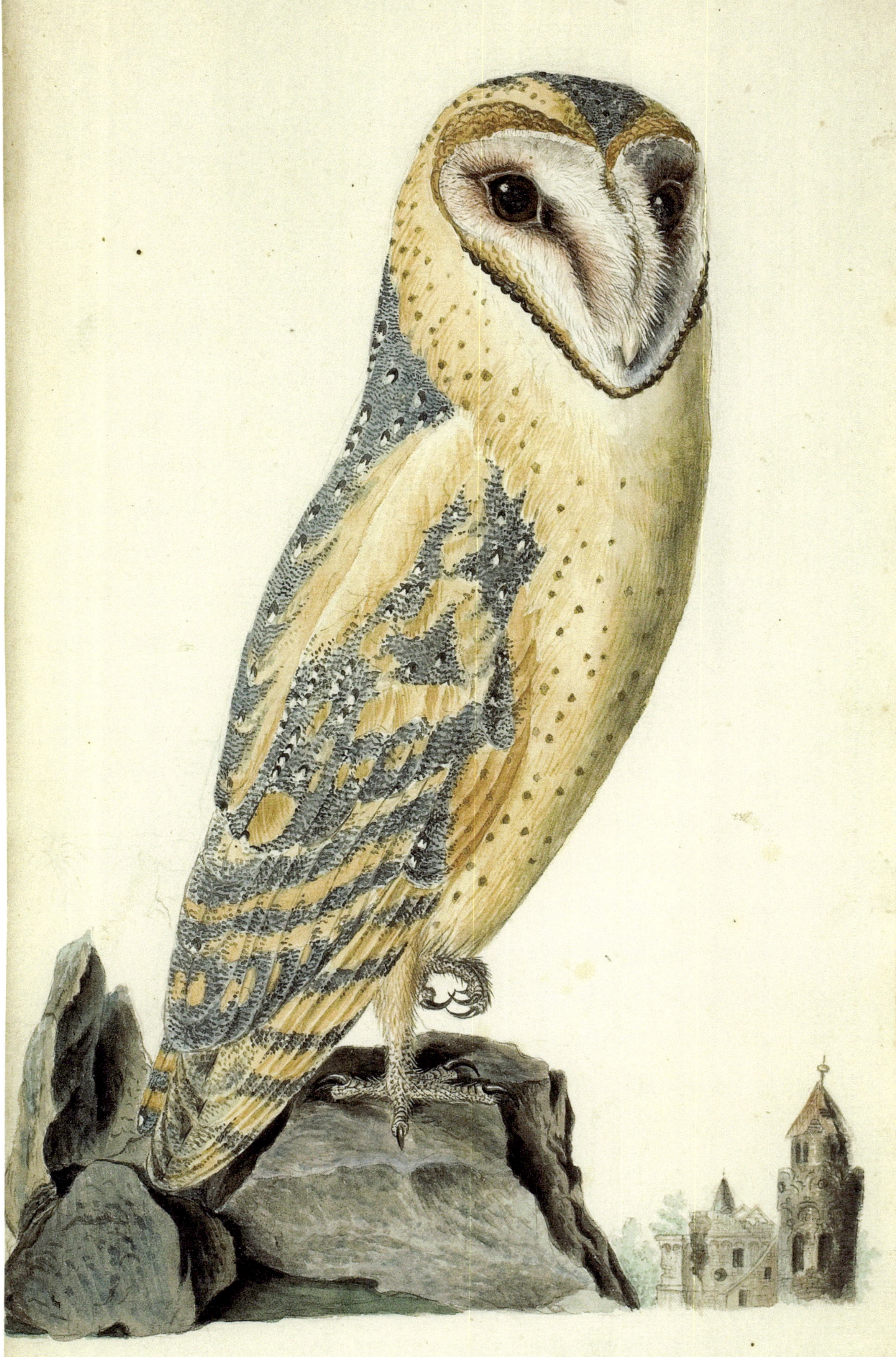
Strix flammea. Schleiereule. alt. ♂
38
TP. 31

Steinkauz (♀)

39

Strix noctua. Steinkauz. alt. ♀

Natürl. Grösse

IV. 32.

Rauhfusskauz (♂)

Strix Tengmalni. Rauchfüss-Kautz. ♂

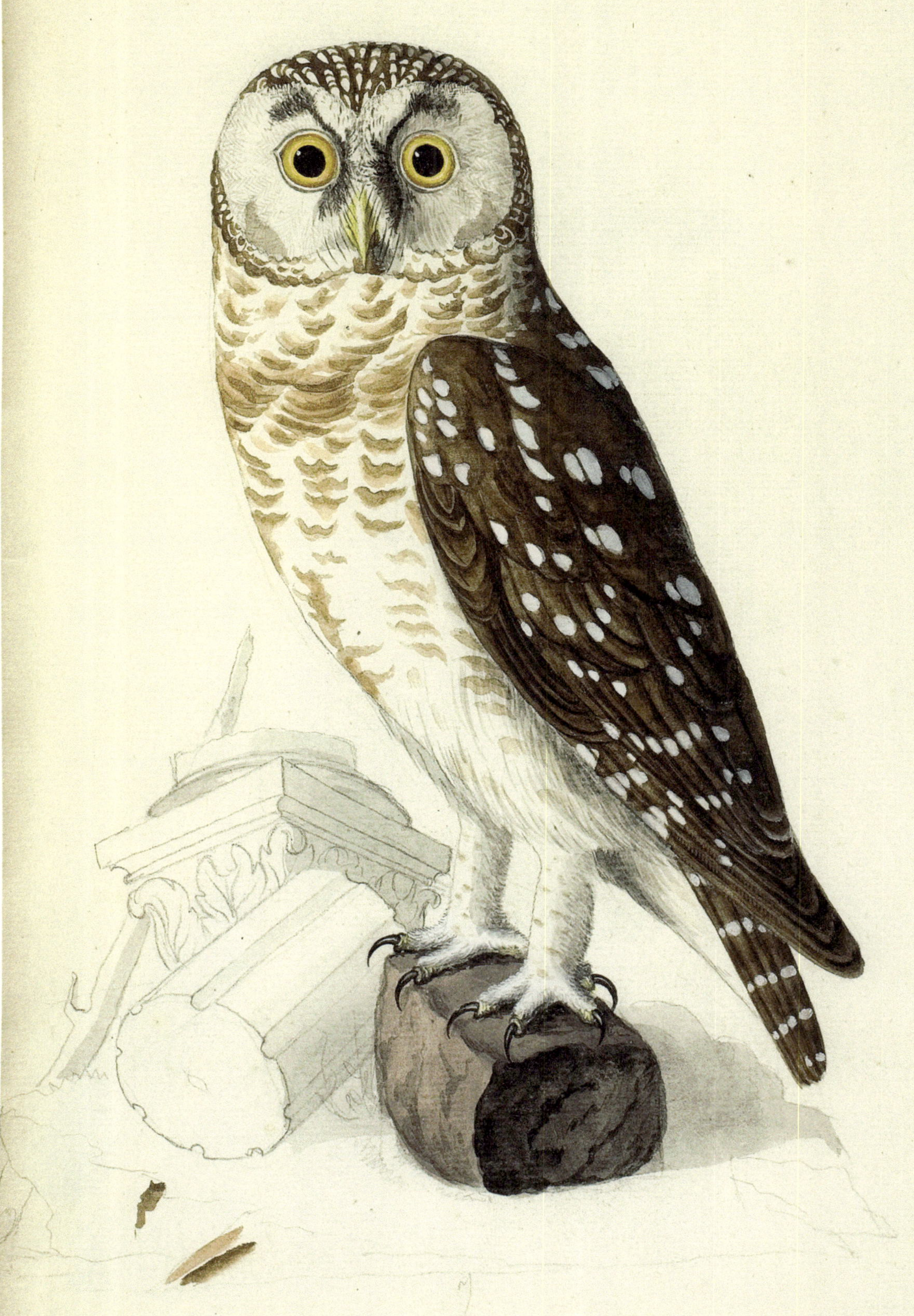

Oben: Schwarzstirnwürger (♂)
Unten: Rotkopfwürger (♂)

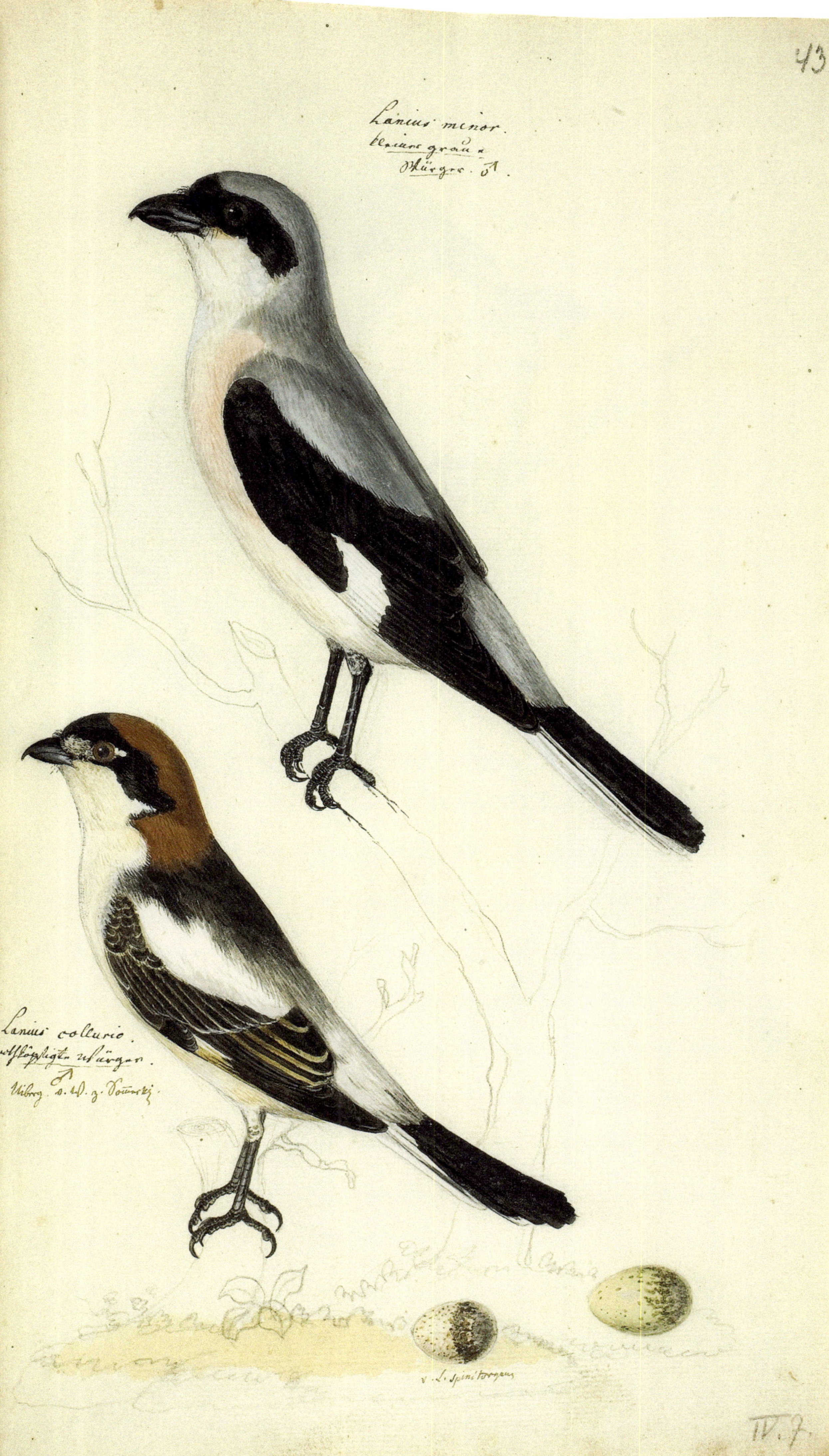

Nebelkrähe

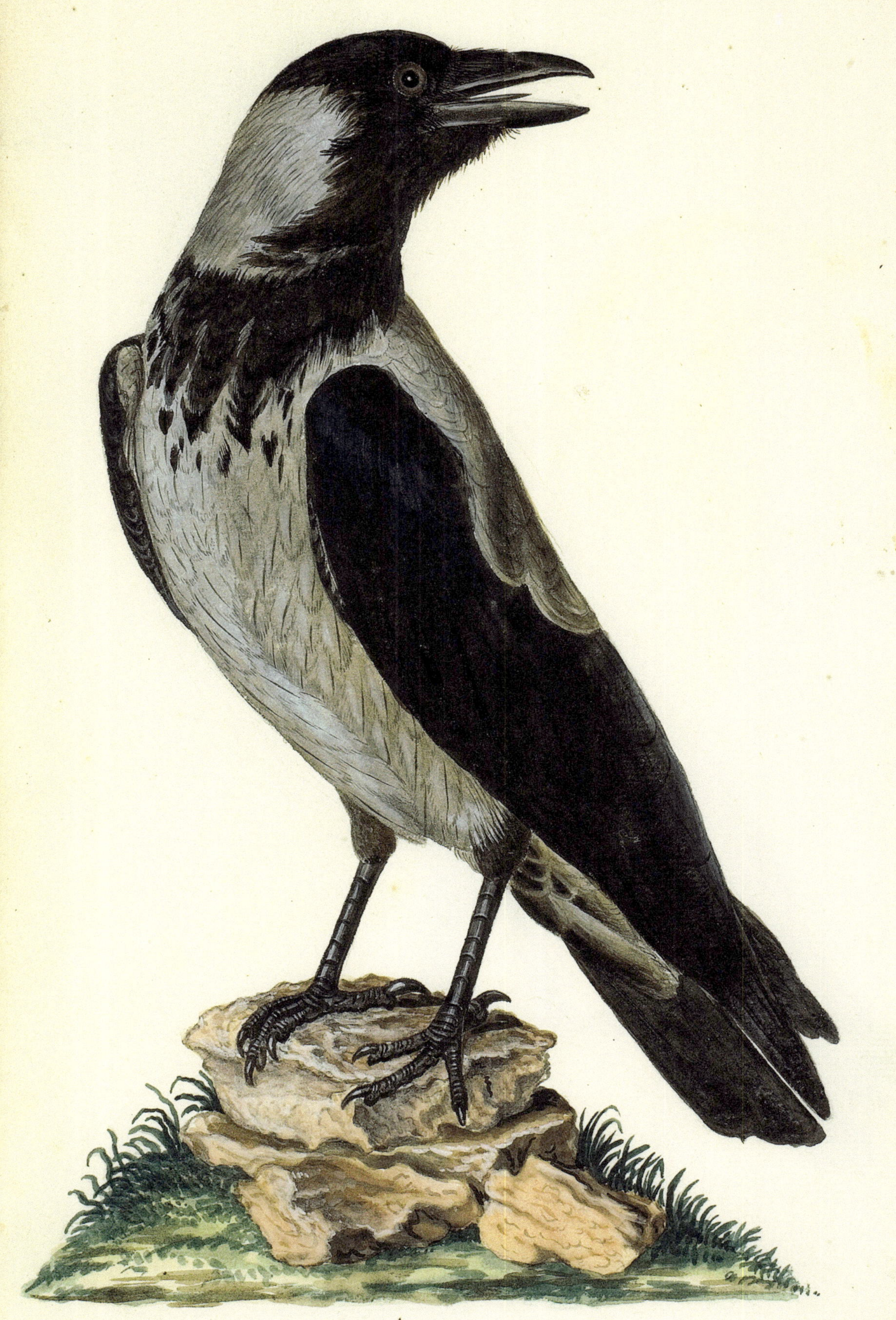
Corvus Cornix.
graüe Krähe.
48
IV. 2.

Dohle (♂)

Corvus Monedula. Dohle. ♂.

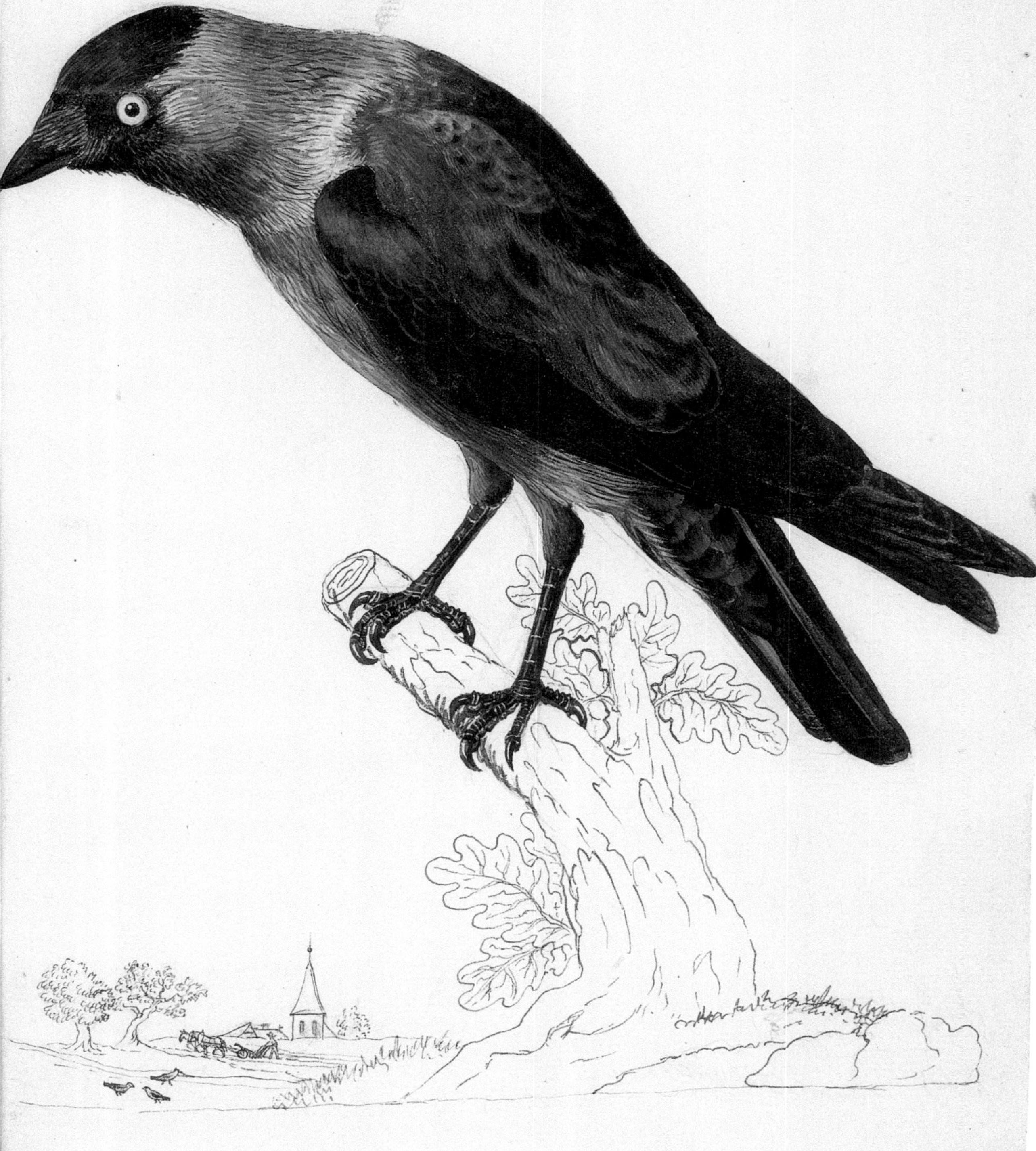

TP. 4.

Tannenhäher (♂)

Corvus Caryocatactes.

Tannenheher. ♂

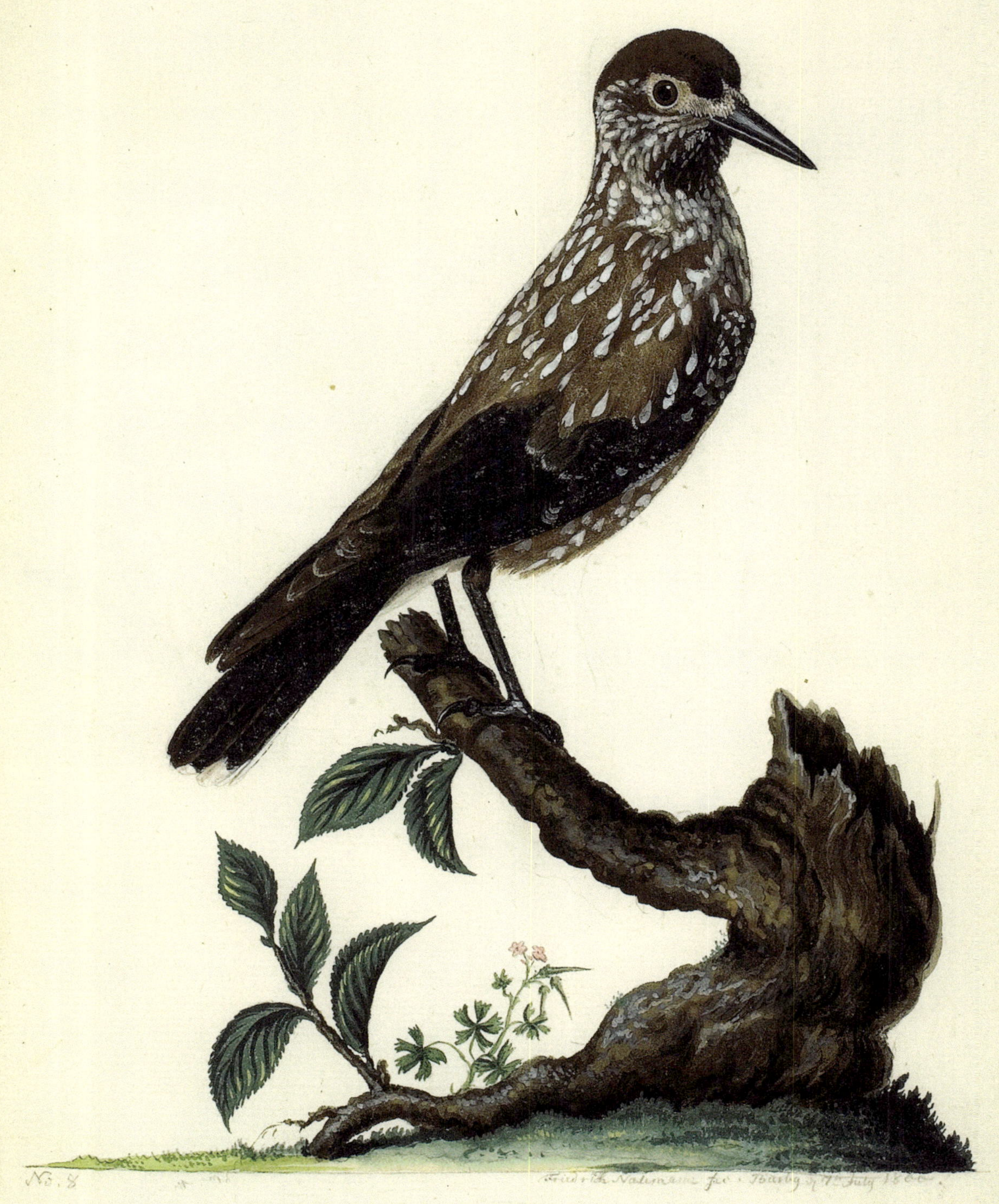

No. 8

Friedrich Naumann fec. … 1800.

IV, 5.

Elster (♂)

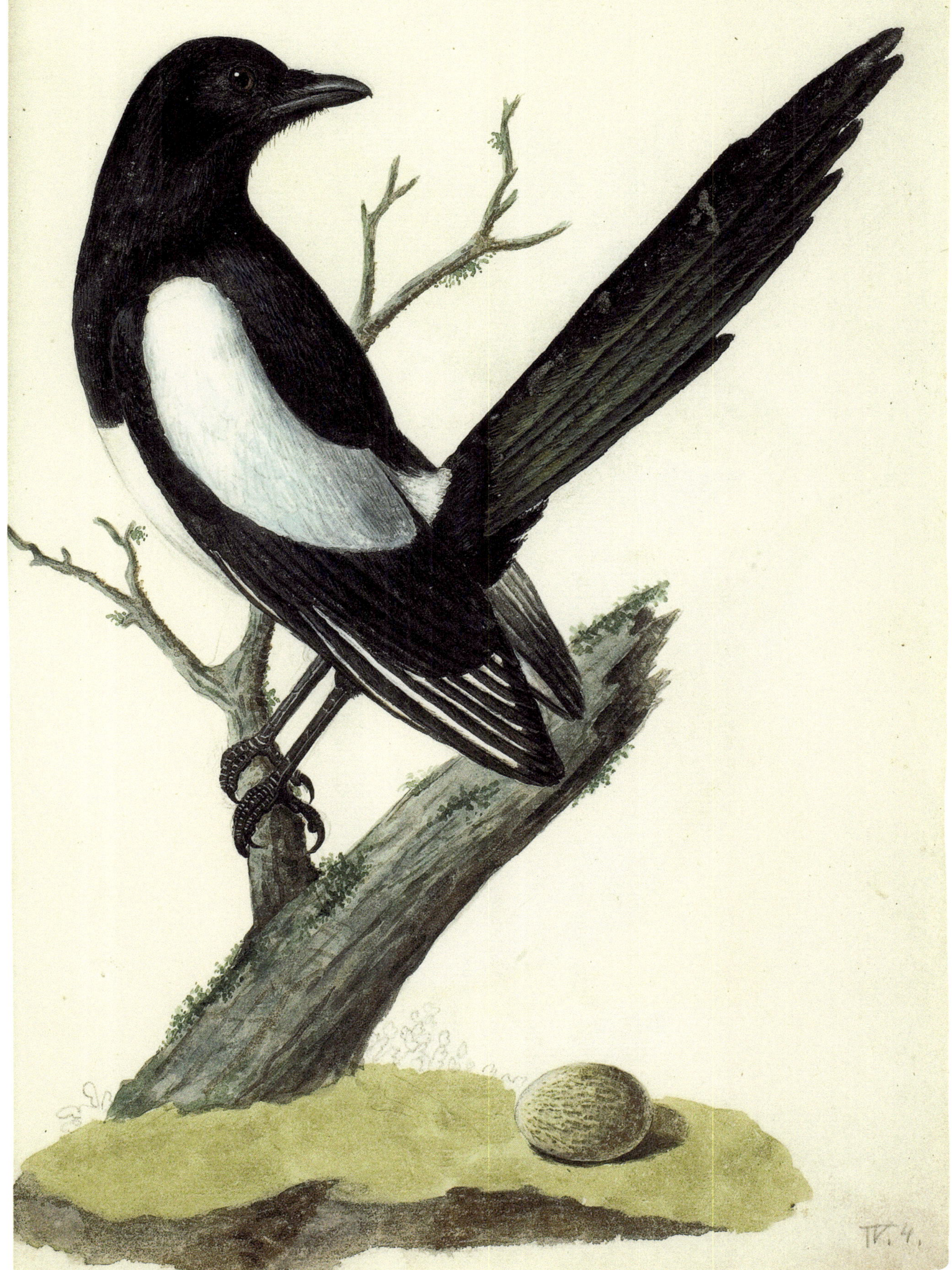
53
Corvus Pica. Elster. ♂
TK. 4.

Oben: Pirol (♂)
Unten: Pirol (♀)

Oriolus Galbula. Pirol, Pfingstvogel.

Tab: XL.

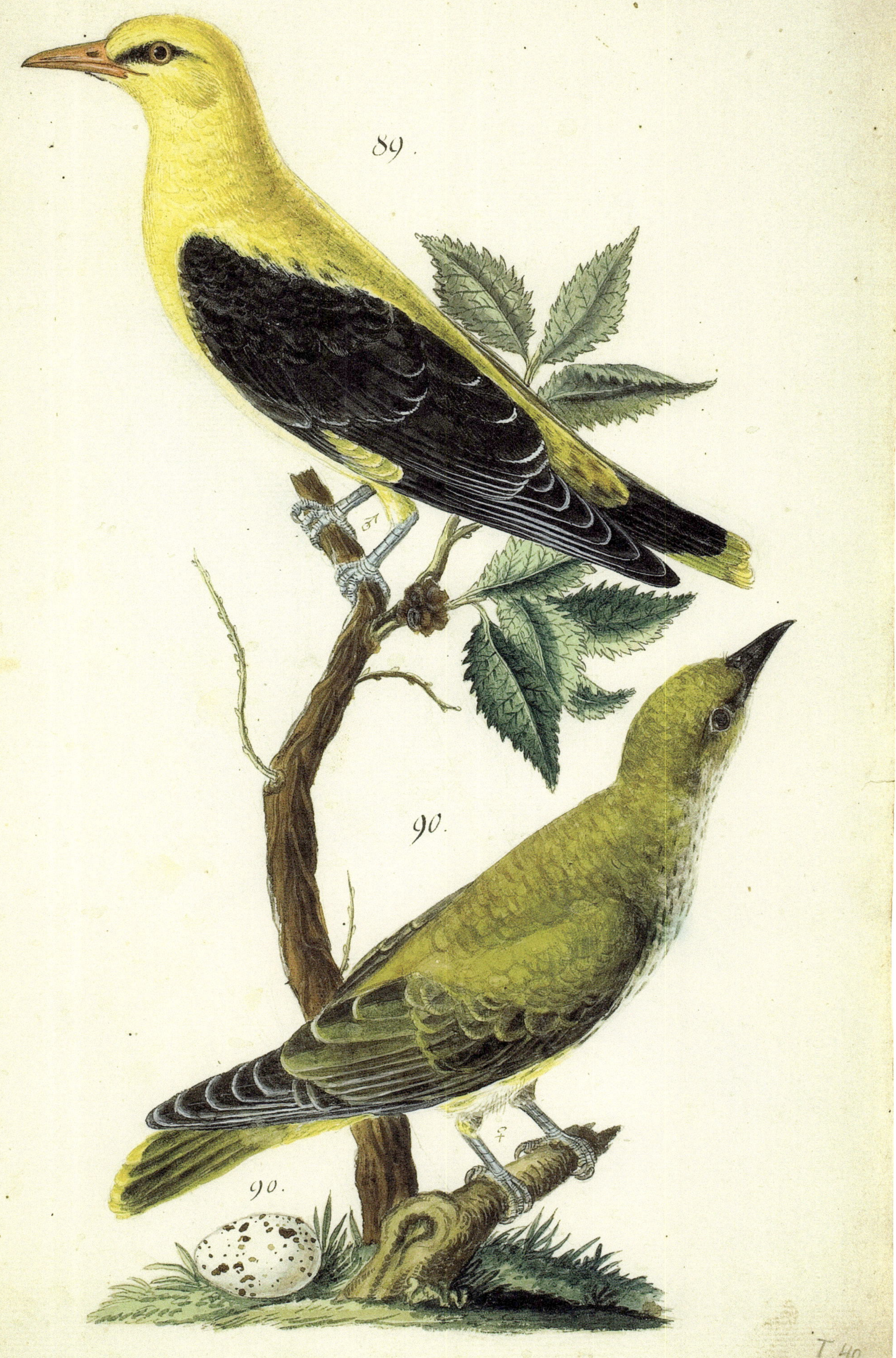

Kuckuck (♀)

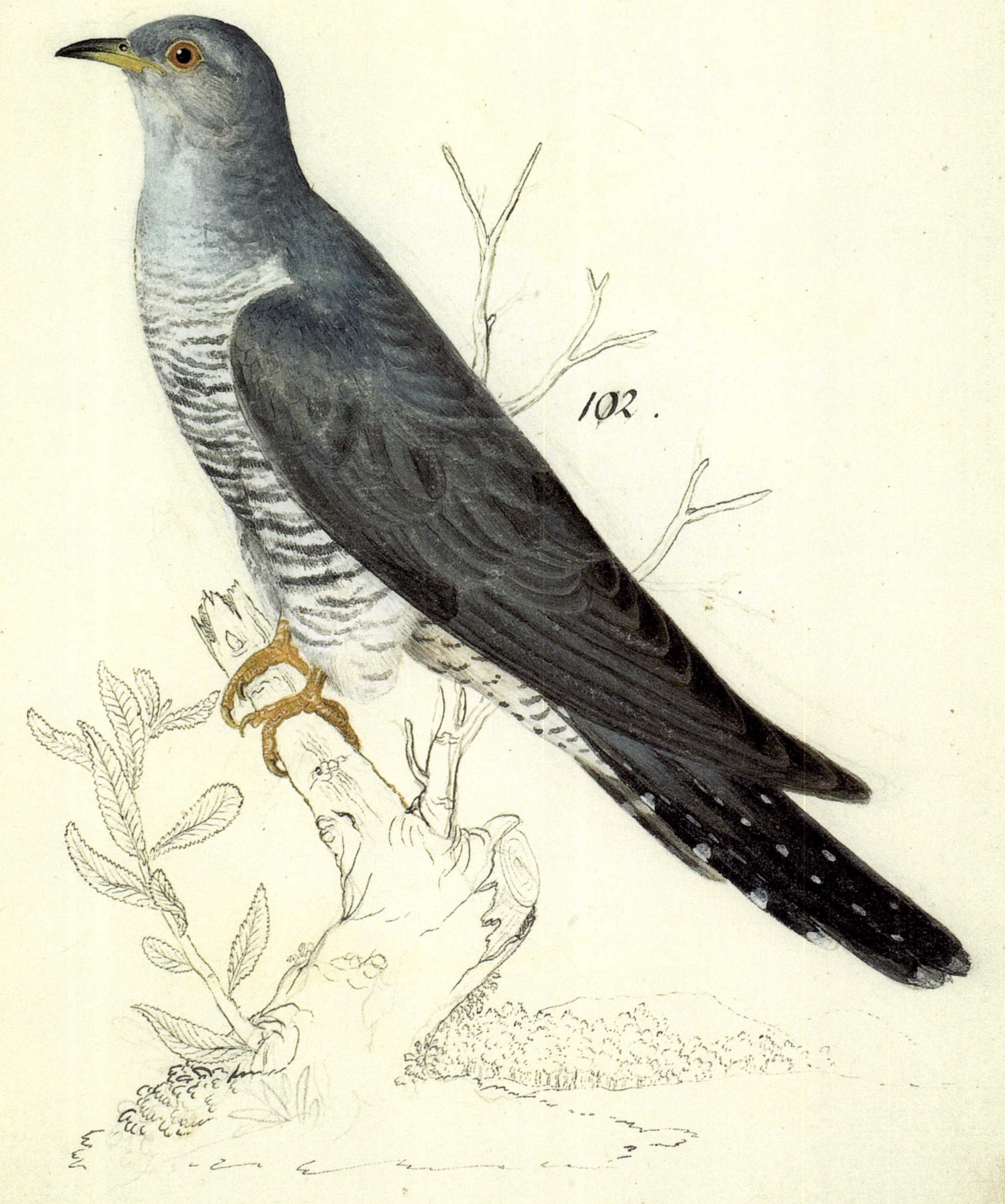
55
Cuculus canorus. Kukuk.
Tab: XLV.
102.
I. 45.

Oben: Wiedehopf (♂)
Unten: Star (♂)

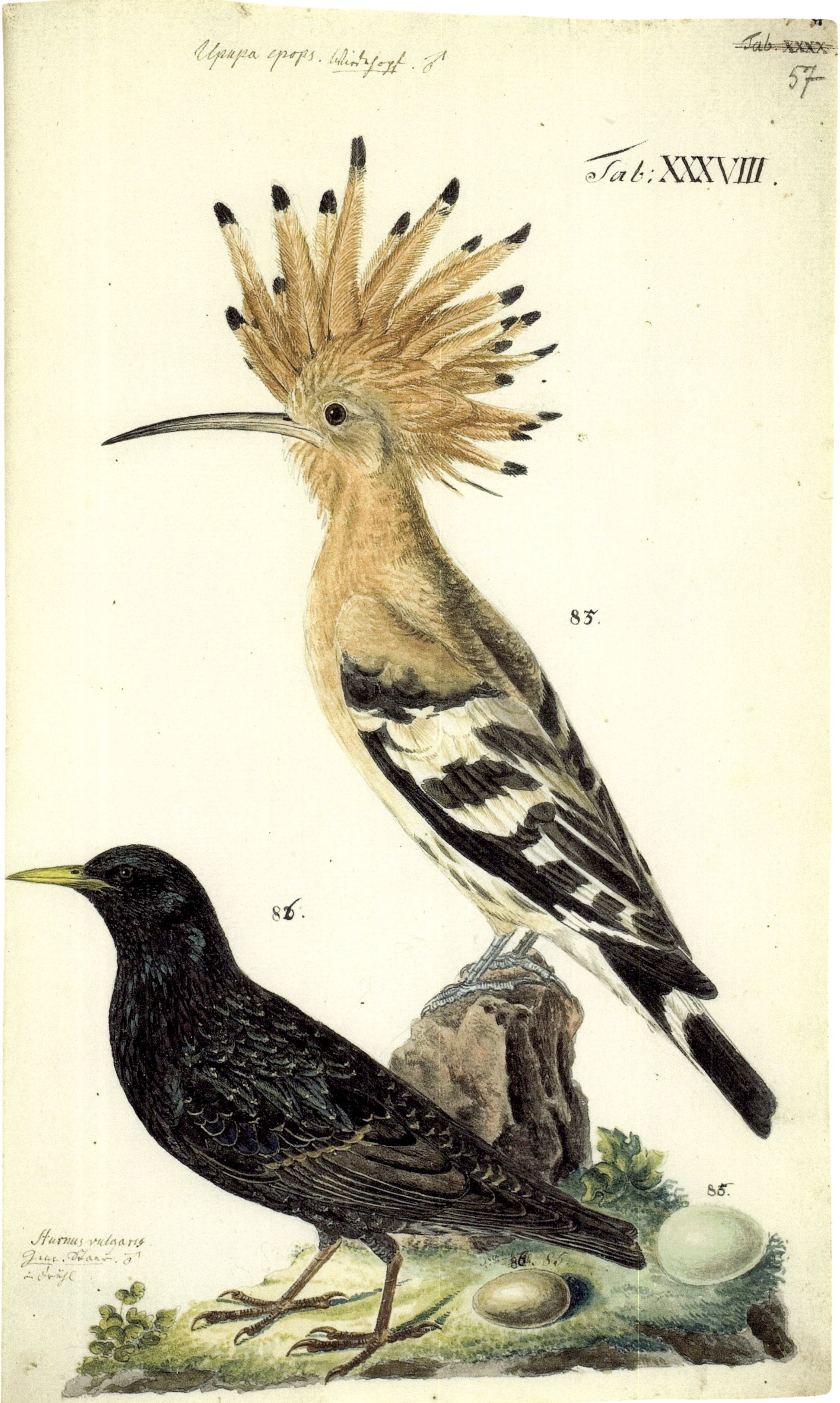

Upupa epops. Wiedehopf. ♂

~~Tab. XXXX~~

57

Tab: XXXVIII.

83.

86.

85.

86. 85.

Sturnus vulgaris

Gem. Staar. ♂

Schwarzspecht (♂)

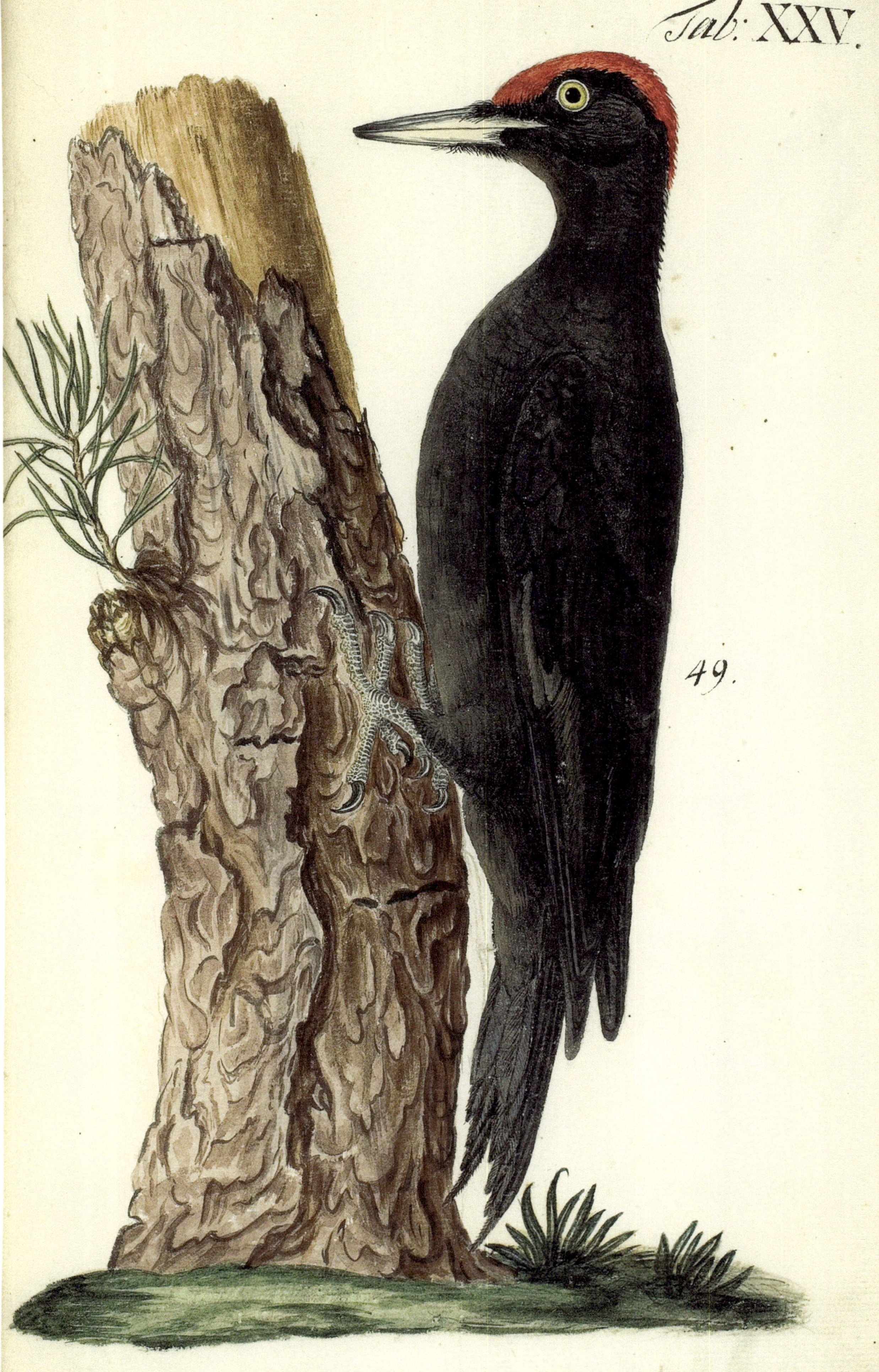
Picus martius
58.
Tab: XXV.
49.

Oben: Grünspecht (♂)
Unten: Grauspecht (♀)

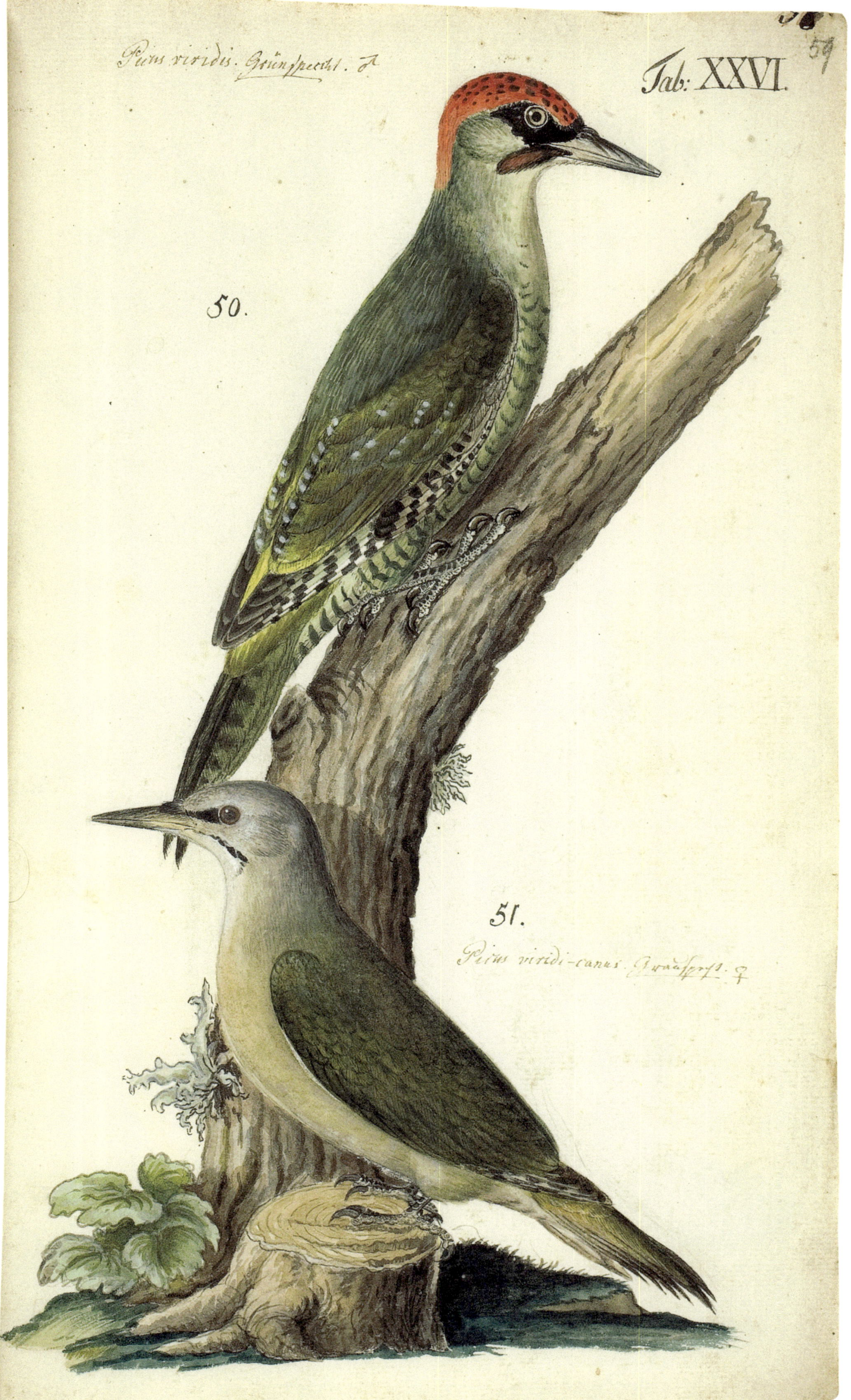
Picus viridis. Grünspecht. ♂
Tab: XXVI.
50.
51.
Picus viridi-canus.

Mittelspecht (♂)

B

61

Picus medius. Mittlerer Buntspecht. ♂

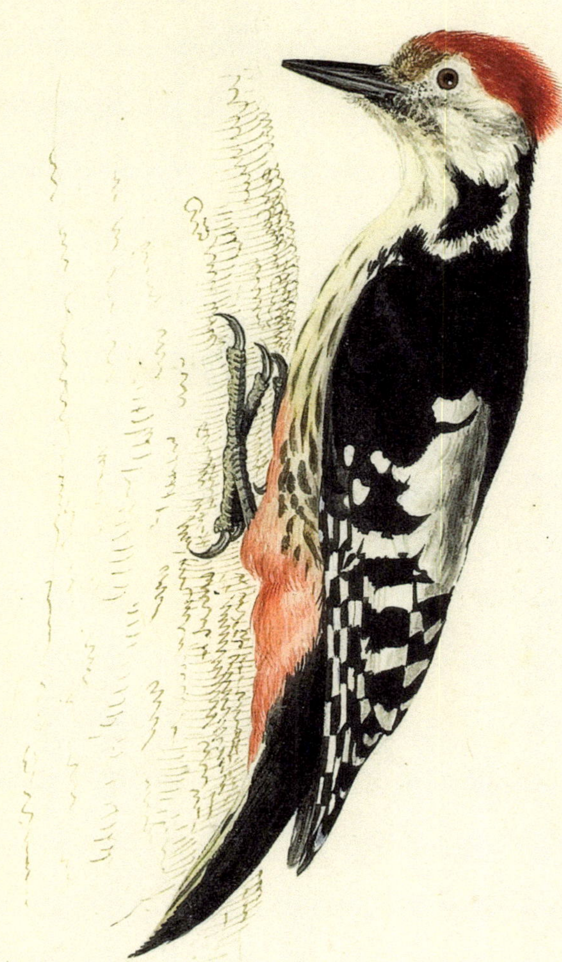

Oben: Grünfink (♂)
Unten: Grünfink (♀)

63

Tabl. VIII.

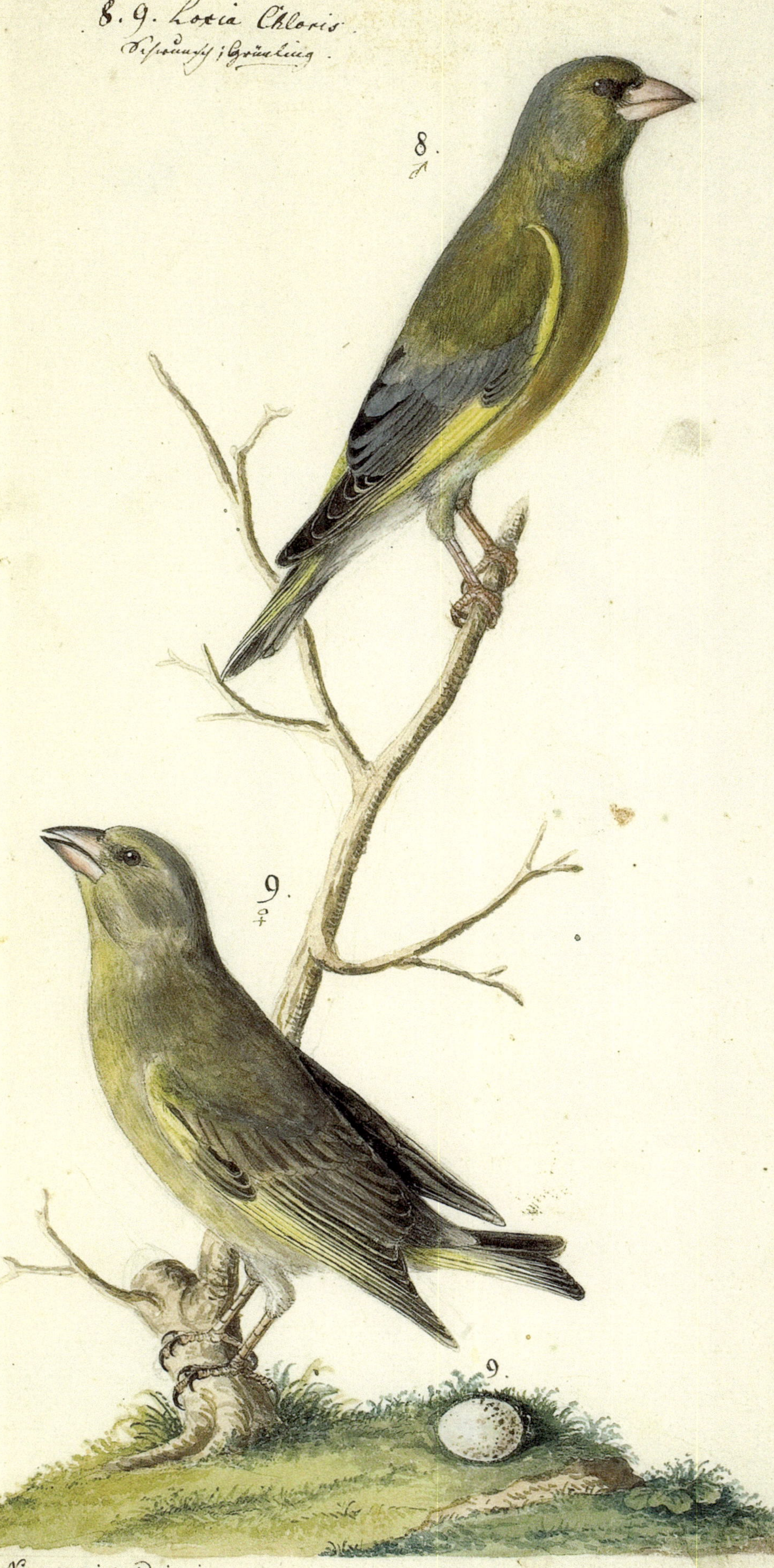

Naumann jun. ad viv. pinx.

Oben: Bluthänfling (♂)
Mitte: Bluthänfling (♀)
Unten: Stieglitz

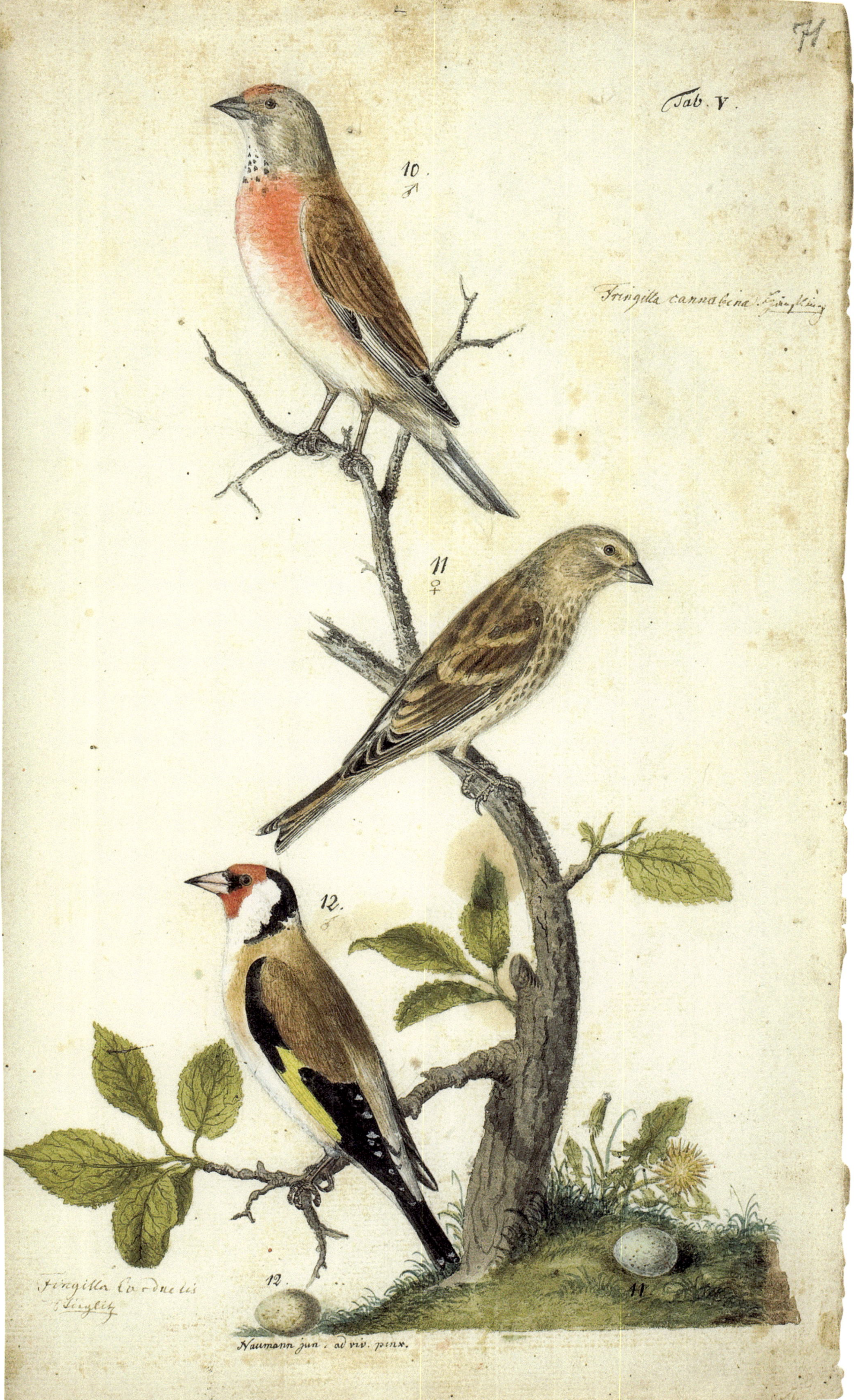
71
Tab. V
10.
♂
Fringilla cannabina
11
♀
12.
Fringilla Carduelis
12.
11
Naumann jun. ad viv. pinx.

Oben: Goldammer (♂)
Unten: Goldammer (♀)

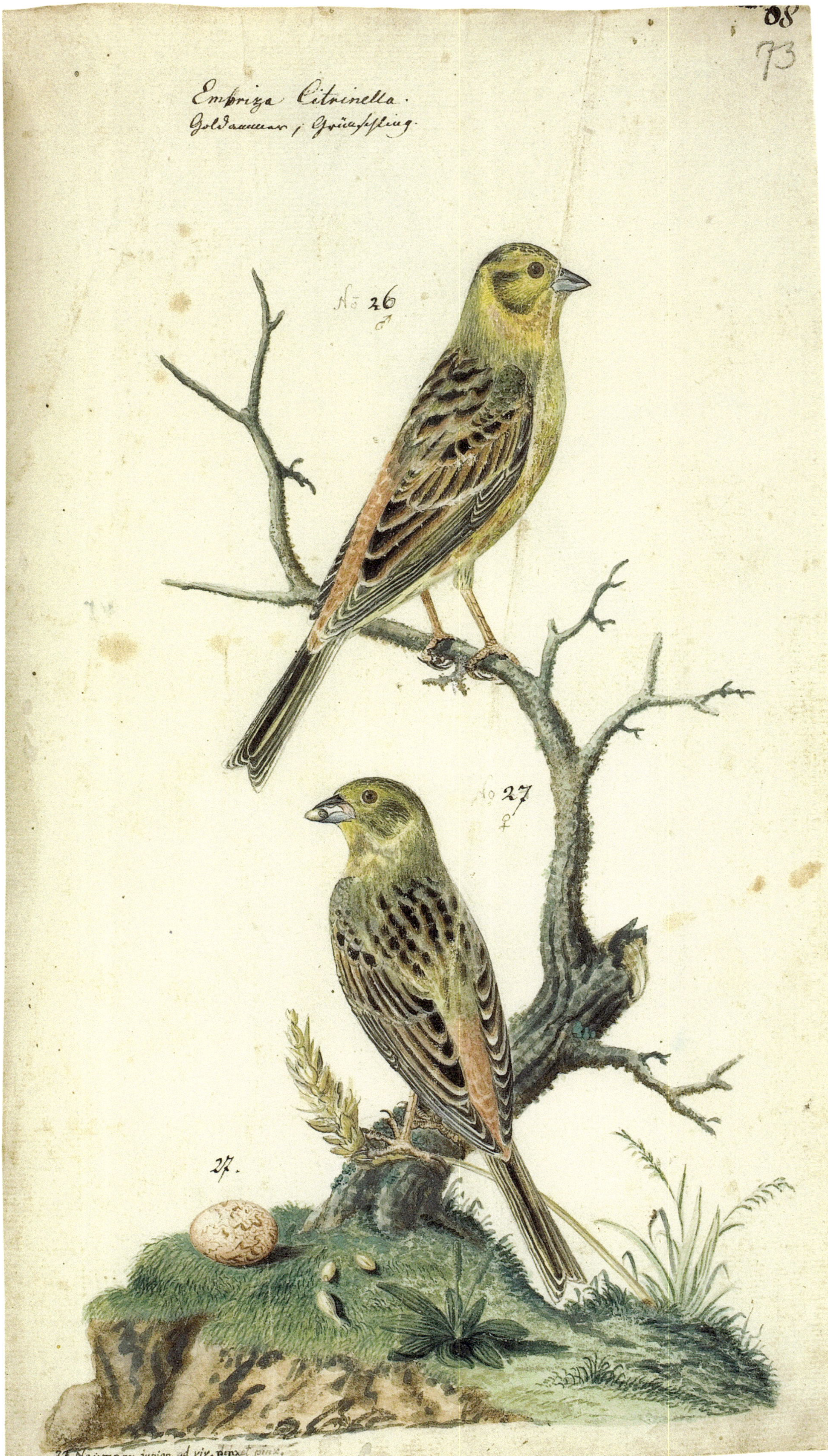

08

73

Emberiza Citrinella.
Goldammer; Grünschling.

No 26
♂

No 27
♀

27.

J.F. Naumann junior ad viv. pinxet pinx.

Oben: Rohrammer (♂)
Unten: Rohrammer (♀)

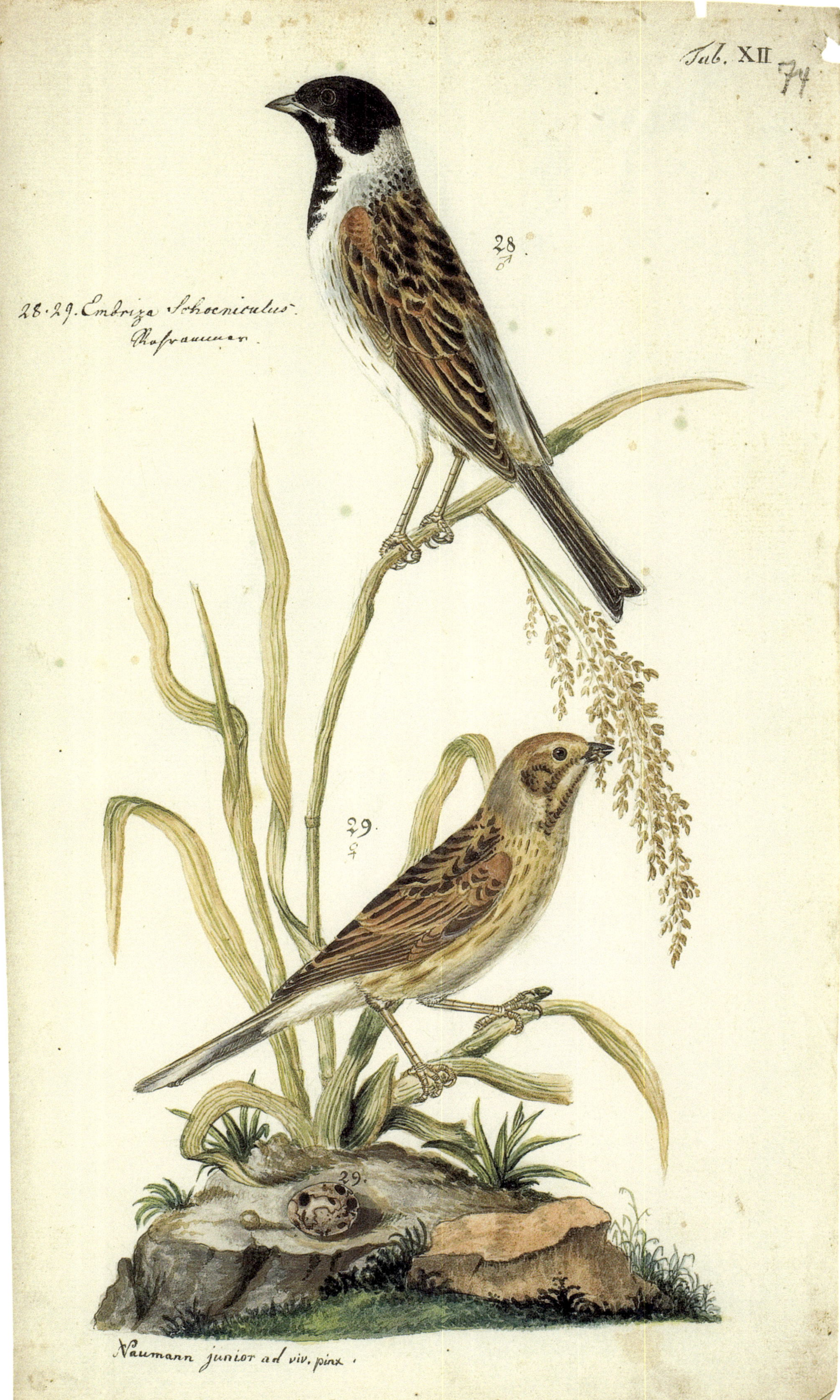
Tab. XII
74
28·29. Embriza Schoeniculus
Rohrammer
28
♂
29
♀
29.
Naumann junior ad viv. pinx.

Oben: Singdrossel (♂)
Unten: Misteldrossel (♀)

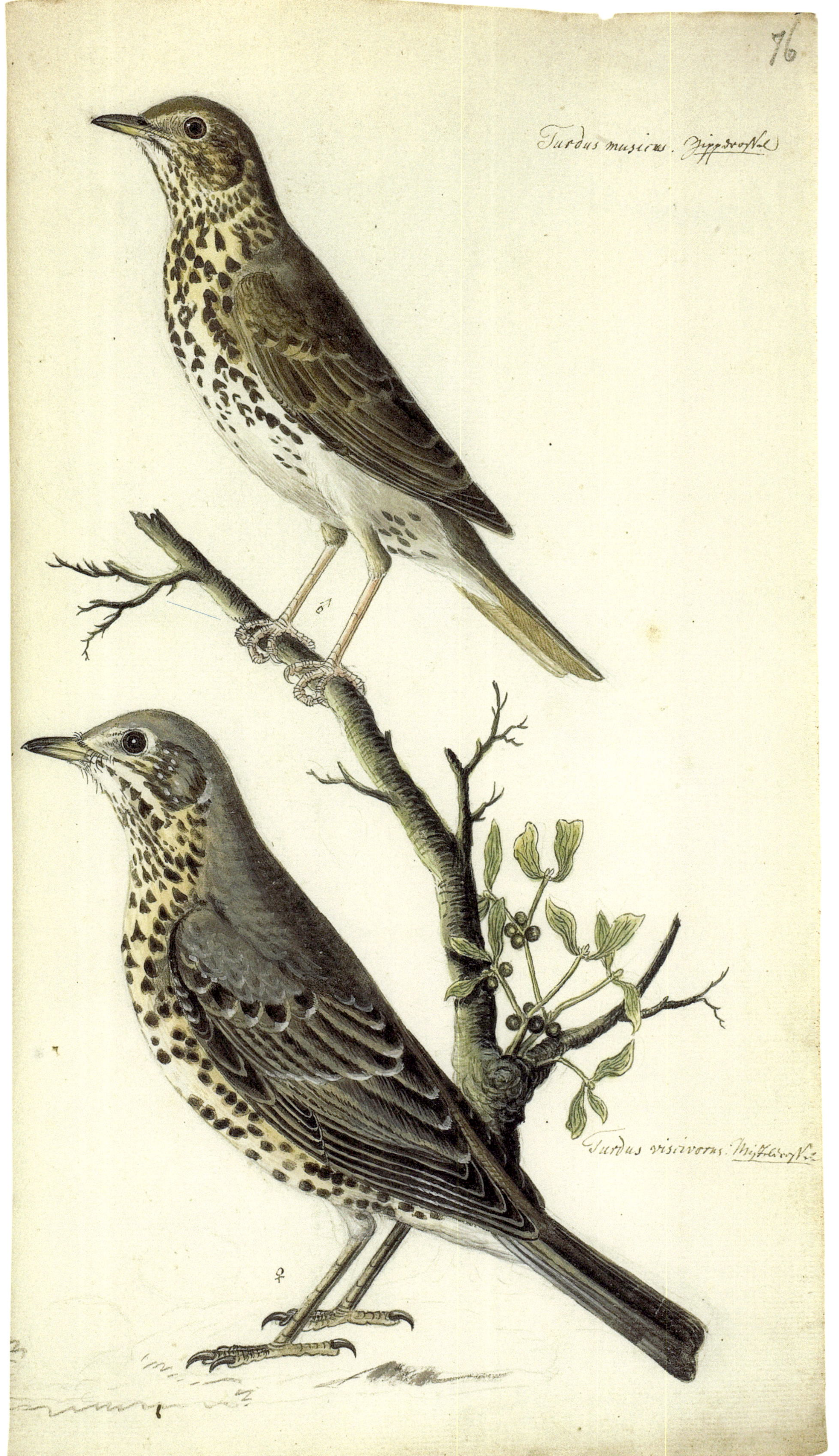
76
Turdus musicus. Zippdrossel
Turdus viscivorus.

Oben: Wacholderdrossel (♂ juv.)
Unten: Rotdrossel (♀ juv.)

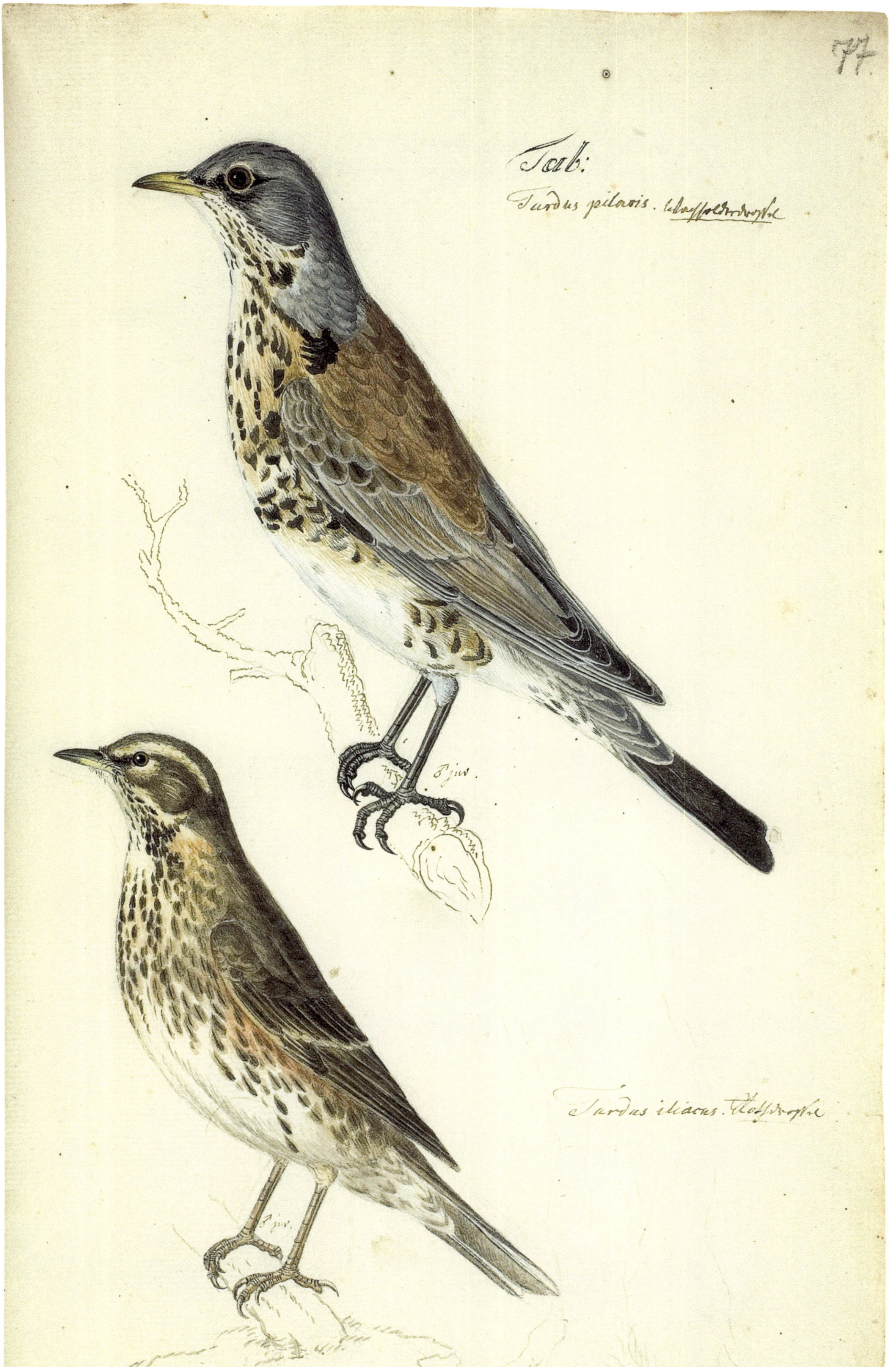

77

Tab:

Turdus pilaris. Wachholderdrossel

Turdus iliacus. Rothdrossel

Wasseramsel (♂)

Cinclus aquaticus. Wasserschwätzer. ♂

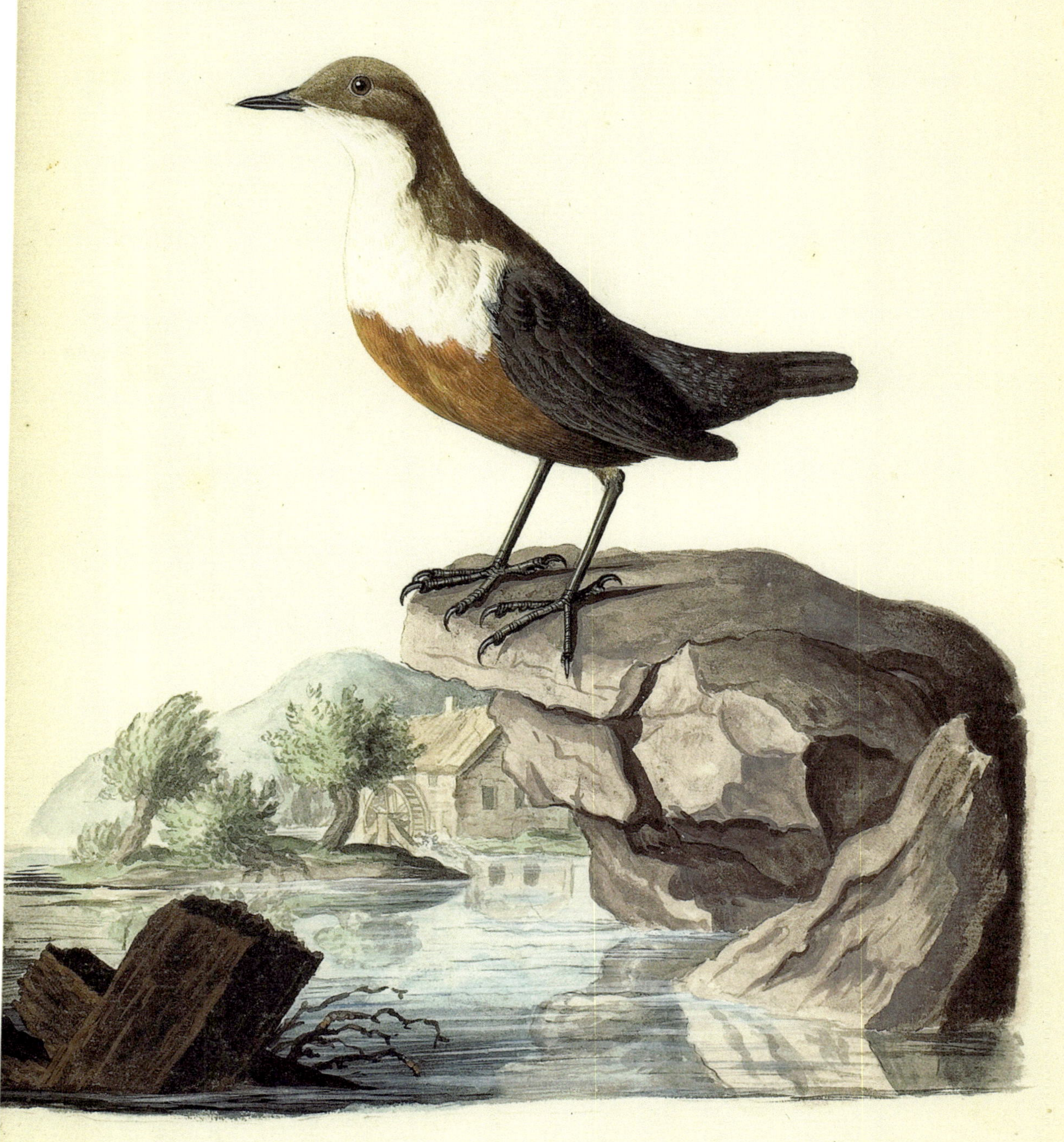

Oben: Klappergrasmücke (♂)
Mitte: Mönchsgrasmücke (♀)
Unten: Mönchsgrasmücke (♂)

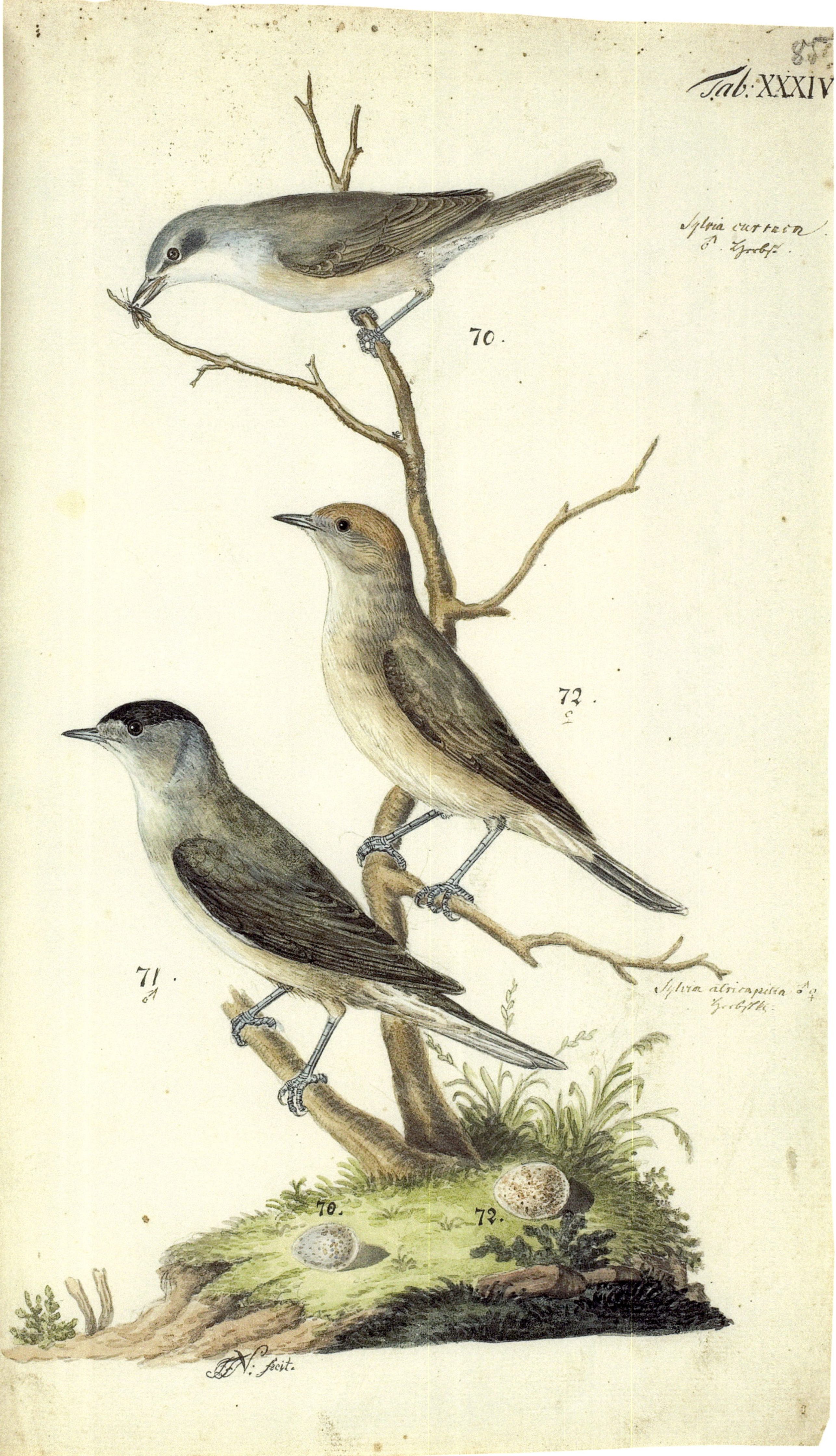
Tab: XXXIV
Sylvia curruca
70.
72.
♀
71.
♂
Sylvia atricapilla ♂ ♀
70.
72.
F.N. fecit.

Oben links: Gartenrotschwanz (♂)
Oben rechts: Gartenrotschwanz (♀)
Unten links: Hausrotschwanz (♀)
Unten rechts: Hausrotschwanz (♂)

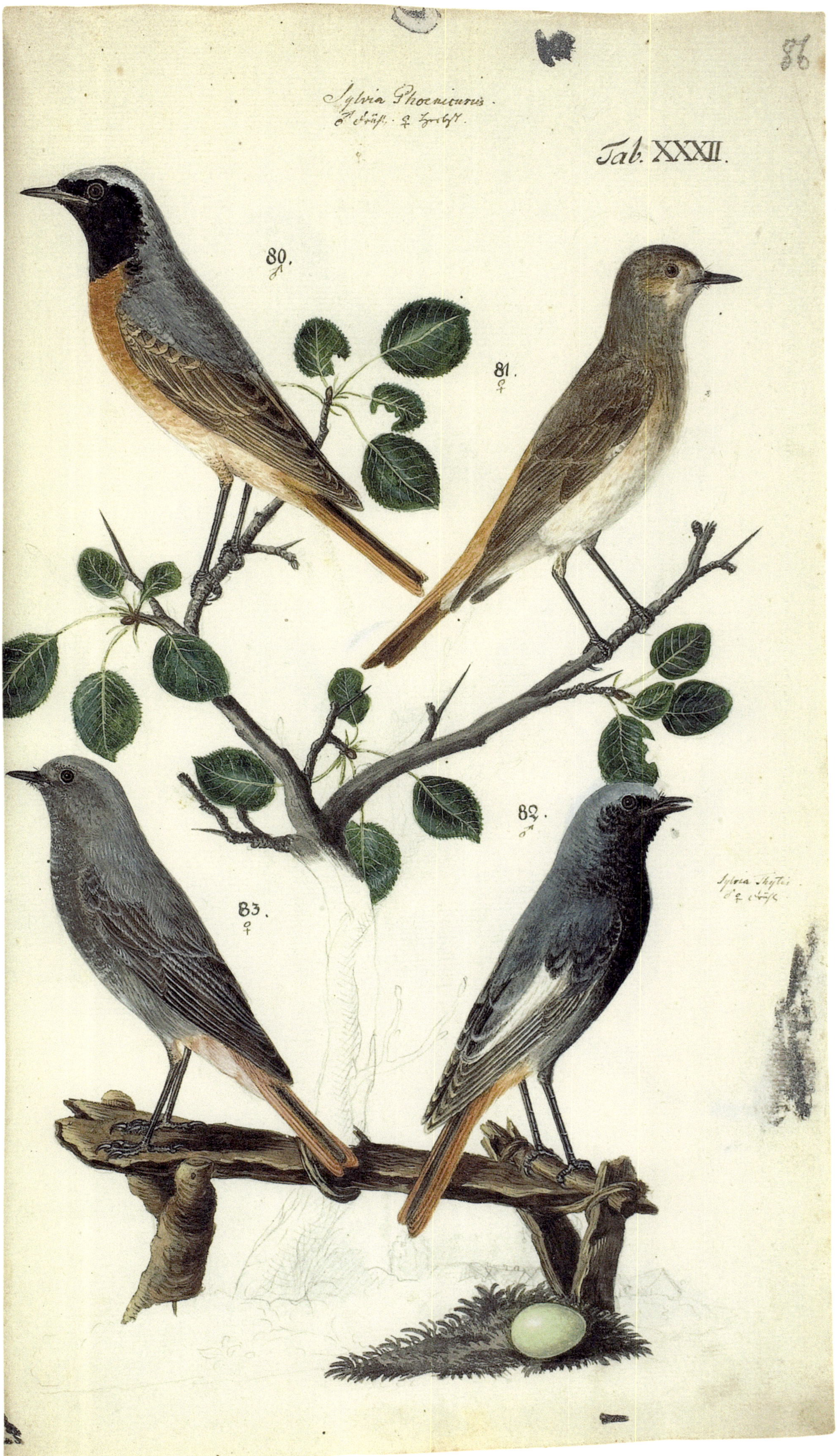

Sylvia Phoenicurus

Tab. XXXII

80. ♂

81. ♀

82. ♂

Sylvia Thytis ♂ ♀

83. ♀

Oben: Drosselrohrsänger (♂)
Unten: Teichrohrsänger (♂)

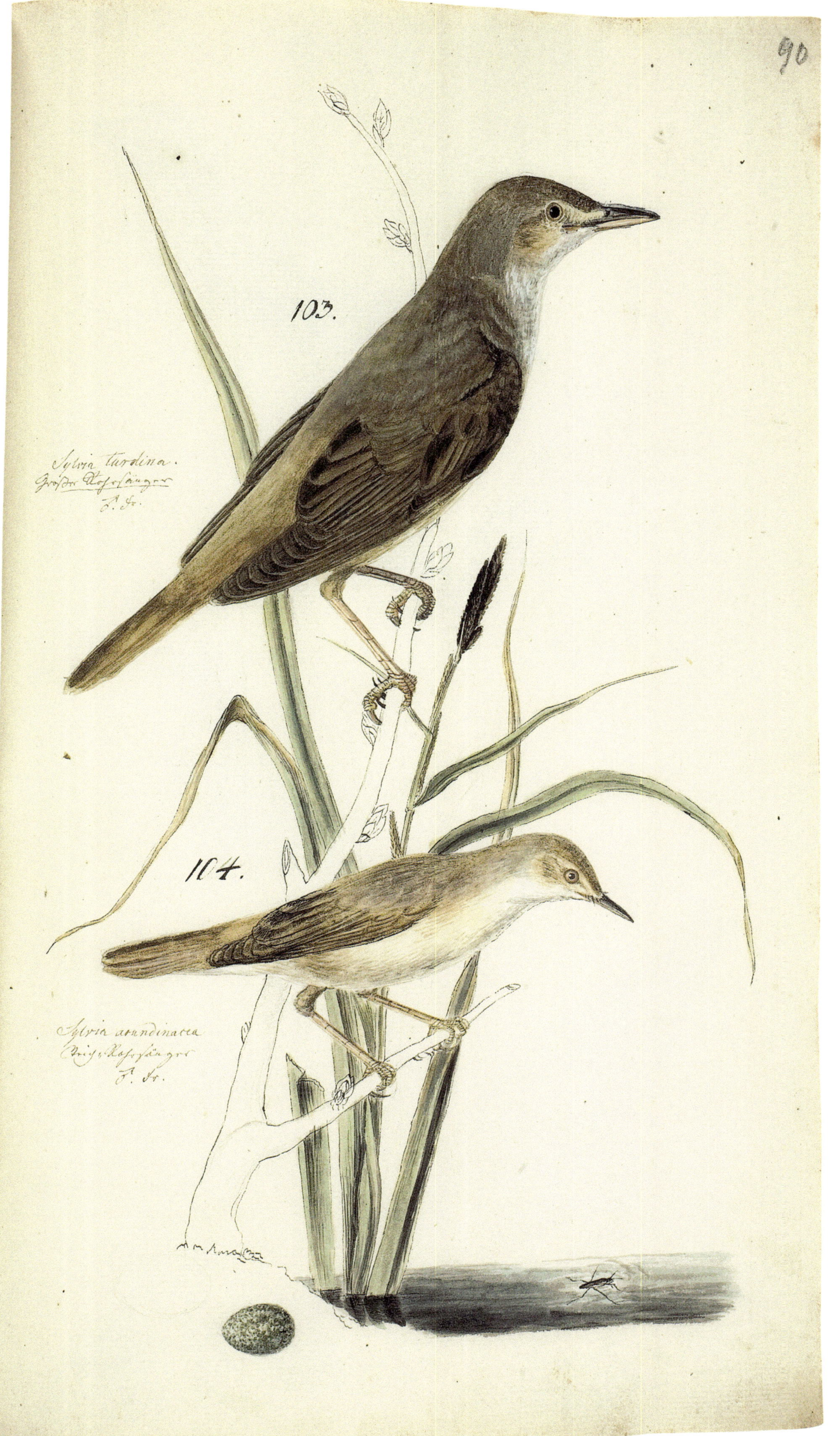
90
103.
Sylvia turdina.
104.
Sylvia arundinacea

Oben links: Braunkehlchen (♂)
Oben rechts: Braunkehlchen (♀)
Unten links: Steinschmätzer (♂)
Unten rechts: Steinschmätzer (♂ juv.)

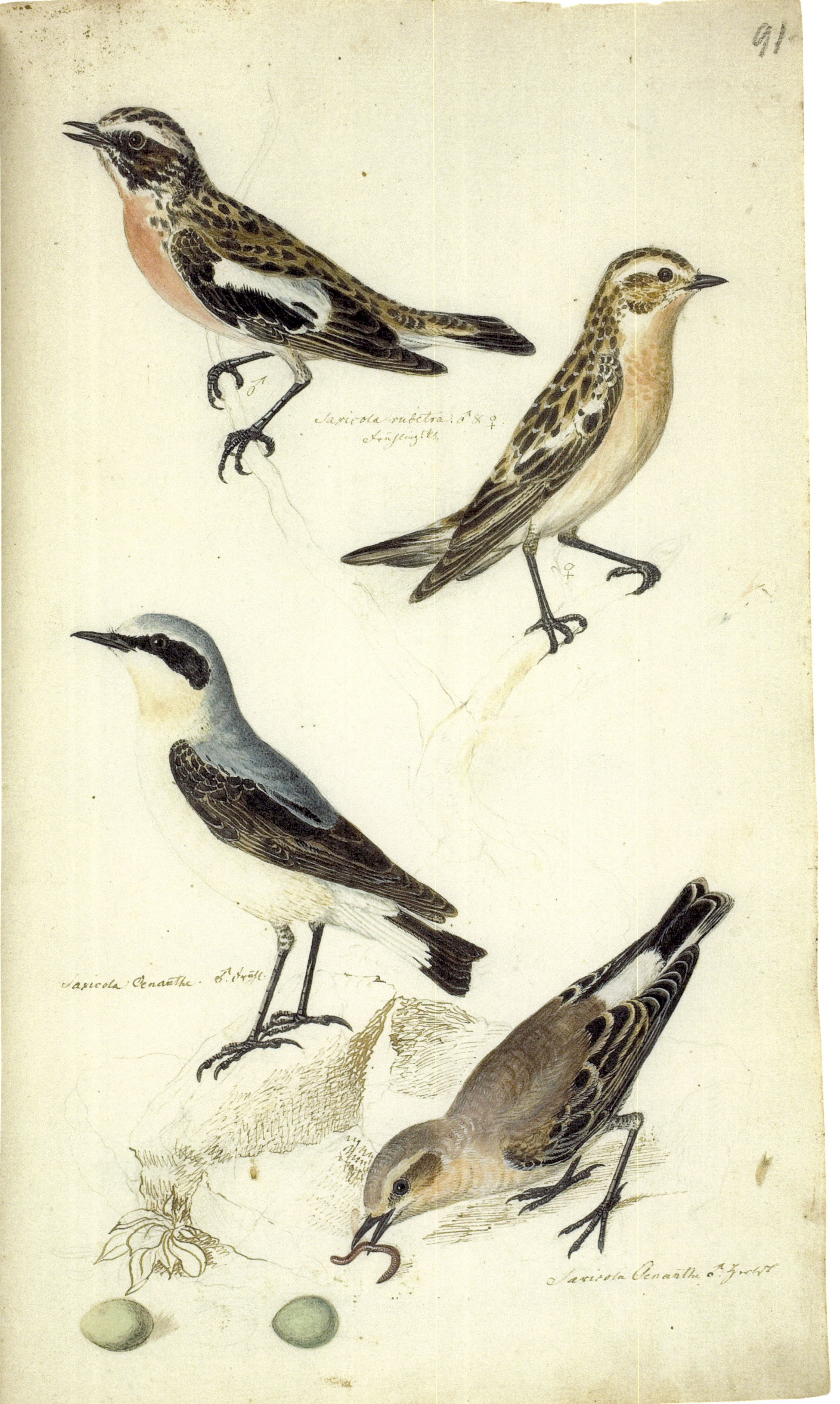
91
♂
Saxicola rubetra ♂ & ♀
♀
Saxicola Oenanthe ♂
Saxicola Oenanthe

Oben: Haubenlerche (♂)
Unten: Schneeammer (♂)

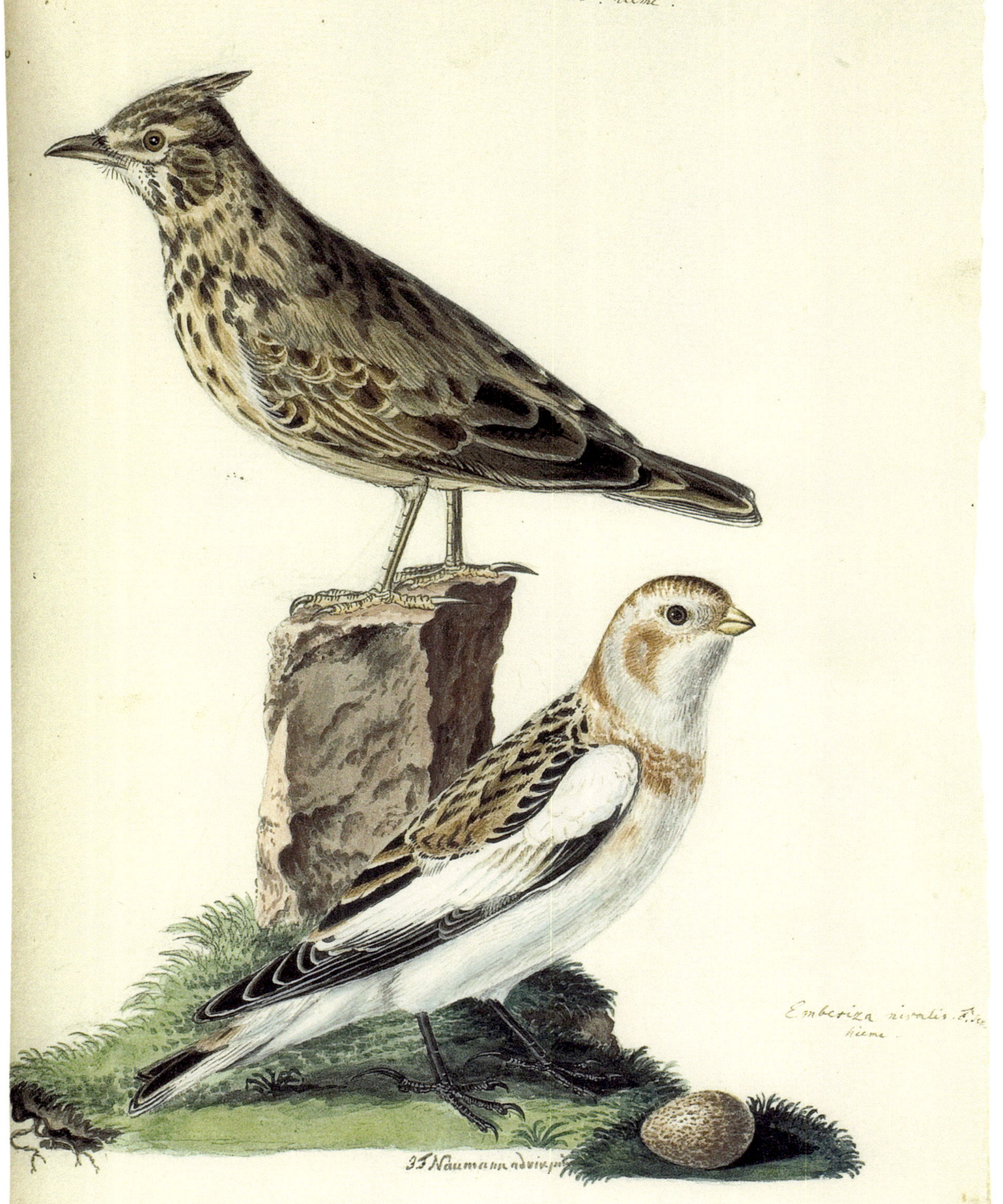
94
Alauda cristata. ♂. hieme.
Emberiza nivalis. ♂.
hieme.

Oben: Sumpfmeise (♂)
Mitte: Blaumeise (♂)
Unten: Kohlmeise (♂)

42. Parus major
43 — coeruleus } P. autumus
44. — palustris

95 87

Tab: XXIII.

44.

43.

42.

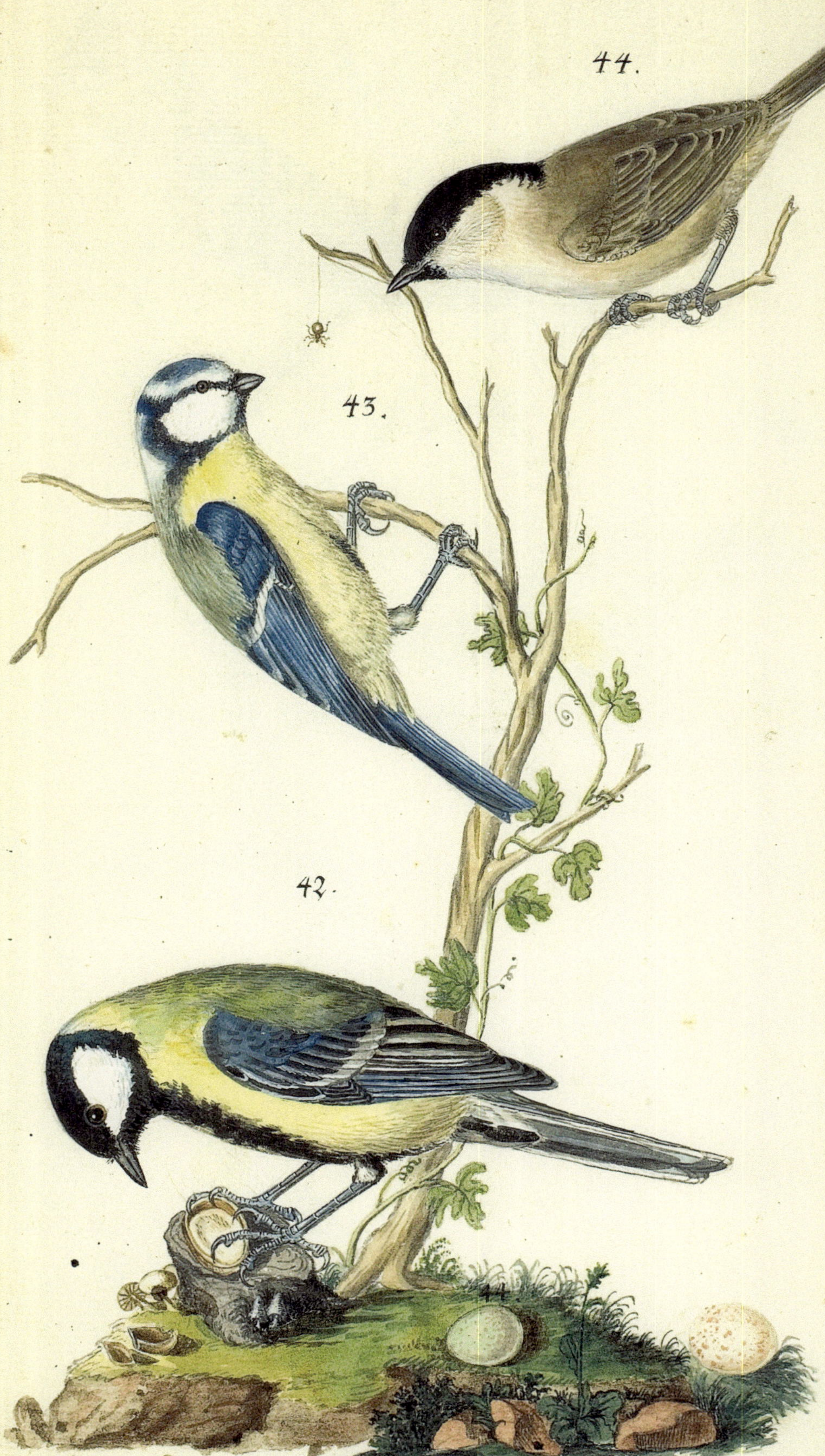

Naumann ad viv. pinx.

Oben: Haubenmeise (♂)
Mitte: Tannenmeise (♂)
Unten links: Schwanzmeise (♂)
Unten rechts: Schwanzmeise (♂ juv.)

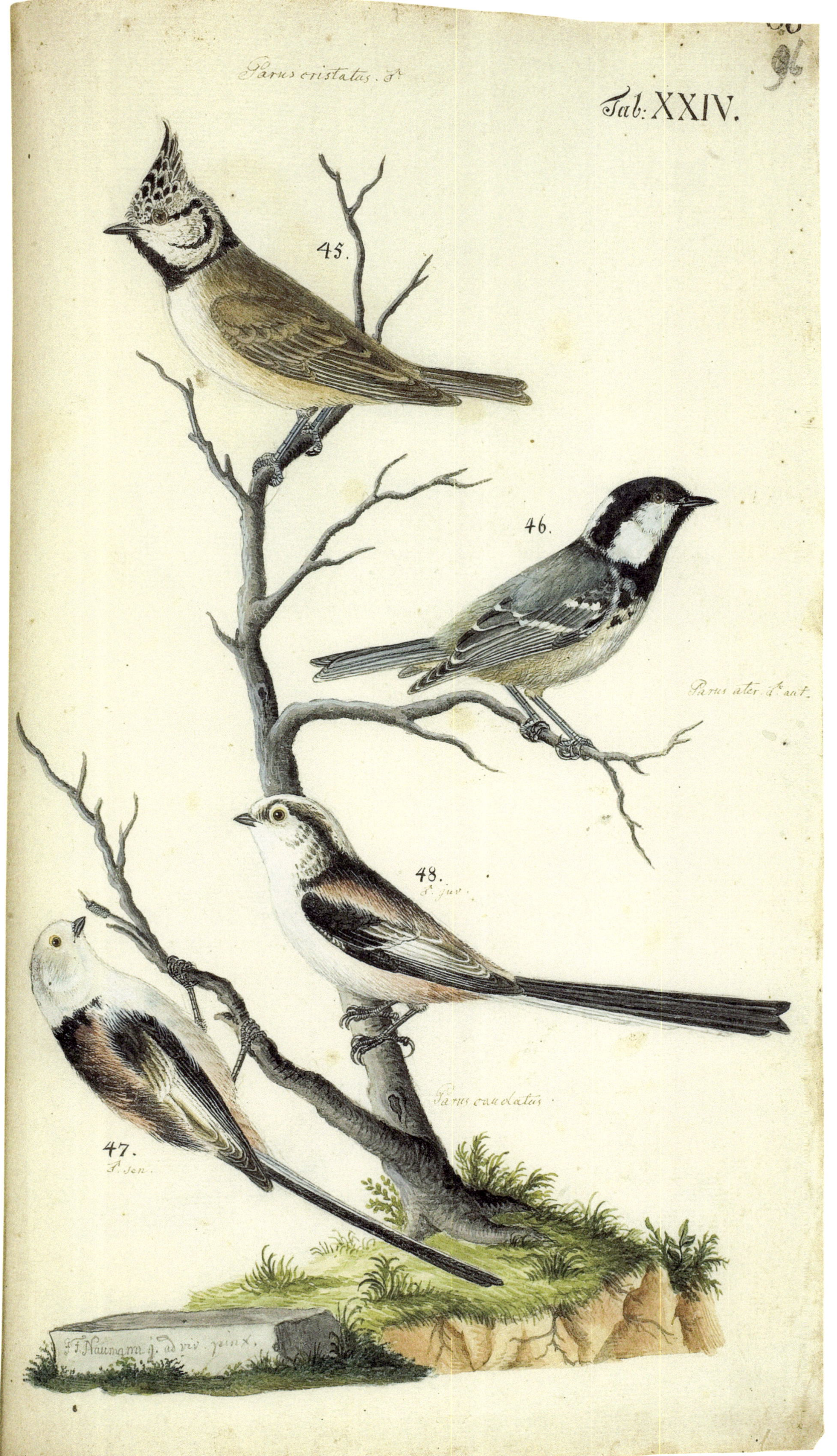
Parus cristatus. ♂
Tab: XXIV.
45.
46.
Parus ater. ♂ aut.
48.
♂ juv.
47.
♀ sen.
Parus caudatus
J. F. Naumann g. ad viv. pinx.

Oben: Rauchschwalbe (♂)
Mitte: Albinistische Rauchschwalbe (juv.)
Unten: Mauersegler (♂)

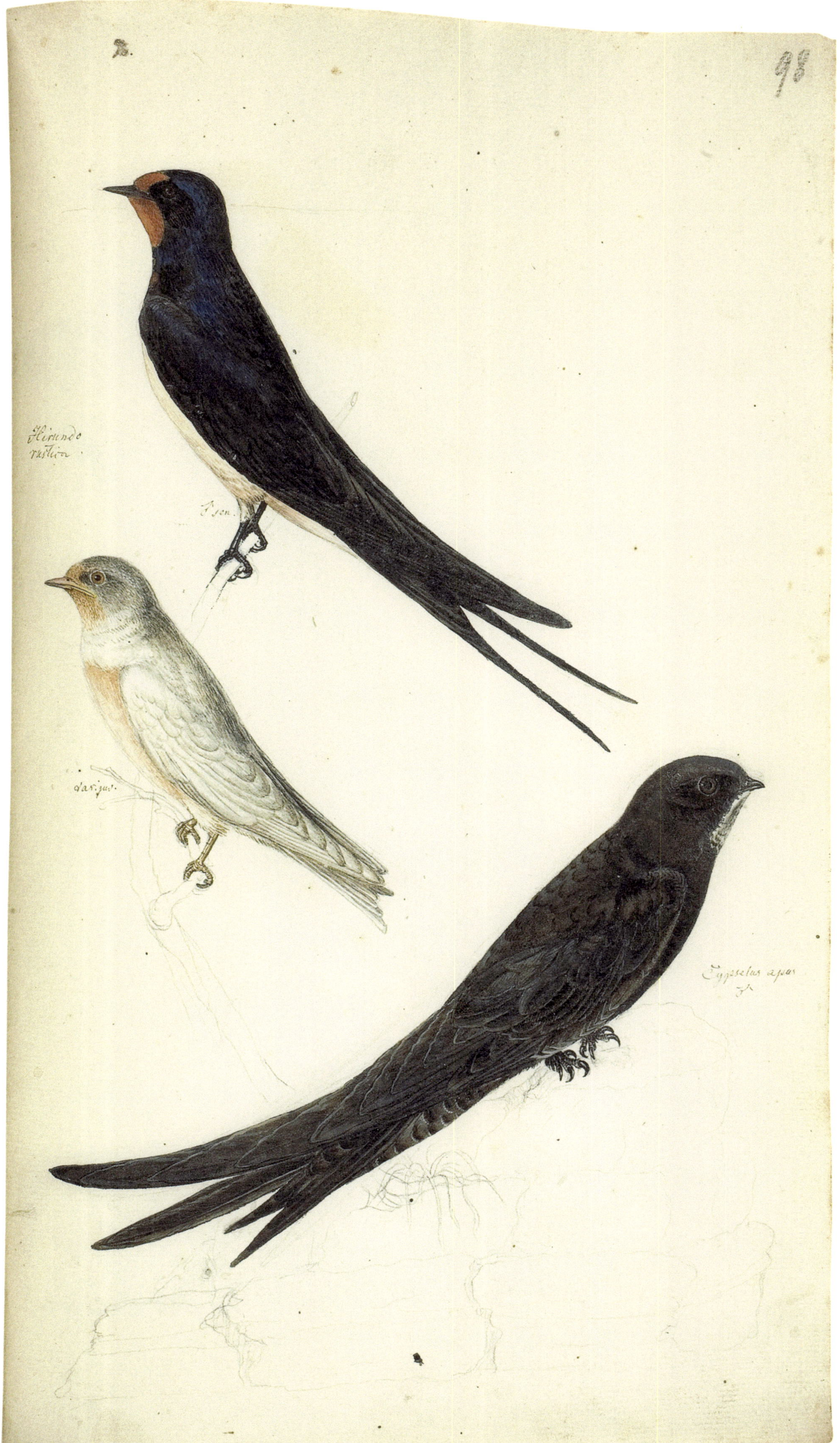

98

Hirundo rustica

F. sen.

d ar. juv.

Cypselus apus

Nachtschwalbe (♂)
mit Birkenspinner

Caprimulgus europaeus.
♂ vere.

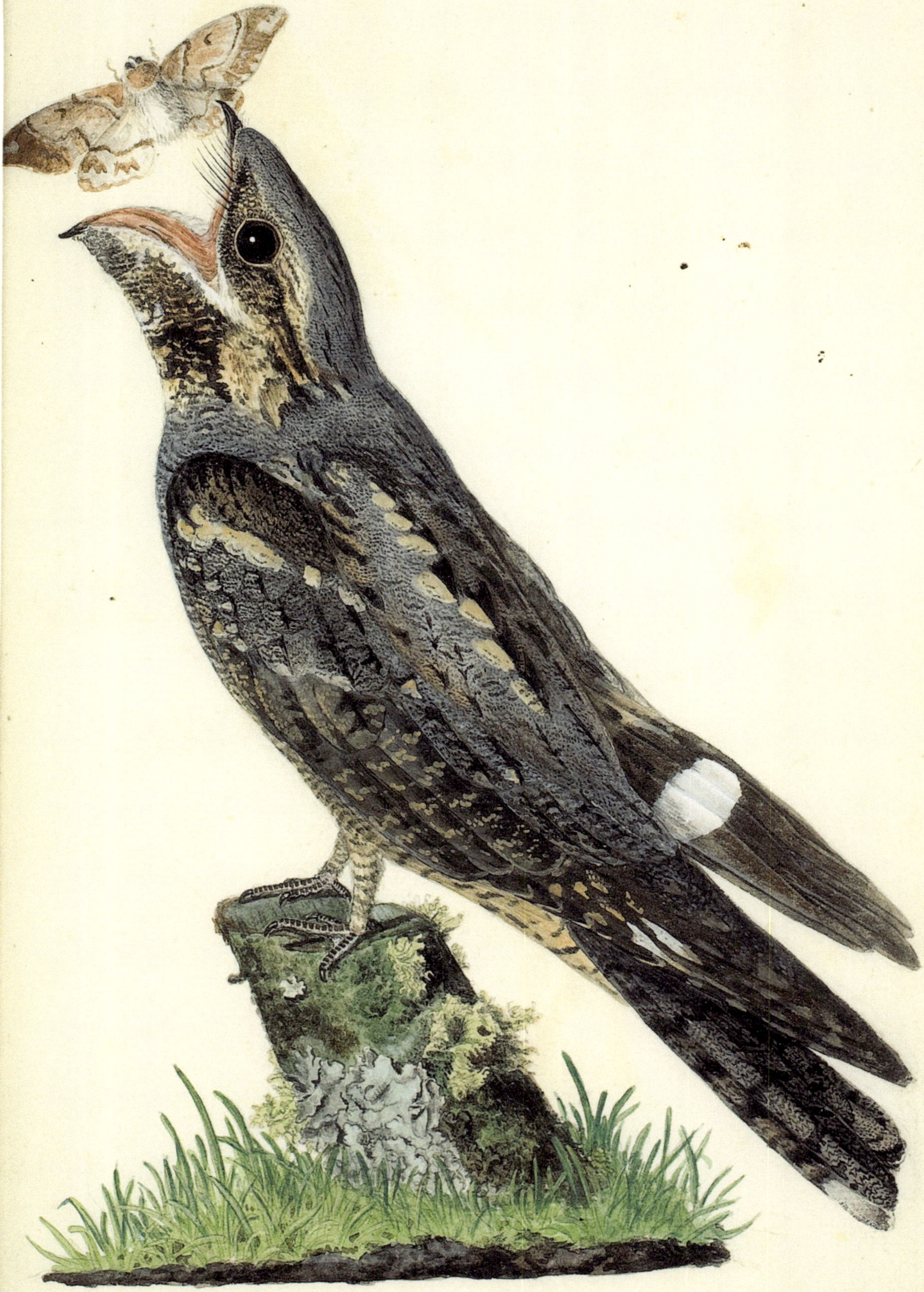

Natürl. Gr.

Hohltaube (♂)

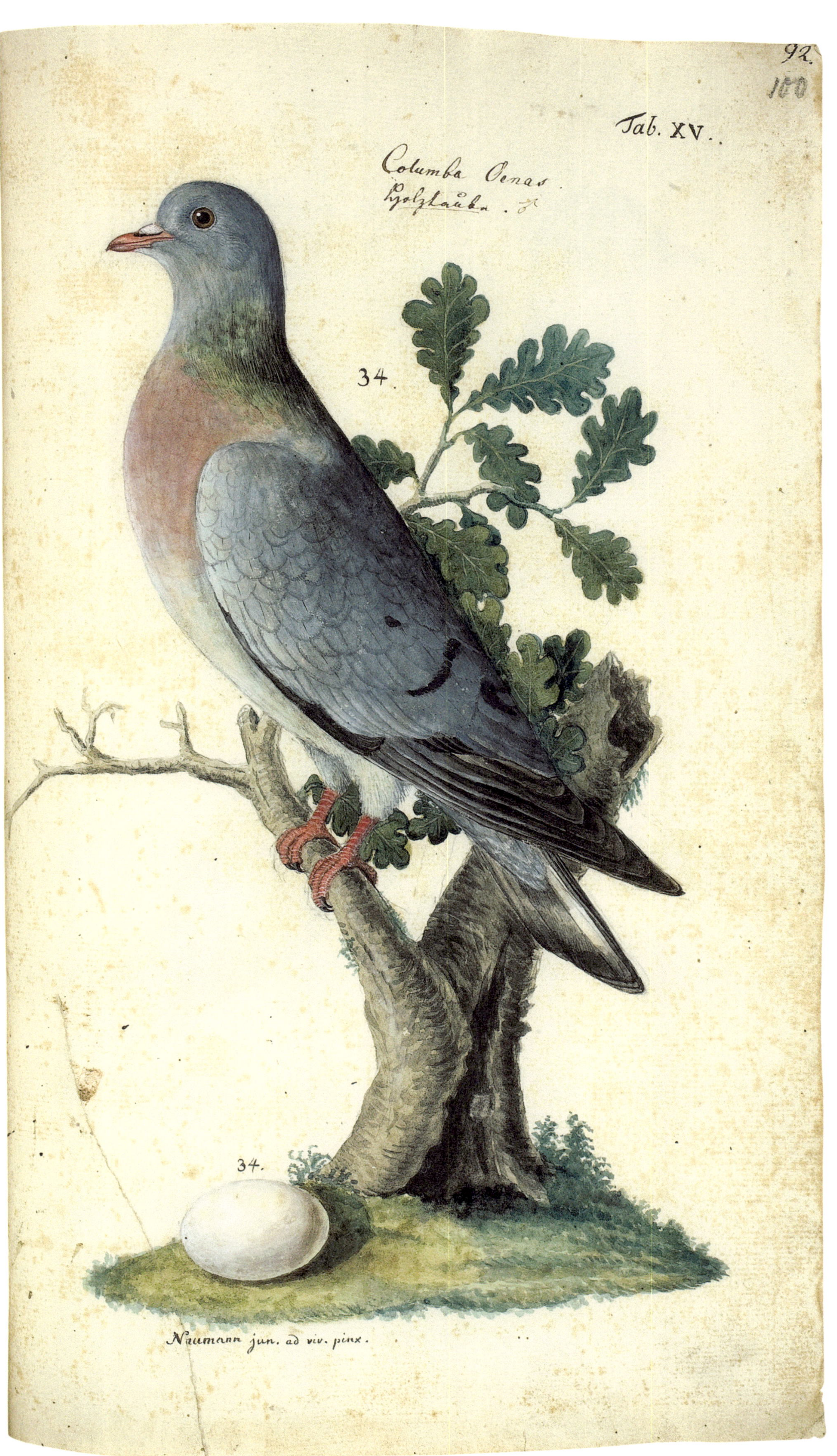
92.
100
Tab. XV.
Columba Oenas
Holztaube. ♂
34.
34.
Naumann jun. ad viv. pinx.

Auerhuhn (♂)

Tab: XVII

104

Tetrao Urogallus.
Auerhahn.

36.

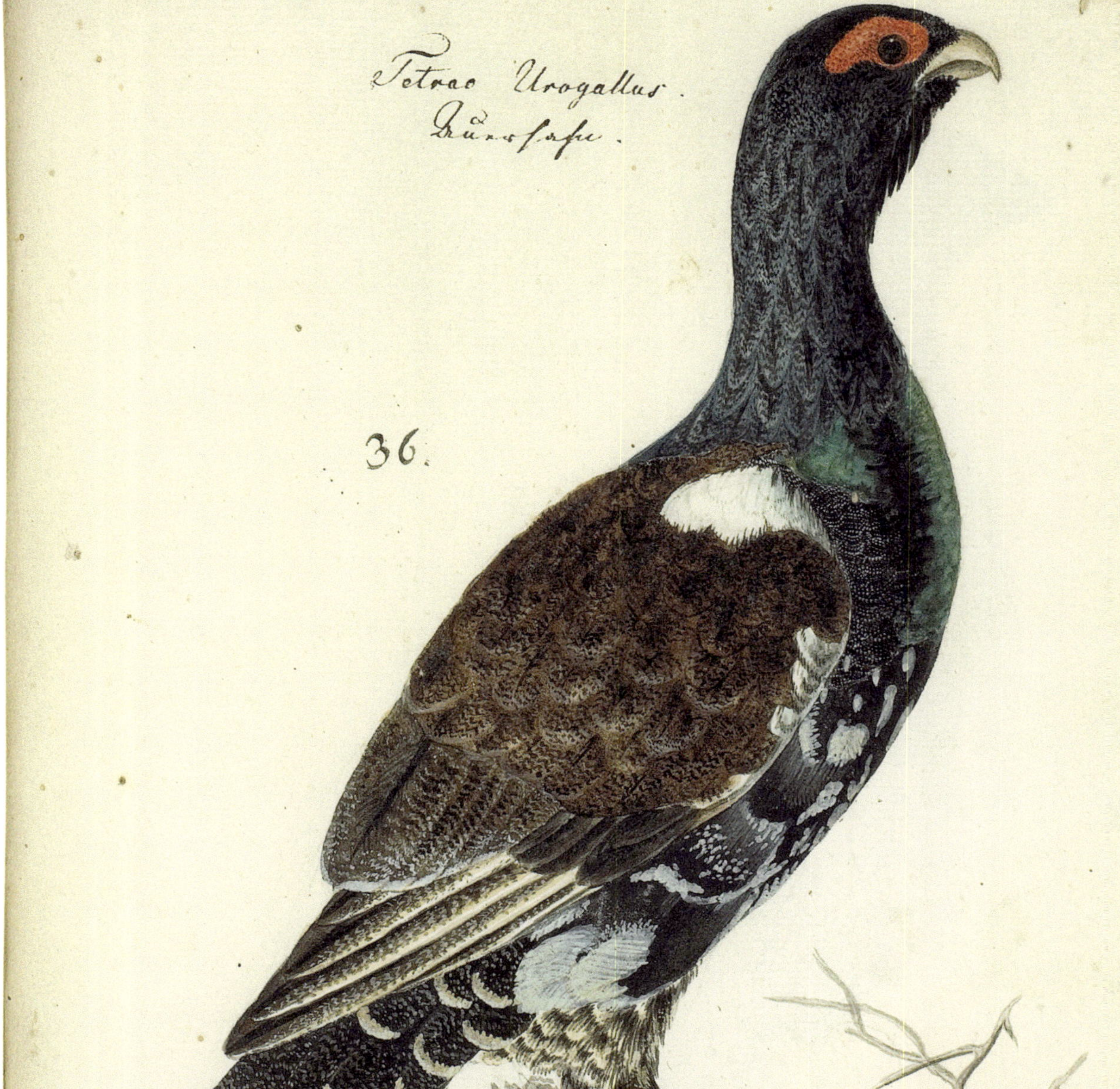

Haselhuhn (♂)

Tab. XX.

Tetrao Bonasia.
Haselhuhn.

39.

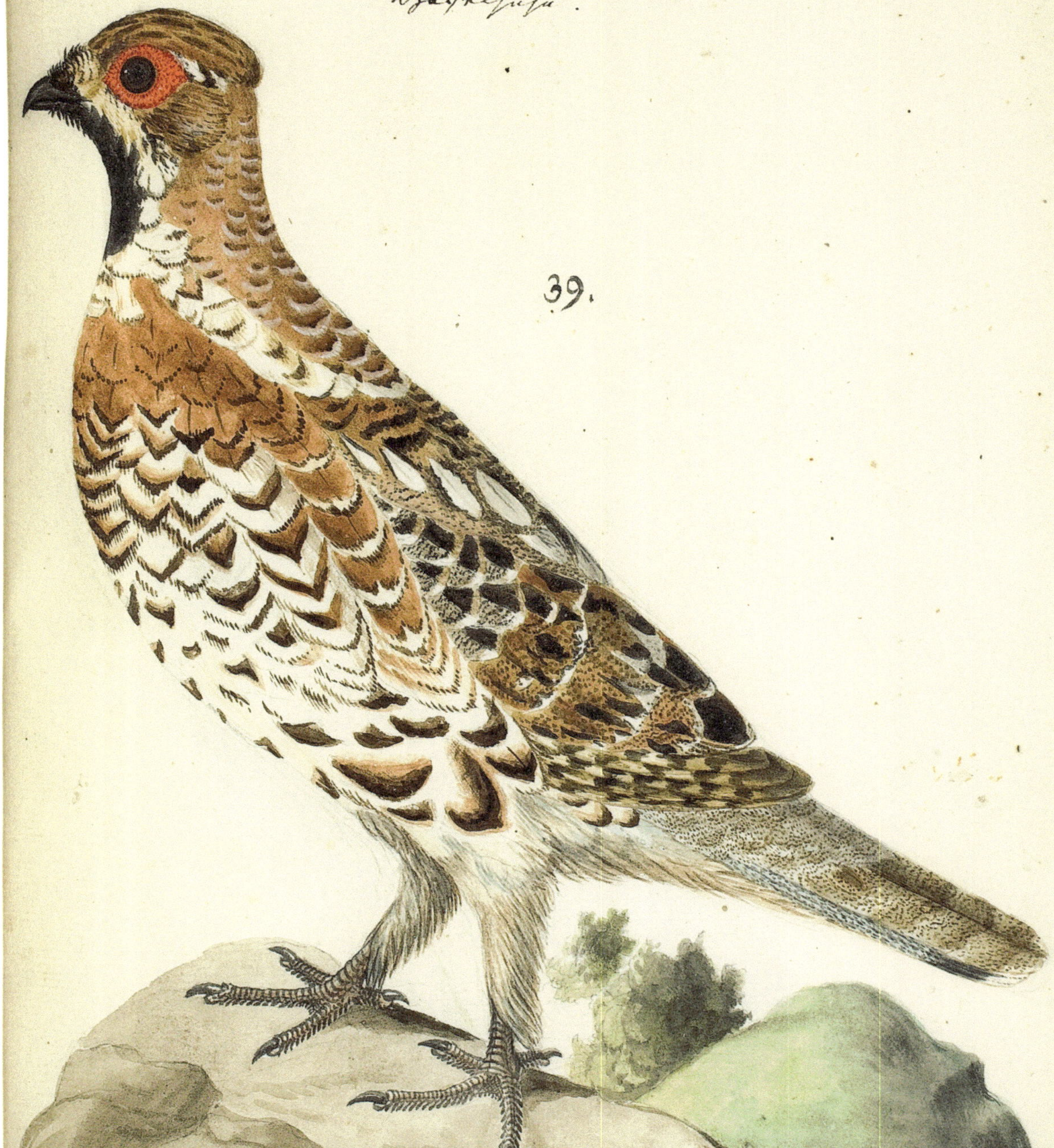

Goldregenpfeifer (♂)

12

Tab. 114
Fig 15

Charadrius auratus. ♂. Vere.

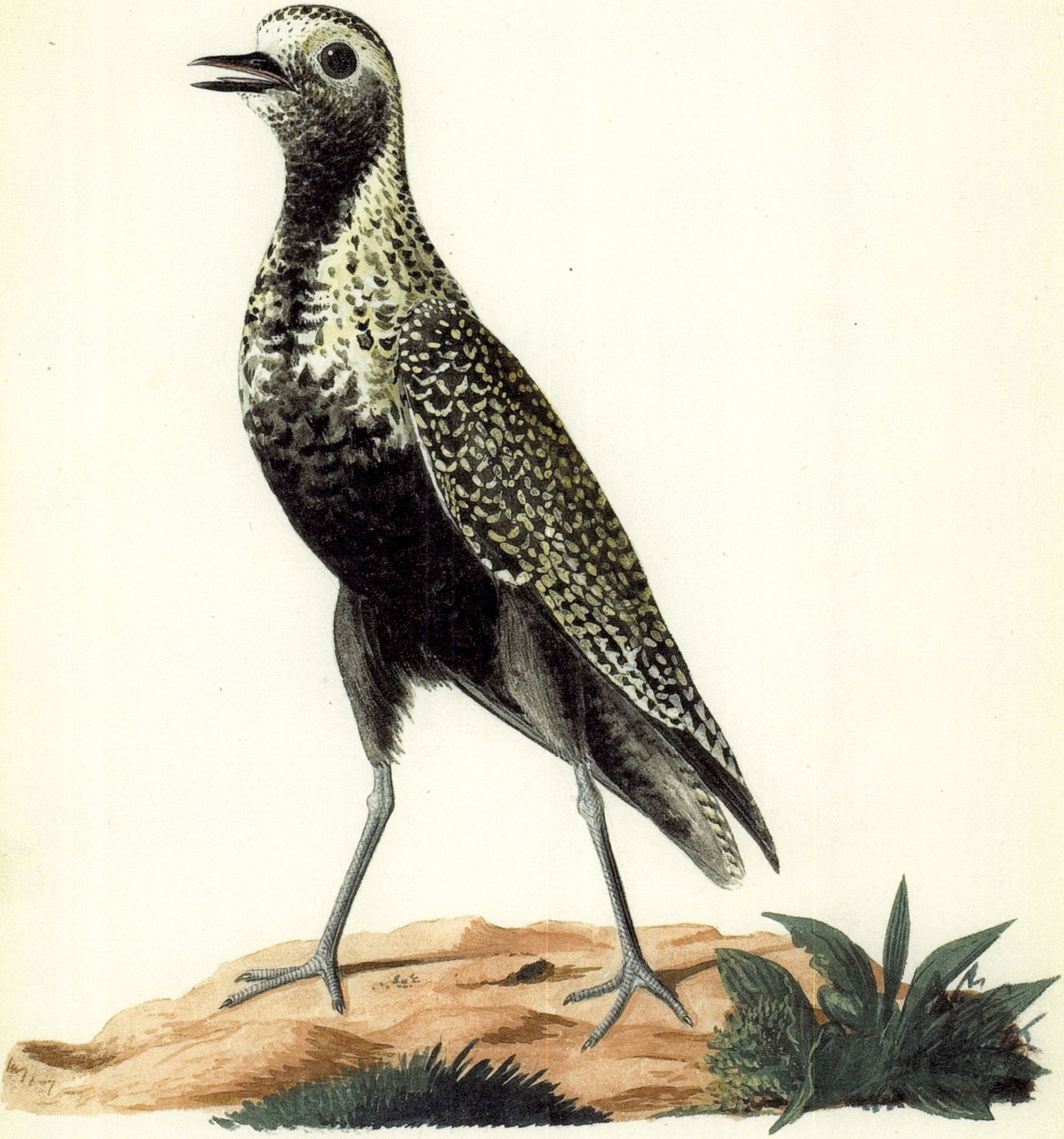

Graureiher (♂)

120

Ardea cinerea.

♂ adultus.

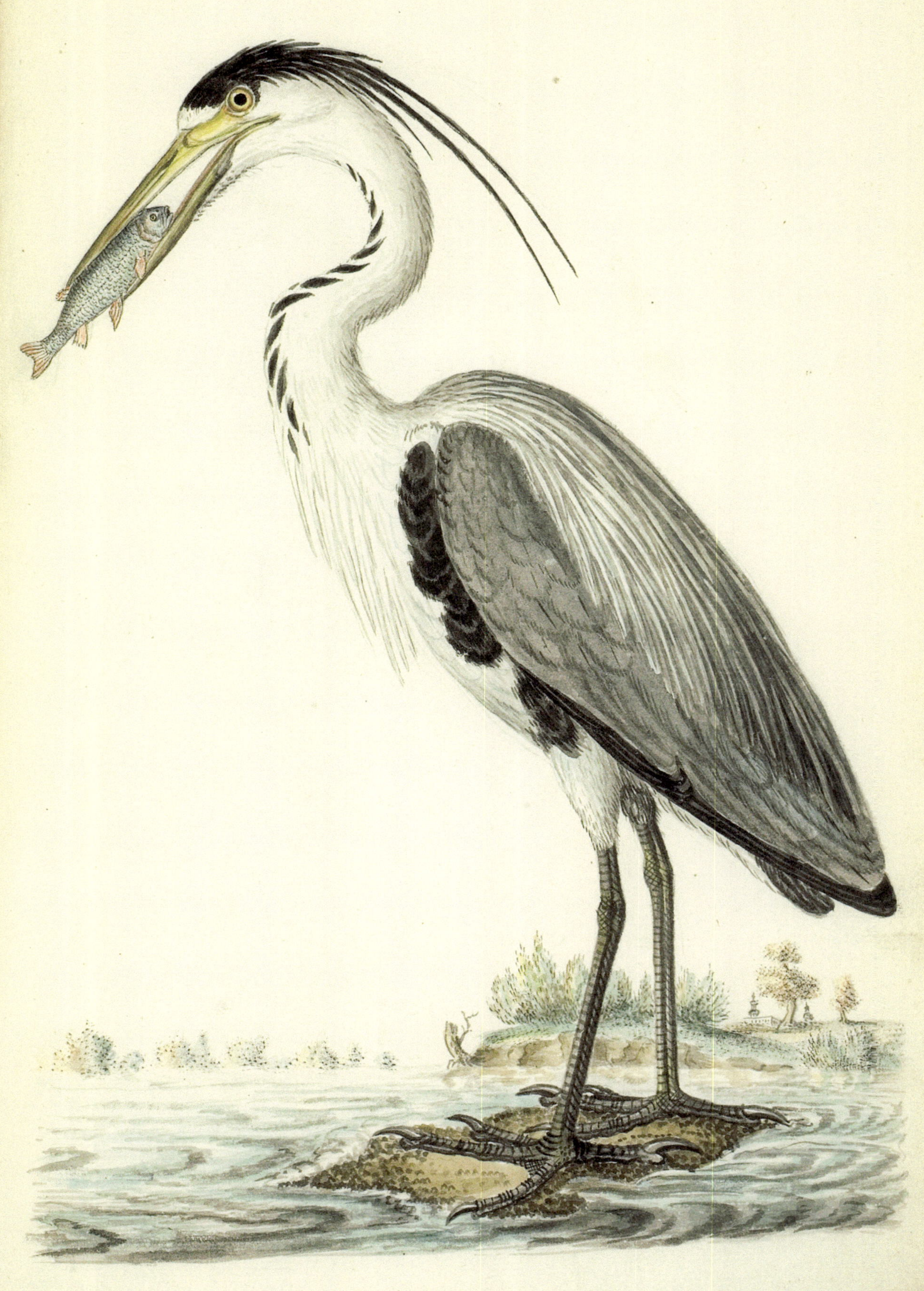

Nachtreiher (♂)

121

Ardea nycticorax.
♂ adultus.

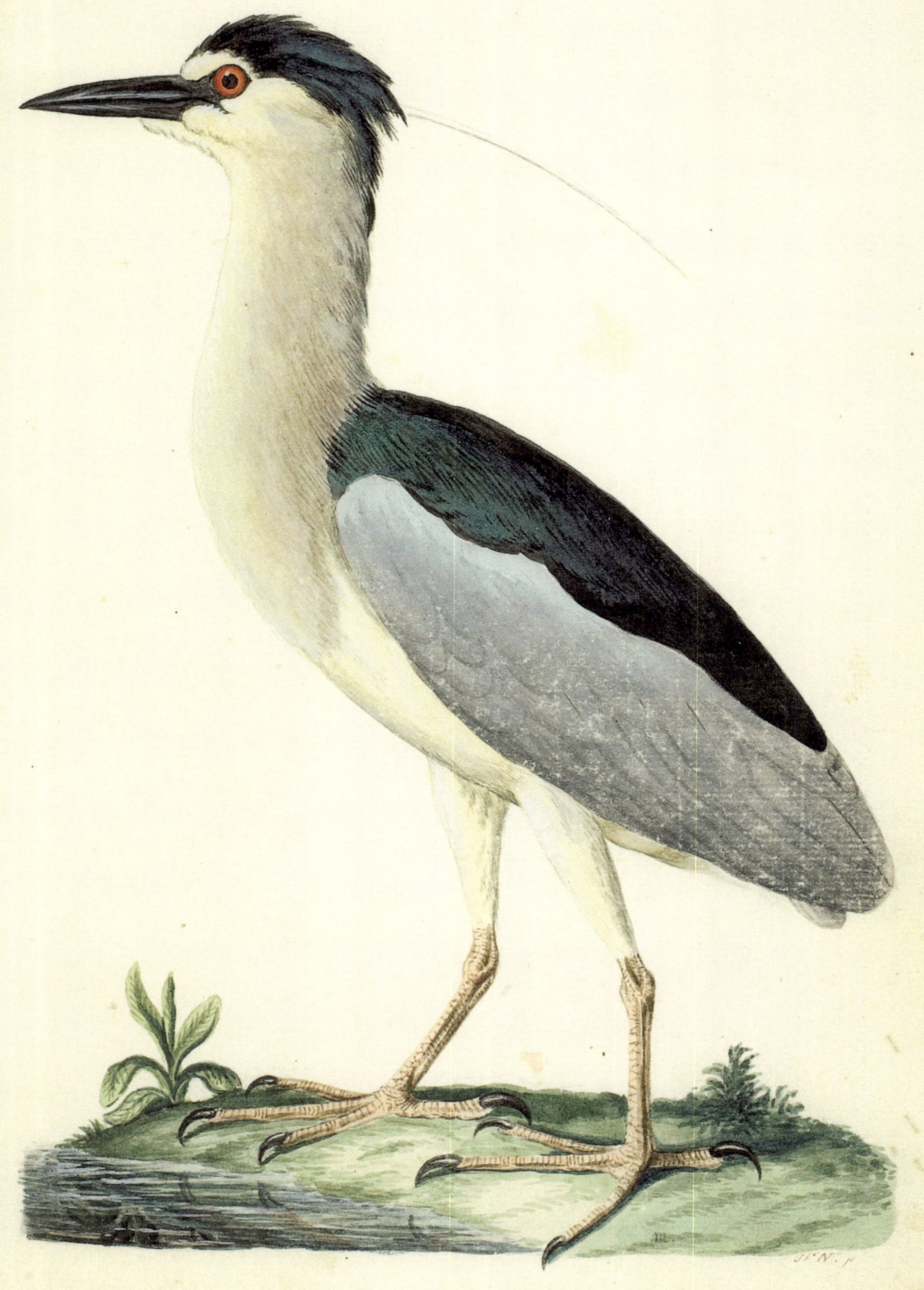

Nach dem Leben gemalt.

Rohrdommel (♀)

Ardea stellaris

♀ sen.

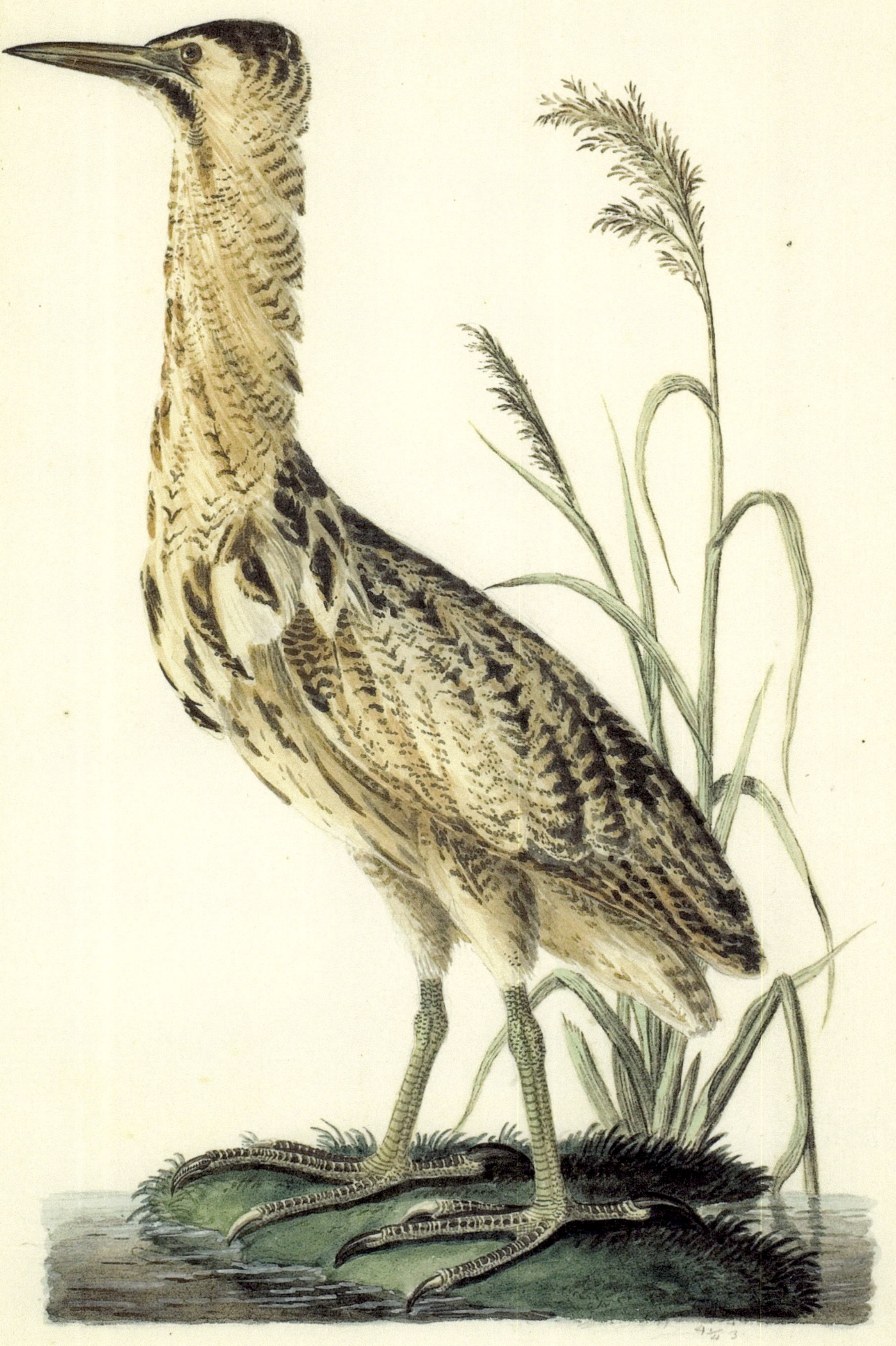

Zwergdommel (♂)

Ardea minuta
f. adulta.

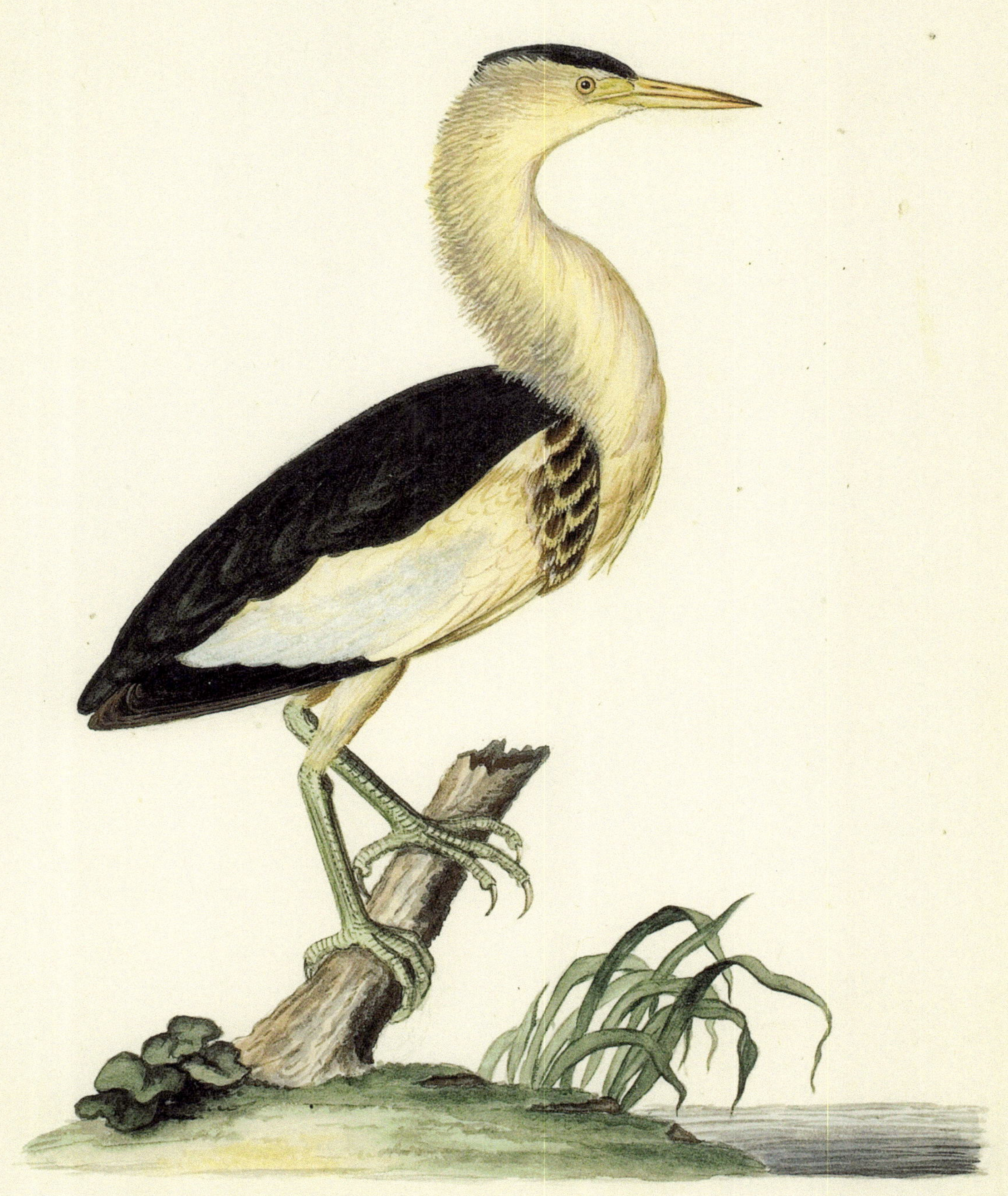

Oben: Zwergdommel (♀)
Unten: Zwergdommel (♀ juv.)

Ardea minuta

1. ♀ sen. 2. ♂ juv.

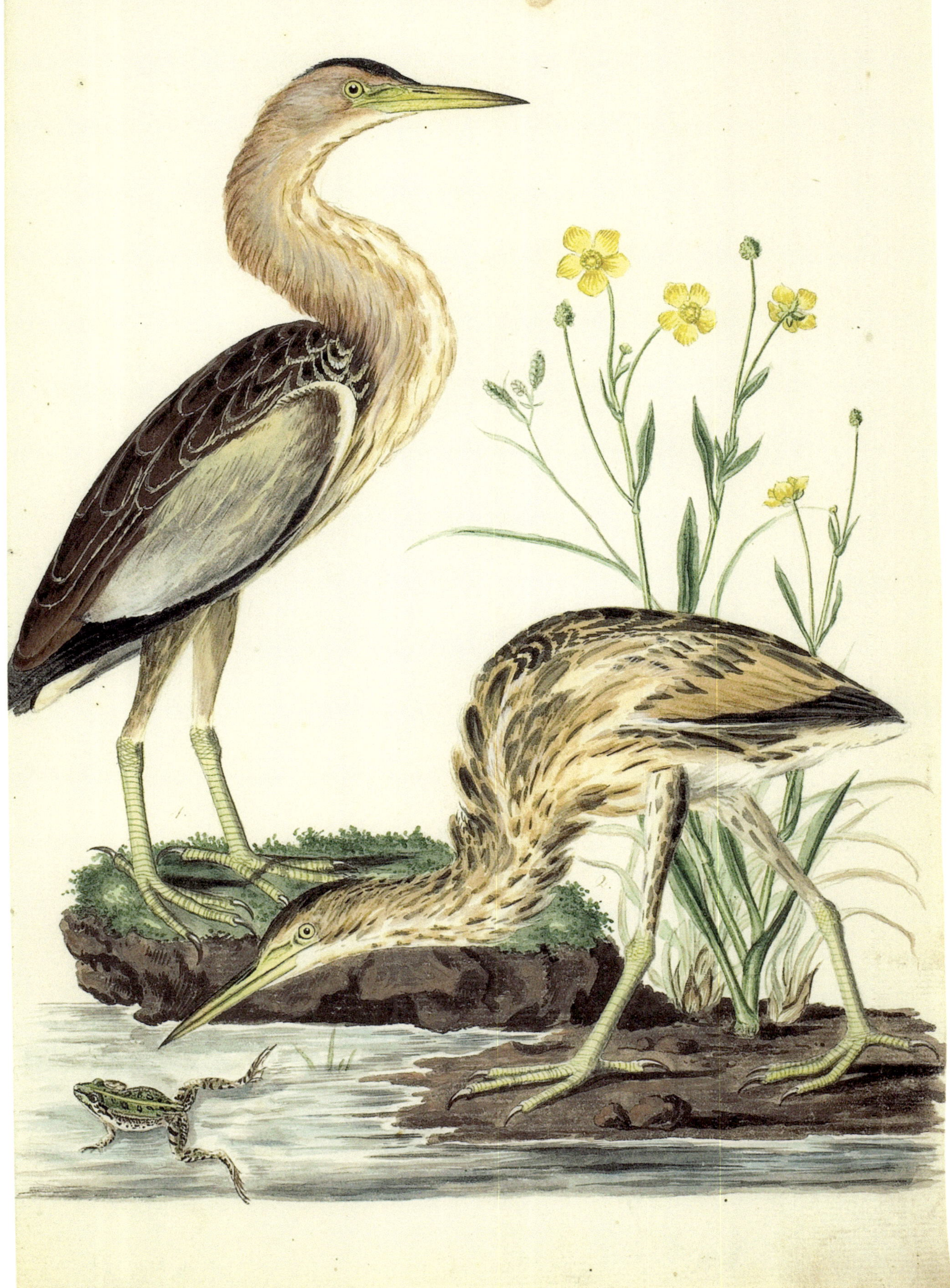

Weißstorch (♂)

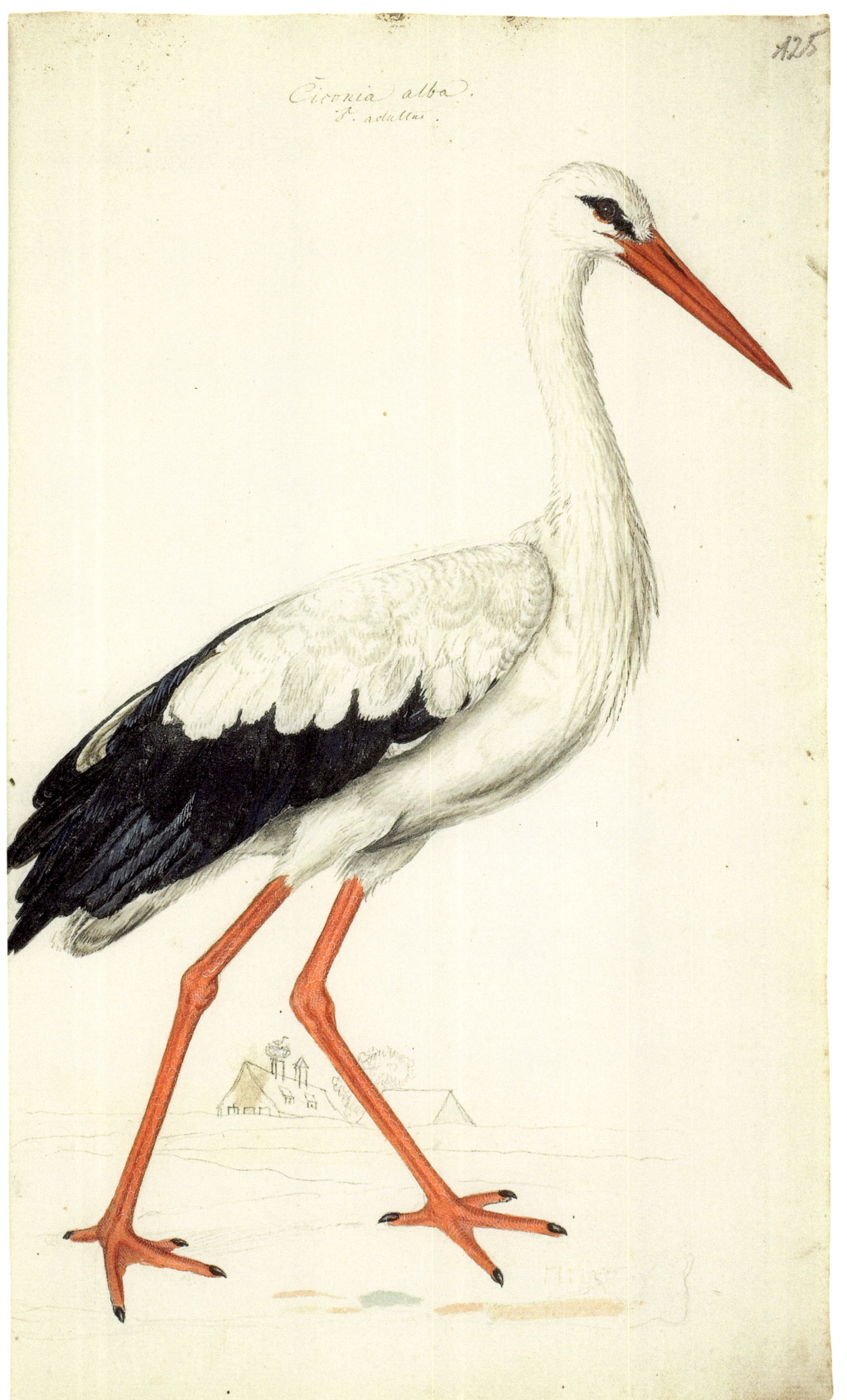
125
Ciconia alba.
♂. adultus.

Kranich (♀)

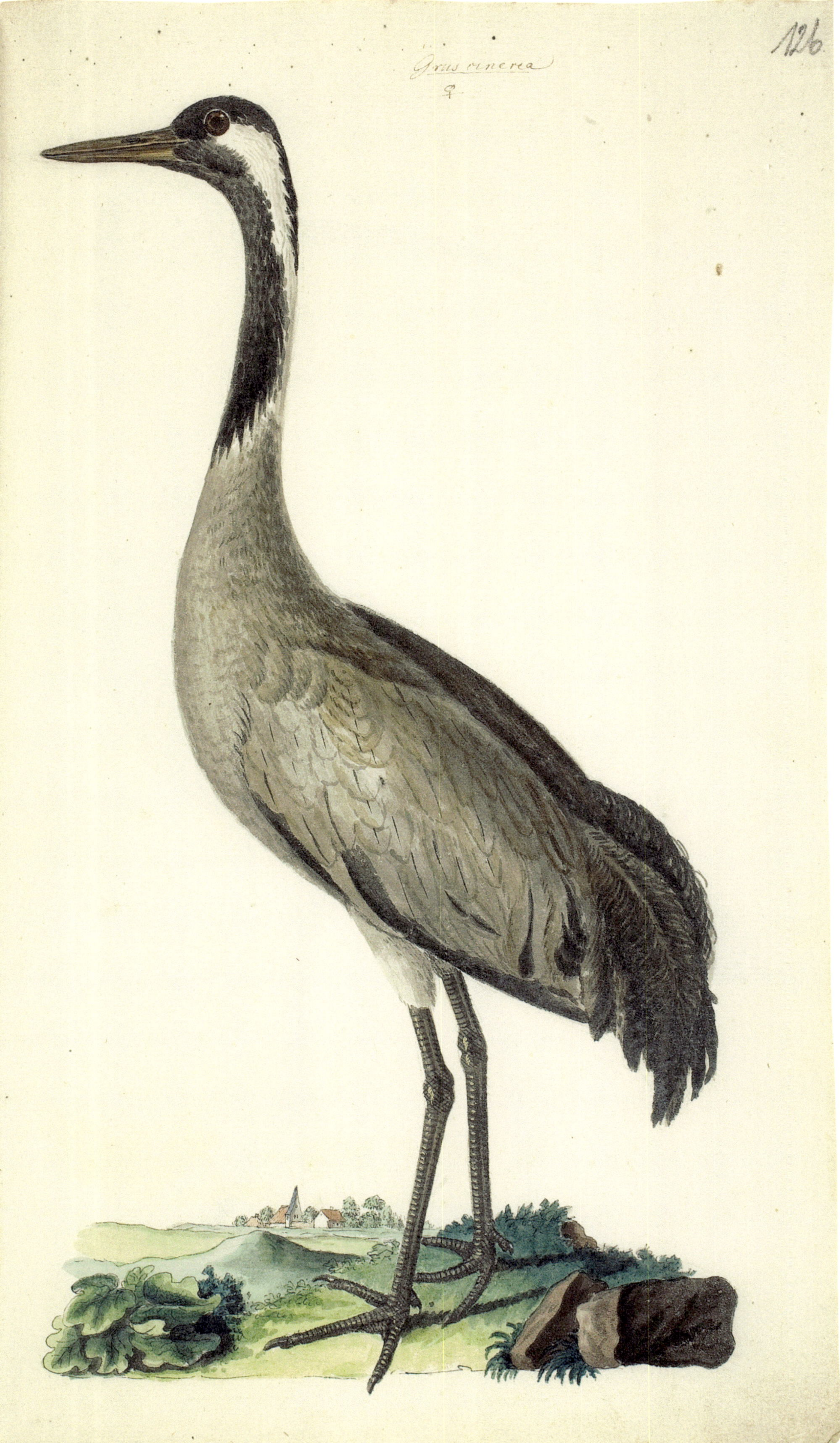
126
Grus cinerea
♀

Großer Brachvogel (♂)

Numenius arquata:

♂ primo autumno.

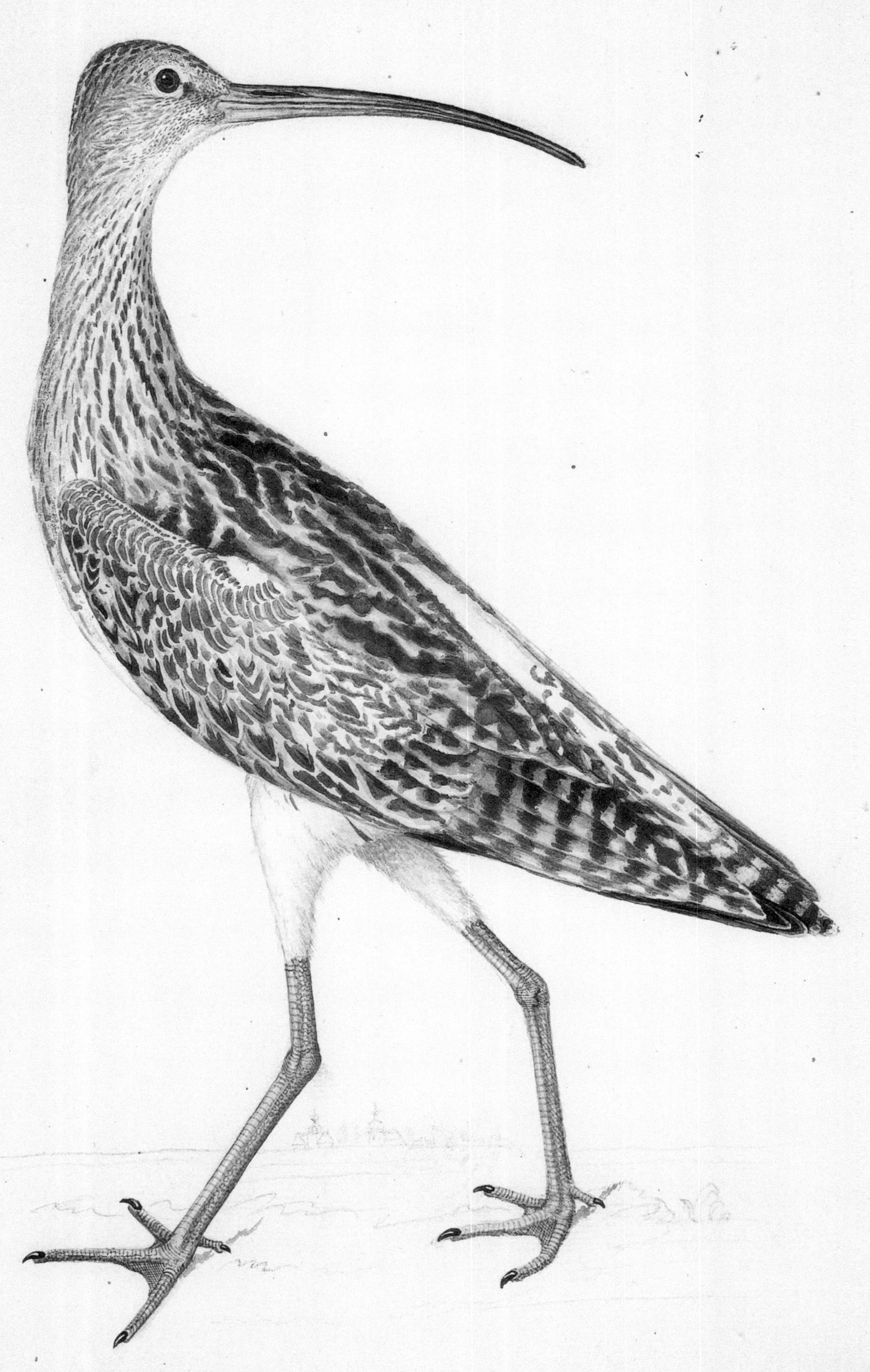

Waldschnepfe (♂)

Scolopax rusticula
♂

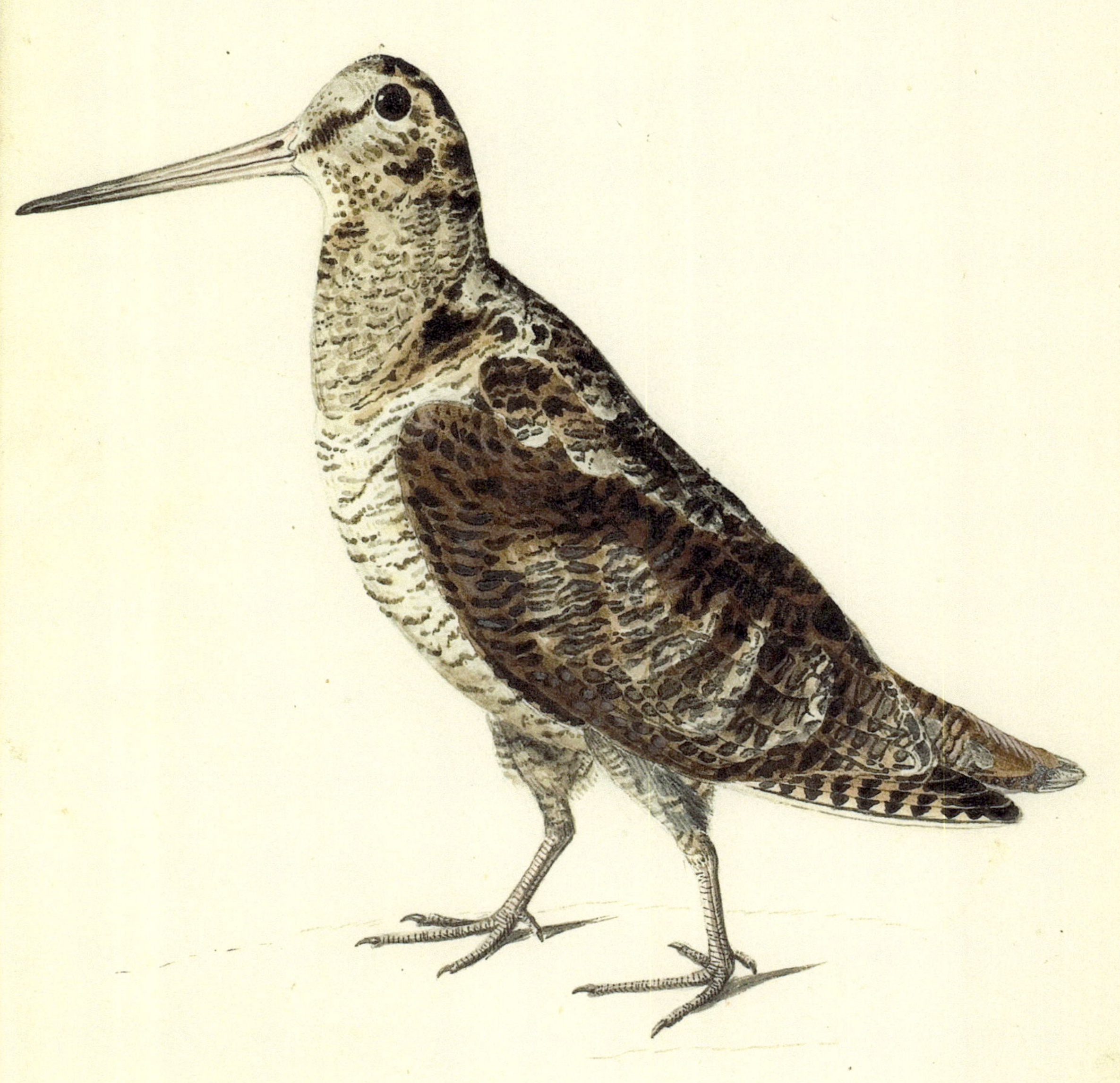

Bekassine (♂)

132

Scolopax gallinago

(St. Vere)

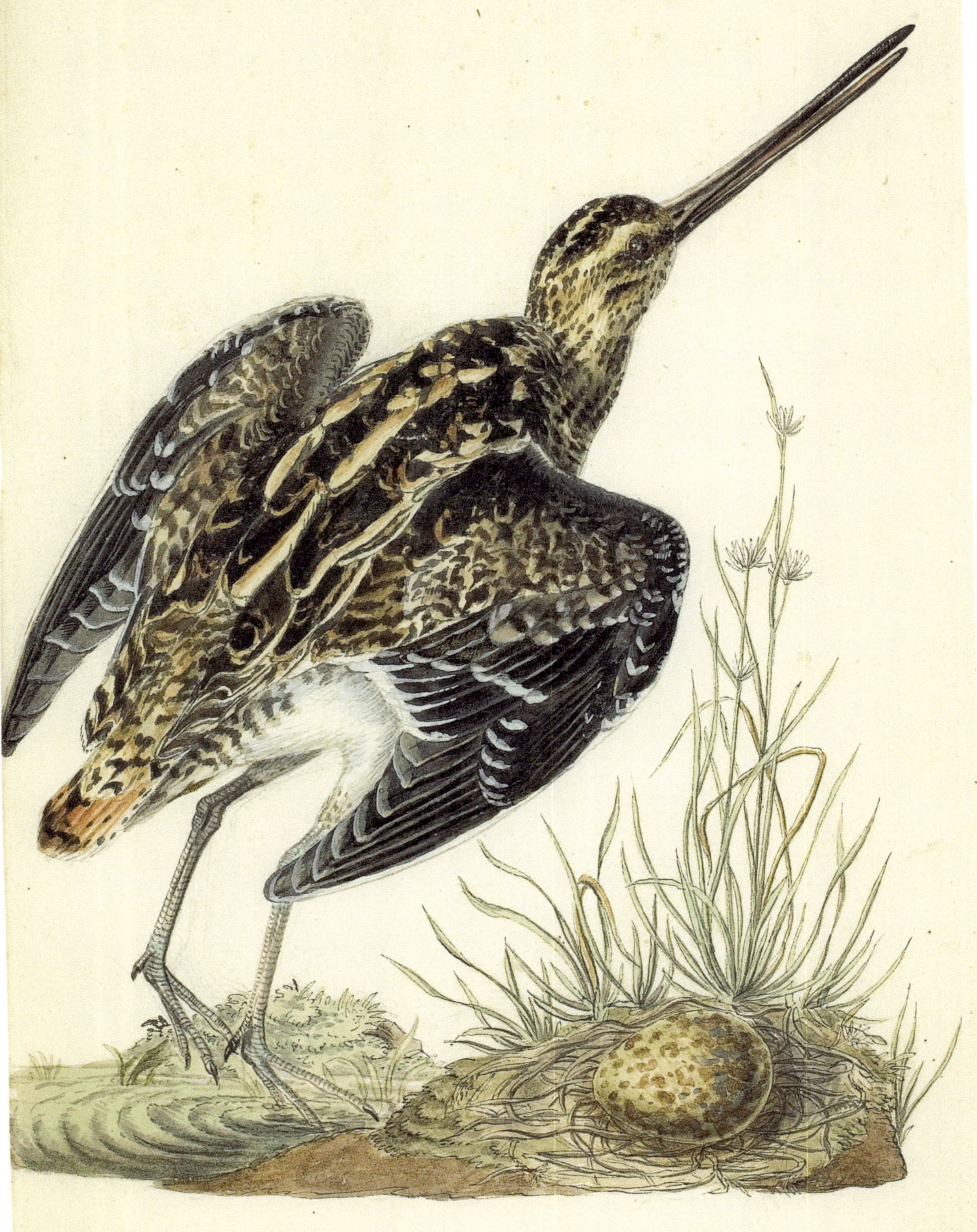

Kampfläufer (♂)

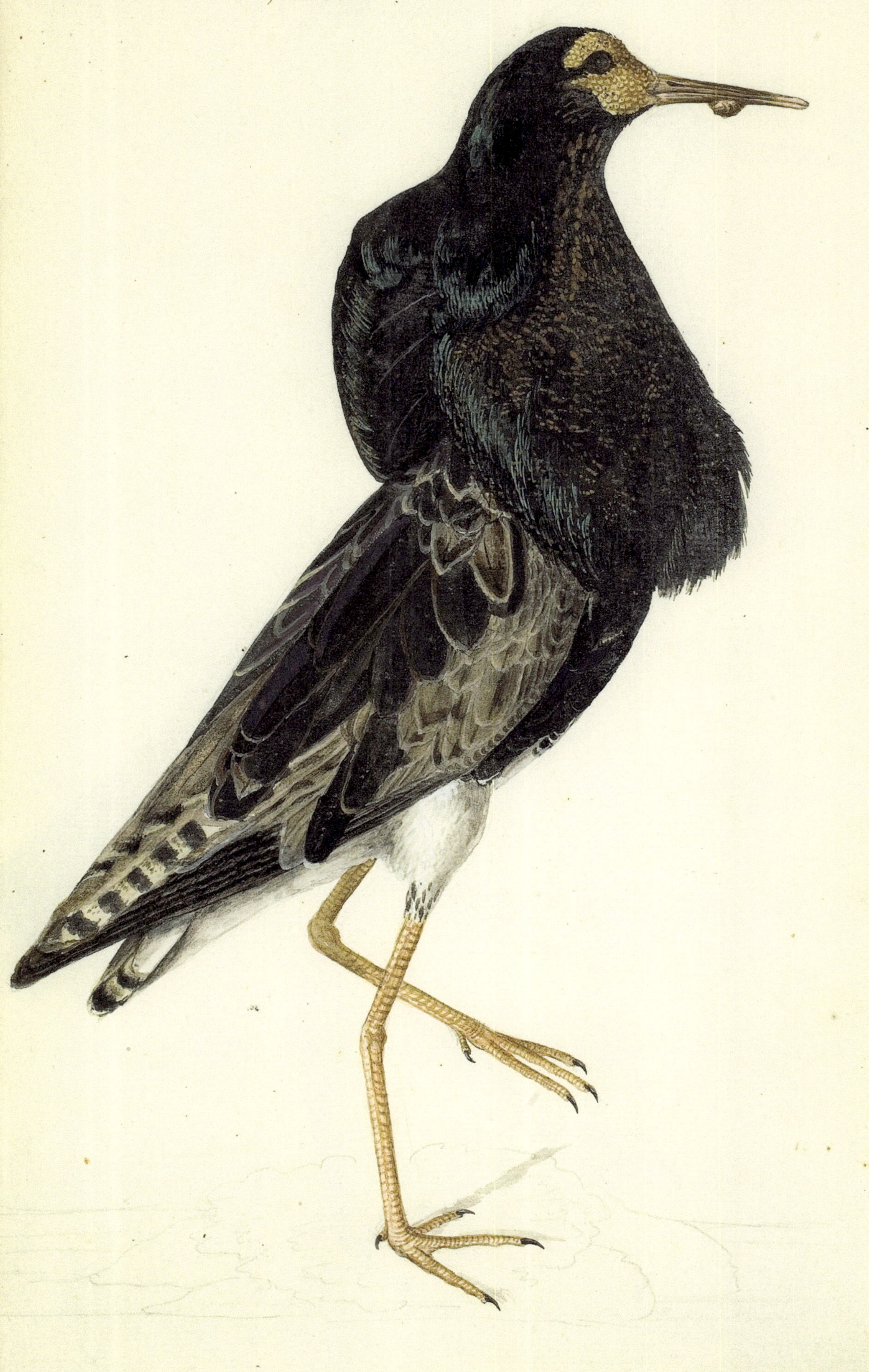
139
Machetes pugnax
♂. ptil. aestiv.

Kampfläufer (♂)

141

Machetes pugnax.
♂. ptil. aest.

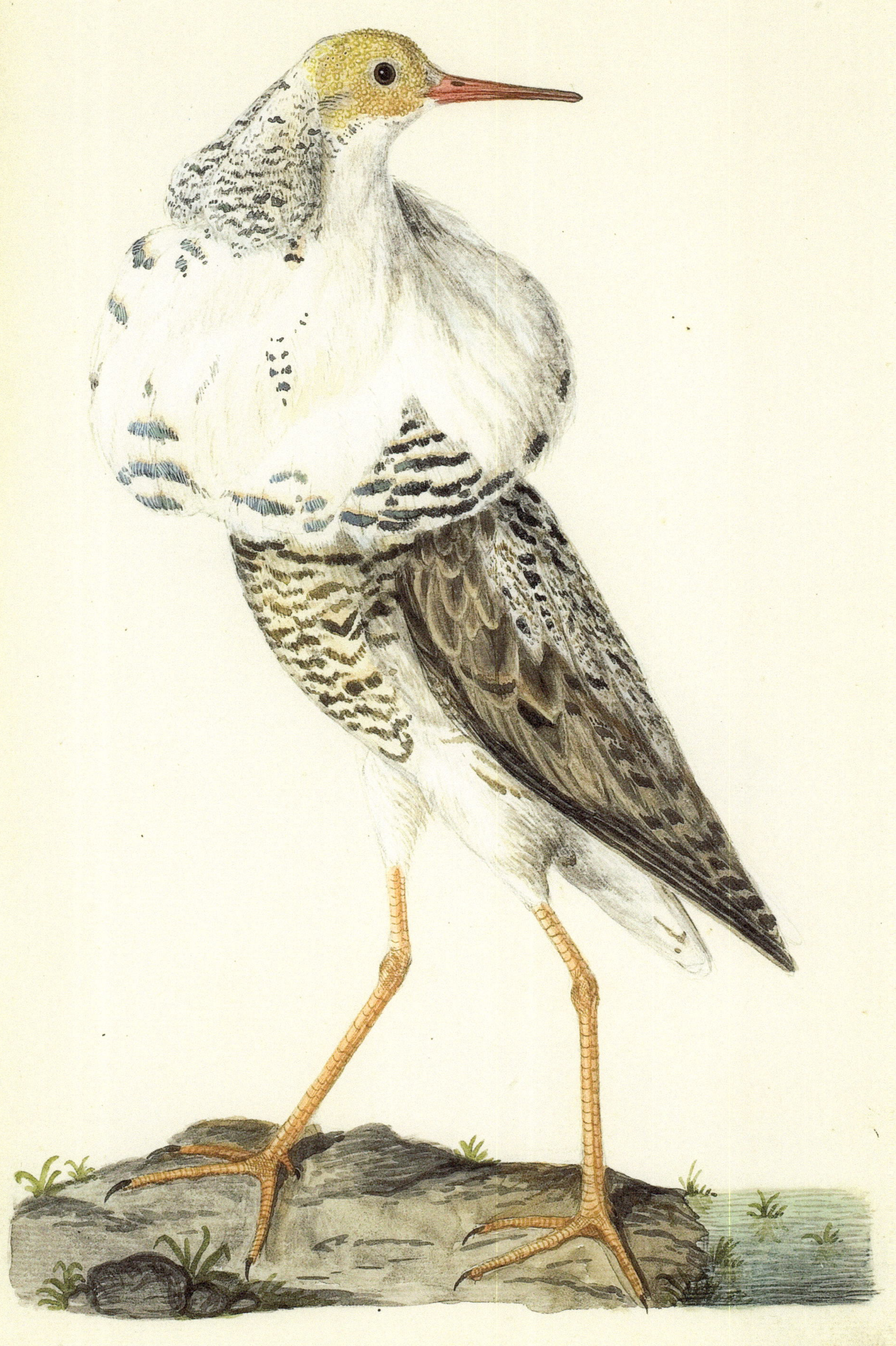

Kiebitzregenpfeifer (♂ juv.)

152

Charadrius Tringa Squatarola [illegible]. varius. [illegible]. ptil. juv.

grau Kiebitz-Regenpfeifer

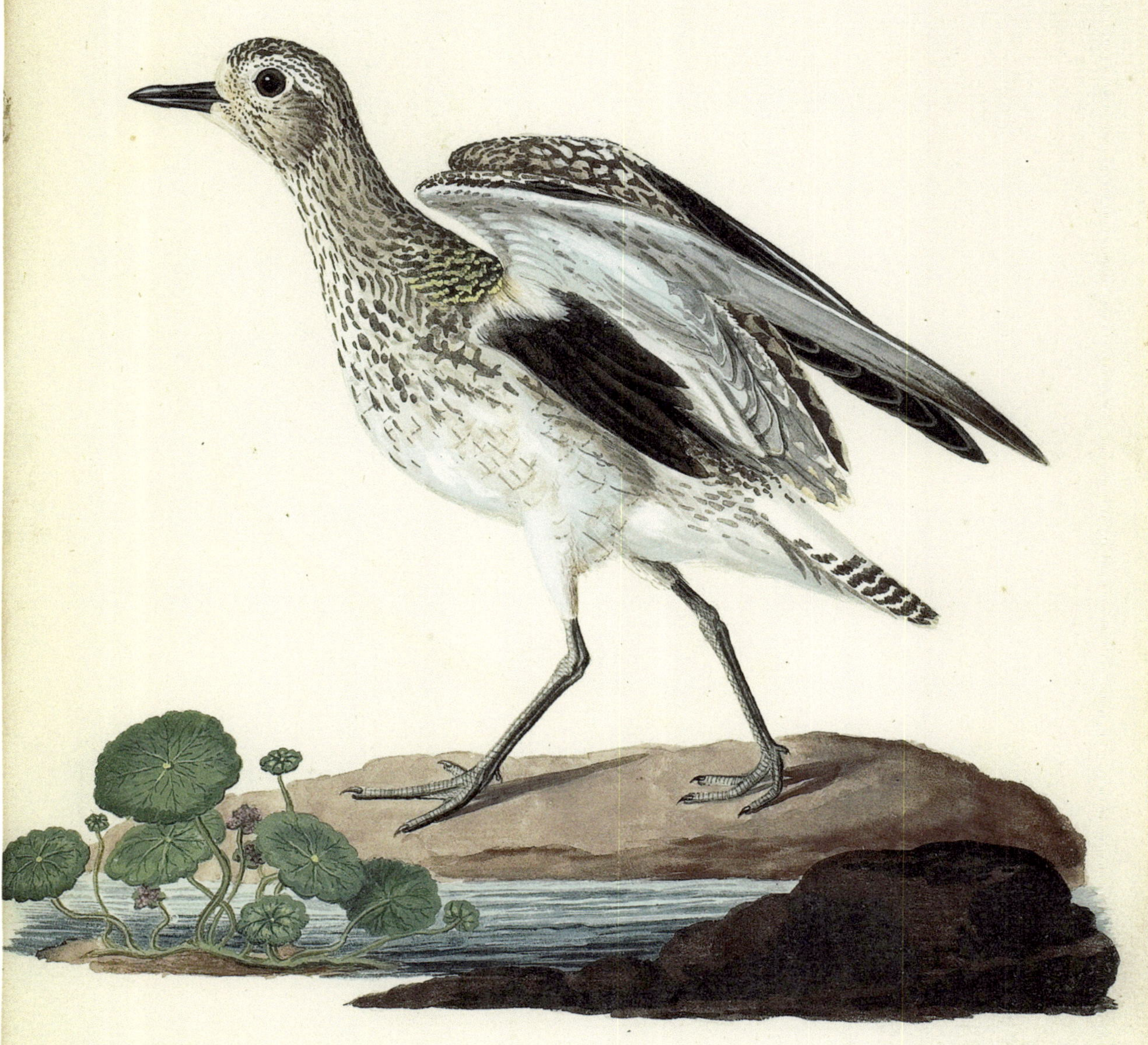

Zwergsumpfhuhn (♀)

Crex pusilla.

♀ ptil. bien. nupt.

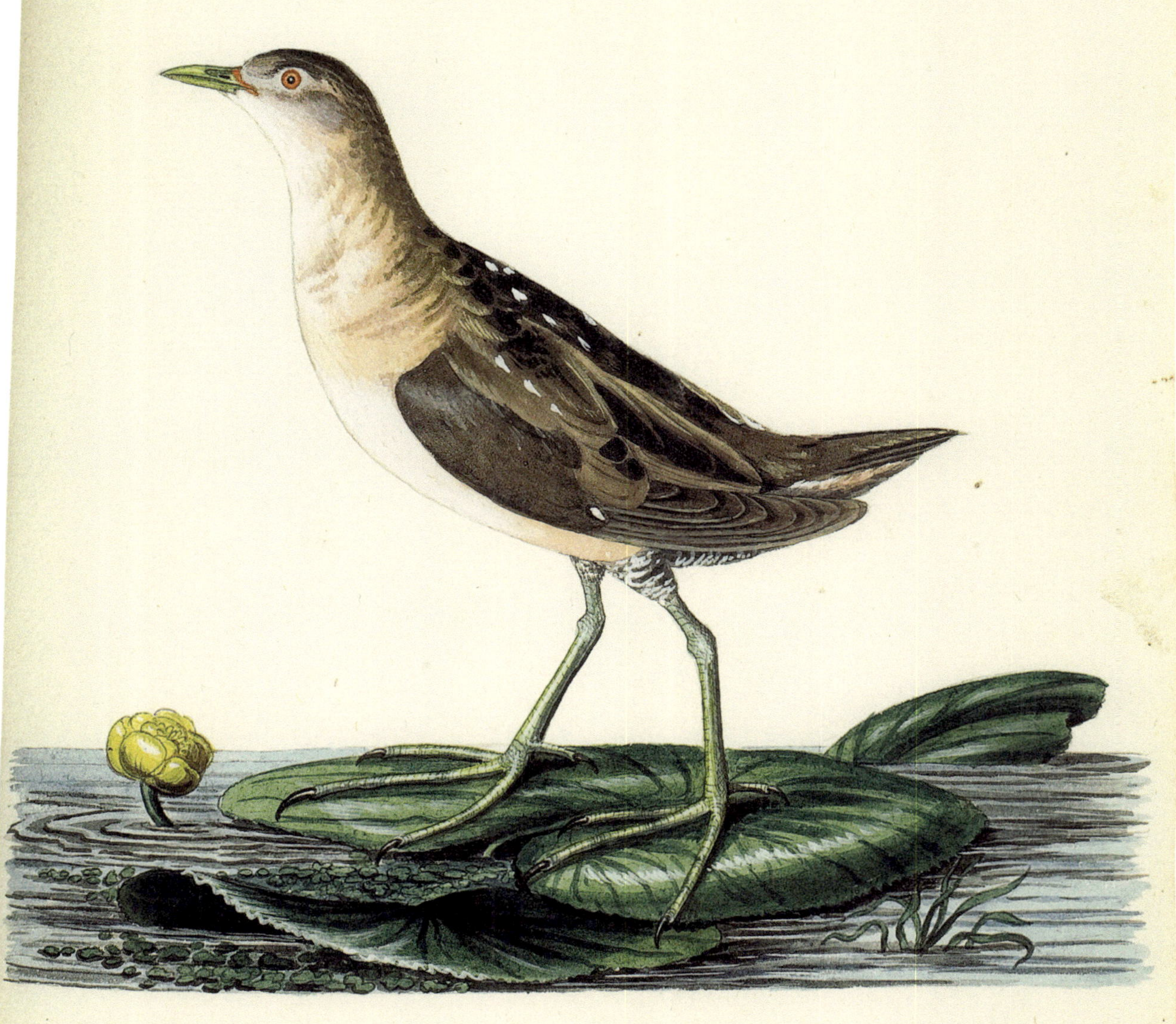

Teichhuhn (♂)

Gallinula chloropus . ♂. adult.

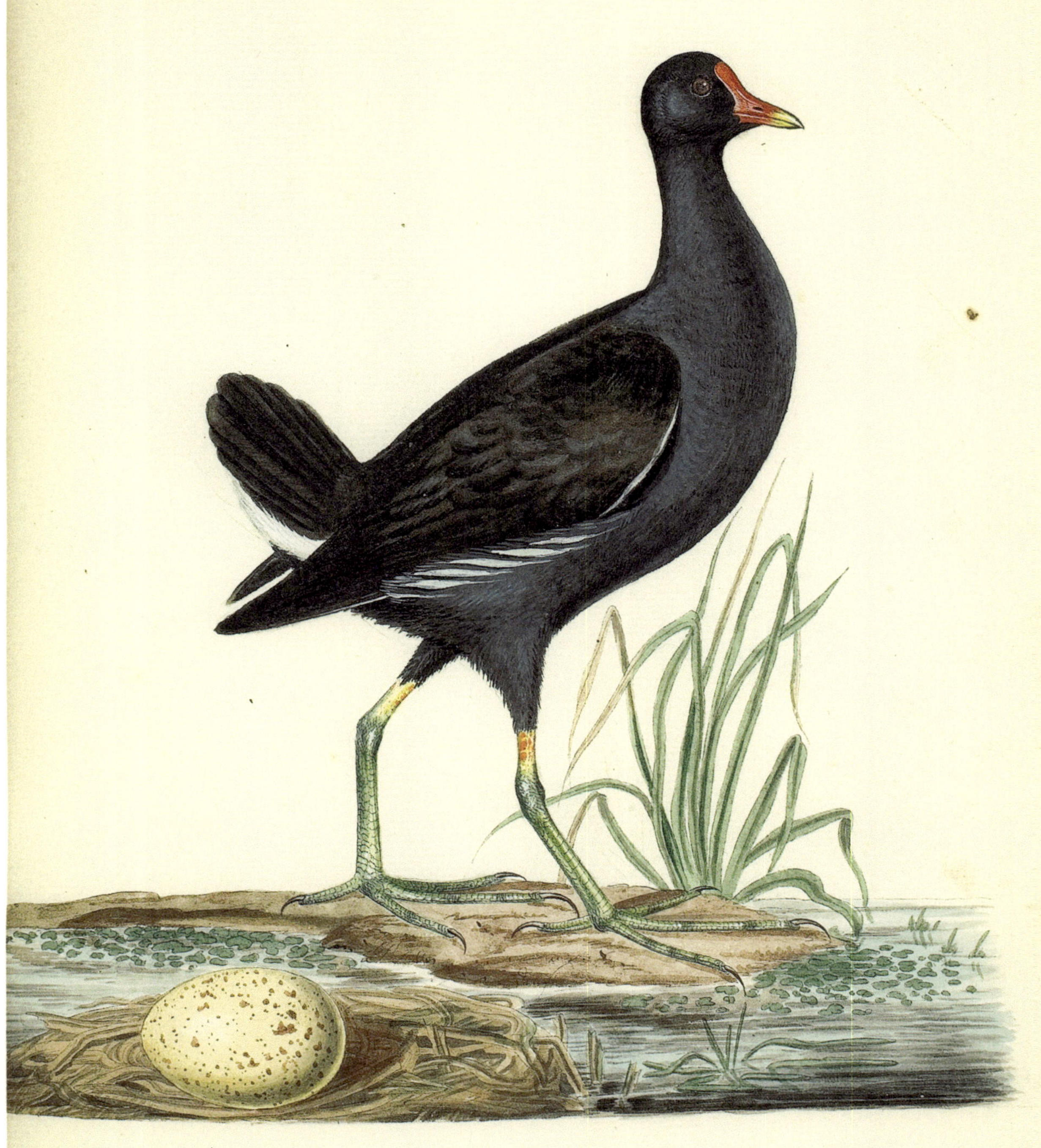

Tüpfelralle (♂)

157

Crex porzana.

♂. adult. pl. nuptial.

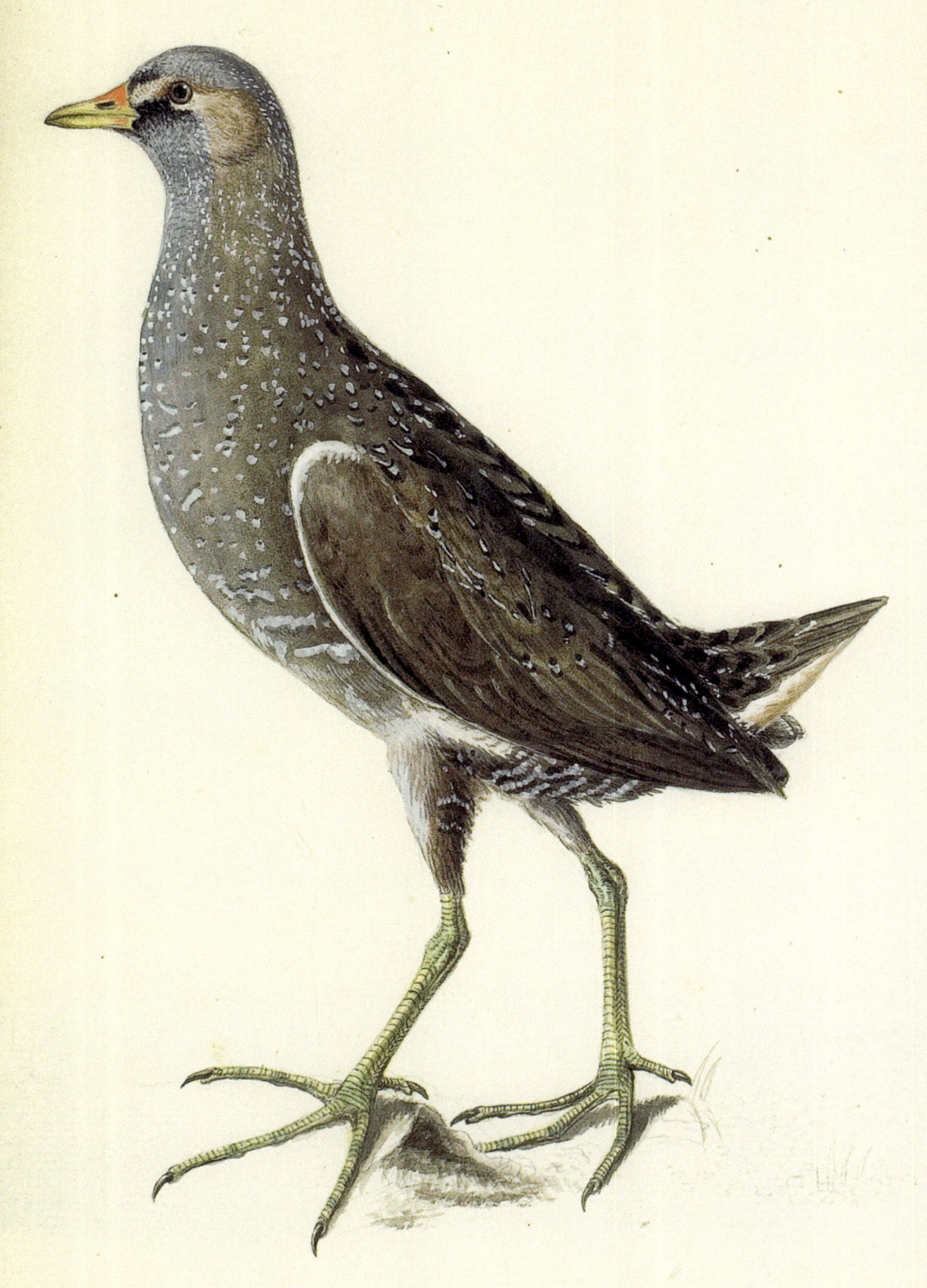

Oben: Odinshühnchen (♂ juv.)
Unten: Odinshühnchen (♀)

159

Tringa lobata

Strandläuferchen mit belappten Zehen, bei [illegible] geschossen.

Phalaropus angustirostris

F. ptil. juv.

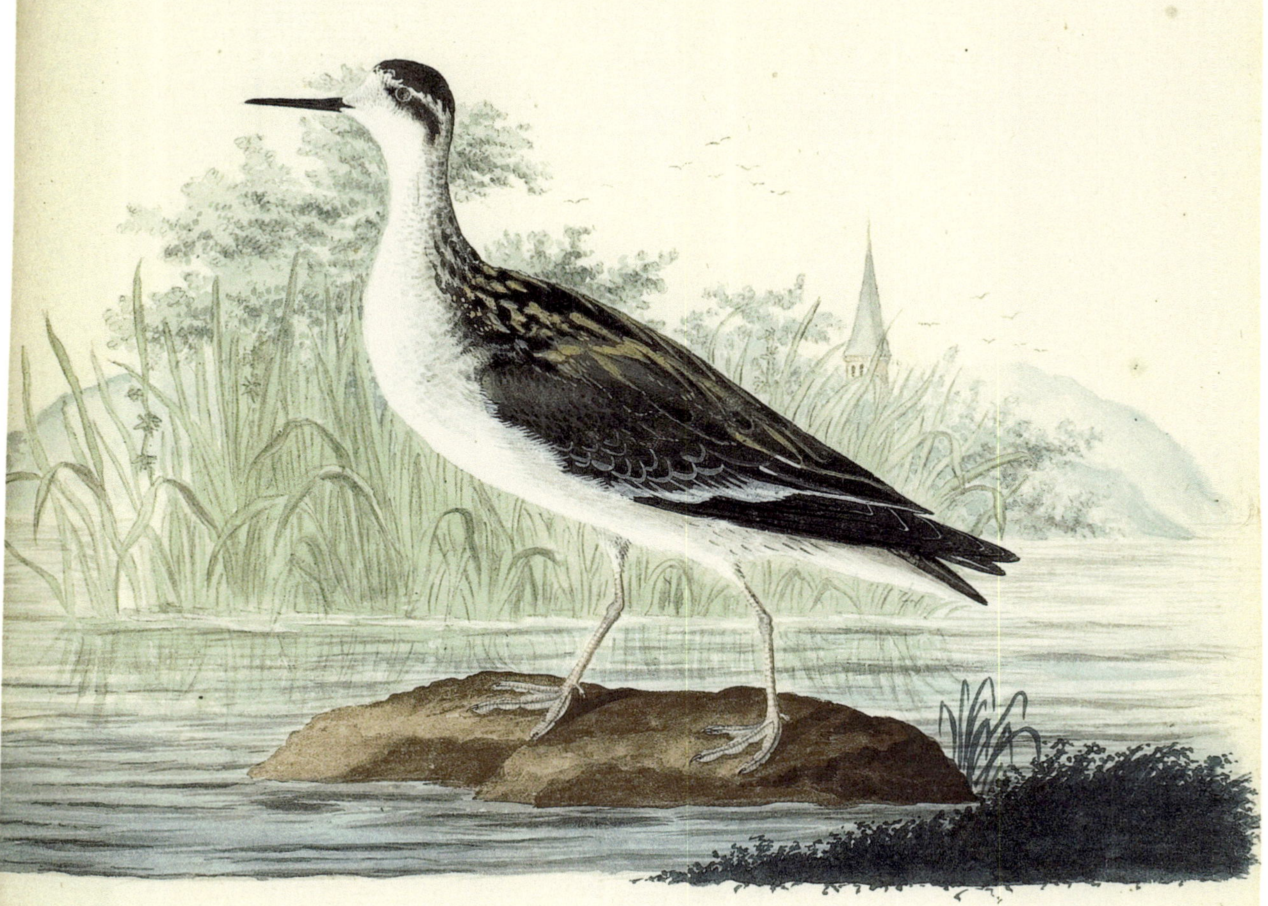

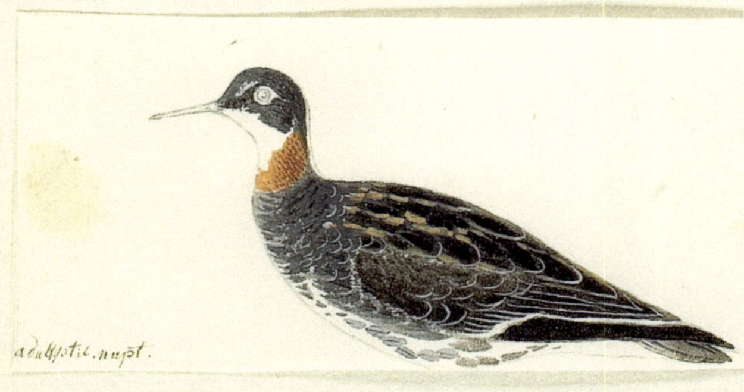

adult. stat. nupt.

Papageitaucher (juv.)

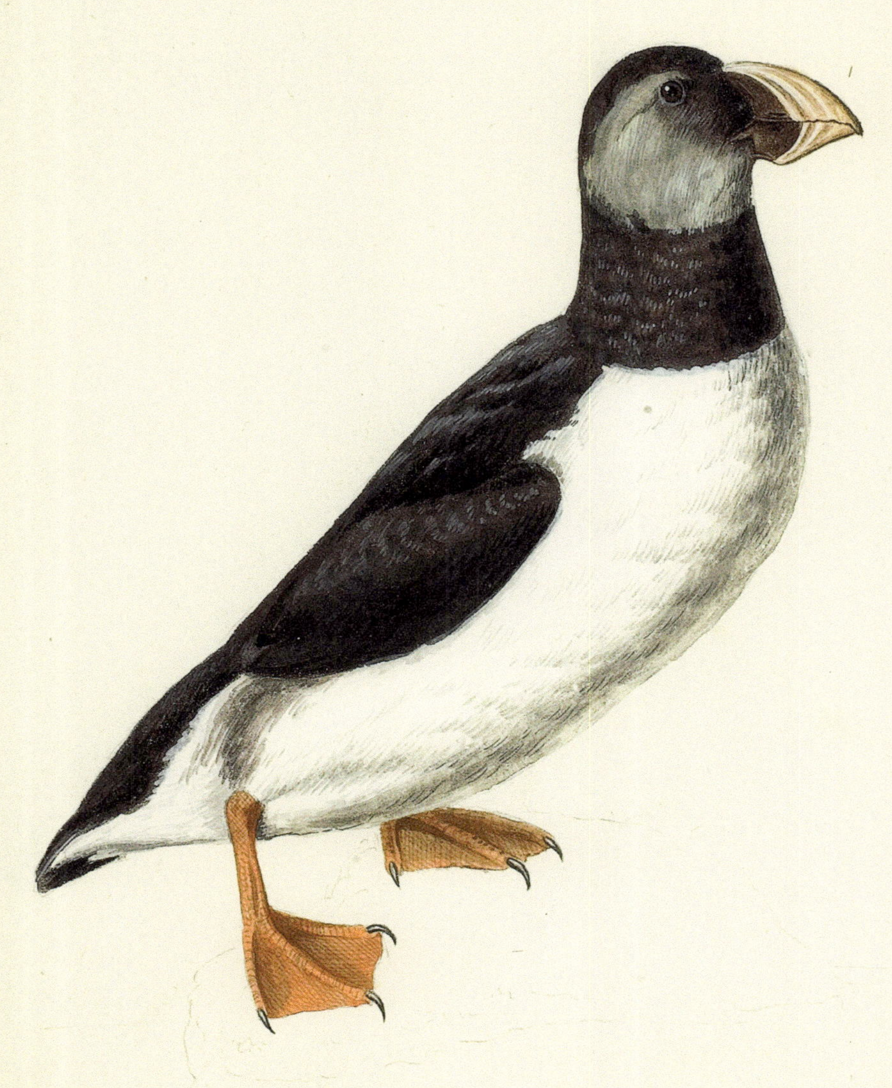
166

Gryllteiste (♂)

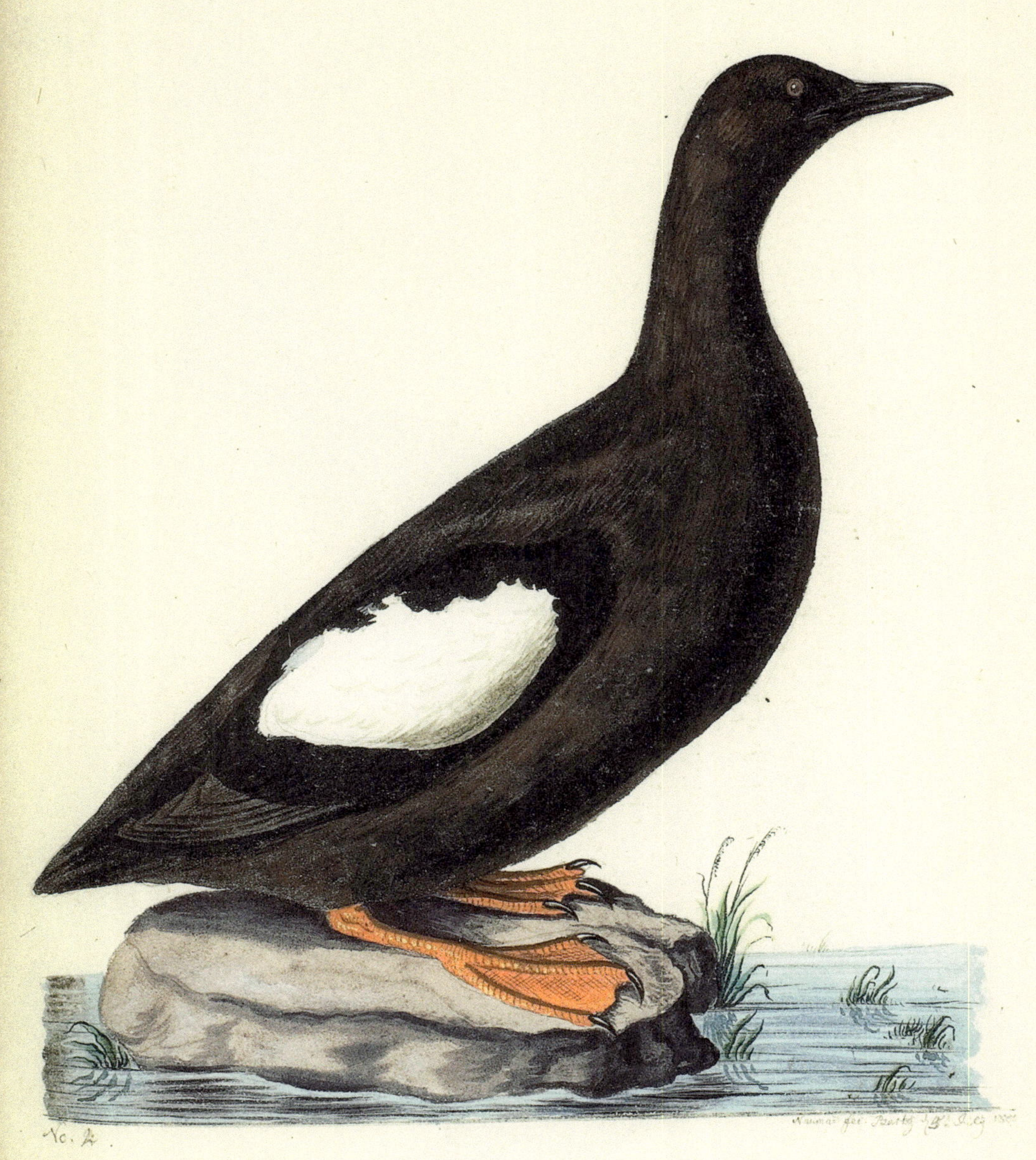
No. 2.

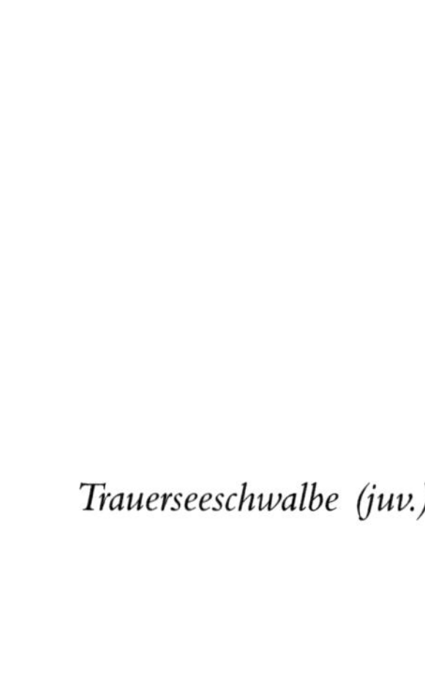

Trauerseeschwalbe (juv.)

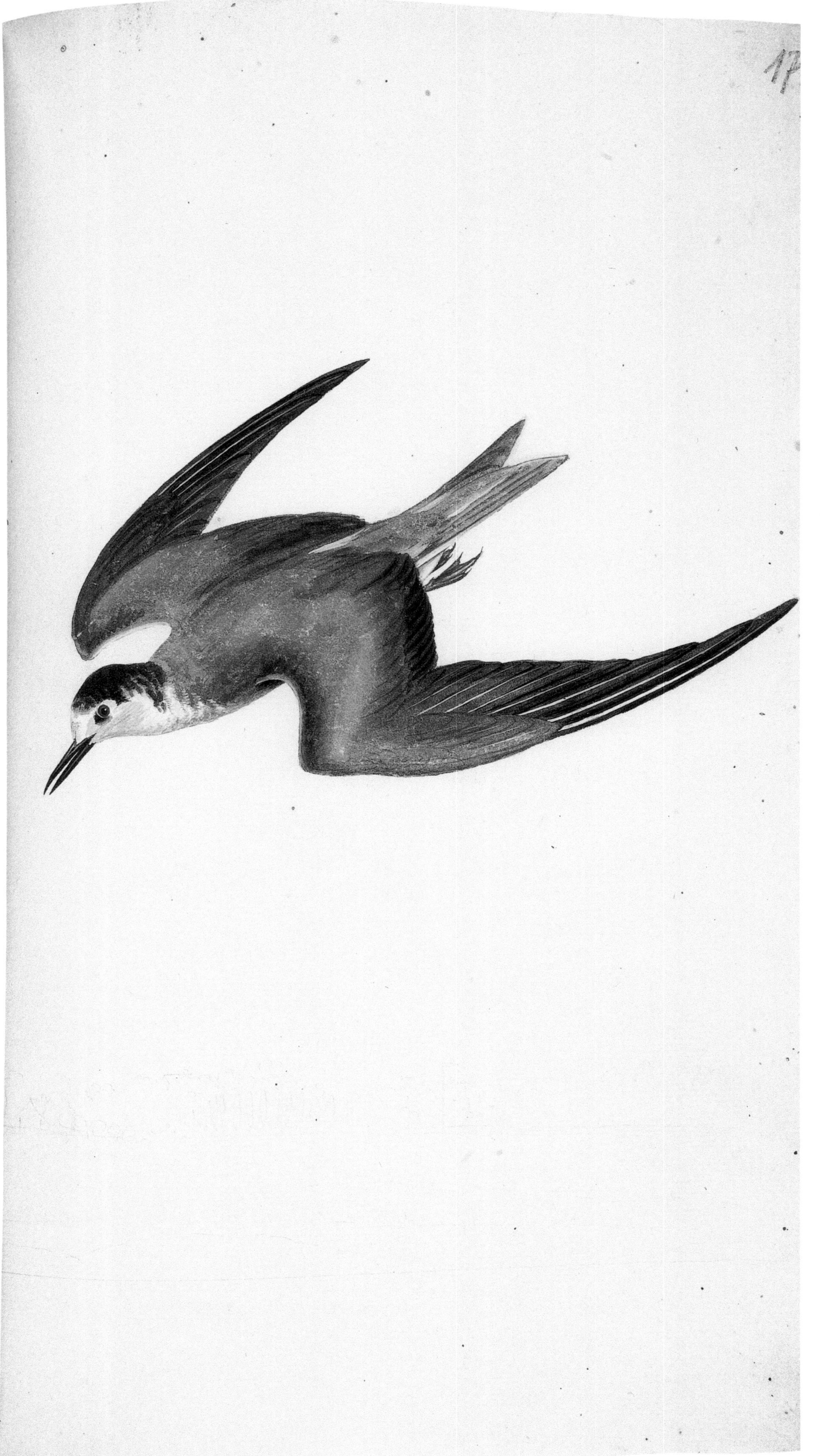

Lachmöwe (♂)

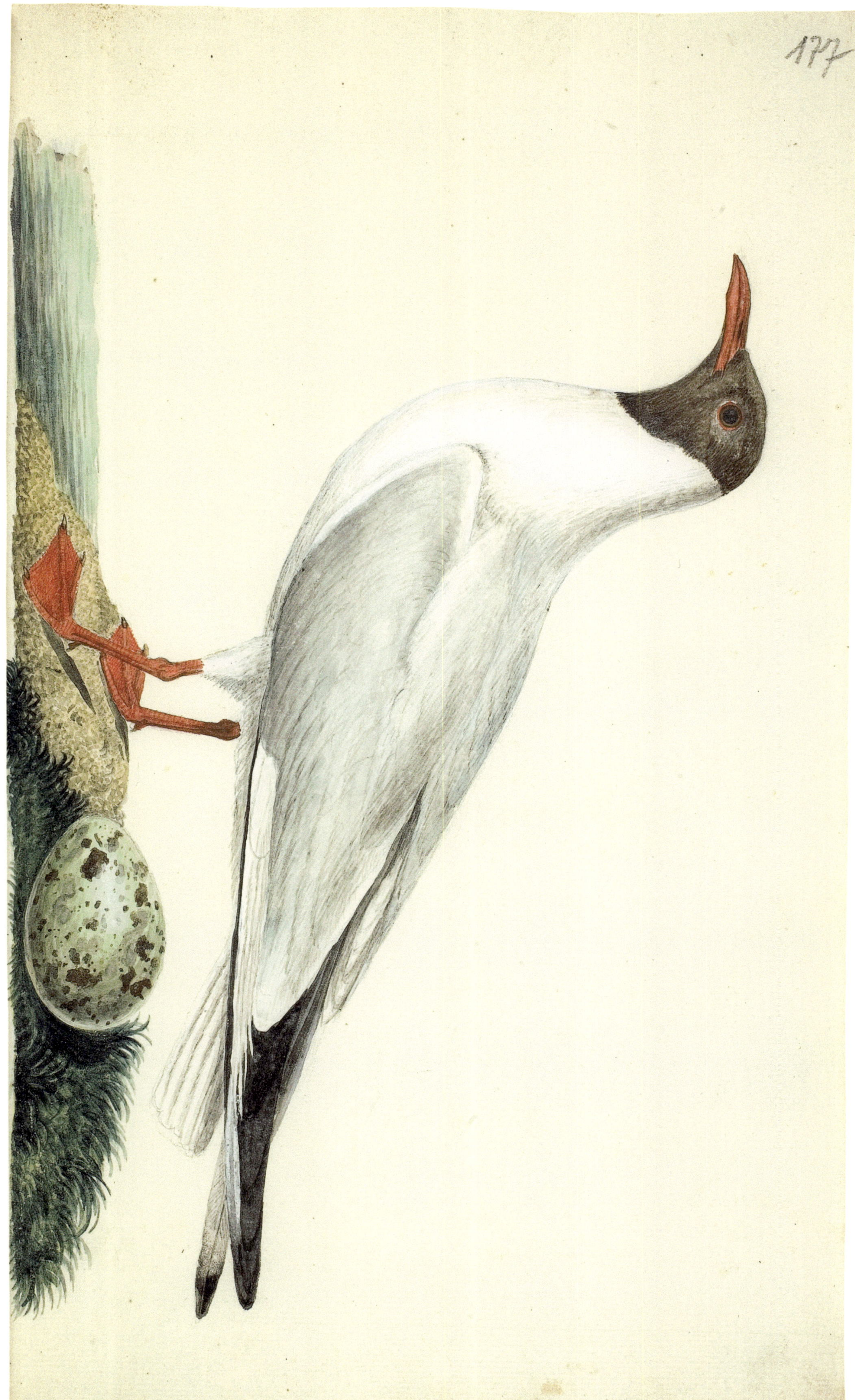
177

Dreizehenmöve (juv.)

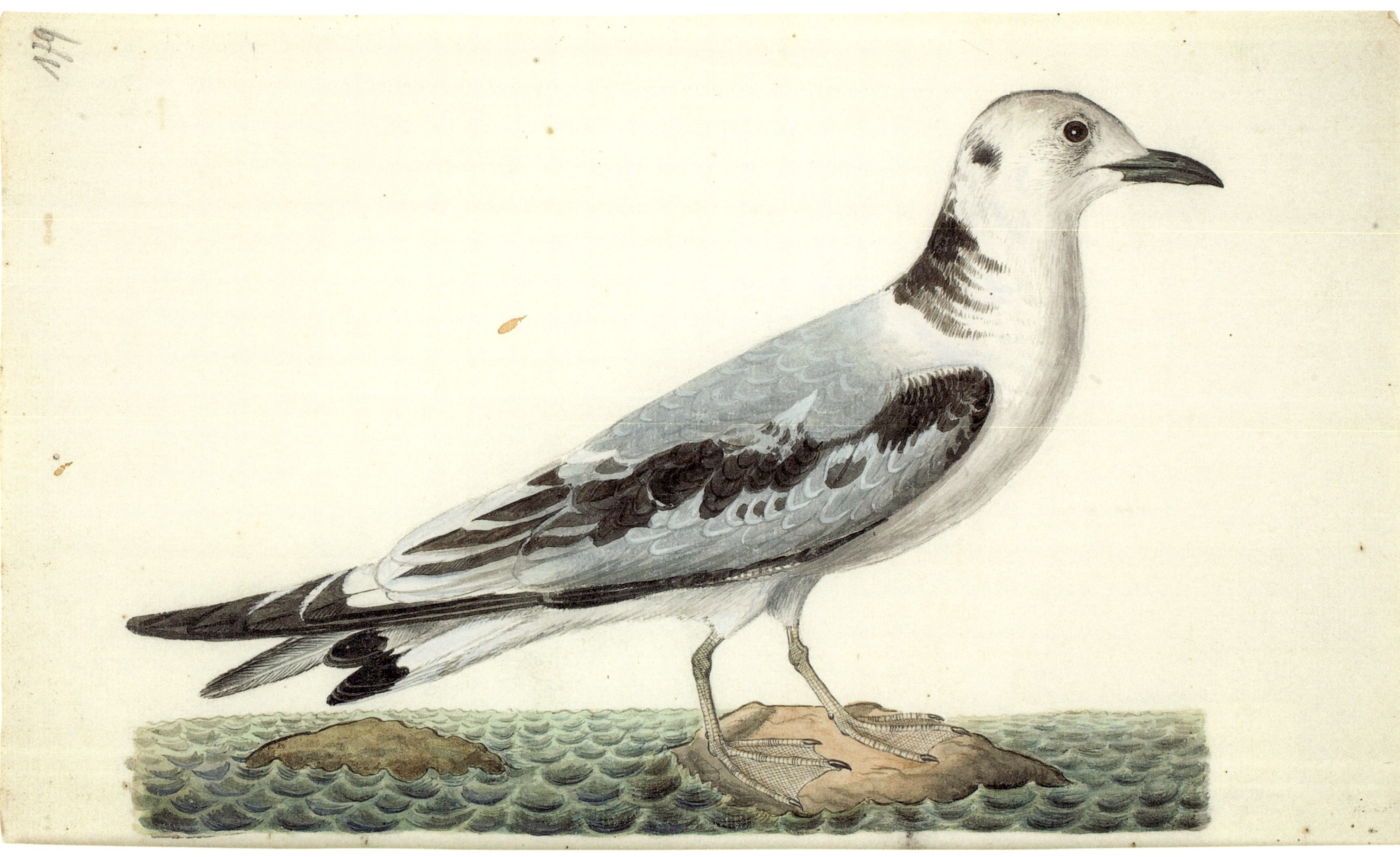
179

Eiderente (♂)

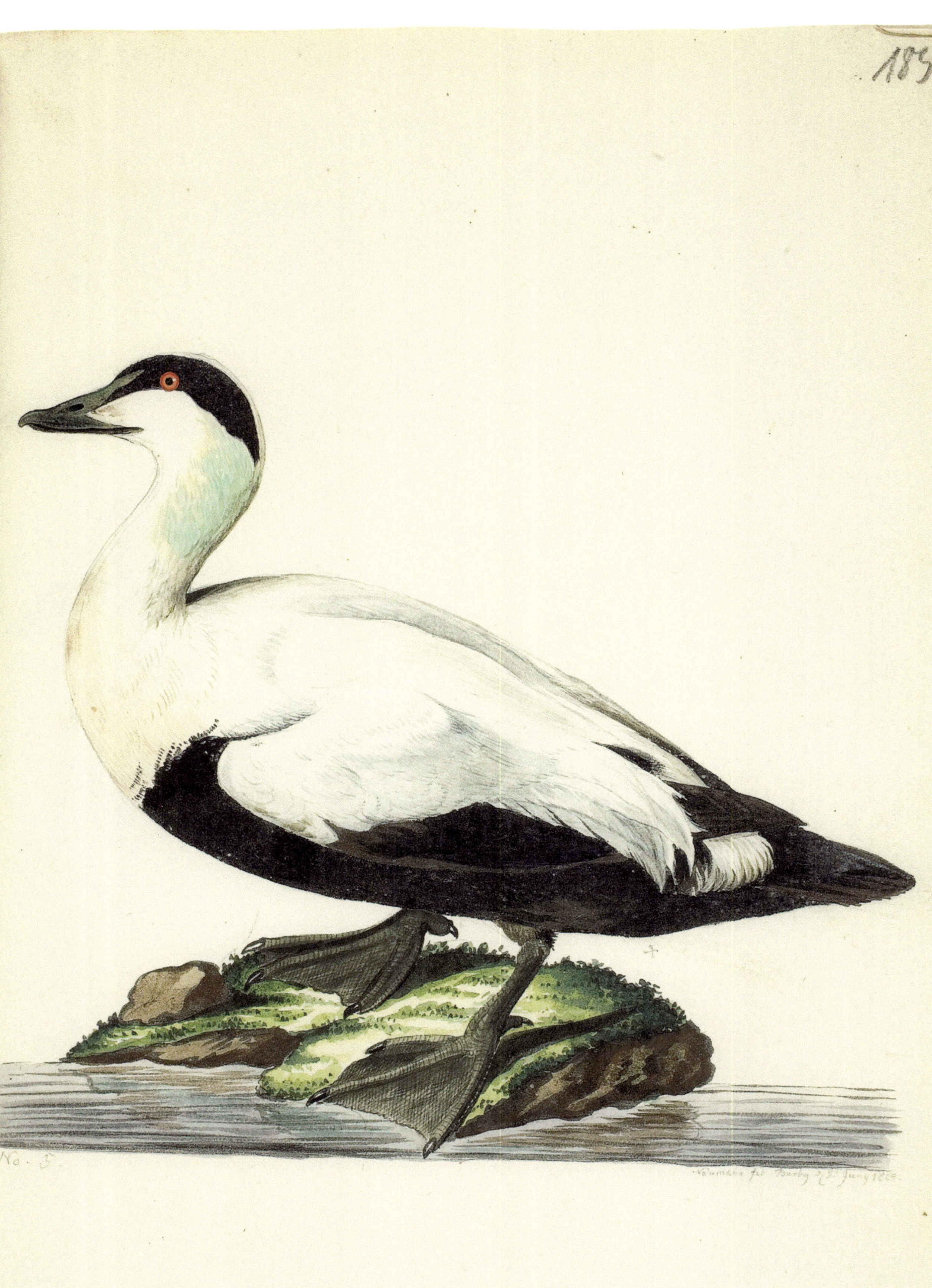
183
No. 5.

Oben: Prachteiderente (♂)
Unten: Prachteiderente (♀)

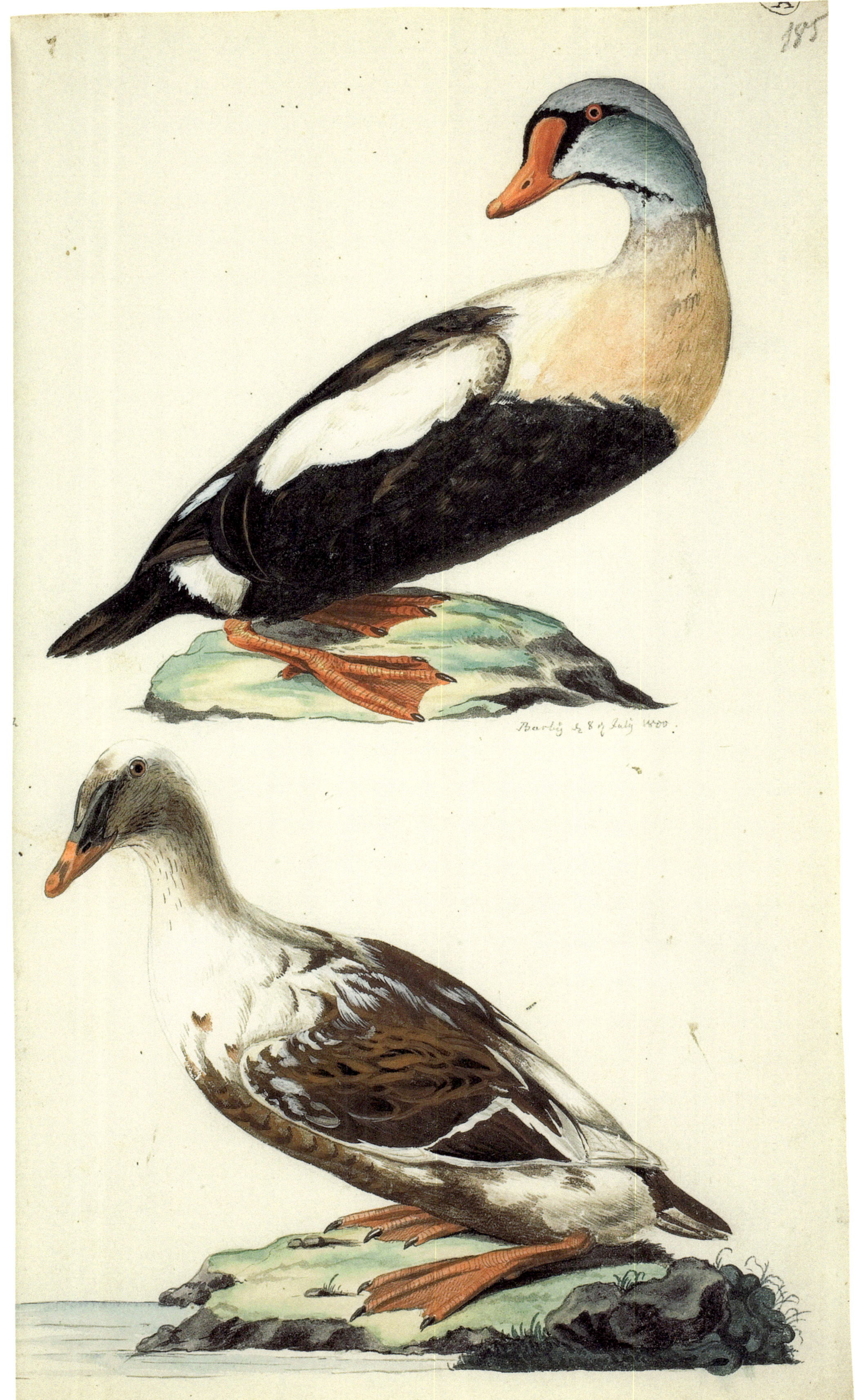

Eisente (♂)

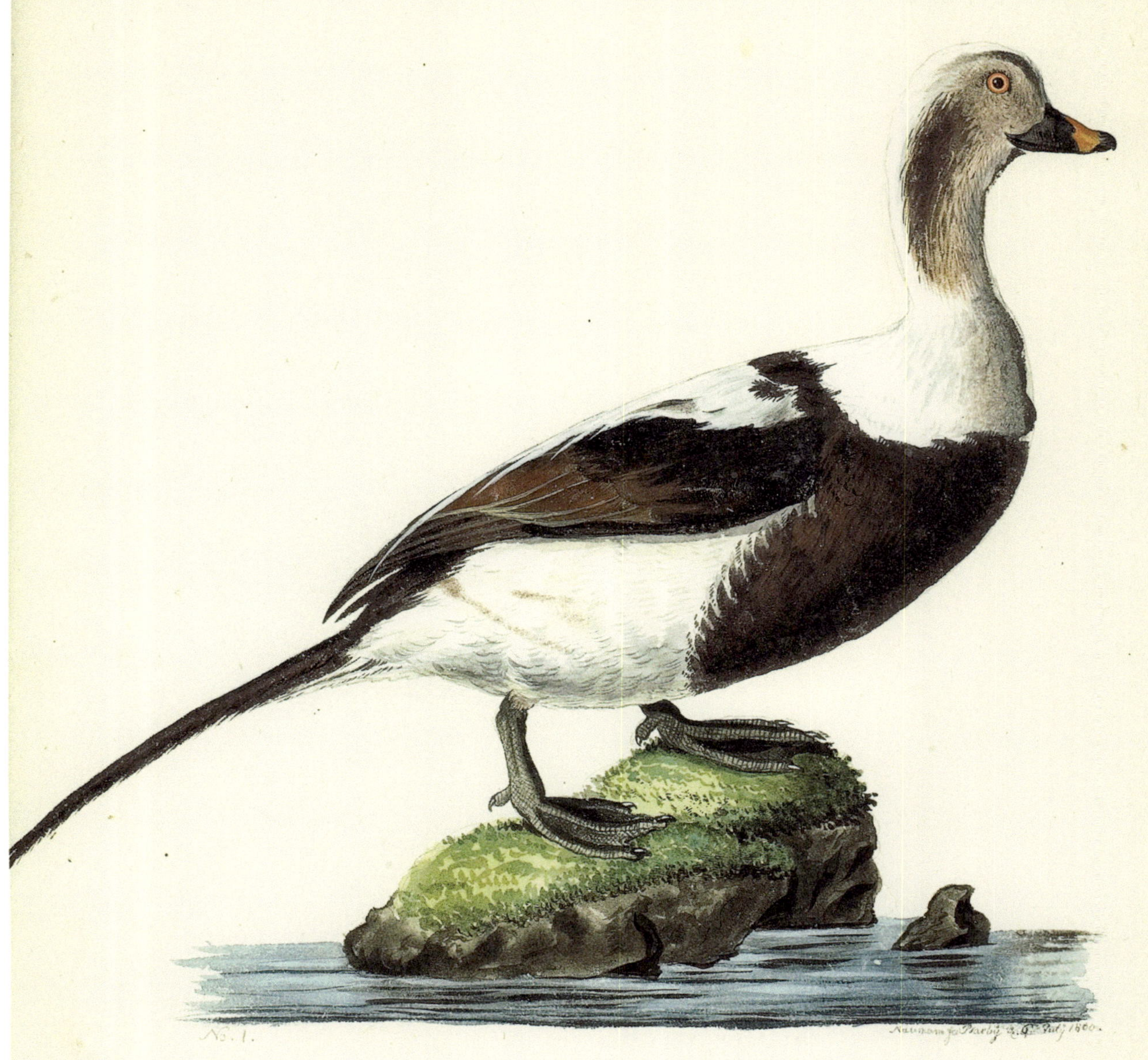
186
No. 1.

Schellente (♂)

190

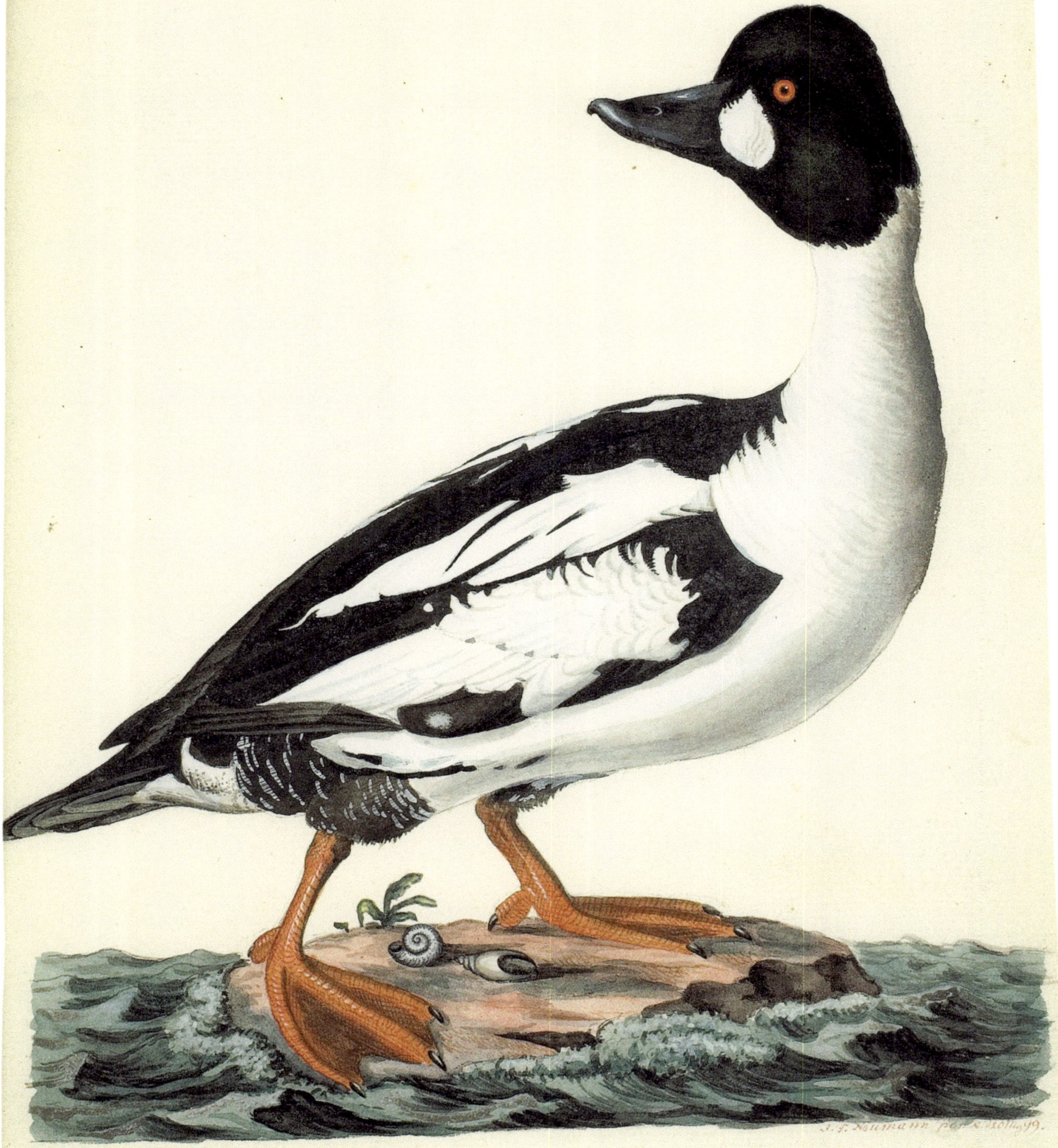

J. F. Naumann

Schnatterente (♂)

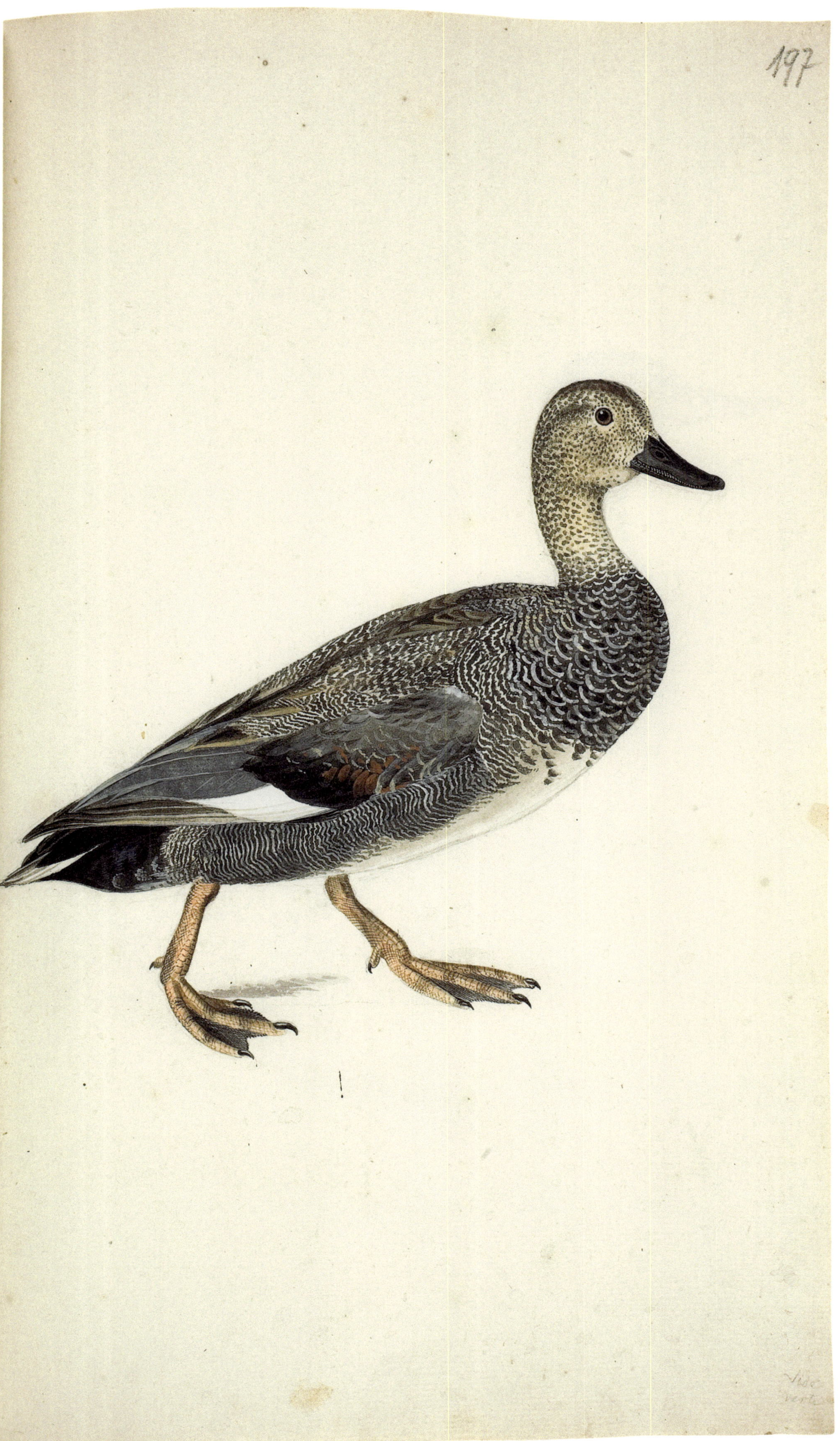

Löffelente (♂)

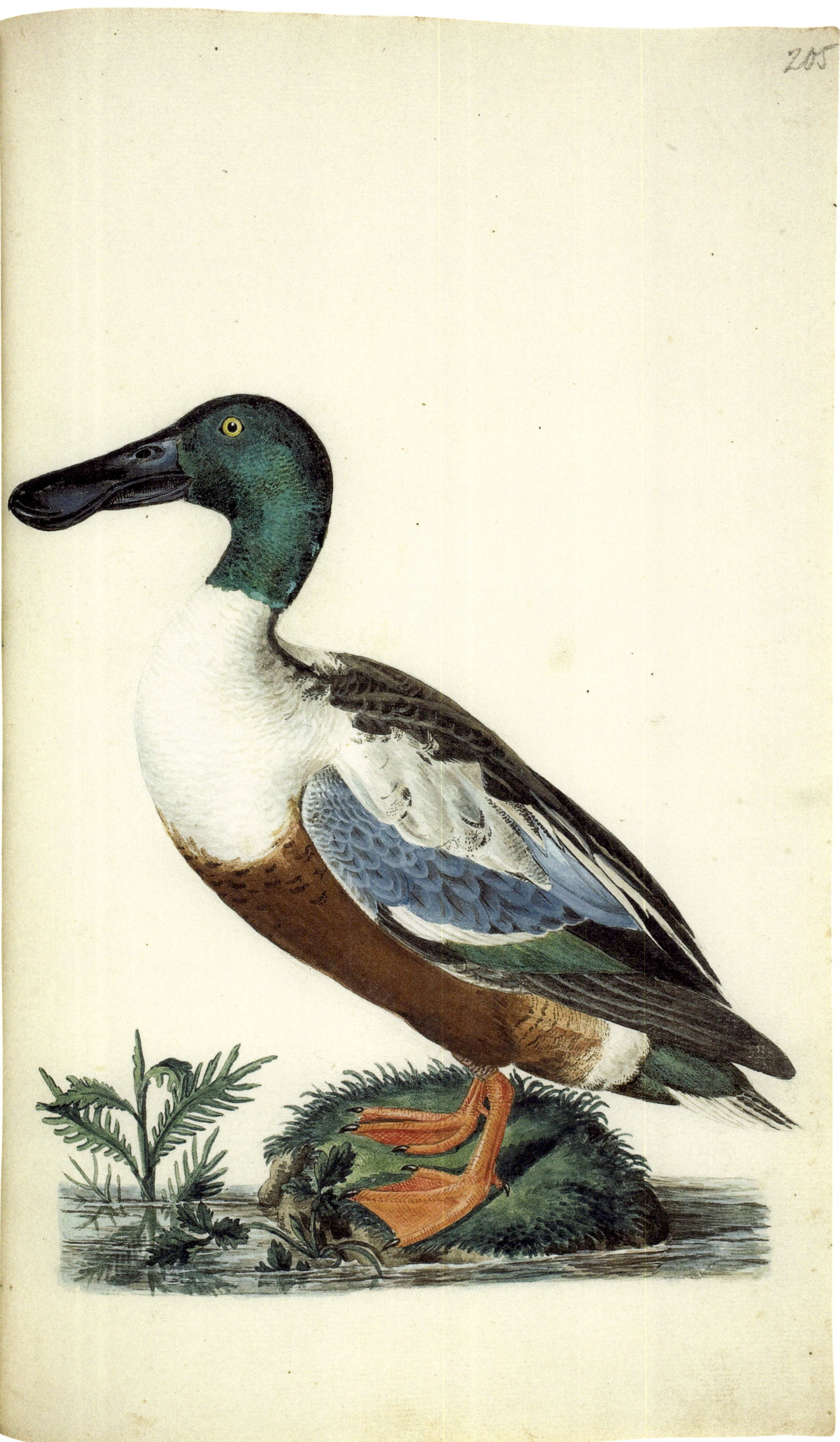
205

Löffelente (♀)

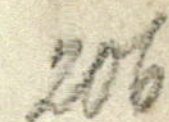
206

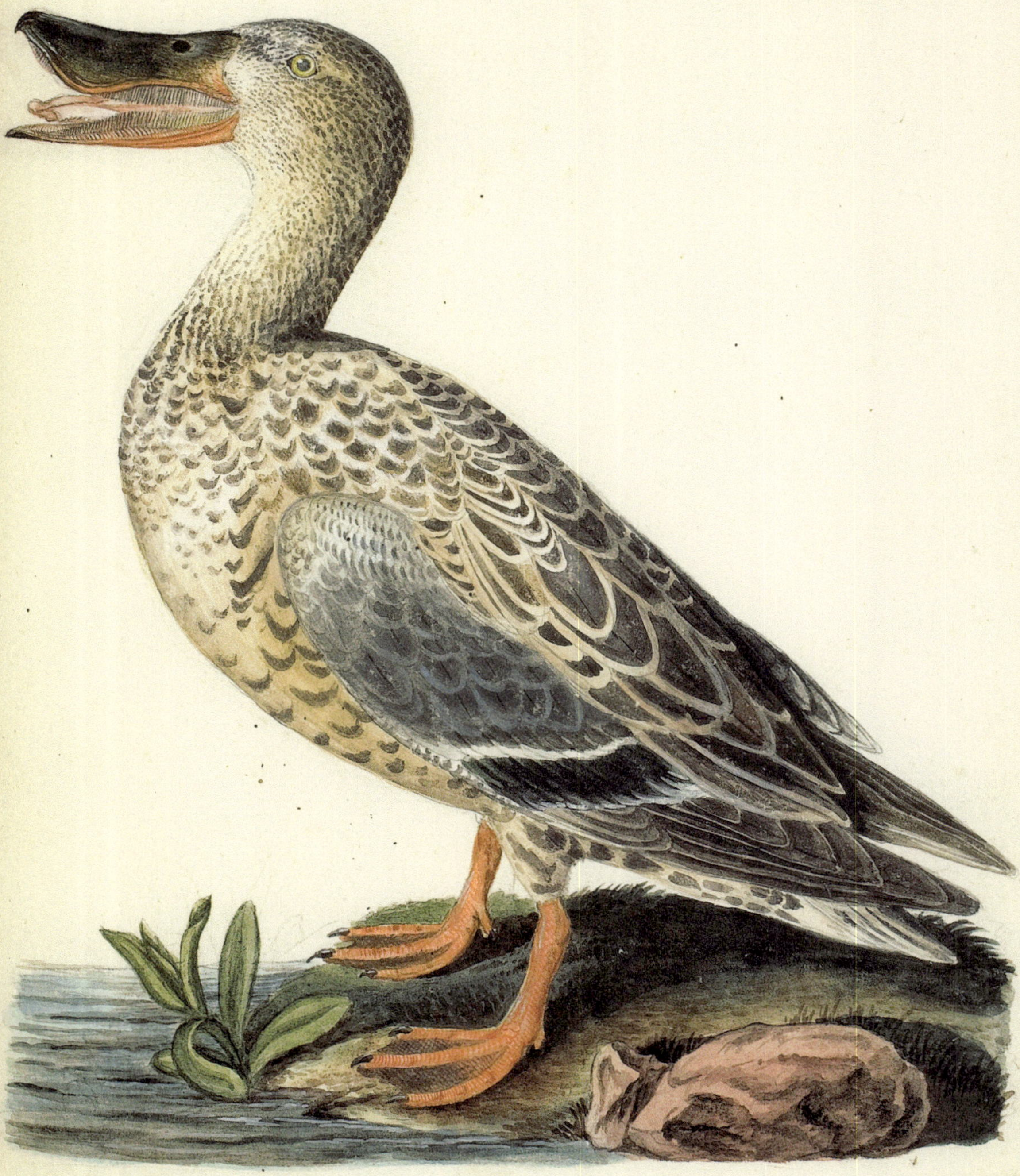

Blässgans

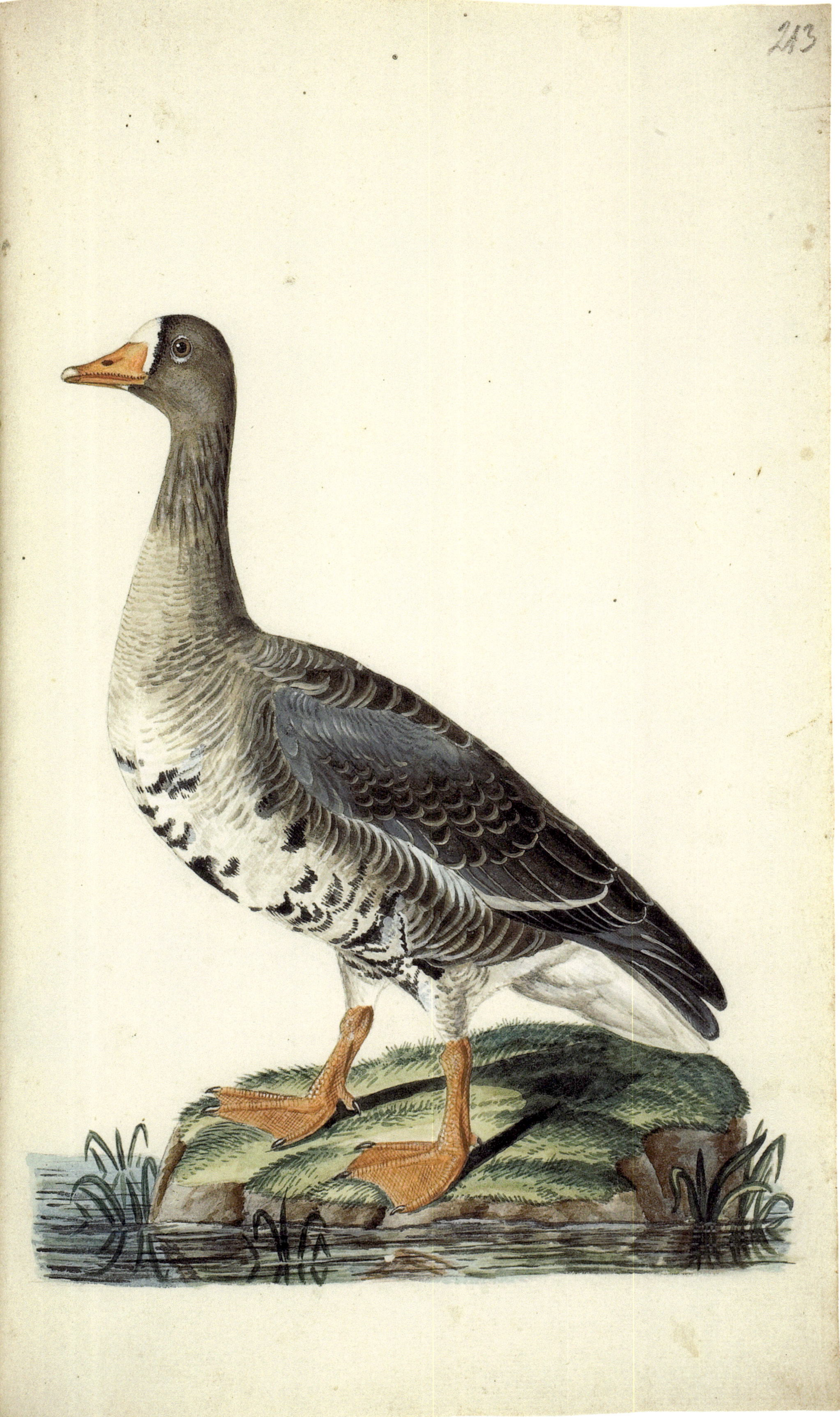
213

Gänsesäger (♂)

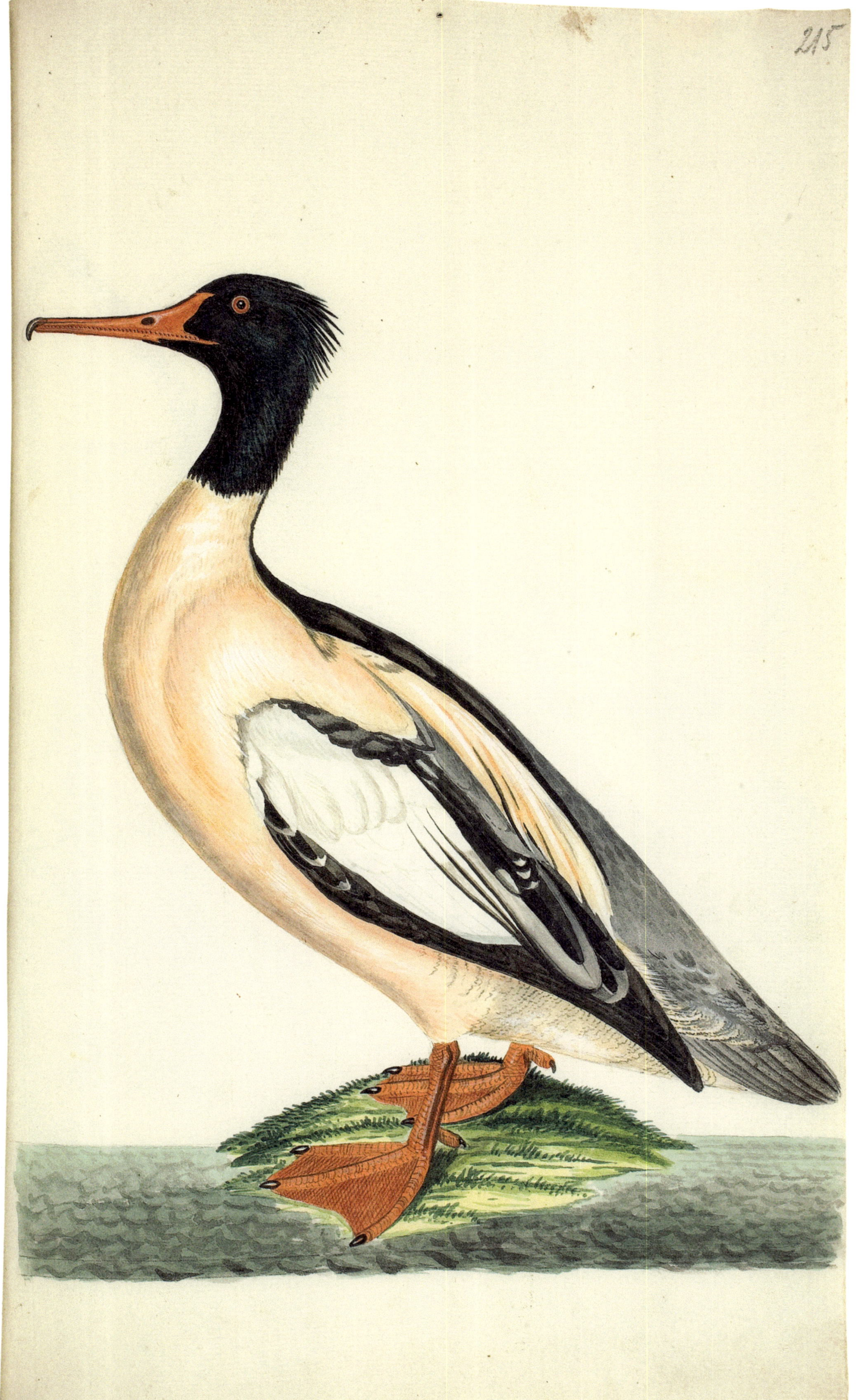
215

Gänsesäger (♀)

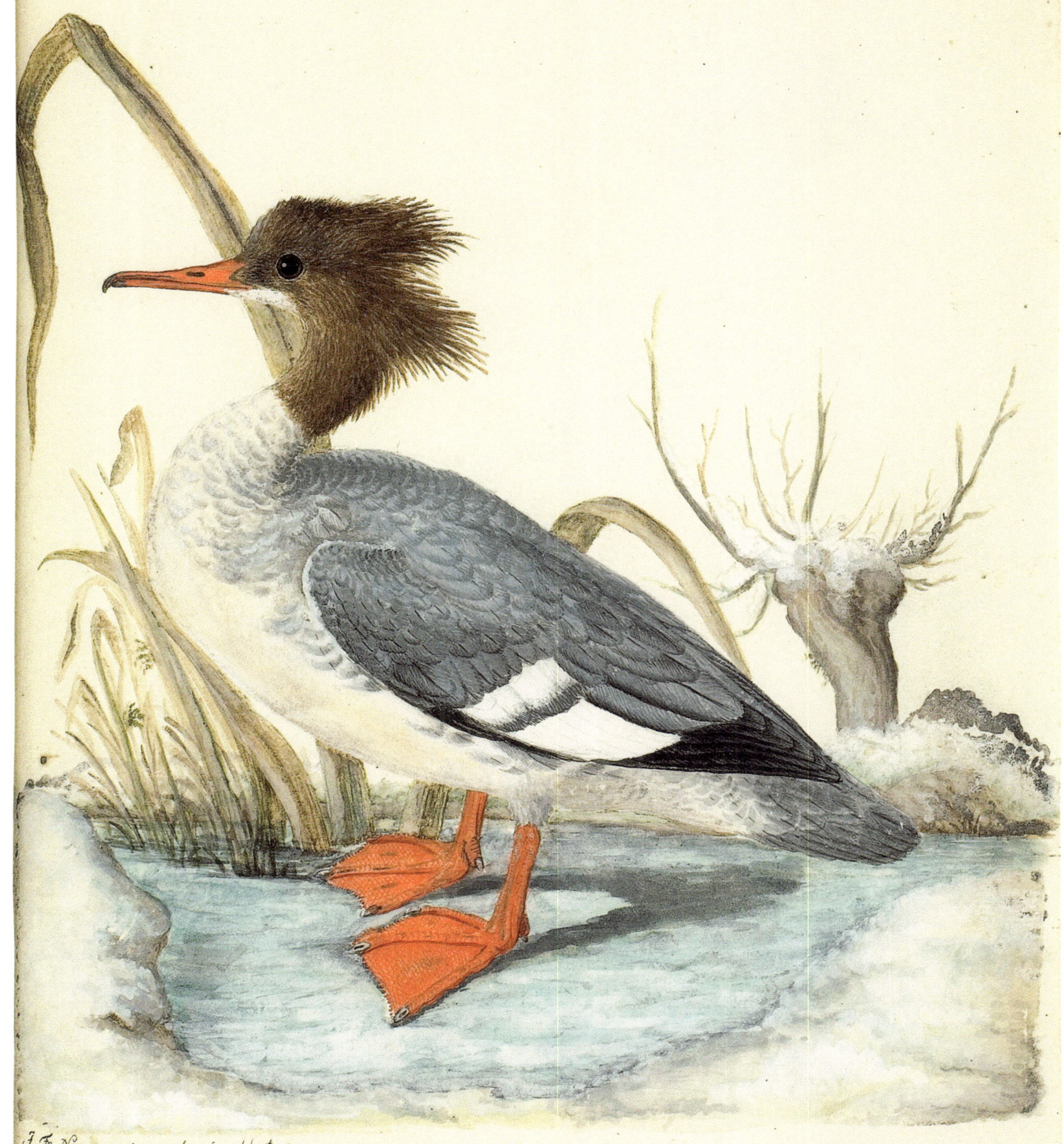

J. Fr. Naumann jun: ad. vir. del. et pix.

Mittelsäger (♂)

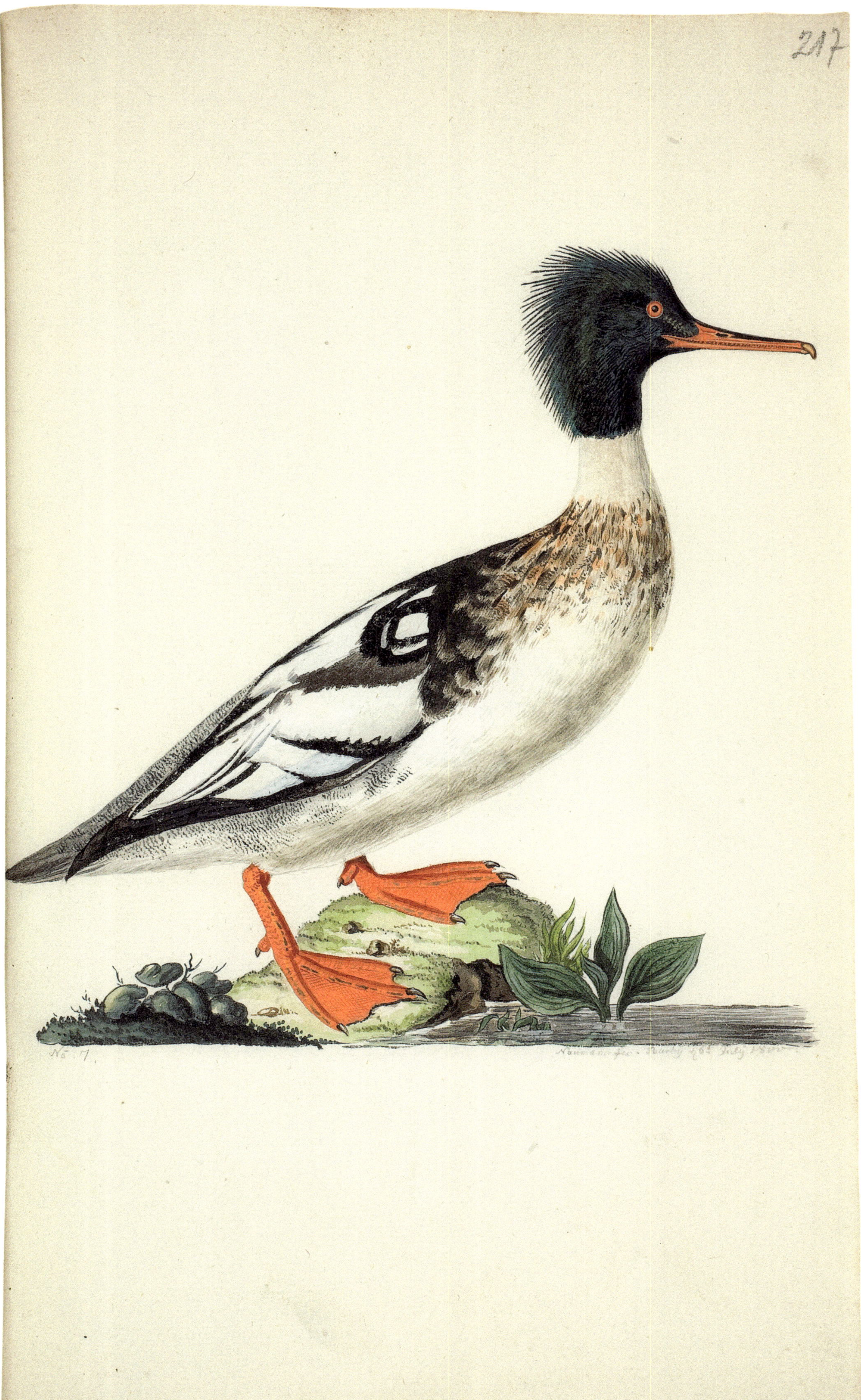

Zwergsäger (♂)

220

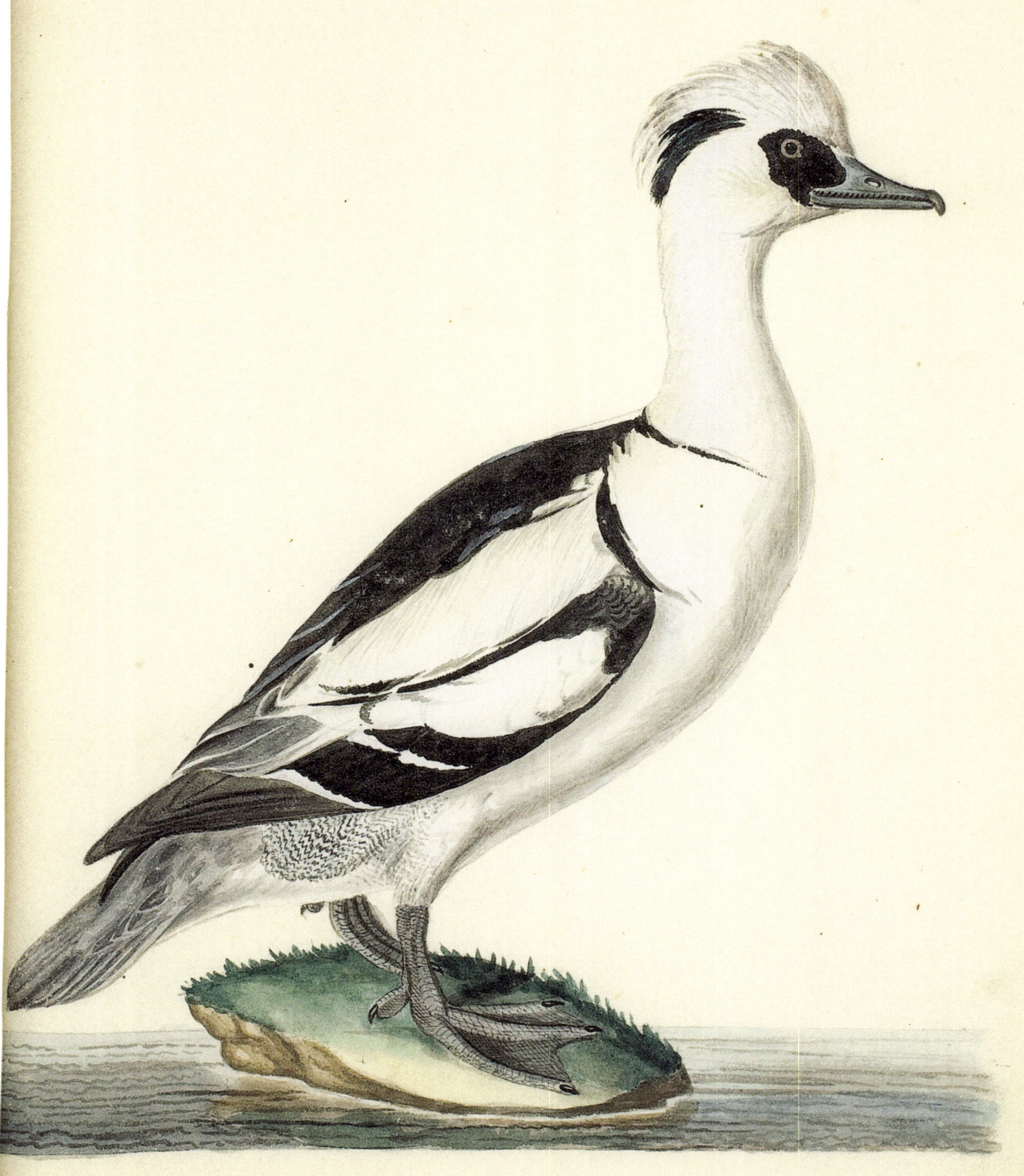

// ÜBER DEN HAUSHALT DER NORDISCHEN SEEVÖGEL EUROPAS //

Gross war in wissenschaftlicher Hinsicht der Genuss, welchen mir meine im Mai und Juni 1819 nach jener interessanten Küste mit ihren für den Ornithologen so wichtigen Inseln unternommene Reise gewährte, von welcher ich schon in OKENS Isis, Jahrg. 1820, St. XII Bericht erstattete. Meine Erwartungen wurden auf jener Reise weit übertroffen; denn ich hoffte wohl, nordische Vögel dort noch auf dem Zuge in Menge, aber nicht so viele daselbst nistend zu finden, und war daher auf das angenehmste überrascht, manche Art ganz so zu sehen, wie ich es mir nur viel höher nach Norden hinauf hatte denken können.

Die Insel **Pellworm** war damals zu einem längeren Aufenthalt bestimmt und gab reiche Beute; allein das zu sehr bewohnte und bebaute fette Ländchen, ringsum mit hohen Deichen umgeben, hatte nur auf der Nordseite ein grosses grünes Vorland, wo es ausser unzähligen daselbst nistenden Vögeln auch noch Zugvögel genug gab, manche in unermesslichen Scharen, z. B. **Ringelgänse** und Myriaden von **Uferschnepfen.** Dies einzige für den Ornithologen wichtige Feld der Insel, dieses Hallig, **Puphever** genannt, musste aber nach einigen Tagen durch das Schiessen und die beständige Störung des daselbst wohnenden zahlreichen Geflügels an Gewinn für mich und meine mich begleitenden Freunde bald verlieren. Es wurde deshalb eine Exkursion von dort nach dem eine Meile südlich gelegenen Eilande **Süderoog** unternommen, welches zwar viel kleiner aber nur von einer einzigen Familie bewohnt war, lauter grünen Rasenboden (bloss zur Viehweide benutzt) und ganz flache Ufer hatte, auch gar nicht eingedeicht war. Niemand störte dort die Vögel als täglich einmal eine Person jener Familie, welche während der Legezeit, etwa zwei Wochen lang, täglich die Eier absuchte, oder zuweilen eine überschwemmende Meeresflut; kein Schuss geschah dort nach ihnen, und lange hatte kein gieriger Sammler dort gewürkt. Als daher die Seichtigkeit des Wassers (es trat eben Ebbe ein) unserem Schiffe Stillstand gebot, wir auf den weiten Watten wohl mehr als tausend Schritt vom Ufer fest lagen, der bestellte Wagen ankam, auf welchem wir vom Bord des Schiffes ohne weiteres hinabgestiegen waren, und so auf dem festen Sande dieser Watten der Insel zufuhren, wurden wir von Tausenden neugieriger Vögel umschwirrt, die uns furchtlos angafften. Da standen kaum zwanzig Schritt vom Wagen die herrlichsten Geschöpfe, z. B. die **Silbermöven** (*Larus argentatus*) Paar bei Paar, uns ruhig ansehend; ihr blendend weisses, oben bläuliches Gefieder, mit den samtschwarzen Flügelspitzen, ihr hochgelber Schnabel mit dem korallenroten Fleck, ihr lebhaft gelbes Auge glänzten in der lebendigsten Pracht. So hatte ich sie noch nie gesehen; ich war vor Freude ausser mir; aber es sollte noch viel besser kommen.

Diese Möven lebten hier grösstenteils von kleinen Krebsen (*Cancer moenas*), wovon ihr Unrat, der durch die Verdauung nie ganz aufgelöster Schalen wegen wie Kalkmörtel aussieht und rosenrot tingiert ist.

Ich fand auf dem Eilande ein ganz mit nistenden Vögeln bedecktes grünes Feld, was voll kleiner Hügelchen war, die aussahen, als wären sie sonst durch Maulwürfe oder Ameisen entstanden (was aber dort nicht möglich ist) und nur wie der übrige Boden mit kurzem Gras bedeckt waren. Die Menge der Vögel war da so gross, dass stellenweise sich fast auf jedem Hügelchen ein Nest befand und diese öfters von ihnen verwechselt werden mochten; denn ich sah ein Ei des **Austernfischers** im Neste und neben den Eiern einer **Silbermöve**, dann wieder im Neste jenes Vogels ein Ei der **Küstenseeschwalbe**. Hier nisteten die Silbermöve, Küstenseeschwalbe, Austernfischer, Säbelschnäbler, Rotschenkel und Alpenstrandläufer friedlich und in Menge bei einander und dazwischen trieben sich noch Schwärme von Knutts und Steinwälzern herum, wodurch ein ausserordentlich buntes Gewirr entstand.

Das Wetter änderte sich während meines kurzen Aufenthalts daselbst und eignete sich keineswegs zu anmutigen Spaziergängen; aber das Inselchen hatte zu viel Interessantes für mich, dass ich nicht bis spät am Abend volle Beschäftigung gefunden, und trotz der kalten Regenschauer und des Sturmes den Aufenthalt daselbst möglichst genutzt hätte. Vorzüglich merkwürdig war hier eine eigene Strasse der **Brandseeschwalben**, die ich entdeckte und natürlich gut benutzte; denn ich erlegte aus einem gewählten Hinterhalt mehr als ein Dutzend dieser schönen Vögel, die sonst ausserhalb dieser Strasse viel seltener und nur hochfliegend über dieser Insel gesehen wurden. Das kleine flache Eiland **Norderoog**, eine Meile von **Süderoog** im Nordwesten gelegen, war nämlich der Brutplatz einer Kolonie dieser Seeschwalben, vielleicht aus einer Million Vögel bestehend, sodass die Insel in der Entfernung von einer Meile gesehen, wenn die Vögel ruhig waren, einen weissen Streifen im Meere bildete, als wenn sie ganz mit Schnee bedeckt gewesen wäre; wenn die unermessliche Schar aber über derselben schwebte, diese einer weissen wirbelnden Wolke glich und ein ganz eigenes, nicht zu beschreibendes Ansehen hatte. Auf jenem Eilande lagen stellenweise die Eier dieser Vögel so dicht, dass man, ohne welche zu zertreten, kaum dazwischen gehen konnte; die brütenden Vögel berühren sich oft und würden nicht Raum haben, wenn sie nicht, wie fast alle an den Meeresküsten gesellschaftlich brütende Seeschwalben, in einerlei Richtung, Kopf und Vorderleib gegen die Wasserseite gerichtet, über den Eiern sässen. Unmöglich kann hier jeder Vogel seine eigenen Eier wieder herausfinden, er muss sich oft auf die ersten besten legen, um den Forderungen der Natur Genüge leisten zu können; so geschieht es denn an solchen Plätzen oft, dass vier, ja fünf Eier beisammen liegen, da die einzelnen Weibchen aller bekannten Seeschwalben nie mehr als drei Stück legen und darauf brüten. Unbeschreiblich der Lärm an solchen Plätzen, denn diese geschwätzigen Vögel machen selbst über Nacht, wo sie eigentlich ruhig auf und neben den Eiern sitzen und schlafen sollten, ein stetes, oft sehr lebhaftes Geschwätz.

Naht man sich am Tage einem solchen Orte, so sieht man sich nach und nach bald von den Schreiern umringt, die Schar wächst schnell zu einer umwirbelnden Masse, ihre tausendfachen Stimmen betäuben die Sinne, ja diese sonst so scheuen Vögel flattern einem so dicht über dem Kopfe herum, dass sie ihn oft mit ihren Flügelspitzen berühren. In dieser Angst entledigen sie sich häufig ihres Unrats, sodass man, als ob sie es aus Rache täten, den Platz mit weissbeklexten Kleidern verlässt und wie mit Kalk bespritzt aussieht. Hier ist es leicht, mit einem Stocke so viel, als man wünscht, zu schlagen oder aus der Luft herabzuschleudern.

Ganz anders zeigen sie sich in geringer Entfernung von den Brutplätzen. So war es auf **Süderoog**; sie flogen dort hoch und waren sehr scheu; nur auf der erwähnten Strasse, wo sie niedriger flogen, war ihnen aus einem Versteck beizukommen. Merkwürdig; diese Strasse war nicht breiter als höchstens fünfzig Schritt, und durchschnitt die Insel in schiefer Richtung, von **Norderoog**, ihrem Brutorte, nach dem festen Lande von **Eiderstedt** zu, wo sie in den seichten Wassern jener Küste fischten, und viele mit kleinen Heringen im Schnabel zurückkehrten. Sie machten demnach ihrer Nahrung wegen Züge von zwei bis sechs Meilen weit vom eigentlichen Wohnorte.

An diesem soll ihnen das Schiessen so zuwider sein, dass sie, wo solches bei ihrem Brutplatze geschah, diesen zwar nicht gleich verlassen, jedoch im folgenden Jahre nicht wieder dorthin kommen, selbst solche kleine Inseln gänzlich meiden. Deswegen erlaubte der Strandvogt auf **Norderoog** (mit seiner Familie die einzigen Bewohner dieses Eilandes) das Schiessen nicht, weil ihm das Sammeln der Seeschwalbeneier eine höchst bedeutende Revenü war, und er sie dadurch zu verlieren befürchtete, was auch der auf **Süderoog**, jetzt unser gefälliger Wirt, bestätigte und versicherte, dass die ungeheure Kolonie von **Norderoog** noch vor wenigen Jahren sein (eingebildetes) Eigentum gewesen sei und hier auf **Süderoog** gebrütet habe, weil er aber gutmütigerweise einigen Leuten das Schiessen in der Brutzeit erlaubt hätte, so habe sie ihn nun verlassen und sei auf jenes Eiland gezogen und wahrscheinlich auf immer für ihn verloren.

Später sah ich auf der Nordseite von **Norderoog** in der Nähe der Insel **Amrum** auf einer Bank im Meere noch eine kleinere Kolonie, wahrscheinlich eine Tochter der ersteren; denn jene Insel schien ihnen genugsam besetzt, und sie mochten die Anzahl, die der jährlich ausgekommenen Jungen wegen doch von Jahr zu Jahr wachsen müsste, nicht weiter vermehrt haben und trieben deshalb die Nachkommenschaft weg.

Auf allen Inseln dieser Küste, wo grosse Kolonien von Seevögeln beisammen nisten, hat immer eine Familie der Bewohner das Monopol, die Eier einer solchen oder eines bestimmten Distrikts sammeln zu dürfen; es muss demnach den Leuten daran gelegen sein, die Vögel oder vielmehr die Eier gehörig zu benutzen, doch jene dadurch nicht zu vermindern; sie suchen demnach, sobald die Legezeit eintritt, täglich die Eier auf, nehmen sie weg und lassen nur hier und da in den Nestern eins liegen, damit die Vögel nicht geschreckt werden und, wenn sie alle sich plötzlich ihrer Eier beraubt sähen, vielleicht einen anderen Brutplatz suchen möchten. Dies Einsammeln geschieht alle Tage regelmässig etwa zwei Wochen lang, bis sie sehen, dass die Vögel das Eierlegen hin und wieder überdrüssig werden; dann hört es gänzlich auf, man lässt den Vögeln ruhig ihre zuletzt gelegten Eier ausbrüten und ungestört ihre Jungen erziehen. Sie kommen bei einer solchen Behandlung gewiss im folgenden Jahre auf diesen Platz zurück. Die Anzahl der Vögel müsste also, hiervon abgesehen, von Jahr zu Jahr wachsen, wenn sie nicht oft durch mancherlei unbekannte Ursachen vermindert oder doch auf einem gewissen festen Punkte erhalten würde. Leider geht den armen Seeschwalben manchmal, meist wie mit einem Schlage, ihre ganze Brut zu Grunde, und für dies Jahr haben sie dann gar keine Nachkommenschaft, weil hohe Springfluten nicht selten jene kleinen niedrigen Inseln oder die flachen Watten und Bänke, wo ihre Eier liegen, überschwemmen und alles vernichten, selbst die schon ausgeschlüpften, aber noch nicht flüggen Jungen mit fortreissen und die allermeisten in den Wogen ihr Grab finden lassen. Solche Unglücksfälle sind für alle nahe am Wasser nistende Seevögel sehr zerstörend und leider nicht selten.

Noch einmal sah ich, als ich von **Pellworm**, an **Hooge** vorbei, nach **Amrum** schiffte, das interessante Eiland **Norderoog** in seinem, von den Myriaden dort brütender **Brandseeschwalben** gebildeten, schneeweissen Mantel gehüllt, wie einen Schneestreif in der grünblauen Flut; und bald nachher, als sich die Schar zufällig als eine grosse, sonderbar bewegte, wimmelnde Masse erhob, war sie einer grossen, wirbelnden, dicht über der Insel schwebenden, schneeweissen Wolke oder Rauchmasse höchst ähnlich.

Die Insel **Amrum**, welche ich jetzt betrat, gewährt schon von weitem einen ganz anderen Anblick als die eben verlassenen Inseln. Dieses dürre, unfruchtbare Land, weder dem Ackerbau noch der Viehzucht hold, hat ungeheure, mit Heidekraut und dürrem Grase nur spärlich bedeckte Sandflächen, einiges schlechte Ackerland, wenig Rasenboden, einzelne Moorplätze, und ein 50 Fuss hohes Dünengebirge bildet eine Vormauer gegen die Gewalt der wütenden Meereswogen auf der ganzen Westseite in einem mondförmigen Bogen von Norden bis Süden. Die Ufer und Watten der meisten jener Inseln waren fetter Schlammboden und sogenannter Schlick, bei **Amrum** aber durchaus Sand, und diese Sandwatten liefen zur Ebbezeit stellenweise eine halbe Meile weit in die See. Die ganze Insel hat einen so nördlichen Charakter, dass ich von einem mühsam erstiegenen Dünenhügel herab, einen grossen Teil derselben überschauend, unwillkürlich an Island erinnert oder mich doch mit einem Male mehrere Breitengrade nach Norden hinauf versetzt glaubte. In den Vertiefungen weideten hin und wieder einzelne, ungeheuer grosse, zottige, schwarze Schafe, Bären nicht unähnlich, dort ein Paar Kühe oder einige Pferde von einer kleinen plumpen Rasse, ja die Pflanzenwelt erhob diese Täuschung, denn unter vielen, im Norden nur prädominierenden Gewächsen ist die Rauschbeere hier schon ungemein häufig.

Brandenten sah man hier in ziemlicher Menge; sie bewohnten zum Teil die zahlreichen Kaninchenhöhlen der Dünenhügel; aber sie waren wild und von den Leuten nicht geachtet; **Sylt** sollte sie mir noch viel häufiger und in einem ganz anderen Zustande zeigen; die Reise dahin ward unternommen und diese bedeutende Insel nach einer langen, unangenehmen und gefährlichen Seefahrt betreten.

Die Insel **Sylt** ist auf der ganzen Westseite, von der südlichen bis zur nördlichen Spitze, von einem fünf Meilen langen, schmalen, meist aus weissem Flugsande bestehenden Dünengebirge begrenzt, was vielen Pärchen des **Grossen Brachvogels** und in seinen begrünten oder mit Heidekraut bedeckten Thälern noch mehreren **Goldregenpfeifern** einen Sommeraufenthalt und Nistplätze gewährte, während der bebaute Teil der Insel von zahllosen **Brandenten** bewohnt wurde, welche hier sogar als halbe Haustiere betrachtet werden können, da man ihnen künstliche Höhlen baut und sie selbst in den Dörfern in Mauer- und Erdlöchern, doch ausserhalb der Gebäude brüten lässt. Dies ist noch weit mehr auf der nördlichen Spitze der Insel bei **List** der Fall. Höchst überraschend war der Anblick, als ich mit meinen Begleitern im Sande auf der Ostseite der Dünen, zwar stellenweise immer von zahlreichem Geflügel umgeben, langsam dahin fuhr (wir waren zu Wagen), als unser Weg plötzlich links abbog, sich uns in den Dünen ein anmutiges Tal öffnete, zwar ohne Baum, aber lauter frische, mit Gräben durchschnittene Wiesen, deren grüner Teppich wie mit weissen, rot und schwarz gezeichneten Blumen gestickt war; diese Blumen aber, genauer besehen, aus lauter **Brandenten** bestanden, die zu Tausenden paarweis auf der Fläche verteilt waren. Ein köstlicher Anblick, diese herrlichen Geschöpfe, eines der schönsten seiner Gattung, in solcher Menge und so zahm zu sehen, dass sie sich auf zwanzig Schritt nahe betrachten liessen, dann zwar aufflogen, sich aber furchtlos bald wieder niederliessen. Ich erstaunte nicht wenig, als ich hörte und sah, mit welcher Industrie hier die Leute mit ihnen verfuhren. Sie hatten ihnen künstliche Höhlen in die kleinen, begrasten oder mit Heidekraut und den kleinen Zwergrosen — welche eben in voller Blüte standen — bedeckten Dünenhügel, bis dicht bei den Häusern, bereitet. Ich untersuchte mehrere solcher unterirdischer Baue und fand selbst in einem derselben sogar **dreizehn** Entennester in den erweiterten Winkeln der verschiedenen Röhren, die alle nur einen gemeinschaftlichen Eingang hatten, sodass, wenn man diesen nur mit dem Hute verstopfte, alle darinnen steckende Enten gefangen waren, was man aber damit keineswegs beabsichtigte; denn man hegte sie nur ihrer Eier und der Nestdunen wegen. Um zu diesen zu gelangen, war über jedem Nest ein Loch senkrecht gegraben; diese Löcher waren etwa zwei bis drei Fuss voneinander entfernt, und unten durch horizontale Röhren miteinander und mit der gemeinschaftlichen Eingangsröhre verbunden, wie es die beigefügte Figur deutlicher machen wird.

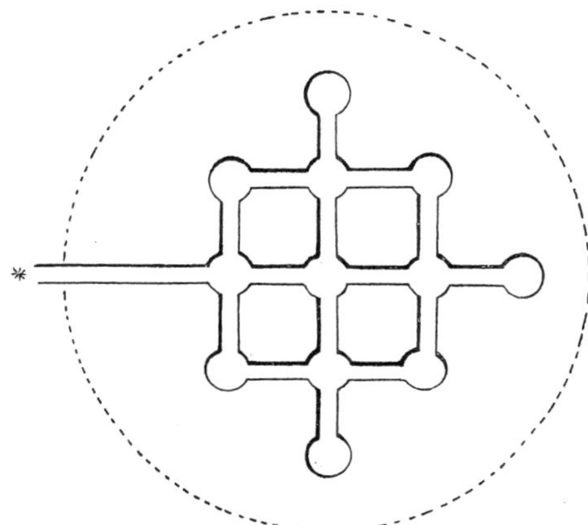

Oben war jedes Loch mit einem Stück Rasen zugedeckt. Man ging zu so einem Bau, hob einen Deckel nach dem anderen auf und sah die Nester mit den Eiern, auch wohl die Weibchen auf diesen, welche so zahm waren, dass sie sich leise streicheln liessen und erst bei etwas unsanfter Berührung sich in den unterirdischen Gängen oder Röhren des Baues verkrochen.

Jeder Einwohner des kleinen Orts hatte einige oder mehrere solcher Entenbaue, holte täglich 20 bis 30 Stück Eier daraus hervor und trieb dies zwei bis drei Wochen lang, wo man dann in jedem einzelnen Neste nur sechs Stück zum Ausbrüten liegen liess, zuvor aber noch die Hälfte der wunderschönen lichtgrauen Dunen, welche die Weibchen, wenn sie brüten wollen, sich ausrupfen und das Nest mit ausfüttern, wegnahm, die ebenso schön als Eiderdunen, aber noch reinlicher und nicht mit so vielem Gras oder gar Tang wie jene öfters vermengt sind.

Die allererst gelegten Eier lässt man gewöhnlich liegen und nimmt immer die frischgelegten. Die Einwohner lieben diese grossen, schön glänzend weissen Eier sehr, und sie sind auch fetter als von allen anderen Seevögeln; allein sie haben einen so ekelhaft tranigen Beigeschmack, dass sie mir immer widerlich blieben. Diesen hässlichen Trangeschmack hat auch das Fleisch dieser schönen Enten, der hier aber noch viel ärger und so stark ist, dass es sogar jene Leute nicht mögen; sogar die Jungen verachtet man deshalb und isst sie dort nirgends. Sonst findet man gewöhnlich diesen ranzigen Geschmack nur bei tauchenden Enten und anderen Vögeln, welche sich auf ähnliche Art nähren; dies ist denn zwar auch hier der Fall, obgleich die **Brandente** zu derjenigen Entenfamilie gehört, deren Hinterzehe nicht belappt ist, und die nie nach Nahrung untertaucht, demungeachtet aber meist von Konchylien, besonders von sehr kleinen Arten, lebt, diese jedoch nur am Strande und auf den Watten bei zurückgetretener See oder zur Ebbezeit aufliest und aus den ausgespülten Wasserpflanzen hervorschnattert. Sie ist deshalb auch sehr gut zu Fuss, und überhaupt mehr Strand- als Seevogel. Daneben frisst sie aber auch Uferwürmer, Regenwürmer und Getreide, wahrscheinlich auch Grassamen und andere Sämereien, letztere aber mehr im Herbst.

Als unser gütiger Wirt von **List** uns endlich seinem grossen Vogelgehege näher brachte, wo keinem anderen als ihm oder seinen Leuten erlaubt ist, Eier zu sammeln, noch viel weniger Vögel zu schiessen, als wir uns nämlich eine Stunde weit nördlich von **List** der nördlichsten Spitze von **Sylt** näherten, wo sich das die Westseite der Insel einfassende Dünengebirge plötzlich östlich wendet, schmäler wird und auf der östlichen Seite des nördlichen schmalen Endes jener, eine kleine Bucht bildet, schienen die graugrünen Hügel der Dünen mit weissen Punkten übersät. »Das sind meine grossen **Möven** dort«, sagte der Mann, und bald überzeugten wir uns, indem wir näher kamen, von der Wahrheit des Gesagten, und die ungeheure Menge der Vögel setzte uns in Erstaunen. Ein eben über sie hinschwebender **Seeadler** brachte die Masse in Aufruhr, der sich jedoch bald wieder legte, und wir fanden sie, als wir in die Dünen und somit mitten unter sie traten, schon wieder vollkommen beruhigt.

Da standen wir von Tausenden umringt, die teils über unseren Häuptern schwebten und ihr heiseres **Hahaha** ausstiessen, teils paarweise ganz nahe vor uns standen, das allzeit grössere Männchen zuweilen seinen Hals ausstreckend und mit weit geöffnetem hochgelben Rachen sein **Giauk jauk jauk** ausrufend, teils das Weibchen ruhig auf dem Neste sitzend, sein Männchen daneben stehend und gleichsam Wache haltend, einzelne niedergekauert, andere schlummernd auf einem Beine stehend, wieder andere sich behaglich dehnend u.s.w., kurz man wusste nicht, ob man die ungemeine Reinheit, Zartheit und einfache Schönheit ihres Gefieders und ihrer Farben oder die ausserordentliche Mannigfaltigkeit und Zierlichkeit in den Stellungen oder die grosse Zahmheit dieser Vögel bewundern, oder ob man über ihre ungeheure Anzahl auf diesen kleinen Räumen erstaunen sollte. Überall, wo man hinsah, oft wenige Schritte voneinander, standen ihre Nester mit den grossen bunten Eiern, in dem dürftigen halbdürren, graugrünen Dünenhafer oder auf graubemoostem oder mit kurzem Heidekraut kümmerlich bedecktem Boden, aus wenigen alten Halmen, Stengeln von Salicornien und trockenem Tang gebaut.

Unser Erstaunen wuchs noch mehr, als wir unter dieser geringen Breite eine Menge (man sagte uns hundert Pärchen) **Eiderenten** antrafen, die aber schon grösstenteils ausgebrütet und ihre Jungen ihrem Elemente zugeführt hatten. Nur einige dieser Bewohner der nordischen Meere, Küsten und Inseln sassen noch über den Eiern, die man ihnen hier nie nimmt, auch erst, wenn sie ausgebrütet haben, die Dunen aus dem Neste holt. Ein Weibchen verliess es erst, als wir uns ihm auf ein paar Schritte genähert hatten, kauerte sich aber in der Nähe an der Erde, und sobald wir uns etwa dreissig Schritt vom Neste entfernt hatten, watschelte es schwerfällig wieder hin und setzte sich ruhig auf seine Eier.

Jene **grossen Möven** gehören alle zu einer Art (**Silbermöve**), die eine der schönsten ihrer Gattung ist; ihre ansehnliche Grösse (der eines **Kolkraben** gleich, doch mit viel längeren Flügeln), ihre angenehme Gestalt, das reinste, blendendste Weiss als Hauptfarbe ihres dichten Gefieders, auf dem Rücken sanft in lichtes Aschblau übergehend, die samtschwarzen Enden des Fittichs mit ihren schneeweissen Federspitzen, das liebliche gelbe Auge, der hochgelbe Schnabel mit seinem korallenroten Fleck, alles dieses gibt zusammen ein wunderliebliches Bild. Allein, man muss sie so im tätigen Leben, in der höchsten lebendigen Reinheit ihres Gewandes muss man diese Unvergleichlichen gesehen haben, um sie in der Tat unbeschreiblich schön zu finden.

Rechts vom Hauptnistplatze dieser herrlichen Vögel schloss sich eine nur kleine Kolonie (man schätzt sie auf zwei- bis dreihundert Pärchen) von **Sturmmöven** an, jenen ganz gleich gefärbt, aber viel kleiner, schmächtiger, mit schwächerem Schnabel ohne Rot. Einzeln mischten sie sich jedoch zuweilen, wenigstens fliegend, auch unter die grossen.

Im süssen Gefühl des höchsten Genusses, im sinnigen Anschauen dieser ornithologischen Herrlichkeiten versunken, sah ich diese sonst und ohne Vögel wohl traurige Gegend. Um sie mir immer frisch im Gedächtnis zu erhalten, entwarf ich die Zeichnung der vorliegenden **ersten Platte**, unterschrieben:

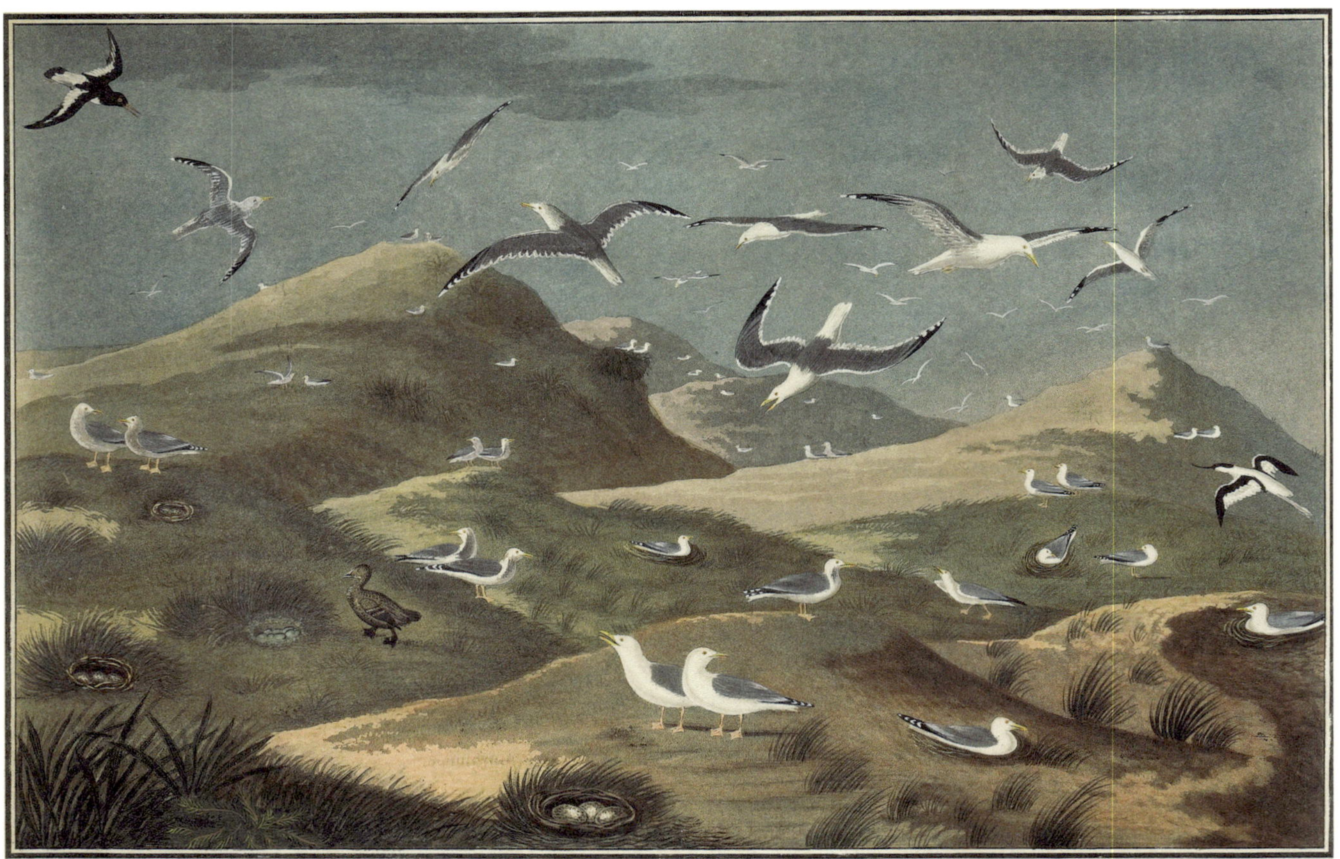

»**Die grossen Möven in den Dünen von List auf der Insel Sylt,** nach der lebendigen Natur.

Ein Teil dieser Dünenhügel, die hier meist fest sind, und woran die Stürme nur stellenweise nagen können, zeigt sich dem Auge in seinem schmutzigen, graugrünlichen und graugelblichen Kolorit. Es scheint, als solle ein Mann aus dem Vor-

Verkleinerung des Naumannschen Originals

dergrunde hervortreten, denn alle näheren Vögel sehen teils aufmerksam herüber, teils sind sie schon in Bewegung, wogegen die im Hintergrunde, noch zu entfernt von der anscheinlichen Gefahr, sich meistens ganz ruhig verhalten. Man sieht sie in vielerlei Stellungen und Bewegungen, fliegend und sitzend, auf und neben den Nestern, naturgetreu kopiert. Die allermeisten sind **Silbermöven**, nur ganz oben rechts zeigt sich eine **Sturmmöve**. Durch ihre kleinere, schlankere Figur, durch ihre schmäleren Flügel und den schmächtigeren, einfarbig gelben Schnabel kenntlich, so auch links ganz oben eine zweite dieser Art.

Die weibliche **Eiderente** im Mittelgrunde links, wie sie zu ihrem Neste mit den zwischen weichen Dunen liegenden Eiern hinwatschelt, ist kenntlich genug.

Ganz oben in der linken Ecke kommt ein schreiender **Austernfischer** geflogen, dergleichen Vögel zwar nicht gerade hier zwischen den Möven, doch auch in keiner grossen Entfernung davon brüteten, öfters durch diese belebten Regionen streiften und das Gewimmel bunter machen halfen.

Nur der **Säbelschnäbler**, welchen wir rechts beinahe im Vordergrunde durchfliegend erblicken, erscheint selten hier; da er aber andere nahe Inseln und Küsten zum Teil häufig bewohnt, so kommt er auch manchmal nach **List** und durchstreift dann auch diese, im Bild vor uns liegende Gegend zuweilen.«

Wir durchschritten diese Dünen von Süd nach Nord, folglich in die Quere, und mit jedem Schritt wuchs der Schwarm uns umschwebender Möven, bis wir nach und nach der Nordseite uns näherten, wo er ebenso wieder abnahm und bis auf wenige schwand, aus der Ursache, weil sie hier keine Nester mehr hatten. Hier sollte sich uns ein anderes, womöglich noch interessanteres Schauspiel eröffnen.

Ruhig zeigte sich jetzt unserem Blicke der jenseitige blaue Ocean; als wir aber unsere Hügel allmählich hinabstiegen und nun auch die jenseitigen Watten oder flachen Sandbänke, als welche die Dünen hier ins Meer laufen, erblickten, erhob sich auf einmal ein unermesslicher Schwarm weisser, flüchtiger Vögel, eine grosse Kolonie **Brandseeschwalben**, sich uns mit ihren tausendfachen Stimmen entgegen wälzend; allein noch zehn Schritte vorwärts, und auch eine mächtige Schar von den so seltenen grossen **Raubseeschwalben**, die dicht unter den Dünen auf dem Sande sich gelagert gehabt hatte und uns deshalb nicht früher ankommen sehen konnte, mischte sich unter jenes zahllose Gewimmel, und kam mit ihm vereint uns mit ihren krächzenden Stimmen entgegen. Wir traten hinab in diese, jetzt von Myriaden Vögeln belebten, sonst toten Sandwatten, auf denen schon manches

Schiff, von wütenden Nordweststürmen hierher geschleudert, seinen Untergang fand, und wandelten über im Sande begrabene Trümmer eines jüngst gescheiterten; aber es war nicht zu verwundern, wenn die freudige Gegenwart die traurige Vergangenheit vergessen machte. Wie konnte jetzt auch ein überstandenes Unglück anderer unsere Freude stören, über unseren Häuptern wimmelte die Luft ja von Tausenden der herrlichsten, schlanken, weissen, noch dazu seltenen Vögel, ihre Stimmen betäubten unsere Ohren und verwirrten unsere Sinne! Wir benutzten die Erlaubnis, uns sechs Stück von der Königin der europäischen **Raubseeschwalbe** schiessen zu dürfen, unglücklicherweise fielen aber mehr als zwanzig Schüsse; auch war es hier kein Wunder, dass ein einziger, auf eine **Raubseeschwalbe** gerichtet, zufällig auch eine Brandseeschwalbe zugleich mit traf. Unser Krieg mit den grossen seltenen Vögeln zog auch eine neugierige Robbe herbei, die dicht am Rand des Wassers auftauchte, uns ein Weilchen zusah, dann verschwand und durch ihr Erscheinen in das Leben des reizenden Bildes noch mehr Abwechslung bringen half. Die armen Vögel hatten gestern das Unglück gehabt, dass die vom Nordwinde aufgeregten Fluten ihre Wogen über die schmalen Watten gewälzt und so die Eier mit in den Abgrund gerissen hatten; heute hatten sich die Vögel erst neue Vertiefungen in den Sand gescharrt, und die Kolonie der **Raubseeschwalben** (doch zwei- bis dreihundert Pärchen stark) hatte nur einige dreissig Eier gelegt. Beide Arten, die **Brandsee-** und die **Raubseeschwalbe**, legten ihre Eier aber nicht an einer Stelle bunt durcheinander, sondern jede Art für sich allein auf einen besonderen Platz.

Die **Raubseeschwalben** waren auch am Brutplatze vorsichtiger als die **Brandseeschwalben**, und sind von jenem entfernt die scheuesten dieser Gattung. Sie scheinen auch nicht so weit herumzuschwärmen, und man sah sie selbst einzeln nicht oft auf der entgegengesetzten Seite dieser Dünen, die hier als Halbinsel eine Bucht bilden, die seichtes Wasser, was sie zum Fischfange lieben, genug hat. Sie fliegen auch schwerfälliger als andere Seeschwalben und ähneln im Fluge den Möven sehr, obgleich sie noch viel gewandter als diese sind. Die Brandseeschwalbe ist dagegen eine der flüchtigsten unter den Seeschwalben, ihr zierlicher, schöner Flug geht reissend schnell vonstatten, bewunderungswürdig sind ihre Schwenkungen, und sie schweift oft sehr weit vom Brutplatze fort.

War schon die Südseite dieser merkwürdigen Dünen mit der Menge schöner Möven und anderer Vögel wert, in einem Bilde dargestellt zu werden, so verdiente die

Nordseite es beinahe noch mehr. Ich entwarf daher die vorliegende naturgetreue Darstellung mit der Unterschrift:

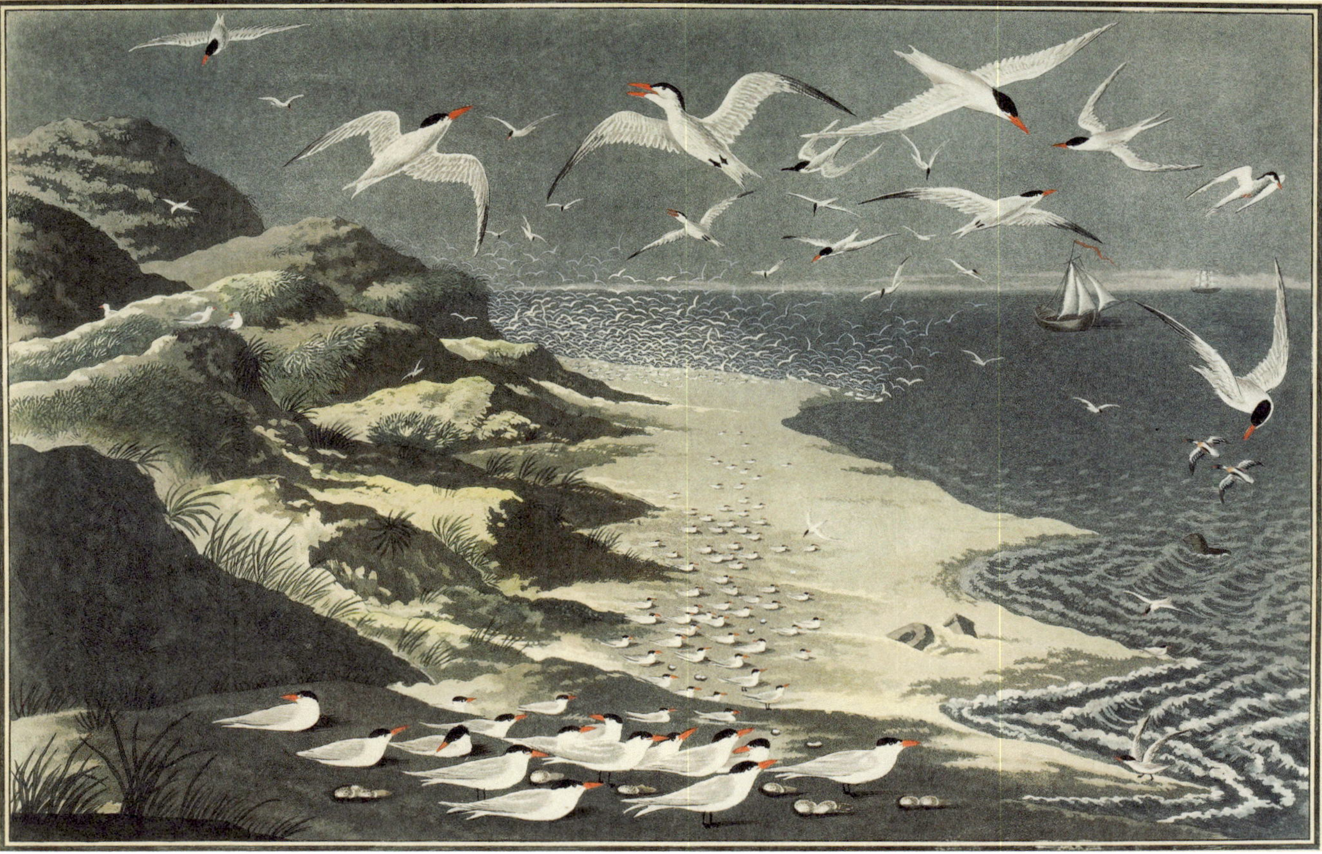

Die grossen Seeschwalben hinter den Dünen von List auf der Insel Sylt.

Die festeren Dünenhügel, welche sich links noch etwas auf diesem Bilde zeigen, lösen sich auf dieser Seite in bewegliche Sandberge auf, deren wandelbare Formen der kümmerlich darin aufsprossenden Dünenhafer noch nicht festzuhalten vermag, und verlaufen bald als schmale Bänke oder Sandwatten ins Meer. Mit ihrem leichten weissgelblichen Sande treiben die Stürme ihr Spiel, daher ragen von den Trümmern jenes, unlängst hier gescheiterten Schiffes nur noch ein paar Fragmente aus dem Sande hervor; was nicht als Brennmaterial davon weggeschafft ist, liegt darunter

---

Verkleinerung des Naumannschen Originals

begraben; man sieht im Mittelgrunde nur noch ein Stück vom Steuerruder und vom Rauchfang der Kajüte.

Vor uns hin dehnt sich der Nistplatz der grossen **Raubseeschwalben** aus; wir sehen diese königlichen Vögel in ihren schneeweissen, oben silbergrauen Gewändern, mit den samtschwarzen Kopfplatten und ihren grossen hellroten Schnäbeln vom Vordergrunde bis weit hinaus, teils sitzend und wie immer mit den Köpfen gegen das Wasser gerichtet, bei und auf ihren, in kleinen Vertiefungen des Sandes liegenden Eiern, teils fliegend in verschiedenen Bewegungen, auch wie sie hier den grossen Rachen weit aufsperren, mit aufgeblasener Kehle und vorgestrecktem Halse ihre krächzende, raben- oder reiherartige Stimme ausstossen; andere, wie sie mit stillgehaltenen, weit ausgebreiteten Flügeln sanft dahinschweben, wieder andere, wie sie in mövenartigem Fluge mit langsamen Flügelschlägen sich aufschwingen, sich schwenken u. s. w.

Im Hintergrunde, wo die Dünen eine stumpfe Ecke bilden, bemerkt man einen Teil des weissen Gewimmels von den in ungeheurer Anzahl dort hausenden **Brandseeschwalben**, von welchen sich einige dieser grossen Kolonie fliegend weiter vorwärts unter den **Raubseeschwalben** befinden, und im Vordergrunde oben rechts fliegt eine solche neben einer grossen, an ihrer viel kleineren schlankeren Figur und dem längeren, schwächeren, schwarzen Schnabel kenntlich.

Gleich neben dieser ganz rechts fliegt auch eine **Küstenseeschwalbe**, an ihrer viel geringeren Grösse, dem sehr langen Gabelschwanz, grauen Bauche und kleinen roten Schnabel leicht zu erkennen. Dieser liebliche Vogel nistet nicht in so grossen Gesellschaften, auch hier nicht, sondern auf anderen Teilen der Küsten dieser Inseln, und zeigt sich hier nur als Herumstreifer.

Weiter abwärts auf der nämlichen Seite, tief im Mittelgrunde, zeigen sich ein paar **Brandenten** durchfliegend, das grössere schönere Männchen folgt wie immer und bei den meisten Entenarten dem kleineren Weibchen. Sie kommen selten hierher, obgleich sie beim Orte **List**, eine halbe Meile von hier, in so grosser Menge hausen. Etwas weiter unter denselben erhebt eine Robbe (Seehund) ihr Haupt aus den Wellen. Links auf den Dünenhügeln, fast im Hintergrunde, sieht man einzelne grosse Möven sitzen, deren Region sich hier von der der Seeschwalben scheidet.«

Die Benutzung eines solchen Vogelgeheges wie das bei **List** ist in der Tat nicht unbedeutend, denn der Besitzer desselben brachte seine Einnahme davon alle Jahre gegen oder noch über 200 Reichsthaler. Er versicherte nämlich, an 30000

Stück grosser Möveneier zu erhalten, die mit Moos in Körbe gepackt nach den Städten des Festlandes geschickt und dort die Stiege (20 Stück) mindestens mit 5 Schilling (etwa 3 Groschen 4 Pfennige) bezahlt wurden. Zum Aufsuchen dieser Eier hält er zwei bis drei Leute, die in dieser Zeit in einer Hütte neben den Vögeln wohnen, von früh 8 Uhr bis nachmittags 3 Uhr vollkommen mit dem Aufsuchen beschäftigt sind und als Lohn alle kleineren Vogeleier, z. B. von **Sturmmöven, Raub-** und **Brandseeschwalben** u.s.w. für sich behalten, deren Zahl sich oftmals auch jährlich auf mehr als 20000 Stück belaufen kann, womit diese, was sie davon nicht in der eigenen Haushaltung verbrauchen, ebenfalls Handel treiben. Alle diese Eier sind sehr wohlschmeckend, besonders die der kleineren Seeschwalben. Die Eier der **Silbermöve** sind übrigens grösser als Puteneier und nur etwas kleiner als Gänseeier; die der **Sturmmöve** und **Raubseeschwalbe** etwa so gross wie die Eier von zahmen Enten; die der **Brandseeschwalbe** von der Grösse kleiner Hühnereier.

Die Zeit des Eierlegens ist für viele Bewohner der nördlichen Küsten und Inseln eine gesegnete Zeit; sie schwelgen im Genuss derselben, weil sie sonst selten Eier zu essen bekommen. Haushühner habe ich auf den bereisten Inseln gar nicht gesehen, und weiter nördlich hält man vollends keine, man begnügt sich mit den Eiern wilder Vögel und geniesst sie so lange, als es ihre Dauer erlaubt. Auf **Amrum** hatte unser Wirt, ein wohlhabender Schiffsherr, auch Strandvogt und Dünenmeister der Insel, Hühnereier vom Festlande mitgebracht und liess sie **Austernfischer** ausbrüten; damit aber diese den Betrug nicht merken sollten, hatte er die Eier mit Tinte beklext und bekritzelt. Es wurde versichert, dass er schon mehrmals dies getan, allein ich habe keine Hühner bei ihm gesehen.

Sehr wichtig ist auf **Sylt** für die dortigen Einwohner ein grosser Entenfang, gewöhnlich die **Vogelkoje** genannt, und wohl wert, dass hier noch ein paar Worte darüber gesagt werden. Diese Anstalt liegt auf dem nördlichen schmalen Teil der Insel an der Ostküste in einer Bucht. Auf der Westseite von den hier besonders hohen Dünen geschützt, gedeiht hier noch einigermassen das dabei nötige Buschwerk von Erlen und hohen Salweiden. Die vielen Flechten, die sich in grossen Klumpen an ihre Stämme und Äste bis in die Zweige angehängt haben, zeugen jedoch von einem kümmerlichen Wuchs, und die hier so furchtbaren Nordweststürme gestatten auch diesen krüppelhaften Bäumen nicht höher zu wachsen als sie unter dem Schutz der Dünen stehen.

Die Einrichtung ist die alte bekannte, in der Mitte ein Teich, aus welchem nach den vier Winden ebenso viele immer schmäler und seichter werdende und zuletzt ganz spitz auslaufende Kanäle gehen, die anfänglich mit hohen Bügeln und weitem Gitterwerk überspannt sind, was weiter hinten enger wird und endlich in einem ganz engen Garnsack ausläuft. An den Seiten der Kanäle sind Rohrwände angebracht, dahinter sich der Entenfänger verbirgt, und die Enten, anfänglich durch hingestreutes Futter mit den Lockenten, dann mittels eines kleinen abgerichteten Hundes u.s.w. eintreibt, bis er sie im Garnsack zuletzt abwürgen kann.

Die Lockenten, welche auf dem Teiche unterhalten wurden, waren teils wirkliche zahme Enten, teils gezähmte **Stockenten**, **Pfeifenten**, **Spiessenten** und **Löffelenten**. Der Entenfänger wohnte in der Koje in einem kleinen, im Buschwerk versteckten Häuschen, dabei auch ein brettern Magazin, die gefangenen Enten aufzubewahren, mit einer so grossen Menge von Fächern, dass Tausende darin Platz hatten. Einer der Eigentümer dieser Anstalt (ich glaube den Besitz teilen ihrer drei) war gerade da, zeigte mir alles sehr genau und sagte, dass hier im Spätherbst manchen Jahres gegen 20000 Stück Enten ihren Tod fänden, ja der alte Entenfänger sprach mit Entzücken vom glücklichen Fange in vergangenen Zeiten, wo er einmal binnen zweier Stunden 300 Stück wilden Enten den Hals umgedreht hatte.

Auf der Insel **Föhr** befanden sich noch zwei solcher Entenkojen, die ich aber nicht selbst sah, weil ich auf dieser sehr bebauten Insel, die in ornithologischer Hinsicht eben nichts Wichtiges hat, mich nur sehr kurze Zeit aufhielt. Es wurde aber versichert, dass beide Fanganstalten nicht so viel Ertrag gäben als die einzige auf **Sylt**.

Die Entenarten, welche man in den Kojen fängt, gehören alle zu der Entenfamilie, welche ihre Nahrung nicht untertauchend sucht und eine unbelappte Hinterzehe hat, mit Ausnahme der **Brandente**, die selten hineingeht, und dann auch, wenigstens auf **Sylt**, wenn es einmal geschieht, wieder freigelassen wird. Die ergiebigste Art ist die **Krickente**, die oft zu Hunderten in einem Tage abgewürgt wird.

So wie dort diese Enten in grossen Massen gefangen und zu Schiffe nach den grösseren Städten gesandt werden, so ist es in den Buchten der Ostsee an der Küste der Halbinsel **Jütland** mit den Entenarten der anderen Familie, die ihre Nahrung untertauchend sucht und eine belappte Hinterzehe hat, der Fall. Dort kommen die nordischen Enten in so ungeheurer Anzahl in die vom Eise freieren Buchten und Fjorde, um daselbst zu überwintern, dass die Scharen ganze Wasserflächen bedecken. Man fängt sie daselbst unter dem Wasser, indem man bei stillem Wetter grosse lange Klebegarne, denen ähnlich, welche man zum Lerchenfange bei Tage gebraucht, ins Wasser hängt, in welchen sich die Enten beim Untertauchen verwickeln und fangen. Sehr berühmt seines einträglichen Fanges wegen ist z. B. der **Kieler Fjord**, wovon mir meine dortigen Freunde berichteten, dass man in einem einzigen Winter allein mehr als 7000 Stück **Bergenten**, aber noch weit mehr **Eisenten** fing, der anderen Arten, wobei auch eine ungeheuer grosse Menge von **Trauerenten** war, nicht zu gedenken, dass man in Kiel und anderen nahen Städten keinen Absatz mehr fand und deshalb mehrere bloss mit Enten befrachtete Wagen nach **Hamburg** abgehen liess. Unter dieser ungeheuren Anzahl auf diese Art gefangener Enten sind hier die **Eisenten**, wie dort in den Entenkojen die **Krickenten** die häufigsten.

So nützt der Mensch die ihm dargebotenen Gaben der gütigen Natur auf die vielfältigste Weise, und etwas, was in einem Lande ganz unbedeutend scheint, macht in dem anderen eine reiche Nahrungsquelle aus. Auch die Vögel nehmen hier eine wichtige Stelle ein, ja im hohen Norden hängt selbst die Existenz mancher Völkerschaften zum Teil vom glücklichen Vogelfange ab; sie benutzen die Eier, das Fleisch, das Fett zur Nahrung, die Federn zu Betten, selbst die Häute zu Kleidungsstücken u. s. w., während die ackerbautreibenden Völker der gemässigten Zone keine Begriffe haben von den Gefahren, mit welchen die Bewohner jener unwirtlichen Gegenden in einem elenden Fahrzeuge sich einem wütenden Elemente anvertrauen, den Meereswogen preisgeben, grässliche Brandungen durchschiffen, dann schroffe Felsen erklimmen, über gähnende Schlünde und schauerliche Abgründe setzen, sich an langen trügerischen Seilen hinablassen oder an solchen von einer Klippe zur anderen gleiten, und so, um ihr Leben erträglicher zu machen, sich zuvor oft den augenscheinlichsten Lebensgefahren aussetzen müssen.

Ich bemerke nur noch, dass alles, was im Vorhergehenden über den Haushalt der Vögel und ihre Benutzung auf jener von mir gesehenen Inselgruppe gesagt ist, eigene selbstgemachte Beobachtungen sind. So merkwürdig sie indessen auch sein mögen, so halten sie doch in mancher Hinsicht noch lange keinen Vergleich mit denen aus, welche andere Beobachter im höheren Norden an der **norwegischen Küste** auf den **Loffoten** und **Islands Vogelbergen**, den **Färöern**, **Orkaden**, **Hebriden** der **schottischen Küste** u. s. w. an den **Alken**, **Lummen**, **Papageitauchern**, **Tölpeln**, **Sturmvögeln**, **Schwarzschnabelsturmtauchern**, **Dreizehenmöven** und anderen machten. Ich war zwar nie selbst dort, erlaube mir jedoch, zum Beweise des eben Gesagten hier einiges mitzuteilen, was uns kenntnisreiche und zuverlässige Beobachter berichten. Zuerst also einige hierher gehörende kurze Auszüge aus der höchst interessanten, unlängst im Druck erschienenen Schrift meines geschätzten Freundes F. BOIE aus Kiel, betitelt: **Tagebuch einer Reise durch Norwegen** im Jahr 1817. Von F. BOIE. Schleswig 1822. Man staunt, wenn man unseren Reisenden, welcher bloss aus Liebe zu den Naturwissenschaften, namentlich der Ornithologie, eine Reise in die rauhen Gegenden des höheren **Norwegens** und seiner gefürchteten Küste mit ihren zahllosen Schären, Klippen und Felseninseln, nicht ohne häufige Gefahren für Gesundheit und Leben, unternahm und seinen Zweck so weit es tunlich rühmlichst verfolgte, wenn man ihn S. 196 erzählen hört:

»Noch bemerkten wir nur das gewöhnliche Seegeflügel, und schon lagen die Gebäude von **Mosta** (auf den **Loffoten**-Inseln zwischen 67 und 68 Grad nördlicher Breite) unter der steilen Felswand vor uns, als wir von unseren Begleitern auf einen grossen dunklen Streif im Wasser aufmerksam gemacht wurden, der aus lauter Vögeln bestehen sollte; das schien uns ganz unmöglich; aber nun setzte sich jener Streif in Bewegung, gerade auf uns zu, und es entwickelte sich ein Schwarm von Seevögeln, aus **Tordalken** und **Trottellummen** bestehend, von dessen Grösse man sich kaum einen Begriff machen wird, wenn ich sage, dass ich meine Doppelflinte zehnmal abdrücken und wieder laden konnte, bevor alle vorüber waren. Dabei nahm der Zug eine Breite von wenigstens tausend Schritten ein, aber die Vögel flogen nicht dicht gedrängt, sondern jeder für sich nahe hinter dem anderen her, und bei der Schnelle ihres Fluges und der geringen Entfernung — denn keine zehn Schritte über unserem Kopf strichen sie hin — waren wir anfangs so verwirrt, dass wir keinen Schuss anzubringen wussten.

Solcher Flüge gab es zwei bis drei in der Gegend, die sich auch auf dem Wasser gelagert, sehr nahe kommen liessen, und man begreift kaum, wie das Gebirge für eine so ungeheure Menge von Vögeln noch Brutplätze genug darbieten kann, und doch hatten wir erst **Alken** und **Lummen** gesehen!«

Dies waren nämlich lange noch nicht alle geflügelte Bewohner jener Gegend, nur zwei Arten derselben; man liest S. 197 wie folgt:

»Nun fuhren wir weiter zur südlichen Spitze der Insel und kamen an eine tiefe Felsspalte, die eine Höhle bildet, in welche wir mit dem Boote fahren konnten, und diese, nebst der ganzen an Absätzen reichen Felswand umher, ward von **Drei-**

zehenmöven bewohnt. Ein aus Seegras gebautes Nest berührte fast das andere so hoch hinauf, als das Auge Gegenstände unterscheidet und so tief herab, dass wir die untersten Nester mit den Händen erreichen konnten; Männchen und Weibchen sassen in lieblichen Stellungen dicht aneinander gedrängt, ohne sich durch unsere am Abhange und in der Höhle selbst gewagten Flintenschüsse aufschrecken zu lassen. Schwärme von ihnen machten ganze Schären schneeweiss, und mit einem Doppelschuss streckte ich neun Stück derselben zu Boden. Sie und die **Lummen** flogen in Schwärmen von Hunderten der See zu, während andere von daher zurückkehrten, **Alken** und **Papageitaucher** bedeckten flächenweise das Wasser unter den Felsen u. s. w.«

Nicht weit von dieser Stelle nisteten die letzteren, ebenfalls in so unbeschreiblich grosser Anzahl, dass sie, in ganz aufrechter Stellung sitzend, ganz grosse Felsenabhänge bedeckten, dass ein Schuss unter sie getan, ihrer sechs Stück tötete u. s. w. Doch mein Freund erzählt S. 199 selbst:

»**Sörlands-Nuppen** (eine ungeheuere Klippe), die sich mit schwindelerregender Steilheit aus der See erhebt, dient so hoch als das Auge reicht den **Scharben** zum Aufenthalt. Überhaupt haben alle erwähnten Vögel einen besonderen Distrikt inne, wobei nur die **Tordalks** und **Trottellummen** durcheinander brüten. Diese haben sich gleichsam in die grosse Kolonie der **Papageitaucher** rechts und links vom Hofe **Mosta** eingedrängt, und zwischen ihnen kommen nur auf einzelnen Vorsprüngen **Scharben** vor. **Gryllteisten** zeigten sich auch hier nur zu unterst über dem Wasser an den Felsen, und so scheinen sie vom südlichen **Schweden** mit Einschluss von **Bornholm** bis hoch nach Norden hinauf an der ganzen Schärenküste vorzukommen u. s. w.«

Es sind hier nun noch verschiedene solcher häufigst besuchten Brutplätze der Vögel jener Gegenden angeführt, auch deren an der isländischen und grönländischen Küste gedacht, und zuletzt die allerdings sehr wichtige Frage aufgestellt, was die Vögel bewegen möchte, in solchen grossen Massen beisammen und dann nur auf besonderen einzelnen Klippen zu nisten. Es heisst S. 201:

»Man fragt sich unwillkürlich nach dem höheren Naturgesetz, welches diese Tiere bestimmen mag, gerade nur einzelnen Felseninseln vor so vielen anderen den Vorzug zu geben, die nicht minder passend für ihren Zweck zu sein scheinen. Offenbar müssen so viele auf dieselbe oder ganz ähnliche Weise lebende Vögel den einzelnen die Auffindung der Lebensmittel erschweren, und es wird also ein anderer Grund vorhanden sein, der allen denselben Ort so anziehend macht; denn zufällig ist, wie überhaupt in der Natur, hier gewiss nichts, und dem Naturforscher kann die blosse Erklärung aus dem Hang zur Geselligkeit dieser Vogelarten nicht genügen! Man müsste alle jene erwähnten Brutplätze besucht haben und aus mehrjähriger Erfahrung genau die Nahrungsmittel und alle äusseren Lebenserscheinungen jedweder Art kennen, um hier mit einiger Sicherheit schliessen zu können; aber was **Vaeroe** anbelangt, so ist es mir nicht unwahrscheinlich, dass die Lage dieser Insel jenen Seevögeln um deswillen so willkommen ist, weil eben hier aus nicht mehr bekannten Gründen unzählige Fische ihren Laich absetzten und die junge Fischbrut jenen eine unerschöpfliche Quelle der Nahrung darbietet. Insofern wären nun freilich alle Küsten von **Loffoten** gleich günstig für einen allgemeinen Brutplatz der Art, aber eigentümlich ist wenigstens an **Vaeroe** die steile Abdachung gegen Süden mit Schutz gegen Nord- und Nordwestwinde, und die ganze Beschaffenheit des Felsens mit seinen vielfachen Höhlungen und Spalten macht ihn für die Vögel unleugbar doppelt günstig. Übrigens scheinen es nicht ausschliesslich Fische zu sein, die den **Alken** und **Papageitauchern** zur Nahrung dienen u. s. w.«

Der dort übliche Fang der letzteren Vogelart wird uns S. 204 erzählt; man liest daselbst folgendes:

»Sehr lieb musste es uns in Bezug auf die Hauptabsicht unserer Exkursion sein, dass uns jetzt eine Frau mit zwei zum Vogelfang abgerichteten Hunden entgegenkam, die sich bereits an einem minder steilen Abhange auf der westlichen Seite des Gebirges zwischen grossen zerstreut liegenden Felsblöcken eine Strecke Wegs hinunter gewagt hatte und mit einem Dutzend gefangener **Papageitaucher**, die sie um den Leib befestigt trug, wieder von der Höhe herabsteigen wollte. Wir überredeten sie, noch einmal mit uns umzukehren und den Fang vor uns zu wiederholen. Die Menge der **Papageitaucher**, die uns hier wie Bienen mit einem dem Stöhnen der **Tordalken** ähnlichen Geschrei umschwärmten oder ganz aufrecht auf Felsen neben uns sassen, lässt sich gar nicht beschreiben, und ich will mich nur bemühen, ein getreues Bild von der Art zu geben, wie diese Vögel hier wohnen, brüten und gefangen werden.

Die Felsart an diesem Platze und an den übrigen der Insel, die der **Papageitaucher** sich vorbehalten hat, ist Schiefer, der schon an sich reich an Vertiefungen, von den Vögeln ganz durchlöchert ist. Jede dieser Höhlen, für ein Pärchen bestimmt, ist bei einer Breite von sechs Zoll im Durchmesser ein bis zwei Klafter tief, und es lässt sich nicht bezweifeln, dass der Vogel sie selbst gräbt mit Hilfe seines grossen harten Schnabels und seiner Klauen, von denen die der inneren Zehen sonderbar horizontal (nach innen) gerichtet ist. Ganz ans Ende solcher Höhle legt das Weibchen **ein** schmutzig weisses ungeflecktes Ei von der Grösse eines Hühnereies, nur an beiden Enden mehr abgerundet.

Die erwähnten Hunde (an Gestalt und Zeichnung den Dachshunden ähnlich, aber höher von Beinen und durch eine doppelte Klaue am Hinterdaumen ausgezeichnet) begannen nun sofort wieder hitzig die Jagd, und wir sahen sie in den Höhlen verschwinden, mit Beute hervorkommen und von neuem andere Löcher durchstöbern. Sie haben im Innern des Lundenbaues einen schweren Stand mit dem sich heftig verteidigenden und bis aufs Blut beissenden und kratzenden Vogel zu bestehen, und die Fängerin, die, wie sie aussagt, zwanzig solche Hunde hält, wollte schon viele derselben eingebüsst haben, die nicht wieder zum Vorschein kamen. Übrigens bringen gut abgerichtete Hunde den Lund noch lebend aus der Höhle, und er wird alsdann, wie es auf Entenfängen mit den gefangenen Enten zu geschehen pflegt, ohne Verletzung der Haut durch blosse Anziehung des Kopfes und Trennung des Atlas vom Hinterhaupte getötet.

Der beschriebene Abhang ist unter die Bewohner von **Mosta** verteilt, welche fast ausschliesslich vom Vogelfange leben. Man verspeist die Vögel frisch und eingesalzen gleich den **Tordalken** und **Trottellummen** — denn nur diese sind ausserdem auf **Mosta** Gegenstand des Vogelfanges — aber so gross auch der Verbrauch derselben sein mag, so wird ihrer doch verhältnismässig nur eine geringe Anzahl getötet, denn gerade die Plätze, welche ihren zahlreichsten Schwärmen zum Aufenthalt dienen, ist der Mensch zu erreichen nicht imstande!«

Es setzt in der Tat in Erstaunen, wenn man diese keineswegs übertriebenen, sondern auch von anderen bestätigten Berichte liest und Beschreibungen ganz ähnlicher Erscheinungen anderer Weltgegenden damit vergleicht. Die ungeheure Menge, in welcher manche Arten Seevögel in vielen Gegenden vorkommen, ist um so wunderbarer, da man weiss, dass jedes Pärchen im Jahr nicht mehr als ein einziges Ei ausbrütet oder ein Junges erzieht, welches gar vielen noch geraubt wird, die also das Jahr ganz ohne Nachkommenschaft bleiben. Die Seevögel haben ausser den Menschen allerdings noch gar viele Feinde, die ihre Zahl vermindern helfen, und doch wird dies, trotz ihrer schwachen Vermehrung, nicht bemerklich; es wohnen und nisten häufig Seeadler und andere grosse Falken in der Nähe grosser Vogelkolonien, welche für sich und zur Atzung ihrer Jungen täglich gar viele verzehren und eine Zeitlang fast von nichts anderem als alten und jungen Seevögeln leben; Silbermöven und Raubmöven saufen die Eier aus und schleppen die kleinen Jungen weg, die Skua füttert ihre Jungen sogar fast allein mit jungen Lummen, Alken, Tölpeln, Sturmvögeln und dergleichen auf, auch Raubtiere stellen hin und wieder der Brut und den alten Vögeln nach, selbst grosse Fische erschnappen manchen Vogel, auch kommen oft Hunderte bei strenger Kälte und heftigen Stürmen der arktischen Winter um, und dazu kommt denn noch, dass, wie gesagt, viele Arten, z. B. Lummen, Alken, Papageitaucher, Eissturmvögel, Basstölpel und Schwarzschnabelsturmtaucher, nur ein einziges Ei legen und bebrüten, was öfters noch faul ist oder ihnen von Menschen oder räuberischen Vögeln genommen wird, in welchem Falle sie zwar ein anderes, auch wohl in wiederkehrendem Falle ein drittes u.s.w. legen, aber am Ende doch nur das zuletzt gelegte einzig ausbrüten. Demungeachtet ist es erwiesen, dass alle diese Vögel, selbst Möven und Seeschwalben, die alle auch nur drei Eier jedesmal legen und auch nur einmal im Jahre brüten, auch öfters nur zwei, sogar nicht selten nur ein Junges aufbringen, in viel grösserer Anzahl angetroffen werden als viele Entenarten, welche sechs bis zehn und wohl noch mehr Eier legen. Es gibt zwar Gegenden, wo Enten- und Gänsearten auch in zahlloser Menge brüten und nachher mit einer weit grösseren Anzahl von Jungen erscheinen als die oben genannten Vögel, aber keine Art hält hinsichtlich der Anzahl an Individuen überhaupt mit jenen einen Vergleich aus.

F. Faber, welcher 2½ Jahre die Vögel Islands an Ort und Stelle beobachtete, teilte uns unlängst die Resultate seiner mühevollen Reise in einem Werkchen mit, was über die Ökonomie der nordischen Seevögel ausserordentlich viel Licht verbreitet und voll der trefflichsten Bemerkungen ist. Unbefangen und mit einer edlen Einfachheit ist darin die Lebensweise jener interessanten Geschöpfe erzählt, die er selbst beobachtete, und unverkennbare Wahrheit leuchtet aus jeder Zeile dieses lehrreichen Büchelchens, betitelt: Prodromus der isländischen Ornithologie oder Geschichte der Vögel Islands von FRIEDRICH FABER. Kopenhagen 1822.

Ein Besuch, den ich von diesem geschätzten Manne vor kurzem erhielt, musste mir um so angenehmer sein, da ausser dem Glück der persönlichen Bekanntschaft ich noch über vieles in jenem Werke nur kürzlich Angeführte mündliche nähere

Aufschlüsse erhielt, und noch manches von ihm erfragen konnte, was dort kaum berührt war.

So wie uns dort Justitiar BOIE von den grossen Kolonien verschiedener Seevogelarten auf den **Loffoten** erzählt, wird es durch FABER von mehreren Gegenden der Küste **Islands** und seiner Inseln und Schären ebenfalls berichtet. S. 91 sagt er z. B. von der **Dreizehenmöve**: »In **Grimsöes** Vogelberg nisten sie in solcher Menge, dass sie die Sonne verbergen, wenn sie auffliegen; die Schären bedecken, wenn sie sitzen; die Ohren betäuben, wenn sie schreien; und den vom Löffelkraut grünen Felsen beinahe weiss machen, wenn sie brüten.« Von den **Papageitauchern**, die um ganz **Island** überall ungemein häufig sind, sagt er S. 50: »Auf den **Westmanöern** bedecken sie in der Brutzeit die Oberfläche der Felseninseln.« Und doch sind diese nicht die einzigen Bewohner jener Inseln, wie wir S. 108 sehen, wo es von den **Eissturmvögeln** heisst: »Ihre merkwürdigsten Brutplätze sind gegen Norden **Grimsöes** Vogelberg, gegen Westen **Lautrabjerg**, gegen Süden **Hafnardbjerg** und **Kryseviks** Vogelberg, vorzüglich aber die **Westmanöer** (Inseln oder Klippen), wo sie von allen dort in den Felsen brütenden Vögeln die häufigste Art sind. Ihre Anzahl auf diesen Inseln kann einigermassen darnach berechnet werden, dass die Einwohner jährlich wenigstens 20000 Junge von diesen Vögeln ausnehmen; da jedes Paar nie mehr als ein Ei hat, so brüten allerwenigstens 40000 Individuen da, welche Anzahl jährlich zunimmt, dort viele Junge nicht erreicht werden, wo die Natur der Felsen dieses nicht erlaubt, obgleich die Einwohner, hier wie bei anderen Vogelbergen in **Island**, sich mit um den Leib gebundenen Gurten an den steilen Felsenwänden hinablassen, wenn sie Vögel aus dem Neste, Junge oder Eier zur Speise ausnehmen wollen.«

Unter den Entenarten ist die **Eiderente** eine der häufigsten bei **Island**. »Sie zieht (nach S. 68) mitten im Mai nach ihren Brutplätzen, die Schären im Meere, wie auch die Inselchen auf den süssen Teichen nahe am Meere oder in den Mündungen der Flüsse von **Grimsöe** an bis zu den **Westmanöern**. Die Insel **Widöe** hat wohl zum grossen Vorteile des Besitzers die grösste Menge brütender **Eidervögel**, da ein grosser Teil der Insel in der Brutzeit ganz von ihnen bedeckt ist. Sie liegen dicht unter den Mauern des Hauses auf Eiern; das zahme Weibchen lässt sich von seinen Eiern abheben und wieder darauf setzen. Diese nebst den Eiderdunen werden jährlich zweimal aus dem Neste genommen.« Und weiter unten: »Im Winter sammeln alle sich im offenen Meere wie in den Buchten in ungeheure Scharen und sind sehr wild. Man kann diese Scharen lange hören, ehe man sie sieht, und man sollte glauben, eine Versammlung von Menschen zu hören, die alle zugleich reden.«

Wir wollen uns jetzt von **Island** weg in eine andere für die Ornithologie wichtige Gegend, nach der Küste **Schottlands** wenden. Welchem Ornithologen wäre dort nicht die in einem Meerbusen (Firth of Forth) liegende Felseninsel **Bass**, von welcher eine Vogelart sogar ihren Beinamen erhielt, wenigstens dem Namen nach bekannt? Schon seit langen Zeiten war sie berühmt durch die Menge der alljährlich dort brütenden **Basstölpel**, die, beiläufig gesagt, nach FABER auch bei **Island** auf den entferntesten Klippen oder Schären, z. B. auf **Grimsöe**, den Vogelschären und auf einzelnen **Westmanöern** häufigst brüten. ERNST FLEISCHER berührte auf einer Reise durch **Albions** merkwürdigste Teile auch jene Gegend, und benutzte diese Gelegenheit, dem berühmten Felsen **Bass** einen Besuch abzustatten. Dies geschah am 30. Juni 1820. Seine höchst interessanten, dort gemachten Beobachtungen sahen wir in einem gediegenen kurzen Aufsatze in OKENS Isis, Jahrg. 1821, St. XII abgedruckt, von dem es mir erlaubt sei, hier einiges auszuheben:

»Der **Bass**, eine hohe, steile Felsenmasse, von der nächsten Landspitze zwei Seemeilen entfernt, in der Mündung der Forth, gleicht aus der Ferne einem Kalkfelsen wegen der ihn bedeckenden unsäglichen Menge **weisser Tölpel** und ihres weissen Unrats, obgleich er aus rotem Porphyr besteht und auf seinem abgeplatteten Rükken begrast, sonst aber ganz kahl ist. Nur an einer Stelle erlauben die tobenden Brandungen das Anlanden, dann ist aber hier der einzige Eingang zur natürlichen Felsenburg durch eine künstliche Thür mit Schloss und Riegel verwahrt. Er enthält eine Seemeile im Umfange und hat wenige beschwerliche Felsenstiege, um eine unbeträchtliche Anzahl von Vogelnestern zu erklimmen; zu den meisten gelangt man nach der auf den **Orkaden** üblichen Methode; ein Mann wird nämlich mit einem Strick um den Leib oder auf einem Querholze reitend zu den Brutplätzen hinabgelassen.

Myriaden dieser Vögel bewohnen den Bass; einen Begriff von ihrer Menge und zugleich von der Wichtigkeit derselben für die Bewohner der Nachbarschaft kann folgendes geben: Der Besitzer der Insel hatte derzeit die Vogeljagd auf derselben an einen anderen Mann für eine jährliche Rente von 35 Pfund Sterling verpachtet. Man beunruhigt die Vögel durchaus nicht, sammelt keine Eier, kein alter Vogel darf geschossen werden, jedes Stück bringt nach den dortigen Jagdgesetzen 5 Pfund Sterling Strafe; in ähnliche Strafe verfällt, wer sich an den Eiern vergreift. Es ist hier bloss auf die jungen Vögel abgesehen. Sind diese ziemlich flügge, so beginnt die Jagd, d.h. man fängt sie grösstenteils mit den Händen oder erschlägt sie mit Stöcken u.s.w. Mit dem ersten Tag des Augustmonats wird damit angefangen und so lange fortgefahren, als man noch Vögel habhaft werden kann; denn sie werden stets von sehr ungleichem Alter gefunden. So fängt man jährlich nicht unter tausend Stück, die man nach Edinburgh und nach anderen Städten zum Verkauf bringt und wovon jedes Stück mit einer halben Krone (20 gute Groschen) bezahlt wird.

Die alten Vögel sind am Brutorte so zahm, dass man sich ihnen auf wenige Schritte nähern kann, und sie sich öfters selbst auf dem Ei oder neben dem Jungen mit Händen greifen lassen.

Die **Tölpel** haben nun zwar die Oberherrschaft auf dem **Bass**, doch nisten daselbst auch eine ungeheuere Menge anderer Seevögel, insbesondere **Sturmmöven**, **Trottellummen** und **Papageitaucher**, minder zahlreich dagegen die **Tordalken** und **Gryllteisten**.«

Die Küsten **Schottlands** sind überhaupt reichlich mit Seevögeln versehen, und an vielen Stellen brüten sie in Myriaden, sodass es demjenigen, welcher nie dergleichen sah, schwer wird, sich einen deutlichen Begriff davon zu machen. Es ist schon erwähnt worden, dass manche Gegenden vielen Arten zugleich zu Brutplätzen dienen, doch halten sich die einzelnen Arten immer näher beisammen an besonderen Stellen auf. Manche sind dabei über viele Teile der nordischen Erde verbreitet, wie wir schon ein Beispiel an den **Gryllteisten** sahen, und hierzu auch noch die **Tordalken** zählen können; denn diese Vögel brüten schon ziemlich zahlreich auf der Insel **Helgoland**, sind an der ganzen Küste **Norwegens**, **Grossbritanniens** und von hier aus an allen felsigen Küsten und auf allen Inseln bis hoch in den arktischen Kreis hinauf überall zahlreich; eine unermessliche Anzahl belebt die nordischen Meere, und ein nach Verhältnis nur kleiner Teil zieht im Winter südlicher und besucht dann auch die Küsten des Festlandes von **Europa**. Ebenso sind die **Papageitaucher** in unglaublicher Menge über viele Teile der nordischen Erde verbreitet.

Manche Arten suchen dagegen nur gewisse kleinere Teile von jenen Gegenden, einzelne Inseln und Klippen auf, wo sie in zahllosen Scharen beisammen leben, wie wir schon von den **Basstölpeln** bemerkt haben. Hierher gehört denn auch der **Schwarzschnabelsturmtaucher**, von welchen nur eine geringere Anzahl auf den südlichen **Westmanöern** bei **Island** brütet. Allein an den nördlichsten

Küsten Schottlands ist er stellenweise sehr häufig; die Insel **St. Kilda** und überhaupt einige der **Orkaden** bewohnt er im Sommer in so unermesslicher Anzahl, dass es daselbst die Hauptnahrung der Einwohner für das ganze Jahr ausmacht. Dieser sonderbare Vogel fliegt auf die höchsten mit Erde bedeckten Felsen und gräbt sich in der wenigen Dammerde lange tiefe Löcher oder Röhren dicht unter der Oberfläche entlang, in welcher er sein einziges Ei ausbrütet. Mit Lebensgefahr erklimmt man die furchtbarsten Felsenmassen, um zu jenen Stellen zu gelangen, wo diese Vögel den Boden durchwühlt haben, und bei Hunderten, ja Tausenden beisammen ihre Fortpflanzungsgeschäfte treiben. Alt und jung, alles was man habhaft werden kann, wird aus den Löchern hervorgezogen und getötet. Gäb es nicht Stellen, welche ein Mensch bei Verachtung aller Gefahr und mit allen ihm zu Gebote stehenden Mitteln dennoch nicht zu erreichen imstande ist, so würde sich die Zahl der Vögel vermindern; allein dergleichen Asyle gibt es für sie noch so viele, dass man die Masse sich jährlich eher vermehren als vermindern sieht oder doch durchaus keine Abnahme spürt. So sorgte die Vorsehung überall weislich für die Erhaltung ihrer Wesen.

Ich schliesse diese kurze Schilderung der Ökonomie der nordischen Seevögel mit dem Wunsche, dass sie hinsichtlich des kunstlosen Vortrags mit gütiger Nachsicht aufgenommen werden möge. Leicht hätte ich das Ganze noch um das Doppelte verlängern können, glaube jedoch, dass das Gelieferte gerade hinreichend sein wird, den Sinn der beiden Zeichnungen gehörig zu verstehen. Enthält es gleich für den Mann vom Fache nicht viel Neues, so wird es doch hoffentlich dem schlichten Liebhaber nicht unangenehm sein, eine kurze Darstellung so merkwürdiger Erscheinungen in der Natur zu finden, die ihn gewiss nicht ohne Interesse lassen werden. Für die Wahrheit des von anderen Entlehnten glaube ich mich übrigens ebenso verbürgen zu können wie für meine eigenen Beobachtungen.

// DIE NACHTIGALL //

LUSCINIA MEGARHYNCHOS

Die Nachtigall, gemeine Nachtigall, Waldnachtigall, Berg-, Wasser- oder Gartennachtigall, Tagnachtigall, kleine oder sächsische Nachtigall, rotgelbe Grasmücke, schlagende Grasmücke, Philomele, Dorling, Waldvogel, Rotvogel, rote Nachtigall.

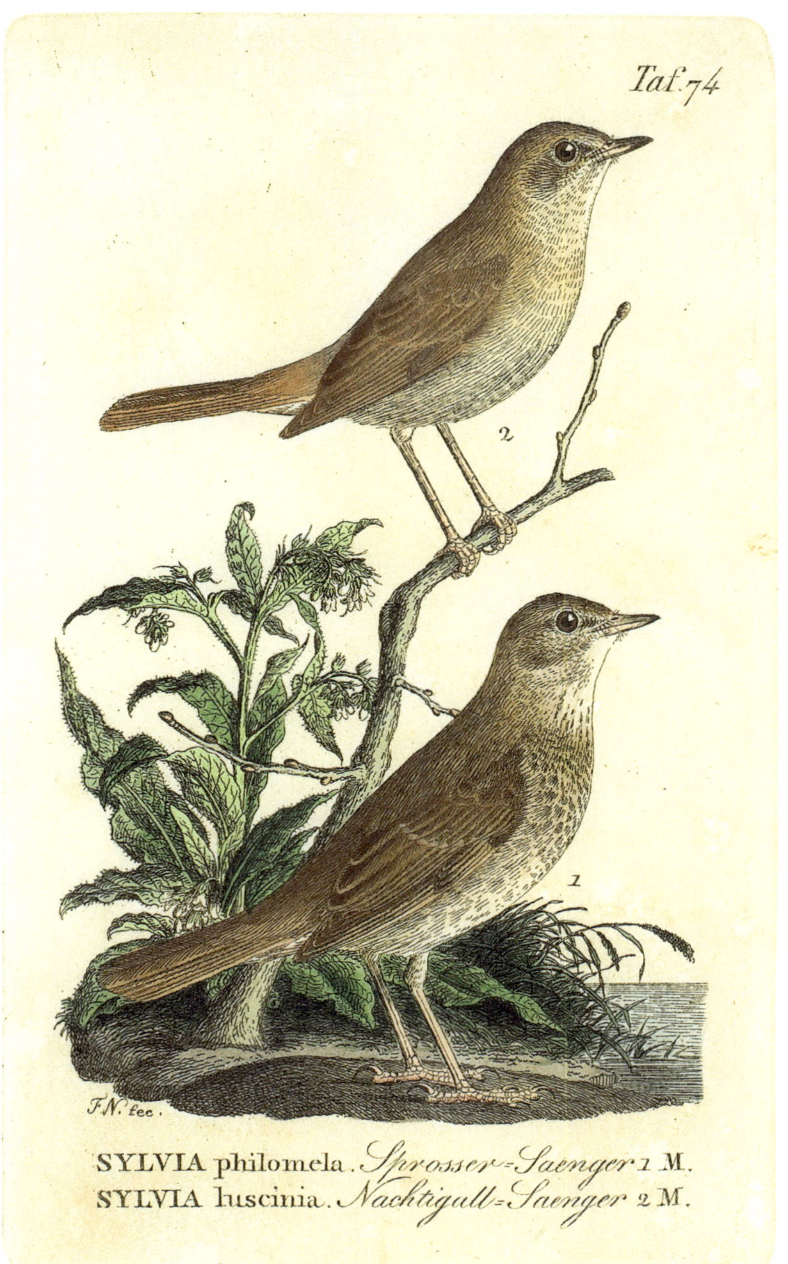

SYLVIA philomela. *Sprosser=Saenger* 1 M.
SYLVIA luscinia. *Nachtigall=Saenger* 2 M.

KENNZEICHEN DER ART

Die oberen Teile sind dunkel rostgrau; der Schwanz rostfarben; die unteren Teile schmutzig graulichweiss. Die erste Schwinge ist kurz, die zweite 6 mm kürzer als die dritte und von gleicher Länge mit der fünften.

BESCHREIBUNG

Dieser unansehnlich gefärbte Vogel, den man seines vortrefflichen Gesanges wegen allgemein schätzt, ist von etwas schlankem Körperbau und sieht daher viel schmächtiger aus als der **Sprosser**, von dem ihn auch die hellere Rückenfarbe und der lichter gefärbte, viel rötere Schwanz, der schwächere, daher länger aussehende Schnabel und andere Merkmale regelmässig unterscheiden. Von dem weiblichen **Gartenrotschwanz**, mit dem er nur von ganz Unkundigen verwechselt werden kann, unterscheiden ihn der einfarbig rostrote Schwanz, die höheren weisslichen Füsse und überhaupt die ansehnlichere Grösse hinlänglich.

Er steht wegen der langen Fusswurzeln etwas hoch auf den Beinen; aber der schlanke Körper erreicht noch nicht die Grösse des **Haussperlings**.

Die Länge beträgt 16 cm, die Flügelbreite 24,7 cm; die Länge des am Ende geraden Schwanzes 6,5 cm, und die ruhenden Flügel reichen mit ihren Spitzen fast bis auf die Mitte desselben.

Der ziemlich gestreckte, vorn pfriemenförmig spitze, hinten etwas breite, fast gerade Schnabel ist 12 mm lang, an der Wurzel merklich breiter als hoch, nach vorn aber sehr zusammengedrückt oder an den Schneiden eingezogen. Von Farbe ist er oben dunkelbraun, unten nur spitzenwärts braun, übrigens blass fleischfarben; Rachen und Zunge gelblich. Die Nasenlöcher sind länglich oval, die Augen gross und lebhaft, mit dunkelbraunen Sternen und weisslich befiederten Augenlidern; über den Mundwinkeln befinden sich einige feine schwarze Borstenhaare.

Die Füsse sind ansehnlich hoch, aber ziemlich dünn, die Krallen mittelmässig und nicht stark gebogen. Die Bedeckung des Laufes ist fast gestiefelt oder nur durch seichte Einschnitte in grosse Schildtafeln geteilt, die Zehenrücken geschildert, die

Sohlen feinwarzig; die Farbe der Füsse schmutzig oder bräunlich fleischfarben, die Nägel etwas dunkler, besonders an den Spitzen. In der Gefangenschaft wird die Farbe der Füsse sehr bleich, rötlich- oder gelblichweiss. Die Höhe der Fusswurzel beträgt 27,5 mm, die Länge der Mittelzehe 19,5 mm, und die der Hinterzehe gegen 14 mm, wovon 7 mm auf die Kralle kommen.

Das Gefieder ist seidenartig weich und trägt sehr einfache, unansehnliche Farben. Der Oberkopf, die Ohrengegend, Nacken, Rücken und Flügeldeckfedern sind dunkel rostgrau oder grau rostbraun, auf dem Scheitel und Oberrücken am dunkelsten, auf dem Bürzel in dunkle Rostfarbe übergehend; Zügel und Augengegend sowie die Seiten des Halses lichter, in weissliches Gelbgrau übergehend, das die ganze untere Seite des Vogels bedeckt und in den Weichen am dunkelsten ist, am After und an den langen unteren Schwanzdeckfedern aber in trübes Rostgelb übergeht; die Mitte der Kehle und die der Unterbrust, der Länge nach, sind schmutzig weiss. Alle Flügelfedern haben auf den Aussenfahnen die Farbe des Rückens, auf dem inneren sind sie nebst den Enden der grossen Schwingen dunkelbraun; die zugerundeten Schwanzfedern sind alle rostfarbig, die mittleren dunkler als die übrigen. Von der unteren Seite ist der Schwanz hell rostfarbig mit rötlich-gelben Federschäften; die Schwingen von unten rötlichgrau, mit einem rötlichweissen Streif längs der Kante der Innenfahne; die unteren Flügeldeckfedern schmutzig rostgelb und grau gemischt.

Zwischen **Männchen** und **Weibchen** ist im Äusseren kaum ein Unterschied zu entdecken; selbst wenn man beide nebeneinander stellt, wird man am ersteren kaum etwas lebhaftere Farben und eine reine weisse Kehle bemerken, was aber gar nicht auffällt, wenn man es allein sieht. Sehr geübte Kenner wollen übrigens in Stellung und Gebärden bei lebenden Vögeln beiderlei Geschlechts einen Unterschied finden, der aber, wie es scheint, auch nicht immer Stich hält, indem sie sich nicht selten täuschen.

Im **Herbst** nach der Mauser, die im Juli statt hat, sind die Farben des Gefieders frischer und dunkler als im **Frühling**, wo sie merklich abgebleicht sind. Das Gefieder nutzt sich indes nur wenig ab. — Im Zimmer werden die Farben meistenteils dunkler oder brauner.

Die **Jungen vor der ersten Mauser** sehen sehr bunt aus; sie haben zwar die Farben der Alten, doch dunkler, und alle Federn an den oberen Teilen haben noch hell rostgelbe Schaftflecke und die Ränder derselben eine schwärzliche oder doch dunklere als die gewöhnliche Farbe; die unteren Teile sind stark mit Bräunlichgelb überlaufen, alle Federn mit graubraun bespritzten Endsäumchen, wodurch hier ziemlich dichtstehende, abgebrochene, nach dem Bauche zu aber undeutliche Wellenlinien gebildet werden. Sie sehen den **jungen Rotkehlchen** ähnlich, sind aber grösser, hochbeiniger, von Farbe röter, und besonders an dem rostroten Schwanze leicht von diesen zu unterscheiden. Sie mausern sich, ehe sie wegziehen, sind aber öfters noch im Federwechsel begriffen, wenn sie sich bereits auf dem Zuge befinden; die von einer späteren Brut oft noch in der Mitte des September.

Im Freien sind **Spielarten** unter diesen Vögeln äusserst selten. Im Zimmer werden sie manchmal **weissgefleckt**, auch wohl **grauweiss** oder **rein weiss**, zuweilen gar **schwarzbraun** oder **rauchschwarz**, doch sind dies ebenfalls nur seltene Fälle. Man will auch in grossen Vogelhäusern von der Nachtigall und dem Rotkehlchen **Bastarde** gezogen haben, die ein scheckiges, von den Farben beider Eltern zusammengesetztes Kleid gehabt haben sollen.

AUFENTHALT

Dieser berühmte Vogel ist über den grössten Teil von **Europa** verbreitet, doch geht er im Norden nicht über das mittlere **Schweden** hinauf. Im Süden ist er fast überall, auch in **Asien**, bis in die Mitte von **Sibirien**, und im nördlichen und mittleren **Afrika**. Hier, namentlich in **Ägypten**, so auch in **Syrien**, soll er überwintern; denn er ist für Europa ein **Zugvogel**. In **Deutschland** ist er überall bekannt und in manchen Gegenden häufig; nur in wenigen vermisst man ihn, und dies sind denn doch immer nur kleine Distrikte. In den meisten deutschen Ländern hegt und schützt man diese angenehmen und nützlichen Vögel.

Als Zugvögel, die nur im Sommer bei uns sind, im Winter aber wärmere Himmelsstriche bewohnen, kommen sie im mittleren Deutschland stets erst um die Mitte des April an, wenn eben die Knospen der Bäume aufbrechen und namentlich der Weissdorn zu grünen anfängt, oder wenn sich die Stachelbeerbüsche völlig belaubt haben und in voller Blüte stehen. Ist nun das Frühjahr zeitig warm genug, sodass die erstarrte Natur früher aus ihrem Winterschlafe erwacht, so tritt dies oft schon in der ersten Woche des genannten Monats ein; im Gegenteil, wenn späte

Fröste und rauhkalte Witterung das Wiederaufleben der Vegetation und der damit in genauester Verbindung stehenden Insektenwelt weiter hinaus verschieben, so geschieht es öfters nicht vor der letzten Hälfte des April.

Sie kommen einzeln an, und immer die Männchen einige Tage früher als die Weibchen, obwohl auch diese Regel ihre einzelnen Ausnahmen hat. Ihre Reisen verrichten sie des Nachts, und es scheint, dass sie sich dabei nicht übereilen. Dies wird besonders auf dem Wegzuge bemerklich, wo sie aber meistens familienweise wandern. Schon in der Mitte des August fangen sie an, wegzuziehen, begeben sich zur Nachtzeit von einem Walde und Gebüsch zum anderen und verschwinden so unmerklich, mit Ablauf der ersten Hälfte des September, gänzlich aus unseren Gegenden. Weil sie um diese Zeit nicht singen, auch sonst stille, ruhige, gern im Dunkel der Gebüsche verborgen lebende Vögel sind, so bemerkt man sie dann auch weniger als im Frühjahr. Selten sieht man einmal zu Ausgang des September oder gar im Anfang des Oktober noch einzelne, von denen man wohl als wahrscheinlich annehmen darf, dass sie durch einen üblen Zufall am früheren Wegziehen verhindert wurden; es sind meistens Junge einer späten Brut, die öfters die Mauser noch nicht völlig überstanden haben.

Es sind Waldvögel, die man vergebens auf dem Freien sucht, selten und nur auf dem Zuge in einzelnen Feldhecken antrifft, die sie auch nur dann zu besuchen scheinen, wenn sie auf ihren nächtlichen Wanderungen grösseres, zusammenhängenderes Buschwerk nicht haben erreichen können. So trifft man sie auch weder im Nadelholze, noch auf hohen Gebirgen an. Sie lieben das niedere Laubholz, besonders wenn es auf feuchtem Boden wächst und Wassergräben, Bäche und Flüsse es durchschneiden. Im Hochwalde sind sie nicht, es müssten denn Stellen sich in demselben befinden, wo die Bäume weniger dicht stehen und unter demselben Unterholz und Buschwerk genug wachsen; dies ist aber selten. In gebirgigen Gegenden bewohnen sie die tiefen, waldigen Thäler und Vorberge, in ebenen Gegenden vorzüglich gern die waldreichen Auen der Flüsse. Aber man findet sie nicht allein hier, sondern auch in allen weniger grossen, mit Wiesenplätzen, Äckern und kleinem Gesträuch versehenen Laubholzwaldungen, in kleinen Feldhölzern, in Lustgärten und Parks, in den Baumgärten bei den Dörfern, wenn sie nur Buschwerk genug haben. Das Weidegebüsch lieben sie nicht so sehr wie der S p r o s s e r, und sie suchen in den grossen Weidenhegern an unseren Flüssen gern solche Stellen, wo auch andere Holzarten wachsen. In tiefliegenden Feldhölzern, wo Eichen, Ulmen, Eschen und andere Laubholzbäume einzeln stehen, unter diesen aber recht viel dichtes Unterholz, aus Haseln, Hartriegel, Faulbaum, Liguster, Salweiden, Schlingbaum, Schwarz- und Weissdorn und anderem Gesträuch bestehend, ein düsteres, schattiges Gebüsch bildet, sind sie ungemein gern. Werden sie hier nicht durch Menschen gestört, zuviel des Holzes in einem Jahre abgetrieben, oder durch andere unbekannte Umstände ihre Zahl vermindert, so besuchen sie solche sehr häufig. Mein eigenes Wäldchen gibt den Beleg hierzu; es hat nur wenige Morgen Flächeninhalt und wird den Sommer über mindestens von sechs, öfters aber wohl von zehn bis zwölf Pärchen bewohnt, die drei bis vier Pärchen, welche teils meine und andere Gärten und Umgebungen des Dorfes bewohnen, ungerechnet. Sie wohnen so nahe beisammen, dass mehr als zwei Pärchen auf einen Morgen Holzung kommen. Höchst merkwürdig bleibt hierbei immer die so sehr verschiedene Anzahl; denn in einem Jahre höre ich oft zwölf Nachtigallen und im darauffolgenden kaum halb so viel schlagen, oder umgekehrt. Es mögen daher zuweilen viele auf der Reise umkommen; denn während ihres Hierseins stört sie niemand, und ich sehe sie jährlich eine Menge Junge ausbringen und aufziehen. Sie sind gern bei den Dörfern und bewohnten Orten, wenn diese nur Buschwerk genug und nicht zu dürren Boden haben; denn Wasser lieben sie sehr. Es ist indessen so bemerkenswert als unerklärlich, dass es Gegenden gibt, die alle Eigenschaften, welche die Nachtigall bei ihrem Aufenthaltsorte verlangt, zu haben scheinen, und doch von keiner bewohnt werden. Unter den verschiedenen Ursachen, die man wohl hiervon angeben könnte, sind keine wahrscheinlicher als der Mangel an gewissen Lieblingsnahrungsmitteln, das Dasein ihnen unangenehmer Ausdünstungen des Bodens oder vielleicht die Lage solcher Gegenden hinsichtlich ihrer nächtlichen Heerstrassen in der Luft; denn dass solche für die Zugvögel wirklich zu existieren scheinen, ist schon früher im allgemeinen Teil erwähnt worden.

Jedes Nachtigallpärchen sucht im kommenden Jahr sein voriges Wohnplätzchen wieder auf, und wenn einer der Gatten davon auf der Reise verunglückt oder bei seiner Ankunft früh genug, ehe die Zugzeit zu Ende geht, weggefangen ist, so sieht man seine Stelle bald wieder ersetzt. Es geschieht dies fast immer durch junge Vögel, welche im vorigen Jahr in dieser Gegend geboren worden sind, was man an der mit der vorigen übereinstimmenden Melodie ihres nur noch weniger ausgebildeten Gesanges bemerken kann. Hat sich während ihrer Abwesenheit die Gegend sehr verändert, besonders wenn das Holz abgetrieben wurde, auch wenn es zu alt und unten zu licht wird, so begeben sich die früher hier wohnenden Pärchen in das zunächst gelegene, ihnen besser zusagende Buschholz und beziehen ihre alten Wohnplätze erst dann wieder, wenn das junge Unterholz etwa Mannshöhe erreicht hat. Jedes Pärchen bewohnt einen gewissen Distrikt von einigen hundert Schritten im Umfange, was besonders da bemerklich wird, wo ihrer viele nahe bei einander wohnen.

Man sieht die Nachtigall fast nie auf hohen Bäumen, schon selten auf denen von mittlerer Grösse, und dann auch stets nur auf den untersten Zweigen derselben. Sie halten sich meistenteils im niederen, dichten Gebüsch nahe an der Erde auf. Sie sind auch sehr gern in solchen Gärten, wo sie beschnittene Hecken von Weissbuchen, Kornelkirschen und dergleichen haben, und in den aus Laubholz und buschigem Nadelholz gemischten Bosketts der englischen Gärten.

EIGENSCHAFTEN

Im Betragen der Nachtigall zeigt sich ein bedächtiges, ernstes Wesen, ihre Bewegungen geschehen mit Überlegung und Würde, ihre Stellungen verraten eine Art Stolz, und sie steht durch diese Eigenschaften nebst ihrem nahen Verwandten, dem **Sprosser**, gewissermassen über alle einheimischen Sänger erhaben. Ihre Gebärden scheinen auch anzudeuten, als wüsste sie es, dass ihr dieser Vorzug allgemein zuerkannt wird. Sie ist dabei sehr zutraulich gegen die Menschen, wohnt gern in ihrer Nähe, zeichnet sich durch ein stilles, ruhiges und gegen andere Vögel friedliches Benehmen aus; auch sieht man sie nur selten mit ihresgleichen zanken. In den Zweigen der Bäume sitzt sie meistens still oder hüpft doch nur wenig und selten durch sie hin; wenn es aber einmal geschieht, dann in grossen Sprüngen und auf starken horizontalen Ästen gern der Länge nach. Immer sitzt sie entweder auf den niederen Ästen der Bäume oder in den Zweigen des Gebüsches nahe über der Erde, um sogleich bei der Hand zu sein, wenn sich auf dieser etwas für sie Geniessbares zeigt, worauf ihre stete Aufmerksamkeit gerichtet ist. Sie trägt die Flügel etwas nachlässig, sodass ihre Spitzen immer etwas unter die Schwanzwurzel herabhängen, schnellt den etwas ausgebreiteten Schwanz bei jeder Veranlassung, die ihre Aufmerksamkeit reizt, wenn sie ihren Platz verändern will oder einen neuen eingenommen hat, hoch aufwärts, trägt ihn auch in Ruhe fast immer horizontal, wippt damit aber stets nur in einzelnen Schlägen und hält grosse Pausen zwischen diesen. Geht sie auf die Erde herab, so sieht sie sehr hochbeinig aus, weil sie die Fersengelenke nur wenig biegt, die Brust sehr aufrecht und den Kopf erhaben trägt; sie hüpft dann, mit über die Horizontallinie erhaben getragenem Schwanze, in grossen Sprüngen stolz dahin, macht aber nach einigen, höchstens zehn bis zwölf schnellen und grossen Sprüngen immer eine Pause, als wenn sie jetzt erst überlegte, was weiter zu tun sei, schnellt den Schwanz in die Höhe und hüpft nun weiter. Oft hüpft sie mit senkrecht emporgehaltenem, etwas ausgebreitetem Schwanze weiter; auf starken, langen, horizontalen Ästen beugt sie dazu manchmal die Brust stark abwärts, und sie hat in dieser Stellung und den damit verbundenen Bewegungen ein ganz eigenes, fremdartiges Ansehen.

Man bildet sich häufig ein, die Nachtigall sei ein sehr neugieriger Vogel, was sie aber in der Tat ebenso wenig ist wie andere ihr nahe verwandte Arten, das **Rotkehlchen, Blaukehlchen** und andere. Lockert man freilich in ihrer Nähe die Erde auf, so wird sie bald herbeikommen, aber nicht aus eigentlicher Neugierde, sondern weil sie hier einen guten Frass zu finden hofft; wirft, hängt oder stellt man aber daselbst ein Stück Papier, ein farbiges Tuch oder andere ihr ungewohnte Dinge hin, so wird sie gewiss nicht kommen, es zu besehen.

Ihr Flug ist schnell, leicht, in steigenden und fallenden Bogen, auf kleinen Räumen flatternd und wankend; sie fliegt aber nur kurze Strecken, von Busch zu Busch, und am Tage nie über grosse freie Flächen. Sehr schnell geht er von statten, wenn sich z. B. zwei rivalisierende Männchen beissend verfolgen, wobei sie sich oft vom Gipfel eines mittelmässigen Baumes bis zu dessen Wurzel herab- und wieder hinaufschwingen und mit einem schirkenden Gezwitscher durch das dichte Gebüsch, selten über kleine freie Plätze jagen. Solche Auftritte sieht man zuweilen im Anfange der Begattungszeit; sonst lieben sie den Frieden, und die Neckereien, welche Männchen und Weibchen auf ähnliche Weise manchmal miteinander treiben, darf man nicht für Zänkereien halten.

Ihre Lockstimme ist ein helles gedehntes **Wid** oder **Wiid**, dem meistens ein schnarrendes **Karrr** angehängt wird, also **wiidkarr** klingt. Wenn sie das **Wiid** schnell hintereinander ausrufen und das **Karrr** nur einzeln anhängen, so zeigen sie dadurch Sorge und Angst an, z. B. wenn ihren Jungen Gefahr droht. Freude und Zufriedenheit suchen sie durch ein tiefes schnalzendes **Tack** auszudrücken, so z. B. wenn sie eine angenehme Mahlzeit entdeckt haben; aber sie rufen dieses **Tack** selten mehr als einmal hintereinander aus. Im Zorn und Ärger oder wenn ihnen etwas Ungewöhnliches aufstösst, geben sie ein rauhes, unangenehmes **Kroäk** oder **Rräh** von sich, was viele Vögel dieser Gattung mit ihnen gemein haben.

Die jungen Nachtigallen rufen anfänglich bloss **fiid**, aber in einem weniger sanften, vielmehr in einem schneidenderen oder zischenderen Tone, wie **st** und nachher **rrr**, woran man sie sogleich von den Alten unterscheiden kann, und dann jenes schnarchende **Kroäk** oder **Schroäk**. — Dies sind denn die Töne, welche beide Gatten gemein haben, und wodurch sie sich ihr Verlangen, ihre Zufriedenheit, Freude, Schreck, Sorge u.s.w. gegenseitig zu erkennen geben.

Der vortreffliche Gesang, welchen bloss das Männchen hervorbringt und den man seiner Stärke und der sprechenden Strophen wegen einen Schlag zu nennen pflegt, ist so ausgezeichnet eigen, es herrscht darin eine solche Fülle der Töne, eine so angenehme Abwechselung und eine so hinreissende Harmonie, wie wir sie in keinem anderen Vogelgesange wiederfinden, daher man auch die Nachtigall die Königin aller befiederten Sänger nennt. Mit unbeschreiblicher Anmut wechseln in diesem Schlage sanft flötende Strophen mit schmetternden, klagende mit fröhlichen und schmelzende mit wirbelnden; wenn die eine sanft anfängt, nach und nach an Stärke zunimmt und sterbend endigt, so werden in der anderen eine Reihe Noten mit geschmackvoller Härte hastig angeschlagen und in der dritten melancholische Töne mit reinster Flötenstimme sanft in fröhlichere verschmolzen. Die Pausen zwischen den Strophen vermehren die Wirkung dieser bezaubernden Melodien, sowie das in denselben herrschende Tempo trefflich geeignet ist, die Schönheiten derselben recht zu begreifen. Man staunt bald über die Mannigfaltigkeit dieser Zaubertöne, bald über ihre Fülle und ausserordentliche Stärke, und wir müssen es als ein halbes Wunder betrachten, wie ein so kleiner Vogel imstande ist, so kräftige Töne hervorzubringen, wie eine so bedeutende Kraft in solchen Kehlmuskeln liegen kann. Manche Strophen werden wirklich mit so viel Gewalt herausgestossen, dass ihre gellenden Töne dem Ohre, das sie ganz in der Nähe hört, wehe tun. Daher hört man auch den Schlag der Nachtigall an stillen Abenden ziemlich weit, ob sie gleich hierin vom **Sprosser** noch übertroffen wird.

Die Anzahl der verschiedenen Strophen im Schlage eines guten Sängers unter den Nachtigallen muss sich auf zwanzig bis vierundzwanzig belaufen; doch findet man auch welche, bei denen diese Abwechselung geringer ist, denn es gibt hier auch, wie unter anderen Singvögeln, gute, mittelmässige und schlechte Sänger. Die mannigfaltigen Töne, aus denen diese Strophen zusammengesetzt sind, lassen sich zum Teil ziemlich gut durch Silben und Worte versinnlichen, aber durch kein Instrument (die kleinen hohlen mit einem Loche versehenen Blechpfeifen, die man ganz in den Mund nimmt, oder ein Stück mondförmig ausgeschnittener Birkenrinde ausgenommen) nachahmen. BECHSTEIN hat den Nachtigallgesang sehr gut beschrieben*, und der eigentümliche Charakter desselben ist in seiner Angabe nicht zu verkennen; demungeachtet wird ein kleiner Vergleich zeigen, dass nicht alle Nachtigallen gerade jene Strophen, Worte und Silben in ihrem Gesange hören lassen. Es herrscht darin ein grosser Unterschied; man weiss, dass sie in manchen Länderstrecken ganz anders schlagen als in den an diese grenzenden, und es gibt ganze Gegenden, die lauter schlechte Schläger, andere, die gute, wieder andere, die nur mittelmässige haben; denn weil die jungen Vögel nachher, wenn sie mündig sind, gern ihre Geburtsgegenden wieder aufsuchen, um sich daselbst anzusiedeln, so wird der vom Vater erlernte Gesang immer wieder fortgepflanzt und erhält sich in seiner ursprünglichen Güte, Mittelmässigkeit oder Schlechtheit von einer Generation zur anderen. So sind z. B. die an den pommerschen Ostseeküsten wohnenden Nachtigallen die schlechtesten Schläger von allen, dagegen die, welche die reizende Gegend von **Wörlitz** im Herzogtum Anhalt-Dessau bewohnen, die besten, die ich je gehört habe; die, welche sich hier bei meinem Wohnorte und in meinem eigenen Wäldchen aufhalten, gehören unter die mehr als mittelmässigen, sie können jedoch noch nicht unter die ganz guten gezählt werden. Je mehr und je längere Strophen ein solcher Schlag hat, je mehr von solchen darunter sind, die im Tone auf- oder abwärts steigen wie die vierzehnte und siebzehnte in der BECHSTEINschen Angabe, und je weniger schirkende Töne oder kurze Strophen dabei sind, desto besser ist der Schlag. Etwas Eigentümliches im Schlage der meinigen sind zwei vielgebrauchte Schlussakkorde einzelner Strophen, die wie **dadahidowitz** und **watiwatiwati** lauten; doch ich will versuchen, die Hauptstrophen mit

---

* Es lautet nach BECHSTEIN wie folgt:
Tiuu tiuu tiuu tiuu,
Spe tiu squa,
Tiō tiō tiō tio tio tio tio tix;
Qutio qutio qutio qutio,
Zquō zquō zquō zquō
Tzü tzü tzü tzü tzü tzü tzü tzü tzü tzi
Quorror tiu zqua pipiqui.
Zozozozozozozozozozozo Zirrhading!
Tsisisi tsisisisisisisi,
Zorre zorre zorre zorre hi;
Tzatn tzatn tzatn tzatn tzatn tzatn tzatn zi,
Dlo dlo dlo dlo dlo dlo dlo dlo dlo
Quoi tr rrrrrrrr itz
Lü lü lü lü ly ly ly ly lî lî lî lî
Quoi didl li lulyli.
Ha gürr gürr quipio!
Qui qui qui qui qi qi qi qi gi gi gi gi;
Gollgollgollgoll gia hadadio.
Quigi horr ha diadiadillsi!
Hezezezezezezezezezezezezezezezeze quarrhozehoi;
Quia quia quia quia quia quia quia quia ti:
Qi qi qi jo jo jo jojojojo qi —
Lü ly li le lä la lö lo didl io quia
Higaigaigaigaigaigaigaigiagaigaigai
Quior ziozio pi.

Buchstaben anzugeben, welche aber die kürzeren, schwer zu beschreibenden und die eigentlich schmetternden und schnurrenden, die sich kaum nachahmen lassen, übergehen.

Ih ih ih ih ih watiwatiwati!
Diwati quoi quoi quoi quoi quoi qui
Ita lülülülülülülülülülü watiwatiwatih!
Ihih titagirarrrrrrrrr itz
Lü lü lü lü lü lü lü lü watitititit;
Twoi woiwoiwoiwoiwoiwoi ih,
Lülülülülülülü dahidowitz,
Twor twor twor twor twor twor twor tih!
Dadada jetjetjetjetjetjetjetjetjet,
Tü tü tü tü tü tü tü qui zatnzatnzatnzi;
Iht iht iht iht iht iht zirhading,
I i i i i i i i a zatn zi,
Rihp rihp rihp rihp rihp rihp rihp rihp rihp ih!
Zezezezezezezezäzäzäzäzäzäzäzäzazazazazazazazazi,
Ji jih güh güh güh güh güh dadahidowitz.

Dies sind ungefähr die vorzüglichsten Modulationen im Gesange der um meinen Wohnort sich aufhaltenden Nachtigallen, unter welchen man die sanft klagenden, melancholischen oft um eine Tertie sinkenden oder steigenden Strophen vermisst, weswegen ich meine lieben Sänger nicht für Virtuosen in ihrer Art halten darf, für solche aber die bei **Wörlitz** sich aufhaltenden erklären muss, weil sie alles, was nur irgend in der Macht ihrer Kehle liegt, aufzubieten scheinen. Wer also etwas Vorzügliches von Nachtigallen hören will, muss dorthin gehen, wo die schöne Natur, mit der Kunst so herrlich vereinbart, die Genüsse erhöhen wird. Ein Hauptgrund liegt nun wohl darin, dass sie dort seit langen Jahren fürstlichen Schutz genossen, das Fangen oder Stören derselben streng verpönt war, und dass es folglich dort sehr alte Vögel geben muss, die jederzeit ihre Melodie vollständiger, reiner und stärker singen als junge, jene dann aber immer wieder für diese die besten Lehrmeister abgeben; unter solchen Umständen konnte sich der Gesang in seiner Reinheit erhalten und nach und nach veredeln.

In vielen anderen Gegenden, wo zwar auch das Verbot des Wegfangens existiert, werden ihrer gar viele von diebischen Vogelfängern weggefangen, und dies hat denn aus den angeführten Gründen grossen Einfluss auf die Schönheit ihres Gesanges.

Man darf übrigens nicht glauben, dass jede Nachtigall sich streng an die Ordnung halte, in welcher BECHSTEIN und ich hier die angeführten Strophen aufgestellt haben; sie wechseln vielmehr nach meinen Beobachtungen darin sehr, und die eine lässt sie so, die andere in einer anderen Reihenfolge, die dritte wieder anders hören. Die ältesten Vögel schlagen nicht nur am regelmässigsten und stärksten, sondern verlängern auch die Strophen, welche die Jungen oft kurz abbrechen, um das Doppelte und Dreifache, sie schlagen auch fleissiger.

Eine Gegend, wo es Nachtigallen gibt, erhält durch den bezaubernden Gesang derselben in den schönsten Frühlingsmonaten einen ganz vorzüglichen Reiz, der durch keinen der anderen einheimischen Vögel ersetzt wird. Mögen alle **Amseln** und **Singdrosseln, Grasmücken** und andere Singvögel ihre Kehlen anstrengen wie sie wollen, die Nachtigall übertrifft sie alle, und es müsste ein ganz rohes Gemüt sein, das ihre himmlische Musik nicht mit Vergnügen hören oder mit Wonne durch sie erfüllt werden sollte. Der Gefühlvolle muss sie daher schätzen und lieben, und er wird ihr gewiss kein Leid zufügen. Gegen Verfolgungen gefühlloser Menschen aber schützen sie fast allenthalben obrigkeitliche Gesetze.

Ein grosser Vorzug dieser lieblichen Sänger ist noch der, dass sie so zahm, so zutraulich gegen die Menschen sind; denn das singende Männchen lässt sich von vorsichtig ihm nahenden Personen lange in der Nähe betrachten und im Gesange nicht stören; fliegt es ja fort, so geht es doch nie weit weg und fährt da im Singen fort. Es sitzt dabei gewöhnlich auf einem etwas freien Zweige oder Aste, meist mannshoch bis zu einer Höhe von drei bis vier Meter, selten höher oder tiefer, auf den unteren Zweigen eines im Gebüsch stehenden Baumes oder im Gesträuch selbst, sodass man es bald entdecken kann. Es verändert während des Schlagens seinen Platz nur wenig, sträubt dabei die Kehle auf und bewegt sie nebst dem Schnabel heftig, bei manchen anstrengenden Strophen auch den übrigen Körper etwas, und lässt dabei den Schwanz fast immer nachlässig herabhängen. Kommen sich zufällig zwei Männchen zu nahe, so bläht sie die Eifersucht mächtig auf, das Gefieder wird struppig, der horizontal aufgerichtete Schwanz sehr ausgebreitet, und die Kraft ihrer Stimmorgane scheint sich zu verdoppeln.

Schon der Name dieses Vogels scheint anzudeuten, dass er auch des Nachts seine gellenden Töne (versteht sich, mit den sanften untermengt, also seinen Gesang) hören lässt. Wenn sie im Frühling bei uns ankommen, so singen beinahe alle auch des Nachts, besonders diejenigen, welche noch kein Weibchen haben; denn diese kommen, wie schon erwähnt wurde, später hier an, und sie wollen den in der Nacht vorüberreisenden höchstwahrscheinlich dadurch ihr Verlangen zu erkennen geben. Manche schlagen die ganze Nacht hindurch und pausieren wenig, man nennt sie ausschliesslich **Nachtvögel**; viele schlagen bloss einzeln, oft nur abgebrochene Strophen, und pausieren viel, ja stundenlang: dies sind die sogenannten **Repetiervögel**; manche sind des Nachts ganz still, und dies sind die meisten von der Zeit an, wenn das Weibchen die ersten Eier gelegt hat, bis zum Ende der Singzeit.

Dass sich übrigens die Nachtschläger wie die Repetiervögel beim Schlagen an keine bestimmte Stunde binden, ist gewiss, und der Aberglaube beim gemeinen Mann, dass sie nie in der Mitternachtsstunde schlügen, ganz grundlos; ich habe sie gar oft in dieser schauerlichen Stunde belauscht.

Unvergleichlich ist indessen der Genuss, einem guten Nachtschläger in einer stillen, mondhellen Nacht des Mai im Walde, wo jetzt alles übrige Geflügel schweigt und in tiefen Schlaf versunken ist, zuzuhören; kein zwitscherndes Getöse minder kunstreicher Sänger stört jetzt den entzückten Zuhörer, und keine Silbe der himmlischen Melodie geht dem lauschenden Ohr verloren; es gewährt ein begeisterndes, ein erhabenes Vergnügen; nur schade, dass um jene Jahreszeit die nächtliche Kühle dem minder abgehärteten Naturfreund nicht so behagt, wie er es wohl wünschen möchte, und dass späterhin, wenn die Abendlüfte milder werden, keine Nachtigall mehr schlägt. Sonst fangen sie gewöhnlich früh, wenn eben die Morgendämmerung beginnt, zu schlagen an und treiben es mit grösstem Eifer, bis es völlig Tag ist, oder eine volle Stunde lang ununterbrochen.

Jetzt suchen sie sich ihr Frühstück; aber es dauert nicht lange, und sie schlagen, doch mit vielen Unterbrechungen, bis früh 8 Uhr; dann pausieren sie noch mehr, und in den Mittagsstunden bis gegen 3 Uhr nachmittags hört man nur selten eine. Gegen Abend fangen sie wieder anhaltender zu schlagen an und treiben dies bis tief in die Dämmerung hinein; doch schlagen sie des Abends niemals mit solchem Eifer als früh, wenn sie den jungen Tag mit ihrem Gesange begrüssen.

Der Wert der Nachtigall wird dadurch ungemein erhöht, dass sie ihren bezaubernden Gesang so häufig auch des Nachts hören lässt; ob aber diejenigen, welche dies besonders tun, die sogenannten Nachtvögel, sich, wie BECHSTEIN behauptet, in dieser Hinsicht als eine besondere Rasse von den Tagsängern unterscheiden sollen, kann ich aus eigener Erfahrung nicht bestätigen. Sie sollen in gebirgigen Gegenden an Bergen wohnen, die Tagvögel aber bloss in Ebenen, und die Eigenschaften, dass jene bei der Nacht wie am Tage, diese aber bloss am Tage singen, auch bei den aufgezogenen Jungen sich unverändert fortpflanzen. Ich glaube indessen kaum, dass dies bei den in Freiheit lebenden Nachtigallen so genau zutrifft; wenigstens kann ich versichern, dass es in hiesiger Gegend nicht so ist. Ich habe die längs den Ufern der Mulde, Elbe und in einem weiten Umkreise um meinen Wohnort wohnenden Nachtigallen genau beobachtet und gefunden, dass davon die meisten Tagvögel, viele Repetiervögel und einzelne Nachtvögel waren; dass ferner gleich nach ihrer Ankunft im Frühling fast alle des Nachts schlugen oder doch repetierten, dass nach ein paar Wochen dieses schon seltener wurde, und dass endlich zu Ausgang des Mai sich nur noch einzelne des Nachts hören liessen. Die Ursachen hiervon sind auch nicht schwer aufzufinden. Sie schlagen nämlich anfänglich gewiss darum des Nachts so anhaltend, um ein vorüberziehendes Weibchen anzulocken; haben sie diesen Zweck erreicht (denn sie leben bekanntlich in Monogamie), so kann sie nur die Erinnerung an genossene oder zu geniessende Freuden und die höchste Üppigkeit dazu anfeuern; diese legt sich aber mit der Zeit, wenn sie die Sorge für die Erhaltung der Jungen beschäftigt, sodass endlich auch am Tage ihr Gesang verstummt. Diejenigen, welche man in der Gefangenschaft unterhält, können hierüber keine befriedigende Auskunft geben, weil dieser Zwang bekanntlich ihre Natur ausserordentlich verändert. Ihr verschiedenes Temperament macht vielleicht hier den Unterschied unter Nachtsängern und solchen, die bloss am Tage singen.

Niemand wird bezweifeln wollen, dass die Nachtigall durch den Trieb der Liebe zum Gesange gereizt wird, dass dieser der Verkündiger ihrer seligsten Empfindungen ist, wenn man weiss, dass er mit der Begattungszeit anfängt und kaum so lange dauert, bis die Geschäfte der Fortpflanzung gänzlich vollbracht sind. Die im Freien lebende Nachtigall, die durch nichts gehindert wird, diesem allmächtigen Triebe Folge zu leisten, schlägt daher auch nur von da an, wo er rege in ihr wurde, bis dahin, wo er, völlig befriedigt, nach ewigen Naturgesetzen wieder erkaltet, um erst nach drei Vierteljahren mit neuer Kraft wieder zu erwachen. Das feurige Temperament mancher Vögel wird oft auch dann laut, wenn andere schlafen. Solche Nachtigallen sprechen ihre Wünsche oder ihre Erinnerungen auch zur Nachtzeit aus. Dies findet endlich, wie vieles in der Welt, seine Nachahmer; die jungen Vögel hören es nämlich von den alten, und so können allerdings die Nachtschläger in einer Gegend gemein werden, die deshalb gerade nicht gebirgig zu sein braucht. Dass es aber in ebenen Gegenden keine solchen Nachtschläger (Nachtschwärmer), sondern lauter kaltblütige Tagsänger geben soll, ist gegen meine Erfahrung.

Ganz anders verhält es sich freilich bei den im Zimmer unterhaltenen Nachtigallen, bei denen wegen Wärme und Überfluss an gutem Futter der Trieb der Liebe früher erwacht und, weil er nicht befriedigt wird, auch länger anhält; daher singen denn diese auch noch einmal so lange als jene; daher sind denn auch hier die sogenannten Nachtvögel wahre Nachtsänger, vom Anfange bis zu Ende der Singzeit.

Man beklagt sich allgemein über die Kürze der Singzeit unserer Nachtigallen, denn sie dauert bei uns selten etwas über zwei Monate, nämlich von der letzten Hälfte des April bis gegen das Ende des Juni, doch vielleicht mit Unrecht. Würden die Nachtigallen länger ihre Lieder hören lassen, so würde sich zur Gewohnheit endlich Gleichgültigkeit gesellen und der uns jetzt so sehr entzückende Gesang dadurch an Interesse sehr verlieren.

In den ersten Tagen nach ihrer Ankunft singen sie noch leise, sie studieren sich ihr Lied erst ein, und es vergehen bei jüngeren Vögeln wohl acht Tage und darüber, ehe sie ordentlich und laut anstimmen. Ist dann vielleicht die Witterung noch rauh, wohl gar mit Nachtfrösten begleitet, so dauert das Stümpern noch länger, und man hört sehr häufig erst nach Ablauf der ersten Woche im Mai ihre vollen Melodien. Am schönsten und fleissigsten singen sie, wenn das Weibchen anfängt, Eier zu legen, bis es ausgelegt und eine Woche lang gebrütet hat; nachher werden sie schon träger, und wenn die Jungen erst ausgeflogen sind, wird der Gesang immer seltener, und endlich verstummt er gegen Johannistag gänzlich. Merkwürdig ist es, dass die jungen Nachtigallen, die den Gesang des Vaters, während sie im Neste sitzen, kaum noch vollständig und nicht einmal oft mehr hören, weil dieser dann schon nach und nach und, wenn sie ausgeflogen sind, gänzlich zu singen aufhört, dennoch seinen Gesang so weit merken, dass sie ihn im kommenden Frühjahr bald vollständig nachsingen lernen. Im ersten Sommer, bald nachdem sie ausgeflogen sind, hört man sie oft leise zwitschern oder, wie die Vogelfänger es nennen, dichten; aber dies hat wenig oder gar keine Ähnlichkeit mit dem eigentlichen Gesange, den sie nicht vor dem kommenden Frühjahr hören lassen, der dann aber ganz dem des Vaters, eine geringere Ausbildung abgerechnet, gleichkommt.

Man darf aber nicht etwa glauben, sie lernten den Gesang in ihrer Abwesenheit, und die Nachtigallen schlügen schon, ehe sie bei uns ankämen, weil die im Käfig eingesperrten viel früher zu schlagen anfangen. Wäre dies der Fall, so müssten sie gleich bei ihrer Ankunft ihr Lied schon vollständig singen können; dagegen streitet aber die Erfahrung, dass man sie, wenn sie hier ankommen, bloss leise dichten hört und wohl acht und mehrere Tage vergehen, ehe sie völlig laut und in der Melodie fest werden.

Man hält die Nachtigallen ihres herrlichen Gesanges wegen häufig in Gefangenschaft, entweder in einer eigenen Kammer allein oder unter anderen Singvögeln frei herumfliegend, wo sie aber nie so gut singen, oder jede einzeln im Käfige. Man fängt sie dazu alt ein, wo sie sich anfänglich zwar wild, ungestüm und oft trotzig zeigen (weswegen man ihnen die Flügel an den Spitzen zusammenbindet, auch wohl das Futter behutsam einstopft), doch aber nachher sich bald in die Umstände fügen lernen und endlich noch ziemlich zahm werden. Man behandelt sie übrigens ebenso wie die **Sprosser**; aber sie sind weichlicher und weniger dauerhaft, ob man gleich auch einzelne Beispiele hat, dass sie sich bei guter Wartung acht Jahre und darüber hielten. Übrigens ist die Behandlung ganz dieselbe, und ich brauche das in der Beschreibung des **Sprossers** Gesagte nicht zu wiederholen.

Die alt eingefangenen Nachtigallen fangen gewöhnlich alle Jahre um Weihnachten zu schlagen an und hören um Ostern wieder auf, doch fangen auch einige schon im November an und fahren damit bis zum Mai fort. Diejenigen, welche man jung aufzog, schlagen jedesmal länger, oft sieben Monate lang, aber selten so gut, weil sie gern fremde Töne nachahmen und in ihren Gesang mit einflechten, wenn man sie anders nicht davor zu bewahren gesucht und ihnen einen schönen singenden Vogel als Lehrer beigesellt hatte. Solche jungen Vögel, die man im ersten Herbst ihres Lebens, wenn sie eben wegziehen wollen, einfängt, sollen am besten einschlagen, weil sie den Gesang ihres Vaters schon vollkommen begriffen haben und diesen vervollkommnen lernen, wenn man sie nachher zu einem schon singenden alten Vogel hängt.

Sie zaubern uns durch ihren vortrefflichen Gesang den rauhesten Winter in einen angenehmen Frühling um; dessenungeachtet ist doch der Schlag der Stubennachtigall, ob er gleich hohen Genuss gewährt, bei weitem nicht so anmutig wie der von einer im Freien schlagenden Nachtigall, selbst wenn es genau dieselbe Melodie wäre. Ich verdenke es daher jedem, in dessen Nähe im Frühjahr Nachtigallen wohnen, wenn er sich, bloss um den Gesang ein paar Monate früher zu hören, mit der mühsamen und kostspieligen Unterhaltung einzelner im Vogelbauer befasst, zumal da oft ihre schmetternde Stimme in kleinen Wohnzimmern beschwerlich wird.*

Hat man mehrere in einem Zimmer, so verraten sie oft ihre Eifersucht im heftigen Schlagen, ja man hat Beispiele, dass eine die andere zu überschreien suchte, die Besiegte dann zuweilen sich gar nicht mehr zu schlagen getraute, ja selbst, dass eine so stark und heftig schlug, dass sie sich Gefässe zersprengte und plötzlich starb. In den Erzählungen hiervon scheint man jedoch manches übertrieben zu haben.

NAHRUNG

Diese besteht mehr in Erdgewürm und Insektenlarven, als wirklichen vollkommenen Insekten; sie hüpfen daher nach diesen fast immer unter dem Gesträuch der Erde herum, suchen die wundgemachten Stellen derselben und in Gärten solche, wo eben gegraben wurde, wodurch Nahrungsmittel für sie an die Oberfläche kommen und von ihnen aufgelesen werden können. Wenn sie, auf einem niederen Zweige sitzend, am Boden etwas Geniessbares entdecken, so fliegen sie schnell hin, schnellen im Niedersitzen den Schwanz aufwärts, ergreifen es aber nicht so hastig, wie viele andere Insektenfresser, sondern sehen es erst ein Weilchen an, und zwar mit seitwärts gewandtem Kopfe und einem Auge, verzehren es gemächlich, hüpfen nun weiter oder begeben sich wieder auf einen Zweig und ins Gebüsch. Im Grase sieht man sie selten forthüpfen, am liebsten und schnellsten dagegen auf glattem und ebenem Boden, wie z. B. in den Gängen der Lustgärten. Da, wo das Gebüsch so dicht steht, dass unter demselben kein Gras mehr wächst, sind sie am liebsten; hier finden sie in dem alten Laube, in der Holzerde und im Moose der alten verfaulten Stöcke kleine Käferchen und vielerlei Larven, besonders in der Erde der faulenden Stämme die lichtgelbe glatte Larve des Schattenkäfers, welche dem sogenannten Mehlwurm (der Larve des *Tenebrio molitor*) täuschend ähnlich sieht, aber etwas kleiner ist und begierig von ihnen aufgesucht wird. Diese und die Puppen der Ameisen (die sogenannten Ameiseneier) sind ihre Lieblingsspeise; sonst fressen sie die Ameisen selbst auch sehr gern und kommen deswegen sehr bald herbei, wenn man einen nahen Ameisenhaufen aufscharrt und ihnen so ein köstliches Mahl bereitet. Überhaupt geben sie auf die in ihrer Nähe hantierenden

---

* Mein Vater hielt von Jugend auf stets eine Menge verschiedenartiger Singvögel, um sich an ihren Gesängen zu ergötzen, aber nie eine Nachtigall; eben darum, und weil sie uns in Menge so nahe wohnen, dass wir in der rechten Jahreszeit, wenn junges Grün den Wald kleidet und die Natur in erneuerter Jugend dasteht, zu jeder beliebigen Stunde und so nahe wir es nur wünschen, ihre göttlichen Lieder hören können.

Menschen genau acht und gehen, wenn diese die Erde wund gemacht und sich etwas entfernt haben, sogleich an solche Stellen, um die daselbst sich vorfindenden Insekten und Würmer aufzulesen. Dass dies nicht aus eitler Neugier geschieht, wurde schon weiter oben gesagt. Sie fressen auch kleine Regenwürmer gern.

Nach fliegenden Insekten sieht man sie selten einmal springen, noch seltener eins im Fluge wegschnappen; eher lesen sie solche, als Fliegen, kleine Motten und dergleichen, auch kleine Räupchen, von den belaubten Zweigen ab, doch auch mehr gelegentlich; denn niemals hüpfen sie, förmlich darnach suchend, in den Zweigen herum; bloss was ihnen da zufällig in den Wurf kommt und behaglich scheint, nehmen sie mit und unterscheiden sich dadurch sehr von den **Grasmücken**. Ihre meisten Nahrungsmittel lesen sie stets vom Erdboden auf und stöbern, wie die **Drosseln**, sehr gern im alten abgefallenen Laube und im Moose an den alten Baumstrünken herum, sitzen aber im Gebüsch auf den Zweigen und Ästen meistens still, ohne sich um die um sie herumschwirrenden Insekten zu bekümmern.

Sobald die Johannisbeeren reifen, suchen sie diese auf und fressen die schwarzen wie die roten gleich gern; besonders begierig sind sie aber nach den roten Beeren des Traubenholunders, und sie können es kaum abwarten, bis diese völlig reif sind. Ich sehe überhaupt in meinem Garten, wo ich sonst noch allerlei Beerenbüsche für die Vögel hege, dass alle kleinen Vögel die roten Holunderbeeren fast allen anderen Beerenarten vorziehen, und ich habe nie die Freude, meinen grossen, schönen Holunderbusch mit seinen hochroten Trauben in voller Pracht zu sehen, weil unzählige Vögel die Beeren, sowie sie nach und nach reif werden, immer abpicken; desto mehr belustigt mich aber das Gewimmel der Vögel zur Zeit der Beerenreife in demselben. Ausser diesen fressen die Nachtigallen auch gern Faulbaumbeeren, die Beeren des gemeinen schwarzen Holunders, des Eppichs oder Attichs und in südlicheren Ländern noch mancherlei andere Beerenarten.

Die Nachtigall ist, wenn es sein kann, gern in der Nähe von Wasser, denn sie badet sich häufig und durchnässt dabei fast ihr ganzes Gefieder; die Zeit des Badens ist in der Regel die Abenddämmerung. Auch den im Käfig gehaltenen darf dies Stärkungsmittel nicht fehlen; sie müssen zum Trinken und Baden täglich frisches Wasser bekommen.

FORTPFLANZUNG

Sobald sich die Nachtigallen bei uns einstellen, sucht jede ihr vorjähriges Wohnplätzchen wieder, und wo davon eine auf der Reise umgekommen ist, nimmt dies bald eine andere, wahrscheinlich eine im vorigen Jahre hier ausgebrütete junge ein. Jede sucht ihr kleines Revier zu behaupten, weswegen es denn auch anfänglich oft wütende Zänkereien unter ihnen gibt, die aber bald aufhören, wenn sich jedes Männchen erst ein Weibchen angepaart hat. Sie suchen dann in Gärten die dichten Hecken, im Walde solche Plätze auf, wo das Unterholz nicht gar zu hoch ist, wo es in demselben kleine Stellen gibt, auf denen niederes Buschwerk und Gras wächst, oder wo alte Stämme stehen, die mit vielen jungen Zweigen umgeben sind, wenn die letzteren auch schon etwas stark wären, selbst in sehr grossen Dornhecken auf dem Freien, wenn sie nur nicht zu weit vom Walde sind oder, besser noch, mit diesem zusammenhängen, und sonst in allerlei dichtem Gebüsch, nur nicht im Nadelholze.

Das Nest steht meistens nahe an oder auf der Erde, auf einem alten Stamme zwischen den aufgeschossenen jungen Zweigen desselben, im dichtesten Gestrüpp nahe an der Erde, in einem Grasbusche auf dieser, an der Seite eines etwas hohen alten Baumstrunks in einer flachen Aushöhlung oder auf einem Büschel Ästen desselben; seltener in dichten Dornen, in einer lebendigen Hecke, in einem Reisighaufen oder in einem toten geflochtenen Zaune, wo es zuweilen mannshoch vom Boden steht, es baute sogar einmal ein Nachtigallpärchen in einem offenstehenden Gartenhäuschen in einem darin liegenden Haufen trockenen Laubes. Meistens findet man es zwischen einem und zwei Fuss hoch vom Boden. Sie wissen es meistenteils sehr gut zu verstecken, und es ist wegen der unansehnlichen Materialien, woraus es gebaut ist, schwer zu finden. Die Grundlage bildet allemal dürres Laub, wenn es sein kann, von Eichen, und dies in ziemlicher Menge; die Rundung geben ihm trockene Halme und Stengel, zuweilen sogar Schilf- oder Rohrblätter, und das Innere ist mit zarten Grashälmchen und Rispen, oft auch bloss mit feinen dunkelbraunen Würzelchen ausgefüttert, dem zuweilen Pferdehaare, aber seltener etwas Pflanzenwolle beigemischt ist. Wo selten Pferde hinkommen, aber Dohnen stehen geblieben sind, zupfen sie die Haare gern aus den Schlingen und tragen sie in die

Nester; dies tun aber auch die Grasmückenarten und andere kleine Waldvögel. Das Nest bildet inwendig einen niedlichen, etwas tiefen Napf, hat aber von aussen ein kunstloses Ansehen und ist meistenteils ein grosser Klumpen.

Das Weibchen legt vier bis sechs Eier von sehr verschiedener Gestalt, nämlich bald von einer kurzen und dicken, bald von einer gestreckten und schlanken Eiform; so findet man denn in einem Neste oft lauter rundliche, in einem anderen wieder lauter längliche Eier. Sie haben eine zarte, glatte, aber wenig glänzende Schale und eine Farbe, die der des grünlich braungrauen Serpentinsteines gleichkommt. Eigentlich sind sie aber, genauer besehen, auf blass meergrünem Grunde mit graubrauner Farbe getüpfelt, sodass die Flecken in der Grundfarbe sich verlieren und mit ihr verschmelzen, daher sie meistens einfarbig erscheinen und wenige den lichteren Grund durch die Flecken, Punkte und Striche durchschauen lassen.

Männchen und Weibchen brüten wechselweise zwei Wochen über den Eiern, doch so, dass das letztere die meiste Zeit brütet, besonders aber in den Mittagsstunden vom Männchen abgelöst wird. Das brütende Weibchen sitzt so fest über den Eiern, dass man es oft mit der Hand fangen kann. Die Jungen erziehen sie ebenfalls gemeinschaftlich mit kleinem Gewürm und Insekten; aber diese verlassen das Nest schon, wenn sie kaum von einem Zweige zum anderen flattern können und ihre Schwanzfedern noch sehr kurz sind. Sie sitzen dann einzeln im Gebüsch umher und lassen sich noch lange von den Alten füttern. Sperrt man sie in ein Vogelbauer, so füttern sie die Alten auf, ja man will Beispiele haben, dass diese dasselbe taten, als man sie samt den Jungen gefangen und eingesperrt hatte.

Diese Vögel brüten übrigens nur einmal im Jahre; werden ihnen das erstemal die Eier genommen, so machen sie eine zweite Brut, welcher Fall dann aber nicht mehr eintritt, wenn sie bereits Junge hatten. Auf solche Weise könnte es wohl zuweilen vorkommen, dass sie in einem Jahre dreimal Eier legten; dass sie aber, ohne verstört zu werden, zweimal Junge ausbrüten und erziehen sollten, ist gegen meine Erfahrung.

Die jungen Männchen fangen schon leise an zu zwitschern und zu dichten, wenn sie nicht lange das Nest verlassen und die Schwanzfedern kaum die Hälfte ihrer Länge erreicht haben; allein dies Zwitschern hat noch wenig Ähnlichkeit mit dem wahren Gesange, den sie erst im künftigen Frühjahre hören lassen; doch ist es hinreichend, die Männchen von den Weibchen zu unterscheiden, und daher für den Liebhaber, der sich junge Nachtigallen auffüttert, von Wichtigkeit.

Die Alten gebärden sich sehr ängstlich, wenn sie Junge haben, und verfolgen ihre Feinde mit unaufhörlichem Angstgeschrei, wobei man das Männchen an dem reineren, flötenden **Wid, wid** vom Weibchen, dessen Stimme schneidender ist, unterscheiden kann.

FEINDE

Sie werden, da sie immer im dichten Gebüsch verborgen leben, nur selten die Beute des **Sperbers** und anderer flüchtiger Raubvögel; aber ihre Brut ist unendlich vielen Gefahren ausgesetzt und wird sehr häufig von **Füchsen, Katzen, Mardern, Iltissen, Wieseln, Ratten** und **Mäusen** selbst zuweilen von **Schlangen**, auch vom **Igel** zerstört, ja oft das brütende Weibchen über den Eiern, besonders von den ersteren, erwischt und aufgefressen. Durch die Menge dieser Feinde wird ihre grössere Vermehrung sehr beschränkt.

NUTZEN

Die Nachtigallen werden uns durch ihre Nahrungsmittel sehr nützlich; denn sie vertilgen eine Menge dem Gartenbau wie der Forstkultur sehr nachteiliger Insektenbrut, und sie verdienten schon deswegen alle mögliche Schonung. Wie höchst angenehm sie uns durch ihren herrlichen Gesang werden, ist jedermann bekannt. Wälder und Gärten beleben in den schönsten Frühlingsmonaten, wenn alles in der Natur neues Leben atmet, ihre bezaubernden Melodien. Allgemein anerkannt ist der Wert derselben, Vornehme und Geringe haben Gefühl für ihre Schönheiten, und man wird nur selten ein Gemüt finden, das gleichgültig bei einem so lieblichen Sänger vorüber ginge, die meisten werden vielmehr mit Entzücken bei ihm verweilen und nicht müde werden, ihm zuzuhören. Wir hören ihn daher nicht allein von den Dichtern, sondern auch vom schlichten Landmann lobpreisen; alles gerät in Entzücken über diese wundervolle Musik, und der, dem es versagt war, die Nachtigall im Freien schlagen zu hören, ergötzt sich an dem Gesange derselben im Käfige. So schafft sie dadurch Erholung, Erheiterung, so weckt sie die reinsten Empfindungen für die Schönheiten der Natur auch in den weniger gefühlvollen Menschen und feuert ihn zum Lobe des grossen Weltregierers an.

Ihr Fleisch ist, wie das anderer kleiner verwandter Vögel, sehr wohlschmeckend; allein wenn es nicht der Zufall einmal in die Küche bringt, so möchte wohl nicht leicht jemand sie um deswillen töten wollen. Die römische Geschichte nennt uns übrigens, wie bekannt, einen berühmten Schwelger, HELIOGABAL, der sich mehrmals ein Gericht aus Pfauen- und Nachtigallenzungen bereiten liess.

SCHADEN

So viel bis jetzt bekannt, schaden sie uns auf keine Weise.

// DAS ROTKEHLCHEN //

ERITHACUS RUBECULA

Das Rotkehlchen, Rotkehle, Rotbart, Rotkröpfchen, Rotbrüstchen, Rottkröpflein, Rottbrüstlein, Kehlrötchen, Rötelein, Winterrötelein, Waldrötlein, Waldrötchen, rotbrüstiger oder rotkehliger Sänger; in hiesiger Gegend: Rotkehlchen.

Taf. 75

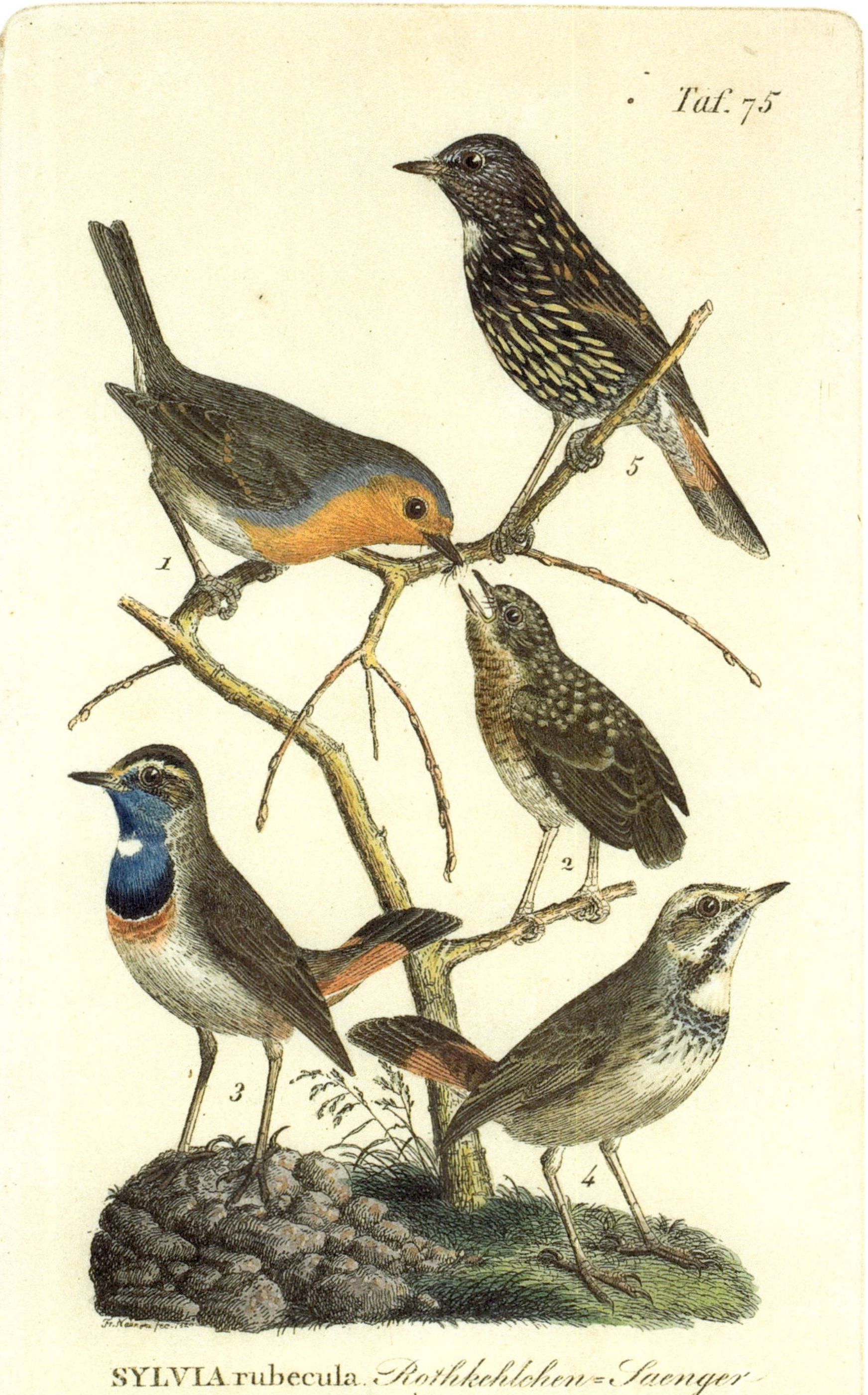

SYLVIA rubecula. *Rothkehlchen=Saenger*
1 M. 2 jung. Vog.

SYLVIA suecica. *Blaukehlchen=Saenger*
3 M. 4 W. 5 jung. Vog.

KENNZEICHEN DER ART

Schwanz und Flügel von aussen olivenbraun; die letzte Reihe Flügeldeckfedern mit rostgelben Spitzenfleckchen.

Alter Vogel: Stirn, Wangen, Kehle und Gurgel gelbrot, mit aschblauer Einfassung.

Junger Vogel: Kehle schmutzig gelblich, mit unordentlichen schwärzlichen Wellen; Oberleib auf olivenbraunem Grunde weisslichgelb getüpfelt und schwärzlich gewölkt.

BESCHREIBUNG

Dieser bekannte Vogel kann alt nicht leicht mit einer anderen Art verwechselt werden. Im Jugendkleide ist es aber schwerer, ihn von anderen jungen Sängern mit gefleckten Gewändern zu unterscheiden, namentlich von den jungen **Nachtigallen**, denen sie täuschend ähnlich sehen; genauer betrachtet sind sie aber kleiner als diese, haben kürzere und dunkler gefärbte Schnäbel und Füsse, und die Schwanzfedern sind olivenbraun, statt dass sie wie bei jenen rostig rotbraun aussehen.

Es steht an Grösse der **Nachtigall** merklich nach, ist 13 bis 13,5 cm lang, 21,2 bis 22,4 cm breit; der Schwanz, der am Ende nur seicht ausgeschnitten ist, misst 5,3 cm, und die ruhenden Flügel reichen mit den Spitzen bis 2,4 cm vor das Ende desselben.

Der braunschwarze, an den Mundkanten und an der Wurzel der Unterkinnlade etwas lichtere, im Frühjahr einfarbig mattschwarze Schnabel ist fast 10 mm lang, an der Wurzel etwas breit, spitzenwärts aber von den Seiten etwas zusammengedrückt, mit erhabener rundlicher Rückenkante. Seiner Gestalt nach ist er dem der **Nachtigall** ähnlich, aber verhältnismässig kürzer und stärker. Das längliche, vorn erweiterte, fast nierenförmige Nasenloch hat oben eine schwielige Decke; die Zunge ist weder sehr breit, noch kurz zu nennen, vorn abgestutzt, in mehreren Zasern zerrissen, hinterwärts mit vorstehenden Eckzähnen versehen, samt dem Rachen rötlichgelb, welche Farbe sich zuweilen auch über die Aussenseite der Wurzel der Unterkinnlade verbreitet. Über den Mundwinkeln stehen jederseits drei starke ab- und vorwärts gerichtete Bartborsten, feinere Härchen sind den Stirn- und Kinnfedern untermischt. Die grossen Augen haben eine dunkelbraune Iris, die bei jungen Vögeln ins Graue fällt.

Die schwächlichen Füsse sind schlank, doch mit etwas niederer Tarse als bei der **Nachtigall** und dem **Blaukehlchen**; die Läufe gestiefelt, die Zehen oben geschildert, unten feinwarzig; die Nägel schwach, mittelmässig gebogen, schmal, unten zweischneidig, übrigens sehr spitz. Die Farbe der Füsse ist ein schmutziges Braun, das an den Läufen, besonders auf der hinteren Seite derselben, immer lichter ist als unten und sich da oft einer schmutzigen Fleischfarbe nähert; im Herbst und bei den jungen Vögeln ist diese Farbe immer lichter als bei den alten; die Nägel sind dunkelbraun. Die Höhe des Laufs beträgt 25 mm, die Länge der Mittelzehe mit der Kralle 17,6 mm, und die der Hinterzehe, ebenso gemessen, 12,5 mm.

Das Gefieder ist an diesem Vögelchen gross, locker und sehr weich, besonders am Unterrücken und an der Unterbrust. Die erste Schwinge ist klein und schmal; die zweite viel länger und die dritte kaum etwas kürzer als die vierte, oft auch von gleicher Länge.

Der Scheitel, Nacken, Rücken, Steiss, die Schenkelfedern und die Flügeldeckfedern sind graulich olivenbraun oder matt grünlichbraun, am Bürzel und an den oberen Schwanzdeckfedern oft mit stärkerem, olivenfarbigem Anstriche; Stirn, Zügel, Augenkreise, Wangen, Gurgel und Kropf bis auf die Oberbrust schmutzig orangerot, eine eigene Farbe, für die es keine recht befriedigende Benennung gibt und die bald mehr ins Rote, bald mehr ins Gelbe spielt. Die Grenze zwischen dieser und der Farbe der oberen Teile bildet ein aschblauer Anflug, der sich über den halben Vorderkopf, an den Schläfen und Halsseiten herab bis auf die Brust verbreitet; alle übrigen unteren Teile sind schmutzig weiss, in den Seiten stark olivenfarbig angeflogen; die grossen Flügelfedern und die Schwanzfedern dunkel graubraun, mit der Farbe des Rückens gesäumt, die Säume der grossen Schwingen am lichtesten, und die grossen Flügeldeckfedern haben an den Spitzen ein dreieckiges, lebhaft rostgelbes Fleckchen, wodurch eine eben nicht sehr in die Augen fallende Fleckenbinde quer über dem Flügel gebildet wird, auch haben einige der hintersten Schwingen oft noch solche Fleckchen oder wenigstens lichtgraue Spitzenkäntchen. Von unten sind Flügel- und Schwanzfedern braungrau, die unteren Flügeldeckfedern grauweiss, mit schmutzig rostgelber Mischung.

Das **Weibchen** ist dem Männchen sehr ähnlich und schwer von ihm zu unterscheiden; es ist etwas kleiner; die Kehle blasser, mehr gelb als rot; die aschblaue Einfassung derselben matter; die Rückenfarbe bleicher und die gelben Spiegelchen auf den Flügeln kleiner, ja sie fehlen ihm zuweilen ganz. Die **jungen Männchen** sehen indessen dem alten Weibchen so ähnlich, dass man öfters keinen äusseren Unterschied auffinden kann.

Das **Herbstkleid** hat viel frischere Farben als das **Frühlingskleid**; denn jene bleichen an dem nämlichen Gefieder, wenn es über ein halbes Jahr alt geworden, sehr ab, ohne dass dabei das Abnutzen der Federn sehr bemerklich würde. Bloss am Kopfe und Halse wird weiterhin das Abschleifen der Federn bemerklich; dies und das immer stärkere Verbleichen der Farben wird endlich gegen den **Sommer** so auffallend, dass sie dann, besonders die vorjährigen jungen Vögel, meist statt der roten eine sehr bleich orangegelbe Kehle und eine sehr unansehnliche blass olivengraue Rückenfarbe bekommen.

Die **Jungen vor der ersten Mauser** sehen ganz anders aus als ihre Eltern; alle oberen Teile sind olivenbraun, mit schmutzig licht rostgelben Schaftflecken nahe am Ende jeder Feder, welche am Kopfe eine fast dreieckige Gestalt haben, auf den Flügeldeckfedern aber grosse dunkel rostgelbe Enden bilden, wobei aber die Rückenfedern noch schwärzliche Endkanten zeigen; Kehle und Vorderhals sind braungelb, mit olivenbraunen Federkanten, welche unregelmässig zerrissene Wellen bilden, die sich mit dem Gelben an der Oberbrust verlieren oder undeutlicher werden, doch noch über die Seiten der Brust verbreiten, aber wenig oder gar nicht an der schmutzig weissen Unterbrust zeigen; der Bauch ist ganz ungefleckt, schmutzig weiss, die Füsse fleischfarben, die Sohlen gelb, die Nagelspitzen schwärzlich, die Augensterne grau, die Mundwinkel gelb. Sie sehen in diesem Kleide sehr bunt aus, legen es aber schon im Juli und August ab, wo sich auch die Alten mausern.

Spielarten sind ziemlich selten; man kennt eine **weisse**, rein oder schmutzig weiss oder oben graulich; eine **weissgefleckte** mit weissem Kopfe, Schwanze, Flügeln oder anderen Teilen, bei übrigens gewöhnlich gefärbtem Gefieder; eine **weissbrüstige** oben grünlich aschgrau, an der Stirn, Kehle, Brust u.s.w. weiss, an den Flügeln und dem Schwanze gelblichweiss; endlich führt man unter den Varietäten noch **Bastarde** an, welche in grossen Vogelhäusern mit der **Nachtigall** oder der **Heckenbraunelle** gezogen worden sein sollen.

AUFENTHALT

Das Rotkehlchen bewohnt ganz **Europa**, vom südlichsten und westlichsten Ende an bis hoch nach **Norwegen** und **Schweden** hinauf, weniger **Russland**, und in **Sibirien** soll es gar nicht vorkommen. Im mittleren Europa ist es, wie z. B. in **Frankreich**, der **Schweiz**, **Holland**, auch in **England**, allenthalben bekannt und in **Deutschland** überall gemein, besonders während seiner Zugzeit; denn es ist bei uns ein **Zugvogel**.

Sie kommen im März, je nachdem die Witterung früher oder später gut wird, bald gleich im Anfange dieses Monats, bald erst nach der Mitte desselben zu uns und sind die Verkündiger des Frühlings, müssen aber doch auch oft bei eintretenden Nachwintern noch viel leiden. Ihr Frühlingszug dauert in der Regel zwei Wochen. Im Herbst begeben sie sich, einzelne schon zu Anfang September, auf die Reise, ziehen aber in dieser Jahreszeit langsamer, und man sieht einzelne noch spät im November. Etwa in der letzten Hälfte des Oktober geschieht der Hauptzug, und dann wimmelt es oft in allen Hecken und Büschen von ihnen. Einzelne werden eben nicht selten, vom Schnee und Frost überrascht, gezwungen, bei uns zu bleiben und hier zu überwintern. Sie können die Kälte gar wohl vertragen, wenn es ihnen nur nicht an Nahrung mangelt, was im Winter, wo es überall noch Beeren gibt, nicht leicht eintritt, dagegen müssen im Frühling, wenn diese fehlen, und dann noch später Schnee und Frost ihnen Würmer und Insekten entziehen, oft viele umkommen. Jedoch nicht alle, die wir im Winter, besonders in den Gärten und in der Nähe von Gebäuden sehen, sind solche, die aus freiem Antriebe hier überwintern, sondern höchstens aus der Stube entflohene, was sie durch ihre geringere Furcht vor den Menschen bald bekunden. Jene sind ungleich seltener als diese. Diejenigen, welche bei tiefem Schnee und strenger Kälte auf die Höfe und Miststätten, selbst in die Ställe kommen, gehören unter die letzteren; die anderen verkriechen sich dagegen in den Zäunen und in an die Gärten stossenden Gebäuden, wo sie meistens umkommen. Ihre Reisen verrichten sie des Nachts und meistens einzeln, wenigstens nicht in grossen und eng zusammenhaltenden Gesellschaften. Zwar hört man des Nachts ihre Stimme nur einzeln in den Lüften, allein die Menge, in der sie zuweilen in einer Nacht ankommen, und der Eifer, mit dem sie bei einbrechender Abenddämmerung einander zurufen, so wie es finster wird aber alle mit einem Male verstummen, lässt vermuten, dass sie nicht ganz ungesellig reisen.

Wenn man in der Zugzeit abends im Zwielichte in einem Walde ist, so erschallen ihre fröhlichen Stimmen aus jedem Strauche, anfangs nahe an der Erde, dann immer höher, bis sie bald die Baumgipfel erreichen, aber nun verstummen; denn so wie der letzte Schein des Tages am Horizonte verschwindet, wird alles im Walde still, und man hört dann eine andere Stimme von ihnen nur in den Lüften, woran man, wenn man auf dem Freien ist, bemerken kann, dass sie von Aufgang der Sonne gegen deren Niedergang ziehen, was im Frühjahr umgekehrt ist. Dass sie niedrig über die Erde hin von einem Gebüsch zum anderen zögen, habe ich nie bemerkt; immer hörte ich hoch in den Lüften ihre Stimmen, und sie setzten ihre Reisen ununterbrochen fort, bis die Morgendämmerung anbrechen wollte, wo man dann auf einmal ihre gewöhnliche Lockstimme in Gebüschen hörte, wo man tags vorher noch keins bemerkt hatte.

Das Rotkehlchen bewohnt im Sommer die düsteren Waldungen, in ebenen wie in gebirgigen Gegenden, doch nicht die hohen Bergrücken, sondern vielmehr die zwischenliegenden Täler und gern wasserreiche Gegenden. In alten Hochwaldungen findet man es nicht, am wenigsten in solchen von Nadelholz; immer muss viel Unterholz und niederes dichtes Gebüsch da sein, wo es lange verweilen soll. Wo das Unterholz so enge steht, dass unter demselben der Boden nur noch wenig Gras und andere niedrige Pflanzen hervorbringt, wo sich selten ein Sonnenstrahl durch die dicht belaubten Zweige stiehlt und den feuchten Boden bescheint, zumal wenn kleine freie Wiesenplätze mit solchem Buschwerk und einzelnen hohen Bäumen abwechseln und Wasser in der Nähe ist, das sind ihre liebsten Wohnplätze in unseren Laubholzwäldern. In den waldreichen Auen unserer norddeutschen Flüsse sind sie daher ungemein häufig. So beschaffene Wälder liebt die **Nachtigall** wie das Rotkehlchen, doch mit dem Unterschiede, dass das letztere die hoch aufgewachsenen Schläge erst dann recht gern bewohnt, wenn sie jener schon zu alt werden. Ganz vorzüglich gern sind sie im hohen Stangenholze, wo es unten viel alte faule Baumstrünke und bemooste Stämme gibt. Sie ähneln hierin den **Amseln**; wo daher diese wohnen, wird man gewiss auch Rotkehlchen antreffen.

In der Zugzeit besuchen sie ausser jenen alles Buschwerk ohne Unterschied von Laubholz oder Nadelholz oder von beiden gemischtes, doch immer am liebsten das erstere. Sie sind dann nicht allein in allen Feldhölzern, in einzelnen Hecken und Gesträuch, sogar zuweilen, wo dieses weit vom Walde auf dem Felde sich findet, im niederen Gebüsch zwischen Wiesen, Äckern und auf Viehweiden und in den mit wildem Gebüsch umgebenen Gärten, sondern selbst in solchen Bauerngärten mitten in den Dörfern, worin nur etwas Buschwerk wächst. Auch in den weniger buschreichen Umgebungen der Städte, selbst oft mitten in denselben in Gärten, wenn das vorhandene Gebüsch auch nur aus einigen Stachelbeerbüschen und einzelnen Holundersträuchern bestände, in den Buschweidengehegen an den Flüssen; kurz, überall wo niederes Buschholz, besonders Beerensträuche wachsen, findet man in der Zugzeit auch Rotkehlchen, und man kann daraus auf die grosse Menge schliessen, in der diese Vögel bei uns vorkommen. Sie lieben die geflochtenen und toten Zäune sehr, zumal wenn etwas lebendiges Holz an selbigen steht, und sind am liebsten auf der Seite derselben, wo sie Schutz vor dem Winde haben oder wo die Sonne vormittags dagegen scheint.

EIGENSCHAFTEN

Dies ist ein munteres, keckes und gewandtes Vögelchen; seine Bewegungen sind abgemessen, aber dabei schnell, leichter und hurtiger als die der **Nachtigall**. Man beschuldigt es, wie diese, der Neugier, und nicht ganz mit Unrecht; sonst zeichnen es noch einesteils Mutwille, anderenteils ein harmloses, zutrauliches Benehmen vor vielen anderen kleinen Vögeln ganz besonders aus.

Es steht immer hoch auf den Beinen, die Brust erhaben tragend, die Flügel etwas hängend, den Schwanz horizontal; schnellt diesen bei jeder Veranlassung aufwärts, macht eine schnelle Verbeugung dazu und ruckt dabei auch meistens mit den Flügeln. Wenn es traurig ist, was selten vorkommt, sträubt es das Gefieder, und der Rumpf wird dadurch fast kugelrund. Nur dann, wenn es einmal ausruht oder wenn das Männchen singt, lässt es den Schwanz abwärts hängen. Es hüpft am Boden in leichten Sprüngen mit häufigen Unterbrechungen oder ruckweise. In den Zweigen des Gebüsches flattert es mehr als es hüpft, ausser auf langen, fast horizontalen Ästen, auf denen es gern in raschen Sprüngen der Länge nach hinhüpft. Obgleich es gern im schattigen Gebüsch verweilt und nicht viele Ruhe an einem Orte hat, so bewegt es sich hier doch jederzeit mehr durch seine Flügel von Ast zu Ast und ruht einige Augenblicke, bevor es seinen Platz verändert, dahingegen die **Grasmücken** ununterbrochen durch dasselbe hinhüpfen und selten flattern. In seinem ganzen Betragen ähnelt es, bis auf eine grössere Lebhaftigkeit, der **Nachtigall**, ebenso sehr auch der **Singdrossel** und der **Amsel**.

In den einzelnen Hecken verbirgt es sich nicht lange, es lässt sich bald am Rande auf vorstehenden Zweigen sehen und fliegt, wenn man ihm zu nahe kommt, auch selten in die Dickung hinein, sondern meistens am Rande derselben hin, auf einen anderen hervorragenden Zweig oder wenigstens nicht tief in die Hecke. Hinter geflochtenen Zäunen hält es sich vorzüglich gern auf.

Es fliegt schneller als die **Nachtigall**, ruckweise und schnurrend, schwenkt sich rasch und geschickt, schnurrt auf sehr kurzen Räumen gleichsam hüpfend fort, wobei es nicht selten auch den Schwanz in die Höhe hält; auf langen Strecken beschreibt es aber im Fluge eine Schlangenlinie von ziemlich kurzen und längeren Bogen, sodass dadurch der Flug sehr unregelmässig wird. Über grosse freie Flächen fliegt es am Tage nie; wird es aber dazu gezwungen, so eilt es niedrig und dicht über der Erde hin, benutzt dabei jedes vorkommende Gebüsch zu einem Ruhepunkte, selbst Distelbüsche, und das kecke Rotkehlchen zeigt sich hier sehr furchtsam und ängstlich.

Es ist ein mutwilliges, zanksüchtiges Geschöpf, besonders gegen seinesgleichen, und das Necken, Jagen und Herumbeissen hat, wenn ihrer zwei sich nahe kommen, eher kein Ende, bis sich eins wieder entfernt hat; besonders hartnäckige Kämpfe gibt es zwischen den Männchen. Nicht selten flattern zwei solche Zänker, die Schnäbel gegeneinander gerichtet und damit klappernd, in senkrechter Richtung eine kleine Strecke aufwärts, ehe eins nachgibt und ausreisst, was von dem anderen aber dann desto ärger von Busch zu Busch verfolgt wird. Sie lassen hierbei häufig einen hohen **tschietschenden** Ton hören, und man hat oft Gelegenheit, hier ihre ausserordentliche Gewandtheit im Fluge zu bewundern.

Die Stimme, womit sie einander locken, Freude und Wohlbehagen zu erkennen geben oder Eulen, Katzen und andere Raubtiere oft dem Jäger verraten, ist eine Reihe hoher, scharfer und kurzer Töne, die wie **schnickschnickschnick** und **schnikkerickickickick** klingen. Wenn sie recht eifrig locken, z. B. des Abends, wenn sie sich auf die Reise begeben wollen, wiederholen sie diese Silben ohne abzusetzen, viel öfter als ich hier angegeben habe, und sie werden so schnell ausgestossen, dass sie von der Mitte an fast trillerartig klingen. Man kann diese Stimme ziemlich gut auf einem einfachen Instrument nachahmen, das man aus einer halben Walnussschale verfertigt, indem man quer über dieselbe einen doppelten Faden spannt, die grössere Spannung desselben durch ein in der Mitte eingedrehtes Hölzchen bewirkt, das dadurch mit dem einen Ende gegen den Rand der Nussschale gedrückt wird, mit dem anderen aber etwas aufwärts steht. Hält man dies Instrument in der einen Hand und streicht mit den Fingern der anderen schnell nacheinander auf das emporstehende Ende des Hölzchens, so hebt sich dadurch das entgegengesetzte und schnellt gegen die Wand der Nussschale, wodurch jene Töne ziemlich täuschend hervorgebracht werden. Ihr Warnungsruf, z. B. bei Annäherung eines Raubvogels, ist ein leises **Sih**, und die Stimme, welche sie bloss auf ihren nächtlichen Wanderungen hören lassen, ein durchdringendes **Tschrietsch**. Die gewöhnliche Lockstimme, **schnickerickick**, hört man zur Nachtzeit nie von ihnen.

Das Männchen singt sehr angenehm, vom März bis tief in den Sommer hinein, sitzt dabei gern hoch, zuweilen nahe am Gipfel kleiner Bäume, lässt Flügel und Schwanz nachlässig hängen und bläst die Kehle weit auf. Der laute, aus mehreren abwechselnden Strophen bestehende Gesang klingt feierlich und etwas schwermütig; er hat viel flötende und trillernde Strophen und nimmt sich besonders an stillen Frühlingsabenden ungemein anmutig aus. Man hört ihn wohl auch am Tage, doch nicht so häufig als am frühen Morgen und gegen Abend bis in die Dämmerung, wo bereits die Lieder vieler kleiner Waldsänger verstummt sind. Doch an schwülen, gewitterschwangeren Sommertagen singt es auch oft sehr anhaltend, hoch im schattigen Gebüsch auf einem dürren Ästchen, nahe am Schafte eines Baumes sitzend, und es verlässt ein solches Plätzchen stundenlang nicht. Geht man behutsam zu Werke, so kann man ihm dabei ganz nahe kommen und lange zuhören, ohne dass es wegfliegt. Es scheint, so lange es singt, ein ganz anderes Naturell angenommen zu haben; das muntere, kecke, unruhige Rotkehlchen sitzt stundenlang still, ein feierlicher Ernst ist an die Stelle des Frohsinns, eine Art Stolz und Würde an die des üppigen Leichtsinns getreten, und nur bei wenigen Vögeln ist dies so auffallend.

Die Rotkehlchen singen zwar auch im Herbst, aber nie anhaltend und nie so laut als im Frühjahr, und man kann dies keinen Gesang, sondern nur ein blosses Zwitschern nennen, was wenig Ähnlichkeit mit dem wahren Gesange im Frühling und gar keine eigentliche Melodie hat. Wer daher dies Zwitschern für jenen halten wollte, würde sehr irren; denn auch die Weibchen zwitschern auf ähnliche Art, doch leiser und seltener, aber den eigentlichen Frühlingsgesang hört man bloss vom Männchen.

Das Rotkehlchen ist ein angenehmer und beliebter Stubenvogel, besonders bei den Landleuten, deren Stuben es, frei herumfliegend, von den lästigen Fliegen und anderem Ungeziefer reinigt. Kein Vogel wird so leicht zahm; denn kaum hat es die Fenster untersucht und die Unmöglichkeit eingesehen, als es sich auch gleich in sein Geschick fügt und bald mit seinen Hausgenossen aus einer Schüssel isst, sich auf den Kopf seines Herrn setzt und ihm wohl gar vorgehaltene Leckerbissen aus der Hand nimmt. Es lässt sich sogar zum Aus- und Einfliegen gewöhnen, ja man erzählt Beispiele, dass im Frühjahr freigelassene im Herbst darauf wieder und durch das geöffnete Fenster in dieselbe Stube kamen, sich durchwintern liessen, und dies mehrere Jahre nacheinander taten. Ihr munteres, zutrauliches Wesen erfreut jedermann, auch zwitschern sie viel, und oft fangen sie schon denselben Tag, da sie in die Stube gebracht wurden, damit an; aber nur selten singt einmal eins so laut wie im Freien. Dies tun sie aber, wenn man sie in ein Nachtigallenbauer steckt und sie gut pflegt; allein sie dauern hier nie so lange, als frei in der Stube herumfliegend, wo man sie mehrere Jahre (man sagt bis acht Jahre) haben kann.

Die Stube, in welcher sie sich indessen lange halten sollen, darf nicht zu niedrig sein (besonders wenn es viel Tabaksrauch und Öldampf darin gäbe), und muss viel Licht und Sonne haben; man muss ihr ferner im Sommer recht oft und lange frische Luft geben können und sonst nichts versäumen, was zum Wohlbefinden dieser Vögel beitragen kann; dahin gehört z. B. täglich frisches Wasser zum Baden und das Darreichen natürlicher Nahrungsmittel, wie sie die Jahreszeiten mit sich bringen. In den düsteren, dampfigen Stuben der Bauern werden diese armen Geschöpfe meistenteils bald das Opfer eines langsamen Todes, das Gefieder beräuchert und kleistert zusammen, und erleben sie ja den künftigen Sommer, so mausern sie aus Mangel an frischer Luft u. s. w. sich nicht und gehen dann drauf; meistens leben sie aber nicht einmal so lange, werden entweder tot getreten oder zwischen Türen gequetscht, ertrinken in der Milch und anderen Flüssigkeiten, verbrennen sich am Licht, fliegen in den Ofen, werden von Katzen erwischt u. s. w. Zu den meisten Arten von Unglücksfällen führt sie fast immer ihre ausserordentliche Zahmheit.

So angenehm es ist, ein so zutrauliches Vögelchen ohne viele Mühe zu besitzen und um sich haben zu können, so unangenehm muss es andererseits dem sein, der auf Reinlichkeit hält; denn sie beschmutzen mit ihrem Unrat das Hausgerät und andere Sachen; kein Plätzchen ist dagegen gesichert. Man darf nur etwas Ungewöhnliches bringen und hinlegen, es wird sogleich von ihnen untersucht, ob nicht etwas

Geniessbares für sie dabei sei, und gewöhnlich dann besiegelt. Für denjenigen, der mit Büchern, Zeichnungen, Schreibereien und dergleichen umgeht, sind sie daher keine angenehmen Gesellschafter.

Ihre Zanksucht zeigt sich besonders in der Stube, wenn man ein frischgefangenes zu einem bringt, das schon in der Stube war; es muss den grimmigsten Verfolgungen und Bissen des letzteren gewöhnlich unterliegen. Will man zwei haben, so muss man sie zu gleicher Zeit in die Stube fliegen lassen; demungeachtet geht es doch nicht immer nach Wunsch damit. Selbst gegen andere ihnen beigesellte Vögel zeigt sich ihr neidischer Charakter, besonders beim Fressnapfe; sogar mit den in Käfigen in der Stube hängenden Vögeln hadern sie gern. Doch ich muss auch etwas zu ihrem Lobe sagen, was sich im folgenden recht schön ausspricht. Ich hatte nämlich einst einen jungen **Hänfling**, den ich selbst auffütterte, der aber, wie gewöhnlich, wenn solchen jungen Vögeln nicht beständig das Maul gestopft wird, viel schrie; das in meiner Stube herumfliegende Rotkehlchen begab sich bald, wie es schien, teilnehmend zum Käfig des jungen Schreiers, der seinen Schnabel aufsperrte und von ihm gefüttert sein wollte; sogleich flog es zum Tisch, holte kleine Brotkrümchen, stopfte ihm damit das Maul und tat dies endlich so oft, als sich der Verwaiste meldete, wodurch mir das Auffüttern desselben sehr erleichtert wurde.

Wenn man sie bei kalter Witterung gefangen hat und zu schnell in die geheizte Stube bringt, so gehen sie meistens drauf, und man pflegt zu sagen: Sie haben den Kopf erfroren, oder die Kälte sitzt ihnen im Kopf; allein der schnelle Wechsel ist hieran bloss schuld, und man kann ihm vorbeugen, wenn man sie zuvor in ein ungeheiztes Zimmer und so nach und nach in das wärmere bringt. Bei solcher Vorsicht bleiben sie leben, wenn es draussen auch noch so kalt wäre.

Man nimmt sie auch jung aus dem Neste und füttert sie auf, tut sie in einen Käfig und hängt sie neben schlagende **Nachtigallen**, von denen sie den Schlag derselben vollkommen nachahmen lernen, doch nicht mit so starker, daher angenehmerer Stimme singen sollen.

Mir ist ein Fall bekannt, dass ein Pärchen, welches vom Herbst an in einer Stube herumflog, gegen das Frühjahr sich begattete, und endlich in einer zu diesem Behuf in einen Winkel gestellten zerbrochenen Flasche ein Nest baute, Eier legte und Junge ausbrütete, diese jedoch nicht aufbrachte. In grossen Vogelhäusern soll dies besser gelingen, und sie sollen sich da zuweilen mit **Nachtigallen** oder der **Heckenbraunelle** verpaaren.

NAHRUNG

Das Rotkehlchen nährt sich meistens wie die **Singdrossel und die Amsel** im Frühling und Sommer auf dem Erdboden, im Herbst in dem Gebüsche. Dort sucht es hüpfend Regenwürmer, kleine nackte Schnecken, kleine Käferchen und allerlei Insektenlarven unter dem Gebüsche, besonders unter dem alten halbverfaulten Laube auf, welches es wie die Drosseln umzuwenden pflegt, oder es fliegt beim Erblicken eines Nahrungsmittels schnell herab, ergreift es und verzehrt es, auf einem Zweige sitzend. So sieht man es oft kleine Heuschrecken, Grasmotten und andere Insekten von mit Gras bewachsenen Stellen der Wiesenränder u.s.w. aufnehmen, doch nicht im langen Grase, überhaupt nicht auf dem Freien darnach herumhüpfen. Von den Blättern des Gebüsches nimmt es auch, wiewohl seltener, kleine Räupchen, öfter Mücken, Fliegen, kleine Nachtfalter und dergleichen hinweg und fängt diese auch zwischen den Zweigen, seltener ausserhalb des Gebüsches im Fluge hinweg. In den Zäunen sucht es Spinnen, sogenannte Ohrwürmer und andere viel kleinere Käferchen und zweiflügelige Insekten auf; auch Asseln und Kellerwürmer frisst es, aber Tausendfüsse nur im Notfall. Es nimmt die sitzenden und kriechenden Insekten stets viel lieber als die fliegenden, weil es im Fangen der letzteren eben keine besondere Geschicklichkeit besitzt, und von **Rotschwänzen, Laubvögeln** und anderen darin weit übertroffen wird.

Sobald es Beeren gibt, sucht es nebenbei auch diese auf, ja sie werden im Herbst endlich seine Hauptnahrung. Die ersten sind die Heidelbeeren, die roten, schwarzen und Alpen-Johannisbeeren, die Beeren vom Seidelbast, und die vom roten oder Trauben-Holunder; dann die Beeren vom Faulbaum, Traubenkirschen, schwarze Holunderbeeren und andere; endlich auch Eberesch- oder Vogelbeeren, und zuletzt die mit einer hoch orangegelben markigen Haut umgebenen Kerne aus den aufgesprungenen Kapseln des Spindelbaums. Sie fressen diese letzteren ungemein gern, und deswegen heissen diese lieblich gebildeten Früchte in hiesiger Gegend allgemein **Rotkehlchenbrot**.

Die grösseren Kerne vom breitblätterigen Spindelbaume fressen sie nicht so gern, auch die Beeren vom gemeinen Hartriegel selten, lieber die vom weissbeerigen Hartriegel, noch seltener Kreuzdornbeeren und nur im höchsten Notfall Wacholderbeeren, die ihnen auch schlecht bekommen. Die Ebereschbeeren sind für ihre Mundöffnung etwas zu gross, es kostet sie daher viel Anstrengung, sie hinein zu würgen, und man sieht sie gewöhnlich von aussen den Schlund hinabgleiten. Fünf Stück solcher Beeren füllen schon ihren Kropf. Ich habe bemerkt, dass sie gern mit den Nahrungsmitteln wechseln, und man muss sie überhaupt für naschhafte Vögel halten; Pflaumenmus und Butter, diese Kunstprodukte, fressen diese Leckermäuler selbst in der Freiheit, wenn sie sich ihnen darbieten, sehr gern, zumal im Frühjahr.

Die harten, saftlosen Flügel und Beine der Insekten, selbst der Fliegen und Mücken, die Erde, welche die Regenwürmer in sich haben, die Kerne vom sogenannten Rotkehlchenbrot nebst den Hülsen oder Schalen und Kernen anderer Beerenarten sondern sich im Magen von den weicheren, verdaulicheren Teilen ab und werden in länglich runden Ballen durch den Schnabel wieder ausgespieen, wobei sie sich meistenteils etwas anstrengen müssen.

Im Zimmer fangen sie anfänglich Fliegen, gewöhnen sich aber bald von selbst, ohne dass man sich um sie zu bekümmern braucht, an alles, was auf den Tisch kommt, an Brot, Semmel, Butter, Käse, Fleisch, Äpfel- und Pflaumenmus, gekochtes Obst und frisches, als weiche Birnen und Pflaumen, wenn sie nur etwas abpicken können, gekochtes Gemüse, kurz, sie naschen von allem, was der Mensch geniesst, und finden darunter bald ihre individuellen Lieblingsspeisen. Sie vergessen darüber meistens das Fliegenfangen, und man sieht daraus, dass ihnen die Einförmigkeit bei ihren Speisen nicht behagen will.

Die Fliegen fangen sie weniger im Fluge, wo sie oft fehlschnappen, sondern mehr die, welche an den Wänden, der Decke, an den Fenstern u.s.w. sitzen, die ihnen doch noch oft genug entwischen. Aber sie suchen auch Spinnen, Flöhe und Käsemaden, alles dem Landmann lästige und in seinen Wohnstuben vorkommende Geschöpfe, mit Begierde auf. An jedes sogenannte Universalfutter gewöhnen sie sich leicht. Sie trinken viel und baden sich ungemein gern und oft, zuweilen täglich zweimal, wobei sie sich meistens so nass machen, dass man keine Farbe am Gefieder erkennt; frisches Wasser darf ihnen daher nie fehlen.

Diejenigen, welchen man einen Käfig zum Aufenthalt anweist, müssen Nachtigallenfutter bekommen, auch fast so sorgfältig wie diese gepflegt werden, öfters einen Mehlwurm, Regenwurm, frische oder gedörrte und wieder aufgequellte Beeren und andere natürliche Nahrungsmittel nebenbei bekommen, wenn sie lange dauern sollen; sonst halten sie eine so enge Gefangenschaft nie lange aus.

FORTPFLANZUNG

Sie nisten in unseren Wäldern in solchen Teilen derselben, wie sie schon oben als ihr Sommeraufenthalt angegeben wurden. In den dichten, schattigen, zu Stangenholz aufgewachsenen Schlägen feuchter Laubholzwaldungen hiesiger Gegenden pflanzen sie sich häufig fort, weniger und seltener in kleineren Feldhölzern. In den waldreichen Auen unserer Flüsse nisten sie in Menge, aber jedes Pärchen hat sein eigenes kleines Revier, in welchem es kein anderes leidet. Man darf nur da, wo man das Männchen immer singen hört, die alten Baumstöcke in einem kleinen Umkreise durchsuchen, besonders wo solche recht im Gestrüpp versteckt sind, um das Nest zu finden; denn dieses steht immer sehr nahe an oder auf der Erde, in der weiten Höhle eines alten ausgefaulten Strunks, zwischen den dicken Wurzeln der Stämme, zwischen mehreren alten Storzeln oder hinter Grasbüscheln an den alten Stöcken, selbst im Moose auf der Erde, in Steinritzen und Mauerlöchern, sogar zuweilen in weiten Erdhöhlen, die von Maulwürfen oder anderen Tieren bereitet wurden. Ist die Höhle zu weit, so wird sie mit dürrem Laube so weit angefüllt, dass bloss für das eigentliche Nest noch Raum genug bleibt. Übrigens muss es immer von oben eine Decke haben, und wenn diese die Höhle oder ein überhängender Stamm nicht bildet, so wird das Nest so gebaut, dass der weite Eingang zur Seite in dasselbe geht. Einst baute ein Pärchen drei Fuss hoch vom Boden in die Mauer meines Vogelstellerhäuschens in ein Guckloch von einem Kubikfuss Weite, welchen grossen Raum es erst mit dürrem Laube ganz anfüllte und dann oben das eigentliche Nest hineinbaute; das Ganze war ein gewaltiger Klumpen, und die Herbeischaffung der Menge von Materialien musste diesen Tierchen viele Mühe gemacht haben.

Übrigens ist das Nest meistens sehr gut versteckt, daher schwer aufzufinden. Seine erste Grundlage sind mehr oder weniger dürre Baumblätter, dann folgt Erdmoos, dann trockene Pflanzenstengel, abgestorbene Grasblätter und Hälmchen, zuletzt Haare und Wolle oder auch wohl einige Federn. Sehr häufig besteht es auch fast einzig aus grünem Erdmoos und nur das Innere ist mit zarten Würzelchen und einzelnen Haaren ausgelegt; dann ähnelt es dem Neste der **Heckenbraunelle**. Es ist meistens ein etwas lockeres oder doch ein ziemlich kunstloses Gewebe.

Man findet in diesem Neste oft schon Ende April, am häufigsten doch Anfang Mai fünf bis sechs, selten sieben, rundliche oder etwas kurzgeformte, zartschalige Eier, die auf gelblichweissem Grunde mit gelblicher Rostfarbe über und über bespritzt und punktiert sind, sodass die Punkte häufig mit dem Grunde verschmelzen; nicht selten zeichnen sich jedoch auch unter diesen einige durch ihre Grösse und dunkle, fast rostrote Farbe aus, die unter den blässeren vorstechen und öfters einen unordentlichen Fleckenkranz am stumpfen Ende bilden.

Die Eier werden wie bei anderen Sängern von Männchen und Weibchen wechselweise — sodass das erstere das letztere, besonders in den Mittagsstunden, ablöst — zwei Wochen lang bebrütet. Durch ein leises Zwitschern beim Füttern verraten sich zuweilen die Jungen, die das Nest schon verlassen, sobald nur die Flügelfedern so weit erwachsen sind, dass sie damit von Zweig zu Zweig flattern können, und wenn die Schwanzfedern noch ganz kurz sind. Sie sehen in ihrem ersten Kleide den Alten gar nicht ähnlich, werden von diesen lange noch, wenn sie schon ausgeflogen, mit Gewürm und Insekten gefüttert und bei herannahender Gefahr durch ein schneidendes **Sih** gewarnt, worauf sie sich gewöhnlich in die Höhe begeben und in den hohen belaubten Zweigen zu verbergen suchen, sodass man sie selten zu sehen bekommt. Sie sind scheuer als viele andere junge Vögel des Waldes und lassen nur, wenn sie sicher zu sein glauben, ein kurzes Zitschen, fast wie ein **Goldammer**, hören. Die Alten zeigen viel Liebe für sie und geben diese durch ein sehr ängstliches Benehmen und heftiges Schnickern zu erkennen. Sind die Jungen erst so, dass sie schon selbst einige Nahrung suchen lernen, was bei guter Witterung in acht bis zehn Tagen, von da an, wo sie das Nest verliessen, sein kann, so schreiten sie zur zweiten Brut, was die meisten tun, obgleich auch einzelne Pärchen nur einmal im Jahre brüten. Wahrscheinlich sind dies die jungen Vögel vom vorigen Jahre.

FEINDE

Ihre Brut wird sehr häufig vom **Fuchs**, vom **Baummarder** und anderen zur Gattung der **Wiesel** gehörenden Tieren, von **Katzen, Igeln** und **Mäusen** zerstört, wobei nicht selten auch eins der Alten sich erwischen lässt; seltener ist dies letztere der Fall durch den **Habicht und Sperber** oder andere kleine **Falken**, weil sie sich im Gebüsch vor diesen meistens gut zu verbergen wissen.

NUTZEN

Unmittelbar nützen sie uns dadurch, dass sie ein sehr delikates Gericht geben, zumal sie im Herbst meistens fett sind. Man fing sie daher früher hin und wieder häufig zum Verspeisen und schickte sie dutzend-, ja wohl schockweise, gerupft und mit den Hälsen in einen langen gespaltenen Stock geklemmt, wie Finken und andere kleine Vögel zu Markte. Sie erfreuen uns ferner durch ihren anmutigen Gesang im Freien wie im Zimmer, wo sie auch durch ihr Betragen sehr angenehm unterhalten. Mittelbar nützen sie aber durch Wegfangen einer Menge schädlicher Waldinsekten und ihrer Brut ausserordentlich; und dass sie in den Stuben die Fliegen wegfangen, auch Flöhe, Spinnen, Käsemaden und anderes Ungeziefer aufsuchen und verzehren, ist eine grosse Wohltat für den Landmann, der sie deswegen auch sehr lieb hat. Hier zu Lande findet man daher im Herbst auf den meisten Dörfern, beim Bauer wie beim Tagelöhner und Handwerker, gewiss nur äussert selten eine bewohnte Stube, in der man nicht wenigstens ein Rotkehlchen anträfe.

Dem Jäger verraten sie durch ihr Schnickern oft Füchse und andere Raubtiere.

SCHADEN

Ist nicht bekannt. Dass sie durch das Drehen die Schlingen in den Dohnen verderben und durch Umhertragen der Beerenkerne schlechte Holzarten dahin verpflanzen, wo wir dergleichen nicht haben wollen, wird ihnen wohl niemand als solchen anrechnen.

// DER GARTENROTSCHWANZ //

PHOENICURUS PHOENICURUS

Rötling (Hausrötling), Rötlein (Hausrötlein), Baumrötlein, Rotschwanz, Rotschwänzchen, gemeines Rotschwänzchen, Gartenrotschwänzchen, Waldrotschwänzchen (Hausrotschwänzchen, Hausrotschweifel), Waldrotschweifel, Rotstärt, Rotsterz, Rotsterzchen, Rotzahl, Rotzagel, Rotzägel, Rotkehlchen mit schwarzem Kinn, Rotbrüstlein, Rotbäuchlein, Sommerrötele, Schwarzkehlchen, schwarzkehliger Sänger, schwarzkehliger Steinschmätzer, Bienenschnappe, Wüstling, Wistling, Hüting, Saulocker, Fritzchen; in hiesiger Gegend: (grauer) Rotschwanz.

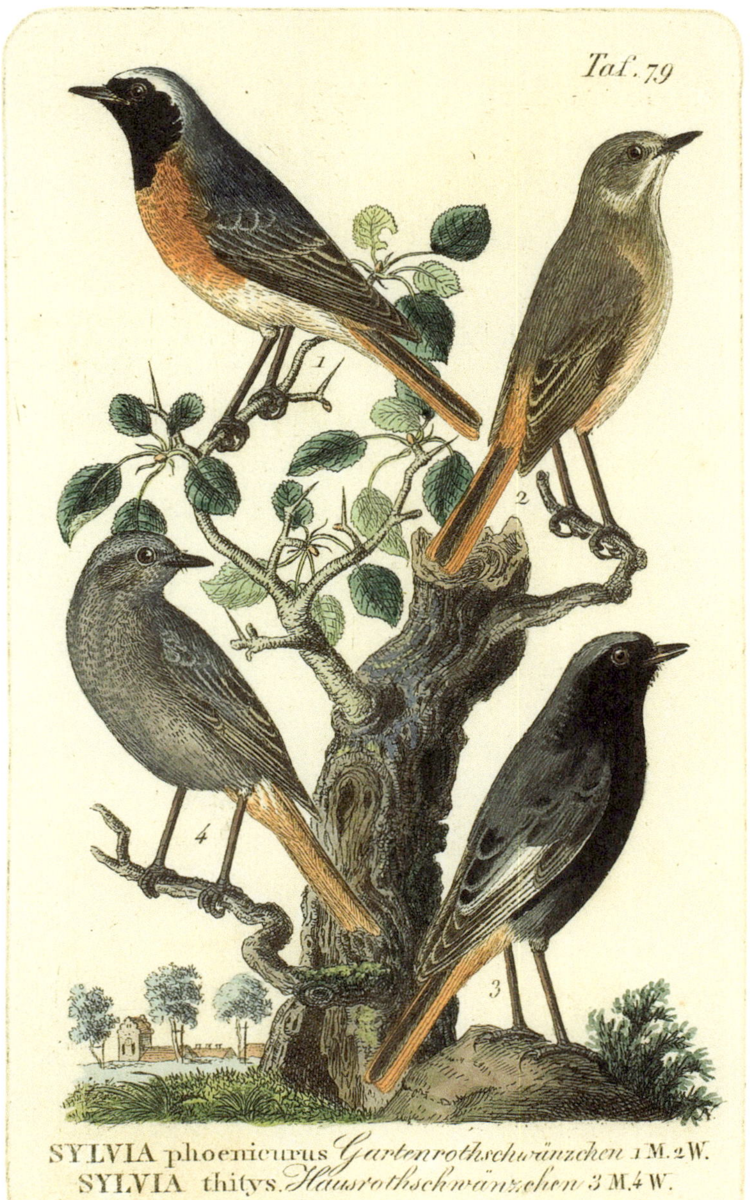
Taf. 79
1
2
3
4
SYLVIA phoenicurus Gartenrothschwänzchen 1 M. 2 W.
SYLVIA thitys. Hausrothschwänzchen 3 M. 4 W.

KENNZEICHEN DER ART

Schwanz lebhaft rostrot mit zwei dunkelbraunen Mittelfedern; die dunkelbraunen Flügelfedern mit hell gelblichbraunen Säumen. Die zweite Schwungfeder ist 0,6 cm kürzer als die dritte und von gleicher Länge mit der sechsten.

Männchen: Die Kehle schwarz; die Brust rostrot.

Weibchen: Die Kehle schmutzig weiss, die Brust in der Mitte weiss, an den Seiten und oberwärts hell gelblichgraubraun; alle oberen Teile matt graubraun.

BESCHREIBUNG

Dieser bekannte Vogel ist sehr häufig mit dem **Hausrotschwanz** verwechselt worden, besonders traf dies die sich sehr ähnlich sehenden weiblichen und jungen Vögel beider Arten. Will man genau auf die hier angegebenen Artkennzeichen acht haben, so wird dieser Fall nicht leicht eintreten können, da doch beide Arten in der Tat eine grössere Verschiedenheit zeigen als sie zwischen manchen anderen dieser Gruppe stattfindet. Es ist ein schlanker, nett gestalteter Vogel, merklich kleiner als das **Rotkehlchen**, auch noch etwas schmächtiger wie der **Hausrotschwanz**.

Seine Länge beträgt gewöhnlich 13,5 cm, selten etwas mehr, die Flügelbreite 22,5 bis 23 cm. Ein Vogel dieser Art von 14 cm Länge und 23,5 cm Breite kommt selten vor. Der am Ende fast gerade Schwanz ist 5,6 cm lang, und die Flügel reichen, in Ruhe liegend, mit ihren Spitzen bis über die Hälfte desselben hinaus.

Der pfriemenförmige, vorn rundliche, hinterwärts breitere Schnabel ist kürzer und runder als am **Hausrotschwanz**, auch sind spitzenwärts die Schneiden weniger eingezogen als an diesem. Seine Länge ist 9 mm, die Breite an der Wurzel 4 mm, die Höhe aber merklich geringer. Er ist hornschwarz, nur beim Weibchen an den Schneiden und der Wurzel der Unterkinnlade licht bräunlich; die Mundwinkel und der Rachen gelb. Das Nasenloch ist klein, oval und, wie in dieser Gattung gewöhnlich, von oben durch eine harte Haut halb bedeckt. Über den Mundwinkeln stehen feine schwarze Borsten, und die Iris ist schwarzbraun.

Die Füsse sind schlank, mittelmässig hoch, die dünnen Zehen haben schwache, sehr zusammengedrückte, flach gebogene Nägel, welche spitz wie Nadeln sind. Die Haut an den Füssen ist ziemlich den ganzen Lauf herab ohne Einschnitt, die Zehen oben geschildert, unten feinwarzig. Füsse und Krallen sind schwarz, mit durchschimmerndem, rötlichem Braun, besonders nach der Ferse zu. Die Höhe des Laufes beträgt ziemlich 2,4 cm; die Länge der Mittelzehe mit der Kralle etwas über 17 mm und die der Hinterzehe 12 mm, ohne Kralle aber nur 7 mm.

Das alte **Männchen** in seinem **Frühlingskleide** gehört unter die schön gezeichneten Vögel. An ihm sind der Anfang der Stirn gleich über dem Schnabel, Zügel, Augen- und Ohrengegend, Wangen, Kehle und Gurgel bis zur Kropfgegend tief schwarz; die Stirn gleich hinter den schwarzen Halftern rein weiss, was bis auf die Mitte des Scheitels reicht und seitwärts über dem Schwarzen bis zu den Schläfen sich hinzieht; der Hinterteil des Oberkopfes, Genick, Hinterhals, Rücken, Schultern und die kleinen Flügeldeckfedern dunkel bläulichaschgrau; die Oberbrust schön gelblich rostrot, welche Farbe sich an den Seiten der Brust bis zu den Schenkeln herabzieht, nur abwärts etwas bleicher wird, in der weissen Mitte der Unterbrust sanft vertuscht, oben aber vom Schwarzen scharf abschneidet. Die Schenkelfedern sind roströtlich und grau gefleckt, die After- und unteren Schwanzdeckfedern bleich rostfarben, mit weisslich rostgelben Enden; der Bürzel, die oberen Schwanzfedern und der ganze Schwanz, die beiden dunkelbraunen, rostfarben gesäumten Mittelfedern ausgenommen, gelblich rostrot oder dunkel fuchsrot. Alle grösseren Flügeldeckfedern, wie die Schwingen, sind schwärzlichbraun, erstere mit bräunlichgrauen Säumen und schmutzig gelblichbraunen Spitzen, letztere mit gelbbräunlichen Säumen. Die unteren Flügeldeckfedern sind schön rostrot; die Schwingen auf der unteren Seite braungrau, mit einer weissrötlichen Kante auf der breiten Fahne; der Schwanz auf seiner unteren Seite licht rostrot.

An **jüngeren Männchen** ist das Weisse am Vorderkopfe von geringerer Breite, die schwarzen Federn an der Gurgel haben weissliche Spitzenränder, die rostrote Farbe an der Oberbrust und am Schwanze ist blasser; das Weisse an der Unterbrust ausgedehnter; das Aschgrau der oberen Teile ist mit gelblichem Braun überlaufen, und die Flügelfedern haben breitere lichtbraune Ränder.

Ganz anders sehen diese Vögel in ihrem **Herbstkleide** nach zurückgelegter Mauser aus, weil da die meisten Federn anders gefärbte Ränder haben, welche die Hauptfarbe verdecken; nur die durchschimmernde schwarze Kehle und rostrote Brust unterscheiden sie dann von den Weibchen ihrer Art. So hat das alte Männchen im September zwar alle oben beschriebenen Farben, allein die Federn an den oberen Teilen haben braungraue, an den unteren breite schmutzig weisse, an Stirn und Wangen aber licht bräunliche Ränder, die jene schönen Farben so weit verdecken, dass Oberkopf, Nacken, Schultern und Rücken schmutzig braungrau, die Zügel bräunlichweiss und schwärzlich gemischt, die Wangen, Kehle und Gurgel grauweiss und schwarz gewölkt, die Oberbrust und Seiten weiss und hell rostrot gewölkt erscheinen; die Flügelfedern haben dann noch ihre vollständigen (viel breiteren) weisslich gelbbraunen Einfassungen, selbst die rostroten Schwanzfedern noch lichtere Säumchen.

Alle diese anders gefärbten Kanten reiben sich nach und nach, ehe sich der Vogel von neuem mausert, an den grossen Federn zum Teil, an dem kleinen Gefieder aber ganz ab, sodass der Vogel kurz vor der Mauser ganz anders aussieht als nach derselben und man kaum glauben sollte, dass ohne eine zweifache Mauser (die doch hier nicht stattfindet) eine so mächtige Veränderung vorgehen könnte.

Bei ihrer Ankunft in unseren Gegenden erscheinen die Männchen, besonders die jüngeren, gewöhnlich mit noch vorhandenen Überresten des Herbstkleides, und bei den letzteren sind jene missfarbenen Federränder so breit, dass sie selbst im Laufe des Sommers bis zur Mauser sich nicht ganz verlieren, was bei ganz alten immer geschieht. In wärmeren Ländern reibt sich jedoch das Gefieder noch weit stärker ab als bei uns, und ich habe in **Italien** geschossene männliche Sommervögel dieser Art gesehen, an welchen dies so stark war, dass selbst das Dunengefieder stellenweise zum Vorschein kam, was an hier lebenden nie vorkommt. Warum bei diesem Vogel, wie auch beim **Hausrotschwanz**, das Abreiben der Federränder weit stärker ist als bei vielen anderen Sängern, lässt sich teils aus ihrer grossen Unruhe, teils und vorzüglich aber aus der Natur ihres Aufenthalts erklären; die rauhen und scharfen Kanten der Felsen, Steine und Baumhöhlen, mit denen sie so häufig in Berührung kommen, selbst vielleicht auch eine etwas verschiedene Textur oder sprödere Masse des Gefieders tragen wahrscheinlich hierzu das meiste bei.

Das **Weibchen** sieht ganz anders aus als der männliche Frühlingsvogel; mit dem Männchen im Herbstkleide hat es mehr Ähnlichkeit, und vom Weibchen des **Hausrotschwanzes** unterscheidet es sich durch ein weit lichteres, bräunlicheres Kolorit und durch das viele mit Rostfarbe vermischte Weiss an den unteren Teilen.

Die Zügel sind rostgelblich, grau gemischt; Stirn, Scheitel, Wangen, Hinterhals, Rücken, Schultern und die kleinen Flügeldeckfedern rötlich braungrau oder matt graubraun; die Kehle und Gurgel schmutzig gelblichweiss, zur Seite graulich, was oft einen Schein wie ein herablaufender Streif bildet; die Kropfgegend und Seiten der Oberbrust rostbräunlich und weiss gewölkt, mit graulicher Mischung, welch letztere an den grau gefleckten Unterschenkeln und in den Weichen herrschender wird; die unteren Schwanzdeckfedern dunkel rostgelb; der Steiss (Bürzel), die oberen Schwanzdeckfedern und der Schwanz wie am Männchen, nur schmutziger oder bleicher, auf der äusseren Fahne der äussersten roten Schwanzfeder nach dem Ende zu aber noch mit einem dunkelbraunen Strich; zuweilen haben auch noch mehrere von den roten Federn vor ihrem Ende eine dunkelbraune Zeichnung. Alle grossen Flügelfedern sind matt dunkelbraun, mit hell gelbbraunen oder schmutzig rostgelben Kanten, und die grossen Deckfedern mit roströtlichen Spitzen; die unteren Flügeldeckfedern sind schmutzig rostgelb, die Schwingen von unten hell braungrau, mit rötlichweissen Kanten an der breiten Fahne.

Manche **Weibchen** bekommen, unabhängig vom Alter, eine schwarzgrau gewölkte Kehle und an der Brust mehr Rostfarbe, sodass sie dann dem jungen Männchen im ersten Herbstkleide sehr ähnlich sehen. Das **Herbstkleid der Weibchen** ist von ihrem Frühlingskleide nur wenig verschieden, ja man kann annehmen, dass letzteres schlechter aussieht als ersteres, weil manche lebhaftere Farbenanflüge desselben sich teils abgerieben haben, teils verbleicht sind.

Die **jungen Vögel** in ihrem Nestgefieder, also vor der ersten Mauser, ähneln ihren Eltern nur in Farbe und Zeichnung der Flügel- und Schwanzfeder, sonst sehen sie ganz anders aus. Alle oberen Teile sind auf braungrauem, ins Olivenfarbige fallendem Grunde schwärzlich gewellt und schmutzig rostgelb getüpfelt, denn die grünlich braungrauen Federn haben einen halbmondförmigen schwarzen Fleck an der Spitze und einen schmutzig rostgelben rundlichen Fleck in der Mitte auf dem Schafte; Kehle und Gurgel sind schmutzig gelblichweiss, schwarzgrau punktiert und bespritzt; an der dunklen rostgelblichen Oberbrust und in den Seiten werden diese dunklen Punkte, welche auf dem Rande jeder Feder stehen, bemerklicher und zusammenhängender, sodass sie undeutliche Wellen bilden, auf der schmutzig weissen Unterbrust verlieren sie sich aber ganz; die After- und unteren Schwanzdeckfedern sind einfarbig dunkel rostgelb, die hell rostfarbigen Bürzelfedern aber schwärzlich gewellt. Flügel und Schwanz sind dunkler als an den Alten, die Einfassungen der Flügelfedern beinahe licht rostbraun, der dunkelbraune Streif auf der äussersten roten Schwanzfeder ist aber nicht immer ein Zeichen des weiblichen

Geschlechts, denn in diesem Kleide sind **Männchen** und **Weibchen** äusserlich nicht zu unterscheiden. Ihr Augenstern ist graubraun; der Schnabel von unten fleischfarben, die Mundwinkel gelb; die Füsse nach der Ferse zu schmutzig fleischbraun, die Zehensohlen gelblich. Sie ähneln den Jungen des **Hausrotschwanzes** sehr, sind aber viel lichter, und ihre vorherrschende Farbe fällt mehr ins Gelbe, bei jenen aber ins Aschgraue. Dem **jungen Rotkehlchen** sind sie bis auf Flügel und Schwanz ganz ähnlich, auch der jungen **Nachtigall**, die aber von oben mehr rotbraun aussieht, auch anders gefärbte Flügel- und Schwanzfedern und stets weissliche Füsse hat.

Dies Kleid legen die Jungen früher Brut schon Ende Juli oder Anfang August ab, die von später Hecke aber erst, wenn sich die Alten mausern, zu Ende August.

Eigentliche **Spielarten** sind mir unter diesen Vögeln noch nicht vorgekommen, und die, welche man in naturgeschichtlichen Werken hierher gerechnet hat, sind keine zufälligen Abänderungen, sondern gehören bloss als Alters-, Geschlechts- und Jahreszeitsverschiedenheiten teils zu dieser Art, teils zum **Hausrotschwanz**, denn beide **Rotschwänze** wurden nur zu oft miteinander verwechselt und ihre Geschichte untereinander gemengt.

AUFENTHALT

In ganz **Europa** wird dieser Vogel angetroffen, im Norden sogar bis zum arktischen Kreise hinauf, im Süden und Osten überall, auch im nördlichen **Asien**. Es ist mir kein Teil des gemässigten Europa bekannt, wo er sich nicht fände, ja er gehört in den meisten Ländern unseres Erdteiles unter die gemeinen Vögel. So ist er auch in **Deutschland** allenthalben gemein; bloss solche Gegenden, die weder Bäume noch Buschwerk haben, im ganzen also doch nur unbedeutende Strecken, vermissen ihn.

Es ist ein **Zugvogel**, als welcher er bloss in der wärmeren Jahreszeit bei uns verweilt und den Winter über in heissen Ländern, vielleicht tief in **Afrika**, wohnt. Er zieht, wie andere Vögel dieser Gattung, bloss des Nachts, im Frühjahr einzeln, im Herbst familienweise, und ist einer von denjenigen Zugvögeln, welche durch ihr Erscheinen den Eintritt warmer Frühlingswitterung bei uns verkündigen. Man hört seine Stimme meistens schon in den letzten Tagen des März, doch geschieht der Hauptzug derjenigen, welche den Sommer über nördlicher wohnen, erst im

April und dauert bis etwa um die Mitte dieses Monats. Im Herbst beginnt ihr Fortzug schon Mitte August, wo sie dann aber nicht sehr eilen und durch den ganzen September hindurch ziehen, sodass man einzelne noch zu Ende dieses Monats oder gar noch zu Anfang Oktober bei uns sieht, was aber gewöhnlich junge Vögel sind. Solche sind dann meistens so fett, dass man glauben möchte, das Fett behindere sie, die Reise zu machen.

Ob man gleich den **Gartenrotschwanz** unter die Waldvögel (Bewohner des Waldes) zählen muss, so darf man dieses doch nicht im strengsten Sinne nehmen; denn sein Lieblingsaufenthalt sind Bäume und Gebüsch in der Nähe menschlicher Wohnorte, besonders Baumgärten. Dabei mag übrigens die Gegend eben oder gebirgig sein, wenn es nur nicht ganz an Bäumen fehlt, so ist er bei Dörfern und Städten überall, selbst in denselben und nahe bei den Häusern. Seine Lieblingsbäume sind die Kopfweiden; er bewohnt daher die Anpflanzungen von diesen Bäumen sehr gern, und in hiesiger Gegend gibt es keine, welche im Sommer nicht von diesen Vögeln besucht würden. Nicht allein bei den Dörfern und Städten, auf Angern und Viehweiden, sondern auch in einsamen Gegenden und tief im Walde, an den Flussufern u.s.w., sucht er mit Kopfweiden bepflanzte Plätze zu seinem Aufenthalt. Einzeln bewohnt er auch den nicht zu dichten Hochwald, aber nicht den von Nadelholz, es müsste denn vielleicht ein mit Laubholz besetzter Bach durch denselben fliessen und auch Kopfweiden hier stehen. Immer zieht er diese Bäume allen anderen vor. Man sieht ihn auch oft auf Häusern und altem Gemäuer, welche an die Gärten und an Buschwerk stossen, doch bei weitem weniger als den **Hausrotschwanz**, dagegen ebenso gern wie diesen in felsigen Gegenden, selbst auf kahlen Gebirgen, und zuweilen in einer Höhe, wo längst die Holzvegetation aufhört. Aber auch in Gebirgsgegenden wohnt er gern in der Nähe menschlicher Wohnorte, in mit Wald, Viehweiden und Dörfern abwechselnden Tälern und hat es gern, wenn sein Aufenthaltsort nicht gar zu wasserarm ist. Man trifft ihn daher auch in ebenen Gegenden gern bei Teichen, Flüssen und Wassergräben an.

Bei ihrer Ankunft im Frühling sieht man diese Vögel meistens nur auf Bäumen und viel mehr an erhabenen Orten, als bei ihrem Wegzuge, wo sie sich auch im niedrigen Gebüsch zu verbergen wissen und sich häufig darin aufhalten, selbst die Beete mit hohen Pflanzen, Bohnen, Samenrüben und dergleichen in der Nähe von jenen besuchen. Sie durchhüpfen es aber nicht so wie die Grasmücken, sondern betragen sich da mehr wie die Erdsänger, durchflattern das Gebüsch, gehen aber seltener auf den Boden unter demselben. Ausser der Zeit ihres Wegzuges, nämlich im Frühling und Vorsommer, leben sie viel freier, am liebsten auf Bäumen von mittlerer Höhe (wie die Kopfweiden), doch sieht man sie auch häufig auf hohen Bäumen. Sie suchen sich da wenig im Inneren der Baumkronen zu verbergen, sitzen vielmehr gern auf freien Ästen, auf den unteren dürren Zweigen der Bäume, auch auf Felsenspitzen und Absätzen an schroffen Felsenwänden, auf alten Mauern und auf den Firsten der Dächer, selbst auf dem Gipfel eines Baumes, fliegen von da auch häufig auf die Erde und wechseln so oft ihren Platz, dass sie sich dadurch bald bemerklich machen. Sie übernachten in hohlen Bäumen oder in Löchern der Mauern und Felsen.

EIGENSCHAFTEN

Unser **Gartenrotschwanz** oder, wie man gewöhnlich diesen Vogel nennt, das **Rotschwänzchen**, ist ein ungemein lebhaftes, unruhiges und fröhliches Vögelchen. Es ist in steter Bewegung; im Hüpfen und Fliegen gleich gewandt, hurtig und munter, neckt es sich gern mit anderen Vögeln, jagt und beisst sich mit seinesgleichen und macht sich immer etwas zu schaffen. Es ist listig und scheu, nur die nahe Umgebung macht es zutraulicher gegen die Menschen, was sich aber verliert, sobald es sich verfolgt sieht. Nur selten sitzt es lange an einer Stelle, dann aber allemal mit hochgebogenen Fersen und erhabener Brust, selbst auf dem Erdboden, wo es in schnellen, grossen Sprüngen hinhüpft und hier, wie auf Zweigen sitzend, stets ein keckes Ansehen hat. In den Baumkronen hüpft es nicht von Ast zu Ast, sondern flattert mehr durch dieselben hin und macht dabei alle Augenblicke Halt, doch auch nur auf sehr kurze Zeit. Dieses Betragen ist von dem der Grasmücken wie der Erdsänger sehr verschieden.

Eine besondere Eigenheit der **Rotschwänze**, die sie vor allen ähnlichen Vögeln auszeichnet, ist eine zitternde oder schüttelnde Bewegung des Schwanzes, von oben nach unten, aber nicht seitwärts. Unser **Gartenrotschwanz** sitzt daher eigentlich niemals ganz still; denn wenn er auch ganz ruhig scheint oder einmal traurig aussieht (was übrigens selten der Fall ist), so macht doch sein Schwanz von Zeit zu Zeit jene schüttelnde Bewegung, die heftiger wird, wenn er etwas Auffallendes bemerkt, wozu er denn auch noch schnelle Verbeugungen mit dem

Kopfe und der Brust macht. Bei jeder Pause im Fortspringen durch die Zweige oder auf dem Erdboden schüttelt er den Schwanz, welcher daher auch fast immer unter den Flügeln getragen wird. Diese Gewohnheit, auch ohne besondere Veranlassung den Schwanz auf eine so eigene Art zu bewegen, macht die kecken **Rotschwänze** schon von weitem kenntlich.

Sein Flug ist sehr schnell und leicht, in kurzen Bogen, fast hüpfend. Im Wanderfluge werden dagegen die Bogen grösser gemacht; aber weil sie überhaupt nicht gleich gross sind, so sieht auch dieser Flug etwas unregelmässig aus. Er ähnelt dem des **Rotkehlchens** oder einiger Meisen.

Seine Lockstimme ist ein heller Pfiff, dessen Ton aber doch sanft und angenehm klingt, wie **füid** oder **hüid**, dem meistens ein schmatzendes **Tick tick** angehängt wird. Ist der Vogel ruhig, so pfeift er bloss **füid**; ist er aber fröhlich oder droht ihm Gefahr, so ruft er **füid tick tick**; nähert sich gar ein Feind, z. B. seinem Neste, so wird das **Tick tick*** schnell und oft wiederholt, ehe einmal das pfeifende **Hüid** ausgerufen wird. Das Pfeifen hat grosse Ähnlichkeit mit dem Lockton des **Fitis** und des **Zilpzalp**, klingt aber stets stärker oder etwas schneidender; der Unterschied ist indessen so subtil, dass er nur dem Kennerohr bemerklich wird. In Not und Angst hört man einen kreischend quäkenden Ton, welchen auch die eben ausgeflogenen Jungen häufiger ausstossen; sonst rufen diese wie die Alten **tick tick tick**. Übrigens lässt dieser Vogel seine Stimme oft hören, und das Männchen gehört auch unter die angenehmen Sänger des Waldes. Es singt ausserordentlich fleissig, von da an, wo es uns dadurch im Frühjahr seine Ankunft ankündigt, bis kurz nach Johannis, anfänglich fast den ganzen Tag bis zur Abenddämmerung, besonders anhaltend und kräftig aber früh schon, wenn sich im Osten kaum erst ein lichter Schein der anrückenden Morgendämmerung zeigt oder, wie man zu sagen pflegt, wenn der Tag zu Grauen anfängt. Es sitzt dabei meistens in den mittleren Zweigen eines nicht gar hohen Baumes, am Tage aber oft ziemlich frei, sogar zuweilen im Gipfel eines Baumes, auf einem Dachfirst und anderen erhabenen Orten oder in den unteren trockenen Zweigen der Weidenbäume. Der Gesang erfreut vorzüglich, wenn man ihn im Frühling zum erstenmal hört, wo er noch nicht so, als späterhin, von besseren Gesängen überschrieen wird. Er besteht höchstens aus drei Strophen, die in kurzen Intervallen aufeinander folgen, und hat etwas Melancholisches, weswegen die Melodie wie aus Moll klingt. Der Ton ist sehr angenehm, sanft, dabei laut genug, fast flötenartig, und die eine Strophe ähnelt einem hellen Wiehern. An

---

* Weil dieses **Tick** Ähnlichkeit mit dem Schnalzen hat, was man hervorbringt, wenn man die Zungenspitze vorn an das Zahnfleisch der oberen Vorderzähne setzt und schnell abzieht, mit welchem Ton man die jungen Schweine zu locken pflegt, so nennt man unseren Vogel in manchen Gegenden **Saulocker**.

schwülen Tagen und bei bevorstehendem Regenwetter hört man diese schwermütige Melodie besonders häufig und anhaltend. Im ganzen hat sie einige Ähnlichkeit mit dem Gesange des **Hausrotschwanzes**, aber der Ton ist viel angenehmer und flötenartiger. Dieser eigentümliche Gesang wird indessen nicht selten noch mit kurzen Strophen aus anderen Vogelgesängen verwebt, und es gibt Männchen, welche eine nicht geringe Fertigkeit hierin zeigen; andere scheinen dagegen nicht auf die um sie lebenden Vögel in dieser Hinsicht zu achten. Besonders angenehm mag jenen der Finkenschlag sein, denn sie verflechten ihn öfters mit ihrem eigenen Gesange, wobei dieser jedoch wenig von seinem eigentümlichen Charakter verliert.

Im gezähmten Zustande zeigt sich dieser Vogel sehr weichlich und hält sich bei der besten Pflege kaum zwei Jahre lang. Man wartet ihn ungefähr wie die **Nachtigall** und steckt ihn auch in einen solchen Käfig, worin man diese zu halten pflegt. Die Bauern halten ihn häufig in ihren Wohnungen zum Fliegenfangen; aber er dauert hier auch nicht lange, höchstens und sehr selten etwas über ein halbes Jahr.

NAHRUNG

Fliegen, Mücken, kleine Schmetterlinge und allerlei kleine zwei- und vierflügelige Insekten fangen sie teils im Fluge, teils im Sitzen, seltener kleine Käferchen. Sie sind im Verfolgen der fliegenden Insekten so gewandt wie die Fliegenfänger und fliegen zuweilen hoch nach ihnen in die Luft, lesen aber auch kleine Räupchen und andere Insektenlarven und Puppen von den Blättern und Zweigen ab oder gehen nach ihnen auf die Erde, wo sie zuweilen ziemlich lange darnach suchend herumhüpfen. Häufig sieht man sie aus der Höhe eines Baumes zur Erde herabfliegen, ein Würmchen aufnehmen und damit wieder auf ihren Baum eilen, wobei man ihr scharfes Gesicht bewundern muss. Auf den Angern, Viehtriften und auf frischgegrabenen Gartenbeeten lesen sie auch kleine Regenwürmer auf. Bei nasskalter Witterung suchen sie die in den Mauerritzen sich verbergenden Fliegen an den Häusern, welche an die Gärten stossen, hervor, sind deshalb auch gern an Gartenmauern und Felsenwänden, die gegen Mittag liegen. Beim Aufsuchen und Fangen ihrer Nahrungsmittel sind sie äusserst behende und gewandt. Sie leben übrigens mehr von vollkommenen und fliegenden Insekten als von Insektenlarven und kriechendem Gewürm.

Gegen den Herbst begeben sie sich mehr ins niedere Gebüsch, woselbst sie Insekten in Menge antreffen, fressen dann aber auch Beeren, als Johannisbeeren, rote und schwarze Holunderbeeren, auch Faulbaumbeeren. Sie leben dann stiller und verborgener als im Frühjahr und Vorsommer.

Im Käfig gibt man ihnen anfänglich Fliegen, Ameisenpuppen, Mehlwürmer, kleine Regenwürmer und im Herbst Holunderbeeren und gewöhnt sie damit nach und nach an das Nachtigallenfutter. Sie werden bald zahm, dauern aber nicht lange. Frisches Wasser zum Trunk und Bade darf ihnen nicht fehlen, denn sie baden sich auch in der Freiheit ungemein gern und oft. Lässt man sie frei in der Stube fliegen, so fangen sie sehr geschickt Fliegen und halten sich, besonders wenn sie mitunter Beeren bekommen, zuweilen recht gut und durch den ganzen Winter, häufig aber auch nicht; denn viele dieser weichlichen Vögel stossen sich gleich anfänglich an der weissen Decke und an den Fenstern den Kopf wund und sterben dann sehr bald. Sie gehen nicht leicht an Brotkrümchen und andere Abfälle von menschlichen Nahrungsmitteln; deswegen sind sie aber auch sehr geschickt, die Stuben von den lästigen Fliegen zu säubern, und eignen sich dazu besser als die allbeliebten **Rotkehlchen**, denen das Fliegenfangen weit schwerer fällt und die sich deshalb gar bald an andere Speisen gewöhnen.

FORTPFLANZUNG

In Deutschland nisten sie allenthalben in Gärten, in Anpflanzungen von Kopfweiden, in Laubholzwäldern und in felsigen Gegenden, wo sich hohle Bäume, Mauer- oder Felsenlöcher befinden. In hiesiger Gegend nisten sie bei allen Dörfern, wo es in den Gärten alte Birn- oder Äpfelbäume, und in den Umgebungen Anger mit alten Weidenbäumen gibt, mag auch sonst weit und breit kein eigentlicher Wald sein. Nicht allein in allen grossen Anlagen von alten Kopfweiden, sondern häufig auch da, wo diese, oft nur in einer Reihe, die Ufer eines von einem Dorfe zum anderen, oft über freies Feld führenden Wassergrabens, Fischteiches u.s.w. bekränzen, in den Umgebungen der Städte, selbst in grossen Baumgärten mitten in Dörfern und kleinen Städten und an vielen anderen Orten, an Waldrändern und mitten im Walde findet man zur Brutzeit auch diese Vögel, doch so, dass jedes Pärchen ein kleines Revier inne hat und darin kein anderes seiner Art leidet. Sie sind daher bei aller Gemeinheit doch nur einzeln über eine Gegend verbreitet. Das Nest steht stets in einer Höhle, die meistens nur einen ganz engen Eingang hat, zuweilen tief unten, zuweilen auch so flach, dass sich einzelne Teile desselben in der Öffnung, die zum Eingang dient, zeigen. Am allerhäufigsten ist es in hohlen Weidenbäumen, und zwar in solchen, wo das Loch zum Einkriechen seitwärts ist, gleichviel, ob dieses weit oder enge, hoch oder niedrig vom Boden sich befindet; doch habe ich es nie in solchen, die unter 56 cm Höhe waren, aber in höheren Bäumen auch nicht über 8,5 m hoch gefunden; bloss in Felsenlöchern steht es zuweilen etwas höher. In hiesiger Gegend findet man es auch häufig in den Löchern und Ritzen der Gartenmauern und in den Wänden und Giebeln an die Gärten stossender Gebäude, in letzteren z. B. in ausgefaulten Balkenköpfen, doch weit seltener als in hohlen Äpfel- und Birnbäumen. Das Schlüpfloch ist zuweilen nicht weiter als nötig ist, um den Vogel durchzulassen, ein andermal aber auch sehr weit, wie z. B. in solchen hohlen Weiden, welche bloss oben offen sind. Das Nest ist ein ziemlicher Klumpen schlecht verwobener dürrer feiner Würzelchen, trockener Hälmchen, mit Wolle, Haaren und Federn vermengt, hauptsächlich besteht das Innere grösstenteils aus vielen Federn, wozu sie am liebsten Gänsefedern nehmen, die sie auf den Viehweiden auflesen. Es scheint ihnen viel Vergnügen zu machen, solche Federn, welche der Wind in die Luft führt, aufzufangen, ja sie zanken sich um solche sogar zuweilen mit den in ihrer Nähe wohnenden **Feldsperlingen**, welche ebenso gern wie die **Haussperlinge** und noch manche andere Vögel, die mit Federn bauen, solche fliegend auffangen. Sieht man daher im Frühling in der Nähe von Bäumen und Gebüsch sich eine Feder in die Luft erheben, so wird man auch bald einen Vogel herbeieilen und sie auffangen sehen.

In dieses weiche und arme Nestchen legt das Weibchen, meistenteils schon in der letzten Hälfte des April, fünf bis sieben Eier; doch findet man auch, aber sehr selten, zuweilen einmal acht Stück in einem Neste. Sie sind von einem lieblichen Ansehen, schön eiförmig, an einem Ende ziemlich spitz, von ungemein zarter, glatter, aber wenig glänzender Schale, und ihre Farbe ist ein schönes, lichtes Blaugrün oder eine helle Grünspanfarbe ohne alle Flecke.

So wie bei vielen anderen Sängern löst auch hier das Männchen sein Weibchen beim Brüten in den Mittagsstunden ab, und nach dreizehn- bis vierzehntägiger Brut schlüpfen die Jungen aus den Eiern. Sie brüten so eifrig, dass sie öfters nicht herausfliegen, wenn man mit einem Stocke an den Baum schlägt, ja sich zuweilen über den Eiern oder den eben ausgeschlüpften Jungen ergreifen lassen. Sie sind überhaupt sehr um ihre Brut besorgt und verraten das Nest, wenn man sich diesem nähert, durch ängstliches Schreien, zumal wenn sie Junge haben, wo sie ihrem Störenfried öfters ganz nahe um den Kopf herum fliegen. Viele leiden es, wenn man ihnen ein Ei nimmt oder die übrigen betastet, andere lassen aber hierauf auch zuweilen das Nest liegen; am wenigsten eigensinnig findet man in diesem Falle diejenigen, welche in der Nähe menschlicher Wohnungen, an gangbaren Wegen u.s.w. nisten. Die Jungen sind, sobald sie sich fühlen lernen, ziemlich scheu und verlassen das Nest auch ohne besondere Störung sehr bald, sitzen dann auf einem horizontalen Zweige alle nahe beisammen und wedeln schon mit den Schwänzen, wenn diese gleich kaum die Hälfte ihrer Länge erreicht haben, und sie eben erst ausgeflogen sind. Sie werden mit kleinem Gewürm, mit Fliegen und anderen Insekten aufgefüttert, und die Alten sind so besorgt um sie, dass jene in den ersten Tagen nach dem Ausfliegen dieser fast nicht ruhig werden, ihr **Füid tick tick tick, ticktickticktick** unter beständigem Hin- und Herfliegen, unter zahllosen Bücklingen und mit stetem Schütteln des Schwanzes, wenn sie sich setzen, ausrufen und so ohne ihren Willen jedem Feinde die Jungen verraten.

Sobald die letzteren selbst Insekten fangen lernen, machen die Alten zu einem zweiten Gehecke Anstalt; doch nisten sie niemals zweimal in einem Jahre in derselben Höhle. Sie suchen allemal eine neue, meistens in der Nähe der ersteren, dazu auf, aber im kommenden Jahre nisten sie häufig wieder in einer von diesen, sodass es Baumhöhlen gibt, in welchen sie, wenn diese nicht früher von anderen Vögeln in Besitz genommen wurden, alle Jahre brüten. Zwei Bruten machen sie alljährlich immer, und wurden ihnen vielleicht früh genug bei der ersten die Eier geraubt, so bauen sie wohl drei Nester, aber es wird dann selten aus der letzten Brut etwas, weswegen es auch nur höchst selten vorkommt.

Der **Kuckuck** legt zuweilen sein Ei in das Nest dieser Vögel; dieser Fall muss aber selten sein, weil er meinem Vater und mir noch nie vorgekommen ist.

FEINDE

Die alten Vögel werden manchmal vom **Sperber** gefangen, und ihre Brut ist der Zerstörung durch **Katzen, Marder, Wiesel, Ratten** und **Mäuse** häufig ausgesetzt. Weil sie in der Nähe menschlicher Wohnorte so oft brüten, wird ihnen auch ihr Nest häufig von losen Buben zu Grunde gerichtet. **Eichelhäher** und **Elstern** fangen die Jungen, ehe sie noch recht flüchtig werden, oft weg.

NUTZEN

Ihr Fleisch ist eine angenehme und wohlschmeckende Speise. Da sie im Herbst meistenteils sehr fett sind, so benutzt man die zufällig gefangenen sehr gern dazu, obwohl man sie eigentlich deshalb nicht fängt oder ihnen deswegen, wenigstens in den meisten Gegenden **Deutschlands**, nicht besonders nachstellt, was aber in **Italien** und anderen südlichen Ländern auf dem Herbstzuge mehr geschehen soll.

Sie nützen übrigens durch Wegfangen vieler beschwerlicher und schädlicher Insekten, weshalb sie auch in den Wohnstuben der Landleute zum Wegfangen der lästigen Fliegen gern gehalten werden. Das Männchen erfreut uns durch seinen anmutigen Gesang und hilft dadurch die Reize des Frühlings erhöhen.

SCHADEN

Sie tun keinen; denn wenn man sie auch des Bienenraubes beschuldigt, so hat man gewiss Unrecht, indem man wahrscheinlich **Drohnen** für Arbeitsbienen angesehen hat und ich für unmöglich halte, dass ein so kleiner Vogel eine **ganze Biene mit dem Stachel** verschlucken kann, ohne sich den empfindlichsten Schaden durch den Stich des herausgedrückten Stachels, welcher noch bei der toten Biene heftig verwundet, zuzufügen, welches sogar den Tod unausbleiblich zur Folge haben würde.

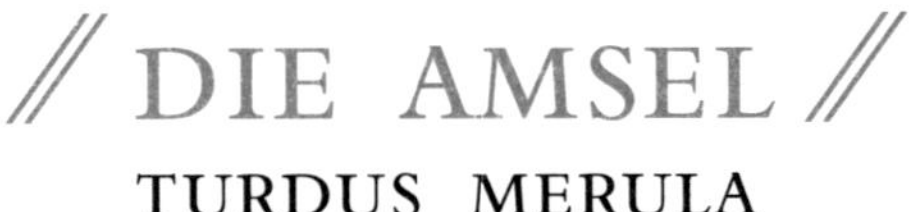

// DIE AMSEL //

TURDUS MERULA

Schwarzdrossel, gemeine, schwarze, gemeinschwarze Amsel, Kohlamsel, Amazl, Amselmerle, Merle, Merel, Merlane, Lyster. Die Weibchen und jungen Vögel: Graudrossel, Grauamsel, Stockamsel, Bergamsel, Braunmerle.

Taf. 71

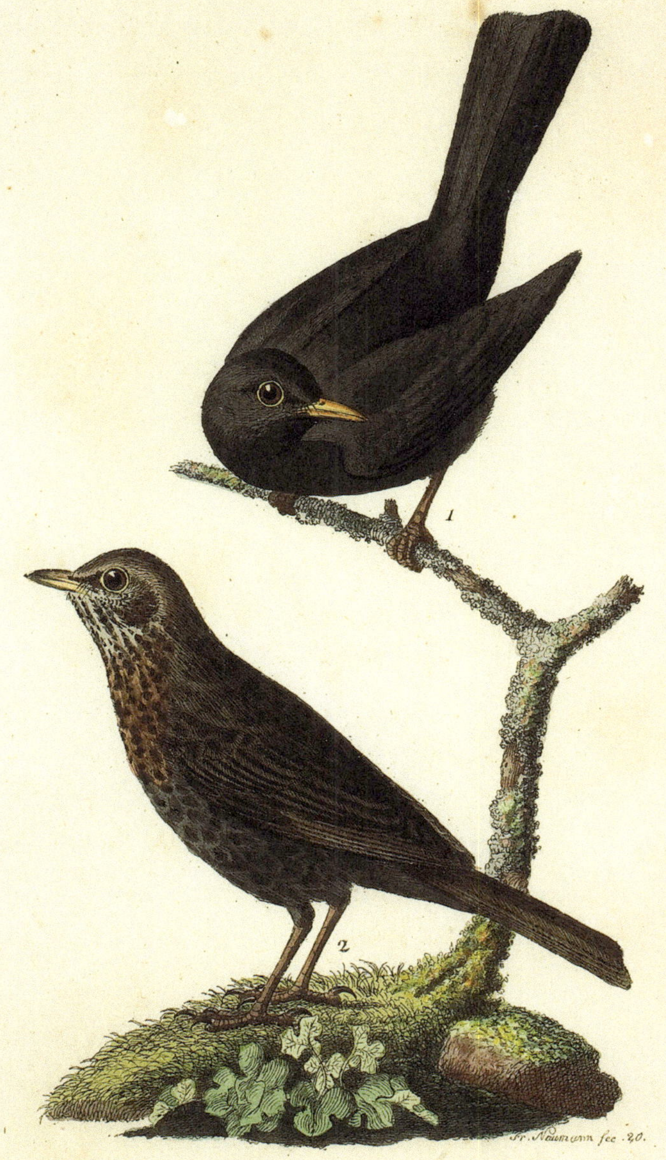

TURDUS merula. *Schwarzdrossel.* 1. M. 2. W.

KENNZEICHEN DER ART

Männchen ganz schwarz, mit gelbem Schnabel- und Augenlidrändchen. **Weibchen** und **junger Vogel** schwarzbraun, mit weissgrauer Kehle und undeutlichen dunklen Flecken am Vorderhalse.

BESCHREIBUNG

Dieser bekannte Vogel ist einer der grösseren unter seinen Gattungsverwandten. Die **Weibchen** sind gewöhnlich etwas grösser als die **Männchen**, und die Farben des Gefieders sind unter beiden Geschlechtern so verschieden, dass sie sonst von vielen, besonders von den Vogelstellern, für zwei verschiedene Arten gehalten wurden, wozu vielleicht noch der merkwürdige Umstand beigetragen haben mag, dass manche **junge Männchen** in der ersten Mauser ein Gewand bekommen, das dem der Weibchen sehr ähnlich sieht, während die Mehrzahl sich den alten Männchen ähnlich färbt.

Die Länge der Amsel beträgt 23,6 bis 24,7 cm, die Flügelbreite 37,7 bis 38,3 cm; der Schwanz ist 10,6 cm lang, am Ende fast gerade, doch die Seitenfedern etwas kürzer, sodass das Ende dadurch eigentlich einen ganz flachen Bogen bildet; die ruhenden Flügel bedecken kaum die Hälfte desselben.

Der Schnabel ist 17 bis 20 mm lang, stark, dem Rücken des Oberschnabels nach sanft gebogen, die Unterkinnlade beinahe gerade; er ist im ganzen nur nach vorn sehr wenig zusammengedrückt, übrigens rundlich. Seine Farbe ist nach Alter und Geschlecht bald ganz hochgelb, bald an der Spitze braun, bald ganz dunkelbraun und nur an den Mundkanten gelb, Rachen und Zunge hochgelb, die Mundwinkel und das kahle Augenlidrändchen gelb; erstere mit grossen schwarzen Bartborsten und die Schnabelwurzel nebst den Zügeln mit untermengten schwarzen Barthärchen besetzt. Das Nasenloch ist wie bei anderen Drosseln, die Iris der ziemlich grossen Augen dunkelbraun.

Die starken Füsse sind schwärzlich, schwarzbraun oder schmutzig braun, die Zehensohlen am lichtesten; ihrer Bedeckung nach sind die Läufe meist gestiefelt, die

Zehenrücken grob getäfelt, die Zehensohlen feinwarzig, und die schwarzbraunen Nägel sind nicht sehr gross und beschreiben nur einen flachen Bogen. Die Höhe des Laufs beträgt fast 3,5 cm; die Länge der Mittelzehe mit dem Nagel 3 cm; die der Hinterzehe mit der Kralle 22 mm.

Das **alte Männchen** ist überall einfarbig schwarz, ohne Glanz, bloss am Unterleibe etwas matter wie oben; die Füsse schwärzlich oder schwarzbraun, mit etwas lichteren Sohlen; der Schnabel und das Augenlidrändchen im **Frühling** einfarbig, brennend hochgelb, eine zu dem kohlschwarzen Gefieder ungemein schön abstechende Farbe, welche sich oft dem Orangegelben nähert; im **Herbst** ist dagegen dieses Gelb matter, und die Schnabelspitze ist meistens braun.

Das **Weibchen** sieht dagegen ganz anders aus; es trägt in der Regel folgende Farben: Stirn, Scheitel, Hinterhals, Rücken, Schultern, überhaupt alle oberen Teile sind sehr dunkel olivenbraun, fast schwarzbraun, die Stirn und Halsseiten am lichtesten, Steiss und Schwanz am dunkelsten, am letzteren die inneren Fahnen der Federn schwarz, die äusserste Feder mit einem feinen lichtgrauen, fast verwischten Aussensäumchen. Die Flügelfedern haben auf den Aussenfahnen die Farbe des Rückens, auf den inneren sind sie matt dunkelbraun, die grossen Schwingen mit bräunlichgrauen lichteren Aussensäumchen, besonders nach dem Ende hin. Die Wangen sind dunkelbraun, mit etwas lichteren Schaftstrichen; das Kinn grauweiss; die Kehle auf grauweissem, schmutzig rostfarben gemischtem Grunde mit dunkelbraunen streifenartigen Flecken; Gurgel und Kropfgegend schmutzig lichtrostbraun, mit einem dunkelbraunen, fast runden Fleckchen an der Spitze jeder Feder, welche Farbe und Zeichnung sich auf der Oberbrust verliert und in ein tiefes (schwärzliches) Aschgrau übergeht, das den ganzen übrigen Unterleib einnimmt, an der Brust meistens aber noch mit lichteren Schaftstrichen und bräunlichen Federspitzen abwechselt; die Unterseite der Flügel ist dunkelgrau. Der Schnabel ist im **Frühling** bei alten weiblichen Vögeln nur an der Spitze braun, übrigens wie das Augenlidrändchen goldgelb, im **Herbst**, zumal bei jüngeren, ganz braun, zuweilen olivenbraun, nur die Kanten und Mundwinkel sowie das Augenlidrändchen sind dunkelgelb oder braungelb. Die Füsse sind schmutzig rötlichbraun, an den Zehensohlen gelbgrau, im Frühling auch dunkler als im Herbst. Nach mehrmaligem Mausern verlieren sich die dunkelbraunen Flecken an der Gurgel und am Kropfe fast ganz, der übrige Unterleib wird reiner dunkel aschgrau, und der Schnabel erscheint bei solchen im Frühling beinahe ganz gelb, bloss am Rücken des Oberkiefers und an der Spitze zeigt sich etwas Braun. Man findet auch, wiewohl sehr selten, **alte Weibchen**, welche beinahe so schwarz wie die Männchen sind, eine dunkelgrau gewölkte Brust, einen braungelben Schnabel und hellgelbe Augenlider haben.

Die **jungen Männchen**, nach dem ersten Federwechsel, sehen den alten Männchen gleich, nur am Unterleibe zeigen sich noch breite dunkelgraue Federränder, und der Schnabel ist schwärzlich, mit durchschimmerndem Gelb, welches jedoch im künftigen Frühjahr mehr zum Vorschein kommt, aber blasser als bei den alten ist.

Höchst merkwürdig bleibt indes der Umstand, dass man auch junge Männchen im Herbst fängt, welche die Farben des Weibchens tragen und diese im Freien bis zur nächsten Mauser, im Juli des kommenden Jahres, ja im Käfig ihre ganze Lebenszeit hindurch, behalten. Wahrscheinlich sind diese Vögel aus einer späten Brut; denn die **Amsel** brütet in der Regel zweimal im Jahr, und, wenn ihr ein Gehecke zerstört wurde, wohl dreimal. Solche junge Männchen haben in der Tat ein ganz eigenes Ansehen, und sie sind es, die man unter verschiedenen Namen, als **Stockamseln, graue Amseln** u.s.w. für eine besondere Art gehalten hat und hin und wieder noch hält. Um dieser Ursache willen und weil sie doch merklich von der gewöhnlichen Zeichnung der Weibchen abweichen, lasse ich hier eine genaue Beschreibung derselben folgen.

Alle oberen Teile des Körpers sind matt schwarz, die hintersten Schwingen und die grossen Flügeldeckfedern braun gekantet; das Kinn weissgrau; die Kehle schwarz, weissgrau gestreift; der übrige Unterleib matt schwarz, an der Gurgel und Oberbrust mit rostbraunen Federkanten, welche nach den Seiten zu und an der Unterbrust ins Weissgraue fallen. Die rostbraunen Federränder bilden in der Kropfgegend eine Art breiter Querbinde. Die grossen Schwingen sind weissgrau gesäumt; Schnabel und Füsse schwarzbraun; der Rachen gelb; das Augenlidrändchen braungelb. Auch im Februar habe ich ein junges Männchen gefangen, das dem eben beschriebenen, im Herbst gefangenen, vollkommen glich, aber schon einen goldgelben, nur an der Spitze schwarzen Schnabel, orangegelben Rachen und hochgelbe Augenlider hatte. Beide unterhielt ich in einer Kammer, bei gutem Futter und hinlänglich frischer Luft und Sonne, wo sie sich im Juli mauserten und schwarz wie das alte Männchen wurden, auch bei den nachfolgenden Mausern immer schwarz blieben, nur im Herbst einen fast ganz schwarzen Schnabel bekamen, welcher aber jedesmal im Frühling schön gelb wurde.

Nun bleibt uns noch die Beschreibung der **jungen Vögel vor der ersten Mauser** übrig. Sie sehen im ganzen den Weibchen ähnlich, sind aber am Kopfe und Halse sehr stark mit Rostfarbe überlaufen, an den unteren Teilen mit vielen dunkelbraunen Flecken bestreut, welche eine mehr nierenförmige als runde Gestalt haben und die man an der Unterbrust sogar Querflecke oder Mondflecke nennen kann. Die Stirn ist ganz rostfarben, und die Federn auf dem Scheitel, dem Hinterhalse, dem Oberrücken, den Schultern und den meisten Flügeldeckfedern haben hell rostfarbene Schaftstriche, wodurch diese Teile sehr bunt erscheinen. Schnabel und Füsse sind rötlichgrau, die Mundwinkel und Augenlider schmutzig orangegelb.

Männchen und **Weibchen** sehen sich in diesem Alter so ähnlich, dass man sie äusserlich nur dann unterscheiden kann, wenn man beide gegeneinander hält, wo dann das erstere immer etwas dunkler als das letztere aussieht.

Diese Vögel mausern im Juli, und nach der Mauser sieht das Gefieder der alten weiblichen Vögel viel frischer aus als im Frühling, wo es schon etwas abgerieben und abgebleicht ist. Die männlichen alten **Amseln** haben gewöhnlich am Unterleibe mehr oder minder auffallende graue Federsäume, welche sich den Winter hindurch nach und nach abreiben, sodass sie meist erst gegen das Frühjahr im rein schwarzen Kleide erscheinen.

Die jungen Vögel von der ersten Brut mausern mit den alten, die von späterer oft erst im August und September, manche sind sogar im Oktober noch nicht rein ausgemausert. In der Gefangenschaft wird der Schnabel und das Augenlidrändchen nie so schön hochgelb, letzteres sieht sogar oft nur weissgelb aus.

Es gibt unter diesen Vögeln auch mehrere **Spielarten**, doch kommen sie eben nicht häufig vor. Man kennt z. B. eine **ganz weisse** mit weissem oder gelblichem Schnabel und Füssen; eine **perlgraue**, hellgrau mit grauen oder weisslichen Füssen, weissgelbem oder weissem Schnabel, auch mit rötlichem Augenstern; eine **bunte**, schwarz und weiss gefleckte, welches noch die gewöhnlichste ist, die dann auch zuweilen bloss **weissköpfig** erscheint, und ausser einem weissen Kopfe und einzelnen Flecken an den Flügeln und anderwärts schwarz aussieht, an welcher, ausser dem Schnabel und den Augenlidrändchen, wohl auch die Füsse gelb oder gelblich sind.

Ausser diesen ist mir noch eine sehr merkwürdige Spielart vorgekommen; sie war von oben her ganz wie ein gewöhnliches altes Weibchen gefärbt, auch alle unteren Teile hatten die gewöhnlichen Farben, doch dunkler, und die Federn an der

Kehle, Gurgel, der Oberbrust und auf der Mitte der Unterbrust hatten an beiden Seiten auf der Kante hellweisse Längsflecke, sodass der dunkle Grund an den genannten Teilen fleckenartig hellweiss gestreift erschien. Dieser Vogel hatte ein sehr auffallendes Ansehen und schien mir weiblichen Geschlechts zu sein.

AUFENTHALT

Die **Amsel** ist fast über ganz **Europa**, das südlichste und nördlichste kaum ausgenommen, verbreitet; auch soll sie sich im nördlichen **Asien**, bis **Syrien** herab, finden. In allen Ländern des gemässigten Europa ist sie häufig und in **Deutschland** ein allgemein bekannter Vogel, obgleich nirgends herdenweise anzutreffen.

Alle Gegenden in den genannten Ländern, wo es Waldungen mit dichtem Gebüsch gibt, mögen sie aus Laub- oder Nadelholz bestehen oder ebenen, sumpfigen oder gebirgigen Boden haben, gewähren ihnen einen Aufenthalt; besonders lieben sie solche Laubwälder, die unter anderem viel dichtes Unterholz und hohes Dorngebüsch haben und an Flüssen liegen, oder die Dickichte, welche junge Nadelbäume in den Schwarzwäldern bilden, am liebsten, wenn sie mit Wacholderbüschen untermengt sind. Auch in sumpfigen Waldungen, wo viele Erlen und Buschweiden sind, halten sie sich gerne auf. Sie scheinen es sehr gern zu haben, wenn es in der Nähe ihres Aufenthaltes Wasser und kleine Wiesenplätze gibt, obgleich sie selten aufs Freie kommen und, wenn sie darüber müssen, ängstlich eilen. In kleinen, trockenen Feldhölzern halten sie sich daher nur selten lange auf.

Die **Amseln** sind **Stand-**, **Strich-** und **Zugvögel** zugleich; das erstere nämlich sind die, welche die mit Wacholdergebüsch versehenen Schwarzwälder bewohnen, denn sie ziehen nicht weg; das zweite sind die meisten alten Vögel, die in Laubhölzern gebrütet haben, weil sie, bei Mangel an Nahrung, ihren Aufenthaltsort im Winter verändern und sich dahin begeben, wo sie hinlänglich Futter finden. Sind Bäche oder warme Quellen in der Nähe, so verlassen viele auch die Laubwälder nicht, zumal die, welche in düsteren Erlenbrüchen wohnen. Viele, besonders die jungen Vögel, sind indessen wahre **Zugvögel**, und ihr Zug dauert von Mitte September bis Anfang November; man fängt sie in dieser Zeit am häufigsten und sieht sie Ende März zurückkehren, während die Alten schon Anfang dieses Monats an den Orte, wo sie brüten wollen, sich hören lassen. So ist es wenigstens, nach meinen selbst gemachten Erfahrungen, im nördlichen **Deutschland** durchgehends.

Ihre Reisen verrichten sie des Nachts. Sie wagen es nie, am Tage über das freie Feld zu fliegen, halten sich vielmehr immer im dichten Gebüsch nahe der Erde auf, und man sieht sie sehr selten auf hohen Bäumen, beinahe einzig nur dann zuweilen, wenn das Männchen singt, oder wenn sie einmal auf einen grossen Beerenbaum nach den Früchten fliegen. An stillen Herbstabenden hört man oft, wenn eben die Nacht anbricht, ihren freudigen Ruf, womit sie einander zur Reise aufmuntern, im Walde erschallen, obgleich sie meistens nur einzeln ziehen. Man sieht sie niemals in grossen Gesellschaften, selbst sehr selten zu dreien und vieren beisammen. Ihre Nachtruhe halten sie im dichtesten Gebüsch nahe an der Erde, zuweilen auch höher im jungen Stangenholze.

EIGENSCHAFTEN

Die **Amsel** ist ein kluger, vorsichtiger und äussert misstrauischer Vogel; immer auf ihrer Hut, entgeht nichts, was ihr gefährlich werden könnte, ihrer Aufmerksamkeit, selbst in der Nacht nicht. Mit hellgellender Stimme begleitet sie ihre schnelle Flucht und reizt dadurch auch die übrigen Waldbewohner, Vögel und Säugetiere, ein Ähnliches zu tun. In ihrem ganzen Wesen verrät sie sehr viel Munterkeit und Kraft; nur wenn sie sich unbemerkt glaubt, hüpft sie gelassen unter dem Gebüsch auf der Erde hin, seltener in den Zweigen selbst, behält dabei aber immer ihr listiges Ansehen.

Obschon sie eigentlich einen hüpfenden, dem anderer **Drosseln** ähnlichen Gang hat, so kommt doch bei allen auch zuweilen und bei manchen recht häufig vor, dass sie schrittweise oft weite Strecken und öfter wiederholt auf dem Erdboden hinlaufen. So sah ich einst bei einem heftigen Sturmwinde — der ihnen auf dem Freien stets sehr zuwider ist, weil ihre Flugwerkzeuge solchem nicht wohl zu widerstehen vermögen — einen solchen Vogel auf dem ebenen Boden einer lichten, zur Zeit noch dazu entlaubten, schmalen Hecke, um so zu Fuss von einem der grösseren Gebüsche zum anderen zu gelangen, einen Raum von einigen hundert Fuss so schnell durchlaufen wie eine Lerche; ebenso später dasselbe Individuum auf dem Schnee stundenlang in meinem Obstgarten von einem Baumstamme zum anderen, beinahe immer bloss schrittweise, laufen, um das unten an den Stämmen befindliche Moos und angehäufte alte Laub, von welchem zunächst der Schnee weggetaut, nach erstarrten Insekten und namentlich Insektenpuppen zu durchsuchen. Beiläufig gingen auch diese **Amseln** (ein gepaartes Pärchen) nur erst bei heftiger Kälte und hohem Schnee an die so einladend aussehenden Beeren vom **Feuerdorn** und an die **Wacholderbeeren**. Dass indessen auch diese Art im Herbst sehr den reifen **Weintrauben** nachgeht und unter diesen, wie andere Drosseln, besonders den kleinbeerigen, mehr oder weniger gefärbten Rieslingssorten den Vorzug gibt, habe ich erst vor kurzem von einem vereinzelten, diesjährigen jungen Vogel täglich in meinem Garten beobachtet; obgleich die sonst schon Anfang September vollständig reifen Trauben dies im gegenwärtigen ungünstigen Weinjahre Ende Oktober noch nicht erreicht hatten.

Stösst ihm etwas Unerwartetes auf, so wippt er mit dem etwas ausgebreiteten Schwanze aufwärts und ruckt dazu mit den Flügeln, wobei er auch meistenteils seine Stimme hören lässt. Fliegt er von der Erde auf einen Baum, so tut er meistenteils noch einige hastige Sprünge durch die Äste desselben, ehe er weiter fliegt. Der Flug ist, der kürzeren Flügel wegen, nicht so schnell wie der vieler anderer Drosseln, doch immer noch rasch genug, meistenteils bloss flatternd, wobei sie den Körper verschiedentlich wenden, beim Niedersetzen aber die Flügel weniger bewegen und in langen Absätzen gleichsam hinschiessen. Diese Eigenheiten des Fluges und die dunkle Farbe des Gefieders machen diese Vögel von weitem kenntlich. Man sieht sie fast immer nur im düsteren Gebüsch, und müssen sie ja einmal eine kurze Strecke übers Freie, über eine Waldwiese oder sonstigen von Holz entblössten Platz fliegen, so sieht man es ihnen an ihrer Eile an, wie ängstlich sie dabei sind. Desto sicherer und gewandter fliegen sie durch das dichteste Gebüsch, und sie wissen sich hier meisterhaft zu schwenken.

Es sind einsame Vögel, die von der Gesellschaft ihrer eigenen Art nicht viel und von der anderer Drosseln noch weniger halten; nur unter den **Singdrosseln**, wenn diese im Gebüsch am Boden herumhüpfen, trifft man manchmal auch eine einzelne **Amsel** an; sonst sieht man nur selten ein Pärchen nahe beisammen, obgleich sie sich das ganze Jahr hindurch eigentlich nicht trennen. Kommen zufällig in der Brutzeit zwei Männchen zusammen, so beissen und jagen sie sich oft heftig und lange herum, wobei sie von Zeit zu Zeit Strophen ihres Gesanges ausstossen und der Sieger dann diesen aus voller Kehle von einem Baume herab ertönen lässt.

Ihre Lockstimme ist ein trillerndes **ssrii** und **ssrissrii**, womit sie einander sitzend und fliegend anrufen und das dem Lockton der **Rotdrossel** ähnelt, aber schnarrender und tiefer klingt. Sonst rufen sie auch oft **tack tack**, was tief, hohl und dumpf, zuweilen fast wie **tuck tuck** klingt, und, wenn sie es ernstlich meinen, schnell **tacktacktacktack**! Sie locken durch diese Stimme, welche der der **Wacholderdrossel** ähnelt, aber hohler oder gedämpfter klingt, zuweilen auch ihre Kameraden, oder sie drücken damit Freude und Wohlbehagen aus; auch zeigen sie damit an, dass etwas im Anzuge sei, was ihre Sicherheit gefährden könnte. Kommt dies allmählich näher, so verwandelt sich die Stimme in ein hohes, weit schallendes **Tix tix tix tix tix tix**, dem sie, wenn sie nun wirklich die Flucht ergreifen, ein durchdringendes, hastiges **Gaigiggiggiggi gaigiggiggiggi** anhängen. Abends, wenn sie zu singen aufhören und sich ins niedere Gebüsch begeben, auch zur Tränke fliegen, rufen sie die Silbe **Tix** in einem weg, oft minutenlang aus. Kommt ihnen aber die Gefahr plötzlich über den Hals, so schreien sie im Fortfliegen in einem hellgellenden Tone **tacktack gaigiggiggiggi tacktack**, wobei die mittleren Silben sehr schnell und hastig ausgerufen werden. Diese Stimme ist das Signal zur Flucht, das auch andere Tiere des Waldes zu verstehen scheinen, und sie sind deshalb dem Jäger, der Wild beschleichen will, recht verhasste Vögel, weil sie ihm dadurch dies oft verscheuchen. In Angst und Not, z. B. wenn sie sich gefangen haben, **schirken** sie laut und hell wie andere Drosseln.

Das **Männchen** hat einen lauten, vortrefflichen Gesang und gehört unter die vorzüglichsten Singvögel unseres Landes. Dieser Gesang hat mehrere Strophen, die sie in kurzen Intervallen aufeinander folgen lassen, worunter aber leider einige zirpende und heisere Töne mit hellpfeifenden abwechseln, aber ein lautes flötenartiges **Tratü-tratätö**, das man auch mit den Worten: **David, Hans David** vergleicht, sich besonders auszeichnet und weit hörbar ist. Sie beleben durch diesen etwas melancholischen Gesang besonders die stillen Abende des ersten Frühlings auf eine höchst angenehme Weise, singen zwar auch am Tage, besonders am frühen Morgen, doch meistens erst recht anhaltend gegen Abend, in der Dämmerung, bis es völlig Nacht geworden, in dieser aber nicht oder doch nur höchst selten. Vom März bis in den Juli singen sie ununterbrochen, am meisten an solchen Abenden, denen ein warmer oder schwüler Tag vorherging. Das Männchen sitzt gewöhnlich hoch, wenn es singt, doch sehr selten so frei wie die **Singdrosseln**; auch singt es zuweilen, wenn es sich von einem Baum oder Gebüsch zum anderen begibt, im Fluge.

So schön übrigens ihr Gesang im ganzen ist, so gibt es doch auch unter den **Amseln**, wie unter anderen Singvögeln, schlechte und gute, fleissige und träge Sänger.

Es gewährt einen unvergleichlichen Genuss, nach einem heiteren Frühlingstage den Abend in einem schönen Laubholzwalde zuzubringen, wo die eben eintretende nächtliche Stille nur noch von den melancholischen Gesängen der **Amsel** und der **Singdrossel** unterbrochen wird; dies Konzert ist so anmutig, dass es manchen erfreut, der sonst nicht gewohnt ist, auf dergleichen Dinge zu achten.

Alt eingefangen, betragen sich diese Vögel anfangs wild und ungestüm, werden auch nie ganz zahm, und nicht alle Männchen singen in der Gefangenschaft laut und schön. In einem grossen Käfige, der am Boden auch Sprossen haben muss, damit der häufige und übelriechende Unrat durchfallen kann, halten sie sich gut, noch besser aber in einer luftigen und sonnigen Kammer, unter anderen Vögeln frei herumfliegend, wo sie zehn und mehr Jahre dauern. Aber sie sind hier sehr zanksüchtig, beissen oft kleinere Vögel tot, und mit einem anderer ihrer Art vertragen sie sich vollends nicht gut. Andere ihnen beigesellte Drosseln leiden sie lieber. Man unterhält sie teils zur Locke auf dem Vogelherd, teils ihres schönen, natürlichen Gesanges wegen, den man dadurch zu verschönern sucht, dass man die Jungen aus dem Neste nimmt, wenn ihnen kaum die Kiele aufgesprungen sind, sie gross füttert und ihnen Arien und andere kurze Melodien vorpfeift, die sie in einem hellen, sehr angenehmen, flötenden Tone nachpfeifen lernen, worüber sie ihren Waldgesang ganz vergessen. Solche Vögel singen das ganze Jahr, die Mauserzeit ausgenommen, und sind oft so gelehrig, dass eine einzige mehrere Arien lernt und behält; auch lernen sie sogar menschliche Worte nachsprechen.

Reinlichkeit ist ihnen besonders erspriesslich, und in einem zu engen Käfige, zumal wenn er einen bretternen Boden hat, verstossen und beschmutzen sie ihr Gefieder, mausern nicht ordentlich, haben dann ein hässliches Ansehen und halten ein so schmutziges Leben nicht lange aus. Sie baden sich gern in Wasser.

NAHRUNG

Sie suchen ihr Futter wie die übrigen verwandten Arten den grössten Teil des Jahres auf dem Erdboden. Sie hüpfen deshalb unter dem Gebüsch, unter Hecken und Zäunen, weniger und selten auf freien Plätzen herum, wenden gern das abgefallene, alte, halbverfaulte Laub um und durchstöbern das Moos, das auf der Erde unter den Bäumen wächst, um hier Regenwürmer, allerlei Maden und Insektenlarven, kriechende Insekten und nackte Schnecken aufzusuchen. Sie fressen auch allerlei unter dem Moos und dürrem Laube versteckte Insektenpuppen, achten aber fliegende Insekten gar nicht, durchsuchen besonders den Boden in Dickichten, wo kein Gras wächst, die alten Stämme und ihre Umgebungen und zeigen sich seltener auf grasreichem Boden im lichten Holze. Hier stöbern sie gern in den Ameisenhaufen und verzehren die Puppen derselben mit sichtlichem Wohlbehagen. Feuchter Boden an Quellen und Waldbächen scheint ihnen vorzüglich viel Nahrung darzubieten, und sie sind besonders im Winter gern da. Sonst fressen sie auch gern Kirschen, saure und wilde Vogel- oder Zwieselkirschen, auch veredelte Süsskirschen. Sie fliegen oft weit nach einem solchen Baume, selbst wenn sie darnach eine kleine Strecke über das Freie müssten, und besuchen ihn des Tages mehrmals.

Sie lieben auch die Beeren vom roten und schwarzen Holunder, dann die Beeren vom Faulbaum und im Herbst vor allen die Ebereschbeeren. Nach diesen letzteren gehen sie aber ungern auf hohe und freistehende Bäume. Werden die Ebereschbeeren endlich seltener, so fressen sie notgedrungen auch die Früchte des Weissdorns, wohl gar Liguster- oder Rainweidenbeeren. Beim Besuch auf den Beerenbüschen sind sie sehr vorsichtig und entfliehen, wenn sie einen Menschen auch nur von ferne gewahren. Im Frühjahr rühren sie keine Beeren an.

Die alt gefangenen Amseln sind anfangs trotzig und wollen nicht sogleich ans Futter, gewöhnen sich aber mit untermengten Beeren oder Regenwürmern doch nach und nach an das gewöhnliche Stubenfutter der Drosseln und halten sich gut dabei. Die Jungen füttert man mit in Milch eingequellter Semmel auf, und diese lernen dann bald auch alles Gemüse, das auf den Tisch kommt, auch klein geschnittenes, gekochtes Fleisch fressen. Aber auch ihnen bekommt ein Futter aus Gerstengrütze, eingeweichtem Weissbrot und klein geriebenen Mohrrüben besser als jedes andere.

FORTPFLANZUNG

Die **Amseln** nisten in unseren Waldungen, vorzüglich da, wo diese am dichtesten sind, in Schwarz- wie in Laubwäldern, in bergigen wie in ebenen, am liebsten in solchen, wo Wasser in der Nähe ist. In Nadelwäldern suchen sie die Dickichte von jungem Stangenholz auf und bauen ihr Nest auf junge Nadelbäume, mannshoch, selten höher oder tiefer; in den Laubhölzern suchen sie die Stellen, wo das dichteste Unterholz wächst, junge Schläge und dichte Dornhecken, auch sumpfige, finstere Erlenbüsche, und bauen hier das Nest bald auf einen mit dichten Zweigen umgebenen, alten Stamm oder auf einen niedrigen alten Weidenkopf, bald in eine oben offene, weite Höhle eines alten abgebrochenen Baumes, in einen Reisholzhaufen oder in einen Haufen Scheitholz, in das dichte Dorngebüsch oder auf die dichten verworrenen Äste nahe am Schafte eines Baumes, besonders an solchen Stellen, wo früher ein starker Ast abgehauen war und Büschel junger Zweige hervorgewachsen sind; bald über Mannshöhe, bald nahe an oder auf die Erde.

Bei guter Witterung zeigen sich die alten **Amselpärchen** schon Anfang März an ihren Brutorten, und das Männchen verkündigt dies durch seinen herrlichen Gesang; doch findet man selten vor Ende dieses Monats Eier, und der Frühling müsste ausserordentlich gut sein, wenn sie dann gar schon Junge haben sollten. Das Nest hat von innen eine bedeutende Weite, obgleich es keine sehr dicken Wände bildet, und die Höhlung ist tiefer als eine Halbkugel, auch ist der obere Rand stark einwärts gebogen. Nach dem Standorte ist es verschieden gebaut; denn in Baumhöhlen, alten Stämmen und an ähnlichen verdeckten Orten besteht es aus einem Gewebe von Erdmoos und dürren Halmen, ohne mit etwas ausgeschmiert zu sein; steht es dagegen freier, auf kleinen Bäumen oder im dichten Gebüsch, so besteht sein Äusseres aus feinen Würzelchen, Stengeln und dürrem Grase, dem nur selten etwas Moos beigemischt ist, und seine innere Fläche ist mit fetter feuchter Erde oder Schlamm (niemals mit faulem Holz) glatt ausgeschmiert. Dies letztere und seine beträchtlichere Grösse unterscheidet es vom Neste der **Singdrossel**.

Man findet in einem solchen Neste, dessen innere glatte Wände, wenn es ausgeschmiert ist, immer feucht sind, vier bis fünf, selten sechs, ziemlich grosse, meist etwas längliche, blass blaugrünliche, mit hell zimtfarbigen oder matt rostfarbigen, kleinen Flecken, Schmitzen und Punkten über und über bestreute Eier. Sie sind fast die grössten unter den Eiern der einheimischen Drosselarten und ähneln in dieser Hinsicht denen der **Elster** und des **Eichelhähers**; den letzteren sehen sie selbst in Farbe und Zeichnung etwas ähnlich.

Sie bebrüten sie fünfzehn bis sechzehn Tage lang, wobei das Männchen sein Weibchen, meist um die Mittagszeit, auf einige Stunden ablöst, und sie füttern die Jungen gemeinschaftlich mit Würmern und Insektenlarven. Wenn sie beunruhigt werden, verlassen diese das Nest bald; sonst warten sie darin so lange, bis Flügel- und Schwanzfedern wenigstens so ausgebildet sind, dass sie notdürftig fliegen können. Bald nachher machen die Alten zu der zweiten Brut Anstalt, denn sie brüten in der Regel zweimal im Jahre, bauen aber jedesmal ein neues Nest und legen dann selten mehr als vier Eier. Nur wenn sie das erste Mal die Eier einbüssen, brüten sie auch noch zweimal; hatten sie aber schon Junge und verlieren diese, so brüten sie nur noch einmal.

Auch ausser der Brutzeit halten sich Männchen und Weibchen zusammen, und man darf da, wo man das eine findet, gewöhnlich nicht lange nach dem anderen suchen. So trennen sie sich, ob es gleich manchmal den Anschein haben möchte, eigentlich das ganze Jahr nicht voneinander.

FEINDE

Von Raubvögeln werden sie, weil sie immer im düsteren Gebüsch versteckt leben und nur wenig aufs Freie kommen, sehr selten gefangen; desto mehr Zerstörer findet dagegen ihre Brut an den kleineren Raubtieren des Waldes, **Mardern, Iltissen, Wieseln, Katzen**, an den Krähenarten, besonders dem **Eichelhäher**, und selbst **Schlangen** sah man mit dem Verschlingen der nackten Jungen beschäftigt. Die Nachstellungen der vielen Feinde, welche im dunklen Gebüsch den Jungen nachschleichen, machen es begreiflich, dass diese Vögel sich nicht stärker vermehren.

NUTZEN

Ihr Fleisch ist eine vortreffliche Speise, weswegen sie schon im alten Rom in grossen Vogelhäusern künstlich gemästet wurden. In Gegenden, wo sie nicht zu einzelnen Stücken verkauft werden, rechnet man ihrer Grösse wegen nur zwei Stück auf eine Kluppe.

Sie vertilgen eine grosse Menge Larven schädlicher Waldinsekten, nackte Schnecken und dergleichen, pflanzen durch das Herumschleppen der Kerne beerentragende Holzarten fort und vergnügen durch ihren herrlichen Gesang, indem sie dadurch teils die Wälder auf die angenehmste Weise beleben, teils den einzelnen Besitzer eines solchen Stubenvogels erfreuen. Eine schön pfeifende **Amsel** im Käfig vor dem Fenster erfreut in Städten oft eine ganze Strasse mit ihrem lauten Gesange.

SCHADEN

Dem aufmerksamen Jäger sind dies höchst ärgerliche und verhasste Vögel; bald ist es der Unfug, den sie ihm im Dohnenstege anrichten, bald ihr fataler hellgellender Warnungsruf, womit sie ihn dem Wilde, auch anderem Geflügel, das er eben beschleichen will, verraten, auch dies dadurch auf seinen Feind aufmerksam machen und zur Flucht reizen. Dies muss ihn gegen sie einnehmen, obwohl es sich auch zuweilen fügt, dass sie ihm dadurch Raubtiere, Raubvögel, auch wohl Wildpret, das er ohne sie vielleicht nicht bemerkt hätte, anzeigen. Schleicht man im Gebüsche, um etwas zu schiessen, und stösst unvermutet auf eine Amsel, so entflieht sie meistenteils mit hellgellendem, einem Hohngelächter ähnlichem Geschrei vorwärts hin, erschreckt dadurch auch den ruhigsten Vogel und setzt alles in Alarm.

Sie besuchen auch die Kirschbäume der reifen Früchte wegen, die sie gern fressen, und tragen dazu bei, die schädliche Mistelpflanze weiter zu pflanzen; doch fressen sie diese Beeren nur, wenn sie keine anderen mehr haben.

Beobachtung. Von der Schlauheit dieser Vögel führe ich hier noch folgendes Beispiel an, das zugleich beweisen wird, dass die **Amseln** nicht überall im nördlichen

Deutschland Standvögel sind. In meinem Wäldchen nistet alle Jahre ein Pärchen, von welchem die ausgeheckten Jungen schon Ende August, die Alten aber erst Mitte September verschwinden. Mein wohleingerichteter Dohnenstieg, der etwa acht Tage vor Michaelis aufgestellt wird, liefert daher anfangs keine **Amsel**; erst wenn der Zug anhebt, mit Anfang Oktober, fangen sich einzelne, wahrscheinlich fern herkommende Strichvögel, worunter auch alte; denn dass keine von den im Sommer hier gewesenen unter diesen war, beweist der Umstand, dass gewöhnlich ein Paar alte **Amseln** etwa um Weihnachten wieder kommt, hier überwintert und durch sein Benehmen, indem es alle Schliche kennt, und durch die Vollkommenheit des Gesanges des Männchens zu erkennen gibt, dass es das meinige oder dasjenige Pärchen ist, das schon oft in meinem Walde gebrütet hatte. Wie sehr muss man aber hier über ihre Klugheit, mit der sie allen Nachstellungen auszuweichen wissen, erstaunen! Auch der Hunger im Winter ist nicht imstande, sie zu bewegen, die Beeren in meinen Dohnen zu versuchen, und selbst den Schlingen bei den Tränkeplätzen, wo ich viele andere Vögel, auch **Amseln**, fange, wissen diese alten Schlauköpfe zu entgehen. So hielt sich ein altes Pärchen wohl sechs und mehrere Jahre, ehe es (doch nicht durch meine Schuld) verunglückte; sein Platz blieb im folgenden Frühjahr unbesetzt, denn das später im April sich zeigende Pärchen, das sicher ein fremdes, hier nicht ausgebrütetes sein mochte, ging, ohne hier zu brüten, weiter. Erst nach einigen Jahren siedelte sich ein neues an, und es ging wie beim ersten. Diesen Fall habe ich nun schon ein paarmal erlebt.

// DIE WACHHOLDERDROSSEL //

TURDUS PILARIS

Krammetsdrossel, Krammetsvogel, gemeiner oder eigentlicher Krammetsvogel, Krammsvogel, Kranwetsvogel, Kranvitvogel, Kranewitsvogel, Krannabetvogel, Krannabeter, Krannabet, Reckholdervogel, Ziemer, Grossziemer, Blauziemer, Blawziemer, grosser Blauziemer, Zimmer, Zeumer, Schomerling, Schacker, Beinauka; im Anhaltischen: der Ziemer.

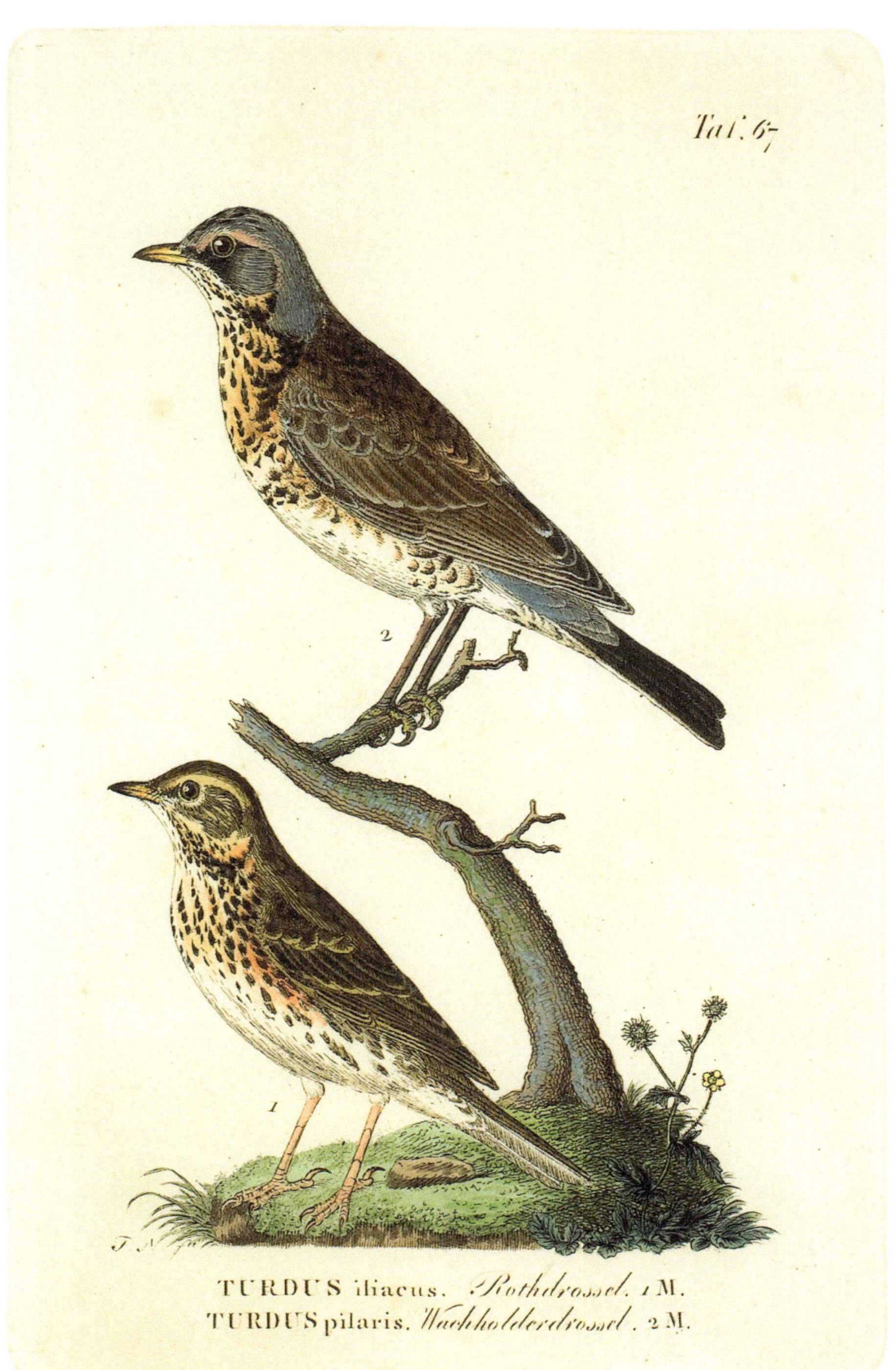

TURDUS iliacus. *Rothdrossel.* 1 M.
TURDUS pilaris. *Wachholderdrossel.* 2 M.

KENNZEICHEN DER ART

Kopf und Bürzel aschgrau; der Oberrücken schmutzig kastanienbraun; der Schwanz schwarz, die äusserste Feder mit einem weisslichen Rändchen; der Unterleib mit länglichen und dreieckigspitzen Flecken; die unteren Flügeldeckfedern weiss.

BESCHREIBUNG

Dieser ansehnliche Vogel ist in vielen deutschen Ländern unter dem Namen **Krammetsvogel** allgemein bekannt, ob man gleichwohl auch in manchen Gegenden mit diesem Namen diese ganze Gattung bezeichnet. Durch seine Farben und Zeichnungen ist er von den übrigen ziemlich auffallend verschieden und wohl nicht leicht mit einer anderen Art zu verwechseln. Seine Gestalt ist etwas schlank, und in der Grösse hält er das Mittel zwischen der **Sing-** und **Misteldrossel.**

Die Länge der Wachholderdrossel beträgt 26 cm, die Breite ihrer ausgespannten Flügel 42 cm, doch gibt es auch Exemplare, welche diese Länge um etwas, und die Breite fast um 2,3 cm übertreffen; der am Ende ziemlich gerade Schwanz ist 10 cm lang, und die in Ruhe liegenden Flügel reichen mit den Enden noch nicht auf die Hälfte desselben.

Der 18 mm lange Schnabel ist weder sehr gross, noch besonders stark, rundlich, doch an der Wurzel beträchtlich breiter als hoch, dem Rücken des Oberkiefers nach sanft gekrümmt, die Unterkinnlade fast gerade; das ovale Nasenloch ziemlich gross. Seine Farbe ist im Frühling orangegelb, mit brauner Spitze, im Herbst braun, nur an den Mundwinkeln und der Wurzel der Unterkinnlade gelb; Zunge und Rachen orangegelb. Über den Mundwinkeln stehen schwarze Borsthaare; das kahle Augenlidrändchen ist gelb, im Frühjahr orange; die Iris dunkelbraun.

Die starken Füsse sind eben nicht hoch, die Läufe fast gestiefelt, die Zehenrücken getäfelt, die Zehensohlen feinwarzig. Die letzteren sind von der Farbe gelbbraun, die Füsse übrigens schwarz, mit durchschimmerndem Rot, oder schwarzbraun. Die Höhe der Fusswurzel ist 3,2 cm, die Länge der Mittelzehe mit dem Nagel 3 cm und die der Hinterzehe, ebenso gemessen, 18,5 mm. Die Krallen sind gross, besonders die hinterste, spitz, aber flach gebogen, unten zweischneidig, von der Farbe schwarz.

Gewöhnlich sind die Farben im Gefieder dieser Vögel folgende: Von der Schnabelwurzel über das Auge hin zieht sich ein verloschener weisslicher Streif; Stirn, Scheitel, Wangen, Hinterhals, Unterrücken und obere Schwanzdeckfedern sind aschgrau, die grössten der letzteren an den Schäften bräunlich und der Scheitel mit schwärzlichen Schaftflecken; Oberrücken und Schultern schmutzig kastanienbraun, mit etwas lichteren Federspitzen. Zwischen dem Schnabel und dem Auge befindet sich eine schwärzliche Stelle; die Kehle ist gelblichweiss und meist ungefleckt; die Seiten derselben, so wie der ganze Vorderhals, bis zur Brust schön rötlich ockergelb, mit braunschwarzen Längsflecken, welche an den Seiten der Kehle herab einige undeutliche Fleckenstreife bilden, an den Halsseiten sich vergrössern und hier, wie an der Seite des Kropfes, so gehäuft sind, dass hier gewöhnlich zwei dunkle Stellen gebildet werden; der ganze übrige Unterleib ist weiss, in den Seiten mit braunschwarzen, rostgelb gesäumten Flecken, welche oberwärts eine dreieckigspitze, unterwärts aber bald eine verkehrt herzförmige, bald mondförmige Gestalt haben; die unteren Schwanzdeckfedern sind weiss, jede nach der Wurzel zu an jeder Seite mit einem schwärzlichen Längsfleck. Die sämtlichen Flügelfedern sind matt braunschwarz, an den Aussenfahnen aschgrau, die Deckfedern nach hinten zu und die hintersten Schwungfedern mit Kastanienbraun gemischt, an den Enden lichtgrau gesäumt; die vorderen grossen Schwingen mit weisslichen Säumchen; die Schwingen auf der unteren Seite hellgrau, die unteren Flügeldeckfedern rein weiss, bloss am Flügelrande schwärzlich gefleckt. Die Schwanzfedern sind braunschwarz, die äusserte am lichtesten, mit einem weisslichen Aussensäumchen.

Das **alte Weibchen** unterscheidet sich im Äusseren ziemlich leicht vom **alten Männchen**, das soeben beschrieben wurde, durch folgende Merkmale: Der Vorderhals ist viel blasser gelb, die braunschwarzen Flecke stehen sparsamer und sind viel kleiner und schmaler; Kopf und Unterrücken bekleidet ein lichteres, sehr sanftes Aschgrau, welches so mit dem schmutzigen matten Kastanienbraun des Oberrückens und der Schultern verläuft, dass für dieses, was auch viel unansehnlicher als am Männchen ist, nur eine kleine Stelle übrig bleibt, wo es rein und ungemischt erscheint; die Flügel überzieht dagegen von aussen auf durchgehends aschgrauem Grunde eine Mischung von gelblichem Braun; der Schnabel ist mehr braun als gelb, und die Farbe der Füsse mehr braun als schwarz.

Im **Frühling** erscheinen die Farben der oberen Teile bei beiden Geschlechtern viel reiner, denn nun haben sich die Ränder der Federn abgetragen, welche das **Herbstkleid** viel unansehnlicher machten, indem die aschgrauen Federn olivengraue und die kastanienbraunen schmutzig lichtbraune Ränder und Spitzen hatten. Bei **jungen Vögeln** sind diese anders gefärbten Ränder noch auffallender, sie verlieren sich, weil sie breiter sind, auch im Frühlinge nicht ganz, und diese sehen daher viel schmutziger aus als die alten, bei welchen auch den Vorderhals und die Kropfgegend stets ein schöneres Gelb ziert, was stärker und dunkler gefleckt ist, als bei den jungen. Männchen und Weibchen lassen sich indes hier nicht so leicht unterscheiden als bei den Alten.

Im verwichenen Sommer [1822] war ein Pärchen **Wachholderdrosseln** in hiesiger Gegend, im Walde bei **Klein-Zerbst**, zurückgeblieben, ein Fall, welcher gewiss unter die grössten Seltenheiten gezählt werden darf; ja es hatte höchstwahrscheinlich dort sogar gebrütet, schien jedoch ohne Nachkommen geblieben zu sein. Mein Bruder, welcher es mehrere Wochen beobachtete, erlegte es endlich auf meine Bitte, weil sich keine Jungen zeigten und zu befürchten war, dass es sich aus der Gegend verlieren möchte. Der Paarungsruf war ganz anders als die bekannte Lockstimme, in einem höheren Tone und den Locktönen der **Ringdrossel** ähnlich; man könnte es ein schnarrendes Schäckern nennen. Anfang Juli, wo das Pärchen erlegt wurde, war sein Gefieder durch Abbleichen und Abreiben so gewaltig entstellt, dass diese Vögel ganz von den gewöhnlichen abwichen, sodass ihre **Sommerkleider**, von welchen überhaupt noch keine Beschreibung bekannt ist, wohl verdienen, dass ich sie hier in der Kürze beschreibe: Die Federn sind so stark abgerieben, dass sie an den Enden ihre Bärte sehr weit herauf verloren haben und an vielen Teilen, vorzüglich am Rücken und auf den oberen Schwanzdecken, die vorn nackten Schäfte wie eine lange borstenartige Spitze vorstehen. Die Schäfte sind fast alle lichter, manche bräunlichweiss geworden, welches auch an den Enden sämtlicher Schwingen, deren Spitzen wie abgenagt aussehen, der Fall ist; am meisten haben jedoch die Oberschwanzdeckfedern an Länge und Umfang verloren, wozu vermutlich das häufige Wippen und Schnellen mit dem Schwanze Veranlassung gegeben; die mittleren Schwanzfedern sind an den Rändern ganz zerschlissen und ihre Fahnen nachenförmig aufwärts gebogen; die übrigen Schwanzfedern und die Federn des Unterleibes haben unter allen am wenigsten gelitten. Am **Männchen** ist der Oberkopf auf aschgrauem Grunde so stark schwarz gefleckt, dass von jenem nur wenig übrig bleibt; Nacken und Hinterhals hell aschgrau; der Bürzel ebenso, aber lichter; Oberrücken und Schultern dunkel kastanienbraun mit schwarzbrauner Mischung; Flügel und Schwanz viel bleicher als im Frühjahr; Kehle und Gurgel gelblichweiss, die Seiten derselben und der Kropf stark mit dunklem Rostgelb oder rötlichem Gelbbraun überflogen, mit vielen braunschwarzen grossen Längsflecken, die an den Seiten des Kropfes in ein grosses braunschwarzes Feld zusammenfliessen, und letztere Farbe nimmt fast ausschliesslich die ganzen Seiten der Brust ein, nur dass sie hier und an den Tragefedern noch durch sehr schmale, hellbraune Federkanten, als Reste jener breiten, lichten Einfassungen vom Herbstkleide, unterbrochen wird; die Mitte der Brust, der Länge nach, und der Bauch sind weiss. Die so sehr dunkle Zeichnung des Kropfes und der Brustseiten gibt dem Vogel ein ganz auffallendes Aussehen. Der Schnabel ist bis auf die braune Spitze des Oberkiefers ganz hochgelb; die Füsse sind sehr licht schmutzig rötlichbraun, die Zehensohlen aber hochgelb.

Das **Weibchen** sieht viel lichter aus, was am Aschgrau der oberen Teile sehr auffällt; der Scheitel ist bleicher und weniger schwarzgefleckt, der Rücken schmutzig rostbraun mit weisslichgelben Federschäften, Flügel und Schwanz sehr bleich mit vorherrschendem Grau; die Halsseiten und die Kropfgegend viel bleicher gelb als beim Männchen, aber deutlicher und klarer schwarz gefleckt; das schwarze Feld an den Kropfseiten nur klein, die Seiten der Oberbrust rostbraun, schwarz gefleckt; die Seiten der Unterbrust noch heller, fast rostfarbig, mit schwarzbraunen Mondfleckchen; die Mitte der Brust und der Bauch schmutzig- oder gelblichweiss. Er unterscheidet sich also gar sehr vom Männchen; auch hat der Schnabel von oben viel mehr Braun und eine braunschwarze Spitze, die Füsse sind auch lichter und die Fusssohlen schön hellgelb. Diese so auffallend abweichende Sommertracht dieser Vögel hätte wohl verdient, durch genaue Abbildung versinnlicht zu werden, was auch geschehen sein würde, wenn ich sie früher gehabt hätte.

Die **junge Wachholderdrossel** vor der ersten Mauser, welche ich in mehreren Exemplaren von GLOGER erhielt, unterscheidet sich nicht so auffallend von den Alten, dass sie nicht sogleich kenntlich wäre; sie hat folgende Farben: Kopf und Hals sind aschgrau, mit olivengrünlichen Federrändern, die die Grundfarbe fast verdecken; der Nacken lichter als der Scheitel; der Oberrücken, die Schultern und zum Teil auch die kleineren Flügeldeckfedern braun, viel schmutziger und lichter als bei den Alten, und alle diese Federn mit hellrostgelben Schaftstrichen oder Flekken, die fast wie Haferkörner gestaltet sind; Unterrücken und Bürzel licht aschgrau, mit olivenfarbigem Anflug. Die unteren Teile vom Kinn bis zum After sind zwar im Grunde denen der Alten an Farbe gleich, doch sind die Flecken ganz anders gestaltet, viel runder und an der Kropfgegend, wo sie bei den Alten jene dreieckige Gestalt haben, von solcher Grösse, dass dieser Teil sehr stark braunschwarz gefleckt erscheint; die Flügel sind ziemlich wie bei den Alten, aber auch grünlicher, und der mattschwarze Schwanz hat ebenfalls einen olivenbräunlichen Anflug. Der Schnabel ist rötlich blassgelb mit brauner Spitze und rotgelben Mundwinkeln; die Augensterne graubraun; die Füsse und Nägel gelblichlichtbraun. Das **Weibchen** unterscheidet sich vom **Männchen** dadurch, dass es, im ganzen genommen, mehr grau als braun aussieht, dass das Rostgelb an der Oberbrust und Gurgel weniger dunkel ist und diese Teile auch nicht so stark gefleckt erscheinen. Wenige Wochen nach dem Ausfliegen fangen sie schon an zu mausern, und erhalten dann das oben beschriebene erste Herbstkleid.

Es herrscht inzwischen unter den alten Vögeln dieser Art eine grosse **Verschiedenheit**, die weniger durch die Jahreszeiten als **durch das Alter** hervorgebracht wird. Je älter sie werden, desto dunkler färbt sich ihr Gefieder; das Aschgrau wird dunkel blaugrau, das dunkle Kastanienbraun verwandelt sich in ein rötliches Dunkelbraun und überzieht dann die ganze Aussenseite der Flügel, sodass von dem vormaligen lichten Grau nichts übrig bleibt als die Säume an den Enden der Federn und an der Aussenkante der vordersten grossen Schwingen; der schwarze Fleck vor dem Auge breitet sich unter demselben bis hinter dasselbe aus; der Augenstreif ist deutlicher und rötlichgelb, ja hinter dem Ohr zeigt sich noch eine so gefärbte Stelle; der Scheitel ist auffallend schwarz gefleckt; Kehle und Vorderhals bis auf die Oberbrust lebhaft dunkel rostgelb und so mit schwarzen Flecken übersät, dass diese Teile sehr dunkel in die Augen fallen, besonders weil die Flecke in ihren Umrissen unbestimmter sind und an den Halsseiten in zwei grosse schwarze Felder zusammenfliessen; die weisse Unterbrust ist rotgelb überlaufen; der Schwanz dunkelschwarz, und die äusserste Feder hat, ausser den weisslichen Aussensäumchen, auf der inneren Fahne, an der Spitze einen hellweissen Saum oder länglichen Saumfleck.* Solche Vögel haben immer einen fast ganz orangegelben Schnabel, dergleichen Augenlider und braunschwarze Füsse, und ich habe immer gefunden, dass es **Männchen** waren, die sich einzeln so von der Mehrzahl auszeichneten. Ich halte sie für **ausserordentlich alte Vögel**. Bei **sehr alten Weibchen**

* Diese Zeichnung der Schwanzfedern findet man nur bei sehr alten Vögeln, die Mehrzahl hat sie nicht; ich konnte sie daher nicht unter die **Artkennzeichen** aufnehmen, wie meine Vorgänger getan haben, zumal da die von mir angegebenen schon hinlänglich sind, den Vogel von anderen leicht zu unterscheiden.

herrscht auf der Aussenseite der Flügel stets mehr die graue Farbe und sie sind jederzeit weniger dunkel gefärbt.

Sonst gibt es auch noch mancherlei **Spielarten** unter diesen Vögeln, welche weder vom Alter und Geschlecht, noch von den Jahreszeiten abhängen, sondern bloss zufällig sind; z. B. die **weisse Wachholderdrossel**, welche entweder rein- und schneeweiss oder gelblichweiss ist oder bei dieser Grundfarbe noch einige dunkle Flecke an verschiedenen Teilen des Leibes hat; so beschreibt man auch eine hierher gehörige ganz weiss, mit einem grossen herzförmigen ziegelfarbenen Flecken auf der Brust. Bei den weissen Varietäten ist der Schnabel gewöhnlich weissgelb, und die Füsse sind fleischfarben oder braunrötlichweiss.

Die **gelbrötliche Wachholderdrossel** ist überall blass rötlichgelb oder lohfarbig, meist mit durchschimmernder dunkler Zeichnung. Diese, wie die weissen, sind indessen viel seltener als die **gefleckten Wachholderdrosseln**, welche, bei übrigens gewöhnlichen Farben, weisse Flecke an verschiedenen Teilen des Körpers haben; so gibt es **weissköpfige**, **weissflügelige** und **weissbunte**, an welchen die weissen Stellen ordnungslos an allen Körperteilen verteilt sind und an welchen die weissen Federn bald grössere, bald kleinere Partien bilden u. s. w. Man beschreibt auch eine **verkehrt gezeichnete Wachholderdrossel**, an welcher der ganze Leib so aussah, wie die gewöhnlichen auf der Brust, und eine merklich kleinere Varietät, die **kleine Wachholderdrossel**, welche ihr Dasein wahrscheinlich einem Erziehungsfehler zu verdanken hat, aber sehr selten ist.

Die Wachholderdrossel **mausert** etwas später als andere dieser Gattung, nämlich im August.

AUFENTHALT

Diese Drossel bewohnt die nördlichen Teile von **Europa** und **Asien** und ist in den meisten Ländern derselben, z. B. in **Norwegen**, **Schweden**, **Polen**, **Russland** und **Sibirien**, bis **Kamtschatka** ein allgemein gekannter Vogel, der aus diesen Ländern gegen den Winter in südlichere Breiten wandert, bei uns in **Deutschland** in grosser Menge ankommt, hier teils überwintert, teils durchzieht und bis in die **Schweiz**, nach **Frankreich** und **Italien** geht, ja selbst in ungeheuerer Anzahl in **Sardinien** überwintert. Auch **Dänemark**, **England** und **Holland** sehen sie in dieser Jahreszeit in Menge, und dieselben Wanderungen finden auch unter den im Sommer das nördliche Asien bewohnenden statt, welche bis **Syrien** herabgehen. Nur strenge Kälte und vieler Schnee scheinen sie aus ihrem rauhen Vaterlande zu vertreiben; denn sie kommen bei harten Wintern häufiger zu uns als bei gelinderen. Finden sie dann bei uns auch noch strenge Winterwitterung, so wandern sie südlicher, wo nicht, so bleiben die meisten in unseren Wäldern, so lange sie nicht Mangel an Nahrung ebenfalls weiter treibt; denn dieser und nicht die Kälte zwingt sie, gelindere Gegenden aufzusuchen.

Sie kommen als **Zugvögel** aus dem Norden einzeln, oft schon in der Mitte des Oktober, im nördlichen Deutschland an, doch erscheinen sie hier in grossen Scharen selten früher als in der ersten Hälfte des November. Sie kommen aus Nordosten zu uns und ziehen von hier weiter in südwestlicher Richtung. Ihr Durchzug durch hiesige Gegenden dauert, von der letzten Hälfte des Oktober an, den ganzen November hindurch. Diejenigen, welche hier bleiben, halten sich da auf, wo sie Nahrung genug finden, und streifen auch wohl in der Nachbarschaft darnach umher; tritt aber vor Mitte Januar noch strenge Witterung ein, so gehen sie ebenfalls weiter, und dieser Januarzug ist für die Vogelfänger hiesiger Gegend oft von ziemlicher Bedeutung.

Bei gelinden Wintern bleiben sie aber hier, bis zum Frühling, wo sie mit den zurückkommenden, im März und April, in ungeheueren Scharen in die nordöstlichen Länder zurückkehren und mit Ende des letzteren Monats uns alle verlassen. Sehr selten sieht man noch welche Anfang Mai bei uns durchziehen, und dies sind gewiss solche, die in südlicheren Ländern, als Deutschland ist, überwintert haben.

In **Schlesien**, **Böhmen**, auf dem **Thüringer Walde** und dem **Harze** überwintern sie da, wo viel Wachholder wächst, in ungeheuerer Menge. Man sieht sie im Frühling stets in viel grösseren Scharen zurückkehren, als man sie im Herbst wegziehen sah, ob ihrer gleich an ihren Winteraufenthaltsorten so viele Tausende als beliebte Speise weggefangen wurden, sodass es mit der Menge eher umgekehrt sein müsste; allein der Grund dazu liegt wohl darin, dass sie sich im Frühling teils durch mehr Lärmen, teils dadurch bemerklicher machen, dass sie weit langsamer ziehen. In solchen Gegenden, wo es ihnen gefällt, liegen sie mehrere Tage still, und sie reisen überhaupt bei widrigem Winde und schlechtem Wetter gar nicht. Auch die Beschaffenheit der Gegend mag mit Ursache hiervon sein; denn eine und dieselbe kann recht schöne Anger und Wiesen mit abwechselndem Gebüsch haben, welches sie im Frühling, wo sie ihre Nahrung auf der Erde suchen, sehr lieben; allein es kann ihr an beerentragenden Holzarten fehlen, und da sie im Herbst die Beeren lieben, so haben sie keine Ursache, sich dann lange in selbiger aufzuhalten, sie durchfliegen sie schnell und werden daher weniger bemerkt.

Sie ziehen am Tage in grossen Gesellschaften, seltener und nur einzeln des Nachts, wo sie sich zuweilen, wenn es finster wird und sie den Wald nicht mehr erreichen können, auf das Feld niedersetzen und daselbst Nachtruhe halten; solche werden dann zuweilen unter dem Lerchennachtgarne gefangen, wie in hiesiger Gegend mehrmals der Fall gewesen ist. Sonst übernachten sie in der Regel in Gesellschaft, bei gelinder Witterung in den Zweigen eines hohen Baumes, bei strenger Kälte suchen sie dagegen das niedrige Holz und dichtes Gebüsch dazu auf, treten aber schon vor Anbruch des Tages ihre Reisen an, und einige ermuntern die Gesellschaft dazu durch ihren lauten Ruf. Sie ziehen in der Dämmerung meist ununterbrochen vorwärts, weniger, wenn es erst Tag geworden, und machen gewöhnlich morgens gegen 9 Uhr Halt, suchen sich Futter und ziehen, wenn sie eilig sind, von Mittag an bis gegen Abend fort, wo sie dann, nach eingenommener Abendmahlzeit, ein stilles Ruheplätzchen suchen; doch machen sie ihre Reisen meist nur in den Frühstunden. Zuweilen habe ich auch im Herbst von früh 7 Uhr bis Nachmittags 3 Uhr ziehende Scharen bemerkt, die, wie andere zu dieser Zeit wandernde Vögel, unaufhaltsam forteilten, und machte dann immer die Bemerkung, dass auf solche Tage schlechte Witterung folgte.

Im Frühling reisen sie, wie gesagt, viel langsamer; denn wenn sie nach einer zurückgelegten Tour sich hinlänglich gesättigt haben, so setzen sie sich auf hohe Bäume, putzen und sonnen sich und führen gemeinschaftlich stundenlange Konzerte auf. Sie reisen dann auch oft in Gesellschaft der **Rotdrosseln**, und diese beiden Arten lieben sich überhaupt mehr, als andere dieser Gattung.

Obgleich die Wachholderdrossel ein wahrer Waldvogel ist, so liebt sie doch nicht solche Wälder, die zu viel dichtes Unterholz haben, und man sieht sie nie so in diesem gleichsam herumkriechen, wie etwa die **Amseln**, sondern immer entweder auf hohen Bäumen, auf Beerenbüschen, oder auf freien Wiesen und Triften, wo Bäume in der Nähe sind, doch auch oft weit von diesen. Sie folgen gern dem Lauf der Flüsse, Bäche und Wassergräben, weil an diesen immer Wiesen liegen, und fliegen auf ihren Zügen höchst ungern über grosse freie Flächen Feld, sondern lieber dem Gebüsch nach, und sollten sie auch bedeutende Umwege machen.

In die grossen, dunklen Nadelholzwaldungen gehen sie nicht, und sie lieben das Nadelholz nur dann, wenn Wachholder darunter wächst.

EIGENSCHAFTEN

Die Wachholderdrossel ist ein harter Vogel und verträgt als solcher die Winterkälte sehr wohl; dagegen ist ihm zu grosse Wärme zuwider, und man sieht oft bei recht warmen Frühlingstagen ganze Herden die Schnäbel aufsperren und keuchen.

Sie ist unter den Drosseln dieser Familie die geselligste, und man trifft sie daher fast immer in grossen Gesellschaften beisammen, und Einsiedler sind selten unter ihnen. Sie werden auch von anderen Drosseln geliebt, und diese folgen gern ihren Locktönen, weswegen ein guter Lockvogel für den Vogelsteller grossen Wert hat, weil alle Arten seine Lockstimme mit Wohlgefallen anzuhören scheinen. Selbst nicht mit ihnen verwandte Vögel finden ihre Gesellschaft behaglich, z. B. die **Goldammern**, und ich habe dies immer mit Vergnügen beobachtet, wenn diese mit einzelnen oder kleinen Gesellschaften von Wachholderdrosseln an meinen Vogelherd kamen und sich oft mit ihnen fangen liessen, ohne dass sie durch einen Lockvogel ihrer Art dazu veranlasst worden wären. Man sieht es aus ihrem ganzen Betragen, wie wohl sie sich in der Gesellschaft der Wachholderdrosseln befinden.

Es sind scheue und vorsichtige Vögel, welche die Nähe der Menschen fliehen. Auf der Erde hüpfen sie in grossen Sprüngen und rucken dabei öfters mit den Flügeln und dem Schwanze. Auch wenn sie auf den Bäumen stillsitzen, rucken sie von Zeit zu Zeit etwas mit dem Schwanze, ohne die Flügel zu rühren; verändern sie aber ihren Sitz, so schnellen sie mit beiden heftiger. Sie suchen am Tage das dichte Gebüsch zu vermeiden; man sieht sie auch niemals in den Zweigen viel herumhüpfen, sondern bloss von einem zum anderen hinflattern und dann stillsitzen. Müssen sie der Beeren wegen ins niedere Gesträuch, so halten sie sich da nur so lange auf, bis sie sich gesättigt haben, und fliegen nun gleich wieder auf einen hohen Baum. Auch auf der Erde halten sie sich nur so lange auf, bis sie ihren Appetit gestillt haben, und setzen sich dann wieder auf hohe Bäume, oft Hunderte auf einen einzigen. Ihr Flug ist mittelmässig, schwankend und flatternd, wenn er nicht weit gehen soll; auf ihren Reisen aber schneller und in sehr flachen Bogenlinien. Ihre schlankere Gestalt macht sie in der Ferne kenntlich, und in der Nähe fallen der hellgraue Unterrücken und Kopf, der dunkle Schwanz und die weissen Unterflügel auch im Fluge auf, um sie sogleich zu erkennen.

Ihre Lockstimme, welche sie sitzend und fliegend fleissig hören lassen und die besonders das Zeichen zum Aufbruch und zur Fortsetzung der Reise ist, klingt laut **schaschaschaschack** (schnell und scharf ausgesprochen), auch wohl einzeln **schack, schack**; wollen sie dagegen näher zusammenrücken oder ein Trupp den anderen einladen, Halt zu machen, so rufen sie hell **quiqui** oder vielmehr **kwrikwri!** Die jungen Vögel rufen jedoch dies letztere seltener als die alten. Ihr Angstgeschrei sind gellend schirkende Töne, wie sie auch andere Drosseln hervorbringen.

Im Frühjahr sitzen sie öfters in zahlreicher Gesellschaft auf einem oder einigen grossen Bäumen und lassen ihren Gesang hören, der aber nicht besonders ist und aus einer Menge eben nicht sehr starker, zwitschernder, schackernder und leise pfeifender, oder vielmehr kreischender Töne zusammengesetzt ist. Die schackernden Locktöne bilden die Basis dieses keineswegs angenehmen Gesanges, der jedoch da, wo sie brüten, lauter erschallen soll, ob er gleich dadurch eben nicht verbessert wird.

In der Gefangenschaft betragen sich diese Vögel anfangs wild und störrig, und sie werden auch nie ganz zahm; doch gibt es hiervon einzelne Ausnahmen unter ihnen. Man hält sie nicht sowohl ihres Gesanges wegen, als darum, weil sie fast alle gute Lockvögel auch für andere Drosselarten sind, für den Vogelherd, wo sie auf den für diese Gattung zu stellenden die Hauptvögel sind, und sperrt sie in etwas geräumige Käfige, die am Boden auch Sprossen haben, damit der Unrat durchfallen kann, mit dem sie sich sonst sehr besudeln würden. Wollte man sie immer in ihrem Käfige lassen, so würden sie nicht viel über ein Jahr aushalten; man tut daher besser, wenn man sie nach der Zeit des Vogelfanges in eine geräumige Kammer fliegen lässt, wo sie Luft und Sonne geniessen, sich frei bewegen und öfters im Wasser baden können, was sie gern und häufig tun. So halten sie sich mehrere Jahre; allein man darf hier nie zwei Wachholderdrosseln zusammenbringen, weil diese sonst so geselligen Vögel diese Eigenschaft in der Gefangenschaft ganz verleugnen und die stärkere nicht eher ruht, bis sie die schwächere umgebracht hat, oder bis gar beide draufgehen. Dagegen mag man ihnen von anderen Drosseln und Singvögeln soviel beigesellen als man will, und sie werden den Frieden mit und unter diesen nie zu stören versuchen.

NAHRUNG

Diese besteht hauptsächlich in Regenwürmern, Insektenlarven und anderen Erdmaden, die man Erdmast zu nennen pflegt, welche sie auf den freien Hutungen, Angern und Wiesen, aber nicht unter dem dichten Gebüsch aufsuchen, sondern, wenn sie ja im Walde darnach gehen, nur im lichten Holze deswegen am Boden umherhüpfen. Sie unterscheiden sich durch diese letztere Gewohnheit merklich von anderen Drosseln; doch habe ich bemerkt, dass sie nur zu Anfang des Frühlings ihre Nahrung meistens auf dem Freien, späterhin, nämlich im April, aber in manchen Jahren auch mit anderen Drosseln unter dem Gebüsch aufsuchen und daselbst, wie diese, das abgefallene Laub umwenden.

Im Notfalle fressen sie auch nackte Schnecken und junge Heuschrecken; aber fliegende Insekten achten sie, so lange sie bei uns sind, gar nicht. Sie sollen auch Spinnen fressen und nach diesen so lüstern sein, dass sie darnach selbst bis in die Walddörfer kommen und früh morgens, wenn die Bewohner derselben noch schlafen, jene sogar von den Gebäuden hinwegfangen.

Regenwürmer lieben sie vor allem am meisten, und wenn zuweilen im Winter oder im Frühjahr der Schnee nur erst stellenweise geschmolzen und der Boden ein paar Zoll tief aufgetaut ist, so wissen sie diese Lieblingskost auch schon in den Maulwurfshügeln aufzusuchen; denn die Regenwürmer fliehen vor dem sie verfolgenden Maulwurf und werden mit dessen aufgestossener Erde ausgeworfen, sie frieren bei starkem Froste samt der Erde ein und werden, wenn es nachher taut, von den Drosseln tot oder lebendig herausgezogen.

Im Herbst sind allerlei Beeren ihre Lieblingsnahrung, unter denen die sogenannten Vogel- oder Ebereschbeeren obenan stehen; doch fressen sie auch die Beeren vom Hartriegel, Schlingbaum, Faulbaum und anderen mehr ziemlich gern. Sie suchen auch die Beeren von den *Arbutus*-Arten, von der **Schwarzen Krähenbeere**, vom Sanddorn, dem Kreuz- und Weissdorn, dem Mistel und Liguster auf und fressen, nächst den **Ebereschbeeren**, die **Wachholderbeeren** am liebsten. Sind jene alle und diese verschneit, so nehmen sie mit anderen, selbst mit den Früchten von wilden Rosen und Schwarzdorn, mit Ligusterbeeren und den saftlosen Früchten des Weissdorns fürlieb, von welch letzteren ihre Exkremente und die ausgespieenen

Butzen, der dunkelroten Schalen jener Früchte wegen, aussehen, als sei zerhacktes rohes Fleisch darunter. In südlicheren Ländern fressen sie auch Oliven und die Beeren des Mastix- und Lorbeerbaumes; überhaupt kenne ich fast keine einheimische beerentragende Holzart, deren Früchte sie nicht mehr oder weniger gern genössen. Wenn gegen Ende des Winters die Erde noch mit Schnee bedeckt ist, dass sie keine Erdwürmer finden können, müssen sie auch noch mit Beeren fürlieb nehmen; weil diese aber jetzt schon seltener und vom Froste ausgetrocknet, kraftloser werden, so magern sie davon ab und werden sichtlich matter. Im Frühling fressen sie, wenn sie nicht der grösste Hunger dazu treibt, gar keine Beeren. Sie achten, wenn erst der Schnee geschmolzen ist und sie wieder Regenwürmer finden können, die Beeren nicht mehr; und wenn man diese den Winter über auch noch so gut aufbewahrt hätte und sie noch so schön und frisch aussähen, so wird doch keine Wachholderdrossel sie angehen; ja selbst in dieser Zeit Gefangene leiden lieber den bittersten Hunger, ehe sie an selbige anbeissen.

In der Gefangenschaft halten sie sich bei dem mehrerwähnten Drosselfutter sehr gut, und man gewöhnt die eben Gefangenen im Herbst mit untermengten Beeren und im Frühling mit Regenwürmern, die man anfänglich in Stücke zerschnitt, daran. Es sind tüchtige Fresser; auch darf ihnen ein frischer Trunk und ein öfteres Wasserbad nicht fehlen, wenn sie sich lange Zeit wohl befinden sollen. Kälte schadet ihnen nicht; dagegen darf man sie nicht dem Ofen nahe bringen, denn das können sie nicht vertragen.

FORTPFLANZUNG

Diese Vögel nisten in nördlichen Ländern, und zwar so hoch nach Norden hinauf, als es noch einigermassen hohe Bäume gibt. In **Norwegen, Schweden, Russland, Livland** und **Polen** nisten sie in Menge, einzeln aber auch schon in **Preussen** und selbst in **Schlesien**. Der Hang zur Geselligkeit, den diese Vögel bei uns auf dem Zuge zeigen, verlässt sie auch in der Brutzeit nicht ganz, und sie nisten im Norden oft in Menge so nahe beisammen, dass man nicht selten mehrere Nester auf einem Baume findet. Aber nicht in Nadelwäldern, sondern in Laubhölzern und einzig wo Birken wachsen, brüten sie. Im nördlichen Norwegen ist jedes kleine Birkenwäldchen voll von ihnen.* Sie brüten zweimal im Jahre, einmal im Mai und

* Diese Nachrichten verdanke ich der Güte meines Freundes BOIE in **Kiel**, der sie auf seiner Reise in Norwegen sammelte und mir auch Nest und Eier in natura mitteilte. Es stimmt fast alles mit dem überein, was wir durch Professor GERMANN in Meyers *Vögeln Liv- und Esthlands* schon früher kannten.

zum zweitenmal im Juni; und da sie meistens vier bis fünf Junge auf einmal aufbringen, so erklärt sich daraus ihre Menge, in der man sie alle Jahre sieht, obgleich ihrer so viele weggefangen werden. Das Nest steht auf Birkenbäumen, bald ziemlich hoch, bald so niedrig, dass man hineinsehen kann; ebenso steht es manchmal im Gipfel, ein andermal in den dichten Zweigen, und dann einmal wieder dicht am Schafte des Baumes, auf daraus hervorgehenden kleinen Ästen. Das Nest ist etwas gross, wenigstens bildet es von innen einen ziemlich weiten und tiefen Napf. Von aussen besteht es aus zarten Reiserchen und dürren Pflanzenstengeln, von innen ist es mit feineren Hälmchen ausgebaut und inzwischen mit Erde oder Lehm zusammen verbunden. Doch nicht in allen Nestern findet sich dieses Bindemittel, wenigstens ist es in so geringem Maße vorhanden, dass man es kaum bemerkt. Ich besitze eins, das von aussen von alten Pflanzenstengeln und Moos gebaut und inwendig mit sehr vielen dürren feinen Grashälmchen und zarten Pflanzenstengeln dicht ausgefüttert ist; es sieht von aussen unkünstlich aus und bildet einen ziemlich tiefen weiten Napf, aber von Erde oder Lehm fand ich wenig oder nichts darinnen. Die Eier, deren man gewöhnlich vier bis fünf, seltener sechs in einem Neste findet, sind stets etwas kleiner als die Eier der **Amsel**, denen sie übrigens in der Farbe ähneln; doch sind die Zeichnungen immer von etwas röterer Farbe. Sie haben eine etwas kurzovale Form und sind auf meergrünem oder sehr blass grünspanfarbenem Grunde rostfarbig oder matt braunrot bespritzt und punktiert, zuweilen auch fein gefleckt, und diese Zeichnungen sind über die ganze Fläche verbreitet, häufen sich jedoch auch manchmal am stumpfen Ende.

In **Livland** sollen sie oft nahe bei den Häusern, in Gärten und Alleen brüten, aber immer nur da, wo es Birken gibt. In Schlesien bei Polnisch Wartenberg, im Territorium meines verstorbenen Freundes VON MINCKWITZ, brütete einstmals ein einzelnes Pärchen in einem kleinen Feldhölzchen, aus Stangenholz von Eichen und Birken bestehend, das kaum tausend Schritte von einem grossen zusammenhängenden Nadelholzwalde entfernt war, in dem man nie nistende Wachholderdrosseln bemerkt hatte; ein Beleg für das oben Gesagte, dass sie nicht in Nadelwäldern, sondern in Birkenwäldern brüten.

Höchst rätselhaft muss uns das erst seit einem halben Jahrhundert beobachtete Auftreten dieser Art als **Nistvogel** auch für **unsere** Gegenden sein. Noch vor dieser Zeit galt die **Wachholderdrossel** unbestritten, nicht allein bei meinem Vater und in allen älteren ornithologischen Schriften, sondern auch bei allen deutschen

Vogelstellern und Vogelkennern als eine Vogelart, die sich bloss im hohen Norden fortpflanze und **Deutschland** nur vom Oktober und November an bis März und April auf dem Durchzuge, oder um bei uns zum Teil zu überwintern, besuche, aber nie hier niste. Jedoch mit Anfang dieses Jahrhunderts vernahm man schon aus mehreren Gegenden **Schlesiens** von dort nistenden Wachholderdrosseln; etwa 20 Jahre später, wo sie nach eingelaufenen Berichten uns schon näher gerückt, traf ich selbst zu meinem nicht geringen Erstaunen und ganz unerwartet eine kleine Gesellschaft dieser Drosseln in den buschreichen Umgebungen eines **sächsischen** Dörfchens, in der Nähe der Stadt **Delitzsch**, nistend an; ein paar Jahre später sah mein Bruder im Herzoglichen Forste **Kleinzerbst**, zuerst im Jahre 1822 und später wieder einmal, ein nistendes Pärchen, und seitdem haben sie sich weniger in einzelnen Paaren, als vielmehr in kleinen Vereinen von mehreren Paaren in einigen Gegenden unseres **Anhalt** völlig eingebürgert. Belege dafür gibt bereits die Zeitschrift: NAUMANNIA II, S. 42 in einem trefflichen Aufsatze von PÄSSLER, und für das Vorkommen nistender Wachholderdrosseln in der **Oberlausitz** ebenfalls die N. IV., S. 30 und folgende noch ausführlicher von O. V. BÖNIGK, zwei herrliche Darstellungen, auf die ich verweisen muss; dem aber noch zuzufügen wäre, dass in den letztverflossenen Jahren nistende Wachholderdrosseln im anhaltischen Forste **Diebzig**, wie in dem angrenzenden preussischen bei **Lödderitz** sich alljährlich in stets wachsender Anzahl einfanden, sodass sie bereits die Aufmerksamkeit der Knaben reizten, die Eier und Junge in Menge ausnahmen, wie denn überhaupt zu bemerken sein möchte, dass Eiersammler vor kaum mehr denn zehn Jahren für ein einziges Ei der Wachholderdrossel noch einen Taler zahlen mussten, während man in jetziger Zeit, mit Auswahl und in beliebiger Anzahl, das Stück für zwei Groschen kaufen kann. Noch wäre vielleicht nachzuholen, dass die Wachholderdrosseln zum Nisten in unseren Gegenden gern solche Waldpartien wählen, die von feuchten Niederungen und Wiesen begrenzt werden, hinsichtlich der Holzarten aber eben nicht wählerisch sind, indem sie nicht allein im vielartigen reinen Laubholz, sondern auch in mit Nadelholz gemischten, selbst in jungen, fast zu Stangenholz aufgewachsenen Nadelbaumansaaten, wo jene Umgebungen jedoch auch nicht fehlen dürfen, oft gesellig nisten, nicht selten so nahe bei einander, dass man von einem Standpunkt aus zuweilen mehrere der stets nur wenig versteckten Nester überblicken kann, die gewöhnlich nicht viel höher als 20 Fuss stehen, nahe dem Wipfel solcher Bäume, oder an grösseren, z. B. an Eichen, auf einem Stummel oder horizontalen Aste, oft weit vom Schafte, in zehn bis zwölf Fuss Höhe, oft auch kaum über Mannshöhe in dem oberen Quirl junger Kiefern, sogar zuweilen auf den Köpfen alter Weiden. Waldteile, wo recht vielerlei Holzarten, wenn auch gerade nicht Erlen und Birken, nicht zu gedrängt beisammen wachsen, zwischen denen auch freie Grasplätzchen vorkommen, ziehen sie zum Nisten dem dichteren Walde vor, zumal wenn Wiesen und feuchte Triften angrenzen, auf denen sie, ohne weit darnach fliegen zu müssen, das Futter für ihre Jungen u.s.w. mit Bequemlichkeit finden.

FEINDE

Während sie bei uns überwintern, sind sie vielen Verfolgungen der Raubvögel ausgesetzt, unter denen der **Habicht** und **Sperber** die ärgsten sind. Kommt ihnen einer derselben nahe, so entfliehen sie mit grässlichem Geschrei und eilen dem dichten Gebüsche zu, wodurch sie sich nicht selten retten.

NUTZEN

Ihr Fleisch ist sehr schmackhaft, und man schätzt es höher als das der anderen Drosseln, teils weil man es länger und auch im Winter hat, teils seines angenehmen, schwach gewürzhaften, etwas bitteren Beigeschmacks wegen, welchen es durch den Genuss der Wachholderbeeren bekommt. Im Frühjahr, wenn sie keine Beeren mehr fressen, verliert sich dieser beliebte Geschmack, aber es bleibt dennoch eine sehr gute Speise. Wenn sie recht fett sind, so sind besonders die jungen Vögel äusserst delikat.

Man verspeist sie alljährlich zu vielen Tausenden, und die Märkte in grossen Städten sind voll von ihnen. Es gibt Gegenden, wo man sie deswegen in ungeheuerer Anzahl fängt. **Ostpreussen** soll alljährlich an 600000 Paar verspeisen und verschicken und **Danzig** mit seinen Umgebungen in manchem Jahr allein gegen 60000 Paar konsumieren. Es gibt Gegenden in **Thüringen**, wo mancher einzelne Vogelsteller in einem Jahr 20 bis 40 Schock fängt. Überall wird ihnen nachgestellt, und könnte man die Listen der in den Städten Deutschlands jährlich zum Verkauf eingebrachten Vögel dieser Art zusammen bringen, so müsste eine ungeheuer grosse Summe heraus kommen. Schon die Alten fanden diese Vögel wohlschmeckend, und die Römer mästeten sie sogar, nebst anderen Drosseln, Ortolanen, Wachteln und dergleichen, in eigens dazu eingerichteten Vogelhäusern.

Sie werden zur niederen Jagd gezählt und entweder einzeln oder in sogenannten Klubbs, wozu man jedes Mal zwei Stück rechnet, verkauft. Sie sind, wie die Misteldrosseln und Amseln, **Ganzvögel** oder, wie man in anderen Gegenden spricht, **Grossvögel** und werden im nördlichen Deutschland das Stück mit einem bis zwei Groschen bezahlt.

Die Federn kann man zum Ausstopfen weicher Kissen, Müffe und dergleichen gebrauchen. In den tief im Gebirge liegenden Walddörfern und ihren Umgebungen, wo es im Spätherbst eine unzählige Menge von Spinnen gibt, sollen sie durch das Aufzehren dieser ekelhaften Geschöpfe noch besonders nützlich werden. Sie vertilgen übrigens eine Menge Larven von schädlichen Insekten.

SCHADEN

Sie schaden einigermassen dadurch, dass sie mancherlei wenig nutzbare Beerensträuche durch die ausgespieenen oder durch den Unrat abgegangenen Kerne fortpflanzen und sie an Orte bringen, wo es vorher keine gab. Auch gehört hierher die schädliche Mistelpflanze.

In Italien sollen sie in den Olivengärten durch Aufzehren der Oliven Schaden tun.

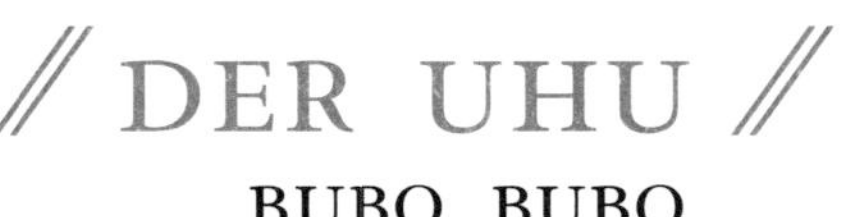

DER UHU

BUBO BUBO

Uhu, Buhu, Schuhu, Schubut, Schuffut, Huhui, Puhuy, Puhi, Bhu, Huo, Hub, Hüru, Auf, Gauf, Berghu, Uhueule, grosse Ohreule, grosse Horneule, grosse gelbbraune Ohreule, Berg- und Steineule, Schubuteule, Adlereule, Grossherzog.

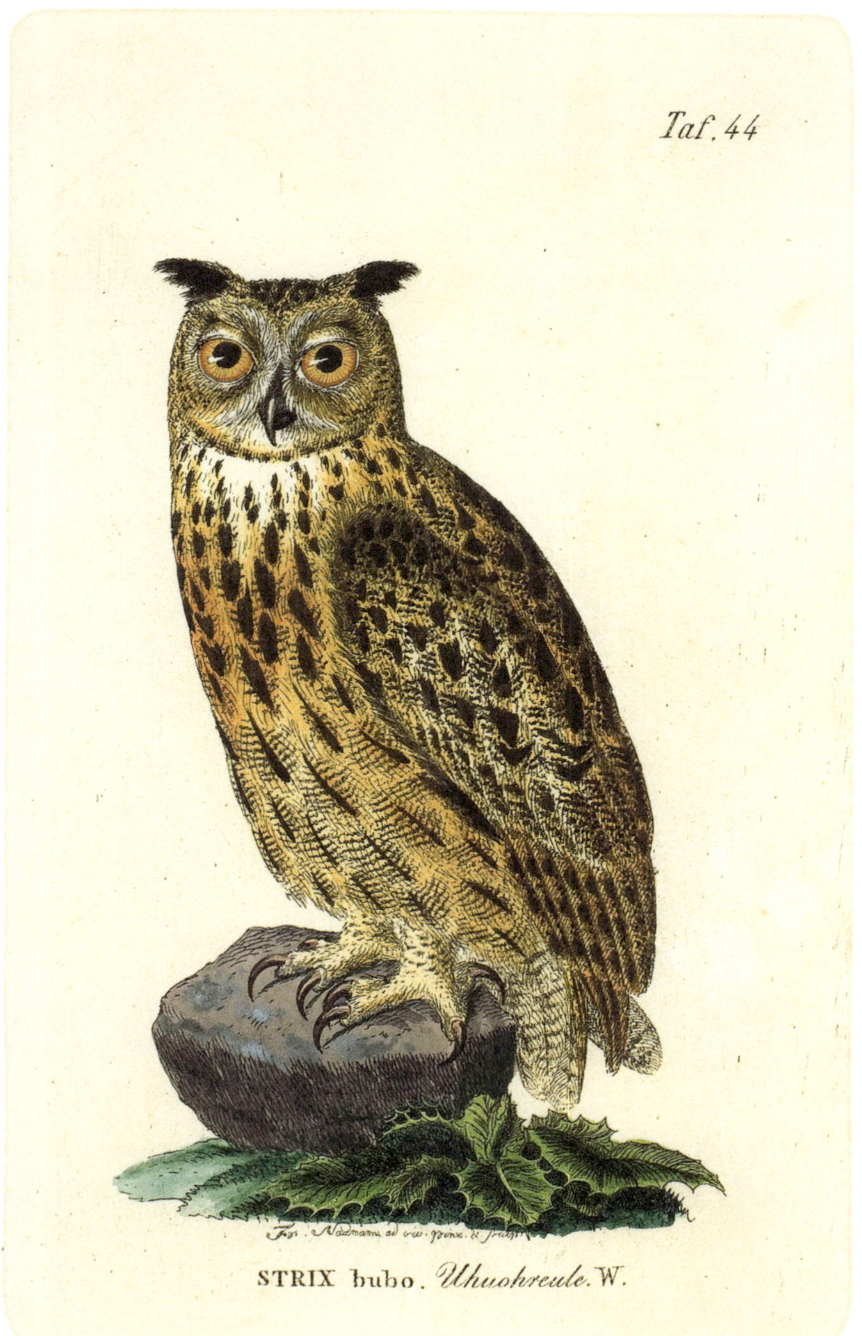

STRIX bubo. *Uhuohreule*. W.

KENNZEICHEN DER ART

Die oberen Teile dunkelrostgelb und schwarz geflammt, die Kehle weisslich, die Federbüsche fast ganz schwarz, die Augensterne orangerot.

BESCHREIBUNG

Der Uhu ist unter den deutschen Eulenarten die grösste. Sein grosses Gefieder, das sehr locker ist und meist vom Körper absteht, gibt ihm eine scheinbare Grösse, die der des Steinadlers oder einer Gans ähnlich wird, ob er gleich einen weit kleineren Rumpf als diese hat. Seine Länge beträgt 57 bis 59 cm, die Flügelbreite 160 bis 165 cm, doch gibt es auch Exemplare, welche diese Grösse noch um mehr als 2,4 cm übersteigen. Der Schwanz ist am Ende gerade, 23,5 bis 24 cm lang, und die zusammengelegten Flügel bedecken ihn bis auf ein Viertel seiner Länge.

Der starke, ungezahnte, in einem Halbzirkel herabgebogene Schnabel ist von der Stirn bis zur Spitze in gerader Linie 4,7 cm, über dem Bogen aber 6 cm lang und schwarz von Farbe. Das sehr grosse feurige Auge hat eine tief schwarze Pupille und eine brennend hochgelbe oder pomeranzenfarbige Iris, eine Farbe, welche sich oft der Feuerfarbe nähert. An diesen grossen schönen Augen bemerkt man sehr deutlich die Verengung und das Erweitern des Sehloches, wie dies mit dem Atemholen abwechselt, wie die Pupille im Dunkeln sehr gross ist und bei plötzlich einfallendem hellem Licht sich schnell zusammenzieht, u.s.f. Die runde Ohröffnung ist verhältnismässig nicht so gross wie bei anderen Eulen.

Die Fusswurzeln und die obere Seite der Zehen sind dicht befiedert, die Zehensohlen rauhwarzig, von Farbe braungrau. Im ganzen sind die Füsse mittelmässig, die Krallen aber gross, schön gekrümmt, stark und dunkelbraun. Der Lauf ist 7 cm hoch; die Mittelzehe 5,9 cm lang, ihre Kralle, über den äusseren Bogen gemessen, 4,7 cm, im Durchschnitt aber 3,5 cm; die Hinterzehe 2,4 cm und ihre Kralle 5,9 cm lang.

Das Gefieder ist mit einem ziemlich unordentlichen Gemisch von gelbbraun oder dunkelrostgelb, dunkelbraun und schwarz bedeckt, so dass es fast unmöglich oder doch unnütz ist, eine ganz genaue Beschreibung aller Flecken und Zeichnungen zu geben.

Die dicken Borstfedern des Gesichtes sind weissgrau, braungelblich und an den Spitzen schwarz; die Einfassung des Gesichts, der Kragen oder Schleier, ist ziemlich unordentlich, gelbbraun mit schwarz gefleckt und punktiert. Auf dem Vorderkopfe erhebt sich über jedem Auge ein Büschel 8,2 cm langer, schwarzer, seitwärts gelbbraun gefleckter und gestrichelter Federn, welche aufrecht stehen, sich jedoch etwas rückwärts krümmen und Ohren oder Hörnern ähnlich sehen. Die Federn auf dem Kopfe sind schwarz und haben gelbbraun gefleckte und gestrichelte Kanten; die Halsfedern rostgelblichbraun mit unregelmässigen breiten schwarzen Streifen in der Mitte; die Rücken- und Schulterfedern, imgleichen die Flügeldeckfedern rostgelblichbraun oder sehr dunkel rostgelb, unordentlich schwarz gefleckt, punktiert und gemischt, die kleinen Flügeldeckfedern am dunkelsten, sodass die letztere Farbe beinahe die Oberhand hat. Die braunschwarze Farbe bildet am Oberteile des Vogels überhaupt auf dem dunkel rostgelben Grunde bald grosse und kleine Flecke, bald Punkte, bald unordentliche Zickzacklinien; alles ist regellos durcheinander gemischt. Die Schwingen sind am Ende abgerundet, der äussere Rand der drei vorderen sägenartig gezähnelt, alle mit bräunlichschwarzen und rostgelben, dunkelbraun bespritzten, gleichbreiten Querbinden durchzogen. Die Steissfedern und Schenkel sind dunkelrostgelb, mit sehr schmalen dunkelbraunen Wellenlinien durchzogen; ebenso, nur etwas heller, sehen auch die dicht befiederten Läufe und Zehenrücken aus. Die Kehle ist weiss, die Halsfedern bis an die Brust braunschwarz mit sehr breiten rostgelben Einfassungen; die dunkelrostgelben Brustfedern haben längs den Schäften einen breiten braunschwarzen Streif und sind mit schmalen dunkelbraunen zickzackförmigen Querlinien durchzogen; die unteren Schwanzdeckfedern schmutzig rostgelb mit bräunlichen Wellenlinien, blasser als die Brust; die mittleren Schwanzfedern schwarzbraun mit schmalen, durchbrochenen, gelbbraunen Querbändern, die übrigen dunkel rostgelb, braun bespritzt, mit neun unregelmässigen, gezackten, schwarzbraunen Binden.

Dies ist die Beschreibung eines **alten Weibchens**. Das **Männchen** ist stets kleiner, seine Gestalt viel schlanker und der Kopf, im Verhältnis zu den übrigen Körperteilen, dicker als am Weibchen. Auch sind die Ohrenfedern viel länger (gegen 9 cm), die Iris dunkler, die Grundfarbe des Gefieders weniger rostgelb, sondern stark mit Weiss gemischt, auch mehr und grösser schwarz gefleckt. Beachtet man diese zwar nicht sehr auffallenden, doch standhaften Unterscheidungsmerkmale, so wird man es nicht mit dem Weibchen verwechseln können.

An den **jungen Vögeln** sind alle Farben dunkler und die Flecke häufiger als bei den Alten; Männchen und Weibchen unterscheiden sich aber dessen ungeachtet auf dieselbe Art voneinander. Die Höhe und Tiefe der Grundfarbe, die grössere oder geringere Anzahl der Flecke und übrigen dunklen Zeichnungen weichen zwar bei diesem Vogel auf mancherlei Weise ab, doch gibt es keine so grosse Verschiedenheiten, dass man sagen könnte, der Vogel variiere auffallend.

AUFENTHALT

Der Uhu ist ein über viele Teile der Erde verbreiteter Vogel. Man findet ihn in ganz **Europa**, im mittleren und nördlichen **Asien**, z. B. in **Astrachan** und in **Kamtschatka**. In **Deutschland** war er 1822 zwar nirgends sehr zahlreich, doch auch keineswegs selten. Er liebt felsige und gebirgige Waldungen und kommt nur selten in die Ebenen. Je einsamer ein solcher Wald ist, je mehr er mit schroffen Felsen und tiefen Bergschluchten abwechselt, desto lieber ist er ihm, zumal wenn sich noch in selbigem Ruinen alter Burgen und sehr hoher verfallener Gebäude befinden, welche er besonders liebt. Im südlichen Deutschland, das mehr solcher Gegenden hat, ist er daher auch häufiger als im nördlichen, wo es meist nur ebene Waldungen gibt. Im **Thüringer Walde** und auf dem **Harz** ist er überall bekannt, in den ebenen sächsischen und brandenburgischen Waldungen aber selten, und noch seltener verfliegt sich einmal einer zu uns in die kleineren anhaltischen Wälder; doch sind mir auch hiervon mehrere Beispiele bekannt. Im Herbst unternimmt er gewöhnlich solche Auswanderungen, die aber nicht Regel sind; denn er ist ein Standvogel und nur unter gewissen Umständen oder zufällig Strichvogel, ob er gleich ein ziemlich weitläufiges Standrevier zu bewohnen pflegt und in selbigem herumstreift.

EIGENSCHAFTEN

In ruhiger Stellung sitzend hat der Uhu ein abenteuerliches Ansehen; aus dem grossen, unförmlich aufgedunsenen Federklumpen sieht man kaum die Spitzen der Extremitäten hervorragen, die halbgeschlossenen Glotzaugen lassen ihr prachtvolles Feuer kaum ahnen; aber plötzlich reisst er sie weit auf, wenn er etwas Unerwartetes bemerkt, biegt den Kopf und Oberleib vor- und seitwärts, hebt einen Fuss nach dem andern und tritt wieder damit auf, indem er die auswendige Zehe bald zur Hinterzehe, bald wieder vor schlägt, fängt an zu zittern, winkt langsam mit den Augenlidern und knappt mit dem Schnabel zusammen. Wird er böse, so scheinen seine grossen Augen zu funkeln, er biegt den Rumpf vorwärts, hält die Flügel etwas hängend vom Rumpfe ab und sträubt das Gefieder so auf, dass er noch einmal so gross aussieht, faucht und knappt mit dem Schnabel gar gewaltig und fährt nun wütend auf seinen Feind los. Es ist überhaupt ein kühner und beherzter Vogel, der im Freien selbst den Steinadler angreift, welcher ihm im Kampfe sogar zuweilen unterliegen soll.* Sein Mut wird durch die Kraft seiner Glieder unterstützt und er lässt, was er einmal gepackt hat, nicht leicht wieder los. Von anderen Eulen unterscheidet er sich vorzüglich darin, dass er am Tage viel munterer ist und dann, in der Gefangenschaft auch oft Nahrung zu sich nimmt; dahingegen die anderen jederzeit die Dämmerung abwarten und den Tag über mit geschlossenen Augen an einer Stelle ruhig sitzen. Er ist daher auch sehr auf seiner Hut, bemerkt alles, was um ihn vorgeht, und flieht schon, wenn die Gefahr nur von weitem droht. Um sich weniger bemerklich zu machen, legt er das Gefieder glatt an den Körper, drückt sich, wenn er auf einem Aste sitzt, an den Stamm des Baumes hart an, wird dann sehr schlank und kann so leicht übersehen werden. Er sucht dazu die dichtesten Bäume und auf diesen die belaubtesten Stellen aus, versteckt sich aber weit lieber in Felsenklüften und in den Ruinen verfallener Gebäude, wenn sich diese im Walde oder in der Nähe desselben befinden, auch wohl in sehr grossen weiten Baumhöhlen, und bringt den Tag über in selbigen zu. Ehedem, als noch der Gebrauch des Schiessgewehrs seine Vermehrung nicht so sehr einschränkte, hauste er selbst auf den abgelegenen Türmen bewohnter Burgen und Waldschlösser. Alte hohe Ruinen, in welchen sich die meisten Eulenarten gern aufhalten, waren

---

* Siehe WAGNER in seiner *Historia naturalis Helvetiae curiosa* p. 195. In wie weit diese Geschichte wahr ist, wage ich nicht zu entscheiden. Der Kampf zwischen Adler und Uhu wird indes von mehreren Schriftstellern erzählt und für wahr gehalten.

daher auch in alten Zeiten als Wohnorte dieser lichtscheuen Nachtschwärmer bekannt, die der Aberglaube für Gespenster hielt. Unser Uhu ist es denn auch, der hierzu mancherlei Stoff gab und in den nächtlichen Zügen des wilden Jägers und wütenden Heeres die Hauptrolle spielte.

Der Uhu lebt meist einsam, nur zur Begattungszeit mit seinem Weibchen und seiner Familie beisammen; doch hat man, besonders zu Anfang des Frühlings, zuweilen auch mehrere beisammen gesehen, welche bei nächtlicher Weile viel Lärm machten und sich wahrscheinlich um die Weibchen stritten. Er fliegt leicht, ohne Geräusch, langsam, schwankend und meist niedrig. Des Abends ist sein Flug nicht nur gewandter als am Tage, sondern er schwingt sich dann auch zuweilen sehr hoch in die Luft. Dass ihn auch das hellste Sonnenlicht nicht blendet, sieht man an der Geschicklichkeit, mit welcher er, ohne anzustossen, am hellen Tage durch die dichten Zweige hindurch fliegt.

Sein gewöhnliches Geschrei ist ein hohles, gedämpftes, aber doch weit hörbares **Puhu!** und **Puhue!** Es klingt um so fürchterlicher, wenn es von mehreren Uhus oft und schnell wiederholt und bei nächtlicher Stille in einsamen Gebirgswäldern oder in den Ruinen verödeter Waldburgen grausend widerhallt. Dass diese grässlichen Stimmen, mit einem etwas höheren **Hu!** untermischt, durch die verschiedene Modulation dieser und anderer, etwas abweichender Töne bald einem schallenden Hohngelächter, bald dem Klaffen und Heulen von Hunden, dem Jauchzen von Jägern, dem Wiehern von Rossen und dergl. ähnlich, ehedem Menschen, welche sich den grausenden Lärm an so unheimlichen Orten nicht naturhistorisch erklären konnten, in Furcht und Schrecken setzte, darf uns nicht wundern. Die Sage vom wilden Jäger und seinen Zügen, vom wütenden Heer, seinen furchtbaren Vorbedeutungen, und was Aberglaube und Unwissenheit eines dunklen Zeitalters Unsinniges und Schreckbares noch ersannen, kommt unfehlbar alles auf Rechnung des nächtlichen Umherschwärmens, der Spiele und Kriege des Uhus, die besonders zur Begattungszeit am lebhaftesten betrieben werden. Das hohe **Hu!** ähnelt in der Tat dem starken Jauchzen eines Menschen und scheint, da man es öfter im Frühling als in einer anderen Jahreszeit von ihm hört, sein Paarungsruf zu sein. Ein grässliches lauttönendes **Kreischen** hörte ich zu dieser Zeit nur von dem Weibchen. Wenn er böse ist, schlägt er den Schnabel so hart zusammen, dass ein lautes **Klappen** dadurch hervorgebracht wird, das im höchsten Zorn noch von einem fauchenden **Pu!** begleitet wird.

Jung aufgezogen wird der Uhu ziemlich zahm, doch auch mit Unterschied, indem es bös- und gutartig Gesinnte unter ihnen zu geben scheint. Wenn auch nicht zu leugnen ist, dass die Behandlung von seiten seines Wärters viel Einfluss hierauf hat, so bin ich doch durch Erfahrung belehrt worden, dass es wirklich sanfte, und im Gegenteil auch unbändige und mordsüchtige Uhus gibt. Mein Vater unterhielt sonst stets einen Uhu für die Krähenhütte, und so hatten wir in vielen aufeinander folgenden Jahren mehrere dieser Vögel. Ihr Betragen war gar sehr voneinander verschieden; denn während mehr als einer jede ihm vorgeworfene lebendige Krähe, sobald er sich unbeobachtet glaubte, ohne Umstände erwürgte und auffrass, auch jedes Mal, wenn ihm die Fesseln für die Krähenhütte angelegt werden sollten, sich fürchterlich zur Wehre stellte, liess ein anderer geduldig mit sich machen, was man wollte, und lebendige Tauben oder Krähen liefen tagelang unangetastet in seinem Behälter herum; ja er litt lieber den bittersten Hunger, ehe er es gewagt hätte, ein ihm vorgeworfenes lebendiges Geschöpf zu töten; sogar von den anderen ihm hingelegten toten Tieren getraute er sich, so lange eine lebende Taube, Krähe, Holzhäher und dergl. in seinem Behälter war, nichts zu fressen.

Die Beispiele von Sanftmut und Feigheit sind indes seltener als die von Bosheit, Widersetzlichkeit und Mordsucht.

NAHRUNG

Diese grosse Eule nährt sich von allerlei kleinen Tieren, als: Hamstern, Wasser- und Wanderratten, Maulwürfen, Wald- und Feldmäusen, Schlangen, Eidechsen, Fröschen und allerlei grossen Käfern. Unter den grösseren Tieren werden dem Uhu aber auch Hirsch- und Rehkälber, Hasen, Kaninchen, und unter den Vögeln Auer-, Birk- und Haselhühner, Fasanen und Rephühner, Krähen, Häher und dergl. oft zur Beute. Auch die kleinsten Vögel verachtet er nicht. Im Winter soll er sich zuweilen den Waldstädten nähern und daselbst die schlafenden Krähen von den Dächern holen; denn Krähenfleisch ist seine liebste Speise, Raubvögel frisst er hingegen sehr ungern. Den kleinen Tieren und Vögeln zerknickt er mit dem Schnabel erst den Kopf und die übrigen grossen Knochen, und verschluckt sie dann ganz, mit Haut und Haar oder mit allen Federn; grösseren Vögeln reisst er den Kopf ab, entblösst die Haut etwas von Federn, reisst nun das Fleisch in ziemliche Stücke und verschlingt es. Die grösseren und härteren Knochenstücke werden im Magen meist in die mit verschluckten Haare und Federn eingewickelt und alles in länglichen Ballen, als sogenanntes Gewölle, durch den Rachen wieder ausgespieen, während nur ein Teil der Knochen mit dem Fleische zur wirklichen Verdauung übergeht. Grössere Tiere frisst er nicht mit Haut und Haar, sondern reisst ihnen die Haut am Bauche auf, frisst bloss das Fleisch heraus, legt, wenn er es auf einmal nicht verzehren kann, das Fell recht artig wieder zusammen und schiebt es in einen finsteren Winkel, aus welchem er es, sobald er von neuem Appetit bekommt, wieder hervorholt. Im Winter geht er auch auf das Aas.

Er fliegt des Abends sehr zeitig, bei trübem Wetter oft noch vor der Abenddämmerung, nach Raub aus und geht auch des Morgens erst spät zur Ruhe.

Die in Gefangenschaft gehaltenen Uhus werden mit allerlei Geflügel, im Notfall auch mit Fleisch von krepiertem Vieh gefüttert, und haben zu ihrem Wohlbefinden nichts nötig als einen geräumigen, nicht zu hellen Behälter oder kleinen Stall mit darin angebrachten Sitzstangen und täglich etwa soviel Futter als eine Krähe beträgt. Zuviel Nahrung ist ihnen nicht gut und es scheint ihnen weit besser zu bekommen, wenn man sie mitunter einige Tage hungern lässt. Sie können viel auf einmal verzehren, aber auch vier bis fünf Wochen ohne Nahrung hinbringen. Doch sie zu lange hungern zu lassen, ist nicht ratsam; auch muss der Behälter oft von dem Abfall ihrer Küche gereinigt werden. Man sagt auch, dass sie Fische frässen; diejenigen, welche ich hatte, wollten jedoch nicht daran. Ihr Behälter muss sich an einem abgelegenen Orte befinden, teils damit sie nicht so oft gestört werden, teils des üblen Geruches wegen, den die Überbleibsel ihrer Mahlzeiten verbreiten. Es ist überhaupt besser und ihrem Wohlbefinden angemessener, wenn man ihnen nicht mehr vorwirft, als sie auf einmal verzehren können; das stinkende Fleisch, besonders wenn es von Maden durchwühlt wird, ist ihnen nicht zuträglich.

FORTPFLANZUNG

Schon in der zweiten Hälfte des März machen sie Anstalt zur Brut, brüten aber dennoch nur einmal im Jahr. Ihr sehr grosses Nest, das auswendig aus vielen Stecken und dürren Reisern und inwendig aus trockenem Laube und Genist unkünstlich gebaut ist, legen sie meistenteils in einer Kluft zwischen Felsen oder alten Ruinen, und nur da, wo sie diese nicht haben, auf einem alten abgestutzten Baum, am seltensten aber auf einem hohen Baum an. Zuweilen bauen sie in Steinhöhlen gar kein Nest und die Eier liegen ohne alle Unterlage da. Das Weibchen legt zwei bis drei, äusserst selten vier, fast runde, weisse Eier, welche eine grobkörnige Schale haben und etwas grösser als Hühnereier sind. Das Weibchen bebrütet die Eier drei Wochen lang, bringt jedoch selten mehr als zwei Junge aus.

Die Jungen sehen anfänglich einem Wollklumpen ähnlich, indem sie mit sehr zartem lockerem Flaum bekleidet sind, welcher auf schmutzig weissem und rötlichgrauem Grunde Punkte und feine Wellenlinien von dunkelbrauner Farbe hat. Sie lassen beständig ein starkes Zischen und zuweilen einige hellpfeifende Töne hören, bleiben so lange im Neste, bis sie völlig fliegen können, und werden von den Alten so reichlich mit Futter versehen, dass man beständig einen grossen Vorrat davon in ihrem Neste findet. Erst in der sechsten Woche werden die Federohren bei den Jungen sichtbar, und sie entdecken sich ihren Feinden durch das erwähnte, weit hörbare Zischen sehr bald. Sehr weit entfernen sich die alten Uhus selten von ihrer Brutstätte; sie finden sich im Frühjahr wieder in der Gegend ein und legen das neue Nest meist an derselben Stelle oder auf dem nämlichen Baum wieder an oder bessern bloss das alte wieder etwas aus. So gibt es Felsenhöhlen, in welchen sie seit langen Jahren alljährlich ihre Brut machten, ob man ihnen gleich alle Jahre die Jungen wegnahm.

So selten der Uhu auch in hiesiger Gegend ist, so liess sich doch vor einigen Jahren ein Pärchen einfallen, in einem Anhaltischen Forste unweit der Stadt **Dessau** zu brüten. Die Gegend war sehr lange von der ausgetretenen Elbe überschwemmt, und es kam natürlich in dieser Zeit kein Mensch dorthin. Als die Elbe wieder in ihre Ufer zurücktrat, entdeckte man den Horst, in welchem zwei Jungen sassen, die ausgenommen und aufgefüttert wurden. Das Nest stand in dem sehr grossen, ausgehöhlten, mit vielen starken Ästen und dichten Zweigen umgebenen Kopfe einer nicht gar hohen, aber sehr alten Hain- oder Weissbuche. Wahrscheinlich dasselbe Pärchen hat nachher wieder einmal in jenem Forste gebrütet.

FEINDE

Alle Vögel hassen den Uhu von ganzem Herzen, jedoch vorzugsweise die Waldvögel; allein die Sumpf- und Wasservögel achten nur wenig, manche sogar gar nicht auf ihn. Er ist deswegen, sobald er sich am Tage sehen lässt, den Verfolgungen und unaufhörlichen Neckereien sehr vieler Vögel ausgesetzt, deren Heldentaten aber nur in Schreien bestehen, und wovon nur wenige es wagen, ihn wirklich zu zwicken. Unter den Tagraubvögeln gibt es viele, welche ihm sehr heftig zusetzen, doch sind vor allem die **Krähen** seine ärgsten und unversöhnlichsten Feinde, welche ihn sogar durch ihren feinen Geruch auswittern.* Sie verraten durch ihr unaufhörliches Schreien um und über ihm oft dem Jäger sein Dasein, wenn sie seinen Schlupfwinkel ausgewittert haben und über demselben herumschwärmen.

NUTZEN

Durch Vertilgung zahlloser Mäuse, Hamster, Maulwürfe und dergl. wird er nützlich. Besonderen Nutzen gewährt er uns noch durch den Gebrauch für die Krähenhütte, indem wir durch dieses Mittel die schädliche Menge mancher Raubvögel- und Krähenarten vermindern können. Für die Fasanerien ist dies von besonderer Wichtigkeit. Die jungen Uhus stehen deshalb an vielen Orten in einem hohen Preise; so in meiner Gegend, wo das Stück meist mit zehn Reichsthalern bezahlt wird.

SCHADEN

Dieser ist für Jagdreviere von nicht geringer Bedeutung, da er sich nicht allein an jungen Rehen, sondern selbst an Wildkälbern vergreifen soll. Soviel ist gewiss, dass ein Pärchen, welches Junge hat, eine unglaubliche Menge von Hasen, Rephühnern und anderem nutzbaren Wildbret diesen zuschleppt. Er ist also in dieser Zeit ein besonders schädlicher Vogel, dem der Jäger mit Recht sehr nachstellt, wozu dieser

---

* Mein Vater pflegte sonst, wenn er in seine etwas entlegene Krähenhütte gehen wollte, den Uhu, um ihn bequemer zu tragen, in einen ganz mit Leinwand überzogenen Handkorb zu stecken; hier trug es sich nun oft zu, dass Schwärme von Krähen, welche von ohngefähr über ihn wegfliegen wollten, plötzlich im Fluge anhielten und meinen Vater eine weite Strecke, zuweilen bis zur Hütte selbst, verfolgten, ob sie gleich nicht das Mindeste vom Uhu sehen konnten.

auch von der Obrigkeit billig durch ein gutes Lösegeld (in manchen Ländern 12 bis 16 Gr.) für ein Paar eingelieferte Fänge [Füsse] aufgefordert wird. Dies ansehnliche Schussgeld und der hohe Preis, in welchem die Jungen stehen, sind auch Ursache, dass die Anzahl der Uhus von Jahr zu Jahr vermindert wird, sodass wir sie in Deutschland bald unter die seltenen Vögel werden zählen müssen.

// DER WANDERFALKE //

FALCO PEREGRINUS

Taubenfalke, Fremdlings- und Pilgrimsfalke, Berg-, Wald-, Stein-, Beiz-, Hühner-, Edel-, Kohl- und Blaufalke, Tannenfalke, grosser Baumfalke, Taubenstösser, Schwarzbacken; edler, ausländischer, schwarzer, schwarzbrauner, schwarzblauer und gefleckter Falke; schwarzbrauner und gefleckter Habicht; in hiesiger Gegend: (sehr uneigentlich) Blaufuss.

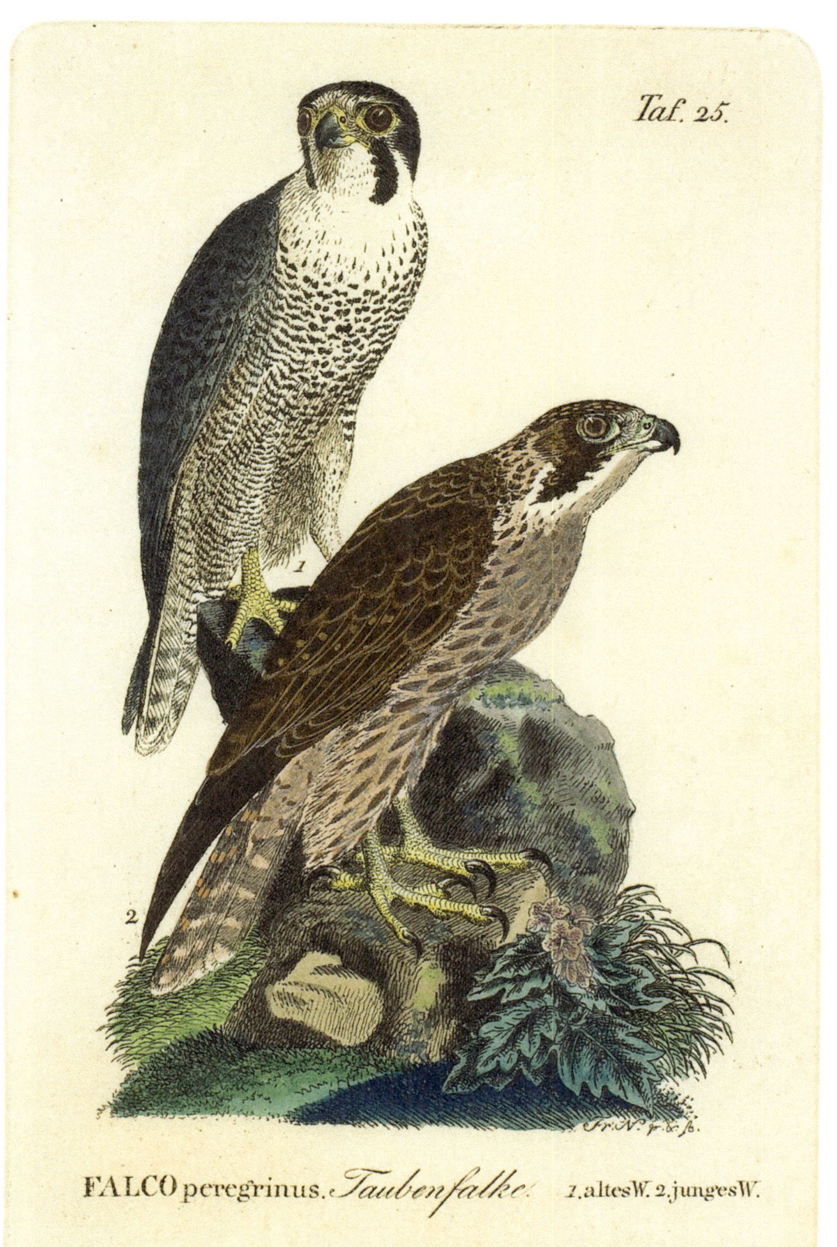

FALCO peregrinus. *Taubenfalke.* 1. altes W. 2. junges W.

KENNZEICHEN DER ART

Wachshaut, Augenkreise und Füsse gelb, in der Jugend grünlich; die Zehen sehr lang; die Flügel lang, mit dem Schwanze von gleicher Länge; der Backenstreif sehr breit und, wie der obere Teil der Wangen, schwarz; das Genick weiss gefleckt. Länge 38–40 cm.

Alter Vogel: Oben aschblau mit schwarzen Querflecken, unten rötlich oder bläulichweiss, mit schwarzen Wellenlinien; Schwanz mit neun bis zwölf schwarzen Querbinden.

Junger Vogel: Oben dunkelbraun mit hellen Federsäumen, unten gelblich- oder bräunlichweiss mit braunen Längsflecken; Schwanz mit sieben bis neun hellen Querflecken.

BESCHREIBUNG

Die Grösse dieses Vogels ist ganz ausserordentlich verschieden; man findet nämlich so kleine männliche Exemplare, die noch nicht die Grösse der **Nebelkrähe** haben, dagegen aber wieder Weibchen fast von der Grösse des **Kolkraben**, sodass diese oft um ein Vierteil grösser als jene sind. Die Männchen messen in der Länge von 39–44 cm, in der Breite von 84–106 cm; die Weibchen findet man von 42,2–49 cm Länge und 99–113 cm Breite.

Die Länge des etwas abgerundeten schmalen Schwanzes steigt von 16–18 cm, und die in Ruhe liegenden Flügel reichen mit ihren Spitzen bis an sein Ende oder doch nahe an dasselbe. Die Länge des Flügels vom Handgelenk bis zur Spitze beträgt 33–36 cm.

Der Schnabel ist kurz, dick, sehr gekrümmt, mit einem scharfen Zahn versehen, welcher in einen eben so scharfen Einschnitt des Unterkiefers passt; im Durchschnitt 2,96 cm, im Bogen 3,32 cm lang und im Durchschnitt an der Wurzel beinahe 2,36 cm hoch; das Nasenloch rund, in der Mitte mit einem kleinen Höcker. Bei alten Vögeln sind Wachshaut, Mundwinkel, die Wurzel des Unterkiefers und die Augenlider nebst einem kahlen Flecke vor und um denselben schön gelb, der

Schnabel übrigens hellblau mit schwarzer Spitze, die Iris nussbraun oder auch dunkelbraun.

Die Füsse sind schön gelb; die Läufe oder Fusswurzeln kurz, stark und geschuppt; die Zehen sehr lang und geschmeidig, oben geschildet, unter den beiden Gelenken der Mittelzehe und dem einen der äusseren und inneren Zehen mit Ballen in Gestalt länglicher loser Warzen besetzt, und zwischen der äusseren und mittleren befindet sich eine kleine Spannhaut. Die Krallen sind krumm, sehr scharf, und schwarzhornfarbig; der Lauf 6 cm, die Mittelzehe 6 cm, die Hinterzehe 2 cm, und die Hinterkralle im Bogen 2 cm lang.

Das zwei Jahre alte **Männchen** hat folgende Farben: Die Stirne ist weisslich, mit schwarzen borstigen Haaren durchmischt, Scheitel und Nacken blauschwarz, im Genick etwas weiss gefleckt; der ganze Rücken, Oberhals und die Deckfedern der Flügel bläulichaschgrau mit schwarzblauen Querstreifen durchzogen, welche eben so breit wie ihre hellen Zwischenräume sind. Die Kehle, der untere Teil der Wangen und der Kropf sind weiss; von der Schnabelwurzel und dem Auge geht ein schwarzer Streif bis auf den halben Hals herab; die Brust ist weiss, oben rötlich überlaufen und nebst den Hosen mit schmalen schwärzlichen Querstreifen bezeichnet, welche gebrochenen oder geketteten Querlinien ähnlich sehen; auf dem Kropfe stehen einzelne runde schwärzliche Flecken; der After ist gelblichweiss, mit schwärzlichen Querlinien einzeln durchzogen. Die Schwingen sind schwärzlich, mit roströtlichweissen Querflecken auf der innern breiten Fahne. Der Schwanz ist etwas zugerundet, von Farbe wie der Rücken, mit neun bläulichaschgrauen und ebenso vielen blauschwarzen breiten Querbändern wechselweise durchzogen, am Ende mit weissen Spitzen. Die unteren Flügeldeckfedern sind weiss mit schwärzlichen Wellenlinien, Schwing- und Schwanzfedern von unten grau und schmutzigweiss gebändert.

So sieht das Männchen aus, wenn es etwa 1 ½ Jahr alt ist oder sich zum erstenmal vermausert hat. Auch das Weibchen trägt ein ähnlich gefärbtes Kleid.

Je älter dieser Vogel wird, desto lichter wird er an den unteren Teilen seines Körpers, die dichten Querstreifen der Brust und Hosen werden schmäler, der gelbliche oder rötliche Anflug verliert sich, die weisse Grundfarbe wird reiner, zuletzt aber hellaschblau überlaufen, vorzüglich in den Seiten und an den Schenkeln; der Rücken wird hingegen mit zunehmendem Alter dunkler. Männchen und Weibchen sind sich in der Farbe jederzeit sehr ähnlich, letzteres ist aber immer grösser als das Männchen, die Brust ist in der Jugend weniger rostgelb und im Alter weniger blau überlaufen, auch der Rücken und die oberen Teile überhaupt nicht so dunkel und weniger schön gezeichnet als am letzteren. In der Grösse ist der Unterschied oft ausserordentlich.

Die jungen Vögel sind ganz anders gefärbt als die alten. Vor dem ersten Federwechsel hat das **junge Männchen** folgende Farben: Der Schnabel ist hellbläulich, die Wachshaut, der Mundwinkel und der kahle Ring um die Augen blaugrünlich, die Iris dunkelbraun. Stirne und Kehle sind weiss, die Backen weiss, etwas rostgelb überlaufen; der Scheitel grauweiss, roströtlich gemischt und schwarzbraun gefleckt, welche Flecken auf dem Hinterhalse grösser werden und vom Auge und dem Mundwinkel am Halse herab einen schwarzbraunen Streif bilden. Die Rückenfedern und die Deckfedern der Flügel sind schwarzblaugrau, hell rostbraun gekantet; die Deckfedern des Schwanzes heller und mit breiteren, an den Spitzen weisslichen Kanten; die Ruderfedern etwas heller als der Rücken, mit licht rostroten gebrochenen Querstreifen und rötlichweissen Spitzen; die Schwingen dunkler mit eben diesen Querstreifen und Spitzen; Unterhals, Brust und Hosen weiss, rostbräunlich überlaufen und jede Feder in der Mitte mit einem breiten dunkelbraunen **Längsfleck**, welche Flecke häufig lanzettförmig zugespitzt und auf den Hosen ganz schmal sind, am Bauche und After sich aber ganz verlieren. Die unteren Deckfedern der Flügel haben weisse und braune gleichbreite Querstreifen. Die Füsse sind grünlichgelb.

Am **jungen Weibchen** sind Wachshaut, Füsse und der kahle Fleck vor dem Auge grüngelb, der Stern im Auge graubraun; die Stirne gelblichweiss, der Scheitel, der obere Teil der Wangen und ein Streif vom Mundwinkel bis zur Hälfte des Halses herab braunschwarz, roströtlich gefleckt; das Genick gelblichweiss, schwarzbraun gefleckt; die Kehle rein weiss, der Rücken und die Flügeldeckfedern dunkelbraun, hell rostgelblich gesäumt, die grösseren, ausser den Säumen noch mit dergleichen Flecken bezeichnet; die Schwingen schwärzlich mit weissen Endkäntchen, die Deckfedern des Schwanzes heller als der Rücken; die Schwanzfedern bräunlichgrau, mit gelblichweissen Spitzen und acht bis neun rostfarbenen Querflecken. Kropf, Brust und Hosen sind gelbbräunlich weiss, auf der Mitte jeder Feder mit einem braunen **Längsfleck**, die Schenkel inwendig gelblichweiss, desgleichen auch die Bauch- und Afterfedern, letztere mit schwarzen Federschäften und einzelnen verloschenen herzförmigen Flecken und Strichen.

Übrigens findet in der Grundfarbe wie in den Zeichnungen unter den jungen Wanderfalken mancher Unterschied statt; sie sind, ehe die Farben von der Witterung abgebleicht werden, sehr dunkel, sodass sie, wenn sie erst das Nest verlassen haben, meistenteils von oben her ganz schwarzbraun aussehen. Sind sie von spät gefallener Brut, so hält sich die dunkle Farbe zuweilen den Herbst und Winter hindurch bis gegen das Frühjahr. Doch gibt es auch noch andere Abweichungen, von welchen uns die Ursachen zur Zeit noch unbekannt sind; denn manche Individuen sind unten mehr, manche weniger, andere dunkler, wieder andere heller gefleckt, bald sind die oberen Teile rötlich-, bald bläulichgrau überlaufen, bald sind sie ganz dunkelbraun, mit breiten oder schmalen, rostfarbenen oder bräunlichweissen Federrändern u. s. w. Besonders dunkel sehen die meisten jungen Weibchen aus, auch fehlen diesen an den oberen Teilen, ausser den lichten Federsäumen, oft alle helleren Flecke. Sie sind am Kopfe, dem Hinterhalse und an dem oberen Teile der Wangen braunschwarz, die Federn am ersteren lichter gesäumt, der Nacken und die Halsseiten weiss gefleckt, der Backenstreif aber sehr breit und einfarbig dunkel braunschwarz. Der ganze Mantel ist schwarzbraun, mit lichtbraunen, ins Weissliche übergehenden sehr schmalen Federsäumen; Unterrücken, Bürzel und Schwanz etwas lichter als der Mantel, und die sieben bis neun lichtrostbräunlichen Querbinden des letzteren sehr schmal, auf der äusseren Fahne nicht sichtbar und auf den Mittelfedern nur als kleine nierenförmige Flecke bemerkbar. Auch auf den in Ruhe liegenden Flügeln bemerkt man ausser den Spitzenrändern der Federn keinen lichten Fleck. Die Kehle ist rein gelblichweiss, alle unteren Teile rostbräunlichweiss, mit grossen schwarzbraunen Längsflecken auf der Mitte der Federn, die an den Schenkeln mitunter in Querstreifen übergehen und an den Afterfedern eine herzförmige Gestalt haben. Am dunkelsten sind die Unterbrust und die Seiten. Die unteren Flügeldeckfedern sind schwarzbraun und weiss gefleckt mit rostgelber und rostbräunlicher Mischung.

Der Zahn im Schnabel ist bei ganz jungen Vögeln oft auch noch nicht so ausgebildet, so gross und scharfeckig wie bei den Alten.

Es soll auch eine ganz weisse Spielart geben, welche aber gewiss äusserst selten ist.

AUFENTHALT

Man findet den **Wanderfalken** durch ganz **Europa** und auch in den nördlichen Teilen von **Asien**, **Afrika** und **Amerika**. In **Deutschland** ist er nirgends selten, am wenigsten im nördlichen, und er gehört bei uns (im Anhaltischen) zwar nicht zu den sehr gemeinen, doch auch keineswegs zu den seltneren Vögeln. Er ist hier ganz einheimisch; denn obgleich die meisten im Herbst fortziehen, so kommen doch immer wieder andere, welche den Sommer über wahrscheinlich nördlicher wohnten, die das Revier eine Zeitlang bestreichen und dann wieder weiter ziehen, an die Stelle der ersteren. Dieses Fortziehen und Ankommen währt den ganzen Winter hindurch, doch sieht man im Winter weniger als im Herbst und Frühling zur eigentlichen Zugzeit. Im Sommer besucht er das Feld wenig, im Herbst, Winter und Frühling ist er aber beständig auf dem Feld, und man sieht ihn dann auf Steinen, kleinen Hügeln und Erdschollen sitzen und sich nach Beute umsehen. In der Fortpflanzungszeit bewohnt er Wälder und felsige Gegenden und liebt dann vorzüglich die waldigen Mittelgebirge. In ebenen Gegenden zieht er die Nadelwaldungen den Laubholzwäldern vor. Er ist zu dieser Zeit mehr Waldvogel, ob er gleich auch die angrenzenden Felder und freien Plätze seiner Nahrung wegen häufig besucht. Mit welcher Zähigkeit ein Wanderfalkenpaar allen Anfechtungen und Verfolgungen zum Trotz dann an der einmal bewohnten, ihm zusagenden Gegend festhält, ist ganz auffallend. Und bestimmte Gegenden, namentlich, wenn sie hohe Felspartien aufweisen, scheinen auf das Wanderfalkengeschlecht eine derartige Anziehung auszuüben, dass immer wieder neue Pärchen die alten abgeschossenen oder gefangenen an den betreffenden Brutplätzen ergänzen. Viele Felsen, die schon seit langen, langen Zeiten den Namen »**Falkenstein**« führen, beherbergen zur Brutzeit das stolze Räubergeschlecht fast Jahr für Jahr, wenn es daselbst auch den grössten Nachstellungen ausgesetzt ist.

EIGENSCHAFTEN

Der **Wanderfalke** ist ein mutiger, starker und äusserst gewandter Vogel; sein kräftiger Körperbau und sein blitzendes Auge beurkunden dies auf den ersten Anblick. Die Erfahrung lehrt uns, dass er nicht vergeblich von der Natur mit so furchtbaren Waffen ausgerüstet ward, und dass er im Gebrauch derselben seinen nahen Verwandten, dem **Jagd-** und **Würgfalken** rühmlichst an die Seite zu setzen sei. Im gezähmten Zustande ist er aber auch gelehrig und folgsam wie sie, daher nach diesen der geschätzte **Beizvogel** der Falknerei. Sein Flug ist äusserst schnell, mit hastigen Flügelschlägen, sehr selten schwimmend, meist niedrig über die Erde hinstreichend. Wenn er sich vom Boden aufschwingt, breitet er den Schwanz aus und fliegt, ehe er sich in die Höhe hebt, erst eine kleine Strecke dicht über der Erde hin. Nur im Frühjahr schwingt er sich zuweilen zu einer unermesslichen Höhe in die Luft. Er ist sehr scheu und so vorsichtig, dass er zur nächtlichen Ruhe meist nur die Nadelholzwälder aufsucht. Hat er diese nicht in der Nähe, so bleibt er öfters lieber im freien Felde auf einem Steine sitzen, und es gehört unter die seltenen Fälle, wenn er einmal in einem kleinen Laubholze übernachtet. Aus Vorsicht geht er auch in letzteren des Abends erst sehr spät zur Ruhe und wählt dazu die dichten Äste hoher alter Bäume. In etwas grösseren übernachtet er gern auf in jungen Schlägen einzeln stehen gebliebenen alten Bäumen, und hier kommt er auch schon mit Untergang der Sonne, meist mit dick angefülltem Kropfe, an. Am Tage setzt er sich ungern auf Bäume. Sitzend zieht er den Hals sehr ein, sodass der runde Kopf auf den Schultern zu stehen scheint, und die weisse Kehle, mit den abstechenden schwarzen Backen macht ihn von weitem kenntlich. Im Fluge zeichnet er sich durch den schlanken Gliederbau, den schmalen Schwanz und durch seine langen, schmalen und spitzen Flügel vor anderen aus. Er fängt schon im August an, seine Federn zu wechseln, mausert aber sehr langsam, oft bis ins Frühjahr hinein.

Seine Stimme ist stark und volltönend, wie die Silben **Kgia, kgia!** oder **Kaja, kaja!** Man hört sie aber, ausser der Begattungszeit, eben nicht oft.

NAHRUNG

Sein Raub besteht bloss in fliegenden Vögeln; den sitzenden kann er nichts anhaben.* Er raubt sie von der Grösse der **Lerche** bis zu der der wilden **Gans** ohne Unterschied, und richtet besonders unter den **Rephühnern** und **Tauben** die grössten Verwüstungen an. Die wilden **Tauben** zieht er den zahmen vor, und da, wo man ihn im Felde auf der Erde sitzen sieht, liegt gewöhnlich eine Kette oder ein Volk (Gesellschaft) **Rephühner** in der Nähe, von denen er, sobald sie auffliegen, eins hinwegnimmt, denen er aber, so lange sie still liegen bleiben, keinen Schaden zufügen kann. Er lauert jedoch gewöhnlich so lange, bis die **Rephühner** glauben, er sei lange fort; sie fliegen dann auf, und er erreicht seinen Zweck. Da wo er keine **Rephühner** findet, müssen die **Tauben** herhalten. Diese wissen kein anderes Rettungsmittel, als in möglichster Schnelle und so dicht aneinander als möglich, die Flucht zu ergreifen. Auf diejenige, die sich etwas vom Schwarme absondert, schiesst er pfeilschnell von oben nieder; stösst er das erste Mal fehl, so sucht ihn die **Taube** zu übersteigen, und glückt ihr dieses nur einige Male, so wird der Falke müde und zieht ab. In der grössten Not rettet sich die Taube zuweilen in ein Gebüsch, in die Zweige der Bäume, ja was noch mehr ist, ich habe eine Taube sich in ein Wasser stürzen und durch Untertauchen glücklich retten sehen. Man sieht hieraus, wozu die Not ein so geängstigtes Tier zwingen kann; es sucht in einem Elemente Rettung, für welches es gar nicht geschaffen ist.

Hat dieser Falke keine **Rephühner** und **Tauben**, so müssen die **Saatkrähen, Dohlen** und auch wohl **Eichelhäher** seinen Hunger stillen. Er raubt auch **Brachvögel, Schnepfen**, wilde **Enten** und wilde **Gänse** und überhaupt alle dergleichen Vögel, die er im Freien fliegend antrifft. Alle Wasservögel suchen sich durch Untertauchen im nächsten Wasser vor seinen Stössen zu sichern, die Waldvögel und andere im Gebüsche. Er verfolgt die Tauben bis nahe an die Dörfer, und seine Kühnheit geht oft soweit, dass er die **Trappe** angreift, doch kann er ihr nichts anhaben.

Er setzt sich mit seiner gefangenen Beute niemals ins Gebüsch, sondern verzehrt sie auf freiem Felde. Grosse Vögel frisst er auf der Stelle, wo er sie gefangen hat; klei-

---

* Diese Tatsache beruht auf den sichersten Beobachtungen, scheint aber durchaus nicht in Mangel an Aufmerksamkeit oder eines guten Gesichts ihren Grund zu haben, sondern darin, dass er, wie alle Edelfalken, mit einem ungeheuren Kraftaufwande in schiefer Richtung von oben herab nach seiner Beute stösst. Er würde sich selbst Schaden zufügen, wenn er mit solcher Gewalt nach einem am Boden sitzenden Vogel stossen wollte.

nere trägt er aber in den Klauen an eine freiere bequemere Stelle. Er fliegt schnell und niedrig an der Erde hin, um so die überraschten Vögel, die meistenteils vor Schrecken das Stillsitzen vergessen und auffliegen, zu überrumpeln. Er stösst allemal auf seine Beute aus der Höhe schief herab.

In grossen oder gebirgigen Waldungen, wo er sich im Sommer aufhält, jagt er **Auer-, Birk-** und **Haselhühner**. Vierfüssige Tiere fängt er in der Freiheit nie, fällt auch nie aufs Aas, ja er ist so ekel, dass er den Raub, den er auf einmal nicht ganz verzehren kann, auch nie wieder anrührt. In der Gefangenschaft aber zwingt ihn der Hunger Nahrungsmittel zu sich zu nehmen, die er sonst nie anrührt, z. B. Mäuse. Er hat immer einen gesunden Appetit. Ich hatte einmal einen solchen Falken über ein Jahr lang in einem grossen Käfige, und dieser frass in zwei Tagen einen ganzen Fuchs auf, desgleichen drei Krähen in einem Tage; er konnte aber auch über eine Woche lang hungern. Er packte oft sechs lebendige Sperlinge, in jeden Fang drei, wobei er auf den Fersen sass, dann einem nach dem andern den Kopf einkniff und beiseite legte. Eine lebende alte **Krähe** machte ihm in seinem engen Gefängnisse viel zu schaffen, desgleichen auch eine **Eule**. Wenn er mich mit einer lebenden **Eule** kommen sah, machte er sich struppig und setzte sich schlagfertig auf den obersten Sitz seines Behälters; die **Eule** legte sich, sobald sie in den Käfig kam, auf den Rücken, stellte ihm ihre offenen Klauen entgegen und zischte fürchterlich; der **Falke** kehrte sich aber hieran nicht, sondern stiess so lange von oben herab, bis es ihm glückte, sie beim Halse zu packen und ihr die Gurgel zuzuhalten; auf seiner Beute sitzend, breitete er jetzt freudig seine Flügel aus, rief aus vollem Halse sein **Kgia, kgia, kgia!** und riss ihr mit dem Schnabel die Gurgel heraus. Mäuse frass er auch, aber bei Hamstern und Maulwürfen verhungerte er.

Er entblösst seinen Raub von den meisten Federn und verschlingt ihn dann stückweise. Die kleinen Vögel verschluckt er samt den Eingeweiden, bei grösseren lässt er aber diese liegen. Faules und stinkendes Fleisch rührt er auch in der Gefangenschaft bei dem grössten Hunger nicht an.

Dieser **Falke** würde bei weitem den Schaden nicht unter dem Geflügel anrichten, wenn er nicht für so viele Faulenzer arbeiten und sie ernähren müsste. Da sitzen die trägen und ungeschickten **Bussarde** auf den Grenzsteinen oder Feldhügeln, geben genau auf den **Falken** Acht, und sobald sie sehen, dass er etwas gefangen hat, fliegen sie eiligst herbei und nehmen ihm ohne Umstände seine Beute weg; der sonst so mutige, kühne **Falke** lässt, sobald er den ungebetenen Gast ankommen sieht, seine Beute liegen, schwingt sich mit einem etlichemal ausgerufenen **Kgia, kgia!** in die Höhe und davon. Ja sogar dem feigen **Rotmilan**, den eine beherzte Gluckhenne von ihren Küchlein abzuhalten imstande ist, überlässt er seine Beute. Er setzt sich auch, wenn er gleich noch so hungrig wäre, denselbigen nie zur Wehre und zankt sich gleichwohl beständig mit seinesgleichen herum. Auch der **Rauhfussbussard** nimmt ihm oft seine Beute ab. Einst hielt ein solcher Falke mehrere Jahre nacheinander zur Herbstzeit die Tauben der Stadt Leipzig im Schach, verfolgte sie hoch über den Häusern und dem Menschengetümmel hin und holte sich in dieser Zeit fast täglich eine, welche er dann in den Klauen fast jedes Mal auf die oberste Gallerie der Sternwarte trug, die ihm regelmässig zur Speisetafel diente, um sie hier zu verzehren, was von vielen Menschen bemerkt wurde und einige junge Leute veranlasste, ihm da oben aufzulauern; weil jedoch bloss mit sogenannten Kugelschnöppern dort zu schiessen erlaubt war, so bemühten sie sich nebenbei, ihm mit allerlei Fangmitteln nachzustellen, doch hat ihnen weder das eine noch das andere gelingen wollen. Nur dann, wenn dieser Falke seine Beute zu weit zu tragen hatte, hielt er seine Mahlzeit auch auf einem hohen Dache einer Kirche oder eines sehr hohen Hauses.

Bei seinen Angriffen auf Taubenschläge bemerkte man, dass er meistens auf die jüngeren **Tauben** geht, die noch unerfahren, sich leichter vom Schwarme absondern lassen, dann mit wenigerem Geschick seinen Stössen auszuweichen wissen, oder aus Mangel an Kraft und Gewandtheit nach einem Fehlstosse sich nicht schnell und hoch genug zu erheben vermögen, daher gewöhnlich nach wenigen wiederholten Stössen in seinen Klauen bluten, während ihm die erfahrneren und gewandteren Alten dennoch oft genug entgehen. Von den **Rephühnern** sehen wir dasselbe; aber es kann diesen das letztere um so seltener glücken, weil schon ihr steteres Fortstreichen ihm hier ein viel sichreres Ziel darbietet; doch kommt es auch vor, durch eine schnelle Seitenwendung das ersehene Schlachtopfer sich ein paarmal retten zu sehen, aber nach wenigen wiederholten Stössen versagt dem Geängsteten doch viel gewöhnlicher die Besonnenheit und Kraft, und es unterliegt ihm viel leichter als jene. Machen zwei Falken zugleich Jagd auf dasselbe Stück, so wechseln sie mit den Stössen, und der Ausgang ist in der Kürze entschieden; sie streiten sich aber dann gewöhnlich um die Beute, wobei, wenn diese nicht tödlich getroffen war, sie ihnen manchmal noch entkommt.

FORTPFLANZUNG

Der **Wanderfalke** horstet in **Deutschland** in grossen Nadelholzwäldern der bergigen und ebenen Gegenden auf den höchsten Nadelbäumen, in Gebirgswaldungen aber auch sehr häufig in den Klüften hoher unersteiglicher Felsenwände, oft in solchen, wo unten gangbare Strassen vorbei führen, und in seiner Höhe scheint ihn das Treiben der Menschen tief unter ihm gar nicht zu stören. Beide Gatten sieht man da, wo sie ihr Nest anlegen wollen, bei schönem Wetter oft im März schon in einer ausserordentlichen Höhe gemeinschaftlich schöne Schwenkungen machen, und hört sie dabei ihr **Kgia!** sehr oft wiederholen. Sein flaches Nest (Horst) besteht aus kleinen und grossen trocknen Reisern; in dasselbe legt das Weibchen seine drei, höchstens vier rundlichen, gelbrötlichen, braun gefleckten Eier, die es binnen drei Wochen ausbrütet.

Während der Brutzeit vergnügt sich das Männchen entweder über dem Neste mit einem hohen schönen Flug und wiederholtem Geschrei, oder es streicht auf Beute für sich oder sein brütendes Weibchen aus, lässt sich aber ausser dem Walde wenig sehen. Er raubt dann allerlei grössere Waldvögel, auch wilde **Tauben, Drosseln, Spechte**, vorzüglich junge Krähen, und ist den **Auer-, Birk-** und **Haselhühnern** und **Fasanen**, so wenig diese auch ausser der Brutzeit von ihm verfolgt werden, sehr gefährlich. Er ist dann ein wahrer Waldvogel. Ausser dieser Zeit hält er sich nur des Nachts im Walde auf und sucht seine Nahrung auf dem freien Felde. Wenn das Feld abgeerntet ist, verlassen alte und junge den Wald, begeben sich auf die Felder und gehen nach Sonnenuntergang in die Wälder zur Nachtruhe. Die Jungen verlassen oft das Nest schon, ehe sie noch Kräfte genug haben, den Alten zu folgen, und sitzen dann zerstreut auf den Bäumen unfern des Nestes umher. Nicht selten werden sie hier von Sturmwinden herabgeworfen und können dann leicht erhascht werden. Auf diese Art habe ich mehrmals junge bekommen.

Wenn dieser **Falke** auch während der Fortpflanzungszeit nach Gelegenheit und Umständen im Walde wohnen muss, so kann er doch hier, ausser auf grossen, freien Plätzen, nirgends mit Erfolg jagen, und die Waldvögel, die er fliegend erwischt, können nur wenige und für den Unterhalt seiner Familie nicht ausreichend sein; er sieht sich daher gezwungen in dieser Zeit, um Futter für die Jungen zu schaffen, täglich Meilen weite Ausflüge auf das Freie zu machen, durchstreicht dann die Felder und Fluren einer weiten Umgegend, nicht selten in der Nähe bewohnter Orte, am häufigsten solcher, wo viele **Tauben** gehalten werden.

NUTZEN

Dieser besteht hauptsächlich darin, dass er sich zum Fange anderer Vögel, zur sogenannten Beize abrichten lässt. Er war von jeher einer der geschätztesten Beizvögel und unter dem Namen **Edelfalke** bekannt, ob man gleich auch manchmal den Habicht mit diesem Namen belegte. Sonst, als die Falknerei noch im Ansehen stand, wurden viel Sorgfalt und grosse Kosten auf die Erziehung oder den Fang dieser Vögel (man schätzte die Wildfänge höher als die aus dem Neste genommenen), sowie auch auf ihre Abrichtung, Pflege und Erhaltung verwendet. Die Einwohner eines Dorfes, **Falkenswerth** bei Herzogenbusch, im ehemaligen Flandern, beschäftigten sich sogar zunftmässig damit und hielten ihre Kunstgriffe geheim. Gegen den Herbst reisten viele in andere Länder, um Falken zu fangen, welche sie nachher abrichteten und in die Falknereien von fast ganz Europa verkauften. Ein gut abgerichteter Falke wurde nicht selten mit 800 holl. Gulden bezahlt. Ein solcher Falkenfänger kam jährlich im Herbst ins Herzogtum Bremen und fing hier von Bartholomäi bis Martini und Weihnachten Falken; hatte er sechs bis acht Stück, so hielt er seine Mühe für reichlich belohnt. Er fing aber oft noch mehr, worunter sich auch manchmal Würgfalken befanden. Die Falkenswerther gingen auch als Falkoniere in fremde Dienste. Aber die Zeit hat alles dies gar sehr verändert, und so sind denn in Deutschland jetzt fast alle Falknereien eingegangen.

SCHADEN

Da er bloss von Geflügel lebt, besonders den nutzbaren **Tauben-** und **Hühnerarten** so nachstellt, diese immer frisch haben muss, auch manches erbeutete Stück, bevor er damit seinen Appetit stillen konnte, den **Bussarden** und **Milanen** zu überlassen gezwungen wird, und sich nun ein anderes zu fangen genötigt sieht, so ist der Schaden, den er den Jagden wie den Flügen zahmer Tauben zufügt, sehr bedeutend. Die Gegend, in welcher sich eine Gesellschaft **Rephühner** oder ein Schwarm **Tauben** aufzuhalten pflegen, von welchem er schon eines oder das andere weggekapert hat, sucht er sehr oft heim und wird hier dem armen Geflügel eine wahre Geissel. Die Jagdherrschaften bezahlen daher dem Jäger ein gutes Schiessgeld für die abgelieferten Fänge eines dieser Falken.

// DER TURMFALKE //

FALCO TINNUNCULUS

Turm-, Mauer-, Kirch- und Mäusefalke. Rotfalke, roter und braunroter Falke, roter Sperber, Lerchensperber, Lerchenhacht, Lerchen- und Sperlingshabicht, Rötel- oder Rüttelfalke, Rotel-, Rötel- und Rüttelweihe, Rötel- oder Rüttelgeier, Rittelweiher, Rötelgeierlein, Rötelhuhn, Rötelweib, Rötelweibchen, Graukopf, Steinschmack, Steinschmatz, Steinschmätzer, Sterengall, Wannen- und Wandweher, Wieg- und Windwehe, Windwehl, Windwahl, Windwachl, Schwimmer; in hiesigem Lande: Rüddelgeier.

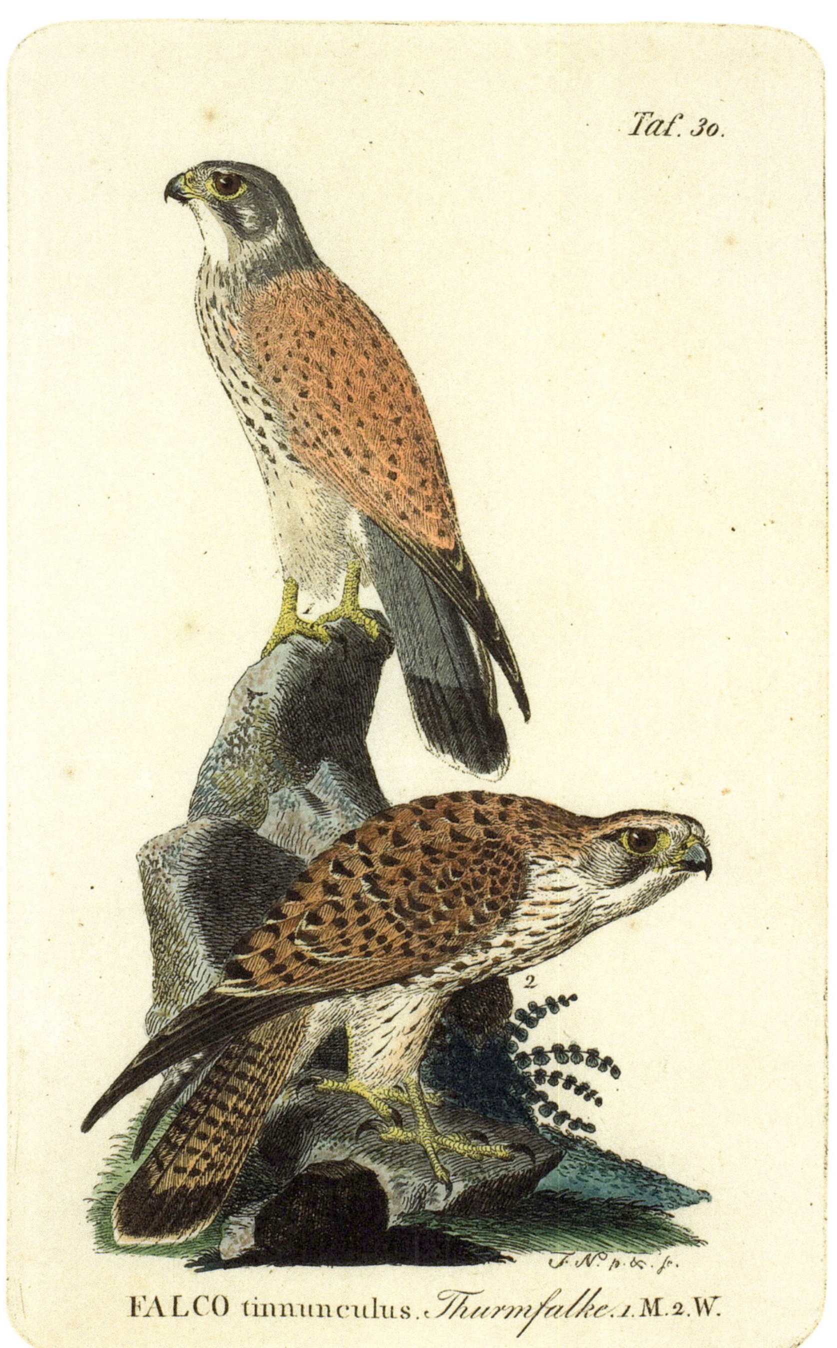

FALCO tinnunculus. *Thurmfalke.* 1. M. 2. W.

KENNZEICHEN DER ART

Mit gelber Wachshaut und gelben Füssen, welche mit **schwarzen Krallen** bewaffnet sind; mit zugerundetem Schwanze, rostfarbenem schwarzgeflecktem Oberleibe; gelblichweissem, mit braunen Lanzettflecken bezeichnetem Unterleibe.

Männchen: Kopf und Schwanz aschgrau, dieser mit einer schwarzen Binde vor der weissen Spitze.

Weibchen und **junger Vogel**: Mit roströtlichem, schwarzbraun geflecktem Kopfe, rostfarbenem, schwarzgebändertem Schwanze.

BESCHREIBUNG

Der Turmfalke ist ein gemeiner, aber angenehm gestalteter und schön gefärbter Vogel. Er gehört unter die kleineren Falken, denn seine Grösse übersteigt nicht die des **Eichelhähers** oder einer **Turteltaube**. Es herrscht in der Grösse, noch mehr aber in der Färbung des Gefieders zwischen beiden Geschlechtern eine grosse Verschiedenheit. Verwechseln kann man ihn nicht leicht mit einer anderen Art, als mit dem ihm in der Tat sehr ähnlichen **Rötelfalken**, von welchem er sich, ausser der ansehnlicheren Grösse, schon durch seine **stets schwarzen Krallen**, die bei **jenem immer weiss sind**, hinlänglich unterscheidet.

Das **Männchen** ist 32 cm lang und 68 cm breit, die zusammengelegten Flügel reichen bis an das Ende des Schwanzes, welcher 14 cm lang ist; das Weibchen ist dagegen 35 cm lang und 73 cm breit. Bei jüngeren Vögeln sind die Flügel immer etwas kürzer und reichen nicht bis an das Schwanzende. Die mittleren Schwanzfedern sind stets länger als die sich stufenweis verkürzenden äusseren, weshalb der Schwanz abgerundet ist.

Der Schnabel ist im Durchschnitt 1,7 cm, im Bogen 1,8 cm lang und an der Wurzel im Durchschnitt 1,2 cm hoch. Er ist vorn scharfeckig gezahnt, sehr krumm, an der scharfen Spitze schwarz, in der Mitte hellblau und an der Wurzel gelb; Wachshaut, Mundwinkel und die kahlen Augenkreise gelb, die Iris dunkelbraun. Das Nasenloch ist rund und hat in seiner Mitte eine kleine runde Erhabenheit, der Unterkiefer da, wo der scharfe Zahn des oberen hinpasst, einen gleichförmigen Ausschnitt.

Die Füsse sind gelb und die nicht gar grossen, nicht sehr stark gekrümmten Krallen schwarz. Die dicht unter dem sogenannten Knie etwas befiederten Läufe sind kurz und stark, desgleichen auch die Zehen, und der Unterschied zwischen diesen und den Füssen des Lerchenfalken, wenn man beide zusammen hält, führt sogleich auf den Gedanken, dass der Turmfalke sich entweder anderer Nahrungsmittel bedienen, oder auf eine andere Art rauben müsste. Der Lauf misst 4,7 cm, die Mittelzehe mit ihrer Kralle 3,6 cm und die Hinterzehe nebst der Kralle 2,4 cm.

Am **alten Männchen** sind Kopf und Hinterhals hellaschgrau, mit feinen schwarzen Federschäften, ein kurzer Streif vom Mundwinkel herab schwarz gestrichelt, Rücken und Flügel schön zimmtfarben oder blassrostrot, mit einzelnen lanzettförmigen schwarzen Flecken. Die Schwingen sind braunschwarz und haben an den inneren Fahnen weisse, mit etwas Braun vermischte Querflecken; die Steiss- und Ruderfedern hellaschgrau, die letzteren am Ende mit einer 3 cm breiten schwarzen Querbinde und weissen Spitzchen. Die Kehle ist ganz weiss, die Brust gelbrötlichweiss, mit kleinen länglichen und lanzettförmigen braunschwarzen Flecken; Hosen und After gelbrötlichweiss und ungefleckt. Flügel und Schwanz sind von unten weisslich, mit durchschimmernder Zeichnung der oberen Seite.

Recht sehr alte männliche Individuen haben an den hell ziegelroten Rücken- und Schulterfedern nur noch einzelne kleine, fast eiförmige, braunschwarze Flecke, auch am Unterleibe sind diese kleiner und runder, nur noch in den Seiten und an der Unterbrust vorhanden; der Kopf ist schön aschblau, der Unterrücken und Schwanz ebenso, doch heller als der Kopf und alle Farben sind ausgezeichnet lebhaft.

Das Aschgrau am Kopfe und Nacken ein- bis zweijähriger Männchen ist gewöhnlich schwach graurötlich überflogen, am bemerklichsten am frischen Gefieder, wovon selbst bei noch älteren etwas sichtbar bleibt, das aber durch Einwirkung der Atmosphäre bei diesem noch viel schneller verschwindet, als dort. Im höheren Alter wird dies Aschgrau nicht bloss reiner, sondern auch **bläulicher**, doch nie so dunkel wie beim männlichen **Rötelfalken**; aber das auf dem Unterrücken, Bürzel und Oberschwanz bleibt stets heller und zarter, als jenes am Kopf und Nacken.

Sehr alte **Weibchen** werden auf dem Kopfe, Nacken und Schwanze grauer, endlich sogar hahnenfedrig, d. h. dem einjährigen **Männchen** ähnlich, doch scheinen solche an dem rötlich-aschgrauen Schwanze, ausser der breiten schwarzen Endbinde, auch alle übrigen schmalen Querbänder, obgleich diese sehr schmal und zum Teil aschgrau überpudert erscheinen, zu behalten; auch die dunklen Flecke auf dem Mantel bleiben zahlreicher und breiter als bei den Männchen.

Das **Weibchen** ist grösser und stärker als das Männchen; Schnabel, Wachshaut, Augen und Füsse sind wie an diesem; Scheitel und Genick sind hellrostfarben, mit braunschwarzen Längsflecken in der Mitte der Federn; die Schulter- und Rückenfedern hell rostfarben, mit helleren Kanten und braunschwarzen, zum Teil halbmondförmigen Querflecken; die Steissfedern rötlich aschgrau mit schwarzbraunen Querflecken. Der zugerundete Schwanz ist rostfarben, mit vielen schmalen, am Ende mit einer breiten braunschwarzen Querbinde und rötlichweissen Spitzen. Die schwarzbraunen Schwingen haben an der inneren oder breiten Fahne breite, gezackte, gelblichweisse, nach den Spitzen zu roströtliche Kanten; die unteren Flügeldeckfedern weiss, schwarzbraun gefleckt, Schwung- und Schwanzfedern auf der unteren Seite grauweiss. Kehle, Wangen und Stirn sind weiss; vom Auge oder Mundwinkel geht ein schwarzbrauner Bartstreif herab; Unterhals und Brust sind gelbrötlichweiss, mit dreieckigen und lanzettförmigen schwarzbraunen Flecken bezeichnet, welche auf den Hosen klein und einzeln werden und sich am After gänzlich verlieren.

Das **junge Männchen** hat, im ersten Jahre, eben die Farben des alten Weibchens, nur sind alle schwarzen Flecke des Mantels kleiner, die Schultern und der Oberrücken noch heller rostrot, und am Kopfe, Steisse und dem Schwanze schimmert ein lichtes Aschgrau durch das Rostrote. Im zweiten Jahre oder nach der ersten Mauser hat es schon die oben beschriebenen schönen Farben, ist aber überall noch stärker braunschwarz gefleckt als jenes, das sich wenigstens zwei- bis dreimal vermausert hat, ehe es in jener Vollkommenheit erscheint.

Die **jungen Weibchen** sind ebenfalls viel dunkler gefärbt als die alten, der rostfarbige Rücken hat auffallend lichtere Federsäume und grössere braunschwarze Querflecke; am Steisse bemerkt man kaum etwas Aschgraues, und die unteren Teile sind gelber, mit grösseren dunkelbraunen Längsflecken.

Die Mauser dieses Vogels fällt eigentlich zu Ende des August und in den September. Sie geht aber sehr langsam von statten, bei manchen, besonders bei jungen Vögeln, so allmählich, dass ich zuweilen im April noch junge Männchen bekam, die noch zur Hälfte das Jugendkleid trugen und sich noch in voller Mauser befanden oder kaum zur Hälfte vermausert hatten. Daraus geht denn hervor, dass solche Vögel, welche ich für Junge späterer Brut halte, volle zwei Jahre alt werden müssen, ehe sie ihr Jugendkleid völlig ablegen oder sich zum erstenmal gemausert haben. Solche in der Mauser begriffene Vögel, an welchen die Federn zweier Kleider untermengt sind, haben ein ganz eigenes Ansehen.

Die meisten **jungen** Vögel mausern in ihrer Abwesenheit im Winter, kommen im Frühjahre oft damit noch nicht fertig zurück, und bei allen bleiben (wie bei anderen Jungen dieser Falkenfamilie) die Schwung- und Schwanzfedern des Jugendkleides bis zur nächsten Mauser zu Anfang des August, wenn sie 1¼ Jahr alt, wo sie nun ausser jenen auch das erst im Laufe des Winters erhaltene, also das sämtliche Gefieder mit einem vollständig neuen Kleide vertauschen; doch waren sie dadurch nicht abgehalten, in jenem gemischten Kleide, folglich im zweiten Frühling ihres Lebens und kaum ein volles Jahr alt, sich bereits fortzupflanzen.

AUFENTHALT

Der Turmfalke ist in ganz **Europa** ein bekannter Raubvogel; auch soll er im mittleren und nördlichen **Asien** überall vorkommen. In gebirgigen Ländern ist er sehr gemein, und in **Deutschland** gibt es wohl keine Gegend, wo er nicht, wenigstens auf dem Durchzuge, angetroffen würde. Im südlichen gebirgigen Deutschland ist er häufiger noch als im nördlichen. Überall liebt er vorzugsweise hohe Gegenden, die mit Felsen und hohen steilen Bergen abwechseln. Auf unserer Ebene ist er daher zwar nicht selten, jedoch wird man ihn in den angrenzenden höheren Gegenden, wie z. B. im **Saalkreise**, im **Mansfeldischen** u.s.f. weit häufiger antreffen. Diese Bemerkung habe ich nicht allein in der Brutzeit, sondern auch selbst in der Zugzeit gemacht; während ich ihn hier nur einzeln sah, traf ich ihn dort ausserordentlich häufig. Bei uns ist er ein Sommervogel; denn er zieht im September von uns, und kommt im März wieder zurück. Sehr selten sieht man einen in gelinden Wintern. Im südlichen Deutschland überwintern dagegen schon mehrere und in der Schweiz soll er fast gar nicht wegziehen. Er liebt das Freie, streift immer auf den Feldern umher und verabscheut die tiefen Waldungen. So wenig er am Tage in den Wäldern gesehen wird, so gern hält er in denselben Nachtruhe; hat er sie aber nicht in der Nähe, so dienen ihm Felsenklüfte, Ritzen und Löcher alter hoher Ruinen zu diesem Behufe. Von den letzteren, besonders wenn sie recht hoch sind und im Felde liegen, scheint er überhaupt ein ausserordentlicher Freund zu sein, denn in der Gegend, wo es dergleichen gibt, wird man auch allemal Turmfalken antreffen. Selbst in vielen grossen volkreichen Städten bewohnt er im Sommer die hohen Türme und Schlösser, wo er aber dies alles nicht haben kann, die kleinen Feldhölzer und Ränder oder grossen lichten Plätze grösserer Wälder, doch immer in der Nähe des Feldes.

Wegen der alten Burgen und vielen Warttürme am östlichen **Vorderharz** entlang sagt ihm vielleicht keine andere Gegend des mittleren **Deutschlands** besser zu, als gerade diese; jedes dieser alten Bauwerke des Mittelalters, selbst manche noch jetzt bewohnte Burg dieses Landstriches, hat im Sommer diesen munteren Vogel aufzuweisen, dazu fast jedes freiliegende Stückchen Wald dieser Gegend, ausser jenen noch seine es bewohnenden Pärchen. Tiefer im Gebirge, wie auf dem Harze selbst, wird er wieder seltener; er liebt also die Ausläufer der Gebirge in hügelige und ebene Gegenden vorzugsweise.

EIGENSCHAFTEN

In Hinsicht seiner Sitten bildet er einen natürlichen Übergang von den **Edelfalken** zu den **Weihen**. Er ist zwar schneller und gewandter als diese, allein bei weitem nicht so mutig, so reissend schnell in seinen Bewegungen als jene, obgleich er übrigens ein unruhiger, lebhafter Vogel ist. Der ihm oft zugeschriebene Mut ist, genau erwogen, mehr Tollkühnheit oder vielmehr Dummdreistigkeit, zu welcher Bemerkung genaue Beobachtungen die entsprechendsten Belege geben. In der Ferne unterscheidet er sich von ähnlichen kleinen Raubvögeln*, namentlich vom Sperber, durch seine längeren und spitzigeren Flügel, vom **Merlin-** und **Baumfalken** aber durch seinen längeren Schwanz und langsameren Flug. Er ist auch weniger edel als Merlin- und Baumfalke, und ähnelt in seiner Lebensart vollkommen den Weihen. Er fliegt übrigens leicht, schnell und mit geschwinder Flügelbewegung, und neckt sich öfters mit anderen Raubvögeln und den Krähen herum. Seine Stimme klingt hell und angenehm, **klih, kli, kli!** Ein sanftes **Kiddrik, kiddrik!** und ein heiseres **Ki, ki!** hört man auch oft von ihm, doch ist das **Kli, kli** oder **Bli, bli, bli**, die gewöhnliche, welche er sehr oft ertönen lässt, zumal im Frühling in der Nähe seines Nestes. Hier schwingt er sich auch zuweilen zu einer ziemlichen Höhe hinauf; auf seinen Jagdstreifereien fliegt er aber mehr niedrig als hoch, wobei

* Auch mit dem Kuckuck, besonders dem rotbraunen, hat er, in der Ferne fliegend, viel Ähnlichkeit, aber dieser macht sich durch seinen geraden Flug, seinen spitzen Kopf und stets schmäler liegenden Schwanz kenntlich. Die Ähnlichkeit beider im Fluge hat vielleicht mit Veranlassung zu dem Märchen gegeben, dass der Kuckuck ein Raubvogel werde.

er das Eigene hat, dass er im Fliegen öfters Halt macht, mit den Fittigen schnell auf- und abschlägt und so eine Zeitlang an einer Stelle bleibt. Dies Hangen und Flattern auf einem Flecke in der Luft nennt man **rütteln** oder **riddeln**, und dies hat dem Vogel zu den meisten Namen verholfen. Er fliegt fast beständig, und man sieht ihn selten sich niedersetzen, um auszuruhen. Ob er gleich scheu und vorsichtig ist, so wird er doch leicht zahm, besonders die Jungen, welche man aus dem Neste geholt und aufgefüttert hat; diese werden ihrem Wärter ausserordentlich zugetan und sollen sich sogar zum Aus- und Einfliegen gewöhnen lassen. Man soll ihn auch zur Beize auf Lerchen und dergleichen mehr abrichten können.

Nur beim Horste und bei recht schönem Wetter steigt er zuweilen bloss schwebend und ohne Flügelschlag in einer Spirallinie zu einer Höhe auf, dass die Sehkraft des besten Auges ihn kaum noch als einen beweglichen Punkt zu gewahren vermag. Sonst fliegt er nie sehr hoch oder doch nicht höher, als seine höchsten Wohnsitze liegen, und wenn er weit weg will, mit schnellen Flügelschlägen und dazwischen nur in ganz kurzen Pausen schwebend, fast wie der **Sperber**.

NAHRUNG

Diese besteht in Mäusen, kleinen oder jungen Vögeln, Vogeleiern, Heuschrecken, Käfern und anderen Insekten, auch kleinen Fröschen und Eidechsen, welches alles er fast immer auf freiem Felde aufsucht. Da er nur im Sitzen raubt, so jagt er die kleineren Vögel, wie: Sperlinge, Lerchen, Goldammern u.a.m. oft so lange umher, bis sie sich setzen, um sie nun erst ergreifen zu können. So jagt er oft die Sperlinge in die Zäune, und an Orten, wo er brütet und viel dreister ist, bis unter die Dächer, und zieht sie da nicht selten aus ihren Schlupfwinkeln hervor. Die Felder durchspäht er im bedächtigen Fluge, macht oft und da Halt, wo er ein taugliches Nahrungsmittel vermutet, indem er sich flatternd so lange an derselben Stelle in der Luft erhält, bis er seine Beute recht aufs Korn genommen hat, um nun schnell und sicher auf sie herabstossen zu können. Er schiesst aber dennoch oft fehl, weil entweder die zu fangende Maus, eben da er zustösst, in ihr Loch schlüpfte oder die die ankommende Gefahr sehende Lerche ihm unter den Klauen weg entflog. Dass er auch so oft und lange vergeblich zielt, mag daher kommen, dass die Feldmäuse, seine vorzüglichste Nahrung, sich spielend oft eben so schnell vor ihren Löchern zeigen, als sie wieder hineinschlüpfen. Ist er des Herumfliegens müde, so setzt er sich auf einen Kloss, Erdscholle, Stein oder Hügel, sieht sich allenthalben um, und sobald sich eine Lerche in seiner Nähe niederlässt, fliegt er hin und macht Jagd auf sie oder ihre Jungen. In dieser Absicht setzt er sich auch gern auf die einzelnen Feldbäume, und zwar auf die höchsten Spitzen derselben. Man sagt auch von ihm, dass er die Tauben oft angreife; allein, ich kann versichern, nie gesehen zu haben, dass ein Turmfalke die Tauben nur verfolgt, viel weniger eine gefangen hätte. Er ist auch viel zu ungeschickt, eine Taube oder andere schnellfliegende Vögel im Fluge zu greifen. Unter den Vögeln, die ihm zur Nahrung dienen, ist die Wachtel, welche er nicht selten erwischt, der grösste. Junge Rephühner von der Grösse der Wachteln werden ihm, da sie die wachsame Mutter mit eigener Lebensgefahr verteidigt, nur selten zur Beute.

FORTPFLANZUNG

Sein Nest findet man in Felsenklüften, in den Löchern hoher steiler Ufer, in den Kirchtürmen mancher Dörfer, selbst in den Löchern sehr hoher Schlösser und Türme grosser volkreicher Städte, in den hohen Ruinen alter verfallener Burgen und Warttürme und, wo sie dieses alles nicht haben können, wie z. B. in unserer Gegend, in hohlen Bäumen oder gar in den oberen Ästen eines hohen Baumes, woselbst aber fast immer ein altes Krähennest die erste Grundlage dazu bildet. In den Wänden tiefer Abgründe und Schluchten nistet er sehr gern, lieber jedoch noch in den Ruinen alter Bergschlösser, besondern wenn sie am Felde liegen; wo er diese vorfindet, wird er sie zur Anlage seines Nestes gewiss allen anderen Gelegenheiten vorziehen. Er begibt sich in der Brutzeit überhaupt nie ohne Not in den Wald, daher er da, wo er einen Platz zum Brüten im Freien auffinden kann, jederzeit diejenigen, die sich ihm im Walde darbieten, verachtet. So findet man oft sein Nest lieber in einem einzelnen hohlen Feldbaume als im Walde selbst, wenn dieser auch nicht weit davon entfernt wäre. Die Eier liegen oft ohne alle Unterlage da, manchmal besteht diese aber auch aus einigen wenigen Strohhalmen, Federn und Tierhaaren. Die freistehenden Nester sind äusserlich von trockenen Zweigen, inwendig von kleinen Wurzeln, Stoppeln, Stroh, Moos und Tierhaaren gebaut; die alten Krähennester werden dagegen bloss inwendig mit wenigen frischen Materialien belegt. Unter den Dächern und in Löchern oder Spalten hochgelegener alter Bauwerke und Türme, meistens an unzugänglichen Orten, nistet er am liebsten und findet sich alljährlich wieder daselbst ein, wo er einmal geduldet oder unbeachtet geblieben war. Merkwürdigerweise horstete einst ein Paar sogar unter dem Dache einer Windmühle. Wo er in einer etwas bewaldeten Gegend wohnt und sich genötigt sieht, auf einem Baume sich selbst ein freistehendes Nest zu bauen, wählt er dazu einen der ältesten und höchsten, gleichviel ob Nadel- oder Laubholzbaum; es steht dann meist nahe am Wipfel und ist ein recht haltbar geflochtener Bau, in der Breite bis gegen 42 cm Durchmesser haltend, mit einer ziemlichen Vertiefung in der Mitte; das Übrige wie beschrieben. Er belegt den Rand desselben häufig mit frisch belaubten Birkenzweigen, die zuweilen mit neuen vertauscht werden; auch fehlen, ausser den angegebenen Materialien zum Ausfüttern der besser als gewöhnlich gebauten Horste, selten Stückchen von Mäusefellen, die ihn sehr kenntlich machen. Das Weibchen legt gewöhnlich vier, seltener fünf bis sechs rundliche, weisse oder rostgelbliche, braunrot gefleckte und überall bespritzte Eier und bebrütet sie drei Wochen lang. Die Alten ernähren ihre Jungen fast mit nichts als Mäusen und jungen Vögeln, und es währt lange, ehe sie imstande sind, sich diese Nahrungsmittel selbst aufzusuchen. Ihre erste Jagd ist dann gewöhnlich die Insektenjagd.

Die Eier verlangen wegen grosser Ähnlichkeit mit denen anderer kleiner Edelfalken und um Verwechslungen vorzubeugen, eine nähere Beschreibung. Sie sind gewöhnlich 3–9 mm lang und 2–7 mm breit, doch aber auch sehr oft etwas grösser oder kleiner. Obgleich denen des **Baumfalken** hierin ganz ähnlich, unterscheiden sie sich von diesen doch leicht genug an der aus der rostgelblichen bis in eine rostrote übergehenden allgemeinen Färbung und daran, dass sämtliche Zeichnungen nicht so scharf von der Grundfarbe getrennt oder mehr verwaschen sind, mehr wolkig oder marmorartig und öfter wie verwischt vorkommen. Die Grundfarbe ist entweder eine weissliche oder rostgelbliche, doch sehr selten ganz ungefleckt — die hellsten nur gelbbraun punktiert und bespritzt — andere dazwischen rostfarbig überwischt — noch andere rostrot und rostbraun gefleckt — wieder andere verwaschen rostrot marmoriert und dazwischen rostbraun gefleckt — die dunkelsten haben so viel von diesen beiden Farben, dass sie den Grund fast ganz bedecken und aus einiger Entfernung wie Ziegelstückchen aussehen, folglich gar gewaltig von jenen hellgelblichen abstechen, sodass man diese Gegensätze kaum für von einer und derselben Vogelart kommend halten möchte, wenn sie sich nicht zuweilen sogar in einem Gelege oder in demselben Horste in diesen Verschiedenheiten vorfänden. Das brütende Weibchen wird vom Männchen mit Futter versorgt, ohne dass letzteres brüten hilft; doch soll es sich manchmal über die noch ganz kleinen Jungen setzen, wenn ersteres eine Ausflucht aufs Feld macht, von wo nachher beide Alten den Jungen unablässig Nahrungsmittel zutragen. Anfänglich sind die kleinen mit zartem, schneeweissem Flaum dicht bekleidet; dieser färbt sich aber, wenn sie grösser werden, an den oberen Teilen ins Hellgraue. Die Jungen, welche in hohem Gemäuer oder Felsenhöhlen ausgebrütet und flügge geworden sind, halten darin länger aus und folgen den Alten erst aufs Feld, wenn sie vollkommen fliegen und sich dann bald selbst ernähren können, wogegen die, welche in freistehenden Nestern auf Bäumen auskommen, ihre Wiege oft schon verlassen, ehe sie noch recht fliegen gelernt haben. Diese sitzen dann zerstreut zwischen den dichten Ästen naher Bäume, bis sie den Alten aufs Feld folgen lernen, da gerne auf einem einzelnen Feldbaume zusammen Platz nehmen, meist auf den obersten Spitzen sitzen und sich von den Alten Futter bringen lassen; sie sind dann schon so scheu, dass sie, durch die Alten gewarnt, nicht leicht schussrecht aushalten, und wenn sie wegfliegen auf einem anderen Baum in dessen Krone sich zu verbergen suchen.

FEINDE

Man sieht **Krähen** und grössere **Raubvögel** sich öfters mit ihm herumzanken. In den Wäldern, wo er in hohlen Bäumen nistet, zerstört der Baummarder zuweilen seine Brut.

NUTZEN

Der Turmfalke zerstört zwar viele Bruten der kleineren Vögel, vorzüglich der **Lerchen**, allein er verzehrt auch eine noch weit grössere Anzahl Feldmäuse und wird dadurch sehr nützlich. Auch speist er so manches schädliche Insekt, z. B. Heuschrecken, Feldheimchen und dergl. Man kann ihn auch zum Lerchenfang abrichten; seiner Ungeschicklichkeit wegen ist jedoch diese Mühe nicht sehr belohnend.

SCHADEN

Er frisst **Lerchen**, ihre Eier und Jungen, verdirbt dem Lerchenfänger sehr oft einen glücklichen Fang, indem er die Lerchen schüchtern macht oder fortjagt, und soll in den Städten zur Brütezeit oft so dreist sein, dass er auf die vor den Fenstern hängenden Vogelbauer stösst und die darinnen befindlichen Vögel erwürgt. Ein seltener und merkwürdiger Fall ist wohl der, wo einmal einer durch ein Fenster flog, um den Kanarienvogel, welcher in einem, in der Stube nicht weit vom Fenster hängenden Käfig sich befand, zu erwürgen, ohne dass er sich durch das Klirren der zerbrochenen Glasscheibe hätte schrecken lassen.

// DIE KÜSTENSEESCHWALBE //

STERNA PARADISAEA

Arktische, nordische, langschwänzige, silberfarbene, silbergraue Meer- oder Seeschwalbe, Böspicker.

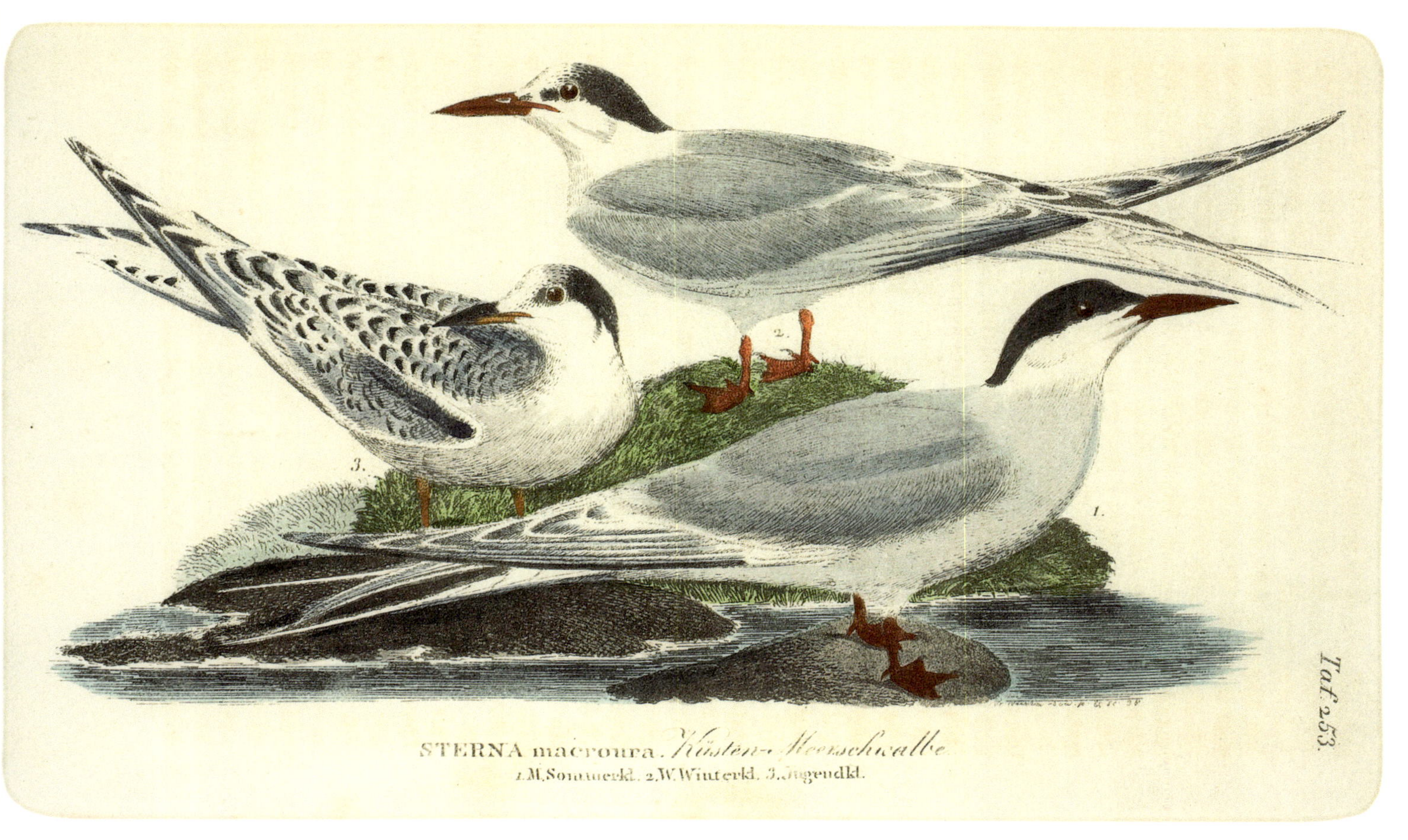

STERNA macroura. *Küsten-Meerschwalbe*

1. M. Sommerkl. 2. W. Winterkl. 3. Jugendkl.

Taf. 253.

KENNZEICHEN DER ART

Die Füsse und der Schnabel hochkarmin- oder zinnoberrot, dieser an der weniger schlanken Spitze gar nicht oder sehr wenig schwarz; der dunkle Streif auf der Innenfahne der ersten Schwungfeder 7 cm von der Spitze nur 2,5 bis 3 mm breit; die Fusswurzel 14 bis 16 mm; das **Jugendkleid** auf dem Mantel mit sehr dunklen Wellen und Mondflecken.

BESCHREIBUNG

Erst seit ein paar Dezennien ist diese Seeschwalbe für das gehalten, was sie unbestreitbar sein muss, für eine von unserer **Flussseeschwalbe** durchaus verschiedene Art. Damals gelang es mehreren Forschern, NITZSCH, TEMMINCK, SCHILLING, BREHM und anderen, wozu ich auch mich zählen darf, fast zu gleicher Zeit, sie dafür zu erkennen; es bleibt indessen sehr gleichgültig, wer von uns ein paar Monate früher oder später hinter das bisherige Geheimnis kam. Schon ein paar Jahre zuvor von NITZSCH, nach in Spiritus erhaltenen Vögeln, aufmerksam auf die zu vermutende Artverschiedenheit dieser Seeschwalben gemacht, sah ich die Küstenseeschwalbe zuerst im Jahre 1819 an der Nordsee in ihrem freien Leben und Wirken, wo mir augenblicklich jene Vermutung zur unumstösslichen Gewissheit wurde, weil sie sich durch ein anderes Betragen, anderen Flug, andere Stimme u.s.w., fliegend durch ihre ganz andere Figur und ganz besonders durch den schmäler gehaltenen und viel längeren Schwanz sogleich unterschied. Ich gab ihr damals auf NITZSCHS Veranlassung den Beinamen *macrura*, **langschwänzige**, weil ihr langer Schwanz das zu allererst in die Augen fallende Unterscheidungsmerkmal ist, wodurch die fliegende Küstenseeschwalbe schon in der Ferne auffällt und die **Flussseeschwalbe** dagegen wahrhaft kurzschwänzig aussieht. Wer gewohnt war, wie ich bis zu jener Zeit, immer nur die letztere gesehen, beobachtet und erlegt zu haben, dem muss sich, wenn er nun auf einmal nur jene sah u.s.w., der Name »langschwänzige M.« gewissermassen aufdrängen. Er ist jedoch ohne Not von mehreren verworfen, aber nicht durch einen bezeichnenderen ersetzt worden, denn *arctica* und *argentata* könnte als Beiname noch viel mehr Arten beigelegt werden als der obigen.

Ausser obigen Artkennzeichen unterscheidet sie sich von der **Flussseeschwalbe** auch im toten Zustande durch den **kürzeren** und nach Verhältnis stärker oder **höher** aussehenden Schnabel und durch die nicht allein niedrigeren, sondern auch viel **kleineren** Füsse. Der mehr oder weniger tiefere Ausschnitt der Schwimmhäute, besonders der **inneren**, bei dieser Art überhaupt nie stark, verdient als etwas Zufälliges so wenig Beachtung wie bei der **Flussseeschwalbe**.

In der Körpergrösse steht sie der **Flussseeschwalbe** merklich nach — man möchte sie mit einer **Wachholderdrossel** vergleichen —, ihr Rumpf ist schwächer und schlanker, wodurch der Schwanz ein noch längeres Aussehen bekommt, und die Flügel sind etwas schmäler. Die **alten Vögel** mit vollständigen Schwanzspiessen messen von 37 bis 39 cm, **jüngere** und **weibliche** stets nur 2 bis 4 cm weniger in der Länge, in der Flugbreite 72 bis 77 cm; die Länge des Flügels von der Handwurzel bis zur Spitze 26 bis 27 cm; die Länge des Schwanzes ist an den Mittelfedern nur 7 bis 7,5 cm, wegen des sehr tiefen Ausschnittes an der äusseren Seitenfeder aber 17 bis 19 cm, auch wohl noch etwas darüber; diese laufen nämlich in sehr lange, schmale Spiesse aus, die bei dem **Weibchen** stets etwas kürzer sind.

Das Gefieder ist noch viel zarter und weicher als das der **Flussseeschwalbe**, auch das im Nacken bei **älteren** Vögeln ein wenig merklicher verlängert, sonst die Gestalt der Schwungfedern, welche ebenfalls sehr starke und straffe, gegen das Ende sanft aufwärts gebogene Schäfte haben, ebenso; allein die Schwanzfedern unterscheiden sich auffallender von denen der **Flussseeschwalbe**. Sie sind sämtlich viel schmäler, nämlich von der Wurzel bis zur Mitte, dann schnell abnehmend zugespitzt; der Gabelausschnitt an seinem Ende bis zu 12 oder mindestens 8 cm tief; die Mittelfedern an den Enden zugerundet, die folgenden von innen nach aussen schräg zugespitzt, das Ende jedoch noch stumpf, stufenweise aber immer schmäler und spitzer, an der dritten von aussen schon etwas, an der zweiten noch weit mehr, an der äussersten sehr lang spiessförmig, sodass Exemplare vorkommen, bei denen trotz der sehr langen Spiesse die äusserste Feder nur 5,5 cm länger als ihre Nachbarin ist.

Die Spitzen der letzteren reichen wenigstens sehr nahe an die Spitzen der in Ruhe liegenden Flügel oder sind mit ihnen von gleicher Länge, oder ragen, wie bei **recht alten** Vögeln immer, über sie oft 5 cm weit hinaus; ein Verhältnis, das dem der **Flussseeschwalbe** zwar ähnlich ist, bei dieser aber wegen grösserer Breite und weniger tiefen Ausschnitts des Schwanzes, bei einem grösseren und stärkeren Rumpf ohne Messung oder vielmehr nach dem Augenmaß noch weit mehr auffällt. Bei der **Flussseeschwalbe** ist auch nur die äusserste Schwanzfeder eigentlich spiessförmig, bei der **Küstenseeschwalbe** sind es aber zwei bis drei, und diese gehen auch schneller in die deshalb viel längere Spiessgestalt über.

Der Schnabel ist etwas kleiner als bei der Flussseeschwalbe, zugleich aber etwas höher, weswegen er kürzer aussieht, obgleich er dies nur sehr wenig ist. Der Oberkiefer ist der Firste nach in einem sanften Bogen abwärts gegen die Spitze geneigt, der jedoch noch schwächer als bei jener ist; der Kiel bis zur Mitte hin, dann ein stumpfes Eck bildend und von hier schräg in die Spitze auslaufend, die, an beiden Schnabelhälften zusammen genommen, weniger schlank ist als bei der vorigen Art. Er ist von den Seiten sehr zusammengedrückt, daher viel mehr hoch als breit, an den scharfen Schneiden etwas eingezogen, dies schwächer als bei jener; der Rachen auch nicht so tief gespalten, kleiner und schmäler. Das schmale, längliche, durchsichtige Nasenloch ist 2 mm von den Stirnfedern entfernt, etwas über 4 mm lang, liegt an einer schwachen Vertiefung, und aus seinem vordersten Winkel läuft ein erhabener Streif vorwärts, der gegen die Schnabelspitze hin sich auf der Schneide verliert.

Die Länge des Schnabels beträgt gewöhnlich 3 bis 3,1 cm, selten darüber; nur bei einem Exemplar fand ich ihn 3,4 cm lang; von der Spitze bis in den Mundwinkel misst er fast 4,7 cm; seine Höhe an der Wurzel ist gewöhnlich 8, selten 9 mm, die Breite daselbst 6 mm.

Die Farbe des Schnabels ist ein prachtvolles Karminrot, wie wenn man feinen Karmin mit dem feinsten Zinnober vermischt, eine herrliche Farbe, wie man sie ganz ähnlich an den Blumen des Armenischen Mohns wiederfindet. Im Tode wird es etwas dunkler, später und wenn die Teile, welche sie tragen, völlig ausgetrocknet sind und dies allmählich geschah, wird es ein mattes Zinnoberrot und bleibt es, wenig ausbleichend, viele Jahre, auch stets röter als das der **Flussseeschwalbe**. Er ist bei **alten** Vögeln und bei der Mehrzahl einfarbig; nur selten, vielleicht bloss bei **jüngeren** Individuen, zeigt sich am Oberschnabel, dicht vor dessen Spitze, ein kleiner schwarzer Längsstrich. Der innere Schnabel, Zunge und Rachen sind hochrot, bei **jüngeren** Vögeln orangerötlich, auch der Schnabel an der hinteren Hälfte, zumal nach unten, ebenso, spitzewärts schwärzlich braun und die Spitze selbst horngelblich; in **frühester Jugend** hat er eine ähnliche, aber noch blassere Färbung.

Das Auge hat stets einen sehr dunkelbraunen Stern, nur in der Jugend ist das Braun desselben lichter, und befiederte Lider.

Die Füsse sind für einen Vogel von dieser Grösse auffallend klein, dabei aber von starkem und stämmigem Bau, niedriger und kleiner als die der **Flussseeschwalbe** im Verhältnis zu ihrer Körpergrösse sind. Sonst haben sie eine ganz ähnliche Gestalt, auch hinsichtlich der Einschnitte ihrer Bedeckung, ebenfalls sehr wenig ausgeschnittene Schwimmhäute; bloss an den inneren wird der Ausschnitt bemerklicher, und sie variieren darin auch individuell etwas. Die Krallen sind mittelgross, aber schwach, sehr gebogen, spitz, unten ausgerinnt, die der Mittelzehe die grösste, mit einer stark vortretenden Schneide auf der innern Seite, die der hinteren Zehe sehr klein.

Die Federn des Unterschenkels decken diesen bis beinahe an die Ferse, selten sieht man über derselben eine 2 bis 4 mm lange nackte Stelle; die Fusswurzel ist 14, seltener bis gegen 16 mm lang; die Mittelzehe misst ohne Kralle 16 mm und diese für sich noch 6 bis 8 mm; die Hinterzehe ist sehr klein, nur 4 mm lang, ihre Kralle ist oft so kurz, dass sie ganz zu fehlen scheint.

Die Füsse nebst den Schwimmhäuten haben ein ebenso prachtvolles Rot wie der Schnabel; es ist auch ebenso dauerhaft und lange Jahre noch an Ausgestopften zu erkennen, aber auch hier stets dunkler als bei der Flussseeschwalbe. Die Krallen sind an den Wurzeln braun oder rötlich, übrigens schwarz. Die Füsse **junger** Vögel sind gelbrötlich, die Krallen hornbraun.

Das **Dunenkleid** ist von dem der Flussseeschwalbe bedeutend verschieden, aber sehr variabel. Schnabel und Füsse sind ungemein klein, ersterer, wenn das weisse Knöpfchen auf der oberen Spitze, das zum Aufbrechen der Eierschalen diente, noch vorhanden ist, zunächst diesem mattschwarz, im übrigen gelblich fleischfarben, die Füsschen mit ihren vollen Schwimmhäuten auch von letzterer Farbe, die Augensterne blaugrau. Die Bekleidung der übrigen Teile besteht in einem langen, dichten und sehr weichen Flaum, der an der Stirn, in einem Fleckchen vor dem Auge und in einem von grossem Umfange an der Kehle schwarzgrau ist; der Kopf von oben und an den Seiten, Hinterhals, alle oberen und seitlichen Teile des Rumpfes sehr hell bräunlichgrau, verschiedenartig schwarz gefleckt; die Flecke bald grösser, bald nur ganz klein, bald dunkler, bald ganz undeutlich, ebenso verschieden jene grauliche Grundfarbe, bis zum ungefleckten Grauweiss; alle unteren Teile vom grauen Kehlfleck an rein weiss. DR. SCHILLING (s. BREHM a.a.O.) vermutet wohl nicht grundlos, dass das gewaltige Abändern des Äusseren der Eier mit dem der daraus hervorgehenden Jungen sich in Verbindung bringen lasse. Die Farbe des Kehlflecks, hier stets nur schwärzlich, ohne rostbraune Beimischung, auch dass dieser noch etwas weiter auf der Gurgel herabreicht, sind Kennzeichen, wodurch sich diese Jungen leicht von denen der **Flussseeschwalbe** unterscheiden lassen.

Sie bekommen bald Federn, und dann unterscheiden sich diese **jungen** Vögel weit auffallender von denen der **Flussseeschwalbe** als die Alten beider, schon durch den kürzeren Schnabel, hauptsächlich aber durch die dunkleren Farben des Mantels, dessen Flecke überhaupt eine ganz andere Farbe haben.

Bei ihrem Fortzuge, also im ganz vollendeten **Jugendkleide**, wo aber der Schnabel nur erst 2,5 cm misst, bis auf die lichte Spitze braunschwarz oder schwärzlich aussieht und meistens bloss auf der Schneide der Unterkinnlade, gegen den Mundwinkel zu einen ziegelroten oder orangefarbenen Streifen zeigt, wie auch Rachen und Zunge gefärbt sind, wo die Füsse nur an den Sohlen orangefarben, übrigens braunrötlich aussehen, ist der Schwanz noch viel kürzer, und die äusserste seiner Federn, nur 11 bis 11,75 cm lang, hat, weil sie wie alle viel breiter ist, noch nicht die spiessförmige Gestalt. Die Farben des Gefieders sind folgende: die Stirn ist weiss, auf der Mitte des Scheitels durch längliche Flecke in die schwarze Platte übergehend, die hier dicht vor dem Auge anfängt, sich an den Schläfen und Ohren hinzieht und auf dem Nacken endet; die Zügel weiss, sehr fein schwarz gestrichelt; Kehle, Wangen, Vorderhals und der übrige Unterkörper, Bürzel und Schwanzdeckfedern, sowie die unter den Flügeln, nebst dem Flügelrändchen rein weiss. Auf dem Mantel herrscht im ganzen ein sehr lichtes sanftes Blaugrau (etwas dunkler als an der **jungen Flussseeschwalbe** mit weissgelblichen und weissen Kanten an den Enden der Federn, die meistens ein matt schwarzbrauner Streifen oder halbmondförmiger Fleck von der Grundfarbe scheidet, dies am schärfsten an den Schulter- und hintersten Schwungfedern — und die auf dem Oberflügel längs der weissen Kante der Unterarmgegend in einen fast schieferfarbigen breiten Streifen zusammenfliessen. Die aschblauen grossen Schwungfedern gehen an den Enden in Schieferfarbe mit weissen Endkäntchen über, haben auf der Innenfahne einen weissen Längsstreifen, weissen Schaft und die vorderste eine schieferschwarze Aussenfahne, dergleichen auch an den äusseren Federn des aschblauen, auf den Innenfahnen und seinen Federschäften weissen Schwanzes sich finden, dessen Federn übrigens auch noch vor der weissen Endkante mit einem dunkelbraunen Halbmond bezeichnet sind.

Wenn sie eine Zeitlang geflogen haben, wo dann Schnabel und Füsse schon etwas röter geworden, werden die dunklen Flecke des Mantels etwas lichter, doch nie so bleich wie bei den **Jungen** der **Flussseeschwalbe**; so haben auch die etwas abgestossenen und in reines Weiss abgebleichten Federspitzen eine kleine Veränderung der Zeichnung bewirkt. Ihre erste Herbstmauser beginnt zwar schon auf dem Wegzuge, wird aber erst in den Winterquartieren beendet. Sie gibt ihnen ein dem der **Alten** ähnliches **Winterkleid**, das sich aber leicht unterscheiden lässt an den vom Jugendkleide verbleibenden Schwung- und Schwanzfedern, von denen die letzteren auch die dunklen Flecke hinter der Spitze durch Abbleichen nach und nach verlieren. Auch ihr **erstes Frühlingskleid** ist noch an den bleibenden Schwingen vom Jugendkleide leicht zu erkennen.

Das **Winterkleid** unterscheidet sich wie bei anderen Seeschwalben hauptsächlich an der Färbung der Kopffedern von dem **hochzeitlichen**. Stirn und Vorderscheitel sind weiss, der Mittelscheitel weiss mit schmalen, hinterwärts breiter werdenden, schwarzen Schaftflecken; ein Fleck vor dem Auge, die Gegend hinter demselben und das Genick bis auf den Nacken hinab tief schwarz; die Augenlider weiss; das frische Gefieder des Mantels von einer etwas dunkleren, aber immer noch sehr lichten und sanften blaugrauen Färbung, der Unterkörper aber viel weniger von dieser Farbe angeflogen als im **Sommerkleid**, bei vielen nur gräulichweiss; das herrliche Rot des Schnabels und der Füsse etwas lichter; sonst alles wie in diesem.

Das **hochzeitliche** oder frische **Sommerkleid** dieser Art, mit den sanft ineinander übergehenden Farben des ungemein zarten Gefieders und seiner samtschwarzen Kopfplatte, wird ausserordentlich gehoben durch das glühende Rot des Schnabels und der kleinen Füsse. Den Oberkopf von der Stirn an, die obere Hälfte der Zügel, die Augengegend und das Genick mit inbegriffen, bedeckt eine samtschwarze Platte, die meistens bis auf den etwas buschigen Nacken hinabreicht, wobei das Auge noch im Schwarzen, aber hart an der Grenze, steht und schwarze Lider hat; diese schwarze Platte begrenzt vom Schnabel an, über die Wangen hin bis an das Genick, ein schneeweisser Streifen, der besonders bei **recht alten** Vögeln am stärksten hervortritt, weil unter ihm gleich eine andere Färbung beginnt; auch das Kinn ist noch rein weiss; Kehle und Vorderhals aber sehr licht bläulichweiss, welches abwärts immer dunkler wird und an der Brust, am Bauch und an den Seiten in ein sanftes, sehr lichtes Blaugrau übergeht. Von eben dieser zarten Färbung, nur ein wenig dunkler (auch in Bezug auf die des Mantels der Flussseeschwalbe) sind der Ober- und Unterrücken, die Schultern, die Flügeldeckfedern und hinteren Schwungfedern, die letzteren und die längsten Schulterfedern mit weissen Spitzen; die Primärschwungfedern dunkel schiefergrau, auf der Aussenfläche hell aschgrau überpudert: alle mit starken weissen Schäften, die vorderste auf der Aussenfahne ohne jenen puderartigen Überzug, schwarz, welches spitzenwärts in Aschgrau übergeht; die Innenfahnen längs dem weissen Schafte mit einem schmalen dunkel schieferfarbenen, gegen die Sitze breiter werdenden Längsbande, von dem sich das Weiss des übrigen Teiles dieser Fahne scharf und in gerader Linie abschneidet; an den etwas lichter grauen Sekundärschwungfedern nimmt das Weiss die Innenfahne fast ganz ein, bildet eine weisse Endkante und läuft von dieser als ein schmales Aussenrändchen noch auf der äusseren Fahne herauf, ist auch nach innen nicht scharf vom Grauen abgeschnitten. Das Flügelrändchen und die ganze Unterseite des Flügels sind weiss, nur die Spitze silbergrau, mit der durchscheinenden dunklen Zeichnung von oben; der After, Bürzel, die oberen und unteren Schwanzdeckfedern sowie der Schwanz rein weiss, die äusserste Spiessfeder desselben mit schieferfarbiger Aussenfahne, die nächste mit aschgrauer, die dritte nur mit grau angeflogener äusserer Fahne, doch ist dies veränderlich, ausser der äussersten oft nur noch die zweite, stets aber etwas blasser grau, alle anderen weiss (dies gewöhnlich an den ältesten Vögeln), bei anderen verbreitet sich dagegen der graue Anflug in stufenweiser Abnahme über mehrere und verliert sich erst auf den Mittelfedern; bei den meisten ist auch die Innenfahne der äussersten Feder silbergrau angeflogen. Die untere Seite des Schwanzes ist glänzend weiss mit silbergrauen Aussenrändchen.

Zwischen beiden Geschlechtern habe ich keinen sehr auffallenden und feststehenden äusseren Unterschied finden können. Zwar sind die **Weibchen** ein wenig kleiner, ihre Schwanzspiesse kürzer und der Unterkörper weniger schön und nicht so dunkel bläulichgrau wie an den gleich alten **Männchen**; allein hierin ähneln jene wieder und bis zum Täuschen den **jüngeren Männchen**. Alle **jüngeren** Vögel unterscheiden sich leicht von den **alten** an der blasseren Färbung der unteren Teile, die oft nur grauweiss oder silberweiss oder bloss grau angeflogenes Weiss, aber von der Kehle bis weit auf die Gurgel herab rein weiss sind; gewöhnlich reicht bei ihnen auch die schwarze Kopfplatte nicht so weit auf den Nacken hinab, und die äussere Einfassung der Seitenfedern des Schwanzes ist blasser grau, aber über mehrere Federn verbreitet.

Stets sind die **ältesten** Vögel an den längsten Schwanzspiessen und an der viel dunkleren Färbung der unteren Teile, besonders der Brust, leicht zu erkennen, und ihre erhöhte Schönheit des Gefieders wird noch durch eine prächtigere Färbung der nackten Teile vermehrt.

Im Laufe des **Sommers** leiden die ausserordentlich sanften Farben ihres zarten Gefieders durch atmosphärische Einwirkung und Reibung sehr bemerklich, am meisten das dem frischen Gefieder nur wie aufgehaucht scheinende lichte Blaugrau des Unterkörpers, das in Silbergrau, bei manchen, besonders dem **Weibchen**, sogar ins Lehmgelbliche abschiesst, und von den längsten Schwanzspiessen ist nicht selten einer oder gar beide abgebrochen; auch die Flügelspitze ist durch das Abreiben des äusseren samt- oder puderartigen Überzugs viel dunkler geworden. Das Gefieder samt seinen Farben hat gegen die Herbstmauser hin an Reinheit und Zartheit auf diese Weise unendlich verloren.

Auch bei dieser Seeschwalbe fängt die Herbstmauser schon im August bei ihrem Wegzuge an und wird erst in fernen Ländern vollendet, weil sie gleichfalls sehr langsam von statten geht. Nur von dorther würde ein frisch und fertig vermauserter Vogel in seinem Winterkleide zu erhalten sein, dessen äussere Umwandlung wir nur durch teilweise erneuertes Gefieder noch während ihres Hierseins erraten können. Gegen das Frühjahr mausern sie zum zweiten Male in ihrer Abwesenheit, behalten aber Flügel- und Schwanzfedern vom Herbst her. Wenn sie dann im Frühling zu uns zurückehren, so haben die allermeisten, namentlich alle **älteren** Vögel, bereits ihr vollständiges **Hochzeitskleide**; nur wenige machen eine Ausnahme hiervon, indem sie noch Spuren des abgelegten Winterkleides, besonders am Kopfe, durch untermischte alte weisse Federn zeigen und zu Ende des Mai den Federwechsel noch nicht beendet haben. Zu den Seltenheiten gehört wohl, dass ich selbst einmal auf Dieksand an der holsteinischen Küste noch am 21. Juni eine Seeschwalbe dieser Art antraf, die noch in vollem **Winterkleid** war.

AUFENTHALT

Die Küstenseeschwalbe ist über viele Teile der Erde verbreitet. Wahrscheinlich lebt sie am nördlichsten von allen, denn man traf sie in den Sommermonaten sogar in der **Baffinsbai**, in der **Davisstrasse**, in **Grönland** und **Spitzbergen**, oft zwischen und auf den **Eisbergen**. Auch die arktischen Küsten **Sibiriens** und **Kamtschatkas** nebst den Inseln in diesen Meeren bewohnt sie.

Im nördlichen **Europa** und **Amerika** ist sie an vielen Küsten und Inseln gemein, so an den Küsten von **Grossbritannien** und **Irland**, von **Dänemark** und zum Teil von **Norwegen**, auf den **Hebriden, Orkaden, den Shetlands**, den **Färoern** und auf **Island** ausserordentlich häufig, auch auf den beiderseitigen Küsten und vielen Inseln der Ostsee wird sie hin und wieder in Menge angetroffen, nicht minder auf und an vielen der deutschen Nordsee, namentlich an der **friesischen** und **holsteinischen** Küste und den vor ihnen gelegenen Inseln der Nordsee*, auf denen ich sie im Jahre 1819 in grösster Anzahl beobachtet habe. Obgleich sie auch an den Küsten des südlichen Afrika angetroffen worden ist, so ist sie dagegen an den **europäischen** Küsten des Mittelländischen Meeres selten und an denen von **Italien** nur einzeln vorgekommen. Da sie als echter Seevogel nie in das Innere der Festländer kommt, auch ihre Wanderzüge nur am Meere entlang macht, so wird jenes klar, wenn man annimmt und, durch Beobachtungen unterstützt, annehmen darf, dass alle den Norden und Nordosten von Europa bewohnenden Scharen längs unseren Küsten der Ost- und Nordsee und des Atlantischen Oceans um die Spitze von **Europa** bis an die West- und Südwestküste **Afrikas** hinab wandern, so können sie immerwährend am Meere bleiben, brauchen nie über Land zu fliegen und kommen, ausser einzelnen durch Stürme verschlagenen auch nicht auf das Mittelländische Meer. Weil sie ferner Binnenwasser nur wenn sie ganz nahe am Meere liegen und Flussmündungen auch selten mehrere Meilen tief ins Land hinein besucht, so ist sie im Innern von **Deutschland** auch noch niemals vorgekommen, wenigstens ist kein Beispiel davon bekannt. An dem **holsteinischen** Strande zwischen den Mündungen der Eider und Elbe ist sie sehr

* Dieser Teil des Meeres gehört wohl unbestreitbar zur **Nordsee**; TEMMINCK nennt ihn aber (a.a.O., wo er meiner, in der **Isis** 1819, Hft. XII beschriebenen Reise dahin gedenkt) Baltique und dies ist in »Ostsee« übersetzt ihm mehrfach blindlings nachgeschrieben worden. Ich sammelte aber nie an der Ostsee — sondern an den Mündungen der Elbe und Eider, die beide in die **Nordsee** fliessen, und auf der interessanten Inselgruppe, die sich an der **Westküste Schleswigs** hinauf zieht und gleichfalls in der **Nordsee** liegt. — Eine Namensverwechselung der Art kann viele Missverständnisse erzeugen.

gemein; allein an letzterer aufwärts sah ich sie nur sehr einzeln noch bis in die Gegend von **Glückstadt** und **Stade**, dann keine mehr, bis auf eine einzige oberhalb **Lauenburg**, im Zanke mit einer **Flussseeschwalbe**, die dort heimisch war und den anderartigen Fremdling zu vertreiben suchte. Ich glaube, dass sie für diese Gegend schon eine höchst seltene Erscheinung ist und sich schwerlich jemals noch weiter stromaufwärts verirrt.

Als **Zugvogel** kommt sie an den Küsten und auf den Inseln der **Nordsee** selten vor Ausgang des April, viel öfter erst im Mai an und verlässt sie wieder im August, sodass höchst selten Nachzügler (gewöhnlich Junge) noch um die Mitte des September dort gesehen werden. Ebenso ist es an der **Ostsee** der **dänischen** Staaten und nicht viel anders auf **Island**, wo sie (nach FABER) um die Mitte des Mai ankommt und einzeln bloss an der Südküste dieser Insel noch bis gegen Ende des September gesehen wird. An der **pommerschen** Küste verliert sie sich allmählich vom Ende des Juli bis Mitte des August, und später wird selten noch eine bemerkt.

Auf ihren Wanderungen fliegt sie sehr hoch, doch zieht sie fast immer bloss des Nachts und in grossen Gesellschaften, oft zu vielen Hunderten vereint, von denen immer einige von Zeit zu Zeit ihre Stimmen hören lassen, woran man dann die Richtung, in welcher der Zug forteilt, und die im Herbst stets eine südwestliche ist, sehr deutlich wahrnehmen kann. Mein Freund FR. BOIE zu **Kiel** hörte einstmals in einer ziemlich finsteren Nacht vom letzten August zum 1. September einen sehr grossen Zug derselben von Nordost nach Südwest durch die Luft streichen, und dem ähnliches ist von mehreren meiner Bekannten an jenen Küsten beobachtet. Im Frühjahr ist die Richtung des Zuges natürlich eine umgekehrte; auch sah man sie dann oft am Tage am vorjährigen Wohnorte ankommen, in solcher Höhe, dass man sie eher hörte als sah, wo sie dann in grösster Höhe unter freudigem Schreien sich in Kreisen über dem Platze schwebend herum drehten, so immer niedriger kamen, aber dazwischen auch mit den anmutigsten Schwenkungen abwechselten.

Der Name: »**Küstenseeschwalbe**« bezeichnet ihren Aufenthalt, der ihr im Äusseren so ähnlichen **Flussseeschwalbe** gegenüber, wie mich dünkt, sehr gut; denn wenn die letztere auch hin und wieder am Meere vorkommt, so ist es doch nicht ihr gewöhnlicher Wohnsitz, und sie schlägt diesen stets nur in der Nähe von süssen Gewässern auf, ja die grosse Mehrzahl lebt einzig an Flüssen, oft in sehr grosser Entfernung vom Meer und tief im Innern der Festländer. Unsere Küstenseeschwalbe gehört dagegen den salzigen Gewässern des Meeres an, entfernt sich nie weit von ihnen, kommt niemals an den Flüssen im Innern der Festländer vor, und wenn sie auf grösseren Inseln und Halbinseln auch an den tiefen Buchten und grossen Landseen, selbst an solchen mit süssem Wasser, lebt, so stehen diese doch gewöhnlich auch mit dem Meer in Verbindung, und wo sie ihre Wasser in dieses ergiessen, lebt sie dann freilich auch am fliessenden Wasser, das jedoch den Namen eines Flusses nicht verdient, z. B. am Abfluss des grossen, von Tausenden der vielartigsten Wasservögel belebten Sees **Myvatn** auf **Island**. Wenn sie die vielgestaltigen Gewässer des oberen **Jütland** so gut wie viele Stellen der offenen Meeresküste in enormer Anzahl bewohnt, so nimmt das kein Wunder, da diese mit dem Meere, wenn auch oft nur mittelbar, in Verbindung stehen, wie z. B. die Seen **Siörring** und **Sperring**, welche diese Seeschwalbe in Myriaden bewohnt; von welchen diese Vögel, sobald sie sich nur etwas höher in die Luft erheben, das offene Meer im Auge behalten und sich schnell dahin begeben können, so oft sie wollen. Das obere oder eigentliche **Jütland** (die Provinz) ist auch vielleicht unter allen in dieser Hinsicht bekannten Ländern der Erde dasjenige, das diese Art am zahlreichsten bewohnt und wo sie sich am weitesten vom offenen Meeresstrande entfernt. Auf kleinen Inseln und Landzungen ist sie stets am Meer, aber nicht auf den hin und wieder vorkommenden Binnenwassern, wenn sie nicht unmittelbar mit jenem in Verbindung stehen und auch salziges Wasser haben. **Pellworm** hatte ein recht ansehnliches süsses Binnenwasser, zahlreich von der **Trauerseeschwalbe**, aber nicht von unserer **Küstenseeschwalbe** bewohnt; sogar bei ihrem beständigen Umherschweifen liess sich äusserst selten eine solche dort sehen, so selten wie jene jenseits der Deiche am Meer. An den obengenannten beiden Seen **Jütlands** leben jedoch beide Arten (nach FR. BOIE) in vertraulicher Nähe, doch auf verschiedenen Plätzen nebeneinander.

Sie bewohnt zwar auch hohe und felsige Gestade, doch viel öfter solche, die allmählich in die See verlaufen, so auch niedrige Inseln mehr als hohe. Auch auf sandigen Inseln und an sandigem Strande kommt sie vor, wenn ihr sonst die Gegend zusagt; doch liebt sie vor allem einen niedrigen grünen Strand mit fettem Boden und schlammigen Watten, die bei der Ebbe mit sogenanntem Schlick bedeckt sind, und kommt, wo sie diese hat, nicht auf die, wenn auch nahe liegenden, Sandwatten und Sandbänke. Auf dem von mir besuchten Teil der Nordsee fällt diese Auswahl so deutlich in die Augen, dass, wenn manche kleine Inseln auf einer Seite Sand, auf der anderen fetten Boden haben, sie immer diesen zum eigentlichen Wohnsitz wählt und jenen nur vorübergehend besucht; ihre Brutplätze sind daher dort nie auf nacktem Sandboden, nie auf ganz sandigen Inseln. Namentlich wohnt sie dort am liebsten, wo sich weite, mit ganz kurzem, gewöhnlich vom Vieh abgeweidetem Graswuchs bedeckte Rasenflächen am Meer hin ausdehnen oder wo viele höhere Salzpflanzen den Boden so weit bedecken, dass solche Flächen in einiger Entfernung ganz grün aussehen; auf sandigem Boden nur dann, wenn er noch Kraft genug hat, einen ziemlich dichten und lebhaft grünen Graswuchs in weiter Ausdehnung hervorzubringen. Dieser Unterschied zwischen totem und nicht ganz unfruchtbarem Sandboden ist vielen Vogelarten wichtig, obgleich von Schriftstellern nicht immer gehörig beachtet worden.

Die Gegenden ihres Aufenthaltes haben meistens ein kahles, wenn auch nicht unfruchtbares Aussehen, keinen Baum und keinen Strauch; oft ist in weiter Ferne nichts hiervon zu sehen. Auch vermeidet diese Art auf Gewässern im Lande hohes Schilf und Rohr. Auch hier sucht sie die mit dem kürzesten Grase bedeckten Stellen auf, lägen sie auch nicht ganz nahe am Wasser.

Selten findet man diese Seeschwalbe vereinzelt oder nur in einzelnen Paaren, denn sie lebt meistens in grösseren Vereinen, mischt sich dann noch gern unter andere Strandvögel und teilt ihren Wohnsitz mit ihnen, doch nicht leicht mit anderen Seeschwalben; namentlich ist dies von den Nistorten zu verstehen, wo im Verein mit jenen oft das bunteste Gewimmel herrscht. Sie schwärmt den ganzen Tag umher, ruht sich zwar oft, aber immer nur auf kurze Zeit auf einem hohen oder flachen Ufer in der Nähe des Wassers, selten auf diesem schwimmend, aus, kommt zwar schon in der Dämmerung an die erwählte Schlafstelle, begibt sich aber erst mit anbrechender Nacht zur Ruhe, ebenfalls nahe am Wasser oder auf dem Brutplatze, selbst wenn dieser weit vom Wasser läge. Mit Anbruch des Tages wird sie wieder rege, und mit Sonnenaufgange beginnt ihr gewöhnliches Herumschweifen.

EIGENSCHAFTEN

Diese Seeschwalbe gibt an einfacher Schönheit den übrigen nichts nach, besonders werden die unvergleichlich sanften Farben des Gefieders durch das glühende Rot des Schnabels und der Füsse so vortrefflich gehoben, dass ihr manche andere Art darin nachstehen muss. Ihr Gefieder ist noch weicher und zarter als das der **Flussseeschwalbe**, von der sie sich durch geringere Grösse, schlankeren Rumpf, schmäleren und längeren Schwanz wie durch sanftere Bewegungen dem geübten Blick auch schon in bedeutender Entfernung unterscheidet. Sieht man beide Arten im freien Leben nebeneinander, so ist der Unterschied so auffallend, dass ihn auch der Bedenklichste augenblicklich zugeben muss und die Identität beider anerkennen wird, während dies an Bälgen und Ausgestopften nicht so sehr in die Augen springt oder strenger abgewogen sein will.

Ihre Stellung im Sitzen ist wie bei anderen Arten, den Hals sehr eingezogen, die Brust etwas tiefer als den Hinterkörper, die Flügel hoch über dem Bürzel gekreuzt, den langen Schwanz zwar etwas unter diesen, aber doch so hoch gehalten, dass er den Flügelspitzen nahe bleibt, und entfernt genug vom Boden, damit seine langen Gabeln nicht beschädigt werden u.s.w.; auch hier sieht dieser, selbst in bedeutender Entfernung, viel länger aus als der bei einem sitzenden Vogel der vorigen Art.

Ihr Gang ist trippelnd, in kleinen Schrittchen und geht nie über ein paar Fuss weit. Noch seltener schwimmt sie, dann sehr oberflächlich, Flügelspitzen und Schwanz hochgehalten; aber sie rudert nicht von der Stelle und erhebt sich von derselben ebenso leicht wieder in den Flug als sie sich aus demselben herabgelassen hatte. Dieses Schwimmen kommt jedoch bei ihr so sehr selten vor, dass ich, obgleich ich mehrere Wochen lang diese Vögel in Menge beobachten konnte, es nur ein einziges Mal gesehen habe.

Sie setzt sich viel öfter als andere Arten, doch immer nur auf eine oder ein paar Minuten, ausgenommen bei stürmischem Wetter, wo sie oft lange an einer Stelle ausruht und dazu, näher oder entfernter vom Meer, meistens solche Plätze aufsucht, die ihr Schutz vor dem Winde gewähren, z.B. hinter den Dünen oder hinter hohen Deichen (Dämmen), auf Äckern u.s.w. So sah ich einst bei einem heftigen Sturme alle auf der Insel **Nordstrand** wohnenden Seeschwalben dieser Art nebst anderen Strandvögeln auf einem frisch gepflügten Acker versammelt, der dicht hinter dem sehr hohen Deiche lag, an dem sich auf der anderen Seite Wind und Wellen brachen und ihn oft überschäumten.

Sie fliegt ungemein leicht und sanft, anscheinend langsamer als manche andere Art dieser Gattung, weil sie darin die Spitzen der grossen, schmalen Flügel nicht weit vom Körper wegstreckt und sie in weit ausholenden Schlägen bedächtig auf und nieder bewegt, wobei der leichte Körper sich abwechselnd ein wenig hebt und senkt, daher in einer schwach wellenförmigen oder doch nicht ganz geraden Linie fortgeschoben wird, hauptsächlich, wenn sie in gerader Richtung fortstreicht und keine Eile bezeigt. Oft beschreibt sie aber auch grosse ungeregelte Bogen, auf-, ab- oder seitwärts und mit den seltsamsten Wendungen, schwenkt sich schnell und leicht, schlägt plötzlich eine andere Richtung ein u.s.w. Gewöhnlich fliegt sie niedrig; allein sie kann sich auch sehr hoch aufschwingen, ohne Flügelbewegung schweben, sich drehen oder sanft fortgleiten, dies besonders bei ruhiger Witterung und heiterem Himmel, wo sie bisweilen so hoch aufsteigt, wie sie es nur auf dem Zuge gewohnt ist. Starker Wind ist ihr sehr unbehaglich; das leicht gebaute und jenem zu grosse Flächen darbietende Geschöpf wird oft ein Spiel desselben; sie muss sich in acht nehmen, dass er sie nicht von der Seite oder gar von hinten ansaust, weil er sie dann ganz aus der Richtung schleudern würde; sie muss ihm vielmehr die Spitze bieten, sich mit sichtlicher Anstrengung ihm entgegenstemmen, kann sich aber dann auch nur langsam fortarbeiten, wobei jener auch das Gefieder knapp auf den Körper andrückt, sie noch schlanker macht und weil auch der Schwanz dann sehr zusammengedrückt wird, eine lange sonderbare Figur aus ihr macht.

Obgleich es bei diesem gemütlichen, gar nicht anstrengend aussehenden Fluge den Anschein haben möchte, als sei sie eine der trägsten ihrer Gattung, so ist sie doch das Gegenteil; denn von einer rastlosen Unruhe beseelt, gestattet ihr diese nirgends ein langes Verweilen und treibt sie unablässig bald hier-, bald dorthin; aber alles wird mit einer wunderlichen Gemächlichkeit und zugleich in so gemütlicher Stimmung ausgeführt, dass man ihrem Treiben mit Wohlbehagen zusehen muss. In ihrem Betragen herrschen Sanftmut und Frohsinn, Mässigung und Vertrauen, und sie scheint geistig viel vorteilhafter ausgestattet als die **Flussseeschwalbe**, bei der stets ein gleichgültiger Ernst die Oberhand behauptet, die überall den Menschen wie anderen Geschöpfen misstraut, sehr ungesellig gegen alle anderen Vogelarten ist, selbst nie in sehr grossen Vereinen der eigenen Art lebt; wogegen die Küstenseeschwalbe ein viel grösseres Talent der Geselligkeit entwickelt, sich nicht genügen lässt, bloss mit sehr vielen von ihresgleichen beisammen zu sein, sondern an den Brutorten sich so auch noch unter anderartige Strandvögel mischt und mit ihnen verträglich und vertraut lebt. Sonderbar genug, dass bei diesem starken Triebe zum geselligen Beisammensein ihre Scharen sich doch nicht so enge verbinden wie viele der grösseren Arten, namentlich der **Brandseeschwalbe**, und zugleich auch sich nie einer anderen Seeschwalbenart innig anschliessen, dies dagegen aber gegen nicht verwandte Vögel tun; ich sah gemeinschaftliche Brutplätze, die ausser ihnen mit **Stelzenläufern, Rotschenkeln, Alpenstrandläufern, Seeregenpfeifern, Austernfischern**, sogar **Silbermöven**, alles bunt durcheinander, besetzt waren, an anderen Orten kommen oft noch viel mehr, sogar auch Entenarten zu solchen Vereinen gehörig vor, und unsere Seeschwalben sind zwischen diesen allen so verteilt, dass zwischen zwei Nestern derselben sich oft mehrere Nester von anderen verschiedenartigen Vögeln befinden. Mit allen diesen Vögeln leben sie höchst verträglich, und diese haben noch den Vorteil von ihnen, dass sie ihre Eier bewachen helfen, weil die Seeschwalben an so einem Platze, wenn sich ein Feind naht, immer zuerst Lärm schlagen und jene aufmerksam machen. Ganz abgesondert und vereinzelt mag keine wohnen; allein an einsam und weit vom Wohnorte Herumschwärmenden fehlt es auch unter ihnen nicht, sowie sie denn ihre Streifzüge immer vereinzelt machen und nur bei gewissen Gelegenheiten sich an Orten zusammen rottieren, die sie sonst nur als Streifer sehen.

Dem, der vorher die **Flussseeschwalbe** fleissig beobachtet hat, muss besonders auch die sanftere Gemütsart der **Küstenseeschwalbe** sehr auffallend sein. Obgleich auch auffahrend und nicht ohne Jähzorn, fehlt es zwar nicht an sich wiederholenden Zänkereien unter diesen Stillvergnügten; aber jene sind von so kurzer Dauer und blossem Mutwillen so ähnlich, dass man sie mehr für vorübergehende Neckereien halten muss. Die erstgenannte ist dagegen viel heftiger, man möchte sagen empfindlicher gegen ihresgleichen, auch ungesellig gegen andere Vögel, und wer weiss, ob nicht diese verschiedene Gemütsart beider sich sonst so ähnlichen Arten Ursache ist, dass sie sich nicht leiden mögen und sich bekämpfen und verfolgen, wo sie zusammentreffen, wobei dann die zärtlichere Küstenseeschwalbe natürlich den kürzeren ziehen muss.

Ein sonderbarer Zug in ihrem Betragen ist eine gewisse Neugier. Wo etwas Neues passiert, kommt bald ein solcher Vogel herbei, beschaut es sich in der Nähe, lässt, darüber herumflatternd, seine Stimme erschallen, und in kurzem ist eine ganze Gesellschaft versammelt, die sich nach gestillter Neugierde nach und nach wieder zerstreut. Wirft man einen frischen Erdhügel auf oder verliert man ein Taschentuch, ein Stück Papier, oder sehen sie einen eben geschossenen Vogel liegen oder einen gefangenen zappeln, so sind sie gleich bei der Hand, flattern und schwenken sich niedrig und schreiend eine Zeitlang über dem Gegenstande ihrer Bewunderung umher, und wenn sie ihn genug begafft und sich mit Schreien ermüdet haben, zieht jede einzelne wieder ihre Strasse.

Bei den **grossen Möven** ist es jedoch mehr als Neugier, was diese Seeschwalben antreibt, die angeschossenen schreiend zu verfolgen oder ihnen wohl gar Schnabelstösse zu versetzen oder über den tot niedergestürzten besonders viel zu schreien oder zu lärmen, weil sie ihnen als Räuber ihrer Eier und Jungen bekannt sind, die Seeschwalben sich aber leider oft gefallen lassen müssen, dass jene, um den Zeitpunkt des Bestehlens recht abpassen zu können, ganz in ihrer Nähe nisten.

Die Küstenseeschwalbe ist harmlos und zutraulich im höchsten Grade, und wo sie nistet und keine Nachstellungen kennt, erregt ihre Vertraulichkeit in der Tat oft freudiges Erstaunen und ein eigenes wohltuendes Gefühl; man meint, diese liebe Einfalt müsse geradewegs aus dem Paradiese stammen. Ohne Furcht fliegt nicht selten das schöne Geschöpf so nahe an dem Menschen vorüber, dass er ihm ins Auge schauen kann, zumal wenn er sich stellt, als bemerke er es nicht. Bei den Nestern und in der Nähe des Brutortes kommt dies oft vor, auch noch an entfernteren, auf mehr als eine Meile im Umkreise. Dort ist diese Seeschwalbe unter allen mit ihr in Gesellschaft lebenden Vögeln der zahmste. Bald scheint sie Furchtlosigkeit allein, bald diese mit Neugier vermischt in die Nähe des Menschen zu ziehen, sowohl wenn er im Boote als wenn er auf dem Lande ist. Bei den Nestern kommt natürlich noch Besorgnis hinzu, und sie kann daselbst so böse über den Störenfried werden, sogar in solche Wut geraten, dass sie nach Hunden und anderen Tieren, selbst nach Menschen, stösst und ihnen nicht selten Schnabelstiche versetzt, weshalb ihr die Bewohner jener von mir bereisten Inseln den Namen **Böspicker** beigelegt haben, den sie aber nur in dieser Bezugnahme verdient. So ungewöhnlich zahm ist sie jedoch nicht allenthalben, und es zeigt dies deutlich, dass jene zu grosse Furchtlosigkeit nicht aus Mangel an Klugheit entspringt. Ich habe sie an manchen Orten so vorsichtig gefunden wie die meisten Strandvögel, und sie wussten daselbst so gut wie **Austernfischer** und andere mehr den Schützen vom Fischer oder Bauer zu unterscheiden, obwohl sie sich immer noch weniger scheu zeigten als die meisten mir bekannten Seeschwalbenarten. Sonderbar genug hält keine Küstenseeschwalbe sitzend die Annäherung des Menschen aus; sie erhebt sich vielmehr bald und meistens über Schussweite, kommt dann aber nicht selten im Fluge nahe an ihm vorüber.

Ihre Stimme charakterisiert diese Art auffallend genug. Sie lassen sich im Fluge oft genug hören, zumal, wenn mehrere beisammen sind, weniger die einzeln herumschwärmenden, in einem eigentümlichen, sanften oder etwas klagenden **Kier** oder **Krier** (meist zweisilbig), einem Ton, welchen man nie von der **Flussseeschwalbe** hört. Begegnet eine der anderen, so begrüssen sie sich gewöhnlich mit einem sanften **Ki, ki ki kieh, krieh** (das E nur schwach hörbar), oder auch **Gib gib, gib gib gib gie gieh**, ebenfalls nie bei jener vorkommend, sowie im Unmut ein schnarchendes **Rrä**, oder beim Zanken und Necken ein heftigeres **Räh räh tetätetetterieh, rieh!** Alle diese Töne mit ihren vielfältigen Modulationen sind so verschieden von denen der **Flussseeschwalbe**, dass sie mir gleich bei der ersten, die ich schreien hörte, als einer anderen Art gehörig auffielen. Weniger ist dies beim Lockton, der Normalstimme der Seeschwalbengattung, einem schleppenden, nicht angenehmen **Kreeäh** oder **Krreäh** der Fall, das allein dem der **Flussseeschwalbe** ähnlich aber doch weniger rauh klingt, sich daher dem geübten Ohr auch etwas unterscheidet. Sämtliche Töne haben, mit denen der eben genannten Art verglichen, wie das Betragen etwas Sanfteres oder Gefälligeres und klingen weniger rauh. GRABA (s. d. *Färöische Reise*, S. 218) bezeichnet sie nicht übel mit folgenden Silben: **Bebereii, eberei, bebebiäh** und **kriäh.** — Die Jungen **piepen** anfänglich, und dies wird, während sie flugbar werden, nach und nach in **kier** oder **krier** umgewandelt, mit dem sie unablässig den Alten nachfliegen.

NAHRUNG

Die Küstenseeschwalbe nährt sich hauptsächlich von kleinen Fischen, namentlich **Stichlingen** (sowohl *Gasterosteus pungitius* als *G. aculeatus)*, auch von Jungen grösserer Arten, besonders der Gattung *Clupea*, von welchen sie, nach FABER, *Clupea sprattus*, wenn sie noch klein, vorzugsweise lieben soll. Kleine Krabben, auch kleine Garnelen und den sogenannten **Strandfloh** frisst sie auch häufig. Ferner gehören auch Insekten, Insektenlarven und Regenwürmer nicht ungewöhnlich zu ihren Nahrungsmitteln, und wo sie den Wattwurm erwischen kann, auch dieser.

Fische scheinen vor allem ihre Lieblingsnahrung zu sein; aber sie frisst nur lebende, die sie sich selbst fängt. Immerfort mit guter Esslust versehen, beschäftigt sie das Aufsuchen der Nahrungsmittel fast den ganzen Tag; sie fliegt nicht nur beständig, sondern oft weit nach ihnen umher, auf meilenweit entlegene Inseln und Küsten oder ganze Strecken ins Land hinein, an fangreiche Gewässer oder auf Wiesen und Äcker. Überall, wo sie Hoffnung hegen darf, etwas für ihren Schnabel zu finden, fliegt sie ganz niedrig, langsam und bedächtig, das Genick so gebogen, dass die Schnabelspitze senkrecht herabgerichtet ist, wobei sie den Kopf bald auf die rechte, bald auf die linke Seite wendet, je nachdem sie das eine oder das andere Auge zum Beschauen eines Gegenstandes gebrauchen will. Nach den Fischen streicht sie niedrig über dem Wasser entlang, den Blick fest auf dieses geheftet, und wenn sie etwas entdeckt, hält sie sogleich an, rüttelt über den Fischchen, bis sich ihr eins von solchen, die der Oberfläche am nächsten stehen, bequem genug gestellt hat; jetzt stürzt sie wie ein fallender Stein auf dasselbe herab, dass das Wasser hoch aufspritzt, und fliegt gleich darauf mit dem Gefangenen im Schnabel davon. Sie taucht indessen dabei nie so tief unter, dass man nicht noch etwas von ihr über der Oberfläche sähe; sie schiesst dagegen in schiefer Richtung oftmals nur mit Kopf und Schnabel durch die Wellen, fischt jedoch nicht gern, wo viel Wellenschlag ist, sondern viel lieber in wenig bewegtem Wasser und kann bei Sturm und hohem Wellengang nichts schaffen, so auch nicht in den Brandungen. Bei solchem Wind und Wetter, welche der **Brandseeschwalbe** gerade recht sind, kann sie nicht in der See fischen; sie sucht dann die stillen Buchten, Binnenwasser oder gar Wiesen und Äcker, um, wenn der Fischfang nicht gehen will, Insekten und Würmer aufzusuchen. Es ist schon oben erwähnt, dass sie zu leicht gebaut ist und nicht Kräfte genug hat, dem Sturm zu trotzen.

Sie verschlingt ihre Beute stets unzerstückelt, gewöhnlich bald nach dem Erheben aus dem Wasser, d.h. im Fluge. Ich habe sie nie im Sitzen verzehren sehen, selbst solche Geschöpfe nicht, die sie von der Erde aufnahm, will jedoch nicht bestreiten, dass sie es vielleicht bei solchen Fischen tue, die etwas zu gross sind, um ohne besondere Anstrengung sogleich verschluckt werden zu können. Mit einem solchen im Schnabel fliegt sie oft lange herum, gewöhnlich so lange, bis er ihr von einer anderen, ihr begegnenden abgejagt wird, der es abermals so geht, bis ihn endlich doch eine recht hungrige hinabwürgt. Kommt eine Raubmöve dazu, so ist es dieser gerade recht, und die Seeschwalbe mag sich einen anderen Fisch fangen. Ein auf dem Wasser schwimmendes Insekt hebt sie gleich auf; es geschah oft vor meinen Augen; aber fliegende sah ich sie nie fangen.

Während der Ebbe ist sie sehr tätig; sie fischt dann aus den auf den Watten zurückgebliebenen Pfützen die Brut von jenen kleinen Krebsen aus den Gattungen *Crangon, Palaemon, Gammarus* und anderen mehr, von denen jene kleine Wasserpfützen an manchen Orten wimmeln, auch blieb wohl hier und da ein Fischchen für sie darin zurück, sowie ihr denn hier auch der Uferwurm zuweilen zu teil wird. Bei schönem, heiterem Wetter sucht sie ihre Nahrung selten anders als auf oder an dem Meere, bei stürmischem und nasskaltem dagegen oft im Lande, hinter Dünen oder hohen Deichen und wo sonst etwas Schutz vor dem Winde ist. Sie schwärmt dann über den Wiesen und fängt die an den Grashalmen sitzenden Insekten oder liest auf Rasenplätzen und frisch gepflügten Äckern Regenwürmer auf. Ich sah sie in Menge dem Pfluge folgen und ausserdem dort auch allerlei Käferlarven aufnehmen. Sie sucht diese nicht etwa zu Fuss, sondern flattert hier über dem Erdboden ganz so wie über dem Wasser, niedrig und immer dicht hinter dem Pflüger her, ergreift den ausgeackerten Wurm oder die Made in demselben Augenblicke als sie sich neben ihm niederlässt, erhebt sich ebenso schnell wieder und verschlingt ihn fliegend. Ich sah mehrmals starke Gesellschaften dieser Vögel sich auf solche Weise beschäftigen. Zuweilen fliegen sie weit vom Meere nach solchen Plätzen, immer aber nur, wenn sie wegen schlechten Wetters dort nicht fischen können.

FORTPFLANZUNG

An den oben genannten Küsten und auf vielen Inseln des Eismeeres, der Nord- und Ostsee, entweder am Meere selbst oder auf den Binnenwassern der Inseln und Halbinseln oder auf nahen Landseen, auch wohl an den Ausflüssen derselben nach dem Meere — aber nie an Strömen und Flüssen grösserer Länder — findet sich diese Seeschwalbe als haufenweise beisammen lebender Vogel im Mai ein, um da bis in den August zu verweilen und währenddessen sich fortzupflanzen. Ein einzelnes, einsam nistendes Paar findet man nirgends; immer nisten mehrere und oft Hunderte beisammen, aber nie so dicht aneinander gedrängt, wie dies von mancher anderen, namentlich von der **Brandseeschwalbe**, bekannt ist. Sehr merkwürdigerweise mischen sie sich hier nicht unter andere Seeschwalben, wohl aber unter andere Strand- und Seevögel aus gar nicht verwandten Gattungen. Ihre Brutplätze können nahe neben denen der genannten Art, auch wohl von der **Trauerseeschwalbe** und anderen liegen, selbst an die verschiedener Mövenarten grenzen, aber ihre Nester mischen sich nicht unter diese; dagegen teilen sie buchstäblich die Brutplätze mit vielerlei **schnepfenartigen** Vögeln und im hohen Norden auch mit vielen **Entenarten**; ihre Nester befinden sich zerstreut zwischen denen dieser, und alle dulden die Seeschwalben gern unter sich, was auch begreiflich ist; denn diese sind von Natur wachsamer, sehen wegen beständigen Herumfliegens jede Gefahr früher nahen und sind zugleich die kühnsten Verteidiger der Eier und Jungen sämtlicher Bewohner eines solchen Brutplatzes, der so viel des Höchstinteressanten bietet, dass auch das kälteste Gemüt beim Zuschauen solch bunten Treibens nicht teilnahmslos bleiben kann. Die Zutraulichkeit der Vögel an solchen buntgemischten Brutplätzen erhöht den Reiz, den sie dem Beobachter gewähren, ganz ungemein; denn an Orten, wo unsere Seeschwalbe ungewöhnlich zahm ist, sind es meistens auch ihre Gesellschafter, obwohl sie darin stets alle übertrifft. FABER (siehe dessen *Prodromus* u.s.w., S. 88) fand sie am See **Myvatn** auf **Island**, wo sie häufig brütet, so zahm, dass ganze Haufen ruhig auf ihren Eiern liegen blieben, während die Einwohner wenige Schritte von ihnen bei einem grossen Feuer und unter lautem Getümmel mit Waschen beschäftigt waren. Auch in **Jütland** gibt es Gegenden, wo man es ganz ähnlich findet; in den von mir bereisten waren sie dagegen im allgemeinen etwas furchtsamer, doch bewiesen einzelne Vorfälle zur Genüge, dass jener Forscher im obigen nicht zu viel gesagt hat.

In den Gegenden, wo ich die Küstenseeschwalbe beobachtete, zieht sie die fruchtbaren Inseln und Küsten, deren Watten aus fettem, schwarzem Schlamm (Schlick) bestehen, den sandigen und weniger fruchtbaren unbedingt vor; nur auf jenen fand ich die am zahlreichsten besetzten Brutplätze, auf sandigen Inseln, wo es wenige Rasenplätze gab, auch nur wenige dieser Vögel nistend, auf nacktem Sandboden gar keine. Ich will zwar nicht bestreiten, dass es anderswo noch anders sein könnte; allein, da gar zu oft bei solcher Gelegenheit in den Angaben anderer die genaue Angabe der Beschaffenheit des Bodens vernachlässigt ist, so muss ich mich vor allem bloss an das halten, was ich mit eigenen Augen sah. Sandige Inseln und Küsten können allerdings auch Rasenstriche und auf diesen unsere Küstenseeschwalbe ihre Brutplätze haben; aber auf nacktem, totem Sande sah ich wenigstens solche nie. Von den an der Westküste **Schleswigs** gelegenen hatten die sandigen Inseln **Amrum** und **Sylt** nur wenige und sehr schwach besetzte, die fetten Inseln **Föhr, Pellworm, Süderoog** und mehrere andere dagegen ganz ungemein belebte Brutplätze, obgleich das letztgenannte Eiland grossenteils sandige Watten hat. Frischer Rasenboden, die Gräser aber von weidendem Vieh kurz gehalten oder ein grossenteils mit niedrig bleibenden Salzpflanzen bedecktes Marschland, wie es sich in der **Nordsee** auf den sogenannten Halligen und Aussendeichen findet und mit wirklichem Rasen wechselt, diese grünen Vorlande dienen ihnen am häufigsten zu Brutplätzen, da wo ich sie nämlich selbst beobachtete.

Wäre dieses allenthalben so, so würde sich diese Art dadurch von der vorhergehenden, die immer nur auf nackten Sand- oder Kiesbänken (oder Felsen) nistet, höchst auffallend unterscheiden. Dagegen wird jedoch versichert, dass die Küstenseeschwalbe an der Ostküste **Jütlands** sowie auf vielen **dänischen Inseln** der Ostsee und auch an der **pommerschen Küste** sehr oft ihre zahlreich besetzten Brutplätze auf nackten Sandbänken habe, wie sie denn an anderen Orten hin und wieder auch auf nackten Felsen, auf **Grimsey** bei **Island** auf Basaltgruppen mehr als 10 m über der Meeresfläche ihre Eier ausbrütet. Dass sie auch an Süsswasserseen, nicht sehr weit vom Meere oder durch ihren Abfluss mit diesem verbunden, häufig nistet, ist ebenfalls erwiesen.

Ihre Brutplätze fand ich oft sehr nahe am Meere und auf so wenig erhabenem Boden, dass bei ungewöhnlichen Fluten Eier und Junge mit fortgerissen werden; manchmal sind die Nester bei gewöhnlicher Flut nur wenige Schritte vom Wasserrande entfernt, an einem anderen Orte liegt der Brutplatz wohl 100 Schritt, an noch anderen mehr als 500 Schritt vom Meer entfernt. Das Plätzchen selbst findet man bald, wenn man auf das ununterbrochene Ab- und Zufliegen der Vögel acht hat, nämlich nicht allein der unruhigen Seeschwalben, sondern auch der mit ihnen in Gesellschaft nistenden **Rotschenkel, Seeregenpfeier, Säbelschnäbler, Austernfischer** und anderer mehr. An den Brutplatz haben alle diese Vögel eine besondere Anhänglichkeit, sie nehmen ihn, wenn man ihnen denselben nicht durch gar zu heftige Verfolgungen verleidete, alle Jahre wieder in Besitz, sogar suchen sie ihn dann noch wieder, wenn er durch besondere Ereignisse ganz und gar umgewandelt wurde. Auf der Halbinsel **Dieksand**, zwischen den Elbe- und Eidermündungen, fand ich z. B. in dem damals neu eingedeichten und in Ackerland verwandelten Teil der grünen Halbinsel einen Nistplatz von jenen Vögeln mit mehreren Pärchen unserer Küstenseeschwalbe vermischt, so vordem ein sehr ausgedehnter gewesen, dieser jetzt aber mit Hafer besät war, der zufällig an vielen Stellen sehr dünn stand; auf einer solchen hatten sämtliche Vögel ihre Nester zwischen handlangem Hafer. Auf der Insel **Nordstrand** hatte eine ziemliche Anzahl, mit jenen Arten vermengt, ihren Brutplatz auf einem Brachfelde, das nicht lange vorher gepflügt war.

Der zahlreichste von allen Vereinen dieser Seeschwalbenart, die ich auf meinen Reisen sah, bewohnte in Gesellschaft von Tausenden anderer Strand- und Seevögel die kleine niedrige Insel **Süderoog**, die ausser dem Strandvogt mit seiner Familie keinen menschlichen Bewohner hatte, und weil sie nicht eingedeicht war, bloss zur Viehweide benutzt wurde. Jener bunte Schwarm hatte zum Brutplatze eine mit kleinen grünen Hügelchen* bedeckte Rasenfläche so besetzt, dass man fast mit jedem Schritte ein Nest, bald von ihnen, bald von einem der erwähnten Vögel fand, an die sich einerseits bis nahe an den sandigen Strand sogar eine ziemliche Anzahl Nester von **Silbermöven** anschloss. Da die Nester aller dieser Vögel sich höchst ähnlich sehen, nichts als eine kleine, sehr wenig vertiefte Aushöhlung des Bodens sind, die sie meistens selbst bereiten, so mag hin und wieder ein Vogel, wenn ihn das zum Legen reife Ei drängt, nicht so schnell sein eigenes Nest wiederfinden, sich deshalb notgedrungen auf dem ersten besten seiner Bürde entledigen, unbekümmert, wem die schon darin liegenden Eier gehören. So erklärt es sich wenigstens mit Wahrscheinlichkeit, dass ich unter diesem Gewirr auch einmal in einem Neste vier Seeschwalbeneier (da sie doch sonst nie mehr als drei legen) fand, oder wie es möglich war, ein Seeschwalbenei mit zweien des **Austernfischers** in einem Neste, oder sogar auch eins von diesem Vogel bei den Eiern einer **Silbermöve** zu finden, was ich dort alles selbst sah und was nach anderen Beobachtern an so stark besetzten Brutplätzen öfter vorkommen soll.

Ich erinnere nochmals, dass ich die Nester dieser Art stets nur auf hartem Boden, aber nicht auf totem Sande, obgleich dieser häufig ganz nahe war, gefunden habe; die allermeisten waren stets auf Rasenboden. Nur ein einzigesmal hatte ein Pärchen am Rande eines solchen Brutplatzes seine Eier auf einen vom Meer auf den Sand geworfenen Streifen von Tang und Meergras, welche alt und trocken waren, gelegt. Wenn sie sich das Nest selbst bereiten, so sieht man auf Rasenboden kaum mehr als das Gras etwas bezupft oder niedergetreten, auf hartem, aber freiem Boden oft

---

* Diese Hügelchen schienen früher durch Ameisen oder Maulwürfe entstanden, obgleich es ein Rätsel bleibt, wie auf einem solchen flachen Eilande, das bei allen hohen Springfluten dem Überschwemmen ausgesetzt ist und mehr als einmal im Jahr überflutet wird, sich jene Geschöpfe so weit sollten vermehrt haben können.

noch weniger, aber häufig ist eine vorgefundene kleine Vertiefung dazu eingerichtet. Die Eier liegen gewöhnlich auf dem blossen Erdboden, sehr selten auf einer ganz unbedeutenden Unterlage von einigen trockenen Pflanzenteilen, Stückchen von Graswurzeln, Blättern oder Hälmchen; vielleicht haben sie solche nicht einmal selbst bereitet, sondern andere neben ihnen nistende Vögel sie ihnen überlassen.

Gegen Ende des Mai oder auch erst im Anfange des Juni findet man ihre Eier, deren ein Weibchen nie mehr als drei für ein Nest, häufig auch nur zwei legt. Unter Hunderten von Nestern sah ich nur ein einziges mit der oben erwähnten Ausnahme, und darf behaupten, dass 3 die Normalzahl für diese Seeschwalbenart ist.

Diese Eier gehören nach Gestalt und Färbung zu den wandelbarsten in der Vogelwelt. Häufig ist erstere zwar eine schön eiförmige, aber diese ist bald bauchiger, bald schlanker, bald kolbiger, bald spitzer und artet auch zuweilen ins Ungewöhnliche aus; ich sah z. B. eine fast walzenförmige, eine sehr verkleinerte, rundliche (sogenannte Spureier) und besitze selbst noch ein solches Ei von der Gestalt einer sehr langen, über der Mitte stark eingedrückten Birne oder ganz so geformt wie die **lange grüne Herbstbirne**. Eine etwas kurze, ziemlich bauchige Eiform ist indessen die gewöhnlichste. Die Schale ist von sehr feinem Korn, ziemlich glatt, aber ohne Glanz. Von ihrer Grundfarbe lässt sich im allgemeinen bloss sagen, dass sie auf ein sehr blasses Olivengrün basiert sei, allein sie geht aus dieser in allen Abstufungen bei einigen in trübes grünliches Weiss, bei anderen in grüngelbliches oder gelbbräunliches Weiss, auch in grünliches Tonweiss, bei noch anderen in grünliches Rostgelb und in blasse Olivenfarbe über. Ebenso variieren die Zeichnungen, von denen die in der Schale bald dunkel aschgrau, bald violett-, bald braungrau, die auf der Schale meistens schwarzbraun, einzeln ganz schwarz, bei anderen sehr dunkel olivenbraun sind, während sie bald als blosse Punkte und Tüpfel sehr einzeln oder sehr gedrängt, bald als Tüpfel und Kleckse sparsamer, bald als wenige Punkte, daneben aber noch als einzelne grosse und sehr grosse Flecke ins Unendliche variieren. Bei feingefleckten und bloss punktierten verbreiten sich die Zeichnungen dichter oder sparsamer, meistens gleichförmig über die ganze Fläche; bei den grobgefleckten hat dagegen gewöhnlich das spitze Ende nur wenig Zeichnung, aber oft häufen sich die grössten Flecke gegen das stumpfe Ende zu einem losen Kranz. Die weissgrünen, wenig oder fast gar nicht punktierten sind die seltensten; die olivengrünlichen, grob und einzeln oder fein und dicht gefleckten die gemeinsten; auch die grünlich rostgelben, stark gefleckten sind nicht selten. Ich habe aus mehreren

Hunderten selbst gesammelter Eier dieser Art ein Dutzend der abweichendsten in Farbe und Zeichnung vor mir, von denen jedes einer besonderen Beschreibung wert wäre, muss mich jedoch auf das oben im allgemeinen Gesagte, das natürlich auch auf diese bezüglich ist, beschränken.

Diese Eier sind denen der **Flussseeschwalbe** ausserordentlich ähnlich, wenn man sie im Kabinette sieht, weniger, wenn sie frisch sind. Sie scheinen im allgemeinen allerdings ein wenig kleiner zu sein als jene, messen aber in der Länge 37 bis 44 mm, in der Breite 27 bis 31 mm, daher die Maße keinen wesentlichen Unterschied machen.

Vergleicht man eine nicht geringe Anzahl beider Arten mitsammen, so wird man bald bemerken, dass es unter denen der **Flussseeschwalbe** viele gibt, die nicht grösser sind als die Mehrzahl von denen der Küstenseeschwalbe, und dass es unter den Eiern dieser ebenfalls wieder welche und zwar nicht wenige gibt, die jenen in der Grösse gleichkommen. Ich kann also ein so sehr schwankendes Kennzeichen nicht für gut halten. Ferner sagt DR. THIENEMANN in seinem Eierwerk, die inneren oder Schalen-Flecke seien bei der Küstenseeschwalbe von einer anderen, mehr braungrauen Farbe und viel kleiner als bei der **Flussseeschwalbe**; ich habe mich aber hiervon nicht nur nicht überzeugen können, sondern möchte fast das Gegenteil behaupten, weil ich an mehreren Eiern, die alle von mir selbst gesammelt, bei der Küstenseeschwalbe so sehr grosse und zum Teil so schön violettaschgraue Schalenflecke finde, als ich bei keinem der der **Flussseeschwalbe**, ebenfalls selbst aus den Nestern genommen, habe finden können. Meine Eiersammlung würde es jedem deutlich vor Augen legen, dass auch dieses Unterscheidungszeichen nicht vorhanden ist oder nicht Stich hält. Endlich bleibt noch ein drittes Kennzeichen, und dies ist das einzige, das sich in den allermeisten Fällen bewährt, am besten freilich nur an frischen, ihres Inhalts noch nicht entledigten Eiern, nämlich die Grundfarbe, die bei der **Küstenseeschwalbe** stets eine viel stärker ins Grüne übergehende ist, wovon auch die rostgelblichen Eier, denen der **Flussseeschwalbe** am ähnlichsten, nicht ausgeschlossen sind. Wenn auch die frischen Eier der letzteren gleichfalls ein wenig ins Grünliche ziehen, so ist dies doch lange nicht so auffallend als selbst bei den am wenigsten grünlichen der **Küstenseeschwalbe**, während die Mehrzahl dieser vom Apfelgrünen bis zum schmutzigen Olivengrün u.s.w. wechselt und auch später immer einen stärkeren grünen Schein behält. Liegen sie eine Zeitlang, wenn auch noch so sorgfältig verwahrt, in der Sammlung, so geht, wie bei allen grünen Eiern, sehr viel von ihrer eigentümlichen Farbe verloren, das Grün verschwindet bist auf einen schwachen Schein, den auch nicht einmal alle behalten, und diese letzteren sind dann durchaus nicht von denen der **Flussseeschwalbe** zu unterscheiden. Einige, deren Grundfarbe im frischen Zustande olivengrün, werden in den Sammlungen olivenbraun und dunkler als jemals welche von der **Flussseeschwalbe**.

Beide Gatten brüten, unordentlich sich ablösend, aber bei Sonnenschein und warmer Witterung wenig oder mit sehr vielen Unterbrechungen, doch liegen sie viel öfter über den Eiern, als man dies von der **Flussseeschwalbe** sieht. Bei schlechtem Wetter brüten sie viel anhaltender, und dann trägt der eine Gatte dem brütenden oft Futter im Schnabel zu. Die Nacht hindurch sitzt das Weibchen ununterbrochen über den Eiern, und das Männchen hält dicht neben ihm Nachtruhe. Es ist ihnen selten vergönnt, die ersten Eier auszubrüten, weil diese von den Menschen aufgesucht und gern verspeist werden. Wiederholt sich das Wegnehmen der Eier aber zu oft und bis über die Mitte des Juni, so hören die Vögel auf zu legen und bleiben für dieses Jahr ohne Nachkommenschaft. Wo indessen ein solcher Brutplatz regelrecht behandelt wird, sucht man die Eier nur zwei Wochen lang alle zwei bis drei Tage ab und lässt nachher die Vögel ruhig ausbrüten.

Das Ausbrüten der Eier dauert 15 bis 16 Tage. Sobald sich die ausgeschlüpften Jungen etwas fühlen, verlassen sie das Nest oder die Stelle, wo die Eier ausgebrütet wurden. An ruhigen Orten bleiben sie wohl auch länger als einen Tag in demselben; jetzt laufen sie zwar fort, das eine hier-, das andere dorthin, doch nie sehr weit weg. Gewöhnlich suchen sie sich solche Stellen, die nicht ganz kahl, hin und wieder uneben, mit allerlei Pflanzen bedeckt sind, auf denen Steine oder Muschelhaufen umherliegen, hinter denen sie sich recht gut zu verbergen wissen, indem sie sich still niederdrücken, oft auch, possierlich genug, bloss den Kopf zu verbergen suchen. Wo Sand genug und dieser trocken ist, wühlen sie sich gern und oft so tief in denselben ein, dass nur der Kopf herausragt; sie bewirken dies mit den Füssen und dem Hinterkörper rückwärts, wie sich Kröten in lockere Erde einzuwühlen pflegen. Sie werden mit Insekten, Würmern und kleinen Fischen aufgefüttert, die ihnen die Alten fleissig zutragen. Mit Regenwürmern, welche diese besonders frühmorgens oder nach Regenwetter auf Rasenplätzen, auch wohl hinter dem Pfluge auf Äckern aufnehmen, werden sie sehr häufig geätzt. Die Alten sind sehr besorgt um sie, kommen gleich herbei, wenn ein Mensch oder ein grösseres Tier in die Nähe derselben kommt, schreien und gebärden sich ängstlich, versetzen Hunden häufig Schnabelstiche, stossen sogar Menschen zuweilen gegen die Kopfbedeckung und sind in Verteidigung ihrer Jungen tollkühner als alle anderen viel grösseren Seeschwalbenarten.

Die Jungen wachsen sehr schnell, bekommen bald Federn, in der bei anderen Arten dieser Gattung gewöhnlichen Folge, und können nach zwei Wochen schon fliegen und den Alten folgen, was sie unter immerwährendem verlangendem Schreien tun, unter solchem auch im Fluge, wie junge Schwalben, das Futter empfangen und sich sehr lange füttern lassen. Es sieht wirklich sonderbar aus, wenn so grosse, dem Anschein nach völlig erwachsene Junge immer noch die elterliche Pflege nicht entbehren können, deshalb unausgesetzt den Alten ihr Verlangen nach Nahrung zu erkennen geben und ihnen in jeder Richtung nachfliegen, aber gar nicht darauf zu achten scheinen, wie diese zu den Nahrungsmitteln gelangen und ihnen dies so oft zeigen, oder nicht den Mut haben, es ihnen nachzumachen.

FEINDE

Die kleinen flüchtigen **Edelfalken**, der **Baumfalke** und der **Merlin**, fangen nicht selten eine solche Seeschwalbe. Ihre Brut hat noch viel mehr Feinde; **Raben** und **Krähen**, auch wohl **Weihen**, z. B. die **Rohrweihe**, stellen ihr nach, sowohl Jungen als Eiern; allein die gefährlichsten dieser Art sind ihnen die grossen Seeschwalben, die **Lach-** und die **Raubseeschwalbe**, die grossen Möven, (**Silber-** und **Mantelmöve** und andere mehr) und im höheren Norden die Raubmöven, weil sie zu oft in ihrer unmittelbaren Nähe wohnen und jeden günstigen Zeitpunkt abpassen können, ihnen Eier oder Junge wegzustehlen. Die Räuber hintergehen die grosse Wachsamkeit der Seeschwalben und üben ihr Vorhaben aus, wenn diese nicht daheim, d. h. allesamt weit nach Nahrung ausgeflogen sind; denn sobald nur eine zugegen ist und ein solches Vorhaben ahnt, so ruft sie durch ängstliches Schreien sogleich um Hilfe, ihre Kameraden kommen von allen Seiten herbeigestürzt, der Räuber wird mit vereinten Kräften angegriffen und gewöhnlich in die Flucht geschlagen; was der einzelnen nicht gelingen würde, erreicht hier die Menge. Dies geschieht unter vielem Lärm, der desto toller ist, je mehr Vögel dieser Art beisammen wohnen, und sich um so öfter wiederholt, als jene Räuber in grösserer Anzahl in der Umgegend hausen. Ihr Hass gegen die grossen Möven geht so weit, dass sie durch einen Schuss verwundete sogleich und zahlreich mit frohlockendem Geschrei verfolgen und so heftig nach ihnen beissen, dass es aussieht, als suchten sie solchen den Gnadenstoss zu geben; stürzt eine, so schwingen sich die Seeschwalben jubelnd noch eine lange Weile über der toten herum.

Die Raubmöven-Arten sind auch zu jeder anderen Zeit ihre heftigen Feinde, weil sie ihnen die gefangene Beute abjagen; sie üben ihr Schmarotzerhandwerk gar gern gegen die schwachen Seeschwalben aus, weil sich diese ohne Widerstand in ihren Willen fügen, ja oft den Fisch früher fallen lassen, als es jenen möglich wird, ihn, ehe er wieder ins Wasser fällt, aufzufangen.

Ungewöhnliche Fluten rauben ihnen oft die Eier oder Jungen, und der Mensch trägt durch zu oft wiederholtes Wegnehmen der ersteren auch viel zur Verminderung dieser Vögel bei.

NUTZEN

Die Vögel isst man gewöhnlich nicht; allein die sehr wohlschmeckenden Eier werden sehr häufig aufgesucht und verspeist. Von den grösseren Brutplätzen sucht man das weidende Vieh abzuhalten und betreibt das Einsammeln der Eier planmässig, wie bei den grösseren Seeschwalbenarten. Dies geschieht indes an sehr vielen Orten nicht, an den meisten dagegen nach Willkür, weil man diese zu kleinen Eier weniger achtet, zumal wo sie nicht in sehr grosser Anzahl gefunden werden.

Einen mittelbaren Nutzen möchten sie dem Menschen vielleicht durch Vertilgen vieler Regenwürmer und anderer lästiger Geschöpfe gewähren.

In ihren Brutgegenden nützen sie dem Schützen dadurch, dass sie ihm durch ihr Betragen anzeigen, ob sein Schuss einen grösseren Vogel, namentlich eine grosse Möve, verwundet hat oder nicht, oder ihm die Stelle anzeigen, wo ein toter herabgestürzt ist. Sollte dies eine grosse Möve sein, so muss man bald hinzueilen, weil zu befürchten steht, dass sie auf obige Weise das zarte Gefieder desselben verunreinigen und sie wenigstens zum Ausstopfen untauglich machen.

SCHADEN

Am Meere fällt es niemandem ein, diesen anmutigen Vögeln die kleinen Fischchen, von denen sie sich meistens nähren, zu beneiden oder sie deshalb für schädlich zu halten, zumal sie vorzugsweise **Stichlinge** fangen, die ihrer Kleinheit wegen nirgends beachtet werden.

// DIE LACHMÖVE //

LARUS RIDIBUNDUS

Grosse, gemeine, rotfüssige, braunköpfige, schwarzköpfige Lachmöve, graue Möve mit dem Mohrenkopf (schwarzköpfige Möve), Braunkopf, Mohrenkopf, Rotschnabel mit schwarzem (oder braunem) Kopf, Rotbein, Pfaff, Lachschwalbenmöve, Hutschwalbenmöve, Hutmöve, Kapuzinermöve, grosse, rotköpfige Seeschwalbe oder Seeschwalm, Seemöve, Fischmöve, aschgraue Fischmöve, Speckmöve, Seekrähe, grosse Seekrähe, graue, gemeine graue, weissgraue, grosse graue, kleinere graue, kleine aschgraue, kleine graue, kleine bunte, kleine, kleinere Möve, Holbrod, Gyritz, in hiesiger Gegend gewöhnlich **Seekrähe**.

Taf. 260.

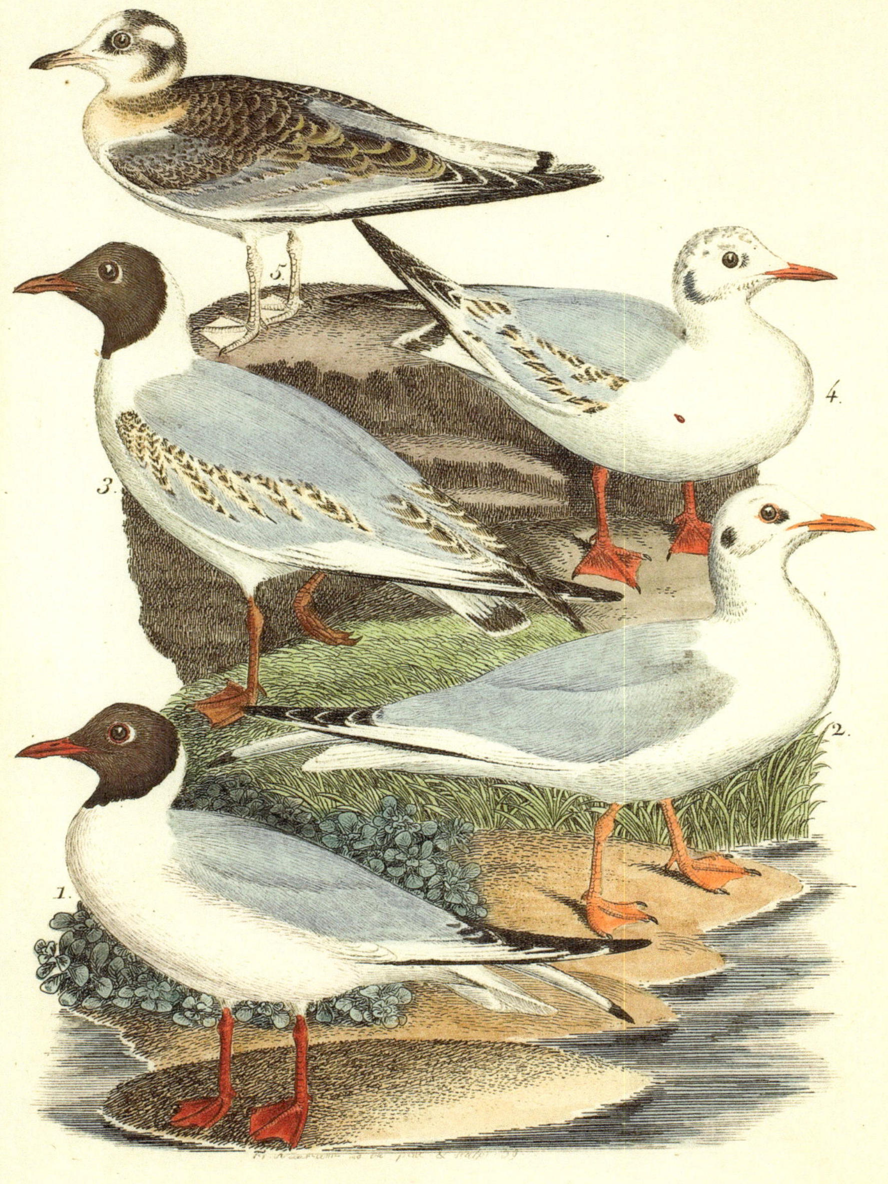

LARUS ridibundus. *Lach-Meve.*

1. M. Sommerkl. 2. M. Winterkl. 3. Erstes Sommerkl. 4. Erstes Winterkl. 5. Jugendkl.

KENNZEICHEN DER ART

Die Schäfte der beiden vordersten Schwungfedern sind bis auf die schwarze Spitze weiss. Taubengrösse.

BESCHREIBUNG

Die Lachmöve, in **Deutschland** die gemeinste, gehört zu den kleineren Arten, übertrifft hierin aber die **Zwergmöve** um vieles. Wenn sie der **Schwarzkopfmöve** auch an Grösse fast gleich kommt, so unterscheidet sie sich doch leicht an dem schwächeren, schlankeren, daher länger scheinenden und weniger hakenförmigen Schnabel wie an den scheinbar niedrigren Füssen in allen Kleidern sehr leicht, und auch diese zeigen in allen Abstufungen nach Alter und Jahreszeiten unterscheidende Abweichungen genug.

Auf der anderen Seite steht ihr die **Sturmmöve** sehr nahe; allein diese ist merklich grösser, robuster gebaut, auch viel stärker an Schnabel und Füssen, im vollkommenen Hochzeitskleide ohne Kappe auf dem Kopf, in anderen viel mehr, dichter und klarer gefleckt und überhaupt in Verteilung der dunklen Zeichnungen des Gefieders sehr abweichend.

Unsere Lachmöve hat ungefähr die Grösse einer **Feldtaube**, aber viel längere Flügel und einen viel schlankeren Körperbau, sodass sie, zumal fliegend, viel grösser aussieht. Wie unter allen Mövenarten, findet man auch in dieser, und zwar an einerlei Orten und in derselben Schar, sehr abweichende Grössenunterschiede; Verschiedenheiten, die nicht das Klima, nicht Mangel an Nahrung hervorbringen, die noch weniger Artverschiedenheit bezeichnen, sondern vom Ei an sich bilden, sodass man schon im Neste sehr grosse und sehr kleine Individuen beisammen findet.

Die Extreme in den Maßen **alter Vögel**, wenigstens zwei Jahre alt, sind folgende: Länge, von der Schnabelwurzel bis zum Schwanzende, 33 bis 39,4 cm; Flugbreite 84,8 bis 100,6 cm; Flügellänge, vom Bug bis zur Spitze, 29,2 bis 33 cm; Schwanzlänge 10 bis 11,8 cm, und die Spitzen der ruhenden Flügel reichen 5,3 bis 6,5 cm über das Ende des Schwanzes hinaus.

Die Extreme in den Maßen **junger, eben flugbarer Vögel** sind von zwei Individuen entnommen, welche Geschwister und beide aus einem Nest waren; sie stellen sich so heraus: Länge 30,6 bis 35,3 cm; Flugbreite 82,5 bis 89,5 cm; Flügellänge 24,7 bis 28,3 cm; Schwanzlänge 9,4 bis 10,6 cm, und die Spitzen der an den Leib geschmiegten Flügel reichen 2,4 bis 3,5 cm über dessen Ende hinaus.

Zwischen diesen **seltenen** kleineren und den grösseren Maßen, die an **frischen** Exemplaren genommen, liegen nun die **gewöhnlicher** vorkommenden in der Mitte.

Wenn nun bei einer Mövenart von dieser Grösse ein Unterschied im Längenmaß von 4,7 bis 7,1 cm vorkommen kann, so darf man sich nicht wundern, wenn es bei den grössten, gerade noch einmal so grossen Arten um 12 bis 14 cm differiert. In diesem Stücke gleichen sich die Mövenarten alle, und jede Mövenkolonie kann den Beobachter davon überzeugen, wenn er es nicht schon in Sammlungen ausgestopfter gefunden oder diesen misstraut hätte.

Das Gefieder ist bei der Lachmöve von derselben Beschaffenheit wie bei anderen, von den grossen Schwungfedern die vorderste wenig, meistens nur um 2 oder 3 mm länger als die zweite, die folgenden dann in grossen Stufen in der Länge abnehmend u.s.w. Die Schwanzfedern sind ziemlich und gleich breit, am Ende sehr wenig, die beiden mittelsten stärker abgerundet, diese sehr oft, zumal bei **jungen** Vögeln, ein wenig kürzer, und wenn sie dieses sind, das Schwanzende sehr unbedeutend ausgeschnitten, bei den allermeisten **Alten** jedoch, sowie bei vielen **Jungen** ganz gerade, wie mit der Scheere verschnitten.

Der Schnabel ist, mit anderen Mövenschnäbeln (die Zwergmöve ausgenommen) verglichen, etwas schwächlich, der abgerundeten Firste nach von der Mitte an im sanften, sehr schwachen Bogen in die Spitze ausgehend, unten am Ende der Kielspalte mit einem ganz schwachen Eck und dann in die etwas schlanke Spitze endend, diese gewöhnlich kaum kürzer als die obere, die sich jedoch bei manchen auch, doch selten, wie ein kleines Häkchen über die untere herab biegt; die geraden, eingezogenen, sehr scharfen Schneiden bei manchen spitzewärts ganz fein gezähnelt, bei vielen auch ganz glatt; übrigens ist er von den Seiten stark zusammengedrückt, doch an der Wurzelhälfte über der Schneide etwas aufgetrieben; die Nasenhöhle lang und schmal; in ihr öffnet sich das ritzförmige, vorn erweiterte, durchsichtige, 6 mm lange Nasenloch nicht weit von der Stirn. Der Rachen ist tief gespalten und ziemlich weit.

Der Schnabel ist auch in der Grösse verschieden, obwohl meistens, doch nicht immer, nach der Grösse des Vogels. Man findet ihn bei **Alten** von etwas über 3 bis 3,4 cm Länge, von der Stirn an, hier von 8 bis 10 mm Höhe und von 6 bis 8 mm Breite; bei **flugbaren Jungen** von 2,6 bis 2,9 cm Länge (vom Mundwinkel zur Spitze von 4,1 bis 5 cm), von 7 bis 10 mm Höhe und 6 bis 7 mm Breite. Von Farbe ist er sehr verschieden, in frühester Jugend ganz fleischfarbig, bei **flugbaren** blass fleischfarbig, an der Spitze schwarz, und dieses zieht auf den Schneiden oft ein ganzes Stück rückwärts; **später** bräunlich fleischfarbig, nachher rotgelb, dann orange- oder ziegelrot, dann braunrot, endlich im **ausgefärbten Frühlingskleide** dunkel karmin- oder hell blutrot. Der Rachen und innere Schnabel hat die Farbe wie aussen, aber stets etwas lichter. Diese Farben werden im Tode alle düsterer und im getrockneten Zustande ganz unscheinlich, heller oder dunkler hornfarbig.

Das eben nicht grosse Auge hat einen sehr dunkelbraunen, fast schwarzbraunen Stern, in der **Jugend** dick und weiss befiederte, im **Alter** nackte ziegel- oder karminrote Lider.

Die Füsse sind weder auffallend hoch noch stark; die Zehen etwas kurz; die Schwimmhäute zwischen den vorderen voll, auch manchmal ein wenig ausgeschnitten; die Hinterzehe kurz und nicht sehr hoch gestellt; die Krallen kurz, wenig gebogen, stark scharfrandig, aber nicht spitz, die mittelste mit vorstehender Schneide nach innen, wie bei den meisten Arten; der Unterschenkel über der Ferse weit nackt; der Überzug der Füsse wie an anderen Arten seicht eingekerbt, vorn herab getäfelt, hinten geschildert, auf den Zehenrücken schmal geschildert, Schwimmhäute und Zehensohlen fein gegittert. Die nackte Tibia misst 12 bis 17,5 mm; der Lauf 4,1 bis 4,7 cm; die Mittelzehe mit der 6 bis 8 mm langen Kralle 3,3 bis 3,8 cm; die Hinterzehe mit der 3 bis 4 mm langen Kralle, 8 bis 10 mm.

Die Farbe der Füsse ist meistens die des Schnabels, in der **Jugend** blass fleischfarbig, später braunrötlich, dann hellrot, endlich bei **ausgefärbten Alten** karmin- oder hell blutrot. Sie wird ebenfalls nach dem Ableben bald düsterer, bei jenen blass rötlichgrau, ausgetrocknet hell hornfarbig, bei letzteren zuletzt rötlich hornbraun. Gewöhnlich wird sie an ausgestopften so hässlich, dass sie nicht mehr zu erkennen ist, am ersten noch das hellere Rot der **alten Herbstvögel**. Die Krallen sind schwarz, bei **jüngeren** braunschwarz, oft an den Spitzen lichter.

Das **Nest-** oder **Dunenkleid** ist ein eben nicht langer, aber dichter und sehr weicher Flaum, von obenher blass gelblichbraun, schwarzbraun verschiedentlich, mehr oder weniger gefleckt; Zügel, Kehle und Wangen sehr dunkel, fast schwarzbraun; der ganze übrige Unterkörper rein weiss; das kleine Schnäbelchen rötlich weiss; die Füsschen bleifarbig, dicht unter der Ferse sehr dick. Dies kleine Geschöpf hat in den ersten Tagen seines Daseins viel Ähnlichkeit mit dem **Jungen** von der **Flussseeschwalbe,** die Kehle ist aber meistens dunkler, der Schnabel kürzer und die Füsse etwas grösser.

Das nach einigen Tagen hervorkeimende ordentliche Gefieder kommt zuerst an den Flügeln und dem Schwanze, zuletzt am Halse und Kopfe hervor; noch sitzen die Dunen auf den Spitzen vieler Federn der letzteren Teile, wenn diese **jungen** Möven bereits fliegen und sich selbst nähren können. Jetzt sind sie in ihrem **vollständigen Jugendkleide** und sehen folgendergestalt aus:

Der Schnabel sieht an diesen **jungen Vögeln** nie gelb (wie man ihn oft beschrieben findet), sondern im Leben blass und etwas schmutzig fleischfarbig oder weissrötlich, bald nach dem Ableben rötlichgrau aus, mit braunschwarzer Spitze; ebenso haben die Füsse jene blasse, im Tode mehr rötlichgraue Farbe, das Auge eine schwarzbraune Iris und dickbefiederte schneeweisse Lider. Das Gesicht ist weiss, an den Zügeln zuweilen bräunlich oder graulich, auf der Stirn oft rostgelb angelaufen; vor dem Auge steht ein halbmondförmiger tief schwarzer Fleck, ein schwärzlich braungrauer viel grösserer fast dreieckiger auf der Ohrgegend, der sich gewöhnlich mit der hinteren Spitze bis auf das weisse Genick zieht; der Scheitel von vorn nach hinten aus dem Weissen in rötliches Braungrau oder Graubraun übergehend, seitwärts über den Schläfen mit einer mehr oder weniger deutlichen weissen Stelle, die sich meistens nur am lebenden Vogel als ein **ovaler** Fleck darstellt; Kinn, Kehle, der halbe Hals ringsum, mit dem oberen Nacken weiss, dieser unterhalb, auf der Halswurzel, mit einem sehr grossen, dreieckigen, braunen, mit hellbraunen, in Rostgelb übergehenden Endkanten der Federn bezeichneten Fleck, dessen seitliche Spitzen, in Rostgelb verlaufend, sich gewöhnlich bis auf die Gurgel herum ziehen oder hier eine Art von Halsband bilden; die Kropfgegend gelblichweiss, an den Seiten in dunkles Rostgelb übergehend, von hier bis an den Schwanz alle unteren Teile weiss, an den Brustseiten oder den Tragfedern mit einem mehr oder weniger starken düster rostgelben Anstrich. Das Gefieder am Oberrücken und an den Schultern ist braun, mit helleren, in Rostgelb übergehenden Endkanten; der Unterrücken mövenblau, auf dem Bürzel in Weiss übergehend; die oberen Schwanzdeckfedern weiss, meistens mit rostgelb angeflogenen Federrändern; das Flügelrändchen schneeweiss; die kleinen Flügeldeckfedern blass mövenblau, mit bräunlichen Endchen; die mittleren braun mit helleren rostgelblichen Endkanten und mit durchscheinendem mövenblauem Grunde der Federwurzeln; die grossen mövenblau mit hellbraunen Spitzchen, die hinteren wie die hinteren Schwungfedern ziemlich dunkelbraun mit hellen, ins Rostgelbe übergehenden Endkanten; die mittleren Schwingen auf der Aussenseite bald schieferschwarz, bald bloss schiefergrau, mit weissen Säumen, übrigens mövenblau; von den Primärschwingen die hintersten noch mövenblau, nach vorn allmählich blasser werdend, die vorderen rein weiss, alle mit schwarzen Enden, und das Schwarze geht auf der Aussenkante nach und nach immer weiter herauf, sodass es an den beiden vordersten fast die ganze Aussenfahne, bis gegen die Wurzel herauf, einnimmt, ihre Schäfte, die schwarze Spitze ausgenommen, rein weiss; oft sind noch schwärzliche Flecke im Weissen der Flügelspitze, und die Spitzen der Federn haben weisse Säumchen; die Fittichdeckfedern weiss, hinterwärts mövenblau, nach vorn mattschwarz; die Daumenfedern weiss, an den Enden schwarz mit bläulichweissen Spitzchen. Von unten ist der Flügel an den kleinen Deckfedern rein weiss, an den grossen silberweiss, an den Schwungfedern das Schwarz von oben bloss glänzendes Schwarzgrau. Der Schwanz ist weiss, mit einem bis 3 cm breiten braunschwarzen Ende und bräunlichweissen Spitzensäumchen; das Schwarz nimmt jedoch, wenn man die Federn einzeln betrachtet, nach aussen stufenweise so ab, dass der äussersten nur ein kleines Fleckchen bleibt, das aber selten ganz fehlt; von unten ist er wie oben, das Schwarze nur blasser.

Kaum sind zwei dieser jungen Möven einander vollkommen gleich gefärbt und gezeichnet, sondern bald heller, bald dunkler, am Kopfe mehr oder weniger weiss, am Kropfe und den Tragfedern mehr oder weniger bräunlichgelb, so das Mövenblau des Oberflügels mit seinen braunen Flecken, selbst die schwarze Zeichnung der Primärschwingen und die Schwanzbinde; aber ein standhafter Unterschied, der das verschiedene Geschlecht bezeichnete, ist darin nicht aufzufinden.

Ungemein bald wird dieses **Jugendkleid** schon mit einem Übergange zum nächstfolgenden Herbstkleide bezeichnet; man erhält diese Jungen nicht selten sogar noch mit Spuren der früheren Dunen auf den Spitzen der Federn des Kopfes und Oberhalses, während sich an anderen Teilen schon der Anfang der Mauser in einzelnen mövenblauen, die braunen des Rückens und der Schultern verdrängenden Federn zeigt; zuvor bleicht aber auch schon das Rostgelb an den Seiten des Kropfes und der Brust wie an den Kanten der Federn in schmutziges Weiss ab, und das Braune wird auch fahler. Rein und vollkommen, in seiner jugendlichen Frische, ist es daher nur in der Nähe des Geburtsortes und kurz nach dem Ausfliegen des Vogels zu erhalten. Dagegen tragen alle jungen Möven dieser Art im **Spätsommer** oder wenn sie bereits auf dem Zuge begriffen sind (mit Ausnahme einzelner von sehr verspätetem Gehecke), ein mit dem folgenden vermischtes Kleid, das sich durch das mehrere Weiss des Kopfes und das Mövenblau des Rückens und der Schultern, dies aber meistens noch mit braunen Federn des jugendlichen Kleides gemischt, kenntlich macht.

Erst im Spätherbst ist dies letztere dann als **erstes Winterkleid** so weit vermausert, dass es folgendergestalt aussieht: Schnabel und Füsse ziehen jetzt schon stark ins Rötliche, mehr oder weniger mit bräunlicher oder gelblicher Beimischung, und die Spitze des ersteren zeigt weniger Schwarz; dicht vor dem Auge (mit seinen weissbefiederten Lidern) steht ein schwärzliches Fleckchen, von dem sich ein graulicher Schein quer über den Scheitel nach dem der anderen Seite zieht; auf dem Ohr ein grösserer dunkelgrauer Fleck, von dem ebenfalls ein stärkerer grauer Schein quer über den Hinterkopf zieht; ausser diesem ist der ganze Kopf und Hals sowie die ganze untere Seite des Vogels rein weiss, ebenso der Bürzel und die obere Schwanzdecke, Rücken und Schultern rein mövenblau; der Oberflügel zwar ebenfalls mövenblau, doch nicht rein, sondern noch mit sehr vielen von den kleinen, mittleren und den hintersten der grossen Deckfedern vom **Jugendkleide** vermischt, an denen das Braun aber sehr abgeschossen ist, die Federkanten sich sehr abgerieben haben und ins Braungelblichweisse übergehen; das Übrige des Flügels und der Schwanz sind vollständig noch die des **Jugendkleides**, das **Schwarze** an ihnen aber schon sehr abgeschossen und die weissen Endkäntchen der grossen Schwungfedern grossenteils abgerieben.

Dieses **unvollkommene Winterkleid** nehmen nun die jungen Lachmöven in den nächsten, ihren **zweiten Frühling** mit hinüber, und die Mauser schreitet dabei, zwar äusserst langsam, immer vorwärts; im Mai sieht man schon einzelne erdbraune Federchen zwischen den weissen am Kopfe hervorstreben, der Schnabel und die Füsse haben sich lebhafter rot gefärbt und die schwarze Spitze an jenem verloren.

Immer langsam fortmausernd, erscheint endlich bei den nun **einjährigen** Lachmöven zu Ende des Juni oder erst im Juli kurz vor Beginn einer neuen Mauser am Kopfe die mehr oder weniger vollständige braune Kappe der **Alten**, hier bloss erdbraun, am Rande herum am dunkelsten, an der Stirn oder um den Schnabel oft nur mäusegrau oder weisslich gemischt, übrigens auch mit dem halbmondförmigen weissen Fleckchen hinter dem Auge; dabei haben sich nicht allein Schnabel und Füsse braunrot gefärbt, sondern auch das Augenlid ist nackt und braunrot geworden; übrigens aber sind die Flügel und der Schwanz wie oben beschrieben geblieben oder durch starkes Verstossen, Abreiben und Verbleichen der Federn bloss dahin verändert worden, dass das Schwarze in ein fahles Schwarzbraun oder Rauchfahl verwandelt ist und die vielen ebenfalls vom **Jugendkleide** verbliebenen Flügeldeckfedern noch unscheinlicher geworden sind, als sie im Winter oder zu Anfang des Frühlings waren. Bei vielen bleibt der Kopf auch bloss braungefleckt oder nicht rein vermausert bis zum folgenden Federwechsel.

In diesem nun, im **zweiten Herbst** ihres Lebens, wird endlich das ganze Gefieder, auch die jetzt einundeinviertel Jahr alten braunen Flügeldeckfedern samt allen Schwung- und Schwanzfedern mit neuen vertauscht, und diese erste **Hauptmauser** wiederholt sich um diese Zeit von jetzt an alle Jahre bis ans Lebensende des Vogels.

Diese erste ganz vollständige Mauser gibt unserer Lachmöve ihr erstes **ausgefärbtes Winterkleid**. In diesem hat sie einen auswendig prächtig mennig- oder orangeroten, inwendig gelbroten Schnabel, auch das nackte Augenlidrändchen und die Füsse haben jene lebhafte Färbung; dicht vor dem Auge steht ein schwärzliches Fleckchen, auf dem Ohr ein grösseres graues, zuweilen ist auch noch quer über dem Hinterkopf ein graulicher Strich angedeutet, aber meistens sehr schwach; übrigens sind der Kopf, der Hals bis an den Rücken, alle unteren Teile des Vogels, auch der Unterflügel und das Flügelrändchen, desgleichen der Schwanz mit seinen unteren und oberen Deckfedern nebst dem Bürzel rein und blendend weiss; der Mantel, das ist Rücken, Schultern, Flügeldeckfedern und hinterste Schwungfedern, sehr zart und rein mövenblau, gesättigter als bei der **Zwerg-** und **Schwarzkopfmöve** und lichter als bei der **Dreizehnmöve**.

Von den Schwungfedern erster Ordnung sind die vier ersten nebst den Schäften von aussen weiss, die Spitzen tief schwarz, an der ersten kurz, an den folgenden zunehmend länger und so weit auch die Schäfte schwarz, die allererste von der Wurzel her auf der Aussenfahne auch schwarz, aber dies nach der äusseren Kante immer schmäler und endlich 5 cm vor dem Ende ganz spitz auslaufend, auch die zweite hat noch auf der Aussenkante 6 cm vor der Spitze einen feinen schwarzen, aber nur bis 2 cm langen Strich; die Innenfahnen der ersten drei Federn sind, an der Spitze ausgenommen, weiss, die erste mit einer schmalen schwarzgrauen Kante, die schon 3,5 cm vor der Spitze ganz schmal ausläuft; an der zweiten ist diese Kante schwärzer, viel breiter, wurzelwärts nach innen aschgrau begrenzt, spitzwärts schmäler und in das Schwarz der Spitze auslaufend; die dritte mit noch breiterem schwarzem Innenrande, der wurzelwärts mit noch mehr Aschgrau nach innen begrenzt ist; die vierte Feder hat eine fast ganz aschgraue, am Rande in mattes Schwarz verlaufende Innenfahne; von der fünften an sind alle übrigen auf beiden Fahnen bläulich aschgrau, mit lichtgrauen Schäften, die zwei längsten mit schwarzer Spitze und schwärzlichem Rande der Innenfahne; die folgende mit schwärzlichem Doppelfleck vor der Spitze und am Rande der Innenfahne schwarzgrau; die übrigen ganz ohne Schwarz; die der zweiten Ordnung mövenblau, die allerletzten weiss an den Enden und auf den Innenfahnen nach dem Rande zu; von den Fittichdeckfedern sind die vier ersten weiss, zuweilen an den Spitzen grau angeflogen, die fünfte blass, die übrigen wenig dunkler mövenblau. Von der unteren Seite sind die Schäfte aller Schwungfedern weiss, die Spitze dieser mattschwarz, der Rand der Innenfahne glänzend schwarzgrau, das übrige weiss; die der zweiten Ordnung silberweiss.

Männchen und **Weibchen** sind im Äusseren einander so gleich, dass sie sich nicht unterscheiden lassen.

Dieses Winterkleid verändert sich nun im Frühjahr durch eine teilweise Mauser in das **hochzeitliche**, und erst in diesem, wenn sie fast zwei Jahre alt geworden, ist die Lachmöve **ausgefärbt** und zugleich **zeugungsfähig**. Dieses **Hochzeits-** oder **Sommerkleid**, in welchem sie im Frühjahr an ihren Brutplätzen erscheint, ist das prächtigste. In ihm sind Schnabel, Füsse und das nackte Augenlidrändchen lebhaft blutrot, fast karminrot, der innere Schnabel und Rachen hochrot; den Kopf ziert eine kaffeebraune Kappe, die hinten nicht weit über das Genick, vorn aber viel tiefer und ein gutes Stück auf die Gurgel herabreicht, während sie sich an den Seiten in einem Bogen nach unten und rundum scharf von dem angrenzenden Weiss des Halses abschneidet; sie ist tief braun, heller oder dunkler, am unteren Rande am dunkelsten, und im Braunen steht dicht hinter dem Auge ein halbmondförmiges weisses Fleckchen, der übrige Hals, Brust, Bauch, Schwanz, dessen Deckfedern unten wie oben und der Bürzel rein und blendend weiss, an Brust und Bauch oft, zumal bei fetten Individuen, mit einer lieblichen Rosenfarbe sanft angehaucht, die mit dem Ableben des Vogels verbleicht und bei ausgestopften nach und nach ganz verschwindet. Der Mantel ist hell mövenblau, wenig lichter als im Winterkleide, die Flügel ganz wie in diesem, weil sie die nämlichen blieben und erst in der nächsten Herbstmauser und, nebst den Schwanzfedern, nur in dieser mit neuen vertauscht werden.

Im folgenden Herbst, dem **dritten** ihres Lebens, legt sie abermals, wie in jedem nachfolgenden Jahr, ein dem oben beschriebenen ähnliches Winterkleid an, das sich von jenem bloss dadurch unterscheidet, dass der rein weisse Kopf nur ein schwärzliches Fleckchen vor dem Auge und ein grösseres graues auf dem Ohre hat und dass die nackten Teile ein noch höheres Rot ziert. Aus diesem Kleide geht dann durch die Frühlingsmauser abermals das **hochzeitliche**, ihr zweites vollständiges hervor, das dem ersten gleicht, kaum prächtiger an den nackten Teilen gefärbt ist und eine etwas dunklere Kappe hat. Diese ist an solchen und noch **älteren** echt kaffeebraun, zuweilen fast schokoladenbraun, am unteren Rande in Schwarzbraun übergehend, letzteres aber oft auch kaum bemerkbar, während viele **jüngere** Vögel vorkommen, bei denen dies auffallender wird, weil hier das Braun der Kappe überhaupt lichter ist und bei manchen am Vorderkopfe, zumal im Sommer, fast in Mäusegrau übergeht. Wenn übrigens diese braune Kappe bei **recht alten** Vögeln manchmal sehr dunkel, vorkommen kann, so darf sie doch nie schwarz genannt werden, und der Beiname »**schwarzköpfig**« passt deshalb durchaus nicht für die Lachmöve.

Im Laufe des Sommers wird das Braun der Kappe etwas lichter, der mövenblaue Mantel auch blasser, und das sämtliche Gefieder hat besonders durch das Abreiben der Spitzen u.s.w. sehr an seiner ursprünglichen Zartheit und Sauberkeit verloren, wenn sie sich einer neuen Mauser nähern.

Das Wechseln des **Sommer-** und **Winterkleides** durch zweimalige Mauser kommt nun alljährlich bis zum Tode des Vogels vor. Die Zeit dieser Federwechsel ist bei **älteren** Vögeln bestimmter als bei **jüngeren**, weil nach einigen Jahren auch die Spätlinge einer Brutzeit nach und nach in die Reihe mit den andern kommen. Die Hauptmauser der **Alten** fängt zwar schon im August an, rückt aber, wie bei allen Möven so auch hier, sehr langsam vorwärts und wird erst spät im Herbst, wenn alle bereits das mittlere Deutschland verlassen haben, vollendet; den Vogel im **reinen Winterkleide** kann man daher nur von den Orten her erhalten, wo diese Art überwintert. So mag es in der Regel sein. Wir wissen jedoch, dass auch gegen Ende des August Gesellschaften von zehn bis zwölf Stück vorkamen und einige davon erlegt wurden, die schon im **vollständigen Winterkleide** waren.

Dies sind nämlich die Jungen vom vorigen Jahr, die dies Kleid zum erstenmal rein bekommen haben.

Die Frühlingsmauser findet ebenfalls dort statt, geht aber viel schneller und geregelter, fängt gegen Ende des Februar an und dauert den März hindurch. Nach Beendigung derselben begeben sie sich auf die Reise nach den Brutorten, wo sie dann im vollständigen hochzeitlichen Kleide erscheinen bis auf einzelne Ausnahmen, wahrscheinlich jüngere oder vielleicht durch Unwohlsein verhinderte Individuen, die noch einzelne weisse Federn zwischen den braunen des Kopfes, sehr selten einen noch fast ganz weissen Kopf als Überbleibsel vom Winterkleide mitbringen, jedoch auch bald mit braunen vollends vertauschen.

Mit den Jungen ist es, wie schon gesagt, anders; sie tragen ihr reines Jugendkleid nach dem Ausfliegen nicht mehr volle zwei Wochen, um welche Zeit ungefähr sich bereits der Anfang ihres künftigen Winterkleides in einzelnen neuen Federn zeigt; dies kann bei zu gewöhnlicher Zeit ausgekommenen Individuen schon mit Ende des Juni, bei denen von sehr verspäteter Brut wohl erst zu Ende des August vorkommen. Sie stehen von diesen ersten Zeichen an ihr ganzes erstes Lebensjahr hindurch im langsamen und fortwährenden Federwechsel, durchlaufen in dieser Zeit noch zwei verschiedene Mauserperioden, ohne dass eins dieser Kleider vollständig würde, und behalten durch alle noch ansehnliche Partien des Gefieders vom Jugendkleide bis zum zweiten Herbst ihres Lebens, wo nun die obige regelmässige Folge des zweimaligen jährlichen Mauserns zum erstenmal, mehr als einen Monat früher als bei den Alten eintritt. Jenes fortwährende Mausern und physische Ausbilden bis über das erste Lebensjahr hinaus ist auch wahrscheinlich Ursache, dass die Periode des erlangten Mannbarwerdens dieser jungen Möven erst im dritten Frühling ihres Lebens, oder wenn sie zwei Jahre alt sind, eintritt. Dies ist bei allen kleineren Mövenarten so; bei den grossen stellt sich diese Periode noch ein bis zwei Jahr später hinaus.

An den Brutorten sieht man daher, ehe die Jungen auskommen, nur Alte im hochzeitlichen Kleide, und diese dulden die Einjährigen in der aus dem Jugend-, Winter- und Sommerkleide gemischten unregelmässigen Tracht nicht unter sich, und diese treiben sich, meist gesellig, an anderen entfernten Orten umher. An den Winteraufenthaltsorten sind dagegen alle beisammen, jung und alt, bunt durcheinander.

AUFENTHALT

Die Lachmöve ist über viele Teile unserer Erde, namentlich deren nördliche Hälfte, verbreitet. Von **Europa** bewohnt sie nicht die hochnordischen Länder, nicht **Island**, auch nicht die oberen Teile von **Norwegen** und **Schweden**. In **Asien** bewohnt sie **Sibirien**, kommt häufig am **Ural**, aber auch in **Syrien** und **Arabien** vor. In den meisten Ländern **Nordafrikas** namentlich in **Ägypten**. In **Europa** geht sie im Sommer, nur in manchen Lagen, höchstens bis zum 65. Grad nördlicher Breite, aber von da ab ist sie durch alle Teile bis zu den westlichsten und südlichsten Grenzen allgemein verbreitet. Sie ist sehr gemein in den Ländern vom Schwarzen Meer herauf, im südlichen **Russland**, der **Moldau**, **Ungarn**, **Italien**, hier in vielen Gegenden, z. B. um **Rom**, in überaus grosser Anzahl, so in **Frankreich**, **Grossbritannien**, **Holland**, der **Schweiz**, in **Dänemark**, dem südlichen **Schweden** und anderen **Ostseeländern**, in **Preussen** und **Polen**, und endlich in ganz **Deutschland**. Sie ist inmitten des Festlandes die gemeinste und zahlreichste Mövenart. Auch unserm **Anhalt** ist sie nicht fremd, zur Brutzeit an manchen Orten im Lande und in der Nachbarschaft sehr gemein, auch in der Zugzeit allenthalben vorgekommen.

In allen nördlichen Ländern ist sie **Zugvogel**, in gemässigten und südlicheren **Strichvogel**. Sie überwintert schon unter einem gemässigten Himmelsstriche, z. B. im **südlichen Frankreich**, in **Italien** u. s. w., viele sogar schon auf dem **Züricher** und anderen Seen der **Schweiz**, in gelinden Wintern bleiben sogar viele in **Holland** zurück, das wohl ihre nördlichsten Winterquartiere enthalten mag. Die in solchen gelinden Wintern an grossen offenen Gewässern in **Deutschland**, namentlich an grossen Flussmündungen, zuweilen zurückbleibenden müssen wir zu den Ausnahmen zählen.

Sobald im Frühjahr nach einigen freundlichen Tagen das Eis zu schmelzen anfängt, hört man hoch oben in den Lüften die bekannten Töne der Lachmöven, oft schon im März, gewöhnlicher aber mit Anfang des April, je nachdem jenes früher oder später eintritt. Sie scheinen den grösseren Gewässern zu folgen und auch, wie zu anderen Zeiten, gewisse Luftstrassen zu haben, bleiben aber auf der Frühlingswanderung selten länger an einem Orte als eben nötig ist, ihren Hunger und Durst zu stillen und Nachtruhe zu halten, denn sie ziehen gewöhnlich am Tage und fliegen dabei sehr hoch. Die Scharen beeilen sich dann, so bald als möglich an den Brutorten anzulangen und sich sogleich daselbst einzurichten. Die alten brutfähigen Vögel sind unter den Ankömmlingen immer die ersten, obgleich man oft im Mai eben solche in kleinen Gesellschaften auf Gewässern und durchwandernd, so einzelne selbst Anfang Juni noch antrifft. Diese scheinen nicht Lust zu haben, in diesem Jahr noch zu brüten; denn in den letzten Tagen des Juni und den ersten des Juli erscheinen die Jungen jener schon wieder, bald in grossen, bald in kleinen Gesellschaften, in denen man aber selten eine Alte bemerkt, auf dem Wegzuge begriffen. Häufig sind jene Verspäteten bei genauerer Betrachtung aber auch bloss **vorjährige** Junge, die in diesem Jahr noch nicht brutfähig sind, in der Ferne aber leicht für Alte gehalten werden können. Weil diese noch nicht vom Fortpflanzungstriebe zu einem bestimmten Ziele hingetrieben werden, so haben sie auch keine Eile, dürfen sich aber auch nicht unter nistende Scharen mischen.

Im Sommer ziehen die Alten viel früher wieder von uns weg als ihre Jungen; sie verlassen den Nistort schon im Juli oder spätestens zu Anfang des August, ebenfalls in grösseren Vereinen, während die Jungen beinahe einen Monat später aus unseren Gegenden wegwandern, meistens in Scharen, oft zu Hunderten, ja Tausenden beisammen, wobei sie vielen Lärm machen und wenig eilen, öfters in der Luft anhalten und sich halbe Stunden lang in grossen Kreisen herumdrehen, wo es ihnen gefällt auch Rasttage halten und sich auf den Gewässern einer Gegend wohl mehrere Tage lang umhertreiben. Wo eine solche Schar auf einem Teiche oder See Halt machte, viel Nahrung fand und keine Nachstellungen erfuhr, wird es ihr oft schwer, ihn wieder zu verlassen; die ersten, denen jetzt das Reisen in den Kopf kommt, erheben sich, schweben und kreisen über den noch sitzenden und mahnen sie durch ihr Schreien zum Aufbruch, haben aber oft viele Mühe, ehe sich alle in Bewegung setzen; endlich erheben sich nach und nach alle in Kreisen zu grösserer Höhe und eilen zuletzt im schnellen Fluge gerade nach West oder Südwest fort. Haben sie viele Eile, so fliegen sie noch höher und bilden dann eine einzige, regelmässige, schräge Linie, oder manchmal auch zwei solche, vorn im spitzen Winkel vereinigte, wie **Kraniche** oder **wilde Gänse**, zerreissen diese Ordnung aber alle Augenblicke, stellen sie auch ebenso schnell wieder her und verschwinden unter solchem Wechseln bald den ihnen folgenden Blicken.

Sehr selten sieht man eine einzelne Lachmöve auf der Wanderung; dies sind gewöhnlich aus verspäteter Brut hervorgegangene, noch zu wenig erstarkte Junge, die auch sehr gemächlich reisen, wo es ihnen gefällt wochenlang verweilen, tagsüber mehrere kleine Gewässer in der Runde wiederholt besuchen und so zuweilen bis zu Ende des Oktober sich bei uns herumtreiben.

Die Lachmöve ist eine Bewohnerin der süssen Gewässer; nicht Seevogel; zu manchen Zeiten zwar gern in der Nähe des Meeres und vorübergehend auch am Strande desselben, niemals aber auf hoher See, oder höchstens nur dann, wenn sie auf der Wanderung darüber hin muss. Nahe Binnenwasser, solche Seen und Flussmündungen, ebenso aber auch weit davon und tief im Festlande gelegene Landseen, grosse Teiche, weite wasserreiche Sümpfe und in Sumpf verlaufende Flussufer, sobald sie stellenweise nicht sowohl mit Rohr als mit Schilf, hohen Gräsern, Binsen und anderen Sumpfpflanzen besetzt oder auch mit grünen Inseln, Halbinseln und Landzungen versehen sind, die viel freie, aber auch viel grün bewachsene Flächen und überhaupt schlammiges Wasser haben, geben ihnen überall, sowohl in ebenen wie in bergigen Gegenden, einen Sommeraufenthalt von gewünschter Beschaffenheit; dagegen werden die klaren, von Pflanzenwuchs entblössten Gewässer mit nackten, zumal sandigen Ufern und die schnell strömenden Flüsse nur auf dem Durchzuge besucht oder dienen in milderen Klimaten dieser Art zu Winteraufenthaltsorten, weil sie dort fast immer vom Eise befreit bleiben. Unsere herrlichen Geschwisterseen im **Mansfeldischen**, der **salzige** und **süsse** (wegen verschiedener Beschaffenheit des Wassers so genannt und beide angeblich über 200 Hufen Fläche bedeckend), sind viel zu weite freie Wasserflächen, ihre nur stellenweise grünen Ufer enthalten zu hohes und dichtes Rohr in viel zu grossen Massen, als dass sie diesen Vögeln weiter etwas sein sollten, als angenehme Erholungsorte auf ihrer Durchreise; dagegen waren ehedem, als die steigende Kultur sie noch nicht verdrängt hatte, die nahe bei diesen Seen gelegenen Teiche mit ihren sumpfigen Umgebungen die wahren Aufenthaltsorte der Lachmöven für längere Zeit und jene grossen Wasserspiegel nur sichere Zufluchtsorte für die dort ausgeflogenen Jungen.

Allenthalben, wo einzelne Gewässer von Lachmöven bewohnt sind, durchstreifen diese, gemeiniglich auf besonderen Luftstrassen, in unsicheren Gegenden jedoch hoch fliegend auch die übrigen, in einem meilenweiten Umkreise täglich und oft wiederholt, aber nicht bloss Brüche, Teiche, Seen und dergleichen, sondern auch die umliegenden Wiesen und Felder. Hier trifft man sie bald auf frisch gepflügten, bald auf brach liegenden Äckern, seltener auf Stoppel- oder Saatfeldern, und bei dieser Gelegenheit besuchen sie auch die kleinsten Feldteiche und Pfützen abwechselnd, weil sie das Wasser nicht lange entbehren können. Auch bei ihrer oft zu voreiligen Ankunft im Frühjahr, wenn sie Teiche und stehende Gewässer noch mit Eis belegt finden, lassen sie sich häufig auf den vom geschmolzenen Schnee in den Vertiefungen der Felder zusammengelaufenen Wasserflächen nieder und folgen in solcher Zeit vorzüglich dem Lauf der vom Eise freien Flüsse.

Sie scheuen sich nicht vor Bäumen, mögen jedoch nicht an Gewässern wohnen, wo Wald ringsum ihnen die Aussicht in die Ferne versperrt, obgleich sie oft auch in waldreichen Gegenden an solchen wohnen, die sich teilweise durch Wald ziehen, anderenteils aber ganz frei liegen und bloss von Wiesen und Feldern umgeben sind. Auf Bäume setzen sie sich nie. Sie lieben die niedrigen grünen Inseln der stehenden Gewässer wie der Flüsse, um so mehr, wenn diese selbst oder ihre seichten Umgebungen mit kurzem Schilf und Gras bewachsen sind. Häufig wohnen sie an belebten Orten, nahe an Wegen und Strassen, kommen jedoch menschlichen Wohnungen nicht zu nahe, ausgenommen, wo sie ihre Winterquartiere aufschlagen, bei starkem Froste, wo, nach SCHINZ, z. B. die des Züricher Sees, wenn dieser sich meist mit Eis bedeckt hat, auf der **Limmat** mitten in die Stadt kommen und dicht bei den Häusern ihre Nahrung suchen.

Ihre Nachtruhe halten sie schwimmend, mitten auf der freien Wasserfläche eines Sees, Teiches und dergleichen. Sie begeben sich spät erst zur Ruhe und sind mit dem grauenden Morgen schon wieder wach. Bei Sturm suchen sie in stillen Buchten Schutz, während sie bei schwachem Luftzuge, ehe sie fest einschlafen, durch geschicktes Rudern dennoch auf derselben Stelle zu bleiben verstehen, in der Nacht aber nicht selten in die Nähe des Ufers getrieben werden. Wo mehrere dieser Möven beisammen sind, haben sie auch eine gemeinschaftliche Schlafstelle, auf der alle einzelnen nahe nebeneinander schwimmen und der Ruhe pflegen.

EIGENSCHAFTEN

Die alte Lachmöve in ihrem **hochzeitlichen** Schmuck ist unbestreitbar eine der schönsten Möven; das ungemein zarte, lichte Mövenblau, die samtschwarze Flügelspitze, die kaffeebraune Kapuze auf dem allerreinsten und allerweissesten Weiss, welches das Auge blendet, oft von unten her mit der lieblichsten Rosenfarbe angehaucht, dazu das prächtige Blutrot der nackten Teile, vereinigen sich zu einem herrlichen und unvergleichlichen Ganzen, wobei nur zu bedauern ist, dass es bloss am lebenden Vogel von so hoher und höchster Schönheit, von dieser unbeschreiblichen Reinheit und Sauberkeit ist, aber im Tode sehr bald so unglaublich an seiner Pracht verliert, dass es mit jenem gar keinen Vergleich mehr aushält, zumal das liebliche Rosa an dem weissen Gefieder der unteren Teile auch bald spurlos verschwindet.

Die **Alte** im reinen **Winterkleide**, ohne braune Kappe, mit hellem rotem Schnabel und Füssen, ist kaum minder schön; aber selten findet sich bei ihr ein leiser Hauch von jener Rosenfarbe, die zwar, wie bei anderen, vom eigenen Fett des Vogels herrührt, aber nicht bei allen, gewöhnlich nur bei **sehr alten in der Begattungszeit**, auch bei den **Weibchen** selten so bemerkbar als bei **Männchen** vorkommt.

Gewöhnlich steht diese Möve auch mit ziemlich eingezogenem Halse, den sie nur etwas mehr in die Höhe reckt, wenn sie auf etwas aufmerksam wird oder fort will; den Rumpf mit dem Schwanz trägt sie dabei ganz waagerecht, die Flügel vorn unter den Tragfedern, an der Spitze über dem breiten Schwanze kaum gekreuzt, die Füsse im Gleichgewicht des Körpers, vom eigentlichen Knie ganz senkrecht gestellt und in der Ferse nicht gebogen. Ist sie in trüber Stimmung, so ist der Hals ganz eingezogen, die Brust nach vorn noch unter die Horizontallinie herabgesenkt und das Gefieder etwas aufgebläht. Sie beharrt zuweilen längere Zeit in solcher Stellung, obgleich sie sonst vom Stillsitzen wenig hält. Zuweilen steht sie nur auf einem Beine und steckt den Schnabel unter die Rückenfedern; dies letztere tut sie immer, wenn sie schläft, auch schwimmend. Unmittelbar nach dem Niedersetzen aus dem Fluge auf festen Boden macht sie eine schüttelnde Bewegung mit dem Schwanze von einer Seite zur andern.

Sie ist sehr gut zu Fuss, schreitet sehr behende unter Kopfnicken bei jedem Schritt vorwärts, fast wie eine **Dohle**, und ist auch imstande, sich so in Lauf zu setzen, dass man z. B. eine flügellahme nicht ohne Mühe einholen kann. An den Ufern (wo sich eine Alte überhaupt selten niederlässt) oder auf kleinen Inseln geht sie noch seltener umher; desto öfter und emsiger sieht man sie aber auf Brachäckern oder in frischgepflügten Ackerfurchen herumlaufen, dabei jedoch auch häufig mit kurzem Fliegen abwechseln. Wenn sie ausruhen will, lässt sie sich gewöhnlich auf den Wasserspiegel, wäre er auch nicht gross, sehr sanft nieder, streckt im Niedersetzen die Füsse vor, wodurch sie dem Fortgleiten vorbeugt, kreuzt dann die langen Flügel hoch über dem auch schon etwas erhobenen Schwanze und Hinterleibe, und ruht so nur vorn bis an die Füsse, aber nur sehr wenig ins Wasser getaucht, auf dessen Fläche. Gewöhnlich fliegt sie bald wieder auf, doch versteht sie auch, wenn sie nach Nahrung herumsucht oder auch vor dem Schlafengehen weiter zu rudern und anhaltend, obwohl langsam umher zu schwimmen. Tauchen scheint sie nicht zu können, ausgenommen die Jungen und eine ihrer Flugkraft beraubte Alte, wenn sie der Jagdhund packen will, wo sie es auch weder tief noch lange vermag, sowie es überhaupt nur selten vorkommt.

Äusserst leicht und sanft erhebt sich diese Möve vom Boden oder Wasserspiegel; ihr Flug ist überhaupt geräuschlos, ihre Bewegungen darin sanft, leicht, gewandt, nicht anstrengend; es leuchtet vielmehr etwas Gemächliches daraus hervor, ohne dass man ihn träge oder nur langsam nennen darf, vielmehr fehlt es ihm nicht an schnellen und kühnen Schwenkungen und mancherlei Abwechslungen. Die Spitzen weit vom Körper weggestreckt, werden die Flügel darin meistens in langsamen, oft weit ausholenden Schlägen auf und nieder bewegt, schneller geschwungen, wenn es eilt, ganz schwebend und grosse Kreise beschreibend, wo sie herab- oder aufsteigen will. Mit diesen Kreisen nähert sie sich zuweilen den Wolken, aber bei ihrem gewöhnlichen Herumtreiben, zumal über dem Wasser, fliegt sie niedrig. Hat sie Eile, namentlich auf dem Zuge, so schwingt sie die Flügel hastig, fast wie eine **Dohle** und streicht dann in grosser Höhe geradeaus, wenn, wie gewöhnlich, mehrere beisammen, in schon oben bemerkter Ordnung fort. Die Luft ist mehr ihr Element als Erde und Wasser, denn von ihrer Lebenszeit bringt sie mindestens zwei Dritteile fliegend hin.

Die Lachmöve ist ein sehr unruhiges Geschöpf, bald hier, bald da, und in einem bedeutenden Umkreise ihres Wohnortes fast unaufhörlich beschäftigt; überall sucht sie etwas, allenthalben bemerkt und findet sie etwas, das ihr Nutzen oder Nachteil bringen könnte, und so geht dies ununterbrochen vom frühen Morgen bis zum späten Abend fort, zumal in der Fortpflanzungsperiode. Es ist schon erwähnt, dass sie vom Wohnorte nach entfernteren Futterplätzen ordentliche Luftstrassen hat, wo den Tag über des Ab- und Zufliegens kein Ende ist, aber die Hinfliegenden sich nicht um die Herkommenden bekümmern. Ihre Geselligkeit ist gross; denn wenn auch auf der Reise sich hin und wieder eine vereinzelt, so ist dies doch bloss Sache des Zufalls, und sie ergreift gewiss die erste beste Gelegenheit, sich mehreren von ihresgleichen baldigst wieder anzuschliessen; dieser Trieb macht, dass sie, wo nur möglich, immer in Gesellschaften, oft zu Tausenden beisammen, lebt und ihre Scharen oft Bienenschwärmen gleichen, die bei den Nestern, in einer dichten Schicht fliegend, die Sonne verdunkeln und mit ihren tausendfachen Stimmen die Sinne betäuben. Sie dehnt indessen diesen Geselligkeitstrieb nicht auch auf andere Arten aus, mischt sich nie unter sie, duldet aber auch keine in ihren Vereinen; obgleich einige, wie die **Trauerseeschwalbe** und, namentlich im oberen **Jütland**, sogar die **Küstenseeschwalbe** und die **Brandseeschwalbe**, ganz in ihrer Nähe wohnen oder sich ihnen unmittelbar anschliessen, so bleibt doch jede Art abgesondert; selbst wenn ihre Schwärme sich in die Luft erheben, fliegt jede Art in einer besonderen Schicht, wovon die Lachmöven die unterste bilden. Auch auf ihren Wanderungen im Herbst dulden sie selten einzelne **Sturmmöven**, noch seltener eine **Heringsmöve** unter sich, im Frühjahr noch weniger, und an den Brutorten dürfen es sogar die **vorjährigen** Jungen nicht wagen, sich ihnen beizugesellen. Während nun kleine Vögel sich schon von selbst hüten, unter diese hämischen Geschöpfe zu geraten, so fallen im Gegenteil diese Möven über alle grösseren sogleich feindselig her, besonders über solche, denen sie nichts Gutes zutrauen, und suchen sie durch Stossen und Zwicken mit vereinter Macht sofort zu vertreiben, sodass ihnen, wie wir mehrmals sahen, sogar der **Schwan** weichen muss.

Sie ist misstrauisch und vorsichtig, besonders während der Zugperiode, weicht daher dem Menschen, der ihr verdächtig vorkommt, weit genug aus, um nicht in Gefahr zu kommen, weiss aber klugerweise einen Unterschied zu machen zwischen diesem und den Fischern, Bauern oder Hirten, gegen die sie mehr Vertrauen zeigt. An den Nistorten macht sie indessen die Liebe zur Brut kecker und tollkühner; sie kommt dort jedem anderweitigen Geschöpf schon mit ängstlichem oder wütendem Geschrei entgegen, selbst dem Schützen und nach wiederholtem Schiessen. An den Winteraufenthaltsorten soll sie ebenfalls wenig scheu sein, zumal, wenn steigende Kälte ihr die Nahrung schmälert, oft alle Vorsicht bei Seite setzen, dann, wie SCHINZ erzählt, z. B. vom **Züricher See** auf der **Limmat** zuweilen bis in die Mitte der Stadt vordringen, nahe bei Brücken und Häusern sich aufhalten, ohne auf die wenige Schritte von ihr verkehrenden Menschen zu achten. Sie verschwanden aber einstens auf mehrere Tage, als man dort einige von ihnen weggefangen hatte. So werden sie auch an anderen Orten durch fortgesetzte Nachstellungen zuletzt ausserordentlich scheu.

Die Lachmöve hat eine keineswegs angenehme, heisere, doch durchdringende Stimme. Ihr Hauptlockton ist ein kreischendes **Kriäh** — krähenartig und dem vieler Seeschwalben ähnlich, doch selten so langgedehnt — wovon sie, auch wohl ihr krähenartiges Betragen dazu genommen, vom Landmann den Namen »**Seekrähe**« erhalten hat. Man hört es besonders, wenn vorüberziehende etwas Auffallendes erblicken, wenn eine von der Schar zurückbleiben will, wenn Entferntere anderen zurufen, aber sonst nicht häufig. Überhaupt schreien sie auf dem Zuge wenig, an anderen Orten dagegen zum Überdrusse viel. Mehrere beisammen unterhalten sich mit einem kurzen, in langen Zwischenräumen wiederholten, einzelnen **Käk** oder **Chräck**, auch **Schärb**. Dieses aus verschiedenen Kehlen und durch besondere Anlässe verschiedentlich moduliert, bei Betrachtung von etwas Verdächtigem auch wohl in **Käckäckäk** verwandelt, hat von mehreren durcheinander Ähnlichkeit mit einem heiseren Gelächter und ihr zu dem Namen »**Lachmöve**« verholfen. In der Wut, wenn sie einen Feind anfallen, schreien sie heftig **Krrr kräck äck äck** oft wiederholt; auch hört man unter den mannigfaltigsten Abwechslungen aller dieser Töne, die aber alle nichts Angenehmes haben, öfter auch ein heiseres **Kirr** und andere noch wunderlicherer Art.

Auf der Wanderung schreit die einzelne selten **Kriäh**; je mehr aber beisammen sind, desto öfters lassen sie es hören, doch ist dies noch lange nicht zu vergleichen mit ihrem unaufhörlichen Toben und Lärmen an den Brutorten. Hier ist es bei Tage nie ganz still, sogar in der Nacht lässt sich dann und wann eine hören, und das Schreien ist um so ärger, je grösser die Anzahl der zu solchem Verein gehörigen Vögel ist, und an denen, wo Tausende beisammen wohnen, wird es wahrhaft unerträglich und so betäubend, dass man sich die Ohren verstopfen möchte. Es macht einen so widrigen und dauernden Eindruck auf das Gehör, dass man es immer noch zu hören wähnt, wenn man sich schon so weit entfernt hat, dass dies gar nicht mehr möglich ist. In der Nähe einer recht grossen Kolonie dieser einförmigen, jämmerlichen Schreier stundenlang aushalten zu wollen, würde eine Qual sein, da sie ihre Anstrengungen verdoppeln, so lange ein Mensch daselbst verweilt. Begibt sich dieser in ein dichtes Versteck, in eine dazu eingerichtete Hütte, um sie besser beobachten zu können, so dauert es sehr lange, ehe der Lärm sich etwas legt; sobald er sich aber wieder blicken lässt, geht das grässliche Toben von neuem los, wie denn ausserdem jeder vorüberfliegende grössere Vogel die ganze Schar in den heftigsten Alarm setzt, wobei sie ihm aus vollem Halse schreiend nachzieht und ihn fortjagt, was nicht allein **Krähen**, **Raben** und **Raubvögeln**, sondern auch **Reihern**, **Störchen**, **Enten** und anderen schuldlosen Wasservögeln widerfährt. Ihr **Kriäh** bildet in dieser hässlichen Musik stets den Grundton, aber auf verschiedene Weise und individuell zwischen halben und viertel Tönen schwankend, in Misstöne überschlagend; dann mit den oben bezeichneten Tönen, endlich mit dem kläglichen **Piepen** und späteren **Kreischen** der Jungen vermischt, überbietet eins das andere an Heftigkeit.

Die Lachmöve lässt sich auch im gefangenen Zustande am Leben erhalten, aber nicht eigentlich als Stubenvogel, besonders weil sie viel Wasser verlangt, sich oft badet u.s.w. Am besten ist es, ihr einen geräumigen, übergitterten Behälter an einem Wasser im Freien anzuweisen. Eines Jahres am 1. August wurde mir eine völlig erwachsene Junge überbracht, die man bei Sturm und heftigem Regen ganz durchnässt im hohen dichten Roggen mit den Händen gefangen hatte. Ich brachte sie in die Stube und ergötzte mich sehr am Betragen dieses netten Geschöpfes. Sie gewöhnte sich sehr bald, stand immer, wie oben beschrieben, steif auf den Füssen, diese weit vorgezogen, liess aber die Flügel, ohne sie zu kreuzen, auf dem sehr breit gemachten Schwanze ruhen, häufig auch ohne sie vorn unter die Tragfedern zu stecken, flog ohne Ungestüm, vielmehr ganz gemächlich in der Stube umher, sass am liebsten hoch auf Schränken und flog von da gewandt, leicht und sehr sanft zu ihrem Wasserbehälter herab, oder auch in der Höhe herum, wobei sie fast nie gegen die Fenster, desto öfter aber gegen die weisse Decke flog, aber weder dort noch hier hart anstiess. Jedesmal, wenn sie sich wieder setzte, wedelte sie mit dem Schwanze schnell hinüber und herüber. Nur einen leisen Ton, **kack — kack**, liess sie manchmal hören, der stärker, aber auch nur einzeln ausgerufen wurde, wenn ein Hund in die Stube kam. Sie hatte schon angefangen zu mausern und trug bereits einzelne Zeichen des ersten Winterkleides. Als ich ihr nach fünf Tagen die Freiheit wieder schenkte und sie an einem Teiche laufen liess, überschwamm sie denselben sogleich, badete sich am gegenseitigen Ufer recht sorgfältig und lange, machte darauf kleine Versuche zum Fliegen, fing Wasserinsekten, badete sich abermals tüchtig, erhob sich endlich in die Luft und flog davon.

NAHRUNG

Die Lachmöve nährt sich meistens von Insekten, sowohl Wasser- als Landinsekten, deren Larven und von Würmern, seltener von kleinen Fischen, auch toten, und anderen Äsern, gelegentlich auch von Mäusen.

Sie fischt zwar vieles, was oben oder sehr flach schwimmt, aus dem Wasser auf, weshalb sie denn auch immerwährend spähend über demselben, bald niedrig, bald höher, in allerlei anmutigen Schwenkungen herumschweift und nach einiger Zeit gewöhnlich auf demselben Striche, den sie anfänglich nahm, wieder zurückkommt oder kleinere Gewässer umkreist; jedoch taucht sie dabei für den Augenblick, wenn sie aus der Luft im Bogen herabfährt, nie tiefer als mit dem Kopfe ins Wasser. Bei solchem Herabschiessen macht sie keinen grossen Bogen, und wenn sie dazu hoch fliegt, dreht sie sich schwebend erst in ein paar Spiralwendungen so weit herab, dass sie das Wasser nun in einem kurzen Bogen erreicht.

Oft fischt sie auch auf seichtem, morastigem Wasser **schwimmend**, zuweilen anhaltend und lange an einer Stelle, im emsigen Picken oder Auflesen begriffen, ohne weiter etwas als den Schnabel dabei einzutauchen. Welches Nahrungsmittel sich ihr an solchen Stellen in solcher Menge darbietet, ist indessen noch nicht bestimmt ermittelt; doch sind es höchst wahrscheinlich sehr kleine Weichtierchen oder Larven von Mücken und anderen kleinen Insekten; denn im Magen bei solcher Beschäftigung Erlegter fand man bloss eine breiartige grüngraue Masse, darin jene nicht deutlich zu erkennen waren, weil man gewöhnlich unterliess, solche Vögel zur Stelle zu öffnen, bald nach dem Tode aber schon Fäulnis eintritt, die jene zarten Geschöpfe sogleich unkenntlich macht.

Auch kleine Fischchen fängt sie auf seichtem, schlammigem Wasser **schwimmend**, besonders wo jene in Pfützen gerieten und das sie bildende Wasser schon grossenteils verdunstet war; hier fährt sie auch, so oft es nötig wird, mit dem ganzen Kopfe unter das Wasser. Bei solcher Beschäftigung haben wir eine erlegt, die Schlund und Magen ganz mit kleinen Fischen angefüllt hatte. Eine Gelegenheit, wo kleine Fische in flache Wasserpfützen geraten oder gewissermassen stranden, lässt sie nie unbenutzt, selbst eine Hand lange ermattete oder tote nimmt sie gierig auf und verschlingt sie ganz oder zerstückelt, hauptsächlich in kalter Jahreszeit, wo sie selbst noch grössere aufgefundene Fische zerhackt und in verschlingbaren Bissen aufzehrt.

Ihre Sommernahrung besteht indessen meistens in Insekten, und sie sind auch die Hauptnahrung der Jungen. Ausser allerlei Wasserkäfern, Wasserwanzen, Libellen und anderen, nebst den Larven derselben, nimmt sie alle im Wasser verunglückten Landinsekten ebenso begierig auf; aber sie sucht die letzteren auch auf trockenem Lande und weit vom Wasser selbst auf, Maikäfer frisst sie sehr gern, und wo sie ihrer habhaft werden kann, in Menge; wir waren mehrmals Augenzeugen, wie ganze Gesellschaften deshalb die Bäume umflatterten, an denen sie welche hängen sahen, und sie eine der anderen vor dem Schnabel wegschnappten. Haben sie sich damit vollgestopft, so fliegen sie zum Wasser, trinken sich satt und kehren nach kurzem Verweilen bald wieder zum Käferfange zurück. Gierig und futterneidisch wird hier in der Hast oft der Käfer samt dem Blättchen, woran er nagte, oder, wenn er herab fiel, mit zufällig gepackten Grasspitzchen verschlungen, was oft auch beim Aufnehmen anderer Nahrungsmittel vorkommt, obgleich sie sonst absichtlich aus dem Pflanzenreiche nichts geniessen.

So sehr sie jene Käfer lieben, ebenso begierig sind sie nach den Larven derselben, den sogenannten Engerlingen. Sie begeben sich deshalb gesellschaftlich aufs Feld, besonders wo eben gepflügt wird, flattern und laufen dort dicht hinter dem Pflüger her und holen aus den frischen Furchen die ausgeackerten Käferlarven, Käfer, Spinnen und Regenwürmer, fangen hier sogar auch manche auf gleiche Weise zu Tage geförderte Feldmaus weg. Ihre Begierde nach allen diesen Geschöpfen zeigt sich hier in ihrer ganzen Grösse, indem sie sich oft, wenn eine der anderen zuvorkommen will oder im Zanke um eine von zweien oder dreien zugleich entdeckte Beute, so in diese Beschäftigungen vertiefen, dass sie vor dem Ackersmann und seinem Zugvieh alle Furcht aus den Augen setzen. Da sie das Wasser nie lange entbehren können, so gibt ihnen ein Ackerstück, das eben gepflügt wird, einen sehr lebhaften Verkehr, und das Hin- und Herfliegen zwischen ihm und dem nächsten Wasser hat kein Ende, so lange dort gepflügt wird. Wasserlachen und kleine Teiche in solchen Feldern sind ihnen dazu sehr gelegen; sie trinken sich satt, schwimmen und schnattern eine Weile im Wasser oder nehmen wohl gar ein Bad, fliegen dann wieder auf den Acker und wechseln so den ganzen Tag über, am lebhaftesten, wenn sie Junge haben und diesen Futter zuschleppen.

Auf anderen Äckern, besonders Brachfeldern, suchen sie Laufkäfer und andere, des Morgens besonders Regenwürmer, diese auch auf feuchten Rasenplätzen und Wiesen, wo sie auch Heuschrecken, Libellen und andere Insekten fangen, doch fliegende nicht zu erhaschen verstehen.

Am Meeresstrande stellen sie auf den bei der Ebbe frei gewordenen Sandwatten dem Wattwurm sehr nach. Auf den Feldern, besonders auf Stoppeläckern, schwärmen sie der Mäuse wegen ganz niedrig hin und erwischen manche, die sie sogleich tot hacken und auf der Stelle verschlingen. Einzelne Mäuse fanden wir gar nicht selten, sogar einige Male zwei zugleich im Magen oder Schlunde erlegter Lachmöven, die gerade vom Felde zurückkehrten.

Im Winter, wo Insektennahrung freilich nicht zureichend vorhanden ist, sollen sie meistens von Fischen, lebenden und toten, und anderen tierischen Überresten leben. Die auf dem Züricher See überwinternden kommen dann bei strenger Kälte auf dem Flusse bis in die Stadt und greifen dort bei den Schlachthäusern gierig nach allen weggeworfenen Fleischabgängen, Gedärmen und dergleichen, mit Hintansetzen aller Furcht, dass sie sich den Leuten, die sich nicht um sie bekümmern, bis auf wenige Schritte nähern und selbst hingeworfene Brocken Brot verschlingen. Als man einstmals solche Bissen, in Krähenaugenabsud eingeweicht, ihnen vorwarf und einige davon Betäubte fing, kamen die anderen lange nicht mehr dahin und wurden in diesem Jahre nicht wieder so zutraulich.

Sie ist, wie fast alle Möven, gierig und futterneidisch in hohem Grade, verdaut sehr schnell und hat daher immer Hunger. Alles Verschluckte wird in der Speiseröhre bald mit Schleim überzogen, ehe es in den Magen rückt, daher auch leicht wieder ausgespieen, was nicht allein beim Füttern ihrer Jungen allemal geschieht, sondern auch oft, wenn sie bei angefülltem Schlunde heftig erschreckt, z. B. unerwartet nach ihr geschossen wird. Ihr Neid gibt oft belustigende Auftritte, wenn eine der anderen etwas wegzuschnappen sucht, noch mehr, wenn ein Schwarm bei seinem Herumschweifen einen Fund entdeckt, z. B. einen toten Fisch. Alle gleich lüstern darnach, umkreisen sie schreiend den Gegenstand, aber keiner Einzelnen gestatten die Übrigen ihn aufzunehmen; der Schwarm zieht schreiend ab, eine Einzelne kehrt um, die anderen sehen dies, kehren sämtlich um und verhindern jene daran; dies wiederholt sich gewöhnlich mehrere Male und so lange, bis es zuletzt doch einer gelingt, verstohlen umzukehren und den Bissen wegzukapern.

Dass sie oft und viel trinken, ist schon erwähnt; sie nehmen dabei den Mund voll, halten den Schnabel in die Höhe und lassen so das Wasser in den Schlund hinabrinnen. So baden sie sich auch sehr oft, nicht selten des Tags zweimal, stellen sich dazu bis an die Fersen ins Wasser, wo es recht klar ist, schlagen dasselbe mit den Flügeln, ohne diese ganz zu öffnen, schütteln sich, tauchen mit dem Kopfe ein und schnell wieder auf, damit das Wasser ihnen so über den Rücken herablaufe, doch so, dass nach tüchtigem Schütteln kein Tropfen an ihnen hängen bleibt; nachdem sie nun bald ihr Gefieder aus der Schwanzdrüse frisch eingefettet, fliegen sie gereinigt weiter. Dieses sorgfältige und oft wiederholte Baden ist allen Mövenarten eigen und erhält eben ihr zartes Gefieder so unvergleichlich sauber und nett.

Will man eine gefangene Lachmöve für längere Zeit im Wohlsein und beim Leben erhalten, so darf man ebenfalls nicht versäumen, sie hinlänglich und oft mit frischem Wasser zu versehen. Die oben erwähnte, die ich mehrere Tage in der Stube hielt, schnurrte oft mit dem Schnabel im Wasser wie eine Ente, nahm am liebsten aus diesem kleine **Fische**, auch grössere, aber zerstückelt, dann Wasserinsekten, namentlich **Rückenschwimmer** und **Schwimmkäfer**, ziemlich gern auch **Regenwürmer**, aber ungern **Blutegel**. Sie fing sehr geschickt Fliegen, sonderbarerweise nicht allein sitzende, durch Beschleichen, sondern auch solche, die, wenn sie still stand, ihr um den Kopf herum summten, schnappte sie sehr geschickt im Fluge weg. Im klaren Wasser einer grossen, flachen Schüssel, die, um das Einsteigen zu erleichtern und Schmutz zu verhindern, aussen bis an den Rand mit Sand umschüttet war, badete sie sich fast alle Tage zweimal, und doch, als ich ihr, wie oben erzählt, die Freiheit schenkte, badete sie auch erst, ehe sie sich gänzlich auf und davon machte.

FORTPFLANZUNG

Auch in **Deutschland** hat die Lachmöve viele Gegenden, in denen sie gegen Anfang des April sich häuslich niederlässt, ihren Fortpflanzungsgeschäften obliegt und sie bald nach Beendigung derselben für dieses Jahr verlässt, sie aber im nächsten und alle Jahre und so lange immer wieder bezieht, als Kunstfleiss und Anbau oder auch Zerstörungssucht der Menschen vor Ort nicht untauglich für sie machen oder sie mit Gewalt vertreiben.

Nicht allein in der Nähe der Meeresküsten, sondern auch mitten im Festlande gibt es der Orte gar viele, wo diese Art in Menge, oft zu vielen Tausenden beisammen nistet. Landseen, umfangreiche Teiche und stehende Gewässer mit grossen freien Wasserflächen, aber auch mit vielem Rohr und Schilf abwechselnd, namentlich mit niedrigen Schilf-, Seggen- und Binsenbüscheln oder sogenannten Kufen auf grossen tiefmorastigen Flächen, mit kleinen, nassen, begrünten Inseln, mit weit in Sumpf verlaufenden, übrigens wenig nackten Ufern, wie auch die tiefsten und wasserreichsten Stellen in grossen Brüchen sind ihre Nistorte; in der Nähe des Meeres auch die süssen Binnenwasser; seltener schilfreiche, morastige Ufer und Inseln langsam strömender Flüsse. Nur an solchen Gewässern — aber nie unmittelbar am Meere — pflanzen sich diese Möven in grösster Anzahl fort, von den Süsswassern mehrerer Inseln des **Kattegats** und vielen anderen der **Ostsee** an, namentlich den sehr ausgedehnten des oberen **Jütland**, wo vorzüglich die Seen **Sperring** und **Siörring** mit ihren sandigen, grösstenteils begrasten, mit Schilf umgebenen Holmen oder kleinen Inseln dadurch berühmt sind — bis zu unzähligen anderen in **Preussen**, **Pommern**, **Mecklenburg**, **Schleswig-Holstein**, **Oldenburg** u.s.w., in der **Mark**, der **Lausitz**, **Schlesien** und auch in **Anhalt**, hier wenigstens in früheren Zeiten, ebenfalls in grosser Anzahl.

Ja, in früheren Zeiten war es freilich für die Vögel unseres Landes im allgemeinen viel besser; überall weniger Menschen, weniger Nahrungssorgen, weniger Anbau, konnten sich die Vogelarten an ihrer Lebensweise angemessenen Plätzen, die sich in Menge fanden, ungehindert fortpflanzen und dies ein Jahr wie das andere. Wir brauchen in diesen Betrachtungen nicht auf Jahrhunderte zurückzugehen; die Beweise davon liegen zum Teil noch im Bereiche unserer Erfahrungen. So waren vor einem halben Jahrhundert zwischen den Dörfern **Langenbogen** und **Cölme**, unfern des in diesem Werke oft erwähnten sogenannten **Eislebener Salzsees**, noch umfangreiche, in tiefem Sumpf verwilderte Teiche, von denen uns alte Leute Wunder erzählen, von den ungeheuren Massen ehedem, als das ganze Tal noch ein einziger freier Sumpf war, dort nistender Möven und anderer Wasservögel; jetzt sind diese Flächen, durch menschliche Kunst und Fleiss entwässert, die trefflichsten Äcker und Wiesen. Nicht weit von diesem Elysium der Lachmöven, dem grossen See noch näher, lag ein zweites: ein sehr grosser, langer, meistens nicht sehr tiefer, flachufriger, einerseits sumpfiger Teich, die **Wietschke** genannt, an und auf dem wir vor vierzig und einigen Jahren noch oft wiederholt die interessantesten Jagden und Beobachtungen machten, von dem damals eine bienenschwarmähnliche Lachmövenschar alljährlich einen grossen Teil zu ihrem Nistplatze inne hatte und sich zu Tausenden vermehrte. Die Entdeckung eines mächtigen Braunkohlenlagers dicht an einem Ende des Teiches erheischte die Anlage eines Bergwerks (jetzt eins der ergiebigsten in der preussischen Monarchie) und machte das Abzapfen des Teiches notwendig, worauf die Fläche in Ackerland verwandelt und somit den Vögeln ein sehr vorzüglicher Aufenthalts- und Brutort für immer geraubt wurde. Aus alter Anhänglichkeit für die Gegend siedelten sich die Lachmöven zwar anfänglich auf ein paar anderen nahen, minder grossen Teichen (den **Dömicken**), aber aus Mangel an Platz in viel geringerer Anzahl, an; doch auch diese vertrieb bald die bis ins Wasser hinab vordringende Kultur.

Der Trieb zum geselligen Beisammenleben wird, wie bei den **Saatkrähen**, an den Brutorten am auffallendsten. Ein einsam brütendes Paar kommt nirgends, ein Verein von sechs bis zehn Paaren schon selten vor; viel öfter sind es Hunderte und Tausende, die eine einzige Gesellschaft bilden und auf einem kleinen Raume nahe beisammen nisten. Es gibt Scharen, die an Zahl und Beweglichkeit Bienenschwärmen, im Aufsteigen einem Rauche zu vergleichen sind, der die Luft erfüllt. Unbeschreiblich ist ein solches Gewimmel, dessen tausendfache Stimmen die Sinne betäuben, wenn ein Mensch sich solchem Platze nähert, wo schon ohnedies des Schreiens kein Ende ist. Es ist schon erwähnt, dass sie jedes feindliche, jedes verdächtige, auch jedes ihnen bloss auffallende, sonst ganz unschuldige Geschöpf unfern vom Nistplatze mit Schreien empfangen, schreiend begleiten und schreiend aus der Grenze ihres Bezirks vertreiben; noch viel weniger gestatten sie einem anderen Vogel, dass er zwischen ihnen niste, höchstens solchen in ihrer Nähe zu wohnen, die in eigenen grossen Vereinen beisammen nisten und sich ihnen gemeinschaftlich zur Wehr stellen können, wie manche Seeschwalbenarten. Übrigens fordern so enorm besetzte Brutplätze noch zu manchen anderen Betrachtungen auf, namentlich ein solcher wie der auf den oben genannten Seen im Nord-Westen der Halbinsel **Jütland**, von FR. BOIE in der ISIS, 1822, St. VIII sehr anziehend beschrieben.

Die Nester einer Schar stehen alle in einem kleinen Umkreise nahe bei einander, am häufigsten auf kleinen, von flachem Wasser und Moraste umgebenen, abgesonderten Büscheln kurzen Schilfes oder Binsen, wo auf jedem nur ein Nest Platz hat, oder auf sogenannten Kufen. Auch auf alten Rohrstoppeln und Haufen vom

Winde zusammengetriebenen alten Geröhrichts kommen diese Nester vor. Auf sumpfigem Boden, nahe am Wasser oder auf kleinen Inseln stehen sie im Grase, eins so nahe wie möglich neben dem andern. Zuweilen sollen sie, besonders bei zufällig verspäteter Brut, ihre Nester auch ins nahe Getreide machen, oder gar (nach PALLAS) auf Bäume, vermutlich in verlassene Reiher- oder Saatkrähennester; beide Nistarten sind uns indessen noch nicht vorgekommen. Zu dem Platze, auf dem die Nester stehen, ist gewöhnlich nicht leicht zu gelangen. Sie wählen ihn in den ersten Tagen ihrer Ankunft im Frühjahr und verraten ihr Vorhaben durch längeres Verweilen, wiederholtes Umschwärmen, vieles Schreien und häufiges Niedersetzen auf denselben. Bald nachher, im April, nach Umständen früher oder später, fangen sie den Nestbau unter vielem Zanken um die einzelnen Nestplätzchen damit an, dass sie einzelne Schilf- und Grasbüschel in der Mitte niederdrücken. Einige Tage später holen sie trockenes Schilf und Rohr, Stroh, dürre Grasstöckchen und dergleichen herbei, häufen es kunstlos, manchmal ziemlich hoch und locker auf einander und lassen oben nur eine geringe Vertiefung. Beide Gatten, die sich schon gepaart zu haben scheinen, wenn sie am Brutorte anlangen, bauen am Neste, auf dem sie auch die Begattung am gewöhnlichsten vollziehen. Manchmal noch im April, doch öfter erst mit Anfang des Mai legt das Weibchen seine zwei, selten drei Eier und nach unseren Erfahrungen nie mehr. Wenn gesagt wird, dass zuweilen vier Eier in einem solchen Neste vorkommen sollen, so sind diese höchst wahrscheinlich nicht von einem Weibchen, sondern ein anderes hat die Überzahl dazu gelegt, ein Vorkommen, das auch bei anderen in solcher Menge und so dicht nebeneinander nistenden Vogelarten nichts Seltenes ist.

Diese Eier sind, wie alle Möveneier, im Verhältnis zur Grösse des Vogels sehr gross, um vieles grösser als die des **Kolkraben**, obgleich die Lachmöve beinahe nur halb so gross ist. Sie sind 43 bis 53 mm lang und 33 bis 37 mm breit, also wie die der anderen Arten in der Grösse sehr verschieden. Noch verschiedener sind sie in der Gestalt, die ebenso oft sehr gestreckt oder schlank als kurz und bauchig vorkommt, an dem einen Ende bald kürzer, bald schlanker zugerundet, an dem entgegengesetzten mehr oder weniger abgerundet ist. Auch ihre Farbe und Zeichnung ist ebenso variabel. Ihre starke, grobkörnige, etwas raue, daher fast glanzlose Schale hat eine bei verschiedenen Stücken sehr verschiedene Grundfarbe, bald ein sehr bleiches, schmutziges Meergrün, bald ein blasses Olivengelb, bald ein ganz mattes Olivengrün, bald ein schwaches Olivenbraun, mit allen möglichen Übergängen von einer dieser Hauptverschiedenheiten zur anderen. Die Zeichnungen sind Flecke, Tüpfel und Punkte, an den hellfarbigen in der Schale rötlichaschgrau oder rein aschgrau, bei den dunklen braungrau; die äusseren Flecke dunkel olivenbraun bis zum Schwarzbraun, am dunkelsten auf hellem Grunde; manche haben über die ganze Fläche zerstreute grössere Flecke und wenig Punkte; andere grosse, oft bleichere, zerrissene Flecke, häufiger am dicken Ende als am entgegengesetzten; wieder andere haben mehr gerundete, aber keine grossen Flecke und desto mehr Tüpfel, über die ganze Fläche zerstreut; noch andere haben viel mehr Punkte, wenig Tüpfel, die gegen das stumpfe Ende kranzartig dichter stehen, sonst aber wenig Zeichnung und gar keine grösseren Flecke; endlich gibt es auch blassmeergrüne, fast ohne alle Zeichnung. Man sieht hieraus, welche grosse Abweichungen unter diesen Eiern vorkommen müssen.

Männchen und **Weibchen** brüten abwechselnd, aber keins lange anhaltend, ausser letzteres die Nächte hindurch. Am Tage, besonders bei schönem Wetter, brüten sie wenig; oft haben sie sich nur soeben auf die Eier gelegt, manchmal auf steifen Beinen bloss über sie hingestellt, so fliegen sie schon wieder weg, weil der Lärm der anderen soeben wächst, vielleicht wegen einer ungewöhnlichen Erscheinung oder bloss, weil sich in dem Augenblicke zwischen zweien ein Zank entspann (unter diesen regsamen Geschöpfen eben nichts Seltenes), woran jede gern Anteil nehmen möchte u.s.w., kurz der Abhaltungen vom Brüten und der Gelegenheiten zum Schreien kommen täglich, ja stündlich so viele, dass nur dann ein Weilchen einige Stille eintritt, wenn die eine Hälfte dieser Vögel auf den Nestern liegt, die meisten der zweiten aber nicht zu Hause und anderswo beschäftigt sind; denn keine schreit, solange sie auf dem Neste liegt oder brütet. Nach 16 bis 18 Tagen schlüpfen die Jungen aus den Eiern.

Wenn ihnen das erste Gelege genommen wird, so legen sie noch einmal; geht auch dies zweite verloren, so legen sie zum dritten, zuweilen wohl gar viertenmal Eier in einem Jahr, aber nur, wenn man ihnen nicht Zeit liess, ein Gelege lange zu bebrüten. Wenn dies der Fall ist, hören sie meistens nach der zweiten Beraubung auf zu legen. Wenn ihnen die Eier frisch weggenommen werden, legen sie schon nach einigen Tagen wieder; haben sie aber schon lange gebrütet, so dauert es auch viel länger, ehe sie wieder legen. In einem zeitig warmen Frühling und wenn sie die Eier des ersten Geleges glücklich ausbringen, können um die Mitte des Juni schon Junge ausfliegen; wenn dagegen über einen Monat später dergleichen Unbehilfliche noch vorkommen, so gehören solche Eltern an, die einige Male ihre Eier eingebüsst hatten. Zweimal in einem Frühling zieht kein Pärchen Junge auf.

Die Jungen sitzen, wo sie nicht gestört werden, zumal wo die Nester mit Wasser umgeben sind, so lange in ihrem Neste, bis sie notdürftig fliegen können. Die Alten bringen ihnen das Futter im Schlunde und würgen es vor ihnen aus; es besteht anfänglich in kleinen Insekten, Insektenlarven und Gewürm. Durch häufiges Betreten und Beschmutzen wird das Nest zuletzt zu einem elenden, dichten, flachen Klumpen, von dem die Jungen oft herabpurzeln und manches umkommt; denn anfänglich können sie nicht schwimmen, und wenn sie dann in den nächsten Umgebungen kein trockenes Plätzchen finden, sterben sie an Erkältung. An grossen Brutplätzen findet man daher viele dem Tode und der Verwesung überlassene herum liegen. Eine Woche alt haben sie jedoch am Unterkörper schon so dichte Federn unter dem Flaum, dass sie das Schwimmen gut aushalten und trockene Ruheplätzchen aufsuchen können; in der zweiten Woche lernen sie schon flattern und bald ein Stück fliegen. Jetzt schwimmen sie viel auf freiem Wasser und lernen bereits selbst Nahrungsmittel aufsuchen. Ununterbrochene Wachsamkeit für das Wohl der Jungen beschäftigt die Alten so, dass anfänglich eins von diesen stets in der Nähe jener bleibt, und das lärmende Getümmel wird an solchen Orten um diese Zeit noch durch das kreischende Piepen der lungernden Jungen vermehrt. Mehr noch als bei den Eiern fallen die Alten dann mit Wut und Ausdauer über jeden sich nahenden Feind her, schon wenn er sich ihnen nur erst in der Ferne zeigt; sie stechen auf Hunde bis zum Berühren und fliegen den Menschen ganz nahe um den Kopf herum. Erst wenn die Jungen selbständig werden, überlassen die Alten sie ihrem Schicksal, verlassen die Brutplätze und wandern sogleich weg. Jene schlagen sich dann in eigene Trupps zusammen, suchen sich anfangs meistens auf dem Wasser zu nähren, gehen aber später auch auf die Felder, verlassen den Geburtsort und zuletzt das Land, dies mehr als einen Monat später als die Alten. An einem reichbesetzten Brutplatze, wo vom April bis in den Juni ein so lärmendes Treiben und Drängen stattfand, wo Ausgelassenheit und überschwengliche Wonne herrschte, wo Freude im Übermass sich überlaut erhob, obwohl zuweilen auch mit Angst und Besorgnis wechselte, hier ist im Juli eine Öde und Stille eingetreten, die jene früheren Herrlichkeiten nicht ahnen lassen; faulende Nester, verwesende Überreste verunglückter Jungen, auch hin und wieder einer lebensmüden Alten, zerstreute Federn und schmutzige Abgänge aller Art bekunden den Wechsel alles Irdischen.

FEINDE

Die Lachmöve wird öfters dem **Wanderfalken** (wahrscheinlich auch anderen grösseren Edelfalken), seltener dem **Habicht** zur Beute. Wenn sie sie überrumpeln, was indessen nur den vereinzelten, namentlich jungen Vögeln, begegnet, so helfen ihr alle kühnen Schwenkungen, mit denen sie den Stössen des Falken auszuweichen sucht, nicht; sieht sie ihn aber früh genug, so beeilt sie sich, ihm die Höhe abzugewinnen, steigt in Kreisen zu Wolkenhöhe auf und ist gerettet.

Die Bruten kleiner Vereine werden oft von **Rohr-, Korn-** und **Wiesenweihen**, von **Raben, Krähen**, auch wohl von **Störchen** und **Reihern** geplündert und ihnen hin und wieder Eier oder kleine Junge gestohlen, weil ihrer zu wenige sind, um sich einem oder dem anderen jener Räuber mit Nachdruck entgegenstellen und ihn von seinem bösen Vorhaben wirklich abhalten zu können; dagegen an zahlreich besetzten Nistvereinen, wo gleich Hunderte über einen solchen Störenfried herfallen, sobald er sich nur blicken lässt, erreicht schwerlich jemals ein solcher seine Absicht. Die erste der Möven, die einen solchen erblickt, schreit sogleich aus allen Kräften Lärm; im Augenblick erhebt sich der ganze Schwarm, stürzt dem Feinde entgegen, umkreist ihn mit grässlichem Geschrei, stösst grimmig und unaufhörlich nach ihm, sodass er an nichts mehr denken kann, als nur so geschwind wie möglich sich den Anfällen dieser Rasenden zu entziehen und schleunigst sich zu entfernen, wobei sie ihm dennoch weit hinaus das Geleit geben. Die **Rohrweihe**, den **Storch**, den **Fischreiher** sahen wir bei solchen Vorfällen in der lächerlichsten Angst, letzteren zuweilen alles Genossene von sich geben und heftig schreien. Auch Hunde und den **Fuchs** verfolgen sie äusserst heftig; letzterer soll sich jedoch zuweilen des Nachts auf den Brutplatz schleichen und dort alles in fürchterliche Verwirrung setzen.

NUTZEN

Ihr Fleisch ist zäh und unschmackhaft, wird daher gewöhnlich nicht gegessen, obgleich sie oft, zumal junge Vögel, sehr fett sind. Dagegen sucht man die wohlschmeckenden Eier, die einen sehr grossen, dunkel orangefarbenen Dotter haben, sehr gern auf und verspeist sie in Menge, obgleich sie nicht jedem Gaumen behagen wollen, weshalb man an Orten, wo man diese Möven nicht leiden will, die Schweine damit füttert, wozu natürlich auch bebrütete Eier, selbst die noch nicht flugbaren Jungen taugen. Planmässig und mit Bedacht auf Erhaltung der Art scheint man sie leider nirgends einzusammeln. Manche Sammler haben eine besondere Fertigkeit, die frischen von den bebrüteten Eiern am Gewicht in der Hand, ohne Hilfe des Schwämmens im Wasser, zu unterscheiden. Ihre Federn sind zum Ausstopfen der Betten Entenfedern gleich.

Mittelbar nützen uns die Lachmöven, wo sie sich in Menge aufhalten, ganz ausserordentlich und vielfältig durch das Wegfangen der Maikäfer und deren Larven, der Maulwurfsgrillen und zahlloser anderer, schädlicher oder beschwerlicher Insekten, durch Verminderung der Regenwürmer und vieler anderer, durch das Wegfangen vieler Feldmäuse, endlich durch Aufzehren der abgestandenen Fische und mancherlei Aases. Dass sie viel Nahrung bedürfen und fast unersättlich sind, vermehrt ihre Nützlichkeit. Unter den Wasservögeln gehören die Lachmöven zuverlässig zu den allernützlichsten; sie verdienen daher eher Duldung und Schutz als Verfolgung, wenigstens sollte man sie nicht gänzlich vertilgen wollen.

Für die Gewässer sind diese herrlichen Vögel eine wahre Zierde.

SCHADEN

Obschon sie lebende kleine Fische gern fressen, so sind sie doch viel zu langsam und zu wenig Taucher, um sich solcher in tiefem Wasser bemächtigen zu können; selten erwischen sie hier eins dieser flinken Geschöpfe, nur wenn es zufällig an die Oberfläche kommt; dagegen aber freilich eine Menge, wo solche in flaches Wasser geraten oder in kleinen Pfützen auf dem Schlamm stehen und schon ermattet sind. Man rechnet ihnen aber auch diese noch viel zu hoch an und verfolgt sie als Fischräuber ungerechterweise, an manchen Orten viel zu hart, wenn man sie zu gewissen Zeiten jedem preisgibt, wie z. B. bei Schleswig, wo im Juni alles zu ihrer Vernichtung ausziehen darf und sie bei Tausenden metzelt, ebenso wie früher in unserer Nachbarschaft das Vernichten der Eier und Jungen erlaubt wurde.

Man beschuldigt sie ferner, dass sie die nützlicheren Enten von ihren Brutplätzen vertrieben oder doch verdrängten, was zwar teilweise wahr, doch auch so arg nicht ist, wie die Entenjagden auf solchen Gewässern oft genug bewiesen haben.

Dass sie dem, der in der Nähe einer ihrer Kolonien wohnt, durch ihr immerwährendes Schreien sehr beschwerlich fallen, ist freilich auch wahr, jedoch nur eine bald genug vorübergehende Unannehmlichkeit.

// DER GROSSE BRACHVOGEL //

NUMENIUS ARQUATA

Brachvogel, gemeiner Brachvogel, Bracher, deutscher Bracher, Brachschnepfe, grosse Brachschnepfe, Kron-, Feldschnepfe, Brachhuhn, grosser Feldmäher, Doppelschnepfe, grosse Wasserschnepfe, braunschnäbelige, krummschnäbelige Schnepfe, Himmelsgeis, Wind-, Wetter-, Gewitter-, Regenvogel, Regenwölp, Regenworp, Regenwulp (Regenwolf), Fastenschlier, Güt-, Güth-, Jüt-, Jutvogel, Geisvogel, Giloch, Grüel, Gruser, Goiser, Louis, grosser Keil- oder Kielhaken; bei hiesigen Jägern: Keilhaken.

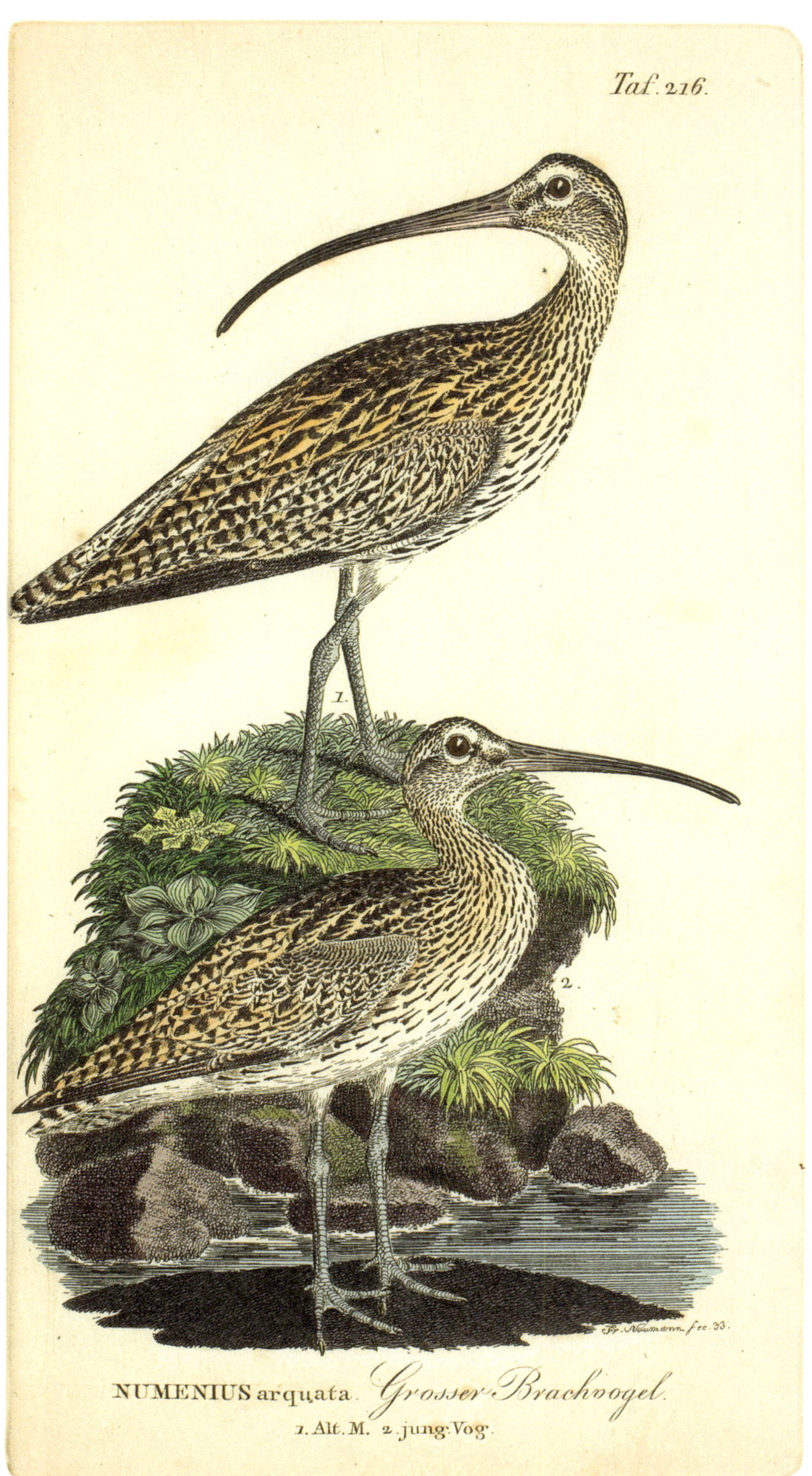

NUMENIUS arquata. *Grosser Brachvogel.*

1. Alt. M. 2. jung. Vog.

KENNZEICHEN DER ART

Der Scheitel rostgelb, schwarzbraun gefleckt; die Weichen weiss mit wenigen dunkelbraunen Schaftstrichen.

BESCHREIBUNG

Dieser Brachvogel ist einer der grössten dieser Gattung; er übertrifft darin die übrigen europäischen Arten seiner Gattung um ein bedeutendes. Auch hat er unter diesen den längsten und stärksten Schnabel, worin er jedoch von einer amerikanischen Art noch übertroffen wird. Mit einem anderen einheimischen Vogel ist er gar nicht zu verwechseln. Da er dem **dunkelfarbigen Sichler** in der Grösse wenig nachgibt, so ist er der grösste Schnepfenvogel unter den inländischen.

In der Grösse gleicht er vollkommen einer **Rabenkrähe,** hat aber eine noch stärkere, rundere Brust und einen längeren Rumpf, dagegen einen kürzeren Schwanz, längeren Hals, kleineren Kopf und viel höhere Beine, sodass er grösser oder doch höher aussieht als jene. Die Grösse schwankt, namentlich zwischen Alten und (erwachsenen) Jungen, sodass manche von jenen eine Länge von 48 bis 49,5 cm oder wohl noch darüber erreichen, unter den Jungen im ersten Herbst aber viele kaum 42 cm lang sind, versteht sich, wie in diesem Werke immer, ohne Schnabel gemessen. Die Flugbreite ist ebenfalls verschieden, von 94 bis 108 oder gar 111 cm; die Flügellänge vom Bug bis zur Spitze 29 bis 30 cm und darüber; die Schwanzlänge 11 bis 13 cm.

Das Gefieder ist wie bei den Wasserläufern und Limosen, ebenso die Gestalt der Flügel, welche einen mondförmig ausgeschnittenen Hinterrand haben. Hierdurch werden zwei verlängerte Teile oder eine vordere und hintere Spitze gebildet, wovon die letztere am zusammengefalteten Flügel bis auf das Ende der vierten grossen Schwungfeder reicht, von den Schwungfedern ist die erste die längste. Das schmale, lanzettförmigspitze, kleine, aber steife Schnepfenfederchen vor der ersten grossen Schwinge fehlt auch hier nicht. Die Schäfte der Schwungfedern erster Ordnung sind stark, ziemlich gerade, die der zweiten etwas schwächer, ein wenig nach hinten gebogen, die der dritten Ordnung ganz gerade und etwas schwach. Dem Umfange nach sind die Federn der ersten Ordnung bis gegen zwei Dritteile ihrer Länge gleichbreit, dann werden sie allmählich schmäler, die letzten an der Spitze der Innenfahne sehen schief ab- und etwas ausgeschnitten aus; die der zweiten Ordnung sind fast gleichbreit, mit auf der Aussenfahne schief ab- beziehungsweise ausgeschnittenem Ende; die der dritten Ordnung sind von einer lanzettförmigen Gestalt und stumpf zugespitzt.

Die zwölf Schwanzfedern sind ziemlich hart, etwas breit, gegen das Ende zugerundet, die mittelsten am meisten, welche auch etwas länger als die anderen sind, die nach den Aussenseiten des Schwanzes allmählich an Länge abnehmen, sodass das äusserste Paar nur 8 bis 12 mm kürzer als das mittelste ist, wodurch ein nur wenig abgerundetes Schwanzende entsteht. Der Schwanz ist im ganzen nicht sehr lang, und die Spitzen der ruhenden Flügel reichen meistens bis an sein Ende.

Der Schnabel des Grossen Brachvogels gehört unter die längsten Vogelschnäbel, ist aber, wie bei anderen langschnäbeligen Arten, bei verschiedenen Individuen von verschiedener Länge, bei jüngeren Vögeln immer viel kürzer als bei den alten, und bei den ältesten gewöhnlich am allerlängsten. Er mag daher, weil er bis gegen die Spitze hin weich ist, mehrere Jahre fortwachsen und an Länge zunehmen, was sonst wohl geleugnet worden, aber doch augenscheinlich genug ist. Dieser Umstand findet sich übrigens bei allen weichschnäbeligen, folglich bei fast allen schnepfenartigen Vögeln und kann nicht bestritten werden, ist aber bei denen mit sehr langen Schnäbeln natürlich am auffallendsten, zumal wenn man sie vom Entschlüpfen aus dem Ei an beobachten kann. Zu diesem Zeitpunkte ist der Schnabel unseres Grossen Brachvogels wenig über 2,3 cm lang, während er beim erwachsenen und die erste Wanderung antretenden **jungen Vogel** wenigstens schon 10 cm misst, und bei **älteren** und **alten** nun von hier an bis zu 16 cm oder gar bis 16,5 cm, in allen dazwischen liegenden Längen vorkommt. So wechselt er auch in der Stärke bei Jungen und Alten verhältnismässig, denn er ist bei jenen an der Wurzel manchmal nur zwischen 12 und 14 mm hoch und gegen 12 mm breit, während er bei Alten gegen 18 mm hoch und fast 14 mm breit vorkommt. Endlich ist er auch seiner Krümmung wegen ziemlich verschieden; er beschreibt nämlich vom zweiten Viertel seiner Länge an bis zur Spitze einen sich sanft herabsenkenden flachen Bogen, dessen Sehne bei alten Vögeln um vieles länger als bei jüngeren ist, und die bei sehr jungen Individuen so gering ist, dass der Schnabel nur wenig von der geraden Linie abweicht.

Der Schnabel ist übrigens höher als breit, nach der Spitze zu jedoch mehr rundlich; seine Firste etwas platt; die Spitze stumpf, am Oberschnabel etwas länger und ein wenig über die untere herabgebogen, dies jedoch fast unmerklich; die Mundkanten stumpf, wurzelwärts etwas wulstig, jederseits mit einer parallelen Furche, die am Oberkiefer fast bis zur Spitze reicht, an der Unterkinnlade aber auf dem letzten Drittel der Länge verläuft. Er ist bis gegen die hornartige Spitze weich und biegsam, an der Wurzel unterwärts fleischfarbig, übrigens rötlichgrau, gegen die Spitze schwarzgrau und endlich schwarz, inwendig nebst Rachen und Zunge fleischfarbig.

Das Nasenloch, ein gegen 12 mm langer, offener Ritz, liegt nahe an der Schnabelwurzel seitlich in einer weichen Haut, welche nicht weit vorgeht und bald in die erwähnte Furche verläuft.

Das Auge ist nicht gross, hat einen tiefbraunen Stern und weissbefiederte Lider.

Die Füsse sind hoch und bedeutend stark, zumal an den Gelenken, ziemlich weit über die Ferse hinauf nackt; die vorderen Zehen nicht lang, etwas stark, an der Wurzel durch Spannhäute verbunden, die an den äussersten bis zum ersten Gelenk reichen, bei den inneren aber viel kleiner sind; die Sohlen etwas breit und ihre Ränder ein wenig vorstehend; die Hinterzehe ist klein, schwächlich, kurz, etwas über den Zehenballen eingelenkt und nicht länger, als dass sie stehenden Fusses mit der Spitze den Boden berührt; der weiche Überzug der Füsse am Lauf und an der Schiene ist nur vorn herab grob geschildert, sonst in lauter kleine achteckige Schildchen gegittert. Die obere Seite der Zehen ist schmal geschildert, die Sohlen sind grobwarzig; die Krallen klein, kurz, wenig gekrümmt, unten etwas ausgehöhlt, scharfschneidig, die Schneide an der Innenseite aller hervortretend, die der Mittelzehe am stärksten und bei alten Vögeln mit mehr oder weniger deutlichen kammartigen Einschnitten, welche allen jüngeren Vögeln fehlen. Der Schenkel 2,9 bis 3,2 cm lang nackt; der Lauf 8,2 bis 8,8 cm hoch; die Mittelzehe mit der 9 mm langen Kralle 4,9 cm, die Hinterzehe nebst der 4 mm langen Kralle 1,8 cm lang. Die Farbe der Füsse ist bei jungen Vögeln, die sich noch besonders durch die stärkeren Fersengelenke kenntlich machen, ein sehr lichtes Graublau, bei alten etwas dunkler, doch immer noch eine helle Bleifarbe oder Aschblau; die der Krallen bei allen schwarz. Im Tode werden die Füsse bald dunkler, aschgrau, endlich völlig eingetrocknet grauschwarz.

Von ihrer ersten Bekleidung, dem **Dunenkleide**, hat man keine genaue Beschreibung und weiss bloss so viel, dass es an den oberen Teilen licht graubraun, schwarz oder dunkelbraun gefleckt und an den unteren Teilen weiss ist, dass die Vögel darin auch noch ein sehr kurzes Schnäbelchen, aber ziemlich lange, an den Gelenken unförmlich dicke und sehr weiche Füsse haben.

Vollständig befiedert oder im **Jugendkleide** haben diese Vögel wie auch in den folgenden Kleidern weder eine schöne Färbung noch sehr auffallende Zeichnungen. Überblickt man einen solchen Vogel bloss oberflächlich, so ist ein gräuliches oder bräunliches Rostgelb mit schwarzbraunen oder erdfarbigen Flecken, in der Ferne dem Lerchengefieder nicht unähnlich, an ihm vorherrschend, von welchem der weisse Bauch, Unterrücken und Bürzel, der weisse, braungebänderte Schwanz und die schwarzen Flügelspitzen eben nicht auffallend abstechen, sodass diese unansehnlichen Farben zusammengenommen und in einiger Ferne gesehen eine Mischung darstellen, die der Färbung des lehmigen Bodens und des trockenen sandigen Erdreiches gleichen, worauf diese Vögel gern herumwandeln. Dies ist auch der Typus im Gefieder der ganzen Gattung.

Doch wir wollen vorerst das **Jugendkleid** im einzelnen mustern. Der ganze Oberkopf von der Stirn bis auf das Genick hinab ist hell bräunlich rostgelb oder lehmgelb, an ersterer und an letzterem mit klaren, auf dem Scheitel gröberen und dunkleren schwarzbraunen Längsflecken; über dem Zügel, dem Auge und den Schläfen ist diese Partie am lichtesten gefärbt; die Zügel sind lehmgelb, dicht schwarzbraun gefleckt und getüpfelt; über und unter dem Auge befindet sich eine gelbweisse, ungefleckte Stelle; Kinn und Kehle sind rein weiss; die Wangen lehmgelb, erdbraun gestrichelt; der ganze Hals ist lehmgelb, an den Seiten etwas lebhafter, in Rostgelb übergehend und auf dem Hinterhalse noch etwas dunkler, allenthalben mit dunkel erd- oder schwarzbraunen Längsflecken, die auf der Gurgel herab am schmalsten und blassesten sind; die Kropfgegend und Brustseiten sind weiss, rostgelb mehr oder weniger überlaufen mit erdbraunen, schmalen Schaftstrichen, welche an ihrem unteren Ende nicht spitz auslaufen, sondern in ein Büschelchen enden; diese Zeichnung setzt sich auf den Tragefedern fort, und es gesellen sich ihr noch einzelne Quer- und Pfeilflecke bei. Die Mitte der Unterbrust, die Schenkel, der Bauch und die Unterschwanzdeckfedern sind weiss, die letzteren mit einzelnen feinen braunen Schaftstrichen. Die Federn des Oberrückens und der Schultern sind dunkelbraun, zunächst den Schäften fast schwarzbraun mit dunkel lehmgelben, ins rötliche Rostgelb spielenden, zackigen Kanten und die grösseren mit ebenso gefärbten grossen dreieckigen Randflecken, an welchen dann die Federsäume ins

Weissliche übergehen. Die grösseren Flügeldeckfedern sind diesen ähnlich, nur etwas lichter; die Federn der hinteren Flügelspitze lehmgelb und dunkelbraun gebändert, doch so, dass ihre dunkelbraunen Binden am Schafte ineinander fliessen; die übrigen Flügeldeckfedern erdbraun mit weisslich lehmgelben Kanten, die an den kleinsten nur schlichte Einfassungen bilden, an den grösseren oft auch Zacken nach innen haben oder an den Federwurzeln in grosse Flecke ausarten. Die Daumen- und Fittichdeckfedern sind schwarz mit weissen Endkanten; die kleine verkümmerte Feder vor den grossen Schwingen schwarz mit weissem Schaft und weisser Spitze; die Schwungfedern erster Ordnung schwarz mit weissen Spitzenkäntchen, die vordersten mit weissen, an den folgenden immer mehr bräunlich überlaufenen Schäften, die ersten zwei oder drei nur mit weisslicher Kante der Innenfahne, die aber bald in grosse weisse Zackenflecke übergeht, welche auf der siebenten auch an der Aussenfahne sichtbar werden, endlich, immer grösser werdend, die Wurzeln der Federn fast ganz einnehmen, auf die der zweiten Ordnung übergehen, sich an den letzten dieser aber nach und nach mit Lehmgelb vermischen und an denen dritter Ordnung in die schon beschriebenen Binden übergehen. Die letzten Schwingen erster Ordnung haben breitere weisse Endkanten als die vordersten, und diese setzen sich auch an den Enden derer der zweiten Ordnung fort. Auf der unteren Seite ist der Flügel an der Spitze glänzend schwarzgrau, der übrige Teil der Schwingen weiss und glänzend dunkelgrau gebändert; die Deckfedern sind weiss mit schwarzgrauen Querflecken; die Achselfedern rein weiss. Der Unterrücken ist hell weiss, der Bürzel und die Oberschwanzdeckfedern ebenfalls weiss, aber mit erdbraunen Längs- und Pfeilflecken, letztere mit rostgelb angeflogenen Enden, welches man auch an denen der Schwanzfedern bemerkt, welche auf weissem Grunde schmale dunkelbraune Querbinden haben, deren Zahl bei verschiedenen Individuen von neun bis zu zwölf wechselt und welche auf den Mittelfedern nach oben in Grau mit der weissen Grundfarbe verlaufen oder nur an der Seite, der Spitze zugekehrt, scharf von jenen abschneiden. Auf der Unterseite ist der Schwanz rein weiss und grauschwarz gebändert.

Ohne anatomische Hilfe sind **Männchen** und **Weibchen** in diesem Kleide nicht zu unterscheiden. Sie nehmen es mit in fremde Länder, da ihre Mauser im Winter erfolgt, währenddessen sie in unseren Gegenden nicht bleiben, und kehren dann erst im Frühling in dem neuen Kleide zurück, welches dem frischen Jugendkleide so ähnelt, dass es keiner weitläufigen Beschreibung bedarf.

Die **alten Vögel**, welche dann mit jenen wiederkehren, sind an dem weniger frischen Gefieder, das sie von der Herbstmauser an, also mehrere Monate länger tragen, leicht zu erkennen, wie denn auch ihr ganzes Aussehen, namentlich ihr längerer Schnabel und ihre schlankeren Füsse, sie von jenen leicht unterscheiden lassen. Ihr Aussehen ist dann eigentlich noch weniger hübsch als das der jungen Vögel, weil ihre Hauptfarbe noch viel mehr ins Lehmgelbe als ins Rostgelbe fällt und die dunkelbraunen Flecke stärker gezeichnet sind, wodurch ihr Gewand viel dunkler und düsterer wird. Hauptkennzeichen, wodurch sie sich sogleich unterscheiden lassen, sind erstens die schmalen Schaftflecke an den Seiten der Brust und an den Tragfedern, welchen nun jene Endbüschel fehlen; sie haben eine richtige, obgleich schmale Lanzettform und auch eine dunklere Farbe; zweitens kommen viel regelmässigere, weisse und dunkelbraune, gleichbreite und scharf voneinander getrennte Schwanzbinden vor. Die Zahl dieser Binden beträgt zehn bis zwölf.

Die meisten Veränderungen erleidet das Gefieder im Laufe der Zeit teils durch Abreiben und Verstossen, besonders seiner Ränder, was bei diesen Vögeln erstaunlich heftig sein muss, teils durch das Verbleichen der Farben unter dem Einfluss der Witterung, der Sonnenstrahlen und dergleichen. Beides kommt hier in einem besonders hohen Grade vor und zeigt sich schon im April und Mai auffallend genug; noch viel mehr aber im **Sommer**, wenn sie einer neuen Mauser näher rücken. Dann ist nicht allein alles Lehm- oder Rostgelbe in schmutziges, bräunliches Weiss abgebleicht, das dunkle Braun zur Erdfarbe, das Schwarze rauchfahl geworden, sondern es sind auch die lichten Farben der Federränder grösstenteils ganz verschwunden, weil sich die Kanten mit ihnen zugleich abgestossen haben, und sonderbar genug, wo sie als grosse Sägezackenflecke vom Rande gegen die Mitte der Federn zu eindrangen (wie an den längsten Schulter- und Flügeldeckfedern nebst den Federn der hinteren Flügelspitze), sind alle diese lichten Randflecke wie aus den Federn herausgebissen, während die dunkel gefärbten Teile dieser Federn mehr Widerstand geleistet zu haben scheinen, stehen geblieben sind und auf diese Weise der Bart solcher Federn einen wirklich tief sägezackig ausgeschnittenen Rand erhalten hat. Ferner haben die Federn, welche nur einen schlichten oder hier und da etwas ausgeschweiften Rand von jener Farbe hatten, ebenfalls so viel am Umfange eingebüsst, dass sie eine Lanzettform erhalten haben, während das gegen Reibungen widerstandsfähigere Ende des Schaftes eine Haarspitze aufweist, sodass diese Federn auf den Schultern und Flügeln eine ganz unnatürliche Gestalt, fast wie

Hahnenfedern bekommen. Durch das Abscheuern der hellfarbigen Ränder muss natürlich das in der Mitte der Federn sitzende dunkle Braun, weil jene nicht mehr so viel davon verdecken können, nun stärker hervortreten; hierdurch bekommen solche Individuen ein viel gleichfarbigeres und dunkleres Gewand, das aber weit weniger schön ist. Ferner treten auch am Unterkörper die dunklen Schaftstriche deutlicher aus dem Weissen hervor, weil sich auch hier die Federränder stark abgerieben haben, wie denn die weissen Endkäntchen an den grossen Schwungfedern auf gleiche Weise verschwanden. Und so ist denn ein alter Vogel, in seinem abgeschabten Kleide, ganz erstaunlich verschieden von einem frisch vermauserten oder einem im Jugendkleide befindlichen.

Auch unter den Alten gibt es keine standhaften Kennzeichen, woran beide Geschlechter äusserlich zu unterscheiden wären, als etwa die verschiedene Grösse und Schnabellänge, indem das **Männchen** gewöhnlich etwas grösser ist und einen etwas längeren Schnabel hat als das gleichalte **Weibchen**. Da sich aber ebenso **jüngere** von **älteren** Vögeln unterscheiden, ohne Berücksichtigung des Geschlechtes, so bleibt ein solches Kennzeichen immer sehr schwankend.

Es soll zuweilen eine **weisse Spielart** vorkommen, mit rein weissem Gefieder, grauem Schnabel und gelblichweissen Füssen. Auch erwähnt BECHSTEIN a. a. O. eine, die auf dem Leibe rosenrot bandierte Federn habe, etwas kleiner, nur von der Grösse der **Waldschnepfe** sein soll. Diese möchte aber wohl schwerlich hierher gehören.

Wie oben erwähnt ist die Mauserzeit der Jungen nicht genau bekannt; dasselbe möchte man auch von den Alten sagen, weil im Sommer, wenn sie durch unsere Gegenden wandern, selten ein alter Vogel dieser Art erlegt wird, an dem sich bereits einzelne neue Federn zwischen den alten finden, was den Anfang des beginnenden Federwechsels andeuten würde. Sie scheinen demnach ebenfalls in ihrer Abwesenheit zu mausern.

AUFENTHALT

Der Grosse Brachvogel hat eine weite Verbreitung. Was von den verschiedenen Ländern **Europas** gesagt werden kann, nämlich dass er in dem einen mehr, in dem anderen weniger oft vorkomme, aber in keinem gänzlich vermisst werde, kann man auch von den verschiedenen Teilen **Deutschlands** sagen, wo er nur in gebirgigen

Strichen unter die seltenen Erscheinungen gehört, sonst aber allenthalben ziemlich bekannt ist und nicht allein die nördlichen Küstenstriche, sondern auch manche ebene und tiefe Lagen in der Mitte unseres deutschen Vaterlandes alle Jahre in nicht geringer Anzahl besucht. Zu den letzteren gehört auch unser **Anhalt** mit seinen nächsten Umgebungen; wir sehen ihn hier alle Jahre, in vielen allerdings nur einzeln, in manchen aber auch in ziemlicher Anzahl und herdenweise.

Dass er zu den **Zugvögeln** gehört, ergibt sich zum Teil schon aus dem eben Gesagten. Er lebt nämlich zur Zeit der Fortpflanzung, im Vorsommer, in nördlichen und nordöstlichen Ländern, wandert dahin und zurück im Frühjahr und Herbst durch die mittleren Länderstriche und überwintert in den südlichen. Letzteres sind in **Europa** die Küsten und Inseln des Mittelländischen Meeres. Ausnahmen hiervon sind selten. So sollen nicht wenige an der Küste **Englands** und einzelne auch in **Deutschland** überwintern; jedoch noch auffallender ist es, dass das nämliche auch auf den **Färöern** stattfindet, wo freilich auch der **gemeine Star** den Winter hindurch bleibt, während er bei uns regelmässig wegzuziehen pflegt. Nur die offen bleibende See kann solchen Vögeln in der strengen Jahreszeit den Unterhalt sichern, wie denn auch die Seeluft das Klima jener Inseln bedeutend mildert.

Sobald die Geschäfte der Fortpflanzung beendigt sind, verlässt der **Grosse Brachvogel** schon seine Brutorte und schwärmt südlicher, in Gegenden, welche ihm die meiste Nahrung und Sicherheit gewähren, sodass selbst in **Mitteldeutschland** um Mitte Juli einzelne Alte und ein paar Wochen später völlig erwachsene Junge erscheinen, die oft bis Mitte August sich in einem Umkreise von einigen Meilen herumtreiben und erst nach mehreren Wochen weiter nach Süden wandern. Der wirkliche Zug, bei dem sie selten länger als einen Tag in derselben Gegend verweilen, wird erst um Mitte August am stärksten, dauert durch diesen Monat bis in den September hinein, wo er sich allmählich verliert. Im Oktober wird bei uns selten noch ein solcher Vogel gesehen, noch später niemals.

Den Rückzug beginnen diese Vögeln im April, er dauert bis anfangs Mai. Diejenigen Alten, welche man noch später, wie zuweilen gar noch anfangs Juni bei uns bemerkt, mögen solche sein, welche aus irgendeinem Grunde sich in diesem Jahre gar nicht fortpflanzen wollen. Alle im Frühjahr durch unsere Gegenden kommenden halten sich selten länger als einen Tag an ein und demselben Orte auf; nur die letzterwähnten machen zuweilen hiervon eine Ausnahme. Vom Frühlingszuge ist übrigens noch zu bemerken, dass diese Vögel in dieser Jahreszeit in einer weit geringeren Anzahl durch unsere Gegenden wandern als im Spätsommer, sodass sie vermutlich entweder eine andere Strasse einschlagen oder an den Winteraufenthaltsorten sehr vermindert worden sein müssen.

Sie wandern selten einzeln, viel öfter gesellschaftlich, meist in kleinen Vereinen von fünf, auch wohl zehn bis zwanzig und noch mehr Stücken, und in Gegenden, durch welche gewöhnlich viele wandern, wie an den Seekanten, schlagen sich oft noch mehrere zusammen, sodass man dort zuweilen Flüge von Hunderten zu sehen bekommt. Sie fliegen dabei oft und am Tage immer sehr hoch, wenn ihrer viele beisammen sind, in einer einzigen schrägen Reihe, wenn sie aber weniger eilen, auch unordentlich durcheinander. Sie wandern nicht allein am Tage, sondern auch einzeln des Nachts, wenn die Nächte nicht zu finster sind.

Der Grosse Brachvogel ist bald See-, bald Sumpf-, bald Feldvogel, so verschieden ist sein Aufenthalt und zwar nicht nur nach den Jahreszeiten, sondern infolge eines immerwährenden Wechsels des Nassen mit dem Trockenen zu jeder Tageszeit. Zugegeben, dass ihm im allgemeinen die Seeküsten am meisten zusagen mögen, weil auf der Wanderung wirklich die Mehrzahl ihrem Laufe zu folgen scheint und auch ihr Winteraufenthalt die Nachbarschaft des Meeres ist, so wird man ihn doch auch an anderen Gewässern, gleichviel ob fliessenden oder stehenden, häufig antreffen, besonders an solchen, welche ganz kahle, flache, sanft in das Wasser verlaufende Ufer und beiläufig sandigen Boden haben. An die Ufer grosser Gewässer, des Meeres, grosser Landseen und Ströme, begibt er sich am gewöhnlichsten bloss des Abends und verlässt sie, wo er es haben kann, erst mit Tagesanbruch wieder; am Tage besucht er dagegen viel lieber die kleineren, im freien Felde liegenden, flachuferigen Teiche und Wasserlachen, selbst unbedeutende Pfützen, die weiten, flachen, sandigen Betten kleiner Flüsse und die seichten Wasserfurten, welche durch Sumpfgegenden führen. Er hält sich aber am Wasser nie lange Zeit, nur Viertel- oder Halbestunden lang, auf; besucht es dagegen mehr als einmal am Tage und kehrt sodann nach trockneren Plätzen zurück, die er nicht immer nahe hat und nach denen er nicht selten sogar weit fliegen muss, weil er viel längere Zeit auf trockenem, ja ganz dürrem Boden, als auf nassem und feuchtem zubringt.

Die trockenen Aufenthaltsorte des Grossen Brachvogels sind Brachfelder und Lehden (des geregelten Anbaues unwerte, deswegen zur Schafweide liegen gebliebene Äcker), grosse, weite Hutungen mit kurz abgeweideten, auch teilweise verdorrten Gräsern und Heidekraut, wüste Sandflächen mit wenigen kümmerlichen Gräsern,

Wolfsmilch und andern erbärmlichen Gewächsen sparsam bedeckt, magere Stoppeläcker oder Ackerstücke mit ganz junger, dürftig gewachsener Saat, endlich auch Anger und feuchte Hutungen; aber niemals nasse Wiesen, niemals die eigentlichen Brüche und nie solche Orte, wo höhere Gräser, Binsen, Schilf, Rohr und Gebüsch wachsen.

Er liebt Sandboden und ist in sandigen Gegenden häufiger als in fetten, geht daher auch gewiss auf keine schlammigen Ufer, wo er sandige in der Nähe hat. Zu seinen Lieblingsgegenden unter den trockenen, inmitten der Festländer, gehören ganz ähnliche, welche dem **Triel** zu Wohnorten dienen, mit Ausnahme derer im oder am Walde und in der Nähe von Bäumen, weil er sich von Bäumen aller Art stets entfernt hält. Allein das öftere Zusammentreffen beider Arten an denselben Orten, einige Ähnlichkeit in Grösse und Farbe und zufällig auch im Geschrei, machen, dass gemeine Leute sie, trotz ihrer entsetzlich verschiedenen Schnabelform, oft verwechselt haben, indem bei ihnen der Name »Keilhaken« oder »Grosser Brachvogel« beide bezeichnet.

Er liebt ferner die Abgeschiedenheit, vorzüglich weite Felder, wie sie in unfruchtbaren Gegenden am häufigsten vorkommen, aber zum Unterschiede von jener Art stets nur solche, auf welchen es nicht ganz an Wasser fehlt oder die nicht zu entfernt von freien Gewässern liegen, weil er das Wasser nicht lange entbehren kann und sehr oft dahin wechselt. Hierdurch unterscheidet er sich nicht allein von dem mehr nächtlichen **Triel**, sondern auch vom **Gold-** und **Mornellregenpfeifer**, welche alle drei, namentlich der erste, und die anderen in der heissen Jahreszeit, nur zweimal des Tages, in der Morgen- und in der Abenddämmerung, zum Wasser gehen und die ganze übrige Zeit auf dem Trockenen hinbringen.

Er hält sich auch in der Fortpflanzungszeit meistens in trockenen, sandigen, aber mit Wasser abwechselnden, moorigen oder von Gewässern begrenzten Gegenden auf, deren Boden nur niedere Pflanzen hervorbringt und mit kurzem Heidekraut, Heidelbeeren, Krähenbeeren und dergleichen nur kümmerlich bedeckt ist, wie solches alles auch oft an der See zwischen den Dünenhügeln vorkommt, wo das Meer Sand ausspült.

In den Brüchen und Sümpfen kommt er allein an den freiesten Stellen am blanken Wasser, aber nie da vor, wo das Wasser zwischen den grünen Pflanzen versteckt ist. Nie kommt er Dörfern und menschlichen Wohnungen zu nahe; er überfliegt sie stets in bedeutender Höhe oder weicht ihnen aus, wo er nur kann. Auch Fluren und solche Gegenden, durch welche viele Wege führen und wo der Verkehr zu lebhaft ist, vermeidet er; daher kennen ihn sehr viele gar nicht, obgleich er in benachbarten Gegenden sich alle Jahre sehen lässt. Auf Feldern und Viehweiden, fern von den Menschen, sieht man ihn in den heissen Mittagsstunden still und untätig lange an derselben Stelle verweilen, weil er an solchen Orten gewöhnlich sein Mittagsschläfchen macht.

EIGENSCHAFTEN

Er ist ein weniger durch seine Farben, als vielmehr durch seine schöne Gestalt und Haltung, durch seine Grösse, sowie noch ganz besonders durch sein Betragen und seine flötende Stimme sehr ausgezeichneter, herrlicher Schnepfenvogel, welcher im ruhigen Stehen und Gehen seinen Leib fast wagerecht, den Hals S-förmig eingebogen, die Schnabelspitze etwas gegen die Erde gesenkt trägt. Er erhält, wenn er, aufgeregt, die Brust mehr erhebt, den langen Hals fast gerade ausstreckt und den Schnabel weniger senkt, ein gar stattliches Aussehen. Leicht und zierlich, in etwas weiten Schritten, pflegt er einherzuschreiten, sein Gang ist so wenig dem rollenden Rennen eines **Regenpfeifers** wie dem geschäftigen Trippeln eines **Wasserläufers** zu vergleichen, ist vielmehr ein geschmeidiges, aber doch ernsteres, anständigeres Einherschreiten, das zwischen dem eines **Dunkelwasserläufers** und dem eines **Reihers** die Mitte hält, jedoch mehr dem der grossen Arten der ersten Gattung sich nähert. Wenn er schnell weiter will, verdoppelt er die Schritte nicht der Zahl nach, sondern in der Weite, und dies macht, dass der Lauf nicht rasch aussieht, aber doch gut fördert.

Dass der Grosse Brachvogel oft nicht allein bis an den Bauch ins Wasser watet, sondern zuweilen ganz ungezwungen auch bei zu grosser Tiefe über dasselbe hinwegschwimmt und das Schwimmen sehr gut versteht, wurde meinem Vater, welcher es zuerst beobachtete, von BECHSTEIN nachgeschrieben, später aber von BREHM bezweifelt. Hierauf muss ich wiederholt versichern, dass es mit dem Schwimmen unseres Vogels allerdings so ist, wie in der alten Ausgabe des Werkes, III, S. 29, Z. 6 und 7 deutlich gedruckt steht; dass wir es, mein Vater und ich, im Beisein meiner Brüder an einem hiesigen Feldteiche in einem Erdloche versteckt, nicht ein-, sondern vielmal beobachtet haben. Oft schwamm von einer Gesellschaft anwesender

Brachvögel, welche am Rande im seichten Wasser hin und her wateten, ganz unerwartet einer oder der andere wie zur Belustigung quer über den ganzen Teich, welcher doch über 100 Schritte breit war, hinweg an das entgegengesetzte Ufer, und wenn es ihm da nicht behagte, auch wieder an das erste zurück; ein Betragen, das uns anfänglich überraschte, später aber oft angenehm unterhielt. Noch mehr vergnügte uns zuweilen die Keckheit dieser Vögel beim Durchschwimmen starker Strömungen zwischen den Enden zweier naher, über dem Wasserspiegel hervorragender Sandbänke im Bette des Elbflusses, wo wir sie nicht selten einen Raum von 6 bis 8 m durchrudern sahen, wobei sie, wie zur Lust, gegen die Strömung kämpften, aber, von ihr getrieben, sich doch gezwungen sahen, am entgegengesetzten Wasserrande tiefer unten zu landen als es wohl anfänglich in ihrem Willen gelegen haben mochte, gerade so wie einem Kahne geschieht, welcher in gerader Linie quer durch den Strom getrieben werden soll.

Allerdings mögen ihm dabei die doppelten Spannhäute zwischen den Zehen sehr wohl zustatten kommen. Das Schwimmen dieser Vögel, das freilich nicht oft vorkommt, ist demnach nicht, wie BREHM meint, aus diesen Spannhäuten gemutmasst worden, sondern eine wirklich in der Natur begründete Tatsache. An eine Verwechselung darf vollends (wie BREHM gar meint mit dem Säbelschnäbler) nie gedacht werden, weil wir einen solchen dort niemals angetroffen, die Brachvögel aber viele Jahre nacheinander daselbst beobachtet haben.

Was von seinem Gange gesagt wurde, passt auch auf seinen Flug. Seine Flügelschläge sind zwar sehr gleichmässig, scheinen aber matt und folgen nicht sehr rasch aufeinander. Will er schneller vorwärts, so schwingt er die Flügel hastiger, streckt sie aber dabei weniger von sich, und dann rückt er wirklich sehr schnell fort. Zuweilen schwebt er auch eine kurze Strecke. Wenn er aus der Höhe schnell herab will, zieht er die Flügel ganz an und schiesst in wenig schiefer Richtung wie ein fallender Stein mit Sausen herab, wobei er nicht selten, schon dem Boden nahe, noch einige besondere Schwenkungen macht, den Körper auf diese und jene Seite wirft, im Bogen sich noch einmal erhebt und dann erst das Niedersetzen gemächlicher vollendet, dem sonst gewöhnlich nur ein kurzes Schweben und Flattern vorangeht. Dieses Manövrieren vor dem Niedersetzen nimmt sich von mehreren zugleich und durcheinander her sehr gut aus. Sonst ist der Vogel im Fluge sehr kenntlich an den grossen, spitzigen Flügeln, den hinten lang und gerade hinausgestreckten Beinen, dem langgedehnten geraden Halse und dem langen Bogenschnabel, in dieser Hinsicht aber auch dem **Braunsichler** sehr ähnlich, gegen welchen er aber etwas spitzere und nach vorn schmälere Flügel hat, wie denn auch in grosser Entfernung seine helle Färbung, namentlich das Weisse des Unterrückens und der unteren Körperteile, sehr in die Augen leuchten.

Der Grosse Brachvogel ist ein äusserst furchtsamer, misstrauischer und scheuer Vogel. Immer auf seiner Hut, bemerkt er schon in weiter Ferne den Feind und erwartet stehend den Augenblick, um zur rechten Zeit in viel grösserer Entfernung als ein Flintenschuss reicht zu entfliehen und sich sehr weit wegzubegeben oder die Gegend ganz zu verlassen, besonders wenn er sich beobachtet und verfolgt sieht. Einem Reiter oder Wagen weicht er zwar nicht sobald aus, unterscheidet aber immer die Personen, welche ihm schaden könnten, von Bauern, Hirten und Kindern, selbst wenn sie sich auf jene Art zu nähern versuchen. Mehrere beisammen sind noch scheuer als einzelne; dass sie sich aber zuweilen, wie BECHSTEIN sagt, vor ihrem Verfolger drücken oder ducken und dann nahe aushalten sollen, streitet ganz gegen unsere Erfahrungen und ist völlig grundlos. Nur dann legen sich diese wachsamen Vögel auf den Bauch nieder, wenn sie einmal ausruhen wollen oder wirklich schlafen; doch auch dies tun nicht alle Glieder einer Gesellschaft zugleich, vielmehr bleiben aus Vorsicht immer einige auf den Füssen oder doch auf einem Beine stehen, gewöhnlich einige Schritte von den anderen entfernt. Sie stellen eine Art von Wache vor, wenigstens geben sie sich nicht mit solcher Sicherheit der Ruhe hin und entfliehen beim Erscheinen von etwas Ungewöhnlichem zuerst. Wie schon beim Aufenthalt bemerkt wurde, sieht man den Grossen Brachvogel immer an ganz freiem Ort, wo ihn nichts behindert, drohende Gefahren von allen Seiten beobachten zu können. Dass er sich im Grase oder irgendwo zu verstecken suchte, kommt niemals vor; sogar angeschossene versuchen dies letzte Rettungsmittel nicht, wohl aber schwimmen und tauchen sie, wo sie das Wasser erreichen können.

Er wird vom Landmann für einen Wetterpropheten gehalten, weil er bei bevorstehender Veränderung der Witterung viel herumschwärmt und sich häufiger hören lässt als zu anderen Zeiten. Er tut dies besonders in den Sommermonaten, wenn die Luft drückend und gewitterschwül ist. Gewöhnlich lärmen jedoch die Brachvögel nur dann recht auffallend, wenn der Regen bereits so nahe ist, dass er ohnehin vorauszusehen gewesen wäre. Ob sie sich vor dem Regen fürchten oder darauf freuen, lässt sich schwer erraten, doch glaube ich das letztere, weil der Regen nackte Schnecken, Regenwürmer und dergleichen hervorlockt, die ihnen zur erwünschten Nahrung dienen, und weil dann bei heftigen Güssen auf dem Felde Pfützen zusammen laufen, in welchen sie gern herumwaten. Sie sind auch bei nicht zu heftigem Regen und bei Gewittern munter und wohlgemut und fürchten das Feuer der Blitze wie das Krachen des Donners, welches anderen scheuen Vögeln oft viel Angst macht, wenig. Uns ist es einigemal vorgekommen, dass sie, aus einem guten Versteck beschossen, vom Blitz und Knall des Gewehres aufgeschreckt, einige Fuss hoch aufsprangen, aber augenblicklich sich wieder neben die niedergeschmetterten Kameraden hinsetzten, vielleicht in der Meinung, es sei Blitz und Donner gewesen.

Der Grosse Brachvogel ist gegen andere Vögel nicht, gegen seinesgleichen sehr gesellig. Der einzelne gibt teils durch vieles Schreien, teils durch williges Folgen der Locktöne anderer seiner Art deutlich zu erkennen, dass er gern bei ihnen ist und sich in ihrer Gesellschaft befriedigt fühlt, ein Hang, zu dem schon Furchtsamkeit, Misstrauen und die daraus hervorgehende Vorsicht auffordern, weil, wie man im gemeinen Leben zu sagen pflegt, vier Augen mehr sehen als zwei. Dieser Trieb ist bei manchem einzelnen Vogel zuweilen so stark, dass er nur auf den nachgeahmten Lockton zu hören scheint und den Menschen, welcher diesen hervorbringt und ihn damit täuscht, so wenig beachtet, dass er näher an ihm vorüber fliegt als seine sonstige Klugheit zugeben sollte, sodass mancher Getäuschte auf diese Weise, selbst wenn der Jäger sich fast gar nicht verbergen konnte, ein Opfer seines blinden Geselligkeitstriebes wird. Selbst der in sehr grosser Höhe still und stumm durch die Luft streichende, auf dem Zuge begriffene einzelne wird durch die von dem ihn Beobachtenden hervorgebrachten Locktöne geweckt und zum Beantworten derselben bewogen, ohne sich übrigens aufhalten zu lassen; aber sein fortgesetztes Beantworten verhallt erst in den Lüften mit dem Entschwinden des Vogels aus dem Gesichtskreise.

Er hat unter allen Sumpfvögeln die angenehmste Stimme; die grossen Wasserläufer, Regenpfeifer und andere mehr, selbst der **Regenbrachvogel** stehen ihm darin nach, weil keiner von allen einen so tiefen Ton hält, alle mehr oder weniger wohlklingend pfeifen, aber keiner so eigentlich flötet wie er. Seine abgerundeten, vollen, herrlichen Töne sind wahren Flötentönen zu vergleichen und dabei so kräftig, dass sie bis in weite Ferne die Luft erfüllen. Sie haben für viele Menschen einen eigentümlichen, für den jagenden Naturforscher aber einen hohen, unvergleichlichen Reiz. Von vielen Vögeln zugleich oder durcheinander ausgerufen, klingen sie wie entfernte Orgeltöne, zumal sie bei verschiedenen Individuen im Tone, in der Modulation und im Ausdrucke verschiedentlich variieren und sich meistens in Halben- und Vierteltönen bewegen. Als pfeifende Vogelstimme und im Vergleich mit den unendlich hohen Tönen der kleinen Strandläuferarten oder gar der Meisen und anderer, scheinen sie allerdings eine bedeutende Tiefe zu haben und gegen diese wahre Basstöne zu sein; allein diese Täuschung schwindet, wenn man sie für sich allein mit den Tönen der bekanntesten Instrumente vergleicht, da sie Fis und G, oder auch Fis, G, Gis in der dreigestrichenen Oktave sind, die für die gewöhnliche Flöte so geschrieben werden müssten.

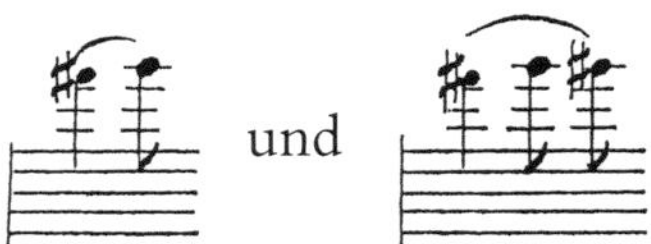

Sie mit Buchstaben zu versinnlichen, hält etwas schwerer; ich würde die erste gewöhnlich vorkommende ein geschleiftes und gezogenes **Taü** und **Taü taü** nennen, die andere, das kräftigere Locken des Vogels **Tlaüid** schreiben, und beim Aussprechen desselben die beiden ersten Buchstaben als einen, die drei Vokale aber jeden für sich etwas hören lassen; sehr oft schiebt aber der Vogel statt des L ein Schnarren ein und zieht das Ende etwas, sodass dieser herrliche Ruf wie **Trraüith** klingt.* Dieses alles sind Locktöne, die letzteren, wenn es mit dem Locken recht ernstlich gemeint ist, auch Ausdruck der Freude, wie denn überhaupt die Modulationen derselben den Kenner manches erraten lassen, was der interessante Vogel damit sagen will. Grössere Gesellschaften, namentlich wenn sie sich niederlassen wollen, verwandeln den erstbeschriebenen Lockton in ein etwas höheres, zärtlich und recht vertraulich klingendes **Twi twi** oder **Twü twi**; es ist der Ton, welchen der versteckte Jäger oder Vogelfänger mit Freuden vernimmt, weil die herbeigelockten Brachvögel, sobald sie ihn vernehmen lassen, nun sicher zu ihm und seinen Verderben bringenden Anstalten herabkommen. Wer nämlich im Pfeifen mit dem Munde geübt ist, kann die anmutigen Töne des Grossen Brachvogels leicht nachahmen und ihn damit an sich locken, wenn er das aber nicht kann, so bedient er sich dazu einer richtig gestimmten Pfeife. Im Sitzen schreien diese Vögeln viel

* Mein Vater schrieb: **Klaüit** und **Kräüit**. — Das französische **Louis** und **Lui**, wovon der Vogel in manchen Ländern den Namen bekommen, versinnlicht seine Stimme ebenfalls nicht schlecht.

seltener als im Fluge beim Wechseln der Futterplätze, am meisten aber beim Auffliegen und beim Niedersetzen, und die einzelnen beim unsteten Umherschwärmen und Suchen nach Gesellschaft. In der Nacht lässt sich selten einer hören. Sonst hört man diese Vögel oft weiter als man sie sieht, besonders wenn sie nicht hoch fliegen. Ausser einem kreischenden **Kräh** oder **Krüh**, das ihm nur zuweilen Angst und Not auspressen, welches wie die obigen Töne beiden Geschlechtern eigen ist, hat das Männchen allein auch einen besonderen Paarungsruf oder Gesang, eine häufigere, hastige Wiederholung der Locktöne, die auch anders moduliert sind. Ich habe ihn aber nur einmal gehört und damals vergessen, ihn aufzuzeichnen, weshalb ich mir ihn jetzt mit Buchstaben nicht richtig zu versinnlichen getraue. Er klingt dem der grösseren Wasserläufer und Schnepfen ähnlich.

Der Grosse Brachvogel, flügellahm geschossen oder sonst eingefangen, gewöhnt sich bald an die Gefangenschaft, wird jedoch selten recht zahm. Er ist dauerhaft und erträgt die Gefangenschaft einige Jahre, empfiehlt sich jedoch seiner Grösse wegen und weil er viel Schmutz macht, nicht zum eigentlichen Stubenvogel. Am besten befindet er sich in einem geräumigen Behälter im Freien oder in einem gut umschlossenen Garten; hier kann er durch Aufsuchen von Würmern und Insekten sogar sehr nützlich werden.

NAHRUNG

Der Grosse Brachvogel nährt sich im allgemeinen von Insekten und Würmern, bald mehr von diesen, bald von jenen, wie sie sich ihm gerade darbieten.

Dass er auch Vegetabilien geniesse und zwar nicht bloss zufällig etwa beim Fangen und Aufnehmen animalischer Nahrungsmittel, was z. B. bezüglich einzelner Grasspitzchen, Stückchen von Blättern und dergleichen wohl vorkommen mag, sondern ganz absichtlich, beweisen die genauesten Beobachtungen und das Öffnen der Magen vieler solcher Vögel. Es hat sich hieraus mehrfach ergeben, dass er **Schwarze Krähenbeeren** und vorzüglich **Heidelbeeren** geniesst. Im Norden sucht er zur Zeit der Reife der Beeren die Plätze besonders auf, wo recht viele wachsen, und verzehrt sie in solcher Menge, dass sich sein Auswurf davon ganz blau färbt, was man, ohne den Vogel zu öffnen, auch von aussen schon an den blau gefärbten Federn, welche den After umgeben, sehen kann.

Ferner fanden wir zwischen anderen Nahrungsmitteln auch ganz kleine Schwämmchen in seinem Magen, und zwar nicht nur einzelne, sondern einmal sogar recht viele. Sie hatten die Grösse einer Erbse bis zu der einer Wolfsbohne, waren noch sehr jung und noch nicht völlig entwickelt. Diese Art wächst häufig auf Feldrainen und Rasenplätzen, wo Schafe weiden und die Brachvögel sich oft aufhalten; es schien mir der Nagelschwamm zu sein, welche Pilzart häufig ist und hier zu Lande **Krösling** (Kreisling) heisst. Noch andere Pflanzennahrung habe ich nie bei ihm gefunden.

Unter den Insekten macht er fast keine Auswahl; er verzehrt sie sowohl als Larven wie im völlig entwickelten Zustande, die harten so gern wie die weichen. Wir fanden den Vormagen oft von Käfern vollgepfropft, ausser Koleopteren aber auch Insekten aller übrigen Klassen, selbst Apteren nicht ausgenommen, nur keine Lepidopteren. So fanden wir oft den Johanniskäfer, den Getreidelaubkäfer und den Gartenlaubkäfer und andere mehr, den Mistkäfer, den Frühlingsmistkäfer (diese namentlich in grosser Menge), mehrere Arten von Dungkäfer und Laufkäfer, den Getreidelaufkäfer und viele andere, dazwischen hin und wieder auch andere Insekten, Spinnen und namentlich viel Weberknechte; mehrmals auch Feldheimchen und kleine Heuschrecken. Alle diese Geschöpfe sucht er auf Brachäckern, Lehden und da, wo öfters Vieh weidet, auf trockenem Boden zusammen, wo er hin und wieder auch die Larven von dieser oder jener Art erwischt, ihnen vielleicht aber nicht so emsig nachspürt, weil man solche gar nicht so häufig bei ihm findet wie Käfer. Doch mögen ihm die Jahreszeiten mancherlei Abwechselungen bringen und in der einen die, in der anderen jene Nahrungsmittel, je nachdem sie häufiger oder seltener vorkommen, den Hauptunterhalt für ihn ausmachen.

Zum Befördern der Reibungen im Magen verschluckt er viele kleine Steinchen und Kieskörner. Wohl möglich, dass ihm auch die Schalen ganz kleiner Schnecken, die er aber mit den Tieren verschluckt, zu gleichem Zwecke dienen.

Er trinkt oft und viel und kann eben deshalb das Wasser gar nicht lange entbehren, sodass er täglich wohl drei- bis viermal, wo es nahe ist wohl noch öfter, vom Felde zum Wasser kommt, um seinen Durst zu stillen und sich abzukühlen. Das letzte scheint ebenfalls ein grosses Bedürfnis für ihn, weshalb er oft ein Bad nimmt, wobei er sich so durchnässt, dass er nur so eben noch fliegen kann. Dann geht er gewöhnlich vom Wasser zu Fuss weg und schüttelt sich auf den flachen, in dasselbe verlaufenden Sand- oder Rasenflächen und trocknet das Gefieder wieder; bald darauf aber fliegt er wieder nach entfernteren trockenen Gegenden hin und bleibt so lange weg, bis ihn dasselbe Bedürfnis abermals zum Wasser lockt. Wir haben ihn fast zu jeder Tageszeit, bei heisser Witterung und Dürre sogar mehr als einmal an einem Tage baden sehen. Wenn eine badelustige Gesellschaft zum Wasser kommt, nehmen niemals alle Glieder derselben zu gleicher Zeit ihr Bad, sondern nur ein Teil derselben, die übrigen folgen einzeln erst nach und nach, wodurch die Schar oft länger daselbst aufgehalten wird, als sonst gewöhnlich ist. Dass nicht alle zugleich baden, scheint eine Vorsichtsmassregel zu sein. Zuweilen baden auch bloss einzelne, andere nicht.

In der Gefangenschaft lässt sich der Grosse Brachvogel mit untermengten Insekten und Würmern leicht an das bekannte Stubenfutter der Schnepfenvögel gewöhnen. Er verlangt auch hier viel Wasser zum Trinken und Baden.

FORTPFLANZUNG

Ob der Grosse Brachvogel sich auch, wie behauptet worden ist, in der Mitte von **Deutschland** oder gar in **Bayern** fortpflanze oder fortgepflanzt habe, scheint nicht recht wahrscheinlich. So viel wir mit Gewissheit wissen, kommt er in der Fortpflanzungszeit nur in der Nähe der Nordseeküsten auf deutschem Boden, ebenso in **Holland** und an den Küsten **Jütlands**, aber nicht an der deutschen Ostseeküste nistend vor. Noch viel häufiger wird er in den vielen Buchten an der Küste **Norwegens**, bis in die Nähe des arktischen Kreises, wie auch im inneren **Schweden** und in **Finland**. Seine Brutorte sind sehr häufig unfern dem Meere, doch nicht immer; denn auch die grossen Landseen, Flüsse und offenen Sumpfgegenden im Innern jener Länder sind gar vielen Pärchen zu Nistorten angewiesen. Gewöhnlich sind es nicht sowohl Sümpfe, als vielmehr dürre und ziemlich unfruchtbare, bloss hin und wieder mit Morast versehene Gegenden, in welchen er nistet. Er liebt die zwischen den Dünen liegenden kleinen Täler mit kümmerlichem Pflanzenwuchs, der jenen elenden Sandboden jedoch ziemlich bedeckt und nicht so leicht mehr vom Flugsande verschüttet wird, wo nicht bloss Sandhafer und Sandgras aufsprossen, sondern sich auch schon kleine grüne Flächen von Heidekraut, Krähenbeere und anderen, mehr holzigen, aber immer ganz niedrig bleibenden Pflanzen bilden, zumal wo die Dünenhügel eine etwas breite Fläche einnehmen und in Heidegegenden verlaufen. Die Dünenreihe der sehr lang ausgedehnten Westküste der Insel **Sylt** hat viele solcher, zugleich einsamer Stellen, an welchen ich mehrfach unseren Vogel bemerkte. Dort sind auch die Wasserränder, sowie die Watten rein sandig, was er ebenfalls verlangt, da er selbst auf den Wanderungen schlammige Ufer zu vermeiden sucht.

Anfangs Mai, in manchen Jahren auch wohl etwas früher, sieht man diese Vögel an den Brutorten fast immer schon gepaart. Das Männchen lässt dann dort im schwebenden und ziemlich hohen Fluge seinen Paarungsruf fleissig erschallen. Die Gatten halten sehr treu aneinander. Wenn das Weibchen auf dem Neste sitzt, ist auch das Männchen in der Nähe anzutreffen, es fliegt dem Ruhestörer mit vielem Schreien entgegen, umkreist und begleitet ihn auch noch ein Stück, wenn er sich entfernt; an solchen Orten ist dann das Nest auch nicht schwer zu finden, weil, wenn auch das Weibchen aufgeflogen ist, die grossen Eier schon in einiger Entfernung in die Augen fallen, obgleich ihre Farbe der der Umgebung ähnelt. Das Nest, gewöhnlich eine selbstgekratzte, kleine Vertiefung, mit wenigen trockenen Pflanzenteilen belegt, ist nämlich sehr oft entweder zwischen dem auf dem Boden kriechenden oder hin und wieder sich nur fingerlang erhebenden Heidekraut und dergleichen oder auf fast ganz kahlem Sande, seltener zwischen einzelnen halbverdorrten Büscheln jener Dünengräser angebracht.

In einem Neste findet man nie mehr als vier Eier, welche zusammen im Neste liegend ein niedliches Kreuz darstellen, weil sie jederzeit mit den stumpfen Enden nach aussen gekehrt sind und mit den Spitzen sich im Mittelpunkte des Nestes begegnen, wie dies auch bei anderen Schnepfenvögeln vorkommt, das hier aber, obgleich fast alle an Zahl und Gestalt sich gleichende Eier legen, schon der Grösse wegen recht auffallend ist. Sie sind im Verhältnis zur Grösse des Vogels ansehnlich gross, fast wie die des **schwarzen Storches**, also grösser als die zahmer Enten, aber von einer ganz anderen Gestalt, nämlich so birnen- oder kreiselförmig wie die Eier der Strand- und Wasserläufer, weshalb sie kurz und dick aussehen, an einem Ende aber sehr spitz, an dem anderen schnell abgerundet sind, während die höchste Bauchwölbung dem letzteren viel näher als der Mitte liegt. Ihre Schale ist stark, wegen der sichtbaren Poren nicht sehr glatt, mit wenigem Glanz, auf schmutzig olivengrünlichem, blassem, bald mehr ins Olivengelbliche, bald ins Olivenbräunliche übergehendem Grunde, mit dunkelgrauen Flecken und Punkten, und über diesen auf der Oberfläche mit zahlreicheren grünlich schwarzbraunen

Flecken und Punkten, mitunter auch kurzen Strichen und Schnörkeln, ziemlich dicht gezeichnet, besonders am stumpfen Ende, wo sich die dunklen Zeichnungen jedoch selten kranzartig häufen, überhaupt auf der ganzen Fläche nirgends so angehäuft sind, dass nicht allenthalben der Grund sichtbar bliebe. Die grössere oder geringere Anzahl der Flecke und die verschiedenartigen Abweichungen des olivenfarbigen Grundes machen, dass mancherlei Varietäten vorkommen. Alle sehen gewissen Eiern der **Silbermöve** sehr ähnlich, sind aber sowohl an der kreiselförmigen Gestalt, wie noch mehr an dem viel feineren Korn der Schale leicht zu unterscheiden.

Aus der Anwesenheit zweier Brutflecke an den Seiten des Unterkörpers bei beiden Geschlechtern hat man gemutmasst, dass beide Gatten abwechselnd brüten; sonst ist davon weiter nichts bekannt. Die Jungen laufen, sobald sie trocken sind, aus dem Neste, die Alten sind ungemein ängstlich um sie besorgt, umschwärmen den Feind, welcher sich ihnen naht, mit kläglichem Schreien, wogegen jene sich zu verstecken verstehen und so festliegen, dass sie sich eher tot treten lassen, als dass sie fortlaufen. Um ihnen das Verstecken zu erleichtern, führen sie die Alten gewöhnlich an Orte mit unebenem Boden und höherem Pflanzenwuchs in der Nähe des Brutplatzes, wo sie ohne Hund fast nie aufzufinden sind, später noch weiter hinweg an einsame Gegenden, wo sie dann, vollends flugbar geworden, von den Alten verlassen werden.

FEINDE

Der **Wanderfalke** und im Norden auch noch andere grosse Edelfalken sind ihre ärgsten Verfolger, weniger der **Habicht**, welcher jedoch auch hin und wieder einen solchen Vogel zur Beute wählt. Von einem dieser Räuber verfolgt, sucht der Geängstete sein Heil in der Flucht und schreit aus vollem Halse dazu, wird aber gewöhnlich so lange gehetzt, bis seine Kräfte nachlassen und er sich ergeben muss, wenn er nicht das Wasser erreichen, sich in dasselbe stürzen und durch Untertauchen retten kann, wodurch er allein sein Leben zu retten vermag. Zwar macht er den Falken in der Luft auch viel zu schaffen, und es nimmt sich herrlich aus, zwei so kräftige gewandte Flieger hoch in der Luft sich herumtummeln zu sehen, allein es glückt dem Brachvogel nur selten, Mut und Kraft zu behalten, den auf ihn gerichteten, immer wiederholten Stössen des Falken stets zur rechten Zeit auszuweichen und ihn dadurch zu ermüden.

Die Feinde seiner Brut sollen **Raben**, **Krähen**, **Elstern** und grosse **Möven**. mitunter auch wohl der Fuchs, also die nämlichen sein, welche auch anderen schnepfenartigen Vögeln nachstellen; genauere Beobachtungen darüber fehlen.

NUTZEN

Sein Fleisch ist von vortrefflichem Geschmack, zumal von jungen Vögeln im Spätsommer, von diesen auch zart, von den Alten im Frühjahr besonders etwas zähe. Recht fett, wie bei vielen anderen Schnepfenvögeln, kommt es selten vor. Wir haben es von sehr verschiedenem Geschmacke gefunden, bald ganz vorzüglich, ein anderes Mal nicht besonders wohlschmeckend. Es wird indessen von vielen für ein leckeres Gericht gehalten und deshalb in grossen Städten ein solcher Vogel mit 3 Mark und mehr bezahlt. Wenn sie lange an der See leben, soll es, vermutlich vom Genusse vieler Schnecken und Wattwürmer, einen ranzigen oder tranigen Geschmack bekommen, worüber ich jedoch selbst keine Erfahrung gemacht habe.

SCHADEN

Sie tun dem Menschen so wenig Schaden wie andere Schnepfenvögel.

// DIE LÖFFELENTE //

ANAS CLYPEATA

Gemeine Löffelente, blauflügelige Löffelente, Löffelente mit rotgelbem oder mit weissem Bauch, Spatelente, Schildente, Schellente, Schallente, Stockente, Moosente, Moorente, Murente, Fliegenente, Mückenente, Muggente, breitschnabelige wilde Ente, grosse breitschnabelige oder langschnabelige Löffelente, Breitschnabel, grosser Breitschnabel, aufgeworfener Breitschnabel, aufgeworfener Breitschnäbler, Breitschnabelkopf, Räschenkopf, Räschen, Taschenmaul, Leppelschnute, Lepelgans, deutscher Pelikan, Seefasan.

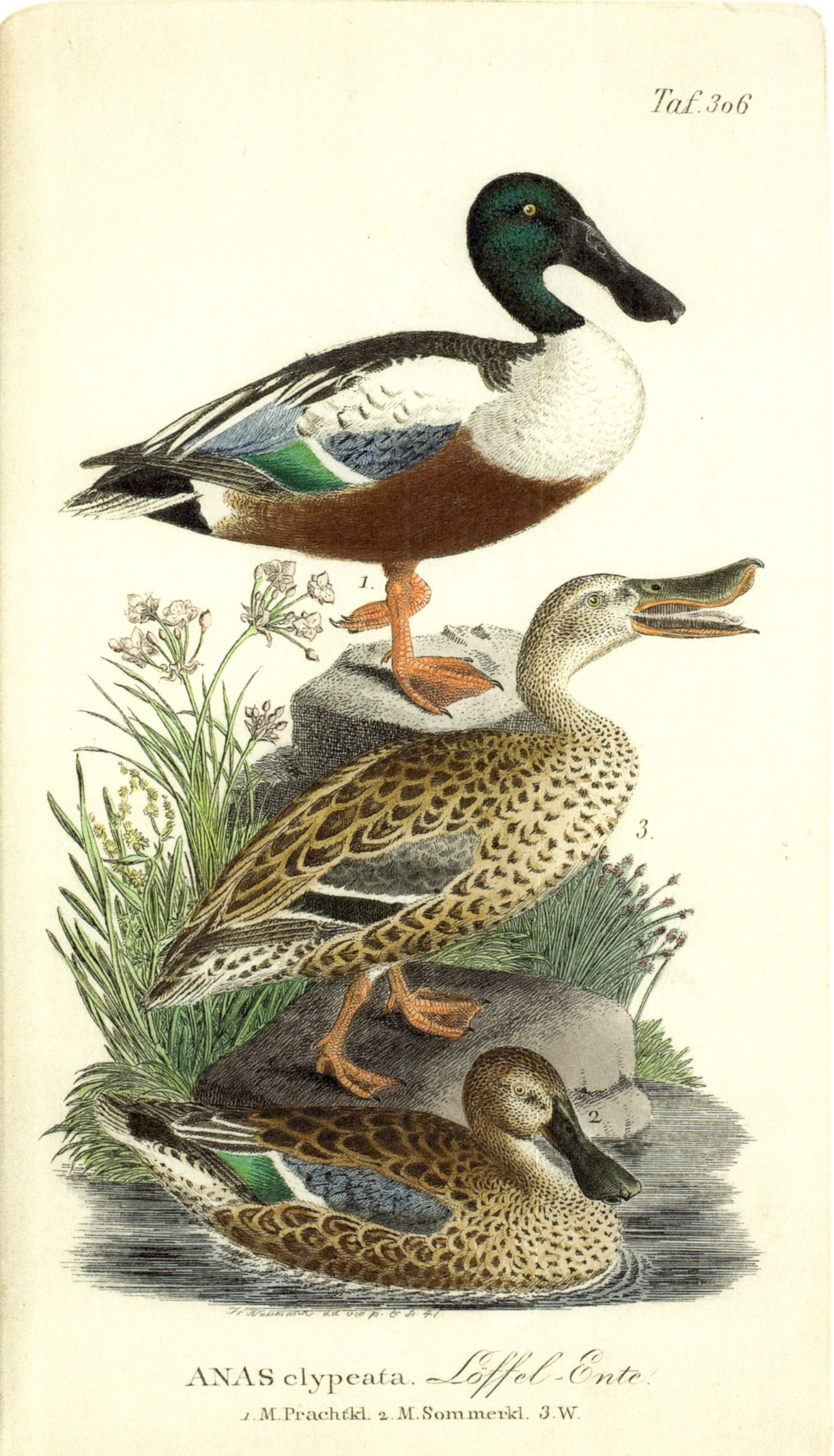

Taf. 306

ANAS clypeata. *Löffel-Ente.*

1. M. Prachtkl. 2. M. Sommerkl. 3. W.

KENNZEICHEN DER ART

Der grosse, breite, vorn sehr erweiterte und stark gewölbte Schnabel dunkel gefärbt; die Füsse orangefarbig. Der Spiegel mittelgross, oben mit einem weissen Streif eingefasst, beim Männchen prächtig grün, beim Weibchen schmutzig dunkelgrün oder grünlichgrau; der Oberflügel bei jenem glänzend himmelblau, bei diesem glänzend aschgrau. Grösse der **Schnatterente**, aber weniger schlank.

BESCHREIBUNG

Der grosse, vorn ausserordentlich erweiterte Schnabel, welcher dieser Entenart den Beinamen verschafft hat, unterscheidet sie von allen einheimischen Arten der Entengattung so auffallend, dass sie mit einer anderen nicht zu verwechseln ist. Allein unter den ausländischen finden sich einige, welche denselben oder doch einen sehr ähnlichen Schnabelbau besitzen und ihr auch hinsichtlich des Gefieders und seiner Zeichnungen mehr oder weniger gleichen. Eine solche ist in **Neuholland** zu Hause; sie hat den Schnabelbau der unserigen, auch ihre Körpergrösse ist im **männlichen Sommerkleide** (in solchem konnte ich sie nur vergleichen) ihr besonders höchst ähnlich, sie ist nur etwas gröber und dunkler gefleckt, aber auf dem Oberflügel mit einer abweichenden Zeichnung versehen, die sie sogleich kenntlich macht; nämlich im Blau desselben, das schöner und glänzender ist, befinden sich hellweisse, dunkelumgrenzte Fleckchen von sehr verschiedener Gestalt, halbmond-, haken-, tropfenförmig u. s. w., die dieser Partie eine sehr niedliche Zeichnung geben.

Unsere Löffelente hat eine mittlere Grösse und würde darin mit der **Schnatterente** übereinkommen, wenn ihr Rumpf nicht etwas kürzer und gedrungener, Kopf und Schnabel aber viel grösser wären. Die Ausmessungen ergeben folgendes: Länge (von der Stirn zur Schwanzspitze): 41 bis 45 cm; Flugbreite: 76,5 bis 81 cm; Flügellänge (vom Handgelenk zur Spitze): 23,5 bis 25,5 cm; Schwanzlänge: 7 bis 8 cm. Die kleineren Maße kommen den **Weibchen** zu.

In der Gestalt ähnelt sie den vorhergehenden Arten, besonders der **Krickente**, aber der Kopf ist noch stärker als bei dieser, und die abnorme Grösse des Schnabels macht das grossköpfige Aussehen noch auffallender, während die Füsse, Flügel und andere Teile mit jenen übereinstimmen. Auch im Bau des Gefieders findet man keinen Unterschied, und die Schwungfedern erster Ordnung scheinen nur etwas lang, weil die der zweiten Ordnung etwas kürzer sind als bei vielen, obwohl sie immer noch einen **Spiegel** von mittlerer Breite bilden. Der etwas kurze Schwanz ist aus vierzehn sehr breiten, kurz zugespitzten Federn zusammengesetzt, von denen nur die etwas spitzeren Mittelfedern etwas mehr über die anderen hinausragen, im übrigen aber das Schwanzende ein stumpf zugerundetes ist, doch von den Spitzen der ruhenden Flügel lange nicht erreicht wird, weil diese meistens nur bis zum Enddritteil der Schwanzlänge reichen. Das **männliche Prachtkleid** ist ausgezeichnet schön und in ihm hat der Oberkopf etwas (doch nicht so sehr wie bei der männlichen **Krickente** in diesem Kleide) verlängerte Federn, die aufgesträubt den Kopf noch dicker machen, doch meistens glatt anliegen, und die hintersten Schwingen mit den grösseren Schulterfedern verlängern sich in schmale Bandspitzen, die sich sichelförmig über dem ruhenden Flügel herabbiegen.

Der Schnabel ist im Vergleich mit denen aller anderen bekannten Entenarten vom grössten Umfange und von einer höchst merkwürdigen Gestalt. Er hat eine beinahe ganz gerade, an der Stirn kaum merklich aufsteigende Firste, einen nach vorn bedeutend aufsteigenden Kiel, ist an der Basis weit höher als breit, hier überhaupt schmal, nach vorn allmählich bis zur doppelten Breite erweitert und im Halbkreis endend, in dessen Mitte der flache und ziemlich kleine Nagel einen wenig vortretenden Zipfel bildet. Hinten, wo der Oberschnabel schmal, sind seine Seiten senkrecht abgeflacht, von den Nasenlöchern an der nach vorn immer mehr erweiterte Teil im flachen oder gedrückten Bogen gewölbt, an den Rändern mit einem schwachen Leistchen umgeben, der innere Rand mit sehr enge stehenden Lamellen, deren **äussere** Ecken in sehr lange, äusserst feine Zähnchen ausgezogen sind, die vom Mundwinkel bis zwei Drittel der Schnabellänge senkrecht gestellt sind und den dichtstehenden Zähnchen eines sehr feinen Kammes gleichen, am Enddrittel aber einwärts gerichtet und niedergedrückt, dort zugleich auch kürzer sind. Die ersteren stehen bei geschlossenem Schnabel gegen 4 mm über den Rand hervor, den ebenfalls senkrechten, nach **innen** in eben solche feine kammartige Zähnchen ausgezogene Querlamellen des eingebogenen Aussenrandes vom Unterschnabel gegenüber, die sie verdecken, schliessen aber in der ganzen Strecke den Schnabel nicht dicht, weil der untere Teil des Schnabels bedeutend schmäler als der obere ist und in diesen hineinschlägt, sodass besonders das sehr abgeflachte Enddrittel sich tief in diesem verbirgt und nur die bogenförmig aufsteigende Unterkante oder Sohle an der Wurzelhälfte des Unterschnabels unten bedeutend vorsteht, wodurch der Schnabel am Wurzelteil sehr an Höhe gewinnt. Von unten gesehen, schliesst der bedeutend schmälere Unterkiefer demnach nur an drei Punkten genau, nämlich gleich an den Mundwinkeln und an dem kleinen flachen Nagel, welcher aber auch tief in den oberen schlägt, während die Seitenränder des umgekehrt löffelartigen Enddrittels vom Oberkiefer bis zu 5,5 mm die Ränder des unteren überragen, weshalb eben die feinen Zähnchen jenes nach innen niedergelegt sein mussten, damit ihre Spitzchen in die korrespondierenden Lamellen des ganz abgeflachten Vorderteils vom Unterkiefer passen sollten, was indessen auch nur unvollkommen geschieht, sodass bis auf jene drei Punkte die ganzen Schnabelränder klaffen oder bloss durch die zarten Zahnspitzen nur ganz lose geschlossen werden. Die Kinnspalte, nur an der Wurzel mit befiederter, übrigens mit nackter Haut überzogen, reicht bis an den Nagel vor, ist ziemlich breit, nach vorn etwas schmäler und stumpfspitz endend.

Die Nasenhöhle ist nicht gross, eirund, nicht weit von der Stirn und hoch oben neben der hier nur etwas über 4,4 mm breiten Firste liegend; die vorn in ihr sich öffnenden ovalen, durchsichtigen Nasenlöcher stehen daher sehr nahe bei einander.

Die fleischige Zunge ist sehr gross, weil sie die innere Höhlung des Schnabels ziemlich füllt, übrigens von Gestalt denen anderer Entenarten ähnlich, in der Mitte entlang mit vertiefter Rinne, an jeder Seite mit einem beweglichen Lappen, vorn mit einem muschelartigen Anhängsel, und das Zungenband, welches sie an die Kinnhaut heftet, reicht bis über die Mitte der Schnabellänge vor.

Dieser Schnabel ist im Leben sehr weich, biegsam, sanft anzufühlen, und unter der weichen Haut, womit er überzogen, liegen eine Menge Nerven, deren Gänge auch nach dem Austrocknen durch die Haut scheinen; nur der Nagel ist hornartig. Die Biegsamkeit des Oberkiefers, **aufwärts**, nicht allein an der Stirn, sondern seiner ganzen Länge nach, wird bei heftigem Schreien sehr auffallend, am allermeisten aber beim Gähnen, wobei er bis zur Spitze einen sanft aufsteigenden Bogen macht. Seiner weichen Beschaffenheit wegen trocknet er im Tode und an Ausgestopften sehr ein und verändert zum Teil seine Gestalt auffallend, namentlich biegt er sich an den Rändern der breitesten Stelle des Oberschnabels stark nach innen, wodurch die Wölbung höher, ihre Basis aber schmäler wird, und der Unterschnabel erscheint viel schmäler, weil, wenn die Zunge herausgenommen oder vertrocknet ist, die Kinnhaut sich zusammenzieht. Ist er dann geschlossen, so klafft er an den Seiten weit stärker als im frischen Zustande oder am lebenden Vogel.

Er ist 6 bis 7 cm lang; an der Stirn 2,2 bis 2,6 cm hoch; an der Wurzel 1,5 bis 1,7 cm, vorn aber 3 bis 3,7 cm breit. Diese Verschiedenheiten in der Grösse sind grösstenteils zufällig und bei manchen Individuen sehr auffallend; die kleineren **Weibchen** haben aber auch gewöhnlich kleinere Schnäbel. Seine Farbe ist nach Alter, Geschlecht und Jahreszeit verschieden, in frühester **Jugend** aschfarbig — dann braunrötlich — erwachsen oben graugrünlich, unten und an den Rändern gelbrötlich; bei alten **Weibchen** ebenso, das Grünliche aber dunkler, das Gelbrote schöner; am **männlichen Sommerkleide** diesem ebenfalls ähnlich, doch von obenher mehr mit Schwarz überlaufen, unten mit weniger Rot oder Saffrangelb; am alten **Männchen** im **Prachtkleide** endlich einfach bläulich- oder tief schwarz, ohne Grün und Rot. Bei letzterem ist auch ausgetrocknet seine Farbe zu erkennen, bei ersterem wird das Grünliche schwarzgrau, das Rötliche hell hornfarbig. Der Nagel ist stets schwarz, Zunge und Rachen blass fleischfarbig.

Das Auge hat ein nach innen nacktes, schwärzlich gefärbtes Lid und bei den **Jungen** einen hellbraunen, nachher und bei den **Weibchen** einen schwefelgelben, bei alten **Männchen** einen hochgelben Stern.

Die Füsse sind ganz gestaltet wie bei der **Schnatterente**, haben aber, mit denen der **Pfeifente** verglichen, etwas längere Zehen, im übrigen aber auch die Zerkerbung des weichen Überzuges, ganz wie bei diesen. Die Krallen sind etwas länger, spitziger und mehr gebogen, sonst denen jener ebenfalls gleich, so auch Grösse und Stellung der Hinterzehe und die Nacktheit über der Ferse. Der Lauf misst in der Länge 3,5 bis 4 cm; die Mittelzehe mit der 8,75 mm langen Kralle 4,75 bis 5 cm; die Hinterzehe mit der 4,5 mm langen Kralle 1,3 cm. Ihre Farbe ist in **frühester Jugend** fleischrötlich und geht nach und nach ins Gelbrote über, wobei die Schwimmhäute schwärzlich überlaufen sind, endlich wird vom zweiten Jahre an, bei den **Männchen** noch früher, alles orangerot, bei letzteren sehr lebhaft, bei den **Weibchen** blasser. Im Tode wird diese Farbe alsbald dunkler und bei den meisten die der Schwimmhäute schwärzlich, nach völligem Austrocknen aber in unscheinbare rotgelbliche Hornfarbe verwandelt, die Mitte der Schwimmhäute schwarzbraun. Die Krallen sind stets graubraun, an den Spitzen ins Schwarze übergehend.

Im **Dunenkleide** ist der Augenstern grau, der Schnabel anfänglich ganz bleifarbig, später an den Rändern und unten rötlich, die Fussfarbe eine blass fleischrötliche; Scheitel und Oberrumpf, auch ein kleiner Strich am Zügel und an den Schläfen grünlich schwarzbraun; die Kehle weisslich; die Kopf- und Halsseiten grüngelblich; Gurgel und Unterrumpf schmutzig lichtgelb. Am grössern und vorn sehr erweiterten Schnabel unterscheidet man diese Jungen leicht von anderen jungen Entchen, obwohl er erst mit dem Zunehmen der Körpergrösse sich nach und nach zu der späteren Gestalt und Grösse ausbildet.

Das nachfolgende **Jugendkleid** sieht in beiden Geschlechtern dem der **alten** Weibchen so ähnlich, dass eine besondere Beschreibung fast überflüssig wird; Farben und Zeichnungen sind nur etwas düsterer, besonders der Spiegel mehr grau als grün, nur beim **Männchen** schöner und glänzender; ebenso der Oberflügel bei diesem bloss aschbläulich, beim andern Geschlecht düster grau; an den Rücken- und Schulterfedern die lichten Kanten, wie überhaupt allenthalben, viel schmäler, daher besonders diese Teile dunkler und schwärzer; Schnabel und Füsse viel blasser als bei den Alten, oft schwarzgrau überlaufen, und die Schwimmhäute stets schwärzlich; auch die braunen Augensterne, sowie die abgebrochenen Spitzen der Schwanzfedern, wo früher der Flaum sass, machen sie kenntlich genug. An der dunkleren Rücken- und Brustfarbe, dem mehr ins Bläuliche ziehenden Oberflügel und grünerem Spiegel sind die **jungen Männchen** nur dann sicher von den gleichalten Weibchen zu unterscheiden, wenn man beide beisammen hat, wo auch schon die verschiedene Grösse auffallend genug wird.

Wie andere Süsswasserenten legen sie dieses **jugendliche** Gefieder bald im Herbst, meistens im Oktober bis auf die Schwung- und Schwanzfedern wieder ab, und die **Männchen** erhalten dann ihr erstes Prachtkleid, dies jedoch vor ihrer Abreise aus den nördlichen Geburtsgegenden nicht vollständig, die **Weibchen** dagegen ihr **ausgefärbtes** Gewand, das sie von jetzt an jährlich nur einmal mit einem gleichgefärbten wechseln.

In diesem hat das **Weibchen** einen oben schwärzlich olivengrünen, an den Rändern, Mundwinkeln und unteren Teilen blass gelbroten Schnabel, orangerote, an den Schwimmhäuten meist schwärzliche Füsse und einen schwefelgelben Augenstern. Kopf und Hals sind auf bräunlich rostgelbem Grunde, welcher in einem Streifen über dem Auge, unter den Zügeln und auf der Gurgel am lichtesten ist und an der Kehle in Weiss übergeht, schwärzlichbraun, teils gestrichelt, teils getüpfelt, dieses besonders an den hinteren Teilen, doch oft auch nur in langen Schaftstrichen bezeichnet, aber auf dem Scheitel, Genick und Nacken graubraun überlaufen; die Kropfgegend auf gleichgefärbtem Grunde mit schwarzbraunen Mondflecken bestreut, weil die Federn hier eigentlich diese Farbe und nur sehr breite, scharfgetrennte bräunlich rostgelbe Kanten haben; die Brust ähnlich, in der Mitte aber in Weiss übergehend, und die dunklen Flecke kleiner und länglicher; Bauch und Unterschwanzdecke in der Mitte weiss, an den Seiten in Dunkelrostgelb übergehend, schwärzlichbraun gefleckt; die Tragfedern wie die der Schultern und des Oberrückens schwärzlichbraun mit dunkelrostgelben, scharf getrennten, aber nicht sehr breiten Kanten, hin und wieder auch mit solchen Flecken in der Mitte der Fahnen; der Unterrücken viel dunkler, mit schmäleren und verlaufenden Kanten; der Bürzel und die Oberschwanzdecke dem Oberrücken gleich. Der mehr zugerundete als zugespitzte Schwanz hat schwärzlichbraune Federn, mit an den Seiten durch Grau und Gelbbraun in Weiss übergehenden, breiten Kanten, der Flügel aber folgende Farben: die Deckfedern rein aschgrau, am Flügelrande am lichtesten, die grosse Reihe mit weissen Enden, welche einen Querstreifen über den Flügel und die obere Einfassung des **Spiegels** bilden, welcher schwärzlich aussieht und etwas metallgrün glänzt und durch die weissen Endsäume der Federn auch unten eine ganz schmale weisse Einfassung erhält; die grossen Schwingen und ihre Deckfedern schwärzlichbraun, an den Kanten in Grau verlaufend; die Tertiärschwingen breit, etwas zugespitzt und von der Farbe der grösseren Schulterfedern; der Unterflügel in der Mitte weiss, an den Rändern grau, die Spitze am dunkelsten. Das ganze Kolorit des weiblichen Gefieders hat mit Ausnahme des Spiegels und der Oberflügeldecke grosse Ähnlichkeit mit dem der weiblichen **Stock-** und **Schnatterente**.

Je älter das **Weibchen** wird, desto lichter wird die bräunlich rostgelbe Hauptfarbe des Gefieders, das Aschgrau des Oberflügels bekommt einen Anflug von Blau und der Spiegel einen stärkeren Glanz in Grün, dieses beides aber doch lange nicht so schön als man es beim **Männchen** findet. In und gleich nach der Begattungszeit erscheint auch dieses weibliche Gefieder ziemlich verbleicht und an den Federenden zum Teil abgerieben. Es wird in der einmaligen Mauser, im Juli und August abgelegt und mit einem neuen vertauscht, wobei es ebenso hergeht wie bei anderen Entenarten, und das neue Gewand trägt wieder frischere Farben, sodass auch diese **Weibchen** im Herbst am schönsten aussehen.

Höchst ähnlich dem **weiblichen** Gefieder ist das des **männlichen Sommerkleides**, aber auffallend dunkler und auf dem Flügel viel schöner und vorzüglich am letzteren nicht schwer vom **Weibchen**, aber viel schwerer vom **männlichen Jugendkleide** zu unterscheiden. Wie bei den vorigen Arten erscheint das **alte Männchen** darin nach beendeter Hauptmauser vom Juli bis zum Oktober und hat dann einen oben mattschwarzen, an den Seiten ins Olivengrünliche verlaufenden, an den Mundwinkeln und hinteren Rändern der Kiefer orangerötlich gefärbten Schnabel, matt orangerote Beine und einen schöngelben Augenstern. Kopf und Hals sind hell rostgelblichbraun, mit schwarzbraunen Strichen und Fleckchen längs den Federschäften, diese Zeichnung auf dem Scheitel und ganzen Hinterhalse, der Ohrgegend und an den Zügeln stark mit einem dunkleren Braun überlaufen; die Kropfgegend hell rostgelblichbraun mit schwarzbraunen Mondfleckchen; Brust und Bauch roströtlichbraun, schwarzbraun gefleckt; die Tragfedern braunschwarz, breit rostbraun gekantet und dies gelblichbraun gesäumt, hin und wieder auch solche Flecke im Schwarzen, und diese dunklere, stark ins Rostbräunliche ziehende Färbung des Unterrumpfes, dem **Weibchen** gegenüber vorzüglich unterscheidend, ebenso der viel dunklere Oberrumpf, indem die schwarzbraunen Oberrücken- und Schulterfedern nur schmale lichtbraune Ränder haben und der Unterrücken, Bürzel und die Mitte der Oberschwanzdecke einfarbig braunschwarz aussehen, wo nur die Seiten der letzteren mit weisslichen Federkanten bezeichnet sind; die Unterschwanzdecke seitwärts weiss, übrigens rostbräunlich gemischt und schwärzlich gefleckt; die mittleren Schwanzfedern schwarzgrau, weiss gekantet, die folgenden weniger grau und breiter weiss, die äusseren in der Mitte bloss dunkelgrau bespritzt, sonst weiss, und das alleräusserste Paar oft noch auf der Kante neben der Spitze mit schwarzen Flecken, von individuell verschiedener Gestalt, aber selten ganz fehlend. Neben diesen gibt der prächtig gefärbte Flügel ein Hauptunterscheidungsmerkmal; denn seine Deckfedern sind schön aschblau, eine zwar etwas dunkle, aber glänzende und an Himmelblau grenzende Farbe, die Enden der grössten Reihe als obere Begrenzung des Spiegels oder eines vorn breiteren, hinten ganz schmal auslaufenden Querstriches über dem Flügel rein weiss, und dies scharf von den Umgebungen getrennt; der mittelgrosse **Spiegel** prächtig goldgrün, sehr wenig in Blau oder Violett glänzend, unten mit sehr feinem, weissem Saum eingefasst; die ihm am nächsten stehende Tertiärschwinge schwarz, fein weiss gesäumt, die übrigen nach aussen mehr grau und ihre schmutzigweissen Einfassungen breiter;

die Primärschwingen und ihre Deckfedern dunkel braungrau, an den Enden in Schwärzlichbraun übergehend. Hat man beide Geschlechter beisammen, so erfordert es wenig Übung, die grösseren **Männchen** an der prächtigen Flügelzeichnung, dem ungefleckten Unterrücken und an dem dunkleren, ins Rostbraune gehaltenen Unterrumpfe von den kleineren Weibchen zu unterscheiden.

Im Oktober beginnt bei den **Männchen** die Schönheitsmauser, bei den **alten** etwas früher als bei den **jungen** desselben Jahres, bei denen sie vor ihrer Abreise gegen Ende November oft noch nicht ganz beendet ist. Wie bei anderen Arten bleiben ihnen vom ganzen Gefieder nur die Flügel- und Schwanzfedern bis auf das mittelste Paar der letzteren, das für das **Prachtkleid** durch ein Paar neue, etwas mehr zugespitzte ersetzt wird.

Zum **ersten Prachtkleide junger Männchen** hat sich bereits ihr Schnabel ganz gleichförmig blauschwarz, der Augenstern gelb, die Füsse lebhaft orangerot gefärbt, der Hinterkopf etwas verlängerte und die Schultern mit einer schmalen Spitze versehene Federn bekommen. An ihnen sind Kopf und Hals, dieser bis über die Mitte seiner Länge herab und hier rundum scharf begrenzt, schwarz, mit bläulich-goldgrünem, etwas ins Purpurblaue schillerndem Glanz, doch lange nicht so schön als beim Männchen der Stockente, vielmehr etwas mit Schwarz geschuppt, überhaupt auf dem Scheitel, zwischen Schnabel und Auge, an der Kehle und auf der ganzen Gurgel fehlend und letztere ausgenommen, die schwarzen Federn auch noch braun gekantet. Der untere Teil des Halses und der Kropf sind rein weiss, jedoch mehr oder weniger mit kleinen braunschwarzen Halbmondfleckchen bestreut, am meisten abwärts, wo die Brust anfängt, wo sie erst in der dunklen Färbung dieser sich verlieren, die vom weissen Kropfe bis zur grünglänzend schwarzen Unterschwanzdecke (hier auch scharf getrennt) ein schönes Kastanienbraun ist, am gesättigtsten und rötesten an der Tragfederpartie, doch an den längsten Federn dieser, nach hinten, und am Ende des Bauches sanft in ein rötliches Rostgelb übergehend und in diesem sehr fein schwarz gepunktet, dies grösstenteils in weitläufigen Wellenlinien quer durchzogen; zwischen Bauch und Bürzel jederseits ein länglicher rein weisser Fleck; der Oberrücken schwarzbraun, mit graubraunen Federkäntchen; der Unterrücken und Bürzel einfarbig braunschwarz; die Oberschwanzdecke tief schwarz, mit schön bläulichgrünem Metallglanz. Die Schulterpartie ist sehr bunt, im Anfang und nach vorn hell weiss, nur viele Federenden schwärzlich bespritzt oder mit einem kleinen schwarzbraunen Querstreifen bezeichnet; in der Mitte nach hinten aus schwarzbraun, an den grösseren Federn in grünliches Schwarz übergehend, die auch sehr verlängert zugespitzt, jede mit einem breiten, spitz auslaufenden, blendend weissen Schaftstrich bezeichnet sind, an welche sich zunächst über dem Spiegel zwei grosse, breite, glänzende, schön himmelblaue Federn anschliessen, von denen die hintere ebenfalls einen schneeweissen Schaftstreifen hat, welcher sehr verlängert in eine zarte Spitze ausläuft. Die sich diesem anschliessende Partie des Hinterflügels oder die lanzettförmig spitzen und ziemlich verlängerten Tertiärschwingen sind tief braunschwarz, die längsten mit breitem, die kürzeren mit schmalem, die allerletzten ohne weissen Schaftstreifen; der Spiegel prächtig goldgrün, viel schöner als das Grün des Kopfes und nur in manchem Lichte schwach violett glänzend, unten mit zartem, weissem Saum, oben mit einem vorn breiten, hinten schmal auslaufenden schneeweissen Querstreifen begrenzt, dieser von den Enden der übrigens tiefgrauen Reihe der grossen Flügeldeckfedern gebildet; die übrigen Deckfedern im Grunde zwar auch von dieser dunkelgrauen Farbe, aber durch die grossen glänzend aschblauen, in Himmelblau spielenden Federenden ist diese völlig verdeckt; die Primärschwingen mit ihren Deckfedern dunkelgraubraun, am dunkelsten spitzwärts und an den Seiten lichtbraungrau gesäumt, ihre Schäfte weiss. Der Unterflügel ist meistens glänzend weiss, nur am Rande etwas braun gefleckt, die Schwingen silbergrau, an den Enden in Rauchfahl übergehend, und ihre Schäfte weiss. Von den breiten Schwanzfedern sind die beiden mittelsten am meisten zugespitzt, doch ragen ihre Spitzen wenig über die der anderen hinaus, schwarzgrau, an den Seiten aschgrau überpudert und weiss gekantet; das nächste Paar auf der Aussenfahne dunkelaschgrau, mit breiter weisser Aussenkante, auf der Innenfahne weiss, grau bespritzt; das folgende Paar auf der äussern aschgrau gemasert, marmoriert oder gesprenkelt, mit breiter weisser Aussenkante, auf der inneren Fahne weiss, nur wenig grau bespritzt; die folgenden noch mehr weiss und weniger grau bespritzt; das äusserste Paar weiss, bloss nach innen grau bespritzt, aber zunächst der Spitze mit einigen braunschwarzen Randflecken von unregelmässiger Gestalt und Grösse, selbst manchmal nicht auf einer Seite des Schwanzes wie auf der anderen, geschweige bei jedem Individuum gleich, doch aber auch selten ganz fehlend; die Unterseite des Schwanzes glänzend weiss, sehr blassgrau bespritzt.

Das **mehrere Jahre alte Männchen** übertrifft an Schönheit das einjährige noch um vieles; sein Schnabel ist am **Prachtkleide** noch schwärzer, die Fussfarbe hoch mennigrot, der Augenstern feurig gelb; Kopf und Hals viel stärker und prächtiger grün glänzend, an den weniger glänzenden schwarzen Stellen des Kopfes und auf der Gurgel auch ohne braune Federkanten; die Kropfgegend blendend weiss, ohne alle Flecken; der Unterrumpf aus dem Kastanienbraunen in schönes Rotbraun übergehend, übrigens am Ende des Bauches und der Tragfedern wie dort; das einfarbige Braunschwarz des Oberrückens läuft gegen den Nacken in einem fingerbreiten Streifen hinauf, hat jederseits vor den Schultern einen heraustretenden Flügel und schliesst sich nach hinten dem gleichgefärbten Unterrücken an, während der schwarze Bürzel und die Oberschwanzdecke stärker grün schillern; der weisse Teil der Schulterpartie ist zuweilen ganz fleckenlos, der hintere schwärzer, mit merklichem, grünem Seidenglanze, reinen weissen und längeren Schaftstreifen, und das Himmelblau der letzten, dem Spiegel zunächst stehenden Schulterfedern, sowie alles auf dem Flügel noch viel prächtiger, hier sowohl das glänzende Himmelblau der Deckfedern, welches jedoch stets dunkler und düsterer bleibt als das der Schulter, wie das Goldgrün des Spiegels; auch der Schwanz hat an den Seiten der Federn mehr Weiss.

Im Juni beginnt die Mauser der **Männchen** und zu Ende dieses Monats oder im Anfange des folgenden verschwinden sie von den freien Wasserflächen, weil sie dann die Schwungfedern verloren haben, an deren Stelle erst gegen Ende Juli wieder neue gewachsen sind, die nun die im vollendeten, oben beschriebenen **Sommerkleide** aus ihren Verstecken hervorkommenden **Männchen** wieder flugbar machen.

Eigentliche **Spielarten** (Ausartungen in Weiss und dergleichen) mögen auch bei diesen Enten äusserst selten vorkommen. FRISCH a. a. O. hat auf Tafel 162 ein sehr schönes **altes Männchen**, im reinen Hochzeitskleide stehend, abgebildet, an welchem Brust und Bauch nicht kastanienbraun, sondern ebenso **weiss** sind als der Kropf; die einzige Ausartung, welche wir gesehen haben. Einer besonderen Art, wie man gemeint hat, gehört sie nicht an. Andere, welche man hierher gezählt hat, waren gewöhnlich mausernde und im Übergange von einem Kleide zum anderen befindliche Individuen.

Eine ungleich interessantere Abweichung traf im Jahre 1796 mein verstorbener Vater auf einem (jetzt längst trocken gelegten) Nebenwasser des Eislebener Salzsees an. Schon von weitem fiel ihm dies Löffelentenpaar auf, dessen **Männchen** ganz anders gezeichnet und gefärbt war als die gewöhnlichen, während das **Weibchen** nur denen dieser glich. Es schien dort brüten zu wollen, und die Gatten waren unzertrennlich, aber auch abgesondert von anderen Enten, eben nicht scheu, doch hinlänglich, um für einen sicheren Schuss nicht nahe genug auszuhalten. Nach langem, vergeblichem Bemühen gelang es endlich, hinter einem kleinen Hügel ankriechend, auf das am Ufer stehende Pärchen schiessen zu können und das Männchen zu treffen; allein es war bloss flügellahm geschossen und stürzte sich ins Wasser, ehe es der herbeispringende Hund greifen konnte, vor dessen Nachsetzen es nun wiederholt tauchte, bis es eine grosse Schilfflur erreichte und in derselben verschwand. Alles war dem Nachsuchen auf frischer Tat entgegen, und am anderen Morgen blieb dies vollends ohne Erfolg, sogar auch das Weibchen war verschwunden. Da mein Vater diesen Enten mehrmals und beim hellsten Frühlingswetter auf 70 bis 80 Schritt nahe war, als er aber das **Männchen** durch den Schuss gelähmt, dieses auf kaum 20 Schritt vor sich hatte, konnte er die Farben und Zeichnungen, die im ganzen denen des männlichen Prachtkleides der Stockente höchst ähnlich sahen, recht deutlich unterscheiden und entwarf demnach folgende Beschreibung davon: »Der Schnabel hatte ganz die Gestalt wie bei der gewöhnlichen Löffelente, allein eine grüngelbe Farbe; die Füsse waren rot; Kopf und Hals schwarz mit prächtigem goldgrünem Schiller; zu Ende dieses umgab den Hals ein schmaler weisser Ring; dann folgte ein glänzendes Kastanienbraun, das den Kropf einnahm und am Anfange der weissen Brust scharf abschnitt; die Tragfedern perlgrau, näher gesehen dicht mit sehr zarten, schwärzlichen und weissen Wellenlinien abwechselnd durchzogen; Rücken und Flügel ganz wie beim Männchen der **Stockente**; der Bürzel schwarz; die Schwanzfedern auch schwarz, an den Seiten weiss gekantet, aber ohne zurückgerollte Mittelfedern.«

Dies merkwürdige Löffelentenmännchen zeichnete sich schon in grosser Entfernung von anderen seiner Art aus, während das mit ihm verpaarte Weibchen anderen gewöhnlichen Löffelentenweibchen so völlig gleich kam, dass, wenigstens aus jener Entfernung, etwas Abweichendes nicht bemerkt werden konnte. Die ansehnlichere Grösse und auffallende Ähnlichkeit der Farben und Zeichnungen dieses Männchens mit dem der **Stockente**, bei völliger Gestalt der Löffelente, machte bei meinem Vater augenblicklich die Meinung rege, dass es aus der Vermischung mit beiden Arten hervorgegangen oder eine Bastarderzeugung sei, weil es, wo beide in der Nähe beisammen nisten, gar so etwas Ungewöhnliches nicht ist, dass man vom Neste abgehende Löffelentenweibchen auch von Stockentenmännchen verfolgt sieht, um sie zu betreten. Es gelang uns indessen nicht, behufs solcher Verpaarung beider Arten, gezählte Löffelenten zu erhalten, um unsere Mutmassung zur völligen Gewissheit zu bringen; auch ist uns seitdem bei fortgesetzter Aufmerksamkeit durch einen so langen Zeitraum ein ähnlich gezeichnetes Löffelentenmännchen nie wieder vorgekommen, weder im Freien noch in Sammlungen.

Die Luftröhre des **Männchens** ist ziemlich gleichweit, nur nach unten etwas mehr erweitert, mit einer kleinen halbkugeligen Pauke auf der einen Seite des untern Larynx und mit etwas langen Bronchien.

AUFENTHALT

Gewöhnlich nimmt man an, unsere Löffelente sei über die ganze nördliche Erdhälfte verbreitet; hierbei muss jedoch bemerkt werden, dass der hohe Norden davon auszuschliessen ist, indem sie zu den weichlicheren Arten gehört und der Winterkälte nach Süden hin ausweicht. Auf **Island** und unter anderen hohen Breiten von **Europa** kommt sie nicht vor, ebenso nur in den gemässigteren Teilen von **Asien** und **Nordamerika**, wie dem südlichen **Norwegen** und **Schweden**, den wärmeren Teilen des europäischen und asiatischen **Russlands**, dem unteren **Kanada** und den **Vereinigten Staaten**. Hier soll sie im Winter bis **Mexiko**, in Asien bis **Japan** und **Ostindien** hinabstreifen. In unserem Erdteil wohnt sie schon häufig in **Preussen**, **Polen**, **Dänemark**, noch häufiger in **England** und am meisten wohl in **Holland**, wie sie denn auch in ganz **Deutschland** bekannt genug ist und in vielen Gegenden ihre Sommerwohnsitze aufschlägt. **Ungarn**, **Italien** und andere südeuropäische Länder gewähren ihr häufig einen Winteraufenthalt, den sie selbst bis über das Mittelmeer ausdehnt, sodass sie im Winter in **Ägypten** und **Nubien** angetroffen worden ist. Sie scheint dabei nirgends in so grosser Anzahl vorzukommen, als viele andere Arten von Süsswasserenten, sodass wir sie hierin nur ungefähr der Knäkente gleichstellen möchten.

In **Deutschland**, wo sie auf dem Zuge zwar ebenfalls nicht in grosser Menge, doch paarweise und in kleinen Vereinen allenthalben vorkommt, bleiben in geeigneten Lagen auch viele, um zu nisten, und dies mag noch mehr in der nördlichen oder vielmehr nordöstlichen Hälfte der Fall sein als in den südlichsten Teilen; so können wir in dieser Hinsicht das **Oldenburgische**, **Holsteinische**, **Pommern**, **Schlesien** u.a. nennen und auch unser **Anhalt** und seine Nachbarländer dazu zählen, weil sie auch hier ziemlich häufig vorkommt.

Im Frühjahr fliegen sie meistens paarweise, im Herbst mehr truppweise, zu 8 bis 20 Stück vereint. Sehr selten kommen hier zu Lande grössere Scharen, im Frühjahr vielmehr öfter nur einzeln durchstreichende Individuen vor.

Sie ziehen fast immer des Nachts, selten am Tage wie die anderen, in eine schräge Reihe geordnet, und bei Tage oft sehr hoch fliegend.

Obgleich die Löffelente das Meer nur als gelegentlichen Zufluchtsort benutzt, so ist sie doch gern auf süssen Gewässern in dessen Nähe. Nur in der Zugzeit trifft man sie unter anderen Süsswasserenten auch in seichten Meeresbuchten und auf schmalen, stillen Meerengen, aus welchen bei der Ebbe das Wasser grösstenteils zurücktritt; zur Flutzeit aber zieht sie dagegen die nächsten Binnenwasser und Sümpfe, wenn sie in einsamen Gegenden liegen, dem Meere weit vor, und in der Fortpflanzungszeit sucht sie dieses gänzlich zu vermeiden.

Grosse, schilfreiche Landseen und Teiche mit flachen und häufig in Sumpf und Wiesen verlaufenden Ufern, die grösseren Wasserflächen und breiten Gräben in ausgedehnten Brüchen sind ihr Lieblingsaufenthalt; aber sie besucht auf der Wanderung auch Teiche und stehende Gewässer jeder Art, gross oder klein, mehr oder weniger mit Schilf oder Binsen besetzt und mit vielen schwimmenden Wasserpflanzen bedeckt, im freien Felde oder mit Viehweiden und Wiesen umgeben, ja selbst in der Nähe der Dörfer und menschlicher Wohnungen liegende, und war daher von jeher auch eine dicht bei meinem Wohnort am häufigsten vorkommende Art, hier jedoch meistens nur vereinzelt.

An allen diesen Orten scheut sie Bäume und Gebüsch nicht; allein auf tief im Walde versteckten Lachen und Tümpeln, welche die **Knäkente** und auch die **Stockente** sehr liebt, trifft man sie sehr selten an.

Seichtes, schlammiges, viel Pflanzenwuchs enthaltendes, aber doch auch mit ganz freien Stellen abwechselndes, nicht durchgängig unter Gräsern, Schilf- und Binsenarten verstecktes Wasser zieht sie den einförmig grünen Brüchen und überschwemmten Sumpfwiesen vor, obgleich ein längeres Verweilen auf grossen freien Wasserflächen, wie auf der Mitte der Teiche und Seen nur vorkommt, wenn es an den Ufern und in den Umgebungen zu unruhig hergeht, und solange Gefahr zu fürchten ist.

Hat sich die Ursache ihrer Furcht entfernt, so schwimmt sie wieder auf die seichten Stellen und nähert sich mehr den Ufern. Auf Flüssen wird sie daher auch nur an grünenden, seichten und schlammigen Uferstellen angetroffen, äusserst selten und nie anhaltend auf der freien Strömung. Wie andere Arten verlässt sie gegen Abend die grösseren Wasserflächen und durchschwärmt die Umgegend, um bis zum Anbruch des folgenden Tages alle kleineren Gewässer, ausgetretene Teiche, überschwemmte Wiesen, im Frühjahr auch die auf Stoppelfeldern zusammengelaufenen Wasserlachen zu besuchen, die letzteren jedoch nicht so gern, wie viele vorhergehende, mehr Körner fressende Arten. Wo vereinzelte in der Nähe der Dörfer erscheinen, zumal auf kleinen Teichen, mischen sie sich oft unter die zahmen Enten, doch ohne sich mit ihnen besonders gemein zu machen. Was sonst noch von ihrem Aufenthalte zu bemerken wäre, kommt dem der **Knäkente** gleich.

EIGENSCHAFTEN

Unsere Löffelente ist schon in weiter Ferne an ihrem grossen Schnabel, welcher dem ganzen Kopf ein grosses Aussehen gibt, von anderen Süsswasserenten zu unterscheiden; selbst von den Tauchenten unterscheidet sie die auffallende Grösse des Schnabels und der nach hinten schlanker zugespitzte Leib. Ungemein auffallend werden vor allen anderen dem Beobachter die Männchen in ihrem **Prachtkleide**, das zu den buntesten gehört und dessen abstrakte Farben, besonders das viele Weiss in grossen Partien beisammen, weit in die Ferne leuchten. Dies Kleid gehört zu den schönsten der Gattung, und man weiss nicht, ob das fliegende Männchen von unten gesehen, das Schwarzgrün des Kopfes und Halses, das reine Weiss des Kropfes und das Kastanienbraun des Unterrumpfes scharf voneinander getrennt, oder von oben gesehen, sich schöner ausnimmt, da hier bei recht alten das Weiss des Kropfes und der Oberschulter der Länge nach durch einen auf den Nacken, am schwarzgrünen Kopfe und Halse schmal anfangenden, auf dem Rücken breiteren und auf den mittleren Schwanzfedern spitz endenden, zusammenhängenden, schwarzen Streifen getrennt wird, welcher demnach bis zum Ende schmäler oder breiter mit Weiss eingefasst ist, während das Himmelblau der ausgebreiteten Oberflügel sich hinterwärts mit dem der Unterflügel vereinigt, und dieses Blau durch den breiten weissen Querstreifen über dem goldgrünen Spiegel wiederum scharf getrennt erscheint. Es hat demnach fliegend und in der Ferne einige Ähnlichkeit mit dem **alten Männchen** der Schellente, ist jedoch an dem blauen Oberflügel und dem kastanienbraunen Unterrumpf, wie an der nach hinten mehr zugespitzten Figur leicht genug zu unterscheiden.

Ihre Stellung im Stehen und Gehen ist ganz wie bei anderen Süsswasserenten, doch erscheint der Rumpf etwas weniger schlank. Sie steht gern anhaltend auf festem Boden, geht auch ziemlich behende und schwimmt wie jene in Ruhe mit ziemlich eingezogenem oder in die S-Form niedergedrücktem Halse und steckt schlafend den grossen Schnabel gewöhnlich zwischen die Schulterfedern, wobei der Körper nur flach auf der Wasserfläche ruht. Das halbe Untertauchen, Gründeln oder Sichaufdenkopfstellen, wenn sie nach Nahrung in die Tiefe und auf den Grund angelt, hat sie mit jenen gemein, und auch sie taucht nur in Lebensgefahr, wenn sie des Flugvermögens beraubt oder spielend ganz unter Wasser ist, dann aber ebenso flink unter demselben wie jene, dies besonders auch bei Gefahren, die Jungen im Dunenkleide.

Ihr Flug ist zwar leicht und gewandt genug, doch mit dem der **Knäkente** verglichen lange nicht so schnell, meistens auch mit etwas Geräusch, zuweilen sogar mit einem sonst nur der **Stockente** eigentümlichen, doch stets viel leiseren, pfeifenden Ton, wie »**wich wich wich**« u.s.w. klingend, verbunden. Beim Aufsteigen oder Niederlassen benimmt sie sich ebenso gewandt wie diese, und man hört dabei nur wenig Geräusch auf dem Wasser.

Unsere Löffelente gehört unter die wenig scheuen Arten, obwohl sie auf grösseren Gewässern dem Menschen, zumal wenn sie sich von ihm beobachtet oder gar verfolgt sieht, immer noch weit genug ausweicht, um nicht in Lebensgefahr zu geraten. Nicht allein zutraulicher, sondern wohl auch einfältiger als andere, zeigt sie dagegen auf Gewässern von geringem Umfange, besonders auf isoliert liegenden kleinen Teichen, so wenig Furcht, dass sie sich sogar auf Stellen wagt, wo Bäume und Gebüsch, ja Zäune, Mauern und dergleichen den lauernden Schützen oder andere Feinde leicht verbergen können, Orte, woselbst sogar **Krickenten** nicht gern, wenigstens nie lange verweilen. Sie scheint auch weniger gesellig als andere, und wenn man in grossen Entenheeren auch Löffelenten in eigenen Abteilungen bemerkt, so sieht man sie doch noch viel öfter abgesondert, ja paarweise oder einzeln umherschwärmen, wie sie denn überhaupt in unserem Lande zu den in grossen Herden vorkommenden Arten nicht gezählt werden kann.

Zu bemerken wäre noch, dass im Frühjahr die **Männchen** (im **Prachtkleide**) weit vorsichtiger sind als zu anderen Zeiten, wenn sie im **Sommergewande** wie ihre **Weibchen** aussehen. Sie halten sich dann mit den angepaarten Weibchen auf grösseren Gewässern auf und schweifen nicht auf weit von den Brutorten entlegenen umher. So haben wir auf hiesigen Teichen, auf der einen Seite dicht am Dorfe gelegen, im Spätsommer und Herbst alte und flugbare junge Löffelenten beiderlei Geschlechts und im Frühjahr auch einzelne Weibchen oftmals angetroffen und erlegt, aber unter sehr vielen in einem langen Zeitraume kaum ein paarmal ein **Männchen** im **Prachtkleide** gesehen, aber nie eins hier erlegt.

Ihre Stimme lässt unsere Löffelente selten hören; sie klingt entenartig quakend, ziemlich laut, beim **Weibchen** wie **Vaak** oder **Vak**, beim **Männchen** in viel heisererem und etwas tieferem Ton, mehr wie **Woak — Woak**, und dieses lässt im Frühjahr beim Auffliegen nicht selten auch einen sonderbaren, nicht sehr lauten Ton, wie **peckn — peckn** klingend, hören. Die Jungen **piepen** auch nur selten und in einem sehr hohen Tone. Ausserdem **fauchen** und **zischen** sie wie andere Enten.

Zu zähmen sind sie so leicht wie andere Arten dieser Abteilung, wenn man sich Eier verschaffen und diese eine **Hausente** ausbrüten lassen kann, die Alte mit den Jungen alsbald auf einen passenden Wasserbehälter bringt, woselbst sie natürliches Futter, zum Versteck hohes Gras und Sumpfgewächse finden, und sich so nach und nach an das ihnen gebotene Futter und an die Menschen gewöhnen können. Wir sahen einst, wie man eine Gluckhenne ein ganzes Gelege solcher Eier hatte ausbrüten lassen, die Jungen, welche sehr schnell wuchsen, mit Brotkrumen und geschroteter Gerste fütterte; als man sie aber auf einen freien Teich brachte, wo sie an der Henne eine zu schlechte Führerin hatten, kam eins nach dem andern weg, ehe sie noch zur Hälfte erwachsen waren. In den nordfriesischen Vogelkojen hielt man auch Alte als Lockenten ohne Schwierigkeit, obgleich ihnen der Teich wenig Grünes darbietet.

NAHRUNG

Aus der abnormen Grösse und Gestalt des Schnabels möchte man wohl im Vergleich mit anderen Entenarten eine sehr abweichende Art sich zu nähren oder eine wesentliche Verschiedenheit der Nahrungsmittel vermuten, allein zur Zeit ist eine solche Entdeckung noch nicht gemacht.

Unsere Löffelente nährt sich wie die **Knäkente** und ähnliche Arten von ganz kleinem Gewürm, von Insektenbrut, Fisch- und Froschlaich, kleinen Froschlarven und Fröschchen, auch wohl von ganz kleiner Fischbrut, von allerlei kleinen Süsswasserschnecken, dann von zarten Vegetabilien, wie Grasspitzchen, Knospen und Blättchen verschiedener untergetauchter Pflanzen und von Sämereien derselben; endlich geniesst sie auch, wiewohl nicht oft, Getreidekörner. Von diesem allen haben wir bald diese, bald jene, mit vielem groben Sand oder kleinen Steinchen vermischt, in ihrem Magen gefunden.

Wie die vorigen Arten durchschnattert sie an den Ufern und auf seichtem Wasser schwimmend, so tief der Hals hinabreicht, den Schlamm, um aus demselben die kleinsten Dinge herauszufühlen, und stellt sich, wo der Hals dazu nicht hinablangen will, sehr häufig auf die oft beschriebene Weise auch auf den Kopf, taucht aber nie mit ganzem Körper darnach unter. Sie durchschnattert besonders gern auch die schwimmenden Wasserpflanzen, zwischen welchen gewöhnlich ganz winzige Geschöpfchen in Unzahl leben, und diese fischt sie auch von der freien Oberfläche des Wassers fleissig auf, indem sie oft in Kreisen oder Schlangenlinien fortschwimmt, den Hals vor sich hinstreckt, den die Fläche durchschneidenden Schnabel schnell öffnet und schliesst, das mit jenem aufgeschlürfte Wasser seitwärts durch die kammartigen Lamellen wie durch ein Filtrum treibt und das Geniessbare zum Verschlucken zurückbehält. Dies alles geschieht gleichzeitig und so schnell, dass dabei, ausser dem Fortrudern, kaum weiter etwas als das schnurrende Plätschern, durch die schnelle Bewegung des Schnabels erzeugt, bemerklich wird. Im Frühjahre, wo es noch an Insektenbrut und kleinen Weichtierchen mangelt, frisst sie auch viele ganz kleine Schnecken; besonders fanden wir solche aus der Familie der Tellerschnecken, von diesen mitunter selbst ziemlich grosse Exemplare, häufig in ihrem Vormagen. Im Spätsommer und zur Samenreife geht sie mehr zum Genusse der Samen von allerlei Sumpfgewächsen über, namentlich ist ihr auch der des Schwadengrases von allen der wichtigste, weshalb sie die Stellen, wo er häufig vorkommt, ebenso fleissig besucht wie andere Süsswasserenten. Zum Genuss des Getreides kommt sie seltener, nur wenn sie solches ganz in der Nähe ihres nassen Aufenthaltes haben kann, fliegt aber darnach nie auf die Felder; dann ist ihr auch Hafer lieber als Gerste.

In einsamen Gegenden sucht sie zwar auch zu jeder Tageszeit nach Nahrungsmitteln und bleibt da nie lange auf freier, tiefer Fläche, sondern schwimmt auf die seichten Stellen und an die morastigen Ufer; allein ihre grösste Tätigkeit beginnt erst beim Eintritt der Abenddämmerung, dauert die Nacht, wenn diese nicht gar zu finster, hindurch und endet mit Aufgang der Sonne. Gleich den anderen wird auch sie beim Untergange der Sonne unruhiger, verlässt bald darauf den Aufenthalt des Tages und fliegt nach den kleineren Gewässern im Umkreise oder nach den Schwadengrasplätzen. Wo sie Futter genug fand und nicht bedeutend gestört wurde, kehrt sie zu solchen alle Abende wieder, solange sie in der Gegend verweilt.

FORTPFLANZUNG

Die Löffelente nistet hin und wieder auch in **Deutschland** in manchen Gegenden, auf mit Wiesen und Sumpf umgebenen Seen, grossen Teichen und in weitläufigen Brüchen; auch auf den süssen Gewässern in der Nähe des Meeresstrandes ist sie gar nicht ungewöhnlich, bei uns wenigstens so häufig als die **Knäkente**. Grosse freie Brüche liebt sie sehr und die hier in dem Winkel, welchen die Saale beim Einfluss in die Elbe bildet, liegenden sind alljährlich so reichlich damit versehen, dass, wenn man dort zehn Entennester findet, die eine Hälfte den Löffelenten, die andere den **Stockenten** und **Knäkenten** zukommt. Sie zeigt sich zwar oft schon zu Ende des März, gewöhnlicher aber erst im April an den Orten, wo sie nisten will, teils schon gepaart, teils bald hierzu schreitend, legt und brütet aber später als andere Enten, sodass sie nicht so leicht wie oft die **Stockente** durch späte Nachtfröste um die beginnende Brut kommt.

An kleinen Gewässern oder auf unbedeutenden zwischen Wald versteckten, wenn auch in der Nähe grösserer vorkommender Lachen, Tümpel und Gräben, wie oft die **Knäkente**, haben wir die Löffelenten nie nistend gefunden; sie liebt ausgedehntere und freiere, nämlich weniger mit Bäumen und Gebüsch versehene, aber auch grösstenteils mit Schilf, Binsen und hohen Gräsern bewachsene Lagen der Gewässer und tieferen Moräste; noch weniger kommt sie auf ganz vom Hochwald umgebenen vor, wenn diese nicht von sehr grossem Umfange sind. Auf den freien und tieferen Stellen des Wassers sieht man dann die sehr verliebten Männchen um die Weibchen buhlen und sich dabei tüchtig herumzausen, weil gewöhnlich um eine Geliebte sich mehrere bewerben, diese dann oft die Flucht ergreift, nun hoch durch die Luft von sämtlichen Bewerbern verfolgt und so lange herumgejagt wird, bis sie sich dem einen ergibt und mit ihm absondert, was aber erst geschieht, wenn sie, müde gejagt, sich wieder aufs Wasser gestürzt haben. Sie zeigen sich hierbei abermals wie die **Knäkenten**, sind jedoch lange nicht so flüchtig, haben weniger

Ausdauer, und das Herumjagen hört auch auf, sobald sich alle gepaart haben, ausserdem, wenn das legende oder brütende Weibchen einmal vom Neste geht. In solchen Fällen wird es gewöhnlich von allen Männchen, deren Weibchen in der Nähe nisten, zugleich verfolgt und so lange gejagt, bis es sich einem, gewöhnlich dem rechtmässigen Eheherrn, ergibt; doch wird der Begattungsakt stets schwimmend (nicht, wie man irrig gemeint, in der Luft) und auf dem Wasser vollzogen. Mit der ehelichen Treue ist es auch bei diesen Enten nicht weit her; ja wir sahen einige Mal ein Löffelentenmännchen sich unter die ein Weibchen ihrer Art verfolgenden Stockentenmännchen mischen und es neben diesen so hitzig verfolgen, als wenn alle nur Löffelenten gewesen wären. Zur wirklichen Begattung so ungleicher Arten mag es denn freilich wohl nicht oft kommen; sie kann aber unter Umständen möglich werden und die oben schon ausgesprochene Meinung von vorkommenden **Bastarden** rechtfertigen, da umgekehrt die Stockentenmännchen nicht selten auch vom Neste abgegangene Löffelentenweibchen in jener Absicht zu verfolgen pflegen. Wie bei anderen Enten ist auch hier die Liebe und Anhänglichkeit des Männchens zu seinem angepaarten Weibchen grösser als umgekehrt, was sich deutlich zeigt, wenn einer der Gatten totgeschossen wird; auch fliegt von einem gepaarten Pärchen das Weibchen stets voran.

Dieses wählt sich allein das Plätzchen für das meist sehr gut versteckte Nest auf einer mit Wasser oder Morast umgebenen Schilf- oder Seggenkufe, im Schilf und Gestrüpp eines Grabenufers, unter dem Strauchwerk auf nassen Wiesen, nahe oder auch ziemlich entfernt vom Wasser, selbst zuweilen auf anstossenden Äckern im Getreide. Einmal ist ein solches sogar dicht am Seestrande in von den Wellen ausgeworfenem und aufgehäuftem Seetang, unfern von süssen Gewässern, gefunden worden. Gewöhnlich ist es aber im Pflanzengestrüpp und unter Gesträuchen so gut versteckt wie das der **Knäkente** und auch aus ähnlichen Stoffen, meistens trockenem Schilf, Binsen, Gras und anderen Pflanzenteilen gebaut, schlecht gewebt, aber ziemlich gerundet und in der Mitte sehr vertieft. Zuweilen ist es in einer kleinen Vertiefung des Bodens angebracht, ein anderes Mal zwischen alten Schilfstoppeln; oft ist es auch nur ein sehr dürftiger Bau von wenigem Material, manchmal dieses wieder ein ziemlicher Haufen. Baumeister ist auch nur das Weibchen, aber während der Arbeit und auch nachher hält das Männchen in seiner Nähe Wache.

Meistens nicht vor Anfang des Mai findet man in solchem Neste die sieben bis zehn, sogar bis vierzehn Eier, welche merklich grösser und kürzer gestaltet sind als die der **Knäkente** und in erster Hinsicht das Mittel halten zwischen denen der genannten und der **Schnatterente**. Sie sind meistenteils etwas kurz eiförmig, an dem schmalen Ende spitzer zugerundet als am entgegengesetzten, von diesen aus die stärkste Wölbung ziemlich in der Mitte liegend; sie haben bei einer Länge von 7 cm eine Breite von fast 3,5 cm, mit Variationen von jener um 2 mm, bei dieser um 1 mm auf und ab. Ihre Schale ist von ungemein feinem Korn, glatt, aber ohne Glanz, einfarbig trübe rostgelblichweiss, frisch kaum bemerkbar ins Grünliche spielend.

Gehen die Eier dem Weibchen zu Grunde, ehe es sie noch zwei Wochen bebrütet hat, so macht es sich ein neues Nest an einem anderen Platz, öfters ins junge Sommergetreide, legt aber dann selten mehr als sechs Eier; hat es aber das erste Gelege schon länger bebrütet, so macht es in diesem Jahre keins wieder.

Beim Brüten verhält sich alles wie bei anderen Enten, und das Nest wird ebenso, von den vorletzt gelegten Eiern an, mit den eigenen Dunen des Weibchens in täglich wachsender Menge ausgefüttert und beim jedesmaligen Abgehen die Eier sorgfältig damit bedeckt. Das auf und sehr tief im Neste sitzende Weibchen würde schon der gleichen Färbung mit den Umgebungen wegen nicht leicht zu entdecken sein, wenn es nicht auch noch Sorge trüge, dass es von oben durch überhängendes Gestrüpp verdeckt würde. Es sitzt sehr fest über den Eiern, poltert endlich meistens ohne zu schreien heraus, geht aber nach solcher Störung nicht leicht wieder aufs Nest, sondern verlässt die Eier, wenn es sie noch nicht lange bebrütet oder gar die Zahl noch nicht vollgelegt hat, gewöhnlich. Hat es aber schon länger gebrütet, so umschwärmt es nach dem Aufscheuchen den Störer in nicht gar weitem Kreise und stösst dazu sein **Vaak** wiederholt, doch nur in grösseren Zwischenräumen aus. Hieran unterscheidet es sich sehr von anderen, unter denen dies manche wohl auch tun, aber, wie z. B. die Stockentenweibchen, ohne zu schreien in ungleich weiteren Kreisen fliegend den Störer nur aus der Ferne beobachten. Es brütet sie in 22 bis 23 Tagen aus, ist dann aber um so anhänglicher an die Jungen und setzt sich, diese zu retten, selbst der augenscheinlichsten Lebensgefahr aus. Das Häuflein um sich versammelt und die ungemein beweglichen Kleinen zum schnellen Verstecken mahnend, hält es oft so nahe bei diesen aus, dass man es mit einem Stocke erschlagen oder wenigstens totwerfen könnte, solange die Jungen erst ein paar Tage alt sind; nachdem diese aber ebensoviel Wochen älter geworden und im Verstecken und Tauchen mehr Übung erlangt haben, hält es auch die Alte nicht mehr für nötig, ihr

Leben dabei sichtlich aufs Spiel zu setzen, indem sie schon früher Reissaus nimmt, jedoch auch zu den Jungen zurückkehrt, sobald sich die Gefahr wieder entfernt hat. Letztere werden nach vier Wochen flugbar und verhalten sich bis dahin im ganzen wie die anderer Süsswasserenten. Im August finden sie sich abends familienweise, doch gewöhnlich ohne die Eltern, auf den Schwadengrasplätzen und an anderen guten Futterstellen ein und rüsten sich allmählich zum Fortzuge.

FEINDE

Diese hat sie mit der **Knäkente** gemein, sowohl den Habicht als auch den Sperber. Die Weihen, Raben, Krähen und Elstern rauben ihr oft die Eier. Die nächtlichen Raubtiere, Füchse, Marder, Iltisse, Wiesel und Ratten zerstören ihre Nester, und ihre grosse Mutterliebe leistet noch manchem der Räuber bedeutenden Vorschub. Dass auch der Fischotter gelegentlich junge Entchen rauben soll, haben wir aus Mangel an Gelegenheit nicht selbst beobachten können, zweifeln aber nicht, dass es damit seine Richtigkeit haben könne.

NUTZEN

Ihr Fleisch oder Wildpret ist von ganz vorzüglichem Geschmack, zumal im Herbst, wo es oft ausserordentlich feist ist und nach dem häufigen oder fast ausschliesslichen Genuss von nahrhaften Sämereien den höchsten Wohlgeschmack hat. Nur in der Begattungszeit ist es mager und anfänglich auch nicht ganz frei von jenem sogenannten wildernden Beigeschmack, weil sich auch diese Enten im Frühjahr häufig von kleinen Wasserschnecken nähren oder solche doch dann in grösserer Menge verschlucken als zu jeder anderen Jahreszeit. Wie bei anderen Arten steht auch bei dieser das Wildpret der älteren Männchen dem der jüngeren und der Weibchen an Wohlgeschmack und Zartheit bedeutend nach.

Die Eier sind ebenfalls sehr schmackhaft, und die Federn können wie die von anderen Enten benutzt werden. Durch Vertilgung vieler lästiger Insektenbrut nützen sie auch mittelbar.

SCHADEN

Dass sie in regelmässig betriebenen Fischereien der jungen Fischbrut nachteilig werden sollten, ist wohl kaum des Erwähnens wert, weil sie nur in Ermangelung anderer Nahrungsmittel an diese gehen und sie nie in Menge verzehren. Sonst nützen sie ungleich mehr als sie schaden.

// DER MITTELSÄGER //

MERGUS SERRATOR

Langschnäbeliger Säger, gemeiner, gezopfter, rotbrüstiger Säger, wahrer Sägetaucher, Sägeente, Sägeschnäbler, Stechente, Tauchente, mittlere, rotbrüstige Tauchente, Tauchergans, Taucherkiebitz, langschnäbelige Halbente, grosse gescheckte Ente, Meerrachen, gezopfter, bunter, schwarzer, braunköpfiger Meerrachen, Seerachen, gemeiner, langschnäbeliger Seerachen, weisslicher Taucher, grosser oder grösserer rotbrüstiger Taucher, Schlichente, Schluchente, Langschnabel, gezopfter Kneifer, Fischtreiber, Nörks, Scharbeje, Seekatz.

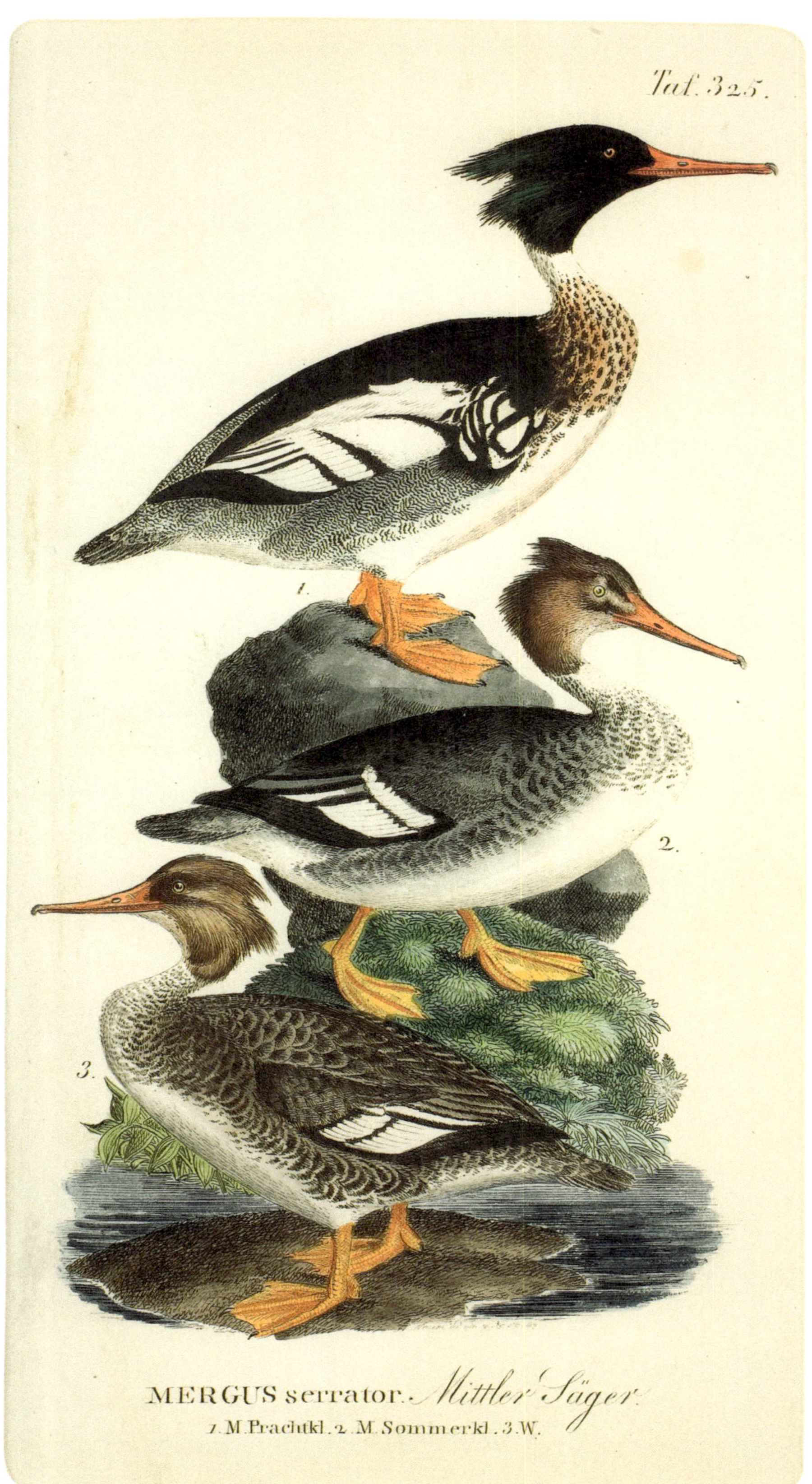

MERGUS serrator. *Mittler Säger.*
1. M. Prachtkl. 2. M. Sommerkl. 3. W.

KENNZEICHEN DER ART

Schnabel stets etwas länger als die Innenzehe; die seitliche Befiederungsgrenze des Oberkiefers bildet einen längeren spitzeren Winkel und der noch spitzere Zwickel des Unterkiefers reicht lange nicht so weit vor, daher nur gleich der Spitze der Horndecke neben der Stirn. Der Flügelspiegel weiss mit vollkommen ausgeprägter schwarzer Querbinde durchzogen, eine zweite, mehr oder weniger auffallend, trennt ihn von den oberen Deckfedern; vom Kopfe herab das Schwarzgrün oder Rostbraun schon auf dem ersten Drittel der Halslänge endend; Schnabel und Füsse rot.

BESCHREIBUNG

So auffallend diese Art sich von dem Zwergsäger unterscheidet, so sehr ähnelt sie im allgemeinen dem Gänsesäger, sodass, wer diese beiden nicht nebeneinander sieht und sich dazu nur aus älteren ornithologischen Schriften Rat zu erholen gedenkt, immer noch im Zweifel über die Art, die er gerade vor sich hat, zu bleiben befürchten muss, da selbst der scharfsichtige LINNÉ nicht ganz frei von Verwechslung beider Arten gewesen zu sein scheint.

Betrachtet man die Farben und Zeichnungen des **Prachtgefieders der alten Männchen beider Arten**, so möchte eine Verwechslung fast unmöglich scheinen, zumal ausser den gegebenen Artkennzeichen im männlichen **Prachtkleide** der rostfarbige, schwarzgefleckte Kropf und die in die Quere zart schwarz und weissgrau gewellten Tragefedern des **mittleren** Sägers gegen das beim **grossen** Säger reine und ungefleckte, bloss mehr oder weniger gelbrötliche Weiss jener Teile gewaltig abstechen, zu geschweigen bei jenem noch obenein des aus weissen, schwarz umrahmten Federn zusammengesetzten Fleckes neben der Oberbrust. Die Färbung der **Weibchen** beider Arten ist ebenfalls so sehr verschieden, dass man nur die der einen Art bestimmt zu kennen braucht, um sie nie mehr mit der anderen zu verwechseln, weil bei der gegenwärtigen die Farbe des Rumpfs eine heller geschuppte und stets in schmutziges Braun, bei der folgenden eine in ein gleichförmiges helles

Schieferblau gehaltene ist. Das **männliche Jugendkleid**, wie das **Sommerkleid alter Männchen**, hat dagegen bei beiden Arten fast gleiche Farben und Zeichnungen, es müssen daher zum Unterscheiden, ausser den Artkennzeichen, auch die verschiedene Körpergrösse, sowie Länge und Stärke des Schnabels zu Hülfe genommen werden, und es wird immer noch viel Übung und Aufmerksamkeit erforderlich sein, ein einzelnes Individuum der einen Art, wenn von der anderen keins zum Vergleichen zur Hand ist, sicher zu bestimmen.

Der mittlere oder langschnäbelige Säger ist viel grösser als der **Zwergsäger**, aber stets bedeutend kleiner und von Gestalt schlanker als der **Gänsesäger**, doch etwas schwächer als die **Stockente**, sodass die **Männchen** ungefähr mit denen der **Spiessente**, auch ihrer schlanken Gestalt wegen, zu vergleichen sind und die **Weibchen** auch denen dieser gleichen. Der Unterschied im Gewicht zwischen Mittelsäger und **Gänsesäger** beträgt gegen 1 Pfund, denn ersterer wiegt selten über 2 Pfund.

Das **Männchen** misst in der Länge (von der Stirn an): 52 bis 55,5 cm; die Flugbreite 79 bis 83,5 cm; die Flügellänge gegen 24,2 cm; die Schwanzlänge 7 bis 8 cm; die kleineren Maße **jüngeren** zukommend; das **Weibchen** in der Länge 46 cm; in der Flugbreite 68 bis 70 cm; die Flügellänge 23 cm; die Schwanzlänge gegen 7 cm.

Die Gestalt ist die einer schlanken und langgehalsten Süsswasserente, ähnlich der **Spiessente** doch mit schwächerem Kopf und viel kürzerem Schwanz; das Gefieder ebenfalls entenartig, aber kürzer, dichter und derber. Der sehr spitze, schmale Kopf mit seiner sehr niedrigen Stirn, die sanft in den ganz abgeflachten Scheitel übergeht, sitzt auf einem sehr schlanken, dünnen Halse und hat ein zartes, zerschlissenes Gefieder, das sich auf dem Hinterscheitel allmählich verlängert, neben und auf dem Genick sich zu einem noch längeren, schmalen, gerade hinausstehenden Federbusch bildet, dem kürzere Federn, dann aber ein zweiter Büschel auf dem Anfange des Nackens folgt, welcher jedoch gewöhnlich etwas kürzer als der erste ist, sodass man den Federbusch einen doppelten nennen kann, den **Männchen** und **Weibchen**, erstere im **Prachtkleide** aber von ausgezeichneter Länge, haben, während bei letzteren die längeren Federspitzen leicht verloren gehen, zumal in der Begattungszeit. Dagegen haben die **alten Weibchen** meist auch auf den Wangen etwas verlängerte, buschige Federn, die man bei den **Männchen** nicht so bemerkt. Die Gestalt des Flügels ist wie bei Enten, nur bilden die Primärschwingen —, von denen die beiden vordersten ziemlich von gleicher Länge und die längsten —, eine etwas schlankere Flügelspitze; die Sekundärschwingen bilden wie dort einen Spiegel, welcher nur etwas kleiner ist oder schmäler als beim **Gänsesäger**; durch die zugespitzten Tertiärschwingen, wovon die ersteren sehr breit, die letzten schmal, stellt sich eine nicht sehr lange hintere Flügelspitze dar, auf welche die längsten schmalen Schulterfedern sich hinablegen. Die Spitzen der ruhenden Flügel reichen nicht viel über die Schwanzwurzel hinaus, und der aus 18 ziemlich horizontal liegenden, etwas starken, zugespitzten Federn zusammengesetzte Schwanz hat ein zugerundetes Ende, weil von den beiden mittelsten Paaren an, welches die längsten, die nach aussen liegenden stufenweise allmählich an Länge abnehmen, sodass das äusserste Paar gegen 2,4 cm kürzer als das mittelste ist.

Von allen Sägern hat diese Art den längsten und schwächsten Schnabel, sodass er in der Ferne und oberflächlich gesehen, seinen Umrissen nach, eine entfernte Ähnlichkeit mit einem Schnepfenschnabel bekommt, eine Idee, die freilich schwindet, sobald man ihn näher sieht und seinen Haken und Zähne unterscheiden kann. Er ist ausgezeichnet schlank, von den Nasenlöchern an etwas schwächer als hinten, aber dann in fast gleicher Stärke bleibend bis auf die abgestumpfte Spitze, die unten wie oben ein harter scharfrandiger Nagel bedeckt, von der Breite des Schnabels, dessen oberer, viel grösser, stärker gewölbt, sich hakenförmig herab biegt und seine schmal zugerundete Spitze gegen 3 mm über den unteren vorstehen lässt. Er ist meistens gerade, zumal in frischem Zustande, nicht selten jedoch auch mit sanftem, fast unmerklichem Aufschwung an seiner vorderen Hälfte; walzenförmig, doch etwas stumpfkantig, die Firste zu einer schmalen Fläche abgeplattet; der Rand des Oberschnabels durch eine vertiefte Linie abgesondert und wulstig, der des unteren ihm ziemlich ähnlich; die Befiederungsgrenze auf und neben der Stirn drei ziemlich spitze Winkel bildend und viel weiter vorgehend als die schmale Federspitze an den Seiten des Unterschnabels, dessen Kielspalte, sehr schmal, sich als vertiefte Linie bis an den Nagel fortsetzt, und vom Kinn aus in einer sehr schmal ausgehenden Spitze tief hinein befiedert ist. Die Mundkanten haben oben eine doppelte, unten eine einfache Reihe äusserst spitziger und mit den Spitzen rückwärts gerichteter Zähnchen, von denen die der äussersten Reihe des Oberschnabels, grösser als die anderen, an Zahl etwa 34 bis 36, auch bei geschlossenem Schnabel von aussen deutlich zu sehen sind, und die der unteren, wohl 42 bis 50 Zähnchen enthaltend, zwischen die Doppelreihe des Oberkiefers eingreifen. Die Nasenhöhle ist schmal und in die Länge gezogen, und das länglichrunde, durchsichtige Nasenloch öffnet sich vorn in ihr, doch nur erst auf der Grenze des ersten Drittels der Schnabellänge vom Mundwinkel aus.

Die Länge des Schnabels von der Stirn bis auf die Kuppe des Nagels beträgt 6 cm, vom Mundwinkel aus 7 cm oder noch 2 bis 4 mm darüber; an der Wurzel ebenso breit als hoch, nämlich 12 bis 13,5 mm, vorn, gleich hinter dem Nagel, nur 5,5 mm hoch und breit; der Nagel des Oberkiefers im Durchschnitt 9 mm, über dem Bogen 12 mm lang. Bei **jüngeren** Vögeln und den **Weibchen** ist der Schnabel oft um einige Millimeter kürzer. Nur der meistens braune oder auch schwarze Nagel und die Spitzen der Zähne sind hornartig hart, das übrige von aussen mit weicher Haut überzogen, welche rot gefärbt ist, hoch zinnoberrot bei **alten Männchen**, am schönsten im **Prachtkleide**; mit einem schmalen schwarzen Streifen längs der Firste, der vor der Stirn am breitesten ist, am Nagel aber ganz spitz ausläuft; bei den Weibchen gelbrot mit schwarzbraunem Streifen auf der Firste; bei **jungen** Vögeln matt gelbrot, der Firststreifen braun und dieses Braun an den Seiten in das Rote verwaschen. Der innere Schnabel ist blass gelbrot, im Rachen in Fleischfarbe übergehend. Beim Austrocknen, zumal wenn dieses zu schnell und heftig geschieht, verwandelt sich das Rot in ein schmutziges Horngelb, von dem der braun gewordene Firststreifen wenig absticht.

Das Augenlid hat nach innen ein nacktes schwärzliches Rändchen, und das kleine lebhafte Auge bei **Jungen** und **Weibchen** eine gelbbraune, bei den **Männchen** später eine braungelbe, dann hellgelbe, endlich eine rotgelbe Iris.

Die Füsse sind mittelgross, ganz wie die tauchender Enten gestaltet, mit vollen Schwimmhäuten, breiten Hautlappen an der inneren Seite der Innenzehe; mit in einen breiten Hautlappen zusammengedrückter Sohle der hochgestellten, kleinen Hinterzehe und mit nicht grossen, flachgebogenen, schmalen, spitzigen Krallen, von denen die der Mittelzehe auf der Seite nach innen eine vorstehende Randschneide zeigt; die Einschnitte der weichen Haut des Überzuges der Füsse wie bei dem Zwergsäger und den Enten. Die Nacktheit der Füsse fängt von der Ferse an, und vom Gelenk dieser bis unter die Einlenkung der Zehen misst der Lauf 4,3 cm; die Mittelzehe mit der 8 mm langen Kralle 6,7 cm; die Hinterzehe mit der 4 mm langen Kralle 1,9 cm.

Die Farbe der Füsse ist bei **alten Männchen**, besonders im **Frühjahr**, ein glühendes Gelbrot, bei **jüngeren** und den **Weibchen** mehr orangerot oder gelblicher; bei **Jungen** desselben Jahres blass gelbrot, an den Schwimmhäuten und Sohlen bräunlich; die Farbe der Krallen ist weisslich mit braunen Spitzen. Die weichen Fussteile bekommen nach völligem Austrocknen ein unscheinbares rötliches Horngelb, welches von der ursprünglichen prächtigen Färbung derselben keinen Begriff gibt oder diese kaum ahnen lässt.

Vom **Dunenkleide** wird bloss bemerkt, dass es dem junger Gänschen sehr ähnele; wir sahen es aber in natura nicht und können demnach eine nähere Beschreibung davon nicht geben.

Das **Jugendkleid** sieht dem der **alten Weibchen**, besonders wenn dessen Gefieder noch frisch und mehr grau als braun ist, sehr ähnlich und ist dann von ihm nur an der blasseren Schnabel- und Fussfarbe, an der kürzeren, meist einfachen Holle und an den abgebrochenen Spitzen der Schwanzfederschäfte zu unterscheiden. Im ganzen hat dies Gefieder folgende Färbung: Der Kopf und Anfang des Halses, die schmutzigweisse Kehle ausgenommen, ist matt rostbraun, an den Zügeln und der Spitze der unbedeutenden Holle am dunkelsten; Vorderhals und Kropf schmutzigweiss, braungrau gewölkt und gefleckt; der Unterkörper bis an den Schwanz weiss; die Seiten des Bauches, der Brust, des Kropfes, der Nacken und alle oberen Teile, nebst den kleinen und mittleren Flügeldeckfedern, dunkel schiefergrau mit schwarzen Schäften und in lichtes Braungrau verwaschenen hellen und breiten Federkanten; der Flügelspiegel, von den Sekundärschwingen und ihrer grossen Deckfederreihe gebildet, nur vorn an einigen Federn schwarz, übrigens weiss mit zwei etwas undeutlichen grauschwarzen Querstreifen, indem die Wurzeln beider Federreihen diese Farbe haben und vom Weissen nicht ganz verdeckt werden; alles Übrige wie beim **alten Weibchen**. Das Gefieder des **gleichalten Männchens** ist am Kopfe etwas dunkler braun und der Oberkörper mehr und dunkler schiefergrau mit nicht so sehr ins Weissbräunliche übergehenden Federkanten, darum dem **Sommerkleide alter Männchen** sich nähernd, von ihm aber ebenfalls durch die abgebrochenen Schwanzfederspitzen, auch an den gelbbraunen Augensternen und an den braun überlaufenen Schwimmhäuten, desgleichen und vorzüglich an dem ganz aschgrauen Oberflügel, leicht zu unterscheiden.

Das **alte Weibchen** hat eine doppelte Holle, einen Federbüschel im Genick, den andern dicht unter demselben, und in beiden Federn mit fast 6 cm langen, sehr dünnen Spitzen, die leicht abbrechen und besonders in der Begattungszeit zum grossen Teil verloren gehen, sonst aber entweder steif hinausstehen oder sich senken — wenn das ganze Gefieder der Holle niedergelegt wird — und auf den

Nacken niederlegen, ohne sich bedeutend zu krümmen. Schnabel und Füsse sind von blasserer Farbe als beim **Männchen**, die Augensterne gelbbraun; Kinn und Kehle weiss, etwas gelbbräunlich überlaufen, das Übrige des Kopfes mit dem Anfang des Halses blass rostbraun, zwischen Schnabel und Auge und in einem verlorenen Streifen über und unter dem letzteren, desgleichen an den Enden der schmal und spitz verlängerten Federn der Holle dunkler braun; die Gurgel meist weiss, braungrau gefleckt; der Kropf, die Tragefedern und Weichen, Rücken und Schultern tief braungrau, am dunkelsten längs den schwarzen Schäften der Federn, an deren Kanten die Grundfarbe, mehr oder weniger schnell, in weissliches Braungrau übergeht, am lichtesten an den äussersten Käntchen; diese hellen Kanten am Kropfe am breitesten, auf dem Flügel und dem Unterrücken stark mit Grau überlaufen, daher undeutlich; der Flügel mit seinem Spiegel wie bei den Jungen, die beiden dunklen Querstreifen desselben aber deutlicher; die Federn der hinteren Flügelspitze auf den Aussenfahnen, längs deren schwärzlichen Aussenkanten, etwas mehr weiss gelichtet, die hintersten aber ganz dunkel graubraun; die grossen Schwingen und ihre Deckfedern braunschwarz; der Unterflügel grau, unter der Achsel weiss; der Schwanz tief braungrau mit schwarzen Schäften und etwas lichter grauen Federkanten; die Mitte des ganzen Unterkörpers bis unter den Schwanz rein weiss.

Die Farben des **weiblichen** Gefieders verändern sich im Laufe der Monate, durch den Einfluss der Atmosphärilien, später auch durch Reibungen, sehr bedeutend; denn das Rostbraun des Kopfes, mit den vollständigen Federenden seines Doppelschopfes, ist im September und Anfang Oktober viel dunkler, vorzüglich auffallend aber am frischen Gefieder der oberen Körperteile eine allgemeine, in Schiefergrau übergehende sehr dunkle Färbung, zwar mit lichtereren Federkanten, aber diese nicht mit weisslichen Rändern; diese bilden sich erst nach und nach aus, während die Schieferfarbe allmählich verschwindet und in Braungrau übergeht, sodass dasselbe Gewand zwei Monate später schon ganz anders aussieht, aber noch später und in der Begattungszeit dem abgebleichten mancher Süsswasserenten gar nicht unähnlich wird, besonders im Mai und Juni, wo dann auch die Doppelholle sehr beschädigt ist, vermutlich vom Packen der **Männchen** mit dem scharf gezähnten Schnabel während des Begattungsaktes. Obgleich nun diese **Weibchen**, im frischen Gefieder, gleich nach vollendeter Mauser, hinsichtlich der Färbung desselben, eine nahe Verwandtschaft mit denen des Gänsesägers zeigen, so unterscheidet sie doch dann schon die viel dunklere Schieferfarbe, die sich weniger zum Blauen als zum Braunen neigt; und da letzteres von Monat zu Monat zunimmt, bald völlig prädominiert und durch weissliche Federränder eine geschuppte oder wenigstens gewölkte Zeichnung bekommt, so unterscheidet es sich bald sehr und höchst augenfällig von der einförmigen, an Mohnblau grenzenden, viel lichteren Schieferfarbe der **Weibchen** des **Gänsesägers**.

Das **Sommerkleid** über ein Jahr alter **Männchen** hat viele Ähnlichkeit mit dem **männlichen Jugendkleide**, aber schon das derbere Gefieder, die vollständig vorhandenen Schwanzfederspitzen, die lebhaftere Färbung der nackten Teile und des Augensterns und anderes mehr machen es kenntlich genug. Die Farbe des Schnabels ist jedoch eine blassere als im Frühjahr, die Firste des Oberkiefers auch mehr braun als schwarz und dies weniger scharf begrenzt, und an den mehr in Pommeranzengelb ziehenden Füssen sind auch oft die Schwimmhäute bräunlich angelaufen; der hochgelbe Augenstern, je nach dem Alter, mehr oder weniger in Gelbrot spielend; der Federbusch zwar doppelt, aber kürzer als an den **alten Weibchen**, samt dem Scheitel und Nacken ziemlich dunkelbraun, die Kopfseiten und der Anfang des Halses lebhaft rostbraun, gegen die Kehle heller, diese, der Zügel und die Umgebung des Auges ins Weissliche schimmernd, über und unter dem weisslichen Zügel ein dunkler, oft bis hinter das Auge fortgesetzter Streifen; der Hinterhals in einem schmalen Streifen bis zum Rücken dunkelschiefergrau; Vorderhals und Kropf weiss, aschgrau gewölkt; die Kropfseiten dunkel schieferfarbig mit helleren Kanten, die an der Stelle, wo im **Prachtkleide** die merkwürdig weiss und schwarz gezeichneten Federn stehen, besonders scharf von der Grundfarbe getrennt und ziemlich breit sind; der ganze Rücken bis an den Schwanz tief schiefergrau, mit schwarzen Federschäften und an der Oberschwanzdecke mit hellerer Schieferfarbe gekantet; die Schultern wie der Rücken, die längsten Federn in Schieferschwarz übergehend; die kleinen und mittleren Flügeldeckfedern dunkelschiefergrau, bei **älteren** Individuen die letzteren mit weissen Federn untermischt oder auch ganz weiss; der vordere Flügelrand dunkel- und hellgrau geschuppt, der obere ein schmales weissliches Rändchen darstellend; die Primärschwingen mit ihren Deckfedern tief schwarz; die Sekundärschwingen mit ihrer grossen Deckfederreihe rein weiss, mit scharf getrennten schwarzen Wurzeln, die zwei schwarze Querstriche des weissen Spiegels bilden, von denen der eine ihn von obenher begrenzt, der andere quer durch das Weisse streicht, gewöhnlich aber nach hinten spitz verläuft, nämlich bei geordneter Lage der Federn, bei verschiedenen Individuen auch nicht ganz gleichförmig schmäler oder breiter; die Tertiärschwingen schieferschwarz, die nächste am Spiegel auf der Aussenfahne weiss, die folgende hellaschgrau, die dritte schiefergrau, und diese drei mit scharf gezeichneter schwarzer Aussenkante, die gegen das Ende der Federn spitz ausläuft; der Unterflügel meist weiss, am Rande herum braungrau, an der Spitze glänzend rauchfahl mit weissen Schwingenschäften, die mittelsten Schwingen ganz weiss. Die Mitte des Unterkörpers bis zu der schwach graulich geschuppten Unterschwanzdecke rein weiss, dies oft etwas gelbrötlich angehaucht; die Tragefedern, Schenkel und Bauchseiten schiefergrau, erstere durch lichtere Federkanten heller gewölkt; der Schwanz schieferschwarz mit schwarzen Federschäften und mit aschgrau überpuderten Federkanten.

Dieses Kleid kommt in unseren Gegenden äusserst selten vor, weil es die **Männchen** in der Hauptmauser, im Juli, wenn sie fern von uns hochnordische Länder bewohnen, anlegen, es nur ein paar Monate tragen und es gegen Ende des September schon wieder mit dem **hochzeitlichen Prachtkleide** vertauschen, sodass bei spät im November erlegten nur selten noch Überbleibsel von jenem, daher lange unbekannt gebliebenen, männlichen **Sommerkleide** in einzelnen Federn vorkommen. Wenn aber in den Wintermonaten **Männchen** erlegt werden, deren **Prachtkleid** noch nicht rein hergestellt oder mit grauen Federn hin und wieder untermischt ist, so sind dies **junge**, die es zum ersten Male anlegen, was bei ihnen um ein paar Monate später erfolgt und langsamer von statten geht, welche man aber auch schon an dem schiefergrauen Oberflügel und an den abgebrochenen Schwanzfederspitzen leicht von den **alten** unterscheiden kann.

Ein prächtiger Vogel ist das **alte Männchen** in seinem vollständigen **hochzeitlichen** Gewande oder **Prachtkleide**. Das glühende Gelbrot der Füsse nimmt auch die Schwimmhäute und Sohlen ein, auf dem prächtig roten Schnabel ist der schwarze Firstenstreif scharf dargestellt, und die hochrotgelbe Färbung des Augensterns ist eine leuchtende. Von der Mitte des Scheitels nach hinten verlängern sich die Spitzen der sehr schmalen, zerschlissenen Federn des Doppelbusches und erreichen auf dem Genick eine Länge von 7 cm, die zweite Abteilung am Anfange des Nackens oft noch darüber bis zu 7,6 cm, und können aufgerichtet strahlenartig sich ausbreiten, stehen aber gewöhnlicher nach hinten in zwei Büscheln steif hinaus. Sie und der ganze Kopf, nebst dem Anfang des Halses, etwa 3,5 cm herab, sind tief schwarz, mit goldgrünem Glanz, der in verschiedenem Lichte hin und wieder auch etwas ins Violette spielt; dann folgt ein 4,75 cm breiter weisser Halsring, der bei **recht alten** jedoch oft mit rostfarbigen, schwarzgefleckten Federchen vermischt, und immer auf dem Nacken entlang durch einen bis zum Rücken herablaufenden schwarzen Strich getrennt ist; den übrigen Teil des Halses mit dem angrenzenden des Kropfes bekleiden bunte Federn, rostfarbig, an den Enden etwas blasser, mit braunschwarzen Schaftstrichen, die in die Spitze auslaufen und an ihren Seiten gezackt oder punktiert sind; weiter hinab ist der Kropf in der Mitte breit weiss, seine Seiten tief schwarz und auf der Grenze des Weissen und Schwarzen zeigen sich noch viele rostfarbige, schwarz gewässerte und punktierte Flecke. An die Kropfseiten schliesst sich abwärts eine Partie grosser, eigentümlich gezeichneter Federn, die sich über das Handgelenk des Flügels legen, wenn dieser unter seinen Tragfedern ruht, auch sie haben in der Nähe ihrer Wurzeln zum Teil rostfarbige, schwarzgewässerte Flecke, die jedoch von anders gefärbten Teilen verdeckt werden, denn jede dieser Federn ist an ihren übrigen zwei Dritteilen in der Mitte rein weiss, dieses Weiss, meistens einen grossen, verkehrtkeilförmigen Fleck vorstellend, in schärfster Begrenzung von einem samtschwarzen Rahmen eingefasst, welcher am zerschlissenen Ende jeder Feder am breitesten ist, sodass durch zufälliges Verschieben dieser Federn die weissen Flecke in allerlei Gestalten aus dem tief schwarzen Grunde hervortreten, immer aber schroff unterschieden und meistens in geraden Linien (auch in die Quere) getrennt. Von der weissen Mitte des Kropfes an bis an den Schwanz ist der ganze Unterrumpf rein weiss, nicht selten mit lieblichem Morgenrot ganz schwach angehaucht; die Tragfedern auf weissem Grunde mit zarten, teilweise auch stärkeren, schwarzen Wellen- und Zickzacklinien quer und dicht durchzogen, sodass diese Teile in einiger Entfernung, wo die hellen und dunklen Linien ineinander fliessen, aschgrau zu sein scheinen; auch die äussere Seite der Schenkel ist so, und die längsten Unterschwanzdeckfedern haben an ihren Spitzen nicht selten auch einen schwachen Ansatz von dieser Zeichnung. Der Oberrücken und die Schultern sind tief und glänzend schwarz, letztere an der den Flügel begrenzenden Seite in einem oben breit anfangenden, aber bald schmäler werdenden, endlich schmal und spitz auf der Mitte der Länge der ganzen Schulterpartie auslaufenden, rein weissen Felde; der Unterrücken braunschwarz, anfänglich ungefleckt, dann lichtgrau punktiert und bekritzelt, auf dem Bürzel und den Oberschwanzdecken in Wellenlinien, in beiden Farben abwechselnd, bezeichnet. Die Wurzel des Flügels und die kleinen Deckfedern, in Gestalt eines fingerbreiten Querstreifs, sind schwarz, nächst diesem bilden die mittleren Deckfedern, welche weiss sind, ein grosses weisses (nur bei **jüngeren Männchen** mit grauen Federn durchmischtes) Feld, dieses von einem tief schwarzen Querstreif begrenzt, welchen die von den Wurzeln herauf bis zu zwei Fünfteilen schwarzgefärbten, von dem reinen Weiss der übrigen Teile scharf begrenzten grossen Deckfederreihen über dem Spiegel darstellen, die gewöhnlich zu ihm gezählt werden; dann folgt der eigentliche Spiegel, von den Sekundärschwingen gebildet, von welchen, was gewöhnlich übersehen worden, die drei ersten Federn (wie die Deckfedern dieser) auf ihren ganzen Aussenfahnen samtschwarz, alle folgenden aber rein weiss, nur am Wurzeldritteil schwarz und beide Farben geradlinig und scharf getrennt, wodurch ein zweiter schwarzer Querstreif gebildet wird. Zählt man nun, wie gewöhnlich, die grosse Deckfedernreihe nebst den Sekundärschwingen zum Spiegel, so fängt dieser der Länge nach mit einem samtschwarzen Streifen an, ist dann aber zu seinem grössten Teile rein weiss, mit zwei scharfgezeichneten schwarzen Querstreifen, der eine seine obere Grenze bezeichnend, der andere durch seine Mitte ziehend; dann schliessen sich hinter ihm, in wachsender Grösse und Länge, vier rein weisse Federn an, an der Kante ihrer Aussenfahnen mit einem samtschwarzen Strich bezeichnet, also vier schwarze Längsstriche auf weissem Grunde; endlich folgen die drei oder vier letzten, schmalen und lang zugespitzten Tertiärschwingen, welche durchaus samtschwarz, auf welche sich die ebenso gestalteten und gleichgefärbten längsten Schulterfedern herablegen. Der Fittich, wozu die Primärschwingen, ihre Deckfedern und die des Daumens gehören, ist tief braunschwarz, der vordere Flügelrand in Braungrau übergehend; der Unterflügel an den Rändern ebenfalls braungrau, in der Mitte weiss, die grossen Schwingen glänzend graubraun, an den Enden in Rauchfahl übergehend, und ihre Schäfte bräunlichweiss. Der Schwanz ist matt braunschwarz, an den Enden der Federn etwas bleicher gekantet, übrigens aschgrau bepudert, auf seiner unteren Seite glänzend graubraun, hier die Federschäfte gelbbraun, von oben schwarz.

Der goldgrüne Schiller des schwarzen Kopfes dieser Art ist an und für sich zwar ein prächtiger, jedoch lange nicht so stark als beim **Männchen** der **Stockente**, sondern nur dem vom **alten Männchen** der **Bergente** oder allenfalls der **Schellente** zu vergleichen, sodass er auch nicht so weit in die Ferne leuchtet wie jener.

Bei den **Männchen**, welche dies prächtige Gewand zum ersten Male trugen, sind die beiden Federbüsche noch kürzer, das grosse weisse Feld zwischen der nur mattschwarzen oberen Flügelkante und dem Spiegel sehr mit Aschgrau gemischt; vorzüglich unterscheiden sie jedoch die abgebrochenen Schwanzfederspitzen, die dadurch entstanden, dass auf ihnen vormals die Dunen des Nestkleides ihren Sitz hatten. Die mehrere Jahre **alten Männchen** sind in den Wintermonaten in ihrem schönsten Schmuck; im Frühjahre verbleicht die schöne Rostfarbe des Kropfes etwas oder verliert doch sehr viel an Lebhaftigkeit, was man am übrigen Gefieder nicht bemerkt; aber die zarten, schlanken Spitzen der Federn des Doppelschopfes verlieren während der Begattungszeit bedeutend, und viele zeigen sich abgebrochen, vermutlich von den Raufereien der **Männchen** um die **Weibchen**.

Die **männliche** Luftröhre unterscheidet sich, wie bereits oben erwähnt, von der des **Gänsesägers** darin, dass sie, ungefähr 4,7 cm unter der Stimmritze, bloss eine einzige, grosse, bauchige, von oben plattgedrückte, 16 mm breite Erweiterung hat, während an der des **Gänsesägers** sich **zwei** solche befinden; und dass die Luftkapsel oder Pauke an der Teilung der Trachea in die beiden Bronchien (am unteren Larynx) in zwei innere und zwei Nebenkammern abgeteilt ist, von denen letztere fast gleichgross sind, die oben voneinander abstehen und aussen **vier** Hautfenster zeigen, wogegen beim **Gänsesäger** nur **drei** solche vorhanden sind.

AUFENTHALT

Alle Länder rund um den Nordpol oder bis hoch in den nördlichen Polarkreis hinauf, von **Island** an durch den Norden von **Europa**, **Asien** und von **Amerika** bis nach **Grönland**, bewohnt der mittlere Säger teilweise in sehr grosser Anzahl und ist in den meisten jener Länder häufiger als der **Gänsesäger**. Aus jenen geht er periodisch in die gemässigte Zone über, in **Nordamerika** bis in die südlichen **Vereinigten Staaten**, in **Asien** bis nach **Japan**, ins südliche **Sibirien** und die **Tatarei**, in unserem Erdteile bis **Südrussland** und die **Türkei**, bis **Polen**, **Preussen**, **Schweden**, **Norwegen**, **Dänemark**, das nördliche **Grossbritannien** und **Irland** und an die diesseitigen Küsten der **Nord-** und **Ostsee**, doch an dieser wie in **Pommern**, **Mecklenburg** und **Holstein** ungleich häufiger als an jener, wo er z. B. im **Oldenburgischen** bloss einzeln vorkommt — ist dann in allen jenen Ländern namentlich im Winter meistens in grosser Anzahl anzutreffen, streicht dann auch weiter nach Süden und Westen, doch nur einzeln oder in viel geringerer Anzahl als der **Gänsesäger**, bis **Frankreich**, **Italien** und **Griechenland**. Im Innern des gemässigteren und wärmeren Festlandes unseres Erdteiles kommt er jedoch nur vereinzelt oder in sehr kleinen Flügen in der kalten Jahreszeit und namentlich bei harten Wintern vor, so in **Holland**, der **Schweiz** und in **Deutschland**. So erschien er auf dem **Rhein**, der **Donau**, der **Elbe** und ihren Nebenflüssen oder anderen nahen Gewässern, aber auch ungleich seltener als der **Gänsesäger**. Immer haben wir in **Anhalt** nur vereinzelte **Mittelsäger** von unseren Flüssen und anderen im Winter offenen Gewässern erhalten, auch auf dem **Salzigen See** unweit **Eisleben** einigemal bloss kleine Gesellschaften bemerkt und einzelne erlegt. Man darf sie bei uns unter die seltenen Erscheinungen zählen, und sie ist auch für das **mittlere Deutschland** überhaupt unter den drei Arten dieser Gattung unbezweifelt die seltenste, obgleich sie in ihrer wahren Heimat viel zahlreicher an Individuen ist als eine von diesen.

Im allgemeinen kann man diese Art wohl zu den Zugvögeln zählen, obgleich ihre weiteren Auswanderungen und die Zeit derselben oft von Zufälligkeiten und namentlich von der Beschaffenheit der Witterung abhängen mögen, indem ihrer viele auch in den heimatlichen Gegenden sich so lange umhertreiben, so lange es Frost und Eis nur gestatten wollen, auch wiederkehren, sobald jene Hindernisse sich wieder entfernt haben, wobei sie zugleich den grössten Gleichmut gegen die heftigste Kälte an den Tag legen. Die grosse Mehrheit wandert indessen bei Eintritt der rauhen Jahreszeit südlich, um in milderen Lagen ihre Winterquartiere aufzuschlagen, desto weiter, je mehr die zunehmende Winterkälte ihnen nachrückt und sie fortdrängt, weil sie ihnen die Gewässer verschliesst. So ist dieser Säger im hohen Norden **Zugvogel**, mehr südlich bloss **Strichvogel** und in uns noch näher liegenden Gegenden wohl gar **Standvogel** zu nennen. Um auszuwandern, versammeln sich die im hohen Norden wohnenden in den Umgebungen ihrer Brutplätze, meistens auf dem Meere, schon im Oktober zu grösseren Flügen, später zu unabsehbaren Scharen an, gesellen sich auch zu denen von anderem Seegeflügel, und so erscheinen sie dann meistens schon im November in grosser Anzahl in Gegenden, in welchen sie im Sommer gar nicht oder nur einzeln bemerkt werden. Die **Jungen** scheinen am frühsten und weitesten auszuwandern, die **alten Männchen** damit viel länger zu zaudern und sich sehr selten und nur einzeln so weit zu verfliegen wie jene. Auch in hiesigen Gegenden sahen wir nur jene zuweilen in kleinen Gesellschaften oder Familien schon zu Ende des November und erhielten einige vereinzelte **Alte** nur mitten im Winter, unter diesen aber von unseren **anhaltischen** Gewässern ein **altes Männchen** im **Prachtkleide** niemals.*

Gegen Eintritt milderer Frühlingswitterung im März verlassen sie unsere und andere Gegenden, in denen sie bloss überwinterten, wieder, um nach dem Norden oder Nordosten zurückzukehren. An den Seeküsten entlang ziehen sie im Spätherbst südwestlich noch weiter und es überwintern selbst in den **griechischen** und **italienischen** Gewässern ihrer nicht wenige, die auch erst im Anfang des Frühjahrs wieder verschwinden und dort wahrscheinlich von Osten her kamen.

Auch sie ziehen meistens des Nachts, wenn sie es bei Tage tun, streichen sie dabei sehr hoch durch die Lüfte und bilden dann gewöhnlich eine einzige, oft sehr lange, schräge Reihe oder, wie die Scharen der wilden Gänse, wahrscheinlich familienweise, viele solcher, seltener eine vorn im spitzen Winkel vereinte, hinten weit ausgespreizte Doppelreihe.

Es ist merkwürdig, doch auch bei anderen Sägerarten so, dass sich die **Weibchen** und gleichgefärbten **jungen Männchen** in Scharen zusammenschlagen, diese aber sehr oft von keinem **alten Männchen** im **Prachtkleide** begleitet werden oder deren verhältnismässig nur sehr wenige in ihrer Mitte haben; dass ferner diese wiederum eigene, ungemischte Vereine, fast ohne jene, bilden, oder sich auch vereinzelt umhertreiben. Unbemerkt mögen unter den übrigen die alten Männchen wohl bleiben, so lange sie im grauen **Sommerkleide**; allein auch im Winter noch, wenn sie dies mit dem hellbunten **Prachtkleide** bereits vertauscht haben und sich schon in weiter Ferne erkennbar machen, scheint es mehr graue als bunte Säger zu geben, obgleich sich nachher an den Brutorten ausweist, dass beide Geschlechter zeugungsfähig in gleicher Anzahl vorhanden sind.

Der Mittelsäger darf wohl Seevogel genannt werden, weil er meistens auf dem Meere lebt, obwohl er in der Nähe der Küsten, zwischen Landengen, in tiefen Buchten und in den Umgebungen der Inseln sich am liebsten aufhält. Aber er liebt auch die grossen Landseen unfern den Meeresküsten, wenn auch mit süssem Wasser, desgleichen Strömungen und Flüsse, vorzüglich an ihren Mündungen ins offene Meer. Auch die hohe See scheut er nicht, vorzüglich wenn das Eis an den Ufern ihn auf sie hinausdrängt. Inmitten des Festlandes muss er freilich im Winter mit allen vom Eise freibleibenden Stellen der Gewässer, der fliessenden wie der stehenden, fürlieb nehmen und oft, um sein Leben zu fristen, die in einem grösseren Umkreise sich bietenden wechselweise besuchen. Im Sommer wohnt er besonders

* Diese musste ich zu meinem Zwecke aus fernen Ländern beziehen und erhielt sie aus den **Vereinigten Staaten von Nordamerika**, aus **Grönland**, **Island**, **Norwegen** und von der Küste **Holsteins**.

gern nicht allein an sumpfigen und schilfreichen, sondern auch an waldigen Ufern und auf den Gewässern waldreicher Gegenden, in unwirtbaren Ländern oft in der Nähe einzelner von Menschen bewohnter Hütten, selbst in mehr bewohnten gar nicht fern von Häusern oder kleinen Ortschaften, obschon er im übrigen eine besondere Vertraulichkeit gegen den Menschen keineswegs verrät.

EIGENSCHAFTEN

In der Ferne hat diese Art so grosse Ähnlichkeit mit dem **Gänsesäger**, dass sie nur dem sehr geübten Beobachter an der kleineren und schlankeren Gestalt kenntlich wird. Sie ist ihr in allen Bewegungen, stehend, fortschreitend, schwimmend, tauchend und fliegend so höchst ähnlich, dass das, was von der einen gesagt werden kann, auch auf die andere passt.

Haltung des Körpers und Gang sind wie bei Süsswasserenten, das Schwimmen wie bei Tauchenten, aber in diesem senken sie den Rumpf noch tiefer in die Wasserfläche, sodass sie darin den Tauchern noch ähnlicher werden, zumal ihr schlanker Hals und dünnspitzer Kopf diese Ähnlichkeit vermehren helfen. In der Fertigkeit und Ausdauer des Tauchens werden sie von den letzteren schwerlich übertroffen. Schnell wie Raubfische durchströmen sie das Wasser zwischen Boden und Fläche nach allen Richtungen, den fliehenden Fischen bis in ihre Schlupfwinkel nachjagend, und fast möchte man diese mittlere Art dabei für noch flinker halten als den **Gänsesäger**, oder sie dem **Zwergsäger** ganz gleich stellen. Wenn, wie gewöhnlich, mehrere beisammen, sind bald alle zugleich oben, bald und ebenso unerwartet alle unterm Wasser verschwunden, und dieses wird teils von den geängstigten Fischen, teils und noch mehr von den ihnen nachschiessenden Vögeln zuweilen in heftige Bewegung gesetzt.

Ihr Flug ist ebenfalls entenartig, äusserst schnell und gewandt, die hastigen Flügelschläge von einem, jedoch nur in geringer Entfernung vernehmbaren, pfeifenden Zischeln begleitet. Sie fliegen, wenn es weit gehen soll, sehr hoch, zu einem näheren Ziel oft auch sehr niedrig, in gerader Linie fort, können jedoch auch mancherlei Schwenkungen machen, den Körper bald auf die eine, bald auf die andere Seite werfen, und das Niederlassen aufs Wasser fängt sehr häufig mit einem kurzen Tauchen an, doch haben sie sich darin mehr in der Gewalt als Taucher und können auch leise aufsitzen und hingleiten. Im Fliegen macht sich diese Art vor allen kenntlich durch ihre schlankere Gestalt und, wenn die Entfernung nicht zu gross ist, an dem ungewöhnlich langen Schnabel, dessen auffallende Länge einem scharfen Auge, selbst wenn sie sitzt oder schwimmt, nicht entgehen kann.

Dieser Säger ist ein sehr scheuer, vorsichtiger Vogel, welcher sich vorzüglich da sehr misstrauisch gegen die Menschen zeigt, wo er nicht sicher vor Verfolgungen zu sein glaubt. Auf dem Wasser entweicht er so lange wie möglich tauchend; ist es aber nicht gross genug, dann schwingt er sich auf und fliegt weit weg, kehrt aber gern auf die erste Stelle zurück, wo ihn der Schütze, wenn er sich gut verbirgt, leicht erlauern kann. In seinen hochnordischen Brutgegenden ist er dagegen ziemlich zutraulich, zumal gegen Leute, die sich nicht um ihn kümmern oder ihm doch nicht mit dem Schiessgewehr nachstellen. Wie oben erwähnt, ist er sehr gesellig, in kleinen wie in grossen Flügen beisammen anzutreffen, und solche trennen sich ungern oder suchen, wenn es geschehen, sehr bald sich wieder zu vereinigen. Enten und anderem Geflügel schliesst er sich zwar, wo ein gemeinsames Interesse, viel Nahrungsmittel sie zusammenführen, jedoch nie innig, an, was man besonders an Vereinzelten bemerken kann, die häufig ganz vereinsamt angetroffen werden, oder ihnen sich aufdringende Gesellschafter gar nicht beachten. Im hohen Norden teilt er indessen oft die Brutplätze mit Enten, Tauchern und anderen.

Seine Stimme ist ein gellendes, schnarrendes **Körrrr** oder **Gerrr**, das meistens im Fluge, zumal beim Aufschwingen, und häufiger vom **Weibchen** als vom **Männchen** vernommen wird, und dieses lässt in der Begattungszeit öfters noch einen besonderen hohlen, dumpfen Ton hören. Die **Jungen** im Flaum **piepen** wie junge Enten.

NAHRUNG

Diese besteht hauptsächlich in kleinen Fischen bis zu der Länge einer Hand, vorzüglich von schmalen Arten; aus Wasserkäfern, Insektenlarven, Würmern, selbst Regenwürmern, seltener aus Fröschen, die auch dieser Säger namentlich im Winter aus dem Schlamme hervorholt. In dieser Jahreszeit findet man wenig und selten Grünes in seinem Magen; dies soll jedoch im Sommer so häufig vorkommen, dass man es nicht bloss für zufällig verschluckt halten darf.

Er verfolgt die kleinen Fische durch Tauchen nach allen Richtungen, schussweise, unter der Wasserfläche und holt sie aus ihren Schlupfwinkeln hervor. Wo dann auf von Fischen sehr belebten Stellen der Gewässer mehrere dieser Säger, wie gewöhnlich, zu gleicher Zeit eintauchen und den geängstigten Fischchen nachjagen, treiben sie die, welche sie nicht sogleich erwischen können, vor sich hin, gewöhnlich gegen die Ufer und auf seichtere Stellen, sie immer rastlos verfolgend, solange welche zu erschnappen sind und bis alle Glieder der Gesellschaft sich gesättigt haben. So treiben sie oft die Schwärme junger Fische eine weite Strecke entlang vor sich her und setzen dadurch besonders stilles und seichtes Wasser gewaltig in Bewegung; allein es ist übertrieben, wenn man ihnen andichtete, dass sie sich dabei im Halbkreise auf der Fläche aufstellten, diese Ordnung beim Eintauchen und unter der Fläche streng beibehielten, so die Fische in die Enge trieben u.s.w. Allerdings schwimmen alle Glieder eines Vereins vor dem Eintauchen nahe beisammen, doch ohne alle Ordnung, und verschwinden in ein paar Augenblicken fast alle zugleich unterm Wasser; allein hier schiesst jedes Individuum seinem erwählten Schlachtopfer nach, welche Richtung dieses auch nehmen möge, sodass, wenn jene wieder auf der Fläche erscheinen, dies einzeln und oft weit von einander entfernt geschieht, und sie nun erst wieder zusammenschwimmen und sich sammeln müssen, bevor sie von neuem eintauchen. Übrigens mag diese Art zu tauchen, worin die Säger den Tauchern und Scharben gleichen, sie abhalten, eher mit diesen als mit tauchenden Enten an derselben Stelle zu fischen, weil die letzteren sich auf andere Weise nähren und beim Tauchen meistens senkrecht bis auf den Grund hinab gehen, die Säger dagegen dies nur selten nötig haben, aber beim schrägen und horizontalen Fortbewegen, unter der Fläche, die fliehenden Fische zu erhaschen, am meisten ihre Rechnung finden.

FORTPFLANZUNG

Der nördliche Polarkreis der alten und neuen Welt scheint den Mittelpunkt der Gegenden zu durchziehen, die der mittlere Säger zur Zeit der Fortpflanzung in grösster Anzahl bewohnt. Über dem 70. Breitengrade wird er seltener; aber, ausser **Grönland** und **Island**, wo er häufig brütet, findet er in der **skandinavischen Halbinsel**, von jenem Kreise südwärts, an den Küsten, wie auf den Landseen und

Strömen des Innern, noch sehr häufig seine Brutplätze, deren Zahl aber von dort südlich immer mehr abnimmt, bis zu den **dänischen** Küsten und Inseln, auf denen er bloss ganz einzeln nistet und diesseits der Ostsee, auf den Gewässern unfern der Küste nur selten, am häufigsten auf **Rügen** noch brütend angetroffen wird. Näher auf **deutschem** Boden ist er nistend niemals gefunden worden.

Seine Brutplätze sind teils unmittelbar am Meer, die grünen Ufer seichter Buchten und Mündungen der Flüsse und Ströme, teils und öfter noch grosse zusammenhängende Landseen und Flüsse, besonders bei reissenden Strömungen, oft weit vom Meere, mit Schilf und anderen Sumpfpflanzen teilweise bewachsen, mit Gebüsch oder gar von Wald umgeben, aber auch mit ziemlich kahlen Umgebungen, jedoch nicht zwischen hohen nackten Felsen versteckte. Sehr gewöhnlich teilt er die Brutplätze mit mancherlei Entenarten, besonders auf den süssen Landseen und Teichen **Islands**, auf denen er (nach FABER) gegen Ende des April und im Anfange des Mai gepaart ankommt, wo man dann die **Männchen** unter wunderlichen Posituren ihre **Weibchen** liebkosen sieht, wobei jenes seinen langen Hals oft hoch in die Höhe reckt, dann plötzlich wieder gegen den Wasserspiegel senkt und einen hohlen Ton dazu auspresst.

Das Nest selbst, ein kunstloses, lockeres Geflecht oder blosse Zusammenhäufung von trockenem Schilf, feinen Reiserchen, Laub, dürren Stengeln und Grashalmen, vom **Weibchen** allein angefertigt, steht an fast so verschiedenen Orten, wie das der Stockente, am häufigsten wohl auf dem Erdboden in einer kleinen Vertiefung desselben, unter dem Schutze einiger Steine, höherer Pflanzen oder eines dichten Gesträuches; dann in horizontalen Erd- oder Steinhöhlen und in solchen von losen Steinen gebildet, bis zu 5,5 m Länge; in hohlen Baumstämmen.

Im Mai, im höheren Norden auch erst in der ersten Hälfte des Juni, legt das **Weibchen** seine neun bis zwölf, selten bis 14 Eier, deren aber bis 30 und mehr, wenn sie ihm, ehe es seine Zahl voll hat, bis auf einige genommen und damit um den anderen oder dritten Tag einige Zeit fortgefahren wird. Diese Eier sind meistens von einer etwas schlanken oder gestreckten Eiform; ihre ziemlich starke und feste Schale von sehr feinem Korne, glatt, aber wenig glänzend; ihre Färbung eine lichtgraugelbliche, ein wenig ins Olivengrünliche spielende, mithin sind sie denen vieler Entenarten zum Verwechseln ähnlich, besonders denen der **Bergente**, welchen sie an Grösse und Gestalt am meisten gleichen, aber eine glattere Aussenfläche und eine Farbe haben, die etwas weniger ins Grünliche fällt, sie also hinsichtlich ihrer

Färbung mehr denen der **Moorente** nahe kommen. Auch manchen der **Reiherente** sind sie ungemein ähnlich. Gegen die der **Stockente** gehalten sind sie bedeutend grösser, oft auch länglicher und ihre Farbe stets eine weniger grünliche. Sie messen in der Länge 61 bis 63 mm, in der grössten Breite, die nicht die Mitte jener erreicht, 43,5 mm.

Das **Weibchen** brütet seine Eier ohne Mithilfe des **Männchens** aus, dies hält sich aber in der Gegend des Nestes auf, bis jenes ernstlicher zu brüten anfängt, den Eiern eine weiche und erwärmende Unterlage von den eigenen Dunen bereitet und auch oben um das Nest einen Kranz von Dunen bildet, welcher die Eier bedeckt, wenn es Bedürfnisse halber vom Neste geht. Wie lange es brütet, ist nicht beobachtet. Nach FABER gibt es auf **Island** in der zweiten Hälfte des Juli Junge, von denen manche Anfang September noch im Dunenkleide sind, Ende dieses Monats aber alle befiedert und flugbar werden. Die Mutter führt sie gleich aufs Wasser, pflegt sie sorgsam, warnt sie in Gefahren und ruft sie mit einem schnarrenden Ton zusammen, wenn sie ein Unfall getrennt hatte. Weiterhin begleitet sie ihre Nachkommenschaft auf das Meer und auf die Reise, aber sehr selten gesellt sich noch vor dem Winter der Vater auch zur Familie; daher jene oben erwähnten kleinen Gesellschaften aus lauter grauen Vögeln bestehen und die alten Männchen einzeln herumschwärmen.

FEINDE

Die grossen **Edelfalken** und **Habichte** verfolgen die Alten, wenn sie von einem Wasser zum andern über Land streichen, können ihnen aber, sobald sie Wasser erlangen, nichts anhaben, indem sie sich hineinstürzen und durch flinkes Tauchen ihren Klauen entgehen. Alle Raubtiere des Nordens suchen ihnen die Eier zu stehlen, was auch **Raben, Krähen** und **Elstern** tun.

NUTZEN

Das Fleisch auch dieser Art schmeckt so sehr nach Fischtran, dass es dem verfeinerten Geschmack des gebildeten Europäers widersteht, wenn ihm derselbe nicht durch künstliche Zubereitung, wenigstens zum grossen Teile, benommen wurde. Den rohen Völkern des hohen Nordens ist es jedoch ein angenehmes Nahrungsmittel. Besser mögen wohl die Eier schmecken, die man im Norden zu erhalten sucht durch planmässiges Wegnehmen nicht der ganzen Gelege, was die Weibchen veranlasst, wohl dreimal so viel Eier zu legen, als ohne das Dazwischenkommen des Menschen geschehen würde. Erst ganz vor kurzem wurde mir von einem in **Lappland** sammelnden Forscher versichert, dass Brutkästen dort allgemein im Gebrauche seien und dass nicht allein der Mittel- und der Gänsesäger, sondern merkwürdigerweise auch vielerlei Entenarten sie gern zum Brüten benutzten, so namentlich auch die **Samtente**, die **Bergente** und andere mehr, von denen man es noch viel weniger erwarten möchte, weil wir von ihnen bisher noch nicht erfahren haben, dass sie von Natur mitunter auch in hohlen Baumstämmen ihre Brut machten.*

Die Federn sind wie Entenfedern zu benutzen und vorzüglich schön sind die reichlich vorhandenen Dunen.

SCHADEN

Weil auch diese Säger grösstenteils von kleinen Fischen sich nähren, so tun sie der Vermehrung derselben grossen Abbruch, zumal wo jene Vögel häufig sind und sich scharenweise aufhalten. Sie vertilgen eine so grosse Menge, dass sie der Fischbrut in geregelten Fischereien kultivierter Länder von grösstem Nachteil sein würden, wenn sie hier auch in so grosser Anzahl erscheinen und für längere Zeit verweilen wollten. Im hohen Norden achtet man aber die kleinen Fischchen nicht, in den **Dänischen** Staaten sind diese Säger dagegen schon als Fischverderber verschrien, und bei uns würde man auch den einzeln zu uns Verirrten die kleinen

---

* Vielleicht sagt ihnen der Instinkt, weil dort die auf dem Erdboden befindlichen Nester der Enten und anderer so viele Verderber an den Raubtieren des Landes finden, dass ihnen jene Kästen mehr Sicherheit vor diesen gewähren; doch scheint ihnen die Fähigkeit abzugehen, zu bedenken, dass sie dadurch dem Menschen, einem in mancher Hinsicht zwar milderen Feinde, in die Hände fallen, also immer nur aus zwei Übeln das kleinste wählen.

Fische nicht gönnen, sie vielmehr als schädliche Vögel verfolgen, wenn man sie auf Streich- und Brutteichen für Karpfen, Forellen und andere geschätzte Fischarten anträfe und gewahr würde, welche Menge kleiner Fische auch schon der einzelne zu seinem Lebensunterhalt bedarf.

// DER SUMPFROHRSÄNGER //

ACROCEPHALUS PALUSTRIS

Sumpfsänger, Sumpfschilfsänger, Rohrsänger, Rohrschmätzer, Rohrgrasmücke, olivengrauer Rohrschirf, olivengrauer Spitzkopf, Weiderich und Weidenzeisig.

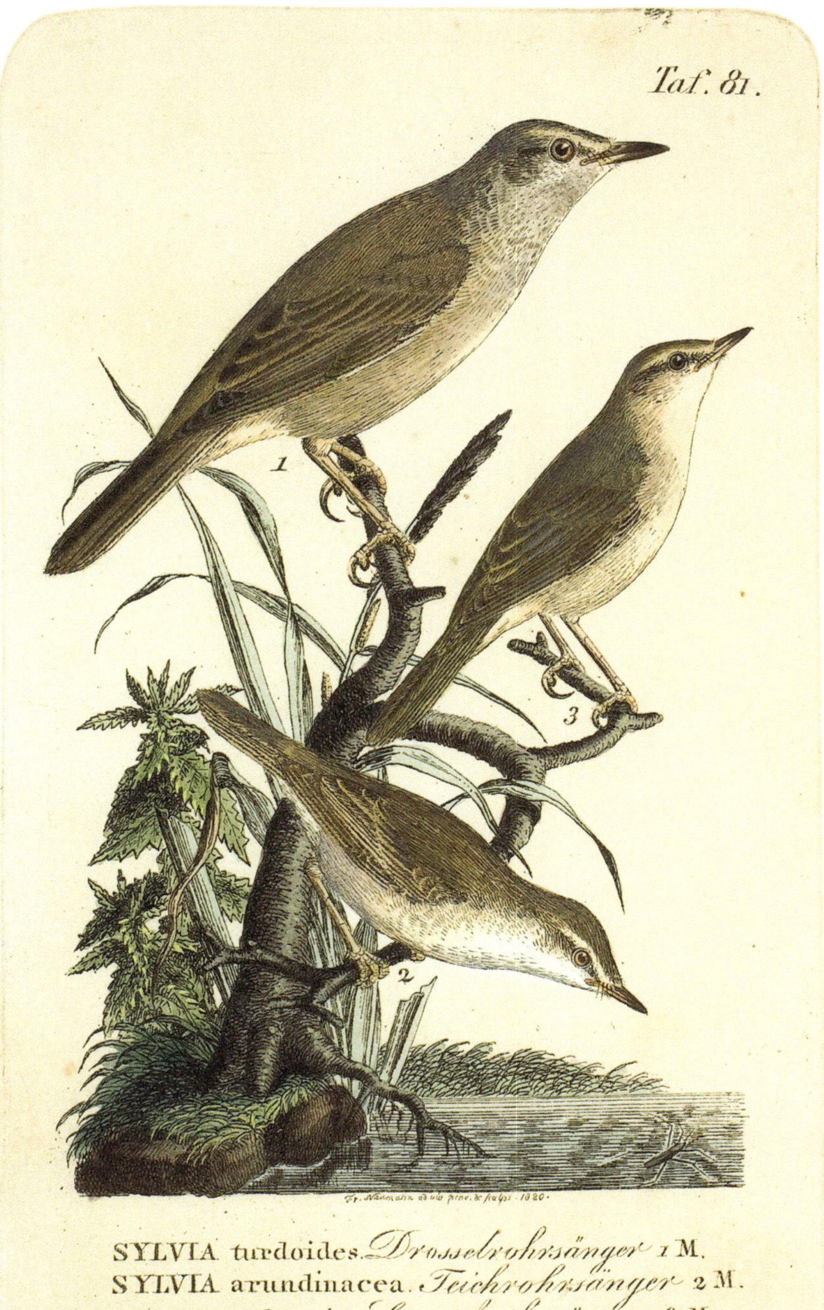

SYLVIA turdoides. *Drosselrohrsänger* 1 M.
SYLVIA arundinacea. *Teichrohrsänger* 2 M.
SYLVIA palustris. *Sumpfrohrsänger* 3 M.

KENNZEICHEN DER ART

Oberleib **grünlich** rostgrau, oder matt olivengrau; ein Strich über dem Auge und der Unterleib weiss, mit ockergelbem Anfluge; Mundwinkel orangegelb. Länge 14,0 cm.

BESCHREIBUNG

Dieser Rohrsänger mag wohl sehr häufig mit dem Teichrohrsänger verwechselt werden, welches Schicksal er früher immer gehabt hatte, bis BECHSTEIN ihn zuerst als eigene Art beschrieb. Es hält auch in der Tat ungemein schwer, beide Arten, den **Sumpfrohrsänger** vom **Teichrohrsänger** zu unterscheiden, zumal wenn beide eine Zeit lang ausgestopft gestanden haben und die Farben etwas verbleicht sind; denn beim ersteren geht der grüne Anflug und beim letzteren der rostgelbe am Oberleibe nach und nach zum Teil verloren, und die bleibende Grundfarbe ist nur wenig verschieden. Der Unterschied im Schnabel- und Flügelbau ist zwar standhafter, aber doch zu subtil, um sehr in die Augen zu fallen. In der Grösse sind sie einander ebenfalls gleich; doch hat der **Sumpfrohrsänger** eine etwas stärkere Brust und sieht daher grösser und nicht so überaus schlank aus wie der **Teichrohrsänger**, obgleich die Längenmaße beider übereinstimmen.

Ganz anders ist es dagegen, wenn man beide Arten in ihrem ganz verschiedenen Leben und Wirken beobachtet; da zeigt sich ein höchst auffallender Unterschied, viel grösser als der zwischen Zilpzalp und Fitis, und wer ihre Wohnorte, ihren Nestbau und den so sehr verschiedenen Gesang der Männchen beider Arten zu beobachten Gelegenheit hatte, wird gewiss nie mehr an der Verschiedenheit dieser an Gestalt und Farbe sich so sehr ähnelnden Arten zweifeln. Sehr verschieden in der Farbe sind die Jungen beider; denn bei denen des **Teichrohrsängers** ist an den oberen Teilen ein sattes Rostgelb, bei denen des **Sumpfrohrsängers** ein ziemlich dunkles Olivengrün vorherrschend.

Wegen des stärkeren Rumpfes nähert sich der Vogel in der Grösse der **Dorngrasmücke**, allein er erreicht die Maße derselben nicht. Seine Länge beträgt 13 bis 13,5 cm, wovon 5,3 bis 5,5 cm auf den weichfederigen, abgerundeten Schwanz abgehen, dessen Federn am Ende alle rund zugespitzt sind und seitwärts so an Länge abnehmen, dass die äusserste Seitenfeder kaum 8 mm kürzer als eine der mittelsten ist. Die Flügelbreite ist 18,8 bis 19,4 cm, die Länge des Flügels vom Bug bis zur Spitze 6,7 bis 6,9 cm (daher ein längerer Flügel als beim Teichrohrsänger), und die ruhenden Flügel lassen vom Schwanze nicht ganz 3 cm bedeckt.

Der Schnabel ist nicht so gestreckt und schlank wie beim **Teichrohrsänger**, sondern etwas kürzer, dicker, runder, an der Wurzel weniger breitgedrückt, nach vorn mehr zusammengedrückt, daher auch die Schneiden des Oberkiefers nicht so stark überstehen, das ovale Nasenloch kleiner, und der halbe Hautdeckel über der Öffnung desselben weniger aufgeblasen; alles zwar merkliche und standhafte Unterschiede, aber nur dann etwas auffallend, wenn man die Schnäbel beider Vögeln gegeneinander halten kann. Im übrigen hat er dieselbe Gestalt und Farbe; denn oben und an der Spitze ist er graulichschwarzbraun, an den Schneiden und beinahe an der ganzen Unterkinnlade gelblichfleischfarben, die aufgeschwollenen Mundwinkel rötlichgelb; Zunge und Rachen orangegelb, blasser als am **Teichrohrsänger**. Seine Länge beträgt nur 10,8 mm (bei Jungen nur 9,8 mm), die Höhe an der Wurzel 3,9 mm, und die Breite daselbst ebensoviel. Über den Mundwinkeln stehen drei bis vier ansehnliche schwarze Schnurrborsten.

Die schlanken Füsse haben fast gestiefelte Läufe, geschilderte Zehenrücken, feinwarzige Sohlen und starke, etwas breit gedrückte, wenig gekrümmte spitzige Nägel, welche immer etwas kürzer und stärker aussehen als beim Teichrohrsänger. Ihre Farbe ist gelblichfleischfarben, die der Nägel etwas dunkler, die Zehensohlen gelb. Bei jüngeren ist die Fleischfarbe schmutziger; aber schwarzbraune Füsse habe ich weder bei einem lebenden noch ausgestopften Vogel dieser Art, überhaupt bei keinem inländischen Rohrsänger jemals gesehen. Die Höhe des Laufes beträgt 23,5 mm, die Länge der Mittelzehe ohne die fast 6 mm lange Kralle 11,8 mm, die der Hinterzehe ohne den 5,9 mm langen Nagel 7,8 mm.

Das Kleid dieses sanft befiederten Vogels ist sehr einfach und unansehnlich gefärbt. Die Zügel, den Hinterteil der Wangen und von der Stirn an alle oberen Teile des Vogels deckt ein mattes grünliches Braungrau, fast wie das der **Gartengrasmücke**, das am Bürzel etwas lichter ausfällt; die dunkelgraubraunen Flügel- und Schwanzfedern sind mit der Rückenfarbe gekantet, doch so, dass an den grossen Schwingen, zumal an den Enden dieser, die Käntchen schmäler und lichter werden, und die vordere Schwinge (eigentlich die zweite, denn die erste ist sehr klein, kurz und schmal) nebst der äussersten Schwanzfeder ein weissgraues Aussensäumchen hat. Vom Nasenloch über das Auge zieht sich ein verloschener gelblichweisser Streifen, welcher wenig bemerkbar ist und hinter dem Auge aufhört; Kinn und Kehle sind weiss, alle übrigen Teile des Unterkörpers trübweiss, mit ockergelbem Anfluge, welcher an den Halsseiten und in den Weichen ziemlich stark wird, unter den Flügeln und an der hinteren Seite der Schenkel aber in die Rückenfarbe übergeht. Die untere Seite der Schwung- und Schwanzfedern ist von einem sehr lichten glänzenden Braungrau; die unteren Flügeldeckfedern sind gelblichweiss.

Zwischen **Männchen** und **Weibchen** ist in der Farbe kein standhafter Unterschied zu finden, es gibt blässere und dunklere Exemplare von beiden Geschlechtern; aber das Weibchen ist meistens etwas kleiner als das Männchen. **Jüngere Vögel** sind gewöhnlich dunkler und grüner als die älteren, was auch von dem noch frischen Gefieder im **Herbste** gilt, denn der grünliche und gelbe Anflug verbleicht im Frühjahr und Sommer sehr. Solche abgebleichten Exemplare sind dann sehr schwer von dem **Teichrohrsänger** zu unterschieden.

Die **Jungen** vor der ersten Mauser sehen ihren Eltern vollkommen ähnlich, nur von oben grüner und von unten gelber. Die Rückenfarbe nähert sich dem Olivengrünen, und dies unterscheidet sie auffallend von den jungen **Teichrohrsängern**, die an den oberen Teilen ein gelbliches Rostbraun tragen und an den unteren Teilen mit einem rötlichen Rostgelb sehr stark angeflogen sind, so dass sie im ganzen röter, jene aber grüner aussehen als ihre Eltern. Von Flecken an der Kehle und sonst wo ist bei beiden niemals eine Spur vorhanden.

Die alten Vögel mausern Anfang August, die jungen einige Wochen später.

AUFENTHALT

Dieser Vogel ist zu lange verkannt und mit anderen verwechselt worden, als dass sich über seine Verbreitung viel sagen liesse. Nur erst neuerdings hat man in Erfahrung gebracht, dass er vornehmlich das mittägliche **Europa** bewohnt, im mittleren weniger häufig ist und im nördlichen wahrscheinlich nicht viel höher als bis **Dänemark** hinaufgeht. Nach TEMMINCK soll er in **Italien** am Po und an den Ufern der Donau von **Österreich** abwärts gemein sein, nach SCHINZ in der **Schweiz** hin und wieder vorkommen; nach BECHSTEIN in **Thüringen** und **Franken** sich selten zeigen; so soll er auch bei **Göttingen** vorkommen. Ich selbst habe diesen Vogel, so lange ich ihn genau kennen gelernt, hier im **Anhaltischen** und dem angrenzenden **Sachsen** und **Brandenburg** alle Jahre eben nicht sehr sparsam bemerkt, in **Holstein**, besonders im **Süderdithmarschen**, aber sehr häufig gesehen und zur Genüge beobachtet.

Er ist gleich den übrigen Rohrsängern ein **Zugvogel**, kommt als solcher erst spät im Frühling zu uns und verweilt auch nicht länger als etwa vier Monate im Sommer hier, worauf er sich wegbegibt und seine Winterwohnung unter einem milderen Himmel aufschlägt. Er kommt selten vor dem Mai hier an, vielmehr sind die ersten Wochen dieses Monats seine eigentliche Zugzeit; allein auch noch zu Ende desselben, bis gegen die Mitte des Juni, habe ich ihn hier, noch auf dem Zuge begriffen, angetroffen. Nur in guten, warmen Frühjahren hört man ihn zuweilen schon in der letzten Woche des April. Auf seinen Herbstreisen zieht er ebenso langsam, nämlich vom Ende des August an, den ganzen September hindurch, wo er sich mit Ende desselben oder Anfang Oktober endlich verliert. Seine Reisen macht er einzeln und bloss des Nachts. Im Herbst streichen sie familienweise weg, sie müssen sich aber auf der Reise bald zerstreuen; denn diejenigen, welche hier ausgebrütet wurden, verschwinden oft mit ihren Eltern in einer Nacht, und doch kommen die, welche nördlicher gewohnt hatten, nur einzeln hier durch.

In den grossen Rohrwäldern, wo man die beiden vorherbeschriebenen Arten fast ausschliesslich antrifft, darf man den Sumpfrohrsänger nicht suchen, und er weicht hierin sehr merklich von dem **Teichrohrsänger** ab. Er ist mehr Waldvogel; doch liebt er auch nur niedriges, sumpfiges Gebüsch und das, was sich an den Ufern der Flüsse, Bäche und Wassergräben, an Seen und Teichen befindet, und in grossen ebenen Wäldern sucht man ihn ebenso vergeblich wie in Gebirgswaldungen. Dagegen ist er sehr gern in solchen Gärten, durch welche ein Bach fliesst, oder die an einem Flusse, Teiche und sonst am Wasser liegen oder wenigstens von Wassergräben durchschnitten werden. Er verlangt aber, dass in dem Wasser oder an dessen Ufern auch Rohr, Schilf und andere hohe Wasserpflanzen wachsen, ob er gleich nur selten sich in solche begibt und, wenn er es haben kann, lieber im niedrigen dichten Buschholze herumkriecht, in den Gärten die Bohnen-, Erbsen- und Samenrübenbeete, die Hanfäcker und in den Marschen die Äcker mit hohem Getreide, Pferdebohnen und besonders die Rapsstücken aufsucht. Weidengebüsch scheint ihm indessen so notwendig, wie dem **Teichrohrsänger** das Rohr. In den

Marschländern traf ich ihn nur da an, wo bei den Gehöften ausser Obstbäumen und anderem Gebüsch auch Buschweiden standen; in den, wie bekannt, mit sich durchkreuzenden Wassergräben im Übermaß versehenen Feldern der Marschen auch immer nur da, wo Weidengebüsch wuchs und einige Bäume standen. War nicht weit von einer Weidenpartie ein Stück Feld mit Raps bebaut, so durfte man daselbst gewiss nicht vergeblich nach ihm suchen. Im Kirchspiel **Brunsbüttel** im Süderdithmarschen ist dieser Vogel sehr gemein, auch um **Meldorf** und anderwärts in den Holsteinischen Marschen. In der **Schweiz** traf ihn DR. SCHINZ in einer ebenen, mit Bächen durchschnittenen Gegend am Vierwaldstädter See in Hanf- und Getreidestücken auch häufig an. In der hiesigen Gegend sah ich ihn auch mehrmals mitten im hohen Getreide, wo ein Wassergraben hindurchlief oder ein Teich nicht zu weit entfernt war, am häufigsten aber in den Buschweidengehegen unserer Flüsse, Saale, Mulde und Elbe, wo er auch nistet; in der Zugzeit aber oftmals nahe bei Dörfern und Städten auf Kopfweiden, in Pflaumen- und Kirschanpflanzungen und sonst auf Bäumen und im Gebüsch, selbst zuweilen weit vom Wasser.

Hinsichtlich seines Aufenthaltes und seines Betragens ähnelt er fast ebenso sehr den **Laubvögeln** wie den Rohrsängern und steht so recht eigentlich, selbst der Farbe nach, zwischen beiden Familien als Bindeglied da, namentlich zwischen dem **Gelbspötter** und dem **Teichrohrsänger**. Dass man ihn selten im Rohre und Schilfe sieht, ist schon erwähnt worden; wenn dies aber geschieht, so ist es gewiss nie mitten in den grossen Wäldern, die das Rohr und Kolbenschilf auf manchen Teichen und Seen bildet, sondern bloss nahe am Ufer und da, wo dieses auch mit Gebüsch von Weiden und dergl. bewachsen ist. Man sieht ihn nicht allein viel öfter als die anderen Arten in dem höheren Buschwerk, sondern häufig selbst in den Zweigen höherer Bäume, in einer Höhe, zu welcher sich fast nie ein anderer Rohrsänger versteigt; auch ist er beinahe mehr und daher wahrscheinlich lieber in den Baumkronen von solcher Höhe, wie z. B. der Pflaumen- oder Zwetschenbäume, als in dem niedrigen Gestrüpp, und er besucht die einzelnen Weiden oder andere Bäume, in deren Nähe er vielleicht im Getreide, Raps und dergl. wohnt, den Tag über ungemein oft, lässt er sich auf freien Ästen oder Spitzen der Zweige, auf hingesteckten, über das Getreide emporragenden Stöcken, auf Pfählen, auf den Stöcken, die man Bohnen, Erbsen und anderen Gemüsepflanzen zu geben pflegt, sehr oft sehen und ähnelt hierin einigermassen dem **Schilfrohrsänger**, welcher jedoch niemals so hoch auf die Bäume geht.

Es ist besonders noch zu bemerken, dass unser Vogel, ob er gleich die Nähe des Wasser liebt, doch nicht gern über demselben verweilt, sondern die meiste Zeit zwar gern neben dem Wasser, doch über dem Erdboden und selbst über trockenem Boden sich aufhält. Trifft man ihn ja einmal im Rohr über dem Wasser, so flieht er, wenn man ihn verfolgt, dem Ufer und dem Gebüsch zu, ganz entgegengesetzt von fast allen übrigen Arten dieser Gruppe, die gewöhnlich nach der Wasserseite zu entfliehen und sich je weiter desto lieber vom Ufer zu entfernen und im Schilf und Rohr zu verstecken suchen.

Ihrer unruhigen aber freieren Lebensart wegen werden sie überall bemerklicher als andere Rohrsänger, doch im Herbst und überhaupt auf ihrem Zuge ebenfalls auch weniger als im Frühjahr. Sie verlieren sich im Herbst auch leichter unter den verschiedenen Laubvögeln und anderen ähnlichen kleinen befiederten Bewohnern der Gebüsche. In wirklichen Brüchen und Morästen habe ich ihn niemals angetroffen.

EIGENSCHAFTEN

Der **Sumpfrohrsänger** ist ein sehr netter, lustiger, unsteter Vogel, hurtig in allen seinen Bewegungen, im Hüpfen und Durchschlüpfen der Gebüsche und des dichtesten Gestrüpps wie im Fluge gleich gewandt, kühn und unternehmend im Streit mit seinesgleichen, was er auch öfters andere ihm nahe wohnende kleine Vögel fühlen lässt, daher es in der Tat eine Lust ist, seinem Treiben und Wirken zuzusehen. Nirgends hat er lange Ruhe; bald hört man ihn soeben hier, in wenigen Augenblicken vielleicht schon hundert Schritte weiter, wobei er aber nicht etwa, wie die anderen Rohrsänger, bloss im Gebüsch forthüpft, sondern vielmehr flattert und fliegt, ja ungezwungen ganze Strecken über das Freie hinstreift. Er hat deshalb auch auf Bäumen und im Gebüsch in seinem Benehmen eine grosse Ähnlichkeit mit dem **Gelbspötter**, doch hüpft er mehr in geduckter Stellung, woran wieder der Rohrsänger nicht zu verkennen ist. Seine Sitten sind überhaupt durchgängig eine Mischung aus denen der Laubvögel und Rohrsänger. Im Klettern und Anklammern ist er ebenso geschickt wie die letzteren, im Fluge aber noch gewandter. Oft stürzt er sich, durch die Luft fortschiessend, aus den Zweigen eines ziemlich hohen Baumes schief herab ins niedere Gesträuch, ein andermal schwingt er sich ebenso aus der Tiefe zur Höhe auf, oder er fliegt gerade fort und ungezwungen eine gute Strecke über das Freie, von Baum zu Baum, oder von einem Busch zum anderen, und nicht etwa ängstlich am Boden hin, sondern meist keck in angemessener Höhe durch die Luft, was man alles von den übrigen kleinen Rohrsängern fast niemals sieht.

Nimmt man an einem Rohrgraben zwei entgegengesetzte Punkte an, wo an jedem etwa ein Baum oder ein Weidenstrauch steht, so lässt sich ein **Teichrohrsänger** im Rohr des Grabens von einem Ende zum anderen treiben, ohne dass man ihn zu sehen bekommt; nicht also der **Sumpfrohrsänger**. Überraschte man ihn ja einmal im Rohre eines solchen Grabens, so würde er, sobald man ihn vor sich hin zu treiben versuchen wollte, sogleich seitwärts heraus und schnell dem Gebüsch zueilen, und scheuchte man ihn aus diesem, so würde er nicht im nahen Rohr, sondern lieber im entfernteren Gebüsch Schutz suchen und, um schnell dahin zu kommen, eher einige hundert Schritte über das Freie fliegen, als im Rohre des Grabens forthüpfen.

Sein Flug ist auch schneller, nicht so hüpfend, sondern in mehr geregelten und grösseren Bogen, auf kurzen Strecken flatternd und fortschiessend und von einem nahen Busch zum anderen, besonders in der Brutzeit, oft verstellt zitternd, wobei der etwas ausgebreitete Schwanz ein wenig herabhängt, was im Fortfliegen fast allemal, doch weniger auffallend, den Rohrsänger in ihm charakterisiert. Nur bei besonderen Veranlassungen zuckt er etwas mit den Flügeln und dem ein wenig ausgebreiteten Schwanze; sonst trägt er den letzteren im ruhigen Forthüpfen, wie die anderen Arten, etwas hängend und den Hals eingezogen.

Seine Lockstimme hört man nur selten; es ist ein schmatzender und schnalzender Ton und klingt wie die fast aller übrigen Rohrsänger, **tschätsch**, im Unwillen oder bei Besorgnis wird auch ebenso ein schnarchendes **Rrr** ausgestossen; allein der Gesang des Männchens übertrifft vorzugsweise nicht allein die Gesänge sämtlicher Rohrsängerarten, sondern auch viele der übrigen Singvögel. Er steht weit über dem des **Gelbspötters** erhaben, dem er zwar etwas ähnelt, dabei aber vielmehr flötende und sanftere Töne, eine grössere Abwechslung und ausserordentliche Mannigfaltigkeit hat, und der letzteren wegen selbst die Gesänge der **Garten-** und **Mönchgrasmücke** übertrifft. Man darf ihn freilich nicht nach dem beurteilen, wie man ihn im Frühjahr von Vögeln, die noch auf der Reise begriffen sind, öfters hört; denn diese singen noch nicht laut, sie können die Melodie noch nicht vollständig, und dieses Stümpern hat sowohl Ähnlichkeit mit dem Gesange des **Gelb-**

spötters, wie des **Teichrohrsängers**, daher man ihn leicht überhören kann, wie selbst manchem Vogelkenner, der diesen herrlichen Sänger noch nicht an seinem Brutorte hörte, begegnet sein mag. Ganz anders ist es, wenn man diesen dort in seiner Vollständigkeit aus voller Kehle hat singen hören und das Thema dieses lieblichen Gesanges hat auffassen können; dann wird man den Sänger auch an jenem Gestümper wieder erkennen.

Der vollständige Gesang ähnelt zwar auf eine entfernte Weise dem des **Gelbspötters**, keineswegs aber dem des **Teichrohrsängers**; doch liegt etwas in den Tönen mancher Strophen, was den Rohrsänger in dem singenden Vogel nicht verkennen lässt. Er besteht aus einer Menge höchst abwechselnder Strophen, wovon viele sanftpfeifend und wirklich flötend sind, manche auch wieder eine täuschende Nachahmung anderer Vogelstimmen zu sein scheinen. Bald flötet die eine Strophe, als wenn sie aus dem Gesange einer **Drossel** entlehnt wäre; bald sind es zwitschernde und schirkende Töne, die auf einmal in hellpfeifende oder sanft lullende, in auf- und absteigende, in kurz abgebrochene oder in geschleifte übergehen; bald folgen Töne, wie aus einem der Gesänge der **Garten-** oder **Mönchgrasmücke** erborgt, dann wieder die wiederholt nachgeahmten Lockstimmen der **Rauchschwalbe**, der **Kohlmeise**, selbst **sperlingsartige** Stimmen in dem buntesten Gemisch durcheinander, dass man nicht satt wird, ihm zuzuhören. Dabei liegt soviel Kraft in seinen Stimmorganen, dass man diesen ausserordentlich anmutigen Gesang, zumal bei der Nacht, ziemlich weit vernimmt; denn er singt von Ende April oder Anfang Mai bis in den Juli hinein, nicht allein vom frühen Morgen bis an den Abend, meist den ganzen Tag über ungemein fleissig, sondern auch die ganze Nacht hindurch.

Er ersetzt daher den Marschgegenden einigermassen die **Nachtigall**; und obgleich sein Gesang dem dieser Königin der Sänger nicht gleich kommt, so klingt er doch in der Stille der Nacht so lieblich und so bezaubernd angenehm, dass man jene einstweilen darüber vergessen kann. Weil dann der herrliche Sänger weniger als am Tage gestört wird, den entzückten Zuhörer aber keine anderen Singvögel mit ihren verschiedenartigen Stimmen in seinen Betrachtungen unterbrechen, so ist der Genuss, ihm in einer warmen Nacht des Brachmonats zuzuhören, für den Naturfreund unvergleichlich zu nennen.

Er sitzt bei Tage während des Singens nur selten still, geht dabei vielmehr häufig seinen Nahrungsgeschäften nach oder neckt und jagt sich singend mit seinen Kameraden oder wohl auch einmal mit einem anderen kleinen Vogel herum. Nur früh morgens sah ich ihn oft frei auf einem Pfahle, einer Brückenlehne, einem freien Aste, auf der Spitze eines Steckens oder eines entblätterten Zweiges, die über dichtem Gebüsch hervorragten, sitzen und ununterbrochen sein liebliches Lied singen. Er lässt dabei die Flügel behaglich hängen, bläst die Kehle auf und richtet den Kopf und den stark bewegten Schnabel etwas aufwärts. Man kann dabei ganz nahe kommen und ihn lange betrachten, ehe er von seinem erhabenen Sitze herabspringt und mit zitternder Flügelbewegung dem Gebüsche, dem Geröhricht oder den hohen Feldfrüchten zuflattert, aber dann hier meistens noch fortsingt. Sind seine Lieblingssitze nahe an Wegen, wie dies in den Marschen häufig die Säulen sind, an welchen daran befestigtes Gitterwerk oder Bretter zur Versperrung der Brücken an den einzelnen Ackerstücken dienen, so gewöhnt er sich so an die vorbeipassierenden Menschen, dass er fast alle Furcht vergisst, und ich bin oft kaum ein paar Schritt an ihm vorbeigefahren. Im Getreide wiegt sich das singende Männchen oft auf hohen starken Getreidehalmen und auf solchen Pflanzen, die etwas höher als die übrigen sind, auf hohen Rapsstauden, Pferdebohnen, Hanfstengeln und dergl. Geht man da auf dasselbe zu, so entschlüpft es in dem übrigen, beunruhigt man es auch hier, so fliegt es meistens heraus und ein ganzes Stück weg.

Den Liebhabern, welche gern singende Stubenvögel halten, würde dieser Vogel gewiss viel Freude machen, wenn sie sich die Mühe geben wollten, ihn zu zähmen und an ein Stubenfutter zu gewöhnen. Dies kann auch für manche, besonders für diejenigen so sehr schwer nicht sein, die den viel weichlicheren **Gelbspötter** zu zähmen und zu erhalten wissen, dass er selbst mehrere Jahr im Käfig ausdauert. Mir sind freilich nur misslungene Versuche der Art von unserem Vogel bekannt; dies beweist aber noch die Unmöglichkeit nicht; vielmehr ist es mir höchst wahrscheinlich, dass er sich viel leichter als der erwähnte Vogel an ein gewisses Futter gewöhnen, bei der Wartung, die beim **Gelbspötter** angegeben wird, selbst länger als dieser halten müsse, weil er lange nicht so zärtlich, vielmehr seiner Grösse nach ein viel derberer Vogel ist. Und hätte es auch hier wirklich ebenso viel Schwierigkeiten wie dort, so würde der herrliche Gesang dieses Vogels die angewandte Mühe doch reichlich vergelten.

NAHRUNG

Vielerlei Insekten, als: Mücken, Fliegen, Schnaken, Hafte, kleine Libellen, Köcherfliegen, Motten und kleine Schmetterlinge, nebst den Räupchen derselben, Spinnen und mancherlei Insekteneier, kleine Rüsselkäferchen, Blatt- und Sonnenkäferchen, Schilfkäfer, verschiedene Arten Blattläuse und mehrerlei andere kleine zwei- und vierflügelige Insekten suchen sie im dichten Gebüsch, in den belaubten Bäumen, im Weidengesträuch und im Geröhricht an den Ufern der Gewässer oder in Gärten und auf wasserreichen Feldern auf und fangen sie teils im Forthüpfen und sitzend, teils auch nach ihnen springend oder sie im kurzen Fluge verfolgend. Oft sieht man sie lange an einem Blatte picken und davon die kleinsten jener Geschöpfchen ablesen, daher sie auch die Blätter sorgfältig von allen Seiten besehen und sich hier beinahe ganz wie die Laubvögel betragen. Aus den Getreidestücken fliegen sie öfters einige Fuss hoch nach vorbeifliegenden Insekten, stürzen sich aber damit sogleich wieder zurück, um sich in den hohen Feldfrüchten zu verbergen. In den Hanfstücken finden sie eine unsägliche Menge kleiner Fliegen, in den Rapsäckern ausser diesen ungemein viel kleine Käferchen, welche ihnen den Aufenthalt daselbst angenehm machen, weil sie sich selbiger zur Speise bedienen.

Sie fressen zuweilen auch Johannisbeeren und im Herbst gern Holunderbeeren, wenigstens diese weit lieber oder öfter als man es von anderen Rohrsängern sieht. Gewiss fressen sie auch die Beeren von Faulbaum und Hartriegel.

FORTPFLANZUNG

Diese Vögel nisten hin und wieder in **Deutschland**, in der **Schweiz** und anderwärts; auch in der hiesigen Gegend hier und da im niedrigen Gebüsch unserer Flussufer, vorzüglich häufig aber in den Marschen **Holsteins**. Sie suchen sich solche Orte, wo an den Ufern der Gewässer ausser Schilf und Rohr viel niedriges Gebüsch, besonders von Weiden, womöglich mit Rohr vermischt, wächst; wo rohrreiche Gräben oder auch blosse Bäche sich zwischen Äckern durchziehen, auf welchen hohe Feldfrüchte, als Raps, Pferde- oder Saubohnen, Hanf, auch wohl Weizen gebaut werden, und wo es auch Weiden gibt; die Gärten, in welchen es nicht an niedrigem Buschwerk und an Wassergräben fehlt; die Ufer grosser mit Buschweiden umgebener Teiche und ähnliche Orte; aber niemals weder die eigentlichen Rohrwälder grosser Teiche und Landseen noch die Brüche und Moräste.

Das Nest steht niemals über dem Wasser, nicht einmal über morastigem Boden. Immer steht es an solchen Stellen, wo unten fester, wenngleich nicht immer ganz trockener Boden ist, wie dies an den Ufern, wo man es oft nahe beim Wasser findet, nicht anders sein kann. Man kann wenigstens jederzeit trockenen Fusses zu selbigem gelangen.

In den Marschländern fand ich es allemal in der Nähe der Gehöfte, besonders in den Gärten, an den bald mit hohem Rohr angefüllten, bald wenig verwachsenen Gräben, allemal am Ufer derselben, bald dicht am Wasser, bald mehrere Schritte davon abwärts, in niedrigem, mit Rohr vermischtem Gebüsch, in einem Nesselbusche, in einem Büschel Wasserampfer und Rohr, auf einem ganz kleinen, mit Rohr, Nesseln, Weiderich, oder auch bloss mit etwas Rohr und hohem Gras umgebenen, niedrigen Bäumchen. In den Rapsstücken soll es an den sie durchschneidenden Gräben an ähnlichen Orten, seltener aber tief im Raps selbst gefunden werden. Der **Teichrohrsänger** nistet oft ganz in der Nähe des **Sumpfrohrsängers**, zuweilen auf demselben Graben, dieser dann jedoch stets am Ufer **neben** dem Wasser, jener aber allemal im Graben **über** dem Wasser; umgekehrt fällt es nie vor.

Das Nest steht meistens zwischen 30 bis 85 cm hoch vom Boden, selten der Erde näher und, soviel ich von glaubwürdigen Personen erfahren konnte, niemals unmittelbar auf dem Erdboden selbst.* Die Bauart ist denen anderer Rohrsänger ähnlich; am Boden nämlich grösstenteils frei, ohne Unterstützung, ist es so zwischen Rohr- und andere Pflanzenstengel, starke Grashalme und dünne, aufrechtstehende Baumzweige befestigt, dass diese das gleichsam schwebende Nest nur an seinen Seitenwänden durchbohren, wo die Materialien desselben so fest um diese gewickelt und wieder mit den Wänden verwebt sind, dass es nicht hinabgleiten kann. An den rauhen und beblätterten Stengeln der Nesseln hält es besonders sehr fest. Einmal fand ich es auch auf einem 85 cm hohen Eschenbäumchen, oben im Gipfel, fast ganz frei. Weil hier das darum stehende Gras und die einzelnen Rohrstengel nicht hinaufreichten, so konnte auch keiner mit dem Neste verwebt werden, und so hing es

---

* Es wäre dies auch ganz gegen die Art und Weise sämtlicher Rohrsänger, die alle etwas Charakteristisches im Nestbau, nämlich in der Befestigung des Nestes an senkrechten Pflanzenstengeln und Zweigen haben, die dann nutzlos wäre. Wenn daher auch das von SCHINZ im I. Heft seiner *Nester und Eier der Vögel Deutschl.* abgebildete Nest mit den Eiern echt ist, so ist es gewiss nicht seine Stellung (es steht auf dem Erdboden), oder man müsste es in dieser Hinsicht zu den seltenen Ausnahmen von der Regel zählen.

sehr kühn an einer Seite des oben in drei zarte Gabelzweige geteilten Gipfels, an welche es, obgleich zwei Dritteile seines Umfangs und der ganze Boden ohne alle Unterstützung waren, wie ein Korb angehängt und gut befestigt war.

Alle Nester dieser Vögel, welche ich teils selbst aufsuchte, teils in den Sammlungen meiner Freunde sah, waren von derselben Bauart wie fast alle Rohrsängernester, als solche sogleich zu erkennen und von anderen ähnlichen, z. B. Grasmückennestern, auf den ersten Blick zu unterscheiden. Übrigens darf man sie nie tief in grösseren Dickichten, sondern näher dem Rande derselben, hauptsächlich in einzelnen kleineren Büschchen, dicht am Rande der Gräben und dergl. suchen. Weiss man dies erst, so finden sie sich leicht auf, ob sie gleich im übrigen nichts weniger als frei stehen. Die meiste Schwierigkeit beim Aufsuchen ist die grosse Unruhe dieser Vögel; denn bald singt das Männchen hier, bald einige hundert Schritt abwärts, und so treibt es sich den Tag über in einem viel grösseren Kreise herum als andere ähnliche Arten. Merkt man sich aber die Stelle, wo es des Nachts oder am frühen Morgen sang, dann findet man auch bald das Nest.

Die Eier, deren man meistens vier und fünf, seltener sechs in einem Neste findet, sind stets etwas grösser als die des **Teichrohrsängers**, und meistens von einer mehr länglichen, sehr niedlichen Eiform. Kürzer geformte, daher denen des letztgenannten Vogels ähnlichere gehören hier ebenso zu den Ausnahmen wie bei jenen die länglichen.

Die Eier haben eine zarte Schale, welche glatt aber nicht glänzend ist, und sind auch hinsichtlich der Farbe und Zeichnungen von den Eiern des **Teichrohrsängers** leicht zu unterscheiden, indem sie stets heller oder weisser aussehen. Der Grund ist schön bläulichweiss und spielt nur bei den dichter gefleckten ein wenig ins Grünliche, wird aber durch ungemein feine graue Pünktchen etwas getrübt; ausser diesen gibt es nun auf denselben noch grössere Punkte und zum Teil grosse umbrabrauner Farbe, und endlich noch in diesen hin und wieder braunschwarze Punkte oder Strichelchen. Manche haben nur sehr wenig vom Braun, und die grossen aschgrauen Flecke sind dann zuweilen Augen ähnlich, in der Mitte mit einem schwärzlichbraunen Tüpfel vertieft; andere haben bloss am stumpfen Ende olivenbraune und schwärzliche Punkte, übrigens einzelne grosse graue Flecke; wieder andere sind, ausser den aschgrauen Flecken, mit einer unsäglichen Menge brauner Pünktchen übersät und bloss am dicken Ende mit grossen braunen, in der Mitte viel dunkleren Flecken bezeichnet; noch andere sind über und über mit aschgrauen und olivenbraunen Flecken bezeichnet, aber die meisten der letzteren haben in ihrer Mitte einen dunkleren Punkt; endlich gibt es welche, wo die Flecke von beiden Farben so gross und häufig sind, dass sie am stumpfen Ende eine marmorartige Zeichnung bilden; dies sind die dunkelsten, die zuerst beschriebenen die hellsten, alle Verschiedenheiten aber stets von denen des **Teichrohrsängers** durch einen viel helleren, weisseren Grund, durch die hellaschgrauen Flecke und die oft Augen ähnliche Zeichnung derselben sehr leicht zu unterscheiden. Überhaupt ist es etwas Charakteristisches, was diese Eier von allen ähnlichen sehr auszeichnet, was sowohl in der Form, wie in der Farbe u.s.w. liegt, was sich aber ohne zu grosse Weitläufigkeit nicht beschreiben lässt.

Eine kranzähnliche Anhäufung der Flecke am stumpfen Ende findet man bei diesen Eiern nicht, wohl aber sind hier die Flecke bei den meisten häufiger, als am entgegengesetzten spitzen Ende. Die Mehrzahl hat stets nur wenige, aber dann desto grössere Flecke.

Beide Gatten brüten abwechselnd, doch sitzt das Männchen nur einige Stunden am Tage, das Weibchen aber die übrige Zeit über den Eiern, und nach dreizehn Tagen schlüpfen die Jungen aus. Sie sind beim Bau des Nestes fast so scheu wie die Grasmücken und lassen ihn, wenn sie einen Menschen in der Nähe desselben herumschleichen sahen, sogleich liegen, selbst wenn er schon ganz vollendet wäre. Die Eier verlassen sie auch leicht, wenn man sich nur irgend unbehutsam dabei benommen hat, weniger die Jungen, die aber dann, sobald sie nur mässig mit Federn bedeckt sind, sich fortmachen. Wenn diese auch nur erst notdürftig ihre kleinen Flugwerkzeuge gebrauchen können, so entschlüpfen sie doch ihren Feinden leicht im Gebüsch durch Behendigkeit im Kriechen und Anklammern, worin sie geborene Meister sind. Sie haben eine quäkende Stimme, welche man von ihnen hört, sobald sie das Nest verlassen haben, bis sie sich selbst nähren können; sie schreien aber nur, wenn sie sich sicher glauben. Vor der Mitte des Juli gibt es nie flügge Junge; denn diese Vögel nisten, wie alle übrigen Rohrsänger, sehr spät, daher auch nur einmal im Jahr. Im Jahr 1819 fand ich erst in der letzten Woche des Juni Eier, und ein Pärchen, dem das erste Nest, noch ehe Eier darin lagen, zerstört worden war, hatte den letzten dieses Monats wieder ein fertiges Nest, aber noch kein Ei. Wird ihnen das Nest mit den Eiern zerstört, so bauen sie in demselben Jahr keins wieder.

FEINDE

Weil sich diese Vögel öfter als andere von ihren Familienverwandten auf dem Freien zeigen, so wird nicht selten einer die Beute des **Sperbers**. Sonst hat ihre Brut noch arge Feinde an den kleinen Raubtieren, an **Iltissen** und **Wieseln**, die an den Ufern der Gräben und Gewässer so gern ihren Räubereien nachgehen; auch zerstören in den Gärten und bei den Gehöften die **Katzen** viele Nester und fangen die eben ausgeflogenen Jungen, selbst zuweilen einen Alten von dem Neste weg. Die **Elstern** zerstören auch manches Nest; selbst die **Würger** fangen bei Regenwetter manchmal ein ermattetes Junges, oder schleppen sie aus dem Neste. Wahrscheinlich bedient sich auch der **Kuckuck** ihrer als Pflegeeltern für sein Junges, worüber ich jedoch nichts mit Gewissheit erfahren konnte.

NUTZEN

Durch Vertilgung einer unzähligen Menge für Menschen und Vieh lästiger und sie plagender Insekten nützen sie gar sehr; auch ist ihr Fleisch so wohlschmeckend wie das anderer kleiner Insektenvögel, es kommt aber, wie billig, bloss zufällig und sehr selten einmal in die Küche. Ihr vortrefflicher Gesang macht sie für die Bewohner wasserreicher Gegenden sehr schätzbar, indem sie damit das wenige Buschwerk daselbst beleben und manchen auch in der stillen Nacht damit erfreuen. Auch dem Liebhaber, welcher sich die Mühe geben und ein singendes Männchen im Käfig unterhalten wollte, müsste dieser Gesang einen hohen Genuss gewähren.

SCHADEN

Diese Vögel nützen bloss, schaden uns aber auf keinerlei Weise.

// EDITORISCHE NOTIZ //

Anmerkung zur Herausgabe — Dieses Buch kann nur einen kleinen Teil des schriftstellerischen und künstlerischen Werkes Johann Friedrich Naumanns wiedergeben. Es soll in das Werk des bedeutendsten deutschen Ornithologen und Vogelmalers einführen und dem Leser einen Eindruck von der sprachlichen Klarheit und Eleganz sowie der künstlerischen Kraft Naumanns vermitteln. Dabei stehen die bisher unbekannten, nie einer Öffentlichkeit gezeigten Aquarelle Naumanns im Vordergrund. Sie stammen aus einem offenbar von Naumann oder dessen Vater selbst gebundenen Arbeitsbuch, das im Naumann-Museum in Köthen liegt. Die Aquarelle dienten als Vorlage für die Kupferstiche der Bücher, vor allem für Naumanns Hauptwerk *Die Naturgeschichte der Vögel Deutschlands*. Mehr noch als die Kupferstiche erweisen die Aquarelle Naumann als großen Künstler in der Vogeldarstellung. Ich bin dem Direktor des Museums, Wolf-Dieter Busching, sehr dankbar, daß er mir den Zugang zu diesen unschätzbaren Aquarellen gewährt hat.

Für den Textteil des Buches habe ich vierzehn der Vogeldarstellungen Johann Friedrich Naumanns aus der *Naturgeschichte der Vögel Deutschlands* ausgewählt. Ein wenig habe ich darauf geachtet, neben den Singvögeln auch Watvögel, Raubvögel und Enten zu berücksichtigen, vor allem aber ging es mir darum, Beispiele von

Naumanns glanzvoller Sprache — insbesondere in der Beschreibung des Federkleides und der Stimmen der Vögel — zu geben. Diese Texte sind reiner Naumann und beruhen auf der Neuausgabe, die um die Wende vom 19. zum 20. Jahrhundert von Carl H. Gericke in Gera — unter dem Titel: *Naturgeschichte der Vögel Mitteleuropas* — veranstaltet wurde. Ihnen wurden die Kupferstiche vorangestellt, die auch die Texte in Naumanns Hauptwerk begleiten. Hinzu kommt — ganz am Anfang des Textteils — ein Aufsatz Naumanns über seinen Besuch Schleswig-Holsteins und der Insel Sylt unter dem Titel ›Der Haushalt der Vögel Norddeutschlands‹. Die Texte sind an manchen Stellen leicht gekürzt. Die Korrekturen und Ergänzungen, welche die zweite Ausgabe enthält, habe ich weggelassen. Entfallen sind auch die Hinweise zur Jagd, die einen heute nur erschaudern lassen, und Bemerkungen zu Parasiten und ähnlichem.

Wo Naumann nur die lateinischen Vogelnamen nennt, sind die geläufigen deutschen Bezeichnungen eingesetzt. Auch wo er von den heute üblichen Vogelnamen abweicht, haben wir statt dessen die uns bekannten Namen verwendet; also beispielsweise statt Naumanns »Schwarzdrossel« die Amsel, statt des »Nachtigall-Sängers« die Nachtigall.

Naumanns Schreibweise und manchmal eigenwillige Grammatik haben wir im allgemeinen so belassen und nur dort, wo der Ausdruck der Lesbarkeit im Wege stand, behutsame Änderungen vorgenommen.

Ich hoffe, daß dieser Band dazu beiträgt, den fast vergessenen Johann Friedrich Naumann wieder auf die Landkarte des europäischen Geistes zu setzen. Sein wissenschaftlicher und mehr noch sein künstlerischer Rang ist in meinen Augen unzweifelhaft.

Arnulf Conradi

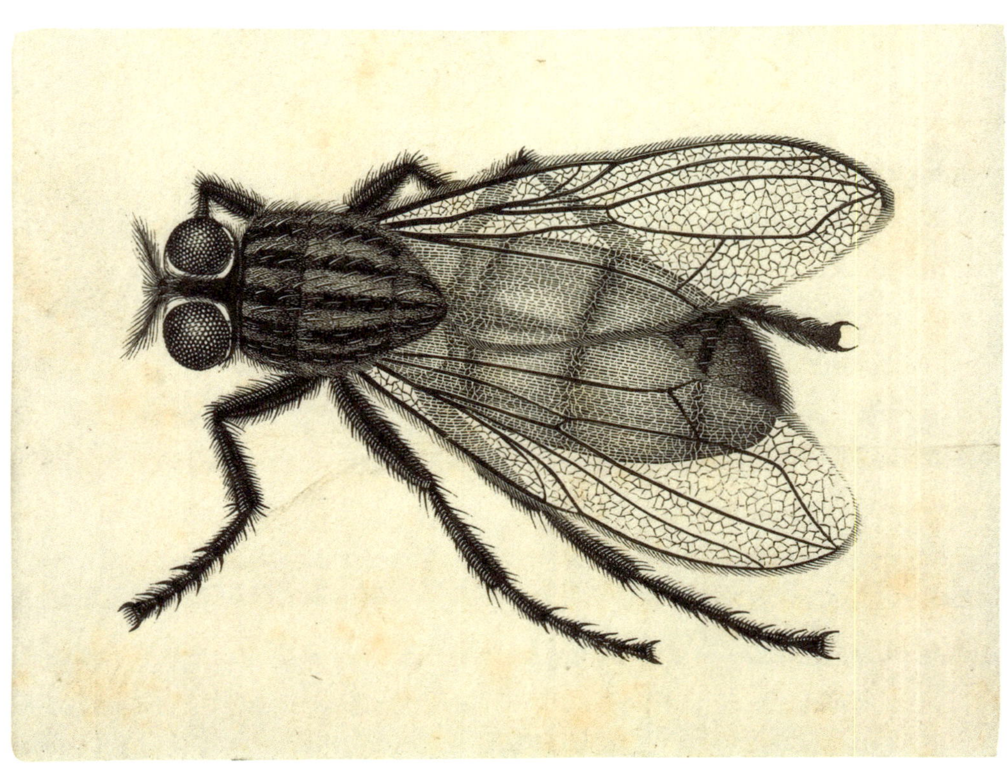

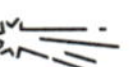

Johann Friedrich Naumann, geboren am 14. Februar 1780 in Ziebigk bei Köthen, Sachsen-Anhalt, gestorben am 15. August 1857 ebendort, war ein begnadeter Vogelmaler und gilt als Begründer der Vogelkunde in Deutschland.

Stubenfliege, Kupferstich von Johann Friedrich Naumann

Die Vögel Mitteleuropas **von Johann Friedrich Naumann** ist im Oktober 2009 als Folioband der ANDEREN BIBLIOTHEK erschienen. Als Sonderband wurde *Die Vögel Mitteleuropas* im September 2020 wiederaufgelegt. Die Erstausgabe von Johann Friedrich Naumanns zwölfbändigem Werk *Die Naturgeschichte der Vögel Deutschlands* wurde in den Jahren 1820 bis 1844 bei Gerhard Fleischer, Leipzig, veröffentlicht.

Die vorliegende Auswahl hat Arnulf Conradi getroffen, ihr liegt die Ausgabe von Carl H. Gericke, Jena, von 1897 bis 1903 zugrunde. Um ein möglichst unverfälschtes Bild des Originals zu geben, wurden die Naumannschen Eigenarten der Schreibungen beibehalten.

Die in dieser Ausgabe erstmals einer Öffentlichkeit präsentierten Aquarelle und auch die Kupferstiche wurden von Tobias Buddensieg, www.tobiasbuddensieg.de, fotografiert.

Der Verlag bedankt sich bei der Kulturmanagement GmbH Köthen und beim Naumann-Museum Köthen, insbesondere bei dessen Direktor Herrn Dr. Wolf-Dieter Busching, für die freundliche Unterstützung.

Das Lektorat lag in den Händen von Palma Müller-Scherf, unter Mitarbeit von Nina Porsch.

Arnulf Conradi war Lektor bei Claassen, dann als Cheflektor und Programmgeschäftsführer elf Jahre beim S. Fischer Verlag tätig. 1993 gründete er den Berlin Verlag, dessen Verleger er bis zu seinem 60. Geburtstag im Jahre 2004 war. Arnulf Conradi, in Kiel aufgewachsen, ist seit Kindertagen ein begeisterter Vogelbeobachter. Zu diesem Thema verfasste, übersetzte und bearbeitete er bereits zahlreiche Bücher und Artikel.

Dieses Buch wurde von Greiner & Reichel in Köln aus der Bembo gesetzt und bei der DZA Druckerei zu Altenburg auf 130 g/m² Schleipen Fly 05 gedruckt und gebunden. Die Reproduktionen stammen von Johann Hausstätter in Berlin. Die Einbandgestaltung lag bei Katja Jaeger nach einem Entwurf von Christina Hucke. Die Typografie gestalteten Susanne Reeh und Cosima Schneider.

1. Auflage 2020 in veränderter Ausstattung

ISBN 978-3-8477-0008-1
AB – Die Andere Bibliothek GmbH & Co. KG
Berlin 2020